D1129565

READINGS IN VERBAL LEARNING

Contemporary Theory and Research

READINGS IN VERBAL LEARNING

Contemporary Theory and Research

Edited by

Donald H. Kausler

Saint Louis University

John Wiley & Sons, Inc. New York · London · Sydney

Library of Congress Catalog Card Number: 66-17628
Printed in the United States of America

Preface

This book of readings has been planned primarily for use in courses directed specifically to the study of verbal learning. I have assumed that the reader has previously completed an introduction to learning terminology, methodology, and basic constructs and, moreover, has had a historical introduction to the problems surveyed in this book.

The book may also be used as a source of supplementary readings for undergraduate students in the later stages of an introductory learning course. Textbooks for the introductory learning course typically concentrate on conditioning phenomena and classical learning theory approaches to these phenomena, particularly as manifested in animal behavior, with verbal learning relegated to a few brief chapters. It is hoped that the present readings will help the undergraduate student develop a more adequate conceptualization of the activities within the contemporary psychology of verbal learning.

As commonly employed, verbal learning is a broad term that encompasses phenomena of transfer and retention, as well as those of acquisition (or learning). The processes and related areas of investigation involved in transfer and retention, of course, bear a relationship to those involved in acquisition. Nevertheless, the literature pertaining to each component of the trichotomy has its own unique characteristics. Consequently, the readings in this book have been organized into three main parts: Acquisition, Transfer, and Retention.

Two important problems were confronted in planning the content of this book. The first problem concerned the selection of general areas or topics which would provide an organizational structure for the individual articles within each of the three main parts. These areas were intended to represent the major categories of theoretical issues and related research extant within contemporary verbal learning. Eleven such categories were devised, seven for Acquisition and two each for Transfer and Retention. These categories, in turn, provide the individual chapter headings. Although it is quite likely that another editor would have preferred a different categorization, I feel that the one presented here fulfills its primary responsibility—the classification of the vast majority of current articles into operationally defined and theoretically oriented issues.

For a number of the eleven categories I attempted a further analysis into subcategories. These subcategories recognize the existence of separate problem areas within more broadly defined phenomena. For example, the chapter entitled "Acquisition as a Function of Similarity" deals with the complex phenomena of primary and secondary generalization as manipulated by dimensions of similarity. A number of distinct areas of investigation have evolved within the rubric of similarity-generalization effects. Included here are the effects of inter-stimulus and/or inter-response similarity (via similarity within the stimulus terms and/or the response terms), stimulus-response similarity (identical items for stimuli and responses), the grouping of similar items during practice, and perceptual or conceptual isolation of task components. Thus, the articles selected for inclusion in this chapter reflect each of these distinct subcategories of investigation.

The second, and more difficult, problem rested in the selection of individual articles. Several hundred excellent articles devoted to verbal learning have appeared during the period of time covered by this book (1951–1965). The criterion established for selection was the fact that the article seemed, in my judgment, representative of the problems, methods, hypotheses, etc., of the designated area of investigation. The reader will discover that most of the articles are concerned with the classical paired-associate and serial-learning tasks. This heavy weighting suggests immediately the dominance of these task variants in contemporary research. Several of the articles, however, particularly in Chapter 7, describe research employing other kinds of tasks, such as free recall, when special task requirements are essential for the problem under study.

The reader will also discover that for many of the articles the nature of the research problem defies a single classification. The placement of these articles corresponds to my interpretation of the primary emphasis of that article. For instance, the study by Underwood, Ham, and Ekstrand has been assigned to "Paired-Associate Learning: Models and Processes" (Chapter 2) in that it provides the reader with a cogent analysis of a process, namely cue selection, operative in paired-associate acquisition (or learning, more narrowly defined). Secondarily, the study could be included under "Transfer: Classical *St-R* Paradigms" (Chapter 8) in that the methodology and design of the study fit those of transfer experiments.

Finally, I have provided both an overview of contemporary theory and research in verbal learning and brief introductions to each of the chapters. The overview serves as a general introduction to recent advances in the areas surveyed throughout the book. The introductory sections present the topics and problems covered in the selected articles and, in addition, summarize other studies relevant to the content of that chapter. References cited in these materials are listed in a bibliography at the end of the book.

On the other hand, an easy problem is the identification and grateful acknowledgment of the many individuals who contributed substantially to the preparation of this book. First and foremost, the authors of the articles kindly permitted the reprinting of their research endeavors. Further consent was received from the Academic Press, the American Psychological Association, the Journal Press, and Psychonomic Science for the reprinting of the articles and from the Academic Press and the American Psychological Association for the inclusion of direct quotations in my introductory materials. Mr. Gordon Ierardi, the Psychology Editor of John Wiley, maintained a highly effective rapport with me through all stages of development. Dr. Charles V. Lair served as a critical reader of my own introductory materials and offered many helpful suggestions. Mrs. Bernice Morris, with an able assist from Miss Jo Ann Haley, made the typing of the manuscript flow steadily and flawlessly. Finally, my wife, Marty, and children, René, Donnie, Jill, and Barry, merit recognition for their patient tolerance and morale boosting during the many disruptions of normal family activity brought about by "that book."

St. Louis, Missouri Donald H. Kausler
February, 1966

Contents

READINGS IN VERBAL LEARNING

Contemporary Theory and Research

Overview

Verbal learning has occupied a central position in the research and theoretical activities of psychology ever since the pioneering studies of Ebbinghaus (1885). The early literature on verbal learning was reviewed by McGeoch (1942) in his classic book, *The Psychology of Human Learning*. A second edition of this book (McGeoch and Irion, 1952) incorporated the theoretical and empirical developments, relevant to human learning in general but devoted largely to verbal learning, that occurred during the period 1942–1950.

In his introduction to the second edition, Irion commented, "The psychology of human learning has undergone great changes since this book appeared in its first edition in 1942" (p. IX). The identical statement may be applied, perhaps to an even greater extent, to human learning for the years 1951–1965. The general purpose of the present book of reading is to familiarize the student of learning with the "great changes" that have taken place during this time period in the verbal component of human learning.

These changes have included a rapid expansion of our understanding of phenomena and processes long within the mainstream of verbal learning. This expansion largely represents the contribution of the "functionalist" psychologists, who are continuing in the tradition of Harvey Carr, Edward S. Robinson, John A. McGeoch, and other early investigators of verbal learning. Most prominent in the contemporary group are Benton J. Underwood and Leo Postman and their colleagues and students. In addition, the contemporary period has been characterized by a multitude of extensions of verbal processes into new problem areas or into older areas that have often been ignored in verbal learning. Here we find the current emphasis on mediation in both acquisition and transfer, categorization and concept formation within the context of verbal acquisition, the effect of formal language approximations on verbal acquisition, and short-term retention. The specific intent of this book is to sample the progress in the traditional areas of research and to convey the excitement of the new directions currently underway in verbal learning.

The Centrality of Verbal Learning

The functional tradition in verbal learning has always accented the phrase "learning as a function of." While carrying on in this tradition, contemporary investigators, whether or not they formally identify themselves as functionalists, have probed deeply into the parametric relationships that account for substantial segments of the variance in verbal learning phenomena. These relationships, or laws, bind together reliable measures (dependent variables) of learning phenomena and their relevant conditions (independent variables). Characteristically, this approach has been guided by the formulation of "miniature" theories which deal with concepts that are restricted to a fairly narrow range of behavior. This is in contrast to the formal learning theory approach of the Hulls, Spences, and Tolmans where the emphasis is placed on more pervasive concepts that enter into wider ranges of behavior.

Nevertheless, verbal learning has progressed to the point where its processes, theories, and findings have widespread implications for many other areas of learning, such as classical and instrumental conditioning, motor skill learning, problem solving, etc. These implications for learning in general are all too frequently misperceived by observers who view the activities of verbal learning psychologists as the epitome of narrow specialization. In response to such observations, Underwood had the following colorful and incisive remarks to make:

> Rote Learning! Let us imagine some free associations which these two words might elicit from people in psychological and educational circles, restricting the responses to those which meet standards of good taste. It is likely that the following would be among the most frequent responses: "dull," "Ebbinghaus," "narrow," "verbal learning," "sterile," "nonsense syllable," "memory drum," "serial list," and so on. Two notions can be culled from such associations. First is the notion that rote learning is closely associated with verbal learning, an association which is quite appropriate. The second notion is that rote learning, identified as the classical area of rote verbal learning, is felt to be dull, narrow, sterile, and, in a manner of speaking, deals with a form of learning that is almost intellectually demeaning. These assumed reactions to rote verbal learning may paint a somewhat exaggerated picture of an attitude toward the areas, but most would probably agree that the core of such an attitude does exist. If a number of research areas in human learning were put into the cruel and grinding dimensions of the semantic differential it seems clear that rote verbal learning would come out with a "bad" profile, perhaps being pressed only by classical conditioning.
>
> Obviously, from the writer's point of view, these attitudes are ill begot. But, perhaps these attitudes are, like so many other attitudes, representative of a cultural lag. Perhaps if the contemporary work in verbal learning were understood by all some change in attitude might occur. Perhaps it is not quite justifiable to view the nonsense syllable as the pedant's playmate. In any event, the position taken here is that the work in verbal learning—rote verbal learning—may stand squarely in the center of all human learning. Research in verbal learning is shooting out phenomena and theories which are touching, sometimes in a very fundamental way, all areas of human learning from simple conditioning to the study of the thought processes (Underwood, 1964a, pp. 51–52).

One example will be given here to illustrate how the problems and advances of verbal learning touch upon other areas of learning. Incidental learning (cf. Chapter 6) is concerned with learning without the deliberate intent to learn. The contemporary period has produced tremendous advances in our understanding of the processes governing learning without intent and how these processes are affected by certain critical independent variables. Verbal conditioning is an area generally considered apart from verbal learning. Nevertheless, verbal conditioning has much in common with incidental verbal learning. In verbal conditioning studies a class of verbal responses (e.g., saying statements that begin with "I" or "we") is selectively reinforced. Whenever the subject

(*S*) responds with a member of that class, he is reinforced by the experimenter (*E*) saying "uh uh," "yes," or some other positive reinforcer. Conditioning is indicated by an increase in the rate of emitting the response class. A critical issue in this area has become that of "awareness"—that is, does conditioning take place without *S*'s conscious awareness of the contingency between the occurrence of the response class and the verbal reinforcer? There is evidence (e.g., Spielberger and Levin, 1962) which suggests that verbal conditioning does not occur without at least some partial awareness of this contingency. Awareness here bears a number of similarities to the recognition of intent to learn in incidental learning studies. Further advances in our understanding of verbal conditioning processes are likely to be made by the application of related processes in incidental learning.

Verbal learning is also an important contributor to areas of psychology other than learning. Theories of psychopathology are frequently tested within the context of verbal learning. For example, Kausler, Lair, and Matsumoto (1964) reported greater negative transfer for schizophrenic *Ss* than for normal control *Ss* on the *A-B*, *A-Br* transfer paradigm but not on the *A-B*, *A-C* paradigm (cf. Introduction, Chapter 8 for a description of these transfer paradigms). They interpreted these differential transfer effects as offering support for Mednick's (1958) learning theory approach to schizophrenia. Motivational theorists have also found verbal learning to be a fruitful milieu for tests of their hypotheses. For example, Spence, Farber, and McFann (1956) employed paired-associate lists varying in their degree of competition between responses to stimuli on groups of *Ss* differing in drive level. Their results were in agreement with predictions from contemporary drive theory. Ideally, a book of readings on verbal learning should include representative articles from these hybrid areas, even though the research itself may have had its impetus from sources extrinsic to verbal learning. Space limitations, however, prohibit this extensive coverage. There are, moreover, a number of reference sources (e.g., Cofer and Appley, 1964) that review these areas.

Chapter Contents

Part One: Acquisition

A large amount of contemporary research has reflected a trend toward the analysis of verbal learning tasks themselves. By this we mean systematic attempts to break down the complex phenomena involved in the acquisition of such tasks into their component subphenomena. These analyses aid in the identification of important independent variables, operating alone or interacting with other independent variables, that are likely to influence the course of acquisition for a given task. Since many of the articles contained within this book require an understanding of task analyses, the readings begin with these general topics.

Three tasks, serial, paired-associate, and free recall lists, have been the ones most frequently used in verbal learning studies. Chapters 1 and 2 are devoted to analyses of the phenomena associated with the acquisition of serial and paired-associate lists, respectively. Free recall lists have been employed primarily in studies investigating the effects of various kinds of organizational variables. For this reason, a separate chapter has not been set aside for free recall; instead, relevant phenomena are treated as part of the content of Chapter 7 (Acquisition as a Function of: Organizational Factors). Illustrative of the content in Chapters 1 and 2 is the important distinction currently being made (e.g., Underwood, 1963) between the nominal and functional stimulus in verbal acquisition. Nominal here refers to the experimenter-designated stimulus, and functional to the subject-designated stimulus. This distinction has become an important one in both serial (cf. Introduction and Article 1, Chapter 1) and paired-associate (cf. Introduction and Article 4, Chapter 2) acquisition.

Verbal discrimination is a fourth possibility for a choice of tasks in verbal learning studies. In this task a list of paired verbal items is presented, one pair at a time, with one member of each pair having been arbitrarily designated "right" by *E* and the other "wrong." The *S*'s task is to learn which member is right in each pair. Verbal discrimination, however, has received little attention during the contemporary period. The few studies available (e.g., Runquist and Freeman, 1960) have indicated that the phenomena involved are far from being understood. Space limitations and the general lack of systematic efforts in this area have forced us to exclude verbal discrimination from further consideration.

Chapters 3–6 deal with independent variables that have had a lengthy history in verbal acquisition. Some of these variables have continued into the present era as part of a step-by-step research effort begun in the preceding era. Much of the research here termed "methodological" (Chapter 3) fits this description. In other instances, contemporary research has benefited greatly from new insights into old problems. For example, research on the meaningfulness–acquisition relationship (Chapter 4) has been largely shaped by recent advances in the scaling of meaningfulness and by the advent of stage analysis as a mode for conceptualizing verbal acquisition (cf. Introduction and Article 2, Chapter 2). The current thinking on incidental learning (Chapter 6) is another example of new insights into old problem areas.

Whereas the articles in Chapters 3–6 pertain largely to so-called rote acquisition, those contained in Chapter 7 treat the more recent attention given to organizational factors that serve to short-circuit acquisition. For example, free recall of items (i.e., recall without regard to serial sequence) is greatly enhanced when the items permit a clustering of meaningfully related items into a conceptual category (Articles 1 and 2). Similarly, acquisition of a serial list of words may be greatly modified when the list begins to take on the syntactic structure of actual language (Articles 5 and 6). These examples are illustrative of what Underwood (1964a) has termed a transitional experiment. In the first example, there is an attempt to bridge the gap between rote acquisition and conceptual activity. The gap in the second example is that between verbal acquisition and psycholinguistics.

Parts Two and Three: Transfer and Retention

Parts Two and Three sample the contemporary literature on transfer and retention, respectively. Two chapters are included in each part, one treating on-going research on traditional problems, the other treating directions that are largely products of the contemporary period. For transfer, the traditional problems have centered on phenomena characteristic of the classical transfer paradigms—that is, paradigms in which the stimulus (*St*) and response (*R*) components of the original and transfer tasks are directly related to one another in some manner (Chapter 8). Here the contemporary period has been characterized by increased methodological sophistication, especially in the control of nonspecific sources of transfer (Introduction), increased precision in identifying the primary and secondary laws of transfer (Articles 1, 2, 5, 6, and 7), and a greater understanding of the mechanisms or processes contributing to transfer effects (Articles 3 and 4). The new (or, more appropriately, reawakened) area of mediated transfer constitutes Chapter 9. The emphasis here is on transfer by means of implicit verbal processes rather than by direct *St-R* relationships as in the classical paradigms. Mediation has also become an issue in verbal acquisition (cf. Introduction and Article 7, Chapter 2) where a distinction is made between the rote acquisition of *St-R* associations by contiguous pairing and mediated acquisition by means of associates common to both stimulus and response. In general terms, mediation may be defined by the symbols A, B, and C, each representing some kind of verbal experience. If A is related to B, and B to C (but A and C are not directly related), then mediation is inferred if the tendency of A to elicit C is greater than expected on a chance basis. Presumably, the common B experience serves to mediate or intervene between A and C.

The traditional area for retention is long-term retention (Chapter 10). Even here there has been a radical break from the traditional view of retroactive inhibition as the dominant source of forgetting. The contemporary stress has been on proactive inhibition, including proaction from "extra-experimental" sources (Article 2). Short-term retention (Chapter 11) is a newer area, but one that has nevertheless been generating a plethora of research and related theorizing. The primary issue examined in the selected articles is the adequacy of the processes held responsible for long-term forgetting to explain forgetting over very short periods of time.

The Functional Approach

An understanding of the functional approach to research in verbal learning is essential for an appreciation of the hypothesizing and research planning found in most of the selected articles. This approach has been well presented elsewhere (Gough and Jenkins, 1963; Hilgard, 1956) and will be given only a cursory review here.

The approach begins with the reliable demonstration of a phenomenon considered to be a contributor to variability in some aspect of verbal learning. This demonstration typically takes the form of what Underwood (1957a) calls "*S-R, E/C* operational identification" in which the effect of some specified degree or level of a variable (the experimental or *E* condition) is contrasted with the effect of an appropriate zero condition of that same variable (the control or *C* condition). Then, according to Underwood, "If there is a reliable difference in behavior resulting from these conditions, the procedures used to derive it define the phenomenon" (1957a, p. 69). However, phenomena defined in this manner may involve a highly complex interaction of subphenomena. These subphenomena are often referred to as processes or mechanisms and are capable of their own operational definition independently of the broader phenomenon in question. Typically, the processes are hypothesized by *E* as being operative within the broader phenomenon. The source of the hypothesis may be the existence of previous data that suggest the presence of the process. The next step is to establish functional relationships between relevant independent variables and the dependent behavioral variable serving to measure the phenomenon. Relevant independent variables are ones that have been previously demonstrated to bear functional relationships with the dependent variables for the suspected subphenomena or processes. Confirmation of hypothesized functional relationships for the broader phenomenon then contributes to the validation of the phenomenon-into-processes analysis.

The phenomenon-into-processes analysis phase of operational identification may be viewed in the following abstract terms. X represents some complex phenomenon, and x_1 and x_2 represent processes hypothesized to be subphenomenal components of X. Assume further that x_1 has previously been demonstrated, outside of the context of the X phenomenon, to be related to an independent variable, J. That is, x_1 = function (J), with the form of the function (e.g., linear, negatively accelerated, etc.) being known. Similarly, assume that x_2 is related to another independent variable, K such that x_2 = function (K), again with the form of the function being known. Empirically, the problem becomes the determination of the "X as a function of J" and "X as a function of K" relationships. If these relationships conform to those found for x_1 and x_2 then we have supportive evidence for the analysis of X into x_1 and x_2 component processes.

One illustration will be given at this point. Many of the articles in the readings will contain further illustrations. The phenomenon in question is the direction of transfer in the *A-B, C-B* transfer paradigm. The paradigm requires the learning of two lists of paired associates, an original list (List 1) and a transfer list (List 2), in which the responses (symbolized as *B* in the paradigm) are identical for the two lists but the stimuli in List 2 (*C* in the paradigm) differ from those in List 1 (*A* in the paradigm). In terms of *S-R, E/C* operational identification, *Ss* in the experimental condition receive *C-B* pairs in List 2 after practice on *A-B* pairs in List 1, and *Ss* in the control condition receive *C-D* pairs (new responses as well as new stimuli) in List 2 after their *A-B* practice. The latter condition (called the *A-B, C-D* transfer paradigm) is the proper control in that it equates the experimental and control groups on nonspecific sources of transfer—that is, transfer from sources, such as "warm-up" and "learning-to-learn," that are outside of the specific stimulus-response content of the two lists. The investigator then determines the performance differential between the experimental and control conditions. This is typically measured by the difference between the mean number of correct responses for the two conditions during a set number of trials on List 2. If there is a statistically significant better performance in the *C-B* than in the *C-D* condition, positive transfer has occurred; if the reverse is true, negative transfer has occurred. The operations used in the experimental condition, namely different stimuli and identical responses, then define the phenomenon.

Several studies (e.g., Twedt and Underwood, 1959; Kausler and Kanoti, 1963) have yielded negative transfer for the *A-B, C-B* paradigm (relative to the *A-B, C-D* paradigm), whereas other studies (e.g., Jung, Article 5, Chapter 8) have yielded either zero transfer or a slight degree of positive transfer. Obviously the transfer phenomenon is a complex one which apparently involves at least two distinct processes. Failure to account for these separate processes obfuscates predictions of the transfer direction for given lists of paired associates. Differential evocation of the two processes could account for the presence of overall positive transfer under some conditions and negative transfer under other conditions if one of the processes contributes a positive transfer effect and the other a negative effect. That is, the overall transfer effect, as measured by the *C-B, C-D* difference, would then be the resultant of two or more separate sources of transfer.

A process that has been linked to positive transfer is that of response learning (cf. Mandler, Article 1, Chapter 2; Jung, Article 5, Chapter 8); a process linked to negative transfer effects is that of competition between the *R-St* or "backward" associations (cf. Jantz and Underwood, Article 5, Chapter 2) of the two lists. Response learning may be viewed as a source of positive transfer via the fact that the responses for *C-B* pairs have already been learned during practice on *A-B* pairs and thus are readily available for associative learning on list 2; on the other hand, the responses for the *C-D* pairs were not learned during List 1 practice and must therefore be acquired during List 2 practice before they may enter into specific associations. As to *R-St* learning, the *R-St* associations of *C-B* pairs in List 2 (i.e., B-C associations) are likely to compete with the *R-St* associations of List 1 (i.e., *B-A* associations) in that they have identical stimulus terms but different response terms. This competitive arrangement is not present for the *C-D* control pairs where the *R-S*t associations are *D-C* and *B-A* for Lists 2 and 1, respectively. In transfer terminology the *R-St* associations of the *A-B, C-B* lists enter into an *A-B, A-C* paradigm—a paradigm long considered to generate interference in List 2 learning, with concomitant negative transfer (cf. Barnes and Underwood, Article 3, Chapter 8).

Response learning and *R-St* learning are distinguishable phenomena, each characterized by well-established functional relationships between independent and dependent variables. For example, the extent of response learning varies inversely with the meaningfulness of response terms in paired-associate learning (cf. Hunt, Article 2, Chapter 4), and *R-St* learning varies directly with the degree of practice on *St-R* pairs (cf. Jantz and Underwood, Article 5, Chapter 2). Consequently, we may hypothesize that if these two phenomena enter as processes into the resultant transfer for the *A-B, C-B* paradigm, the direction and amount of transfer will similarly vary as a function of response meaningfulness and degree of practice on List 1. In fact, these are among the research hypotheses proposed by Postman (Article 6, Chapter 8) in his experiment dealing, in part, with the *A-B, C-B* paradigm.

Part One

ACQUISITION

CHAPTER 1

Serial Learning:

The Functional Stimulus, Serial Position Effects, and Remote Associations

Serial learning (SL) or, more appropriately, serial acquisition consists of the sequential (generally in temporal order) acquisition of a set of items or verbal units. Thus the items symbolized as *A, B, C, D, E, F,* and *G* (which represent whatever the formal units are—nonsense syllables, adjectives, etc.) constitute a serial list whenever *Ss* are required to learn them in a specified (temporal) sequence, such as *A-B-C-D-E-F-G*. Procedurally, the items are exposed individually via a standard device (memory drum, slide projector, etc.) at a controlled rate. The anticipation method, in which *S* attempts to anticipate the next term in the list during the exposure of the preceding term, is usually employed. A trial consists of one complete presentation of all of the terms, with, of course, the identical order being replicated on each trial. The dependent variable is likely to be either the number of trials needed to reach some predetermined criterion of mastery or the number of correct anticipations (or, conversely, the number of errors) committed during a fixed number of trials. With errors as the dependent variable, several categories of error are typically included in ancillary analyses of total errors for paired-associate learning as well as SL. One category consists of omission errors—that is, failures to respond with any kind of overt response at the appropriate time. A second category consists of intrusion errors. Intrusions may be further subdivided into intralist and extralist intrusions. In both cases a response is given (rather than the no response of omission errors), but it is either misplaced within the list (intralist intrusion) or is entirely outside the content of the list (extralist intrusion). In addition, a dependent variable unique to SL, namely, performance proficiency at each of the serial or ordinal positions in the list, is involved in those experiments that are directed toward serial position effects.

Serial learning has served as a standard laboratory task for investigating a wide range of learning phenomena and related independent variables (e.g., "isolation" effects as described in Chapter 5). Many of the functional relationships reliably demonstrated in verbal learning have been established within the context of SL. In this chapter, however, we are concerned with the nature of SL per se and the processes operative during SL. Three subphenomena of SL (defined as the broad phenomenon) have received considerable attention and will be the subjects of this chapter. They are: The Functional Stimulus, Serial Position Effects, and Remote Associations.

The Functional Stimulus

Traditionally, SL has been viewed as the acquisition of a chain of *St-R* associations, with the discrete *St-R* links of the chain being closely akin to paired associates (cf. Chapter 2). The chaining hypothesis, by definition, assigns a "double function," stimulus and response, to each item within the list. When applied to our symbolic *A-B-C-D-E-F-G* list, the separate links are *A-B*, *B-C*, *C-D*, etc. These links are eventually integrated into the continuous chain.

The chaining hypothesis perceives the stimulus term for a given item (as a response) to be the specific prior item and, for this reason, is also commonly labeled the specificity hypothesis. In terms of the distinction between the nominal and functional stimulus (Underwood, 1963) made in the Overview the specificity hypothesis implies a complete overlap between the nominal and the functional stimulus. In other words, what is designated as the stimulus by the experimenter, the prior item, actually serves as the discriminable cue, or functional stimulus, for the individual *S*. For many years this conceptualization of the stimulus in SL was accepted, either overtly or covertly, as being valid by the vast majority of verbal learning psychologists without experimental tests of its implications. An occasional dissident voice could be heard, however. Most significantly, Woodworth and Poffenberger in 1920 (cf. Article 2 by Jensen) proposed a variant of what now bears the appellation of the "ordinal position" hypothesis. The functional stimulus postulated in this hypothesis is that provided by an item's ordinal or numerical position in the list. For example, the functional stimulus for Item *D* in our list would be *S*'s discrimination of *D*'s position as the fourth item in the list.

The contemporary period of research on SL has been characterized by a systematic reappraisal of the specificity hypothesis and its alternatives, particularly the position hypothesis denoted above and the cluster hypothesis. The cluster hypothesis is basically a variant of specificity in which a cluster of two or more items, rather than a single item, serves as the functional stimulus. For our list, the simplest cluster possible for Item *D* would be a composite of Items *B* and *C*. More complex clusters are, of course, conceivable.

Experimental tests of these three hypotheses have usually been conducted within the rubric of operational identification and its application to a transfer phenomenon. Suppose we request *Ss* to learn a List 1 that contains clearly delineated stimuli and responses, identified in transfer terminology as *A-B* pairs. Following practice to a criterion of mastery on List 1, our *Ss* practice on a List 2 that contains the same *A-B* pairs found in List 1. We would obviously expect to find a high degree of positive transfer for these *Ss* relative to other *Ss* who receive *C-D* pairs (new stimuli and new responses) in List 2 after practice on the *A-B* pairs of List 1. The positive transfer found in the former group would then be defined in terms of the operations used to define the phenomenon, namely identical stimuli and responses for the sets of pairs in the two lists. The reader may well ask why this procedure is apropos to the testing of hypotheses about the functional stimulus in SL. The study by Young, Patterson, and Benson (Article 1) nicely illustrates the analogy to our transfer phenomenon and the corresponding research strategy. They structured their research problem by having *Ss* learn two serial lists as Lists 1 and 2, with List 1 (the original list) being a standard list like our *A-B-* . . . *-G*, and with List 2 (the transfer list) being a list identical in content to List 1 but with the items in a reverse or "backward" order (i.e., *G-F-* · · · *-A*). If the functional stimulus for List 1 is ordinal position, then the stimulus for the middle item (Item *D*) becomes "fourth in the list" or some representation of that position. Moreover, the functional stimulus for Item *D* in List 2 must also be "fourth in the list" in that the item occupies the same ordinal position in the backward list that it does in the forward list (List 1). Therefore, if the stimulus-response relationship for Item *D* in List 1 is labeled "*A-B*," then the comparable relationship for List 2 is also "*A-B*." We are then ready to predict greater amounts of positive transfer for this item than for other items in the list where the position stimulus changes from List 1 to List 2 (e.g., Item *B* is second in List 1 but sixth in List 2).

Another variation of this procedure is to have *Ss* learn a serial list as List 1 and a paired-associate list as List 2. If, for example, experimental pairs in List 2 are composed of serially linked items from List 1 (such as *E-F*) and control pairs are composed of completely new items (such as *J-K*), then positive transfer may be predicted for the linked items to the extent that the specific item *E* is the stimulus in both lists for response *F*. Studies by Young (1962) and Horowitz and Izawa (1963) are among those that have employed this strategy.

The reader may be surprised to discover that the research in this area has failed to provide unequivocal support for any single view of the functional stimulus in SL. The Young et al. study suggested that the stimulus may well be ordinal position in the middle of the list but the specific preceding item in the ends of the list. Further evidence for this Type of Stimulus × Locus in the List interaction was given earlier in three separate experiments by Young (1962). On the other hand, Horowitz and Izawa (1963) provided evidence for the cluster hypothesis when the items of the serial list are independent of one another—that is, their associative hierarchies (Deese, 1961) do not overlap. Ebenholtz (1963) has added to the impossibility of taking a resolute stand, at the present stage of research, on the nature of the stimulus by postulating a Type of Stimulus × Locus interaction that is opposite in direction to that postulated by Young. According to this view, position is the functional stimulus at the ends of the list and specificity in the middle.

A study by Battig, Brown, and Schild (1964) lends some support to the Ebenholtz interpretation. Battig et al. found clusters of items to be the most likely stimulus in the middle of their list, with simpler units (either the immediately preceding item or ordinal position) being most efficacious in the beginning of the list. In an attempt to reconcile their findings with those of Young (1962) and Young et al. (Article 1), they hypothesized that list difficulty may be a critical factor influencing the nature of the functional stimulus. Their rationale implies that with increasing difficulty of learning increasing amounts of intralist interference (most likely through the mechanisms of stimulus and response generalization; cf. Chapter 5) are generated, thus making it hard for *S* to utilize simpler, but more generalized, stimulus components. It should be noted that the lists of Battig et al. were difficult ones in that they were composed of low meaningful bigrams (such as "JV") whereas the lists of Young et al. were composed of easier-to-learn meaningful words. If Battig et al. are correct, then the interaction between the nature of the stimulus and the locus in the list should be broadened into a higher order interaction that would incorporate difficulty as a third factor.

Thus, the "Case of the Missing Stimulus" seems far from being solved, and interest in the search for the stimulus is likely to continue. Jensen (Article 2, 1962a), however, seems to be suggesting that the searchers may be pursuing a phantom stimulus. Of particular interest in his study is the finding of a nearly zero correlation between proficiency in learning a serial list and proficiency in learning a paired-associate list derived from that list. This, together with other findings in this and other studies by Jensen (1962b; 1962c; Jensen and Rohwer, 1965), has prompted him to interpret SL as a phenomenon requiring response learning only (cf. Mandler, Article 1, Chapter 2). In other words, the list in his view is not learned as a sequence of *St-R* associations that would require separate stimuli for each component item as a response but rather as a single, integrated total response. During recall of the list, the stimulus that triggers the integrated massive response is likely to be some extra-list cue within the learning environs.

Serial Position Effects

Now that we have managed to impart the confusion extant on the identification of the functional stimulus, we are ready to confront another puzzling issue in SL—the existence of serial position effects. By serial position effects we are referring to two phenomena found in the distribution of errors (or correct responses) over the ordinal positions of a rotely learned serial list when *Ss* practice to some specified criterion of mastery. The two phenomena have been observed in countless experiments and seem to be parts of the facts of life for SL.

The first phenomenon is that of the "bowness" of the error distribution, with the concentration of errors being most dense in the middle positions and decreasing progressively in density toward both ends of the list. The second phenomenon, "skewness," calls attention to the fact that the peak of the error concentration is commonly *not* in the middle position of the list but is displaced toward the right of middle (i.e., toward the end of the list). Suppose, for example, that the mean number of errors to criterion by a group of *Ss* on our *A-B-* · · · *-G* list is 100. A typical distribution of errors for the seven ordinal positions, reflecting both bowness and skewness, would be the following:

	Item						
	A	*B*	*C*	*D*	*E*	*F*	*G*
Mean number of errors	6	10	15	20	25	15	9

Theoretical attempts at explaining serial position effects (i.e., hypothesizing processes accounting for the effects) have had a long history. The important theories in existence before the period covered in this book have been given an excellent summary by McGeoch and Irion (1952, Chapter 3). In most cases the earlier theories stressed either inhibitory or interfering processes which distibute themselves unevenly over the ordinal positions of a list. The inhibition theory which has stimulated the greatest amount of research has undoubtedly been that of Lepley (1934) and Hull (1935). The contemporary period of research, however, has been marked by a preponderance of evidence that has failed to support some basic tenets of the theory. Because of the great impact of this theory on SL research, we shall discuss its more important facets below.

The Lepley-Hull theory proffers a classical conditioning model of SL, with serial position effects as a by-product. The conditioned stimulus for a given item as a response is assumed to involve both an attribute of the immediately preceding item (as in the specificity hypothesis described earlier) and traces of these attributes for all other preceding items in the list. For example, in our *A-B-* · · · *-G* list, Item *A* as a stimulus enters into the direct forward conditioning of Item *B* as a response, via a positive excitatory tendency, and as a trace stimulus for all other items (as responses) in the list. For Item *A* to evoke Item *B* as a response, the trace conditioning of *A* to Items *C*, *D*, *E*, *F*, and *G* must undergo an inhibition of delay. That is, the evocation of these other responses must be delayed until the appropriate points in the list are reached. There would then be five sources of inhibition present during the evocation of *B*. For Item *B* to evoke Item *C* as a response, the traces of *B* to responses *D*, *E*, *F*, and *G* must be inhibited (i.e., the responses must be delayed until the appropriate time) but so must the traces of *A* to responses *D*, *E*, *F*, and *G* in that the trace of *A* is part of the compound stimulus (namely, item *B* plus the trance of *A*) being conditioned to *C* as a response. In other words, there are eight sources of inhibition for Item *C* as a response. Similarly, we could identify nine sources of inhibition for Item *D* (three from *C*, three from *B*, and three from *A*), eight for Item *E* (two each from *D*, *C*, *B*, and *A*), and five for Item *F* (one each from *E*, *D*, *C*, *B*, and *A*). Item *A* and *G* would have no source of inhibition in that traces do not enter into their conditioning. The bowness of the error distribution is therefore explained by this postulated symmetrical distribution of inhibition. The theory, however, does have difficulty in accounting for the empirically established skew.

Proponents of the Lepley–Hull theory have reasoned that inhibition of delay, like reactive inhibition (cf. Kimble, 1961), is sensitive to temporal variables, such as the rate of exposing items to *S*. Since inhibition of delay is assumed to be greatest in the middle of the list, the effects of rate of exposure should be reflected more in that part of the list than in other parts. As the rate of exposure is increased from 2 seconds to 4 seconds per item, we would expect to find not only a corresponding decrease in the total number of errors but also a greater decrease in the middle positions than in the end positions; that is, the gradient or slope of the distribution of errors would be expected to be steeper, or more peaked, under 2 seconds than under 4 seconds of exposure. For many years, the presence of these differential gradients (e.g., Hovland, 1938) has been cited as the primary evidence supporting the Lepley–Hull theory.

In an important methodological article, McCrary and Hunter (1953) stated the need to consider the gradient of relative errors as well as that of absolute errors (the error measure employed by Hovland and other earlier investigators) when examining serial position effects. Temporal variables may well alter the gradients for absolute errors but not for relative errors by simply raising or lowering the number of errors by some constant factor throughout the list. Previously we gave a hypothetical distribution of 100 total errors over seven positions. Suppose another group of *Ss* averaged 50 errors on the same list and that these errors averaged 2.5, 5, 10, 15, 10, 5, and 2.5 for positions 1 through 7, respectively. A plot of these two absolute distributions would reveal a far steeper gradient for the first group than for the second. If, however, we determine the per cent of the total number of errors separately for each ordinal position (a relative measure), we may see that the percentages are the same at each position for the two distributions (5%, 10%, 20%, 30%, 20%, 10%, and 5%). As to the Hovland finding of differential gradients for varying exposure rates, McCrary and Hunter discovered that temporal variables altered the gradients when errors were expressed absolutely but not when they were expressed relatively. A comparable finding was later reported by Braun and

Heymann (1958). Evidence of this kind strongly suggests that inhibition of the Lepley–Hull variety, if present at all in SL, is *not* distributed unevenly over ordinal positions as demanded by the theory.

Additional reasons for questioning the validity of the Lepley–Hull theory were provided by Jensen (1962c) and Bowman and Thurlow (1963). Jensen, in a study employing geometric forms rather than conventional verbal materials, reasoned that theories based on conditioning concepts should predict bowness only when the temporally sequential aspects of SL are preserved. In a series of clever experiments, he discovered that the classical features of error distributions over serial positions remain largely unchanged when methods other than temporal ordering (e.g. spatial ordering in which *S* is exposed to a specific order in its totality and then asked to reconstruct the order) are used. He concluded that the Lepley–Hull type of theory is either incorrect or is not general enough to explain the occurrence of bowness under methods other than temporal ordering. Bowman and Thurlow felt that the Lepley–Hull type theory should not predict bowness when serial position qua position is systematically varied over trials but the relative serial order is held constant (e.g., *A-B-C-D-E-F-G* as the order on Trial 1, *B-C-D-E-F-G-A* on Trial 2, *C-D-E-F-G-H-A-B* on Trial 3, etc.). According to these authors, the theory should now predict equal sources of inhibition at each position. However, their error frequencies when plotted against position on Trial 1 closely resembled the classically bowed distribution, again refuting the conditioning theory.

The reader may well be wondering what, if anything, seems to be replacing the Lepley–Hull theory. In the editor's opinion, the trend has been toward more empirically oriented explanations that place less reliance on theoretical constructs borrowed from other learning phenomena. The Deese and Kresse (Article 3) and Glanzer and Peters (Article 4) studies are illustrative of this approach, with the former analyzing the kinds of errors made during SL and their separate distributions and the latter analyzing the characteristics of beginning and end points of a list.

The Glanzer and Peters study is especially relevant to the recent emphasis on explaining position effects in terms of either response integration (Jensen, 1962c; see p. 14) or forward and backward learning occurring at differential rates (Ribback and Underwood, 1950). According to Jensen, the first item serves as the anchoring point for beginning the response integration of the separate items. The *S* then learns new component responses (items) by attaching them to previously learned ones in an all-or-none manner. This procedure is likely to progress around the anchor item in both the forward (toward the second item, then third, etc.) and backward (toward the last item, then next to last, etc.) direction. Thus, for our *A-B-* · · · *-G* list, Item *A* is likely to be learned first, with Item *B* then attached to *A*, followed by Item *G* attached to *A*, Item *C* attached to *A-B*, Item *F attached to G-A*, etc. From this point, Jensen's further empirical analysis leads to an explanation of both bowness and skewness. The Ribback and Underwood analysis is less thoroughly developed than that of Jensen. It postulates the existence of two separate learning processes, forward and backward, during SL. Forward learning is initiated at the beginning of the list and backward learning at the end. If forward learning is assumed to take place at a faster rate than backward learning, the skew in the error distribution may be understood. The finding by Glanzer and Peters of anchoring effects associated with the beginning and end points of a list may then be taken as support for the interpretation of either Jensen or Ribback and Underwood.

Finally, we should note that not all of the contemporary attempts to explain position effects have relied upon learning processes as explanatory devices. Murdock (1960), for example, reviewed the literature on position effects and concluded that processes other than learning-related ones are likely to be involved. He speaks of the "distinctiveness of stimuli," a concept which seems to have psychophysical undertones. By assuming a logarithmic progression of distinctiveness with ordinality in a serial list, he was able to account for some position effects.

Remote Associations

The third subphenomenon, the purported existence of remote associations, dates back to the pioneering work of Ebbinghaus (1885). Remote associations refer to the establishment of associations between an item (e.g., *D*) in a serial list as a stimulus and items other than the immediately adjacent items (e.g., *C* and *E*) as responses. The adjacent *D-E* association, of course, takes us back to a chaining position, and the adjacent *D-C* association is comparable to the backward learning discussed previously in connection with the Ribback and Underwood hypothesis (1950). Remote associations have been postulated as existing in both the forward (e.g., *D-F*) and backward direction (e.g., *D-B*).

The reader by now suscepts a close relationship between the concept of remote associations and the issues at stake in the other subphenomena of SL—and how right he is. Fortunately, for both the reader and the editor, this relationship has been given an exceptionally fine analysis by Slamecka (1964a; Article 5) and will not be extended here. The Slamecka article also contains an historical review of the remote association concept and the methodologies related to the study of the concept. Most importantly, the article contains empirical evidence which weighs heavily against the existence of remote association. For further obviation of the concept, the reader is referred to a study by Hakes, James, and Young (1964).

As is often the case in psychology, including the psychology of verbal learning, critical issues are not easily resolved, and the door to complete closure remains ajar. Such is the case with remote associations. Both Dallett (1965) and Bugelski (1965) have identified what they feel are logical and empirical errors in the Slamecka analysis. Bugelski states it firmly:

> It is my contention that Slamecka has concocted an ingenious and plausible, but incorrect, account of the process of serial learning. Much of what he has to say is indisputable, and, granting his assumptions, much of his argument appears unassailable. Closer examination, however, suggests that the attack is directed at a series of straw men, and that the traditional views Slamecka hopes to deny are hardly affected. It is, however, proper to point out that the fresh approach taken by Slamecka has produced a number of dividends in our understanding of serial learning. . . . (Bugelski, 1965; p. 169).

Bugelski offered evidence of his own for the existence of remote associations. His procedure involved the single presentation of a serial list, followed by recall in the serial order. He found a large number of forward associations, mostly of first-order remoteness, with fewer second-order, still fewer third-order, etc. Considerably fewer backward associations were yielded.

One may well anticipate a counterattack by the antiremote association forces in the near future. In fact, Slamecka (1965) has already provided a battle strategy. Only through the process of careful examination of methodological differences, the refinement of procedures, and continuing empirical analysis will closure be attained on this issue.

ARTICLE 1

Backward Serial Learning

ROBERT K. YOUNG, JUDITH PATTERSON, AND WILLIAM M. BENSON

The University of Texas, Austin, Texas

While research concerned with backward learning in a paired-associate task has attracted a great deal of interest, similar research using serial lists has been virtually ignored.

Only three studies of backward learning in which serial lists were used have been conducted (Ebbinghaus, 1913; Garrett and Hartman, 1926; Trowbridge, 1938). Positive transfer was obtained by Ebbinghaus and by Garrett and Hartman when a serial list (symbolized A-B-C-D-E-F) was learned and then relearned with the items arranged in reverse order (symbolized F-E-D-C-B-A), while zero transfer was obtained by Trowbridge. It should be noted that in the studies by Ebbinghaus and by Garrett and Hartman the effects of practice, warm-up, and item learning were all uncontrolled and these variables may have been related to the positive transfer obtained in the two studies. In the Trowbridge study, which employed an alphabet-learning task, when such controls were introduced, positive transfer was not obtained and no differences were found between experimental and control conditions.

Recently a series of studies (Young, 1959, 1961, 1962) has investigated the hypothesis that the functional stimulus in serial learning is the item immediately preceding the response to be given. This hypothesis, called the specificity hypothesis, assumes that associations are formed between the items of a serial list. The cited research has, however, been unable to find consistent support for such a position.

A second hypothesis also dealing with the functional stimulus in serial learning, called the serial-position hypothesis, assumes that the position an item holds in the list is the effective stimulus. Evidence in support of this position has been found (Young, 1962).

Predictions about backward serial learning may be made by both the specificity and serial-position hypotheses. The specificity hypothesis assumes associations have been formed between adjacent items during first-list learning and, as a consequence, positive transfer should occur from the first to the second list. The serial-position hypothesis, on the other hand, must restrict its predictions to the learning of specific items within the list, basing these predictions on the similarity of serial positions between the first and second lists.

Suppose a serial list is learned and then relearned with the items arranged in reverse order. The items in the middle of the list hold similar serial positions in both the first and second list, while items at the extremes hold dissimilar positions. Under these conditions, the position hypothesis would predict that positive transfer would occur for those items in the middle of the list and that this transfer would decrease the closer an item is to the extremes of the list.

The present study investigates backward serial learning. We will attempt to gain information about transfer from one serial list to another and, in addition, compare the results obtained to those predicted by the specificity and the position hypotheses.

Reprinted with permission of the authors and the publisher, the Academic Press. The article appeared originally in the *Journal of Verbal Learning and Verbal Behavior*, 1963, **1**, 335–338.

Method

Each of the 40 *Ss* learned two serial lists of 12 items each (with the first item serving as the cue symbol). The *Ss* in Group EE ($N = 20$) learned a serial list and then relearned it with the items arranged in reverse order, while the *Ss* in Group CE ($N = 20$) learned a dissimilar serial list (List C) and then learned one of the two lists learned by Group EE. The lists learned in Group EE were counterbalanced and each of the two EE lists was learned by half the *Ss* of Group CE. The C list may differ in difficulty from the two EE lists and the proper measure of transfer is a comparison of second-list learning. This analysis would then be based on a 2×2 factorial design in which Group would constitute the row variable and List would constitute the column variable.

The *Ss* were selected from introductory psychology classes at The University of Texas and randomly assigned to groups. Each *S* learned serial lists of two-syllable adjectives taken from Melton's lists (Hilgard, 1951). With the exception of the independent variable, the lists were so constructed that intralist and interlist similarity were as low as possible. Each list was presented by a projector at a 2-sec. rate of presentation with a 6-sec. inter-trial interval, and all lists were learned to a criterion of one perfect recitation. Approximately 1 min. elapsed between the learning of the two lists.

Results and Discussion

The mean numbers of trials to learn the lists are presented in Table 1. Analysis of

TABLE 1
MEAN NUMBERS OF TRIALS TO LEARN THE TWO LISTS

	List 1		List 2	
Group	Mean	SD	Mean	SD
EE	18.7	7.50	8.1	5.07
CE	19.0	7.14	9.7	3.86

the first list learned failed to yield a significant *F* and this gives some support to the assumption of equivalent groups. Analysis of the second list did not result in a significant difference between Groups EE and CE ($F = 1.11$, $df = 1/36$), failing to support the hypothesis of positive transfer when a serial list is relearned in reverse order. The second list was learned faster than the first ($F = 87.19$, $df = 1/36$, $P < .001$), apparently reflecting the influence of practice and warm-up effects.

Means of errors per trial are presented in Table 2. Analysis of the results for the

TABLE 2
MEAN NUMBERS OF ERRORS PER TRIAL

	List 1		List 2	
Group	Mean	SD	Mean	SD
EE	.96	.37	.72	.50
CE	1.03	.47	.77	.42

second list learned failed to yield a significant difference between groups ($F < 1.00$).

For the first list learned by Group EE the mean number of correct responses per trial at each successive serial position was as follows: .88, .69, .67, .44, .35, .37, .43, .38, .44, .58, .57. These points do not differ from what would be expected of a plot of serial position effects. The intent here is to indicate that the particular samples of *Ss* and items used do not result in a serial-position curve which can be described as atypical, at least during first-list learning.

The prediction that the items in the middle of the second list would be easier to learn for Group EE than for Group CE has been derived from the serial-position hypothesis. On this basis, it would be expected that the serial-position curves for the two groups would differ. This prediction was tested by an analysis of the quadratic component of the group by serial-position interaction. The two serial-position curves presented in Fig. 1 were found to differ ($F = 6.27$, $df = 1/36$, $P < .05$). As can be seen from Fig. 1, the items in the middle of the EE list were more often correct than the CE control items. Items at Positions 4, 5, 6, and 10 were more often correct in Group EE than in Group CE with *F*s of 12.32 ($df = 1/36$, $P < .01$), 4.32 ($P < .05$), 8.00 ($P < .01$), and 4.55 ($P < .05$), respectively. Each of these analyses constituted a 2×2 factorial design, with the rows being the group variable and the col-

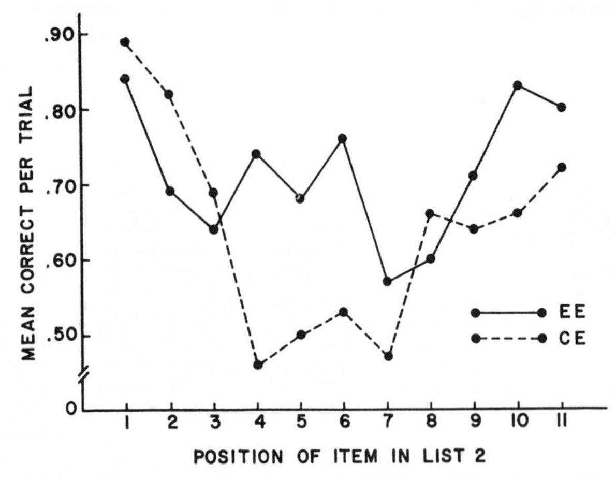

FIG. 1. Serial position curves for the second list learned by Groups EE and CE.

umns being the item variable. Within each analysis the same item served both as experimental and as control item, and any difference observed between groups must be attributed to the independent variable.

Transfer during early learning of the second list was also investigated as a function of serial position. The trial on which an item was first given correctly was analyzed. Although there seems little reason to suspect that the graph of these results would differ from the usual bowed curve, there is even less justification in making a prediction as specific as that made about the relationship between the two serial position curves. For this reason, the simple interaction between groups and serial position was computed and was found to be significant ($F = 2.83$, $df = 10/360$, $P < .01$). Despite the fact that the same items were learned at identical serial positions in both groups, the items in the middle of the EE lists were given earlier than the comparable CE items. Items at Positions 4, 5, 6, and 7 were given earlier in Group EE than in Group CE, with *F*s of 11.05 ($df = 1/36$, $P < .01$), 6.29 ($P < .05$), 7.11 ($P < .05$), and 8.81 ($P < .01$), respectively. No other *F*s approached significance.

In terms of trials to learn, little, if any, transfer obtains when a serial list is learned and then relearned with the items arranged in reverse order. Although the second list takes less than half as many trials to learn as the first list (confirming the results of Garrett and Hartman, 1926), this transfer may be accounted for in terms of warm-up and practice effects and is not attributable to the specific relations between items within the serial list.

The specificity hypothesis assumes that the nominal stimulus is the functional stimulus in serial learning (Young, 1961, 1962). If this assumption is valid, then backward learning should be no more difficult to demonstrate in serial learning than in paired-associate learning where it appears that the nominal stimulus is the functional stimulus. On the basis of the results of the present experiment, such backward learning appears to be difficult to demonstrate and the magnitude of the phenomenon, if present, appears to be minimal. The transfer data of the present experiment fail to provide evidence favorable to a specificity interpretation.

It was noted that the usual bowed serial-position effects were obtained from the first list learned by Group EE. At the end of first-list learning the end items had been given correctly more often than the middle items and, from the specificity hypothesis, the end items should have stronger associations than the items in the middle. On this basis, transfer, when compared to the control, should be greater for the end items than for the items in the middle of the list. Contrary to such a prediction, positive transfer was observed in the middle of the list but not at the ends.

The data found in the present study tend to support the hypothesis that the functional stimulus in serial learning is the position the item holds in the list. Items holding similar ordinal positions in the first and second lists were learned faster and given correctly more often than those items which did not hold similar ordinal positions. It should be noted, however, that other conceptions of the nature of serial learning can also be employed to interpret the results of the present experiment. For example, it has been shown that generalization of serial position (serial confusion) occurs to the greatest extent in the middle of the list (Schulz, 1955). On this basis, the bowed curve commonly observed in serial learning can be interpreted in terms of stimulus generalization (i.e., generalization of serial position). This interpretation in turn may be used to explain the atypical curve observed in the learning of List 2 by Group EE. If during first-list learning greater reduction of generalization occurred in the middle than at the ends of the list and if this differential reduction in generalization transferred to the second list, then the middle of the second list would be easier to learn than a suitable control.

Summary

An experiment was conducted which investigated backward serial learning. The basic design was such that *S* learned a serial list and then relearned it with the same items arranged in reverse order. Positive transfer was not obtained when it was measured in terms of trials to learn. The items in the middle of the list being relearned in reverse order were learned faster and given correctly more often than the same items in the control list. These results were interpreted as favorable to an hypothesis which assumes that the functional stimulus in serial learning is the position the item holds in the list.

References

Ebbinghaus, H. *Memory: A contribution to experimental psychology* (1885). Trans. by H. A. Ruger and C. E. Bussenius. New York: Teachers Coll., Columbia Univer., 1913.

Garrett, H. E., and Hartman, G. W. An experiment on backward association in learning. *Amer. J. Psychol.,* 1926, **37**, 241-246.

Hilgard, E. R. Methods and procedures in the study of learning. In S. S. Stevens (Ed.) *Handbook of experimental psychology.* New York: Wiley, 1951. Pp. 517-567.

Schulz, R. W. Generalization of serial position in rote serial learning. *J. exp. Psychol.,* 1955, **49**, 267-272.

Trowbridge, M. H. A study of backward and forward remote associations. *J. exp. Psychol.,* 1938, **22**, 319-337.

Young, R. K. A comparison of two methods of learning serial associations. *Amer. J. Psychol.,* 1959, **72**, 554-559.

Young, R. K. The stimulus in serial verbal learning. *Amer. J. Psychol.,* 1961, **74**, 517-528.

Young, R. K. Tests of three hypotheses about the stimulus in serial learning. *J. exp. Psychol.,* 1962, **63**, 307-313.

(Received August 27, 1962)

ARTICLE 2

Transfer between Paired-Associate and Serial Learning[1,2]

ARTHUR R. JENSEN

University of California, Berkeley, California

The psychological differences between paired-associate and serial learning are probably far more profound than their formal differences would seem to suggest. Indeed, among S-R oriented psychologists the reaction to a number of studies which compare these two forms of rote learning has generally been one of surprise. The principal experimental investigations of the problem have been carried out by Young (1959, 1961a, 1962). Underwood (1961) recently reviewed the literature on the problem, including a number of unpublished studies, and has indicated their theoretical importance.

The traditional S-R conception of serial learning, which Young (1961a) refers to as the *specificity hypothesis,* represents serial learning as the acquisition of a chain of S-R associations. The stimulus for each successive response is assumed to be the item which immediately precedes it in the list. Thus, each item in the chain (except the first and last) is considered to have a *double function,* serving in turn as a response and as a stimulus.

This hypothesis that a serial list is learned essentially as a chain of paired associates (PA) implies that there should be a high degree of positive transfer from a previously learned serial list, A-B-C-D, etc., to learning a PA list, A-B, B-C, C-D, etc., even when the pairs are presented in a different order on each trial, as is usually done in PA learning. Conversely, a similarly high degree of transfer should be expected from a previously learned set of PAs, A-B, B-C, C-D, etc., to learning a serial list, A-B-C-D, etc. Now the main point of interest is the fact that the evidence clearly does not support these expectations. Briefly, as of now, the research presents the following points.

Transfer from a Serial to a PA List. Only a negligible amount of transfer has been found in going from a serial to a PA list in which the S-R elements are common to both tasks (Young, 1959, 1961a, 1962). For example, in Young's 1959 study, despite the fact that all the S-R elements were common to the serial and the PA tasks, there was only 8% transfer, a statistically nonsignificant amount. This is typical of Young's later findings. A significant amount of transfer appeared only in the first few learning trials, but the over-all transfer in these studies was practically nil. It was also found that 10 trials of overlearning of the serial list still did not result in significant transfer to the PA list (Young, 1962).

Transfer from PA to Serial List. Here the picture is quite different. There has generally been found a moderate degree of transfer from PA to serial learning when the S-R elements are common to both lists. Primoff (1938) found 35% transfer; Young (1959) found 55%. Since even this amount of transfer is less than one might expect, considering that the PA list was always learned to a criterion of mastery, Underwood (1961, p.

1 This research was aided by a National Science Foundation grant to the Center for Human Learning.

2 An abstract of this article was presented at the annual meeting of the Western Psychological Association, San Francisco, California, April, 1962.

Reprinted with permission of the author and the publisher, the Academic Press. The article appeared originally in the *Journal of Verbal Learning and Verbal Behavior*, 1962, 1, 269–280.

18) has suggested that learning serial lists in the manner of a chain of PAs, though possible, may not be "natural" for the *S*. Transfer from the PA to the serial list is far less than perfect, perhaps, because in going through the serial list as if it were a chain of the previously learned PAs, the *S* must overcome some tendency to relearn the list in a different manner which is peculiar and "natural" to serial learning. The amount of transfer may reflect mainly the extent to which the *S* is successful in maintaining the *set* for responding to the serial task as if it were a PA task.

The present experiment is directly concerned with this problem. The main question is whether there is greater transfer from PA to serial learning when it is made relatively easy for the *S* to maintain the set for PA learning when going to the serial list than when it is made more difficult for the *S* to maintain his set for PA learning.

One other finding in the literature is quite relevant to the design of the present experiment. This concerns the difference between *double-function* and *single-function* PA lists. In a double-function list each item serves both as a stimulus and as a response, e.g., A-B, B-C, C-D, etc. In an single-function list the S and R terms are entirely separate, e.g., A-B, C-D, E-F, etc. Primoff (1938) was the first to note the great difference in difficulty of learning these two forms of PA task. The *Ss* required two to three times as many trials to learn the double-function lists as they needed for the single-function lists. Young (1961b) performed an experiment which substantiated Primoff's findings and permitted a more generalized explanation of the phenomenon in terms of the known effects of intralist similarity on rate of learning: the rate of PA learning is inversely related to the degree of stimulus-response similarity. Primoff attributed the greater difficulty of learning the double-function than the single-function lists to the inhibitory effect of backward associations. This is also an empirically valid observation. In learning PAs such as A-B, B-C, etc., *Ss* often give A rather than C as the response to B. These first-order backward associations rarely occur in serial learning, where the order of presentation is constant, probably because the *S* can remember the item one position back, since it has so recently been given as a response. Consequently, when *S* goes from a serial to a PA list of the double-function type, he is plagued by a source of errors—first-order backward associations—which he did not have to overcome during serial learning, with the result that positive transfer appears only on the first few trials of serial learning. Soon the errors of backward association overtake any initial transfer effect, and the total amount of transfer at the end of learning is practically zero.

That the inhibitory effect of backward associations in the double-function PA list is not the sole cause of poor transfer from serial to PA learning, however, is shown by an unpublished study by Young and Benson (cited in Underwood, 1961, p. 19), in which only a small amount of transfer occurred even when the PA task was a single-function list.

Findings such as these, which run counter to the expectations of the specificity hypothesis, have given rise to two alternative hypotheses: the *compound-stimulus hypothesis* and the *serial-position hypothesis*.

According to the compound-stimulus hypothesis, the functional stimulus in serial learning is not a single item but a compound of two or more items preceding the response term. Thus, the functional stimulus for D in the list A-B-C-D might be BC or ABC. Under investigation this hypothesis has fared no better than the specificity hypothesis. When *two* items in the learned serial list were used as the stimulus term in the PA transfer task, there was still no positive transfer (Young and Benson, unpublished, cited in Underwood, 1961, p. 19; Young,

1962). In the latter study there was even negative transfer!

According to the serial-position hypothesis, originally proposed by Woodworth and Poffenberger (1920, pp. 71-72), the functional stimulus in serial learning is the ordinal position, or some symbolic equivalent thereof, of each item in the list. The results of experimental investigations of this hypothesis seem to be conflicting [Rehula (Unpublished Ph.D. dissertation cited in Underwood, 1961, p. 21); Jensen and Blank, 1962; Young, 1962; Newman and Saltz, 1962]. Yet it appears from this evidence that whatever cue function serial position per se may possibly have, it is probably of minor importance, and Underwood's conclusion that the functional stimulus in serial learning has not as yet been identified still seems valid (Underwood, 1961, p. 22).

The purpose of the present experiment was to test the hypothesis that the "natural" way of learning a serial list is psychologically different from PA learning in that serial learning does not consist of chaining together successive pairs of S-R elements. According to this hypothesis, whatever transfer to serial learning results from the prior learning of a derived PA list (aside from generalized transfer effects such as warm-up, stimulus differentiation, and response integration) is due to the *S*'s tendency to carry over the "set" for PA learning to the serial list. Thus, there should be relatively less transfer from a PA list to a serial list when it is made difficult for *S* to maintain the "set" for PA learning. The *S* will then tend to learn the serial list in a manner peculiar to serial learning, resulting in less transfer from the prior PA learning than if the PA set were maintained.

Method

Design

Two experimental groups were compared for relative transfer from PA to serial (S) learning. Group PA(Odd)-S first learned a single-function list of PAs having the odd-numbered items of the derived 9-item serial list as the stimulus terms, thus: 1-2, 3-4, 5-6, 7-8. Group PA(Even)-S learned first the even pairs: 2-3, 4-5, 6-7, 8-9. The second task for both groups was, of course, the same serial list: 1 2 3 4 5 6 7 8 9. It was hypothesized that the Odd Group, for whom the serial list begins with a pair already learned (1-2), should find it easier to maintain the PA set than would the Even Group. Thus, if a different strategy exists for serial than for PA learning, the Even Group should be more prone than the Odd Group to lose the set for PA learning and to adopt the strategy of serial learning.

A Control Group learned the serial list first. In order to assess transfer from the serial to the PA list, some of these *S*s then learned the odd PA list.

Transfer due to response integration and acquisition per se was minimized by composing the serial and PA lists of colored forms, which in previous experiments have been shown to attain high response availability as soon as they have been described in the preliminary instructions to the *S*. Thus, practically all the learning that occurs with these stimuli involves only the associative phase of PA or serial learning. Since a preliminary study indicated that the PA task would have been too difficult for most *S*s if the pacing interval had been the same as in the serial learning (3 sec.), and since it was desired to have *S*s overlearn the first task to a rigorous criterion and yet not be unduly fatigued or suffer a motivational slump by the beginning of the second task, it was decided to use self-pacing in the PA task.

An aspect of procedure that is probably unique in PA-serial transfer experiments is that the *S*s here were clearly informed of the method by which the PA list was made up from the serial list (and vice versa), and in going from the first to the second task they were explicitly instructed to try to use the S-R connections they had acquired in the first task. The experiment was represented to the *S*s as a test to determine how well they could transfer what they learned in one situation to another. This procedure more or less insured that any failure of transfer to occur could not be attributed to the *S*'s failure to perceive the possibility for transfer from the first to the second task.

Subjects

The *S*s were 171 juniors and seniors (35 men and 136 women) recruited from an introductory course in educational psychology at the University of California. Three women were eliminated from the experiment for refusing to persist in the first task until they attained the criterion. Of the remaining 168 *S*s, all attained the criterion on both the first and second tasks. The number of *S*s in each treatment group was as follows: 25 in Group S—PA (Odd); 54 in Group PA(Odd)—S; 54 in Group PA(Even)—S. The serial learning data from a control group ($N = 35$) which learned only the serial list was combined with the serial data of Groups S—PA(Odd), and these combined data were used as the control (with $N = 60$) against which relative transfer was measured in the two groups (Odd and Even) going from PA to serial learning.

Procedure

The PA and serial lists were presented by two different apparatuses. The *S* sat a few feet in front of the apparatuses and could change from the apparatus used in the first task to that used in the second merely by turning 90 degrees in a swivel chair.

The stimulus items common to all tasks were colored forms—squares, triangles, and circles colored red, yellow, and blue. In the serial list from which the PAs were composed, each form appeared once in each of the three colors, and items of the same shape or the same color were never adjacent in the list. The color-forms appeared approximately 2 in. in size on the screen and the colors were vivid.

Instructions. All *S*s were told five things: (*a*) all the items to be learned would consist of color-forms (as described above) and items of the same shape or the same color would never be adjacent in the list; (*b*) the *S* was to learn by the anticipation method, by saying, for example, "red triangle," "blue square," etc., and guessing was encouraged from the first trial on; (*c*) *S* had to learn to a criterion of three consecutive errorless trials; (*d*) the serial task would be paced at a 3-sec. rate and the PA task would be unpaced (or self-paced); (*e*) the second task would be made up of the same S-R connections learned in the first task, for this was a test to see how well the *S* could transfer the first-task learning to the second task.

The procedure for PA learning or serial learning was exactly the same whether it was the first task or the second.

PA Task. The paired stimuli, first one and then the two together, appeared in two side-by-side ground-glass windows about 2 in. apart. On each trial the stimulus item was first presented alone in the left-hand window until the *S* made his anticipation and then the response term appeared in the right-hand window; the two items were displayed simultaneously for approximately 2 sec. and then the screen went blank for approximately 2 sec. before the next stimulus item appeared. The interval between the S and R terms was governed by each *S*'s own rate of responding. The order of presentation of the four PAs was different for every *S* and was random on every trial, with two exceptions: (*a*) the same pair was never repeated in immediate succession; and (*b*) every pair was presented once within each set of four presentations. The *S*s learned to a criterion of three successive errorless trials, each trial consisting of all four PAs.

When the PA task came first, immediately on attaining the criterion the *S* was told to turn to the other display panel and was reminded to try to transfer the PAs he had just acquired to the serial list about to be presented. The *S* began anticipating the serial list on its first presentation.

Serial Task. The 9-item serial list was always preceded by a green light as the signal for the first anticipation. The items were presented at a 3-sec. rate, with a 6-sec. intertrial interval. The *S*s learned to a criterion of three successive errorless trials.

When the serial task came first, immediately upon attaining the criterion, the *S* was told to turn to the other display panel and to try to transfer the S-R connections he had just acquired to the PA list.

RESULTS

Since the primary concern was the *relative* amounts of transfer in the two experimental conditions [PA(Odd)—S and PA(Even)—S], no attempt was made to equate the experimental and control groups for generalized transfer effects such as warm-up and learning-to-learn, as would be necessary in order to establish the absolute amount of specific transfer. Since the two experimental groups did not differ in the first-task learning (PA), it can be safely assumed the generalized practice effects were the same for both groups.

Two measures of performance were used: number of trials to criterion (of three successive errorless trials) and the percentage of errors (100 $\times$ the ratio of errors to all opportunities for error).

The principal results of the experiment are summarized in Tables 1 and 2.

Transfer of Serial-Position Effect to Paired-Associate Learning

As shown in the lower half of Table 1, Group S-PA(Odd) learned faster than the corresponding control group (PA Odd); the differences both for trials to criterion and for percent errors are significant beyond the .001 level ($t = 3.34$ and 5.74, respectively).

TABLE 1
SUMMARY OF DATA ON LEARNING UNDER THE DIFFERENT CONDITIONS

Group	Trial 1 errors		Trials to criterion		Per cent errors	
	M	*SD*	*M*	*SD*	*M*	*SD*
			Serial Learning			
Control	7.83	1.10	24.98	7.73	43.49	7.31
PA(Odd)—S	5.70	1.49	16.50	6.91	36.69	9.90
PA(Even)—S	7.02	1.48	22.48	8.40	42.87	9.01
			PA Learning			
PA(Even)			17.48	5.97	43.99	12.80
PA(Odd)			18.54	7.28	48.02	12.21
S—PA(Odd)			12.24	7.83	30.97	12.02

The relative amounts of transfer to PA learning for the individual pairs is a function of the serial position held by the items during serial learning, as shown in Fig. 1. Note how perfectly the serial-position curve emerges in the transfer to the PA learning, even though the pairs were always presented in a different order. The control group pairs would form a practically straight horizontal line in Fig. 1. Analysis of variance yielded a Groups $\times$ Positions interaction significant beyond the .001 level. Apparently by the end of serial learning the items differ in associative strength according to serial-position, with the earliest learned items being the most overlearned and consequently having the greatest associative strength.

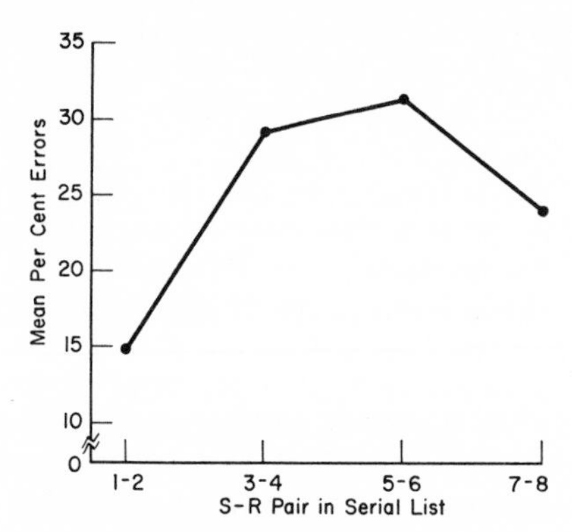

FIG. 1. Mean percentage of errors made on each of the pairs in the PA transfer task. The numbers on the abscissa indicate the serial positions occupied by the S and R members of the pair during the serial learning which preceded the PA task, in which the S-R pairs were presented in a random order.

It seems clear that *S*s, after learning (or overlearning) a serial list, are to some extent able to respond to the appropriately derived paired-associates as if the serial list had been learned in accordance with the specificity hypothesis. The basic question, however, is whether the acquisition of a chain of S-R associations is *essential* to serial learning or is merely *incidental* learning.

Transfer from Paired-Associate to Serial Learning

PA Learning. As shown in Table 1, the means and standard deviations of the two transfer groups, PA(Odd)—S and PA(Even)—S, do not differ significantly on either of the measures in the first-task PA learning. The Odd and Even pairs are quite equivalent. For trials and for percent errors the t's are 1.00 and 1.66, respectively.

Serial Learning. Group PA(Odd)—S showed significantly faster learning of the serial list than Group PA(Even)—S. For trials to criterion, $t = 4.01$, for percent errors $t = 3.36$; for both, $P < .001$. The Odd Group differs significantly from the Control Group at the .001 level ($t = 6.11$ and 4.10 for trials and percent errors, respectively), while the Even Group does not differ significantly from the Control Group ($t = 1.63$ and < 1.00 for trials and percent errors, respectively).

TABLE 2
RESULTS FOR ITEMS PREVIOUSLY LEARNED AND ITEMS NOT PREVIOUSLY LEARNED IN TRANSFER FROM PA TO SERIAL LIST

Group	Trial 1 errors		Errors		Per cent errors	
	M	*SD*	*M*	*SD*	*M*	*SD*
			Previously Learned Items			
Control (Odd)	3.41	0.71	41.12	15.53	46.80	11.43
Control (Even)	3.56	0.64	42.32	16.85	47.90	8.61
PA(Odd)—S	1.50	1.17	17.02	12.07	29.30	13.54
PA(Even)—S	2.33	1.17	34.72	19.50	43.63	12.67
			Not Previously Learned Items			
Control (Odd)	4.42	0.74	45.48	17.50	41.45	7.42
Control (Even)	4.27	0.93	43.83	16.26	39.97	8.04
PA(Odd)—S	4.20	0.83	28.22	16.31	42.14	11.19
PA(Even)—S	4.69	0.57	41.57	18.14	44.12	6.02

As shown in Table 2, transfer is considerably greater for the associations specifically learned in the PA task than for those that were not a part of the PA task, and this is true for both the Odd and Even Groups. The Odd Group showed significantly faster learning than the Even Group both for items previously learned and for items not previously learned (in terms of number of errors to criterion, $t = 5.62$, $P < .001$, for previously learned items, and $t = 3.98$, $P < .001$, for not previously learned items).

First-Trial Data. Is the transfer from PA to serial learning an immediate effect or is it more a "savings" effect which shows up only later in the course of serial learning? Comparison of the first-trial data of the transfer and control groups, shown in Table 1, provides the answer. (The first-trial responses of the Control Group were pure guessing, since *S*s were required to begin anticipating on the very first presentation of the list.) The amount of transfer on the first trial is comparable to that for the entire course of learning. Again, the Odd Group shows significantly more transfer than the Even Group ($t = 4.57$, $P < .001$). Note, however, that on the first trial the Even Group is also significantly better than the Control Group, but this advantage is mostly lost in later trials. As one would expect, the only significant transfer on the first trial occurs on the associations previously learned in the PA task.

Failures to Respond. Did the Odd Group tend to carry over the PA "strategy" into serial learning to a greater extent than did the Even Group? That is, did the Odd Group tend more than the Even Group to regard the serial list as a chain of S-R pairs? If so, it would seem reasonable to expect a relatively greater percentage of failures to respond for the Odd Group on those items which were stimulus terms in the PA task. The items that *preceded* each of these in the serial list, having been response terms in the PA list, had thus never functioned as stimuli. Some change in the *S*'s "set" would seem necessary for these terms to elicit anticipations, as required by the serial task. The question, then, is, does the Odd Group change "set" less readily than the Even Group?

Since the Odd and Even Groups differ in total error rate, it is necessary, to examine this point properly, first to determine the percentage of all errors that are failures to respond. This was done separately for each position in the serial list, except for the items that never appeared in the PA list, i.e., the last item of the serial list for the Odd Group and the first item for the Even Group (these items were omitted from this analysis). From these data, on which the Odd and Even Groups were now, in effect, equated for total errors at each serial position, it was possible to compare the percentage of *failures* on the items that had been *stimulus* terms and on those that had been *response* terms in the PA list. The PA stimulus terms (Positions 1, 3, 5, 7) for the Odd Group account for 60% of the failures to respond in serial learning; the response terms account for 40%. The PA stimulus terms (Positions 2, 4, 6, 8) for the Even Group account for 48 per cent of the failures in serial learning; the response terms account for 52 per cent. (When the percentage of failures is not corrected for total error rate, the PA stimulus terms for the Odd and Even Groups account for 68% and 53% of the total failures, respectively.)

These results are highly consistent with the notion that the Odd Group tends to regard the serial list as a chain of PAs and therefore experiences relatively greater difficulty in making responses to the *response* terms carried over from the PA task. The *S*s tended simply to *wait* for the next stimulus item, as they had done in the PA learning, rather than to anticipate the next item, as required by the serial task. The Even Group, on the other hand, showed practically no difference in failure rate between the PA stimulus and response terms in serial learning.

Serial-Position Effects. The serial-position curves show the differences between the Odd and Even Groups most strikingly. The curves in Fig. 2 plotted in terms of mean errors at each position, clearly show the effects of the prior PA learning for the Odd Group, while the Even Group produced an almost typical serial-position curve. (Since the curve for the Control Group was quite typical, it was not entered in this graph.) It appears that the Even Group tended to lose its paired associations in going to the serial list, while the Odd Group was able to some extent to

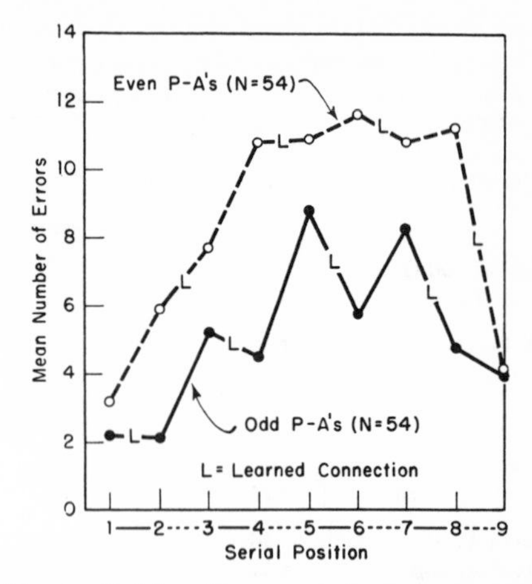

FIG. 2. Serial-position curves showing mean errors at each position for the serial transfer groups PA (Odd)—S and PA(Even)—S. The S-R connections that had been learned in the prior PA task are indicated by the letter *L*, and by the solid (Odd) and dotted (Even) lines connecting the numbers on the abscissa.

transfer the PA connections to the serial learning. In order to get a closer look at this phenomenon, it was decided to plot the serial-position curves in terms of each one-fourth of the trials to criterion. Figures 3, 4, and 5 show the serial-position curves of the Control, Odd, and Even Groups, respectively, when the curves are plotted in terms of the mean errors made in each quarter.

It is evident in Fig. 4 that the serial-position curves of the Odd Group continue to reflect the marked transfer effects of the previously learned items through at least the first half of the trials-to-criterion. In the Even Group (Fig. 5), on the other hand, the effects of the PA learning are reflected only in the first fourth of the trials, after which the serial-position curve begins to assume a more or less typical appearance. By the last fourth of learning, the curves of both groups are fairly typical serial-position curves and resemble closely that of the Control Group (Fig. 3). These results seem to suggest that the Odd Group may show greater transfer mainly because they were better

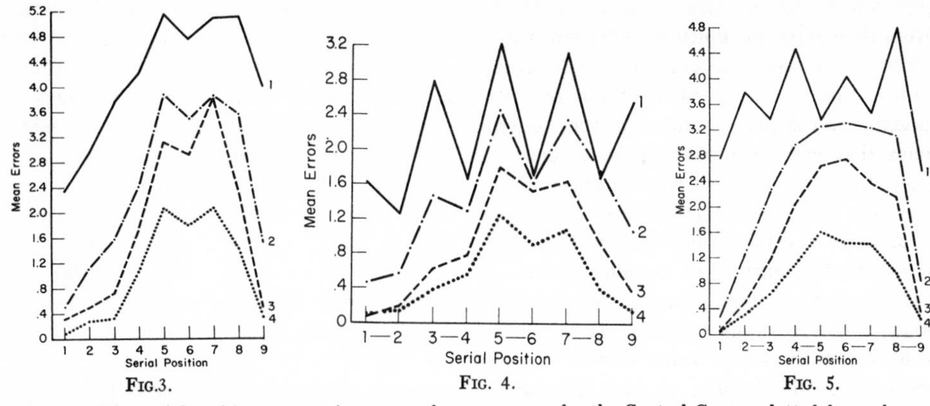

FIG. 3. The serial-position curves, in terms of mean errors, for the Control Group, plotted for each one-fourth of the trials to the criterion of three successive errorless trials.

FIG. 4. The serial-position curves, in terms of mean errors, for the PA(Odd)—S group, plotted for each one-fourth of the trials to the criterion of three successive errorless trials. The lines connecting the numbers on the abscissa indicate the S-R connections learned in the PA task.

FIG. 5. The serial-position curves, in terms of mean errors, for the PA(Even)—S group, plotted for each one-fourth of the trials to the criterion of three successive errorless trials. The lines connecting the numbers on the abscissa indicate the S-R connections learned in the PA task.

able to retain the PA set in the serial learning. The fact that they were not completely successful in this is shown by the less than perfect transfer even on the previously learned items and by the emergence of rather typical serial-position curves in the last half of learning.

The "Fate" of a Single, Learned Paired Associate. Was the Even Group more or less forced into abandoning the PA associations in order to be able to learn the list in accordance with some different strategy peculiar and "natural" to serial learning? To get at this, learning curves were plotted for single items. Figure 6 shows a typical set of such curves. It shows the percentage of errors (or the percentage of *S*s who fail to give the correct response) made on each of the first 11 trials (which is approximately half the mean number of trials to criterion) on the item nearest the middle position in the list which had been learned as a response in the PA task. Thus, for the Odd Group is shown the learning curve for Position 6 (which had been learned as the response term of the

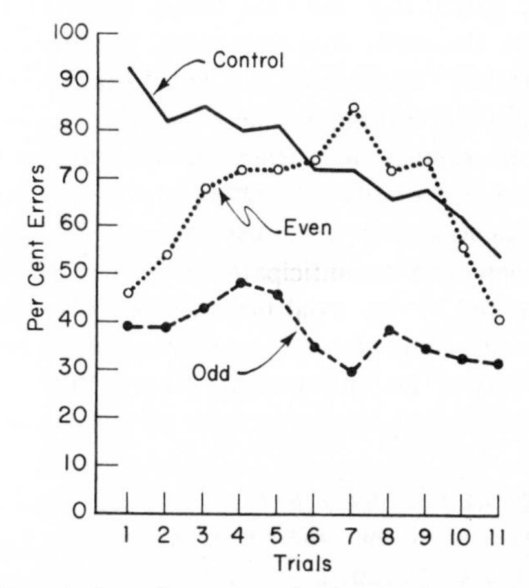

FIG. 6. Learning curves, in terms of percentage of errors (or percentage of *S*s making errors) on each of the first 11 trials of serial learning, for the item nearest the middle of the list which had been acquired in the PA task. The Control Group curve represents the mean percentage of errors on each trial for Positions 5 and 6 in the serial learning. The curve for the PA(Odd)—S group is for Position 6, which had been learned in the PA task as the response to the item in Position 5. The curve for the PA(Even)—S group is for Position 5, which had been learned in the PA task as the response to the item in Position 4.

pair 5-6 in the PA task). The curve of the Even Group is for Position 5 (the response term of the paired-associate 4-5). The curve of the Control Group is the mean of Positions 5 and 6. The results for the Control Group, of course, reveal a typical learning curve, with a fairly regular decrease in errors as a function of trials. The Odd Group shows an advantage from the very first trial, but there is practically no improvement in performance on this item through approximately the first half of learning. (This is reflected, too, in Fig. 4.) The Even Group shows an initial advantage, but it quickly fades, and by Trial 6 they perform no better than the Control Group.

These results are clearly in accord with the hypothesis that the PA strategy breaks down for the Even Group, which then abandons the previously learned PA connections and learns the list in a fashion peculiar to serial learning.

Correlations Between Serial and Paired-Associate Learning

If serial and paired-associate learning involve essentially the same kind of learning process, one should expect a fairly high correlation between individual differences in the two forms of learning, especially when the learning materials are the same in both modes of presentation. Table 3 presents the correlations between PA and serial learning for the various groups and conditions in this study. None of the correlations is significantly greater than zero at the .05 level, although all are positive, which suggests that there might be some true correlation, albeit slight. The variance the two tasks share in common, however, seems surprisingly small, considering their formal similarity. Scores based on the previously learned items show no higher correlations than items not previously learned.

TABLE 3

CORRELATIONS (PEARSON r) BETWEEN PAIRED-ASSOCIATE AND SERIAL LEARNING, BASED ON TOTAL ERRORS TO CRITERION[a]

Tasks	r
(*a*) S—PA(Odd)	.295
(*b*) PA(Odd)—S (Total List)	.035
(*c*) PA(Odd)—S (Learned Items)	.035
(*d*) PA(Odd)—S (Not-learned Items)	.034
(*e*) PA(Even)—S (Total List)	.207
(*f*) PA(Even)—S (Learned Items)	.129
(*g*) PA(Even)—S (Not-learned Items)	.265

[a] *Note*: for *a* (23 *df*) a correlation of .396 would be significant at the .05 level; for *b* through *g* (52 *df*) the required value is .268.

It is unlikely that these low correlations are due to low reliability of the learning measures. Some idea of the reliability of the serial learning measures is suggested by the correlations between error scores on the odd and even items in the serial list. These "split-half" reliabilities for the Odd, Even, and Control Groups were .88, .89, and .92, respectively. The "split-half" reliabilities of the paired-associate learning was obtained for the Odd Group and Control Group by correlating the errors made on pairs 1-2 and 3-4 with errors on 5-6 and 7-8; for the Even Group the errors on pairs 2-3 and 4-5 were correlated with pairs 6-7 and 8-9. The reliabilities thus obtained for paired-associate learning in the Odd, Even, and Control Groups were .90, .84, and .89, respectively.

DISCUSSION

These findings, along with those reviewed from the literature, invite the following generalizations and speculations. (*a*) Serial and paired-associate learning depend upon different processes or strategies of learning which psychologically have little in common, if paired-associate learning is viewed as the formation of S-R associations. (*b*) A serial list is not normally learned as a chain of S-R associations. (*c*) The slight transfer that occurs from serial to PA learning, when they formally have S-R elements in common, may be due to incidental learning of the PA connections in the serial list rather than to a fundamental similarity between serial and PA learning. In the present experiment there is no way of evaluating the degree of transfer attributable to generalized transfer effects, but even if there were a good deal of such transfer, the remarkable thing, considering the conditions of the experiment, is the relatively small degree (about 50%) of over-all transfer from the serial to the PA list. The conditions for producing specific transfer seemed close to maximal: *S*s were told they were supposed to transfer; only four single-function PAs were derived from the serial list; the serial list was overlearned to a criterion of three successive correct trials; and the PA presentation was unpaced, so that the *S* could have run through the serial list in his memory to find the terms that followed each stimulus item in the PA list. Under these conditions, if what is learned in serial and PA learning is essentially the same, it seems surprising that transfer was not close to 100 per cent. (*d*) In transfer from PA to serial learning, *S*s who are enabled to carry over their *set* for PA responding into the serial task learn the serial list faster than do *S*s for whom the congruence, or lack of it, between the PA and serial list is not such as to facilitate continuance of the PA response set.

Other evidence that different processes are involved in PA and serial learning are the negligible correlations between individual differences in the two forms of learning and the difference in difficulty of learning the PA and serial lists. The latter point can only be surmised from the present data, since the number of items in the PA and serial lists differed as well as the pacing of their presentation. But consider the following facts, based on first-task (control group) data: On a 9-item *serial* list presented at a 3-sec. rate, *S*s required on the average approximately 25 trials to attain criterion, while on a 4-pair *paired-associate* list (which involved learning only four-ninths as many connections as in the serial list) presented at a self-paced rate, *S*s required approximately 19 trials to attain the same criterion. [In a previous experiment (Jensen, 1962b) in which *S*s learned the same kind of 9-item color-form test with an unpaced rate of presentation, the average number of trials needed to attain one errorless trial was between 3 and 4.] Since the PA task was the single-function type, there was not the added interference which would have resulted had a double-function PA list been composed from these color-form materials. It is doubtful if the majority of *S*s could have mastered a double-function list in any reasonable amount of time. If the same kind of learning were going on in the two forms, why should they differ so greatly in difficulty?

But the really central question is exactly how serial learning differs from PA learning. To use Underwood's term (1961, p. 18), what is the "natural" manner in which a serial list is learned? One possible answer is suggested in the writer's tentatively formulated theory of serial learning (Jensen, 1962a). The hypothesis is not essentially an S-R conception of serial learning; it even suggests that a search for the "functional stimulus" in serial learning may be a vain pursuit. The theory holds that the "natural" process of learning a serial list consists of "attaching" responses to an anchor point (the first item, the intertrial blank space, or the signal preceding the first list-item) in both a forward and backward direction. What the *S* is doing is not linking up a chain of S-R associations, with each item acting as the stimulus for the next, but is *integrating* a number of responses. All that is meant by the term *integrated responses* is that the response elements (e.g., words or nonsense syllables) can be emitted by the *S* in a particular sequence without their being individually dependent upon specific eliciting stimuli or cues. This applies to either external stimuli or to response-produced stimuli. An example in the motor realm is a pianist's execution of a rapid passage of notes. There is a definite sequence of finger movements, but it is known that these movements can take place so rapidly as to make it impossible that they could be guided by external stimuli such as the printed score or the preceding sounds, or by proprioceptive feedback from the finger muscles. This complex response apparently issues from some centrally integrated process, and its sequential elements are not dependent upon eliciting stimuli for their execution. Another example of centrally integrated response elements is the immediate memory span; an *S* can make a series of responses, such as repeating a sequence of digits, after a single presentation of the series. There seems to be no specific stimulus for each digit. The units of a serial list can be thought of as being integrated in the same sense that a shorter series, comprehended by the memory span, is integrated. Through repeated trials the *S* can integrate a longer series of response elements than can be comprehended by his memory span. The items of a serial list might be conceived of as serving not essentially as the stimuli for anticipations, but as *reinforcers* of the *S*'s responses. Of course, the items also provide the *S*'s repertoire of responses that become integrated as the serial list. Thus, psychologically, the list is not composed of S-R connections; the items never really take on functional stimulus properties in the sense that they must do in PA learning. In PA learning the largest unit of integrated response is only two items, and thus each S-term is crucial to performance. In serial learning, on the other hand, the *S*, after a certain number of trials, is able on request to recite the serial list without being given any formal stimulus whatsoever. The list has become an integrated response without the need for specific stimulus cues along the way. An heuristic analogy might be to consider the groove in a phonograph record, which for its initial formation depends upon a sequential "stimulus" input, but which on later playings, once the stylus has been set in the groove, gives off the sequence of tones without any sequence of "stimuli" being involved at all. Certainly each successive tone is not the "stimulus" for the next. A similar sort of thing may be true for human sequential acts, such as playing a piece on the piano, assembling an apparatus, or learning a list of nonsense syllables. A pattern for an integrated response is laid down in the nervous system, likened to the groove on the phonograph record, rather than a sequence of discrete S-R associations, which might be likened to the chain reaction in a row of dominoes when the first one is tipped over. This conception of serial learning should suggest many experiments capable of further testing its validity.

Summary

It was hypothesized that serial learning takes place by a different process or strategy than PA learning and does not normally consist of the chaining together of S-R connections. It was also hypothesized that specific transfer of S-R pairs from PA to serial learning would be facilitated under conditions that make it relatively easy for the *S* to carry over his *set* for PA learning into the serial task as compared with conditions that make it relatively difficult to maintain the PA set. To test this hypothesis two experimental groups learned a PA list followed by a serial list with common S-R elements. A control group learned only the serial list. The two experimental groups, labeled Odd and Even, learned different pairs of items derived from the serial list. The Odd Group learned pairs 1-2, 3-4, 5-6, 7-8; the Even Group learned pairs 2-3, 4-5, 6-7, 8-9. The second task consisted of learning the serial list 1 2 3 4 5 6 7 8 9. The Odd Group, for whom the set for paired-associate responding in serial learning was facilitated by the fact that the first items in the serial list had already been learned as a paired associate, learned the serial list significantly faster than the Control Group. Though the Even Group showed some advantage over the Control Group in the first few trials of serial learning, this advantage disappeared completely by the sixth or seventh trial. This was true even of the adjacent serial items that had been previously learned as paired associates. This result was interpreted as being due to a loss of the PA set and the adoption of a strategy peculiar to serial learning. Other evidence that quite different processes are involved in serial and PA learning was the lack of a significant correlation between individual differences in the two forms of learning.

It appears that a serial list is not learned as a chain of S-R connections and that what the *S* learns in the serial task is somehow quite different from what he learns in the PA task, even though both tasks formally have the same associative elements in common. An hypothesis was suggested to account for these findings, viz., that in PA learning the S-terms serve primarily a cue or stimulus function, while in serial learning the subject integrates a number of responses (supplied by the items in the list) and the items serve primarily as reinforcers without acquiring a cue function, except possibly by incidental learning when the list is overlearned.

REFERENCES

JENSEN, A. R. An empirical theory of the serial-position effect. *J. Psychol.*, 1962, **53**, 127-142. (a)

JENSEN, A. R. Temporal and spatial serial-position effects. *Amer. J. Psychol.*, 1962, **75**, 390-400. (b)

JENSEN, A. R., AND BLANK, S. S. Associations with ordinal position in serial rote-learning. *Canad. J. Psychol.*, 1962, **16**, 60-63.

NEWMAN, S. E., AND SALTZ, E. Serial position as a cue in learning. *Amer. J. Psychol.*, 1962, **75**, 102-108.

PRIMOFF, E. Backward and forward association as an organizing act in serial and in paired associate learning. *J. Psychol.*, 1938, **5**, 375-395.

UNDERWOOD, B. J. Stimulus selection in verbal learning. Paper for the Second Office of Naval Research Conference on Verbal Learning. June, 1961.

WOODWORTH, R. S., AND POFFENBERGER, A. T. *Textbook of experimental psychology.* Mimeographed ed. New York: Columbia Univer., 1920.

YOUNG, R. K. A comparison of two methods of learning serial associations. *Amer. J. Psychol.*, 1959, **72**, 554-559.

YOUNG, R. K. The stimulus in serial verbal learning. *Amer. J. Psychol.*, 1961, **74**, 517-528. (a)

YOUNG, R. K. Paired-associate learning when the same items occur as stimuli and responses. *J. exp. Psychol.*, 1961, **61**, 315-318. (b)

YOUNG, R. K. Tests of three hypotheses about the effective stimulus in serial learning. *J. exp. Psychol.*, 1962, **63**, 307-313.

(Received August 8, 1962)

ARTICLE 3

AN EXPERIMENTAL ANALYSIS OF THE ERRORS IN ROTE SERIAL LEARNING[1]

JAMES DEESE AND FREDERICK H. KRESSE

The Johns Hopkins University

The present experiment is an attempt to analyze the familiar bowed serial-position effect found in rote verbal learning in terms of the kinds of errors *S*s make. It is, in this sense, an empirical approach to the problem of serial position in anticipation learning. The present experiment, however, differs from the previous experiments that make use of an analysis of intrusive errors in that, in the major experimental conditions, *S*s were unpaced during learning. Together with the instructions given the *S*s, this condition allowed every opportunity for *S*s to verbalize any errors that they might have had a tendency to make during learning. Failures to respond were a result of an inability on the part of *S*s to make a response with unlimited time. The *S*s were not forced to guess, so that the number of times failure to respond occurred at each position could be tabulated.

PROCEDURE

Three different experiments were performed, and the procedure for each of these will be described separately. The following general procedures apply to all of the experiments, however: All *S*s were instructed to learn by the method of anticipation and to spell all of their responses. All *S*s learned a preliminary list of six nonsense syllables consisting of two consonants with a vowel in between (hereafter called "vowel" syllables). These were presented to *S*s by means of flash cards. This list was learned to a criterion of two consecutive errorless trials. The *E* used this opportunity to correct the learning technique of *S*. It was anticipated that the preliminary learning might give *E* an opportunity to discard unsatisfactory *S*s at this point, but the occasion never arose. After a brief rest, *E* proceeded to the body of the experiment, which in every case consisted of learning, by the method of anticipation, a 12-item list of nonsense syllables. In Exp. I and II, a projection exposure device was used. Because of the limitation of alterations in the order of the film strips, however, in Exp. III a Gerbrands memory drum was used. All *S*s were tested individually, and were instructed that *E* was interested in the kind of mistakes made during learning. In all experiments *S*s were brought to a criterion of two consecutive correct trials.

Experiment I.—Ten *S*s learned vowel syllables chosen from those with Glaze (1) association-values between 40% and 13%. The syllables were chosen so that no consonant appeared in either the first or third location more than once, and no vowel was duplicated more than twice. A 6-sec. interval was interpolated between each trial. The *S*s were signaled the beginning of a trial by *E*. Each syllable appeared at the exposure window for a period of 2 sec., and there was a 2-sec. blank exposure between each syllable.

Two orders of list presentation were used. In the second order, the two halves of the list were exchanged and turned mirrorwise so that the syllables previously at the middle were now at the ends.

Experiment II.—Thirty *S*s were used in this experiment. The procedure was exactly the same as in Exp. I except that *S*s were not paced. The syllables were exposed in the window for 2 sec., as before, but the interval between syllables was prolonged until *S* responded or said that he could not think of the next syllable. The *S*s were not forced to guess. The lists of Exp. I were used in this experiment.

Experiment III.—Twelve *S*s learned lists of Witmer (4) consonant syllables of 13% to 42% association value which were presented on a memory drum. The order of the items in the list was different for every *S* (randomized in a latin-square design against *S*s). The syllables were so devised that no consonant appeared in any one of the three locations more than once.

Scoring errors.—All responses were recorded and subsequently analyzed into three categories: (*a*) failures to respond, (*b*) errors or "intrusions" coming from other syllables within the list, and (*c*) overt errors not attributable to items within the list. The intralist intrusions were of two types, "complete intrusions" and "partial intru-

[1] The authors are indebted to Miss Elizabeth Ormond who gathered a portion of the data.

Reprinted with permission of the authors and the publisher, the American Psychological Association. The article appeared originally in the *Journal of Experimental Psychology*, 1952, **44**, 199–202.

sions." Complete intrusions were complete spellings of syllables from other locations at an incorrect point. Partial intrusions were intrusions of two consecutive letters contained in syllables at other locations. Thus, for example, if *S* gave "Q-E-__" or "Q-E-T," and there was a syllable in the list, "Q-E-Z," this would be counted as a partial intrusion.

The validity of partial intrusions was checked by comparing their frequency at each position with complete intrusions, and they follow each other very closely. Because of necessary duplication in the vowel position in the vowel syllables, partial intrusions for these syllables were more equivocal than in the case of the all-consonant syllables. The results for the two cases were almost exactly the same, however (as can be inferred from an inspection of Fig. 2, 3, and 4). Therefore, the partial and complete intrusions were combined for the present analysis. In Exp. I the partial intrusions represented nearly 60% of the total intrusions, and in Exp. II and III about 40%. The higher figure for the first experiment is due to the fact that under conditions of pacing, *Ss* frequently gave a blank for the last letter.

RESULTS

The results of Exp. I are presented in Fig. 1. A classical serial-position curve was found for total errors which was rather steep because of the comparatively rapid pacing. The intralist intrusions were of low frequency and bow shaped, as you can see in the

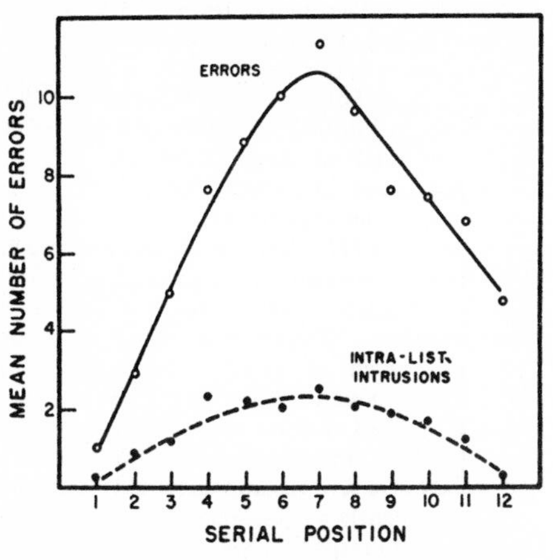

FIG. 1. Serial-position curve and frequency of intralist intrusions per syllable in Exp. I (paced learning of vowel syllables)

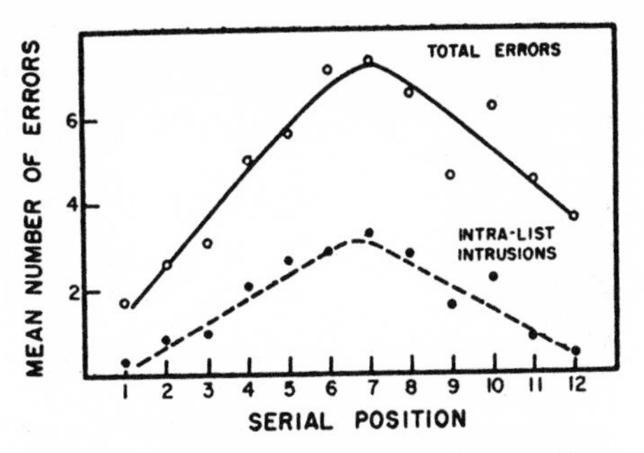

FIG. 2. Serial-position curve and frequency of intralist intrusions per syllable in Exp. II (unpaced learning of vowel syllables)

bottom curve of Fig. 1. A striking fact appears, however: unlike the serial-position effect itself, the distribution of intralist intrusions is almost symmetrical. The frequency of such errors is just as great at the twelfth position as at the first. The highest frequency of such errors occurs at the seventh position and the next highest at the fourth. It cannot be unequivocally said that the distribution of intralist intrusions is perfectly symmetrical, but it is certainly more symmetrical than the distribution of total errors. It cannot be concluded that the remaining empirical sources of errors lead to the skewing effect, however, because no account is taken of implicit errors or errors that *S* almost made but couldn't because of the time. It is widely agreed, with data from many sources, that conflict between correct and incorrect responses produces long latencies of responses, so it was decided to repeat the experiment giving *S* unlimited opportunity to respond to each syllable.

The serial-position curve of total errors for Exp. II is shown in Fig. 2. Again we have the familiar curve, but this time much reduced in slope because of the longer average time between syllables. The intralist intrusions are about of the same order of magnitude as in Exp. I, but they account for a

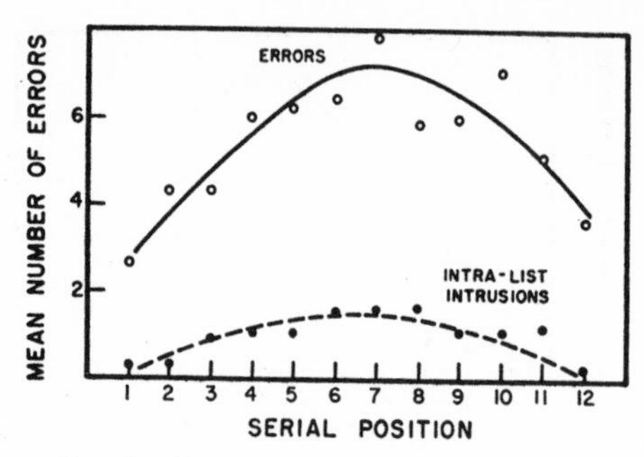

FIG. 3. Serial-position curve and frequency of intralist intrusions per syllable in Exp. III (unpaced learning of consonant syllables)

much larger proportion of errors (Fig. 2). Again the striking fact is that the the serial-position effect is, as usual, skewed, but the intralist intrusions are almost symmetrical. The slope of the curve for the last half of the list appears to be a little steeper than that for the first half, but it is not nearly so skewed as the curve for total errors. This time, however, if we now tabulate the remaining two categories of errors, we come up with an additional interesting fact. The failure-of-response errors are very low at the beginning of the list, rise rapidly through the first half of the list, and are approximately level through the second half of the list. This can be seen in Fig. 4. The overt errors coming from without the list (source unknown, perhaps "guessing," perhaps from the practice list) show no consistent pattern as a function of serial position. The mean frequencies of such errors per position, in order, are as follows: .76, 1.24, 1.34, 1.13, 1.43, 1.23, 1.33, .83, .46, .87, .90, .90.

Thus it appears that the skewed serial-position effect found in this experiment can be accounted for largely by two empirical factors: (*a*) intralist intrusions that are almost symmetrically bowed, and (*b*) failures to respond that increase through the first half of the list and reach a plateau during the second half. There are several features about this experiment that left us with the desire to pursue the matter further, however. The scoring of partial intrusions was not altogether unequivocal (because of necessary duplication of vowels in a 12-item list) and the list was presented in two orders, which did not clearly eliminate any confounding factors due to intrinsic difficulty of syllables. Therefore, the experiment was repeated using all-consonant syllables and a completely randomized order of items in lists.

The serial-position curve of Exp. III is again the classical curve (Fig. 3). Also, as in the case of the two previous experiments, the intralist intrusions are almost symmetrical about the middle. This distribution is more heavily skewed towards the end of the list than those of Exp. II, however. Also, as in Exp. II, the failure-of-response errors increase through the first half of the list and are approximately level through the last half (Fig. 4). The principal difference between this experiment and Exp. II is in the larger frequency of extralist overt errors in Exp. III, although they again show little consistent pattern. The mean frequencies per syllable are as follows: 2.08, 1.83, 3.00, 2.66, 3.50, 1.92, 2.16, 3.00, 1.07, 1.00. The larger frequency of these errors is responsible for making

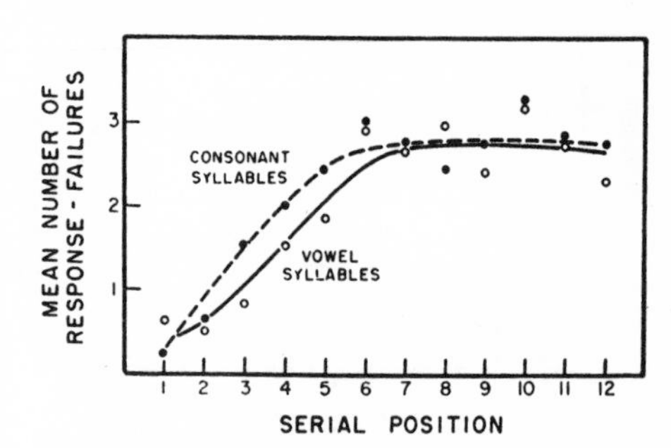

FIG. 4. Frequency of failure-of-response errors per position in Exp. II and III (unpaced learning of vowel and consonant syllables)

the serial-position curve itself flatter in Exp. III than in Exp. II. The bowness and skewness of the curve are entirely accounted for, however, by the intralist errors and the failures of response.

Discussion

It appears that there are two empirical factors responsible for the skewed serial-position curve obtained with unlimited recall times. One is the almost symmetrical distribution of intralist intrusions and the other is the growth of failures to respond through the first half of the list to reach an asymptote during the second half. These facts suggest a two-factor theory of the serial-position curve in unpaced learning. A factor of associative inhibition would be indicated by the intralist intrusions, and a second factor, that might be identified with either the notion of response-induced inhibition or the immediate memory span, would be indicated by the failure-to-respond curves.

The serial-position curve obtained with paced learning appears to be more complicated. Failures of response, instead of growing in frequency through the first half of the list, show a bow-shaped, skewed curve. Further experimental work will be necessary to establish the reason for this difference.

Summary

Three experiments on rote verbal learning by the method of anticipation were performed. In two of the experiments *S*s were allowed unlimited time between each syllable to anticipate, though they were not forced to guess. Under these conditions the skewed serial-position effect seems to be accounted for by the simple sum of two empirical factors. Intralist intrusions (mistakes based upon other items in the list) form a distribution about the middle of the list that is almost symmetrical. Failure-of-response errors are low at the beginning of the list, mount rapidly through the first half of the list, and reach a somewhat variable asymptote during the second half of the list. These two sources of errors, summed together, produce the classical serial-position curve. Response errors coming from the outside of the list form no consistent pattern as a function of serial position. By and large, they serve merely to flatten the serial-position curve.

(Received February 2, 1952)

References

1. Glaze, J. A. The association value of nonsense syllables. *J. genet. Psychol.*, 1928, **35**, 255–267.
2. Hull, C. L. The conflicting psychologies of learning—a way out. *Psychol. Rev.*, 1935, **42**, 491–516.
3. Hull, C. L., Hovland, C. I., Ross, R. T., Hall, M., Perkins, D. T., & Fitch, F. B. *Mathematico-deductive theory of rote learning.* New Haven: Yale Univer. Press, 1940.
4. Witmer, L. R. The association value of three-place consonant syllables. *J. genet. Psychol.*, 1935, **47**, 337–359.

ARTICLE 4

RE-EXAMINATION OF THE SERIAL POSITION EFFECT[1]

MURRAY GLANZER

Department of Psychiatry, University of Maryland

AND STANLEY C. PETERS[2]

Walter Reed Army Institute of Research

Existing generalizations about the serial position effect in rote learning have recently been challenged as based on artifacts. McCrary and Hunter (1953) presented evidence that the different curves produced by experimental variables, such as presentation rate, distribution, and list difficulty, are a single curve multiplied by different numbers of errors. Their contention was borne out by the findings of Braun and Heymann (1958). A re-examination of the serial position effect seems necessary. Since any statement about serial position effects must refer to the beginning and end of a series of items, the first step in the re-examination is to analyze the meaning of the terms *beginning* and *end*. The analysis consists of three steps: to determine what characteristics *E* points to as defining the beginning and the end of a list, to analyze these characteristics, and to determine their effect on *S*'s performance.

In a rote learning experiment, *E* presents to *S* a continuous and repetitive cycle of events: the series of syllables, a gap; the series of syllables, a gap. The terms *beginning* and *end* are used to refer to the characteristics associated with this gap. They are the following: (*a*) Primacy-recency: The first item *S* sees, and the last item he sees before the cycle repeats itself, appear on either side of the gap, because *E*s usually present the list starting from the gap. (*b*) Spacing: The appearance of the gap coincides with a period in which *S* is not required to anticipate syllables. (*c*) Association break: Every item in the series is both a stimulus and a response item, except the two on either side of the gap. The *S* is not required to form an association across the gap. The first item in a list is usually a pure stimulus item. The last item is a pure response item, in that it does not function as stimulus for the first item.

The purpose of the following experiments was to separate the factors that make up the complex called *the beginning* and *the end* of the list, and to determine the part these factors play in the serial position effect.

EXPERIMENT I: PRIMACY-RECENCY

Mitchell's (1934) evidence that the usual bowed curve appears in lists that have neither spacing nor association breaks would indicate a considerable role for primacy-recency effects. In Exp. I, the role of primacy-recency was evaluated by varying *S*s' starting positions: starting some *S*s at the normal position in the list, and starting other *S*s at what would ordinarily be called the middle of the list. The normal position in the list is that part which has the gap followed by the asterisk, or other starting cue; this may be called the *structural beginning*. The *temporal*

[1] This work was carried out under Contract DA-49-007-MD-1004 between the Office of The Surgeon General and the University of Maryland.

[2] Now at the University of Illinois.

Reprinted with permission of the authors and the publisher, the American Psychological Association. The article appeared originally in the *Journal of Experimental Psychology*, 1962, **64**, 258–266.

beginning, a term which may be used to refer to the first syllable exposed to *S*, may or may not coincide with the structural beginning. The two experimental conditions here were one in which the structural and temporal beginning coincided, and one in which they did not coincide. If the temporal starting point (the primacy-recency factor) plays an important role in determining the serial position effect, then groups starting at the structural middle should show a flattened or indented serial position curve.

Method

Subjects.—The *S*s were 32 Army medical service enlisted men. They were average or above average in their scores on Army intelligence tests (General Technical score of the Army Classification Battery).

Materials.—Two six-syllable lists (Glaze 20% association value) were used: List I: *, ZID, NUK, WEF, QAM, TUH, BEJ; List II: *, QAM, TUH, BEJ, ZID, NUK, WEF. The two lists consist of the same series of syllables, with the structural beginning placed at different positions.

Procedure.—The *S*s were first given two three-syllable practice lists (Glaze 100% association value). One practice list was started from the structural beginning, i.e., the asterisk. The other was started from the structural middle. Half the *S*s were started from the structural beginning in their first practice list; the other half were started from the structural middle in their first practice list. After learning both practice lists to a criterion of one perfect trial, *S* learned one of the six-syllable lists.

The presentation rate was 3 sec. per syllable, with a 6-sec. interval (two blank spaces on the drum) between successive cycles of the list. All groups received the same instructions: to try to anticipate each syllable before it appeared. No reference was made to either the beginning or the end of the list. The list was learned to a criterion of three consecutive errorless trials. Half the *S*s learned List I; the other half, List II. Half the *S*s started at the structural beginning with the asterisk exposed. The other half started at the structural middle of the list, with either WEF or BEJ exposed. Trials were counted as starting at the structural middle of the list for the *S*s who started at that point.

Results

Since the work of McCrary and Hunter (1953) and Braun and Heymann (1958) showed that the total number of errors has a multiplicative effect on the shape of the serial position curve, here, and in the subsequent experiments, error scores were translated into logarithms. This translation converts the multiplicative effect to an additive factor and permits direct comparison of the shapes of the curves. This procedure was adopted instead of dividing through by the total number of errors, as in the work mentioned above.

The groups that started in the structural middle had a slightly higher serial position curve (see Fig. 1) than those starting at the structural beginning. The overall differences between the two experimental groups

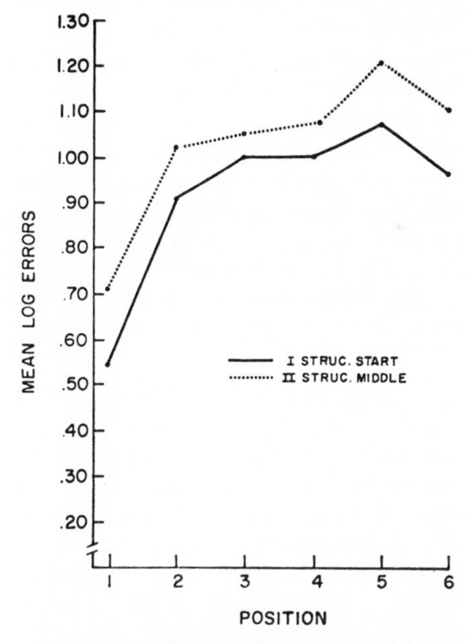

FIG. 1. Serial position curves with primacy-recency varied: Exp. I. (Group II started in the middle of the list.)

TABLE 1

Analysis of Variance of Log Error Scores: Exp. I

Source	df	MS	F
Between Ss			
Condition (C)	1	.5645	1.69
Lists (L)	1	.3934	
C × L	1	.1068	
Error (between)	28	.3331	
Within Ss			
Position (P)	5	.9834	42.76***
P × C	5	.0171	
P × L	5	.0193	
P × C × L	5	.0384	1.67
Error (within)	140	.0230	

*** $P < .001$.

were not, however, statistically significant (see Table 1). For the group starting at the asterisk, the overall mean of the converted error scores was 5.5 ($SD = 1.4$); the mean number of trials to criterion was 19.7 ($SD = 9.2$). For the group starting at the structural middle, the mean of the converted errors was 6.1 ($SD = 1.4$); the mean number of trials to criterion was 22.9 ($SD = 9.4$). The experimental operation had no discernible effect on the shape of the serial position curves, and of course the Position × Experimental Condition interaction was not significant. List structure was the sole effective factor, significant at the .001 level.

Greenhouse and Geisser (1959) have pointed out that the significance levels used in analyses of variance in repeated measurements designs are incorrect, if the assumption of equal covariances is not met. In that case, the usual test, presented in Table 1, overestimates the significance level. A lower bound test that underestimates the significance level can be obtained by appropriate reduction of the degrees of freedom. The effect of list structure remains significant at the .001 level ($df = 1/28$).

The lists used in this experiment were shorter than the 10- to 12-syllable lists usually used in serial position studies. However, the curves (Fig. 1) show the same skewed bow shape as the curves obtained with longer lists (Hovland, 1938a). They are also similar to the family of curves obtained by Robinson and Brown (1926) for lists that range from 5 to 17 syllables. There is no basis, therefore, for assuming that different factors are at work in 6-syllable lists than those in longer lists.

The type of scoring used above (based on the total number of errors before the criterion was met) may conceal an early effect of primacy-recency that is swamped by the repeated effect of list structure. To check on this possibility, the number of the first trial on which a correct anticipation occurred was scored for each position in the list. With the starting position at the asterisk, the means for the six positions were 2.38, 5.00, 8.06, 8.50, 9.75, and 6.62. With the starting position in the middle of the list, the means were 3.81, 6.38, 6.31, 7.81, 11.31, and 8.50. There is an indication of flattening of the curve for the lists started at the middle. The Position × Condition interaction, however, was not significant ($df = 5/140$, $P > .10$).

It is clear that the structure of the list, rather than a primacy-recency effect, is the major determinant of the serial position effect; the same serial position effect appears with or without primacy-recency. The results do not contradict Mitchell's (1934) results, since in her lists the structural characteristics of spacing and association break were absent. As will be pointed out below, when the structural characteristics are removed, primacy-recency effects can be seen. For the usual type of list presentation, however, the important factor seems to be the structure of the list. The next step was to examine the two factors associated with the structural beginning and end of the list: spacing and the association break.

Experiment II: Spacing

If spacing is a factor determining the appearance of serial position effect, then changing the amount of spacing should affect the shape of the serial position curve. More specifically, if the confounding multiplicative effect of total number of errors is eliminated, then increasing the spacing should give more pronounced serial position effect. McCrary and Hunter (1953) and Braun and Heymann (1958) have presented evidence that contradicts this hypothesis, but they compared only 6-sec. and 126-sec. intertrial intervals. Intervals between 0 and 16 sec. were included in the experiment below. Perhaps more important than the range of spacing values is the fact that in the Hovland (1938b, 1940) studies re-analyzed by McCrary and Hunter, and also in the Braun and Heymann study, the long and short spacing intervals were not completely comparable. In those studies, an interpolated task was given during the 126-sec. interval, but not during the 6-sec. interval.

Method

Subjects.—The *S*s were 90 Army medical service enlisted men. The group was above average on Army intelligence tests (General Technical score on the Army Classification Battery).

Materials.—Two 10-syllable (Glaze 20% association value) lists were used: List I: *, RUW, GIY, POH, WEF, QAM, ZIX, NUK, BEJ, XOC, KAZ; List II: *, ZIX, NUK, BEJ, XOC, KAZ, RUW, GIY, POH, WEF, QAM.

Procedure.—The *S*s were assigned in equal numbers to each of the two list conditions and the five spacing conditions. They first learned two 3-syllable practice lists (Glaze 100% value) to a criterion of one perfect trial, under the same spacing condition as their main list. They then learned one of the 10-syllable lists to a criterion of two errorless trials. The criterion was set as high as possible within the time available, so that the serial position curves would represent final, stabilized performance.

The lists were presented at a 2-sec. rate, with zero, one, two, four, or eight blank spaces (0, 2, 4, 8, or 16 sec.) between the end of the list and the reappearance of the beginning. There were 9 *S*s who were unable to reach the criterion within the 75 min. available: 2 each in the zero- and one-space condition, 1 each in the two- and eight-space condition, and 3 in the four-space condition. These *S*s were replaced by others.

Results

The mean log error curves show an orderly change from a relatively flat curve for the zero-spacing condition, to a sharply peaked curve for the maximum spacing condition (see Fig. 2). The statistical evaluation (see Table 2) of the effect with the usual tests, however, does not find the Spacing $\times$ Position interaction significant ($.10 > P > .05$). This analysis does not, of course, reflect the orderly nature of the changes in the curves. For example, there is a progressive increase in the slope of the curve between Positions 1 and 6 as the spacing increases. The rank order correlations for the difference between Positions 1 and 6 with the amount of spacing is 1.00 for both the List I and List II groups. In both groups, there is a corresponding, but less marked, decrease in slope between

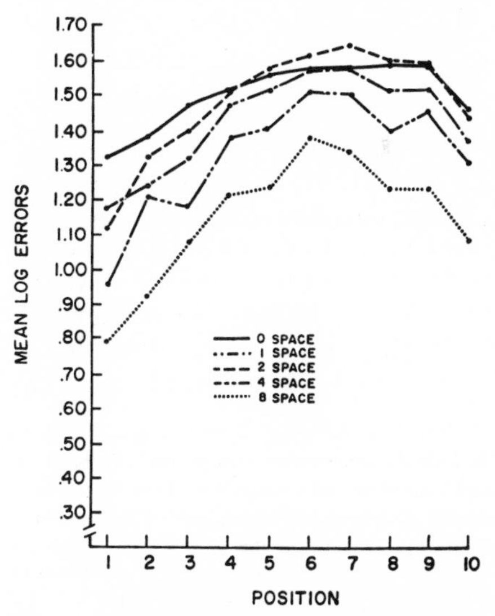

FIG. 2. Serial position curves with spacing varied: Exp. II.

TABLE 2

ANALYSIS OF VARIANCE OF LOG ERROR SCORES: EXP. II

Source	*df*	*MS*	*F*
Between *S*s			
Spacing (S)	4	3.5962	7.00***
Lists (L)	1	0.0059	
S × L	4	0.3396	
Error (between)	80	0.5138	
Within *S*s			
Position (P)	9	2.0380	90.18***
P × S	36	0.0315	1.39
P × L	9	0.0437	1.93*
P × S × L	36	0.0168	
Error (within)	720	0.0226	

* $P < .05$.
*** $P < .001$.

Positions 6 and 10 as spacing increases. The rank order correlation for the difference between Positions 6 and 10 with the amount of spacing, is .70 in both groups.

The analysis demonstrates the expected overall differences between the spacing conditions, the means declining ($P < .001$) with increased spacing, except for a reversal between the one- and two-space conditions. The overall means of the converted errors for the zero- to eight-space conditions, in order, were as follows: 15.0 ($SD = 2.1$), 14.3 ($SD = 2.1$), 14.8 ($SD = 1.9$), 13.4 ($SD = 2.7$), 11.6 ($SD = 2.2$). The means of the number of trials to reach criterion were, in order, as follows: 58.4 ($SD = 21.8$), 54.4 ($SD = 19.6$), 60.3 ($SD = 21.4$), 47.7 ($SD = 22.1$), 35.0 ($SD = 18.0$).[3] The Position × Lists interaction reflects differences in the difficulty of the syllables. The absence of a significant third-order interaction indicates that the effect of the spacing on the serial position curve does not differ for the two lists. The position effect is significant ($P < .001$) and remains at that level under the Greenhouse-Geisser lower bound test.

[3] The contribution of intrusion errors to the total error score may be of interest. The number of complete intrusions was tallied and expressed as a percentage of total errors for each *S*. The mean percentage of intrusion errors for the zero- to eight-space conditions, in order, was as follows: 5.3 ($SD = 6.1$), 4.7 ($SD = 6.5$), 3.0 ($SD = 2.5$), 4.2 ($SD = 2.7$), 7.7 ($SD = 6.7$).

The results lent some support to the hypothesis that the serial position curve changes in an orderly fashion as a function of spacing. The statistical support was, however, not satisfactory.

EXPERIMENT III: SPACING AND ASSOCIATION BREAK

In this experiment, the aim was to retest the effect of spacing on the serial position effect and also to evaluate the effect of the association break. The expectation was that spacing would increase, and that associative chaining across the gap would decrease, the serial position effect.

Method

Subjects.—The *S*s were 120 college students. They were paid for their participation.

Materials.—In order to insert associative chaining between successive presentations of the list, the lists were constructed in quasi-paired-associates format. Ten chained lists were constructed by rotating the syllables systematically through the 10 available positions. Two of the chained lists are shown below.

Chained 1: * ZIX NUK * NUK BEJ * BEJ XOC * XOC KAZ * KAZ RUW * RUW GIY * GIY POH * POH WEF * WEF QAM * QAM ZIX (Space 0, 2, or 8) * ZIX NUK * (etc.)

Chained 2: * NUK BEJ * BEJ XOC * XOC KAZ * KAZ RUW * RUW GIY * GIY POH * POH WEF * WEF QAM * QAM ZIX * ZIX NUK (Space 0, 2, or 8) * NUK BEJ * (etc.)

To break the chaining, the initial syllable in each of the 10 chained lists was replaced with a substitute syllable, i.e., LEB for ZIX in Chained 1; CIW for NUK in Chained 2; and TIV for BEJ, HUQ for XOC, VEP for KAZ, FOJ for RUW, LEQ for GIY, JAT for POH, YUS for

WEF, and FUP for QAM, in the other 8 chained lists.

All syllables, including the substitute syllables, were from the Glaze 20% association value list.

Procedure.—The presentation rate was 1 sec. per syllable. Three spacing conditions were used: 0, 2, and 8 spaces, or seconds, between lists. The 10 lists, 3 spacing conditions, and 2 chaining conditions formed a 10 × 3 × 2 factorial design. Two *S*s were assigned to each of the 60 experimental conditions.

The drum displayed an asterisk, followed by a stimulus syllable and then the response syllable. A stimulus syllable, therefore, appeared every 3 sec. After learning two 3-syllable practice lists in the same quasipaired-associates format to a criterion of one errorless trial, each *S* learned a 10-syllable list to a criterion of two successive errorless trials.

Results

Spacing has the expected effect of decreasing total errors during learning. The effect is significant at the .01 level (see Table 3). The overall means of the converted errors for the zero-, two-, and eight-space conditions, in order, were as follows:

TABLE 3

ANALYSIS OF VARIANCE OF LOG ERROR SCORES: EXP. III

Source	*df*	*MS*	*F*
Between *S*s			
Spacing (S)	2	2.5434	6.09**
Chaining (C)	1	0.0097	
Lists (L)	9	0.3966	
S × C	2	0.2680	
S × L	18	0.3114	
C × L	9	0.7316	1.75
S × C × L	18	0.2184	
Error (between)	60	0.4175	
Within *S*s			
Position (P)	9	1.0312	56.35***
P × S	18	0.0609	3.33***
P × C	9	0.0250	1.37
P × L	81	0.0584	3.19***
P × S × C	18	0.0261	1.43
P × S × L	162	0.0172	
P × C × L	81	0.0178	
P × S × C × L	162	0.0184	1.01
Error (within)	540	0.0183	

** $P < .01$.
*** $P < .001$.

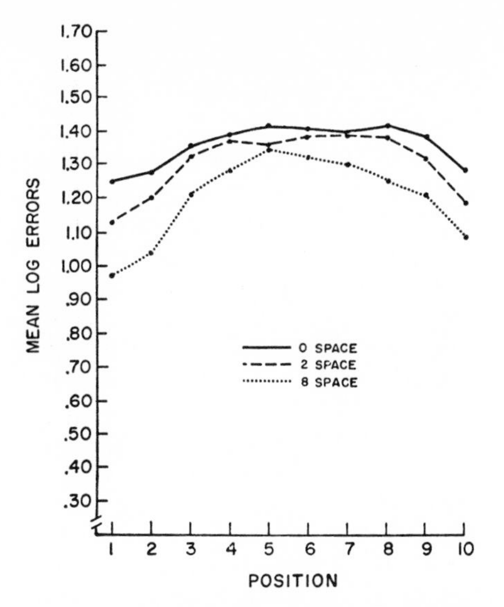

FIG. 3. Serial position curves with spacing varied: Exp. III.

13.6 ($SD = 2.1$), 13.0 ($SD = 2.0$), 12.0 ($SD = 1.7$). The means of the number of trials to reach criterion were, in order, as follows: 44.7 ($SD = 18.2$), 39.6 ($SD = 15.0$), 31.9 ($SD = 11.1$). Chaining does not have any significant overall effect. The serial position effect was significant ($P < .001$), with the Greenhouse-Geisser lower bound test leaving the significance level unchanged.

The effect of spacing on the serial position curve is shown in Fig. 3. As spacing increases, the curve moves toward a markedly bowed shape of classic form, with the beginning lower than the end. The effect, as evaluated by the Position × Spacing interaction, is significant at the .001 level. Use of the Greenhouse-Geisser lower bound test with 2 and 60 *df* leaves the effect significant, at worst, at the .05 level. The effect of chaining on the serial position curve was not significant. The significant interaction of Lists and Serial Position ($P < .001$) reflects differences in the difficulty of individual syllables, which were in different positions in the 10 lists.

The plots of the mean unconverted error scores display the same progression toward a more peaked serial position curve, with increased spacing. Plots of percentages of total errors, of course, give essentially the same picture, with respect to the shapes of the curves, as that obtained with mean log of errors. The data were also converted into ranks. Thus, if *S* had the following raw error scores for the 10 positions: 6, 8, 15, 21, 18, 22, 19, 24, 13, 17, his scores were converted to the following ranks: 1.0, 2.0, 4.0, 8.0, 6.0, 9.0, 7.0, 10.0, 3.0, 5.0. Examination of the mean ranks for each position showed the same progression found with the mean log scores. Using the ranks, coefficients of concordance were computed for each group. For both the chained and unchained groups, the coefficients increased as spacing increased. In the chained group, they were .18, .30, .48; in the unchained group, they were .11, .42, .48. All the coefficients are significant ($P < .05$). The regular progression of the coefficients indicates that the increase in the bowing of the serial position curve as a function of spacing is independent of the particular conversion used.

Figure 3 shows a slight serial position effect in the zero-space condition. Separate analysis of the zero-space condition finds the effect significant ($F = 7.39$, $df = 1/60$, $P < .01$). The chained zero-space condition by itself also demonstrates a significant serial position effect ($F = 4.94$, $df = 1/60$, $P < .05$). The factor underlying this effect is the primacy-recency variable. Evidently, as in Mitchell's (1934) study, when spacing is absent, the primacy-recency factor affects the shape of the curve. The effect is, however, too slight to account for the usual serial position effect.

Discussion

The preceding experiments indicate that of the three factors listed initially as possible determinants of the serial position effect (chaining, spacing, and primacy-recency), the most important factor is spacing, the appearance of a gap in the list. Experiment I eliminated primacy-recency as a major factor in the usual serial learning situation, since a full, unaffected serial position effect was shown even when opposed by the primacy-recency factor. Experiment II gave some evidence that the serial position effect was a function of spacing. Experiment III completed the case in support of the effect of spacing and eliminated chaining as a major determinant of the serial position effect. Experiment III also indicated a slight effect for primacy-recency when it is not opposed by spacing.

McCrary and Hunter (1943), in their re-analysis of Hovland's (1938b, 1940) data, and Braun and Heymann (1958) display curves that remain unaffected by spacing, once the multiplicative effect of total number of errors is eliminated. Evidence has been presented here that spacing does have an effect. The apparent contradiction probably stems from differences in procedure. In the previous studies, the intertrial intervals were 6 and 126 sec.; in the present experiments, they ranged between 0 and 16 sec., with large changes appearing between the 0- and 2-sec. conditions. In the previous studies, an interpolated task was used, but only during the long interval. This could have counteracted the spacing effect by slowing the learning of the beginning and end syllables of the long interval lists.

Inhibition (Hull, Hovland, Ross, Hall, Perkins, & Fitch, 1940) and interference (Atkinson, 1957) constructs have been popular in the explanation of the serial position curve. From one point of view, the results above fit in with inhibition or interference explanations of the serial position effect. Spacing could function as a barrier to protect the items near the beginning and the end of the list. With the demonstration of a systematic effect of spacing on the serial position curve, however, another type of explanation becomes possible: a facilitation explanation. With this type of explanation, interference or inhibitory effects between list items are considered homogeneous within the list. The serial position curve is viewed as a result of the facilitative effect of spacing on the learning of the first and last items of the list. These, in turn, facilitate the learning of their neighbors. The skewing of the curve can be explained by an effect demonstrated by Ribback and Underwood (1950). They showed that once an association is learned between a pair of syllables, it is easier to attach a third association to the second member of the pair than to the first. In other words, once the association X-Y is learned between syllables X and Y, it is easier to learn the triplet of syllables X-Y-Z than it is to learn A-X-Y. The Ribback-Underwood mechanism by itself is not sufficient to generate the serial position curve, since the mechanism does not determine the syllables from which it will spread. This determination could be made by spacing, which would facilitate the syllable pairs bordering the gap. These anchor syllables would in turn generate the serial position effect forward and backward from the gap.

Summary

Serial position effects are usually defined on the basis of the beginning of a list. In rote learning, the term "beginning" may be analyzed into three factors associated with a repetitively-appearing gap that separates the "end" from the "beginning" of the list: (*a*) Primacy-recency. The first item the *S* sees, and the last item he sees before the cycle repeats itself, appear on either side of the gap, because *E*s usually start the list from the gap. (*b*) Spacing. The appearance of the gap coincides with a period in which the *S* is not required to anticipate syllables. (*c*) Chaining versus association break. Every item in the series functions as both a stimulus and a response item (chaining), except the two on either side of the gap. One of these is solely a stimulus item; the other is solely a response item.

Three experiments were carried out to determine the role of these three factors in generating the serial position effect. In Exp. I, primacy-recency was opposed to both spacing and association break by varying *S*'s starting position in conventional lists. No effect of the variation was found, indicating that primacy-recency was not a major factor. In Exp. II, spacing was varied, using intertrial intervals of 0, 2, 4, 8, and 16 sec. With the multiplicative effect of total number of errors held constant, some evidence was obtained indicating that the serial position curve became more peaked as spacing increased. In Exp. III, both spacing (intertrial intervals of 0, 2, and 8 sec.) and chaining or association break were varied. To vary chaining, the lists were given in quasipaired-associates form. Some lists required that an association be formed between the end and the beginning of the list; other lists did not. Experiment III showed clearly the effect of spacing in determining the serial position effect. There was no evidence for the effect of association break or chaining. Experiment III also indicated a slight effect for primacy-recency when it is not opposed by spacing. On the basis of these findings, it is concluded that the major factor determining the serial position effect is the amount of space between the end and the beginning of the list, with an increase in spacing producing a more marked serial position effect.

References

Atkinson, R. C. A stochastic model for rote serial learning. *Psychometrika*, 1957, **22**, 87–96.

Braun, H. W., & Heymann, S. P. Meaningfulness of material, distribution of practice, and serial-position curves. *J. exp. Psychol.*, 1958, **56**, 146–150.

Greenhouse, S. W., & Geisser, S. On methods in the analysis of profile data. *Psychometrika*, 1959, **24**, 95–112.

Hovland, C. I. Experimental studies in rote-learning theory: II. Reminiscence with varying speeds of syllable presentation. *J. exp. Psychol.*, 1938, **22**, 338–353. (a)

Hovland, C. I. Experimental studies in rote-learning theory: III. Distribution of practice with varying speeds of syllable presentation. *J. exp. Psychol.*, 1938, **23,** 172–190. (b)

Hovland, C. I. Experimental studies in rote-learning theory: VII. Distribution of practice with varying lengths of list. *J. exp. Psychol.*, 1940, **27,** 271–284.

Hull, C. L., Hovland, C. I., Ross, R. T., Hall, M., Perkins, D. T., & Fitch, F. B. *Mathematico-deductive theory of rote learning.* New Haven: Yale Univer. Press, 1940.

McCrary, J. W., & Hunter, W. S. Serial position curves in verbal learning. *Science,* 1953, **117,** 131–134.

Mitchell, M. B. The effect of serial position in the continuous memorization of numbers. *Amer. J. Psychol.*, 1934, **46,** 493–494.

Ribback, A., & Underwood, B. J. An empirical explanation of the skewness of the bowed serial position curve. *J. exp. Psychol.*, 1950, **40,** 329–335.

Robinson, E. S., & Brown, M. A. Effect of serial position upon memorization. *Amer. J. Psychol.*, 1926, **37,** 538–552.

(Received July 27, 1961)

ARTICLE 5

AN INQUIRY INTO THE DOCTRINE OF REMOTE ASSOCIATIONS [1]

NORMAN J. SLAMECKA

University of Vermont

The essential validity of the doctrine of remote associations was assessed. The findings of three original derived-list experiments supported a hypothesis of perception of list patterning, and were incompatible with predictions based upon remote associations. A fourth experiment supported the hypothesis that the association method produces its results through an artifact of serial position. Findings based upon the method of anticipatory and preservative errors were explained consistently by an alternative rationale that excluded remote associations. It was concluded that the doctrine of remote associations is of doubtful validity, and that serial memorization involves acquisition of the items per se, and then the learning of their positions in the list.

In his now classic monograph on rote verbal learning and retention, Ebbinghaus (1885) established the concept of remote associations. His investigations led him to believe that during the memorization of a serial list of items, functional associative bonds were established not only between immediately adjacent items but also directly, and at the same time, between items farther separated from each other in the list. These latter direct connections between noncontiguous items were designated as remote associations. They presumably arose automatically as part of the ordinary process of serial memorization, with no special effort on the part of the subject to bring them about. They were conceptualized as being formed both in the forward and backward directions, that is, an item in the middle of the list could develop a forward connection with the last item and a backward connection with one of the first items. As memorization of the series proceeded, it was thought that each and every item tended to form such a connection with every item in the list, thereby resulting in a complex bundle of associative interconnections among all the individual members of the series, as depicted in Figure 1. Numbers represent the sequential positions of the items as they occur in the list and arrows indicate associative bonds, with remote forward asociations lying above, and remote backward lying below the item sequence.

Furthermore, the strength of any given associative bond was asserted to be a negative function of its degree of remoteness. The bond between Items 1 and 5, above, represents a third degree of remoteness (since it spans three intervening items), and it would be of lesser strength than the bond from 1 to 3, a first degree of remote-

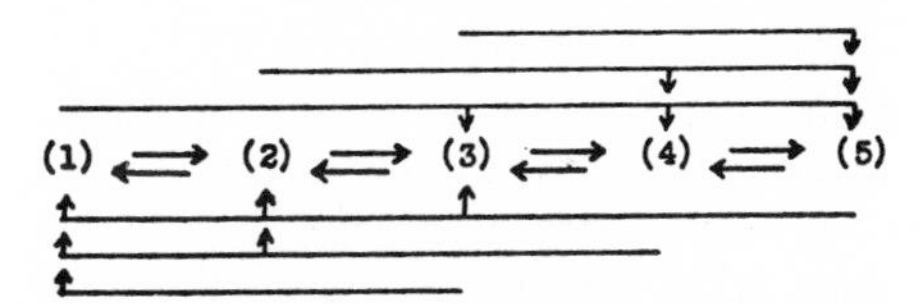

FIG. 1. Schematic illustration of associative bonds among the items of a memorized serial list, according to the concept of Ebbinghaus.

[1] This work was aided by National Science Foundation Grant No. G-14, 721. The author is grateful for the assistance rendered by Ernest Lemay and Muriel Whalen.

Reprinted with permission of the author and the publisher, the American Psychological Association. The article appeared originally in the *Psychological Review*, 1964, **71**, 61–76.

ness (since it spans only one intervening item). Also, all backward associations were considered to be much weaker than their counterparts in the forward direction. Thus, the remote backward linkage from 4 to 1, above, would be weaker than the remote forward linkage from 1 to 4. To summarize our description of the essential properties of his concept, here is a statement from Ebbinghaus (Woodworth & Schlosberg, 1954):

> With repetition of the syllable series not only are the individual terms associated with their immediate sequents but connections are also established between each term and several of those which follow it. . . . The strength of these connections decreases with the number of the intervening (syllables). . . . Certain connections of the members are . . . actually formed in a reverse as well as in a forward direction. . . . The strength . . . was however considerably less for the reverse connections than for the forward ones [p. 710].

Since its inception some 77 years ago this formulation has remained, for all intents and purposes, essentially unchanged and has been accorded rather solid and widespread recognition in the conceptual armamentarium of the verbal learning theorist. Contemporary reference works in the experimental area discuss remote associations as an important part of the phenomena of serial learning (Hovland, 1951; McGeoch & Irion, 1952; Woodworth & Schlosberg, 1954), and recognition of the concept is also given in several introductory psychology texts (Geldard, 1962; Kimble, 1956; Morgan, 1961).

After a close appraisal of the pertinent literature and after conducting several experiments of our own, we have been forced to the conclusion that such widespread acceptance is definitely ill-advised, since there is much room for reasonable doubt about the validity of the remote associations doctrine (in our estimation it has indeed become a doctrine), and that it serves no necessary purpose in the conceptualization of serial verbal learning.

Experimental data from the remote associations literature have usually been regarded as proof that there indeed are such functional connections between each item and all others in a serial list. However, it will be demonstrated that certain necessary deductions from the remote associations position are not borne out empirically, and that these data are susceptible of other equally (if not more) plausible interpretations. Further, it will be shown that phenomena previously attributed to the necessary influence of remote associations can be produced in the absence of any serial learning whatever. We shall present our supporting evidence in the sections to follow, sections delimited on the basis of the three types of experimental methods which have been utilized in the study of remote associations.

Method of Derived Lists

This method, originated by Ebbinghaus, provided the sole source of the data which he presented as evidence for remote associations. An original list is memorized, then the same items are arranged in a different serial order and presented to the same subject again for learning. The latter is the derived list, and it usually involves a patterned rearrangement of the items with respect to their original arrangement. A first-order derived list is formed by skipping every other item from the original list, a second-order list skips two items at a time, and so on. If the sequence of appearance of items in the original list is designated as 1, 2, 3, 4, 5, 6, 7, 8, 9, then a first-order derived list would have a sequence of 1, 3, 5, 7, 9, 2, 4, 6, 8, and a second-order list would be 1, 4, 7, 2, 5, 8, 3, 6, 9. The first-order list brings together items which were linked by a first degree remote association in original learning, and the second-order arrangement brings together items which were previously related by a second degree association. Keeping in mind that remote asociations of the lowest orders are strongest, it then follows that a first-order list should be learned faster than one of second-order, and the latter still faster than a scrambled or control list whose items are in a random sequence. Ebbinghaus (1885) tested such a hypothesis and, indeed, found it supported by his data in terms of percentage savings in learning time.

We cannot agree, however, that his experiment proved the existence of remote associations, for at least three reasons. First, Ebbinghaus learned by the method of whole presentation, wherein the entire list was always in view. It is possible that, inadvertently, he formed "remote" associations directly, by attending to nonadjacent items in direct succession. Secondly, he read the lists in a regular rhythmical manner, and such an imposed organization itself probably influenced the ease with which certain associations were formed, as shown by Müller and Schumann (Woodworth & Schlosberg, 1954). Third, and perhaps the more important objection, Ebbinghaus was his own subject. Since he prepared his own lists and was fully aware of the principle of their construction, it is quite possible that such knowledge could have produced the results, in spite of whatever other precautions he did take.

We turn, then, from this pioneering work to the subsequent experimental literature on remote associations using the method of derived lists, and find relatively few references.[2] Cason (1926) found no significant facilitation in the learning of first-order lists and concluded that "when a series of items is well learned and practiced until the recitation is very smooth, the forward associations between the adjacent items are the only associations that are formed [p. 316]." But we are left with some misgivings since the materials used were very long prose passages and a poem, and it is possible that the sequential dependencies and contextual constraints found in such material served to mask any effects of remote associations. A study by Hall (1928) must be ruled out of serious consideration because her peculiar method of constructing derived lists precluded any meaningful conclusions about remote associations. (McGeoch and Irion [1952] are also of this general opinion.) By far the best designed and controlled study was carried out by Lepley (1934), who used first-order lists and comparable control lists of 12 nonsense syllables at six different retention intervals. Unfortunately, in no case was any first-order list easier to learn than its original list, and the same applied to a majority of the control lists as well. Such heavy and consistent negative transfer, resulting in a finding of no savings, renders the meaning of the results inconclusive for our purposes. Lepley (1934) himself wrote: "Apparently, the potent factors at work in the present study are factors of interference of some sort and the only evidence of remote excitation we have results from a lesser degree of interference in the test lists at the

[2] Since we are concerned only with derived-list studies in which remote associations were sought, we are not including a discussion of two studies in which the focus was upon adjacent backward associations, even though derived lists were used.

end of the thirty minute forgetting interval [p. 16]." Such words are hardly calculated to convince the disinterested reader of the reality of remote associations.

Goldstein (1950), with relatively naive subjects, reported substantial savings over the original list in the learning of both a first-order list and a control list, but failed to find any savings advantage of the former over the latter arrangement, contrary to the results of Ebbinghaus. Apparently, degree of acquaintance with the materials used is a factor in the outcomes to be expected.

We will now describe our own experimental efforts to clarify the question of the meaning of derived list data. One common characteristic of all materials used in previous studies is that, with the exception of the control condition, there was always a rigidly patterned arrangement of items in the derived lists. That is, the ordering of the items in a derived list with respect to their original order was always regular or systematic. It is therefore conceivable that the subject, given a derived list, might actually perceive the orderly relation that it bore to the original (such as skipping every other item), and proceed to "learn" it by (for instance) a process of mediation. This might take the form of uttering aloud every other item, and bridging the gaps by silent utterance of the intervening items. If his retention of the original list was perfect he could "learn" the derived list on the first recitation trial and earn an impressive savings score. If such were the case, his behavior certainly would not constitute proof of remote associative bonds, but only of perceptual alertness. Degrees of remoteness beyond the first would be progressively more difficult to perceive, and thus progressively fewer savings would be the inevitable result. Certain statements from previous studies are provocative in this regard. Cason (1926), who found no savings, wrote: "When the third and last part of the procedure had been completed, the subject was asked a number of questions about the experiment. None of the subjects noticed the way the lists had been constructed . . . [p. 309]." On the other hand, in a report where substantial savings were obtained in a study of adjacent backward associations, Garret and Hartman (1926) commented: "When the reversed lists appeared, every *S* immediately guessed the order of the new arrangement, while the order of the reversed-pairs was at once evident to three *S*s . . . [p. 245]."

Clearly, what is needed is some way of minimizing the possibility that the subject will have such an insight, while at the same time permitting savings due to truly remote associations. There is nothing whatever in the general rationale of the derived list method that requires the use of a regularly patterned list, just so long as it allows remote associations to demonstrate their facilitating effects upon learning. Therefore, a modified type of derived list which is of the first-order *on the average,* should produce just as much savings as the regularly arranged first-order list, but without allowing the subject to benefit from perception of patterning. But if perception of patterning is the critical variable, then the modified first-order list should be learned just as slowly as a control list.[8] Experiment I was designed to test these divergent hypotheses.

[8] The importance, in a learning situation, of identifying patterns of events is attested to in a paper by Bruner, Wallach, and Galanter (1959) when they write: "learning and problem-solving may be more profitably viewed as identification of temporarily

TABLE 1

MEAN TRIALS FOR OL AND DERIVED LISTS FOR EXPERIMENTS I, II, AND III

Experiment	OL		Patterned list		OL		Modified list		OL		Control list	
	M	*SD*	*M*	*SD*	*M*	*SD*	*M*	*SD*	*M*	*SD*	*M*	*SD*
I	1.06	.23	4.94	3.22	1.06	.23	7.61	3.59	1.06	.23	7.94	2.51
II	20.45	8.22	13.30	4.40	19.95	8.01	12.95	7.31	20.60	6.27	13.55	5.17
III	19.90	4.42	10.90	4.71	20.25	7.32	12.05	3.28	20.80	4.81	14.10	5.02

EXPERIMENT I

A total of 36 students served as subjects as part of the general psychology course requirements. Each subject learned one original list and then three derived lists in immediate succession, all to a criterion of one perfect recitation. The order of the derived lists was counterbalanced across subjects. Learning was by serial anticipation on a memory drum with a 3-second rate of presentation and a 6-second intertrial interval. The original list items were 14 letters of the alphabet in alphabetical sequence, from A to N for half the subjects, and from M to Z for the other half. The three derived lists were: (*a*) a control list with items in haphazard order, (*b*) the usual patterned first-order list with every other item skipped, and (*c*) a modified first-order list with 0, 1, and 2 items skipped in an irregular fashion, but with an overall mean of one skipped item. For the A to N list, it looked like this: A, D, E, G, H, K, M, B, C, F, I, J, L, N, corresponding to a skip sequence of 2, 0, 1, 0, 2, 1, (2), 0, 2, 2, 0, 1, 1. The necessary gap from M to B (indicated by the number in parentheses) also occurred in the regularly patterned arrangement, and is a common feature of derived list construction, in order that all the items be used. All lists retained the same first and last items of the original arrangement. The results presented in terms of mean total acquisition trials are found in the top row of Table 1. Original learning (OL) was 1.06 trials because, oddly enough, two subjects needed two trials each to recite the alphabet, in spite of the fact that all subjects were told the initial letter and that there was an alphabetical sequence. The overall F of 10.43 was significant beyond the .01 point ($df = 2/35$), and Tukey's test showed that the patterned list was more rapidly learned than either the modified first-order, or the control list (.01 level gap = 1.86), with no difference between the latter two lists. Furthermore, 10 subjects learned the patterned list on the very first recitation trial, but this did not occur even once for the other two lists! It seems undeniable that such extremely rapid acquisition must have been the result of perception of the pattern. We feel that these data definitely provide strong support for the perception of patterning hypothesis, and at the same time stand against the remote associations doctrine, since the latter would maintain that the modified list should have produced savings equivalent to those of the patterned list.

The fact that savings were not consistently obtained in all past studies

or spatially extended patterns . . . [p. 209]." Also, the well-known "discrimination hypothesis" is based upon the organism's perception of regular sequences of events (Tyler, Wortz, & Bitterman, 1953).

may be attributed to the subject's failure to perceive the particular derived list patterning. The familiar alphabet series used for OL in Experiment I was deliberately chosen in order that it would facilitate rapid perception of the derived list pattern. On the other hand, we would predict that an original list of relatively unfamiliar items, such as nonsense syllables, would not produce facilitation in either type of first-order derived list. Although Ebbinghaus used nonsense syllable lists and reported savings in accord with remote association expectations, it can hardly be said that, for him, those materials were unfamiliar, since he invented them and was fully cognizant of their patterning. A truly naive subject would less likely have insight into the systematic rearrangement used for the patterned list, and consequently would show no savings over the control or modified lists. The remote assocations position would predict that since the original list was learned, remote associations must have been formed, and subsequent savings of equal degree should be obtained for both the patterned and modified lists, over the control. Experiment II tested these hypotheses.

Experiment II

A total of 60 naive subjects drawn from the same source as before was divided into three groups of 20 subjects each. Each subject learned a single original list to a criterion of two successive correct recitations, followed immediately by acquisition of a single derived list to the same criterion. The same presentation rate and intertrial interval were used as before. The lists were made up of 12 nonsense syllables with m' values from 3.03 to 3.12 (Noble, 1961). Two forms of the original list were made up, using the same syllables but in different order, to lessen inadvertent sequence effects. The three derived lists were of the same types as those used before: (*a*) a control list, (*b*) a patterned first-order list, and (*c*) a modified first-order (on the average) list with the following sequence of skipped syllables: 2, 0, 1, 2, 0 (2), 0, 2, 1, 0, 2. Prior to exposure to the derived list, each subject was told that it consisted of the same items as those in the original list, but in a different order. (The subjects of Experiment I were also told this.) Results of Experiment II are shown in the second row of Table 1. It requires no statistical analysis to conclude that there were no significant differences in the rates of learning among the three derived lists. No subject gave any evidence of having detected the principle of arrangement of List *b*. Goldstein (1950) also found that a patterned list was learned no more rapidly than a control list.

It is clear that simply arranging a derived list in patterned low-order form for learning by a naive subject does not automatically produce more rapid acquisition in comparison to the random or control arrangement. This fact is in contradiction to the specific expectation from the doctrine of remote associations, as is the finding of no savings for the modified list, as well. Some knowledge of the patterning must be present, it would seem, before facilitation can reasonably be expected.

What would the outcome of Experiment II have been if each subject did have knowledge of the principle of construction of his second list? We would predict that such knowledge would most benefit the group having the regularly patterned list, would least benefit the control group (knowing that the list is a haphazard rearrangement does not reduce much uncertainty), and might conceivably benefit the modified list group to some extend (knowing that the next item is either 0, 1, or 2 items away in the original list should reduce some uncertainty). Experiment III was performed to answer this question.

Experiment III

Another 60 naive subjects were used from the same source as before. Essentially, Experiment II above was repeated, with the identical nonsense syllable lists, the three types of derived lists, and the same presentation conditions and acquisition criteria. But these subjects were given full knowledge of the nature of their respective derived lists. This was achieved by: numbering each syllable on the original list in consecutive order from 1 to 12 and retaining these same numbers when the list appeared in derived form, and informing the subject, just before presentation of the second list, of the precise principle underlying its rearrangement. Results are shown in the bottom row of Table 1. Duncan's Multiple Range Test indicated significantly faster learning of the patterned list than of the control list ($Rp3 = 3.02$, $df = 57$, $p < .05$). The modified list occupied an intermediate position in mean trials but was not significantly different from either of the other two lists ($Rp2 = 2.86$, $df = 57$, $p > .05$). Thus, with knowledge of the arrangement principle available to them, the subjects did best on the traditional Ebbinghaus type of list. Without such knowledge, as shown in Experiment II, they did no better than control subjects, favorable "remote" associations notwithstanding. Such a distinction would be foreign to the remote associations position, since it views formation of remote bonds as an *automatic* accompaniment of serial learning.

For purposes of control it was necessary to check that the three types of derived lists used in Experiments II and III were of equal difficulty in and of themselves, apart from any transfer effects from the original learning. Thirty naive subjects, from the same source as before, were each given one of the three list types to learn to a criterion of one errorless trial. Mean trials and subjects *SD*'s for the patterned, modified, and control lists, respectively, were: 18.3 (5.14), 20.1 (5.90), and 19.2 (5.81). The F was .23 ($df = 2/27$), certainly not significant. It can be concluded that the derived lists per se did not differ in difficulty.

We conclude from the above experiments that the derived list method in fact fails to provide convincing support for the doctrine of remote association, and instead, serves to give plausibility to an alternative account based upon the subject's perception of list patterning. We will next consider the second method of studying remote associations.

Association Method

This method was introduced by Wohlgemuth (McGeoch & Irion, 1952) and later elaborated by others. After having learned a serial list, the subject is presented with each item individually and required to react with the first response that occurs to him. In order to reduce extraneous responses the subject may be instructed to restrict his associations by responding only with a list item. In any event, the production of an item response which was not adjacent to the stimulus item in OL is taken prima facie as representing a remote association established through serial learning. If Item 2 is the stimulus and the subject responds with Item 6, this is construed as a third degree remote forward association. McGeoch and Irion (1952) appear to have no doubts about the essential superiority and validity of this technique when they assert that:

> Results obtained by the association method provide a more direct picture of the specific remote associations formed, are freer than the method of derived lists from the possible masking influences of associative inhibition, and leave no doubt that forward remote associations occur in relatively large numbers [p. 96].

McGeoch (1936) conducted an experiment using this technique, where, in addition to the associations, he also measured the reaction times of each. His results showed that there was a fairly steady decrease in the absolute number of associations (both backward and forward) as their degree of remoteness increased. Such a finding is in accord with expectations, since more remote associations are presumed to be weaker than less remote ones, and consequently less probable of emission. However, the forward reaction latencies themselves clearly contradicted such a position, since they tended to have shorter durations as they became more remote. Thus there is a nagging inconsistency in the findings as they relate to the doctrine of remote associations.

Later, Raskin and Cook (1937) added a logical refinement to the analysis of data generated by this method, and their paper appears to be the last significant word on the development of the technique. They pointed out that it is improper to tabulate only the absolute number of remote associations given, since the opportunities for their occurrence necessarily lessen as the degree of remoteness increases. A correction for opportunity must be made on the absolute totals. In their experiment they found, in agreement with McGeoch, that the absolute totals showed a steady decline with increasing degrees of remoteness, but when corrected for opportunity there was a rise starting at the fourth degree, resulting in an overall U-shaped function. They attributed this rise to summative effects of both backward and forward remote associations impinging upon the same item. They concluded that:

> remote forward associations are formed in the learning of a series of nonsense syllables, but . . . backward associations, also, are formed during the learning of such a series. As in the case of forward associations, the associations in a backward direction are formed between nonadjacent as well as adjacent syllables . . . [p. 393].

We vigorously dispute this conclusion and challenge the validity of the technique on which it was based, on the grounds that the association method involved a serious artifact which renders the results at least ambiguous with respect to the interpretation to be placed upon them. This flaw consists in completely neglecting the decisive implications of the serial position function. It is a well-established empirical fact that the initial items of a list are most easily learned, the last items next most easily, and those just beyond the middle are the last to be mastered. Since serial learning proceeds by complete trials, wherein the entire list is always run through in succession, it follows that the subject will have differential amounts of practice in giving the correct responses to different items. That is, by the time the list is mastered the subject will have had considerable overlearning on the first items, less so on the last items, and only bare mastery of the middle ones. Now, generalizing from the important work of such authors as Goldiamond and Hawkins (1958) and Underwood and Schultz (1960, Ch. 6), a relationship between the prior frequency of a response and its degree of availability may be stated as follows. Prefamiliarization of a response, or the degree to which it has been previously emitted, determines the probability of its emission in a subsequent free-responding situation. We suggest that the association method embodies the essential aspects of such a prefamiliarization procedure, in that the subject gets differential practice on the various OL items (because of their different serial positions), and is later tested for the relative dominance or availability of his responses. Such a state of affairs should logically, in and of itself, produce the pattern of results commonly reported with the use of the association method, and heretofore singly attributed to the operation of true remote associative bonds. We contend that results such as those of McGeoch (1936) and Raskin and Cook (1937) could be obtained with no serial learning entering into the picture whatever, and that therefore they would not bear critically upon the question of whether remote associations are a valid by-product of serial learning. Experiment IV tested this hypothesis.

Experiment IV

Fifty-four naive psychology students participated as subjects. Each subject was given a controlled amount of differential practice on six nonsense syllables. The syllables, ranging in *m′* value (Noble, 1961) from 3.51 to 3.53, were: CIV, LAT, KEN, DIS, MOR, HAL. Each syllable was typed on a separate card, and after the deck of cards was well shuffled, the subject went through it, looking carefully at each card, spelling the syllable aloud and then pronouncing it. The frequencies of appearance in the deck of the six syllables were 25, 10, 3, 1, 3, 10. This was an approximation to the general shape of a serial position curve, and the subject went through this deck of 52 cards just once. There were three different arrangements of syllable-frequency pairings in order to control for idiosyncratic properties of any given syllable. Upon completion of this differential practice, the subject was tested by the association technique. In order to avoid the emission of unusable, extraneous responses, the subject was asked to respond with the first syllable that came to mind from those he had seen, but not to repeat the stimulus term he was being given. He was presented with each of the six syllables in haphazard order, one time each. The results are displayed in Table 2.

We may regard the items across the top margin of Table 2 as representing the sequence of items in a serial list which had, respectively, 25, 10, 3, 1, 3, and 10 mean total correct anticipations in OL. Along the left-hand margin are the stimuli presented during the association test, and the cells contain the total frequencies of particular responses given as associates. One diagonal row of cells is blank, since instructions forbade responding with the given stimulus syllable. Entries in the top row were not obtained empirically but were derived from the marginal totals of 54, divided according to the proportions required by the obtained column totals and are not included in the grand totals. The (X) represents what would have been the starting symbol for a serial list, that tells the subject to anticipate item number one. Since we lacked the foresight to include such an item during the association test, we decided, for completeness' sake, to synthesize its effect in the controlled manner described in order to provide one more level of forward remoteness for the presentation in Table 3.

The frequencies within any column

TABLE 2

TOTAL FREQUENCIES OF ASSOCIATIONS OBTAINED IN EXPERIMENT IV

Stimulus items	Response items						Total
	1 Practiced 25 times	2 Practiced 10 times	3 Practiced 3 times	4 Practiced 1 time	5 Practiced 3 times	6 Practiced 10 times	
(X)	15	11	7	4	8	9	
1		21	8	2	9	14	54
2	24		7	4	8	11	54
3	14	9		6	14	11	54
4	13	14	10		9	8	54
5	26	8	6	5		9	54
6	17	13	12	6	6		54
Total	94	65	43	23	46	53	324

in Table 2 display some degree of unaccounted-for variability, but an inspection of the overall column totals shows that the attempt to achieve a serial position function through manipulation of the practice frequencies alone was reasonably successful. By the same token, our original statement relating degree of prefamiliarization to the subsequent degree of response availability was confirmed. Table 3 shows the distribution of these same remote associations arranged in degree of remoteness, according to the customary analysis of association method data. For instance, to obtain the total immediate forward responses (zero degree of remoteness), the frequencies in Table 2 running from the upper left corner down to the right through 15, 21, 7, 6, 9 and 9 were summed and appear as an absolute total of 67 in Table 3. To obtain the immediate backward responses, the frequencies running from the lower right corner of Table 2 up to the left through 6, 5, 10, 9, and 24 were summed and appear as a total of 54 in Table 3. The corrections suggested by Raskin and Cook, and the resulting totals, are also presented. The "absolute totals" columns show steady decreases in the totals of remote associations as degree of remoteness increases, in good agreement with McGeoch (1936) and Raskin and Cook (1937). The

TABLE 3

ABSOLUTE TOTALS AND CORRECTED TOTALS OF ASSOCIATIONS IN EXPERIMENT IV, ACCORDING TO DEGREES OF REMOTENESS

Forward associations				Backward associations			
Degree of remoteness	Absolute totals	Correction factor	Corrected totals	Degree of remoteness	Absolute totals	Correction factor	Corrected totals
0	67	6/6	67	0	54	5/5	54
1	45	6/5	54	1	40	5/4	50
2	28	6/4	42	2	33	5/3	55
3	24	6/3	48	3	39	5/2	97
4	22	6/2	66	4	17	5/1	85
5	9	6/1	54				

"corrected totals" columns also tend to approximate the U-shaped function described by Raskin and Cook.

Since it has now been shown that the overall results of the association method can be brought about without any previous serial learning, it follows that data gathered by that method are not at all conclusive with regard to the question of remote associations, and constitute no clear proof of their existence. Although the responses obtained in Experiment IV may be said to be associations to the stimulus items, they are certainly not the result of any *serial* learning procedure, and are not, therefore, remote associations in the true meaning of the term.

The last of the three methods used in the study of remote associations is discussed below.

Method of Anticipatory and Perseverative Errors

When one attempts to recite a serial list from memory, he may omit a few items and give a response further ahead in the sequence, or he may repeat an item that occurred earlier in the sequence. These responses are customarily designated, respectively, as anticipatory and perseverative errors. The method of anticipatory and perseverative errors consists essentially in analyzing the pattern of such errors committed during serial memorization. It has been presumed, rather uncritically, that such errors represent genuine remote associations formed by serial learning. The apparent advantages of this method, according to McGeoch and Irion, (1952), are:

> The anticipatory error method has certain advantages over the two other methods. The remote associations, whatever their degree of remoteness, are overt and specific, which is not the case under the method of derived lists, though it is by the association method. Remote associations may be observed as a function of amount of practice in a single group of subjects. This cannot be done with the method of derived lists, and can be done with the association method only if an association test is made after each practice trial or after selected blocks of trials [p. 98].

Studies by Lumley (1932), Mitchell (1934), and Bugelski (1950) are representative of the use of this method, and their major findings may be summarized as follows: (*a*) anticipatory errors are much more frequent than perseverative errors, (*b*) frequency of such errors is inversely related to their degree of remoteness, even when corrected for opportunity of occurrence, and (*c*) as learning progresses, the number of far remote associations declines both absolutely and in proportion to the number of near remote assocations.

In order to verify such findings from some of our own data, we present in Table 4 an analysis of the OL performance, up to one perfect trial, of the 60 subjects from Experiment II, above. Our data do indeed show the same pattern as those of previous reports: (*a*) out of a total of 1077 remote errors, only 62, or 5.8%, are in the backward direction; (*b*) there are fewer errors the higher their degree, even after correction; and (*c*) as fourths of learning increase, far remote errors drop off faster than near remotes. There is even a tendency, as Lumley (1932) observed, for near remotes to increase somewhat, at least up to the second fourth of learning.

However, as may by now be suspected, our view of the meaning of data such as these is quite different from the usual interpretations that have been put upon them in the past. We choose, in order to test the strength of the traditional doctrine, to reject the assumption that these responses are true remote associations,

TABLE 4

Total Number of Remote Associations (Forward and Backward Combined) According to Degree of Remoteness for each Fourth of Learning, from OL of Experiment II

Fourths of learning	Degree of remoteness									Total
	1	2	3	4	5	6	7	8	9	
1st	110	67	40	31	18	11	7	9	3	296
2nd	188	86	26	24	11	2	5	2	1	345
3rd	160	61	15	14	5	1	1	2	2	261
4th	128	27	14	4	1	1	0	0	0	175
Total	586	241	95	73	35	15	13	13	6	1077
Corrected total	586	265	116	100	55	28	29	36	22	

according to the sense of that concept. Simply because the subject makes an intralist error does not necessarily mean that it represents an association that has been built up specifically through *serial* learning any more than if he were asked to utter the first number between 1 and 10 that occurs to him when the stimulus "go" is given. It might be a response made prepotent through much prior practice of it alone. The presumption that such errors indicate serially learned, *direct* connections between spatially and temporally separated items is gratuitous and highly questionable. Rather, they can be more simply and compellingly explained as being the joint result of serial position effects and educated guesses on the part of the subject in the following manner.

As he learns, the subject must acquire the responses themselves (the "response-learning" phase of Underwood and Schultz, 1960), as well as their *relative* positions in the list (somewhat akin to the "hookup" phase of Underwood and Schultz). During the early stage of acquisition the subject has probably mastered only the first few (and possibly the last) items, thus reflecting the serial position influence, and has but a very sketchy grasp on the identity of the remaining items. There is, for him, an uncertain region in the central area of the list, the order of whose items has as yet not been fixed. However, the subject does his best to follow instructions and occasionally makes a guess as to the next item, uttering any one he happens to know except those he has just seen (therefore, very few backward associations), and those (probably the first ones) whose identity and position have been fixed. At this early stage he is more likely to emit remote associations of higher degree than later, since his ignorance of the list is maximal, and his guesses are less constrained. As learning proceeds, the uncertain region of the list shrinks in extent, leaving fewer unplaced items to be guessed, thus logically insuring that the resulting total errors, as well as their degrees of remoteness, will be smaller. It can be seen in Table 4 that the error total for the second fourth of learning is higher than for the first fourth, and yet, according to the account thus far, it should be lower. This may readily be understood on the presumption that the response-learning phase has reached completion during the second fourth of learning, and therefore the subject has more responses available to him for potential guesses than he has during the first fourth.

The preceding rationale predicts the obtained overall pattern of errors in Table 4 and in those of other studies of this type, without drawing upon any dubious assumptions concerning the development of any remote associations. Such a rationale seems to us more parsimonious and somehow more promising than its alternative. For instance, it would be forced to predict that the distribution of the actual serial position sources of intralist errors would show a tendency, as learning proceeded, toward a greater concentration beyond the middle of the list, because of the progressive shrinking of the uncertain region. In other words, the variability of these errors should show a steady decline across successive fourths of learning, as acquisition progressed. The remote associations doctrine would, of necessity, be silent on this question, since it could deduce nothing specific from its premises alone.

A test of this prediction was made from the OL data (up to a criterion of one perfect trial) of Experiment II. The variances of the distributions of intralist errors from the first to the last fourths of learning were, respectively: 7.29, 6.07, 5.20, and 3.91. Thus, the predicted decline in variability was obtained, and the mean location in the list from which the errors came was about the eighth item, which lies precisely in the region last to be mastered. That part of our hypothesis which asserts that the subject guesses at items he has not yet learned, but refrains from naming items that have already gone by, has received empirical confirmation from a recent study by Peterson, Brewer, and Bertucco (1963). Those authors tested the possibility

> that the occurrence of remote associations is strongly influenced by a guessing strategy on the part of the Ss. In the ideal case, after the S had learned what the responses were, if he could remember what items had already appeared on a given trial, then he could confine his guesses to the remaining items [p. 258].

Their experimental results supported such a hypothesis.

At this point we are convinced that data generated by the method of anticipatory and perseverative errors yield more fully to the above stated rationale than to the alternative account invoking remote functional connections.

Discussion

The major conclusion to be drawn is that the classical doctrine of remote associations is doubtful, in the sense that the data upon which the doctrine was dependent do not in fact unequivocally support it, but rather tend to support more strongly other explanatory hypotheses. These other hypotheses must be regarded, at the very least, as being strong alternatives to the classical doctrine in the light of the experiments described above. Nevertheless, what heuristic benefits has the classical doctrine been able to achieve? The main noteworthy use that has been made of it has been its application toward an explanation of the serial position function. Thus, Hull (1935) used it when he spoke in terms of trace-conditioned responses, and later Bugelski (1950), when he made direct use of the method of anticipatory and perseverative errors in developing a serial position rationale. We must maintain, however, that since the premise upon which such explanations rest (that is, the asumption of the existence of true remote associations) has been shown to be open to question it follows that such explanations themselves are not highly likely to survive future investigation. Judging by the evidence already marshalled above, it might be more prudent to say that the serial position function goes a long way toward explaining data usually attributed to the operation of remote associations, and not the other way around. Whatever the ultimately accepted explanation of the serial position curve will be (and papers are still being published about that problem), is is unlikely that remote associations will play any part in it.

What more positive statements can be made at this time about the conceptualization of serial memorization? Certainly, we feel that remote associations are out of the question, but it would be tempting at least to agree that adjacent connections between items are formed. However, even such an assumption cannot be made with confidence, since recent developments have rendered it highly questionable. Young (1961, 1962) has presented a great deal of convincing data to the effect that the stimulus for an item in a serial list is not the preceding item at all, but that it may instead be the serial position of that item. Also, Ebenholtz (1963) has demonstrated clearly that a serial list *can* be learned quite satisfactorily without the necessity of forming adjacent sequential connections in the list, but rather through associating the items with their spatial positions. With these developments to guide us, the most promising (and challenging) statement we can offer to describe serial learning is that it involves acquiring of the items per se, and then the fixing of their relative positions in the list, through associating them, not with each other, but with a self-generated sequential or spatial symbol (such as first, second, etc.). Both of these processes probably overlap in time, with the response-learning stage being initiated first, and the position-learning stage starting shortly thereafter, in much the same manner as the two phases discussed by Underwood and Schultz (1960). It should be emphasized that this position does not deny the existence of associative bonds, but it does deny that serial learning proceeds by a process that results in simple chaining whereby one item is the stimulus for the next, and it also denies the necessity for postulating any remote associations. Rather, the associations formed are more likely to be between the item and some distinctive symbol designating its relative position in the list, and are the result of an active searching process on the part of the subject. An apposite summarization of the serial learning situation was made many years ago by Woodworth (1938):

> We may well be struck also with the importance of perception or apprehension in the learning process—perception of relations, patterns and meanings. To look at a list of number or nonsense syllables, you would think that the thing to be done was to forge links between the adjacent terms, but the actual learning proceeds largely in quite another way. It does not start with elements and unite these, but it starts with groups, or even with the whole series, and proceeds largely by analysis and the finding of parts and relations [p. 35].

Summary

Previous studies relating to the doctrine of remote associations were reviewed, and several new experiments testing the validity of the concept were presented.

The overall results of Experiments I, II, and III served to support an hypothesis based upon perception of derived-list patterning, and were essentially incompatible with predictions based on the doctrine of remote associations.

Experiment IV gave support to a hypothesis that the association method produces its results because of an artifact, namely, differential practice on the correct responses because of the serial positions of list items. It was concluded that the association method was totally inconclusive with regard to the question of the reality of remote associations.

Findings based upon the use of the method of anticipatory and perseverative errors were consistently accounted for by a rationale based on serial position effects and the subject's guessing pattern, and a further prediction based on that rationale was confirmed.

It was concluded that the doctrine of remote associations is doubtful, and that other alternative hypotheses merit serious consideration. It was suggested that serial memorization involves the acquiring of the items per se, and then the fixing of their positions in the list through associating them with self-generated sequential or spatial symbols.

References

Bruner, J. S., Wallach, M. A., & Galanter, E. H. The identification of recurrent regularity. *Amer. J. Psychol.*, 1959, **72**, 200–209.

Bugelski, B. R. A remote association explanation of the relative difficulty of learning nonsense syllables in a serial list. *J. exp. Psychol.*, 1950, **40**, 336–348.

Cason, H. Specific serial learning; a study of remote forward association. *J. exp. Psychol.*, 1926, **9**, 299–324.

Ebbinghaus, H. Memory: A contribution to experimental psychology. (Trans. by H. A. Ruger, & C. E. Bussenius.) New York: Teachers College, Columbia University, 1913.

Ebenholtz, S. M. Position mediated transfer between serial learning and a spatial discrimination task. *J. exp. Psychol.*, 1963, **65**, 603–608.

Garrett, H. E., & Hartman, G. W. An experiment on backward association in learning. *Amer. J. Psychol.*, 1926, **37**, 241–246.

Geldard, F. A. *Fundamentals of psychology.* New York: Wiley, 1962.

Goldiamond, I., & Hawkins, W. F. Vexierversuch: The log relationship between work-frequency and recognition obtained in the absence of stimulus words. *J. exp. Psychol.*, 1958, **56**, 457–463.

Goldstein, N. Saving in the learning of scrambled lists as influenced by degree of familiarity with nonsense syllables. *J. gen. Psychol.*, 1950, **42**, 87–96.

Hall, M. E. Remote associative tendencies in serial learning. *J. exp. Psychol.*, 1928, **11**, 65–76.

Hovland, C. I. Human learning and retention. In S. S. Stevens (Ed.), *Handbook of experimental psychology.* New York: Wiley, 1951.

Hull, C. L. The conflicting psychologies of learning: A way out. *Psychol. Rev.*, 1935, **42**, 491–516.

Kimble, G. A. *Principles of general psychology.* New York: Ronald Press, 1956.

Lepley, W. M. Serial reactions considered as conditioned reactions. *Psychol. Monogr.*, 1934, 46,(1, Whole, No. 205).

Lumley, E. H. Anticipation as a factor in serial and maze learning. *J. exp. Psychol.*, 1932, **15**, 331–342.

McGeoch, J. A. The direction and extent of intra-serial associations at recall. *Amer. J. Psychol.*, 1936, **48**, 221–245.

McGeoch, J. A., & Irion, A. L. The psychology of human learning. (2nd ed.) New York: Longmans, Green, 1952.

Mitchell, M. B. Anticipatory place-skipping tendencies in the memorization of numbers. *Amer. J. Psychol.*, 1934, **46**, 80–91.

Morgan, C. T. *Introduction to psychology.* New York: McGraw-Hill, 1961.

Noble, C. E. Measurements of association value (a), rated associations (a′), and scaled meaningfulness (m′) for the 2100 cvc combinations of the English alphabet. *Psychol. Rep.*, 1961, Monograph Supplement 3-V8, 487–521.

Peterson, L. R., Brewer, C. L., & Bertucco, R. A guessing strategy with the anticipation technique. *J. exp. Psychol.*, 1963, **65**, 258–264.

Raskin, E. & Cook, S. W. The strength and direction of associations formed in the learning of nonsense syllables. *J. exp. Psychol.*, 1937, **20**, 381–395.

Tyler, D. W., Wortz, E. C., & Bitterman, M. E. The effect of random and alternating partial reinforcement on resistance to extinction in the rat. *Amer. J. Psychol.*, 1953, **66**, 57–65.

Underwood, B. J., & Schultz, R. W. Meaningfulness and verbal learning. New York: Lippincott, 1960.

Woodworth, R. S. *Experimental psychology.* New York: Holt, 1938.

Woodworth, R. S., & Schlosberg, H. *Experimental psychology.* (Rev. ed.) New York: Holt, 1954.

Young, R. K. The stimulus in serial verbal learning. *Amer. J. Psychol.*, 1961, **74**, 517–528.

Young, R. K. Tests of three hypotheses about the effective stimulus in serial learning. *J. exp. Psychol.*, 1962, **63**, 307–313.

(Received December 10, 1962)

CHAPTER 2

Paired-Associate Learning:

Models and Processes

In paired-associate (PA) learning, *Ss* are required to associate together clearly defined stimuli (*St*) and responses (*R*). As in SL, the usual method of presentation is the anticipation method in which *St* is presented alone for a predetermined interval (e.g., two seconds) on a memory drum or its equivalent and is followed by the simultaneous presentation of *St* and *R* in juxtaposition for an equal interval. The *S* is instructed to anticipate the *R* component during the exposure of the *St* alone, with the subsequent occurrence of *R* serving as an informative feedback or reinforcement for *S*'s response. A PA list then consists of some specified number of such pairs. The dependent variables are likely to be identical with the ones found in SL experiments, supplemented, perhaps, by ancillary measures described on pages 65–66.

If we label the stimuli in a PA list *A* and the responses *B*, then a six-pair list would contain the following pairs: A_1-B_1, A_2-B_2, . . . , A_6-B_6. To avoid the possibility of having *Ss* learn the *R* terms serially, that is, as a chain of responses without direct association to the appropriate *St* terms (cf. introductory section and Article 3 of Chapter 3), the specific pairs are usually presented in a different order on each trial. For example, if the previously stated order had been employed on Trial 1, the order for Trial 2 might be A_3-B_3, A_6-B_6, A_4-B_4, etc.

The presence of extrinsically defined and independently manipulatable stimuli, as well as responses, in PA tasks has important heuristic and analytical advantages for PA learning over SL. In fact, PA tasks have become increasingly the counterpart in the verbal learning laboratory of the Skinner box in the animal conditioning laboratory. As one illustration of the relative merits of PA tasks, suppose the problem in question is the functional relationship between the meaningfulness of verbal materials and rate of acquistion (cf. Chapter 4). By means of a factorial research design the investigator could determine the orthogonal effects on acquisition of the meaningfulness of the stimulus component, the response component, and the interaction of the two components. From Chapter 1, the difficulty in interpreting comparable effects in SL should be apparent to the reader. The advantages of PA over SL in many other problem areas could likewise be delineated.

Interest in PA learning, however, has been carried far beyond its pragmatic value in the laboratory. Contemporary psychologists have been particularly interested in the identification of subphenomena or processes that enter into PA learning as a grossly defined phenomenon. Moreover, great strides have been attained in this direction. That this interest is a product of the contemporary period is evident from a pronounced hiatus in the earlier survey of the literature by McGeoch and Irion (1952). In contrast to the detailed examination of SL processes conducted by these authors, scant mention is made of PA learning. The purpose of the present chapter is to familiarize the reader with the models and processes that have been recently introduced by psychologists into their conceptualizations of the PA learning phenomenon. An understanding of these conceptualizations is requisite to the understanding of many of the research areas covered in the remainder of this book.

Conditioning Models

A starting point is to approach PA learning as a possible variant of classical conditioning. This approach would have the distinct advantage of placing PA learning within the continuity of a vast array of other learning phenomena. Efforts of this kind have, in fact, been made, particularly at the procedural or operational level. That is, an analogy is drawn between the procedures and operations of classical conditioning and those of PA learning. In this analogy, Goss, Morgan, and Golin (1959) noted that the *St* component of a single pair corresponds to the conditioned stimulus, the presence of the *R* component (i.e., its physical presentation—visually or aurally—to *S*) corresponds to the unconditioned stimulus, and *S*'s response (such as, overt or covert pronunciation) to *R* corresponds to the unconditioned response. The elicitation of *R* by *St* is not present initially in the conditioning sequence and is therefore analogous to the formation of a conditioned stimulus–conditioned response association.

A procedural model implies that the variables related to classical conditioning should enter into comparable relationships with the new phenomenon in question (here being PA learning). Supportive evidence for these common relationships is then a form of operational identification (cf. Overview), and the evidence partially validates the conceptualization of the new phenomenon as a variant of classical conditioning. This procedural model has been fairly successful in other areas of psychology. A prominent example is the application of classical conditioning principles to the r_g-s_g mechanism of incentive motivation (Lachman, 1960; Spence, 1956). In the case of PA learning, the variable most frequently selected for testing the classical conditioning–PA analogy has been percentage of reinforcement (e.g., Goss, Morgan, and Golin, 1959; Schulz and Runquist, 1960). These studies have tested primarily the effect of partial reinforcement, with reinforcement being defined as the occurrence of the *R* component (the unconditioned stimulus) in the usual *St*, *St-R* sequence of the anticipation method. Thus, 100 per cent reinforcement refers to the occurrence of *R* following every presentation of *St*; 50 per cent reinforcement refers to the occurrence of *R* following half of the *St* components and its omission following the other half. Unfortunately, the available evidence fails to demonstrate a relationship between percentage reinforcement and PA acquisition parallel to that found for more commonly accepted conditioned behaviors. Similarly, Kintsch and McCoy (1964) investigated the delay of informative feedback (i.e., the joint presentation of *St-R*) as a parallel of delay in the conditioned stimulus–unconditioned stimulus interval of classical conditioning. The outcome of their study again accentuates the negative for the application of a classical conditioning procedural model.

Perhaps an instrumental or operant conditioning model would serve more efficaciously for interpreting PA learning. Indeed, both Grant (1964, pp. 26–28) and Wickens (1964, pp. 86–87) alluded to PA learning as a variant of instrumental conditioning but made no systematic attempt to establish the PA procedural analogues of instrumental conditioning. The basic requirements of the instrumental conditioning procedure are the freedom of responding by *S* in the presence of a stimulus complex and the differential reinforcing by *E* of a selected response. These critical elements appear to be lacking in the constrained responding that ordinarily takes place in laboratory studies of PA learning (and, most likely, outside of the laboratory as well—as in the learning of English-foreign language equivalents). This, of course, does not mean that the incorporation of instrumental conditioning procedures into PA tasks is impossible. Underwood and Schulz (1960a, pp. 273–278) described an experiment by Mattocks in which *Ss* supplied their own *Rs* to the *St* components of a truncated PA list. This procedure, which continues until consistent *Rs* are given to the same *St* components on two consecutive trials, closely approaches that of instrumental conditioning.

Stage Analysis

An alternative to analysis of PA learning in terms of conditioning procedures is analysis in terms of the logical stages or phases that are observable during *S's* progress toward the mastery of a PA list. This approach has been led by Underwood and his colleagues and has dominated the contemporary period of PA research. A significant predecessor to the advent of Underwood's version of stage analysis was the careful consideration given by Mandler (1954; Article 1) of the process entering into the integration of the units of a verbal response into a unified response aggregate. Thus, in learning a nonsense syllable, like QAZ, as the *R* component of a single pair, *S* integrates a series of pre-experimentally learned (i.e., in the experiences of daily living) letters into a previously unfamiliar sequence, with Q functioning as a stimulus for A and A for Z. Eventually the three units become available for recall as an entity.

The study by Underwood, Runquist, and Schulz (1959; Article 2) includes a brief summary of the basic tenets of stage analysis. The first stage is that of response learning. If the responses contain disconnected sequences of units, then response learning consists of the integration of these units as discussed by Mandler. If, however, the units are already integrated (e.g., as in meaningful words) prior to PA laboratory practice, then response learning is the differential strengthening of these integrated units to the various situational cues (e.g., the memory drum) in the PA context, whereas other integrated units in *S*'s repertory that are excluded from the list are unaffected (Underwood and Schulz, 1960a, p. 93). This latter function has been called the selector mechanism. In the second or associative stage the responses are "hooked-up" with the appropriate stimuli of the list such that *St* becomes capable of eliciting *R*. The primary role of the stimulus in stage analysis is in the associative stage and will be discussed in greater detail below. It should be noted that stage analysis is intended for application to SL (e.g., Keppel, 1964a) as well as to PA learning. In practice, however, the application has centered on PA learning, largely because of the complications in the associative stage of SL revolving around the complexity of *St* identification.

Methodologically, stage analysis lends itself nicely to the development of criterial measures of acquisition that supplement the customary trials to mastery criterion. For a given *S* the response learning stage is measured by the number of trials taken to emit all of the *R* components whether they are correct associations to the *St* components or whether they occur as intrusions in the list. The associative stage is then measured by the additional number of trials needed to anticipate correctly all *Rs* to the appropriate *St* components. The locus of influence for an independent variable that is to be related to PA phenomena may then be identified. For example, Postman and Schwartz (1964), using this method, found that the nonspecific transfer ("learning-to-learn"; cf. Chapter 8) resulting from previous practice on a list unrelated in content to the test list is concentrated in the associative stage of the test list. This, in turn, led them to hypothesize specifically about the nature of the process affected by prior unrelated practice.

Stage analysis, however, is more than a mere description of the logical phases that *S* completes in mastering a PA list. Extensions of stage analysis that embody the differential roles of the *St* and *R* components in the separate stages represent rigorous attempts at explaining the nature of PA phenomena. The remainder of this introductory section will be devoted to the conceptualization of PA processes within the framework of stage analysis.

Extensions of Stage Analysis

The Stimulus

Of special interest in the extensions of stage analysis is the question, "At what point does the stimulus enter into the stages of acquisition?" Empirically, certain variations in *St* conditions (e.g., intra-list similarity; cf. Chapter 5) yield greater fluctuations in performance proficiency than do comparable variations in *R* conditions. Obviously, the *St* component cannot be ignored in any theory of PA processes. One solution is to conceive of *St* as the origin of the first of a three-link chain of habits that intervene between *St* and *R*. The second and third links are the construct-equivalents (i.e., habits) corresponding to the associative and response learning stages, respectively. McGuire's (1961; Article 3) multiprocess model for PA learning provides a carefully reasoned translation of this first link into the terminology and constructs of modern learning theory. According to McGuire, there is associated with each *St* of a PA list an implicit stimulus-producing reponse *r*. The *rs* serve to encode those parts of the *St* components that are discriminable from one another. These identifying or "labeling" *rs* are, according to the theory, capable of evoking their own stimuli *st*, which mediate habit acquisition for the second link of the chain. In other words, the sequence is

$$St \rightarrow [r \rightarrow st] \rightarrow R.$$

The brackets symbolize the fact that the labeling–mediating sequence is a hypothetical, inferred chain of events. This reliance on labeling and stimulus-producing responses is closely identified with the learning theory constructs of Dollard and Miller (1950), Goss (1955), etc.

In their original consideration of the *St* component Underwood and Schulz (1960a, pp. 292–296) largely ignored labeling responses to *St* components as a separate link in the chain of PA processes. Rather, they preferred to emphasize the role of *St* as a contributor to the associative stage. It should be noted, however, that Underwood and Schulz were analyzing meaningfulness as a dimension of *St*. Comparable attention to similarity as a dimension may well have called for a greater stress on recognition responses or on labeling responses to *St* as a distinct stage of acquisition. Within their conception of the associative stage *St* may provide links that aid in "hooking-up" with *R*. These links are viewed as associates of *St* which hold some commonality with associates of *R*. Suppose, for example, that *S* is faced with the learning of KAG-DRINK as a nonsense syllable (*St*)-word (*R*)-pair in a list. The syllable KAG could elicit the word "keg" as an associate, and this associate may then provide a link to "drink," especially for more wordly *Ss*. Underwood and Schulz are quick to point out (p. 296) that the source of such mediators may rest in the *R* component as well as in the *St* component. In other words, *R* functions in both the response learning and associative stages, whereas *St* functions only in the associative stage.

Lest the reader feel that stage analysis has doomed the *St* component to the minor leagues (while elevating the *R* component to the majors), it should be realized that stage analysts have recently devoted a great deal of interest to stimulus processes other than those entering into the associative stage. Underwood and Schulz (1960a, p. 298) themselves reported that *Ss* frequently select a single unit of a nonsense syllable (e.g., the "Q" of QAZ) to serve as their discriminable *St*. From the Overview and Chapter 1 the reader may recognize selection of this kind as involving the nominal-functional stimulus distinction. The total *St* as actually presented on the memory drum is the nominal *St*; that portion selected by *S* as his effective cue is the functional *St*. In many respects "cue-selection" could be interpreted as demanding the kinds of responses McGuire (1961; Article 3) describes in his first habit link. The importance of the cue (or *St*) selection process to extensions of stage analysis is epitomized by the study of Underwood, Ham, and Ekstrand (1962; Article 4).

The research strategy in the Underwood et al. study and other related studies is to manipulate cue selection by constructing an original list in which the stimulus is a compound containing two or more discrete parts. The investigator then tests for transfer effects, following mastery of the original list, by introducing a second list with the same *R* components (*B* terms) as the original list and either one part or the other of the *St* in the original list as the new *St*. If we visualize the original list as made up of *A-B* pairs, with *A* symbolizing the cue actually selected by *S* as the functional *St*, and *B* the *R* components, then the second list which has these specific cues as the new *St* components would also be made up *A-B* pairs. Consequently, the transfer situation becomes *A-B*, *A-B*, and a large amount of positive transfer is to be expected (cf. Introduction to Chapter 1). On the other hand, the other second list would contain something other than the selected cue from the original list, and would enter into an *A-B*, *C*(new *St*)-*B* relationship with the original list. A reduced amount of positive transfer would then be predicted for the second list (cf. Overview and introduction to Chapter 8).

Underwood et al. employed verbal units as one part of the *St* compound and a distinctive color context as the other part. Earlier studies by Dulsky (1935) and Weiss and Margolius (1954) indicated that the presence of contextual cues facilitates PA learning when the primary *St* part (i.e., the part designated by *E* as the nominal *St*) is a nonsense verbal element. Underwood et al. found a propensity for the more meaningful part of the compound (e.g., the color context when combined with a low meaningful trigram as the other part) to be selected as the functional cue. Cohen and Musgrave (1964) carried this procedure one more step by employing a compound *St* in which both elements are verbal terms. Again, when the elements were of differential meaningfulness, there was a propensity for the one of higher meaningfulness to be selected as the cue. Finally, Saufley and Underwood (1964) found convincing evidence for the fact that cue selection may be manipulated to produce interference rather than facilitative effects under appropriate conditions.

The Associative Stage

The associative stage of PA learning has been the center of several lively and, at points, abstruse issues in the contemporary period. One that has been especially intriguing to the editor concerns the "directionality" of association. By now a number of studies have yielded highly convincing evidence for the fact that many of the *St-R* associations in PA learning are bidirectional; that is, not only does the *St* elicit *R* in the direction *S* is instructed to practice, but also *R* frequently elicits *St* in the backward or noninstructed direction. Although some early psychologists (e.g, Wohlgemuth, 1913) were aware of the existence of these *R-St* or backward associations, systematic interest in this subphenomenon of the associative stage is a product of the contemporary period, beginning with Umemoto (1951) in Japan and Feldman and Underwood (1957) in the United States. During this period the issue at stake has become one of incidental learning (cf. Chapter 6 for a general discussion of incidental learning) versus associative symmetry as alternative explanations for the subphenomenon.

Underwood (1957, pp. 237–238) originally proposed that *R-St* associations be interpreted as a variant of incidental learning. This view is the one espoused in the study by Jantz and Underwood (1958; Article 5). Evidence for this position has generally been that of operational identification; that is, the functional relationships for *R-St* learning are similar to those for incidental learning (e.g., as involving meaningfulness in Jantz and Underwood). When viewed in this manner, *R-St* learning would appear to be a variant of Type II incidental learning (cf. Chapter 6). The Type II situation is characterized by the simultaneous learning of both intentional and incidental components of a complex task. When extended to PA tasks, *R-St* learning becomes analogous to Type II in that *R-St* associations are learned incidental to but simultaneously with *St-R* associations.

An opposing view of *R-St* learning has been presented by Asch and Ebenholtz (1962) in terms of a Gestalt-like principle of associative symmetry. According to this principle, all associations acquired during *St-R* practice are bidirectional by their very nature. Thus, recall in the backward direction would be expected to be as efficient as recall in the forward direction. Support for this position is beginning to accumulate (e.g., Houston, 1964a; Leicht and Kausler, 1965; Murdock, 1962).

In the typical *R-St* study, *R-St* learning is measured by presenting *R* components individually to *S* and asking him to recall the *St* component that had been paired with it. Accordingly, *S* is scored as being correct if he recalls the *nominal St*. Consequently, *Ss* who employed something other than the completely integrated *St* as their functional *St* are unlikely to earn credit for learning the *R-St* association in question, unless they had incidentally integrated the remaining elements of the nominal *St*. For this reason, *R-St* learning, as measured by the above method, is likely to reach an asymptote that is considerably below that for *St-R* learning. The asymptotic differential is one of the main points raised by Jantz and Underwood (Article 5). With nonsense syllables as *St*, the amount of *R-St* learning appears to increase monotonically with *St* meaningfulness (as in Jantz and Underwood and also Cassem and Kausler (1962)), but, even with 100 per cent meaningfulness (as defined by association value; cf. Chapter 4), the amount of *R-St* learning rarely exceeds 50–60 per cent of asymptotic *St-R* learning. From a cursory examination the low degree of *R-St* learning relative to *St-R* favors an incidental learning view and detracts from associative symmetry. Incidental learning is generally less than the intentional learning of the same materials (in the case of PA tasks, of course, incidental and intentional refer to similar rather than identical tasks) unless special kinds of orienting instructions are incorporated into the incidental situation (cf. Chapter 6). In the standard PA procedure such orienting instructions are not present, and an incidental learning interpretation would predict less *R-St* than *St-R* learning.

Ekstrand (personal communication) has elaborated further on an incidental learning view of *R-St* associations in the framework of stage analysis. In this elaboration *R-St* learning is analyzed into two stages—the stimulus integration stage, an incidentally learned counterpart of response integration, and the *R-St* associative stage, the incidental counterpart of the *St-R* associative stage. Although this view may seem to be a natural elaboration to the proponents of stage analysis, it may nevertheless be adding an unnecessary complexity that dimidiates the most attractive feature of stage analysis—its parsimony.

On the other hand, associative symmetry should predict virtually identical amounts of *St-R* and *R-St* learning. Although *R-St* learning with nonsense syllables as stimuli falls considerably short of equality with *S-R* learning, *R-St* learning with words as stimuli seems to come closer to fulfilling this prediction. In a study by Dron and Boe (1964), *Ss* in one condition were given ten trials on a list of seven paired adjectives, followed by a standard *R-St* recall trial. The mean *St-R* score on Trial 10 was 6.53, and the mean *R-St* score was 5.73. Thus, *R-St* learning averaged 87.7 per cent of *St-R* learning. Similarly, Kausler and Lair (1965) reported *R-St* learning to be 85.1 per cent of *St-R* learning with a list composed of unrelated words. In a previous section it was noted that the standard method of *R-St* recall measures *R*-nominal stimulus associations only. It is conceivable that with nonsense syllables there is considerable disparity between the nominal and functional stimulus, with the disparity increasing inversely with meaningfulness; with meaningful words, there is likely to be less disparity between the nominal and functional stimulus. *R-St* recall, as measured nominally only, would be expected to reflect this effect.

A recent study by Leicht and Kausler (1965) introduced two innovations to *R-St* methodology that are especially pertinent to the present analysis. Both innovations deal with the functional stimulus in *R-St* recall. First, they followed practice on *St-R* pairs by a recognition task in which *S* was asked to identify among three alternatives (all nonsense syllable stimulus terms from the list) the stimulus that had been paired with a given response from the list. Under these conditions, the experimenters were essentially measuring response-functional stimulus ($R\text{-}St_f$) recall rather than the response-nominal stimulus ($R\text{-}St_n$) recall of other studies, with *S* being free to recognize whatever element within the stimulus that provided his functional stimulus. Second, the *Ss* were given a sheet containing all of the stimulus terms from the list and were instructed to encircle the letter or letters in each term that had actually served as the cue for identifying the stimulus within the context of the paired-associate list and for associating it with the paired response.

The authors found that $R\text{-}St_f$ recall, unlike $R\text{-}St_n$ recall, slightly exceeded the amount of $St\text{-}R$ acquisition early in $St\text{-}R$ practice and, again unlike $R\text{-}St_n$ recall, eventually reached the same asymptote as $St\text{-}R$ acquisition. This finding was true for stimuli of both high and low meaningfulness. However, the letter identification procedure indicated that more letters are utilized as the functional stimulus in nominal stimuli of high meaningfulness than in nominal stimuli of low meaningfulness. The frequently found relationship between stimulus meaningfulness and $R\text{-}St_n$ recall may then be accounted for in terms of the disparity between the nominal and functional stimulus previously discussed in this section. With nonsense syllables of high meaningfulness there seems to be a propensity for *Ss* to utilize most if not all of the letter content from the nominal stimulus as the functional stimulus. For stimuli of low meaningfulness, the nominal unit is less fully integrated prior to exposure to the learning materials, and, consequently, less of the full unit enters into the functional stimulus.

The tendency of associations to be predominantly unidirectional (stimulus to response) as reported in numerous previous studies would thus appear to be resultant of the failure to distinguish between the nominal and functional stimulus. When this distinction is made, the evidence favors bidirectionality (or associative symmetry) between the functional stimulus and the response. Within the framework of contemporary stage analysis, the $St_f\text{-}R$ and $R\text{-}St_f$ bidirectional concept refers to the associative phase. There is also the strong possibility that many *Ss* may integrate elements of St_n even though the integration may involve elements not directly incorporated into St_f. The processes likely to be involved here are probably akin to those involved in the response learning phase of stage analysis. Surplus stimulus integration of this kind may well be considered as incidental learning in that it occurs incidental to, but simultaneously with, the intentional discrimination of functional cues. The variables related to surplus integration are beyond the present scope of this introductory section. However, it seems plausible to expect that conditions favoring integration of this kind will be negatively related to $St\text{-}R$ proficiency. This expectation follows from the increasing competition between incidental and intentional components of the paired-associate task occuring during the time available for attention and rehearsal.

A second issue concerning the associative stage is one that has been debated in classical learning theory for many years (e.g., Hayes, 1953) but only recently in verbal learning. The problem is whether $St\text{-}R$ associations accrue strength in gradual increments or in sudden all-or-none spurts. If we examine the issue in terms of the probability of St eliciting R, an incremental view stresses the gradual change, with repetition over a number of trials, in probability from 0 to 1.0, with various intermediate values like 0.20, 0.30, etc. Associations can accrue strength without being overtly evident in performance as long as the magnitude of strength is below some presumed threshold value. On the other hand, an all-or-none view insists that the probability shifts immediately from 0 to 1.0 without intervening steps. Underwood and Keppel (1962a; Article 6) have presented a clear exposition of this theoretical issue and further elaboration in this section seems redundant. For still another evaluative essay the reader is referred to a review by Postman (1963).

The incremental versus all-or-none controversy was introduced into verbal learning by Rock (1957) in a now-famous experiment. Rock contrasted the performance of *Ss* who had the same items (letters as *St* and numbers as *R* components) paired randomly from a pool of items and presented repeatedly on each trial, whether answered correctly or incorrectly, with other *Ss* practicing without item repetition; i.e., having new items substituted on each trial for items answered incorrectly on the previous trial. He found no difference in these two performances and concluded that repetition does not facilitate learning—a conclusion consonant with all-or-none theory. A follow-up study by Williams (1961), however, strongly suggested that Rock's finding may well have resulted from a methodological artifact. Namely, the elimination of incorrect items succeeded in removing originally difficult pairings from the list. These difficult pairings are then gradually replaced in the list by easier pairings. In another follow-up study, Taylor and Irion (1964) employed Rock's procedure, with some modifications and extensions, and managed to find strong support for an incremental theory.

A second methodology for contrasting the two views attained prominence in a stimulating article by Estes (1960). Estes interpreted the findings reported with this method as convincing evidence for the validity of all-or-none theory. A brief synopsis of Estes' approach and findings are given in the Underwood and Keppel article (Article 6) and will not be duplicated here. Underwood and Keppel also give a thought-provoking critique of the Estes-type evidence for an all-or-none view. Although the evidence summarized in Underwood and Keppel seems to weigh heavily against all-or-none thinking, Estes (1964) continues to probe the issue and concludes that the evidence for incremental theory is a facade resulting from incomplete analysis of the learning situation.

A third and final issue in the associative stage returns us to the use of mediators as mnemonic devices. Although *Ss* frequently report (e.g., Underwood and Schulz, 1960a, pp. 296–300), when interviewed postexperimentally, the use of such devices in aiding *St-R* hook-up, the reader should realize that mediators are not ubiquitous in the associative stage. Underwood and Schulz (1960a, pp. 302–303), among others, observed that their *Ss* seemed to learn some associations rotely—that is, without benefit of an active mediator (or, minimally, without *S* being cognizant of mediation). Moreover, the acquisition of nonmediated rote pairs is typically at a slower rate than that for mediated pairs. Underwood and Schulz (1960a p. 302) implied that mere contiguity of *St* and *R* may be sufficient for acquisition to take place. This point has received further support in a study by Spear, Ekstrand, and Underwood (1964).

At the other extreme, *St-R* pairs exist in which there is a pre-experimental association (as determined by *S*'s natural language habits which accumulate with verbal experience) between *St* and *R*. The pre-existing associative strength may be great enough that *S* does not need to search for a mediator—the natural habit per se effectively mediates the hook-up. Example of word pairs of this kind are pairings selected from the Minnesota word norms (Russell and Jenkins, 1954; Palermo and Jenkins, 1964a) which are contemporary restandardizations of the old Kent–Rosanoff word norms. Associative strength is measured by the percentage of *Ss* in a normative sample who report a given word as their association to a stimulus word. Thus for the word "lamp" as a stimulus, the word "light" is by far the dominant response among college students (70.6 per cent of the normative sample giving "light" as their response; Palermo and Jenkins, 1964, p. 183). The word "table" is a weaker associate of "lamp" (5.5 per cent of the normative sample giving the response), but the word "oil" is not an associate at all (0 per cent). Common sense would lead us to expect that the greater the pre-experimental strength of a *St-R* pairing, the easier the acquisition when incorporated into a PA list. Still, the evidence (Jenkins, in press) indicates that this is only partially true when studied in college level populations. As long as some pre-experimental associative strength exists, the degree does not markedly affect PA acquisition. In other words, strongly and weakly associated pairs are learned more readily than unrelated (0 per cent response) pairs, but they do not differ from one another. With children as *Ss*, however, Wicklund, Palermo, and Jenkins (1964) found a monotonic relationship between associative strength of pairings and rate of acquisition. These authors attributed this finding to differential *absolute* strengths of natural language habits between children and adults. That is, associatively related pairs may well have comparable *relative* strengths as measured by dominace of responses to stimuli but different *absolute* strengths as a function of fewer exposures to the pairings in children than in adults. Consequently, word norms in children are likely to reflect both relative and absolute strengths, whereas similar norms in adults reflect primarily relative strength.

The situation described in the preceding paragraph applies to pairings in which associative strength is evaluated by free associations to word stimuli in the sense that no restrictions are placed upon the attributes of responses selected by *S*. A study by Underwood and Schulz (1960b) suggests that the associative strength–acquisition rate relationship in college level *Ss* becomes positively monotonic for a broad range of associative strengths when restrictions are placed upon the associative process. In their study *Ss* were restricted (in the normative phase of the study) to sense impressions (e.g., words denoting color, shape, etc.) as responses to the word stimuli. Conceivably, restrictions of this kind tap associations of differential absolute, as well as relative, strengths.

In between the zero strength pairings of rote learning and the related pairings of natural language habits are the vast majority of pairings contained in standard laboratory PA lists. It is here that the concept of a mediator as a mnemonic device is most apropos. Research specifically directed toward mediation in PA learning has taken two different directions. The one approaches mediation through the study of transfer phenomena and will be treated extensively in Chapter 9. The other approaches mediation through the acquisition of a single PA list. It is this approach that concerns us presently. Unfortunately, systematic research in this area is just beginning to appear, and there is little to review in this section. A safe prediction though is that a myriad of studies will appear in the near future.

The study by Dallett (1964a; Article 7) will serve to introduce the reader to the kinds of problems subjected to experimental investigation in the mediated learning of a single list. For other studies the reader is referred to studies by Jensen and Rohwer (1963), Houston (1964b), and Runquist and Farley (1964). The study by Jensen and Rohwer, with retardates as *Ss* in order to minimize pre-experimental habits, is particularly interesting in that it suggests the utilization of mediators as a primary factor distinguishing PA learning from SL.

ARTICLE 1

RESPONSE FACTORS IN HUMAN LEARNING[1]

GEORGE MANDLER

Yale University[2]

Theoretical treatments of human learning phenomena have been largely confined to an analysis of stimulus variables. In recent years, however, more attention is being paid to response factors, especially in the investigations of Underwood (28), Morgan and Underwood (20), and Osgood (22). This paper will present a theoretical framework, applicable to human learning and thinking problems, which will stress response factors. Attention will also be paid to the point, made by McGeoch (18) and others, that most "new" learning in human adults is at least partly a transfer phenomenon. The paper will be particularly concerned with the differentiation of stimulus conditions depending on the evocation of responses made by the organism, the relationship between overt and symbolic responses, and the transfer and overlearning of these responses. Thus, stimulus factors will be viewed as dependent upon the particular response repertory and previous experiences of the individual. This is in line with the position of Sperry (27) who has recently argued, from a neurological point of view, for a response approach to problems of perception and thinking.

The definitions and assumptions which represent the theoretical structure will be specified and some applications will be given, with particular reference to the effect of overlearning on transfer. The reader will note that some of the assumptions are deductive corollaries of others, or are related to other theoretical systems. For the present purposes they will be stated as assumptions.

Definitions

Stimulus. The term stimulus will be used as defined by Hull (15), essentially in terms of receptor input. Hull defined as "actual stimuli" those events which activate a receptor.

Overt response. This term will refer to any observable activity of the organism.

Symbolic response. A human organism will be considered to have made a symbolic response analogous to the overt response if he reports the perception of the overt response without performing the overt response.

Reinforcement. The term reinforcement will refer to an event in the environment which indicates to an individual the correct performance of a response. (No position is taken in this paper as to the specific mechanism of reinforcement. Presumably the above formulation is consistent with all current theories of reinforcement.)

Assumptions

The Differentiating Response

1. A stimulus is differentiated from other stimuli when it evokes a response different from the response evoked by other stimuli. This differentiating response will be designated as R_g. The

[1] This paper is part of a dissertation submitted to the Graduate School, Yale University, in partial fulfillment of the requirements for the degree of Doctor of Philosophy. The writer wishes to thank Drs. F. D. Sheffield, C. I. Hovland, and N. E. Miller for their suggestions and help in the preparation of this paper.

[2] Now at Department of Social Relations, Harvard University.

Reprinted with permission of the author and the publisher, the American Psychological Association. The article appeared originally in the *Psychological Review*, 1954, **61,** 235–244.

R_S can belong to any class of responses, i.e., it can be verbal, motor, or symbolic, depending on the original learning experiences of the individual.

2. When identical R_S responses have been frequently reinforced for two or more different stimuli, these stimuli, other things being equal, will be perceived as identical. Conversely, when different R_S responses have been reinforced to two or more different stimuli, these stimuli will be perceived as different. Identity or difference of stimuli, qua stimuli, depends solely on receptor stimulation, but identity or difference in the perception of these stimuli depends upon the differentiating responses. Thus identical stimuli cannot be perceived as different, but different stimuli can be perceived as identical. Another important implication is that two stimuli which differ in receptor stimulation, but do not evoke any differentiating responses, cannot be perceived as different.

3. Several different differential responses can be associated with any one stimulus and, other things being equal, they will differ only in terms of the probability of their evocation, which is a function of their reinforcement history, as in Hull's "habit family hierarchy" (14).

It will be noted that the present concept of differentiating responses is closely related to Dollard and Miller's (7) concept of cue-producing responses. Their description of attaching the same (or distinctive) cue-producing responses to distinctive (or similar) stimulus objects does not differ from the present treatment. The present statement does imply, however, that stimuli cannot be differentiated unless different responses are evoked.

The adult human organism responds to complex stimulus situations with a variety of previously learned responses which in turn become the stimuli in the learning of new responses, i.e., they "mediate" the new associations. Thus, in a concept-formation experiment, the learning of a nonsense syllable response to all "green" stimuli is an example of mediated learning. On the other hand, a child's learning to differentiate the colors "red" and "green" (different stimuli) by differentially attaching the two verbal responses would be considered original learning.

Response Integration

1. Many responses performed by human organisms consist of aggregates of several subresponses which may be innate or acquired.

2. With successive repetitions of a response aggregate, the separate responses eventually become stimuli for each other such that any part of the response aggregate will tend to evoke the whole response aggregate. This process will be referred to as integration of the response.[3]

3. Integration is an increasing function of reinforced repetitions of the response aggregate.

4. The growth of integration is dependent upon the elimination of responses which prevent or delay reinforcement (as in "anticipatory errors").

5. The integration or association of two responses proceeds more rapidly than the association of a response with a stimulus. Thus, it is easier to learn a new response to a stimulus which already evokes a differentiating response than to a new unfamiliar stimulus.

6. The integration of a response aggregate proceeds more rapidly when the response units belong to the same effector modality. Differences in effector

[3] Integration as used here does not refer to the simple chaining of responses, but rather to the simultaneous elicitation of an aggregate of responses. Responses that occur as overt chains very often are integrated, in the present sense, at the symbolic, perceptual level.

modality refer to differences in effector organs utilized in making the response. Thus it would be easier to integrate two verbal responses than a verbal and a motor response.

This conception of integration is closely related to Hollingworth's (11) concept of redintegration. Guthrie (9) has modified Hollingworth's concept in terms of parts of a response tending to condition each other.

Symbolic Responses

1. Any overt response which is perceived by a human organism evokes a symbolic response analogous to the overt response.

2. The symbolic response tends to be activated whenever the overt response is performed. Evocation of the symbolic response, however, tends to elicit the overt R_S only if motivation to perform the response is present.

3. Whenever a stimulus evokes two separate integrated responses, the two symbolic analogues may also be activated and associated so that, on future presentations of a stimulus which evokes only one of the responses, both symbolic responses will be activated.

4. Symbolic responses can be associated with other symbolic or nonsymbolic responses. In particular, they can be associated with verbal responses.

5. Previously learned verbal responses can have inhibiting effects which prevent occurrence of an overt response. When a particular overt response no longer leads to reinforcement, verbal statements as to its incorrectness can be attached by this experience to the symbolic analogue. On future occasions when the symbolic response occurs anticipatory to performing the overt response, the inhibiting verbal response can effectively forestall the error.

6. In a learning task, the symbolic analogue of a response aggregate will differ from one trial to the next as long as irrelevant overt responses are still present and errors are still made. Thus, irrelevant responses which do not prevent, but are also not correlated with, reinforcement will from time to time be represented in the symbolic analogue. Necessary overt responses will continue to be represented and reinforced, while the irrelevant responses will drop out. In particular, the symbolic analogue is expected to be most distinctive and constant after many contiguous repetitions of the same response aggregate, i.e., after errors have been eliminated and overt performance has reached an asymptote.

The actual modality of the symbolic response is not relevant to the applicability of this concept. It appears advisable to leave stipulation of modality unspecified, which makes it possible to extend the concept of symbolic responses to both verbal and nonverbal behavior.

Applications

In this section an attempt will be made to integrate, in terms of the present theoretical framework, some of the empirical results that have been obtained in studies of human learning. The studies quoted are intended to be representative of the empirical data in a particular area rather than exhaustive listings of these data.[4]

Learning of Differentiating Responses

It is to be expected that complex stimuli will evoke several differentiating responses previously learned to different parts of the stimulus pattern. At the same time, however, differentiating responses can be learned to the total stim-

[4] In the present discussion, no statements have been made about the effects of differential motivation and related concepts. Such phenomena are presumably operative in addition to the effects discussed here.

ulus. Rossman and Goss (24) found that, while subjects used recently acquired verbal differentiating responses to distinguish stimuli in new paired-associates tasks, they looked for "identifying parts" of stimulus terms more frequently and found these more helpful. We would expect such a preference since highly overlearned responses to the identifying parts presumably have a higher degree of probability of evocation than recently learned nonsense syllables.

On the other hand, adult human behavior also provides many examples of the association of identical differentiating responses to different stimuli. Thus, the same word written in several different handwritings or in print will evoke the identical response and will be perceived as identical unless differentiating responses referring to the stimulus differences are actually evoked.

Differentiating responses will be associated not only with the experimentally controlled stimulus but also with other aspects of the total situation. The integrated response is reinforced in the context of the experimental situation, particularly in regard to the experimenter, the apparatus, and so forth. A recent study by Bilodeau and Schlosberg (3) showed more retroactive inhibition when the experimental room was the same for both tasks than when the interfering task was learned in a different room.

Prior training with attendant integration of a differentiating response is expected to shorten the learning process on future occasions when that response is used. Hovland and Kurtz (12) found that prior familiarization with nonsense syllables facilitated learning of lists using those nonsense syllables.

Concept Formation

Under this heading will be discussed only those aspects of so-called concept formation in which a subject is required to learn a common response to a class of stimuli. The experimental situation has most frequently been exemplified by Heidbreder's experiments (10).

It is assumed that in the presentation of a number of stimuli, many differentiating responses will be evoked by each stimulus. The stimuli will have been predifferentiated to varying degrees, and different aspects of each stimulus will evoke different responses. In most cases these responses are verbal responses which also elicit their symbolic analogues. At the same time, the subject learns to make the new paired-associates response (nonsense syllables in Heidbreder's experiments). These new responses, which have never before been evoked in the presence of these particular stimuli, are now associated with the already learned symbolic responses. In the process of successive presentations, the symbolic response which corresponds to the "concept" will be associated more frequently than any other with the new response. Thus, if one of the prior differentiating responses is "face," then the new response (the nonsense word) will be associated with the symbolic analogue "face." In successive presentations of instances of this concept, this association will be reinforced so that, eventually, the evocation of the symbolic response "face" will also evoke the new *name* of the concept—the correct nonsense response. Figure 1 shows a schematic representation of this process; R_{S_x} is the symbolic response common to the stimuli, and will be more frequently associated with the concept response than other differentiating responses. This is similar to Hull's (13) theoretical description of concept formation. The difference is that, in the present formulation, the concept response is (at least at first) associated with the respective differentiating responses rather than directly with the stimulus components.

A recent study by Baum (2) indicates

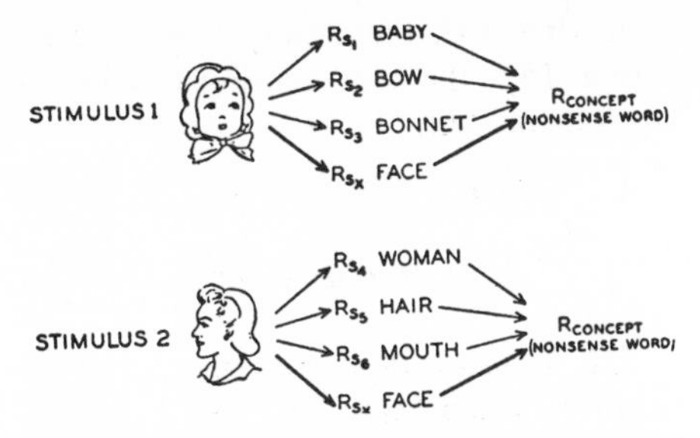

FIG. 1. Two instances of the same concept (Stimuli 1 and 2) eliciting one common ("face"), and several different, differentiating responses

that ease of concept attainment is a function of the discriminability of the stimuli. Her findings imply that degree of previous learning of the differentiating response determines ease of concept learning. In the extreme case, it would be expected that a stimulus which evokes no previously learned differentiating responses—the completely "unfamiliar" stimulus—could not be one of a class of "similar" stimuli. On the other hand, stimuli which have been maximally differentiated, i.e., with a high probability of evocation of a differentiating response, provide highly integrated responses, potent symbolic responses, and easy association with the new response.

Response Generalization

The general statement of this phenomenon usually implies that the learning of a response to a particular stimulus will facilitate the learning of similar responses to the same stimulus. This similarity can be specified in two dimensions. It can be either a similarity of overt parts of the two responses or a similarity of symbolic responses, as in the use of synonyms in Morgan and Underwood's experiment (20). An attempt will be made to show that response integration and symbolic responses are sufficient to explain the phenomena usually described as response generalization.

Similarity in terms of elements involves a communality of some of the parts of an integrated response. Substituting a new unit for one of the original units of the integrated response does not affect the integration of the units which are common to both aggregates. If it is assumed that the replaced unit can be dropped out fairly efficiently, this situation should produce faster learning than one in which all the units have to be integrated.

Similarity of symbolic responses, i.e., in the meaning realm, is comparable to the concept formation situation. The two synonymous responses both evoke a common symbolic response. As a concrete example, two of the synonyms used by Morgan and Underwood (20) were "dirty" and "unclean." To the extent that these two responses are associated with a common symbolic concept such as "filth," paired associate learning of the second response will be mediated by the common concept. Figure 2 diagrams this process. The common symbolic response, however, need not be as specific as the one used in the example, and it may be nonverbal. Morgan and Underwood also found that different degrees of synonymity are reflected in the degree of response generalization. The position taken here is that synonymity is a function of common symbolic representation of the two differentiating responses, which in turn would affect response generalization as found. A similar point of view, describing meaning as a function of commonly associated re-

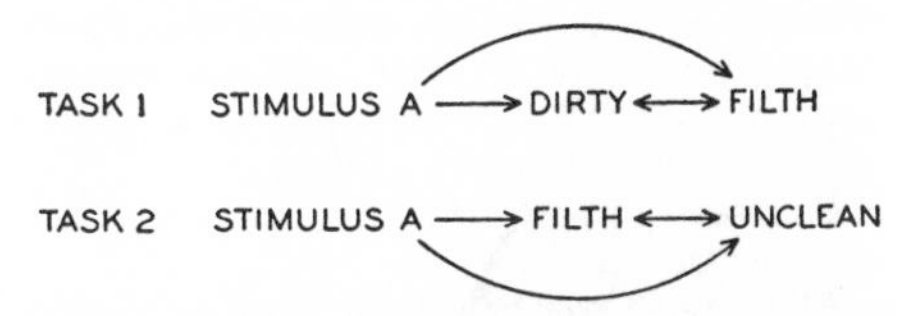

FIG. 2. The mediating and facilitating effect of a common symbolic concept in the response generalization of two synonymous responses

sponses, has been advanced by Noble (21).

Implicit Trial and Error

Dashiell (6), and others, have pointed out the importance of implicit trial and error in facilitating problem-solving behavior in human subjects. The facilitating mechanism is provided by the attachment of an implicit "yes" or "no" to the symbolic analogues of the various courses of action. A symbolic response sequence that leads to the anticipation of an unwanted consequence could produce one-trial inhibition in human subjects. The subject continues with such trial and errors—at the symbolic analogue level—until he hits upon the desired outcome; this sequence can then be translated into overt behavior.[5]

Transfer of Training[6]

Given an original learning situation, subsequent transfer situations can contain either new or the old stimuli, and either new or the old responses. "New" and "old" indicate whether or not the particular stimulus or response has been previously paired with any response or stimulus used in the experimental situation. Thus, a *new* stimulus is that stimulus which has not been previously used to elicit any of the responses used in the experiment, and a *new* response is a response or response aggregate which has not been previously reinforced in the experiment; *old* stimuli and responses are those which have been presented, or elicited and reinforced, in the original learning task.

[5] The inhibiting "no" response would also produce other, primarily motivational, effects. Mechanisms such as fear and anxiety are probably additional factors in this inhibition phenomenon. It appears, however, that for the present purposes the more simplified conceptualization is adequate.

[6] This topic will be treated more extensively than preceding applications, partly because relevant implications of the present theoretical approach have been explored experimentally (19) in a study to be published separately.

In line with the terminology used by Bruce (4), the four possible conditions of transfer are:

I. Making a new response to an old stimulus.

II. Making an old response to a new stimulus.

III. Making an old response to an old stimulus when these have not been previously paired.

IV. Making a new response to a new stimulus. This is considered chiefly as a condition in which the effect of previous training on new learning can be controlled; the kinds of "transfer" observed in this condition are not relevant to the present theoretical framework.

In order to schematize all four conditions, two *S-R* pairs are necessary in the training situation. This is forced by the third condition, where making an old response to an old stimulus requires more than one original pair. Thus, to make the other conditions comparable, two training pairs will be considered in each of the conditions. The schema is shown below, in which the original learning is S_1-R_1 and S_2-R_2. New stimuli and responses are indicated by S_3, S_4 and R_3, R_4 respectively.

	Conditions			
	I	II	III	IV
Training	S_1-R_1	S_1-R_1	S_1-R_1	S_1-R_1
	S_2-R_2	S_2-R_2	S_2-R_2	S_2-R_2
Transfer	S_1-R_3	S_3-R_1	S_1-R_2	S_3-R_3
	S_2-R_4	S_4-R_2	S_2-R_1	S_4-R_4

For the present purpose, only familiar stimuli will be considered, i.e., stimuli with a high probability of evocation of a differentiating response. With less familiar stimuli, the predictions would be similar, but would involve the learning either of a response specific to the stimulus as its differentiating response or, with relatively unfamiliar stimuli, the adoption of the experimental response as the differentiating response. In the present analysis, the experimental response is added to, and integrated with, the previously established differentiating responses to the stimulus.

In the original training task (i.e., in the acquisition of S_1-R_1 and S_2-R_2), response integration and generation of symbolic analogues proceed as a function of degree of training. Similarly, the probability of evocation of the response is increased. In the transfer situation, degree of training will produce differential facilitation or interference effects. Predictions for the three transfer conditions, schematized above, follow:

1. *Learning to make a new response to an old stimulus.* The relevant processes during original training are the integration of the response, the attendant formation of the symbolic analogue, and the increasing probability of evocation of the correct response. At high degrees of learning, the symbolic analogue will be distinctive enough so that on the first trial of the transfer task, i.e., the first time the subject makes the now incorrect old response, an "inhibitory" response will be attached to the symbolic response and will tend to decrease the probability of evocation of the now interfering response. Thus, at high degrees of overlearning on the original task, we would expect less negative transfer than at previous stages of training. Attaching the inhibiting response to both the overt response and its symbolic analogue on the first and succeeding transfer trials will tend to evoke the symbolic response and the inhibiting response before the overt response on subsequent presentations of the stimulus, and may thus avoid the overt response entirely. In this way the highly overlearned response has a sufficiently distinctive symbolic analogue so that the inhibiting response is readily associated, and the usual effects of associative interference between the old and the new response are much less in evidence. The present analysis therefore predicts less interference with high degrees of learning.

A study by Underwood (29) confirms this prediction. Using adjectives (highly integrated responses) as stimuli and responses, he found a decrease in associative inhibition as the degree of prior learning was increased, and marked facilitation when the original task had been learned to a high degree. The present model would predict no facilitation when familiar stimuli are used, and Underwood's experiment is not crucial in this respect since he did not control for the effect of high degrees of learning on warm-up. Otherwise, the only effect to be expected is a decrease in associative interference.

In this transfer condition the latter effect would be expected to be less pronounced when nonintegrated responses are utilized, in which case more trials on the original task would be needed to show the decrease in negative transfer. Bruce's data (4), using nonsense syllables (rather than meaningful adjectives), do not show the decrease in interference at higher degrees of learning if his data are corrected for the positive transfer that he found in the new-stimulus new-response condition.

In the area of motor learning, Lewis, McAllister, and Adams (17) have shown that prior learning can produce both facilitation and interference. The task consisted of learning to manipulate controls which could be operated to superimpose two separate lights on a screen. On the transfer task, the controls were reversed so that, for example, a previously correct movement which had moved the light to the right now moved the light to the left. In this type of task, we would expect the similarity of the responses to produce some facilitation, while the reversal of the controls would produce interference. The data suggest that, with increasing training on the original task, the number of correct responses on the reversal transfer task increases (response facilitation through transfer of a previously integrated response), but that specific errors also increase (interference due to previous reinforcement of the now incorrect response).

2. *Learning to make an old response to a new stimulus.* In this condition, the primary factor is assumed to be the integration of the response, i.e., the subject learns how to perform the response. Since the response has been learned not only in the presence of its original stimulus, but also is associated with all other constant aspects of the experimental situation, the probability of its evocation is high, and once evoked and reinforced in the transfer situation, the rate of learning of the new association will be partly a function of the integration of the response and its association with the context cues. It should be pointed out, however, that measurable transfer will reach a maximum before response integration does. For example, if the new association is learned on the first or second trial of the transfer task, increased integration of the response on the original task will show little measurable transfer effects. The prediction in this situation would be increasing positive transfer as a function of correct repetitions of the response on the original task.

The earliest relevant study is that of Bair (1), whose subjects learned to press specific colored typewriter keys to color stimuli. When a new list of stimuli was presented, with the responses remaining identical to the ones previiously used, he obtained positive transfer. Bruce's data (4), again corrected for warm-up effects, show increasing positive transfer as degree of original learning is increased. Bunch and Winston (5) obtained clear positive transfer effects when a previously learned nonsense syllable response had to be learned to a new stimulus.

The paucity of data in the literature relevant to this problem is compensated for by their unequivocal direction. However, one important implication from the present position has been given little experimental verification: if the response on the original task is already highly integrated (e.g., in the use of adjectives), then transfer effects should be minimal. In other words, amount of positive transfer in this situation is partly a function of degree of integration of the response at the beginning of the original task. The evidence that is available, however, is confirmatory (25).

3. *Learning to make an old response to an old stimulus when these have not been previously paired.* Three factors influence learning in the transfer task:

a. The integration of the response in the original task: facilitating effect.

b. The probability of evocation of the response, now incorrect, learned in the original task: interfering effect.

c. The symbolic "inhibition" of that incorrect response: counteracts the interfering effect of *b*.

At low degrees of learning, up to maximal strength of the original association, we would predict variable positive or negative transfer effects, depending on the relative strength of the facilitating and interfering effects *a* and *b*. When the symbolic analogue has become stable (at high degrees of overlearning), there would be an increasing tendency toward positive transfer as the interfering effect of *b* is counteracted by *c*.

One additional factor, however, is important in this particular condition. The differentiating responses evoked by the stimulus may be integrated to a greater or lesser degree with the response learned in the original task. In Conditions 1 and 2, this factor is presumably of minor importance. In Condition 1, the old response is never reinforced in the transfer situation, and the integration would be additive to the general interference effect so that like-modality responses would lead to greater initial interference. In Condition 2, the effect might delay the increasing positive facilitation since part of the integrated response (the previously correct differentiating response) has to be eliminated. In Condition 3, however, these two effects would not only be additive, but the constant re-evocation of parts of this integration would interfere with the elicitation of either part alone. A recent study by Porter and Duncan (23) has shown greater negative transfer in Condition 3 than in Condition 1, when the stimulus and response elements were both verbal, which would favor integration of stimulus and response elements. In their discussion, the authors point to the possibility of the response re-evoking the stimulus and thus leading to greater interference.

If the differentiating response is verbal and the newly learned response (in the original task) motor (i.e., if the two responses belong to different effector modalities), we would predict that the integration of these two components would be minimal and would show less negative transfer than Condition 1. Siipola and Israel (26) have presented data bearing on this latter expectation. Subjects were pretrained to learn a series of responses on telegraphic keys. They were then presented with the original task in which these codes had to be associated with letters of the alphabet. In the transfer task, the same stimuli and responses were used, but their combinations were changed. The data, measuring transfer as a function of training on the original task, show slight initial negative transfer followed by a large positive transfer effect.

Kline's (16) subjects paired authors' names with book titles. He found that, with greater degrees of prior knowledge of the *correct* authors' names, paired-associates learning was easier even when the correct response was to give wrong authors' names to the book titles. His evidence for decreased interference as a function of increasing familiarity is consistent with our prediction.

Conclusion

Further empirical verification of the above predictions should precede the application of this theoretical framework to more complex problems. The general emphasis on the model presented here has been on the importance of response factors in activities of the human organism prior to its introduction to an experimental situation. Phenomena such as stimulus discriminability are assumed to be a function of such previous experiences. In these terms, the differentiation of stimuli varies from individual to individual, and any general description of the discriminability of a stimulus only refers to the communality of experiences a group of individuals has had in learning differentiating responses to that stimulus. Thus, statements about stimuli, other than those referring to receptor stimulation, are limited to common social and learning experiences of subjects. In the past, studies such as Gibson's (8) have used stimuli and responses (with relatively homogeneous groups of subjects) which were most likely to result in similar differentiating learning experiences.

In reference to transfer effects, Guthrie's warning (9) that transfer is specific and not general has been taken account of. Particular attention has been paid to the fact that most human activities involve highly overlearned responses and response aggregates, and to the relevance of this phenomenon to transfer effects. If the predictions made concerning the differential effects of a subject's experiences with the stimuli and responses are borne out, then such long-accepted generalizations as Wylie's

(30), that "the transfer effect is positive when an old response can be transferred to a new stimulus, but negative when a new response is required to an old stimulus," need re-examination.

REFERENCES

1. BAIR, J. H. The practice curve: a study in the formation of habits. *Psychol. Monogr.,* 1902, **5**, No. 2 (Whole No. 19).
2. BAUM, MARIAN H. A study in concept attainment and verbal learning. Unpublished doctor's dissertation, Yale Univer., 1951.
3. BILODEAU, INA M., & SCHLOSBERG, H. Similarity in stimulating conditions as a variable in retroactive inhibition. *J. exp. Psychol.,* 1951, **41**, 199–204.
4. BRUCE, R. W. Conditions of transfer of training. *J. exp. Psychol.,* 1933, **16**, 343–361.
5. BUNCH, M. E., & WINSTON, M. M. The relationship between the character of the transfer and retroactive inhibition. *Amer. J. Psychol.,* 1936, **48**, 598–608.
6. DASHIELL, J. F. *Fundamentals of general psychology.* Boston: Houghton Mifflin, 1937.
7. DOLLARD, J., & MILLER, N. E. *Personality and psychotherapy.* New York: McGraw-Hill, 1950.
8. GIBSON, ELEANOR J. A systematic application of the concepts of generalization and differentiation to verbal learning. *Psychol. Rev.,* 1940, **47**, 196–229.
9. GUTHRIE, E. R. *The psychology of learning.* (Rev. Ed.) New York: Harper, 1952.
10. HEIDBREDER, EDNA. The attainment of concepts: I. Terminology and methodology. *J. gen. Psychol.,* 1946, **35**, 173–189.
11. HOLLINGWORTH, H. L. General laws of redintegration. *J. gen. Psychol.,* 1928, **1**, 79–90.
12. HOVLAND, C. I., & KURTZ, K. H. Experimental studies in rote-learning theory: X. Pre-learning syllable familiarization and the length-difficulty relationship. *J. exp. Psychol.,* 1952, **44**, 31–39.
13. HULL, C. L. Quantitative aspects of the evolution of concepts. *Psychol. Monogr.,* 1920, **28**, No. 1 (Whole No. 123).
14. HULL, C. L. The concept of the habit-family hierarchy and maze learning. *Psychol. Rev.,* 1934, **41**, 33–52.
15. HULL, C. L. *Principles of behavior.* New York: Appleton-Century-Crofts, 1943.
16. KLINE, L. W. An experimental study of associative inhibition. *J. exp. Psychol.,* 1921, **4**, 270–299.
17. LEWIS, D., MCALLISTER, DOROTHY E., & ADAMS, J. A. Facilitation and interference in performance on the modified Mashburn apparatus: I. The effects of varying the amount of original learning. *J. exp. Psychol.,* 1951, **41**, 247–260.
18. MCGEOCH, J. A. *The psychology of human learning.* New York: Longmans, Green, 1942.
19. MANDLER, G. Transfer of training as a function of degree of response overlearning. *J. exp. Psychol.,* 1954, **47**, in press.
20. MORGAN, R. L., & UNDERWOOD, B. J. Proactive inhibition as a function of response similarity. *J. exp. Psychol.,* 1950, **40**, 592–604.
21. NOBLE, C. E. An analysis of meaning. *Psychol. Rev.,* 1952, **59**, 421–430.
22. OSGOOD, C. E. The similarity paradox in human learning: a resolution. *Psychol. Rev.,* 1949, **56**, 132–143.
23. PORTER, L. W., & DUNCAN, C. P. Negative transfer in verbal learning. *J. exp. Psychol.,* 1953, **46**, 61–64.
24. ROSSMAN, IRMA L., & GOSS, A. E. The acquired distinctiveness of cues: the role of discriminative verbal responses in facilitating the acquisition of discriminative motor responses. *J. exp. Psychol.,* 1951, **42**, 173–182.
25. SHEFFIELD, F. D. The role of meaningfulness of stimulus and response in verbal learning. Unpublished doctor's dissertation, Yale Univer., 1946.
26. SIIPOLA, ELSA M., & ISRAEL, H. E. Habit interference as dependent upon stage of training. *Amer. J. Psychol.,* 1933, **45**, 205–227.
27. SPERRY, R. W. Neurology and the mind-brain problem. *Amer. Scientist,* 1952, **40**, 291–312.
28. UNDERWOOD, B. J. *Experimental psychology.* New York: Appleton-Century-Crofts, 1949.
29. UNDERWOOD, B. J. Proactive inhibition as a function of time and degree of prior learning. *J. exp. Psychol.,* 1949, **39**, 24–34.
30. WYLIE, H. H. Transfer of response in the white rat. *Behav. Monogr.,* 1909, **3**, No. 5.

(Received August 10, 1953)

ARTICLE 2

RESPONSE LEARNING IN PAIRED-ASSOCIATE LISTS AS A FUNCTION OF INTRALIST SIMILARITY[1]

BENTON J. UNDERWOOD, WILLARD N. RUNQUIST,[2] AND RUDOLPH W. SCHULZ

Northwestern University

Paired-associate learning of verbal lists can be divided logically into two phases. These two phases will be called the response-recall or response-learning phase, and the associative phase. The response-learning phase is conceived of as the learning required to make the responses readily recallable. This first phase must necessarily precede the second phase, the associative phase, since the response must be available before it can be associatively connected (second phase) to a specific stimulus in the paired-associate list. It is possible, of course, that certain components of the response (e.g., the first letter) may develop associative strength to the stimulus before the entire response is available.

This division of rote learning into two phases is not new (e.g., Hovland & Kurtz, 1952), but so far as is known it has not been used systematically as an analytical device. Certain considerations suggest that variables which are known to affect the over-all rate of learning operate differentially during the two phases. For example, the fact that meaningfulness of responses in paired-associate learning influences the rate of learning to a greater extent than does stimulus meaningfulness (Sheffield, 1946) could be interpreted to indicate that as response meaningfulness increases both the response-recall phase and the associative phase are enhanced, whereas, when stimulus meaningfulness increases through a corresponding range only the associative phase is facilitated.

The present studies are concerned with intralist response similarity and its role in the two phases of learning as outlined above. The general hypothesis to be tested is that the higher the intralist response similarity the greater the facilitation of the response-learning phase. Since it is known (Feldman & Underwood, 1957) that with the type of lists to be used high intralist response similarity impedes over-all paired-associate learning (as compared with low intralist response similarity), it must follow from the hypothesis that the negative or interference component of high response similarity occurs primarily in the associative phase.

That the response-recall phase would be enhanced by high intralist response, similarity could be expected on at least two somewhat independent bases. First, it is known that high inter-item similarity (at least meaningful similarity) and associative connection are almost perfectly correlated (Haagen, 1949). Thus, if *S* recalls one response, the recall of other similar responses should be facilitated. The clustering effect of items of high similarity shown by Bousfield and Cohen (1955) suggests the operation of this principle. A second way of viewing the situation would suggest simply that if all responses in a paired-associate list are similar, *S* merely has to remember a single con-

[1] This work was done under Contract N7onr-45008, Project NR 154-057, between Northwestern University and the Office of Naval Research.

[2] Now at Hobart College.

Reprinted with permission of the authors and the publisher, the American Psychological Association. The article appeared originally in the *Journal of Experimental Psychology*, 1959, **58**, 70–78.

cept and then give instances of that concept in the response-recall phase. If all responses are dissimilar, however, as many different "concepts" as there are responses must be learned. Either way of viewing the situation suggests that the response-recall phase will take place more rapidly with items of high similarity than with items of low similarity.

In the major conditions of the present studies two 10-item paired-associate lists are used. In one list the 10 responses are dissimilar adjectives, and in the other they are adjectives all of which have a more or less common meaning. In one set of conditions, *S*s are taught the 10 responses *before* they become responses in a standard paired-associate list. Teaching *S* the responses may be thought of as isolating the response-learning phase. The hypothesis stated above leads to two predictions about the results of these procedures. First, when *S*s are taught the responses before they become a part of a paired-associate list, it must be predicted that acquisition of the 10 similar responses will take place more rapidly than the acquisition of the 10 dissimilar responses. Secondly, having taught *S* the responses before they become a part of a paired-associate list, it must be predicted that when they do become responses in this paired-associate list the initial learning process will occur more rapidly than will learning in control conditions where the initial learning of the responses has not taken place. This prediction must be limited to the early trials corresponding to the period during which response learning is believed to occur. While it might appear that if response learning is facilitated the associative phase would "get started sooner" and that over-all learning would thereby be facilitated, there is nothing in the hypothesis which asserts this. Teaching *S* the responses before these responses become a part of a paired-associate list is assumed merely to remove the bulk of the response-learning phase in paired-associate learning.

In another set of conditions standard paired-associate learning is used but *S*s are stopped at various points in learning and are asked to give all the response items they can remember. The prediction is that more responses will be given from the high-similarity list than from the low-, (at least early in learning) even though the over-all rate of learning is slower for the high-similarity list.

Method

Materials.—For the basic learning task two lists of 10 pairs were used in which the stimulus items were nonsense syllables and the response items were two-syllable adjectives. The stimuli were taken from a previous study (Underwood, 1953a) and were of from 46–53% association value (Glaze, 1928) and of low intralist similarity. The responses were also taken from a previous study (Underwood & Goad, 1951). In one list all responses were more or less synonymous in meaning (*cheerful, sunny, carefree, pleasant, gleeful, laughing, happy, genial, jolly, smiling*). In the other list the responses were unrelated in meaning (*spicy, rounded, hairy, equal, modern, tiresome, fiery, faithful, plastic, guilty*). On the average both sets of responses have about the same Thorndike-Lorge (1944) frequency. In pairing a syllable and an adjective an attempt was made to avoid any apparent connections between the two.

General design.—Three basic conditions each involved paired-associate learning of the high-similarity list and the low-similarity list, with separate groups learning each list in each condition. In one condition of response learning (Cond. RL), *S* learned the responses alone before learning the paired-associate list. In this RL procedure the responses were presented in varying order from trial to trial for five trials with a recall test being given after each trial. One group learned the high-similarity responses and another the low-similarity responses before proceeding to their respective paired-asso-

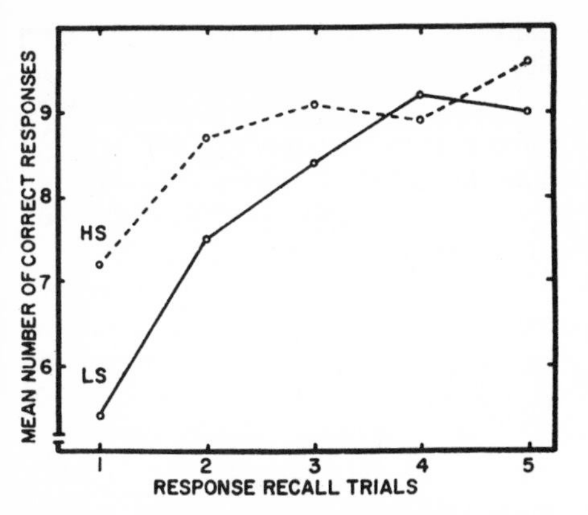

FIG. 1. Mean correct responses on each response-recall trial as a function of high similarity (HS) and low similarity (LS).

ciate lists. A control condition (Cond. C) involved no pretraining. A comparison of learning the paired-associate lists for RL and C conditions should indicate the effectiveness of learning the responses prior to paired-associate learning. The third condition (Cond. PA-RL) was designed to determine the extent of response learning (RL) during paired-associate learning (PA). Various groups were stopped at different points during paired-associate learning and given a single free recall of the responses. This response learning was tapped at six points, namely, after 1, 2, 3, 5, 8, and 13 exposures of the paired-associate lists. Since each *S* was stopped only *once* during learning, the PA-RL conditions involved 12 groups, six for each of the paired-associate lists.

Subjects and procedure.—A total of 320 *S*s served in the experiment, 20 in each of the 16 groups. Condition RL involved 2 groups; Cond. C, 2 groups; and Cond. PA-RL, 12 groups. The *S*s were assigned to one of the 16 groups randomly with the restriction that one *S* was assigned to each group before there were any replications. All *S*s were naive to verbal learning experiments.

In the standard paired-associate learning 15 anticipation trials were given under all conditions. Lists were presented on a memory drum at a 2/2-sec. rate, with a 4-sec. intertrial interval. Five different orders of the pairs were used to minimize serial learning with an equal number of *S*s being started on each order.

For the response-learning phase of the two RL groups, the list of responses was presented in five alternate learning and recall trials. The *S* was clearly instructed that he was not to learn the adjectives in order since they would be in a different order on each trial. The recall period after each learning trial was 1.5 min. The *S* simply wrote down on a sheet of paper as many responses as he could remember. Since there were five trials and five orders, an equal number of *S*s was started on each order to avoid any possible serial position bias. None of these orders was the same as subsequently used in paired-associate learning. For the paired-associate learning for these RL groups the *S* was provided with a card on which all the responses were listed. The intent of this was that if any of the responses were forgotten of those just learned, or if learning had been incomplete on five trials, the responses would still be available. However, few *S*s appeared to use the information on these cards; the majority reported that they simply did not have time to make use of the information during paired-associate learning.

In the PA-RL conditions, *S* was stopped after the appropriate number of trials on the paired-associate list, read the instructions for response recall, and then given 1.5 min. to write down all the responses he could remember. The *S* did not know beforehand that such a recall would be asked for. The instructions made it clear to *S* that he was to write down all the adjectives he could remember without regard to order. After the recall period he was informed that he would not be interrupted again and the standard learning of the paired-associate list continued until 15 anticipation trials were completed.

RESULTS

Response learning.—The mean number of correct responses on each of the five response recall trials for the RL groups is shown in Fig. 1. Initially the similar responses are recalled better than the dissimilar responses, although by Trial 4 performance is approximately equal on both lists and asymptotic for a majority of *S*s in both groups. The *t* on the total correct responses over all five trials for the two groups was 3.09 ($P < .001$). Thus, relatively pure response learning occurs more rapidly for responses of high similarity than for those of low similarity.

The results from the response recall trials for the PA-RL groups are plotted in Fig. 2. A comparison of Fig. 1 and Fig. 2 shows that response learning is much higher when occurring independently (Fig. 1) than when measured as a component of standard paired-associate learning (Fig. 2). Nevertheless, the same general relationship between the recall of high- vs. low-similarity responses still obtains. The curves are again initially separated, with recall best for high-similarity items, although the performance becomes equivalent after only a few trials. An analysis of variance was performed using data from the groups with 1, 2, 3, and 5 previous learning trials (since the prediction concerns only initial learning), making a 2 × 4 factorial design with trials and similarity being the two variables. The F's for trials (21.18, 3 and 152 *df*) and similarity (10.51, 1 and 152 *df*) are both significant beyond the .01 level, while the interaction is not significant ($F = 1.32$).

It can be shown that response learning measured during paired-associate learning (Fig. 2) is considerably higher than over-all paired-associate learning as such. While this would be expected from the general conception being evaluated (response learning precedes the associative phase), the data of the present experiment do not allow a satisfactory conclusion concerning this matter. This is because in the measurement of response recall during paired-associate learning essentially unlimited recall time was given, while in paired-associate learning only 2-sec. per item were allowed.

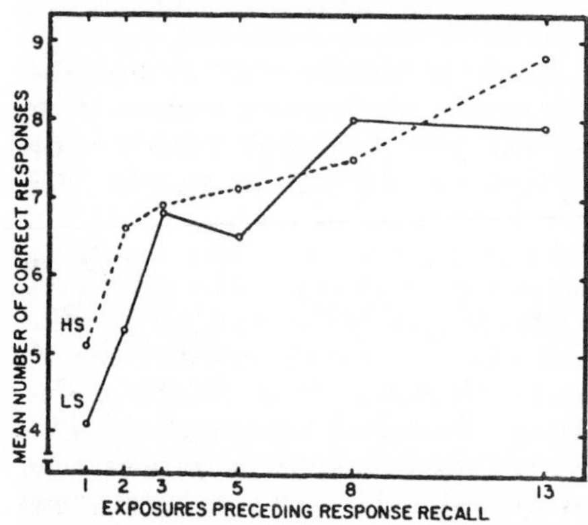

FIG. 2. Mean correct responses on response recall during paired-associate learning as a function of similarity (HS vs. LS) and number of exposures preceding response recall.

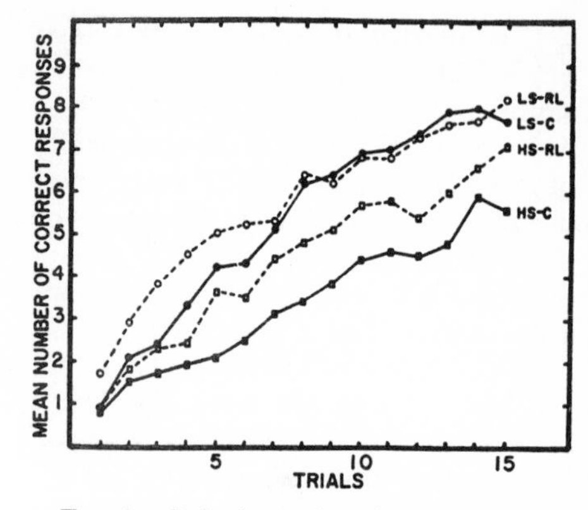

FIG. 3. Paired-associate learning in Exp. I as a function of preresponse learning (RL vs. C) and intralist response similarity (HS vs. LS).

Paired-associate learning.—The acquisition curves during paired-associate learning for the RL and C groups for both high- and low-similarity lists are presented in Fig. 3. In both kinds of lists there is evidence of facilitation due to the prior learning of the responses. The facilitation in the high-similarity list is apparent throughout the 15 trials, while facilitation in the low-similarity list is restricted to early trials. Again, since the prediction only involves the early trials, statistical evaluation of these results was made on the total correct responses over the first six trials. Analysis of variance showed that response learning was significant beyond the .02 level ($F = 6.35$, 1 and 76 *df*), similarity beyond the .001 level ($F = 16.00$, 1 and 76 *df*), and a nonsignificant interaction ($F < 1$). There was some evidence of heterogeneity of variance; however, *t* tests were used to compare the performance on the RL and corresponding C groups on the high- and low-similarity lists separately. The *t* was 1.90 for the high-similarity condition and 1.77 for the low. These are both significant beyond the .05 level if one assumes a single-tailed alternative.

Other evidence on response learning.—From the above comparisons it may be inferred that response learning of similar items occurs more rapidly than response learning of dissimilar items. Thus, early in learning a paired-associate list, *S* should have more responses available if the responses have high similarity than if they have low similarity. If this is true, evidence for it might be found in actual paired-associate learning. The point at which such evidence would be least contaminated by the associative phase would be the first anticipation trial. The *S* would be expected to give more *different* responses on this trial if the responses have high similarity than if they have low similarity. Such an analysis ignores the question of whether the response was appropriately paired with its stimulus; rather, a simple count is made of the number of different responses occurring. Five such comparisons are available from the PA-RL conditions; that is, there are five conditions in which a low-similarity list was taken through at least one anticipation trial by standard procedures and five comparable conditions for high-similarity lists. There is an additional comparison which can be made using the C groups, and one further comparison from a second experiment to be presented shortly. The comparisons were between the mean number of different responses given on the first anticipation trial of the high-similarity and low-similarity lists. In six of the seven comparisons, the mean was larger for the high-similarity lists. The over-all mean was 2.31 for the high-similarity lists and 1.76 for the low-similarity lists.

In contrast to the above expectations, if *S* has been taught the responses before paired-associate learning (as was true in the RL conditions) the high-similarity list should not show a superiority in number of different responses. Two tests of this can be made, one from the present RL groups and another from two comparable groups appearing in Exp. II. In both of these comparisons the mean number of different responses was higher for the low-similarity lists than for the high-similarity lists.

Discussion.—The prediction that response recall will be initially greater when the responses are similar in meaning than when they are dissimilar is clearly supported in all of the above data. This is true whether the response recall is taken during paired-associate learning, whether a response-learning procedure is used, or whether the responses in paired-associate learning as such is examined. The prediction that the initial performance during the learning of a paired-associate list will be facilitated by the prior learning of the responses is not supported as clearly. The differences, while small, are in the predicted direction and closely approach statistical significance. However, it is possible to attribute this small facilitation to some kind of warm-up or learning-to-learn (or both) produced by response learning and which is independent of the particular responses which were learned. Therefore, Exp. II was run which duplicated the RL and C conditions with the exception that the C groups in this second study were given irrelevant response learning prior to paired-associate learning. Thus, if relevant response learning facilitates paired-associate learning over and above that produced by irrelevant response learning, the differences found in Exp. I cannot reasonably be attributed to warm-up and practice effects.

Experiment II

Method.—The RL conditions of the previous experiment were replicated exactly, with both the high- and low-similarity lists being used. The C groups in Exp. II, however, were given five response learning and recall trials on irrelevant lists before being given the paired-associate lists. The lists were irrelevant in the sense that none of the items appeared in the paired-associate list. Such irrelevant learning should produce the same warm-up and practice which the RL groups might get in learning a relevant list. The irrelevant responses learned in the response-learning phase for the group subsequently learning the paired-associate list with high similarity among responses were: *shifty, crafty, expert, cunning, cagey, wily, foxy, clever, skillful,* and *tricky.* For the group learning the paired-associate list with low similarity among responses the items for the irrelevant response learning were: *hybrid, crumbling, vulgar, fiscal, worldly, inform, warlike, neuter, sterile,* and *flashy.*

A total of 60 *S*s served in the experiment, 15 in each group. All *S*s were naive to verbal learning experiments. All procedures were exactly the same as those in Exp. I, except as noted above, and except for the fact that during paired-associate learning the RL groups were not provided the card on which the correct responses were written.

Results.—The response-recall data showed essentially the same results as did Exp. I. The difference between high and low similarity was somewhat less than in Exp. I, but still significant statistically on the first recall trial.

As may be seen in Fig. 4, the results of the learning of the paired-associate list duplicate almost exactly those of the first study. For both high- and low-similarity lists the RL group exhibits better performance than the C group. The only clear difference between the results for the two studies is that in the present results the RL group is facilitated throughout all 15 trials on the low-similarity list; this was not true in the first study. Direct comparisons between the results of the two studies are not justified since the *S*s in Exp. II, as a group, were faster learners than those in Exp. I.

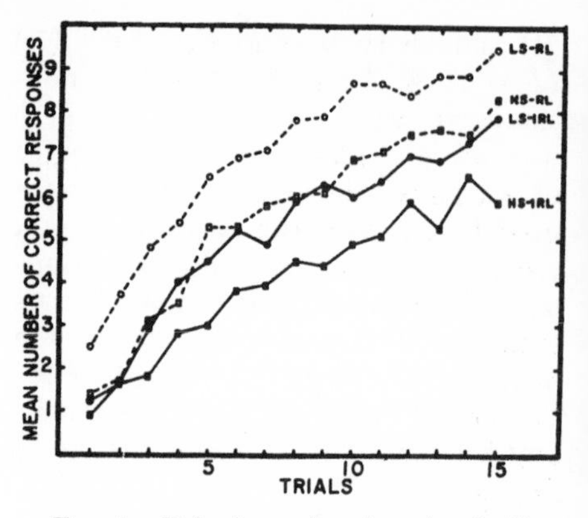

Fig. 4. Paired-associate learning in Exp. II as a function of preresponse learning (RL vs. IRL) and intralist response similarity (HS vs. LS).

Analysis of variance of the total correct responses on the first six trials gave significant *F*'s for both similarity (7.53) and relevance of response learning (9.81). With 1 and 56 *df*, the *F* at the .01 level is 7.12. Separate *t* tests between the RL and C groups gave values of 2.32 for high similarity and 2.23 for low similarity, both of which are significant at the .05 level with 28 *df*. The conclusion seems justified that prior learning of the responses facilitates paired-associate learning over and above any nonspecific effects, such as warm-up or learning-to-learn.

Discussion

The results are consonant with a two-phase conception of verbal learning. It should be clear that the present results are directly relevant only to the first phase—the response-learning phase. Nothing is given in the present findings as to how the associative phase—the second phase—takes place. Nor is there any intent to suggest that, all items considered, the two phases can be clearly separated in the over-all learning process. It has been asserted only that the early trials have a heavy component of response learning and the present results show that response similarity may be viewed as a variable influencing the rate at which this response learning takes place. Furthermore, the results indicate that if the necessity for response learning in paired-associate learning is removed by teaching *S* the responses before they become a part of the paired-associate list, paired-associate learning is facilitated. Concerning this latter finding it should be noted that Hovland and Kurtz (1952) have shown that familiarization training will facilitate serial learning. However, serial learning tends to confuse stimulus and response functions of the items. While stimulus learning before paired-associate learning (given in the same manner that response learning was given here) might influence subsequent paired-associate learning, it would be through other mechanisms (e.g., stimulus differentiation) than those being dealt with here for response learning.

It might be suggested that the response-learning procedures used produced a differentiation among the responses (reduced intralist similarity), hence facilitated learning. A number of facts argue against this interpretation. (*a*) If differentiation among responses is involved, response learning of the lists of low similarity should have little or no effect in paired-associate learning. (*b*) If differentiation among responses is the critical factor, it should have produced a much greater facilitation in the learning of the paired-associate lists for responses with high similarity than for responses with low similarity. The results showed that there was no appreciable difference between the effect for responses of low similarity and responses of high similarity. In fact, the mean differences for the initial part of learning favored the lists with low response similarity. (*c*) Finally, there is no reason to believe that the *method* used for response learning would produce a differentiation among responses in the sense that associations were differentially reinforced. All facts considered, therefore, it does not seem likely that response differentiation is of much moment in the present studies.

The present materials probably do not allow an optimum effect to be produced by response learning. That is, since adjectives were used, response learning should take place much more rapidly than if, say, nonsense syllables of low-association value had been employed. (It will be recalled that pure response learning in the RL groups took place very rapidly.) It would be expected that if response learning were given before paired-associate learning with material of low meaningfulness, subsequent paired-associate learning would be facilitated more than was true in the present results.

What is the stimulus for the recall of each item in the response-learning phase? There is no satisfactory answer to this question. But, it should be pointed out that the question is relevant not only to the present procedures but also to any learning situation in which *S* is shown a group of items and is then asked to recall them in any order. The stimulus for such recall may be the gross stimulus complex of the laboratory room, the memory drum, the instructions, etc. No resolution of this systematic problem seems possible. At the same time it must not be inferred that the initial recall of a given response is never instigated by the particular stimulus with which it is paired in the list. The fact that it is possible to set up pairs in which already established associations obtain between the stimulus and response, and that learning is very rapid in such situations, suggests that response recall can be tied to the specific stimulus and that this is a very effective arrangement. It is therefore quite possible that in the present experiment the initial recall of some items by some *S*s is entirely tied to a specific stimulus.

The present findings on the role of intralist response similarity have some implications for the role of both stimulus and response similarity in over-all paired-associate learning. Although available data are not completely conclusive on this matter (Underwood, 1953a; 1953b), the best evidence is that a given range of intralist stimulus similarity produces a greater variation in learning than does a corresponding range of response similarity. Such a finding is understandable in light of the present results and the conception of two stages in learning. It could be assumed that increasing interference produced by increasing similarity would affect the associative phase of learning and would have an equal effect in this phase for stimulus and response similarity. But, increasing response similarity has an increasing positive effect for response learning in the first phase (as seen in the present results) which has no counterpart in stimulus similarity. Therefore, the over-all effect of stimulus similarity should be greater than the effect of response similarity.

Summary

Verbal learning may be conceptualized as a two-stage process. In the first phase *S* must learn the responses, in the second he must attach them to specific stimuli. The present experiments dealt directly with the first stage only. It was hypothesized that: (*a*) response learning is initially more rapid the higher the response similarity in a paired-associate list; and (*b*) teaching *S* the responses before he learns a paired-associate list would initially facilitate the learning of this list.

Two paired-associate lists were used. The stimuli for both lists were nonsense syllables, the responses, adjectives. In one list the adjectives were all similar in meaning, in the other, dissimilar. In one set of conditions (control), *S*s merely learned the paired-associate lists by standard procedures for 15 trials. In a second set of conditions, *S*s were taught the responses prior to learning the paired-associate list for 15 trials. In the third set of conditions standard paired-associate learning was used but different groups of *S*s were stopped after 1, 2, 3, 5, 8, and 13 trials and were asked to write down all the responses they could remember. These three sets of conditions required 16 groups of *S*s. There were 20 in each group, all naive to verbal learning experiments.

The results show that:

(a) Teaching *S* the responses prior to paired-associate learning facilitates the learning of lists with both high and low similarity among the responses. A second experiment showed that this effect cannot be ascribed to warm-up or learning-to-learn resulting from the procedure of teaching *S* the responses before paired-associate learning. In both experiments the positive effect was evident throughout the entire 15 trials for lists of high response similarity. For low similarity the effect was only in initial learning for one comparison but present throughout learning in the other.

(b) In response learning (prior to paired-associate learning) items with high similarity are learned initially more rapidly than are items of low similarity, although for both lists learning was very rapid. When *S*s are tested for free recall at various points in learning a paired-associate list, more responses are given from a high-similarity list than from a low-similarity list even though over-all level of paired-associate learning is higher for the low-similarity list. The difference in this response recall was clearly evident for the first few trials.

The results confirm the expectation that high intralist response similarity would facilitate response learning. Thus, the results are consistent with the two-stage conception of learning. Furthermore, the present results aid in understanding certain previous findings on the roles of stimulus similarity and response similarity in verbal learning.

References

Bousfield, W. A., & Cohen, B. H. The occurrence of clustering in the recall of randomly arranged words of different frequencies of usage. *J. gen. Psychol.*, 1955, **52,** 83–95.

Feldman, S. M., & Underwood, B. J. Stimulus recall following paired-associate learning. *J. exp. Psychol.*, 1957, **53,** 11–15.

Glaze, J. A. The association value of nonsense syllables. *J. genet. Psychol.*, 1928, **35,** 255–269.

Haagen, C. H. Synonymity, vividness, familiarity, and association-value ratings of 400 pairs of common adjectives. *J. Psychol.*, 1949, **30,** 185–200.

Hovland, C. I., & Kurtz, K. H. Experimental studies in rote-learning theory: X. Pre-learning syllable familiarization and the length-difficulty relationship. *J. exp. Psychol.*, 1952, **44**, 31–39.

Sheffield, F. D. The role of meaningfulness of stimulus and response in verbal learning. Doctoral dissertation, Yale Univer., 1946.

Thorndike, E. L., & Lorge, I. *The teacher's word book of 30,000 words.* New York: Columbia Univer. Press, 1944.

Underwood, B. J. Studies of distributed practice: VIII. Learning and retention of paired nonsense lists as a function of intralist similarity. *J. exp. Psychol.*, 1953, **45**, 133–142. (a)

Underwood, B. J. Studies of distributed practice: IX. Learning and retention of paired adjective lists as a function of intralist similarity. *J. exp. Psychol.*, 1953, **45**, 143–149. (b)

Underwood, B. J., & Goad, D. Studies of distributed practice: I. The influence of intra-list similarity in serial learning. *J. exp. Psychol.*, 1951, **42**, 125–134.

(Received August 14, 1958)

ARTICLE 3

A MULTIPROCESS MODEL FOR PAIRED-ASSOCIATE LEARNING [1]

WILLIAM J. McGUIRE [2]

Yale University

The present study synthesizes several recent theoretical trends bearing on paired-associate learning by postulating that learning a single pair may involve, not just a single link between the stimulus member, S, of the pair and its response member, R, but rather a chain of habits involving at least three links.

The first postulated link in this habit chain involves associating with each S a mediating, stimulus-producing response, r. This r is a partial representation of the S to which it becomes connected, encoding some aspect of the S which discriminates that S from the others in the list. Evidence that *S* does tend to encode the S only partially and, more specifically, only with respect to aspects that usefully distinguish it from other Ss in the list, is found in the stimulus predifferentiation studies. Prelearning a set of Rs to a set of Ss is found to result in positive transfer when a new set of Rs are then learned to the Ss provided the Ss are distinguished by the same aspects on both tasks (Goss, 1953). If they are distinguished by a new aspect, however, there is no transfer if the old aspect is missing on the new task (Hake & Ericksen, 1956); and negative transfer results when the old aspect is present and interferes with the encoding of the alternative aspect that has been made significant on the new task (Kurtz, 1955).

The difficulty of this first habit component (S-r) can be manipulated by varying the physical similarity (primary generalization) of the set of Ss, as is done in the present study and, in principle, by Goss (1953), or by varying the number of irrelevant dimensions, as in the typical concept-attainment study (Pishkin, 1960) in which *S* must learn which is the relevant dimension along with the Ss can be discriminated.

The second link in the habit chain involves learning to make the appropriate gross response, R, to each stimulus, s, produced by the mediating, labeling response. That the R of the pair tends to become associated with this mediating s rather than to the S itself has been demonstrated by Bugelski and Scharlock (1952) for experimentally established mediators and by Russell and Storms (1955) for those provided by language habits. That the mediators tend to be the discriminating labels attached to the Ss is demonstrated by McAllister's (1953) finding that stimulus predifferentiation results in positive transfer to the extent that the differentiating labels (r) are "relevant" to the new Rs to be learned for the Ss.

The third link in the habit chain which we postulate involves the possibility that the response member of the pair, R, may itself be a chain of habits that have to be learned. The importance of this "response learning"

[1] This paper is based on a dissertation submitted in partial fulfillment of the requirements of the PhD degree at Yale University in 1954. The author is greatly indebted to Carl I. Hovland for his advice and guidance and also to C. E. Buxton, R. P. Abelson, and N. E. Miller.

[2] Now at the Department of Social Psychology, Columbia University.

Reprinted with permission of the author and the publisher, the American Psychological Association. The article appeared originally in the *Journal of Experimental Psychology*, 1961, **62**, 335–347.

has been reviewed by Mandler (1954) and most recently demonstrated by the response-meaningfulness (*m'*) studies (Hunt, 1959; Nobel & McNeely, 1957) and the response-similarity studies (Feldman & Underwood, 1957; Underwood, Runquist, & Schulz, 1959) which deal with two somewhat different aspects of R learning—within-R synthesis, and between-R discrimination.

In summary, learning each pair in a paired-associate task involves, not a single S-R connection, but rather three component habits. The first involves S and r; the second, s and R; and the third (which may be a chain of habits) the R elements, R_a, R_b, $\cdots R_n$. Hence, learning a pair may involve the following habits:

$$S \rightarrow r \rightarrow s \rightarrow R_a \rightarrow s_a \rightarrow R_b \rightarrow s_b \rightarrow \cdots \rightarrow R_n$$

We are ignoring here the remote associations that probably get formed and which may account for some slight discrepancies from the predictions reported below.

The materials used in the present study were designed to enable us to identify in each erroneous instance (that is, a failure by the *S* on any trial to respond to a given S with the correct R) which of the links in the chain failed in that instance. By such an analysis of the errors we can determine the practice functions, not only of the usual H_c (the proportion of pairs correctly anticipated on a given trial), but also of H_1 (the proportion of correct S discriminations, i.e., S-r habits, on a given trial), of H_2 (the proportion of correct associations, i.e., s-R_a habits), and of H_3 (the proportion of Rs correctly synthesized, i.e., $R_a \rightarrow s_a \rightarrow \cdots \rightarrow R_n$ habits).

Besides indicating processes involved and sources of difficulty in paired-associate learning, these separate indices enable us to compute independently the curves for stimulus generalization and for intrusion errors, the confusion between which has given rise to that hardy perennial among verbal learning controversies, the temporal trend of stimulus generalization during practice, which has recently blossomed again among Murdock (1958, 1959), Battig (1959), Gibson (1959), and Runquist (1959).

Method

Materials and experimental variations.—The Ss and Rs in this study were designed to allow independent manipulation of the difficulty of each of the three sets of habits, H_1, H_2, and H_3.

Each *S* learned, by the anticipation method, a list of nine paired associates. The Ss of these pairs were nine, solid black circles of varying diameters. Two different sets of circles were used for different groups of *S*s. In Set I the diameters ranged from .37 to 1.49 cm. in .14-cm. steps; in Set II, from .37 to .93 in .07-cm. steps. The difficulty of learning the S-discrimination habits (H_1) was defined as being greater for Set II than for Set I.

The Rs were numbers. For some *S*s these Rs were the numbers from 1 to 9. For other *S*s the Rs were 3-digit numbers, each beginning with a different integer between 1 and 9, and with the second and third digits assigned by a random procedure. The difficulty of learning the R-chaining habits (H_3) was defined as being greater for the 3- than the 1-digit Rs. In fact, for the 1-digit numbers, H_3 was defined as having a value of 1.00 from the outset of the experiment; that is, it was assumed that *S* would always perform perfectly at this segment of the task.

The difficulty of learning the s-R_a association habits (H_2) was manipulated by the manner of assigning Rs to Ss. An advantage of using sets of Ss that differ along a single linear dimension, size in this case, is that it permits hypothesizing what the discriminating labeling rs will be. With the nine different-sized but otherwise similar Ss used here and with the instructions to *S* described below, it was assumed that *S* would use a numerical-type labeling response; for example, he would tend to label the smallest circles as "one" the next larger as "two," etc., up to the largest which he would label as "nine." For some *S*s the Rs were assigned consecutively so that the successively larger numbers were assigned

TABLE 1

DESCRIPTION OF DIFFICULTY LEVELS OF COMPONENT HABITS IN THE SIX CONDITIONS, WITH FORMULAS FOR PROPORTIONS OF CORRECT ANTICIPATIONS (H_c) AND OF INTRUSION ERRORS (IE)

Cond.	Task			H_c[a]	IE[a]
	H_1	H_2	H_3		
$H_1H_2H_3$	easy	easy	easy	H_1	$1 - H_1$
$H_1'H_2H_3$	hard	easy	easy	H_1'	$1 - H_1'$
$H_1H_2H_3'$	easy	easy	hard	$H_1 \cdot H_3'$	$H_3'(1 - H_1)$
$H_1'H_2H_3'$	hard	easy	hard	$H_1' \cdot H_3'$	$H_3'(1 - H_1')$
$H_1'H_2'H_3$	hard	hard	easy	$H_1' \cdot H_2'$	$1 - H_1' \cdot H_2'$
$H_1'H_2'H_3'$	hard	hard	hard	$H_1' \cdot H_2' \cdot H_3'$	$H_3'(1 - H_1' \cdot H_2')$

[a] These H_c and IE formulas are based on the general equations $H_c = H_1 \cdot H_2 \cdot H_3$ and $IE = H_3(1 - H_1 \cdot H_2)$ and the assumptions that the values of H_2 and H_3, without primes, equal 1.00 from the beginning of practice.

to progressively larger circles. For other groups, Rs were assigned at random to Ss so that no simple system related size of numbers and size of circles. The difficulty of learning the association habits (H_2) was, of course, defined as being greater with the latter, random method of assignment. In fact, in the conditions with consecutive assignment of the numerical responses, H_2 was defined as equaling 1.00 from the outset of practice; that is, it was assumed that *S* always performed this segment of the task perfectly.

Experimental design.—An incomplete 2^3 factorial design (minus one quadrant) was employed. The three variables were difficulty of learning the H_1, H_2, and H_3 sets of habits, there being an easy and difficulty level of each as defined above. Table 1 shows the levels of each of these factors in the six conditions used, with primes (e.g., H_1') indicating the difficult condition and no primes (e.g., H_1) indicating the easy condition on the given link. Ten *S*s served in each of the six conditions, and each *S* served in only one condition.

Apparatus.—A Hull memory drum with 1-in.-square windows was used. The Ss were presented in the left window, and the Rs in the right window. The anticipatory method was employed, S appearing alone for 2 sec. and then S and R appearing together for 2 sec. after which both windows closed again. Almost immediately, the left window reopened, showing the next S on the list. The *S* was required to anticipate the R within the first 2-sec. period. The pairs came in a different order on each trial.

Instructions to S.—The *S*s were given the usual instructions for a paired-associate task regarding how the materials would be presented and what they were to try to do. In addition, they were told that all Ss were solid black circles, differing only in size, and that there were nine different pairs in all. Further, those in H_3 groups were told that the Rs would be the 1-digit numbers from 1 to 9, while those in H_3' groups were told that the Rs would be nine 3-digit numbers, each beginning with a different integer from 1 to 9. Subjects in H_2 conditions were given the additional information that progressively higher numbers were assigned to successively larger circles, while those in H_2' conditions were told that the magnitudes of the Rs of the pairs were randomly related to the sizes of the circles. All *S*s were instructed to try to give some response to each S after the completion of the first trial. Those in H_3' (3-digit R) conditions were further directed to respond with at least the first digit even if they could not give the other two. As a further measure to keep omissions at a minimum, all *S*s were told that when they were not sure of a correct R they should guess.

Length of the learning session.—The experimental session for each *S* consisted of 80 continuous trials without any intertrial pause (48 min.). Only 1 *S* asked to be relieved before completing 80 trials; he was replaced by the next *S* in the pool.

Subjects.—The 60 *S*s were selected on the basis of availability from a pool of several hundred college students in an introductory psychology course and assigned to one of the six conditions in accordance with a random order. The writer served as *E* for all *S*s.

RESULTS AND DISCUSSION

Correct anticipations (H_c): *Group means.*—The manipulation of the difficulty of each of the three postulated sets of habit links (H_1, H_2, and H_3) did produce the predicted difference in the mean proportion of correct anticipations per trial (H_c) over the 80 trials.[3]

The difficulty of forming the first set of habit links (S-r), involving S discrimination, was manipulated by using .14-cm. steps between the Ss in some conditions (H_1-) and .07-cm. steps in other conditions ($H_1'-$). Insofar as this set of habits is involved in learning the paired associates, performance (H_c) in Cond. $H_1H_2H_3$ should have been superior to that in Cond. $H_1'H_2H_3$ since the only difference between the two tasks was that the S discrimination was more difficult in the latter conditions. For like reasons, performance on Cond. $H_1H_2H_3'$ should have been superior to that in Cond. $H_1'H_2H_3'$. Both of these predictions are confirmed by the results. The mean H_c value for the 10 *Ss* over all 79 anticipatory trials is significantly higher (see Table 2) in Cond. $H_1H_2H_3$ than in $H_1'H_2H_3$ ($P < .001$) and in Cond. $H_1H_2H_3'$ than in $H_1'H_2H_3'$ ($P = .02$).

The difficulty of learning the habit chains of R elements was varied by

[3] The H_c symbol has been deliberately selected in the present model for its resemblance to the Hullian habit strength symbol, $_SH_R$, because the constructs are similar in that both are negatively accelerated increasing functions of the number of reinforced S-R pairings. However, the H_c differs quantitatively from the Hullian $_SH_R$ in three respects. First, the present H_c is a direct one-to-one function of the probability of correct response, whereas $_SH_R$ is an intervening construct that is an exponential function of this probability. Secondly, $_SH_R$ is the strength of a single S-R habit, while H_c is the mean strength of a set of as many habits as there are pairs. Thirdly, the present H_c need not be zero when $N = 0$ since, unlike Hull (1943, 1952), we allow the a and c parameters in the equation $H_c = c - ae^{-bN}$ to assume different values (Lewis, 1960).

TABLE 2

PROPORTION OF CORRECT ANTICIPATION PER TRIAL (H_c) IN EACH OF THE SIX CONDITIONS

Cond.	Mean	*SD*
$H_1H_2H_3$	.793	.048
$H_1'H_2H_3$	.635	.057
$H_1H_2H_3'$	.618	.090
$H_1'H_2H_3'$	.491	.116
$H_1'H_2'H_3$	.462	.105
$H_1'H_2'H_3'$	.340	.098

Note.—Each mean is based on 10 *Ss* over 80 trials, 9 pairs per trial.

using 1-digit Rs in some conditions ($-H_3$) and 3-digit Rs in others ($-H_3'$). Hence, higher H_c scores are predicted in Cond. $H_1H_2H_3$ than in $H_1H_2H_3'$; in Cond. $H_1'H_2H_3$ than in $H_1'H_2H_3'$; and in $H_1'H_2'H_3$ than in $H_1'H_2'H_3'$. All the obtained H_c differences (see Table 1) are in the predicted direction and the three differences are significant at the .001, .001, and .01 levels, respectively.

The difficulty of forming the third set of habit links, the s-R_a or "association" habits, was manipulated by assigning Rs to Ss consecutively in some conditions ($-H_2-$) and randomly in others ($-H_2'-$). Hence, the H_c scores should be higher in Cond. $H_1'H_2H_3$ than $H_1'H_2'H_3$ and in Cond. $H_1'H_2H_3'$ than $H_1'H_2'H_3'$. Both mean differences are in the predicted direction (see Table 2) and are significant at the .001 and .01 levels, respectively.

So far only the directions of the differences in H_c scores between the conditions have been considered, but the relative sizes of these differences are also of interest. In Table 1 the equations of H_c in each of the six conditions are given. Solving for H_3' in each of the equations where it appears, it is found that in Cond. $H_1H_2H_3'$, $H_3' = H_c \div H_1$; in Cond. $H_1'H_2H_3'$, $H_3' = H_c \div H_1'$; and in

Cond. $H_1'H_2'H_3'$, $H_3' = H_c \div (H_1' \cdot H_2')$, the value of H_c in each case being that for the given condition. But the divisors of the right hand members of each of these three equations can be seen in Table 1 to be the H_c values of, respectively, Cond. $H_1H_2H_3$, $H_1'H_2H_3$, and $H_1'H_2'H_3$. Since each of the three fractions is equal to the same thing, H_3', then the following equation can be derived:

$$H_3' = \frac{H_c \text{ of Cond. } H_1H_2H_3'}{H_c \text{ of Cond. } H_1H_2H_3} = \frac{H_c \text{ of Cond. } H_1'H_2H_3'}{H_c \text{ of Cond. } H_1'H_2H_3} = \frac{H_c \text{ of Cond. } H_1'H_2'H_3'}{H_c \text{ of Cond. } H_1'H_2'H_3}$$

Substituting the obtained mean H_c values (shown in Table 2) in this equation, the values of these three fractions are found to be .779, .773, and .736, respectively.

We would expect these three quotients to be equal to the extent that the learning of any one of the three postulated sets of habits proceeded independently of the difficulty of the other two sets of habits being acquired simultaneously. The closeness of the three obtained quotients suggests that there is considerable independence. The closeness of the .779 and .773 values, particularly, suggests that the difficulty of learning the response chains is only negligibly affected by the difficulty of the S discriminations being learned concurrently. The third value, .736, is slightly (about 5%) lower than the other two. While the first two values give a derived measure of H_3' in consecutive S-R assignment conditions, this third gives an H_3' value in a condition where the numerical values of Rs are randomly related to the size of Ss to which they are assigned. Hence, the learning of the response chain may be (very slightly) impeded by the difficulty of the s-R association habits being learned concurrently. This interaction might be expected in view of the similarity of the s-R habits and the $R_a \rightarrow s_a \rightarrow \cdots R_n$ habits in the present study (both involve linking numbers) and of the usual finding that difficulty of learning is a positively accelerated function of amount of material (Hovland, 1940).

These derived estimates of H_3' in Cond. $H_1H_2H_3'$ and Cond. $H_1'H_2H_3'$ can be checked by an independent method of computing H_3' which requires us to anticipate the classification of errors discussed below. Briefly, the sum of Categories A and C in Table 3 should yield a running measure of H_3', the number of R chains correctly learned. The mean H_3' for Cond. $H_1'H_2H_3'$ computed in this way is .778 (as compared to the .773 mean yielded by the quotient method just discussed). The mean for Cond. $H_1H_2H_3'$ is .800 (as compared with the .779 mean yielded by the quotient method). The slight discrepancy in each condition, between the summation and the quotient method of deriving H_3', falls far short of conventional significance levels.

The H_c learning curves.—We can obtain a more analytic understanding of the effect of manipulating H_1, H_2, and H_3 on proportion of correct anticipation (H_c) if the group trends during practice in each of the six conditions are considered. To calculate these practice functions, the group mean H_c values in each condition over the 80 trials were used to determine 13 practice points, as follows. Trial 1 was omitted in the determination of the fitted curves, since this trial constituted an initial presentation to allow *S* to see each pair at least once before being required to anticipate. The first point (point "2") is based on scores on Trials 2 and 3, the next point (point "5") is based on Trials 4, 5, and 6; the next (point "8") on Trials 7, 8, 9, and 10; and each of the next 10 points (called 14, 21, 28, 35, 42, 49, 56, 63, 70, and 77, respectively) on successive blocks of seven trials. For example, point 77 is based on the means of Trials 74 through 80. More points were calculated in the case of the earlier trials in order to determine more accurately the shape of the function near the beginning of practice, when improvement was most rapid. The scores at each practice point for each of the six groups are plotted in Fig. 1, which also shows the fitted function for each condition.

All of the functions shown in Fig. 1 are of the inverse exponential family; $H_c = c\text{-}ae^{-bN}$, where H_c is the proportion of the nine possible anticipations given correctly on any trial, *c-a* is the proportion of correct anticipations at the outset of practice, *c* is the asymptote, and *b*, the growth parameter. Exponential functions were used because they described the data more accurately than any straight line in each of the six conditions by an amount that was significant at the .05 level in all cases except Cond. $H_1'H_2H_3$. In Cond. $H_1H_2H_3$ and $H_1'H_2H_3$ we also fitted hyperbolic and Gompertz functions to the data, but these functions were found to describe the data somewhat less adequately than the exponential. Cond. $H_1H_2H_3'$ was the only one of the six in which the data deviated from the fitted exponential function by an amount that approached the .05 level. The test for goodness of the fit was based on Lindquist's Case 8 (1947) with $df = 10$ (i.e., 13 − 3, the number of trial blocks minus the number of parameters calculated for each function).

Some criticism has been published by Sidman (1952) and Bakan (1954) regarding the practice of inferring the shape of the individual functions from that of the group functions, especially in the case of exponential functions. The criticism has no bearing on the results reported in the

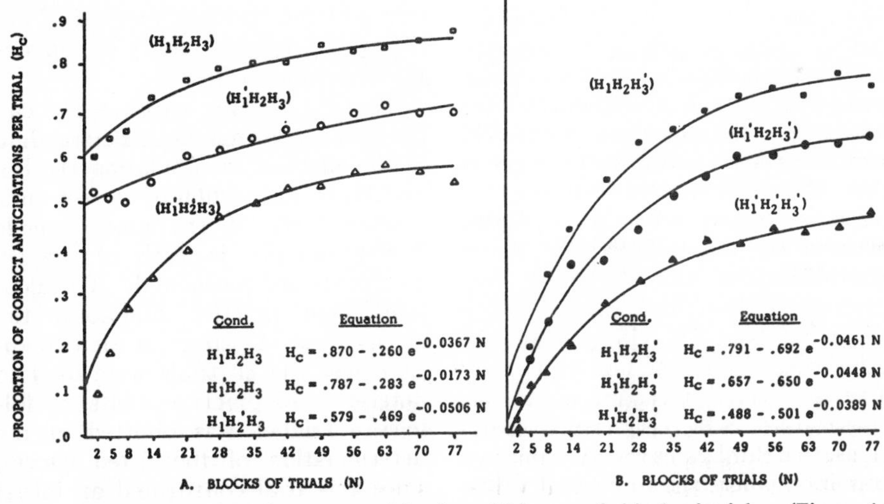

FIG. 1. Mean proportion of correct anticipations (H_c) on each block of trials. (Figure 1a shows curves for one-digit, and Fig. 1b, for three-digit response conditions.)

present experiment since no inference is made regarding the exact shape of the individual curves. The objection is relevant at all, only when there is an appreciable variance among the growth parameters (b) of the individual curves, and when the $b \cdot N$ products are large. The second condition does obtain in the present study, but whether there is a significant variance among the individual b values has not been computed (because of labor involved in fitting exponential curves to the data of each of the 60 individuals). In the absence of more information on the b parameters, caution should be exercised in inferring the shapes of the individual *S* curves in the present study.

Effect of the experimental variables on the different parameters of the H_c learning curves.—Several conclusions can be drawn from the functions obtained in the present study. Each of the three hypothesized sets of habits is found to play a consistent part in determining both the initial level of performance (the H_c-intercept, equal to c-a) and the asymptote (c) of the functions. This conclusion follows from the obtained effect of increasing the difficulty of either the H_1, H_2, or H_3 task, which is found in all cases to lower both of these parameters. There are seven nonredundant pairs of conditions between which such a comparison is possible, and for both the c and the c-a parameters, the above stated effect was obtained in all seven comparisons.

The growth parameter (b) of H_c appears to be related to the difficulty of the component sets of habits, H_1, H_2, and H_3, in a more complex way. In the first place, it seems that where the source of greater difficulty derives from the greater similarity between the *S*s, so that there are more generalization errors, then the rate of learning of the paired-associate task is slower as the difficulty increases (compare b parameters in Cond. $H_1H_2H_3$ and $H_1'H_2H_3$ and in Cond. $H_1H_2H_3'$ and $H_1'H_2H_3'$). As regards the effect on the growth parameter of increasing the difficulty of the R-chains (H_3) or of the s-R associations (H_2), the b parameters shown in Fig. 1 suggest that increasing the difficulty of one or both of these increases the rate of learning (compare Cond. $H_1H_2H_3$ with $H_1H_2H_3'$; and Cond. $H_1'H_2H_3$ with $H_1'H_2H_3'$, with $H_1'H_2'H_3$, and with $H_1'H_2'H_3'$), but that increasing the difficulty of just one (H_2 or H_3) increases the learning rate more than does increasing the difficulty of both H_2 and H_3 (compare Cond. $H_1'H_2H_3'$ with $H_1'H_2'H_3'$; and Cond. $H_1'H_2'H_3$ with $H_1'H_2'H_3'$). These interpretations are post factum, however, and call for further investigation.

Practice curves of stimulus discrimination and of intrusion errors.—An intrusion error is defined as the giving of an R that is in the list but giving it to an S other than the one with which it is actually paired in the list as presented. Hence, the probability of an intrusion (IE) is directly proportional to the learning of the R chains (H_3) and inversely proportional to the learning of the S discrimination (S-r) habits (H_1) and of the association (s-R_a) habits (H_2); that is:

$$IE = H_3(1 - H_1 \cdot H_2)$$

An S-generalization error, on the other hand, was defined as giving the wrong r to an S and measured by $1 - H_1$, a value that will tend to differ from IE when either H_2, H_3, or both are less than 1.00. The practice of defining stimulus generalization during paired-associate learning has, as was pointed out above, led to considerable controversy. An *E* may be allowed a certain liberty in defining his terms, as long as he does so clearly. However, this definition that S discrimination has occurred only when *S* discriminates the Ss with the Rs that *E* has arbitrarily assigned becomes misleading, particularly as regards the practice curve of the generalization function and particularly when the Rs themselves or their relations to the Ss must be learned (that is, when H_3 or H_2 increases with practice). Eleanor Gibson (1940, 1942), whose provocative research using the IE definition of S generalization has given rise to this controversy, has herself pointed out (Gibson, 1959; Gibson & Gibson, 1955) the inadequacy of this definition.

The materials used in this study were designed to allow the responses given by *S*s in each instance to be classified into separate categories in terms of which the practice curves of H_1, H_2, and H_3, as well as of H_c, could be calculated. In this way, we could test the above formulations. Each of *S*'s 711 responses (9 pairs × 79 trials) was put in one of the following five categories:

A. A first digit appropriate to the given S (indicating a correct discrimination) and the second and third digits appropriate to the first (indicating a correct R). The proportion of responses in this category equals, by definition, H_c, the usual measure of a correct response in paired-associate learning.
B. A first digit appropriate to the given S (indicating a correct discrimination) and second or third digits not appropriate to the first (indicating a wrong R).
C. A first digit not appropriate to the given S (indicating a wrong discrimination or a wrong s-R association or both) and second and third digits appropriate to the first (indicating a correct R). The proportion of responses that falls in this category equals, by definition, IE.
D. A first digit not appropriate to the given S (indicating a wrong S discrimination or a wrong s-R association or both) and second or third digit not appropriate to the first (indicating a wrong R).
E. An omission, no response given.

The proportions of responses falling into each of these five categories for Cond. $H_1H_2H_3'$ and $H_1'H_2H_3'$ during successive practice intervals are shown in Fig. 2 and Table 3. Only for those two conditions are all categories used unambiguously. In Cond. $H_1H_2H_3$, $H_1'H_2H_3$, and $H_1'H_2'H_3$ where initial $H_3 = 1.00$, i.e., the Rs are one digit numbers, no Category B or D responses would occur. In Cond. $H_1'H_2'H_3$ and $H_1'H_2'H_3'$ (where Rs are randomly assigned to Ss), a wrong first digit indicates that either the S discrimination, or the s-R association, or both, are wrong. Hence, in these two conditions the interpretation of Category C and D responses is ambiguous, and separate measures of H_1' and H_2' are not possible.

Representing the proportion of responses that fall into these categories by the letters A, B, C, D, and E, respectively, then in all six conditions, the pro-

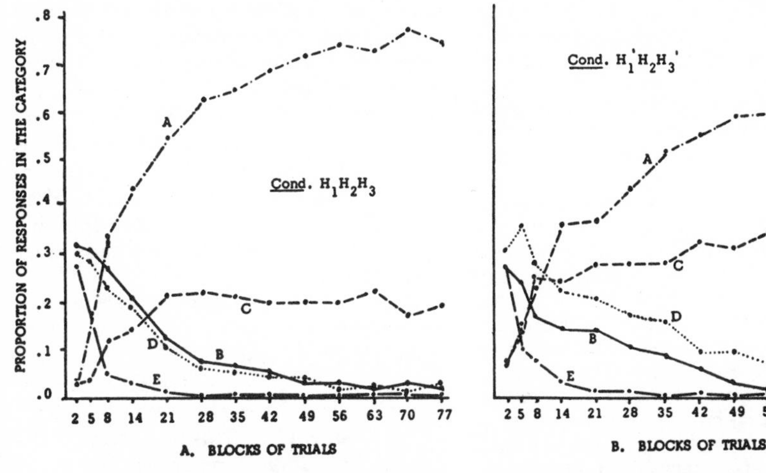

FIG. 2. Practice trends of the mean proportion of responses in each of the five categories (as discussed in text) for Cond. $H_1H_2H_3$ (Fig. 2a) and Cond. $H_1'H_2H_3'$ (Fig. 2b).

TABLE 3

PROPORTION OF THE OBTAINED RESPONSES THAT FELL IN THE FIVE RESPONSE CATEGORIES IN EACH CONDITION

Category	Conditions					
	$H_1H_2H_3$	$H_1'H_2H_3$	$H_1H_2H_3'$	$H_1'H_2H_3'$	$H_1'H_2'H_3$	$H_1'H_2'H_3'$
A. Correct Response	.793	.635	.618	.491	.462	.340
B. Correct S-r and s-R but inadequate R chain	—[a]	—	.094	.079	—	.020
C. Incorrect S-r or s-R, but adequate R chain (=IE)	.207	.365	.182	.287	.436	.330
D. Incorrect S-r, and inadequate R chain	—	—	.083	.118	—	.118
E. Omission	.000	.000	.023	.025	.002	.192
Total	1.000	1.000	1.000	1.000	1.000	1.000

Note.—Each mean is based on 10 *Ss* over 80 trials.
[a] Category B and D responses cannot occur in the three 1-digit R conditions.

portion of correctly learned R chains, H_3, equals A and C and the proportion of pairs that have been mastered to the extent of both correct S-r discriminations and s-R associations, $H_1 \cdot H_2$, equals A and B. Since, as discussed above, the proportion of intrusion errors, $IE = H_3(1 - H_1H_2)$, we find by substitution that $IE = (A + C)(1 - A - B)$.[4]

[4] These equations apply in conditions where there are no omissions or where it is assumed that such omissions as do occur represent responses which, had they occurred, would all have been Category D responses, that is, completely wrong. In the present study a different assumption has been made, namely, that omissions represent responses that, had they been made, would have divided among the other error categories (B, C, and D) in the same proportion as the erroneous responses that were made. Hence, the B and C values used in the subsequent discussion are "corrected" values (represented by the symbols B′ and C′), equal to the obtained B and C values, plus a proportional amount of the E values, yielding the "corrected" equations of $H_1 \cdot H_2 = A + B'$ and $IE = (A + C')(1 - A - B')$. There are still other assumptions regarding omissions that might have been made. This discussion of omissions is important mainly in connection with Cond. $H_1'H_2'H_3'$, since the number of omissions was negligible in Cond. $H_1H_2H_3$ and $H_1'H_2H_3$ and occurred in appreciable numbers in the other three conditions, only during the first few trial intervals.

With these preliminaries understood it is possible to test the hypotheses concerning stimulus discrimination and intrusion errors as a function of practice. In Cond. $H_1H_2H_3$ and $H_1'H_2H_3$ (the two conditions with consecutively-assigned one-digit Rs) the test is a direct one since initial H_2 and $H_3 = 1.00$ and there are not omissions. Hence, $H_o = H_1 \cdot H_2 \cdot H_3$ becomes $H_o = H_1$, i.e., in these two conditions the overall performance score on the paired associates (H_o) is identical with that of stimulus discrimination (H_1). In both of these conditions there is a clear tendency for H_1 to increase monotonically throughout practice. The trends in both conditions are well fitted by rising, negatively accelerated, exponential functions (see Fig. 3). These results tend to confirm the hypothesis that discrimination increases monotonically during practice with a set of paired associates and to infirm the opposing hypothesis that this function first rises, then falls.

Since initial H_2 and $H_3 = 1.00$ and no omissions occur in these two conditions ($H_1H_2H_3$ and $H_1'H_2H_3$), the equation, $IE = H_3(1.00 - H_1 \cdot H_2)$, simplifies to $IE = 1.00 - H_1$, or its equivalent, $IE = 1.00 - H_o$. This congruency between the stimulus generalization curve and the intrusion error curve is a special case that occurs, as described by the

TABLE 4

PROPORTION OF CORRECT S DISCRIMINATIONS PER TRIAL (H_1) IN THE FIRST FOUR CONDITIONS

Cond.	Mean	*SD*
$H_1H_2H_3$	.793	.048
$H_1'H_2H_3$	.635	.057
$H_1H_2H_3'$	.712	.101
$H_1'H_2H_3'$	.570	.123

Note.—Each mean is based on 10 *S*s over 80 trials, pairs per trial.

TABLE 5

PROPORTION OF INTRUSION ERRORS (IE) PER TRIAL IN EACH CONDITION

Cond.	Predicted Mean	Obtained Mean	Obtained *SD*
$H_1H_2H_3$	.207[a]	.207	.048
$H_1'H_2H_3$	.365[a]	.365	.057
$H_1H_2H_3'$	.199	.182	.058
$H_1'H_2H_3'$	.305	.287	.114
$H_1'H_2'H_3$	.436[a]	.436	.109
$H_1'H_2'H_3'$	.348	.330	.092

Note.—Each obtained score is based on 10 *S*s over 80 trials, 9 pairs per trial. Predicted scores were derived from the equation: $IE = (A + C')(1 - A - B')$.

[a] In the three 1-digit R conditions, the "predicted" means necessarily coincide with the obtained means.

model, when initial H_2 and $H_3 = 1.00$ and there are no omissions. When the IE curve does coincide with that of stimulus generalization, it, as well as the latter, falls throughout practice.

In the two conditions with consecutively assigned 3-digit Rs, $H_1H_2H_3'$ and $H_1'H_2H_3'$, the equation $H_1H_2 = A + B'$ reduces to $H_1 = A + B'$ on the assumption that $H_2 = 1.00$ in the consecutive assignment conditions. (This assumption may be somewhat extreme, in which case the values of H_1 shown in Table 4 and Fig. 3 would slightly underestimate the true values.) Figure 3 shows the practice curves for S discrimination in these two conditions, which can be seen to follow the predicted monotonically rising trend, well fitted by negatively-accelerated exponential functions, rather than the sometimes reported rising, then falling curve.

The intrusion error values (Table 5) are given by the formula $IE = (A + C')(1 - A - B')$. These predicted practice functions for IE in Cond. $H_1H_2H_3'$ and $H_1'H_2H_3'$ are shown in Fig. 4, where the obtained values (that is, number of category C responses) are also shown.

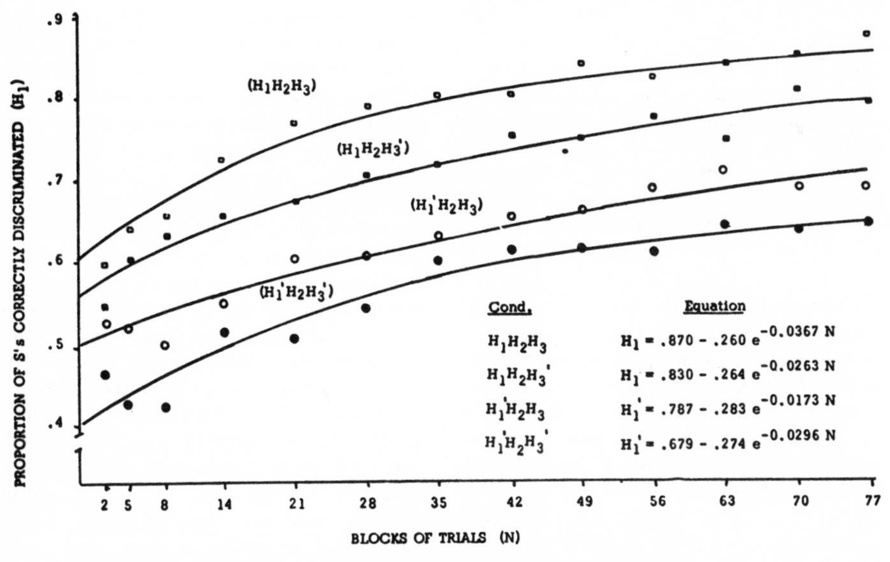

FIG. 3. Mean proportion of correct S discriminations (H_1) on each block of trials for the four conditions in which this information was available.

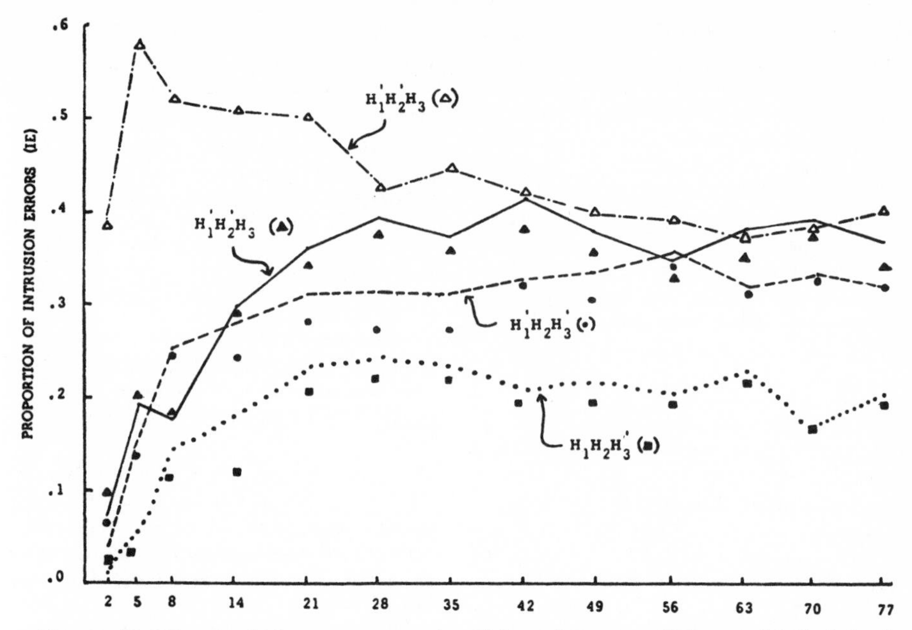

FIG. 4. Practice trends for mean proportion of intrusion errors (IE) per trial block in the four conditions in which Category B or E responses occurred. (Lines indicate predicted trends; symbols, the obtained values in the given condition.)

It can be seen that in each condition there is good agreement between predicted and obtained scores, with respect to practice trend and maximum point, as well as to height. There is a slight tendency in both conditions for the predicted values of IE to overestimate the obtained values but these discrepancies yield *F* values of only 1.14 and 0.61 in the two conditions (using the *S*s × Trials interaction as the error term), and therefore such discrepancies as these are can be attributed to chance. These IE curves in both conditions show an initial rise, followed by a leveling off and a slow decline, while the stimulus generalization trend has just been seen to follow a falling course throughout practice. This disagreement demonstrates that, while the shape of the IE function does coincide with that previously reported (Gagné, 1950; Gibson, 1942; Underwood & Goad, 1951) for S generalization, it does not coincide with S generalization more logically defined.

For the final two conditions, $H_1'H_2'H_3$ and $H_1'H_2'H_3'$, with randomly paired Ss and Rs, the response categorization possible with the present materials yields separate values of H_3 and of $H_1 \cdot H_2$, but not of H_1 and H_2 separately, as discussed above. Hence, it is not possible to test the hypotheses regarding S discrimination with the results from these conditions. The hypotheses regarding IE, however, can be tested since for this a composite value for $H_1 \cdot H_2$ suffices.

Since in Cond. $H_1'H_2'H_3$, initial $H_3 = 1.00$, the predicted $IE = 1.00 - A - E$. The values for IE so calculated necessarily coincide with the obtained values since there are no category B or D responses in this condition. The practice trend shows a brief initial rise followed by a subsequent decline (see Fig. 4). Here again it can be seen that intrusion errors do not furnish a valid measure for stimulus generalization: first, because it is influenced also by omissions (which account for the brief initial rise); and secondly, because aside from the omissions which become infrequent after the first few trial intervals, the

IE = 1.00 − $H_1 \cdot H_2$ while stimulus generalization = 1.00 − H_1. Hence, since in this condition initial H_2 is less than 1.00, IE overestimates the amount of stimulus generalization.

In Cond. $H_1'H_2'H_3'$, the "corrected" equation is again used to determine the predicted IE scores. These calculated scores are shown, together with the obtained scores, in Fig. 4. Here again is seen the initial tendency to rise, followed by a leveling off and perhaps slight decline as practice continues. There is close agreement between the magnitudes and the trends of predicted and obtained scores ($F = 0.70$). In this condition the invalidity of using the IE score as a measure of stimulus generalization is more obvious still, since it is determined not only by H_1 but by H_2, H_3, and the number of omissions as well.

Hence, the present model has proved adequate to predict the IE curves over a wide range of conditions. It has also shown that stimulus generalization falls monotonically during paired-associate learning and that intrusion errors constitute a valid measure of S generalization only when initial $H_3 = 1.00$; otherwise, the IE curve tends to rise at first and then fall with continued practice.

Summary

A stimulus-response analysis of paired-associate learning is described, postulating that the learning of each of the pairs involves the formation of three different connections: (*a*) between the stimulus member of the pair and a mediating, labeling response which discriminates it from the stimulus members of the other pairs; (*b*) between the stimulus produced by that labeling response and the response member of the pair; and (*c*) between the stimuli produced by each successive subelement of the response member and the following subelement. A quantitative model which relates the strength of these component habit connections to various aspects of performance on paired associates is described.

Deductions from the model were tested by means of an experiment involving 10 *S*s in each of six conditions. The antecedent variables were the difficulties of forming each of the three component habits described above, manipulated by using different stimulus members and response members in the pairs, and by assigning the responses to the stimuli in varying ways. With these materials it was possible to analyze the responses given by the *S*s so as to obtain separate measures of the strength of the three component habits during learning. A typical paired-associate learning situation was employed, using a Hull memory apparatus and the anticipatory method of performance.

It was found that the relations between the gross learning scores in the different conditions predicted from the model agreed closely with the obtained results in direction and magnitude. The obtained practice curves for intrusion errors agreed closely over a wide variety of conditions with those predicted from the model which postulates that the number of intrusions is a function of the strengths of all three of the habits described above, and not just of that of the discrimination habits as assumed in some studies. The intrusion error curves tended to first rise, then fall slightly with practice under most conditions. The practice curve for stimulus generalization during paired-associate learning was found to have a monotonically falling slope rather than the first rising, then falling shape sometimes inferred.

References

Bakan, D. A generalization of Sidman's results on group and individual functions and a criterion. *Psychol. Bull.*, 1954, **51**, 63–67.

Battig, W. F. Comment on "intralist generalization in paired-associate learning." *Psychol. Rev.*, 1959, **66**, 338–339.

Bugelski, B. R., & Scharlock, D. P. An experimental demonstration of unconscious mediated association. *J. exp. Psychol.*, 1952, **44**, 334–338.

Feldman, S. M., & Underwood, B. J. Stimulus recall following paired-associate learning. *J. exp. Psychol.*, 1957, **53**, 11–15.

Gagné, R. M. The effect of sequence of presentation of similar items on the learning of paired associates. *J. exp. Psychol.*, 1950, **40**, 61–73.

Gibson, E. J. A systematic application of the concepts of generalization and differentiation to verbal learning. *Psychol. Rev.*, 1940, **47**, 196–229.

Gibson, E. J. Intra-list generalization as a factor in verbal learning. *J. exp. Psychol.*, 1942, **30**, 185–200.

Gibson, E. J. A re-examination of generalization. *Psychol. Rev.*, 1959, **66**, 340–342.

GIBSON, J. J., & GIBSON, E. J. Perceptual learning: Differentiation or enrichment? *Psychol. Rev.*, 1955, **62**, 32–41.

GOSS, S. E. Transfer as a function of type and amount of preliminary experience with task stimuli. *J. exp. Psychol.*, 1953, **46**, 419–428.

HAKE, H. W., & ERICKSEN, C. W. Role of response variables in recognition and identification of complex visual forms. *J. exp. Psychol.*, 1956, **52**, 235–243.

HOVLAND, C. I. Experimental studies in rote learning theory: VII. Distribution of practice with varying lengths of lists. *J. exp. Psychol.*, 1940, **27**, 271–284.

HULL, C. L. *Principles of behavior.* New York: Appleton-Century-Crofts, 1943.

HULL, C. L. *A behavior system.* New Haven: Yale Univer. Press, 1952.

HUNT, R. G. Meaningfulness and articulation of stimulus and response in paired-associate learning and stimulus recall. *J. exp. Psychol.*, 1959, **57**, 262–267.

KURTZ, K. H. Discrimination of complex stimuli: The relationships of training and test stimuli in transfer of discrimination. *J. exp. Psychol.*, 1955, **50**, 283–292.

LEWIS, D. *Quantitative methods in psychology.* New York: McGraw-Hill, 1960.

LINDQUIST, E. F. Goodness of fit of trend curves and significance of trend differences. *Psychometrika*, 1947, **12**, 65–78.

MCALLISTER, D. E. The effect of various kinds of relevant verbal pretraining on subsequent motor performance. *J. exp. Psychol.*, 1953, **46**, 329–336.

MANDLER, G. Response factors in human learning. *Psychol. Rev.*, 1954, **61**, 235–244.

MURDOCK, B. B. Intra-list generalization in paired-associate learning. *Psychol. Rev.* 1958, **65**, 306–314.

MURDOCK, B. B. A reply to Battig, Gibson, and Runquist. *Psychol. Rev.*, 1959, **66**, 345–346.

NOBEL, C. E., & MCNEELY, D. The role of meaningfulness (*m*) in paired-associate verbal learning. *J. exp. Psychol.*, 1957, **53**, 16–22.

PISHKIN, V. Effects of probability of misinformation and number of irrelevant dimensions upon concept identification. *J. exp. Psychol.*, 1960, **59**, 371–378.

RUNQUIST, W. N. Remarks on "intra-list generalization in paired-associate learning." *Psychol. Rev.*, 1959, **66**, 343–344.

RUSSELL, W. A., & STORMS, L. H. Implicit verbal chaining in paired-associate learning. *J. exp. Psychol.*, 1955, **49**, 287–293.

SIDMAN, M. A note on functional relations obtained from group data. *Psychol. Bull.*, 1952, **49**, 263–269.

UNDERWOOD, B. J., & GOAD, D. Studies of distributed practice: I. Influence of intralist similarity in serial learning. *J. exp. Psychol.*, 1951, **42**, 125–133.

UNDERWOOD, B. J., RUNQUIST, W. N., & SCHULZ, R. W. Response learning in paired-associate lists as a function of intralist similarity. *J. exp. Psychol.*, 1959, **58**, 70–78.

(Received July 21, 1960)

ARTICLE 4

CUE SELECTION IN PAIRED-ASSOCIATE LEARNING

BENTON J. UNDERWOOD, MARGARET HAM, AND BRUCE EKSTRAND

Northwestern University

Consider a paired-associate list in which the stimulus term for each response consists of two distinct components, A and B. Both components are consistently present on each learning trial. Assuming that learning occurs in this situation, there are many possible interpretations which may be given as to what the effective stimulus or cue is for each response. It might be said that the effective cue is a configuration formed by A and B. Or, it might be said that each component is independently a cue for the response; that one or the other components is the effective cue, but not both, and so on.

The present study is predicated on the notion that when a complex stimulus is presented to *S* a selection process may occur so that the effective cue for the response is some component of the complex stimulus that is actually presented. Thus, the assumption is that there may be a discrepancy between the nominal stimulus (the stimulus actually presented *S*) and the functional stimulus (the component of the nominal stimulus which becomes the effective cue for response elicitation). That such discrepancies may exist is suggested by the reports of *S*s that they have used only a single letter of a three-letter stimulus as the effective cue (Underwood & Schulz, 1960). Such discrepancies might also be inferred from the so-called context experiments (e.g., Weiss & Margolius, 1954) in which the removal of a component of a compound nominal stimulus produces a decrement in recall, although such studies offer other interpretative possibilities, e.g., the functional stimulus is a configuration and the removal of any component reduces the effective associative strength.

If cue selection occurs—if only a part of a compound stimulus becomes the functional stimulus—certain variables should influence the selection. The hypothesis tested in the present experiment is that given two components of different classes as the nominal stimulus, the more meaningful component will become the functional stimulus. This hypothesis seems very close to the notion of differences in discriminability as a variable determining stimulus selection, a notion suggested by Sundland and Wickens (1962), and for which some experimental support was obtained.

The particular predictions for the present study may now be specified. Two lists for original learning were constructed. The stimulus compound for one list consisted of colors and low-meaningful trigrams; for the other list the compound consisted of colors and common three-letter words. For the first list it was assumed that the colors were more meaningful than the trigrams; therefore, the functional stimuli should be the colors. In the case of the word-color compound it was assumed that the words were more meaningful than the colors, hence, the functional stimuli should be the words. (It would have been more precise to have used two sets of verbal units of known meaningfulness for the compounds, but the use of colors was recommended by the desire to keep the experiment continuous with the context experiments.) Given the

Reprinted with permission of the authors and the publisher, the American Psychological Association. The article appeared originally in the *Journal of Experimental Psychology*, 1962, **64**, 405–409.

above assumptions, it was predicted that following the learning of the list with the trigram-color compounds, very little decrement would be observed if the trigrams were removed on a transfer test, but that a great loss would appear if the colors were removed from the compound. Contrariwise, in the case of the word-color compounds, removal of the words on a transfer test would result in a large loss but removal of the colors would have little effect on transfer performance.

METHOD

The general procedure required that half the *S*s learn an original list with trigram-color compound stimuli, and half learn a list with word-color stimuli. To test for each component separately on a transfer list required four groups. However, to determine precisely the amount of decrement occurring required two control groups for which the stimuli on the transfer test were the same as on original learning. Thus, the design called for six groups. Let W stand for words, T for trigrams, and C for colors, and the symbols before a hyphen designate the stimulus during original learning, those after the hyphen the stimulus on the transfer test. The six groups are, therefore: WC-WC and TC-TC (the two control groups); WC-C and TC-C (only color stimuli on transfer test); WC-W and TC-T (the verbal units appear alone as the stimuli on the transfer test).

Lists.—The materials for the lists are shown in Table 1. Each list consisted of seven pairs. The three-letter words all have AA ratings in the Thorndike-Lorge (1944) list except the word GAS, which is rated A. The trigrams have quite low associative con-

TABLE 1

STIMULUS COMPONENTS USED IN THE LISTS

Words	Trigrams	Colors
GAS	GWS	Red
DAY	DWK	Brown
NEW	NXQ	Yellow
DIE	DHX	Blue
BAD	BWD	Orange
GOT	GVS	Black
BED	BXD	Green

TABLE 2

MEAN NUMBER OF TRIALS TO CRITERION ON ORIGINAL LEARNING AND MEAN NUMBER OF ITEMS LOST ON FIRST TRANSFER TRIAL

Cond.	Original Learning		Transfer	
	Mean	σ_m	Mean	σ_m
WC-WC	8.80	.97	—	—
WC-W	8.00	1.18	1.20	.44
WC-C	9.20	1.14	2.50	.47
TC-TC	11.55	.95	—	—
TC-T	10.00	1.20	2.85	.36
TC-C	10.00	1.21	.05	.37

nections between letters as based on the Underwood-Schulz (1960) tables. It should also be noted that the trigrams have relatively high formal similarity as indexed by repeated letters. The purpose of this was to minimize the possibility that a single letter (such as the first letter) might become the functional stimulus. The frequency of repeated letters in the word list is about the same as for the trigrams and the repetitions are in the same positions. Both lists have the same initial letters.

The color components were made of construction paper and pasted on the vellum tape. Rectangular frames of color completely surrounded the verbal unit, the width of the frame being approximately ¼ in. When the color was the only component on the transfer test the frame appeared exactly as it had during original learning, the verbal unit having been removed. The particular colors paired with particular verbal units appear in the same row in Table 1. The response terms were the single digit numbers 2 through 8.

On both learning and transfer trials the rate of presentation was 2 sec. for the stimulus alone, and 2 sec. for the stimulus and response together. Four different orders of the pairs were used. Anticipation learning was used throughout.

Procedure.—The original learning was carried until the *S* achieved one perfect recitation of the list. The transfer tests were carried for 10 trials with *S* instructed to give as many correct responses as possible on the first transfer trial. The usual paired-associate instructions were given prior to original learning. In addition, *S* was told that both the word (or trigram) and color would appear consistently together from trial to trial. The intent of these instructions was to inform *S* of the nature of the stimulus compound with-

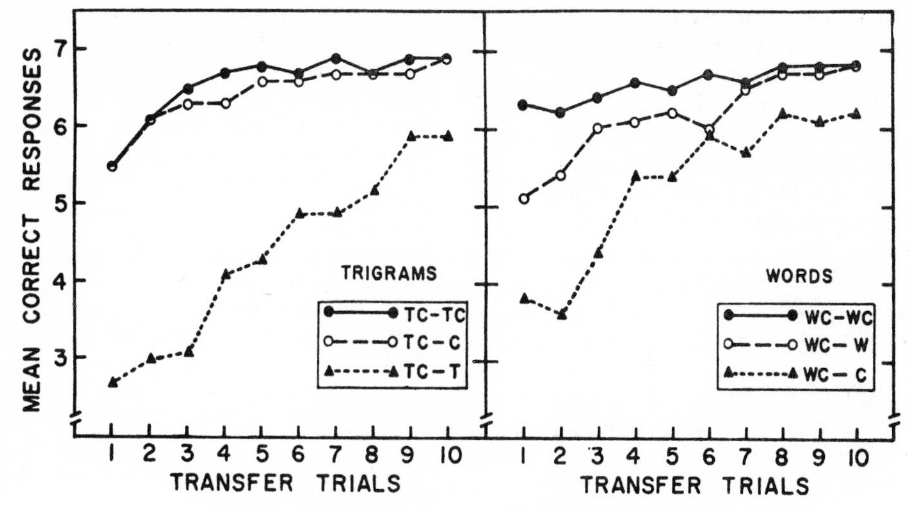

FIG. 1. Acquisition curves on the 10 transfer trials.

out, at the same time, biasing him toward "using" one or the other components. Prior to the transfer trials *S* again was fully informed as to the nature of the stimulus which would be present on these trials. Approximately 45 sec. elapsed between original learning and the first transfer trial.

Each of the six groups contained 20 *S*s. Twenty blocks were made up such that each condition occurred once within each block, with the order of the six conditions within a block being randomly determined. The *S*s were then assigned to the schedule in terms of their appearance at the laboratory. No *S* was lost for failure to learn.

RESULTS

The mean numbers of trials to attain the criterion on original learning are shown in the left portion of Table 2. Differences among the three WC groups and among the three TC groups represent random variation, the *F* being less than 1 in each case. For the 60 WC *S*s the mean is 8.67 ± .63, and for the 60 TC *S*s, 10.52 ± .65. The difference (1.85 ± .90) gives a *t* of 2.06, which is just past the 5% significance level.

The mean performance on each transfer trial is shown in Fig. 1. The left-hand section refers to the TC groups, the right-hand section to the WC groups. For the TC groups it can be seen that when the colors alone were used as stimuli, transfer was virtually complete; the performance of this group is only slightly below the control (TC-TC), thus indicating that the colors alone were completely effective functional stimuli. If *only* the color component was the functional stimulus, performance of Group TC-T should start at zero. It does not. For at least some *S*s the trigrams were also functional stimuli for at least a few responses.

The right-hand section of Fig. 1 shows that for the WC groups neither the words nor the colors developed complete effectiveness. The colors are less effective than the words, but the words alone show some loss as compared with the control.

The clearest inferences concerning the functional stimuli in original learning can be made from the performance on the first transfer trial. Since Group TC-TC showed a larger criterion drop than did Group WC-WC, loss scores have been calculated. To do this, each *S*'s score on the first trial was subtracted from the mean score of the appropriate control group. These loss scores are shown in the right section of Table 2. A 2 × 2 analysis of variance was performed on these scores, using as one classification variable TC and WC as identified in original learning, and as the other, colors and verbal units on transfer. Only the interaction F was significant, being 25.31; with 1 and 76 *df*, the F needed for the 1% significance level is approximately 7.00. Thus, the predictions that for the TC lists the colors would become the functional stimuli and that for the WC lists the words would become the functional stimuli, are given some support.

Discussion

The transfer tests for the TC compounds showed that color alone was a completely effective functional stimulus. This fact precludes an interpretation of the functional stimulus as being a configuration. However, it was noted that the trigram stimuli were not completely ineffective on the first transfer trial. There are at least two possible interpretations of this finding. First, it may mean that some trigrams, quite independently of the color component, become associated directly with the response term. Secondly, it may mean that some associative connection may have developed between the color and trigram components of the stimulus compounds. Thus, when the trigram is presented, the correct anticipation is mediated by associations running from the trigram to the color to the response term. The present data do not allow a choice between these two alternative interpretations.

The transfer data following learning of the WC lists raise three interpretative problems. First, it was noted that transfer was greater when the words became stimuli than when the colors became stimuli. Two circumstances could lead to this finding. (*a*) Most *S*s in original learning used words as stimuli for *all* associations but a few *S*s used colors as stimuli for all associations. (*b*) All *S*s used words as stimuli for *most* associations during original learning but used color as stimuli for a few associations. Given a large number of *S*s a choice between these two alternatives could be made by examining the distributions of scores on the first transfer trial. If the first of the two possible explanations is appropriate, the distributions should be bimodal when words alone or when colors alone are stimuli on the first transfer trial. If the second alternative is appropriate, each distribution should be continuous. Actually, bimodality is suggested in the present distributions but with only 20 cases in each this may be quite fortuitous.

The second interpretative problem is the same as that posed for the TC compounds where the data show that for some associations for some *S*s both the trigram and the color elicited the response. Such dual functionality may also be deduced from the data for the WC compounds. On the first transfer trial a mean of approximately 5.0 correct responses occurred when the words were presented alone and 3.8 when the colors were presented alone. These two values sum to 8.8, which is appreciably higher than the mean of 6.3 shown by the control *S*s on the first transfer trial. Clearly, dual functionality of the two components obtained for at least some *S*s. However, just as in the case of the TC compounds, this apparent duality may result from direct associations between the components and the response term or it may result from mediation between the stimulus components.

The third interpretative problem presented by the results of the WC compounds is the fact that the words showed greater transfer than did the colors. As stated in the procedure section, it was believed that the words would be more meaningful than the colors. We have no independent evidence for this and it may not be valid. The *S*s, being much more practiced in dealing with word stimuli than with patches of color as stimuli, may be biased toward the selection of the verbal stimuli. The data are quite in harmony with such a notion. However, a somewhat different approach may be taken to the problem. An empirical test can be made to determine which stimulus compound leads to most rapid learning when this learning is not preceded by learning in which the compound is present. To determine this three new groups of 15 *S*s each were run. One group learned the trigram-number pairs, a second the word-number pairs, and the third the color-number pairs. The mean total correct responses in 10 trials were 38.80 ± 3.61, 51.20 ± 3.52, and 50.40 ± 2.19, respectively. While the F is significant far beyond the 1% level it is clear that most of the variance is produced by the trigram-number pairs. The words and colors do not differ appreciably in their effectiveness as stimuli. The small difference in favor of the words occurred primarily on the first three trials. Thus, it seems quite reasonable to conclude that when *S* is given a compound consisting of common words and colors, he is likely to select the words as functional stimuli, not necessarily because they are more meaningful, but because he is more accustomed to dealing with such stimuli.

Finally, it may be stated that the results of the present experiment, taken in conjunction with the study by Sundland and Wickens (1962), would seem to indicate that it may be more fruitful to view the so-called context experiments as experiments investigating the variables determining cue selection.

Summary

This experiment was based on the assumption that when *S* is presented a compound stimulus in a verbal-learning experiment, cue selection may occur. Word-color or trigram-color compound stimuli were used in learning original paired-associate lists with numbers as responses, followed by a transfer test in which one or the other components alone was presented as the stimulus. Control groups were also used, these groups being given further trials with the original compound stimuli.

The results show:

1. For the trigram-color compounds, color was a completely effective stimulus on the transfer test. The trigrams, however, also produced a small positive transfer effect. The selection of the color component as the primary functional stimulus was assumed to be due to its higher meaningfulness.

2. For the word-color compounds, transfer was higher when the words appeared alone than when the colors appeared alone. This may be due to a bias *S*s have toward dealing with verbal material (as compared with the color patches used) rather than to higher meaningfulness of the words.

It was concluded that experiments dealing with the effects of context changes on retention may be viewed as representing cases of cue selection.

References

Sundland, D. M., & Wickens, D. D. Context factors in paired-associate learning and recall. *J. exp. Psychol.*, 1962, **63**, 302–306.

Thorndike, E. L., & Lorge, I. *The teacher's word book of 30,000 words.* New York: Teachers College, Columbia University, 1944.

Underwood, B. J., & Schulz, R. W. *Meaningfulness and verbal learning.* Chicago: Lippincott, 1960.

Weiss, W., & Margolius, G. The effect of context stimuli on learning and retention. *J. exp. Psychol.*, 1954, **48**, 318–322.

(Received September 15, 1961)

ARTICLE 5

R–S LEARNING AS A FUNCTION OF MEANINGFULNESS AND DEGREE OF S–R LEARNING

ELEANORE M. JANTZ AND BENTON J. UNDERWOOD

Northwestern University

It is an established fact that, when *S* learns a list of paired associates, not only does he learn S-R (forward) associations according to instructions given him, but he also learns some R-S (backward) associations without having been instructed to do so. Thus, if A-B is the forward association being learned, B-A may be being learned at the same time. The development of such R-S associations may be inferred from transfer studies (**4**, **6**), but can be shown directly by presenting *S* with B and asking him to recall A (**2**, **9**).

In a previous study (**2**) it was suggested that the operations defining R-S learning may simply be another way of producing what is commonly called incidental learning. If this is true it would be expected that the variables which influence incidental learning would influence R-S learning in a comparable manner. Such comparability for a number of variables would make it likely that the different operations are producing essentially the same learning process. With regard to number of presentations and incidental learning, two studies (**1**, **8**) have shown a direct relationship. Concerning meaningfulness, the data are conflicting. Brown (**1**) found no appreciable difference in the incidental learning of words and low association-value nonsense syllables. Postman, Adams, and Phillips (**7**), on the other hand, found an increase in amount of incidental learning as association value of syllables was increased from 0% to 100%. In the present study the S-R learning consists of nonsense syllables as stimuli and adjectives as responses. Since the association value of the syllables is varied, the present study will give evidence as to whether or not R-S learning is a function of the meaningfulness of the stimuli during S-R learning. In addition, the number of S-R learning trials is varied.

Since the present study was completed, a summary in English of the results obtained by a Japanese investigator, Morikawa, (**5**) has become available. In Morikawa's study both meaningfulness and number of S-R trials are reported to show a positive relationship to R-S learning. As will be seen, the present investigation confirms these results.

Method

General.—When R-S learning is measured by recall there is no need for a control condition. That is, if a control group, not having S-R learning, were asked to respond on an R-S recall trial it is highly unlikely that any correct responses would be given. However, if R-S learning is to be measured by transfer effects over a number of trials, a control group is essential. This control group must be at the same practice and warm-up level as the experimental group at the initiation of the transfer trials. In the present procedure three experimental groups were given 4, 12, or 24 trials on S-R learning and then 10 trials on R-S learning. Three control groups were given 4, 12, or 24 S-R trials on a comparable but different list from that given the experimental group. These groups were then given 10 trials on the same R-S list as the experimental groups. Differences between these groups on the 10 transfer trials must be attributed to R-S learning which took place as the experimental groups learned the S-R list.

Specific.—Six groups of 24 college students each, all naive to verbal-learning experiments, served as *S*s. The *S*s were assigned to the six groups in an ascending-descending order, i.e., to Groups, 1, 2, 3, 4, 5, 6, 6, 5, etc.

Reprinted with permission of the authors and the publisher, the American Psychological Association. The article appeared originally in the *Journal of Experimental Psychology*, 1958, **56**, 174–179.

There were two lists of eight pairs each. The major list was learned by the experimental groups as their S-R list and, when "turned over," by all groups as the R-S list. Four association values were represented in the eight stimuli, there being two syllables each from 0%, 33%, 67%, and 100% values as determined by Glaze (**3**). The syllables and their association values are as follows: TEX, NAR (100%); POF, SUZ (67%); VOQ, KIW (33%), YUD, CIJ (0%). The eight adjectives were as follows: agog, hearty, laughing, inert, massive, equal, brutal, glassy. In S-R learning the syllables were stimuli, the adjectives were responses. Therefore, for the R-S trials the adjectives became stimuli and the syllables became responses. Four different sets of pairing of syllables and adjectives were used to minimize the possibilities of getting a pairing that might be particularly easy or particularly difficult. In actual fact the results have shown that the four different pairings were not a significant source of variance.

The S-R list given the control groups was constructed in the same manner as the one given the experimental groups except that different syllables and adjectives were used. This list was learned as the S-R list by the three control groups merely to make practice and warm-up equivalent to the experimental groups at the time the R-S list was learned by all groups. Preliminary testing showed that the two S-R lists did not differ significantly in difficulty. Similarity between the two lists was made as low as possible to minimize negative transfer when the control *S*s shifted to the R-S list.

In S-R learning, one experimental group was given 4 trials, another 12, and the third, 24 trials. The corresponding control groups also received 4, 12, or 24 trials on their S-R list. Immediately after completing the S-R trials, all groups were given 10 trials on the R-S list. The experimental groups were instructed concerning the nature of the R-S list and were further instructed to give as many syllables as possible on the first presentation of the R-S list. They had not been told previously that they would have to learn an R-S list so there is no reason to believe that they intentionally learned R-S associations during S-R learning. The control groups were also instructed concerning the nature of the R-S list (as compared with the list that had just been presented) but were given one study trial since all items were completely new to the *S*s in these control groups.

In presenting the lists on a Hull-type drum, the syllables were printed in capital letters, the adjectives in lower-case type. The presentation rate was 2 sec. for the stimulus and 2 sec. for the stimulus and response pair together. Three different orders of the pairs were used to minimize serial learning. A 4-sec. interval occurred between trials. Anticipation learning was used throughout, and in R-S learning the syllables were spelled.

Results

S-R learning.—The mean number of total correct responses over 4, 12, and 24 trials for the experimental groups was 5.75, 53.21, and 131.83, respectively. Corresponding values for the control groups were 6.42, 39.67, and 121.13. An analysis of variance showed that the six groups did not differ significantly in performance on the first four trials. However, considering the total correct responses over all trials, the F between experimental and control groups was significant at the 5% level. As might be expected when degree of learning is manipulated, the variance was heterogenous (Bartlett's test). The calculation of t's between the control and experimental groups for each of the three degrees of learning showed that only the two 12-trial groups differ more than would be expected by random assignment of *S*s. The difference between these two groups was significant at the 1% level. Since the lists were shown to be not different in difficulty, the difference in performance between these two groups must represent a sampling deviation. Adjustment for these differences will be made in presenting the data on R-S learning. Meaningfulness of the stimuli was also a significant variable during S-R learning for both experimental and control groups; the higher the meaningfulness the greater the number of correct responses. However, the functions were by no means smooth, a result which might be expected since only two syllables were used as samples at each level of meaningfulness.

R-S learning measured by recall.—Immediately after learning the S-R list the experimental *Ss* were given the R-S list in which the adjectives were now the stimuli, the syllables the responses. The *Ss* were asked to anticipate as many syllables as possible on the first presentation. Following 4, 12, and 24 S-R trials, the total number of items correct on R-S recall was 30, 79, and 95, respectively. As a function of 0%, 33%, 67%, and 100% association values, the total number of items recalled was 34, 29, 60, and 81, respectively. Very marked heterogeneity of variance was present in these recall data, but since both variables were significant far beyond the 1% level by analysis of variance it seems reasonable to conclude that both variables are positively related to R-S recall. No evidence existed for an interaction between the two variables.

It may be noted above that the syllables having 33% association values resulted in slightly lower recall than those having 0% association values. This same small difference existed in S-R learning. However, such data should not be taken to indicate a reversal of the expected relationship between association value and learning since, as noted above, two syllables from each association-value level is too small a sample to expect a precise relationship. The present data are clear in showing only that in both S-R learning and R-S recall there is a gross positive relationship between meaningfulness and performance.

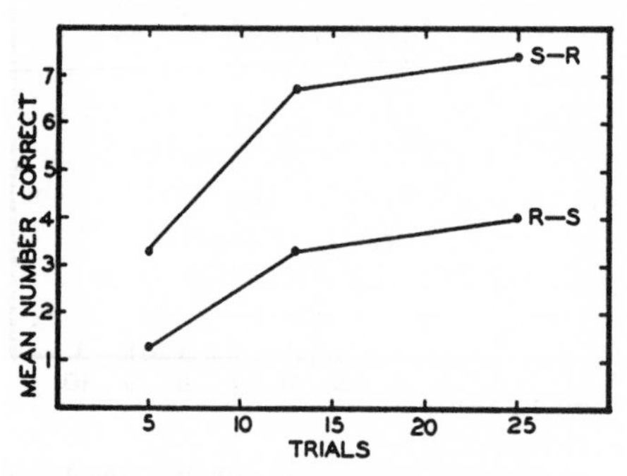

Fig. 1. Comparison of S-R and R-S learning as a function of number of S-R trials.

The increase in number of associations as a function of trials for both S-R and R-S learning is shown in Fig. 1. The R-S function simply represents the mean number of syllables correct on R-S recall. The S-R function was obtained by visual extrapolation of the S-R learning curves. For example, the acquisition curve for the 4-trial S-R group was plotted and then extrapolated to determine the approximate number of responses this group would have anticipated correctly had it been given an additional trial. The same procedure was followed for the 12-trial group to obtain an estimate of their performance on a 13th trial, and for the 24-trial group to estimate performance on a 25th trial. Since R-S recall for the three groups may be considered to have taken place on the 5th, 13th, and 25th trials, the two functions are coordinated at these three trial points. It would have been possible to use the actual performance of the 12-trial S-R group on the 5th trial to estimate the performance of the 4-trial group had they been given another trial, and the 24-trial group to estimate the 12-trial group's performance had they been given a 13th trial. However, in view of the differences in learning rate of the groups (as noted earlier) the extrapolation method would seem to be preferable and it allows comparison of S-R and R-S learning for the same *Ss* at a given point.

It is clear from Fig. 1 that the increase in number of correct associations as a function of trials is greater in S-R learning than in R-S learning. For both types of associations the greatest increase takes place during the first half of the learning period. During the second half of the trials, S-R learning, when measured by the number of correct associations, cannot increase much more since it has almost reached the maximum of eight correct responses. This is not true for R-S learning; yet, there is only a small increase in number of responses recalled between the 13th and 25th trials. The R-S curve suggests an asymptote considerably below that of the S-R curve.

R-S learning measured by transfer.—The performance of the control and experimental groups on the ten transfer trials is shown in Fig. 2. Since the transfer list was a new list for the control groups, the first trial was a study trial. The first-trial performance of the experimental groups represents R-S recall as discussed above. An analysis of variance of total correct responses over all transfer trials allows the following conclusions: (*a*) performance of the experimental groups is superior to that of the control groups; (*b*) the higher the degree of S-R learning the greater the transfer; (*c*) the higher the meaningfulness the greater the transfer. If the performance curves for the control groups are subtracted from those for the experimental groups for each degree of learning it can be seen that the difference following 12 and 24 trials on the S-R list is maintained throughout all transfer trials. Furthermore, the difference for the 24-trial groups is greater than for the 12-trial groups. This is true in spite of the fact that earlier evidence indicated that the 12-trial experimental group was a faster-learning group and the 12-trial control group a slower-learning group than the two 24-trial groups. With

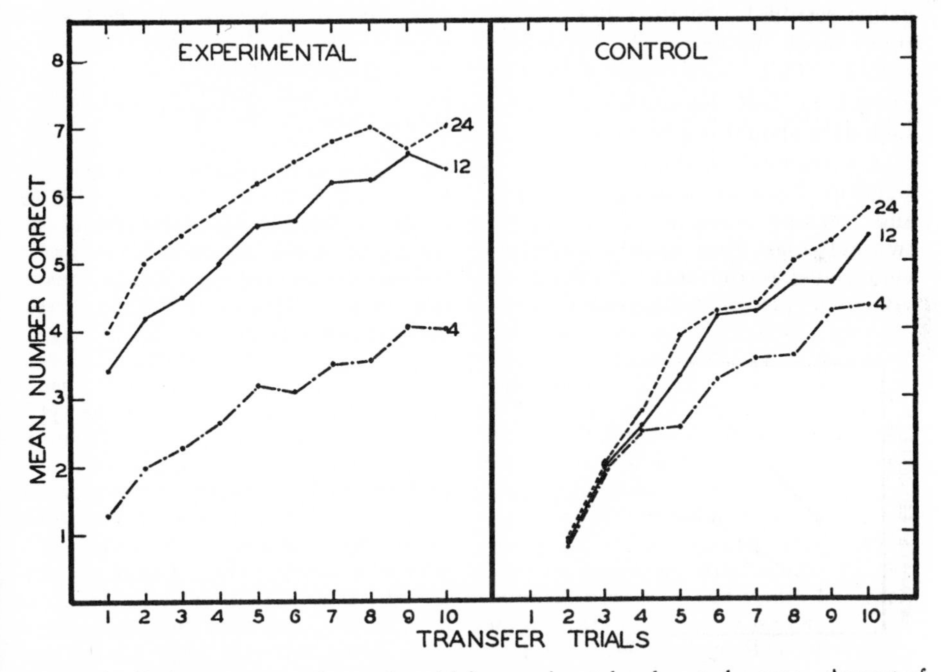

Fig. 2. Performance on each transfer trial for experimental and control groups. Amount of R-S learning is indicated by the superiority of the experimental group over the control group having had the same number of S-R trials.

only 4 trials on the S-R list the experimental group shows a clear superiority over the 4-trial control group on only the first few trials.

The need for the control groups in measuring the transfer effects is clearly apparent. Since the 12-trial control group is a slower-learning group than the 24-trial control group, these two groups may be considered roughly equivalent on these transfer trials. However, it is not possible to interpret clearly the differences in the performance of the control groups from the present data. Learning-to-learn differences, warm-up differences, and even temporary negative transfer may all influence the performance of these control groups.

Discussion

The results have shown that R-S or backward learning is a direct function of both meaningfulness of stimuli during S-R learning and degree of S-R learning. Measurements of R-S learning by recall and by transfer effects yielded essentially the same results.

With 24 trials, S-R learning had apparently reached a near asymptote of about 93% correct responses on a given trial. However, at this same point, R-S learning as measured by recall was about 50% correct responses. Furthermore, Fig. 1 indicated that the amount of R-S learning would never approach the amount of S-R learning even with a great many more trials beyond the 24 actually given. It appears that during S-R learning some R-S associations are learned and some are not and those that are not will never be established even if an extended number of S-R trials are given. Some pairings rather easily and quickly result in bidirectional associations and others result in only unidirectional (S-R) associations. Although the number of bidirectional associations is directly related to meaningfulness of the stimuli during S-R learning, the lack of evidence for interaction between degree of S-R learning and meaningfulness indicates that even with the most meaningful stimuli used here some bidirectional associations will not be formed. The situation appears analogous to results from free-association tests when it is shown that for some pairs A has a high probability of eliciting B, and B an equally high probability of eliciting A, whereas for other pairs A may have a high probability of eliciting B, but B a low probability of eliciting A.

The results of the present study would give some support for the incorporation of R-S learning into the body of data associated with what is commonly called incidental learning. The increase in R-S learning as a function of degree of S-R learning parallels the results on incidental learning as a function of number of trials (**1**, **8**). The direct relationship between R-S learning and meaningfulness of stimuli during S-R learning conforms to the incidental-learning results of Postman, Adams, and Phillips (**7**). Indeed, these investigators used the same association values as used in the present study and the incidental recall curve as a function of meaningfulness is remarkably similar to that found in the present study, including the slightly poorer performance on the syllables having 33% association values as compared with those having 0%. The one known conflicting study is Brown's (**1**). He found no difference in the incidental learning of low-association syllables and monosyllabic nouns. This was true after 4 presentations of a serial list of 12 items or after 8 such presentations. Brown's study differed somewhat from the usual incidental learning study. In the typical study *S*s are exposed to a group of items without instructions to learn and then are asked to recall as many of the items as possible without regard to order. Brown, however, required his *S*s to reproduce the order. The amount of incidental learning in Brown's study is extremely low, less than one item per *S* being given correctly after 4 trials and an average of about 1.5 after 8 trials. It may well be, therefore, that differences in meaningfulness would emerge if many more trials were given on the list than were actually given. As the data stand, however, Brown's results are contradictory to one other study on incidental learning and to the present study if R-S learning is considered incidental learning.

Summary

This study was designed to determine R-S or "backward" learning of paired associates as a function of number of S-R trials and meaningfulness of the stimuli in the S-R list. Three experimental groups were given 4, 12, or 24 trials on a list of eight paired associates having nonsense syllables for stimuli and adjectives for responses. Four different association values were represented by the stimuli. Following the specified number of trials on the S-R list, all groups were given 10 transfer trials on the R-S list which consisted of the same items as were in the S-R list but the syllables were responses and the adjectives stimuli. Three control groups had 4, 12, or 24 trials on an irrelevant list and then were given 10 trials on the same R-S list given the experimental groups.

The results show that, whether measured by recall or by positive transfer over the 10 trials, both degree of S-R learning and meaningfulness were positively related to amount of R-S learning. The data strongly suggest that R-S learning would never be complete when measured by recall even if the number of S-R trials was greatly extended over the maximum of 24 used here.

A consideration of evidence from incidental-learning studies reveals a high correspondence between the functions of meaningfulness and number of trials for incidental learning and the present results for these two variables in R-S learning. This may be used to support an argument that R-S or backward learning is essentially a form of incidental learning.

References

1. Brown, G. H. Factors influencing incidental learning. *J. exp. Psychol.*, 1954, **47**, 163–169.
2. Feldman, S. M., & Underwood, B. J. Stimulus recall following paired-associate learning. *J. exp. Psychol.*, 1957, **53**, 11–15.
3. Glaze, J. A. The association value of nonsense syllables. *J. genet. Psychol.*, 1928, **35**, 255–269.
4. Harcum, E. R. Verbal transfer of overlearned forward and backward associations. *Amer. J. Psychol.*, 1953, **66**, 622–625.
5. Morikawa, Y. Studies in paired-associate learning (1). Forward-backward recall gradient. *Jap. J. Psychol.*, 1955, **26**, 156–171.
6. Murdock, B. B., Jr. "Backward" learning in paired associates. *J. exp. Psychol.*, 1956, **51**, 213–215.
7. Postman, L., Adams, P. A., & Phillips, L. W. Studies in incidental learning: II. The effects of association value and of the method of testing. *J. exp. Psychol.*, 1955, **49**, 1–10.
8. Saltzman, I. J., & Atkinson, R. L. Comparisons of incidental and intentional learning after different numbers of stimulus presentations. *Amer. J. Psychol.*, 1954, **67**, 521–524.
9. Stoddard, G. D. An experiment in verbal learning. *J. educ. Psychol.*, 1929, **20**, 452–457.

(Received October 21, 1957)

One-Trial Learning?

BENTON J. UNDERWOOD[1] AND GEOFFREY KEPPEL

Northwestern University, Evanston, Illinois[2]

A controversial theoretical issue has arisen in very recent years over the manner in which associations are formed. Controversies are not new in interpretations of learning phenomena, but it is a signal historical event when the controversies are based primarily on the interpretation of data from the verbal-learning laboratory rather than on data from the animal-learning laboratory. The history of verbal learning shows few instances in which the learning of a list of nonsense syllables became the center of affectively tinged and opposed conceptual assertions. But such seems to be the case in the current assertions which place in opposition what is called *incremental* or *gradual* development of associations and *one-trial* or *all-or-none* formation of associations.

As an illustration of the central points of disagreement, we may consider the learning of a single paired associate, VOF-CAT, which is one of several pairs in a list. The list is presented to a subject for alternate study and recall trials. That is, the subject is presented each pair singly for three or four seconds on a study trial under instructions to learn to associate the two members of each pair. Then he is given a test trial on which the stimulus terms are shown singly and he is asked to try to give the response word that was paired with each. Thus, when VOF is shown on a test trial, the subject should try to give the response CAT. He is never shown the response terms on test trials. After the first test trial he is given another study trial, followed by another test trial, and so on. Now, let us assume that on the fourth test trial when VOF is shown, the subject first correctly gives the response in the time allowed him for this item.

We may now show schematically how "what has happened" is interpreted by a theory of one-trial learning as opposed to an incremental theory. In Fig. 1 the four study trials are shown along the baseline, with associative strength on the ordinate. An incremental theory would say that with each successive study trial there has been a gradual increase in the associative strength between the stimulus and response term for the single pair under consideration (the linear relationship between trials and associative strength is used merely to simplify matters). The one-trial notion, on the other hand, says "nonsense"; no learning occurred until the fourth study trial at which time the association was established at maximum strength. Thus, Fig. 1 represents the interpretation of the learning of a single paired associate by the two contrasting notions.

Two investigators have independently put forth the notion that associations are formed in one trial. One is Irwin Rock, who first published his ideas on the matter in 1957, and the other is William Estes who advanced his ideas in his Division-3 Address in 1959, the substance of his remarks subsequently being published in the *Psychological Review* (Estes, 1960). An evaluation of the methods used by Rock to investigate one-trial learning has been presented elsewhere (Underwood, Rehula, and Keppel, in press), the conclusion being that since the methods used

[1] The substance of the Psi Chi address by the senior author at the meetings of the Midwestern Psychological Association, Chicago, May, 1961. Prof. W. K. Estes was chairman of the session.

[2] The experiments were supported by contract Nonr-1228 (15) between Northwestern University and the Office of Naval Research.

Reprinted with permission of the authors and the publisher, the Academic Press. The article appeared originally in the *Journal of Verbal Learning and Verbal Behavior*, 1962, **1**, 1–13.

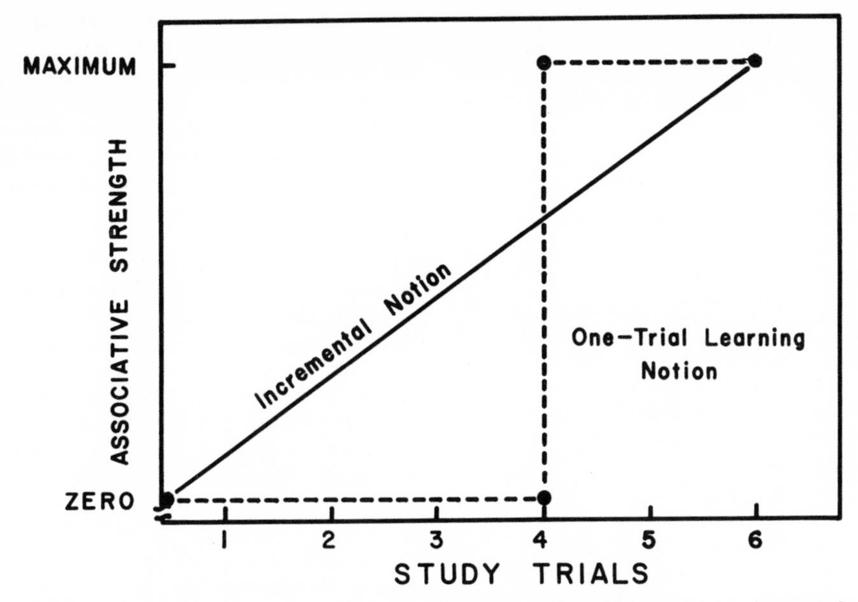

FIG. 1. Schematic representation of the learning of a single paired associate as interpreted by a one-trial theory and by an incremental theory. The single item was first given correctly following the fourth study trial.

by Rock did not control for item selection, hence item difficulty, the results of his investigations could not be used to arbitrate between one-trial and incremental-learning notions. Other investigators have also questioned the adequacy of Rock's procedures (Lockhead, 1961; Postman, in press). Therefore, the present paper will be concerned with the Estes version of one-trial learning. Our approach to the problem can best be understood by referring to a statement in the article by Estes, Hopkins, and Crothers (1960, p. 338):

> "Assuming that possible artifacts have been adequately handled by our various control measures, the results on acquisition appear incompatible with any theory which expresses learning in terms of increments in associative strength, excitatory potential, or simply response probability in individual *Ss*."

The initial part of the present paper revolves around two main points. First, we do not believe that critical artifacts have been removed in the procedures of Estes *et al.* Secondly, even if the artifacts could be ruled out, we believe that the data presented could be interpreted handily by certain extant incremental theories. Before elaborating these two points, we wish to make our position clear on certain matters to avoid any possible misunderstanding. It will be seen that we are critical of the methods of research of a very small segment of the great amount of research with which Estes has been associated since the early 1940's. We may well be wrong in our assessment of these methods; if we are, we are sure that replies will be given in the same spirit as the present critique, namely, to try to get at the true state of affairs concerning the experimental facts. Our interest in the issues stems not from a strong theoretical commitment but from a commitment to the use of the best methods of research available. We have probably always accepted implicitly the validity of an incremental theory; indeed, the results of experiments we shall report tend to support such a theory. In spite of this, it is not the major purpose of this paper to promulgate an incremental theory nor to deny a one-trial theory. But, we *will* look critically at the methods of research from which data are obtained to support one or the other theories.

The Criticisms

Procedures Used by Estes et al. (1960)

We will evaluate the first experiment presented in this article since it is implied that the results of this experiment provide the most critical data for separating one-trial and incremental-learning theories. A list of eight paired associates was used. The stimulus terms were consonant syllables, the response terms single-digit numbers. The list was presented first for a single study trial, followed by a test trial. Then, for each subject, four of the pairs were drawn randomly from the eight. These four pairs were given a second study trial, and finally, a second test trial was given for all eight items. From these simple procedures the data to deny incremental learning and to support one-trial learning were derived. We will look first at the data.

The first fact is that on the first test trial 49% of the stimuli were responded to correctly. This fact has no immediate theoretical implications. Of course, it might be said that for the average subject about half the items were indeed learned on one trial. But the issue before us is not whether one trial learning ever occurs but whether or not this is typical of *all* learning. And yet, as a baseline, the 49% figure becomes important. For now, the investigators ask the question of whether this value means that for a given item the probability of being correct is approximately .5 for each subject, or whether it represents a probability of 1.0 for half the subjects and zero for the other half. The former interpretation, namely, that it represents a .5 probability for each subject, is asserted to be an interpretation made by incremental theories, whereas the latter would be expected by a one-trial theory. So, of course, the intent is to make a choice between the two conceptions. The choice, according to these investigators, is made as follows. Assume there are four subjects. The fact reported earlier showed that approximately 50% of the items were correct. If the all-or-none notion is correct, each of two subjects had a probability of 1.0 for a given item and the other two subjects each had a probability of zero for the item. If this is true, a second test trial should demonstrate this state of affairs. Items which were correct on the first test trial should be correct on the second (without intervening study), and those not correct on the first should not be correct on the second (without intervening study). The data show that 71% of the items which were correct on the first test trial were also correct on the second, and only 9% of those not correct on the first test trial were correct on the second. Strictly speaking, from a one-trial theory the values should be 100% and 0%. These are matters for later discussion. For the moment it is sufficient to report that Estes *et al.* conclude that the one-trial position is supported, the incremental position is not.

Application of an Incremental Theory

Let us consider how the above data may be handled by an incremental theory. Certain incremental theories do not set associative strength and performance isomorphic. More particularly, these theories make use of a threshold notion. This threshold is said to be reached at a certain level of associative strength, and it is only at this point that excitatory potential, necessary for a response to occur, comes into use; or, to keep the language consistent, only after the threshold is attained do these theories start considering probabilities of performing a response. Zero probability is set at threshold, not at zero associative strength. Thus, for the results of the experiment by Estes *et al.*, it could be said that if an item were incorrect on the first test trial then it was below the performance threshold; there is no reason why it should be correct on the second test trial with no intervening study. Likewise, an item above threshold on the first test trial has a high probability of being correct on the second. Items which were correct on the first test trial but not on the second, and those which were not correct on the first but correct on the second, would be handled by some incremental theories via the notion of *oscillation*.

It is apparent that the incremental theory which we think can handle the data of Estes *et al.* is a Hull-type theory. The threshold notion, which implies a distinction between associative strength and performance has always been a part of Hull's system building. A single quotation may be used to make this point (Hull, 1952, p. 12): "The reaction threshold stands at an appreciable distance above the absolute zero of reaction potential."

The failure of Estes to attempt to interpret his data in terms of such a theory is puzzling. It is as if he is setting a trap for the unwary, and we may be the first quarry. By this we do not mean that Estes must use such a theory but rather, if assertions are made that incremental theories cannot handle the results, it is puzzling why a Hull-type theory did not enter into his thinking. For it seems to us that such a theory can readily accommodate the results of the original experiment.

To make an incremental theory more complete, one may add an individual-difference variable; both Hull (1952) and Spence (1956) have done this. While it does not seem that either of these theorists have firmly set their systems as to the method of handling individual differences, one method is to keep the threshold for a given association constant across all subjects and vary the rate of growth of the association to incorporate differences in rate of learning among subjects. A schematic presentation of such a conception is given in Fig. 2. The display shows four subjects of different learning abilities and the rate of growth of the associative connection for each as a function of a single study period. It will be noted that two ordinates are drawn. The one to the left is the same as that in Fig. 1 and represents associative strength running from zero to some maximum strength. The other ordinate represents a performance measure; this measure starts at threshold with a probability of zero and increases as associative strength increases beyond the threshold. According to Fig. 2, two subjects have developed associative strength above threshold and two have not. This conception leads to exactly the same prediction as that given by Estes *et al.*

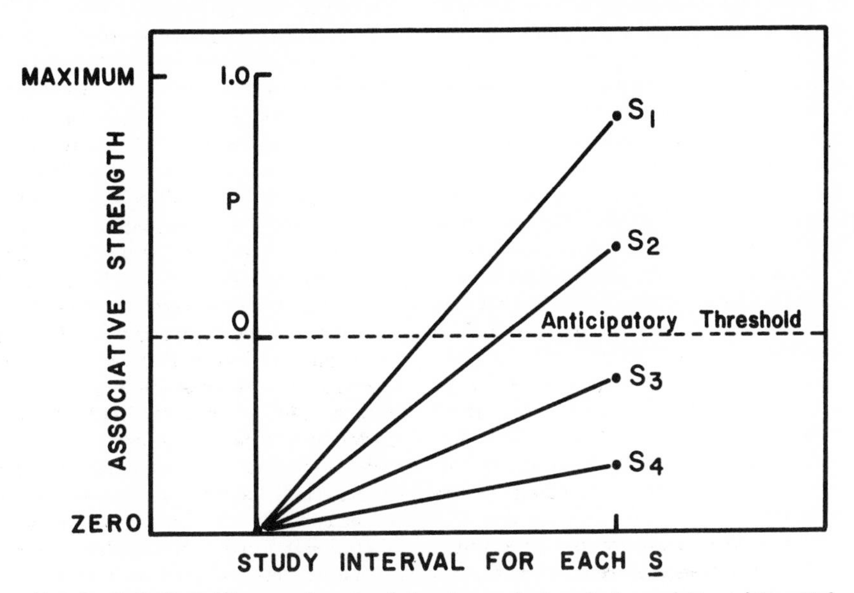

FIG. 2. Individual differences in rate of learning a single paired associate as interpreted by an incremental theory using an anticipatory threshold.

based on an all-or-none theory, namely, that without intervening reinforcement, the two items which were correct on the first test trial are likely to be correct on the second, and the two that were incorrect on the first test trial are likely to remain incorrect on the second.

It can also be seen that an incremental theory could handle differences in difficulty of items in the same manner that individual differences are handled in Fig. 2. Thus, the four curves of Fig. 2 could be thought of as representing four items of different difficulty for a single subject. With a constant period of study for each item the rate of growth varies because of differences in difficulty.

To summarize, we have been unable to see why a Hull-type incremental theory cannot handle the data Estes *et al.* present from this experiment. Furthermore, we have not found that any of the data presented by Estes (1960) from other experiments are resistant to interpretation by a theory of this type.

Questions of Procedure

We turn next to procedural matters in an effort to show that artifacts have not been ruled out of the simple experiment outlined earlier. Two facts seem apparent. First, those items which were not gotten correctly on the first test trial must inevitably represent more difficult items on the average than those which were given correctly. Secondly, more incorrect items are represented in the protocols of slow-learning subjects than in those of fast-learning subjects, and, contrariwise, more correct items on the first test trial must be given by fast-learning subjects than are given by slow-learning subjects. Under these circumstances it seems quite out of the question that even Estes' interpretation of an incremental theory (i.e., that items which were incorrect and correct on the first test trial have equal probabilities of being correct on a second test trial), could receive confirmation.

Estes *et al.* were quite aware of the possibility of item differences producing the results we have discussed. But, in our opinion, their test of this was simply inappropriate. It will be remembered that after the first study trial four of the eight items were drawn at random for each subject, and the subject was given a second study trial for these four items, after which a second test of all eight items was made. Estes *et al.* show that 46% of the items which were incorrect on the first test trial, and then were given a second trial, were correct on the second test trial. Since the proportion correct on the first test trial was 49%, and since 46% is very close to that value, it is concluded that the two sets of items on which these values were determined are equivalent in difficulty. This comparison *assumes* that the first study trial produced no associative strength for items missed on the first test trial. But, an incremental theory could say simply that a certain amount of subthreshold strength had developed for these difficult items and that the second study trial resulted in about half of these being above the performance threshold. The fact that 49% and 46% are quantitatively about the same may well be an irrelevant, indeed, misleading fact, for theoretical inference. However, this is not the major point we wish to make, since we are concerned with methods.

It will be remembered that four items were given a second study trial. About half of these were incorrect on the first test trial, and it is these incorrect items to which attention is still directed. We have assumed that these items must necessarily be more difficult items than the full population of items, but no data are presented by Estes *et al.* which will test this assumption directly. However, such data would be available in their records. There were 48 subjects and by the nature of the design each subject learned two eight-item lists so that records on sixteen different pairs of items are available for each subject. The 48 subjects could be divided randomly into two subgroups of 24 subjects each. For each subgroup the number of times each of the sixteen items was responded to correctly on the first test trial could be determined. Finally, a correlation could be calculated between these two arrays for the sixteen items. The correlation must not differ significantly from zero to conclude that differences in item difficulty were of little relevance for the interpretation of the results of this experiment. Unless the experience in the Northwestern University laboratory is completely atypical, it seems clear that a significant positive correlation will be found. The implication of such a correlation is that the items missed on the first test trial *were* more difficult than those given correctly and were consistently more difficult across subjects.

The second artifact of the experiment by Estes *et al.* concerns individual differences. Four items were drawn randomly from the eight presented on the first study trial, and those that were incorrect on the first test trial were examined to see what happened after a second study trial; the result was that 46% were correct. To take two extreme cases of individual differences, suppose first that a very slow subject got no items correct on the first test trial. On the second study trial he contributes four items to the pool from which the 46% statistic was derived. Secondly, suppose that a very fast learner got all items correct on the first test trial; such a subject will contribute no items to the pool from whence the 46% value came. It seems inevitable that the pool of missed items must be made up of the more difficult items and that these are more frequently represented in the protocols of slower-learning subjects than in the protocols of faster-learning subjects.

The third artifact contributing to the value of 46% comes from the method used to give the second study trial—the second reinforcement. The length of list was reduced from eight to four items; for the average subject two of these items were correct on the preceding test trial and two were incorrect. It is necessary, of course, to define operationally what is meant by a reinforcement. Estes *et al.* do this by specifying that a reinforcement is a single exposure of a given pair for a given time interval. These operations were identical for the first study trial where eight items were given and for the second where four were given. Thus, the two trials differed only in terms of the number of items in the list. The assumption which underlies the evaluation of the 46% statistic made by Estes *et al.* is that the likelihood of an item being learned when in an eight-item list is equivalent to the likelihood of it being learned when in a four-item list. This is probably contrary to fact; the shorter the list into which an item is placed the greater is the likelihood that it will be given correctly. Two of the senior author's students (Fred Brown and Stephen Avard) have recently collected some data relevant to this point. Two conditions of a larger experiment will be considered. In one condition five pairs of items (consisting of bigrams as stimulus terms and common three-letter words as responses) were given a single study and test trial. For another group of subjects the same five items occurred as the first five items in a ten-item list which was also given a single study and test trial. What is the proportion correct for the five items common to both lists? The values were 75% for the five-item list and 59% for the ten-item list. It is conceivable that if the retention tests for the five-item lists had included five filler items (to make a ten-item list and thus more nearly simulate the Estes procedure), the recall of the five common items might have been equivalent for both lists, but this seems very doubtful.

To summarize: because of the problems of method outlined, we do not think the experiment by Estes, Hopkins, and Crothers is capable of deciding between an incremental theory and a one-trial theory.

How can investigation assess the merits of the two opposed conceptions? From the work of Estes *et al.*, and also from the work of Rock (1957), it would appear that there are at least three potential points or phases in learning an association where the insertion of empirical tests may be of value.

(1) The first phase occurs during a trial or trials during which an item is presented but is not given correctly on the test trial, i.e., no evidence of learning is given in the performance of the subject. The one-trial theory asserts that no associative strength has developed for such an item. An incremental theory would say that subthreshold associative strength may have developed, although we see no reason why an incremental theory

is compelled to say that associative strength has developed for all such items.

(2) The second sensitive phase or point concerns the situation after an item has first been correctly anticipated. An unmodified one-trial theory must say that the probability of such an item being correct on a second test trial is 1.0; an incremental theory, using the oscillation principle and perhaps others, would expect variable probabilities depending upon the suprathreshold strength of the item.

(3) The third phase may be identified in classical terminology as the effect of overlearning on retention. One may not be able to measure changes in probability of performing an association over a series of trials simply because it is correct on every trial. Again, an unmodified one-trial theory would say that such overlearning is of no consequence, whereas an incremental theory might say that appropriate measures (e.g., long-term retention) would detect differences as a function of overlearning. Now, in fact, Rock (1957, p. 193) has said that "repetition *after* the association is formed is effective in strengthening it." He denies only that repetition was responsible in an incremental manner of forming the association. Thus, tests of Rock's one-trial theory versus an incremental theory must be confined to the first phase. Estes (1960), however, appears to make no such concession and intends to have his theory applied to all three phases.

Each phase will now be considered in turn, with major emphasis placed on the first phase.

Phase 1

Have items given one or more study trials but never given correctly on test trials developed any associative strength? If the answer is "yes," support is given to an incremental theory; if the answer is "no," support is given to a one-trial theory. It is simple to pose the empirical question, but to get an unambiguous answer empirically is not so simple. At a philosophical level we tend to eschew the crucial experiment for the simple reason that they rarely turn out to be crucial. However, our philosophy was not quite strong enough to prevent our trying the two experiments which will be reported now.

Experiment I

Procedure. Twenty-two pairs of items were constructed. The stimulus terms were two letters with low associative connection between the two letters according to the Underwood-Schulz (1960) tables. The response terms were single letters. Each of 22 letters was used once as the first letter of a stimulus term, once as the second letter, and once as a response letter, with no letter repeated in a given pair.

Two groups of 44 *S*s each were run, and a member from each group may be thought of as being run in pairs, an Experimental *S* and a Control *S*. For each of the 44 pairs of *S*s the procedure was as follows. Eleven pairs were randomly selected from the 22-pair pool. These 11 pairs were presented to the Experimental *S* for a single study trial followed by a test trial. Those items that were missed (no response or an incorrect response) were now given immediately to *S* for a second study and test trial. We were asking, of course, whether or not any associative strength had developed on the first study trial for those items that were missed on the first test trial; the plan was to let such associative strength, if it existed, manifest itself by determining the influence of a further study trial. But what is the appropriate control for the learning which is shown by the second test trial? We need to compare the recall of the shortened list of items originally missed by the Experimental *S* with the recall of the same items when they had not been given the original study trial. A Control *S* must be presented the shortened list of items for a study and recall trial, but the study trial must be the first exposure the *S* has to the critical items. In addition, the Control *S* cannot be given the list "cold"; he must be at the same practice and warm-up level as the Experimental *S*. To accomplish this the Control *S* was given a study and test trial on the 11 items remaining in the pool after drawing 11 for the Experimental *S*. Immediately after the test trial, the Control *S* was given the shortened list given the Experimental *S*.

As noted, 11 pairs were drawn randomly from the pool of items and given to the first Experimental *S*. The remaining 11 items were given the Control *S* to equate practice and warm-up for the two *S*s. For the next pair of *S*s, the two groups of 11 items were reversed so that the 11 given to the Control *S* of the first pair of *S*s were now given the Experimental *S* in the second pair of *S*s, and the 11 pairs given the first Experimental *S* were used as the warm-up and practice list for the second Control *S*. Thus, each item was used equally often as a control and experimental item when the results for the procedure for the four *S*s are considered. Successive blocks of four *S*s were handled in exactly the same way except that a new random drawing of 11 items was made for each block.

Items were presented by hand on cards at a 4-sec. rate, with 2 sec. between each card. On test trials only the stimulus was presented for 4 sec., with *S* instructed to give the response paired with it. All *S*s were urged *not* to guess. Approximately 1 min. elapsed between the test trial for the first list and the start of the study trial for the shortened list. Any *S* was dropped if eight or more of the 11 items were given correctly on the first test trial. The reason for this was to avoid giving second lists so short that no discrimination between Control and Experimental *S*s would be expected. The order of the items on the shortened-list study trial was different from the order in which these items had been presented the Experimental *S*s on the original study and test trial but was the same for both Control and Experimental *S*s. The test order for the shortened list was different from the order on the study trial but was again identical for both Control and Experimental *S*s in a given pair of *S*s. All *S*s were given a second retention test on the shortened list immediately after the first.

Results. The results for the shortened list show a higher recall by the Experimental *S*s than by the Control *S*s. The Experimental *S*s recalled 3.65 items, the Control, 3.10. This difference of .45 items is not significant statistically. However, it was noted that the Control *S*s had better performance on the first list than did the Experimental *S*s, the values being 3.75 and 3.63 for these 11-item lists. The use of covariance to adjust for the difference in learning of the first list produced a t of 2.19 for recall of the second list, a value which is beyond the 5% significance level. On the second test trial Experimental *S*s gave an average of 3.40 items correct, the Control *S*s gave 2.90 correct.

Another way to view the results is in terms of pairs; that is, let the 22 items rather than *S*s be the entry. While these occurred with different frequencies in the shortened list the frequency of each was identical for Experimental and Control *S*s. Using the direct-difference method of determining the t gave a value of 2.22, with greater frequency of recall by the Experimental *S*s. It was noted that the 22 items were not equally represented in the second list. The reason is that there were consistent differences in item difficulty. The number of times each item was given correctly on the first test trial was determined for each subgroup of 44 *S*s. The product moment correlation between these two arrays of 22 scores was .74. This high relationship was attained in spite of the fact that some attempt was made to construct homogeneous pairs.

Discussion. These results would tend to support an incremental theory; it appeared that the first study trial for the Experimental *S*s was not irrelevant for the items missed on the first test trial. But we should not be too quick in reaching the conclusion that the relevancy of the first study trial comes about because of the subthreshold tendencies developed on that trial. One can always find fault with these crucial experiments and since the critical difference between the recall of the Experimental and Control *S*s on the shortened list is not, in either an absolute or statistical sense, great, the effect of a possible confound cannot be gainsaid. For example, it is possible that the Control *S*s may have suffered some interlist interference in learning the shortened list since each had been exposed to 11 stimuli in addition to the number of stimuli in the shortened list while the Experimental *S*s had only been exposed to 11 different stimuli. However, if such differences in interlist similarity were operative it did not show up in the number of overt errors made in recalling the second list since both groups made exactly the same number, namely 89, or approximately two per *S*. (These errors were made in spite of the fact that *S*s were instructed not to guess.) Still, it could be argued that errors are not an infallible index of amount of interference. Thus, the possibility that poorer performance of the Control *S*s could be attributed to greater interlist interference cannot be entirely ruled out. On the other hand, there is a factor which would tend to favor the Control Group. We know that the missed items for an Experimental *S* are more difficult for him than are the items he anticipated correctly. But, in an absolute sense, the missed items for an Experimental *S* may be more difficult for him than would the same items be for a Control *S*. If any items are especially difficult for idiosyncratic reasons (which is quite possible since the intersubject agreement on item difficulty was not perfect), such items would not be as difficult for the Control *S*; or, to put this another way, some items which are difficult for an Experimental *S* for whatever reason may be easy for the Control *S* because of idiosyncratic reasons. This would facilitate the learning of the Control *S*s. Our conclusion is that while the results tend to support an incremental theory we cannot be completely sure that the test is adequate. We therefore designed another experiment to avoid the difficulties noted.

Experiment II

Procedure. A single list of 11 pairs was used, with two-letter stimuli and the digits 1 through 11 as responses. No letters were duplicated among the 22 letters used in the stimuli. Eleven different lists were constructed such that each stimulus term was paired once with each response term. Of course, no given stimulus term nor a given response term appeared twice within a list. The eleven different lists represent 121 different pairs. Two Experimental Groups of 44 *S*s each were run. Since 11 lists were available, and since no pair was repeated in the 11 lists, each list and each item was given to four different *S*s in each group.

One Experimental Group (E1) was treated in exactly the same manner as was the Experimental Group in the previous experiment. That is, they were first given the 11 pairs for a study and test trial and then a study and test trial on the items missed on the first test trial. The second group (E2) provided the new twist. They were also given a study and test trial on the 11 items, and again the missed items became the critical ones. However, the stimulus and response members of the pairs of items missed by *S*s in E2 were re-paired for the second study and test trial. Thus, the second list given the E2 *S*s constituted a negative transfer paradigm. That is, it constituted a negative transfer paradigm if any associative strength had developed on the first study trial for the items missed on the first test trial. In short, we thought that a comparison of the performance of the two groups on the shortened list would maximize the effect of any associative tendencies developed on the first study trial, these tendencies pushing the performance of E1 up and the performance of E2 down.

Our basking in the beauty and simplicity of this experiment was abruptly terminated when we suddenly realized that this design possessed a very likely confound. By avoiding the difficulties produced by the design of the first experiment we had admitted a new problem. Consider the group (E2) in which the missed items are re-paired for the second study trial. The original items that were missed were difficult, relatively; we know this simply because they were missed. By re-pairing the stimulus and response terms we may very well be providing the *S*s with easier pairs than would be the case for *S*s in E1 who are "stuck" with the original pairs they missed. Thus, a direct comparison between the two groups on the recall of the shortened lists would be biased against an incremental theory. Nevertheless, we proceeded with the experiment as planned since we saw a way to test independently the difficulty of the shortened lists.

Details of the experimental procedures were the same as for Experiment I except that 2 min. elapsed between the test trial of the first list and the start of the study trial of the shortened list, this time being necessary for the experimenter to re-pair the missed items according to a prearranged random schedule.

Results. The two groups of 44 *S*s each gave identical mean performance on the first list. This is important for it avoids having different lengths of lists as second lists for the two groups. The mean recall of the first list was 4.61 items out of the 11 presented. Therefore, the average length of the second list for both groups was 6.39 items.

In the recall of the shortened list the E1 *S*s averaged 4.07 items, the E2 *S*s averaged 3.75. This difference is not significant, giving a t of just over 1, but the difference is in the direction which would favor an incremental theory. On the second test trial the mean recall was 3.98 for E1 and 3.55 for E2. Our next step was to evaluate item difficulty for the two shortened lists.

Item difficulty was determined by evaluating the first recall—the recall of the 11 items presented initially. There are 121 different pairs. Each pair was given to four different *S*s in each of the two groups of 44 *S*s each. For each group separately we determined the number of times (out of a possible four times) that each item was correctly given on the first recall trial. The correlation between these two arrays of scores for the 121 items was .31, with .23 needed for the 1% significance level. This correlation, it should be clear, was obtained despite the fact that only four different *S*s determined the score for an item in each group of *S*s. When the items were grouped into 24 categories (23 groups of 5 items and 1 group of 6 items) to give more stability, the correlation became .61. But, by either value we may conclude that there is some intersubject agreement on easy and difficult items.

The next step was to assess the difficulty of the re-paired items given the E2 *S*s as compared with the item difficulty of the second list given the E1 *S*s. To make the determination a value was assigned each item in each list, and a mean list difficulty index determined for each *S*. The value assigned a given item was the number of times it was given correctly on the first study trial; these values could range from 0 to 4, since only 4 *S*s determined the difficulty of an item within a group of *S*s. Hence, a high mean list value indicates relatively easy items (easy list) and a low mean value indicates relatively difficult items. For the E1 *S*s the mean list difficulty of the shortened list, consisting of pairs that had been missed on the first test trial, was 1.20. For the re-paired lists of the E2 *S*s the mean list value was 1.51. The difference between these two means gives a *t* of 3.48, far beyond the 1% significance level.

The above comparison on item difficulty may not be quite fair. Item values for E1 *S*s cannot be above three for a given item in the second list. For an item to appear in the second list for an E1 *S*, it had to be missed by that *S* on the first list; hence, a maximum value of three is all that is possible. For E2 *S*s, on the other hand, a re-paired item in the second list could receive the maximum value of four. Indeed, for the 44 *S*s in E2, there were 14 re-paired items which received a value of four. While this fact supports our contention that the re-paired items for E2 *S*s are easier than the second-list items for E1 *S*s, the comparison of mean list values may be biased by the admission of these items with values of four in determining mean list values for E2 *S*s. Therefore, we rescored all re-paired lists in which items receiving a value of four appeared, assigning a value of three to all such items. Our earlier conclusion does not change; the mean value for the second lists for E1 *S*s is 1.20, that for the E2 *S*s, 1.46. The difference produces a *t* of 3.13.

Discussion. From these analyses we conclude that the second or shortened lists learned by the E2 *S*s (the re-paired lists) were constituted of easier items than the shortened lists learned by the E1 *S*s. If no associative strength had developed for the missed items on the first study trial we would have expected the E2 *S*s to learn their shortened re-paired lists significantly better than the E1 *S*s would be expected to learn their shortened lists, since the E2 lists were easier than the E1 lists. In spite of this, the E1 *S*s got more items than did the E2 *S*s. Thus, it could be inferred that some associative strength had developed for items which were missed on the first test trial; the evidence could be interpreted as consonant with an incremental theory and as not supporting a one-trial theory.

In Experiment II we attempted to eliminate possible objections to procedures in Experiment I. We believe this was accomplished. And, although the interpretation of the results of Experiment II involved an indirect step, we can see no methodological problems which prevent this interpretation. Perhaps others can. In any event, we are not so untutored as to believe that these two experiments have settled a theoretical issue.

PHASES 2 AND 3

Phase 2 represents another point which may provide an evaluation of the two theoretical positions. The question is simply—what happens on a second recall trial to an item given correctly on the first, with no study intervening? As noted earlier, an unmodified one-trial theory must say that such items will be correct 100% of the time after they are first given correctly. In the study of Estes *et al.* (1960), discussed in detail earlier, the percentage repetition was 71%. In another study which Estes (1960) cites, the repetition value was 54%. Estes is quite aware of this disparity between his theory and the data; indeed, it causes him no little theoretical agony. His two mechanisms for resolving the contradiction are *guessing shrinkage* and *forgetting*. By guessing shrinkage is meant that if the subject guesses and gets a response correct on the first test trial no learning has occurred and this response is not likely to be given on the second test trial. We will not deny that some *S*s may guess and that some of the guesses are correct. We do not see, however, that one can assign quantitative estimates to guessing shrinkage unless the *S* is *forced* to respond to all stimuli.

That forgetting may occur between two test trials seems clear, and certainly Estes *et al.* (1960) make matters difficult for themselves when they use the same *S*s in more than one condition. If one uses naive subjects and lists of low intralist similarity the percentage of repetition increases appreciably. For example, in our Experiment I the percentage repetition of correct responses for the two test trials was 84% for the Experimental *S*s, and 83% for the Control *S*s. In Experiment II the values were 89% and 88% for E1 and E2, respectively. In the Brown-Avard experiment (mentioned in connection with the length of list issue), the percentage repetition was 91% for the 5-item list and 94% for the 10-item list. These values are much closer to the 100% than is shown in the studies of Estes. And yet, even under the most favorable circumstances (namely, subjects naive to the material in the laboratory, instructions not to guess, and low intralist similarity), the percentages do not attain 100%. In short, the Phase-2 facts do not give support to a one-trial learning theory. These facts do not, of course, require that the basic notion of one-trial learning be abandoned. But modifications seem necessary, and when these are made the basic postulate loses its uniqueness since these modifications must account at least for incremental changes in performance if not in learning. At this point the two opposed conceptions will not differ as starkly as they do when the basic notions are set in opposition as they were in Fig. 1.

The question of Phase 3 is whether or not reinforcements (study trials) beyond the trial on which an item is first given correctly influences retention. The data presented by Estes *et al.* (1960) in their second experiment indicates that there is little effect of such further study. We shall not analyze this experiment nor attempt to defend a position that overlearning does influence retention. However, it should be noted that in the experiment the retention interval used by Estes *et al.* is a matter of a few minutes. It remains to be seen whether or not with longer retention intervals the same facts obtain, and hence that they may be considered as contradictory to the classical principle (as exemplified by Krueger's work, 1929) that overlearning enhances retention.

Summary and Final Comments

We have taken the position that the data which have been used to support one-trial learning postulates have come from experiments with faulty methods. This position does not disavow the theory of one-trial learning. We have also taken exception to statements that the data of these experiments cannot be interpreted by available incremental learning theories. In addition, two experiments were reported which could be interpreted as supporting an incremental theory and as not supporting a one-trial theory, but we are under no illusions that these experiments settle the issue in the sense that they are crucial experiments. The consideration of the performance of subjects in verbal learning experiments after a response is first given correctly led to the conclusion that if one-trial learning is occurring, a system which uses this basic postulate must be modified to such an extent that it will closely approximate the incremental theories. In conclusion, certain additional statements are judged to be relevant.

(1) What constitutes "one trial" is quite an arbitrary matter. An 8-sec. rate of presentation for a pair of items constitutes four trials at a 2-sec. rate. We feel confident that shortening the anticipation interval on test trials will give data which, superficially at least, conform even more to an incremental notion than is the case when slow rates of presentation are involved (as has been the case in most of the experiments from which notions of one-trial learning have stemmed). Again, it should be clear that if such is true

it does not mean a disproof of the one-trial theory, but rather it means that modification of it is needed. It is perhaps quite possible to add modifying performance factors to the one-trial theories; if so, accounting for performance will become a major part of the theories. There is nothing wrong with this except that there will remain little difference between the theories which are now set in opposition.

(2) We have spoken earlier of the difficulties of deriving crucial experiments. Certain theories simply are not capable of disproof. Certain aspects of the incremental theory seem to be of this nature. To disprove the incremental theory in Phase 1 (to show that an item not given correctly has gained *no* associative strength) essentially requires proof of the null hypothesis. As long as experiments show a small, consistent, even though statistically insignificant effect in Phase-1 experiments, the incremental theory remains tenable. To disprove the incremental theory in this phase requires that a series of experiments show results which represent a random dispersion of effects around zero. This is not a virtue for a theory, but this characteristic seems to be inherent in the incremental theory.

(3) In the experiments dealing with one-trial learning the emphasis has been on the single association between a stimulus and a response term. The responses used have been readily available to the subjects; little if any response learning as such is involved. Learning a verbal list under these conditions takes place very rapidly. But, it should be clear that the association between the stimulus and response term in fact may not be representative of the other learning which occurs when heavy response learning is involved (e.g., integration of the letters of difficult syllables); certainly when heavy response learning is involved it requires the major portion of the learning time (Underwood and Schulz, 1960). One-trial theories have not included response learning in their discussion. It is quite possible that a theory of one-trial learning could be extended to cover response learning as well as learning the association between the stimulus term and response term, but we believe it will be a very difficult job. In any event, the point we wish to make is that the issues as drawn by the one-trial theories cover only a small portion of the associations which must be established in many verbal-learning tasks.

(4) As noted in the introduction, the theoretical issues represent a curious twist in theorizing about learning in that the data to support the theories are sought in the verbal-learning laboratory. Not since Thorndike has the human subject been used consistently as a source of data to test basic theoretical notions about learning. The memory drum seems to have replaced the T-maze, at least temporarily. This may or may not be an appropriate trend. There is some evidence (Postman, in press) that human subjects may adopt certain strategies in learning which may completely prohibit theoretical tests of propositions of the kind discussed in this paper. For example, supposing a subject adopts a strategy to concentrate on one or two pairs out of a list of eight on a given trial, ignoring all the others. If this does happen, the arbitrary definition of "one trial" is sadly deficient for the theoretical purposes intended. Now in fact we do not really know in any systematic way how frequently such strategies, as well as others, may be adopted by a subject. But, if such strategies do occur, and if they make tests between alternative theoretical positions absurd, then perhaps the verbal-learning laboratory is not the place to seek data in support of so-called fundamental postulates of learning.

References

Estes, W. K. Learning theory and the new "mental chemistry." *Psychol. Rev.*, 1960, **67**, 207-223.

Estes, W. K., Hopkins, B. L., and Crothers, E. J. All-or-none and conservation effects in the learning and retention of paired associates. *J. exp. Psychol.*, 1960, **60**, 329-339.

Hull, C. L. *A behavior system*. New Haven: Yale Univer. Press, 1952.

Krueger, W. C. F. The effect of overlearning on retention. *J. exp. Psychol.*, 1929, **12**, 71-78.

Lockhead, G. R. A re-evaluation of evidence of one trial associative learning. *Amer. J. Psychol.*, 1961, **74**, 590-595.

Postman, L. Repetition and paired-associate learning. *Amer. J. Psychol.*, in press.

Rock, I. The role of repetition in associative learning. *Amer. J. Psychol.*, 1957, **70**, 186-193.

Spence, K. W. *Behavior theory and conditioning.* New Haven: Yale Univer. Press, 1956.

Underwood, B. J., and Schulz, R. W. *Meaningfulness and verbal learning.* Philadelphia: Lippincott, 1960.

Underwood, B. J., Rehula, R., and Keppel, G. Item selection in paired-associate learning. *Amer. J. Psychol.*, in press.

(Received December 4, 1961)

ARTICLE 7

Implicit Mediators in Paired-Associate Learning[1]

KENT M. DALLETT

University of California, Los Angeles, California

The fact that paired-associate learning is influenced by the number of associations elicited by both stimulus and response items led Underwood and Schulz (1960, pp. 295ff.) to propose the *associative probability hypothesis*. This hypothesis maintains that *S*s generate associations to the items on a verbal list, and that the greater the number of such associations, the greater the likelihood that one of them will serve as a functional mediator for the pair to be learned. An added inducement for considering this hypothesis is that *S*s are typically eager to volunteer information to the effect that the seeking of meaningful mediators is, indeed, an important part of their learning process.

Unfortunately, the associative probability hypothesis raises a theoretical problem which Underwood and Schulz call the *interference paradox* (1960, p. 143). The paradox is that the greater the number of associations available to serve as a source of mediating responses, the greater the possibility that they will interfere with the association to be learned. The associative probability hypothesis and its attendant paradox can best be explained in terms of an example. Referring to Fig. 1, consider the trigram BAC as a potential stimulus in a paired-associate list. This trigram, when given to *S*s with instructions to give the first word it makes them think of, elicits several associative responses. The most popular of these responses are listed in Fig. 1, together with the proportion of times each response appeared in association data gathered from 140 *S*s. Now, consider the case in which the response EGGS happens to be assigned to BAC in a paired-associate list.

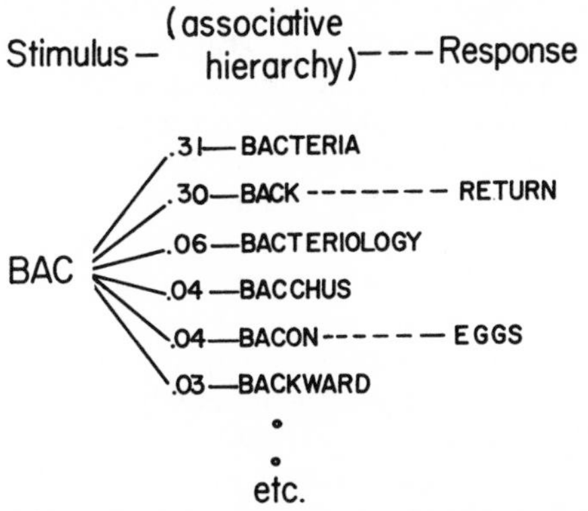

FIG. 1. Conceptual model of a paired-associate item, including the stimulus, its associative hierarchy, and two possible response words.

Because both BAC and EGGS have many associative connections with other items, the mediating link *bacon* happens to be available, together with several stronger associates of BAC (e.g., *bacteria*, *back*, etc.) which might interfere with elicitation of the mediator *bacon*. The response word EGGS will also have a number of associative connections (not shown in Fig. 1) which might interfere with learning. For any randomly selected pair, the probability of there being both facilitating and interfering associations available is a direct function of both stimulus and response association value. Clearly, if the mediating link

[1] This investigation was supported by U. S. Public Health Service research grant MH 06589-01 from the National Institutes of Mental Health. The author is grateful to Paula Tobin for her competent assistance in collecting the data.

Reprinted with permission of the author and the publisher, the Academic Press. The article appeared originally in the *Journal of Verbal Learning and Verbal Behavior*, 1964, **3**, 209–214.

BAC (*bacon*) is to be of any effectiveness, it must be possible for *S* to suppress the effects of the stronger, unwanted associates apparent in Fig. 1. Initially, such suppression might result from the associative context provided by the response word. The response *bacon* might be the strongest associate to the compound BAC-EGGS. However, unless the presence of EGGS on the list produces a relatively persisting change in the associative strength of *bacon,* it will be unlikely for *bacon* to occur as a mediator in the presence of the stimulus BAC alone, and it is to BAC alone that *bacon* must occur if it is to aid *S* in arriving at the desired response EGGS. That an association such as *bacon,* having once occurred for whatever reason, is likely to occur again, can be considered as similar to the phenomenon of *associative priming* (Storms, 1958). Underwood and Schulz (1960, p. 143) propose a theoretical *selector mechanism* to accomplish a similar priming operation in which *S*s learn what the relevant overt responses are. The concept as they use it seems readily applicable to the priming of mediators.

While all that has been said seems reasonable on the theoretical level, there appear to be no experiments which directly demonstrate that the selection and priming of implicit mediators can occur. Hence, an attempt was made to prime specified associative responses which might mediate learning in a paired-associate list.

METHOD

Design. The priming was carried out by showing *S* a trigram together with a word which was an associative response to that trigram. In terms of the example presented in Fig. 1, *S* might be presented BAC, and with it, in parentheses would appear *back* or *bacon,* half of the *S*s seeing one word, and half the other. The assumption is that *S* reads the word, and that this strengthens (primes) the associate designated by the word. For half of the *S*s who saw BAC (*back*), the word *back* was a relevant mediator: when the response item appeared, it was RETURN. For the other half of the *S*s, *back* was an irrelevant mediator: the response which appeared was *EGGS.* Relevance and irrelevance was analogously defined for *S*s who saw BAC (*bacon*), so that the Relevant and Irrelevant conditions (Group R and Group I, respectively) have the same response items and the same primed mediators. A Control group was given no priming, and it was predicted that the Control *S*s would implictly give relevant mediators to some items and irrelevant mediators to other items, and would fall between the two main experimental groups. To cast some light on the associations which Control *S*s might have produced, an Association condition was included, in which *S*, the first time the stimulus item appeared (in the interval in which other groups were given a relevant or irrelevant associate) gave his own association. Finally, an added control group, designated the Practice group, was added to evaluate the possibility that *S*s who saw BAC (*bacon*) were in effect learning a prior list which would facilitate BAC-EGGS by virtue of an A-B,A-B′ transfer paradigm. Put another way, the Relevant group was getting added practice on a closely related list during a brief interval of time in which other groups were seeing only the stimulus item. If this were the case, they should do less well than a group which got added practice on the critical list itself. Hence, the Practice group was primed with the response word itself, seeing BAC (*eggs*) before the response word EGGS appeared.

All of the experimental manipulations described apply only to the first exposure of the list. On subsequent exposures, only the stimulus and response items appeared, in the usual manner.

Materials. Twenty-four CVC trigrams of 93–100% Glaze association value were given in four different orders to four groups of 35 *S*s each as a free-association test. From the resulting association norms, 12 trigrams were selected by *E* so as to have at least two associative responses which, in turn, were associatively related to two other words in such a way that the two associative chains were not themselves related. An example of the relationships involved appears in Fig. 1: the responses to BAC are obtained from free-association norms, but the selection of two such mediators, and the overt responses RETURN and EGGS depend upon *E*'s judgment. The trigrams used, together with the assumed mediators and response items, appear in Table 1. Two lists were made up, each using the same trigrams and one of the two sets of responses. Each list appeared on two memory-drum tapes, and appeared in four different orders. The tapes were arranged in such a way that *S* could be shown a list with relevant or irrelevant priming for one trial, and then shown the same list without priming on subsequent trials, simply by moving the window on the memory drum.

Procedure. The *S* was seated before the memory drum, and given instructions for paired-associate

TABLE 1
MATERIALS USED IN THE EXPERIMENT

Stimulus	Mediator	Associative Strength	Response
WEV	weave	0.414	CLOTH
	weather	0.021	SNOW
TAL	talent	0.042	SCOUT
	talcum	0.043	POWDER
YAR	year	0.200	SEASON
	yarn	0.085	KNIT
RUJ	rouge	0.121	LIPSTICK
	rug	0.107	CARPET
BAC	bacon	0.036	EGGS
	back	0.300	RETURN
KAF	calf	0.171	PASTURE
	cough	0.071	SYRUP
DEP	depth	0.121	OCEAN
	deputy	0.078	SHERIFF
MOD	mode	0.150	FASHION
	mood	0.086	SAD
PIC	picture	0.421	FRAME
	picnic	0.393	BASKET
SAV	savage	0.143	NATIVE
	save	0.403	MONEY
LUN	lunch	0.243	FOOD
	lunatic	0.107	CRAZY
TIR	tire	0.321	AUTO
	tiger	0.071	JUNGLE

learning. Then, if *S* was in one of the priming groups he was told that for the first presentation only, "an extra word will appear (for the Practice group, "the word" instead of "an extra word") at the same time the syllable appears. The extra word will be in small letters and in parentheses. It will not appear again, and you will only be asked to learn the pairs that appear in capital letters. Only the pair in capital letters will appear after this first presentation." For the Control group, no such instructions were given. For the Association group, *S* was told "each time a syllable appears try to tell me the first word it suggests to you. Then you will see the syllable paired with the word you are to learn. You will not have much time, so tell me the word that the syllable suggests as quickly as possible." After one presentation, the drum was stopped, the window adjusted to show only the list without priming, and *S* reminded that from this point on he was to try to anticipate each word before it appeared. Throughout the experiment, the drum was operated at a 2:1 rate.

When *S* had attained a criterion of one perfect recitation of the list, the drum was stopped, and *S* was given a dittoed list of the pairs that had just been learned. At the top of the list were instructions to write, next to each pair, any "associations, mnemonic aids, or memory 'tricks'" which they had used in learning. One or two *S*s who did not spontaneously give this information were asked to indicate whether the syllables had been interpreted as words, and if so, what words they were. Virtually all *S*s gave this information without such prompting.

Then, a new list was put on the memory drum consisting of the same stimuli paired with the alternate set of responses. This second list was learned to a criterion of one perfect trial, with no difference in treatment among groups. The main reason for the second list, as it turned out, was to provide further evidence concerning the mediators which *S*s arrived at without overt prompting. Furthermore, in the second list previously relevant mediators become irrelevant, and vice versa; the effects of this reversal of relevance are of lesser interest, however, because they are confounded with the effects of differential relevance on first-list learning.

Subjects. The *S*s were students in the first and second semester introductory psychology classes at UCLA and were, in most cases, naive with respect to laboratory learning tasks. They were assigned to conditions and lists in rotation. The *S*s were obtained from regular spring semester classes, and from two summer sessions: in each experimental condition, there were 6 *S*s from each of these three populations for a total of 18 *S*s per group, and 90 in the entire experiment.

RESULTS AND DISCUSSION

Relevance of the Assumed Mediators. In all instances, *S*s were asked after learning a list to specify the associations which they thought

TABLE 2
MEDIATORS REPORTED AFTER LEARNING

Condition	List	Total reported	Relevant	Irrelevant
Control	1	178	144	4
	2	174	141	3
Association	1	171	136	3
	2	175	140	2
Relevant	1	189	176	1
	2	171	136	3
Irrelevant	1	177	147	5
	2	190	170	2
Practice	1	183	155	2
	2	170	139	5

they had used in learning. In Table 2 appears a tabulation of (a) the number of associations reported on the post-criterial questionnaire;

(b) the number of relevant mediators among them; and (c) the number of irrelevant mediators among them, an irrelevant mediator being the mediator specified for the *other* response used, and not simply a mediator which was not designated as relevant before the experiment. It will be noted in Table 2 that *S*s in each condition reported using some association in 78–88% of the 216 opportunities. Of these associations, approximately 80–90% were the mediators selected by *E*, or words scored as functionally equivalent, (e.g., "deep" for "depth": these amounted to only 90 of the 1778 associations). Very few associations were specified irrelevant mediators. It is of interest to note that while Group R on their first list, and Group I on their second list, each report a greater number of relevant associations than do *S*s who have not been told what the relevant mediators are, the difference is not great, amounting to an advantage of 1.6 such associations per *S*. While in most cases *S*s reported approximately 7.9 of the 12 relevant mediators without being told about them, the priming of the R and I groups makes it possible for them to give 9.5 of the relevant mediators.

The Effects of Priming. Two performance scores were analyzed: performance on the first anticipation trial, and trials to the criterion of one perfect recitation of the list. In Table 3 will be found the means and *SD*s of first-trial performance. An analysis of variance was carried out, with the five experimental conditions as one variable, and the three sets of *S*s as another. Only the difference between conditions was significant, with $F(4,75) = 11.435$, $p < 0.001$. A multiple range test (Duncan, 1955) shows that the Relevant priming group was not significantly different from the Control condition; the Control and Practice groups did not differ, while the Association and Irrelevant priming groups did worse than the controls, and did not differ from one another. Hence, the differences, while all in the right direction, favor the inhibitory but not the facilitative effect of priming. It was not expected that the Association group would be similarly inhibited. An explanation of these results might depend upon the ease with which Control *S*s apparently arrive at the relevant mediators: since the relevant mediators are spontaneously identified by most *S*s, providing them overtly might not appreciably hasten their availability. The irrelevant associations, however, are less likely to occur spontaneously, so priming them blocks the appearance of a relevant mediator. In the Association group, any explanation must be *ad hoc,* but in terms of that given for the R and I groups, we must assume that in those instances in which the Association group does not spontaneously hit upon the relevant mediator at first, the requirement to overtly associate slows attainment of the relevant mediator—either because of the time required to associate overtly, or because an overt association has a greater priming or strengthening effect than a covert association, or because Control *S*s do not generate associations until the response has appeared.

TABLE 3
MEANS AND *SD*s OF CORRECT ANTICIPATIONS ON THE FIRST ANTICIPATION TRIAL

	First List		Second List	
Condition	*M*	*SD*	*M*	*SD*
Control	6.44	2.87	2.94	1.86
Association	4.11	2.82	4.00	1.78
Relevant	7.55	1.79	3.55	2.15
Irrelevant	2.72	2.36	4.78	3.47
Practice	6.61	2.43	3.61	2.52

The mean trials to criterion are summarized in Table 4. An analysis of variance parallel to the one reported for first-trial performance again revealed a significant difference between conditions; $F(4,75) = 3.166$, $p < 0.05$. A Multiple Range test shows that this significant *F* reflects the differences between the Irrelevant group, which learned most slowly, and the Relevant and Practice groups, which learned most quickly. Other differences are not significant at the 0.05 level. The finding is less clear-cut than that reported for first-

TABLE 4
MEANS AND *SDs* OF TRIALS TO CRITERION

Condition	First List *M*	First List *SD*	Second List *M*	Second List *SD*
Control	7.38	4.50	7.78	3.93
Association	7.72	5.06	6.50	2.36
Relevant	5.22	3.09	7.83	3.81
Irrelevant	10.22	5.71	8.67	5.08
Practice	6.50	3.48	9.94	5.25

trial performance, but does not contradict those results, and suggests that the effect of the experimental manipulation is washing out during learning.

Second-List Performance. Unfortunately, the differences between groups in first-list learning make differences on the second list hard to evaluate. Hence, second-list learning was not analyzed extensively. When first-trial performance (Table 3) and trials to criterion (Table 4) for the first and second list learned are compared, however, it is apparent that second-list scores are closer to one another than are first-list scores, as would be expected since all groups were treated alike on the second list. Every S, as a result of completing the first list, has acquired irrelevant mediators for second-list learning, and it is of interest to note that except for groups A and I (who have presumably primed second-list mediators during first-list learning), the other groups show absolute negative transfer in List-2 learning.

Analysis of the Association Group. Within the Association group, items eliciting relevant associations should be more easily learned than items eliciting irrelevant associations. To determine the relevance of an association given in the Association group, norms were developed using the associations reported by *Ss* after learning. This tabulation included reports given after both the first and second list; the number of associations reported, the specific responses given, and the identity of the dominant response being virtually identical for the two lists. Excluded were those cases in which a relevant mediator had been specified for *S* (the first list for the Relevant group, the second list for the Irrelevant group), and also excluded was the first list of the Association group, to which the results of the tabulation were to be applied. For each S-R pair used in the experiment, there were altogether 63 possible reports of mediating associations used in learning, and hence each association given by a member of the Association group on the first trial, could be assigned a relevance score ranging from 0 to 63. This procedure was designed to take into account such unforeseen but obviously relevant mediators as TAL-(*tall*)-SCOUT which was reported with a frequency of 30% after learning, in place of the expected TAL-(*talent*)-SCOUT which was given 46% of the time. On the basis of these relevance scores, three categories of associations were established. One category included items for which no association was given (NA). These NA items were a minority, but at least one such item was contributed by each of 15 of the 18 *Ss*. The other categories were designed so that roughly equal numbers of items could be contributed by as many as possible of the 18 *Ss*: the division decided upon placed items with a relevance score of zero or one in one category (IA), and items with a relevance greater than one in the other category (RA). Since the number of relevant associations given depended systematically upon items and randomly upon *Ss*, a control was needed for artifacts of item and *S* selection. The Association, Control, and Practice *Ss* were each ordered, within their own group, on the basis of (a) which of the two sets of responses they had learned and (b) speed of learning. This established a matching of *Ss* in the Association group with *Ss* in the Control and Practice groups. Next, each item learned by an *S* in the Control or Practice groups was designated NA, IA, or RA, depending upon the designation given the association for that item for the corresponding *S* in the Association group. All subsequent comparisons made within the Association group could then be made within the Control and Practice groups as well.

For the 15 *Ss* who had contributed at least one NA item, a comparison was made between mean correct anticipations for NA and for IA items. The predicted outcome of such a comparison was unclear, since the NA items have, by definition, a lower association value than the IA items, while the IA items suffer the disadvantage of an irrelevant association. As it turns out, knowing whether an item elicited no association or an irrelevant one makes no difference in these data, the within-*S* difference in mean correct anticipations per item for these two classes of items being the same in the Association groups as in the Control and Practice groups (Table 5). Comparing the Association with the combined Control

TABLE 5

MEAN DIFFERENCE SCORES, IN CORRECT ANTICIPATIONS PER ITEM, COMPARING ITEMS WHICH ELICITED NO ASSOCIATION (NA), AN IRRELEVANT ASSOCIATION (IA), OR A RELEVANT ASSOCIATION (RA) ON THE FIRST TRIAL IN THE ASSOCIATION GROUP, AND MATCHED ITEMS IN THE CONTROL AND PRACTICE GROUPS

	(NA)-(IA)		(RA)-(IA)	
Group	*M*	*SD*	*M*	*SD*
Association	—0.460	1.64	1.162	1.26
Control	—0.695	1.92	0.124	1.58
Practice	0.565	1.82	0.337	1.80

and Practice groups yields an F of less than one. This lack of significance may result in part from unreliability, since in 10 of the 15 *Ss* there were no more than two NA items, while 11 of the 15 *Ss* had 4 or more IA items. A similar analysis was carried out on the 17 *Ss* who contributed both IA and RA items. In this analysis, the difference between the Association group and the other two is significant; $F(1,48) = 4.518$, $p < 0.05$, and favors the RA items as expected. The Means and *SDs* of these difference scores appear in Table 5.

The results support the implications of the associative probability hypothesis, and make it appear likely that *Ss'* verbal associations to stimulus and response items play an important role in learning. In a sense, however, it can be argued that the findings apply only to materials which are specially selected to have exactly those associative properties which the hypothesis requires. Hence, the present experiment might not be relevant to situations for which obvious mediating responses are not available. However, (and this seems untestable at present), the selection of materials could also be regarded not as an attempt to guarantee the *presence* of relevant mediators, but merely as an attempt to guarantee their *commonality,* so that they could be experimentally manipulated for randomly selected *Ss*. In cases in which association norms do not suggest a possible mediator, we do not know whether *Ss* can provide idiosyncratic mediators of equal effectiveness.

SUMMARY

On the first trial of paired-associate learning, when the stimulus trigram appeared and before the response word was shown, an attempt was made to alter *S*'s associative response to the stimulus trigrams by presenting a word which was (a) an associate of the trigram according to free-association norms, and (b) judged by *E* to be either relevant or irrelevant to the response which *S* was to learn. If a relevant association was primed in this way, *S* learned faster than if an irrelevant association was primed. An unprimed Control group did not differ from the Relevant group: together with other evidence, this was taken to mean that the relevant mediating associations were readily available without priming. Priming with the response word itself led to performance equivalent to that of the Controls. Another group of *Ss* gave an associate of their own on the first trial, and were retarded in subsequent learning relative to the Control group. Within this Association group, however, items which elicited relevant associations were easier to learn than items which happened to elicit irrelevant association. The results support the associative probability hypothesis of Underwood and Schulz.

REFERENCES

DUNCAN, D. B. Multiple range and multiple F tests. *Biometrics,* 1955, **11**, 1-42.

STORMS, L. H. Apparent backward association: A situational effect. *J. exp. Psychol.,* 1958, **55**, 390-395.

UNDERWOOD, B. J., AND SCHULZ, R. W. *Meaningfulness and verbal learning.* Philadelphia: Lippincott, 1960.

(Received September 11, 1963)

CHAPTER 3

Acquisition as a Function of Methodological Variables

Chapters 1 and 2 examined the basic processes believed to be involved in the acquisition of verbal tasks, particularly PA and SL. In this chapter we begin our consideration of the important independent variables related to acquisition, most likely via their effects on these basic processes. We will lead off with a class of variables that may be called methodological in the sense that the variables in question commonly enter into decisions concerning the methodology to be employed by *E* in his verbal learning experiment. As such, the variables are part of what ordinarily constitutes experimental control. In most verbal learning studies the variables in the present grouping are held invariant under the careful scrutiny of *E*. Conceivably, their variation could, if uncontrolled, interact with the independent variable(s) deliberately introduced by *E* and therefore confound the interpretation of the independent variable-acquisition relationship.

Suppose an investigator finds that his research or independent variable relates in some demonstrated manner to acquisition when all of his *Ss* perform under a constant level X of a methodological condition. The problem of special interest in this chapter is whether the relationship would be grossly altered if the experiment had been conducted under a different (but equated for all *Ss*) level, say *Y*, of that methodological variable. For example, meaningfulness could be the independent variable and rate of exposing the *St* and *R* components on a memory drum could be a control factor. The investigator may have selected a two second rate and then made certain that all components for each level of meaningfulness are exposed at this constant rate. How well may he generalize his results (i.e., for the effects of meaningfulness on acquisition) to other rates of exposure? Is there a possible interaction between meaningfulness and rate? If there is, is the interaction due to differential effects of rate on the response stage or on the associative stage? These are the kinds of questions posed by a consideration of methodological factors. To answer them we need to depart from the control procedure of holding the factors constant. Rather, we need to introduce them as variables *qua* variables—that is, as independent variables in their own right. The methodological variables that have been of greatest interest in contemporary verbal learning belong to three distinct subclasses: Sensory Modality, Presentation Conditions, and Temporal Conditions. Each of these will be considered.

Sensory Modality

In practically every contemporary study of SL and PA acquisition (and, for that matter, on transfer and retention as well) the learning materials have been exposed visually, as on a memory drum. In a study by Martin and Schulz (1963; Article 1) the paucity of data on aural presentation of materials was noted, and an attempt was made to help fill the void. Their study contrasted the acquisition of trigrams of low and high pronunciability as *St* and *R* PA components when presented aurally. Their study did not include a condition in which the same materials were presented visually. Nevertheless, their results substantiated what had been previously found under visual presentation, namely that pronunciability and meaningfulness both affect acquisition but with the effect being greater for the *R* than for the *St* component (cf. Chapter 4). A subsequent study by Schulz and Martin (1964), again employing aural presentation alone, found an effect of stimulus familiarization consonant with that previously found under visual presentation (cf. Article 5, Chapter 4). Thus, modality does not appear to be a critical factor in terms of an interaction with meaningfulness and prior familiarization of learning materials. However, another study (Williams and Derks, 1963) contrasted aural with visual presentation and both individually with the two combined into a simultaneous presentation. Their results indicated a consistent superiority for the combination over either one separately at each point of a wide continuum of meaningfulness. In addition, visual presentation alone was superior to aural alone when the materials were high in pronunciability and high in meaningfulness (but not meaningful words). When the materials were low in pronunciability and low in meaningfulness or when they were high in pronunciability and were meaningful words as well, the two modalities did not differ in their effectiveness.

A less putative research area for incorporating the visual–aural distinction is that of similarity of learning materials, particularly when similarity is manipulated in terms of synonymity of meaning (cf. Chapter 5). Mediated generalization (i.e., involving meaning as the dimension of similarity) has been demonstrated largely by means of aural presentation of stimuli (e.g., Mednick, 1957). It is conceivable that intra-list generalization effects from similarity may be greater for aural than for visual presentation. This problem remains relatively unexplored.

Presentation Conditions

Anticipation versus Recall Method

In Chapter 2 we discovered that most studies on PA acquisition present *St* and *R* components by the anticipation method. This method features the presentation of *St* alone, followed by *R*, usually in juxtaposition with *St*. During the exposure of an isolated *St*, *S* is instructed to anticipate the *R* paired with that *St*. Battig and Brackett (1961) pointed out that in the anticipation method learning is inherently confounded by the measure of performance. In the anticipation method *S* must learn (i.e., recognize the *St* and attempt to hook-up *St* and *R*) at virtually the same time he is called upon to perform or emit the *R* component. This dual responsibility could generate considerable interference on acquisition and thereby reduce *S*'s overall learning proficiency.

An alternative way of presenting *St-R* pairs is the recall or blocking method.

In this method the *St-R* components are presented together as a block, one block (pair) at a time, for a study period set at some predetermined rate. Following the study of all pairs in the list, a test trial is given in which each *St* component is exposed individually without its accompanying *R*, and *S* attempts to name the associated *R* component. Usually the sequential order of presentation (see below for a discussion of the serial versus random order issue) on a test trial differs from that of the order on the preceding study trial. For a list of A_1-B_1, A_2-B_2, ... , A_6-B_6 pairs, the first study trial might begin with the A_1-B_1 block, then the A_2-B_2 block, and on through the A_6-B_6 block. The first test trial could then begin with A_3, followed by A_5, etc. Successive study-test trial cycles continue until the specified criterion is attained.

Battig and Brackett (1961) noted that the source of confounding that is conspicuously present in the anticipation method is absent in the recall method. That is, the recall method provides a separation of learning and performance —thanks to the clearly partitioned study (learning) and test (performance) trials. But, alas, the recall method introduces its own built-in brand of confounding by requiring a delay of reinforcement (in the sense of informative feedback) to intervene between a test trial and the subsequent study trial when *S* receives information as to the correctness of his responses (Battig and Brackett, 1961; Lockhead, 1962). However, research in other areas of human learning, such as perceptual-motor skills, has not revealed any large deleterious effects from delayed informative feedback (e.g., see Bilodeau and Bilodeau, 1958), and delayed feedback may not necessarily be detrimental to verbal learning as well (Lockhead, 1962).

Contrasts of the relative efficiencies of the anticipation and recall methods have failed to yield consistent advantages for one over the other. Although Battig and Brackett (1961) found a statistically significant advantage for recall, a follow-up study by Battig, Brown, and Nelson (1963) did not replicate this finding in one experiment (but did in another experiment in the same study). Lockhead also failed to find an advantage for recall over anticipation. Moreover, the Battig et al. (1963) study suggested that the method of presentation does not interact with the nature of verbal learning materials. It seems apparent, at least for college students (as in the previous studies), that the difference, if any, in effectiveness between the two methods is not great. However, with special populations of *Ss*, like the elderly neuropsychiatric *Ss* employed by Kausler (1963), the utility of fractionating learning and performance in the recall method may be enhanced greatly.

Confirmation versus Prompting

In the anticipation method of PA acquisition *S* emits his response and then receives immediate confirmation as to the correctness of this response by way of the appearance of the *R* component in the aperture of the memory drum. Frequent errors in responding are likely to occur in the early trials under this method. Suppose, however, that *E* prohibits errors from occurring by prompting S as to what the correct *R* is on each trial. Acquisition could then be measured by inserting test trials (as in the recall method) between prompted trials. Prompting closely resembles the recall method in that *S* in the blocking phase of the recall method rehearses the *St-R* pairing in the direct presence of *R*. Prompting is also a direct descendant of the maze guidance studies of a past era (e.g., Carr, 1930).

The research of Cook (Cook, 1958; Cook and Spitzer, 1960) has suggested a superiority for prompting over confirmation in PA acquisition, but subsequent studies (cited in Hawker, 1964a; Article 2) have been more ambiguous. The Hawker study (Article 2), which nicely illustrates the special techniques used to manipulate prompting versus confirmation, did find the aforementioned superiority for prompting, but only in the early acquisition trials. In another study by Hawker (1964b) a confirmation versus prompting contrast was made for SL. He found no real difference between the two methods and concluded that the two methods require a more thorough investigation in a variety of learning situations before generalizations regarding superiority of one method are possible. The research literature indicates that this conservative conclusion is definitely warranted.

Serial versus Random Ordering of PA Lists

In Chapter 2 the exigency for randomly varying the order of PA pairs from trial to trial was stated as a defense against the learning by *S* of a chain of *R* components rather than sets of *St-R* associations. What this means is that a constant order of exposing *St-R* pairs across trials makes possible, at least in theory, the reduction of a PA list to the equivalent of a serial list, with serial position serving as a discernible cue for responding. Early studies by McGeoch and McKinney (1937) and McGeoch and Underwood (1943) reported a facilitative effect for a constant, serial ordering of pairs within a PA list. These two studies undoubtedly convinced a cautious generation of following researchers to avoid PA chaining effects by routinely varying, by random assignment, the ordering of pairs from trial to trial. Thus, randomization became a standard part of PA methodology.

Interest in the serial-random ordering issue was rekindled by Newman and Saltz (1962) in a contemporary study in which they replicated the basic methodological features of the older studies but with an additional control condition (this condition is described in Article 3). Their results supported the superiority of a serial order over a random order but were inconclusive regarding the use of fixed serial positions as the source of this positive effect. The Newman and Saltz study was extended by Martin and Saltz (1963; Article 3), but this time no apparent facilitating effect for serial ordering was found. Perhaps the ordering of pairs, as a varying condition of PA methodology, contributes a relatively minor segment of the total variance in PA acquisition. At any rate, variation of this presentation condition, like the preceding two conditions, does not seem to play a major role in PA acquisition.

Whole versus Part Method

Given a verbal list of *n* items, the usual practice procedure is to present the list to *S* as an entity, or whole, in which all *n* items are repeated on each trial until mastery of the entire list is attained. An alternative procedure is to split the *n* items into two or more parts, with each part containing *n*/2, etc., items. Practice commences with one part and continues until that part is mastered. Then practice proceeds to the next part, then on to any other remaining parts. Following the consecutive mastery of the separate parts, *S* is presented with the integrated parts (i.e., the "whole" list), and he practices on this entity until it is mastered. The question is: Is it more efficient for the acquisition of a whole list to practice by the whole method or by the part method? In their summary of the early literature on this problem, McGeoch and Irion (1952, pp. 506–507) concluded that there are advantages to both methods, and that, overall, neither method is to be considered grossly advantageous.

Postman and Goggin (1964) pointed out that McGeoch and Irion's analysis of whole and part methods revealed three sources of differences. The first is the fact that increasing the length of a list disproportionately increases the difficulty of learning the list (e.g., Lyon, 1917; Wilcoxon, Wilson and Wise, 1961). For example, in the Wilcoxon et al. study (1961, their Experiment III), groups of *Ss* were trained on PA lists containing 4, 6, or 8 pairs at varying rates of presentation. At each rate, the mean number of trials to criterion was more than twice as large for the 8-item list than for the 4-item list. In other words, we may well expect the summated time required to learn the separate parts to be considerably less than the time taken to learn the whole list. This should be a decided advantage for the part method. The second source results from the time needed to unite the parts into an integrated whole. This source should reduce the initial advantage of the part method. Finally, the third source rests in transfer and interference effects that are likely to occur in the part method. The first part learned may have an interfering effect (negative transfer) on the acquisition of the second part, etc., and retroactive and proactive inhibitory effects (cf. Chapter 10) may take place in the retention of the separate parts. The relative advantage of one method over the other may therefore be regarded as the resultant (i.e. net effect) of these three sources.

Postman and Goggin's (1964) study contrasted SL with the whole and part (in this case, two $n/2$ parts) in the light of the aforementioned three sources. They found a pronounced gain for the part method in terms of summated presentations to learn the whole list. This gain was largely offset by the large number of additional presentations needed to combine the parts into the whole. Nevertheless, the net effect was slightly in favor of the part method, and, moreover, the slight advantage remained consistent over widely divergent levels of item meaningfulness and similarity.

Jung (1964) introduced a variation of the part method for PA acquisition that he calls the cumulative method. In this method, *S* begins practice with a single pair. This pair is repeated on the next trial together with an added second pair, followed on the next trial by repeating both pairs and adding a third pair, etc. Jung compared this method with the standard anticipation (whole) method and failed to find a difference in acquisition between the two. Once more, the evidence indicates that presentation conditions are not especially potent contributors to variance in verbal acquisition.

Temporal Conditions

Intra-trial

Intra-trial temporal variables refer to the rate of exposing the components of a verbal learning list. Historically, rate of exposure has been a variable of critical importance in SL theory, particularly with regard to serial position effects. As noted in Chapter 1, the absolute gradient of error distribution over serial positions steepens markedly with shortened exposure rates. The relevance of this and related findings to the Lepley–Hull theory was discussed in the introductory section of Chapter 1. More importantly for present purposes, overall proficiency in SL acquisition, as measured by trials to mastery, decreases with faster rates of exposure of individual items (e.g., Braun and Heymann, 1958). At the risk of redundancy, we need to emphasize once more the problems inherent in the identification of processes within SL. These problems engender a great risk in trying to relate the rate phenomenon (i.e., slower acquisition with faster exposures) to specific processes. A more patent course of action is to gravitate toward the rate-acquisition relationship for PA materials. This does, in fact, seem to be a contemporary trend.

Several studies (e.g., Carroll and Burke, 1965; Goss, Morgan, and Golin, 1959; Wilcoxon, Wilson, and Wise, 1961) have demonstrated an inverse relationship between PA acquisition and exposure rate with the traditional anticipation method, but without attempting to partial out the separate effects of rate on the *St-R* components. A study by Bugelski (1962; Article 4), however, has triggered off a series of more analytically oriented experiments. Bugelski's methodology involved a fixed rate of exposure for the *St*-alone phase of the anticipation method but a varied rate for the *R*-alone phase. The most important finding of this study is the apparent fact that Presentation Time multiplied by Trials (or, in other words, total time taken to reach a criterion of mastery) equals a constant. Stated in another way, lengthening the rate of exposure increasingly reduces the number of trials to mastery but leaves the total learning time relatively invariant. This principle, if it withstands the test of replication, has sweeping implications for PA theory. For example, the concept of a "trial," as Bugelski astutely recognizes, needs a cautious interpretation when it enters into such issues as the one-trial (all-or-none) learning controversy (cf. Chapter 2, Introduction).

A number of other analytical studies have appeared since the Bugelski study. Bugelski and Rickwood (1963) provided a further generalization for the Bugelski constancy principle by including a self-pacing condition (i.e., *S* sets his own learning pace by controlling the rate of exposure). Two studies by Nodine (1963; 1965) varied both *St* and *St-R* exposure rates (anticipation method) within a factorial design that included other variables as well. In his first study Nodine (1963) found that both the duration of exposure to *St* alone and to *St-R* together had statistically significant effects on the number of correct responses made over a fixed number of trials, but the effect of *St-R* duration was more potent than that for *St*-alone duration. His supplementary analyses also revealed that the potent effect of *St-R* duration probably resulted from the opportunity to integrate *Rs* during this exposure period, rather than from any increased opportunity to rehearse the *St-R* associations. In the second study (Nodine, 1965) *Ss* were carried to a criterion of mastery. The *St-R* duration was found to be an important determiner of learning rate with Bugelski's constant total time principle again applying, but *St* duration was not invariant with respect to total time. In fact, increasing *St* exposure beyond 1 second inflated total learning time without enhancing rate of acquisition (trials to criterion). Newman (1964a) tested the Bugelski principle in a recall method of presentation in which exposure rates for the study period and the test period were factorially combined. With the number of trials held constant, he found both sources to facilitate performance with increasing durations of exposure. Finally, Keppel and Rehula (1965) tested the Bugelski principle on SL and found support for its generality to this kind of learning task.

Inter-Trial

Two separate subphenomena are subsumed under the effects of variations of the temporal period intervening between successive presentations of a verbal learning list. The first is called "reminiscence." By reminiscence we mean an improvement in *performance* that may follow a rest pause inserted into a practice sequence at a point prior to the attainment of mastery on the task in question—the improvement, of course, being relative to a control group performing without such a pause. The second may be called, for lack of a better name, the "distributed practice" effect. This effect consists of an improvement in performance during acquisition when a temporal gap is inserted between the end of one trial and the beginning of the next trial. The control condition is the massing of practice, that is, beginning a trial immediately after the end of the preceding trial.

Reminiscence was a very popular area of research in verbal learning prior to the Second World War, with a number of studies lending support to its reality (cf. McGeoch and Irion, 1952, pp. 138–193). Empirical support has been more difficult to come by in the postwar years. The article by Underwood (1961a; Article 5) contains a review of the contemporary research on reminiscence as well as a discussion of the methodological and theoretical issues involved.

Distributed practice has been closely identified in recent years with the research of Underwood and his colleagues. (Much of this research is summarized in Article 5.) In general, a distribution of practice effect has been more easily established in SL than in PA acquisition. Lippman and Denny (1964) have convincing evidence that suggests a critical factor in this SL-PA difference is the presence of order cues in SL that are lacking in the usual random sequence of PA presentation. That is, spacing of trials in SL generates specific primacy–recency cues which determine, in turn, the ordering of learning items as responses within a serial list. This interpretation of distribution of practice in SL fits neatly within the conceptualization of SL given by Glanzer and Peters (1962; Chapter 1, Article 4). The transitory nature of a distributed practice effect in PA acquisition is treated by Underwood (Article 5) within the framework of stage analysis. Here the emphasis is on the response learning stage as a critical factor in determining the presence or absence of a facilitating effect. However, it should be pointed out that Marshall and Runquist (1962) found evidence for the importance of the associative stage in determining the distributed practice effect.

ARTICLE 1

Aural Paired-Associate Learning: Pronunciability and the Interval between Stimulus and Response[1]

EDWIN MARTIN AND RUDOLPH W. SCHULZ

State University of Iowa, Iowa City, Iowa

Verbal learning and communication can be accomplished via either the visual or aural modality. Thus a comprehensive empirical description and theoretical analysis of verbal-learning processes must make provisions for the potential necessity of including a "modality parameter" in the statement of the laws which govern these processes. Moreover, there is the distinct possibility that certain variables will be uniquely aural or uniquely visual. For reasons that are not immediately obvious, however, relatively little research in verbal learning has been done with aurally presented stimuli, the overwhelming majority of the studies having involved visual rather than aural presentation of the verbal units which were to be learned by *S*. In light of the foregoing it is evident that more studies of learning under conditions of aural presentation are needed. Therefore, the present study investigated the learning of *aurally* presented paired-associate (PA) lists as a function of the following variables: (1) pronunciability (PR) of stimulus units; (2) PR of response units; and (3) length of the interval between the presentation of the stimulus and the presentation of the response (intra-SR interval).

METHOD

Design. Half the *S*s learned a list of trigram-number pairs (variation of stimulus PR), the other half number-trigram pairs (variation of response PR). Of the eight trigrams in each list, there were two at each of four PR levels representing the entire range of scaled PR. The *S*s in the above conditions were further divided so that half the *S*s learned with a 2-sec. intra-SR interval and half with a 6-sec. interval. The *S*s, 30 per condition, were assigned randomly to conditions with the restriction that the *N*th *S* not be assigned to a given condition until *N* — 1 *S*s had been assigned to all other conditions. The 120 *S*s were introductory psychology students who had not had prior experience with trigram lists, though some of the *S*s had served previously in verbal learning experiments.

Lists. Following the practice of Underwood and Schulz (1960), two comparable lists of trigrams were selected and three different random pairings of the numbers 2 through 9 were employed with each list to increase the generality of the results and avoid bias due to a fortuitous pairing. The trigrams were selected from among those which were scaled for PR and used under conditions of visual presentation in Exp. 15 by Underwood and Schulz (1960). The following are the two lists (A and B) of trigrams and the mean PR value of the two items representing each of the four PR levels which were used: (List A) *RZQ, KBV* (8.55), *UNH, EKL* (6.84), *ITE, CED* (3.24), *MOP, BUG* (1.96); (List B) *XFH, ZJM* (8.53), *TRC, NUW* (6.02), *DOK, JAD* (3.44), *MEL, SAY* 1.90).

Procedure. All *S*s were given 15 study and 15 test trials in alternating order. On study trials, *S* studied the pairs *silently* as *E* spelled the trigrams and said the numbers. The intra-SR interval (onset of stimulus unit presentation to onset of response unit presentation) was either 2 or 6 sec. The inter-item interval (onset of response unit presentation to onset of next stimulus unit) was 1 sec.

On test trials, all *S*s were allowed 2 sec. to respond to each stimulus unit with the appropriate response unit. At the end of 2 sec. the next stimulus unit was presented. Knowledge of results was not given. The *S*s responded by either spelling the trigrams or saying the numbers, depending on the list to which

[1] We are grateful for the assistance of the State University of Iowa Computing Center in carrying out the statistical analysis of the data. The article is based upon an M.A. thesis done by the first author under the second author's direction.

Reprinted with permission of the authors and the publisher, the Academic Press. The article appeared originally in the *Journal of Verbal Learning and Verbal Behavior*, 1963, **1**, 389–391.

they were assigned. The *S*s were not required to articulate the stimulus units.

The intertrial interval was 4 sec. During this interval *S* was told whether the next trial would be study or test. The pairs were presented in four random orders on study trials; a different set of four orders was used for presentation of the stimulus units on test trials. Start order was varied from *S* to *S* within each condition.

The lists were presented through earphones with a Norelco (Model EL 3542A) tape recorder. Timing was accomplished by having *E* read the units onto tape from a Gerbrands Memory Drum. The tape was played into a voice key connected to an appropriate recording device to check the adequacy of the timing. It was found to be satisfactory.

Results and Discussion

The relationships between PR and performance for the two loci of trigrams and two intra-SR intervals are shown in Fig. 1. The means shown in Fig. 1 are based on the total number of correct responses per pair per *S* over 15 trials.

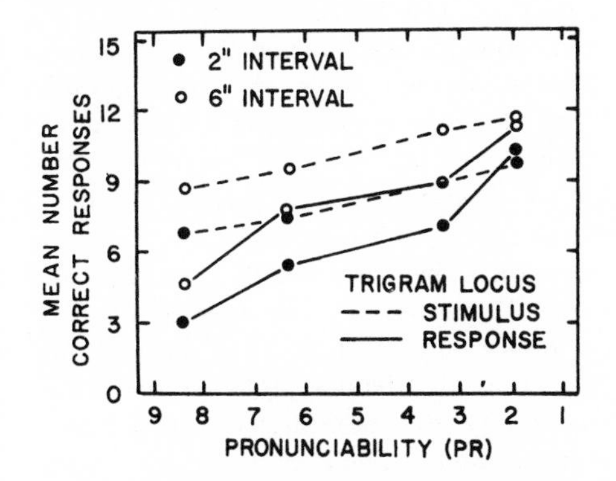

Fig. 1. Learning of aurally presented PA trigram-number and number-trigram lists as a function of length of intra-SR interval and PR. The means represent total number of correct responses over 15 trials per pair per *S*.

In Fig. 1 there is a positive relationship between PR and performance for both loci of trigrams. It is also apparent that PR had a greater effect when trigrams were responses than when they were stimuli. If the curves of Fig. 1 are regarded as linear, the slopes of the functions for response PR are approximately 2.4 times as great as those for the stimulus-PR functions. Statistically, for both loci of trigrams, PR effects are significant beyond the .001 level ($F = 27.64$ for stimulus PR and 119.57 for response PR; $df = 3/168$).

Though the overall level of performance is lower in the present study, the relationships between PR and performance under conditions of aural presentation are highly similar to those observed by Underwood and Schulz (Exp. 15, 1960) with visual presentation of the same material. In the present study, the product-moment correlations between PR and total number of correct responses per pair over 15 trials are .91 and .90 for response PR at the 2- and 6-sec. intervals respectively. For stimulus PR, the correlations for the 2- and 6-sec. intervals are .78 and .75. These may be compared with correlations of .96 for response PR and .73 for stimulus PR computed from the Underwood-Schulz data.[2] The agreement between the two studies is rather striking, particularly so in light of the several differences between the two studies, namely (*a*) modality (aural versus visual); (*b*) method of presentation (study-test versus anticipation); (*c*) stimulus-response presentation (successive versus simultaneous). Thus, the relationships between rated ease of pronunciation and PA performance appear to have considerable generality.

Returning to Fig. 1, it can be seen that performance was better with a 6-sec. than with a 2-sec. intra-SR interval and about equally so for both loci of trigrams. These differences in performance are statistically reliable ($F = 6.64$ and 4.88 for trigrams as stimuli and responses, respectively; $df = 1/56$, $P < .05$). It is also clear, both statistically and from Fig. 1, that PR and intra-SR interval did not interact ($F = 1.20$ for re-

[2] The correct response data for these items reported by Underwood and Schulz (1960) in their book were for 20 trials. For the present purposes the means based on 15 trials were used.

sponse PR and $F < 1$ for stimulus PR; $df = 3/168$).

Since satisfactory procedures for the control of rehearsal in the present situation have not been developed, *S*s were free to use the intra-SR interval to rehearse. Accordingly, it would be appealing, from the standpoint of simplicity, to attribute the superior performance under a long interval to the fact that *S*s had more time to rehearse. However, such an interpretation is difficult to reconcile with the absence of interaction between interval and PR. That is, it seems highly unlikely that *S* would be able to rehearse with equal facility over the wide range of PR represented by the present items. Similarly, it is not readily apparent how a simple rehearsal hypothesis would account for the fact that a 6-sec. intra-SR interval appeared to be equally beneficial for both loci and trigrams.

There have been a number of studies of intra-SR interval with visually presented material. These studies have found performance facilitated (Froeberg, 1918, Exp. 2; Guthrie, 1933), unaffected (Froeberg, 1918, Exp. 1; Grier, 1961) and inhibited (Froeberg, 1918, Exp. 3) by lengthening the intra-SR interval. Aside from the lack of agreement among these studies, there are a variety of reasons (e.g., counterbalanced designs, type of material, the number of trials prior to a test, etc.) which make a direct comparison of the present results with the results of these studies difficult. However, the conditions of study (W. E. Walther and R. Somnapan, unpublished, 1961), conducted in our laboratory with 12-item lists of consonant syllable-number pairs of low meaningfulness and intervals of 2, 4, and 6 sec. intervening between the termination of a 2-sec. stimulus-unit exposure and the onset of a 2-sec. response-term exposure, do come close to being comparable to the present conditions where trigrams rated as difficult to pronounce were stimuli. Yet, in the Walther-Somnapan study, intra-SR interval failed to affect performance. Moreover, rehearsal was not controlled; unless the fact that intra-SR interval was manipulated "within lists" somehow discouraged rehearsal.

In brief, it is clear empirically that a long intra-SR interval facilitated performance in the present study. A precise assessment of the role that rehearsal and/or other factors play in producing this facilitation will evidently require further research.

Summary

Aurally presented (tape recorded) trigram-number or number-trigram eight-item paired-associate lists were learned by two groups of 60 *S*s. The trigrams varied in rated pronunciability from easy to difficult. On study trials, half the *S*s in each group learned their list with a 2-sec. interval between the onset of the stimulus and response unit (intra-SR interval), the other half with a 6-sec. interval. Acquisition consisted of 15 alternating study and test trials. All *S*s had 2 sec. to respond on test trials.

In terms of mean total number of correct responses on test trials, the following was found. (1) Performance and rated ease of pronunciation are directly related for both loci of trigrams with a greater effect of pronunciability when trigrams are responses than when they are stimuli. (2) A 6-sec. intra-SR interval was accompanied by better performance than a 2-sec. interval for both loci of trigrams. Interval and pronunciability did not interact either when trigrams were stimuli or when they were responses.

References

Froeberg, S. Simultaneous versus successive association. *Psychol. Rev.*, 1918, **25**, 156-163.

Grier, J. B. Stimulus-response asychronism in paired-associate learning. Unpublished Masters thesis, North Carolina State College, Durham, 1960.

Guthrie, E. R. Association as a function of time interval. *Psychol. Rev.*, 1933, **40**, 355-367.

Underwood, B. J., *and* Schulz, R. W. *Meaningfulness and verbal learning*. Philadelphia: Lippincott, 1960.

(Received October 8, 1962)

ARTICLE 2

The Influence of Training Procedure and Other Task Variables in Paired-Associate Learning[1]

JAMES R. HAWKER[2]

The University of Texas, Austin, Texas

A series of studies by Cook and his colleagues (Cook, 1958; Cook and Kendler, 1956; Cook and Spitzer, 1960) has indicated that a prompting procedure results in faster learning of paired-associate material than does a confirmation procedure. A prompting procedure is one in which the *S* is prohibited from making erroneous responses by having the correct response to each stimulus shown to him just before he responds, while confirmation refers to trial-and-error responding. The *S* follows one of the two procedures with performance measures taken on test trials interspersed among the prompting or confirmation trials.

Several related studies have appeared recently, but the results have been equivocal. Silberman, Melaragno, and Coulson (1961) compared confirmation with two methods of prompting in the learning of connected discourse and found no difference among the three procedures on a post-training test. Sidowski, Kopstein, and Shillestad (1961) compared six different procedures, which were variations of prompting and confirmation, in the learning of English-Russian paired associates. The results indicated that prompting generally resulted in fewer errors than did confirmation. Battig and Brackett (1961) compared two different methods of presenting paired-associates which they called "anticipation" (cf. confirmation) and "recall" (cf. prompting). Their results showed prompting to be superior to confirmation in terms of both number of errors and trials to criterion. Lockhead (1962) performed an experiment similar to Battig and Brackett's, but found no difference between the two procedures as measured by trials to criterion or number of correct responses. Peterson and Brewer (1963) also compared the anticipation and nonanticipation methods of presenting paired-associates and found that the prompting procedure yielded significantly more correct responses than did the confirmation method, with the difference especially evident during the initial five test trials.

Thus, it can be seen that the differences obtained between the two training procedures have not been consistent. Moreover, most of the preceding studies have been concerned primarily with comparing the two procedures and have not investigated the interaction of the training variable with other task variables. Consequently, it was felt that additional information was needed concerning the operation of the training variable under different conditions and with different materials. Also, as Cook and Spitzer (1960) have pointed out, the comparison of these two procedures is quite relevant to the preparation of material for programmed instruction.

[1] This paper is based on a dissertation submitted in partial fulfillment of the requirements for the Ph.D. degree at The University of Texas while the author was a University Fellow. The author wishes to thank Dr. Robert K. Young for his advice and assistance, and for serving as chairman of the doctoral committee.

[2] Present address: University of Pittsburgh, Pittsburgh, Pennsylvania.

Reprinted with permission of the author and the publisher, the Academic Press. The article appeared originally in the *Journal of Verbal Learning and Verbal Behavior*, 1964, **3**, 70–76.

METHOD

Design and Subjects. A 2 × 2 × 2× 2 factorial design was employed in which the four variables were training procedure (prompting or confirmation), stimulus similarity (high and low), response similarity (high and low), and method of presentation (figure-word or word-figure).

The 96 *S*s were volunteers from introductory psychology classes at The University of Texas, and all were naive to verbal learning experiments. The *S*s were randomly assigned to one of the 16 experimental conditions upon appearing at the laboratory, with the restriction that there would be an equal number of *S*s in each cell, and each *S* was run individually. Ten additional *S*s had to be discarded (four because of equipment failure and six because of failure to understand instructions), and when an *S* had to be dropped, another *S* was randomly assigned to that particular group so as to keep an equal number of *S*s in each cell. The discarded *S*s were evenly distributed over the various experimental conditions.

Materials. Each group of *S*s learned a list of eight pairs of adjectives and nonsense line-figures. The line-figures consisted of a square matrix of nine dots (3 × 3) with three of the dots connected by two straight lines, and were constructed for the purpose of having unfamiliar items. Prior to the experiment, they were classified and judged as to similarity by a group of 10 judges, with similarity determined by the physical resemblance between items. After the figures had been judged, high- and low-similarity lists were constructed and used in a pilot study in which stimulus and response similarity were the only variables. The results showed significant differences in learning as a function of both variables, indicating the apparent reliability of the rating procedure. Two adjective lists reflecting high and low similarity were used, and were obtained from the lists of Underwood and Goad (1951) and Melton and Safier (Hilgard, 1951), respectively. The two nonsense-figure lists and the two adjective lists in combination produced four different paired-associate lists which, for ease of identification, can be labeled as follows: *List A*: low similarity figures and low similarity adjectives; *List B*: low similarity figures and high similarity adjectives; *List C*: high similarity figures and low similarity adjectives; and *List D*: high similarity figures and high similarity adjectives.

The same four lists were used throughout the experiment, but the order of the pairs was dependent upon the method of presentation; that is, under method figure-word (F-W), the line-figures were stimuli and the adjectives were responses, while under the other method (W-F), the items were reversed.

Apparatus. The apparatus was basically a self-paced memory drum constructed by the *E*. The front of the machine contained two apertures through which the learning material was exposed. A stimulus term would appear in the aperture on the left and four response terms would appear in the aperture on the right. Below each of the positions on the right was a pushbutton switch and above each of them was a jewelled pilot light. A control unit operated by the *E* permitted the lights and switches to be connected in several ways. On the extreme right side of the apparatus was a lever that the *S* pulled to advance the drum and, hence, each set of items to be learned. The learning materials were put on paper tapes and attached directly to the drum. A wired program plate attached to the drum provided the necessary circuitry for connecting each position on the left with the correct position on the right.

Procedure. The task utilized in the present study differed somewhat from the classical paired-associate paradigm since it had some of the features of verbal-discrimination learning as well. Instead of the typical anticipation method used in paired-associate learning, the material was presented as follows: S_1–R_1, R_2, R_3, R_4; S_2–R_1, R_2, R_3, R_4; etc. The *S* was presented with the stimulus term and four response terms simultaneously, and his task was to select the correct response to go with the stimulus. The alternative responses in each group were legitimate responses to other stimuli in the list, and varied from trial to trial for a given stimulus. However, the alternative responses were arranged in such a fashion that, over all the trials, each response term appeared an equal number of times as an alternative response (e.g., in one presentation of the eight items, each response term would appear once as a correct response and three times as an alternative response). Eight different orders of presentation were used to preclude any serial learning.

During the practice trials, the *S* following a confirmation procedure would receive a set of items and was required to push the switch under the response term which he thought was correct. If he were correct, the light over the item would come on confirming his response. If he were incorrect, the light would not come on and he would have to continue responding until he did make the correct response. Under the prompting procedure, however, each time the *S* turned the drum, the light over the correct response term would come on automatically; he was required to push the switch under that item and then advance to the next set of items. Hence, the *S* was shown the correct response each time and made the correct response with no opportunity for making errors.

Since the practice trials for the prompting groups entailed error-free responding, it was necessary to interpolate test trials to get measures of learning. Thus, each series consisted of two practice trials and a test trial. During the test trials, the lights were covered so that the *S* received no knowledge of results. Each of the eight sets of items was presented and the *S* was required to select the correct response. The test trials were identical for all *S*s and the measures recorded were the number of correct responses on each test trial and the amount of time required to complete each test trial. All *S*s were given seven series of trials unless they registered two consecutive errorless test trials at which time the experiment was concluded. In such cases, the *S*'s score and time on the last perfect trial were recorded as the data for the remaining test trials.

Five min. after the end of the experiment proper, the *S* was given a "free-recall" test which consisted of the eight stimulus terms printed on a sheet of paper, and he was required to reproduce the correct response term for each stimulus.

RESULTS AND DISCUSSION

The mean number of correct responses made on each of the seven test trials is presented in Fig. 1. An analysis of variance was performed on the total number of correct responses and indicated significant effects due only to stimulus similarity ($F = 11.93$, $df = 1/80$, $p < 0.001$), response similarity ($F = 7.95$, $df = 1/80$, $p < 0.01$), and to the interaction, R $\times$ M, between response similarity and method of presentation ($F = 8.63$, $df = 1/80$, $p < 0.005$). As stimulus similarity increased, the total number of correct responses decreased. Likewise, there was

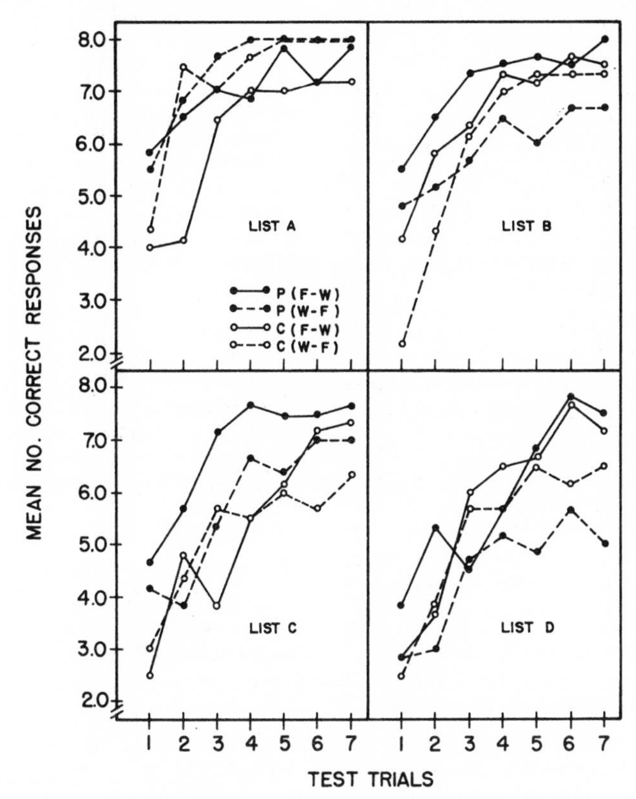

FIG. 1. Mean number of correct responses on each test trial.

a decrease in the number of correct responses as response similarity increased. Similar results have been reported by Feldman and Underwood (1957) in paired-associate learning, and by Underwood and Archer (1955) in verbal-discrimination learning. The R $\times$ M interaction indicated that increasing response similarity had little effect when the words were used as responses (method F-W), but produced a marked decrease in the number of correct responses when the figures were the response terms (method W-F).

To see if the variables were affected differently over trials, a second analysis was done by combining the scores on the first three test trials (Block 1), and comparing them with the combined scores on the last three test trials (Block 2) by means of a repeated-measures analysis of variance. The variance due to trial blocks was, of course, highly significant; moreover, by isolating the variance associated with trials, other relationships became apparent. In addition to the significant factors noted in the first analysis, there was an interaction between trial blocks and stimulus similarity ($F = 5.43$, $df = 1/80$, $p < 0.025$) which indicated that the differences due to low and high similarity stimulus terms decreased over trials; that is, the effect of increasing stimulus similarity served to retard learning only during the early trials. There was also a significant interaction between training procedure and trial blocks ($F = 6.12$, $df = 1/80$, $p < 0.025$) which showed that prompting generally produced more correct responses than confirmation during the first block of trials, but that the two procedures were equally effective during the last block of trials. A similar effect was seen in the data reported by Peterson and Brewer (1963).

Underwood and Schulz (1961) and Wilcoxon, Wilson, and Wise (1961) have shown, using nonsense syllable-adjective lists, that the lists are more difficult to learn when the order of presentation is adjective-nonsense syllable than when the order is reversed. There was some evidence in the analysis of total correct responses for poorer performance under method W-F than under F-W, but the obtained F-ratio ($F = 3.02$, $df = 1/80$, $p < 0.10$) was not sufficiently large. The failure of this variable to reach significance could be due to the fact that the S was required only to recognize the correct response each time rather than recalling it as in regular paired-associate learning. Consequently, the analysis of the free-recall data should indicate whether or not method of presentation affected the amount learned. The mean number of items correctly reproduced under each of the various conditions is presented in Table 1. Analysis of variance indicated significant effects due to response similarity ($F = 16.62$, $df = 1/80$, $p < 0.001$), method of presentation ($F = 27.48$, $df = 1/80$, $p < 0.001$), and to the interaction between these two variables ($F = 13.55$, $df = 1/80$, $p < 0.001$). More low- than high-similarity responses were correctly recalled, and more word than figure responses were correctly recalled. The R $\times$ M interaction reflected the same relationship noted in the analysis

TABLE 1

NUMBER ITEMS CORRECT ON FREE-RECALL TEST

Method of presentation	List A	List B	List C	List D
Method F-W				
Prompting[a]				
Mean	7.83	7.67	6.83	6.67
SD	0.41	0.82	1.60	1.51
Confirmation[a]				
Mean	7.67	6.67	6.00	6.67
SD	0.52	1.75	2.28	2.81
Method W-F				
Prompting[a]				
Mean	6.67	6.17	4.17	4.00
SD	2.16	2.86	2.32	1.26
Confirmation[a]				
Mean	7.17	5.83	2.33	3.17
SD	1.33	2.32	1.37	2.93

[a] Training procedure.

of the total number of correct responses. Neither stimulus similarity nor training procedure had any appreciable effect on the number of items correctly recalled. Thus, the results do support previous findings that the method of presentation is a significant variable.

The final analysis made was concerned with the time required to complete each test trial, or "performance speed," and these data are represented in Fig. 2. Since the task utilized in the present study was self-paced rather than automatically paced, speed of performance could have been affected by the experimental conditions. Consequently, a repeated-measures analysis of variance similar to that done for total correct responses was performed on the average performance speed for the first three test trials and for the last three test trials. In general, the results were similar to those for total correct responses. Increasing stimulus similarity decreased performance speed ($F = 9.44$, $df = 1/80$, $p < 0.005$) as did increasing response similarity ($F = 26.20$, $df = 1/80$, $p < 0.001$). There was again a significant R $\times$ M interaction ($F = 7.67$, $df = 1/80$, $p < 0.01$) which showed the same phenomenon noted earlier, i.e., that increasing response similarity had a much more pronounced effect under method

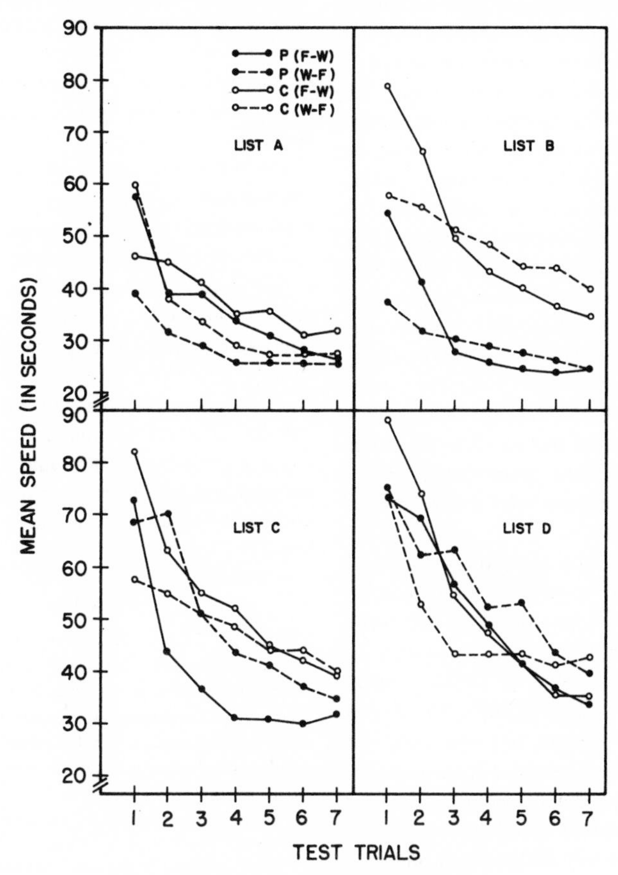

FIG. 2. Mean time to complete each test trial.

W-F than under method F-W. Perhaps the most interesting result of this analysis was the finding that prompting resulted in significantly faster performance than confirmation ($F = 6.80$, $df = 1/80$, $p < 0.025$). As can be seen from Fig. 2, the prompting groups were superior to the confirmation groups under almost all of the experimental conditions. However, there was an $S \times R \times T$ interaction ($F = 4.61$, $df = 1/80$, $p < 0.05$) which indicated essentially that with low stimulus similarity, increasing response similarity accentuated the difference between prompting and confirmation, while with high stimulus similarity, increasing response similarity produced negligible differences between the two training procedures. Whether or not time measures such as these constitute a measure of verbal learning is not clear, but it is interesting to note that these results are in direct opposition to those found in motor-learning tasks. For example, Wang (1925) carried out a series of studies on the effectiveness of response-guidance (cf. prompting) in maze learning and found that while such guidance did facilitate learning, it also resulted in a slower final performance speed. Similarly, Hawker (1964) found no differences in learning an electrical punchboard maze as a result of the training procedure followed, but did find that the final performance speed was significantly slower for the prompting group than for the confirmation group.

It appears, then, that prompting does have a facilitating effect during the early part of training but loses such an effect as training progresses. Moreover, there appears to be no over-all superiority of either prompting or confirmation since the total number of correct responses over all test trials did not differ significantly under the two procedures. However, the fact that prompting resulted in a faster performance speed than confirmation is an interesting finding and deserves additional attention.

Summary

The present study was designed to investigate the effects of training procedure, stimulus similarity, response similarity, and method of presentation in the learning of paired-associate material. A 2^4 factorial design was employed with two levels of each of the four variables, and 6 *S*s were run under each of the resulting 16 experimental conditions. The *S*s were given seven series of practice and test trials to learn a list of eight paired adjectives and line figures, with the number of correct responses on each test trial taken as the primary measure of acquisition.

The results supported previous findings in paired-associate learning concerning the effects of stimulus similarity, response similarity, and method of presentation, but did not clearly support those regarding the effectiveness of prompting and confirmation. There were no significant differences as a function of training procedure in either the total number of correct responses or in the number of responses correctly reproduced in a post-session free-recall test. However, an analysis of correct responses over blocks of trials did indicate that prompting was superior to confirmation during the first block of trials, but that the two procedures were equally effective during the last block of trials. In addition, it was found that prompting resulted in faster "performance speeds" under almost all of the experimental conditions.

References

Battig, W. F., and Brackett, H. R. Comparison of anticipation and recall methods in paired-associate learning. *Psychol. Rep.*, 1961, **9**, 59–65.

Cook, J. O. Supplementary report: Processes underlying learning a single paired-associate item. *J. exp. Psychol.*, 1958, **56**, 455.

Cook, J. O., and Kendler, T. S. A theoretical model to explain some paired-associate learning data. In G. Finch and F. Cameron (Eds.), *Symposium on Air Force human engineering, personnel, and training research.* Washington: Nat. Acad.

Sci.—Nat. Res. Counc. Publ. 455, 1956. Pp. 90–98.

Cook, J. O., and Spitzer, M. E. Supplementary report: Prompting versus confirmation in paired-associate learning. *J. exp. Psychol.*, 1960, **59**, 275–276.

Feldman, S. M., and Underwood, B. J. Stimulus recall following paired-associate learning. *J. exp. Psychol.*, 1957, **53**, 11–15.

Hawker, J. R. Supplementary report: Effects of prompting and confirmation in a serial learning task. *J. exp. Psychol.*, 1964, **67**, 99-101.

Hilgard, E. R. Methods and procedures in the study of learning. In S. S. Stevens (Ed.), *Handbook of experimental psychology*. New York: Wiley, 1951, Pp. 517–567.

Lockhead, G. R. Methods of presenting paired-associates. *J. verb. Learn. verb. Behav.*, 1962, **1**, 62–65.

Peterson, L. R., and Brewer, C. L. Confirmation, correction, and contiguity. *J. verb. Learn. verb. Behav.*, 1963, **1**, 365–371.

Sidowski, J. B., Kopstein, F. F., and Shillestad, I. J. Prompting and confirmation variables in verbal learning. *Psychol. Rep.*, 1961, **8**, 401–406.

Silberman, H. F., Melaragno, R. J., and Coulson, J. E. Confirmation and prompting with connected discourse material. *Psychol. Rep.*, 1961, **9**, 235–238.

Underwood, B. J., and Archer, E. J. Studies of distributed practice: XIV. Intralist similarity and presentation rate in verbal-discrimination learning of consonant syllables. *J. exp. Psychol.*, 1955, **50**, 120–124.

Underwood, B. J., and Goad, D. Studies of distributed practice: I. The influence of intralist similarity in serial learning. *J. exp. Psychol.*, 1951, **42**, 125–134.

Underwood, B. J., and Schulz, R. W. Studies of distributed practice: XX. Sources of interference associated with differences in learning and retention. *J. exp. Psychol.*, 1961, **61**, 228–235.

Wang, T. L. The influence of tuition in the acquisition of skill. *Psychol. Monogr.*, 1925, **34**, No. 154.

Wilcoxon, H. C., Wilson, W. R., and Wise, D. A. Paired-associate learning as a function of percentage of occurrence of response members and other factors. *J. exp. Psychol.*, 1961, **61**, 283–289.

(Received July 9, 1963)

ARTICLE 3

SERIAL VERSUS RANDOM PRESENTATION OF PAIRED ASSOCIATES [1]

CLESSEN J. MARTIN AND ELI SALTZ

Center for the Study of Cognitive Processes, Wayne State University

The effect of constant serial order in presentation of paired associates was investigated in 2 experiments. Experiment I (100 Ss) found that constant order resulted in serial associations between the response items of the pairs (significant beyond .01) but, contrary to other studies, did not facilitate paired-associate learning. Experiment II (72 Ss) tested the hypothesis that facilitory effects due to constant order were a function of S-R presentation rate. Contrary to prediction, no facilitory effect occurred at any presentation rate. Results indicate that, contrary to previous belief, serial presentation of paired associates does not necessarily facilitate learning.

Studies by McGeoch and McKinney (1937) and by McGeoch and Underwood (1943) have reported that presentation of S-R pairs in the same serial order on each learning trial will facilitate learning. However, it was not possible to determine the exact source of such facilitation in these studies. Newman and Saltz (1962) have attempted to identify more clearly the source of serial facilitation in paired-associate learning.

To test the hypothesis that facilitation is produced by serial position cues, these investigators, following the procedure of McGeoch and McKinney, employed a condition in which S-R pairs were presented in a constant serial order for five trials, then on the sixth trial *S*s were tested with the stimuli presented in random order. Contrary to the hypothesis that facilitation is produced by serial cues, this group performed no worse on the sixth trial than a group in which pairs were presented in a constant serial order for the five learning trials and also the sixth, *test*, trial. Both serial groups performed better than a random presentation group on the sixth trial.

The purpose of Exp. I in the present paper is to investigate the possibility that the lack of difference between the serial presentation-serial test, S(S) and the serial presentation-random test, S(R), groups in the Newman and Saltz study was due to the fact that their test situation was not sufficiently sensitive to permit an adequate test of the serial position cue hypothesis. Since the degree of learning over five trials was low due to competing S terms in the Newman and Saltz investigation, the S terms in the present study were noncompeting and of higher association value in order to increase the degree of learning over the first five learning trials. In addition, after the test on Trial 6, an additional five learning trials and a final test trial were administered to *S*s to determine if the Newman and Saltz results held up over greater numbers of trials. A 10-sec. interval was used for each presentation of an S term during the retention test in the Newman and Saltz investigation. A 2-sec. interval was used in the present study.

[1] The present study is part of a program of research, concerned with the influence of differentiation on verbal processes, supported by the National Science Foundation under NSF G-9068 to the junior author.

Reprinted with permission of the authors and the publisher, the American Psychologic Association. The article appeared originally in the *Journal of Experimental Psychology*, 196 **65**, 609–615.

It was thought that the 10-sec. interval for each presentation of the S terms reduced the sensitivity of retention measurement and that there may have been differences between the S(S) and S(R) groups which failed to emerge because of the reduced sensitivity of the 10-sec. interval.

The procedure, employed by Newman and Saltz, of presenting the S-R pairs for five trials before the first test trial, was retained in the present study. This procedure was considered critical for a test of the hypothesis that serial position cues were responsible for the facilitation of the constant order conditions. The crucial aspect of the present study is the performance of the group trained on a constant order of presentation when shifted to a random order. The results of the McGeoch and McKinney and the McGeoch and Underwood studies suggest that the use of the standard anticipation method during the first five training trials should lead to a history of more successful anticipations during these training trials for the constant order group than for the random presentation group. When the serial position cues are eliminated for the constant order group by randomizing the order on Trial 6, a failure of this group to fall to the level of the random presentation group might be attributable to the greater history of successes during learning trials.

Finally, to determine if serial presentation of pairs resulted in learning the serial order of responses, after paired-associate learning, *S*s learned a serial list composed of the R terms of the original S-R pairs.

Experiment I

Method

Subjects.—The *S*s were 100 introductory psychology students at Wayne State University. The first 80 of these were assigned randomly to the experimental conditions with the limitation that subgroup *N*s be equal. After the data had been analyzed a new set of materials was developed and the additional 20 *S*s were randomly assigned to an S(S) or an R(R) treatment involving these materials.

Materials.—List 1, the 10 S-R pairs learned by the first set of 80 *S*s, consisted of the same 10 R terms used in the Newman and Saltz study, high *M* value nouns from Noble's (1952) list; the S terms were nonsense syllables having a 47% association value (Hilgard, 1951). The actual pairs were: YAT-JEWEL, TIS-DINNER, ZUG-MONEY, KEM-VILLAGE, SOZ-INSECT, QUN-GARMENT, XOW-HEAVEN, NOL-WAGON, RUH-OFFICE, BEK-KITCHEN. Two different random orders, an A and a B order, of the above pairs were employed such that half the *S*s in a serial learning condition learned Order A, half learned Order B. An additional five random orders were developed for the random presentation condition learning trials. For all 80 *S*s, the A or B orders were used during test trials. Thus half the *S*s in a random presentation group were tested on Order A, the other half on Order B.

List 2, the materials developed for the 20 additional *S*s, consisted of the identical R terms as for the 80 *S*s, but a new set of 47% association stimuli: FAZ-JEWEL, KOR-DINNER, WAH-MONEY, YOB-VILLAGE, BEW-INSECT, RUV-GARMENT, NAC-HEAVEN, MEP-WAGON, QIG-OFFICE, TAJ-KITCHEN. Material was presented on a Lafayette memory drum.

Procedure.—All *S*s received 10 learning trials in which the stimulus and response members of each pair appeared simultaneously in the window of the memory drum at a 2-sec. rate with 6 sec. between trials. Test trials were presented after the fifth and tenth learning trials. The separation of learning and test trials is consistent with the procedure used by both McGeoch and McKinney (1937) and Newman and Saltz (1962). A test trial consisted of presenting each stimulus member alone for 2 sec. and requiring the *S*s to emit the appropriate response to each stimulus within the 2-sec. interval. In the instructions it was suggested that *S* not attend to the order in which the S-R appeared during the learning trials.

There were four experimental groups.

1. Group S(S)S(S) received the S-R pairs in the same serial order on all learning and test trials.

2. Group R(R)R(R) received the S-R pairs in a different order on each of the first five learning trials and the test trial (i.e.,

six different orders). This sequence of six random orders was then repeated for the second five learning trials and the second test trial.

3. Group S(S)S(R) received the S-R pairs in the same serial order during all 10 learning trials and Retention Test 1, but during Retention Test 2 (twelfth trial) the S terms were presented in a different random order.

4. Group S(R)R(R) received the S-R pairs in the same serial order during the first five learning trials but during Retention Test 1 the S terms were presented in a different random order. In the second five learning trials the S-R pairs were presented in different serial order on each trial. The S terms during Retention Test 2 were presented in the same order as during Retention Test 1.

5. Group S(S) consisted of 10 of the additional 20 *S*s. This group learned List 2. Procedure was identical with that of Group S(S)S(S) except that the *S*s received only five learning trials and one test trial.

6. Group R(R) consisted of the remaining 10 of the additional 20 *S*s. This group also learned List 2. Procedure was identical with that of Group R(R)R(R) except that *S*s received only five learning trials and one test trial.

For Groups 1, 3, and 4, following the second retention test the *S*s were presented with a serial list consisting of the 10 R terms that had been presented during the paired-associate learning trials. Half of the *S*s in each experimental group received the R terms in the identical order in which they had been presented during the learning trials, and the other half received the R terms in an order different from any used during the learning trials. Each *S* was given five trials on the serial list. Each word in the serial list was presented at a 2-sec. rate with a 6-sec. interval between trials. The number of correct anticipations was recorded on each of the last four trials.

Results

Table 1 reveals that serial position did not facilitate the learning of the S-R pairs. The R(R)R(R) group learned more S-R associations than did the S(S)S(S) group as measured by either Retention Test 1 or 2. Additional evidence concerning the effects of serial presentation is provided by the S(S)S(R) group which, through Retention Test 1, also is a serial presentation condition. As can be seen in Table 1, on Retention Test 1 the means for the S(S)S(R) group are close to those of the S(S)S(S) group, and indicate poorer performance than the random group, R(R)R(R). These results are not in accord with those found by previous investigators.

In order to determine whether the difference between the serial and

TABLE 1

MEANS AND *SD*s OF NUMBER OF CORRECT RESPONSES FOR EXP. I ON RETENTION TESTS 1 AND 2

Groups	Order	Retention Test 1			Retention Test 2		
		M	*SD*	Group *M*	*M*	*SD*	Group *M*
1. S(S)S(S)	A	4.4	2.22	4.55	7.3	2.26	7.50
	B	4.7	2.75		7.7	2.59	
2. R(R)R(R)	A	5.5	2.27	5.80	7.5	1.90	7.90
	B	6.1	1.52		8.3	1.34	
3. S(S)S(R)	A	4.9	2.08	4.95	6.9	2.47	7.10
	B	5.0	3.19		7.3	3.20	
4. S(R)R(R)	A	4.2	2.90	4.60	7.0	2.45	7.55
	B	5.0	1.95		8.1	1.45	
5. S(S)	List 2	—	2.26	5.7			
6. R(R)	List 2	—	2.38	6.1			

TABLE 2

MEANS AND *SD*s OF CORRECT RESPONSES IN SERIAL LEARNING OF R TERMS OF PREVIOUSLY LEARNED PAIRED-ASSOCIATE LISTS

Groups and Orders in Original Paired-Associate Learning		Relationship between Serial Order of R Terms in Paired-Associate and Serial Learning					
		Identical			Different		
		M	*SD*	Group *M*	*M*	*SD*	Group *M*
S(S)S(S)	A	16.0	7.07	16.6	11.4	5.59	10.5
	B	17.2	4.32		9.6	4.16	
S(S)S(R)	A	18.6	1.14	18.2	10.2	8.35	10.0
	B	17.8	3.27		9.8	6.22	
S(R)R(R)	A	15.8	6.98	16.4	5.8	4.55	8.6
	B	17.0	7.07		11.4	6.80	

random groups in Exp. I was significant a t test was performed. The mean number of correct responses made on Retention Test 1 for the serial groups, Groups 1 and 3, which received the S-R pairs in the same serial position on the first five learning trials was compared to the number of correct responses made by the random group, Group 2, which received the S-R pairs in a different random order on each of the first five learning trials. The mean for the serial groups was 4.75 compared to a mean of 5.80 for the random group. The resulting t (58) = 1.65 was not significant at the .05 level. A similar comparison of Groups 1 vs. 2 on Retention Test 2 also failed to prove significant.

Groups 5 and 6 were run on a new list, List 2, to determine if the effects reported above were due to idiosyncracies of the S terms employed. (It will be recalled that R terms were those used by Newman and Saltz who found facilitation as a function of serial order.) The findings for Groups 5 and 6 are consistent with the findings for List 1.

With the combined data from Lists 1 and 2, there was a total of 50 *S*s who had received the S-R pairs in a constant serial order during the first five learning trials and had received the S terms in the same serial order on Retention Test 1. There was a total of 30 *S*s for whom each S-R pair appeared in a different serial position during each of the first five learning trials, and during Retention Test 1 the S terms were presented in an order different from any used during the learning trials. The mean number of correct responses on Retention Test 1 for all the R(R) groups was 5.90 as compared to 4.93 for all the S(S) groups. The resulting t (78) = 1.80 was not significant at the .05 level.

The second phase of Exp. I investigated whether constant order of paired associates leads to serial associations between the R terms of the pairs. Consequently, only *S*s in Groups 1, 3, and 4 were involved in this phase, since these were the only groups in which constant order of pairs was utilized during the earlier, paired-associate phase. Following paired-associate training, *S*s in these three groups were presented a serial list of the 10 R terms they had learned in original paired-associate training. Half the *S*s in each group learned the items in the same serial order in which the items had appeared during paired-associate training. The remaining *S*s learned the items in a new random order. The *S*s received five trials on the serial list, with instructions to anticipate on the last four of these trials. Table 2 gives the means and *SD*s for the correct anticipations made by the various groups on the four anticipation trials.

A 3 × 2 analysis of variance indicates that *S*s receiving the R terms in an identical order to that used during the paired-associate learning task made significantly ($p = .001$) more correct R term anticipations on the serial learning task than did *S*s who received the R terms in an order different from any used during the paired-associate learning task. None of the other effects approached significance.

Originally, the S(S)S(R) and S(R)R(R) groups in Exp. I were run because it was thought that the comparison of these groups with the S(S)S(S) group would give an indication as to the mechanisms involved in facilitation of serial presentation of S-R pairs. However, since no such facilitating effect occurred in Exp. I, the results of the S(S)S(R) and S(R)R(R) Groups of Exp. I become of minor interest.

Experiment II

The results of Exp. I are contradictory to the findings of McGeoch and McKinney (1937), McGeoch and Underwood (1943), and Newman and Saltz (1962). Presentation of the S-R pairs in the same serial position at every repetition did not lead to a greater degree of learning than presentation in a different serial position each time as measured by Retention Tests 1 and 2. In fact, the group which received the S-R pairs in a changing order learned more S-R associations as measured by Retention Tests 1 and 2 than the group which received the S-R pairs in an unchanging order. Although there was no significant difference between the groups in the mean number of correct responses on Retention Tests 1 or 2, the results were certainly not in the expected direction and are not in accord with other findings. However, the studies reporting facilitation due to serial presentation of S-R pairs involved either easier materials than the present study (McGeoch & Underwood, 1943) or a longer time for recall during the test trials (McGeoch & McKinney, 1937; Newman & Saltz, 1962). Experiment II was designed to determine if a variable related to facilitating learning in general would also act to differentially facilitate learning of S-R pairs in a constant serial order over a random order. The factor chosen for manipulation was rate of presentation, since this permitted using the same paired-associate lists in easy and difficult conditions.

Method

Subjects.—The *S*s were 72 students in introductory psychology at Wayne. The *S*s were randomly assigned to conditions with the limitation that all subgroups have equal *N*s.

Materials.—The three basic lists of Exp. I were used.

Procedure.—A 2 × 3 × 3 factorial design was employed with two rate presentations (a 1-sec. rate and a 4-sec. rate), three sets of materials, and three presentation conditions: S(S), S(R), and R(R), as described in Exp. I.

All *S*s received five learning trials in which the stimulus and response terms were presented simultaneously, followed by a test trial in which only stimulus terms were presented.

Results

Table 3 presents the mean number of correct responses on the retention

TABLE 3

MEAN NUMBER OF CORRECT RESPONSES ON THE RETENTION TEST FOR SERIAL AND RANDOM PRESENTATION GROUPS LEARNING AT 1- AND 4-SEC. RATES

Groups	1-Sec. Rate		4-Sec. Rate	
	M	*SD*	*M*	*SD*
S(S)	2.83	2.25	8.25	2.05
R(R)	2.25	1.24	7.75	2.34
S(R)	1.67	1.43	7.75	1.87

test (Trial 6) for each group. Each mean is based on 12 *S*s. A 2 × 3 × 3 analysis of variance indicates a significant difference in the number of correct responses between the 1- and 4-sec. time intervals, $F(1,54) = 147.44$ but there is not a significant difference between the S(S) and R(R) groups nor between lists. The interactions did not approach significance. A *t* test was used in order to determine whether the S(S) 1-sec. group, was significantly different from the R(R) 1-sec. group. The resulting $t(46) = .79$ was not significant. A *t* test between the S(S) 4-sec. group, and the R(R) 4-sec. group, did not yield a significant *t* value. Thus, although the mean number of correct responses in the S(S) groups was greater than the mean number of correct responses in the R(R) groups, there was no evidence which would support a rejection of the null hypothesis between the means of the S(S) and R(R) groups at either the 1- or 4-sec. interval.

Examining the comparable data relevant to serial vs. random presentation obtained in Exp. I and II yields a relationship of serial to random presentation across three rates of presentation. The 1-sec. and 4-sec. groups of Exp. II each consisted of one third of the *S*s on List 1, Order A; one third on List 1, Order B; and one third on List 2. To provide a similar distribution of materials from Exp. I, Groups 1 and 5 of that experiment were used to determine the mean for serial presentation at 2 sec., and Groups 2 and 6 were used to determine the mean for random presentation at 2 sec. A 2 × 3 × 3 factorial design was used to analyze the results. Again a highly significant effect due to rate of presentation was found. However, there was no significant effect due to serial vs. random presentation ($F < 1.00$) nor did any of the interactions approach significance.

DISCUSSION

Experiment I in the present paper clearly shows that presentation of pairs in a constant order led to formation of serial association between the response items of the pairs. Clearly these serial associations must have been present during paired-associate learning; nevertheless, they did not facilitate that learning. Newman and Saltz (1962) found that constant order of pairs during five learning trials facilitated performance on the test trial (Trial 6) even when pairs were presented in a random order during the test trial eliminating serial position cues. Taken together, the present studies and the Newman and Saltz study indicate that serial position cues are not an important factor in learning paired associates in a constant order.

An unexpected finding arose in connection with the R term serial learning. In the S(R)R(R) condition, the block of five serially presented pairs was followed by five trials in which the R terms appeared in five different orders. There is no evidence, in Table 3, that this random presentation interfered with the subsequent serial learning of the R terms.

The most important conclusion from the present studies is that, contrary to previous belief, it is not necessarily true that serial presentation of S-R pairs will facilitate learning. Nor is it clear under what conditions such facilitation will occur.

REFERENCES

HILGARD, E. R. Methods and procedures in the study of learning. In S. S. Stevens (Ed.), *Handbook of experimental psychology.* New York: Wiley, 1951. Ch. 15.

MCGEOCH, J. A., & MCKINNEY, F. Studies in retroactive inhibition: The influence of the relative order of presentation of original and interpolated paired associates. *J. exp. Psychol.*, 1937, **20**, 60–83.

MCGEOCH, J. A., & UNDERWOOD, B. J. Tests of the two-factor theory of retroactive inhibition. *J. exp. Psychol.*, 1943, **32**, 1–16.

NEWMAN, S. E., & SALTZ, E. Serial position as a cue in learning. *Amer. J. Psychol.*, 1962, **75**, 101–108.

NOBLE, C. E. An analysis of meaning. *Psychol. Rev.*, 1952, **59**, 421–430.

(Received August 8, 1962)

ARTICLE 4

PRESENTATION TIME, TOTAL TIME, AND MEDIATION IN PAIRED-ASSOCIATE LEARNING[1]

B. R. BUGELSKI

University of Buffalo

The present experiment deals with a neglected variable in the systematic study of memorization; namely, item presentation time per trial in relation to total learning time. This variable is obviously important in the interpretation of claims such as that of Rock (1957) for one-trial learning, claims that were based on an interitem time of 8 sec. For Rock, a trial consisted of 96 sec. during which 12 nonsense pairs were exposed. During this period *S* was free to repeat any item for the entire period, but even if he merely used the 8-sec. per item interval, he could still repeat any item quite frequently. The claim that repetition has no merit is obviously improperly drawn from such a study. Time per trial is also involved directly in studies of massed vs. spaced learning where massing is defined as a rapid interitem rate (Hovland, 1938). Using a rate of 2 sec. per item Hovland found learning inferior (14.89 trials) to a rate of 4 sec. per item (6.78 trials). A simple multiplication of trials by time, however, shows the two procedures to involve about the same total time (29.98 and 27.12 sec.). Even when a long intertrial interval is employed, total times appear to be about the same (22.36 and 23.40 sec.) for 2-sec. and 4-sec. presentation rates although the number of trials differed significantly (11.18 and 5.85).

[1] This study was supported by United States Public Health Research and Fellowship Branch Grant M-3489. The writer wishes to acknowledge the aid of N. Carriero and J. Rickwood in gathering the data.

It is the present hypothesis that in at least some areas of memorization, and under some conditions of presentation, the degree of learning will be a function of total time, regardless of the duration of the individual trials or interitem times. The hypothesis does not appear to be without support. Murdock (1960), employing free recall of words in lists of varying length, found total time to be a determining factor in how much was learned regardless of presentation rate. Attempts to compute total learning times from published studies have also proved suggestive for a variety of learning situations but the many variations in kinds and length of material and associated learning conditions prevent adequate comparisons. It is hoped that the present study will focus more attention on the various temporal factors in learning such as exposure time per item, interitem interval, intertrial interval, and total learning time. The essence of the problem is: what is a learning trial?

METHOD

Apparatus.—The Hunter Card Master was used to expose pairs of nonsense syllables at varying presentation times. The stimulus syllable was always exposed for 2 sec. and remained visible while the response syllable was exposed for either 2, 4, 6, 8, or 15 additional sec. Two seconds always elapsed before a new stimulus syllable appeared. Eight pairs of syllables which had been used by Rock, 1957 for his control group (see Table 2), were presented in three different random orders. The total time available to *S* for reacting to or learning a given pair, including the time before a new stimulus was presented,

Reprinted with permission of the author and the publisher, the American Psychological Association. The article appeared originally in the *Journal of Experimental Psychology*, 1962, **63**, 409–412.

varied, therefore, from 6 sec. for the 2-sec. response to 19 sec. for the 15-sec. response, with the other times lasting 8, 10, and 12 sec. per pair. The time allowed for anticipation of the response term was, of course, always 2 sec.

It will be noted that the total time for presentation of eight pairs of syllables, i.e., one trial, would last either 48, 64, 80, 96, or 152 sec. depending upon the exposure time of the response syllable. There was no rest period between trials.

Procedure.—Each *S* learned the same eight pairs of syllables to a criterion of two successful anticipations of the complete list. The apparatus used did not allow for the elimination of pairs as they were learned, but this was done in the computations so that the total learning times reported are based on the time taken to learn each pair to the criterion. Upon completion of learning each *S* was asked specifically how he happened to learn each pair, what made him think of the correct response, why some pairs were easy and some difficult.

Subjects.—One hundred sophomore students in experimental psychology courses, naive with respect to nonsense syllable learning, were assigned to one of the five experimental conditions, thereby making up five groups of 20. Assignment to groups depended only on order of arrival at the laboratory; the first *S* was assigned to Group 1, the next to Group 2, etc.

TABLE 1

MEAN TRIALS AND TOTAL TIMES TO LEARN LISTS

Presentation Time	*N*	Trials		Total Exposure Time	
		Mean	*SD*	Mean	*SD*
6 sec.	20	10.2	4.1	61.2	24.3
8 sec.	20	8.8	3.8	70.1	30.4
10 sec.	20	5.8	1.9	57.9	19.0
12 sec.	20	4.7	2.5	56.1	29.6
19 sec.	20	3.3	1.2	62.2	22.2

RESULTS

Both trials and total time to learn are shown in Table 1 for each of the five different presentation times. The total times are obtained by multiplying the total number of trials to learn each pair in the series by the presentation time. As expected, the longer the presentation time per pair, the fewer the number of trials to criterion. Analysis of variance for the trials yields $F = 18.53$ ($P = .01$, $df = 99$). Total time, however, is not significantly different among the five conditions ($F = 0.845$). The correspondence between total times for the most rapid presentation time and the longest presentation time is striking. Although the former required more than three times as many trials as the latter, the mean time difference is hardly more than 1 sec. Extrapolating roughly from these findings, it might be possible for similar *S*s to learn all eight pairs in one trial with a presentation time of about 25 sec. per pair. Within the limits, then, of the intervals and conditions used, the conclusion appears reasonable that presentation time multiplied by trials amounts to a constant value, $T_p \times T = k$.

During the postexperimental interrogation every *S* reported spontaneously that one kind of association, mediator or bridge occurred to him and was used to fix the responses. They did not, of course, use such terms and their explanations were ordered into a tentative and arbitrary classification of five seemingly discriminable groups such as the following:

I. The *S* formed one word of the two syllables, as, for example, from DUP-TEZ, he would create DEPUTIZE; from GAC-QET, he would form RACQUET or JACKET.
II. The syllables would be formed into two separate words or a phrase that could be initiated by the stimulus syllable: CEZ-MUN becomes SAYS MAN or C'EST MAN or SEND MONEY.[2]
III. The *S* would manufacture or imagine appropriate phrases or words that sound like the syllables, e.g., GEY-NUR becomes

[2] Categories I and II appear to be "sound bound." The associations appear to derive from the sounds of the syllables. The sounds are modified into words.

TABLE 2

MEAN TRIALS TO LEARN EACH PAIR OF ASSOCIATES AND THE CORRESPONDING NUMBER OF MEDIATORS VOLUNTEERED BY *S*s, WITH BREAKDOWN BY TYPE OF MEDIATOR

Syllables	Trials		Total (out of a possible 100)	Mediators					
				Types					
	Mean	*SD*		I	II	III	IV	V	None
GEY-NUR	5.02	5.2	81	54	12	8	2	5	19
KAR-WEH	5.51	5.8	84	7	68	4	3	2	16
BIH-XIR	5.53	4.6	73	18	2	16	29	8	27
CEZ-MUN	6.79	6.2	70	6	31	13	4	16	30
FAX-SOQ	6.94	4.7	57	1	11	26	15	4	43
TOF-LAH	7.13	5.6	54	5	19	7	9	14	46
DUP-TEZ	7.16	5.8	52	2	1	32	5	12	48
GAC-QET	8.24	5.6	66	25	0	15	21	5	34

A GENERAL NURSE or KAR-WEH becomes KAREN-WAYWARD. This category involves largely personal experience.

IV. Some *S*s would attempt abstract analyses of the syllables to get at some lead to the response, e.g., BIH-XIR becomes BI = 2, *X* = 10, ONE NUMBER GOES WITH ANOTHER NUMBER, or THEY BOTH HAD AN "I."

V. The *S*s would report some vague association with one part of the combination, e.g., GAC-QET becomes translated into TOURNIQUET, BIH-XIR becomes SOMETHING LIKE BICEPS.

Not all pairs aroused reportable mediators for all *S*s (see Table 2). Some mediators were forgotten after being used. Useless mediators were also commonly mentioned but those were impossible to classify and frequently forgotten. Many *S*s reported inability to learn until a mediator of some type did occur. The longer the interitem interval the more likely the occurrence of a mediator. The five intervals in order from shortest to longest aroused respectively 94, 96, 109, 111, and 127 mediating associations.

DISCUSSION

The findings support the original hypothesis that total learning time is a significant variable to consider in at least some kinds of learning. While it may be convenient to break up a learning session into some kinds of units of time, and label these as "trials," it may be a questionable practice in trying to get at an appreciation of what *S* is actually learning or doing. If a presentation time is anything upwards of 1 sec., he may very well repeat the material to himself within the trial. To count the period as one trial may be quite inappropriate. To conclude, where *S* learns after one such interval, that he learned in one trial (implying no repetition) may be quite incorrect.

On the other hand, the reports from *S*s support the interpretation that on many of the trials nothing effective is learned. Wrong responses may occur because inadequate mediators occurred to *S* or the mediators misled *S* into an inappropriate response. After varying amounts of search, which takes more or less time, an appropriate mediator might be generated or stimulated into functioning. Once this occurs, *S* might be able to respond correctly and meet the learning criterion. In a sense, then, learning does occur in one trial in such situations. It must be remembered that about a third of the time *S* is unable to report any mediator. On such occasions he reports "working on the pair" with a "it just came to me" type of answer. It may be that such unassignable associations are of an unconscious nature, as suggested by Bugelski and Scharlock (1952), Russell and Storms (1955), and Ryan (1960).

The vast amount of research done on lists of pairs and on serial lists must be viewed from the limited viewpoint of how *lists* are learned, and not how pairs or other units are learned. From the viewpoint of a learning theory, it is the latter question that is of greater importance, however practical the former may be.

While the present study was not directed at the question of massed as opposed to spaced learning it does suggest that such studies too might take into consideration the question of total time involved in the learning sessions. Typically such studies provide some rest interval between trials for the spaced group while the massed *S*s carry on with the activity. Commonly enough it is found that the spaced group performs at a higher level than the massed group after the same number of trials. When the spaced group's rests are included, however, it might be found that the total time was far in excess of the apparent advantage in trials, and the massed *S*s have learned proportionally more than the spaced.

The present finding must be interpreted as restricted to the experimental conditions involved, particularly with respect to the time intervals employed, the method of exposure, and the nonsense material task. This report must be considered more suggestive than conclusive and other tasks must be examined before greater confidence can be placed in the constant time principle.[3]

[3] It has been suggested to the writer by the linguist, Henry Lee Smith, that there is a striking similarity in the ages at which children of different nationalities learn to speak their native language to about the same level of efficiency.

Summary

Five groups of 20 *S*s learned eight pairs of nonsense syllables under conditions where the stimulus syllable was always presented for 2 sec. while the response syllable was presented for an additional 2, 4, 6, 8, or 15 sec. depending on the group. A 2-sec. interval preceded each new stimulus. The total exposure times for the several groups were 6, 8, 10, 12, or 19 sec. per syllable pair. A significant difference was found between trials to learn with the fastest learning occurring with the longest presentation times. When presentation time was multiplied by trials, however, no significant differences were found. It was concluded that T_p (presentation time) $\times$ T (trials) is a constant value.

Interrogation of *S*s after learning revealed that in 67% of the total possible learning units, *S*s made use of mediational devices. Those pairs that lent themselves most readily to translation into two meaningful words or could be combined into one word, or could initiate some imagery were most easily learned. These findings are discussed in terms of their significance for studies of "one-trial" learning.

References

Bugelski, B. R., & Scharlock, D. An experimental demonstration of unconscious mediation. *J. exp. Psychol.*, 1952, **44**, 334–338.

Hovland, C. I. Experimental studies in rote-learning theory. III. Distribution of practice with varying speeds of syllable presentation. *J. exp. Psychol.*, 1938, **23**, 172–190.

Murdock, B. B. The immediate retention of unrelated words. *J. exp. Psychol.*, 1960, **60**, 222–234.

Rock, I. The role of repetition in associative learning. *Amer. J. Psychol.*, 1957, **70**, 186–193.

Russell, W. A., & Storms, L. H. Implicit verbal chaining in paired-associate learning. *J. exp. Psychol.*, 1955, **49**, 287–293.

Ryan, J. J. Comparison of verbal response transfer mediated by meaningfully similar and associated stimuli. *J. exp. Psychol.*, 1960, **60**, 408–415.

(Received February 21, 1961)

ARTICLE 5

TEN YEARS OF MASSED PRACTICE ON DISTRIBUTED PRACTICE[1]

BENTON J. UNDERWOOD
Northwestern University

For the past 10 years a series of studies dealing with the influence of distributed practice on verbal learning has been carried out in the Northwestern University laboratories. The purpose of the present paper is twofold: to present the critical variables which have emerged from this series of studies, and to suggest certain conceptual notions which at the present time seem useful in trying to understand the effects of distributed practice and related phenomena.

The primary empirical goal at the time this series of studies was initiated was a straightforward one, namely, to determine the range of conditions and materials within which distributed practice facilitated learning or retention. The fact that 10 years have passed since this goal was established indicates that it has proven to be an elusive objective to attain. Indeed, no implication should be drawn from the present paper that the goal has now been reached; the pursuit continues. Therefore, the "critical variables" to be presented, while representing a considerable experimental distillation over the years, may yet change with continuing work and new perspectives.

To say that certain variables are more critical than others necessarily implies some evaluation. For the phenomenon being dealt with in this paper, the evaluation is based on three criteria. First, and fundamentally, the positive effects of distributed practice are not found unless a critical variable is involved. Second, the effects of other variables can be shown to be a consequence of the simultaneous change in a critical variable. Finally, using the particular critical variables chosen, conceptual notions are suggested which in turn lead to further testable propositions.

There should be no misunderstanding about the conceptual notions to be presented in this paper. They are a posteriori notions; the sifting of the facts of massed versus distributed practice led to an assertion about critical

[1] The substance of this paper constituted the Presidential Address given before Division 3, American Psychological Association, Chicago, 1960.

Most of the work reported here was supported by Contracts N7onr-45008 and Nonr-1228(15) between Northwestern University and the Office of Naval Research. Over the 10 years of this work five extraordinarily capable research associates have been involved: Ross L. Morgan, E. James Archer, Jack Richardson, Rudolph W. Schulz, and Geoffrey Keppel. The author is deeply indebted to them all. For certain analyses and data first presented here, the aid of Schulz and Keppel has been invaluable, and the manuscript has benefited by their critical readings.

Reprinted with permission of the author and the publisher, the American Psychological Association. The article appeared originally in the *Psychological Review*, 1961, **68**, 229–247.

variables, and then it was found possible to cast these variables into a theoretical scheme which had some generality. The theory was not originated as a deductive one, but neither was it ad hoc. Its usefulness, no matter how momentary, can be justified on the grounds that it makes some sense out of a number of phenomena and, in addition, yields a number of testable propositions.

Because the theory has emerged from the various analyses leading to the selection of the critical variables, the order of the argument in this paper will maintain some historical integrity as follows: the nature of the data leading to the selection of the critical variables, the theoretical notions by which these critical variables are asserted to produce the phenomena associated with the massed-distributed problem, and a consideration of other phenomena which may be incorporated within the system. However, before initiating the central arguments, it is necessary to dispose of certain preliminary matters.

The Basic Operations. The basic procedures used in the Northwestern studies, procedures which are quite comparable to those used by other investigators, are as follows. A trial is defined as the single presentation of all items in a list of verbal units. The list may be presented for a constant number of trials or until the subject achieves some arbitrary level of performance, such as one perfect recitation. The central variable is the length of the interval between trials. If the interval is short, say 2 seconds to 8 seconds, learning is said to be by massed practice (MP). If the interval is longer—15 seconds or more—learning is said to be by distributed practice (DP). In actual practice the DP interval has not exceeded 3 minutes. The simple empirical problem is to determine under what conditions learning under DP differs from learning under MP. Several studies have also dealt with the effect of MP and DP on long-term retention. However, because of the scope of the material to be covered on the effects of MP and DP on learning, their effects on retention will not be covered in this paper.

Magnitude of the Effects. When DP is introduced in the acquisition of a motor task, such as a pursuit rotor, enormous facilitative effects on performance are observed. There is no comparison to be made between the magnitude of such effects and those which occur as a consequence of DP in verbal learning. Facilitation by DP in verbal learning occurs only under a highly specific set of conditions, and the magnitude of the effect when it does occur is relatively small. The reliability of certain DP effects must, in some cases, be based upon consistency from experiment to experiment rather than upon a strict statistical criterion for any given experiment. If one wishes to use an efficiency measure for learning, it would be very inefficient to learn by DP; the subject would be much further ahead to learn by MP if total time to learn (including the rest intervals in DP) is the criterion. Even under the most favorable conditions for facilitation by DP, one could not recommend its use in an applied setting where verbal materials are to be mastered.

First Critical Variable: Response-Term Interference

In this section evidence will be summarized which has led to the conclusion that a certain amount of response-term interference must be present before DP will facilitate acquisition. However, some background preparation is necessary.

Two-Stage Conception

In recent years it has been found useful to view verbal learning as occurring in two stages. The first stage is the response-learning stage during which the subject must acquire the responses as responses; they must become readily recallable units. The second stage is the associative stage during which the response must be attached or hooked up to a specific stimulus. A more complete elaboration of these two stages has been given elsewhere (Underwood & Schulz, 1960); not only do these stages seem to be logically necessary but the behavior of subjects in mastering lists appears to correspond closely to the two stages. Furthermore, variables may have different effects during the two stages. For example, high similarity among responses in a paired-associate list facilitates response learning but retards associative learning (Underwood, Runquist, & Schulz, 1959).

The relevance of the two-stage conception for understanding the effects of DP is this: when DP facilitates verbal learning the evidence points strongly toward the fact that it does so because of interference operating during the response-learning stage. This would *exclude* interference in attaching responses to particular stimuli. It would *include* any interference which impedes the learning of responses as responses. This is most clearly seen in learning low-meaningful units, such as consonant syllables. The interference may prevent the ready learning of the correct sequences of the letters of the consonant syllables. Or, to say this another way, the interference may retard response integration.

The evidence leading to this conclusion will now be given in summary form.

1. In a recent study (Underwood & Schulz, 1961a), it was shown that if interference was built up among responses across paired-associate lists, DP facilitated learning. However, if interference was built up among stimuli across lists (with minimum interference in acquiring responses), DP actually retarded learning.

2. In a study of verbal-discrimination learning and DP (Underwood & Archer, 1955), intralist similarity and rate of presentation of the pairs was varied. Under conditions which would normally produce facilitation by DP in serial or paired-associate learning, no effect was found. In verbal-discrimination learning the subject does not have to acquire the response terms in the sense that he does in serial or paired-associate learning. Rather, he is presented a pair of items and he merely has to indicate which member of the pair is correct; no response integration is required.

3. In a study of concept recognition (Underwood, 1957a) where the response was a common word, no facilitation by DP was found in spite of the fact that heavy interference was produced because of the overlap among concept stimuli.

4. Paired-associate lists of 16 pairs were constructed in which interference was varied in amount by using very familiar words representing the same concept (Underwood & Schulz, 1961b). Although widely different rates of learning were observed as a consequence of the differential interference, DP did not facilitate learning at any level of interference. In this task there was no problem of integrating responses; they were common words which were quickly acquired as responses. The interference occurred in attaching them to particular stimuli.

Such evidence as the above has led to the conclusion that DP will facilitate acquisition only when the interference impedes the integration of the response as such. In most of the situations occurring in our studies this has involved the integration of letters forming verbal units which are not words. However, an argument will be advanced later that if interference occurs among syllables in words, DP may also facilitate acquisition.

Types of Interference in Response Integration

The available evidence indicates that as long as interference attains a certain level in the response-acquisition stage, the source of the interference is irrelevant. The interference may derive from formal similarity by duplicating letters among nonsense and consonant syllables (e.g., Underwood & Schulz, 1959). It may stem from habits developed in learning previous lists in the laboratory (e.g., Underwood & Schulz, 1961a). Finally, the interference may come from letter sequence habits which have been built up during the lifetime of the subject. Thus, if the response required of the subject involves sequences of letters which run counter to strongly established letter-sequence habits, DP may facilitate acquisition (Underwood & Schulz, 1961b).

Analytical Implications

The evidence summarized above strongly suggests that interference in response integration is responsible for facilitation by DP. Furthermore, it has been shown that similarity among stimulus terms may actually retard learning by DP. Certain implications for analysis follows from this state of affairs.

1. In serial learning the functional stimulus for any given item in the list is essentially unknown. It may be serial position, the immediately preceding item, several preceding items, or some complex of all of these. Therefore, serial learning is not a task providing sufficient isolation between stimulus and response functions to produce critical theoretical decisions. This does not mean, of course, that serial learning will not respond to DP. Indeed, it has been found generally "easier" to get positive effects of DP for serial than for paired-associate lists, probably because of differences in rate of presentation usually employed (Hovland, 1949). But, if the inferences made earlier are correct, when the investigator cannot specify the locus of interference (among stimulus terms or among response terms), the worth of a task is much reduced for the study of DP.

2. The paired-associate task is most suited for decisive testing of hypotheses about how DP produces its effect. However, if interference occurs among stimulus terms, among response terms, and among stimulus and response terms—all simultaneously—the analytical capabilities of the task are greatly reduced. The use of counterbalanced designs may well "throw in" interference of an unspecifiable nature across lists. Thus, when such designs are used and when interference is ostensibly independently manipulated among stimulus terms and among response terms within lists, interlist interference may completely eliminate the analytical usefulness of these studies; that this seems to have been the case has been detailed elsewhere (Underwood, 1954).

Second Critical Variable: Length of Intertrial Interval

The length of intertrial interval is, obviously, a critical variable since it is an integral part of the defining operations for the phenomenon under consideration. So, therefore, the question asked about this variable concerns phenomena which may be correlated with variations in the intertrial interval.

If one asks the beginning student in elementary psychology what would happen if a rest interval were introduced as he was endeavoring to learn a list of words, a likely response would be that he would forget some of what he had learned. The logic of this position seems unassailable if we use rest intervals of an hour, a day, or a year. The line of evidence to be pursued is that measurable forgetting occurs over the short intervals used to define DP.

1. A study has been reported (Underwood & Schulz, 1961a) in which interference among stimuli in paired-associate lists was built up across four lists. In learning this fourth list, DP (1-minute interval) was somewhat inferior to MP. Since the responses in these lists for both studies were adjectives of low intralist and interlist similarity, the effect observed appears to result from interference in the associative or hook-up stage of learning. It is presumed that the DP interval results in more proactive interference than the MP interval. The effect of this interference on short-term forgetting may be indexed by determining on which trial responses were first correctly paired with their stimuli. A tally was made of the trial on which each response was first correctly paired with its stimulus (combining all subjects). Then, the percentage of total items first given correctly on each trial was determined; for presentation here, blocks of two trials have been combined. As seen in Figure 1, a greater percentage of responses was first paired correctly on

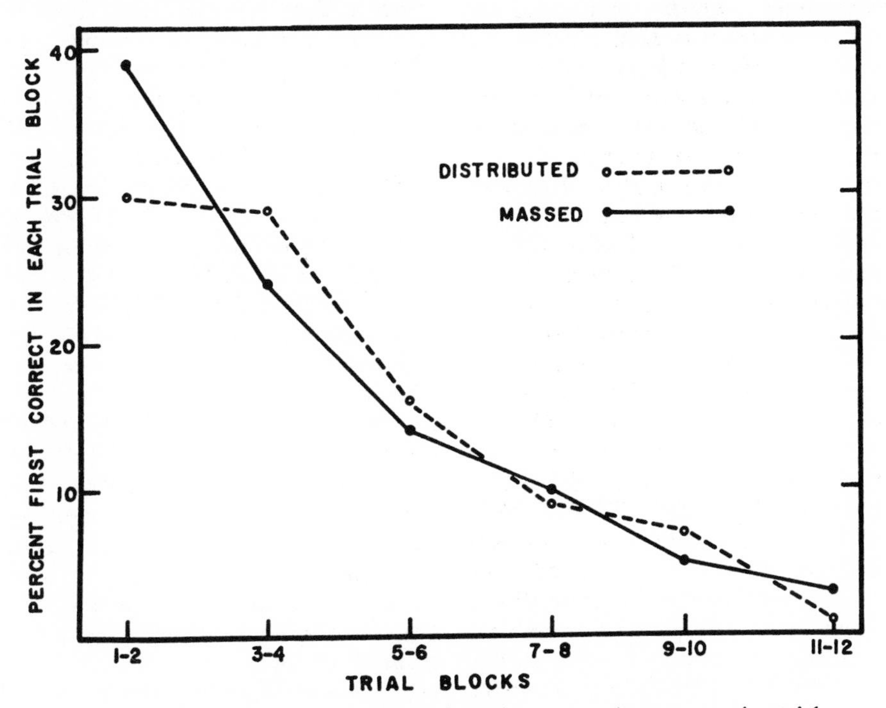

FIG. 1. Proportion of adjective responses first given correctly on successive trial blocks when learning was by massed practice and by distributed practice.

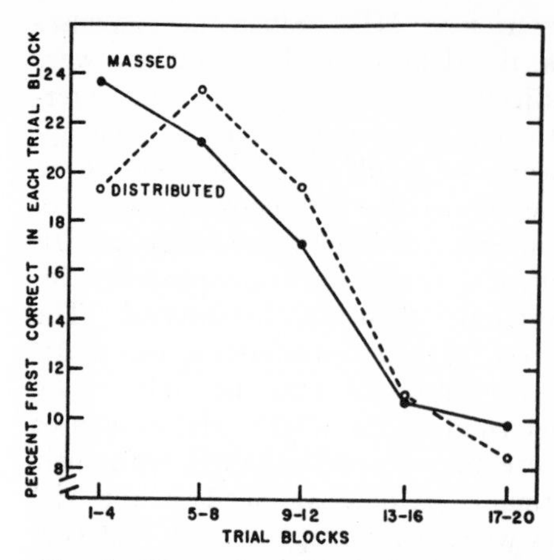

FIG. 2. Proportion of trigram responses first given correctly on successive trial blocks when learning was by massed practice and by distributed practice.

Trials 1 and 2 when learning was by MP than when it was by DP. There were 48 subjects in each condition; the t between the mean number of different items correctly anticipated on the first two trials is 2.03, which meets the 5% significance level. Of course, it must be remembered that for such short intervals no great amount of forgetting would be anticipated.

2. A comparable analysis has been made for quite a different kind of paired-associate list (Underwood & Schulz, 1961b). The response terms in these lists consisted of three-letter units (trigrams) constructed so as to have very low-associative connection between letters as determined by the Underwood-Schulz tables (1960). One of the three sets of response terms used is as follows: DSU, RZL, CFY, XBN, IGW, TPM, OVJ, KHQ. The learning of such responses appears to be heavily interfered with by well-established letter associations. Stimuli were single-digit numbers. Altogether, 70 subjects learned such a list under DP (30-second interval) and 70 with MP (4-second interval) for 20 trials. The learning under DP was not appreciably better than under MP (a matter for later discussion). The percentage of responses first given correctly in successive blocks of four trials is shown in Figure 2. This figure indicates that under DP the responses on the average are first given correctly at a later point in learning than under MP. The mean difference between MP and DP on the first block of trials fails to achieve an acceptable level of statistical significance, but that a true difference in forgetting is occurring is suggested by the next set of data.

3. A list was made up of single-digit numbers as stimuli and the eight above listed trigrams as responses. Thirty-six subjects, naive to verbal-learning experiments, were assigned on a random basis to one of two groups. Each group received 20 acquisition trials. One of the groups was given a 2-minute rest after Trial 9, and the other group a 2-minute rest after Trial 18. The rest interval in each case was filled by a symbol cancellation task commonly used to fill DP intervals (Underwood, 1952a).

The performance curves for these two groups are shown in Figure 3. Not only do the two groups differ significantly on Trial 10 ($t = 4.42$), but loss from Trial 9 to Trial 10 for the group given the rest interval is highly significant ($t = 3.05$). However, differences in performance on Trial 19, or the loss between Trials 18 and 19 for the group given the rest interval, do not even approach statistical significance. The fact that forgetting occurs after Trial 9 and not after Trial 18 would be anticipated on the basis of differences in level of learning attained at those two points. The major point to be made by these data, however, is that forgetting can be measured over short intervals early in learning when the response terms are

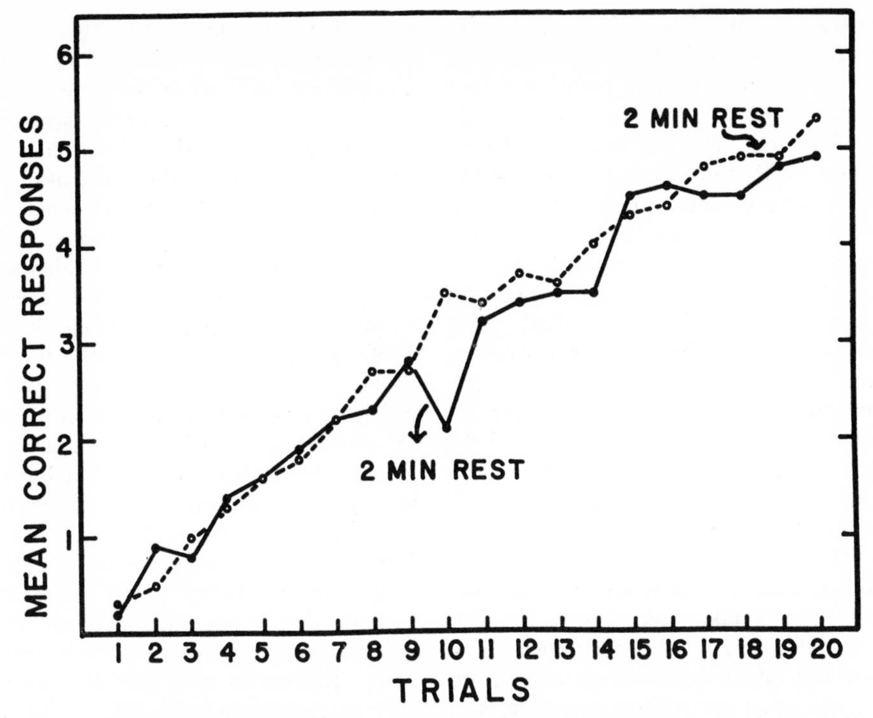

FIG. 3. Forgetting of trigram lists over a 2-minute interval when the interval is introduced after the ninth trial and after the eighteenth trial.

difficult ones to learn (presumably because of interference from stronger letter-association habits). That forgetting may occur over a 2-minute interval is quite in line with previous results using serial lists of consonant syllables (Underwood, 1957b).

4. In a published study (Underwood & Schulz, 1959) data have been presented on the learning of a serial list with high formal intralist similarity among consonant syllables. Four different intertrial intervals were used, namely, 2, 8, 17, and 38 seconds. Over an interval the subject may forget the response as such, or he may forget its proper position in the serial list. There is no evidence in this experiment that the syllables as such were forgotten over these short intervals, but the initial retention of the proper positions of the items in the list was impaired as a consequence of the interval. The measure used to demonstrate this is simply the mean number of items incorrectly positioned when first given. This measure is related to the length of the interval in Figure 4. The longer the interval the

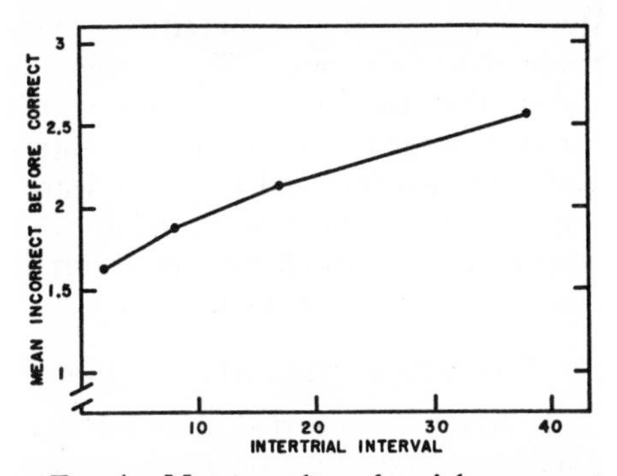

FIG. 4. Mean number of serial consonant syllables placed incorrectly before being placed correctly as a function of the length of the intertrial interval.

greater the number of items given incorrectly before being given correctly.

5. Finally, it may be mentioned that in a number of published studies (e.g., Underwood & Richardson, 1958) where DP did facilitate acquisition there was evidence during the initial trials that DP resulted in inferior performance. This effect may be attributed to proactive interference in cases where other lists had been learned previously. But the phenomenon has also been found with 38-second intervals in serial learning by naive subjects. The effect could be due to loss of warm-up over the interval during the early trials, but it is more likely due to forgetting.

The above evidence has been presented merely to demonstrate that forgetting has taken place over the DP interval in many of the studies. The purpose of demonstrating this is to suggest that in trying to understand how DP produces a positive effect the understanding of processes producing forgetting must be given a central role. To attain this goal, the evidence presented above is no substitute for extensive systematic studies of short-term retention using different materials for which interference possibilities are known. Since such studies are not available, certain assumptions will have to be made about how forgetting occurs over short intervals. The position is taken that the very processes which produce forgetting over the short intervals are also involved in better learning by DP. The resolution of these superficially contradictory positions is the next matter for discussion.

The Interaction Hypothesis

It has been asserted that DP will facilitate acquisition only when some minimal level of interference is present in the response-acquisition phase of learning. An interference theory of forgetting presumes that this same interference will produce forgetting. Forgetting will occur because interfering tendencies recover in strength over the interval; if the recovery is great enough, and if the intial association defining the correct response is weak, the recovered tendencies will block or replace the correct tendencies.

Evidence from recent experiments (Barnes, 1960; Barnes & Underwood, 1959) give firm support to the notion that verbal associations are extinguished or weakened by the occurrence of conflicting associations. There is also evidence that a process analogous to spontaneous recovery of extinguished associations occurs; this is fairly clear over long periods of rest (e.g., Briggs, 1954). But it is also evident that some such process may occur over very short intervals when error tendencies are initially strong and correct tendencies weak. In almost all of our studies of DP it has been found that more overt errors are made early in learning under DP than are made under MP. The one assumption which must be made, and it is an assumption for which direct independent evidence in the learning of verbal units is lacking, is that extinction of associations following recovery attains a greater "depth" than when such recovery does not occur. Under highly MP conditions such recovery is presumed not to occur (at least to any extent). Under DP there is successive recovery of error tendencies and successive extinctions. Under MP the error tendencies essentially remain suppressed but, at the same time, reduce the effective strength of the correct response tendency. Early in learning this reduction in effective strength of the correct response tendency may be less than that produced by the recovered tendency in DP; hence, forgetting under DP may be shown to be greater than under MP over the short intervals. But, as interfering associations are weakened by successive extinctions in DP—and not in MP—the situation becomes reversed as trials continue.

With the above conception in mind it can be seen why obtaining facilitation by DP is dependent upon a highly specific set of conditions. If DP is to produce facilitation, the following conditions must be met: (*a*) there must be some minimal amount of interference in response acquisition so that the integration of the components of the correct response by the subject is slow, (*b*) error tendencies must recover enough so that successive extinctions can be effective, but (*c*) the recovery must not be so great as to block or replace the correct association over several trials. The situation is most delicate early in learning when correct response tendencies are relatively weak and error tendencies relatively strong. Thus, the two critical manipulable variables are amount of interference and length of DP interval because these two variables allow indirect manipulation of strength of error tendencies and amount of recovery of error tendencies.

One of the implications of the above conception is that given at least some minimal amount of interference in response integration, a DP interval could be found which would facilitate acquisition. Data already published and data to be published do not completely conform to this expectation so that considerable evaluation is necessary.

Length of Interval

An examination of studies in which length of DP interval is varied does not give much support to the idea that length of DP interval is critical, given a certain level of intial interference. This is true in our studies and also in those of other investigators (e.g., Wright & Taylor, 1949). However, note can be taken of certain studies where there is suggestive evidence that longer DP intervals result in poorer learning than do shorter ones. For example, in one study (Underwood, 1953c) two independent experiments were done in which 60-second and 120-second DP intervals were used. The performance in both studies was poorer with 120 seconds than it was with 60 seconds. Such a result also occurred in another study where the intervals were 30 seconds and 60 seconds (Underwood, 1952a), but not in another of near comparable design (Underwood, 1952b). In still another study (Underwood & Richardson, 1955) there was no inversion in the relationship between length of DP interval and rate of learning up to 3 minutes. However, the present belief is that this relationship was confounded by a subject selection. The learning of difficult lists was carried until the subject achieved a criterion of one perfect trial. Total learning time was limited to a 50-minute period. If the subject did not achieve the criterion within that period he was dropped. The number of subjects dropped was directly related to length of DP interval. It is possible, therefore, that the longer the interval the greater the selection of subjects who could learn under the long DP intervals. It may be that those selected represent subjects whose short term memory was good.

The Wright-Taylor study, noted above, used DP intervals up to 8 minutes. Performance under the 8-minute condition was as good as under the shortest DP interval, which was 75 seconds, and all DP conditions were superior to MP (2 seconds). There are possibilities of rationalizing the results of this study so that it does not stand in such apparent contradiction to the position stated earlier. Interference involved would be fairly low and entirely of an intralist nature, since the subjects were apparently naive. It is possible that all recovery of intralist error tendencies that would occur had taken place in the shortest DP interval (75 seconds). Forgetting which might occur because of interference from outside sources would be slight for these naive subjects over the longest DP interval (8 minutes). Finally, cartoon reading was used to fill the DP intervals; this may be quite an ineffective method to prevent rehearsal.

In short, there is no evidence available which denies the possibility of full exploration of the notion that the critical interaction involved is that between amount of interference and length of DP interval.

Degree of Response Integration

Three paired-associate lists were made up in which response terms were trigrams of three different degrees of integration (Underwood & Schulz, 1961b). The list of initially low integration was made up of items comparable to those presented earlier in this paper. The higher the degree of integration, the easier it is to learn the list. A DP interval of 30 seconds did not produce positive effects for any of the three lists. However, the list of poorly integrated trigrams showed evidence of forgetting (as indicated in Figure 2) with an indication that DP was producing some facilitation near the end of the 20 trials given. This suggests that a shorter DP interval, perhaps 15 seconds, would result in significant facilitation in learning. If this is the case, however, why did the list of somewhat higher integration not show facilitation over 30 seconds? There are two possibilities. This list was much easier to learn than the list of low integration. It may not have met the minimum requirements for amount of response interference. If a list were constructed which is in between the low and medium list in terms of degree of integration such a list might show facilitation with a 30-second DP interval. The other possibility is that the relatively weak error tendencies in the medium list require a longer DP interval for recovery, such recovery being necessary for DP to facilitate.

It can be seen that in making the above predictions it is again necessary to specify a highly particular set of conditions before DP will facilitate learning. One strong reason for confidence in such predictions lies in the results of the following experiment, an experiment which was viewed as a method of manipulating initial response interference (Underwood & Schulz, 1961b).

Two paired-associate lists in which two-letter units were the response terms were constructed. In one list each of these bigram responses had low integration between the two letters, and in the other the integration was high. The units having low integration were: EY, CF, XV, DS, QW, JH, MK, RZ. Those having high integration were: MN, RA, CO, QU, XY, ET, JK, DI. The stimuli for both lists were single-digit numbers. The list of low initial integration was much more difficult to learn than the one with high integration. Furthermore, DP (30 seconds) significantly facilitated the learning of the list with poorly integrated items and had no effect on the list in which the bigrams were well integrated.

Thus, with a 30-second DP interval, the learning of the lists in which trigrams were responses was not facilitated, but the learning of bigrams was facilitated. That the number of letters is not the critical variable is shown by the fact that with single letters as responses DP did not facilitate (Underwood & Schulz, 1961b). The conclusion from these experiments is that there is a very sharp interaction between length of the DP interval and the amount of initial response interference. With the poorly integrated bigrams, the 30-second interval may have been about optimal; with the poorly integrated trigrams, this interval may have been too long. It is also possible that if response interference is too high, DP will never facilitate acquisition if the DP intervals are introduced at the start of learning. That is to say, any recovery of error tendencies may so retard learning that MP will be superior. However, this is not expected to be the case; rather, when interference is heavy, the expectation is that the DP interval must be short in order for facilitation to occur.

Words

To maintain that DP facilitates acquisition only when interference occurs in acquiring the responses as such requires a consideration of instances in which words have been used and in which DP has facilitated acquisition. The problem provided by these instances is simply this: if the interference must obtain during the response-integration phase, why should words ever be facilitated by DP? Before considering possible answers to this question, the facts concerning the effects of DP in the learning of word lists need to be reviewed.

Serial lists of adjectives, with relatively low intralist meaningful similarity, have been shown to be learned faster under DP than under MP (Underwood, 1951, 1953b; Underwood & Goad, 1951; Wilson, 1948). The differences have not always been statistically significant, but the consistency argues that DP is having some effect. In one study (Underwood & Goad, 1951) in which all adjectives within the serial list had the same core of meaning the effects of DP were greater than if the adjectives had relatively low meaningful similarity. In another study (Underwood, 1953b), where similarity was manipulated among clusters of words within serial lists, the effects of DP were small and did not differ as a function of the degree of similarity. No effect of DP has been noted when paired-associate lists of adjectives have been used (Underwood, 1953a).

All of the above studies used two-syllable adjectives. The position is taken here that difficulties may occur in integrating two-syllable adjectives in the same sense that these difficulties may occur in integrating two letters within a nonsense syllable or a consonant syllable. For example, consider a list in which two of the words are ROUNDED and CRUMBLING. Interference in integration could be indexed by the subject responding with ROUNDING and CRUMBLED. Thus, when syllables are interchangeable and the interchange still makes words—whether of the same part of speech or not—interference in response integration may occur. Such merger responses do in fact occur in the record sheets.

It would be presumed that when interference occurs among syllables of the words it would occur most severely when the correct syllable sequence has relatively weak associative connection and the incorrect relatively high. The situation may be viewed in exactly the same way as was done previously for letter sequences. It would be possible to construct lists in which the likelihood for interference varied from low to high among the syllables making up the words within a list. So far as is known, however, no such systematic data are available. Therefore, only the assertion can be made that syllabic interference is responsible for instances in which DP has facilitated the learning of word lists. Two sets of data are available, however, which indirectly support the position. These data have not been published elsewhere.

It was noted above that in one study (Underwood & Goad, 1951), learning of serial lists was facilitated by DP when all items in the list had the same core of meaning. In this counterbalanced study subjects learned a total of eight lists so that interlist syllabic interference could be built up. If the source of the interference is largely of an interlist nature, DP should not facilitate the acquisition of these lists if the subjects were relatively naive. A test of this implication was made. Two of the original high-similarity lists were used, each being learned by 12 subjects under MP (2 seconds) and 12 subjects under DP (30 seconds). Thus, 24 subjects learned under DP and 24 under MP. The lists were presented for 20 acquisition trials. While learning was more rapid under DP than under MP, the difference was far from being significant statistically. This finding, therefore, argues that the original results were at least in part an interlist effect; since several lists had been learned the possibilities of syllable interchange was much greater than in the present study.

In another study a serial list was constructed of 14 words. The 14 words, seven pairs of highly associated words from the Minnesota free-association norms (Russell & Jenkins, 1954), were as follows: TABLE, CHAIR, BED, SLEEP, NAIL, HAMMER, GIRL, BOY, SCISSORS, CUT, LOW, HIGH, LONG, SHORT. The words were randomized in terms of serial position within the list presented to the subject. The notion was that such a list would have rather high internal interference because of the strong associative connections existing between pairs of words. However, there should be low syllabic interference because many of the words have only one syllable. Response learning should take place very quickly but the existing associative connections should retard the associative phase of learning. Thirty naive subjects were presented the list (for 20 trials) under MP and 30 subjects under DP (2 seconds and 30 seconds, respectively). Learning by MP was not superior to that by DP. Thus, a word list with rather heavy interference, but an interference that did not prevail among syllables, was not facilitated by a 30-second DP interval.

It should be clear that the above two studies only indirectly support the idea that syllabic interference of a certain amount must be present before DP will facilitate the learning of word lists. Only studies specifically designed to vary syllabic interference will give a decision as to whether or not the position taken here is appropriate.

Related Variables and Phenomena

Serial Position Curve

In a recent study (Underwood & Schulz, 1959) it was noted that when DP facilitated the acquisition of serial lists the shape of the serial position curve differed for MP and DP. Learning under MP gave the classical bowed curve, clearly skewed so that the point of maximal difficulty was past the center of the list, and with the last few items in the list clearly being learned more slowly than the first few items. Under DP, however, the curve was almost symmetrical: very little skew was evident and the last items in the list were learned almost as rapidly as the first items in the list. The difference in the shapes of these curves led to the conclusion that DP facilitated learning in a direct relationship to the position of the item in the serial list: those items near the end of the list were greatly facilitated, those near the beginning were facilitated very little. The question raised here is whether or not this phenomenon should be given any theoretical importance in trying to understand how DP produces its effect. The conclusion is that it should not be given such status. The reason for this is that it is a phenomenon limited entirely to subjects naive to serial learning as experienced in the laboratory.

An examination has been made of a number of our previous studies in which subjects served for several days and learned several lists (e.g., Underwood & Richardson, 1955). In every case it was found that in learning the first list the above described difference in the shape of the serial position curve as a function of MP vs. DP was found, but after the subjects were practiced the differences disappeared and both the MP and DP serial position curves assumed the shape of the classical curve. This was true in spite of the fact that DP had facilitated learning at all stages of practice. Furthermore, with naive subjects learning lists which were not facilitated by DP, the last few items in the list were learned more rapidly under DP than under MP but at the expense of inferior performance on other items in the list, primarily those at the beginning.

Because of these facts it seems most reasonable to interpret this phenomenon as a side effect resulting from the introduction of the DP intervals to naive subjects. It may represent a short-term memory effect based on recency, or it may be that naive subjects adopt a different strategy of learning when given DP than when given MP. In any event, at the present time there seems to be no necessity to attach theoretical importance to the phenomenon when the theoretical interest is in understanding how DP produces its facilitating effect on learning.

Rate of Presentation

Previous investigators have shown that the faster the rate of presentation of a serial list (Hovland, 1938b), or of a paired-associate list (Hovland, 1949), the greater the facilitation by DP. This relationship (as well as others) has always been a compelling one for the introduction of an inhibitory construct in explanatory attempts. With such a construct it can be said that the faster the rate of presentation the greater the amount of inhibition built up, hence, the greater the positive effect of allowing the inhibition to dissipate over the DP intervals. The question for the moment, however, is how can the rate-of-presentation effect be handled by the present conception?

The slower the rate of presentation the greater the amount of response learning which occurs on any one trial. The greater the amount of response learning the less likely it is that recovered error tendencies will interfere, hence, the less the "need" for extinction. Presenting (at a relatively slow rate) a list in which considerable response integration is required is comparable to presenting a list of fairly well integrated responses at a fast rate. However, the present conception also leads to a prediction in which a slower rate of presentation would give greater facilitation by DP than would a faster rate. If a list of responses is used in which there is very heavy interference in response integration, the fast rate of presentation will allow so little learning to occur that with certain DP intervals the amount of forgetting would be greater than the positive effects of successive extinctions. A slower rate of presentation—allowing for greater response learning per trial—would give greater facilitation for this DP interval. So far as it is known, there are no data available for this test. To make the test, the following requirements must be met. First, a paired-associate list in which the responses are poorly integrated must be employed. As a guess, a list of poorly integrated trigrams (as presented earlier) would probably be satisfactory, perhaps with the inclusion of a small amount of formal similarity (duplicated letters). Second, the reduction in the rate of presentation must occur in the response inspection period, not in the anticipation period. Thus if the "slow" rate of presentation is 2 seconds for the anticipation period and 2 seconds for the stimulus and response together, a fast rate would be 2 seconds and 1 second, respectively. A reduction in the anticipation interval introduces differences in performance factors which are not included in the present conception. Finally, because of the sharp interaction presumed to occur between amount of interference and the DP interval, several DP intervals should be included. If the above suggested list is used, intervals of 15, 30, and 120 seconds should give full opportunity for the expected reversal in the rate-of-presentation relationship to occur. That is, if it does not occur at 30 seconds, it should occur at 120 seconds.

Length of List

Hovland (1940) has also shown that as the length of a serial list of nonsense syllables increases, a given DP interval facilitates acquisition more and more. One of the inevitable consequences of increasing the length of lists made up of such materials is to increase the amount of formal similarity, and with an increase in amount of formal similarity the greater the likelihood that DP will facilitate acquistion (e.g., Underwood & Richardson, 1958; Underwood & Schulz, 1959). If the amount of interference in response integration was below the optimal amount for the given DP interval, increasing the length of the list would increase the amount of interference toward the optimal. It is apparent that this conception immediately leads to a prediction in which length-of-list relationship as found by Hovland would break down. For, if the shortest list used had the amount of response interference that was optimal for a given DP interval, increasing the length of the list (thus increasing the amount of interference) would lead to less facilitation by DP than was true for the shorter list. No data are available to test this expectation.

Reminiscence in Recall

Reminiscence is demonstrated when recall following a short interval of rest is greater than if no rest occurred. As is well known, this is one of the most elusive phenomena extant in the whole area of verbal learning. Many investigators have been unable to produce the effect. Its magnitude, when found, is very small. For example, in Hovland's (1938a) first study the reminiscence at various points in learning varied from one-third to one-half an item out of a 12-item list. The appearance of the phenomenon is also acutely dependent upon the length of the rest interval (Ward, 1937). Just as the facilitation by DP is dependent upon a highly specific set of conditions, so too is the phenomenon of reminiscence. The present paper has attempted to integrate facts relating DP and learning through the use of certain notions about retention over short intervals. It is reasonable to expect, therefore, that these notions may have some relevance to reminiscence in recall.

When reminiscence is found it is under conditions of rather heavy interlist interference. With serial or paired-associate lists, there is no reason to believe that potential proactive interference tendencies, established by the learning of many earlier lists, are specific to only one item or one association in the list for which reminiscence is demonstrated. That is to say, a proactive error tendency may interfere with more than one item in a list. If this error tendency recovers over a reminiscence interval, it may reach a strength that will interfere with a response but not prevent its correct anticipation. However, with such an error tendency having recovered a certain amount, but with the correct response being anticipated correctly in spite of the recovery, some extinction of that error tendency should occur. If, as presumed above, this error tendency could interfere with other items in the list, especially ones near the anticipatory threshold, a consequence of this partial extinction is to reduce the interference on these near-threshold items. This should give them a slightly higher probability of being correct, thus producing reminiscence.

Again it is clear that this conception of how reminiscence may ocur necessitates a highly specific set of circumstances. The amount of recovery of the error tendency must be "just right," hence the amount of interference and length of interval again become the critical manipulable variables. Furthermore, the interfering tendency must potentially interfere with more than one item so that its partial extinction (when it occurs in conjunction with one response) will reduce the likelihood that it will interfere with other responses. Finally, a single extinction of the interfering tendency must reduce its actual interference effects for other items below those effects which prevail for the same error tendency under the no-rest (control) condition. To suggest that this extraordinarily specific set of conditions must be met before reminiscence can be demonstrated does not seem entirely unreasonable in view of the ephemeral nature of the phenomenon.

Two other comments should be made about reminiscence in recall. First, the above notions have been applied to the situation in which there is interlist interference. In studies of DP, both interlist and intralist interference can produce a positive effect for DP. There appears to be no reason why reminiscence could not be demonstrated with intralist interference with naive subjects, as long as the above mentioned set of conditions are met. That is, there must be interfering tendencies which are not specific to a given response unit, and the amount of interference and length of interval must be coordinated. The present belief is that once these more critical relationships are plotted for DP, it will be a much easier task to specify the exact conditions necessary for the production of reminiscence than is possible at the present time.

The second point to be made is that it is still barely possible that reminiscence is an artifact of the color-naming activity used to fill the interval in many studies. The rationale for this has been outlined elsewhere (Archer, 1953), and in spite of the negative results of Archer's test of this notion, it is conceivable that the conditons necessary to produce this artificial reminiscence are also specific and that these conditions were not met in the test made.

Reminiscence in Relearning

Certain studies have shown that whereas a single rest interval introduced during the acquisition of a list may not produce enhanced recall after the interval, subsequent learning will be facilitated. Studies of this type are illustrated by the work of Riley (1953, 1954, 1957). In Riley's studies, subjects learned two lists of paired-associate nonsense syllables of low meaningfulness. Since intralist formal similarity was low, interlist similarity among responses was appreciable. A single 2-minute rest interval introduced during the learning of the second list produced some facilitation in subsequent learning although no reminiscence was apparent on the recall trial. No effect was noted when only a single list was learned; therefore, it seems evident that the presence of interlist interference was a critical component for the phenomenon. Furthermore, since the effect occurred whether the two lists had the same stimuli and different responses or different stimuli and different responses, it may also be concluded that the critical interference is not in the stimulus-response relationships. In line with previous work on DP, therefore, it seems likely that the critical locus of interference is in response integration. If this is the case, the single-trial extinction hypothesis can be applied; the interval allows recovery of errors which are extinguished a certain amount; hence, interference with subsequent learning is less than if the interval had not been introduced.

Why does not reminiscence occur on the recall trial immediately after the interval? The reason for this may be that the interference is specific between a response term in the first list and one in the second, e.g., those that begin with the same first letter. If this is the case, extinction of this specific interfering tendency cannot influence the recall of other items on the recall trial since they are interfered with by other specific tendencies.

If this interpretation of Riley's work is appropriate, it would obviously be predicted that no reminiscence effect would be found if the response terms were common one-syllable words. This prediction would hold regardless of the materials used for stimuli and regardless of the relationships between the stimuli in the two lists.

Meaningfulness

There is some evidence that the lower the meaningfulness of the materials the greater the likelihood that DP will facilitate learning. Tsao (1948) concluded this as a result of his experiment, but it is possible that meaningfulness and formal intralist similarity were confounded in his study (Underwood & Richardson, 1958). Nevertheless, in terms of the conception advanced here, meaningfulness should be a variable determining DP effects because in general the lower the meaningfulness the lower the degree of response integration (Underwood & Schulz, 1960). And, as stated several times earlier, the lower the degree of response integration the greater the susceptibility of these responses to interference effects. However, if experiments are performed in which the complete range of meaningfulness is used, but with a single DP interval, the results are not likely to meet expectations. This failure would result from the interaction between amount of interference and length of DP interval. Finally, it should be mentioned again that when interference in integrating responses is very heavy—as it may be with material of very low meaningfulness—it is possible that amount of forgetting occurring over even a short DP interval will be too great to expect overall facilitation.

SUMMARY

This paper presents a conception of how distributed practice facilitates the acquisiton of verbal lists. The evidence indicates that distributed practice will enhance learning only when interference occurs in the response-learning phase. This interference reduces the effective response strength of the correct response. With the introduction of a rest interval, error tendencies recover in strength, but with subsequent occurrences of the correct response the error tendency is extinguished. Thus, distributed practice allows for successive extinctions of error tendencies and the assumption is that such a process results in a more effective elimination of the deleterious effects of interference than occurs under massed practice. Under massed practice error tendencies are assumed to be suppressed rather than extinguished.

This conception makes amount of response interference and length of the distribution interval the two critical variables in determining whether or not distributed practice will facilitate learning. In general, the greater the interference the shorter must the distribution interval be for facilitation to occur. If interference is high, and the interval too long, forgetting will occur because of the weak development of the associative strength of the components of the correct response on any one trial and the recovery of the error tendencies will persistently block or replace the correct response. Therefore, for distributed practice to facilitate learning when response interference is heavy, the distribution interval must be short. It is possible that when interference is very heavy, distributed practice will never facilitate learning.

The effects of several other variables, including length of list, rate of presentation, single short rest intervals (reminiscence), and meaningfulness were evaluated. Certain predictions were advanced concerning the effect of these variables when more thoroughly explored.

It should be noted that there are certain "soft" spots in the conception as presented.

1. At the present time the minimal amount of initial interference necessary before a distribution interval of any length will facilitate acquisition cannot be independently specified. The same is true with maximal amount of initial interference.

2. It has been noted that the necessary interference must occur in the response-learning stage; interference in associating the stimulus term with the response term is irrelevant. There is no apparent logical or theoretical reason why the effect of these two sources of interference should be different; however, the data overwhelmingly support the generalization that the interference must be localized in the response term.

3. While the ideas that error tendencies recover with rest, and that they can be extinguished, have independent empirical backing, the notion that recovered error tendencies are more effectively extinguished than nonrecovered tendencies has been developed merely to fit the demands of the data.

The dissatisfaction with these matters may disappear in the research of the next 10 years.

REFERENCES

ARCHER, E. J. Retention of serial nonsense syllables as a function of rest-interval responding rate and meaningfulness. *J. exp. Psychol.*, 1953, **45**, 245–252.

Barnes, Jean M. "Fate" revisited. Unpublished PhD dissertation, Northwestern University, 1960.

Barnes, Jean M., & Underwood, B. J. "Fate" of first-list associations in transfer theory. *J. exp. Psychol.*, 1959, **58**, 97–105.

Briggs, G. E. Acquisition, extinction, and recovery functions in retroactive inhibition. *J. exp. Psychol.*, 1954, **47**, 285–293.

Hovland, C. I. Experimental studies in rote-learning theory: I. Reminiscence following learning by massed and by distributed practice. *J. exp. Psychol.*, 1938, **22**, 201–224. (a)

Hovland, C. I. Experimental studies in rote-learning theory: III. Distribution of practice with varying speeds of syllable presentation. *J. exp. Psychol.*, 1938, **23**, 172–190. (b)

Hovland, C. I. Experimental studies in rote-learning theory: VII. Distribution of practice with varying lengths of list. *J. exp. Psychol.*, 1940, **27**, 271–284.

Hovland, C. I. Experimental studies in rote-learning theory: VIII. Distributed practice of paired associates with varying rates of presentation. *J. exp. Psychol.*, 1949, **39**, 714–718.

Riley, D. A. Reminiscence effects in paired-associate learning. *J. exp. Psychol.*, 1953, **45**, 232–238.

Riley, D. A. Further studies of reminiscence effects with variations in stimulus-response relationships. *J. exp. Psychol.*, 1954, **48**, 101–105.

Riley, D. A. The influence of amount of prerest learning on reminiscence effects in paired-associate learning. *J. exp. Psychol.*, 1957, **54**, 8–14.

Russell, W. A., & Jenkins, J. J. The complete Minnesota norms for responses to 100 words, from the Kent-Rosanoff Word Association Test: Studies on the role of language in behavior. Technical Report No. 11, 1954, University of Minnesota, Contract Nonr-66216.

Tsao, J. C. Studies in spaced and massed learning: II. Meaningfulness of material and distribution of practice. *Quart. J. exp. Psychol.*, 1948, **1**, 79–84.

Underwood, B. J. Studies of distributed practice: III. The influence of stage of practice in serial learning. *J. exp. Psychol.*, 1951, **42**, 291–295.

Underwood, B. J. Studies of distributed practice: VI. The influence of rest-interval activity in serial learning. *J. exp. Psychol.*, 1952, **43**, 329–340. (a)

Underwood, B. J. Studies of distributed practice: VII. Learning and retention of serial nonsense lists as a function of intralist similarity. *J. exp. Psychol.*, 1952, **44**, 80–87. (b)

Underwood, B. J. Studies of distributed practice: IX. Learning and retention of paired adjectives as a function of intralist similarity. *J. exp. Psychol.*, 1953, **45**, 143–149. (a)

Underwood, B. J. Studies of distributed practice: X. The influence of intralist similarity on learning and retention of serial adjective lists. *J. exp. Psychol.*, 1953, **45**, 253–259. (b)

Underwood, B. J. Studies of distributed practice: XI. An attempt to resolve conflicting facts on retention of serial nonsense lists. *J. exp. Psychol.*, 1953, **45**, 355–359. (c)

Underwood, B. J. Intralist similarity in verbal learning and retention. *Psychol. Rev.*, 1954, **61**, 160–166.

Underwood, B. J. Studies of distributed practice: XV. Verbal concept learning as a function of intralist interference. *J. exp. Psychol.*, 1957, **54**, 33–40. (a)

Underwood, B. J. Studies of distributed practice: XVI. Some evidence on the nature of the inhibition involved in massed learning of verbal materials. *J. exp. Psychol.*, 1957, **54**, 139–143. (b)

Underwood, B. J., & Archer, E. J. Studies of distributed practice: XIV. Intralist similarity and presentation rate in verbal-discrimination learning of consonant syllables. *J. exp. Psychol.*, 1955, **50**, 120–124.

Underwood, B. J., & Goad, D. Studies of distributed practice: I. The influence of intralist similarity in serial learning. *J. exp. Psychol.*, 1951, **42**, 125–134.

Underwood, B. J., & Richardson, J. Studies of distributed practice: XIII. Interlist interference and the retention of serial nonsense lists. *J. exp. Psychol.*, 1955, **50**, 39–46.

Underwood, B. J., & Richardson, J. Studies of distributed practice: XVIII. The influence of meaningfulness and intralist similarity of serial nonsense lists. *J. exp. Psychol.*, 1958, **56**, 213–219.

Underwood, B. J., Runquist, W. N., & Schulz, R. W. Response learning in paired-associate lists as a function of intralist similarity. *J. exp. Psychol.*, 1959, **58**, 70–78.

Underwood, B. J., & Schulz, R. W. Studies of distributed practice: XIX. The influence of intralist similarity with lists of low meaningfulness. *J. exp. Psychol.*, 1959, **58**, 106–110.

Underwood, B. J., & Schulz, R. W. *Meaningfulness and verbal learning.* Chicago: Lippincott, 1960.

Underwood, B. J., & Schulz, R. W. Studies of distributed practice: XX. Sources of interference associated with differences in learning and retention. *J. exp. Psychol.*, 1961, **61**, 228–235. (a)

Underwood, B. J., & Schulz, R. W. Studies of distributed practice: XXI. The effect of interference from language habits. *J. exp. Psychol.*, 1961, in press. (b)

Ward, L. B. Reminiscence and rote learning. *Psychol. Monogr.*, 1937, **49** (4, Whole No. 220).

Wilson, J. T. The formation and retention of remote associations in rote learning. Unpublished PhD dissertation, Stanford University, 1948.

Wright, S. T., & Taylor, D. W. Distributed practice in verbal learning and the maturation hypothesis. *J. exp. Psychol.*, 1949, **39**, 527–531.

(Received September 9, 1960)

CHAPTER 4

Acquisition as a Function of Meaningfulness and Familiarization

If one were to conduct a popularity poll among contemporary verbal learning psychologists for the general research area of greatest interest, a leading contestant would undoubtedly be the area covered in this chapter. There are a number of reasons for this popularity. Perhaps the greatest is the fact that, outside of the nebulous variable of aptitude (or plain old "individual differences" in learning ability), variation of meaningfulness, or related dimensions, seems to account for more of the variance in acquisition than any other single variable.

Meaningfulness of learning materials, and its relationship to learning phenomena, is by no means a new area of study. Ebbinghaus (1885) introduced the problem of meaningfulness, actually in absentia, so to speak, by attempting to study (with himself as the only *S*) the acquisition and forgetting of materials *devoid* of meaningfulness. His goals were to investigate the acquisition of verbal learning lists under various conditions and then, particularly, to relate the condition-acquisition relationships to the course of forgetting over time. Accomplishment of these goals required, he believed, learning materials for which there were no previously acquired associations. Thus, the associative processes of acquisition and forgetting could be investigated from scratch—that is, the associations would begin with a prelaboratory strength of zero. His solution to the learning materials requirement took the form of an invention of great import on the future of verbal learning. The invention was that of the nonsense syllable—a three letter combination which in toto does not form a meaningful world. Most nonsense syllables in current use are three letter sequences (trigrams) in the order of consonant–vowel–consonant (CVC syllables).

The fact that many nonsense syllables are *not* devoid of associations became apparent years later when Glaze (1928), in standardizing the association-values (see the following section) of CVC (including "y" as a vowel) syllables, discovered that their meaningfulness (as association-value) actually ranged from 0 to 100 per cent. Gradually a new era of interest in meaningfulness began growing, albeit a bit amorphously until the contemporary period. This interest has centered largely on the empirical relationships between meaningfulness and acquisition, with frequent excursions into explanations of these relationships.

The contemporary period has also been graced by an intensive interest in a concept related, but nevertheless differing in many respects, to meaningfulness. This is the concept of "meaning" and its implications for verbal learning.

Meaning, as used here, encompasses the kinds of mediating processes closely identified with Hullian learning theory (pure stimulus acts, conditioned fractional responses and their response-produced stimuli, etc.). The work of Osgood (e.g., Osgood, Suci, and Tannenbaum, 1957) on the semantic differential measure stands out in this approach. The nature of any overlap between meaningfulness, as discussed in this chapter, and meaning of the Osgood variety is considered by the editor to lie outside of the scope of this book. The reader will profit greatly, however, from reading an excellent article by Staats and Staats (1959) on this issue.

For pedantic purposes the topics covered in this Introduction and reflected in the selected articles are organized into four components of the broader meaningfulness–acquisition problem. If subjected to a factor analysis, the components would most likely be identified as having some commonality of variance, but they seem sufficiently pure to demand separate consideration. The four components are: Methods of Measuring Meaningfulness, Meaningfulness and Acquisition, Other Variables Related to Meaningfulness, and Familiarization.

Methods of Measuring Meaningfulness

Assuming, with obvious face validity, that verbal learning materials run the gamut from very low to very high degrees of meaningfulness, the psychologist is still confronted with the formidable task of measuring differences in meaningfulness. One approach is to begin with an operational definition of meaningfulness that is generally accepted by psychologists, select a heterogeneous group of related materials for which the definition applies, and finally, scale psychometrically individual differences among representative *Ss* in response to these materials. The individual difference measures are then interpreted as reflecting varying degrees of meaningfulness within the selected materials. This broad strategy was initiated by Glaze's (1928) early standardization of nonsense syllables and has continued full steam into the contemporary period. A second approach is to define meaningfulness in terms of prior exposure to materials and then subject groups of *Ss* to varying degrees of such exposure under rigorous laboratory conditions. This is the method of familiarization that will be treated in a subsequent section of this Introduction.

Individual difference measures have at their operational base some description of the number of associations an item has attached to it. Three specific strategies have evolved from this base. Each one provides an assessment, via a different route, of the extensity of these associations (i.e., degree of meaningfulness). The first strategy, attributable originally to Glaze, computes association-values as normative percentage scores.

Association Value

Glaze employed a group of fifteen *Ss*, with each *S* being exposed to every one of over two thousand CVC syllables for approximately 2 seconds. The *Ss* were asked to tell, in a word or two, if a given syllable meant something to them. Consider a syllable like VIP. We would most likely find that all 15 *Ss* in a sample comparable to that of Glaze's would quickly blurt out a word or two in response to the syllable. In Glaze terminology, 100 per cent of the sample responding to a syllable constitutes "100 per cent association value," or, in other words, a very high degree of meaningfulness. On the other hand, a syllable like XEJ might encounter a complete vacuum of responding by the *Ss* and be assigned an association-value of 0 per cent. Similarly, another syllable might elicit associations from five *Ss* but none from the remaining ten *Ss*. Its association value becomes 33 per cent in Glaze-like norms. In this manner, the entire continuum from 0 to 100 per cent may be represented by specific syllables.

Following Glaze, several other standardizations of association values have appeared (Hull, 1933; Krueger, 1934; Trapp and Kausler, 1959; Witmer, 1935), including one (Witmer) in which the universe of items was expanded into the realm of CCC syllables. A monumental restandardization of Glaze's CVC syllables appeared in 1960 (Archer, 1960). The Archer values have recently been supplanting the out-of-date (largely as a consequence of the influx of alphabetization within our society) Glaze values in most of the post-1960 studies relating association value to acquisition.

Within the current Zeitgeist of meaningfulness calibration has become highly contagious, with association-value type measures spreading to materials other than verbal items. Association values are now available for nonsense shapes (Vanderplas and Garvin, 1959), and rated association values (see below) have been established for the numbers 0 to 100 (Battig and Spera, 1962). Thus, the verbal learning psychologist is beginning to accumulate an arsenal of calibrated materials that spans a wide range of verbal involvement.

Production Value (*m*)

Noble (1952a; Article 1) introduced a second methodology, and a related new conceptualization of meaningfulness, that served to incorporate meaningfulness into a broader learning theory framework. His conceptualization conformed closely to the Hullian concept of habit strength (Hull, 1943), but in terms of the number (i.e., extensity) of *St-R* associations evoked by a verbal item as a stimulus rather than the more restrictive use of habit strength as an index of intensity of a single *S-R* bond (see Noble, 1963, pp. 82–86, for a further account of his rationale). Unlike the association-value method, where the mere presence or absence of an association is recorded for each *S*, the production method assesses the number of continued (i.e., successively elicited) associations *S* has to a given item during a standard time period (e.g., 60 seconds in Noble's 1952a study). A production value, or index of meaningfulness (designated *m* by Noble), is computed for each of the scaled items by finding the mean number of associations for the total N of the normative sample (i.e., the arithmetic mean). In this way, Noble (1952a) computed *m* for 96 two-syllable items, ranging from paralogs of low meaningfulness (e.g., gojey) to highly meaningful words (e.g., kitchen).

The major advantage of production values over association values rests in the applicability of the former to variations in meaningfulness of formal words. Association value is insensitive to the nuances of meaningfulness at the high end of the scale. Most words of our everyday language are likely to elicit at least one association, which is all that is called for in the association-value method, but they may still vary greatly in the total number of associations they arouse. The association-value method would by necessity classify all such words in the 100 per cent category. Finer gradations of classification are accessible by the production method.

The production method may also be more sensitive than the association-value method for nonsense syllables at the upper end of the meaningfulness continuum. Mandler (1955) determined the *m* values for 100 syllables selected from the Glaze (1928) and Krueger (1934) standardizations. His *m* values correlated only moderately (*r* of .65) with conventional association values. Noble (1963) has pointed out that the covariation between *m* and association value is curvilinear, due to the insensitivity of association value at the upper range of meaningfulness (just as it is for words). Nevertheless, most psychologists relating meaningfulness to verbal learning seem to prefer association value as their index when they employ nonsense syllables as components of their learning tasks.

Rated Value

A third approach to measuring meaningfulness is to have *Ss* rate a series of items along some specified dimension. The rated value of an item is then its mean rating for a normative sample. This technique was introduced by Noble, Stockwell, and Pryor (1957). Their *Ss* were asked to rate 100 nonsense syllables on a five point scale in terms of the number of things or ideas the item made them think of. Noble (1963) has shown that rated values correlate moderately (*rs* of about .72) with production values for nonsense syllables. Rated values are also available for dissyllabic nouns (Noble, 1963). These ratings appear to correlate highly (*r* of .92) with *m* values for the same nouns. Finally, Noble (1961) has provided rated values transformed to a Thurstone interval scale equivalent for 2100 syllables. However, rated values, for either words or syllables, have not been widely used as an index of meaningfulness in verbal learning studies.

Meaningfulness and Acquisition

Glaze's standardization opened the door for entry into the area of the meaningfulness-acquisition relationship, but the psychologists of the 1930's infrequently set foot inside. A few studies with association value as the independent variable were conducted on SL (Davis, 1930; Sauer, 1930) and on free recall (items presented serially but recalled during performance in any order; McGeoch, 1930). The effect of meaningfulness was found by these investigators to be positive and, when more than two levels of meaningfulness were employed (McGeoch, 1930), roughly linear in form. An early study of special importance was that of Cason (1933). This was the first study to employ PA lists in order to contrast the relative effects of *St* and *R* meaningfulness on acquisition. Cason's results suggested that meaninfulness of the two components had comparable effects on acquisition. The contemporary period was ushered in by Noble's (1952a; Article 1) new approach to the measurement problem and his parallel laboratory studies on acquisition (see below). In between the Cason and Noble efforts the output of research on meaningfulness-acquisition was sporadic. One important intervening milestone was Sheffield's (1946) repetition of the Cason procedure. This time the outcome revealed a greater effect for variation in *R* meaningfulness than in *St* meaningfulness. The differential effects of *St* and *R* meaningfulness, and explanations for such differences, have become central contemporary issues.

We shall survey the literature on SL first and then turn to the more analytical studies on PA acquisition. The studies surveyed have typically employed one of the group-normative measures of meaningfulness described earlier. The curious reader may wonder if it may not be more advantageous for the psychologist to use meaningfulness scores based on individual measures of the specific *Ss* learning the list rather than to rely on norms from a distant standardization sample. Actually, there is evidence (Cochran and Wickens, 1963) which suggests that group measures are superior to individual measures in predicting rate of acquisition. Further probes into the likely causes of this superiority have not yet been reported in the literature.

Serial Learning

Noble (1952b) related his *m* values to SL, with *m* being sampled at three widely disparate levels. He found difficulty of SL to be a negatively accelerated function of increasing *m* that may be expressed mathematically as a decreasing exponential function. In other words, from low to moderate *m* there appeared to be a pronounced reduction in learning difficulty; from moderate to high *m* the reduction was considerably less pronounced.

In the same study, Noble also related *m* to individual differences in learning ability and to serial position effects. His results suggested that slow learners are more sensitive to variations in *m* than are fast learners. As to absolute serial position effects (see introductory section of Chapter 1), he found an increasing flattening of the error distribution over positions as *m* increased. McCrary and Hunter (1953) and Braun and Heymann (1958) also related meaningfulness (nonsense syllables versus words in the former and differential *m* items in the latter) to serial position effects. In both studies the authors reported an effect comparable to Noble's for absolute error distribution, but they found no effect for *m* on relative error distribution.

Paired-Associate Learning

Contemporary research on "PA acquisition as a function of meaningfulness" began with a study by Kimble and Dufort (1955). They selected pairs of words from the complete range of Noble's *m* scale and inserted the pairs into a mixed list (a mixed list is one of heterogeneous content—in this case, *m* is matched within a pair for *St* and *R* components, but the matched *m* value varies from pair to pair). Their results indicated that difficulty of acquisition increases as *m* decreases *up to a point*. With pairs of very low *m*, they found evidence for a facilitative effect on acquisition which they interpreted in terms of a Gestalt-like isolation phenomenon (cf. Chapter 5); that is, low *m* pairs seemed, to Kimble and Dufort, to be "perceptually isolated" from the other pairs in the list. Kimble and Dufort (1955) conducted a second experiment in the same study which placed the isolation phenomenon primarily in the *St* component of the pairs.

The Kimble and Dufort procedure was soon replicated by Noble and McNeely (1957) but with more pairs included at each point sampled along the *m* continuum. This time a more regularly increasing difficulty with decreasing *m* was detected, leading Noble and McNeely to conclude that the perceptual isolation effect of the previous study may have been an artifact resulting from inadequate sampling of the pairs at the low end of the *m* scale. At any rate, perceptually oriented explanations of meaningfulness-acquisition relationships have not attracted many adherents.

The Cason-Sheffield problem area (see p. 185) of *St* and *R* as separate loci of meaningfulness effects has been frequently revisited in recent years. Although both Cason (1933) and Sheffield (1946) found an overall beneficial effect of increasing meaningfulness, regardless of locus, they disagreed as to the relative contributions of *St* and *R*. Mandler and Campbell (1957) further compounded the disparity with results which disagreed with both of the earlier studies! They found high meaningfulness to be more potent when varied in the *St* component than in the R component, rather than vice versa as in Sheffield's findings.

Subsequent studies (e.g., Cieutat, Stockwell, and Noble, 1958; Hunt, 1959; Article 2) have been more consistent in that they have reported findings in closer agreement with those of Sheffield. The Hunt study (Article 2) is illustrative of the research design typically employed in this problem area. Low (*L*) and high (*H*) meaningful (as defined by any one of the standard measures) *St* components are factorially combined with *L* and *H* response components to yield *H-H*, *L-H*, *H-L*, and *L-L*, *St-R* combinations. (Hunt also related meaningfulness to *R-St* learning; for a discussion of this problem area the reader is referred to the introductory section of Chapter 2.) The fact that ease of acquisition generally falls into the precise order listed above (i.e., *H-H*, easiest to *L-L*, hardest) supports the contention that variation in *R* meaningfulness is more prodigious than variation in *St* meaningfulness.

Explanations of the positive function between meaningfulness and PA acquisition, with the issue of *St* and *R* contributions as a significant by-product, have traversed two major dissident paths. One stresses motor-patterning concepts; the other fits meaningfulness into the broader perspective of stage analysis (cf. Introduction, Chapter 2 for a discussion of stage analysis).

According to a motor-patterning concept (Cieutat, Stockwell, and Noble, 1958; Goss, Nodine, Gregory, Taub, and Kennedy, 1962; Noble, 1955), verbal units of high meaningfulness are likely to be better integrated, in the sense of consistent pronunciation and/or spelling than are units of low meaningfulness. When the *R* component of a PA list is in question, a highly meaningful *R* will probably elicit from *S* only one form of "saying" or spelling that *R* (i.e., responses to the *R* component as a stimulus-like term). On the other hand, a component of low meaningfulness will probably elicit a number of qualitatively different pronouncing, spelling, etc. responses. Consequently, the overall rate of acquisition should be faster in the former case in that fewer responses are required to be associated with the discriminable cues of the *St* component. Moreover, responses to *R* components of high meaningfulness are likely to have shorter latencies and shorter durations than are responses to *R* components of low meaningfulness. This would provide more available time for rehearsal (in this instance, covert practice) of the *St-R* association during the brief exposures of paced practice when *R* is of high rather than low meaningfulness. Similarly, high and low meaningful *St* would differ in the stability and consistency of their recognition responses (cf. introductory section and Article 3, Chapter 2).

The stage analysis view of the meaningfulness-acquisition relationship, parts of which have already been touched upon in the Introduction to Chapter 2, has been elegantly presented by Underwood and Schulz (1960a). In this view, one vehicle by which meaningfulness relates to PA acquisition is by way of a frequency of prior experience-rate of emission-availability for association-chain of events. This chain is of direct concern to the first or response learning stage of PA acquisition. *R* components of differential meaningfulness, as measured, say, by association-value, are presumed to reflect variations in prior frequency of experience with these components—the higher the meaningfulness, the greater the degree of prior frequency. In turn, the order in which *R* components are emitted or "spewed" (hence the name spew hypothesis given by Underwood and Schulz (1960a, p. 86) to the frequency-order of emission effect) during acquisition is a direct function of frequency. High meaningful *R* components are regarded as being emitted earlier in practice than are low meaningful components, and are also available for hook-up with *St* components at an earlier point in practice. In the associative stage of acquisition, meaningfulness of both *St* and *R* components is hypothesized to be a factor through the number of associates to the components that are accessible for mediating the hook-up of *St* and *R* (cf. Introduction, Chapter 2, p. 67). This is known as the principle of associative probability. To recapitulate, *R* meaningfulness is a factor in both stages of acquisition, but *St* meaningfulness is involved in only the second or associative stage—thereby accounting for the supposedly greater effect of variation in the meaningfulness of *R* than of *St*.

Stage-analytic research of the post-Underwood and Schulz period has attempted to sharpen our understanding of the relative contributions of *St* and *R* meaningfulness. Illustrative of this research is the study by Epstein and Streib (1962; Article 3) in which the response learning stage was presumably eliminated from acquisition by means of a recognition procedure which obviated the response recall feature of the conventional anticipation method. Epstein and Streib found that under these conditions *St* meaningfulness contributed a more potent effect on the associative stage of acquisition than did *R* meaningfulness. A literal interpretation of the Underwood and Schulz position would predict that there should be little difference between *St* and *R*, with regard to meaningfulness, in this stage. However, subsequent studies by Epstein himself (Epstein, 1963; Epstein and Platt, 1964) have "muddied the waters" a bit and have left us with a less than unequivocal acceptance of the position that *St* meaningfulness is definitely more important than *R* meaningfulness in the associative stage. The oft-cited conclusion in verbal learning seems in order once more—more research is obviously needed.

Other Variables Related to Meaningfulness

There are several other variables which, though generically related to meaningfulness, are sufficiently distinctive to require a separate discussion. Although meaningfulness has been placed squarely in the center of the research arena, these other related variables have been displaced to a more peripheral position. Nevertheless, periodic activity has revolved around two of these variables: familiarity and pronunciability.

Familiarity

The familiarity of a verbal unit is generally used in verbal learning to indicate the frequency with which *Ss* have experienced that unit. Frequency here refers to prelaboratory, everyday experience as opposed to deliberate laboratory familiarization (see the following section). Psychometrically, familiarity may be measured by a rating-scale method similar to the rated value measure of meaningfulness (see p. 185 of this introduction); that is, *Ss* are asked to rate words or nonsense syllables in terms of how frequently they have experienced them. Familiarity ratings of the words in Noble's *m* scale have been compiled by Noble himself (1953). The fact that familiarity, defined in the foregoing manner, is closely related to meaningfulness, defined by the number of associates, is attested to by the high but slightly curvilinear correlation (a coefficient of correlation of .92; Noble, 1953) between them. Noble (1953, 1955) has traced the covariation between familiarity and meaningfulness to their common dependence on frequency of prior experience. But to Noble (1963), and probably to most other psychologists active in this area, there is an important difference between the two. Noble's distinction is the fact that familiarity is the consequence of frequency alone, whereas meaningfulness is the product of both frequency *and* multiple associations. To the reader, the word "and" is assuredly a highly familiar one (via frequent experience)—but it is likely to have few associations directly elicited by it. The word "Istanbul" has probably been read and/or heard relatively infrequently. Still it may arouse a wide range of exotic associations. There would seem to be a pressing need for verbal learning psychologists to tuck both familiarity and meaningfulness into their independent variable bag of tricks. The problem remains, however: What effect on acquisition is attributable to which variable?

An alternative approach to scaling familiarity by ratings is to conduct, tediously and compulsively, formal counts of the frequency with which verbal units actually occur in written expositions (or, perhaps, in oral communications). The procedure requires a definition of the verbal unit to be counted and a selection of representative materials upon which to base the count. Thorndike and Lorge (1944) performed an invaluable service to psychologists, and other vested interest groups, by determining estimates of the frequency of meaningful words in written text. The Thorndike-Lorge count classifies words into categories, identified by letters of the alphabet, which signify frequency per standard unit of printed text (e.g., per million words). A similar service has been provided by Underwood and Schulz(1960a) in their now famous counts of bigram (2-letter sequences) and trigram (3-letter sequences) frequencies per unit of printed text.

Thorndike-Lorge count, as an index of differential familiarity, has proved to be reliably related, positively, to verbal acquisition (e.g., Hall, 1954, with free recall). Judging from the work of Underwood and Schulz (1960a, p. 281), we have less reason to feel confident about bigram and trigram frequency as reliable predictors of acquisition proficiency. The impact of this negative finding on the thinking of Underwood and Schulz will be discussed later.

Studies which have tried to tease out the separate effects of familiarity and meaningfulness on acquisition are quite rare. In one, Lindley (1963a) found that familiarity, defined primarily by trigram count, did not affect acquisition (in agreement with Underwood and Schulz), whereas meaningfulness did. Surprisingly, though, Lindley's further analyses revealed that the beneficial effect of high meaningfulness was concentrated in the response learning stage, with little effect on the associative stage. Noble's emphasis on meaningfulness differing from familiarity in terms of multiple associates implies that meaningfulness should exert a greater influence than familiarity in hooking-up. However, the commonality of both variables with prior frequency suggests that the two should not differ in their influence on response integration.

Pronunciability

If the reader examines the two nonsense syllables MEF and QOW, he is looking at two syllables of fairly comparable association-values. However, if he now tries to pronounce each one, he will discover that they differ markedly in facility. Underwood and Schulz (1960a) discovered that nonsense syllables and other trigrams display a wide range of ease of pronunciation. To evaluate these differences, they employed a conventional rating scale procedure in which *Ss* were asked to rate the ease of pronouncing each of 178 three-letter units along a nine-point scale that ranged from one (easy) to nine (hard). The mean rating was then computed for each unit (with the means being given in the appendix of their book). For example, the mean ratings for MEF and QOW are 3.28 and 6.29, respectively. In addition, they found that the pronunciability ratings of the nonsense syllables included in their materials correlated moderately high (*r* of .78) with *m* values obtained for the same syllables. This suggested to them the existence of some common underlying denominator, as for familiarity and meaningfulness. Again the common denominator is inferred to be frequency of prior experience, but this time frequency is that of emitted sound or spoken frequency. Unfortunately, sound counts are not part of the repertory of standardizations, and they do not seem to be just around the corner. Until standardized, sound units remain no counts.

Underwood and Schulz found, apparently to their surprise, that pronunciability was a remarkably good predictor of response learning in PA acquisition, in fact, considerably better than trigram frequency. This finding was incorporated into a variation of their spew hypothesis. For a general critique of the Underwood and Schulz position on pronunciability as related to acquisition the reader is referred to a study by Johnson (1962). Further evidence for the pronunciability-acquisition relationship was previously encountered by the reader in the Martin and Schulz study (Chapter 3, Article 1).

Familiarization

As we have noted several times, familiarization means laboratory pre-exposure to the components that will enter into the learning task; that is, familiarization is an artificial means of generating varying degrees of frequency of experience. In SL the overall positive effects of prior familiarization with the items of the list have been well established. However, the tremendous variations in the specific procedures of familiarization make it hard to synthesize the research in this area. For example, Noble (1954) familiarized his *Ss* with the items by having them pronounce the items during the familiarization trials, whereas Underwood and Schulz (1960a, their Experiment III) familiarized their *Ss* with the items by having them learn the items as PA *R* terms during familiarization training. In both cases, familiarization facilitated SL acquisition, but some contrasting findings were reported. The Underwood and Schulz procedure most likely promotes response integration to a greater extent than the Noble procedure, but the Underwood and Schulz procedure also introduces the possibility of interference from *R-St* associations acquired during familiarization training. Another common procedure is to familiarize via free recall, as in the Underwood, Runquist, and Schulz study (Article 2, Chapter 2).

The contemporary period has featured familiarization as related to PA acquisition, and especially the relative effects of *St* versus *R* familiarization. The studies by Gannon and Noble (1961; Article 4) and Schulz and Tucker (1962; Article 5) convey the history of this problem area, important methodological problems (especially the need for including an irrelevant familiarization control), and an adequate sampling of the empirical findings and discussions of theoretical issues. Three other studies which have appeared since the one by Schulz and Tucker should be of some interest to the reader. One (Simon and Wood, 1964) raised the important question of *R-St* associations as a confounding factor when PA components are familiarized via the prior learning of other PA lists. The second (Horowitz and Larsen, 1963) extended the class of verbal units for such studies to foreign (Japanese) words and noted the advantages of this extension to the verbal learning psychologist. The third (Baker and Noble, 1965) obtained further support for Schulz and Tucker's finding that *St* familiarization facilitates PA acquisition when *S* is required to pronounce the *St* component during acquisition.

ARTICLE 1

AN ANALYSIS OF MEANING [1]

BY CLYDE E. NOBLE [2]

State University of Iowa

INTRODUCTION

Intimately related to the production of research data and to the formulation of theory in psychology is the procedure of identifying and quantifying the relevant variables within its various domains. Concerning the field of verbal learning, such writers as Carr (5), Robinson (24), McGeoch (22, 23), Dashiell (8), Melton (19, 20), and Underwood (28) have emphasized the continuing need for this type of analytic research.

The analysis of the attributes of verbal material has, moreover, a more general application. The training of human perceptual and motor skills is often accompanied by verbal instructions intended to facilitate performance on such tasks. One factor which may determine the effectiveness of instructions is the nature of the verbal stimuli which are introduced. For example, particular words may vary in *meaningfulness*. Evidence reviewed in such sources as McGeoch (23), Underwood (28), and Woodworth (31) indicates this to be a potential relevant variable in verbal learning. Historically, however, there has been little agreement on the precise definition of meaning, with the result that few consistent scaling procedures have been developed with which its actual relevance may be evaluated.

The objective of the present study is a theoretical-experimental analysis of the attribute of meaning in verbal stimulus material. Defining operations will be designed in accordance with rational considerations about this concept. In addition, quantitative analysis will provide the scale values necessary to the discovery of accurate functional relationships among this and other better-known psychological variables.

AN ANALYSIS OF MEANING

The many problems of *meaning* have occupied the attention of philosophers and of psychologists for a long time. Some of these problems have been genuine, others spurious. Inasmuch as its necessary and sufficient operations are both logically possible and empirically feasible, it may be shown that at least one of these alleged issues constitutes a genuine problem. Such is the requirement of an analysis of meaning in verbal learning theory.[3]

Within the framework of Hull's (14) behavior theory this is a relatively straightforward task. Consider a stimulus element S_x, a class of conditioned responses R_1, R_2, R_3, $\cdots$ R_n, and a

[1] This report forms a part of a dissertation submitted to the faculty of the Department of Psychology of the State University of Iowa in partial fulfillment of the requirements for the Ph.D. degree, June 1951. The author is indebted to Prof. Kenneth W. Spence for his advice and criticism. A portion of this paper was read before the Midwestern Psychological Association, April 1951.

The experimental work was conducted during the writer's temporary appointment as research psychologist with the Human Resources Research Center during the summer of 1950. The opinions or conclusions contained in this report are those of the author. They are not to be construed as reflecting the views or endorsement of the Department of the Air Force.

[2] Now at the Human Resources Research Center, Lackland Air Force Base, San Antonio, Texas.

[3] For a set of criteria to determine the status of a given problem, *cf.* H. M. Johnson (16). It is of historical interest that Watson's position on the meaning issue in 1925 was that the term was then unnecessary but that, should the need arise, behavioristic definition and explanation could be given (29, p. 201).

Reprinted with permission of the author and the publisher, the American Psychological Association. The article appeared originally in the *Psychological Review*, 1952, **59**, 421–430.

class of corresponding habit strengths H_1, H_2, H_3, · · · H_n, forming hypothetical bonds between them. Assume that these Rs have, by virtue of prior training, been connected at various times to S_x, and that, for simplicity, the Hs of these connections are severally equal. This hypothetical situation may be represented by the schema in Fig. 1, where the broken-shafted arrows denote learned connections, and where the dotted line following D denotes a continuing need or motivational state. It will be seen that this model depicts an ordinary competing response situation, in which each R has an equal probability of occurrence (R_p) following the presentation of S_x, and in which, given a wider range of observations, such phenomena as alternation, blocking, and increased reaction latency (R_t) are predictable (*cf.* **15**). Should the Hs be altered considerably in value the principle of competition would still hold, except that to refer to the habit structure under such conditions one would use the term *hierarchy of habits*.

Since, by logical anaylsis, *meaning* is a relation between terms, let us define the meaningfulness of this *situation* as the number of Hs subsisting between S and the several Rs taken together. More specifically, the *particular* meanings of S_x are: H_1, H_2, H_3, · · · H_n, and different conceptual combinations of these Hs yield different *numbers* of meanings.

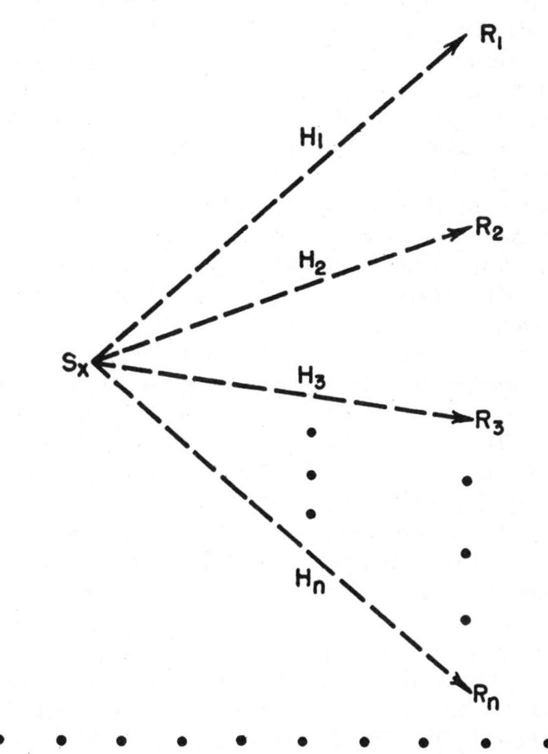

FIG. 1. Schema illustrating the development of stimulus meaning.

In this definition the author presupposes, of course, that the system *S–H–R* is isomorphic with the system α-*means*-β.

Various possible *logical* "meanings" of meaning—e.g., signification, denotation, connotation, equality, equivalence, definitional equivalence, material implication, strict implication—are not at issue here. Throughout the present analysis one must clearly and persistently distinguish between logical and psychological notions about meaning; the former class of notions is conceptual (hypothetical), the latter empirical (categorical). Further, no confusion should result from referring to relations between *S* and *R* as *psychological* (empirical) meanings, since such relations are (a) purely empirical constructs, and (b) presently to be coordinated with an operational index, *m*.

The present analysis does not assert meaning and habit strength to be identical concepts, although they have some common properties. Meanings are postulated to increase in number not as an exponential growth function of the number of *particular S-particular R* reinforcements—as *H* in Hull's theory—but rather as a simple linear function of the number of *particular S-multiple R* connections established. Now in terms of excitatory strength (*E*), where $E \equiv H \cdot D$, a specific "energized" meaning may best be regarded as an unspecified supraliminal value of effective excitatory strength ($\bar{E}$), where $\bar{E} \equiv E - I$. To strengthen $\bar{E}$ beyond the value of the limen (*L*) required for reaction evocation (*R*) may alter R_p, R_a, R_n, or R_t, but the qualitative fact that *S sometimes evokes R* is unaltered. This is the psychological connotation of the assertion: *S means R*.

From an historical point of view it may be interesting to note that the present analysis is formally analogous to certain notions advanced by the British philosophers of the 18th and 19th centuries—especially by Berkeley and by James Mill. Later, from the standpoint of introspectional psychology, Titchener taught that meaning is the conscious context which, under certain conditions, accrues to a "core" of sensory or imaginal content. This is his context "theory" of meaning, which Boring (2, pp. 185, 408) has implemented by suggesting the principle of 'accrual' to be that of association; i.e., learning. In terms of the Titchener-Boring viewpoint, then, *context* (or associated content) $\equiv$ *meaning*. Boring has also attempted to describe Titchener's doctrine in *S–R* terminology by identifying *S* with "core" and *R* with "context" (2, p. 588; 4, p. 18); hence with "meaning." However, since they can be shown to state infeasible demands (*cf*. 16), these and allied considerations —such as whether meaning is "palpable," "unconscious," or only "potential" —are of no scientific concern to modern (behavioristic) psychology.

An interesting approach to a contextual theory of meaning at a more complex level of analysis is provided by the recent paper of Miller and Selfridge (21). Defining meaningfulness in terms of dependent probabilities in successive free-association observations, these investigators have developed lists of varying orders of approximation to the structure of English.

So much for the formal definition of the concept of psychological meaning in terms of habit. Like habit, meaning is here a purely empirical construct. In order to impart significance to this notion—i.e., to relate it systematically to other constructs in behavior theory—it is first necessary to exhibit certain operations by means of which it may be given empirical verification. In other words, one must specify an empirical *index* with which the formal concept of meaning may be placed in correspondence. A few such indices are already available in the field of verbal learning.

They are defined by the various operations used for calibrating the "association values" of stimulus items. The work of Cason (6), Glaze (9), Haagen (11), Hull (13), Kreuger (18), and of Witmer (30) represent important contributions to this problem. However, most of these indices are unsatisfactory either because they involved (a) very short response intervals, (b) free association techniques, (c) relative frequency measures, or (d) because their reliabilities were not reported. Since theoretically the number of *R*s is proportional to the number of supraliminal $\bar{E}$s, frequency of response is proposed as a rational index of stimulus meaning (*m*). Therefore, the appropriate association value for the present analysis would be denoted by the central tendency of the frequency distribution of *continued* associations given by *S*s per unit time.[4]

Following these considerations an operational index of the attribute of stimulus meaning (*m*) was sought for each member of a list of 96 dissyllables, as indicated by the following definition:

$$m_s \equiv \frac{1}{N} \sum_{i=1}^{N} R_s, \qquad (1)$$

where $S \equiv$ verbal stimulus; $R \equiv$ unit written response; $N \equiv$ number of subjects.

Procedure

A provisional list of 120 two-syllable nouns was taken from the Thorndike-Lorge tables (26), the principal selection criterion being the *G* (general) frequency count. These items were drawn with the intention of representing (a) nearly all of the alphabet in the initial letters and (b) an extreme frequency-of-use range. It was hypothesized that frequency of occurrence in the written language would be highly correlated with *m* and therefore should provide a useful approximate ranking of the sample of stimuli to be calibrated.

The words from the Thorndike-Lorge list were supplemented by 18 artificial words which were also dissyllabic and in the form of nouns. They were selected from Dunlap's list (*cf.* 31) or invented by the author. The purpose of including these paralogs was to insure a low-*m* extreme on the final scale, as well as to calibrate such items empirically on a scale continuous with that of actual words.

After a number of arbitrary and systematic rejections, the final list was reduced to 96 items. This list contained approximately 20 per cent paralogs, 35 per cent infrequent items ($<$ 1 per 4 million), and 45 per cent frequent items ($>$ 1 per million). The last two frequency classes are defined by their Thorndike-Lorge relative frequency counts indicated in parentheses. The number 96 was selected because it was associated with a convenient maximum testing time for the prevailing military research schedules at the Human Resources Research Center. The time interval of 60 sec. was chosen because (a) preliminary tests showed that *S*s reported 60 sec. to be an optimal interval, and (b) to insure a reliable time sample of the *S*s' response hierarchy.

The stimulus items were administered in test booklet form with attached answer sheets. A uniform set was maintained by printing only one stimulus per page and by instructing *S* to return to the stimulus each time before responding anew. Furthermore, a given stim-

[4] *Continued* associations are those which are successively elicited by the same stimulus, as distinguished from *free* or *controlled* associations. The present procedure is analogous to one reported by Cattell and Bryant (7) and called, apparently by Woodworth (31), the *method of continued association.* Krueger (18) later used written responses in determining the association values of nonsense syllables, although the instructions to his *S*s would seem to define their responses as *free* associations.

ulus item was reproduced on each line in an effort to reduce *S*'s inveterate tendency to free-associate. The sequence and order of presentation of the stimuli were varied by shuffling the answer sheets during the assembly of the test booklets. This device served to minimize constant errors due to fatigue, decreasing motivation, and inter-item interaction. After administering a pilot list to 15 *S*s, in order to standardize the procedural variables, the final list of 96 items was given to a sample of 131 basic airmen from two flights undergoing routine classification testing at the Human Resources Research Center. These *S*s were group-tested in four separate units of approximately half-flight size (about 33 men) in order to reduce inter-individual interaction. This source of variance was further reduced by varying the order and sequence of stimuli per *S*, as indicated. Two examiners tested two groups each, and the testing periods were held during the morning hours of two days one week apart. Response periods were of 60 sec. duration per stimulus, with an inter-item interval of 15 sec. Rest periods were given as follows: 5 min. at the end of the first 45 min. of testing, 10 min. at the end of the second 45 min. period, and 5 min. at the end of the next 30 min. period.

Instructions to the *S*s were as follows:

> This is a test to see how many words you can think of and write down in a short time.
>
> You will be given a *key* word and you are to write down as many *other* words which the key word brings to mind as you can. These other words which you write down may be things, places, ideas, events, or whatever you happen to think of when you see the key word.
>
> For example, think of the word, *KING*. Some of the words or phrases which *KING* might bring to mind are written below:
>
> | | |
> |---|---|
> | queen | Kingdom |
> | King Cole | England |
> | ruler | imperial |
> | Sky-King | kingfish |

*S*s were then given two practice sessions, using as stimuli the words HAM and KOREA. They were permitted to use two-word phrases, slang, long words or short words, provided they were associates of the stimulus words.

Instructions regarding motivation and set were as follows:

> No one is expected to fill in all the spaces on a page, but write as many words as you can which each key word calls to mind. Be sure to think back to the *key* word after each word you write down because the test is to see how many other words the key word makes you think of. A good way to do this is to repeat each key word over and over to yourself as you write.

E also gave supplementary motivating instructions during the three rest periods.

The method of recording *S*'s responses was sufficiently objective to require very little evaluation on *E*'s part. However in terms of the analysis of meaning proposed, it was decided to set up three objective criteria for unacceptable responses. These were:

1. *Illegible responses*: $S_x \rightarrow ?$
2. *Perseverative responses*:
$$S_x \rightarrow R_1(s_1) \rightarrow R_1(s_1) \cdots$$
3. *Failures of set*: $S_x \nearrow R_1$; $S_x \searrow R_2(s_2)$, with $R_2(s_2) \nearrow R_{2_1}$, $R_2(s_2) \rightarrow R_{2_2}$, $R_2(s_2) \searrow R_{2_3}$

This last class of unacceptable responses was further classified into:

(a) *Free or tangential associations:* e.g., LEMUR→Dorothy, Hope, faith, charity. . . .

(b) *Clang or alliterative associations:* e.g., KAYSEN→caisson, Casey, casein, casement. . . .

Finally, a general rule of giving *S* the benefit of the doubt was adopted. This was occasionally necessary in the case of category 3 above, although free and

TABLE I

LIST OF DISSYLLABLE WORDS (NOUNS) IN RANK ORDER OF INCREASING MEANINGFULNESS (m) AS DEFINED BY MEAN FREQUENCY OF CONTINUED ASSOCIATIONS IN 60 SEC. ($N = 119$)

Rank	Word Number	m-Value	σ	Word	Rank	Word Number	m-Value	σ	Word
1	24	0.99	2.05	GOJEY	49	58	2.69	3.43	OVUM
2	53	1.04	1.60	NEGLAN	50	72	2.73	3.24	ROSTRUM
3	49	1.05	1.85	MEARDON	51	84	2.76	2.92	VERTEX
4	8	1.13	1.89	BYSSUS	52	5	2.80	3.27	BODICE
5	4	1.22	1.95	BALAP	53	76	2.89	3.20	TANKARD
6	86	1.22	2.17	VOLVAP	54	60	3.06	3.04	PALLOR
7	77	1.24	2.03	TAROP	55	74	3.21	2.85	SEQUENCE
8	90	1.24	2.20	XYLEM	56	1	3.34	3.34	ARGON
9	41	1.26	2.16	LATUK	57	68	3.36	3.22	RAMPART
10	66	1.26	2.01	QUIPSON	58	35	3.51	3.50	JITNEY
11	25	1.27	2.20	GOKEM	59	17	3.55	3.19	ENTRANT
12	52	1.28	1.96	NARES	60	59	3.62	3.26	PALLET
13	96	1.28	2.19	ZUMAP	61	51	3.64	3.48	NAPHTHA
14	63	1.30	1.98	POLEF	62	62	3.77	3.45	PIGMENT
15	73	1.33	2.06	SAGROLE	63	57	3.91	3.42	ORDEAL
16	55	1.34	2.37	NOSTAW	64	94	4.44	3.19	ZENITH
17	6	1.39	2.12	BODKIN	65	91	4.60	3.82	YEOMAN
18	81	1.50	2.78	ULNA	66	67	4.68	3.13	QUOTA
19	88	1.53	2.05	WELKIN	67	64	5.10	3.45	QUARRY
20	29	1.54	2.84	ICON	68	15	5.13	3.19	EFFORT
21	40	1.55	2.45	KUPOD	69	83	5.32	3.24	UNIT
22	13	1.60	2.46	DELPIN	70	18	5.33	3.46	FATIGUE
23	3	1.71	2.55	ATTAR	71	37	5.47	3.11	KEEPER
24	48	1.73	2.69	MATRIX	72	38	5.52	3.70	KENNEL
25	12	1.74	2.69	DAVIT	73	47	5.61	3.32	MALLET
26	89	1.78	2.77	WIDGEON	74	42	5.94	3.17	LEADER
27	7	1.79	2.65	BRUGEN	75	65	5.98	3.16	QUARTER
28	36	1.82	2.95	KAYSEN	76	69	5.98	3.70	REGION
29	46	1.84	2.85	MAELSTROM	77	28	6.02	3.33	HUNGER
30	79	1.84	2.95	TUMBRIL	78	95	6.15	3.05	ZERO
31	70	1.86	2.85	RENNET	79	30	6.24	3.50	INCOME
32	71	1.90	2.35	ROMPIN	80	82	6.57	3.79	UNCLE
33	22	1.95	2.55	GAMIN	81	92	6.75	4.12	YOUNGSTER
34	19	2.09	3.11	FEMUR	82	80	6.83	3.29	TYPHOON
35	45	2.09	3.42	LOZENGE	83	10	6.88	3.11	CAPTAIN
36	20	2.13	2.77	FERRULE	84	93	7.12	3.75	ZEBRA
37	75	2.14	2.75	STOMA	85	23	7.17	4.48	GARMENT
38	26	2.15	3.09	GRAPNEL	86	85	7.28	4.05	VILLAGE
39	21	2.19	3.25	FLOTSAM	87	31	7.39	3.09	INSECT
40	11	2.26	3.35	CAROM	88	34	7.58	3.69	JEWEL
41	54	2.26	2.65	NIMBUS	89	32	7.70	3.53	JELLY
42	43	2.28	3.06	LEMUR	90	27	7.91	3.86	HEAVEN
43	9	2.41	3.13	CAPSTAN	91	56	7.95	3.66	OFFICE
44	61	2.43	2.88	PERCEPT	92	87	8.12	3.67	WAGON
45	44	2.48	2.96	LICHENS	93	14	8.33	4.21	DINNER
46	33	2.54	3.53	JETSAM	94	50	8.98	4.27	MONEY
47	16	2.59	3.08	ENDIVE	95	2	9.43	4.30	ARMY
48	78	2.63	3.04	TARTAN	96	39	9.61	4.30	KITCHEN

clang associations were usually easily identified by the three scorers. Of the original 131 *Ss* tested, 12 protocols were rejected for persistent violations of the criteria cited. This brought the effective sample to 119 *Ss*.

Results

The index of meaning (m) of a particular stimulus was defined in equation [1] as the grand mean number of (acceptable) written responses given by all *Ss* within a 60 sec. period. Therefore, the scale values of the stimuli were determined directly by the average response frequencies of the 119 *Ss*. These m-values with the σ's of their distributions are shown in Table I, ranging in rank order from dissyllables of low response-evocation value (e.g., No. 1: GOJEY) to those of high response-evocation value (e.g., No. 96: KITCHEN). The empirical range is from 0.99 to 9.61. It will be noted that there is no discrete gap between the paralog items and the actual words. In fact, there are a few actual words low on the scale (e.g., No. 4: BYSSUS), while one paralog (No. 32: ROMPIN) appears at the third-way point. It is also to be noted that response variability tends to increase with increasing m-value.

It was found that the m-values of particular items were quite stable from group to group. Intercorrelations of the four sets of mean m-values per word were carried out among all six combinations of groups. These Pearsonian r-values appear in Table II. All are significantly different from zero ($P < 0.01$). Since the sampling distribution of r is skewed for large values, Fisher's Z-transformation was used to estimate the mean intergroup reliability coefficient of the m-scale: $\bar{r}_{mm} = 0.975$. It may be pointed out that a between-groups reliability coefficient [5] is the appropriate statistic to compute in this case since it was *E*'s aim to determine the consistency of *different response samples* to the *same stimuli*. A more conventional reliability coefficient —such as one defined by the test-retest, split-half, or the alternate form procedure—would not have evaluated this particular relationship.

TABLE II

INTERGROUP RELIABILITY COEFFICIENTS (r) FOR m-SCALE BASED ON MEAN m-VALUES FOR FOUR GROUPS OF *Ss*

Group	I	II	III	IV	n
I	—	—	—	—	27
II	.98	—	—	—	30
III	.98	.98	—	—	30
IV	.96	.97	.98	—	32

N = 119.

Of some interest in this investigation was the extent to which the assumptions of the product-moment correlational method were met. The family of response frequency distributions associated with the stimulus items exhibited skewness at the low-m extreme of the scale, but throughout the central and upper portions they were approximately symmetrical. Hence, means were retained as measures of central tendency. When the six intercorrelations of the m-scale were plotted, it was found that the requirements of linearity of regression and of homoscedasticity were reasonably satisfied.

DISCUSSION

Meaning. After reviewing the analysis of meaning, one properly may ask whether responses may acquire meanings also, or whether only stimuli do so. As has been indicated, meanings are considered relations between *Ss* and *Rs*.[6]

[5] Rather than a "reliability" coefficient, some might prefer to call this statistic a coefficient of "objectivity," "agreement," or of "consistency."

[6] Not all writers would agree to construe meaning thus (*cf.* 2, 3, 4, 17, 27). Some of the divergences of opinion are reflected in the following successive quotations from Boring's

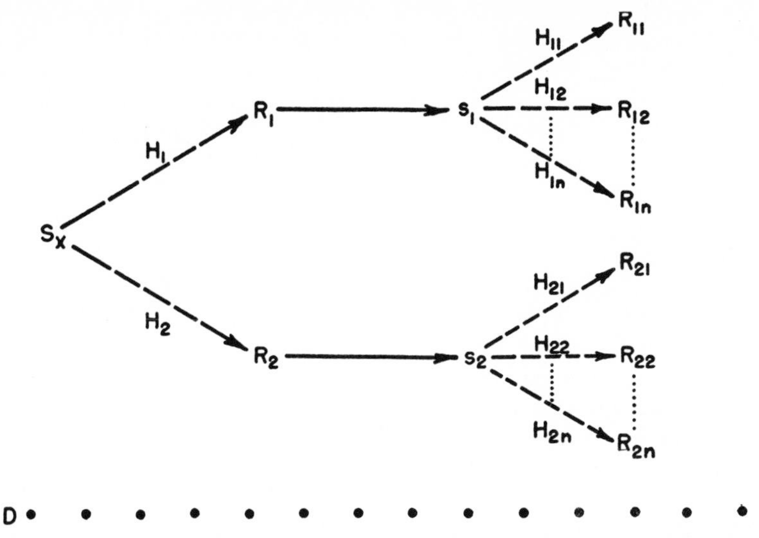

FIG. 2. Schema illustrating the development of more complex degrees of meaning.

It is for convenience that, instead of referring to *m*, one speaks of "the meaning of a stimulus" or of "stimulus meaning," just as one speaks of "reinforcing a conditioned response," when more precisely it is the *S–R* connection, or *H*, which strictly is reinforced. To speak of *stimulus* meaning is to imply an asymmetry in the empirical meaning relation. Indeed, common linguistic usage seems to concur that meaning, like causation, be regarded as a property of stimuli rather than of responses.[7]

Under certain conditions, however, it is appropriate to refer loosely to the meaning of a *response*. One such condition would arise if analysis should indicate that a certain class of responses results in proprioceptive stimulation (*s*) to an organism. This is the well-known response-produced stimulus situation, or feedback mechanism. Kinesthesis is perhaps the best example. The descriptive schema outlined in the section on meaning applies equally well, as shown in Fig. 2. Here the situation becomes more complex, but no different qualitatively. *H*s develop between initial *R* ($\rightarrow s$)s and subsequent *R*s, thereby permitting more complex degrees of development of meaning.

The serial anticipation learning situation, for example, fits this schema well in that each successive response functions as a stimulus to the next response in the series, while the verbal stimuli appearing serially in the memory drum aperture serve as secondary reinforcing agents. This type of analysis also suggests an explanatory approach for the relationships Miller and Selfridge (21) have found between reproductive recall and contextual dependencies. The work of Thorndike (25) on "belonging" may be similarly regarded.

The result of this analysis of meaning and its incorporation into learning theory is twofold: (a) it establishes

---

1933 text (3): "The correlation between stimulus and ultimate response *is* a meaning . . ." (p. 153); ". . . the data of consciousness are meanings" (p. 222); ". . . a meaning is a relation" (p. 222); "Meaning is response" (p. 223).

[7] This is not to be interpreted as bearing any relation to the Gestalt doctrine of meaning as immediately given in the external world (*cf.* 17), but simply as a clarification of a familiar idiom.

a highly reliable, unequivocal new attribute of variation in learning, and (b) it provides an operational basis for explicating the common-sense notion of "meaning." Thus, if one were to ask a layman what he intended by saying that "home" to him *means:* "family, spouse, children, friends, love," etc., he would doubtless reply, "I think of these things when 'home' is mentioned." It is a simple matter to fit this statement to the model proposed in Fig. 1. A learning theorist would explain that to the auditory (or visual) *S home,* these various verbal *R*s have become conditioned during our imaginary layman's previous experience, and that under appropriate conditions (e.g., adequate *D* level, sufficient reinforcements to each *L*) these *R*s are elicited. The meaning of *S* subsists in the *H*s developed to it —nothing more.[8] A neutral *S,* by the present definitions, is meaning*less*; an *S* conditioned to twenty *R*s is more meaning*ful* (i.e., has more meanings) than is one conditioned to ten, and so on. Speaking quite non-technically, meanings are habits. And as more habits accrue to a particular stimulus situation, so does its meaningfulness increase.

In the final analysis the index *m,* like *H,* emerges as a statistical concept. It is a function of the number of particular *S*-multiple *R* connections which are formed, and it enjoys an existence independent of the cited operations no more than does any other empirical construct.

In view of its theoretical status and exceptional reliability, the *m*-scale is regarded with especial interest for research in verbal and in perceptual-motor learning. Using the *m*-scale, research may now be directed toward the solution of such current problems as the relationship between difficulty and meaningfulness, the effect of meaningfulness upon reminiscence, and the rôle of verbal instructions in the acquisition of motor skills.

[8] In view of the fact that the class of responses defining the *m*-scale represents a set of individual-difference variables, one should properly denote the meaning relation in this case by the symbol *U* rather than by *H*. From a genetic standpoint, certain learning theorists preserve a distinction between innate *or* previously-acquired connections ($_sU_r$'s) and laboratory-established connections ($_sH_r$'s). However, in Hull's theory both *U* and *H* are considered habit or associational concepts, hence the proposed coordination with meaning is unimpaired. A similar argument holds for conditioned generalized connections ($_s\bar{H}_r$'s).

Summary and Conclusions

This paper has presented a theoretical-experimental analysis of the attribute of meaning in verbal stimulus material. A word list of 96 dissyllables consisting of nouns and paralogs was presented to a sample of 119 USAF recruits in order to establish a quantitative scale for this attribute. The results of this analysis were as follows:

1. Meaning was formally defined as a relation between *S* and *R*. It was coordinated with Hull's theoretical construct *H* by postulating that meanings increase as a simple linear function of the number of *S*-multiple *R* connections acquired in a particular organism's history.

2. An index of stimulus meaning (*m*) was operationally defined in terms of the mean frequency of continued written associations made by subjects within a 60-sec. time interval.

3. A psychological performance scale of *m*-values was developed which exhibited a range extending from 0.99 to 9.61. The mean product-moment intergroup reliability coefficient was $\bar{r}_{mm} = 0.975$.

4. The significance of these findings for human learning theory was discussed.

References

1. Bergmann, G., & Spence, K. W. The logic of psychophysical measurement. Psychol. Rev., 1944, 51, 1–24.

2. BORING, E. G. *A history of experimental psychology*. New York: D. Appleton-Century Co., 1929.
3. ——. *The physical dimensions of consciousness*. New York: D. Appleton-Century, 1933.
4. ——. *Sensation and perception in the history of experimental psychology*. New York: D. Appleton-Century, 1942.
5. CARR, H. A. *Psychology: A study of mental activity*. New York: Longmans, Green, 1925.
6. CASON, H. Specific serial learning: a study of backward association. *J. exp. Psychol.*, 1926, **9**, 195–227.
7. CATTELL, J. McK., & BRYANT, S. Mental association investigated by experiment. *Mind,* 1889, **14**, 230–250.
8. DASHIELL, J. F. A neglected fourth dimension to psychological research. PSYCHOL. REV., 1940, **47**, 289–305.
9. GLAZE, J. A. The association value of non-sense syllables. *J. genet. Psychol.*, 1928, **35**, 255–269.
10. GUILFORD, J. P. *Psychometric methods*. New York: McGraw-Hill, 1936.
11. HAAGEN, C. H. Synonymity, vividness, familiarity, and association value ratings of 400 pairs of common adjectives. *J. Psychol.*, 1949, **27**, 453–463.
12. HEBB, D. O. *The organization of behavior*. New York: John Wiley & Sons, Inc., 1949.
13. HULL, C. L. The meaningfulness of 320 selected nonsense syllables. *Amer. J. Psychol.*, 1933, **45**, 730–734.
14. ——. *Principles of behavior*. New York: Appleton-Century, 1943.
15. ——. *Elementary theory of individual behavior*. (In preparation.)
16. JOHNSON, H. M. Are psychophysical problems genuine or spurious? *Amer. J. Psychol.*, 1945, **58**, 189–211.
17. KÖHLER, W. *The place of value in a world of facts*. New York: Liveright, 1938.
18. KRUEGER, W. C. F. The relative difficulty of nonsense syllables. *J. exp. Psychol.*, 1934, **17**, 145–153.
19. MELTON, A. W. The methodology of experimental studies of human learning and retention: I. The functions of a methodology and the available criteria for evaluating different experimental methods. *Psychol. Bull.*, 1936, **33**, 305–394.
20. ——. Learning. In W. S. Monroe (Ed.), *Encyclopedia of educational research*. New York: Macmillan, 1950, 668–690.
21. MILLER, G. A., & SELFRIDGE, J. A. Verbal context and the recall of meaningful material. *Amer. J. Psychol.*, 1950, **63**, 176–185.
22. McGEOCH, J. A. The vertical dimensions of mind. PSYCHOL. REV., 1936, **43**, 107–129.
23. ——. *The psychology of human learning*. New York: Longmans, Green, & Co., 1942.
24. ROBINSON, E. S. *Association theory today: An essay in systematic psychology*. New York: Century, 1932.
25. THORNDIKE, E. L. *Human learning*. New York: Century, 1931.
26. ——, & LORGE, I. *The teacher's word book of 30,000 words*. New York: Columbia Univ. Press, 1944.
27. TOLMAN, E. C. *Purposive behavior in animals and men*. New York: Century Co., 1932.
28. UNDERWOOD, B. J. *Experimental psychology*. New York: Appleton-Century-Crofts, Inc., 1949.
29. WATSON, J. B. *Behaviorism*. New York: Norton & Co., 1925, 2nd Ed.
30. WITMER, L. R. The association value of three-place consonant syllables. *J. genet. Psychol.*, 1935, **47**, 337–359.
31. WOODWORTH, R. S. *Experimental psychology*. New York: Holt, 1938.

[MS. received September 4, 1951]

ARTICLE 2

MEANINGFULNESS AND ARTICULATION OF STIMULUS AND RESPONSE IN PAIRED-ASSOCIATE LEARNING AND STIMULUS RECALL [1]

RAYMOND G. HUNT [2]

University of Buffalo

It seems fairly well agreed that the general effect of meaningfulness is to facilitate the acquisition of verbal materials. However, the question of the relative effects of meaningfulness of the stimulus and response members in paired-associate learning remains an open one. The empirical literature bearing upon it is by no means clear. Noble and McNeely (1957) Cieutat, Stockwell, and Noble (1958) have found both stimulus and response meaningfulness to facilitate learning but conclude that response factors are of greater importance. Kimble and Dufort (1955) report similar data but arrive at the opposite conclusion. Sheffield (1946) found response meaningfulness, but not stimulus meaningfulness to facilitate learning. Mandler and Campbell (1957) found consistent and clear-cut effects only in regard to response meaningfulness or association value. Further investigation in this area is clearly in order.

Linked to the question of the roles of stimulus and response factors in paired-associate learning is the question of what psychological mechanisms may be responsible for the effects observed. Noble has suggested that variations in the motor skill of pronunciation may be one of the gross variables underlying the relative ease of learning meaningful verbal material. Such a notion is consistent with Noble's emphasis upon the primary role of response factors in paired-associate learning and suggests the hypothesis that practice in pronouncing the stimulus words during the learning of paired-associates might facilitate their acquisition. Such facilitation could occur by virtue of the pronunciation process providing more stable internal cues which then mediate the acquisition of "associations."

Finally, Bugelski (1957), for one, in an effort to further specify the role of stimulus members of paired associates, has proposed that, in the paired-associate procedure, the stimulus term plays only a minimal role. From his theoretical analysis Bugelski suggests that its usual function is simply to provide a "cue" occasioning the performance of the response term. Given such a state of affairs, any discriminable portion of the stimulus term can suffice. In other words, *S* need not learn the term completely nor even pay much attention to it as a word. As a simple and preliminary test of this hypothesis Bugelski proposes a "backward" recall procedure like that used by Feldman and Underwood (1957) to demonstrate the acquisition of R-S associations in the course of learning S-R associations. It would be expected that *S* will be unable to recall stimuli

[1] This paper is based upon a dissertation submitted to the Department of Psychology at the University of Buffalo in partial fulfillment of the requirements for the degree of Doctor of Philosophy. The author wishes to thank B. R. Bugelski, chairman, and the other members of his doctoral committee for their advice and assistance. Thanks are also due K. H. Kurtz for his help in preparing this paper.

[2] Now at Washington University, St. Louis, Missouri.

Reprinted with permission of the author and the publisher, the American Psychological Association. The article appeared originally in the *Journal of Experimental Psychology*, 1959, **57,** 262–267.

of low meaningfulness since they are initially unfamiliar and are not learned as units during the acquisition trials. On the other hand, meaningful stimuli should be recalled readily as these have already been learned prior to the experiment and so will tend to be associated as wholes with the response members.

METHOD

Experimental design.—Three main experimental variables formed the basic structure of the experiment: (*a*) stimulus meaningfulness (high or low); (*b*) response meaningfulness (high or low); and (*c*) articulation or nonarticulation of the stimulus word (response words were necessarily articulated in all conditions).

Four main experimental conditions were employed as follows: High-High (high stimulus meaning—high response meaning; Low-Low (low stimulus meaning—low response meaning); High-Low (high stimulus meaning —low response meaning); Low-High (low stimulus meaning—high response meaning).

Each of these conditions was divided into two subconditions, in one of which *S*s overtly verbalized the stimulus words during learning and in the other of which they did not. While it is likely that some *S*s in the nonarticulation conditions verbalized the stimulus subvocally, it is unlikely that anything approaching the 100% vocalization of the articulation groups obtained. It is questionable in any case whether subvocal articulation is equivalent to overt vocalization.

Apparatus.—A device adapted to the presentation of verbal materials for paired-associate learning and previously described by Bugelski and Scharlock (1952) was used. This apparatus consists essentially of a screen with an aperture behind which revolves a sectioned disk. The revolving disk exposes words at predetermined intervals. All words were block printed in India ink on 5 × 8-in. white cards with letters 4 mm. high by 3 mm. wide. The cards bearing the paired words were stacked behind the aperture and were changed manually. Individual S-R pairs were withdrawn when the criterion of two successive correct anticipations was attained, thereby controlling overlearning.

The stimulus word of each pair was first exposed alone for 2 sec., then both words of the pair were exposed for 2 sec.; the interval between successive pairs was 4 sec.

Material.—Eight paired-associate lists were used, two in each of the four main experimental conditions. Each consisted of 10 pairs drawn from Noble's (1952) list of disyllabic nouns and paralogs scaled for meaning (*m*). A High-High list was constructed by selecting 20 words at random from the 34 in Noble's list having *m*-scale values greater than 5.50. In one such list the odd-numbered words formed the stimulus units and the even-numbered words the response units. A second High-High list was formed by reversing these positions.

Two Low-Low lists were derived in identical fashion from the 25 words in Noble's list having *m*-scale values less than 2.00.

Two High-Low and two Low-High lists were constructed by appropriate combinations of the words in the High-High and Low-Low lists.

The usual precautions were taken to avoid possible biasing effects peculiar to individual pairs.

Finally, a six-pair practice list was constructed. This consisted of geometric figures as stimuli and colors as responses. It was assumed that such a list would effectively acquaint *S* with the procedure and apparatus. Each *S* received a minimum of five practice trials.

Subjects.—Eighty volunteer undergraduate students (54 men, 26 women) enrolled in summer session courses at the University of Buffalo served as *S*s. They ranged in age from 17–30 yr. (mean 21, *SD* 3 yr.). Approximately one-fourth of these *S*s had participated previously in verbal-learning experiments.

Procedure.—Twenty *S*s were assigned to each of the four main experimental conditions. Within each condition 10 *S*s vocalized both S and R terms while the remaining 10 *S*s vocalized only the R terms. Five *S*s in each of these subconditions learned one of the two experimental lists for that condition. All *S*s were assigned randomly to the experimental conditions and no *S* served in more than one condition.

Learning was by the anticipation method with correction on all but the first run through the list, during which *S* simply pronounced the appropriate terms as they appeared. Common pronunciation was agreed upon at this time. The technique of correction varied according to *S*'s treatment condition. The *S*s in the articulation conditions corrected by pronouncing both the S and R words whereas *S*s in the nonarticulation conditions corrected by pronouncing only the correct R word. The *S*s were instructed to avoid wild guessing.

One run through a list of 10 pairs constituted a trial, the cards being shuffled after each trial to control serial effects. The intertrial interval was about 15 sec.

Learning was measured in terms of median trial to criterion for each *S*. This score was obtained by determining the trial on which each of the 10 pairs making up the experimental list was learned, placing these in rank order and then determining their median.

Immediately following the learning trials each *S* was tested for recall of the *stimulus* words of the pairs just learned. The response words of these pairs were presented for 4 sec. each. The *S*s in the articulation groups pronounced each word as it was shown and then attempted to reproduce, either by pronouncing or by spelling, the word which had been paired with it. The *S*s in the nonarticulation groups simply viewed the word without pronouncing it. Recall was measured in terms of number of errors, an error being defined as anything less than perfect reproduction. Each *S* was encouraged to report whatever he could recall of the stimulus term in the event he was unable to reproduce it completely.

Results

Acquisition.—The mean acquisition scores for the four main experimental groups were 3.19, 5.10, 7.18, and 8.31 for the High-High, Low-High, High-Low and Low-Low groups, respectively. These mean scores are consistent with the hierarchy of effects predicted by Noble and McNeely (1957) and reported by (Cieutat, Stockwell, and Noble (1958).

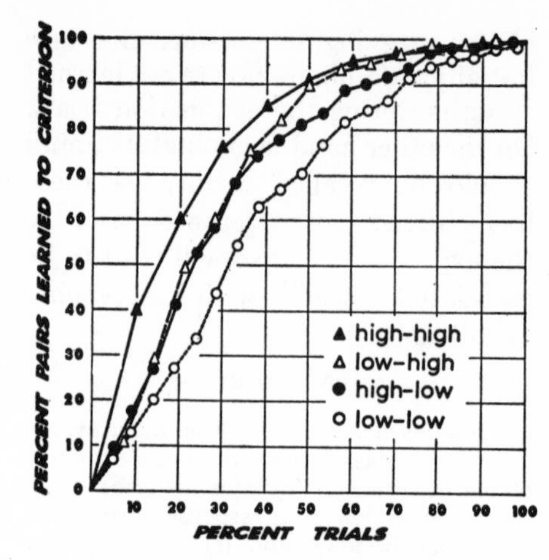

FIG. 1. Cumulative acquisition curves for the four main experimental conditions.

A similar conclusion might be drawn from the learning curves presented in Fig. 1. Because of the procedure used in the learning, not

TABLE 1

ANALYSES OF VARIANCE OF STIMULUS, RESPONSE, AND ARTICULATION FACTORS IN PAIRED-ASSOCIATE ACQUISITION

Analysis	Source[a]	*df*	Acquisition		Recall	
			MS	*F*	*MS*	*F*
Response	Treatment	1	265.72	141.34**	40.61	16.78*
	Error (Lists within treatments)	2	1.88		2.42	
Stimulus	Treatment	1	25.66	1.85	374.11	239.81**
	Error (Lists within treatments)	2	13.88		1.56	
Articulation[a]	Treatment	1	0.00	—	.12	—
	Error (Lists × Articulation)	4	82.21		13.66	

* .05 < *P* < .10.
** *P* < .01.
[a] Only the sources of interest for present purposes are selected from the complete analysis for presentation.

all *S*s received the same number of trials. Consequently the curves in Fig. 1 are "Vincent-type" adjusted for unequal trials by a method described by Woodworth and Schlosberg (1954). It can be seen that each of these curves conforms to the usual negatively accelerated growth curve and that the respective steepness of slope of the four curves is consistent with the Noble-McNeely hypothesis.

However, as reported in Table 1, analyses of variance of the effects of stimulus and response meaningfulness reveal that only variations in response term meaningfulness produced a statistically significant effect upon acquisition rates. Neither stimulus meaningfulness nor articulation had any significant effect in the present experiment. The data reported in Table 1 were obtained by performing independent analyses of the effects of the three main experimental variables.

In the case of the stimulus and response analyses the error term used to test experimental effects is based upon sampling variation among lists of similar *m* value. Since the same lists were used under articulation and nonarticulation conditions, the list-by-articulation interaction was employed as an error term for evaluation of the effects of articulation. Inasmuch as *S* variability was confounded with list variability, each of these analyses permits generalization both to a population of *S*s and to a population of lists.

Recall.—The mean numbers of errors in stimulus recall were 1.80, 5.70, 2.80, and 4.30 for the High-High, Low-Low, High-Low and Low-High groups, respectively. Results of analyses of variance of errors in stimulus recall are presented in Table 1. As predicted by Bugelski, variations in stimulus meaningfulness produced a statistically significant effect upon stimulus recall. Similar variations in response meaningfulness produced an effect which approaches significance. Stimulus articulation, however, had no significant effect upon stimulus recall.

Discussion

The main results of the present study are consistent with those presented by Sheffield (1946). Differential acquisition rates appear to be associated primarily with response dimensions of the paired-associate process. It seems quite possible that the diverse findings reported in the literature concerning the effects upon acquisition of varying stimulus meaningfulness may be a function of variations from experiment to experiment in sampling from the range of meaningfulness, or association values. Preliminary analysis (not reported) of the present data revealed as untenable any assumption of an absence of variance in the data attributable to differences among stimulus materials of similar *m* value. It is essential that this variance be accounted for in the error term used to test experimental effects. The positive effects upon acquisition sometimes obtained by increasing the meaningfulness of the stimulus member of the paired associate may reflect sampling variations attributable to materials rather than true effects. Further experimentation in this area should probably involve careful sampling from a wide range of *m*, or association, values, while at the same time closely controlling variations on the response side of the paired associate. In any case, judging from the results presented here, in conjunction with those of Sheffield, and in view of the inconsistent effects reported by Mandler and Campbell (1957), it seems likely that variations in the meaningfulness of the stimulus member are not apt to produce consistent effects upon paired-associate acquisition.

The fact that recall is better for meaningful stimuli is consistent with Bugelski's hypothesis of the "minimal cue" function of the stimulus member in such learning. Moreover, the fact that increasing response term meaningfulness appears to produce greater facilitation of paired-associate learning than does increasing stimulus meaningfulness can also be accommodated within the Bugelski hypothesis. Such a finding would be expected since it is postulated that only the response member of the pair need be performed in its entirety. Therefore, meaningfulness of that unit would be expected to aid learning more than would comparable degrees of stimulus meaningfulness.

Some further support for the Bugelski hypothesis can be taken from the frequency of partial recall in the high- and low-stimulus-meaning conditions. Partial recall, defined as some part of the appropriate term but less than the whole, accounted for 37% of the errors in recall for the low-stimulus-meaning condition but only 8% in the high-stimulus-meaning condition. These differences were primarily a result of a decrease in the percentage of intrusion errors from 49% in the high-stimulus-meaning condition to 17% in the low-stimulus-meaning condition (the percentage of failures was 46% in both). These findings would be expected from Bugelski's thesis which assumes *S*s in the low meaning condition to be discriminating as a cue only a fragment from the general topography of the total stimulus. The *S* would thus be expected to be prepared to perform only that fragment rather than the whole word.

The present failure to demonstrate any facilitation of learning as a function of stimulus articulation does not necessarily contradict an emphasis upon motor factors as mediating the facilitative functions of meaningful material. It may simply be that *S* discriminates fragments of the stimulus word with which he is "familiar"; a process which could operate along linguistic lines. The larger process of "integrating" an instrumental response to the stimulus word could be a process concomitant with but largely independent of the formation of an association between some fragment of that word and some other unit (the response word).

Finally, the present data bear upon the "backward" recall findings of Feldman and Underwood (1957). These investigators reported the correct recall of stimulus items following paired-associate learning to be of the order of 50%. Nonsense syllables were used as stimuli and adjectives as responses. Their experimental lists, therefore, were comparable with the Low-High condition in the present experiment. The percentages of stimulus items correctly recalled (perfect reproduction) in the present study were 99, 80, 54, and 32 for the High-High, High-Low, Low-High and Low-Low conditions, respectively. The percentages of stimuli recalled by comparable groups in the two studies are almost identical, indicating the generalization that stimulus recall will be approximately 50% following the learning of similarly constituted paired associates. As the stimulus or response terms vary in meaningfulness, a concomitant increase or decrease, respectively, in recall may be expected.

Summary

Eighty *S*s learned lists of paired associates in which the stimulus and response terms varied in meaningfulness (*m*). Four main experimental conditions were employed (High-High, High-Low, Low-High, and Low-Low). In addition half of the *S*s in each condition articulated the stimulus word during learning while the other half did not.

Each *S* learned by the anticipation method with correction to a criterion of two successive errorless anticipations. Immediately after the acquisition trials *S*s were given a "backward" recall test.

The main results were:

1. Variations in response meaningfulness produced a significant effect upon acquisition. Stimulus meaningfulness and articulation produced no significant effects.

2. Stimulus meaningfulness produced significantly greater *stimulus* recall, and the effect of response meaningfulness on stimulus recall approached significance. Stimulus ar-

ticulation had no significant effect upon stimulus recall.

3. Learning curves for each of the four main experimental conditions were negatively accelerated and conformed to the hierarchy of effects predicted by Noble and McNeely.

It is concluded that the results of the present experiment generally support an S-R motor patterning view of paired-associate learning.

References

BUGELSKI, B. R. The role of familiarity in the transfer of training situation. Paper read at Amer. Psychol. Ass., New York, Sept., 1957.

BUGELSKI, B. R., & SCHARLOCK, D. F. An experimental demonstration of unconscious mediated generalization. *J. exp. Psychol.*, 1952, **44**, 334–338.

CIEUTAT, V. J., STOCKWELL, F. E., & NOBLE, C. E. The interaction of ability and amount of practice with stimulus and response meaningfulness (*m*, *m'*) in paired-associate learning. *J. exp. Psychol.*, 1958, **56**, 193–202.

FELDMAN, S. M., & UNDERWOOD, B. J. Stimulus recall following paired-associate learning. *J. exp. Psychol.*, 1957, **53**, 11–15.

KIMBLE, G. A., & DUFORT, R. H. Meaningfulness and isolation as factors in verbal learning. *J. exp. Psychol.*, 1955, **50**, 361–368.

MANDLER, G., & CAMPBELL, E. H. Effect of variation in associative frequency of stimulus and response members on paired-associate learning. *J. exp. Psychol.*, 1957, **54**, 269–273.

NOBLE, C. E. An analysis of meaning. *Psychol. Rev.*, 1952, **59**, 421–430.

NOBLE, C. E., & MCNEELY, D. The role of meaningfulness (*m*) in paired-associate verbal learning. *J. exp. Psychol.*, 1957, **53**, 16–22.

SHEFFIELD, F. D. The role of meaningfulness of stimulus and response in verbal learning. Unpublished doctoral dissertation, Yale Univer., 1946.

WOODWORTH, R. S., & SCHLOSBERG. H. *Experimental psychology.* (Rev. ed.) New York: Holt, 1954.

(Received May 8, 1958)

ARTICLE 3

The Effect of Stimulus Meaningfulness and Response Meaningfulness in the Absence of Response Learning

WILLIAM EPSTEIN AND RACHEL STREIB

University of Kansas, Lawrence, Kansas

Almost all studies of the effects of independent variations of stimulus meaningfulness (*M*) and response meaningfulness on associative learning have concurred in showing that variations in response *M* have greater effects than comparable variations in stimulus *M* (cf. Underwood and Schulz, 1960, pp. 35-42, for a review). This finding fits in well with the two-stage analysis of associative learning discussed by Köhler (1941), Hovland and Kurtz (1952), and elaborated recently by Underwood and Schulz (1960). The two phases are the response-learning stage and the associative stage. Response *M* has a greater effect because variations of response *M* can influence both stages of learning, while variations of stimulus *M* presumably affect the associative stage only. One obvious implication of this analysis is that "if the response-recall phase could be completely eliminated [then] the effect of *M* on the stimulus and on the response side would be equivalent, for both effects would be limited entirely to the associative stage" (Underwood and Schulz, 1960, pp. 95-96).

An experiment was performed to test this implication. The general aim of the experiment was to compare the facilitating effects of stimulus *M* and response *M* when response learning was necessary with the effects obtained when response learning was unnecessary. For this purpose, pairs consisting of low-*M* stimuli and high-*M* responses (List L-H) were compared with the same pairs in reverse order (List H-L) under three conditions of learning. Condition *A* followed the conventional procedures of the method of anticipation. Anticipatory learning requires both response learning and association formation and should yield a difference in favor of List L-H. Conditions *Re* and *Rd* were two different conditions of recognition. The procedure for these conditions was similar to that of Condition *A* with one major difference. The test exposures for Condition *A* were presentations of the stimulus without any accompanying response, while under Conditions *Re* and *Rd* the test exposures presented the stimulus accompanied by three alternative responses. The *S* was instructed to select the correct response from the set of three available responses. This procedure eliminated the necessity of response recall since the responses were available to *S* at the time of testing. Under these circumstances, the effects of stimulus *M* and response *M* should be equivalent, and no difference between the learning of Lists L-H and H-L should be obtained.

METHOD

Subjects

Ninety-six undergraduate students in an introductory psychology course, with no prior experience as *S*s in experiments on serial or paired-associate learning, were assigned to one of the six experimental conditions, thereby comprising six groups of 16 *S*s each. Assignment to experimental conditions was determined by order of arrival in the laboratory. The running sequence was *Re*, H-L, L-H; *A*, H-L, L-H; *Rd*, H-L, L-H, for each successive block of six *S*s.

Materials

Sixty paralogs ranging in *m*-value from 0.99 to 9.61 were selected from Noble's list (1952, p. 426). Twenty of these were combined into ten pairs. The

Reprinted with permission of the authors and the publisher, the Academic Press. The article appeared originally in the *Journal of Verbal Learning and Verbal Behavior*, 1962, **1**, 105–108.

differences between the value of *m* for the stimulus and response members comprising the ten pairs were comparable. The mean difference was 5.28 ($SD = 1.03$). The remaining 40 paralogs served as the incorrect alternatives for Lists L-H and H-L under Condition *Re*. Two of these paralogs were assigned to each of the response members in a manner intended to meet the following two requirements: (1) The *m*-values of the correct response and the two incorrect alternatives within a given set of choices should be similar. The mean range of the value of *m* within a set of alternatives was 0.20 ($SD = 0.40$). (2) Obvious associative linkages between stimuli and responses (correct or incorrect) should be avoided.

Procedure

Easy Recognition (*Re*). The lists were presented in a memory drum at a 2:2-sec. rate with a 4-sec. intertrial interval. After the initial learning trial, each trial consisted of 2-sec. presentations of the stimulus accompanied by a set of three alternative responses, followed by a 2-sec. exposure of the correct pairing. The *S* was instructed to select the correct response and pronounce it aloud. Three different random orders of presentation were used. The same order was never used on successive trials. Learning continued to the criterion of one perfect trial.

In preliminary work we were surprised to observe that three out of five *S*s learned the list of 10 pairs in one trial. Granting that recognition is an easier task than correct anticipation, one-trial acquisition of the entire list is unusual. Postexperimental questioning revealed the basis for this performance. The *S*s were not acquiring associations. Instead, they were able to select the correct response solely on the basis of differential familiarity. Thus, if the pair TARTAN-LEMUR appeared on the initial learning trial and TARTAN-NIMBUS-PERCEPT-LEMUR appeared in the test on the next trial, *S* selected LEMUR because it was the only one of the three alternatives which he remembered as having appeared previously. This is an interesting accomplishment, but it is not associative learning.

In order to eliminate the differential familiarity of the correct response, familiarization training was introduced prior to associative learning. Each stimulus and each correct response received two familiar ization exposures, and each incorrect response-alternative received three exposures. The third exposure of the incorrect alternative was intended to compensate for the preliminary presentation of the correct alternative during the initial learning trial. The familiarization procedure consisted of a serial presentation of the 40 items in random order. Each stimulus and each correct response appeared twice in the series and each incorrect alternative appeared three times. The *S*s were asked to read the items aloud, and they were informed that items from this list would be used in a task which would follow immediately.

Difficult Recognition (*Rd*). The conditions were very similar to those prevailing for *Re*. The main difference concerned the set of responses available to *S* during the test. The alternative responses for *Re* were items which never served as the correct responses for any stimuli in the list. For *Rd* the incorrect alternatives were selected from the pool of correct responses. Each response served twice as an incorrect alternative. To enhance the comparability of the two recognition conditions, each of the 20 items was given two familiarization exposures in the manner described above. No pretraining on irrelevant responses was introduced since Underwood *et al.* (1959) obtained comparable results with *S*s who received pretraining on irrelevant responses and those who received no pretraining.

Anticipation (*A*). The *S*s in these two groups began with two familiarization trials with the 20 items in the list. Following pretraining, *S*s learned List L-H or H-L according to the customary procedures for the method of anticipation. A 2:2-sec. rate of presentation was used with an intertrial interval of 4 sec. The responses were pronounced aloud, and learning continued to one perfect trial.

Results

The mean number of trials to criterion for Lists L-H and H-L under the three conditions of testing are given in Table 1. An over-all analysis of variance of these data showed that the main effect for lists was not significant ($F = 0.34$). However, the effects of conditions of testing ($F = 42.89$, $df = 2/90$) and the interaction of lists with conditions of testing ($F = 13.94$, $df = 2/90$) were significant ($P < .01$).

Table 1 shows that List L-H was learned more rapidly than List H-L under Condition *A*. The difference of 9.56 trials is statistically significant ($t = 2.81$, $df = 15$, $P < .02$).[1] This result confirms the findings of earlier investigators as well as the suitability of our particular selection of items.

[1] Because of the presence of a significant difference between the two sample variances, the obtained *t* value was evaluated in terms of half the number of *df* available. The rationale for this procedure is discussed by Edwards (1960, cf. Chapter 8).

TABLE 1
MEAN NUMBER OF TRIALS TO MASTERY FOR LISTS L-H AND H-L UNDER THREE CONDITIONS OF TESTING

List	Condition *A*		Condition *Re*		Condition *Rd*	
	Mean	*SD*	Mean	*SD*	Mean	*SD*
H-L	23.56	12.96	3.31	1.36	7.40	4.69
L-H	14.00	4.79	3.31	1.90	15.18	7.00
diff.	9.56	—	0.00	—	7.78	—

The results of Condition *Re* will be considered next. The two-stage analysis of associative learning suggests that with the elimination of response learning the effect of stimulus *M* and response *M* will be equivalent. In the present case, the prediction was that under Condition *Re* the rates of learning Lists L-H and H-L would be equivalent. Table 1 shows that the mean trials to mastery were identical for both lists.

Finally, the results for Condition *Rd* will be examined. In *Rd* the incorrect alternatives were responses from within the list instead of extra-list items as in *Re*. The purpose of introducing this condition was to test the main hypothesis under more difficult recognition conditions. That difficulty was indeed increased may be seen by comparing the results for *Rd* with those for *Re* (see Table 1). However, in respect to our main hypothesis the results were completely unexpected. List L-H required twice as many trials to mastery as List H-L. The difference between the two lists was significant ($t = 2.10$, $df = 30$, $P < .05$). An analysis of the individual pairs showed that each of the ten L-H pairs was more difficult than the corresponding H-L pair.

DISCUSSION

This experiment has demonstrated that the superior effectiveness of response *M* is restricted to the conditions of anticipatory learning. Under Condition *Re* the lists did not differ in ease of learning, and under Condition *Rd* List L-H was more difficult than List H-L.

The results for *Re* were expected, although they contradicted the usual finding of response-*M* superiority. The two disparate findings are theoretically congruent in the terms of the two-stage analysis of associative learning. However, the results for *Rd* were unexpected. They are inconsistent with all previous findings regarding this question, and do not appear to be directly derivable from any specific theoretical proposals advanced by earlier investigators.

One way to explain the results for *Rd* is to assume that stimulus *M* facilitates the formation of associations in the associative stage. This facilitation may be ascribed to the greater associative probability of high-*M* stimuli as Underwood and Schulz (1960, pp. 294-296) have suggested. High-*M* stimuli elicit a greater number of associates and one of these may successfully mediate the prescribed association. The presumed facilitating effect of stimulus *M* is masked by differences in response learning under Condition *A* and is not discernible under Condition *Re* due to the rapid acquisition of both lists.

Supportive evidence for this interpretation is provided by comparing the learning of both lists under Conditions *A* and *Rd*. List H-L, which is presumed to be favored by high stimulus *M*, required less than 1/3 the number of trials to criterion under Condition *Rd* than under Condition *A*. On the other hand, List L-H which derived no special advantage from meaningfulness required an equivalent number of trials under both conditions.

An experiment which compared the acquisition of L-L and L-H (or H-L and H-H) lists, with the need for response learning eliminated, would be instructive. The interpretation proposed above would predict that the two lists of constant stimulus-*M* should fare equally well under these conditions. The occurrence of differences in favor of the high response-*M* list would have interesting implications for the stage-analysis of associative learning.

Summary

The two-stage analysis of associative learning suggests that with the elimination of response learning, stimulus *M* and response *M* should have equivalent effects. This expectation was tested by comparing a low stimulus *M* and high response M list (L-H) with its reversed version (H-L) under three conditions. Condition *A* was anticipatory learning. Since this involved both response learning and association formation, a difference in favor of List L-H was expected. Conditions *Re* and *Rd* were recognition tests of two levels of difficulty. Under these conditions no response recall was necessary and the two lists were expected to be learned at comparable rates.

The results showed that List L-H was superior under Condition *A*. The two lists required an identical number of trials to mastery under Condition *Re*. These findings supported the two-stage theory. However, the results for *Rd* were unexpected. For *Rd*, List H-L was learned in significantly fewer trials than List L-H.

The findings were discussed, and an effort was made to explain the paradoxical results of Condition *Rd*.

References

Edwards, A. L. *Experimental design in psychological research.* New York: Rinehart, 1960.

Hovland, C. I., and Kurtz, K. H. Experimental studies in rote-learning theory: X. Pre-learning syllable familiarization and the length-difficulty relationship. *J. exp. Psychol.*, 1952, **44**, 31-39.

Köhler, W. *Dynamics in Psychology.* New York: Liveright, 1940.

Noble, C. E. An analysis of meaning. *Psychol. Rev.*, 1952, **59**, 421-430.

Underwood, B. J., and Schulz, R. W. *Meaningfulness and verbal learning.* Philadelphia: Lippincott, 1960.

Underwood, B. J., Runquist, W. N., and Schulz, R. W. Response learning in paired-associate lists as a function of intralist similarity. *J. exp. Psychol.*, 1959, **58**, 70-78.

(Received April 19, 1962)

ARTICLE 4

FAMILIARIZATION (*n*) AS A STIMULUS FACTOR IN PAIRED-ASSOCIATE VERBAL LEARNING[1]

DONALD R. GANNON AND CLYDE E. NOBLE

Louisiana State University *Montana State University*

The Law of Acquaintance is currently enjoying a scientific revival among human learning psychologists. According to Robinson: "the act of reading or reciting . . . may . . . influence the facility with which that act enters into new associations" (1932, p. 118). Despite its premature announcement nearly thirty years ago, very little evidence favoring this principle was available until the past decade when the quantitative effects of frequency of stimulation (n) upon recognition behavior and familiarity judgments were discovered (Arnoult, 1956; Noble, 1954, 1960; Solomon & Postman, 1952; Underwood & Schulz, 1960, Exp. I). In general, the facilitation functions for a variety of materials are negatively accelerated in the range $n=0$ to 40, with returns diminishing rapidly around $n = 20$. Serial learning proficiency (R%) is similarly affected by n (Hovland & Kurtz, 1952; Noble, 1955; Riley & Phillips, 1959; Underwood & Schulz, 1960, Exp. III), but paired-associate learning presents a maze of contradictions.

One of G. E. Müller's students (Winzen, 1921) made an early attempt to determine whether familiarization is more influential in the stimulus (S) or in the response (R) position. Learning pronounceable syllables which they had seen either 0 or 20 times the day before, *S*s practiced by the method of right associates (Treffermethode) at a presentation rate of about one S-R pair every 9 sec. Winzen reported that the combination S_{20}-R_0 produced more correct responses than the combination S_0-R_{20}. Unfortunately, the control pairs S_0-R_0 and S_{20}-R_{20} were not included in the experimental design, nor was the statistical treatment adequate by modern standards to permit any definite conclusions. Two recent studies (Cieutat, 1960; Morikawa, 1959, Exp. II) lend partial support to Winzen's observations, but other investigators have either found null results (Bailey & Jeffrey, 1958; Mandler & Campbell, 1957; Waters, 1939) or contradictory evidence (Sheffield, 1946; Underwood & Schulz, 1960; Weiss, 1958). These experiments will be discussed later.

The present study was designed to evaluate an hypothesis based on data pertaining to *meaningfulness* (Noble, 1952a) available in 1957. Two independent experiments by Cieutat, Stockwell, and Noble (1958), confirmed since by others (Cieutat, 1959; Hunt, 1959; Morikawa, 1959, Exp. I), showed significant effects of meaningfulness on both the S term and the R term but a greater influence

[1] This paper is based upon a master's thesis performed by DRG under the guidance of CEN. An abridged report was made to the Southeastern Psychological Association, April 1958. We are grateful to Blaine L. Baker, Victor J. Cieutat, and Charles H. Koski for checking the statistical analyses; to Irmgard Taylor for assistance in translation of the Winzen article; and to Margaret B. Koch, Donald J. Lewis, and Ruth H. Preston for helpful suggestions.

Preparation of this report was facilitated by a contract between the Office of Naval Research and Montana State University. Reproduction in whole or in part is permitted for any purpose of the United States Government.

Reprinted with permission of the authors and the publisher, the American Psychological Association. The article appeared originally in the *Journal of Experimental Psychology*, 1961, **62**, 14–23.

on R than on S. Mindful of the serial learning data, they reasoned that if differences in the learning of paired associates varying in meaningfulness are due primarily to the positive transfer effects of *n*, an appropriate experiment

> might reveal that meaningfulness is a secondary phenomenon derivable from the same basic variable that controls all learning. This coordination would be demonstrated neatly if one could produce similar acquisition curves by manipulating either (frequency or meaningfulness). The empirical question [they concluded] is whether familiarization would affect the S and R terms differentially (1958, p. 201).

Since it is known that R% is a function of meaningfulness in serial and paired-associate learning (Noble, 1952b; Noble & McNeely, 1957); that R% is a function of familiarization in serial learning; and that the meaningfulness of the R term in paired associates contributes more to learning proficiency than the S term, it follows that if familiarization is the *sole* basis of the meaningfulness effect, then familiarization should facilitate the learning of paired associates in a similar manner. In symbolic terms, the following three implications were drawn by analogy to the two experiments by Cieutat, Stockwell, and Noble (1958): (*a*) $(S_{20}\text{-}R_{20}) > (S_0\text{-}R_{20}) > (S_{20}\text{-}R_0) > (S_0\text{-}R_0)$. (*b*) All main effects due to the stimulus term (S), the response term (R), and number of practice trials (N) should be significant. (*c*) Given enough practice, there ought to be significant two-factor interactions ($S \times R$, $S \times N$, $R \times N$) and a three-factor interaction ($S \times R \times N$).

Should the main effects and interactions turn out radically different from the predictions above, it would incline one toward the alternative hypothesis that familiarization (*n*) cannot be used to explain all of the variance in R% scores thought to be due to meaningfulness (*m*), and that there must be more to meaningfulness than sheer frequency of experience, e.g., number of associations (Noble, 1961; Parker & Noble, 1960). The latter is the view of *m* originally espoused by the second author (Noble, 1952a); hence the present investigation is at once an indirect test of the associationistic concept of meaningfulness and a direct test of Winzen's stimulus-familiarity hypothesis.

Method

Design considerations.—The experiment consisted of two phases: familiarization and learning. In the familiarization phase *S*s received either 0 or 20 independent exposures (*n*) of items of low meaningfulness (*m*) and familiarity (*f*). The "words" later to be designated as S and R terms were never paired; each was presented as a single stimulus to which *S* made the identifying response of pronunciation. This insured stimulus reception as well as exercise of the response. The learning phase was designed to determine whether *n* facilitated learning, and if so, whether familiarization differentially influenced the relative contributions of S and R to the learning of five pairs of the previously isolated items. Four experimental groups were formed by all combinations of locus (S vs. R) and amount (0 vs. 20) of familiarization, while a control group received no familiarization training. All *S*s practiced the same five S-R pairs during the learning phase, so any observed differences in R% scores among the experimental groups would have to be attributed to effects of the familiarization phase.

Several methodological points must be considered. First, high *m* theoretically requires high *n*, but not conversely (Noble, 1953); familiarization effects in this study may not, therefore, be explained as changes in meaningfulness. One experiment consistent with this view (Riley & Phillips, 1959) found that although serial learning of CVC material was accelerated by prior familiarization, the *m* values of the CVCs were unaffected. Second, it is important in the present investigation to use independent groups of naive *S*s in a constant-trials design. The purpose of this is to study acquisition phenomena including interactions, to avoid interference effects, to permit unbiased tests of S-R interaction, and to provide controls for generalized familiarization influences. Finally, in the interest of standardization, the familiarization and transfer operations are similar to those employed in earlier studies in this series.

Apparatus.—Instrumentation consisted of a Viewlex Viewmatic automatic slide projector (No. RCP-1) for the familiarization phase and a Patterson memory drum (No. 1-A) for the learning phase. The projector was equipped with a circular slide cartridge having a capacity of 30 2 × 2 in. slides. Four cartridges were required, each of which contained the familiarization items for a single experimental group. The memory drum was fitted with a white tape containing the paired associates typed in capital letters. A sliding shutter over the aperture permitted *S* to view either the left or the right side of the drum. The projection and tachistoscopic functions were controlled by two Hunter electronic timers set to expose each slide for 1 sec., and to provide a 1.4-sec. interstimulus period.[2] This gave a presentation rate of one slide every 2.4 sec. in the familiarization phase. For the learning phase, the intertrial interval was 8 sec., and the S item appeared for 2 sec. followed by the S and R items together for 2 sec.

TABLE 1

Familiarization Lists for the Four Experimental Groups Appearing in Each Projector Cartridge

	S_{20}-R_{20}		S_0-R_{20}		S_{20}-R_0		S_0-R_0
I	DELPIN		DELPIN	I	DELPIN		DELPIN
	BYSSUS		BYSSUS		BYSSUS		BYSSUS
	ULNA		ZUMAP		ULNA		JETSAM
	TAROP		JETSAM		TAROP		ZUMAP
	GOKEM		DELPIN		GOKEM		BYSSUS
	NOSTAW		QUIPSON		NOSTAW		QUIPSON
R	SAGROLE		BYSSUS	R	SAGROLE		ZUMAP
	NOSTAW		ZUMAP		NOSTAW		DELPIN
	GOKEM	I	DELPIN		GOKEM		QUIPSON
	TAROP		JETSAM		TAROP		JETSAM
	ULNA		QUIPSON		ULNA		BYSSUS
	SAGROLE		BYSSUS		SAGROLE		DELPIN
	JETSAM		JETSAM		JETSAM		JETSAM
	ZUMAP		ZUMAP		ZUMAP		ZUMAP
I	QUIPSON		QUIPSON		QUIPSON	I	QUIPSON
	BYSSUS		BYSSUS		BYSSUS		BYSSUS
	ZUMAP		ZUMAP		ZUMAP		ZUMAP
	DELPIN		DELPIN		DELPIN		DELPIN
	VOLVAP		VOLVAP		ZUMAP		QUIPSON
	XYLEM		XYLEM		JETSAM		DELPIN
	MEARDON		MEARDON	I	DELPIN		ZUMAP
	KUPOD		KUPOD		QUIPSON		JETSAM
R	LATUK	R	LATUK		BYSSUS		DELPIN
	KUPOD		KUPOD		ZUMAP		BYSSUS
	MEARDON		MEARDON		DELPIN		QUIPSON
	XYLEM		XYLEM		JETSAM		JETSAM
	VOLVAP		VOLVAP		QUIPSON		BYSSUS
	LATUK		LATUK		BYSSUS		ZUMAP
I	QUIPSON	I	QUIPSON		QUIPSON		QUIPSON
	JETSAM		JETSAM		JETSAM		JETSAM
I	5@2 ea.		5@4 ea.		5@4 ea.		5@6 ea.
R	10@2 ea.		5@2 ea.		5@2 ea.		none
Σ	30		30		30		30

Note.—R = relevant items, I = irrelevant items.

Learning materials.—Fifteen dissyllabic "words," mostly paralogs, were used for familiarization training. Ten of these (relevant items) also appeared as the S-R elements of the paired-associate lists in the learning phase, while the remaining five (irrelevant items) were used only as fillers in the familiarization phase in order to equate the total number of exposures for *S*s in the four experimental conditions. All items were chosen from the low end of the *m* and *f* scales (Noble, 1953) so that the mean median *m* value was .30, and the mean *f* value was .41. Low scale values were used in order to reduce the number of possible S-R connections formed outside the experimental situation and to insure comparability with the previous serial learning study (Noble, 1955). The four familiarization lists are reproduced in Table 1.

Subjects.—The *S*s were 120 male and female college students obtained on a voluntary basis at Louisiana State University in 1957. Ages ranged from 17 to 43 yr. (mean = 19.3 yr.), and all *S*s were naive with respect to paired-associate learning. Twenty-four *S*s were assigned to each of the four experimental groups in a counterbalanced order of arrival at the laboratory. An additional 24 *S*s were used as a special control group which received no familiarization training. The *E* engaged these *S*s in conversation for an amount of time equivalent to the familiarization phase, then proceeded to the learning phase.

Procedure.—Four experimental groups were formed in terms of locus and amount of familiarization, as follows: S_{20}-R_{20}, S_0-R_{20}, S_{20}-R_0, S_0-R_0. In the familiarization phase, *S* was instructed to pronounce each dissyllable aloud as it was projected on the screen. The *S*s were not informed of the subsequent learning phase. As shown above in Table 1, the relevant items were separated by irrelevant items in order to reduce the formation of any initial S-R connections before the learning phase. The ratios of relevant to irrelevant items in the S_{20}-R_{20}, S_0-R_{20}, S_{20}-R_0, and S_0-R_0 groups, respectively, were 20/10, 10/20, 10/20, and 0/30. Since each relevant item was exposed

[2] The present exposure duration is from 1.3 to 2.0 sec. briefer than those used in earlier studies (Noble, 1954, 1955), but the interstimulus period is the same.

twice in each cartridge, 10 revolutions were required to obtain 20 exposures. There were 300 exposures in all.

In the learning phase, *S* was instructed to anticipate the R term after the first trial. As is standard in this series, both S and R were pronounced and the correction method was used. Seventeen learning trials were given, with the two groups of five relevant items constituting the S and R terms. Responses were scored as correct (R+) or erroneous (R−). The criteria for an erroneous response were as follows: (*a*) omissions, (*b*) late responses, (*c*) mispronounced responses, (*d*) the same response repeated three times in succession during a single trial. The *Ss* had to maintain a uniform pronunciation of the paralogs in order to receive R+ scores by the third error criterion. To neutralize accidental order effects, two lists of S-R pairs were formed. The Forward list, mounted on the left side of the memory drum, consisted of pairs formed from the 10 relevant items. The Reverse list, mounted on the right side of the drum, transposed these items so that S_1 became R_1, S_2 became R_2, etc. The *E* constructed four random trial sequences to minimize serial learning effects. These learning lists are reproduced in Table 2. There were three Forward and three Reverse *Ss* assigned to each of the four trial sequences, making a total of 24 *Ss* per condition. The familiarization and learning phases required 12 min. each, separated by a 1-min. rest interval during which *E* engaged *S* in conversation. Total time, including instructions, was approximately 27 min. for all *Ss*.

Instructions.—The familiarization instructions were given verbatim as follows:

This is an experiment on verbal learning. We are interested in the general learning process common to all people and are not testing your intelligence or personality. In the first part of the experiment you will be shown slides to get you acquainted with the procedure. With this projector, I am going to flash on the screen some two-syllable words similar to actual words. Probably you have never seen any of them before so there is no standard or correct pronunciation. All you have to do is say each word out loud before it leaves the screen. Whichever way you pronounce each word when we start is all right, but try to say it the same way each time the word comes up. Do *not* try to memorize the order of the words because this will change constantly. Please say each word loudly and clearly enough so I can hear and understand you. In this way I will be sure to give you credit for a response. Try to say the word before it leaves the screen, since the words come in rapid order. Are there any questions? Now remember, if you see "dinner," say "dinner." Ready?

The learning instructions were given verbatim as follows:

TABLE 2

PAIRED-ASSOCIATE LISTS AND TRIAL SEQUENCES FOR ALL GROUPS DURING THE LEARNING PHASE

Trial Sequences	Learning Lists			
	Forward		Reverse	
I	TAROP	XYLEM	XYLEM	TAROP
	SAGROLE	LATUK	LATUK	SAGROLE
	GOKEM	MEARDON	MEARDON	GOKEM
	ULNA	VOLVAP	VOLVAP	ULNA
	NOSTAW	KUPOD	KUPOD	NOSTAW
II	ULNA	VOLVAP	VOLVAP	ULNA
	GOKEM	MEARDON	MEARDON	GOKEM
	TAROP	XYLEM	XYLEM	TAROP
	NOSTAW	KUPOD	KUPOD	NOSTAW
	SAGROLE	LATUK	LATUK	SAGROLE
III	GOKEM	MEARDON	MEARDON	GOKEM
	NOSTAW	KUPOD	KUPOD	NOSTAW
	ULNA	VOLVAP	VOLVAP	ULNA
	SAGROLE	LATUK	LATUK	SAGROLE
	TAROP	XYLEM	XYLEM	TAROP
IV	NOSTAW	KUPOD	KUPOD	NOSTAW
	ULNA	VOLVAP	VOLVAP	ULNA
	SAGROLE	LATUK	LATUK	SAGROLE
	TAROP	XYLEM	XYLEM	TAROP
	GOKEM	MEARDON	MEARDON	GOKEM

This is the second part of the experiment. Here is a memory drum. Shortly after the apparatus starts, you will see a word in the window. You are to pronounce this word and those that follow it as you see them. First, a word will appear alone, then the shade will rise and you will see another word. You are to pronounce them both. After you have seen this entire list once, your job will be to call out each single word and then to anticipate the word with which it was paired. In other words, as you see the *single* word, you are to pronounce it, and then immediately you are to pronounce the word with which it was paired *before* the second word appears. If you fail to anticipate an item, pronounce it when it appears anyway. If you think you know what a word will be but are not sure, *guess*. It will not hurt your score any more than to say nothing, and if you get it correct it will count as a success. If you anticipate a word *incorrectly*, correct yourself as soon as the word appears. Remember to pronounce each item *aloud*. Do not try to think ahead more than one step at a time or to count, because the *order* of the pairs will change as the list is repeated. Do not try to use any special system in your learning. Simply associate each single word with the word with which it is paired. Please try to pronounce all words the same way each time they appear so that I can give you credit for a correct response. Any questions?

RESULTS

The major results of the experiment are shown in Fig. 1. Percentages of correct responses (R%) are plotted as a function of amount of practice (N) grouped in blocks of two trials for the five conditions. The influence of S-term familiarization is greater

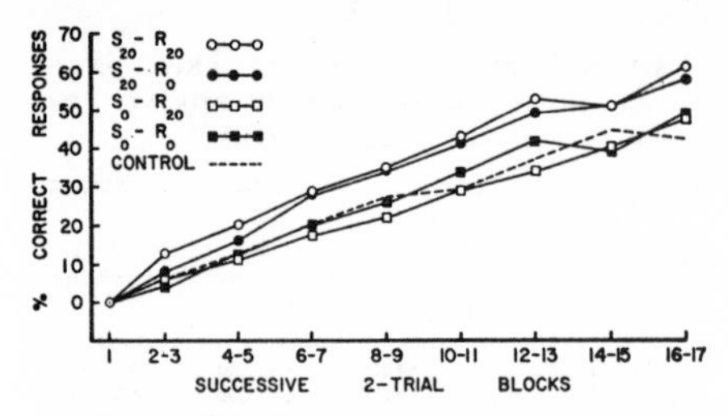

FIG. 1. Acquisition curves for a list of five paired associates as a function of practice under four different combinations of low ($n = 0$) and high ($n = 20$) frequency of stimulus (S) and response (R) term familiarization. (The Control group received no prior familiarization experience. Each curve contains 24 *Ss*.)

than that of R-term familiarization, while the effect of the latter treatment is little different from having no familiarization at all. Total R+ scores for the various groups during the 17-trial period, given in parentheses, were ordered as follows: S_{20}-R_{20} (735), S_{20}-R_0 (689), S_0-R_0 (542), Control (524), S_0-R_{20} (504). The S-term difference is (1424 − 1046 =) 378 units, contrasted with an R-difference of only (1239 − 1231 =) 8 units. An 8 × 5 Type I mixed-factorial analysis of variance (Lindquist, 1953, p. 267) was performed on the R+ scores from which Fig. 1 was constructed. There were significant main effects of Practice ($F = 157.29$; $df = 7/805$; $P < .001$) and Conditions ($F = 2.69$; $df = 4/115$; $P < .05$), but the interaction was not significant ($F < 1.00$; $df = 28/805$).

In order to test for a learning-to-learn familiarization effect, the Control group may be considered a baseline from which to measure possible generalized influences of the familiarization phase on the learning phase. A 3 × 1 simple-randomized analysis of variance (Lindquist, 1953, p. 47) was therefore applied to the overall R+ scores of the Control group and the two S_0 groups, omitting both S_{20} groups. The result gave no evidence of any nonspecific familiarization effect ($F < 1.00$; $df = 2/68$; $P > .20$), so the three lowest curves in Fig. 1 may be regarded as the same except for sampling fluctuations. There is neither a relevant response effect (S_0-R_{20} vs. S_0-R_0) nor an irrelevant stimulus-response effect (S_0-R_0 vs. Control) that can be attributed to the 300 trials of stimulation and pronunciation experienced during the familiarization phase.

To evaluate possible two-factor and three-factor interactions, a 16 × 2 × 2, N × S × R Type III mixed-factorial analysis of variance (Lindquist, 1953, p. 281) was performed on the individual trial R+ scores for the four experimental groups only. The summary, shown in Table 3, indicates significant main effects of Practice (N) and Stimulus Familiarization (S). Neither the Response Familiarization (R) factor nor any of the interactions were significant sources of variance.

Because R+ scores do not reveal any Practice × Conditions interactions, the facilitation due to S-term familiarization must be largely an initial effect followed by latter paral-

TABLE 3

ANALYSIS OF VARIANCE OF CORRECT RESPONSES (R+) OF THE EXPERIMENTAL GROUPS DURING TRIALS 2–17

Source	*df*	*MS*	*F*
Between *Ss*	95		
Stimulus (S)	1	93.02	7.86*
Response (R)	1	.04	.00
S × R	1	4.60	.39
Error (*b*)	92	11.83	
Within *Ss*	1440		
Trials (N)	15	57.99	84.30**
S × N	15	.70	1.03
R × N	15	.44	.63
S × R × N	15	.54	.78
Error (*w*)	1380	.69	
Total	1535		

* $P < .01$.
** $P < .001$.

lelism. This hypothesis is confirmed by comparing the average number of trials or errors (R−) preceding the first correct anticipation of each S-R pair in all groups. Most of these R− scores were omissions rather than late or overt incorrect responses, so no qualitative analysis of errors will be made. Mean R− scores required to attain this reaction-threshold criterion (averaged over *S*s not S-R pairs) were ordered as follows: S_{20}-R_{20} (5.20), S_{20}-R_0 (5.33), Control (6.28), S_0-R_{20} (6.88), S_0-R_0 (6.95). A 5 × 1 simple-randomized analysis of variance (Lindquist, 1953, p. 47) of these data gave an F ratio of 2.79 ($df = 4/112$; $P < .05$) which is significant. Again, the major difference favors the two S_{20} groups over the S_0 groups, with the Control group in the middle. Employing t tests of the deviations of each pair of extreme groups from the Control group based on the within-groups σ^2 (Lindquist, 1953, p. 91), we find significantly more errors under the S_0 (irrelevant n) combination and fewer errors under the S_{20} (relevant n) combination ($t = 3.31$; $df = 112$; $P < .01$); however, the two component ratios are not significant individually ($t \ngtr 1.69$; $df = 112$; $P > .05$). By the second correct (reinforced) anticipation all five groups have converged ($F < 1.00$; $df = 4/110$), and the speed of error elimination is essentially constant thereafter in agreement with Fig. 1. Observed group trends in R+ scores thus probably reflect unequal levels of proficiency (number of associates attained per trial) rather than differential rates of learning (growth of habit strength).

The results lead us to state that n has a facilitative influence on paired-associate learning only when familiarized items become the S members. Prelearning familiarization with the R members fails to produce any significant result, and except for initial error effects there is no further interaction between locus of familiarization (S vs. R) and amount of practice (N). In the light of these data, a simple stimulus-frequency theory of meaningfulness (Cieutat et al., 1958; Underwood & Schulz, 1960) must be rejected as untenable. We conclude that familiarization (n) does not produce effects which are equivalent to those produced by meaningfulness (m), and that m and n are therefore independent variables affecting verbal behavior.

Discussion

Two principal questions are raised by this experiment: (*a*) Are the results comparable with those obtained by other investigators? (*b*) Assuming no artifacts, what is the most reasonable interpretation of the current data?

Comparability.—Eight laboratories have followed up Winzen's (1921) work. Negative results in the Waters (1939), Mandler and Campbell (1957), and Bailey and Jeffrey (1958) experiments seem to be contingent on the use of CVC or CCC materials and very brief amounts or durations of familiarization. Contradictory findings reported in the Sheffield (1946), Weiss (1958), and Underwood and Schulz (1960) experiments are also associated with trigram material; in addition, the types and amounts of familiarization as well as the transfer tests are different. In opposition to Winzen, the hypothesis coming from this second group of studies suggests that familiarization is effective only in the R position. Occasionally there were signs of decremental influences of S-term familiarization (Sheffield, 1946; Underwood & Schulz, 1960, Exp. I, IV), but these trends were neither significant nor consistent (Underwood & Schulz, 1960, Exp. II). Although the latter experiments contain many ingenious features, there are difficulties in evaluating the R-facilitation and S-interference phenomena because of rather complex familiarization techniques, sophisticated *S*s, and incomplete factorial designs. Statistical tests of interaction among the S, R, and N factors are frequently lacking. As Underwood and Schulz say of their Exp. I, II, and IV: "they have raised more issues than they have settled regarding the effects of stimulus familiarization" (1960, pp. 125–126).

In support of Winzen, on the other hand, are the present data together with those of Morikawa (1959, Exp. II) and Cieutat (1960). Morikawa noted definite S-facilitation in Japanese *S*s when the R term was unfamiliar but little difference when the R term was familiar. A different procedural approach was tried by Cieutat in that pronounceable items of low *m* value were used, but he varied exposure duration (0 vs. 60 sec.) of the two terms (S vs. R) rather than frequency and did not require verbalization. Another difference is that his *S*s served in all four combinations of duration and locus; however, both S and R were pronounced in the transfer period, as in this experiment, and the *S*s were from the same population. Cieutat found significant effects attributable to N and to the $S \times R$ interaction, the latter being observed as a weak S-term decrement under R_0, a strong S-term increment under R_{60}, and an overall main effect favoring stimulus familiarization. (Referring to his Table 2, mean R+ scores for the S_0 and S_{60} conditions were 2.31 and 2.50, respectively, whereas means for R_0 and R_{60} were both exactly 2.41 units.) Sustained viewing, possible intertreatment interferences, and failure to require articulation during the familiarization period may account for the slight (statistically marginal) inhibitory S-effect under irrelevant R-term familiarization; the absence of a reference level provided by an unfamiliarized control group precludes firm inferences. This peculiarity is also characteristic of the Sheffield and Underwood-Schulz experiments. In one crucial respect, however, Cieutat's data are quite consistent with Winzen's and ours; namely, the significant superiority of his S_{60}-R_0 treatment combination over that of S_0-R_{60}.

The use of confounded and incomplete designs, unrelated or inadequate control procedures, *S*s of heterogeneous experience, diverse types or amounts of familiarization, different learning materials, and varied methods of testing for transfer renders impossible any comparative evaluation of the present findings in the same context with the above studies. About all that can be done from a constructive point of view is to urge that the reader be cautious in trying to resolve these conflicting reports, and to judge each set of experimental data in the light of its own methodology. With the reminder that our procedure was standard in this research program (e.g., specific familiarization technique), and that it was designed to meet certain boundary conditions (e.g., two-term articulation during learning), we turn now to a tentative explanation of the results.

Interpretation.—The data permit three unequivocal statements: (*a*) relevant S-term familiarization produced significant superiority in total R+ scores whereas relevant R-term familiarization had no influence; (*b*) when compared with the unfamiliarized Control condition, initial R− scores increased after irrelevant S-term familiarization and decreased after relevant S-term familiarization; (*c*) acquisition rates of correct responses and extinction rates of incorrect responses both became independent of original familiarization following the first reinforcement in the list.

Recalling the introductory discussion, a two-factor hypothesis may be suggested to account for the differential effects of *m* and *n* in paired-associate learning under these conditions. The evidence indicates that *n* is sufficient to influence behavior via the S term alone (stimulus predifferentiation) whereas *m* is *jointly* necessary to affect behavior via the R term (response patterning). One possible explanation of S-term facilitation, considered earlier by the second author in connection with the complex familiarization effects in serial learning (where the "perceptual" and "motor" aspects of verbal learning are confounded), is provided by the principle of stimulus constancy (Noble, 1955, p. 336). The core assumption, derived from the conditioning literature, is that repeated exposure-articulation sequences during the familiarization phase will attenuate variability in *S*'s perceptual (e.g., orientation, fixation) and identifying (e.g., pronunciation) responses to the paired-associate S terms when the learning phase is encountered. Assuming further that the stability of these perceptual and identifying responses grows in some negatively accelerated fashion with increasing n (like habit strength or familiarity), their facilitative influences ought to be maximal early in the learning phase then subside later as paired-associate training progresses. Although less parsimonious than a simple frequency explanation, this notion helps to understand the consistent (but weak) S-effects of m which have been observed in a number of studies (Cieutat, 1959; Cieutat et al., 1958, Exp. I, II; Hunt, 1959; Morikawa, 1959, Exp. II; Underwood & Schulz, 1960).[3]

Our two-factor hypothesis implies a systematic view of the verbal learning process which is somewhat at variance with that held by Underwood and Schulz (1960). Their two-stage analysis of "response-recall" followed by "associative hook-up" (reminiscent of Thorndikean selecting and connecting) postulates that frequency alone (e.g., n without reinforcement) is important for the first stage of learning, the second being related to meaningfulness (or pronunciability). So far we might agree, but they proceed from their "spew" hypothesis, which is based on free-recall phenomena, yet considered "not relevant for stimulus familiarization" (p. 100), to predict that (*a*) "rate of paired-associate learning should be an increasing function of amount of familiarization training given the response units of the list," and (*b*) that "response familiarization should facilitate learning considerably more than stimulus familiarization" (pp. 100–101). The emphatic lack of any R-term effect or of an R > S relation in the present data is clearly embarrassing to the Underwood-Schulz hypothesis.

But is our evidence relevant? A sophisticated critic might object that this investigation (using pronounceable words and paralogs) is not a fair test of the "spew" hypothesis because it fails to satisfy some of the Underwood-Schulz boundary conditions (e.g., CVCs and the spelling method). Unfortunately, these writers are neither very specific nor consistent about such matters (cf. the familiarization procedures, transfer tests, and *S*s in Exp. I vs. Exp. IV), but in one chapter (p. 95) they describe a hypothetical task where, even though the responses are "well integrated" (pronounceable), prior differences in n are definitely expected to alter the "availability" (reaction threshold?) of the R terms. The present procedure appears to conform to these general requirements; only the data are recalcitrant, paradoxically. Considering their repeated emphasis on the first stage process, incidentally, we find it curious that Underwood and Schulz are less interested in initial performance and rate measurements than in overall analyses.

A second possible objection to this experiment turns on our custom in this series of having *S*s articulate both terms in the paired-associate learning phase. It may be claimed that this requirement either (*a*) produces an unusual amount of S-term familiarization, or (*b*) shortens the effective anticipation interval for the S_0 groups as contrasted with the S_{20} groups. Briefly (aside from the standardization issue), our rejoinder to (*a*) is that we believe double articulation is necessary both to guarantee stimulus reception and to provide an unbiased test of differences between the manipulated properties of the antecedent (S) and consequent (R) events. Since all factors except temporal succession should be equated when evaluating the effects

[3] This tentative explanation does not presume to account for the initial decrements in the S_0-R_0 and S_0-R_{20} groups (relative to the Control), but it would not be inconsistent with a theory of stimulus variability to hypothesize that irrelevant familiarization in the S-position produces interference via stimulus trace generalization.

of *S*'s built-in response to an S term upon his ability to anticipate its paired R term, it seems elementary to have the former occur just as frequently as the latter during the learning phase (cf. also the rationale of the correction method on erroneous trials). This Underwood and Schulz did not do, hence it constitutes yet another difference between our procedures. Such a criticism could be turned around and directed at those who introduce biases favoring R-term familiarization.

The distributed-practice argument (*b*) is more plausible, though it loses force in view of Hunt's (1959) report of null results in a Cieutat-Stockwell-Noble (1958, Exp. I) type of experiment in which half the *S*s in each group articulated the paralogs while the other half did not. It is important to note that Hunt's material, the same dissyllables of the *m* scale used herein, can be pronounced faster than CVCs can be spelled. Of course, no one can be sure without experimenting that S-R familiarization effects do not interact with distributional factors, but the likelihood appears slim in the present case because *S*s in all groups except the Control were trained for 300 trials to pace their pronunciation responses at a 1-sec. rate during the familiarization phase. Furthermore, the S_0-R_0 group is slightly superior to both the Control and the S_0-R_{20} groups on R+ performance throughout the learning phase. The same phenomenon occurs in Cieutat's (1960) study. Both "spew" and distributional hypotheses imply the exact opposite of these observations. Appropriate experiments to settle this question will occur readily to most readers; meanwhile, the second author has some research in progress which indicates that type and tate of *n* are also relevant. The S-articulation factor is yet to be explored.

Our best judgment at the present writing is that no serious artifacts or procedural errors are contaminating the interpretation presented above. To repeat, however, the familiarization issue is not yet definitely settled. Much undoubtedly remains to be learned about the experimental control of *n* and the measurement of its effects.

Summary

The role of familiarization (*n*) in paired-associate verbal learning was investigated. One hundred twenty *S*s, divided into five independent groups of 24 each, were used. Four experimental groups were formed by all combinations of locus (S vs. R term) and amount (0 vs. 20 exposures) of familiarization, while a Control group received no familiarization experience. All groups then practiced a five-unit paired-associate list of dissyllables of low initial familiarity (*f*) and meaningfulness (*m*) for 17 trials.

The influence of relevant S-term familiarization was positive and significant ($P < .01$), but not that of relevant R-term familiarization. Analyses of correct responses (R+) revealed no evidence of an irrelevant (learning-to-learn) familiarization effect, nor of any interactions between S or R and amount of practice. The initial effects of familiarization on incorrect responses (R−) were also significant ($P < .05$), causing decrements in the (irrelevant) S_0 groups and increments in the (relevant) S_{20} groups when compared with nonfamiliarized controls. After the first correct (reinforced) anticipation, acquisition rates of R+ and extinction rates of R− were uniform for all groups.

It was concluded that familiarization (*n*) and meaningfulness (*m*) operations do not produce equivalent effects on verbal behavior under these conditions. Contradictory results from other laboratories were discussed, and a tentative two-factor hypothesis was presented as an attempted synthesis of the differential roles played by *m* and *n* in paired-associate learning.

References

Arnoult, M. D. Familiarity and recognition of nonsense shapes. *J. exp. Psychol.*, 1956, **51**, 269–276.

Bailey, J. H., & Jeffrey, W. E. Response strength and association value in stimulus predifferentiation. *Psychol. Rep.*, 1958, **4**, 715–721.

Cieutat, V. J. Supplementary report: Stimulus and response meaningfulness (*m*′) in paired-associate learning by hospitalized mental patients. *J. exp. Psychol.*, 1959, **58**, 490.

Cieutat, V. J. Differential familiarity with stimulus and response in paired-associate learning. *Percept. mot. Skills*, 1960, **11**, 269–275.

CIEUTAT, V. J., STOCKWELL, F. E., & NOBLE, C. E. The interaction of ability and amount of practice with stimulus and response meaningfulness (*m*, *m'*) in paired-associate learning. *J. exp. Psychol.*, 1958, **56**, 193–202.

HOVLAND, C. I., & KURTZ, K. Experimental studies in rote-learning theory: X. Pre-learning syllable familiarization and the length-difficulty relationship. *J. exp. Psychol.*, 1952, **44**, 31–39.

HUNT, R. G. Meaningfulness and articulation of stimulus and response in paired-associate learning and stimulus recall. *J. exp. Psychol.*, 1959, **57**, 262–267.

LINDQUIST, E. F. *Design and analysis of experiments in psychology and education.* Boston: Houghton Mifflin, 1953.

MANDLER, G., & CAMPBELL, E. H. Effect of variation in associative frequency of stimulus and response members on paired-associate learning. *J. exp. Psychol.*, 1957, **54**, 269–273.

MORIKAWA, Y. Functions of stimulus and response in paired-associate verbal learning. *Psychologia*, 1959, **2**, 41–56.

NOBLE, C. E. An analysis of meaning. *Psychol. Rev.*, 1952, **59**, 421–430. (a)

NOBLE, C. E. The role of stimulus meaning (*m*) in serial verbal learning. *J. exp. Psychol.*, 1952, **43**, 437–446; **44**, 465. (b)

NOBLE, C. E. The meaning-familiarity relationship. *Psychol. Rev.*, 1953, **60**, 89–98.

NOBLE, C. E. The familiarity-frequency relationship. *J. exp. Psychol.*, 1954, **47**, 13–16.

NOBLE, C. E. The effect of familiarization upon serial verbal learning. *J. exp. Psychol.*, 1955, **49**, 333–338.

NOBLE, C. E. Supplementary report: Familiarity and frequency. *J. exp. Psychol.*, 1960, **59**, 432–433; **60**, 418.

NOBLE, C. E. Verbal learning and individual differences. In C. N. Cofer (Ed.), *Verbal learning and verbal behavior.* New York: McGraw-Hill, 1961, in press. Ch. 6.

NOBLE, C. E., & MCNEELY, D. A. The role of meaningfulness (*m*) in paired-associate verbal learning. *J. exp. Psychol.*, 1957, **53**, 16–22.

PARKER, G. V. C., & NOBLE, C. E. Effects of experimentally-produced meaningfulness (*m*) on paired-associate learning. *Amer. Psychologist*, 1960, **15**, 451. (Abstract)

RILEY, D. A., & PHILLIPS, L. W. The effects of syllable familiarization on rote learning, association value, and reminiscence. *J. exp. Psychol.*, 1959, **57**, 372–379.

ROBINSON, E. S. *Association theory today.* New York: Century, 1932.

SHEFFIELD, F. D. The role of meaningfulness of stimulus and response in verbal learning. Unpublished doctoral dissertation, Yale University, 1946.

SOLOMON, R. L., & POSTMAN, L. Frequency of usage as a determinant of recognition thresholds for words. *J. exp. Psychol.*, 1952, **43**, 195–201.

UNDERWOOD, B. J., & SCHULZ, R. W. *Meaningfulness and verbal learning.* Chicago: Lippincott, 1960.

WATERS, R. H. The law of acquaintance. *J. exp. Psychol.*, 1939, **24**, 180–191.

WEISS, R. L. The role of association value and experimentally produced familiarity in paired associate verbal learning. (Unpublished doctoral dissertation, University of Buffalo, 1958) *Amer. Psychologist*, 1958, **13**, 386. (Abstract)

WINZEN, K. Die Abhängigkeit der paarweisen Assoziation von der Stellung des besser haftenden Gliedes. *Z. Psychol.*, 1921, **86**, 236–252.

(Early publication received August 17, 1960)

ARTICLE 5

SUPPLEMENTARY REPORT: STIMULUS FAMILIARIZATION IN PAIRED-ASSOCIATE LEARNING

RUDOLPH W. SCHULZ AND IRVING F. TUCKER

State University of Iowa

When *S*s are familiarized with the stimulus units but not the response units of a list prior to paired-associate (PA) learning, it has generally been found that stimulus familiarization (SF) has a slight inhibitory effect or no effect at all on PA performance (Underwood & Schulz, 1960). Recently, Gannon and Noble (1961) have reported significant facilitation of performance on a list of paired dissyllables following 20 trials of SF. Since the latter result is the one to be expected if frequency of prior experience is the vehicle through which stimulus meaningfulness has its effect on PA performance, it is a result with considerable theoretical significance (e.g., Cieutat, Stockwell, & Noble, 1958; Underwood & Schulz, 1960). However, the finding of a positive effect from SF is also conspicuously inconsistent with the results of previous studies. Therefore it seemed especially important to further assess the reliability of this result and consider potential alternative explanations for it.

One such alternative is that Gannon and Noble's procedure of having *S* articulate the stimulus unit during the PA anticipation interval, when combined with variation in amount of SF, may have inadvertently produced simultaneous variation in the *effective length* of the anticipation interval. Since practice in articulation of stimulus units is directly related to amount of SF, familiarized *S*s might spend relatively less of the 2-sec. anticipation interval for stimulus articulation than nonfamiliarized *S*s. On the basis of the presumed direct relationship between PA performance and length of the anticipation interval Gannon and Noble's results would then be expected. The present experiment tested this hypothesis by comparing the performance of *S*s instructed to pronounce the stimulus units during PA anticipation with performance of *S*s instructed *not* to pronounce. A significant interaction of PA instruction and amount of SF will be required to support the present contention.

Method.—A 2 × 3 factorial design with 2 levels of PA instruction—articulation (A) vs. nonarticulation (NA) of stimulus units—and 3 amounts of SF (0, 20, and 60 trials) was used. The six respective conditions will be referred to in terms of the values of the independent variable associated with them (e.g., Cond. A_0 articulation instructions and O familiarization, Cond. NA_{60} nonarticulation instructions and 60 trials of familiarization, etc.).

The materials and procedures were identical to those used by Gannon and Noble (1961) with the following exceptions: (*a*) A .85-sec. rate of presentation was used during familiarization; (*b*) PA performance consisted of 17 anticipation trials.

A total of 144 *S*s, 24 per condition, taking introductory psychology at the University of Iowa were randomly assigned to conditions as they appeared at the laboratory. The *S*s had not served in prior verbal learning experiments.

Results and discussion.—Performance on the PA list under the six conditions, in terms of mean total number of correct responses during 17 anticipation trials, is shown in Fig. 1. The predicted interaction between PA instructions and amount of SF was obtained, and is shown by an analysis of variance to be the only significant effect ($F = 3.78$, $df = 2/138$, $P < .05$). In agreement with the results of Gannon and Noble (1961), performance was a monotonic increasing function of number of familiarization trials when *S*s were required to pronounce the stimulus terms of a PA list prior to anticipation of the response terms. However, with

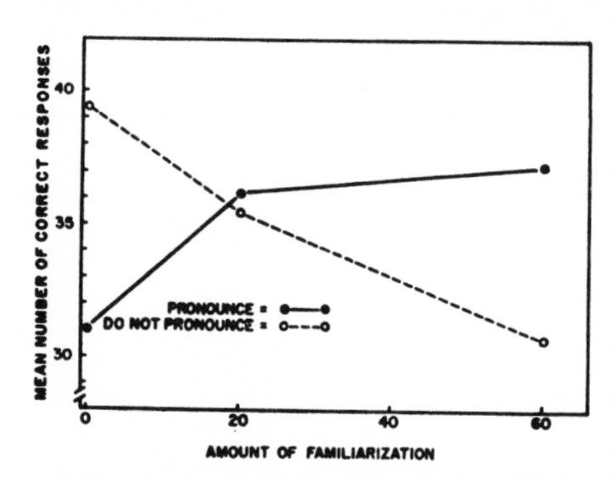

FIG. 1. Mean total number of correct responses during 17 anticipation trials as a function of PA instructions and number of stimulus familiarization trials. (The standard error of the means in Fig. 1, as estimated from the within-groups *MS* of the overall analysis of variance, was 2.71.)

Reprinted with permission of the authors and the publisher, the American Psychological Association. The article appeared originally in the *Journal of Experimental Psychology*, 1962, **64,** 549–550.

nonarticulation PA instructions, performance was inversely related to amount of familiarization. It can also be seen from Fig. 1 that, even though the facilitating effects of familiarization appear to be approaching an asymptotic level under Cond. A_{60}, performance under Cond. NA_0 was slightly better than under Cond. A_{60}. Irrespective of how proficient *S* becomes at pronouncing the stimulus units, it takes longer to pronounce than not to pronounce; it takes longer to say something than to say nothing.

Intercomparison of the various conditions via the critical difference technique (Linquist, 1953) revealed two significant ($P < .05$) differences, Cond. NA_0 vs. Cond. A_0 and Cond. NA_0 vs. Cond. NA_{60}. Inspection of acquisition as a function of trials for each of the conditions did not reveal evidence of interaction between treatments and trials.

In conclusion, it is apparent that PA instructions regarding *S*'s response to the stimulus term during the anticipation interval can determine whether SF facilitates or inhibits PA performance. We believe that these effects are attributable to covariation of the effective length of the anticipation interval with amount of familiarization. Furthermore, it may be expected that such factors as word length, pronunciability, and meaningfulness will also, depending on the length of the anticipation interval, interact with PA instructions and amount of familiarization.

References

Cieutat, V. J., Stockwell, F. E., & Noble, C. E. The interaction of ability and amount of practice with stimulus and response meaningfulness (*m*, *m'*) in paired-associate learning. *J. exp. Psychol.*, 1958, **56**, 293–302.

Gannon, D. R., & Noble, C. E. Familiarization (*n*) as a stimulus factor in paired-associate verbal learning. *J. exp. Psychol.*, 1961, **62**, 14–23.

Linquist, E. F. *Design and analysis of experiments in psychology and education.* Boston: Houghton Mifflin, 1953.

Underwood, B. J., & Schulz, R. W. *Meaningfulness and verbal learning.* Chicago: Lippincott, 1960.

(Received September 14, 1961)

CHAPTER 5

Acquisition as a Function of Similarity

If the reader is given a PA list containing the nonsense syllable VOJ as one of the *St* components, and if we insert, as a second *St* component, the nonsense syllable VOK, he will notice immediately that these two nominal stimuli overlap a great deal in their letter content. That is, the two stimuli have a high degree of *formal* or *primary* (physical) similarity. If the inserted *St* had been VEC, instead of VOK, there would be less primary similarity (defined in terms of letter commonality) between the two components. Operationally, variations in the primary similarity of verbal materials are accomplished by these kinds of manipulations in the commonality of letter contents. Similarity, however, also exists along another major dimension, that of *semantic* or *secondary* (mediated) similarity. Here similarity is defined in terms of commonality of meaning, especially as it involves implicit mediating responses (Cofer and Foley, 1942; Osgood, 1953, pp. 695–698) evoked in common to discrete verbal units. Several systematic scalings along a semantic dimension have been accomplished (Haagen, 1949; Melton and Safier, 1951) for pairs of adjectives, thus permitting the selection of verbal units from a broad continuum of similarity. For example, Melton and Safier (1951) had a group of college student *Ss* rate 300 pairs of adjectives on a 3-point scale of similarity in meaning, and they then determined the mean rating for each pair. The adjectives "perfect" and "faultless," "vicious" and "spiteful," and "erect" and "fancy" are examples of pairs rated high, moderate, and low, respectively, within the Melton and Safier norms.

When two or more primarily or secondarily related *St* components are incorporated into the same PA list, there is a pronounced tendency, especially in the early acquisition trials, for one *St* to evoke the *R* that is becoming associated with a related *St*. If we designate the association for the related *St* as St'-R_2 and the association for the reference *St* as St-R_1, then the tendency noted above becomes St'-R_1. The occurrence of R_1 as a response to St' is, of course, an error, and, more specifically, an overt intrusion error (see introductory section of Chapter 1). Another intrusion error would be the occurrence of R_2 as a response to *St*. This kind of error is an instance of stimulus generalization, a highly important and widely studied phenomenon (Kimble, 1961, pp. 328–360) which the reader has undoubtedly encountered previously in the context of other discourses on learning. In addition, the tendency to evoke the inappropriate *R* (but appropriate to the similar *St*) diminishes progressively with decreasing similarity between the related *St* components. This is an example of another well-known phenomenon in learning—the stimulus generalization gradient. In verbal learning, both primary and secondary stimulus generalization and their gradients are commonly accepted as valid phenomena.

Just as *St* components may vary in their primary or secondary similarity, so may *R* components. The accompanying generalization effects are those of primary and secondary response generalization. In response generalization, there is a tendency for a similar *R* component to be evoked in lieu of its related member when the *St* for that related member is given. If the reference association is designated as St_1-R and the association involving the related *R* as St_2-R', then St_1-R' represents a generalized tendency. Again the consequence is the occurrence of an intrusion error.

In this chapter we shall deal with the overall problem of the effects of similarity on acquisition, together with three more specialized subphenomena within the broader similarity-acquisition relationship. The specialized topics are: Grouping Similar Stimuli, Double Function Lists, and Isolation Effects. In each case, we shall limit ourselves to intra-list similarity, that is, similarity as varied within a single list. We shall return to similarity in Chapter 8 when we meet the problem of inter-list (i.e., between two lists) similarity as related to transfer effects.

Similarity and Acquisition

Differentiation Theory in Verbal Learning

Stimulus similarity became an important independent variable in verbal acquisition, and transfer and retention as well, largely through the effort of Eleanor Gibson (1940, 1941, 1942) to formulate a comprehensive theory of verbal learning based largely on stimulus generalization and differentiation concepts. The theory stressed the discriminability of stimuli, and the attainment of differentiation between the stimuli of verbal lists was identified as the essential task of *S* in acquiring verbal associations. According to the theory, as similarity increases, the demands of differentiation become more and more pronounced in that generalization tendencies correspondingly increase. Generalized responses to similar stimuli, however, are not reinforced, whereas correct responses are. Through this process of differential reinforcement Gibson viewed acquisition as the extinction of the generalized tendencies and the progressive strengthening of the differentially reinforced correct responses.

One of the important corollaries of Gibson's theory specifies that differentiation lapses over a period of time, thus allowing for the spontaneous recovery (note the parallel to conditioning concepts throughout the theory) of the generalized tendencies. As a result, retention should be adversely affected by intra-list similarity to the extent that these generalized tendencies recover. Also, long inter-trial intervals (as in distribution of practice; cf. Chapter 3, Article 5) should engender some degree of spontaneous recovery. Another important corollary hypothesizes that generalization during acquisition should show an initial *increase* during the early practice trials, followed by a *decrease* as the differential reinforcement of correct and incorrect responses sets in. In her own test of this hypothesis, with geometric forms rather than verbal units as *St* components of a PA list, Gibson (1942) did find an increase of overt intrusion errors (the index of generalized tendencies) during the early trials, followed by a steady decline.

Gibson's theory was restricted to stimulus similarity and, more specifically, to primary similarity. Others (e.g. Osgood, 1949; Underwood, 1951a) have extended Gibson-like concepts to include secondary stimulus similarity and both primary and secondary response similarity. In spite of its widened perspective, Gibson's theory has been the subject of several lively reappraisals during the contemporary period. Murdock (1958a) questioned the utility of the concept that generalization tendencies first increase and then decrease during acquisition. He pointed out that in the ordinary PA task *S* begins by learning what the *Rs* are (the response learning stage). The early trials are characterized by an absence of *R* availability for associations. Consequently, overt errors can logically show only an increase from this zero initial point. With the advent of the associative stage, overt errors would be expected to decline. In other words, the Gibsonian function is a natural product of the sequence of acquisition. Murdock presented data of his own with a procedure in which *Ss* were told in advance what the *Rs* were and were then forced to respond from the first trial on. Under this condition, generalization tendencies, as measured by overt errors, showed only a *decrease* with progressive practice. Others (Battig, 1959; Gibson, 1959; Runquist, 1959) rushed adamantly to the defense of Gibson's theory. For example, Runquist insisted that the occurrence or nonoccurrence of errors for a given association is determined by many factors in addition to the strengths of a correct and an interfering incorrect (generalized) response. Runquist further exclaimed that the strength of generalized, interfering responses and the number of overt intrusion errors are not expected to covary perfectly. He added that the presence of a generalized tendency may be more adequately indicated by the occurrence of omission (failure to respond) errors than by intrusion errors. Acceptance of Runquist's rationale requires a broad, and perhaps overly broad, modification of Gibson's original position on intrusions as *the* index of generalization tendencies.

A more polemic and a far more sweeping criticism of Gibson's theory has been offered by Underwood (1961) who found major shortcomings in the ability of data accrued from acquisition, transfer, and retention experiments to fit various predictions from the theory. For example, in his own series of studies on distributed practice (cf. Chapter 3, Article 5), he failed to find any substantial support for the spontaneous recovery of generalization tendencies as differentially related to the degree of intra-list similarity—a differential relationship that is a cardinal prediction from Gibson's theory. Underwood offered some tentative starting points for alternative approaches to the similarity problem. Among these alternatives is one previously stated in the Underwood, Runquist, and Schulz study (Chapter 2, Article 2). Namely, with increasing similarity of *Rs* in a PA list, response learning is expected to be increasingly facilitated via a clustering effect (see also introductory section of Chapter 7). Underwood (1961, 1964) also suggested that *St* similarity may affect acquisition by means of the ease of establishing discernible representational (recognition-labeling) responses (cf. introductory section and Article 3 of Chapter 2), with increasing similarity bearing an inverse relationship to the ease of these establishments. We should note that still another alternative, but one that is probably related to the recognition-response hypothesis, stems from the fact that with increasing *St* similarity *S* is likely to be forced to rely on more precise elements of the nominal stimulus for use as a discriminable functional stimulus. In other words, high *St* similarity should demand finer cue discriminations, and concomitantly more practice trials, than low *St* similarity.

A theoretical attempt to explain an even broader range of learning phenomena by means of differentiation concepts has been evolving in the work of Saltz (1961a, 1961b, 1963; Saltz and Riach, 1961; Saltz and Youssef, 1964 Uhlmann and Saltz, 1965). When applied to PA acquisition, the approach includes both *St* and *R* differentiation, but, more importantly, it emphasizes what Saltz calls "cognitive" differentiation. Apparently, cognitive differentiation, at least in PA acquisition, refers to the formation and maintenance of "boundaries" between specific *St-R* associations. Single associations are here viewed as being easily acquired. The major problem for *S* is to prohibit associations from intruding on one another—that is, to prevent breakdowns of the boundaries. Saltz and his colleagues have presented evidence which suggests that the stability of boundaries is related to such variables as perceptual field-independence (Witkin, Dyk, Faterson, Goodenough, and Karp, 1962) and anxiety.

St and R Intra-list Similarity

The deleterious effect of increasing item similarity on SL seems well substantiated (e.g., Underwood, 1952). For analytical purposes, however, the effects of similarity as an independent variable have been tested largely on PA acquisition. High primary similarity between *St* components yields less proficient acquisition than does low primary similarity (Feldman and Underwood, 1957, Article 1; Levitt and Goss, 1961; Newman and Buckhout, 1962; Underwood, 1953a). The Feldman and Underwood study (Article 1) demonstrates the techniques commonly employed to manipulate primary similarity (and secondary similarity for *R* components as well). In addition, this study, together with that of Newman and Buckhout (1962), indicates that another effect of increasing primary *St* similarity is to decrease the amount of *nominal R-St* recall (cf. introductory section to Chapter 2). A possible interpretation of this finding is that with high primary similarity *S* is forced to rely on a single letter as the sole discriminating feature (i.e., the functional stimulus) between a given nominal *St* and its related members. As a result, the remaining elements of the nominal *St* may be loosely integrated for highly similar *St* components. Secondary similarity for *St* components has been less widely explored. Underwood (1953b), however, did find that intermediate degrees of similarity seem to result in more proficient acquisition than either low or high similarity.

Turning to the *R* component, studies on increasing similarity, both primary and secondary, have produced conflicting findings. Underwood (1953a) failed to find a significant effect for primary similarity, whereas Levitt and Goss (1961) and Newman and Buckhout (1962) found an inverse relationship between primary similarity and acquisition. Similarly, Underwood (1953b) did not find a statistically significant effect for secondary similarity on acquisition, but Feldman and Underwood (1957) found the expected inverse relationship.

Although *St* similarity is expected to adversely affect only the associative stage of acquisition, most likely through generalization effects, *R* similarity should affect both the associative *and* the response learning stages. Moreover, high *R* similarity should aid the response learning stage but hinder the associative stage (cf. Underwood, Runquist, and Schulz, Chapter 2, Article 2). The net effect is that increasing *R* similarity should have a less pronounced negative effect on PA acquisition than should the comparable variation in *St* similarity. Using the factorial design characteristic of the Cason-Sheffield type studies on meaningfulness, Levitt and Goss (1961) found some support, though statistically nonsignificant, for this *St*, *R* similarity differential effect. Horowitz (1962) and Jung (1965a), both employing an associative matching procedure rather than the standard anticipation method, have provided additional evidence for the twofold role of *R* similarity as predicted by stage analysis.

Grouping Similar Stimuli

Granted that lists with *St* components of high similarity are more difficult to learn than lists with *St* components of low similarity, is there any modification of the usual practice conditions that might produce a diminution of this difficulty effect? Gagne (1950) introduced a "grouping" procedure which appeared to be very effective. To illustrate his procedure, we will make use of a symbolic list in which there are three different reference stimuli (St_1, St_2, and St_3) and two similar (primary dimension) stimuli for each reference stimulus (e.g., St_1' and St_1'' as related to St_1), along with nine unrelated responses ($R_1, R_2, \ldots, R_9$). Gagne's procedure consisted of grouping together (i.e., consecutively following one another), during the training trials of one group of *Ss*, the *St-R* pairs for each set of similar stimuli. Thus, during the training trials, St_1-R_1, St_1'-R_2, and St_1''-R_3 were grouped together, followed by St_2-R_4, St_2'-R_5, and St_2''-R_6, and then S_3-R_7, St_3'-R_8, and St_3''-R_9. For another group of *Ss*, sets of dissimilar stimuli were grouped together during the training trials. We might have as one unrelated set, St_1-R_1, St_2''-R_6, and St_3'-R_8 with the remaining sets being equally unrelated. In other words, for this second group of *Ss* the related stimuli were deliberately separated from one another during training. These two groups were then contrasted on a series of test trials in which the *St* components were presented in a random order. Gagne found that the group of *Ss* given training with grouped similar stimuli performed at a significantly higher level on the test trials than the group of *Ss* trained with grouped dissimilar stimuli. His explanation for this superiority followed the lines of Gibson's differentiation theory, stressing the opportunity for early generalization effects in the *Ss* with grouped similar stimuli and the accompanying early differentiation that follows through differential reinforcement. For the other group of *Ss*, generalization is delayed by the separation of similar stimuli, leading to an eventually slower rate of differentiation.

In Gagne's study the *St* components were nonsense forms comparable to those used earlier by Gibson (1942). A later study by Rothkopf (1958), with elements of the Morse code as *St* components, however, failed to replicate the finding of a superiority for the grouping of similar stimuli—in fact, the grouping of dissimilar stimuli was found to be superior. The difference in the findings of these two studies suggests the importance of verbal involvement as a critical factor in determining the effectiveness of grouping similar stimuli. In reopening this area of investigation, Rotberg and Woolman (1963; Article 2) tested the verbal involvement factor by employing formal verbal units (4 letter nonsense syllables) as *St* components. Their findings agreed with those of Gagne, in terms of the superiority of grouping similar stimuli (they also failed to find any effect for the grouping of similar *R* components), but their evidence also suggested the operation of another mechanism, "coding," to supplement any differentiation advantage for grouping similar stimuli. By coding, they apparently mean some kind of implicit, categorizing response (akin to those described in Chapter 7) that is acquired during the training trials. The grouping of similar stimuli encourages the acquisition of these coding responses, but the grouping of dissimilar stimuli does not. Further evidence for the existence of this coding mechanism has been provided by Keefe (1965).

Double Function Lists

Maximum Double Functioning

Thus far we have considered intra-list similarity only as it involves between-stimulus and/or between-response similarity. In these cases there is a deliberate attempt to exclude any relationship between the *St* and *R* components. However, intra-list similarity may also be defined in terms of intra-list stimulus-response relationships; that is, the *St* components are related to the *R* components, in some specified manner, rather than to themselves. In its maximum form, stimulus-response similarity becomes what we have previously called a double function list (cf Chapter 1, Introduction, p. 12). Double functioning of PA items as both *St* and *R* components becomes apparent if we label any six items entering into a list as *A*, *B*, *C*, *D*, *E*, and *F* and then construct pairs from these items like the following: *A-D*, *B-F*, *C-A*, *D-B*, *E-C*, and *F-E*. Each item will thus be functioning as both an *St* and an *R* component. Primoff (1938) introduced the double function list in a study of transfer effects from SL to PA when the same items form both lists. The results of that study, together with those of Young (1959), revealed the extreme difficulty of learning double function lists. This difficulty was attributed by both writers to the probable interference of backward (*R-St*) associations as they compete with forward (*St-R*) associations. As an example, consider the pairs *A-D* and *D-B* from our above representative double function list. With *A* as the forward *St* component of *A-D*, *D* is elicited as the forward *R* component; simultaneously, for the same pair, there should be some tendency for *D* as the backward *St* component to elicit *A* as the backward *R* component. With *D* as the forward *St* component of *D-B*, *B* is elicited as the forward R component; however, as we noted above, *D* is also the *St* component (in the *R-St* direction) for *A* as a response. Consequently, we should expect to find some degree of competition between *B* and *A* as responses to *D* as a stimulus, leading to an overall interference in the learning of the pair *D-B* in the forward direction. A comparable pinpointing of sources of interference could be made for each of the double function pairs.

Experiment I of the Umemoto and Hilgard study (1961; Article 3), in addition to demonstrating the methods of double function experiments, offers strong support for the *R-St* competition hypothesis as an explanation of the pronounced difficulty found in learning such lists. Further support for the hypothesis has been given in studies by Newman (1964b) and Young and Jennings (1964). The latter study also offered some evidence of other factors that serve to increase the complexity of the role of *R-St* associations in double function list acquisition.

Partial Double Functioning

Less than maximum degrees of double functioning have also been investigated in the laboratory. By this we mean that the *St* and *R* components are related to each other, but we avoid the complete identity of the two. One method of accomplishing partial double functioning is to have only a portion of the *St* components within the list repeated as *R* components and have unrelated *St* and *R* components serve as filler pairs for the rest of the list. In Experiment I of the Umemoto and Hilgard study (Article 3) this condition was included (their List 2), with four of the eight *St* components serving double duty as *R* components. They found that the difficulty of this list, as measured by trials to criterion, fell in between that of the 100 per cent (all eight *Sts* serving as *Rs;* their List 1) and 0 per cent (unrelated *Sts* and *Rs;* their List 3) lists. They also discovered that their partial (50 per cent) list was actually more difficult than the 100 per cent list during the early stages of acquisition. A factor contributing to the difficulty of 50 per cent lists that is missing in 100 per cent lists is that *S* may be unable to differentiate, particularly early in practice, between those items that are double in function and those that are single. Consequently, single function *St* components may erroneously intrude as response errors through the failure of this differentiation. In 100 per cent lists, intrusions of *St* components as responses, as Umemoto and Hilgard point out, may actually increase the number of correctly scored anticipations.

Another method of constructing partial double function lists is to relate the *St* and *R* components to one another by means of some similarity dimension. For example, Underwood (1951b) made use of secondary similarity by constructing sets within his PA list in which highly synonymous adjectives functioned as both *Sts* and *Rs*. He found that lists of this kind are learned slowly, relative to lists with components of low synonymity. Young (1961) and Newman (1964b) found comparable effects when partial lists were constructed along the dimension of primary similarity (i.e., *Sts* and *Rs* had considerable commonality in the letter content of nonsense syllables, but they were not identical). Finally, Experiment II of the Umemoto and Hilgard study (Article 3) shows that with partial lists acquisition may be facilitated, as well as hindered, depending on the nature of the relationship between the relevant *St-R* and *R-St* associations.

Isolation Effects

Serial Lists

A classical experiment by von Restorff (1933) demonstrated that a dissimilar item placed in the context of an otherwise homogeneously cloistered set of serial items is learned much more readily than is another item of the same ilk as the cloistered set placed in the same position within the list. For example, we might have a list of nonsense syllables, minimally related to one another in terms of primary similarity, with one of the serial position assigned a critical role. At this critical position we insert an item that is somehow isolated from the items at the other positions; that is, it is distinctive in some way. The isolated item could be from an entirely different class of verbal materials, such as a 2-digit number, or it could simply be made unique by changing its sensory attributes, such as printing it in red ink while printing all the other items in black ink. The *Ss* practicing on the altered list with the isolated item constitute an experimental group; the *Ss* practicing on the unaltered or homogeneous list constitute a control group. These carefully spelled out manipulations, together with the observed superiority of the experimental group over the control at the critical position, provide us with an operational definition of a phenomenon called the isolation or von Restorff effect. The effect was originally explained by von Restorff (1933) as an example of the Gestalt principle of figure and ground perception. We have previously noted (introductory section of Chapter 4) that others have applied the same explanation to the inordinate ease of learning items of low meaningfulness embedded in a list of items otherwise high in meaningfulness.

One of the high lights of the contemporary period has been the effort by some investigators (e.g., Newman and Saltz, 1958; Article 4) to incorporate isolation effects into an extended version of Gibson's differentiation theory. The extension is one that includes response generalization-differentiation in addition to stimulus generalization-differentiation. Newman and Saltz (Article 4) conducted an exceptionally fine analysis of the isolation effect in the light of differentiation theory. Their analysis leads us to expect a threefold consequence of isolation on serial acquisition. First of all, the isolated item is a response that has a fixed position in the list. Being isolated in the list, this response should not fall within the response generalization gradients of other items as responses, nor should the other responses fall within its generalization gradient. As a result, the isolated item should both be easily learned as a response in the appropriate position, and it should not readily intrude as an error at other positions in the list. Second, assuming at least partial validity of the specificity hypothesis (cf. Chapter 1, Introduction), the isolated item should be an effective stimulus for the response that follows it in the list. That is, it should fall outside of the stimulus generalization gradients of the other stimuli, and vice versa. Therefore the response following the isolated item should be learned more readily than the response following the comparable item in the control group. Third, the fact that both stimulus and response generalization effects throughout the list are reduced by the presence of the isolated item, leads us to expect that the entire list for the experimental group should be learned more proficiently than the entire list for the control group.

Newman and Saltz found evidence to support only one of these predictions, the first, and then only in part. As in von Restorff's earlier study, the isolated item was indeed learned readily as a specific response. However, contrary to the prediction, the isolated item occurred more frequently as a response intrusion than did the control item. The failure to find a stimulus effect should not surprise us in view of what we know about the speciousness of the specificity hypothesis. As to the third prediction, the possibility remains that one isolated item is not enough to affect markedly the overall course of acquisition for the entire list. Roberts (1962) tested this hypothesis by using three isolated items in a serial list rather than one. Still no overall superiority for the experimental group was found.

A study by Saltz and Newman (1959) suggested that some basic revisions are required in order to incorporate isolation into differentiation theory. In their revised version, the effect of isolation is assumed to be that of increasing the likelihood of the isolated item being emitted as a response per se without any pronounced tendency for increasing its attachment to its intra-list stimulus—thus accounting for the stepped up intrusion rate, as well as the rate of correct responses in the appropriate list position. As they point out, this conceptualization is outside of the current framework of differentiation theory.

Other evidence for the emitted-response approach was given by Rosen, Richardson, and Saltz (1962).

Two other approaches to isolation effects in SL are worthy of the reader's consideration. One (Green, 1956) proposes that the mechanism responsible for the isolation effect is that of surprise. That is, the surprise of being unexpectedly exposed to a distinctive item arouses an emotional feeling that somehow mediates the learning advantage. The second (Jensen, 1962b) proposes an approach that fits neatly into some of the current thinking on SL in general. We noted earlier (Chapter 1, introductory section) the view that serial position effects are governed solely by the order in which items are learned, but the difficulty of learning any one item is invariant with respect to this ordering, Jensen's study (1962b) provided some evidence favoring the interpretation that the effect of isolation is to provide an anchoring point for learning the isolated item earlier in the ordering sequence than the comparable item in the control condition. This should lead to more correct responses for the former than for the latter as practice continues to a criterion of mastery.

Paired Associates

Finally, we need to recognize that studies on the isolation effect have not been the exclusive property of SL. Earlier in this section (pp. 227–228) we discovered that variation in *St* similarity affects PA acquisition to a greater extent than does variation in *R* similarity. Correspondingly, we might anticipate isolation to be more advantageous to acquisition when it enters the *St* component than when it enters the *R* component. This should follow if isolation functions through a reduction of generalization tendencies. On the other hand, the previously discussed studies on SL lead to the conclusion that isolation involves response emission only. Accordingly, isolation may be more advantageous for the *R* component than for the *St* component in PA acquisition. Little experimental evidence has been accumulated in this area, and what is available suggests the need for greater empirical activity. A study by Nachmias, Gleitman, and McKenna (1961) found isolation of both *St* and *R* components to facilitate acquisition and to an equal extent. Erickson (1965) also found isolation to be facilitative in both components, but this time *St* isolation was considerably more facilitative than *R* isolation.

Erickson (1963) introduced an additional PA isolation method in which neither *St* nor *R* isolation was directly involved. Instead, the source of isolation rested in the relationship of the *St* and *R* components to one another in the critical (isolated) pairs, relative to the comparable relationships in the control (nonisolated) pairs. The critical pairs had either nonsense syllables as both *St* and *R* components or digits as both *St* and *R* components, whereas the control pairs had either nonsense syllables as *Sts* and digits as *Rs* or digits as *Sts* and nonsense syllables as *Rs*. Erickson found a superiority for pairs isolated relationally, leading him to conclude that there are mechanisms above and beyond stimulus and response generalization-differentiation tendencies. In other words, for relationally isolated pairs the *St* and *R* components are similar to those of the nonisolated pairs, with only the nature of the *St-R* pairing distinguishing between the two kinds of pairs ("like" components for isolated and "unlike" components for nonisolated pairs). More recently, Newman and Forsyth (1965) obtained additional evidence for the learning advantage of relational isolation. Explanation for this phenomenon remains highly speculative. Perhaps Saltz's concept of *St-R* boundaries (see p. 227) will eventually have applicability, both theoretically and heuristically.

Shortly after the completion of the above section a detailed review of the research on the isolation effect appeared (Wallace, 1965). Wallace also contrasted the Gestalt and stimulus-response approaches to explaining the effect. He concluded that neither approach in its present stage of development is solely adequate for explanation and suggested that isolation effects most likely involve a complexity of different processes.

ARTICLE 1

STIMULUS RECALL FOLLOWING PAIRED-ASSOCIATE LEARNING

SAMUEL M. FELDMAN AND BENTON J. UNDERWOOD

Northwestern University

In the present experiment *S* learned a list of verbal paired associates by standard procedures. Immediately after learning he was presented with the response words, one at a time, and was asked to give the stimulus word with which that response had been associated during learning. Thus, if during learning *S* was required to anticipate B when A was presented, on the recall he was asked to give A when B was shown. So far as is known, results of such operations have not been reported previously. The basic question, therefore, is whether or not *S* learns the R-S association when instructed merely to learn the S-R association. Thornton performed a study (unpublished) in the Northwestern University laboratory which answers this basic question. A list of 10 paired adjectives was learned to a criterion of two consecutive perfect trials. Immediately afterward *S* was shown each response word separately and was asked to give the stimulus word. On the average 83% of the stimuli were correctly recalled. This finding clearly suggested that *S* does learn R-S associations while learning S-R associations and learns them rather well. The present study will, first of all, endeavor to confirm Thornton's findings and will, secondly, explore the influence of stimulus and response similarity on this recall phenomenon.

The phenomenon in question may be associated with what is called, commonly, *incidental learning*. In incidental learning (e.g., **2**) *S* learns material when he is not specifically instructed to do so. In the present situation *S* appears to learn associations which he is not instructed to learn but during a period when he is learning other associations which he has been instructed to learn. The fact that he is instructed to learn something differentiates the operations from those commonly used to study incidental learning. The high recall shown by Thornton's *S*s might argue against incidental learning and suggest something more fundamental. It might, for example, suggest that in learning S-R connections the acquisition of R-S associations takes place as an integral part of the learning. Ideas of direction of association ($S \rightarrow R$) which are used to conceptualize experimental operations may not at all reflect the learning which is taking place. Nevertheless, in initiating the present study R-S learning was viewed as essentially a form of incidental learning as a basis for exploring the influence of variables of which it might be a function.

In order to minimize associative interactions between stimulus and response words, nonsense syllables were used as stimuli and adjectives as responses. In one case high intralist stimulus similarity was used, and in another low. It was believed that with high intralist similarity *S* would be forced to attend more carefully to the stimuli than when similarity was low, thus facilitating R-S learning. Response similarity was also high in one list and low in another. If this high-response similarity forced *S* to pay careful attention to the responses,

Reprinted with permission of the authors and the publisher, the American Psychological Association. The article appeared originally in the *Journal of Experimental Psychology*. 1957. **53,** 11–15.

R-S learning might be inhibited as compared to the case of low-response similarity.

Method

Materials and subjects.—Four lists of seven paired associates each were constructed. The stimuli were nonsense syllables taken from Glaze (1) with an average association value of 11.4%. The adjectives used as responses came from a previous study (5). The lists are shown in Table 1. For high similarity among stimuli, two consonants were repeated four times and two others were repeated three times each. For low similarity, no consonants were repeated. In the case of responses, high similarity was produced by having a commonality of meaning among all seven words; for low similarity, words were used which had little commonality of meaning.

A total of 120 undergraduate students served as *S*s. Thirty *S*s were assigned to each of four groups, the groups being differentiated only by the list which they learned. These groups will be referred to by the symbols given above the lists in Table 1; e.g., HS-HR, indicates the list had high stimulus similarity and high response similarity. The 24 permutations of the order of the four lists were used as a basis for assigning *S*s to a given list. An *S* who failed to learn the list assigned was replaced immediately by the next *S* coming to the laboratory. One *S* assigned to the HS-HR group failed to learn as did one assigned to LS-LR group.

Procedure.—Lists were presented on a Hull-type drum at a 2:2-sec. rate, i.e., 2 sec. for the stimulus and 2 sec. for the stimulus and response together. Three different orders were used to minimize serial learning. Learning was taken to two successive perfect trials. Immediately after attaining the criterion, *S* was presented the responses (adjectives) at a 4-sec. rate (the adjective was seen for only the first 2 sec. of the 4-sec. period) and was asked to give the stimulus (syllable) which went with each adjective. During this stimulus recall *S* spelled the syllables. The *S* never saw the original stimuli during this recall period. Following this drum recall, *S* was presented with the list of adjectives on a sheet of paper and again was asked to call out the syllables (stimuli) for each. No time limit was imposed.

Results and Discussion

Learning.—The mean number of trials to learn each list, and the mean number of errors per trial in learning are shown in Table 2. Looking first at trials to learn, performance varies significantly as a function of both stimulus similarity and response similarity, the *F*s being 35.13 and 17.21, respectively. An *F* of 6.84 is needed for significance at the .01 level. The interaction term did not approach significance. (Unless otherwise noted, all analyses of variance were based on distributions for which the variance was not significantly heterogeneous.) In terms of *t*s, using the within-groups error term (1.92), any difference in mean trials of 5.36 or larger is significant at the .05 level. While differences in learning as a function of stimulus similarity have frequently been reported, so far as is known this is the first clear demonstration of differences in learning as a function of response similarity. A previous study, while showing large differences

TABLE 1

Lists Used

(H refers to high similarity; L to low similarity; S to stimulus and R to response)

HS-HR	HS-LR	LS-HR	LS-LR
WEZ-Gleeful	WEZ-Agog	CEF-Gleeful	CEF-Agog
GYK-Genial	GYK-Neuter	MIB-Genial	MIB-Neuter
GOK-Pleasant	GOK-Pretty	GUK-Pleasant	GUK-Pretty
KIG-Smiling	KIG-Worldly	TIV-Smiling	TIV-Worldly
GUW-Blissful	GUW-Irksome	NUX-Blissful	NUX-Irksome
ZOW-Elated	ZOW-Vulgar	JUH-Elated	JUH-Vulgar
ZYW-Laughing	ZYW-Equal	ZER-Laughing	ZER-Equal

in error frequency as a function of response similarity, failed to show appreciable differences in trials to learn (**3**).

Error frequency reflects similarity differences almost perfectly; that is, the higher the similarity the greater the frequency of errors per trial. Although heterogeneity of variance prevents exact statements of significance, the *F*s for both response similarity and stimulus similarity are beyond the .01 significance level with interaction again being far from significant. In terms of *t*s, both comparisons (one with stimulus similarity low and one with it high) for influence of response similarity are significant beyond the .05 level. Comparable comparisons for stimulus similarity shows one *t* significant beyond the .05 level and one not significant. The latter occurs when response similarity is high.

Recall.—It will be remembered that recall of the stimulus items took place in two ways, first a controlled *drum* recall, and then an *unlimited* recall. The basic results are given in Table 3. For both drum and unlimited recall, two response measures are presented, namely, total correct syllables recalled and total number of letters correct, where correctness is defined as the correct letter in the correct position. As can be seen in Table 3, unlimited recall averaged 10–15% higher than drum recall; however, the correlations between these two types of recall ranged from .54 to .70.

TABLE 2

MEAN TRIALS TO LEARN AND MEAN ERRORS PER TRIAL

List	Trials		Errors	
	Mean	σ_M	Mean	σ_M
HS-HR	34.20	2.04	1.28	.12
HS-LR	28.53	1.65	.91	.07
LS-HR	25.17	2.21	1.02	.11
LS-LR	15.13	1.60	.66	.09

For drum recall, analysis of variance for syllables recalled shows only stimulus similarity to be significant, *F* being 6.73 with 6.9 necessary for the .01 level. The same variable approaches but does not reach significance for total letters recalled. The *F*s for response similarity and interaction between response and stimulus similarity fall far short of significance.

While Table 3 shows that for unlimited recall the mean differences are in the same direction as for drum recall, none of the variables achieves the .05 level. It is concluded, therefore, that stimulus similarity has a small but consistent effect on recall,

TABLE 3

MEAN NUMBER OF SYLLABLES RECALLED AND MEAN NUMBER OF LETTERS RECALLED ON DRUM AND WITH UNLIMITED TIME

List	Syllables				Letters			
	Drum		Unlimited		Drum		Unlimited	
	Mean	σ_M	Mean	σ_M	Mean	σ_M	Mean	σ_M
HS-HR	2.90	.35	4.07	.32	11.80	.92	15.80	.62
HS-LR	3.33	.30	4.40	.28	14.33	.84	16.33	.61
LS-HR	3.70	.32	4.40	.29	13.10	.74	16.20	.54
LS-LR	4.13	.27	5.00	.29	13.67	.74	17.53	.59

with the higher the similarity the poorer the recall.

It may be noted that in the case of total syllables recalled (drum) the over-all recall represents 50% of the items, while for letters the value is 61%. These values are considerably below those found by Thornton (83%) when he used adjectives for both stimuli and responses. Nevertheless, the present results essentially confirm the phenomenon that *S* does learn a number of R-S associations when asked to learn S-R associations.

Further analyses.—It has been shown that R-S learning does occur in paired-associate learning, but that it is not highly affected by stimulus or response similarity. It is assumed that if (as a control) *S* had never learned the S-R associations before being asked to recall the stimuli, he would have been unable to give any appreciable number correctly; certainly he would not have gotten 50% correct. On the other hand, if S-R recall had been taken following learning, it would probably have been 90–100% correct. The data thus indicate that R-S learning took place, but at a lower level than S-R learning. The relationship between R-S learning and other variables is now examined.

First, is R-S recall related to speed of learning the S-R associations? The *S*s in each group were divided into two subgroups based on speed of learning. The division was made on the basis of median trials to learn, so that 15 *S*s were in each subgroup. The fast learners were then compared with slow learners on R-S recall; none of the four *t*s approached statistical significance. Even allowing for differences in slope of S-R acquisition curves for fast and slow *S*s, the recall differences still would be small.

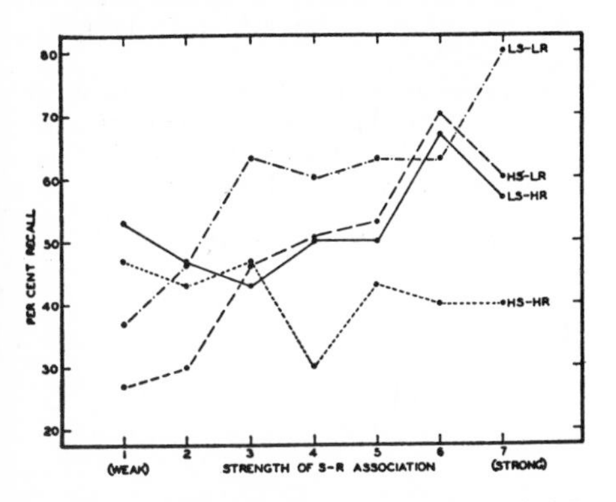

Fig. 1. R-S recall as a function of S-R strength. Strength of S-R association increases from Rank 1 through 7.

Recall of the S-R association has been shown to be directly related to number of correct anticipations during learning (4). The next question is, therefore, whether or not R-S recall is related to strength of S-R associations when the strength is measured by number of correct anticipations. The results of this analysis show that whether plotted separately for each list or whether all lists are combined, there was very little relationship. The recall of R-S associations started at about 50% when the items had been correctly anticipated twice (the lowest strength resulting from the criterion of learning used) and remained at about 50% irrespective of number of correct anticipations. This, then, is not in line with what has been found with S-R recall. However, this method of plotting recall as a function of strength is not very sensitive when wide differences are involved in trials to learn. Furthermore, all *S*s are not represented at all points. Another method utilizes the idea of the Vincent curve. For each *S* the strengths of the seven items for learning were rank-ordered, assigning Rank 1 to the item which had been given correctly the fewest number of times (weakest), and 7 to the item which had been anticipated correctly the greatest number of times (strongest). For each item it was noted whether or not the R-S recall was correct. Thus, the percentage correct at R-S recall can be plotted as a function of S-R strength and each *S* is represented once at each of the seven strengths. The results of these analyses are shown in Fig. 1. As can be seen, there is some relationship between recall of R-S and strength of S-R association for the two lists with low response similarity. However, there is little if any relationship when response similarity is high. Looking at the data as a whole, R-S recall appears to be much less clearly related to strength of S-R learning than is S-R recall. At the present time there is no wish to speculate on these differences in R-S recall as a function of response similarity.

The fact that R-S recall is not strongly and unambiguously related to S-R strength will obviously require further work for clarification. If this is a form of incidental learning, it may be a simple and direct function of number of exposures of the S-R pairs. Since *S*s were taken to a performance criterion in the present experiment, it cannot be determined if frequency of exposure (as contrasted to number of correct S-R anticipations) is related to R-S recall.

In view of Thornton's findings (discussed earlier) and the present results, the phenomenon of R-S learning seems to be a reliable one. The scope of the theoretical problem it represents can best be assessed after more is known of variables which affect it. It may well fit into the literature on incidental learning, and the generalizations which Postman and his students (e.g., **2**) are obtaining about incidental learning may also suffice for the phenomenon of R-S learning.

Summary

Subjects learned a list of seven paired associates. Immediately after learning they were presented the response items, one at a time, and were instructed to give the stimulus items associated with them during learning. The basic question was whether or not *S* could give the stimuli correctly. Does *S* learn an R-S association when instructed only to learn the S-R association? Four groups of 30 *S*s each were used. Each group learned a different list. The four lists made up a 2 × 2 design in which stimulus similarity and response similarity were both high and low. For each list the stimulus items were nonsense syllables and the response items adjectives.

The results show:

1. In terms of syllables correct, recall of the stimuli (R-S) was 50% correct. In terms of correct letters in correct positions the recall was 61%.
2. While both stimulus and response similarity markedly effected rate of learning the S-R associations, only stimulus similarity produced significant differences on recall.
3. R-S recall was not strongly related to strength of S-R associations; when response similarity was high, there was virtually no relationship.

The results establish the existence of a phenomenon not hitherto reported but probably long suspected to exist. Whether or not it is a form of incidental learning requires further analyses.

References

1. Glaze, J. A. The association value of nonsense syllables. *J. genet. Psychol.*, 1928, **35**, 255–269.
2. Postman, L., & Phillips, L. W. Studies in incidental learning: I. The effects of crowding and isolation. *J. exp. Psychol.*, 1954, **48**, 48–56.
3. Underwood, B. J. Studies of distributed practice: IX. Learning and retention of paired adjectives as a function of intralist similarity. *J. exp. Psychol.*, 1953, **45**, 143–149.
4. Underwood, B. J. Speed of learning and amount retained: a consideration of methodology. *Psychol. Bull.*, 1954, **51**, 276–282.
5. Underwood, B. J., & Goad, D. Studies of distributed practice: I. The influence of intralist similarity in serial learning. *J. exp. Psychol.*, 1951, **42**, 125–134.

(Received November 10, 1955)

ARTICLE 2

VERBAL PAIRED-ASSOCIATE LEARNING AS A FUNCTION OF GROUPING SIMILAR STIMULI OR RESPONSES [1]

IRIS C. ROTBERG AND MYRON WOOLMAN [2]

Human Resources Research Office, George Washington University

Verbal paired-associate learning was measured when similar or dissimilar stimuli were grouped, and when similar or dissimilar responses were grouped. The following measures were employed: number of correct responses; type of errors made, i.e., errors indicating confusion between similar items and those indicating confusion between dissimilar items. The results indicated that learning was better when groups of stimuli were composed of similar items rather than dissimilar ones. The findings were interpreted in terms of discrimination and coding of the similar items.

The ability of *S*s to learn to associate pairs of items was measured (*a*) when similar or dissimilar items were grouped, and (*b*) when the similar or dissimilar groups of items were used either as stimuli or responses.

Gibson's (1942) research demonstrated that confusions between stimuli are a function of the degree of similarity between the stimuli. Subsequent studies have indicated that the manner in which similar stimuli are grouped affects the ease with which they are learned. In this connection, Gagné (1950) compared similar and dissimilar stimulus groups. Using nonsense forms as stimulus material, Gagné found that *S*s given learning groups composed of similar stimuli did better during testing than did those given dissimilar groups. He interpreted the finding in terms of the hypothesis that similar learning groups provide an earlier opportunity than do dissimilar groups for learning the cue relevant to the response. For the similar groups, earlier stimulus generalization is followed by relatively rapid discrimination and, therefore, superior test performance occurs.

Because of the nature of the response words that he used, Gagné could not demonstrate, for the majority of items, whether the errors resulted from confusion between similar items or dissimilar items. Therefore, his study used, as a measure of generalization, the number of overt errors, regardless of the type of confusion errors occurring.

It should be noted that Rothkopf (1958), using Morse Code stimuli, found the dissimilar groups superior. As a possible explanation, he noted that the stimuli in his study, unlike Gagné's, were not amenable to verbalization.

In the present study, the following measures were employed: (*a*) number of correct responses; (*b*) type of errors made, i.e., errors indicating confusion between similar items and those indicating confusion between dissimilar items. Each of these

[1] The research reported here was conducted by the authors while they were employed by the Human Resources Research Office, George Washington University, operating under contract to the Department of the Army. Opinions and conclusions are those of the writers and do not necessarily represent views of the university or the Department of the Army. The authors wish to thank their colleagues at HumRRO for their valuable comments and suggestions.

[2] Now at the Institute of Educational Research, Washington, D. C.

Reprinted with permission of the authors and the publisher, the American Psychological Association. The article appeared originally in the *Journal of Experimental Psychology*, 1963, **65**, 47–51.

measures was compared for (*a*) *S*s given groups of stimuli composed of similar or dissimilar items and (*b*) *S*s given groups of responses composed of similar or dissimilar items.

METHOD

Three experiments were conducted. In Exp. I, each stimulus and each response presented were displayed for 4 sec. To allow more time for responding, each stimulus and response were displayed for 8 sec. in Exp. II and III. Experiments I and II used the same operational definition of similarity. Experiment III used a second definition.

Subjects.—The *S*s were 154 male and female high school student volunteers from the District of Columbia. Fifty-six *S*s participated in Exp. I, 55 in Exp. II, and 43 in Exp. III.

Word list.—The nine-word paired-associate list of nonsense and English words and the organization of the list into similar and dissimilar groups are illustrated in Table 1.

The list of nine nonsense terms consisted of three similarity categories. The three words within each category had three letters in common (nondistinctive letters) and one letter differing (distinctive letter). No letter in any category was repeated in any other category.

Two types of similarity were employed. For Exp. I and II, nonsense terms were used in which the first three letters of each term within categories were nondistinctive letters. As may be noted from Table 1, these letters were identical in content and sequence. The fourth letter of each term was the distinctive letter. For Exp. III, the nonsense terms used the same three nondistinctive letters within each category. However, the letters differed systematically in sequence and position. The distinctive letter also varied in position.

Words were combined for learning into three-word groups composed of either similar or dissimilar nonsense terms. The nonsense terms were randomly paired with common four-letter English words.

Experimental design.—Similarity was manipulated only in the nonsense term. Therefore, stimulus similarity was studied under a paired-associate procedure with English responses. Response similarity was studied under a procedure with nonsense responses.

The *S*s in each experiment were assigned to one of the following learning groups:

1. Similar Stimulus group—grouped presentation of similar stimuli (example, VKIW, VKIH, VKIF).
2. Dissimilar Stimulus group—grouped presentation of dissimilar stimuli (example, VKIW, LDAQ, BJER).
3. Similar Response group—grouped presentation of stimuli for which the correct responses are similar (example, YARD, STAR, ROAD).
4. Dissimilar Response group—grouped presentation of stimuli for which the correct responses are dissimilar (example, YARD, MEAT, DOOR).

Procedure.—For each experiment, *S*s were randomly assigned to treatment, and treatments were randomly assigned to day and hour. The same *E* and room were used for each experimental group. The word lists were presented by means of filmstrips projected on a screen facing the group.

First, a stimulus (nonsense or English) was flashed on the screen. While the stimulus was on the screen, *S*s were to write the response (English or nonsense) which they considered correct. The correct response was shown immediately after the presentation of the stimulus. The *S*s were directed to write their responses on every trial except the first trial of each three-word group.

During learning, each three-word group was presented for five trials. Words were rerandomized within groups each time they were repeated. The five trials for each three-word group were completed before the next group was presented.

Following learning, *S*s were given a test consisting of the nine words presented in random order for five trials. During the test period, correct responses were not shown.

TABLE 1

SIMILAR AND DISSIMILAR LEARNING GROUPINGS

Exp. I and II		Exp. III	
Similar	Dissimilar	Similar	Dissimilar
VKIW-YARD	VKIW-YARD	VKIW-YARD	VKIW-YARD
VKIH-STAR	LDAQ-MEAT	HVIK-STAR	DLAQ-MEAT
VKIF-ROAD	BJER-DOOR	KFIV-ROAD	BJER-DOOR
LDAQ-MEAT	VKIH-STAR	DLAQ-MEAT	HVIK-STAR
LDAT-TREE	LDAT-TREE	LTAD-TREE	LTAD-TREE
LDAX-COAT	BJEG-BOAT	XDAL-COAT	GBEJ-BOAT
BJER-DOOR	VKIF-ROAD	BJER-DOOR	KFIV-ROAD
BJEG-BOAT	LDAX-COAT	GBEJ-BOAT	XDAL-COAT
BJEN-HOUR	BJEN-HOUR	JNEB-HOUR	JNEB-HOUR

TABLE 2

MEAN NUMBER OF CORRECT RESPONSES FOR EACH EXPERIMENTAL TREATMENT DURING TESTING

Exp.	Stimulus Groups		Response Groups	
	Similar	Dissimilar	Similar	Dissimilar
I	19.17	10.93	4.93	6.53
II	28.57	20.79	23.43	18.15
III	37.40	27.44	13.08	13.91

RESULTS

The mean number of correct responses during testing is presented in Table 2 for each experimental treatment. The differences were evaluated by means of two-tailed t tests.

The Similar Stimulus groups made more correct responses than did the Dissimilar Stimulus groups. The difference was significant in Exp. III ($p < .02$), and approached the .05 significance level in Exp. I ($p < .057$) and Exp. II ($p < .051$). Differences between the Similar and Dissimilar Response groups were not significant.[3]

Errors were classified into inside-category (similar) and outside-category (dissimilar) substitutions. In the stimulus groups, an inside substitution is defined as the use of a response word appropriate to a term from the same similarity category. An outside substitution is the use of a response word appropriate to another similarity category. For example, if the stimulus is VKIW, an inside substitution is STAR or ROAD, and an outside substitution is MEAT, TREE, COAT, DOOR, BOAT, OR HOUR. (See Table 1.)

For the response groups, an inside substitution is defined as the substitution of a letter from the same similarity category. An outside substitution is the substitution of a letter from another category. The measure used is number of erroneous occurrences of the distinctive letters, regardless of position. For example, if the stimulus is YARD, the response KFBT includes one inside substitution (F) and one outside substitution (T).

The mean number of errors of each type for each experimental group is presented in Table 3.

[3] It can be noted from Table 2 that the groups whose responses were English words made more correct responses than did the groups whose responses were nonsense terms. These differences were significant for the similar ($p < .01$) and dissimilar ($p < .02$) groups in Exp. I and for the similar ($p < .001$) and dissimilar ($p < .02$) groups in Exp. III.

TABLE 3

MEAN NUMBER OF INSIDE AND OUTSIDE SUBSTITUTION ERRORS FOR EACH EXPERIMENTAL TREATMENT DURING TESTING

Exp.	Substitution Errors	Stimuli				Responses			
		Similar		Dissimilar		Similar		Dissimilar	
		Weighted Mean	Raw Mean	Weighted Mean	Raw Mean	Weighted Mean	Raw Mean	Weighted Mean	Raw Mean
I	Inside	20.76	6.92	39.99	13.33	13.92	4.64	23.19	7.73
	Outside	14.42	14.42	16.47	16.47	10.00	10.00	12.73	12.73
II	Inside	20.13	6.71	29.79	9.93	25.50	8.50	22.62	7.54
	Outside	9.00	9.00	13.29	13.29	7.50	7.50	13.38	13.38
III	Inside	9.30	3.10	19.32	6.44	37.38	12.46	21.54	7.18
	Outside	3.70	3.70	9.56	9.56	16.54	16.54	14.64	14.64

The inside substitutions were weighted by 3 because their chance probability of occurrence was one-third the probability of outside substitutions. The raw number of substitutions for each treatment is also presented in the table.

Comparisons indicate the following significant differences:

Within stimulus groups.—More inside (weighted by 3) than outside substitution errors were made by the Similar ($p < .05$) and Dissimilar ($p < .01$) Stimulus groups in Exp. I and II, and by the Dissimilar Stimulus group in Exp. III ($p < .05$).

Across stimulus groups.—The Similar Stimulus group made fewer inside substitutions than did the Dissimilar Stimulus group in Exp. I ($p < .01$), and fewer outside substitutions than did the Dissimilar Stimulus group in Exp. III ($p < .05$).

Within response groups.—More inside (weighted by 3) than outside substitutions were made by the Dissimilar Response group in Exp. I ($p < .01$), by the Similar ($p < .02$) and Dissimilar ($p < .01$) Response groups in Exp. II, and by the Similar Response group in Exp. III ($p < .001$).

Across response groups.—The Similar Response group made more inside substitutions than did the Dissimilar Response group in Exp. III ($p < .01$).

Discussion

The results of this study show that learning is better when groups of stimuli are made up of similar items rather than dissimilar ones. As previously described, Gagné (1950) suggested that groups of stimuli consisting of similar items provide a discrimination advantage. This explanation would be sufficient in the present study if the Similar Stimulus groups were superior only because they made fewer inside errors. However, this explanation does not account for the fact that the Similar Stimulus groups made fewer outside errors as well, in Exp. II and III. Only in Exp. I can the overall superiority of the Similar Stimulus group be attributed primarily to fewer inside errors.

We suggest that the Similar Stimulus groups made fewer outside errors for the following reasons: Similar stimulus grouping provides stimulus categories that can be learned readily. The responses paired with the stimuli within categories will also, to some degree, be associated with each other. During testing, *S* can assign each stimulus to one of the categories. To the extent that he has also linked responses to each other and to the similarity category, *S* can reduce the number of alternatives from which he must choose. Thus, for example, although there are nine possible responses to the stimulus VKIW, *S*s from the Similar Stimulus group are more likely to limit their responses to YARD, STAR, or ROAD—all of which belong to the appropriate similarity category. When dissimilar stimuli are grouped, stimuli belonging to similarity classifications are separated and, therefore, no easily identifiable categories are available.

Rothkopf (1958) explained the superior performance of the Dissimilar Stimulus group in his study by noting that *S*s were unable to verbally describe the stimuli (Morse Code). The apparent inconsistency between these results and the results of Gagné (1950) and those cited in the present paper may be in part resolved by noting that the inability to verbalize might reduce the coding advantage provided by the Similar Stimulus group.

In summary, stimulus similarity results in learner generalization, manifested both in discrimination difficulty and coding opportunity. Thus, similar stimulus grouping is superior to dissimilar grouping because it decreases discrimination difficulty, while increasing the opportunity for coding. Within the present research structure, an inability to discriminate has been measured in terms of *S*s' confusions between similar items (inside substitution errors). An inability to code, that is, an inability to assign responses to the proper similarity category of items, has been measured in terms of *S*s' confusions between dissimilar items (outside substitution errors).

Generalization between similar responses is evident from the error analyses. However, the present results do not indicate that grouping similar responses (as distinguished from similar stimuli, described above) is effective for error reduction.

Grouping similar responses apparently does not provide the possibility either for accelerated discrimination or for coding. Accelerated discrimination might not be evident because the role of the distinctive cue is not so sharply delineated. Coding probably does not occur because *S*s have not classified stimuli and, therefore, cannot assign them to similarity categories during testing.

We have hypothesized that discrimination and coding can operate most effectively when the grouped similars are in the stimulus position. The similar items can be functionally placed in this position by the appropriate use of stimulus and response correction procedures.

In the stimulus correction procedure, *S*s are shown the stimulus, make their responses, and then are shown the correct stimuli for the responses they made. This procedure functionally places responses in the stimulus position. Therefore, a stimulus correction method should be more effective than a response correction method for reducing errors under similar response grouping.

In the response correction procedure, *S*s are shown the stimulus, make their responses, and then are shown the correct response for the stimulus presented. This is the usual procedure and the one employed in the present experiments. A response correction method should be more effective under similar stimulus grouping (Shepard, 1958).

References

GAGNÉ, R. M. The effect of sequence of presentation of similar items on the learning of paired associates. *J. exp. Psychol.*, 1950, **40**, 61–73.

GIBSON, E. G. Intra-list generalization as a factor in verbal learning. *J. exp. Psychol.*, 1942, **30**, 185–200.

ROTHKOPF, E. Z. Stimulus similarity and sequence of stimulus presentation in paired-associate learning. *J. exp. Psychol.*, 1958, **56**, 114–122.

SHEPARD, R. N. Stimulus and response generalization: Tests of a model relating generalization to distance in psychological space. *J. exp. Psychol.*, 1958, **55**, 509–523.

(Received January 20, 1962)

ARTICLE 3

PAIRED–ASSOCIATE LEARNING AS A FUNCTION OF SIMILARITY: COMMON STIMULUS AND RESPONSE ITEMS WITHIN THE LIST

TAKAO UMEMOTO[1] AND ERNEST R. HILGARD

Stanford University

Although in serial learning the same item serves as both stimulus and response, when a paired-associate list is arranged in comparable fashion (e.g., A-B, B-C, C-D, etc.), learning is more difficult than in simple serial learning (Primoff, 1938). It has been found, further, that familiarity with the items as a result of prior serial learning facilitates the learning of a specially constructed paired-associate list in which the same items appear as stimuli and as responses, but this facilitation is lost when the list is half-mastered (Young, 1959). The interferences that account for the difficulties within such paired-associate lists have been attributed by Primoff and by Young to backward association, an interpretation coherent with the findings of Murdock (1956) and Feldman and Underwood (1957).

In the two experiments to be reported we manipulated the similarity between stimulus and response items in a manner to demonstrate circumstances under which the phenomena shown by Primoff and by Young are likely to be found, and some circumstances under which they will not be found. Such manipulation has been done in somewhat different contexts by Underwood (1953a, 1953b, 1954) and by Morikawa (1959b). While there are several possible approaches to the manipulation of S-R similarity in paired-associate learning, we have chosen to take the approach in which similarity between S and R is controlled by the number of items in common between S and R.

EXPERIMENT I

In Exp. I, paired-associate lists were constructed with three degrees of S-R similarity: complete similarity, in which all S items appear as R items; half similarity, in which half the S items are found as R items, the other S and R items all being different; complete dissimilarity, in which all S items and R items are unlike.

What kind of effect can be expected in such a situation? Two contradictory outcomes appear plausible:

1. The first hypothesis can be stated as follows: the more common items there are, the more competitive and conflicting

[1] Now at Kyoto University, Japan. The experiments were performed while a visiting scholar at Stanford University, 1959–60.

Reprinted with permission of the authors and the publisher, the American Psychological Association. The article appeared originally in the *Journal of Experimental Psychology,* 1961, **62,** 97–104.

TABLE 1

LISTS USED IN EXPERIMENT I

List 1	List 2	List 3
BAF-JOC	BUF-RAQ	BEF-SUC
DEX-SIV	CAG-MUZ	CIM-ROX
JOC-WEY	DOX-FID	DAT-FEN
LIG-HOK	LIY-JOW	JUP-HIB
PUM-DEX	WER-CAG	KIR-JAD
HOK-BAF	SOK-BUF	WOV-ZEK
WEY-LIG	QAL-DOX	TOG-PIQ
SIV-PUM	MUZ-HEV	HAC-LUV

responses will occur, hence more trials will be required for mastery. When *S* tries to learn a pair A-B in a list, and there is another pair C-A which has a common item as its response, a backward association, that is the association A-C, will also be acquired. Hence when the stimulus item A appears, there might be a competition between A-B and A-C, thus increasing the difficulty of learning.

2. The second possible hypothesis is: The ease of learning a list is inversely proportional to the number of different items in the list. Thus the list with more common items will have fewer different items to be acquired, and may lead to more rapid learning.

The first experiment tests these hypotheses, and should permit a choice between them. They are not mutually exclusive, but one effect should be stronger than the other, even if both effects are found.

Method

Lists.—Three experimental lists and one practice list were used. Each experimental list consisted of eight pairs of nonsense syllables, having a Glaze (1928) association value of 73%. The three lists are given in Table 1.

In List 1, each of the eight syllables is used both as S and R. In List 2, half of the eight syllables used are in common to S and R, so that there are 12 different syllables in this list. In List 3, none of the eight syllables is repeated, so all 16 syllables are different. In these lists similarities within the S and R items were equalized as well as possible. Some repetition of vowels is inevitable but each consonant and vowel appears no more than twice in the stimulus or the response side of these lists. In pairing syllables also an attempt was made to avoid any apparent connection between them.[2] The practice lists consisted of three pairs of nonsense syllables, with association values of 100% in Glaze's table.

Conditions and Ss.—Three groups of eight *S*s served in this experiment. All *S*s were students in introductory psychology at Stanford University, and all were naive with respect to verbal learning in the Laboratory.

After general instructions to memorize, *S*s were told:

> . . . pairs of nonsense syllables will be presented in the window of the memory drum, such as JIN-TAK, etc. The presentation time for each pair is 2 sec. Then the recall trial will begin in which the stimulus syllable on the left side is presented, such as JIN. You must recall the other item which was on the right side. . . . The order in which the syllables are presented varies from trial to trial. . . . Please *spell out loud* the correct answer (only) in the recall trial, e.g., TAK. Since the time allowed for recall is only 2 sec. please answer as quickly as possible. If you cannot remember the syllable, you may guess or keep silent, just as you wish. The learning trials and recall trials will alternate until you are able to remember *all* the items. There are two kinds of lists. The first is for your practice and composed of only three pairs. The second list is the main list, which is composed of eight pairs. Do not be in too much of a hurry to succeed. University students usually need 40 or more trials to memorize a list of eight nonsense pairs.

Lists were presented on a memory drum at a 2-sec. rate, with a 4-sec. intertrial interval. The learning trials and recall trials were alternated. The serial orders of the stimulus syllables were changed in each learning trial and in the recall trials in order to minimize serial learning.

The *S* learned the practice list to one errorless trial, then learned the experimental list

[2] There is one unintentional peculiarity in the construction of List 2 that may be noted. While half the S items recur also as R items, in only one pair (CAG-MUZ) are both members of a pair repeated in other parts of the list. This produces an unfortunate asymmetry in design. Because this relation is universal in List 1 (all items appearing both as S and as R) any contrast between results in Lists 1 and 2 cannot be attributed to the CAG-MUZ pair in List 2.

to one errorless trial, after which S was asked to make a backward recall. The response syllables typed on cards were presented to S; he was asked to write down each stimulus syllable previously attached to the response syllable. Ten seconds were allowed to recall each stimulus syllable in this test. The *S*s were not informed beforehand about the later backward recall.

Results

The mean numbers of trials required to memorize the three pairs in the practice list were 3.38, 3.50, and 4.13 for Groups 1, 2, and 3, respectively. The differences between the scores are not statistically significant ($F = 0.46$, $df = 2/23$).

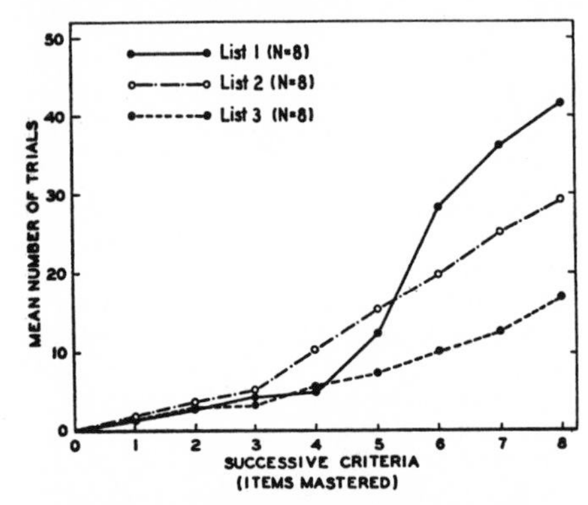

FIG. 1. Mean number of trials to successive criteria (Exp. I). (List 1 has all items common to both S and R, List 2 has half of the items in common, List 3 has none in common.)

The mean numbers of trials to reach successive criteria on the three experimental lists are shown in Fig. 1. In terms of the number of trials required to reach 8/8 correct responses, List 1 is most difficult and List 3 is easiest ($F = 19.25$, $df = 2/23$, $P = .01$). However, Fig. 1 also shows that in the early stage List 2 is rather more difficult than List 1. After the stage of 50% learning (4/8 criterion) the success with List 1 is delayed as shown by the rising curve. The learning process is somehow interrupted when the list is half learned, in agreement with Young (1959). This disruption is evident also when the average number of errors per list is similarly plotted. Table 2 shows the cumulative errors in the first half stage and later half stage. An analysis of variance based on this error score is shown in Table 3. The differences are significant not only with reference to List and Stage, but also in the interaction of these two variables.

TABLE 2

MEAN CUMULATIVE ERRORS IN EARLY AND LATE STAGES OF LEARNING

List	N	Stage I (0–50% Learning)	Stage II (50–100% Learning)
1	8	27.75	141.25
2	8	57.63	62.50
3	8	28.50	30.13

The individual data for List 1 show that learning develops smoothly at the first stage and *S*s easily reach the criteria of 4 or 5 out of 8 items. Thereafter almost every S suddenly shows confusion. They need a number of trials to acquire even one more correct response. This is also evident in the types of errors made (Table 4). The *S*s who learned List 1 not only show an extraordinarily high proportion of overt errors (51% vs. 23%

TABLE 3

ANALYSIS OF VARIANCE OF ERRORS FOR STAGES OF LEARNING (EXP. I)

Source	*df*	*MS*	*F*
Between lists (L)	2	12,288.9	12.62*
Between *S*s in same group	21	973.9	—
Total between *S*s	23		
Between stages (S)	1	19,280.1	31.55*
S × L	2	16,340.9	26.73*
Pooled *S*s × S	21	611.2	—
Total within *S*s	24		
Total	47		

* $P < .01$.

TABLE 4

ERRORS CLASSIFIED BY TYPE

List	*N*	Overt Errors		No Response	Total Errors
		Backward Associations	Other		
1	8	51.2	34.0	83.8	169.0
2	8	3.6	20.8	95.7	120.1
3	8	0.0	12.0	46.6	58.6

and 20% for Lists 2 and 3) but also show a predominance of errors classified as backward associations on the basis of possible mediation by common items. The difficulty experienced by *S*s learning List 1 in overcoming their trouble in the middle of the process was striking. To fill the most difficult gap (between the fourth and fifth, or fifth and sixth item recalled) took at least 15 trials for every one of these 8 *S*s. Only one of the remaining *S*s took that long. This effort to gain one item in recall required for List 1 *S*s more than a third of their total trials to mastery.

These deadlocks with List 1 almost always originated in perseverative repetition of wrong responses, which were mediated by common items in S and R. If there were A-B and B-C pairs in a list, and if *S*s learned A-B at first, it happened quite often that they responded B-A instead of B-C when B was later presented. Such a backward association mediated by common items in S and R is probably one of the interference sources in this situation, as proposed in our first hypothesis.

The mean numbers of correct responses in backward recall were for List 1, 5.38, for List 2, 5.75, and for List 3, 3.13. The prevalence of backward recalls in Lists 1 and 2 suffices to make our hypothesis plausible. The fact that there were about an equal number for the two lists is immaterial, for the opportunity to interfere is twice as great for List 1 as for List 2. The relatively lower number of backward recalls for List 3 calls for a comment. The backward associations tend to develop with fully practiced responses, as proposed by Umemoto (1951) and Morikawa (1959a). Because there was much less overlearning of the items of List 3 than of the items of List 1 and 2, the lower number of backward associations within List 3 is understandable.

The results thus give support to our first hypothesis. The relationship between our results and the second hypothesis is more complex. It was proposed that the fewer different items there were the easier the learning might be. There is some slight support for this hypothesis in the early trials, in which List 1 is easier than List 2, but List 3 is never at a disadvantage, and the hypothesis is clearly contradicted later in learning. We shall return to an interpretation of these findings after reporting Exp. II.

EXPERIMENT II

The results of Exp. I have been tentatively explained by the competition between right and wrong associations in Lists 1 and 2 which seem to have been mediated by backward associations. However, mediated backward associations need not always produce inhibition. If, for example, the mediated responses are the same as the correct response these mediated responses may facilitate

TABLE 5

LISTS USED IN EXPERIMENT II

List 1	List 2	List 3
YAV-perfect	YAV-perfect	YAV-perfect
noonday-GID	noonday-GID	noonday-GID
ZOT-clumsy	ZOT-vacant	ZOT-clumsy
empty-KEB	empty-KEB	empty-KEB
GID-midday	GID-midday	GID-vacant
faultless-YAV	faultless-YAV	awkward-YAV
KEB-vacant	KEB-clumsy	KEB-midday
awkward-ZOT	awkward-ZOT	faultless-ZOT

learning instead of interfering with it. When the mediated responses are quite different from the correct ones, we would expect competition, as in Exp. I. Experiment I controlled the possible frequency of mediated responses by adjusting the number of common items between S and R, and all the mediated responses (if any occurred) were incorrect. In Exp. II the possible frequency of mediated responses remained the same for all three lists, but the relation of the mediated responses to the correct response differed; that is, the items of the three lists were all alike except that the lists were so constructed that some backward associations would facilitate, some interfere. Thus any differences in results are unlikely to be attributable to the *number* of mediated backward associations, although they may be due to the *arrangement* whereby the mediated response is inhibitory or facilitating.

Method

Lists.—Three experimental lists and one practice list were used. Each of the experimental lists consisted of eight pairs of items, in every case a nonsense syllable paired with an adjective. Four out of eight pairs in each list had nonsense syllables on the stimulus side and adjectives on the response side; the remainder were in the reverse order. The nonsense syllables were all of low association value (Glaze 13%). The adjective pairs were taken from the Melton and Safier table (Hilgard, 1951), all from the 10 pairs highest in similarity. The three lists are given in Table 5.

As shown in Table 5, the three lists all have the same components, but differently paired. In List 1, each member of the four pairs of similar adjectives was connected to the same nonsense syllable, one member of the pair on the stimulus side, one on the response side, for example: noonday-GID, GID-midday. In List 2 this arrangement holds only for two pairs of adjectives, while the other two similar adjective pairs are connected to unlike nonsense syllables. Thus "faultless" and "perfect," "noonday" and "midday" have the same syllable for each member of the pairs, while "awkward" and "clumsy," "vacant" and "empty" have different syllables. Two dissimilar adjectives, however, are paired with a common syllable (empty-KEB, KEB-clumsy). In List 3 similar pairs were in no case connected with the same syllable. As before, different orders of presentation were arranged for each list. In these arrangements an attempt was made to avoid presentation of the same item (whether syllable or adjective, stimulus or response) twice in succession. The practice list consisted of three pairs of nonsense syllables and meaningful nouns, avoiding transfer effects which might have been caused by using adjectives in the practice list.

The conjecture being tested is that the mediated responses based on backward association in List 1 will be facilitating, those in List 3 will be inhibiting, and those in List 2 will fall between. Thus we would expect errors of recall in increasing order from List 1 to List 3.

Conditions and subjects.—Groups of 11, 12, and 13 *S*s, comparable to those used in Exp. I, served in Groups 1, 2, and 3, respectively. Essentially the same instructions as in Exp. I were used. A substitute for the memory drum was improvised from a copy holder used in typing (Remington-Rand Line-a-Time). All lists, including the practice one, were printed on a paper fastened to the copy holder. The copy holder was covered with a panel board having a narrow slit window (⅛ in. by 24 in.) through which the stimulus was presented. The exposures were made manually, the rate being controlled by a click from a 2-sec. interval timer. Exposure time was 2 sec., and 2 sec. elapsed between trials. The learning proper took place after the short practice session and was followed, as before, by backward recall from the response items typed on cards.

Results

The mean number of trials required to memorize the three pairs composing the practice list was 4.15, 4.50, and 4.55 for Groups 1, 2, and 3, respectively. The differences between these groups were not significant ($F=0.29$, $df = 2/35$).

The mean number of trials to reach successive criteria with the lists is shown in Fig. 2. The mean number of trials to reach a criterion of one perfect trial is significantly different among lists ($F = 5.07$, $df = 2/35$, $P = .05$). In terms of t ratios, there were significant differences between

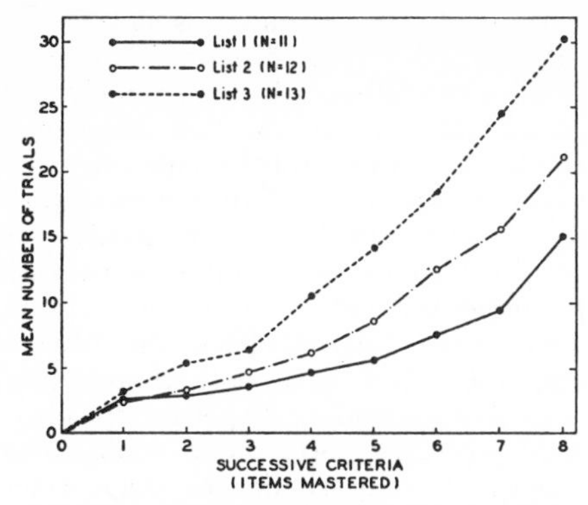

FIG. 2. Mean number of trials to successive criteria (Exp. II). (In List 1 both members of similar adjective pairs are associated with the same nonsense syllable, in List 2 half the pairs have both members associated with the same nonsense syllable, in List 3 no similar adjective pair has its members associated with the same syllable.)

Lists 1 and 3 ($t = 2.14$, $P = .05$) and between Lists 2 and 3 ($t = 2.30$, $P = .05$), though the difference between Lists 1 and 2 was not significant ($t = 1.48$).

The mean numbers of errors in the first half and second half of learning are shown in Table 6. An analysis of variance similar to that shown in Table 3 revealed only Lists as a significant effect ($F = 6.225$, $df = 2/33$, $P < .01$). The order of increasing errors by list is from List 1 with fewest errors to List 3 with most errors, as predicted.

The number of correctly reproduced responses in backward recall was 5.54 for List 1, 5.25 for List 2, and 5.07 for List 3. Thus there were no significant differences between the lists in backward recall. Even *S*s who learned List 1, which would seem quite easy to recall backward, were confused in recall, and were not protected from error by the similarities between the adjectives from the stimulus side and from the response side. All *S*s, regardless of list learned, made more backward recall errors from syllable to adjective (Means = 2.5, 2.6, and 2.1, respectively, for Lists 1, 2, and 3) than in the direction from adjective to syllable (Means = 0.0, 0.1, and 0.3, respectively).

Thus our prediction that the lists would fall in the order of difficulty from List 1 to List 3, with List 1 the easiest, is borne out, and gives further support to the interpretation that the results are mediated by backward associations.

DISCUSSION

In Exp. 1 the more common items there were on the stimulus and response sides in paired-associate learning the more difficult it was to master a list. However, early in learning this was not so, and it was in fact easier to learn the first few items of a list having more common items in S and R. We interpreted the interference as due to the formation of backward associations, and left unaccounted for the early advantage of the common-item lists.

The early advantages of the common-item lists have been found before. Umemoto (1958), in a somewhat similar experiment using group learning, found that the list with all items in common (similar to our List 1 of Exp. I) was easy early in learning, while the list with half of the items similar (corresponding to our List 2) was more difficult early in learning. This correspondence between the two studies, one done in Japan and one in the United States, implies that the result is not accidental. Hence it is

TABLE 6

MEAN CUMULATIVE ERRORS IN EARLY AND LATE STAGES OF LEARNING

List	N	Stage I (0–50% Learning)	Stage II[a] (50–100% Learning)
1	11	25.09	28.73
2	12	34.75	48.83
3	13	68.85	63.31

[a] Stage II vs. Stage I for pooled *Ss*, $df = 1/33$, $F = 514/641 = 0.8$, *ns*.

necessary to postulate some difference in process between what is going on in the early stages of learning and what is going on in the later stages. One possibility is that before the association between S and R has progressed there is a false appearance of association because of the intrusion of some stimulus items into the responses. It has been suggested that in paired-associate learning the first stage consists in the acquisition of response items before associations between S and R develop (Morikawa, 1959a; Umemoto, 1951; Underwood, Runquist, & Schulz, 1959). If that is the case, the "familiar" item is likely to be offered as a response, regardless of the presented stimulus. But the stimulus items are also "familiar" through incidental learning, and not yet differentiated from response items. Hence some stimulus items will appear as responses. In this stage, if some of the stimulus items are the same as the response items, the independent acquisition of response items will be obscured by the intrusion of stimulus items, some of which, by chance, may get scored as "correct" acquisitions, although most of them are, in fact, interferences with learning. If there is no common item between S and R (as in List 3), evocation of the response items will not be subject to interference through the intrusion of an occasional stimulus item. This is a tentative hypothesis to explain the early advantage of List 1 over List 2, although they later cross and List 2 comes to have the advantage. Later in acquisition, the backward associations take over, and the intrusion of stimulus items becomes more generally interfering with the correct response. Thus, in retrospect, we have abandoned the second hypothesis of Exp. I in favor of the hypothesis that early in paired-associate learning some stimulus items intrude as response items not through backward association, but through failure of discrimination between stimulus and response items at this early stage.

In Exp. II, the hypothesis of mediated backward association is tested in a situation in which the backward association may facilitate learning instead of inhibiting it. This situation, however, implies two different factors, namely, the occasional facilitation and occasional inhibition by backward mediating associations. In List 3, all the backward associations, mediated by similar or identical items, are inhibiting because responses evoked by mediation are in every case different from the correct response. List 1 is more complex, in that some intruding responses are identical with the correct one while some others are only similar to the correct one. For the pairs which have adjectives in their stimulus side, such as noonday-GID in List 1, backward association will be clearly facilitating, because the response items mediated by similar adjectives from the response side (such as a backward association leading to midday-GID) are just the same nonsense syllables as the correct ones. For the pairs which have nonsense syllables on their stimulus side in List 1, such as GID-midday, the problem is rather complex, because the response adjectives mediated by identical nonsense syllables from the response side, such as the backward association GID-noonday, are only similar to the correct ones. Does a similarity between two responses facilitate the learning of a pair having the same stimulus or is it inhibiting? According to the surface of Osgood (1949) the point of the present scheme is located slightly under the zero point, hence ought to be inhibiting. According to Underwood (1949), however, the result was rather facilitating. Ishihara and Kashu (1953) also found in the A-B, A-C paradigm, in which B and C are similar, neutral, and opposite, that there were some facilitating effects when the responses are similar. From these results it is a reasonable inference that a similarity between two responses does not inhibit learning. Thus there is no inhibiting situation in List 1. Of course in List 3 of Exp. II, there are the conflicting arrangements of A-B, A-C (backward association), with no similarity between response items B and C for either nonsense syllables or adjectives, so there is no problem when we compare the *relative* difficulties of List 1 and List 3 in Exp. II.

Summary

Two experiments were reported here. In Exp. 1, three lists, each consisting of eight pairs of nonsense syllables, were used. The number of common items between stimulus and response was 8 (all) for List 1, 4 (half) for List 2, and none for List 3. The more common items there were the more trials to mastery though in an early stage there was a tendency for learning a list having half common items to be more difficult than learning a list having all items of S and R in common. A hypothesis of backward mediated association was proposed.

In Exp. II, the hypothesis is tested in a situation in which the backward association facilitates learning as well as inhibiting it. The materials used were three lists all of which had the same items on the stimulus and response sides, differing only in arrangement. These lists consisted of eight pairs, half of which had adjectives as stimuli and half of which had nonsense syllables as stimuli. List 1 was so arranged that all backward mediated responses would be the same or similar to correct responses. For List 2 half of the backward associations would be facilitating, while for List 3 all backward associations were designed to be inhibiting. The results confirmed the hypothesis. The mediation through backward association thus accounts both for the inhibition in Exp. I and the facilitation and inhibition in Exp. II.

References

Feldman, S. M., & Underwood, B. J. Stimulus recall following paired-associate learning. *J. exp. Psychol.*, 1957, **53**, 11–15.

Glaze, J. A. The association value of nonsense syllables. *J. genet. Psychol.*, 1928, **35**, 255–269.

Hilgard, E. R. Method and procedures in the study of learning. In S. S. Stevens (Ed.), *Handbook of experimental psychology*. New York: Wiley, 1951.

Ishihara, I., & Kashu, H. Learning of responses having relations of similarity, oppositeness, and neutrality. *Jap. J. Psychol.*, 1953, **24**, 1–12.

Morikawa, Y. Function of stimulus and response in paired-associate verbal learning. *Psychologia*, 1959, **2**, 41–56. (a)

Morikawa, Y. Studies in paired-associate learning: IV. On the influence of intra-stimulus and intra-response similarity upon learning and recall. *Jap. J. Psychol.*, 1959, **3**, 116–127. (b)

Murdock, B. B., Jr. "Backward" learning in paired-associates. *J. exp. Psychol.*, 1956, **51**, 213–215.

Osgood, C. E. The similarity paradox in human learning: A solution. *Psychol. Rev.*, 1949, **56**, 132–144.

Primoff, E. Backward and forward association as an organizing act in serial and paired-associate learning. *J. Psychol.*, 1938, **5**, 375–395.

Umemoto, T. On the relative weight of stimulus versus response words in rote learning. *Jap. J. Psychol.*, 1951, **21**, 46–55.

Umemoto, T. Similarity between stimulus and response words in paired-associate learning. *Tohoku J. exp. Psychol.*, 1958, **2**, 95–102.

Underwood, B. J. Proactive inhibition as a function of time and degree of prior learning. *J. exp. Psychol.*, 1949, **39**, 29–43.

Underwood, B. J. Studies of distributed practice: VIII. Learning and retention of paired-nonsense syllables as a function of intralist similarity. *J. exp. Psychol.*, 1953, **45**, 133–142. (a)

Underwood, B. J. Studies of distributed practice: IX. Learning and retention of paired-adjectives as a function of intralist similarity. *J. exp. Psychol.*, 1953, **45**, 143–149. (b)

Underwood, B. J. Intralist similarity in verbal learning and retention. *Psychol. Rev.*, 1954, **61**, 150–166.

Underwood, B. J., Runquist, W. N., & Schulz, R. W. Response learning in paired-associate lists as a function of intralist similarity. *J. exp. Psychol.*, 1959, **58**, 70–78.

Young, R. K. A comparison of two methods of learning serial associations. *Amer. J. Psychol.*, 1959, **72**, 554–559.

(Received June 27, 1960)

ARTICLE 4

ISOLATION EFFECTS: STIMULUS AND RESPONSE GENERALIZATION AS EXPLANATORY CONCEPTS [1, 2]

SLATER E. NEWMAN

North Carolina State College

AND

ELI SALTZ

Wayne State University

The present experiment on the von Restorff isolation effect has two purposes: (*a*) to examine the extent to which the concepts of stimulus and response generalization can be used to predict isolation phenomena in serial learning; and (*b*) to investigate the inconsistency between some of the results reported by Kimble and Dufort (**7**) and the results of other studies of isolation reported in the literature.

Von Restorff (**20**) found that an isolated term, such as a number in the midst of a list of nonsense syllables, was learned very quickly. Many explanations arising from entirely different theoretical frameworks have been proposed for the isolation effect. Thus, von Restorff used the gestalt concepts of figure and ground to predict her results, Green (**4**) refers to a "surprise" factor, while Smith and Stearns (**17**) have proposed that presence of the isolated item leads to reorganization of the serial list, the isolated term serving as an orienting device for the learner.

S-R psychologists have, in general, employed the notion of reduced intralist competition as an explanatory device (**1**; **2**; **8**, p. 384; **11**, p. 504; **13**). In addition, McGeoch and Irion (**8**), Osgood (**11**), and Underwood (**18**) suggest that the concepts of stimulus and response generalization may provide the basis for a theory of competition in verbal learning. Thus, the effects of isolation might be explained in terms of its effects on the tendencies for stimulus and response generalization to occur. The reasoning is this. The typical operational manipulation of stimulus generalization is to increase the similarity among *stimulus* members of a list. The typical operational manipulation of response generalization is to increase the similarity among *response* members of a list. In von Restorff-type experiments, the isolation of an item consists of inserting a dissimilar item into a list of similar items. Thus, the isolation manipulation can be expected to lead to a reduction in within-list stimulus and response similarity, and a consequent decreased likelihood that stimulus and response generalization will occur. On the

[1] This report is based on work done under ARDC Project No. 7709, Task No. 77304, in support of the research and development program of the Air Force Personnel and Training Research Center, Lackland Air Force Base, Texas. Permission is granted for reproduction, translation, publication, use and disposal in whole or in part by or for the United States Government. The opinions or conclusions expressed herein are those of the authors. They are not to be construed as necessarily reflecting the views or endorsement of the Department of the Air Force or of the Air Research and Development Command.

[2] A paper, based on the results of this study, was read at the 1957 meeting of the Midwestern Psychological Association.

Reprinted with permission of the authors and the publisher, the American Psychological Association. The article appeared originally in the *Journal of Experimental Psychology*, 1958, **55**, 467–472.

basis of generalization theory, then, it is possible to state a set of predictions concerning the effects of isolation on the learning of a serial list.

The isolated term as a response.—The most consistent finding of isolation studies is that the isolated term is well learned as a response. Can this be predicted from generalization theory? Consider two serial lists which are identical except for the item in the Xth serial position. In the first (isolated) list, the item in the Xth position is dissimilar from the remaining items, although these remaining items are similar to one another. In the second (homogeneous) list, the item in the Xth position is similar to all the other items in the list. First consider the operation of response generalization. Since the isolated term in the Xth position of the first list is dissimilar from the other items, the tendency for other responses to be inappropriately elicited in place of the isolated response should be less than the tendency for such items to be inappropriately elicited in place of the corresponding Xth item in the second (homogeneous) list. Thus, the isolated term should be learned more quickly as a response than its nonisolated counterpart. The concept of response generalization, then, can be used to predict the typical von Restorff effect in serial learning.

A second prediction can also be generated using response generalization. It was pointed out above that in the isolated list there should be a reduced tendency for other responses in the list to compete for elicitation with the isolated term. In a like manner, there should be a reduced tendency for the isolated term to be elicited inappropriately in place of any of the other responses in the list. This prediction is more crucial than the first, since it does not represent a post hoc rationalization of known data.

The isolated term as a stimulus.—Consider again the two hypothetical serial lists discussed above. Since the isolated term is dissimilar from other items in the list, there should be less tendency for the isolated item, as a stimulus, to elicit responses which are appropriate for other stimuli in the list than would be true for the corresponding Xth item in the homogeneous list. Thus, by using the concept of stimulus generalization, it would be predicted that isolation should reduce competition of responses to the isolated term as a stimulus. Consequently, isolation should facilitate the learning of a response to the isolated term as a stimulus.

Effect on learning the entire list.—Since the isolated term is dissimilar from the other items in the list, there should be a lessened tendency for stimulus and response generalization to occur throughout the isolated as contrasted with the nonisolated list. Thus, total errors during learning of the isolated list will be fewer than for the nonisolated list, even when the learning of the Xth items and their responses are not considered.

These predictions were evaluated using materials employed by Kimble and Dufort (7) in their Exp. III. Kimble and Dufort attempted to test the utility of conceptualizing "meaningfulness" as a dimension on which similarity could be manipulated. Thus, they attempted to manipulate isolation by placing a term low in Noble's (**10**) "meaningfulness" scale within a list of highly meaningful terms. Kimble and Dufort succeeded in obtaining the typical von Restorff effect: The isolated term was learned quickly as a response. However, contrary to the prediction made above, the response to the isolated term was learned more slowly than the response to the corresponding item in the homogeneous list. While the results of previous studies have not been conclusive on this issue (**5, 6, 17, 22**), the Kimble and Dufort results appear to be inconsistent with those studies which are methodologically most relevant (**6, 17**). Consequently, one of the purposes of the present study was to investigate the possibility that the Kimble and Dufort results were a peculiarity of the particular isolated items they employed.

It should be pointed out that evidence

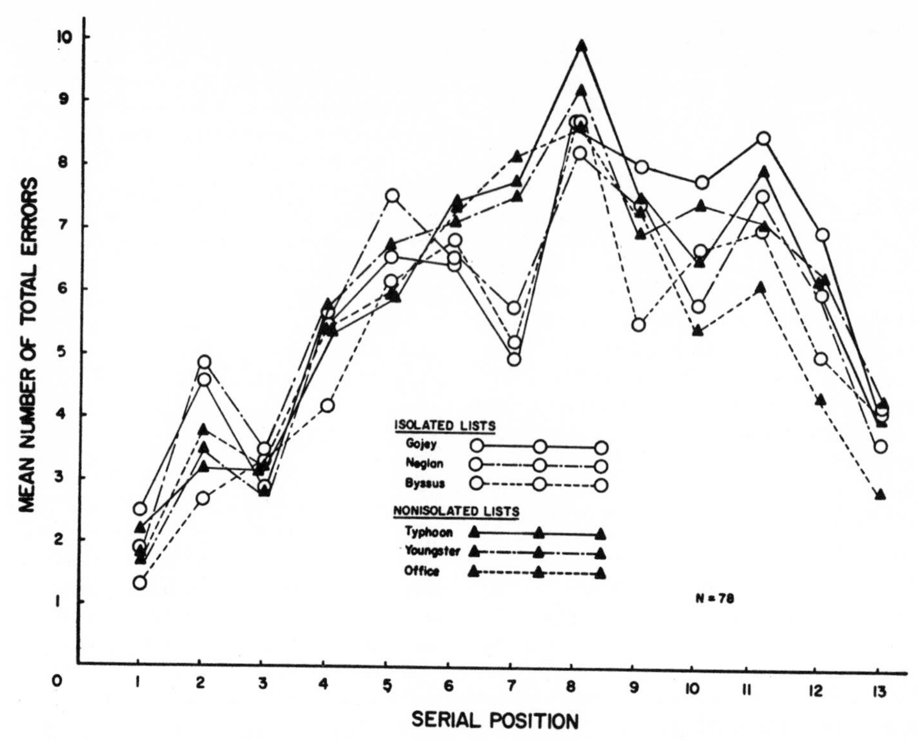

FIG. 1. Mean number of total errors as a function of serial position.

exists, from experiments reported in the literature, relevant to several of the predictions in this paper (**1, 3, 4, 5, 6, 7, 9, 12, 13, 14, 15, 16, 17, 19, 20, 21, 22**). However, this evidence arises from several studies which used different procedures both for learning and for producing isolation. In the present experiment the predictions were tested within a single type of learning situation, using a single isolation technique.

METHOD

Learning materials.—The materials were similar to those used by Kimble and Dufort (**7**) in their serial learning study. Six 13-word lists, identical except for the seventh word, were constructed. The 12 words common to all lists were from the high end of Noble's meaningfulness scale (**10**) their *m* values ranging from 7.12 to 9.61. For the three nonisolated lists, the words in the seventh position also had high *m* values: youngster (6.75), typhoon (6.83), and office (7.95). For the isolated lists, the terms in the seventh position were paralogs of low *m* value; gojey (.99), neglan (1.04), and byssus (1.13). Each list was preceded by a double asterisk which served as the stimulus for the first term.

Subjects and procedure.—The *S*s were 78 airmen waiting to attend an Air Force technical school. Thirteen *S*s were randomly assigned to each group, a different list being learned by each group. Data from one *S* were discarded since he reported learning the list in narrative fashion.

After instructions describing the serial learning task were read to *S*, learning of the list was begun and proceeded to one errorless repetition of the list. The terms were exposed on a memory drum at a 2-sec. rate. Trials were separated by 12 sec.

RESULTS

Prediction 1.—The isolated term will occur more frequently as a correct response than will a nonisolated term occupying the same serial position. Figure 1 demonstrates that there are fewer errors at Position 7 for the isolated lists than for the nonisolated lists. Table 1 presents an analysis of variance of the proportion of correct responses at this position divided by total correct responses at all positions. The F for treatments is significant at beyond the .001 level. This finding is consistent with Prediction 1 and with the results of other isolation studies showing that the isolated term is more effective as a response term than its nonisolated counterpart.

Prediction 2.—The isolated term will occur less frequently as an overt intrusion than will its nonisolated counterpart. Since the isolated item was learned more quickly than its nonisolated counterpart, and since also there is a complicated relationship between stage of learning and the tendency for intrusions to occur, an analysis of intrusions occurring in the first learning trial was performed. Application of Fisher's exact test to those data gave a P of .05, when a two-tailed test was employed. The results were, however, opposite in direction from those anticipated on the basis of Prediction 2. Thus, significantly more overt intrusions occurred involving the isolated terms than involving the nonisolated terms.

Prediction 3.—More correct responses will be made to an isolated term as a stimulus than to a nonisolated term occupying the same serial position. The serial position curves presented in Fig. 1 indicate

TABLE 1

Analysis of Variance of Ratio of Correct Responses at Position 7 to Total Correct Responses at All Positions

Source	*df*	*MS*	*F*
Treatments	1	120.78	21.32*
Groups/Treatments	4	6.68	1.18
Within groups	72	5.66	

* $P = .001$.

TABLE 2

Analysis of Variance of Ratio of Correct Responses at Position 8 to Total Correct Responses at All Positions

Source	*df*	*MS*	*F*
Treatments	1	11.85	3.04*
Groups/Treatments	4	6.60	1.69
Within groups	72	3.90	

* $.10 > P > .05$.

that fewer errors were made to the isolated terms as stimuli than to the corresponding nonisolated terms. Table 2 presents an analysis of variance based on these data, using the proportion, correct responses at this position divided by total correct responses at all positions. The F for Treatments is 3.04 with 1 and 72 *df*. On the basis of a two-tailed test, this F is significant between the .05 and .10 levels. Since a directional prediction was made, it appeared legitimate to evaluate the results using a one-tailed test; on the basis of a one-tailed test the F is significant at beyond the .05 level.

Prediction 4.—Total errors during learning of isolated lists will be fewer than for nonisolated lists, even when the isolated terms as stimuli and as responses are not considered.

Results of an analysis of variance of the number of errors (excluding those at Positions 7 and 8 which involve the isolated term as stimulus and as response), indicate that 59.74 errors were made in learning the isolated lists and 58.15 errors were made in learning the nonisolated lists.[3] The F for Treatments is less than 1.00 indicating that the difference is not significant. Thus, Prediction 4 fails

[3] Mean number of trials to learn the isolated lists, *including the isolated item*, was 12.9, to learn the nonisolated lists, 13.0. This lack of difference occurs despite the relatively rapid learning of the isolated term.

of verification. The F for Groups within Treatments was also less than 1.00.

Discussion

The results of the present experiment do not strongly support the utility of stimulus and response generalization as explanatory concepts for the effects of isolation. The stimulus generalization concept proved useful for predicting the facilitated learning of a response to an isolated stimulus; however, this effect was weak, and was statistically significant only when a one-tailed test was employed. The strongest isolation effect in the present experiment and in previous research was the tendency for an isolated item to be rapidly learned as a response. The writers found it necessary to employ the concept of response rather than stimulus generalization to make the essentially post hoc prediction of this phenomenon.

Although the concept of response generalization effectively handles the above results (i.e., the tendency for the isolated item to be rapidly learned as a response), it does not handle the intrusion data. Specifically, and contrary to prediction based on the response generalization concept, the data indicated that the isolated term occurred significantly more, rather than less, frequently as an intrusion error early in learning.

As was predicted earlier in this paper, a consequence of both stimulus and response generalization should be fewer errors during learning of isolated lists than of nonisolated lists. In the present study no such tendency was observed, the results being opposite in direction, although not significantly so, from those predicted. It may be argued that reduction of within-list similarity by one item may have only a very small effect on the learning of the entire list. It is interesting to note, however, that an examination of the data of three other studies also indicates poorer learning of the remainder of the isolated lists (**6, 7, 17**), although significance levels are not indicated in any of these studies. The writers are aware of no studies in which over-all facilitation has been reported.

One of the purposes of the present study was to investigate an inconsistency between results reported by Kimble and Dufort (**7**), and results reported by others (**6, 17**). Specifically, Kimble and Dufort reported that more errors were made to the isolated term as a stimulus than to the corresponding nonisolated term. The writers felt that this result might have been a function of the particular isolated term (i.e., "gojey") and the particular nonisolated term (i.e., "office") used by Kimble and Dufort. Consequently, in the present study three isolated and three nonisolated lists were constructed. "Neglan" and "byssus" were used as isolated items, in addition to "gojey"; while "youngster" and "typhoon" were used as nonisolated items in addition to "office." As was reported earlier in this paper, the isolated terms, as stimuli, elicited more correct responses than their nonisolated counterparts. However, fewer correct responses were elicited by "gojey" than by "office," which, as a stimulus, was the most effective of the three nonisolated terms (cf. Fig. 1). Thus, the Kimble and Dufort results on this point may be an artifact of the particular items they employed.

The present results suggest that the concepts of stimulus and response generalization may not be adequate to account for the effects noted. The alternatives, then, are these: (*a*) to identify additional processes, which, together with those of stimulus and of response generalization, can be used to explain the effects noted, or (*b*) to reject stimulus and response generalization as explanatory concepts, and to identify other processes which may handle more effectively the results obtained in the present study. At any rate, the view that all the effects of introducing an isolated term into a serial list are due to a reduction in intraserial interference may demand revision.

Summary

This study examined the extent to which the concepts of stimulus and response generalization can be used to predict isolation phenomena in serial learning. Four predictions based on those concepts were evaluated.

The learning materials were six 13-word lists, identical except for the seventh word. The 12 words common to each list had high meaningfulness. For the three nonisolated lists, the word in the seventh position was also of high meaningfulness; for the three isolated lists, they were low in meaningfulness. Each list was learned by a different group of 13 *S*s. A serial anticipation procedure was employed.

As predicted, the isolated terms occurred correctly more frequently as responses than did the nonisolated terms and also tended, as stimuli, to elicit more correct responses than the nonisolated terms. Contrary to expectation, however, over-all learning of the isolated list was not facilitated; also the isolated terms occurred significantly more, rather than less, frequently as overt intrusions than the nonisolated terms. It is concluded that the concepts of stimulus and response generalization may not be adequate to account for the effects of isolation.

References

1. Buxton, C. E., & Newman, E. B. The forgetting of 'crowded' and 'isolated' materials. *J. exp. Psychol.*, 1940, **26**, 180–198.
2. Gibson, E. J. A systematic application of the concepts of generalization and differentiation to verbal learning. *Psychol. Rev.*, 1940, **47**, 196–229.
3. Gibson, E. J. Intra-list generalization as a factor in verbal learning. *J. exp. Psychol.*, 1942, **30**, 185–200.
4. Green, R. T. Surprise as a factor in the von Restorff effect. *J. exp. Psychol.*, 1956, **52**, 340–344.
5. Jenkins, W. O., & Postman, L. Isolation and 'spread of effect' in serial learning. *Amer. J. Psychol.*, 1948, **61**, 214–221.
6. Jones, F. N., & Jones, M. H. Vividness as a factor in learning lists of nonsense syllables. *Amer. J. Psychol.*, 1942, **55**, 96–101.
7. Kimble, G. A., & Dufort, R. H. Meaningfulness and isolation as factors in verbal learning. *J. exp. Psychol.*, 1955, **50**, 361–368.
8. McGeoch, J. A., & Irion, A. L. *The psychology of human learning.* New York: Longmans, Green, 1952.
9. McGourty, M. C. Serial position effects in learning as a function of interfering associations. Unpublished M.A. thesis, State Univer. of Iowa, 1940.
10. Noble, C. E. An analysis of meaning. *Psychol. Rev.*, 1952, **59**, 421–430.
11. Osgood, C. E. *Method and theory in experimental psychology.* New York: Oxford Univer. Press, 1953.
12. Pillsbury, W. B., & Raush, H. L. An extension of the Köhler-Restorff inhibition phenomenon. *Amer. J. Psychol.*, 1943, **56**, 293–298.
13. Postman, L., & Phillips, L. W. Studies in incidental learning: I. The effects of crowding and isolation. *J. exp. Psychol.*, 1954, **48**, 48–56.
14. Saul, E. V., & Osgood, C. E. Perceptual organization of materials as a factor influencing ease of learning and degree of retention. *J. exp. Psychol.*, 1950, **40**, 372–379.
15. Siegel, P. S. Structure effects within a memory series. *J. exp. Psychol.*, 1943, **33**, 311–316.
16. Smith, M. H., Jr. The influence of isolation on immediate memory. *Amer. J. Psychol.*, 1949, **62**, 405–411.
17. Smith, M. H., Jr., & Stearns, E. G. The influence of isolation on the learning of surrounding materials. *Amer. J. Psychol.*, 1949, **62**, 369–381.
18. Underwood, B. J. *Experimental psychology.* New York: Appleton-Century-Crofts, 1949.
19. Van Buskirk, W. L. An experimental study of vividness in learning and retention *J. exp. Psychol.*, 1932, **15**, 563–573.
20. von Restorff, H. Über die Wirkung von Bereichsbildungen im Spurenfeld. In W. Köhler and H. von Restorff, Analyse von Vorgängen im Spurenfeld. I. *Psychol. Forsch.*, 1933, **18**, 299–342.
21. Young, C. W., & Supa, M. Mnemic inhibition as a factor in the limitation of the memory span. *Amer. J. Psychol.*, 1941, **54**, 546–552.
22. Zirkle, G. A. Success and failure in serial learning: II. Isolation and the Thorndike effect. *J. exp. Psychol.*, 1946, **36**, 302–315.

(Received June 10, 1957)

CHAPTER 6

Acquisition as a Function of Instructions to Learn

An assortment of problem areas, research hypotheses, methodologies, and procedures have been covered in the acquisition-related articles of the preceding five chapters. Yet there is one common condition or factor appearing in all of them. The *Ss* in each study were fully informed by *E* that their "job" during their tenure in the laboratory consisted of learning, as an active endeavor, the assigned task. In other words, *E* established an intent for *S* to acquire the new skills represented in the task. This intent was most likely communicated to *S* by a few simple but pointed phrases from *E*, such as : "I am going to show you a list of words which I would like to have you learn." All such instances of acquisition may be grouped together into what is commonly called intentional learning. In the laboratory intent is mediated in some way by *E*'s instructions. Away from the laboratory intentional learning of this kind is most likely to take place in the classroom, in which the teacher, like *E*, serves as the point of origin for the extrinsically aroused intent to learn.

The reader must realize that in his ordinary activities a veritable deluge of stimuli impinge on him. Only a minor segment of these stimuli are captured for reception by a deliberate intention induced externally and then assigned some kind of labeling response for future recall. Nevertheless, he manages to learn the color of an acquaintance's eyes, some details of an accident he just happened to witness, the floor plan of a friend's house he recently visited, etc. In fact, much of our everyday learning would seem to be learned in this incidental—that is, without deliberate instructions to learn—manner. Obviously, something serves to direct our attention to these stimuli and to make possible registration for future recall. Psychologists interested in the phenomenon of incidental learning have come to call these "somethings" orienting tasks or activities. The orienting task brings about sufficient exposure to stimuli to accomplish their learning.

Incidental learning, like most of our other phenomena, has had a lengthy research history. The early investigators (e.g., Myers, 1913) were concerned mainly with the simple demonstration of the reality of acquisition without an *E*-induced intent to learn and with the demonstration that such learning is greatly inferior to acquisition with intent. Early attempts to explain the intentional-incidental differential stressed the vaguely formulated concept of a "set," or readiness to learn, presumed to be present with intent to learn.

Contemporary research was influenced greatly by the important study of Postman and Senders (1946). Postman and Senders continued to employ the rather ambiguous concept of set. However, they stressed the fact that sets to learn may generalize to instructions other than intent instructions. These uncontrolled, generalized sets thus account for the phenomenon of incidental learning. So regarded, set becomes a molar response composed, conceivably, of a number of separate component responses to *E*'s instructions as a stimulus. The phenomenon of stimulus generalization (cf. Chapter 5) leads us to expect that varied instructions, including incidental learning instructions, may fall along the generalization gradient for intent instructions as the stimulus in question. This conceptualization has been gradually refined and modified by Postman and his colleagues to a position recently summarized by Postman (1964a). In this conceptualization, instructions are viewed as the stimulus for a number of cue-producing (mediating) responses which govern activity during acquisition—including labeling the stimulus component, encoding (cf. Chapter 7), rehearsal, etc. Instructions may differ widely in the extent to which they elicit these cue-producing responses essential for acquisition. Intent instructions, of course, are highly effective in this elicitation process. Other kinds of instruction are effective to the degree they arouse the appropriate cue-producing responses. The amount of incidental learning then becomes a function of the degree factor. In the laboratory, incidental learning instructions take the form of requesting *S* to perform orienting tasks which direct *S* to the learning materials but which may vary in their tendency to elicit appropriate cue-producing responses. Acquisition may then be considered a function of instructions. Like most of the other independent variables we have examined, instructions interact with other variables, for example, meaningfulness, in ways which often modify the basic relationship with acquisition.

Fortunately, for both the edification of the reader and the belabored output of the editor, an excellent review of the literature on incidental learning has just appeared (McLaughlin, 1965; Article 1). Consequently, the reader will be spared further redundancies in content. McLaughlin's article reviews the important theoretical and methodological issues in this area. Included in it are a discussion of the major research designs employed in incidental learning experiments, one of which (Type II) we have already encountered in our previous discussion of *R-St* learning (cf. introduction to Chapter 2), an analysis of the processes presumed affected by instructions, and a massive review of the research literature relating instructions to other independent variables. Special attention is devoted to motivation as one of the interacting variables, and the theoretical implications of the motivation-incidental learning relationship are carefully scrutinized.

To familiarize the reader directly with the flavor of research in this area, two other articles are included. One (Postman, Adams, and Philips, 1955; Article 2) is illustrative of research with the Type I design (see Article 1). The reader should note how an orienting task serves to direct *S* to the learning materials in the absence of instructions to learn. The other article (Mechanic, 1962a; Article 3) demonstrates how a Type II design (see Article 1) may be applied. The reader should note the features of this design that distinguish it from Type I. Readers who are interested in Mechanic's approach to incidental learning phenomena are referred to two other studies by him (Mechanic, 1962b, 1964).

ARTICLE 1

"INTENTIONAL" AND "INCIDENTAL" LEARNING IN HUMAN SUBJECTS:

THE ROLE OF INSTRUCTIONS TO LEARN AND MOTIVATION [1]

BARRY McLAUGHLIN

Harvard University

This paper reviews research on the phenomenon of incidental (INC) learning with particular attention to differences in degree between the functional relations pertaining to INC and intentional (INT) learning. The nature of orienting instructions and resultant differential cue-producing responses are seen to be critical to the study of INC learning. The importance of studies dealing with properties of stimulus items is stressed and the differential cue-producing hypothesis examined in the light of research involving variations in motivational level. It is suggested that this conceptualization be extended to include theoretical formulations based on cue utilization as a function of motivation. Defining operational procedures are criticized for providing no clear distinction between INT and INC learning.

Recently Postman (1964) reviewed the literature on short-term memory and incidental (INC) learning in human subjects. His discussion highlighted the points of similarity between the two phenomena and he argued that there are important continuities between the theoretical and methodological problems involved in research on short-term memory and INC learning. Both types of studies were seen to be concerned with the initial disposition of a learner as determining the reception and immediate storage of information. Experimental procedures are directed therefore at the determination of those factors which limit and bias a subject's responses in a learning situation rather than at the laws which govern response integration.

Deese (1964), in his discussion of the Postman paper, argued that the basic problem in the study of INC learning is that of the nature of the differences in behavior under instructions to learn compared with no instructions to learn when exposed to the same materials. The central problem in such studies "is not in the conditions of incidental learning per se but in determining what alterations in behavior are induced by the formal instructions to learn something [Deese, 1964, p. 203]." The variables mediating such alterations are subsumed by Postman under the general concept of "differential responses" which "include categorizing responses such as naming or labeling, other responses elicited by the items through stimulus generalization, and responses serving as associative links among the members of a series [Postman, 1964, p. 190]."

The main force of Postman's argument was that the observed differences between intentional (INT) and INC learning result from the effect of the instruction stimuli which influence the amount and characteristics of learning by determining the differential cue-producing responses occurring during a period of practice. Deese (1964) simplified this explanation somewhat and stressed the role of "representational responses" which are either overt "encoding responses" or implicit "unarticulated phonemic equivalences of some potentially overt response [p. 204]." Instructions to learn produce appropriate representational responses during presentation of the material, whereas under INC-learning conditions this is the case to a lesser degree.

Deese (1964) also pointed out that Postman's review made almost no mention of any possible direct effects of motivation in the differences between conditions of INC and INT learning. This was consistent with the emphasis Postman placed on the nature of the re-

[1] The preparation of this review was facilitated by a grant, 1-F1-MH-22, 445-01, from the National Institute of Mental Health.

The author is indebted to D. H. Kausler, R. W. White, and B. A. Maher for their valuable suggestions and critical reading of the manuscript.

sponses elicited by instructions and with his argument that effects resulting from changes in incentive or drive conditions are merely correlates of the pattern of responding introduced by differences in instructions (Deese, 1964).

The present review differs from Postman's discussion in that it will be concerned specifically with the functional properties of INC-learning phenomena and the factors bearing upon the determination of differential cue-producing responses during the period of practice. Explanations of INC learning which depend upon such mediating constructs as differential responses and representational responses have an ad hoc ring to them and it is imperative that the functional properties of the manipulated variables be specified. The importance of establishing such functional relationships in INC-learning research has been stressed by Estes (1956).

Second, the question of motivation as a variable affecting INC and INT learning will be treated in more detail in the present review than was the case in Postman's discussion. Thus, while it will be impossible to avoid some repetition, the aim of the present review is to complement Postman's paper by concentrating on areas deemphasized by that author because of a theoretical concern with the relationship between short-term memory and INC learning.

Although the investigations reviewed in this paper are experimental studies of human learning in laboratory situations, work in the area of INC learning has important implications for clinical and social psychology. Aborn (1953), for example, has demonstrated that the INC-learning procedure is more sensitive to the effects of anxiety-produced repression than are traditional (intentional) procedures. Bandura and Huston (1961) reported an experiment in which identification in children was conceptualized as a process of INC learning. Bousfield, Cowan, and Steward (1963) and Yavuz (1963) reported evidence that connotatively meaningful evaluative responses are incidentally learned to stimulus objects. This confirms clinical and everyday experience which indicates that failure to recall the name of a person or a verbal label of an object does not necessarily preclude the possibility of making valid evaluative statements regarding the person or object (Yavuz, 1963). In general, it is likely that Berlyne (1960) was correct in feeling that by far the greater part of man's learning experience involves what is technically INC learning.

Definitional Questions and Experimental Procedures

The early studies of INC learning were directed primarily at demonstrating that the phenomenon did in fact occur and that such learning is inferior to INT learning (e.g., Chapman, 1932; Mulhall, 1915; Myers, 1913; Poppelreuter, 1912). Concern with the functional properties of the variables affecting INC and INT learning is a more recent development in the experimental literature. To a great extent such systematic analysis was neglected because of difficulties in the formulation of a clear operational distinction between INT and INC learning (Postman, 1964).

Definition of INC Learning

The Concept of Set. In the early investigation of INC learning the concept of set was employed as a central explanatory construct. In the INC-learning situation the subject apparently learned in the absence of an experimental set to learn. In contrast, a set to learn always characterized INT learning. Admittedly, the concept of set was very loosely, and often ambiguously, defined (Gibson, 1941). It was felt necessary, however, to use this construct to refer to the apparent preparedness or state of readiness (usually experimentally induced by instructions to the subject) which is an important determinant of the formation of associations (Postman & Senders, 1946). Even in recent experimental work the selector mechanism which produces differences between relevant (INT) and irrelevant (INC) learning is sometimes classed under the general heading, set (Underwood & Schulz, 1960).

Merely not instructing subjects to learn does not, however, preclude the possibility of a set to learn (Bahrick, Fitts, & Rankin, 1952; Bitterman, 1956; McGeoch & Irion, 1952; Shellow, 1923). Sets are habits and are themselves the results of previous learning (Bruner, 1957). Brown (1954) has pointed out that a situation similar to a situation in which learning has occurred in the past may evoke a set to learn through stimulus generalization. Postman and Senders (1946) also cited generalization, as potentially determinant of uncontrolled sets to learn, operating in what appears to be INC learning. They suggested that since all learning involves activity, and hence some kind of preparatory set, it is more economical to waive the INT-INC distinction in favor of a distinction based on explicit sets to learn (experimentally and self-induced) and covert sets (derived from sets of greater generality).

It is difficult even in this context, however, to speak operationally of intent to learn. Often introspective reports reveal awareness of irrelevant cues (McGuigan, 1958). This may result from varied self-instructions, from habitual interests, or from characteristics of the stimuli (McGeoch & Irion, 1952). But whether this awareness is self-induced (explicit set) or an extension of a more general set to learn (covert set) is impossible to determine at an operational level. In addition, awareness of irrelevant cues does not necessarily imply intent to learn and lack of awareness does not exclude the possibility of "unconscious" (Brown, 1954) motives to learn.

Operational Definitions. Because of the difficulty of handling the concept of set operationally, it seemed preferable not to define INC learning in terms of set, intent, or motive to learn (McGuigan, 1958). One approach has been merely to regard learning as INC if there are no formal instructions to learn the particular (INC) material, and as INT if there are formal instructions to learn the (INT) material (whether it be the same or different material). In this way investigators have explored the INC-learning phenomenon by establishing relationships among experimental variables with one variable, incentive to learn INC material, held as constant as possible at some unspecified (though admittedly poorly approximated) low value (Goldstein & Solomon, 1955).

Postman (1964) argued that INT and INC learning can be operationally distinguished by the use of different classes of instruction stimuli. The effect of instructions on learning varies as a function of the intensity and specificity of the verbal communications given to subjects. These effects may be maximal in the case of subjects who are prepared by the instructions for a test of retention, or minimal in the case of subjects who are not so prepared by instruction stimuli. These stimuli are seen to be integral parts of the experimental conditions and can themselves be specified. It is the manipulation of this dimension of the learning situation that determines the amount of information given to the subject about test-performance expectations (Postman, 1964).

The adequacy of such operational procedures for INC learning is open to question. Nevertheless, such procedures are ordinarily employed in the research which has accumulated in this area. Criticism of these defining procedures will therefore be held in abeyance until a review of the literature has been presented. For purposes of discussion the customary definitions will be employed. Learning is called INT when there are instructions to learn the relevant material and INC when there are no instructions to learn the relevant material.

Experimental Designs

Two basic experimental methods have evolved in the study of INC learning (Kausler & Trapp, 1960), and a third method which combines these two basic designs has been used in recent studies. There are a number of other research designs concerned with the effect of irrelevant or incidental cues upon performance in a perceptual or learning situation (e.g., Hammer, 1955; Lepley, 1935; Prentice & Asch, 1958; Saltzman, 1957) which will not be discussed here. Furthermore, the present review will not deal with studies in the area of concept attainment wherein subjects learn incidentally a common defining property (INC concept attainment) in a task seen as rote memorization of stimulus labels (Bruner, Goodnow, & Austin, 1956; Reed, 1946), nor with various experimental designs concerned with peripheral learning without awareness (e.g.,

Bitterman, 1956; Hirsch, 1957; Porter, 1957a, 1957b; Postman & Adams, 1954, 1955, 1957a). Rather, this discussion is restricted to studies employing the following designs.

Type I Design. The first procedure requires subjects in the INC group to learn material when they are not specifically instructed to do so. These subjects are directed toward the task by some orienting instructions—such as encircling the items or making free associations—but are given no instructions to learn. The subjects in the INT group, on the other hand, learn the task with specific instructions to learn. After exposure to the material, subjects in the INC condition are given an unexpected test of retention. Postman (1964) has argued that a postexperimental inquiry should be employed and those subjects who anticipated the test of retention or who deliberately rehearsed the material should be discarded and replaced. This insures a sharpening of the effect obtained between experimental groups.

The Type I design is characteristic of "classical" investigations of INC learning (e.g., Biel & Force, 1943; Myers, 1913; Prentice, 1943; Shellow, 1923) and of many more recent studies. Earlier studies in this framework, however, may be seriously criticized for their failure to require subjects in the INT group to perform the orienting task (e.g., Biel & Force, 1943; Jenkins, 1932; Mulhall, 1915). When this is the case, the superior performance of the INT learners may be ascribed to both the intention to learn and to freedom from activities interfering with the formation of associations (Postman & Adams, 1956b; Saltzman, 1953).

Type II Design. In the Type II design INC learners appear to learn associations which they are not instructed to learn during a period when they are learning other assocations which they have been instructed to learn (Feldman & Underwood, 1957). In this design each subject serves as his own control for both INT and INC learning. The Type I procedure allows INT learners to surpass INC learners only insofar as their instructions orient them towards dimensions of the stimuli which are relevant to performance on a test of retention. In the Type II design an INT subject becomes at the same time an INC learner with respect to characteristics towards which he has not centrally focused.

Postman (1964) noted that the Type II situation may be further subdivided into two classes on the basis of the relationship between relevant (INT) and irrelevant (INC) components to the total learning situation. In one case the irrelevant material is directly related to the material to be learned under INT conditions. For example, if the subject has been instructed to learn a list of geometric forms which are of different colors (e.g., Bahrick, 1954), then the colors are a feature of the learning material which is irrelevant, but intrinsic, to the task toward which the subject was oriented by the instructions. On the other hand, the irrelevant component might be materials or cues which bear no direct relation to the learning task, such as is the case when the instructions are to learn a series of words which have additional items such as digits or geometric forms exposed along with the words (e.g., Fischer & Cook, 1962). The difference between the two classes of Type II design therefore refers to the INC learning "of intrinsic and extrinsic components of the experimenter-defined learning task [Postman, 1964, p. 187]."

Mixed Design. Several recent studies have used a "mixed" design employing both Type I and Type II procedures. Rosenberg (1962), for example, was interested in the generalization of learning instructions which presumably occurred in the Type II design and investigated this phenomenon by employing both the Type II design and a control Type I procedure in which subjects were exposed to both INT and INC materials without instructions to learn. Similarly, Fischer and Cook (1962) used the Type II method in a study of distribution of practice and presentation rate with the added control of groups exposed to both INT and INC materials without instructions to learn (Type I INC learning). Miller and Lakso (1964) also used the mixed design in a study of the effects of presentation rate and number of exposures.

The mixed design allows comparison within single studies of INC learning with and without instructions to learn INT material. Fischer and Cook (1962) found that such a comparison showed INC learning to be superior in the Type I design, even though the groups receiving no instructions to learn had on the average only half as many trials as groups in the Type II condition. The authors interpreted these findings in terms of the hypothesis that the amount of INC learning is inversely related to the degree of constriction of the field of perception. Assuming a motivational state induced by instructions to learn the INT materials, a greater constriction of perception would result in the Type II situation than in the Type I situation where no such motivational state was present. Consequently, the amount of INC learning would be greater in the Type I than in the Type II design, while the opposite would hold for the INT materials.

Mechanic (1962a) proposed an alternative interpretation of differences in INC learning found in the Type I and Type II designs. This author noted that the Type II design is in principle more favorable than the Type I procedure because cue-producing responses may be presumed to generalize to irrelevant features of the presented materials. However, the Type II situation also involves task competition between relevant and irrelevant materials, which is not the case in the Type I design. Such variables as difficulty of the material, exposure time, and instruction stimuli will determine the extent to which the advantages accruing from generalization in the Type II situation are offset by the effects of competiton. For example, Rosenberg's (1962) failure to obtain a generalization of learning is possibly the result of a cancellation of this effect by task competition in the Type II procedure.

An added complication was introduced by the work of Miller and Lakso (1964). In a test of Mechanic's (1962a) hypothesis that performance of the INT task in a Type II design interferes with INC learning, these authors increased the exposure interval in an attempt to reduce the amount of interference. It was expected that with a longer exposure interval, more time would be available for the INC material and more INC learning would occur. The data failed to support this. Recognition of the INC material was not better with 8-second than with 2-second intervals when presentation of the materials was constant. However, when the order of the INC material varied from trial to trial, INC learning showed improvement. This suggested that:

> even though more time may be available for responding to the incidental material, *S* will not necessarily utilize that time unless some variable is introduced which serves to focus *S*'s attention on the incidental material [Miller & Lakso, 1964, p. 261].

Varying the order of the INC items had this "attention-focusing" effect in their experiment.

In general, a comparison of the various experimental designs involves several considerations. Because the amount of INC learning can be evaluated without the complications resulting from generalization and task competition, the Type I situation is to be preferred where emphasis is on the associative processes in INC learning as determined by the nature of the materials and the conditions of presentation (Postman, 1964). On the other hand, investigators concerned with INC learning as a function of generalized drive and incentive conditions have employed the Type II situation. In this case the focus of attention has been on the question of how variations of drive and incentive conditions affect generalization and competition of responses. The mixed design has the advantage of allowing a comparison of results obtained under the two procedures and has been profitably employed for this purpose in more recent work.

Orienting Tasks

Postman (1964) discussed the various types of orienting tasks, employed in INC-learning studies, for both the Type I and Type II designs, and the methodological problems raised by variations in orienting tasks. Two points touched upon by this author deserve elaboration. These have to do with the effects of orienting tasks in minimizing the difference between INT and INC learning and with the differential effect of orienting tasks on INT and INC learning.

Minimization of Differences. The great

majority of studies in INC learning have been concerned with discovering properties that differentiate INC from INT learning and with measuring the amount of material incidentally learned. It is generally thought that the differences between INT and INC learning and variations in amount of INC learning are a function of differences in the orienting tasks required of subjects (unless otherwise specified, the studies cited have employed the Type I methodology). Saltzman (1956), for example, produced different degrees of INC learning by the manipulation of orienting instructions over several levels "intuitively" designed to inhibit INT learning or facilitate INC learning. The inhibition of INT learning supported the findings of earlier studies (Neimark & Saltzman, 1953; Saltzman, 1953) and is readily explained on rational grounds. That is, requiring the INT subjects to perform various orienting tasks (sorting cards, circling numbers, etc.) while learning insures restricted observation of the materials presented as well as consequent interfering response tendencies. In fact, Saltzman's work demonstrated that under certain conditions the orienting task could actually interfere with INT learning to such a degree that INC learning would be superior to INT learning (Neimark & Saltzman, 1953). In such cases orienting instructions to INC learners are such as to direct attention to the INC materials although no overt instructions are given to learn these materials.

Postman and Adams (1956b) also demonstrated that changing the nature of the orienting task can effect changes in the degree of INT and INC learning. These investigators found that when the task was relatively favorable to learning (giving meaningful associations to stimulus items) there was an increase in the difference between INT and INC learners in favor of INT subjects, and when the task was relatively unfavorable (matching stimulus items with geometric forms) there was less difference between the two groups of learners.

Mechanic's (1962b) research with Type II conditions also indicated that differences in orienting instructions (number of pronouncing responses required of the subject) produced differential INC learning. This author's findings indicated that variations in orienting instructions determined the amount of Type II INC learning in a manner consistent with that obtained in Type I situations. Mechanic also noted that differences in orienting tasks are important for understanding the results of studies with apparently contradictory findings. On the basis of such differences, he was able to reconcile his own research (Mechanic, 1962a) with that of Postman and Adams (1958) and Bahrick (1957; Bahrick, Fitts, & Rankin, 1952).

To explain experimental findings in which the difference between amount of INT and INC learning was minimal, Postman (1964) conceptualized a continuum of orienting tasks, ranging from those requiring responses maximally favorable to learning to those requiring responses maximally unfavorable. At either extreme on the continuum the differences between INT and INC learning are minimal. Thus, at the favorable extreme INC learning increases through generalization, while at the unfavorable extreme INT learning decreases because of interference from the orienting activity.

Differential Effects of Orienting Tasks. Learning may be seriously hindered or substantially facilitated by the orienting task. The experimental data on this point are extremely conclusive. However, Postman's (1964) generalization that intent per se has no significant effect on learning is possibly too sweeping. This author argued that instructions to learn activate responses to the materials which are favorable to acquisition and that "the same results could be obtained by appropriate orienting tasks without instructions to learn [Postman, 1964, p. 189]." It has not been empirically demonstrated, however, that merely orienting the subject toward material without instructing him to learn can, in fact, produce learning as effectively as that which results under normal conditions when instructions to learn are administered. When the INC learning approaches or surpasses INT learning this is the result of orienting tasks which interfere with INT learning.

Postman's (1964) concern was apparently to avoid any explanation which posits a "set" or "intent" on the part of a subject to learn the material. He argued, consequently, that the difference between INT and INC learning reduces to zero when learning is either seriously hindered or maximally facilitated by the orienting task regardless of intent. Empirical data support the first part of this contention, but not the second. When INT learning is maximally facilitated it is possible that INC learning will also be facilitated, but not to the same degree (Neimark & Saltzman, 1953; Saltzman, 1956). Postman could, however, account for this without recourse to the concept set or intent to learn on the part of the subject. In his own terms it is possible to say that instruction stimuli activate cue-producing responses which are favorable to acquisition. These are maximally favorable when they orient the subject to learn the material, which is the case specifically in the INT condition. Instruction stimuli administered to subjects in the INC group will facilitate learning to a lesser degree, although INC subjects may even surpass INT subjects when these INT subjects have been given additional instructions which interfere with learning.

Several attempts have been made to state the effects of orienting tasks upon learning in general terms. Postman and Senders (1946), for example, suggested that specific instructions to learn may have three possible effects: (*a*) a gradient effect which strengthens the memory for items which are adjacent to the explicitly learned ones on the continuum of generality, (*b*) an inhibition effect if items are too similar to each other, and (*c*) a compensatory effect whereby instructions to learn highly specific details causes the subject to emphasize general comprehension in his learning of the stimulus material. Postman and Tuma (1954) suggested that the establishment of selective orientations provides an analogue to the manipulation of drive. In this conceptualization, stimuli conforming to the subject's orientation toward the task serve as relevant "incentives," while stimuli which are inappropriate to the relevant task serve as irrelevant incentives. The tendency in recent work, however, has been to avoid such generalizations and to determine empirically the relationship between specific orienting tasks and learning.

Functional Properties of Incidental Learning Phenomena

The customary procedure followed in INC-learning studies has been to employ one of the three designs—Type I, Type II, or Mixed—and to study differences which obtain under various conditions between subjects given instructions to learn relevant material and subjects given no such instructions to learn relevant materials. The variables manipulated relate to experimental conditions, to stimulus properties, or to intrasubject differences. By studying the functional properties of these variables to learning it was hoped that empirical laws could be established to account for differences between INT and INC learning.

Experimental Variables

Number of Presentations. In an early formulation of his differential response hypothesis, Postman (Postman, Adams, & Phillips, 1955) conceived on such responses as habits attached to stimulus items through previous experience or stimulus generalization. In the case of INC subjects, differential responses tend to be reactions strongly associated with learning items. Such responses are readily evoked and are likely to occur during initial exposure to the materials. It follows that further presentations of the materials have limited effects upon INC learning since initial differentiations presumably reflect strong habits which benefit little from further exercise. On the other hand, INT subjects do not limit their differential responses to highly familiar items, but utilize additional trials to increase the number of differentiations and connections among items. This line of argument received experimental support from the work of Postman and Adams (1958). Koyanagi's findings (1958) were in agreement. In both cases INT learners showed a significant upward trend as a function of presentations, while INC subjects did not.

Other studies of the effects of exercise under INT and INC conditions have not produced conclusive results. Brown (1954) failed to secure a differential effect as a function of frequency of presentations. His findings may be criticized, however, since his comparison was between INT subjects who learned by the anticipation method from the beginning of practice and INC subjects who were first introduced to this method at the time of the test (Postman & Adams, 1958). Saltzman and Atkinson (1954) found little difference between the two kinds of learners until 16 presentations. Their method of testing retention (recognition), however, is relatively insensitive to differences between INT and INC learners (Postman, Adams, & Phillips, 1955). They may also be criticized for not controlling for exposure time (Postman & Adams, 1958). The findings of Gleitman and Gillett (1957) are more difficult to explain. Their results indicated that levels of greater frequency of presentation led to better recall scores for both INT and INC subjects.

Employing the Type II design to investigate INC learning at five stages of INT learning, Bahrick (1957) found that INC learning was greatest in the very early (0%–25%) and late (100%–150%) stages of INT learning. Little or no INC learning was found to occur between the 50% and the 100% level of INT learning, indicating that during this stage of practice the efforts of subjects were directed almost exclusively toward mastery of the task set by the experimenter. These results agree with the Postman and Adams (1958) hypothesis that a great percentage of INC learning occurs during very early trials, and also indicate that overlearning (when it occurs) may be a source of a large percentage of INC learning. If this is true it is very possibly the key to the Gleitman and Gillett (1957) study, since in their experiment the orienting task (rating a speaker's voice on a 2-point scale) was extremely simple, and 14 presentations of a series of 12 two-place numbers conceivably led to overlearning and permitted subjects to attend to a great deal of the stimulus material. Hence there was an increase in INC learning with exercise and the differential effect was not found.

In line with this interpretation are the experimental findings of Mechanic (1962a, 1962b) and Miller and Lakso (1964). In the Mechanic studies, INT and INC learning were found to increase with practice. As in the Gleitman and Gillett study, however, the lack of a differential effect was most likely the result of the nature of the orienting task required of subjects. Mechanic required INC subjects to pronounce INC items in order to rate their phonetic similarity or to perform similar tasks which made it necessary for INC subjects to respond to nonsense syllables differentially. In contrast, Miller and Lakso found that relevant (INT) learning varied directly with number of presentations whereas irrelevant (INC) learning did not. This is in agreement with the differential effect obtained by Postman and Adams (1958). However, under one condition, where exposure time and number of trials were both maximal, Miller and Lakso found that INC learning did improve with practice. Under such conditions, subjects most likely arrived at the late stages of INT learning (Bahrick, 1957) and were able to respond differentially to the INC materials. In short, the effects of practice on INC learning are a function of the characteristics of the learning materials, the nature of the orienting task, and the resultant degree of INT learning.

Amount of Material. In (INT) learning experiments increasing amounts of material create more opportunities for intraserial interference and consequently relative efficiency varies inversely with the length of the list (e.g., Calhoun, 1934; Woodworth, 1915). In INC learning, however, the effects of intraserial interference have been found to be less severe (Postman & Adams, 1957b), and therefore Postman and Adams (1958) hypothesized that increases in amount of material should have a less adverse effect on INC than on INT learning. Their hypothesis was supported. These investigators found, in addition, an interaction between length of the list and meaningfulness of the material. While INC learners retained fewer nonsense syllables than INT learners, they were less subject to increases in intralist interference with the addition of new items to the list. With familiar meaningful items the pattern of differential responses made by INT and INC learners became more similar. Consequently, the differences in amount recalled were reduced when meaningful material was employed, and the two conditions of learning produced parallel trends in retention scores with changes in the length of the list.

Exposure Time. Saltzman (1953) suggested that an important variable in studies comparing INT and INC learning is the rate of presentation of the learning material. His investigations indicated that in the Type I procedure the magnitude of the difference between INT and INC learning was greatest with slow and least with fast rates of presentation. The findings of Neimark and Saltzman (1953) supported this contention. The results of both experiments are open to criticism, however, because the use of the recognition method of retention which has been shown (Postman, Adams, & Phillips, 1955) to be relatively insensitive to differences between INT and INC learning. Unfortunately, the method of recognition has been used in even recent experiments comparing INT and INC learning, and results such as those of Miller and Lakso (1964), who failed to find an effect of variations in exposure time on INC learning, may be simply the product of the type of retention measure employed. This is not to say that the recognition method has no place in the study of INC learning, but that only a testing procedure (free recall) sensitive to differential associative habits is legitimate where such associative habits are critical to the comparison of INT and INC learning.

In the Type II design experimentation has indicated that an increase in presentation interval significantly facilitates both INT and INC learning (Fischer & Cook. 1962; Kausler & Trapp, 1961; Rosenberg, 1959). It is quite possible that a task-difficulty variable is responsible for such results. That is, a slower rate of presentation lessens task difficulty, decreases the degree of concentration required of subjects, and consequently affects the range of attention for simultaneously presented irrelevant cues (Kausler & Trapp, 1960).

In this connection Broadbent (1963) reported experimental evidence that pronouncing material aloud was, under certain conditions, more harmful to learning than rehearsing to oneself. This suggests that there is a maximum as well as a minimum time factor for the flow of information in the learning subject. Too much time spent on rehearsing aloud tended to interfere with learning. Broadbent criticized Postman and Phillips (1961) for interpreting their results as indicating that rehearsal was harmful to learning. What these investigators demonstrated, Broadbent argued, was that pronouncing the verbal material aloud was detrimental to recall. There was no evidence that rehearsal as such was harmful to learning.

Proactive and Retroactive Inhibition. There is strong evidence of proactive and retroactive inhibition effects for INC material (Gleitman & Kamrin, 1957; Postman & Adams, 1956a; Prentice, 1943; Rosenberg, 1961). In a typical study, Rosenberg (1961) gave two groups of subjects three original learning trials on a list of 12 common words each, accompanied on the left with a 2-digit number (Type II design). The control group was subsequently given a puzzle, while the experimental group was required to learn three more lists of words without digits. The control group was shown to recall significantly more INT words and INC numbers than the experimental group.

Postman and Adams (1956a) employed the notion of differential response tendencies to explain findings obtained in INC-learning studies concerned with retroactive inhibition. Original learning is typically higher under INT than under INC-learning conditions. Since degree of original learning and amount of retroactive inhibition are inversely related (McGeoch & Irion, 1952), the expectation is that less interference would be obtained in the case of INT than INC learners. However, the distribution of habit strengths differs under conditions of INT and INC learning. The few items learned by INC subjects are likely to have high associative strength (Postman, Adams, & Phillips, 1955). The items learned by INT subjects are more numerous but include more items of low strength. Consequently, among those items learned by INT subjects a greater proportion are susceptible to interference. The two effects tend to cancel each other out, and no major differences are found in the relative amounts of retroactive inhibition following INT and INC learning.

Serial Position Effects. There is strong evidence that INT and INC learning are mediated by the same processes from studies of the serial-position effect in INC learning (Goldstein & Solomon, 1955; Postman & Adams, 1957b, 1960; Postman & Phillips, 1954). However, the functional relations which characterize INC learning differ in degree from those found in INT learning. Those subjects given INT instructions show relatively greater primacy than recency effects, while the opposite is true of INC learners. In fact, Postman and Adams (1957b) found that, in spite of a lower overall level of retention, INC subjects surpassed INT subjects in recall of the final section of the list. The advantage of the INT group was, therefore, limited to the beginning and middle of the series where instructions to learn favored the establishment of sequential associations between responses to successive items (Postman & Adams, 1960).

Postman (1964) has generalized these findings and concluded that sequential associations are discriminated less effectively by INC than by INT subjects. That is, the absence of a primacy effect in INC learning indicates both a low degree of sequential organization and a tendency instead to respond to items on the basis of sheer strength. This is consistent with the differential response hypothesis that uninstructed subjects respond to fewer features of the learning situation than do instructed subjects. Nevertheless, it should be pointed out that these differences between INT and INC subjects result from variations in instruction stimuli and consequent differential cue-producing responses rather than from qualitative differences between the two types of learning.

With the Type II procedure, Kausler and Trapp (1962, 1963) found that the serial-position curve in INT learning was flattened in the middle of the list when irrelevant or INC cues (2-digit numbers) were added to relevant cues (nonsense syllables). This effect was attributed to variations in cue distinctiveness of the relevant cues, as a function of the presence of irrelevant cues, and was most marked when irrelevant cues were peripherally placed. Thus, differential learning of irrelevant cues altered distinctiveness (Murdock, 1960) of relevant cues and consequently flattened the serial-position curve. Because of the small amount of INC learning which occurred in these studies, no conclusions were possible concerning primacy versus recency effects in the Type II design.

Stimulus Variables

Relatively little experimental interest has been shown in determining what material will be amenable to INC learning (Berlyne, 1960). Murdock's (1960) work with the distinctiveness of stimuli in serial-position learning and Kreezer's (1958; Agnew & Pyke, 1963) approach to the attention-demand value of stimuli provide operational techniques for the measurement of stimulus properties. However, no application of methods of this level of sophistication has been made in studies concerned with INC learning. One interesting finding was that of Mechanic (1962b) who reported that stimulus items most frequently learned intentionally were also most frequently learned incidentally. This is additional evidence that the same responses underlie both INT and INC learning and that the stimulus properties facilitating these responses are the same.

Meaningfulness. The stimulus property which has received most experimental attention in INC-learning research is that of meaningfulness. Verbal stimuli vary widely in the frequency with which they elicit differential responses in a sample of subjects (Glaze, 1928; Hull, 1933; Mandler, 1954). Empirical evidence indicates a positive relationship between associative value (the index of readiness with which an item elicits differential responses) and recall (McGeoch & Irion, 1952; Mandler, 1955; Noble, 1952; Underwood & Schulz, 1960). Again a somewhat different functional relationship characterizes INT and INC learning. The slope of the functions relating meaningfulness to recall is consistently steeper under INC than under INT conditions (Mayzner & Tresselt, 1962; Mechanic, 1962a; Postman & Phillips, 1961), indicating low-association-value stimuli evoke less effective differential responses from INC than from INT subjects. Consequently, the lower the association value of stimuli, the greater the differences in amount retained by INT and INC learners. Karen's (1956) conflicting results are puzzling, but Postman (1957) has argued that procedural differences are responsible for the discrepancy. Brown (1954) also offered conflicting evidence, since he found no difference in INC learning of low-association syllables and monosyllabic nouns. He required his subjects to reproduce the order of the syllables, however, and in this respect his method differed from the usual scoring procedure employed in INC-learning studies. Brown's subjects also showed extremely low INC-learning scores, suggesting that with the more customary procedure of free recall a greater differential effect would have been found (Jantz & Underwood, 1958).

Postman (1964) pointed out that studies of R-S learning provide an important confirmation of the generality of the relationship between meaningfulness and INC learning. Feldman and Underwood (1957) described R-S (backward) learning as merely a variant of INC learning since the R-S associations are not part of the task specified by instructions. Experimental work comparing the functional properties of R-S and INC learning (Cassem & Kausler, 1962; Jantz & Underwood, 1958; Morikawa, 1959) supports this contention. Particularly significant here is the study of Jantz and Underwood (1958) in which the function relating meaningfulness and R-S learning corresponded exactly to that obtained by the method of free recall for INC learning (Postman, Adams, & Phillips, 1955).

There is evidence for an interaction between the meaningfulness of the stimulus materials and the nature of the orienting task (Mechanic, 1962a; Postman & Adams, 1956b). This follows from the assumption that the amount of learning depends on the frequency of effective differential responses made to stimulus items (Postman, 1964). Meaningful items evoke differential responses more readily than do nonsense syllables for both INT and INC learners, and hence the differential responses of meaningful items are less susceptible to interference from the orienting task.

Intralist Similarity. Postman and Adams (1957b) and Koyanagi (1957b, 1957c) have demonstrated that there is a decrease in the differential effects of INT- and INC-learning conditions as a function of intralist similarity. Since an increase in intralist similarity interferes with sequential associations, and since sequential associations are more critical in INT than in INC learning, intralist similarity is more detrimental to INT than to INC learning. That is, the INC learner acquires not only fewer correct responses but fewer incorrect ones as well. Consequently, increased similarity of items has a more adverse effect upon INT than upon INC learning. Research in R-S learning supports this finding (Feldman & Underwood, 1957; Morikawa, 1959).

Isolation Effect. Postman and Phillips (1954) investigated the learning of "crowded" and "isolated" items presented under conditions of INT and INC learning. They felt that from the point of view of Gestalt psychology isolated items should be particularly well learned under conditions of INC learning—that is, when results depend upon spontaneous organization of the experimental series. Their findings, however, did not support this hypothesis. Instead, it was only under conditions of INT learning that recall of isolated items was superior. Postman and Phillips (1954) attempted to explain their findings by arguing that since there is less intraserial interference under INC conditions, the isolation of an object brings about less reduction in INC than in INT learning. Koyanagi (1957a) and Gleitman and Gillett (1957) reported similar results (with some slight facilitation appearing in INC learning).

Saltzman and Carterette (1959) presented evidence that isolation had no effect upon INT or INC learning, even when isolated materials were circled in red. The explanation proposed by Postman and Phillips (1954) may be applied to these results—namely, that isolation will favor retention only to the extent that the stimulus features producing isolation are relevant to the learner's task. However, Saltzman and Carterette (1959) were reluctant to accept an ad hoc explanation, arguing that no technique for assessing the extent of such relevance was as yet available. Instead they felt that experimental investigations should ascertain empirically when isolation will affect learning and when it will not.

Studies on stimulus relevance are a step in this direction.

Relevance. Quartermain and his associates (Quartermain & Mangan, 1959; Quartermain & Scott, 1960) attempted to assess the relevance of stimuli in INC learning. Quartermain and Scott (1960), for example, gave their subjects the task of finding a key amid the objects in an experimental room. They then asked subjects to recall the objects in the room and found that those objects that might conceal a key (relevant objects) were recalled best, while less relevant and irrelevant objects were not recalled as well. They concluded that the relevance of environmental features to the goal that is directing behavior is an important determinant of what is learned by INC subjects. Their procedure represents a novel and significant contribution to research directed at ascertaining how it is that some material is amenable to INC learning and other material is not.

Experimental evidence lends credence to Deese's (1958) statement that differences between INT and INC learning can be examined in terms of the nature of the task to be learned and the nature of the learner's orientation to the task. Bousfield, Cowan, and Steward (1963) proposed that a basic consideration applying to both these factors is "the extent to which each of the given stimulus items evokes a distinctive meaningful response pattern [p. 329]." This pattern they saw to vary positively with its association value and inversely with the interference produced by competing responses. The design of INC-learning experiments insures the presence of competing responses, since such responses are necessary for the performance of the orienting task. However, Bousfield et al. (1963) were able to control the degree of competition, thereby maximizing the "distinctive meaningful response pattern" or relevance of the stimulus items. Under such conditions INC learning was high and varied from 36 to 48%. Similarly, under beneficial conditions in R-S learning, a 50% asymptote was obtained (Hunt, 1959; Jantz & Underwood, 1958). This degree of INC learning is unusual and suggests that the responses given by subjects in a learning situation are not necessarily veridical indices of the amount of material learned. Lawrence (1958) suggested that instructions merely insure that the material learned corresponds to the response measures used by the experimenter, and that subjects actually learn equal amounts under INT and INC conditions. Possibly studies concerned with effect of the relevance of stimulus items will permit more parsimonious treatment of INT and INC learning.

Subject Variables

Individual Differences. Frequently individual differences in INC learning are larger than comparable differences in INT learning (e.g., Postman & Phillips, 1954). Upon analysis this finding is not surprising. Plenderleith and Postman (1956) found empirical evidence that two characteristics of individual subjects were especially related to success in INC learning: (*a*) the ability of the subject to maintain attention to multiple aspects of the stimulus, and (*b*) the availability and effectiveness for subjects of differential responses to the stimulus items. There are wide intersubject variations in INC learning because under INC conditions subjects are not motivated to use their discriminative and verbal skills to differentiate and integrate the stimulus items. Hence only differential responses which are strong and readily available will be evoked by the stimuli, and there are great individual differences in the repertoire of such responses. Consequently, response habits with which the INC learner enters the experimental situation are the chief determinants governing the selectivity of INC learning (Postman, Adams, & Phillips, 1955), and—the other side of the coin—the determinants of selectivity in human learning are most readily accessible to experimental investigation under INC conditions (Plenderleith & Postman, 1957).

Mechanic (1962a) failed to find any relationship between intelligence and amount of INC learning. Mentally retarded children learned some INC material, although they were significantly inferior to gifted children on more complex INC tasks (Goldstein & Kass, 1961), and organic retardates learned less INC material than familial retardates or normal children (Hetherington & Banta, 1962).

Motivation. A few studies have employed the Type I design to investigate the effect of manipulation of motivational level on INC learning. Spielberger, Goodstein, and Dahlstrom (1958) found that high-anxious subjects showed more INC learning than low-anxious subjects on easy tasks, whereas low-anxious subjects recalled more of the INC material on harder tasks. In this study, however, only INC conditions were employed with no subjects given corresponding INT instructions. Johnson and Thomson (1962) varied motivational levels and found that low motivation facilitated INC learning more than medium or high levels. In their design, INC learning consisted in recognition of syllables learned by a partner. Aborn (1953) studied the influence of experimentally induced failure on retention of INT and INC material and found that the introduction and alleviation of threat produced marked differential effects upon INT and INC learners. Threat had no marked inhibitory effect upon INT subjects, but the introduction of threat significantly depressed the recall scores of the INC subjects and alleviation of the threat resulted in some recovery. This would seem to indicate that INC-learning conditions are superior to the typical INT-learning design employed in the experimental study of the clinical phenomenon of repression.

Studies employing the Type II design have provided the basis for theoretical discussion on the relation of level of motivation to cue utilization (Easterbrook, 1959; Kausler & Trapp, 1960). These studies (e.g., Bahrick, 1954; Kohn, 1954; Silverman, 1954; Silverman & Blitz, 1956) have yielded empirical evidence that, with an increase in drive, the amount of INC learning has been reduced, although task (INT) learning has remained constant or been improved. Easterbrook (1959) interpreted these findings as indicating a restriction or funneling of cue utilization with increase in drive. The findings of Kausler, Trapp, and Brewer (1959), however, yielded conflicting results. In this study the performance of the high-drive group was superior, but no difference was found between the two groups on the INC-learning task. The drive condition in this experiment, however, was generalized drive (as conceptualized by the Iowa group—e.g., Farber, 1955) and not an incentive-oriented set (as in the Bahrick, 1954, study with which Easterbrook was chiefly concerned). Kausler and Trapp (1960) have argued that Easterbrook's treatment of motivation as a variable in cue utilization fails to distinguish generalized drive from motivational states aroused by specific sets. These authors proposed that a general restricting function of increased motivation on attention to irrelevant cues, regardless of the nature of other determinants, be limited to emotional variants of motivation. It is only on this basis that conflicting empirical evidence, such as that found in the Kausler et al. (1959) study, can receive adequate theoretical explanation.

Kausler and Trapp (1960) also argued that there is an interaction effect between level of motivation and cue positioning. This explains why the study of Kausler et al. (1959) yielded evidence which conflicts with that of Silverman (1954; Silverman & Blitz, 1956). In the Kausler et al. study, irrelevant cues were embodied within relevant cues. In the Silverman studies, relevant and irrelevant cues were widely spaced within the perceptual field. This is very similar to Postman's (1964) distinction between intrinsic and extrinsic components of a Type II learning task and suggests that spatial characteristics of stimulus material are important variables in the study of INC learning.

Referring to this distinction between intrinsic and extrinsic components, Mechanic (1962a) pointed out that the Type II procedure in which relevant and irrelevant items are intrinsically associated (Bahrick, 1954; Kausler et al., 1959) permits no control over the subject's response to the INC material although its sensory reception is insured. When the irrelevant items are extrinsic to the relevant ones (Mechanic, 1962a; Silverman & Blitz, 1956), the responses to the INC material can be manipulated by means of different orienting tasks. Postman argued that contradictory findings fall into place when such differences in degree of control over a subject's responses and differences in orienting tasks in INT and INC learning are considered. In themselves, "incentives do not influence either type of learning [1964, p. 190]." Similarly, variations in generalized drive, like incentive, are expected to influence the relative frequency of the subject's responses to relevant and irrelevant stimuli. The more directly these responses are brought under experimental control through orienting tasks, the more predictable the relative amounts of INT and INC learning (Postman, 1964).

Postman's explanation may be criticized for not taking into account the study of Kausler et al. (1959) in which relevant and irrelevant items were intrinsically associated and where, in contrast to Bahrick's findings (1954), variations in motivational level produced no systematic effects on INC learning. Although Postman (1964) attempted to explain these and other (Silverman, 1954; Silverman & Blitz, 1956) contradictory findings on the basis of the distribution of responses to relevant and irrelevant stimuli, greater precision would be achieved by enlarging the differential response explanation so as to encompass theoretical formulations regarding the restriction or channeling of cue utilization (Easterbrook, 1959) which occurs or does not occur in INT and INC learning under variations in generalized drive or incentive conditions (Kausler & Trapp, 1960).

Evidence from other studies introduces further complexity into theoretical formulations relating motivational variables to INT and INC learning. The study of Spielberger et al. (1958) showed task difficulty and motivational level to interact, and Johnson and Thomson (1962) found that excessive motivation disrupted performance on the INT task while INC learning decreased with motivational level. The nature of the population studied is also important, and evidence that different results are obtained with different populations limits the generality of the functional relations found to occur. Kausler, Laughlin, and Trapp (1963), for example, found that with children instructions to learn relevant (INT) cues were generalized to irrelevant (INC) cues as well. This is in contrast to the finding that college students restrict attention to irrelevant cues under increased incentive conditions (Bahrick, 1954; Johnson & Thomson, 1962).

Discussion

In conclusion, several points should be underscored because of their importance for future research in INC learning. There is, first of all, a methodological point which requires reiteration. The test of retention employed in INC-learning studies is of critical empirical importance. The study of Postman, Adams, and Phillips (1955) demonstrated that effects obtained by means of a free-recall test of retention disappear when the method of recognition is used. They argued that only the free-recall method is adequately sensitive to differences between INT and INC learning. While there are exceptions to this rule, such as the use of the serial-anticipation method for measuring the differential effects of intralist similarity (Postman & Adams, 1957b), recent studies have perhaps been too indiscriminant in their use of the recognition method, and comparison of the findings of such studies (e.g., Johnson & Thomson, 1962; Miller & Lakso, 1964) with other studies becomes a hazardous undertaking.

Second, concern with the properties of stimulus items represents a potentially significant line of investigation. Methodological advances in this direction have been made in a number of areas (Agnew & Pyke, 1963; Kreezer, 1958; Murdock, 1960). Investigations by Quartermain (Quartermain & Mangan, 1959; Quartermain & Scott, 1960) on relevance and by Bousfield et al. (1963) on distinctive meaningful response patterns have to do expressly with INC learning and indicate the importance of stimulus properties and contextual relations for INC learning.

A third point concerns Postman's argument that the differential cue-producing response hypothesis provides the most adequate theoretical explanation of results found in INC-learning studies. According to this hypothesis what is learned depends on responses—such as categorizing, responses elicited by stimulus generalization, and responses serving as associative links among members of a series—to the stimuli in the experimental situation. It is the frequency and intensity of these responses which vary as a function of instruction stimuli and which provide the essential cues mediating recall on a test of retention

(Postman, 1964). The theory has been criticized, however, for providing an ad hoc explanation for findings in INC-learning studies (Saltzman & Carterette, 1959). It is particularly vague when the manipulated variable is motivational level, since its generality allows for no critical test. Any research findings may be explained as correlates of the pattern of responding introduced by differences in instructions. The formulations of Easterbrook (1959) and Kausler and Trapp (1960) regarding motivational level and cue utilization lend more precision to the differential cue-producing response hypothesis. If such amendments are made to the theory and are empirically substantiated, it may be possible to give an adequate account in theoretical terms for differences between INT and INC learning.

A final point is that any such differences are quantitative, and not qualitative, in nature. The review of the literature supports Postman's (1964) contention that:

> Except for purposes of convenient reference to experiments in which the instruction stimulus is manipulated, there is little or no reason to maintain a conceptual distinction between intentional and incidental learning [p. 193].

This is no startling conclusion, however, in view of the logic of research in the INC-learning literature. The operational procedures by which INT and INC learning are distinguished typically involve the comparison of performance under instructions to learn the relevant material and no instructions to learn this material. Data from research show quantitative differences between the instructions and no-instructions groups, but all that can be concluded on the basis of such data is that learning is more difficult under disadvantageous (no-instructions) conditions. The no-instructions procedure does not preclude the possibility of sporadic self-instructions, and consequently intergroup differences are attributable only to the functional relations of a number of parameters of efficient and inefficient INT learning. There is no justification for the implication that two types of learning—defined by different operational antecedents—are being investigated in this research. Strictly speaking, "INC learning," as operationally defined in most research, is a misnomer. There is no experimental evidence demonstrating INC learning in the strict, traditional sense—namely, a distinct learning process which occurs when there is no motive, self-instruction, or set to learn (McGeoch & Irion, 1952). Whether such learning does occur is an unanswered, and perhaps unanswerable, question.

REFERENCES

Aborn, M. The influence of experimentally induced failure on the retention of material acquired through set and incidental learning. *Journal of Experimental Psychology,* 1953, **45**, 225–231.

Agnew, N. M., & Pyke, S. Attention-demand value of stimuli. *Perceptual and Motor Skills,* 1963, **16**, 843–846.

Bahrick, H. P. Incidental learning under two incentive conditions. *Journal of Experimental Psychology,* 1954, **47**, 170–172.

Bahrick, H. P. Incidental learning at five stages of intentional learning. *Journal of Experimental Psychology,* 1957, **54**, 259–261.

Bahrick, H. P., Fitts, P. M., & Rankin, R. E. Effect of incentives upon reactions to peripheral stimuli. *Journal of Experimental Psychology,* 1952, **44**, 400–406.

Bandura, A., & Huston, A. C. Identification as a process of incidental learning. *Journal of Abnormal and Social Psychology,* 1961, **63**, 311–318.

Berlyne, D. E. *Conflict, arousal, and curiosity.* New York: McGraw-Hill, 1960.

Biel, W. C., & Force, R. G. Retention of nonsense syllables in intentional and incidental learning. *Journal of Experimental Psychology,* 1943, **32**, 52–63.

Bitterman, M. E. Information and effect in incidental learning. *American Journal of Psychology,* 1956, **69**, 410–416.

Bousfield, W. A., Cowan, T., & Steward, J. R. The incidental learning of associative responses to given stimulus words. *Journal of General Psychology,* 1963, **68**, 325–331.

Broadbent, D. E. Flow of information within the organism. *Journal of Verbal Learning and Verbal Behavior,* 1963, **2**, 34–39.

Brown, G. H. Factors influencing incidental learning. *Journal of Experimental Psychology,* 1954, **47**, 163–169.

Bruner, J. S. Going beyond the information given. In, *The Colorado symposium: Contemporary approaches to cognition.* Cambridge: Harvard Univer. Press, 1957. Pp. 45–70.

Bruner, J. S., Goodnow, J. J., & Austin, G. A. *A study of thinking.* New York: Wiley, 1956.

Calhoun, S. W. Influence of length of lists upon ability immediately to reproduce disconnected word series auditorily presented. *Journal of Experimental Psychology,* 1934, **17**, 723–738.

Cassem, N. H., & Kausler, D. H. Supplementary report: The effects of stimulus association value and exposure duration on R-S learning. *Journal of Experimental Psychology,* 1962, **64,** 94.

Chapman, D. W. Relative effects of determinate and indeterminate *Aufgaben. American Journal of Psychology,* 1932, **44,** 163–174.

Deese, J. *The psychology of learning.* New York: McGraw-Hill, 1958.

Deese, J. Behavioral effects of instructions to learn: Comments on Professor Postman's paper. In A. W. Melton (Ed.), *Categories of human learning.* New York: Academic Press, 1964. Pp. 202–209.

Easterbrook, J. A. The effect of emotion on cue utilization and the organization of behavior. *Psychological Review,* 1959, **66,** 183–201.

Estes, W. K. Learning. *Annual Review of Psychology,* 1956, **7,** 1–38.

Farber, I. E. The role of motivation in verbal learning and performance. *Psychological Bulletin,* 1955, **52,** 311–327.

Feldman, S. M., & Underwood, B. J. Stimulus recall following paired-associate learning. *Journal of Experimental Psychology,* 1957, **53,** 11–15.

Fischer, G. J., & Cook, M. B. Influence of distribution of practice and varying speeds of stimulus presentation on incidental learning. *Psychological Reports,* 1962, **10,** 539–545.

Gibson, J. J. A critical review of the concept of set in contemporary experimental psychology. *Psychological Bulletin,* 1941, **38,** 781–817.

Glaze, J. A. The association value of nonsense-syllables. *Journal of Genetic Psychology,* 1928, **35,** 255–267.

Gleitman, H., & Gillett, E. The effect of intention upon learning. *Journal of General Psychology,* 1957, **57,** 137–149.

Gleitman, H., & Kamrin, R. Proactive and retroactive inhibition in intentional and incidental learning. *Psychological Reports,* 1957, **3,** 155–160.

Goldstein, H., & Kass, C. Incidental learning of educable mentally retarded and gifted children. *American Journal of Mental Deficiency,* 1961, **66,** 245–249.

Goldstein, R., & Solomon, R. J. A serial position effect in "incidental learning." *Journal of General Psychology,* 1955, **53,** 293–298.

Hammer, M. The role of irrelevant stimuli in human discrimination learning. *Journal of Experimental Psychology,* 1955, **50,** 47–50.

Hetherington, E. M., & Banta, T. J. Incidental and intentional learning in normal and mentally retarded children. *Journal of Comparative and Physiological Psychology,* 1962, **55,** 402–404.

Hirsch, J. Learning without awareness and extinction following awareness as a function of reinforcement. *Journal of Experimental Psychology,* 1957, **54,** 218–224.

Hull, C. L. The meaningfulness of 320 selected nonsense-syllables. *American Journal of Psychology,* 1933, **45,** 730–734.

Hunt, R. G. Meaningfulness and articulation of stimulus and response in paired-associate learning and stimulus recall. *Journal of Experimental Psychology,* 1959, **57,** 262–267.

Jantz, E. M., & Underwood, B. J. R-S learning as a function of meaningfulness and degree of S-R learning. *Journal of Experimental Psychology,* 1958, **56,** 174–179.

Jenkins, J. G. Instructions as a factor in "incidental" learning. *American Journal of Psychology,* 1932, **44,** 471–477.

Johnson, R., & Thomson, C. Incidental and intentional learning under three conditions of motivation. *American Journal of Psychology,* 1962, **75,** 284–288.

Karen, R. L. Recognition as a function of meaningfulness and intention to learn. *American Journal of Psychology,* 1956, **69,** 650–652.

Kausler, D. H., Laughlin, P. R., & Trapp, E. P. The effects of incentive-set on relevant and irrelevant (incidental) learning in children. *Child Development,* 1963, **34,** 195–199.

Kausler, D. H., & Trapp, E. P. Motivation and cue utilization in intentional and incidental learning. *Psychological Review,* 1960, **67,** 373–379.

Kausler, D. H., & Trapp, E. P. The effects of position and exposure duration on irrelevant cue learning. Paper read at the Southwestern Psychological Association Meeting, Little Rock, Arkansas, 1961.

Kausler, D. H., & Trapp, E. P. Effects of incentive-set and task variables on relevant and irrelevant learning in serial verbal learning. *Psychological Reports,* 1962, **10,** 451–457.

Kausler, D. H., & Trapp, E. P. Irrelevant cues and serial learning effects. *Psychological Reports,* 1963, **12,** 798.

Kausler, D. H., Trapp, E. P., & Brewer, C. L. Intentional and incidental learning under high and low emotional drive levels. *Journal of Experimental Psychology,* 1959, **58,** 452–455.

Kohn, H. Effects of variations of intensity of experimentally induced stress situations upon certain aspects of perception and performance. *Journal of Genetic Psychology,* 1954, **85,** 289–304.

Koyanagi, K. Studies in incidental learning: I. Intention of learning and isolation effect. *Japanese Journal of Psychology,* 1957, **27,** 270–278. (a)

Koyanagi, K. Studies in incidental learning: II. Intraserial interference. *Tohoku Psychologica Folia,* 1957, **15,** 1–11. (b)

Koyanagi, K. Studies in incidental learning: III. Clustering responses and associative responses. *Bunka,* 1957, **21,** 172–182, 266–267. (c)

Koyanagi, K. Studies in incidental learning: VI. The effects of rate and number of stimulus-presentations. *Japanese Journal of Educational Psychology,* 1958, **6,** 100–105, 134–135.

Kreezer, G. L. A threshold-method for measuring the attention-demand value of stimuli. *American Journal of Psychology,* 1958, **71,** 111–122.

Lawrence, D. H. Learning. *Annual Review of Psychology,* 1958, **9,** 157–188.

Lepley, W. M. A gradient in incidental learning. *Journal of Experimental Psychology,* 1935, **18,** 195–201.

McGeoch, J. A., & Irion, A. L. *The psychology of human learning.* (2nd ed.) New York: Longmans, Green, 1952.

McGuigan, F. J. Incidental learning in the formation of concepts. *American Journal of Psychology,* 1958, **71**, 539–547.

Mandler, G. Response factors in human learning. *Psychological Review,* 1954, **61**, 235–244.

Mandler, G. Associative frequency and associative prepotency as a measure of response to nonsense syllables. *American Journal of Psychology,* 1955, **68**, 662–665.

Mayzner, M. S., & Tresselt, M. E. Incidental learning: A function of associative strength and distance between S-R pairs. *Journal of Psychology,* 1962, **53**, 155–160.

Mechanic, A. The distribution of recalled items in simultaneous intentional and incidental learning. *Journal of Experimental Psychology,* 1962, **63**, 593–600. (a)

Mechanic, A. Effects of orienting task, practice, and incentive on simultaneous incidental and intentional learning. *Journal of Experimental Psychology,* 1962, **64**, 393–399. (b)

Miller, M. E., & Lakso, V. Effects of constant versus varied pairing of simultaneous intentional- and incidental-learning materials with different rates and number of exposures. *Journal of Experimental Psychology,* 1964, **67**, 256–262.

Morikawa, Y. Functions of stimulus and response in paired-associate verbal learning. *Psychologia,* 1959, **2**, 41–56.

Mulhall, E. F. Experimental studies in recall and recognition. *American Journal of Psychology,* 1915, **26**, 217–228.

Murdock, B. B. The distinctiveness of stimuli. *Psychological Review,* 1960, **67**, 16–31.

Myers, G. C. A study of incidental memory. *Archives of Psychology,* 1913, **4**(No. 26).

Neimark, E., & Saltzman, I. J. Comparison of incidental and intentional learning under different rates of stimulus presentation. *American Journal of Psychology,* 1953, **66**, 618–621.

Noble, C. E. An analysis of meaning. *Psychological Review,* 1952, **59**, 421–430.

Plenderleith, M., & Postman, L. Discriminative and verbal habits in incidental learning. *American Journal of Psychology,* 1956, **69**, 236–243.

Plenderleith, M., & Postman, L. Individual differences in intentional and incidental learning. *British Journal of Psychology,* 1957, **48**, 241–248.

Poppelreuter, W. Nachweis der Unzweckmässigkeit die gebräuchlichen Associations experimente mit sinnolsen Silben nach dem Erlernungs- und Trefferverfahren zur exakten Gewinnung elementarer Reproduktionsgezetze zu verwenden. *Zeitschrift für Psychologie,* 1912, **61**, 1–24.

Porter, L. W. The effect of "right" in a modified Thorndikian situation. *American Journal of Psychology,* 1957, **70**, 219–226. (a)

Porter, L. W. Effect of shock-cessation as an incidental reward in verbal learning. *American Journal of Psychology,* 1957, **70**, 421–426. (b)

Postman, L. Karen's study of incidental learning as a function of meaningfulness. *American Journal of Psychology,* 1957, **70**, 465–466.

Postman, L. Short-term memory and incidental learning. In A. W. Melton (Ed.), *Categories of human learning.* New York: Academic Press, 1964. Pp. 145–201.

Postman, L., & Adams, P. A. Performance variables in the experimental analysis of the law of effect. *American Journal of Psychology,* 1954, **67**, 612–631.

Postman, L., & Adams, P. A. "Isolation" and the law of effect. *American Journal of Psychology,* 1955, **68**, 96–105.

Postman, L., & Adams, P. A. Incidental learning studies: III. Interserial interference. *Journal of Experimental Psychology,* 1956, **51**, 323–328. (a)

Postman, L., & Adams, P. A. Incidental learning studies: IV. The interaction of orienting tasks and stimulus materials. *Journal of Experimental Psychology,* 1956, **51**, 329–332. (b)

Postman, L., & Adams, P. A. On recent studies of the law of effect in incidental learning. *American Journal of Psychology,* 1957, **70**, 642–646. (a)

Postman, L., & Adams, P. A. Studies in incidental learning: VI. Intraserial interference. *Journal of Experimental Psychology,* 1957, **54**, 153–167. (b)

Postman, L., & Adams, P. A. Studies in incidental learning: VII. Effects of frequency of exercise and length of list. *Journal of Experimental Psychology,* 1958, **56**, 86–94.

Postman, L., & Adams, P. A. Studies in incidental learning: VIII. The effects of contextual determination. *Journal of Experimental Psychology,* 1960, **59**, 153–164.

Postman, L., Adams, P. A., & Phillips, L. W. Incidental learning studies: II. The effects of associational value and of the method of testing. *Journal of Experimental Psychology,* 1955, **49**, 1–10.

Postman, L., & Phillips, L. W. Incidental learning studies: I. The effects of crowding and isolation. *Journal of Experimental Psychology,* 1954, **48**, 48–54.

Postman, L., & Phillips, L. W. Studies in incidental learning: IX. A comparison of the methods of successive and single recall. *Journal of Experimental Psychology,* 1961, **61**, 236–241.

Postman, L., & Senders, V. L. Incidental learning and generality of set. *Journal of Experimental Psychology,* 1946, **36**, 153–165.

Postman, L., & Tuma, A. H. Latent learning in human subjects. *American Journal of Psychology,* 1954, **67**, 119–123.

Prentice, W. C. H. Retroactive inhibition and the motivation of learning. *American Journal of Psychology,* 1943, **56**, 283–292.

Prentice, W. C. H., & Asch, S. E. Paired association with related and unrelated pairs of nonsense-figures. *American Journal of Psychology,* 1958, **71**, 247–254.

Quartermain, D., & Mangan, D. Role of relevance in incidental learning of verbal material. *Perceptual and Motor Skills,* 1959, **9**, 255–258.

Quartermain, D., & Scott, T. H. Incidental learning in a simple task. *Canadian Journal of Psychology,* 1960, **14**, 175–182.

REED, H. B. Factors influencing the learning and retention of concepts: I. The influence of set. *Journal of Experimental Psychology,* 1946, **36**, 71–87.

ROSENBERG, S. Exposure interval in incidental learning. *Psychological Reports,* 1959, **5**, 675.

ROSENBERG, S. Retroactive inhibition in incidental learning. *American Journal of Psychology,* 1961, **74**, 283–286.

ROSENBERG, S. The influence of intentional learning on incidental learning. *Journal of General Psychology,* 1962, **67**, 181.

SALTZMAN, I. J. The orienting task in incidental learning. *American Journal of Psychology,* 1953, **66**, 593–597.

SALTZMAN, I. J. Comparison of incidental and intentional learning with different orienting tasks. *American Journal of Psychology,* 1956, **69**, 274–277.

SALTZMAN, I. J. Incidental and intentional memory for lifted-weights. *American Journal of Psychology,* 1957, **70**, 253–257.

SALTZMAN, I. J., & ATKINSON, R. Comparison of incidental and intentional learning after different numbers of stimulus presentations. *American Journal of Psychology,* 1954, **67**, 501–524.

SALTZMAN, I. J., & CARTERETTE, T. S. Incidental and intentional learning of isolated and crowded items. *American Journal of Psychology,* 1959, **72**, 230–236.

SHELLOW, S. M. Individual differences in incidental memory. *Archives of Psychology,* 1923, **10**, 1–77.

SILVERMAN, R. E. Anxiety and the mode of response. *Journal of Abnormal and Social Psychology,* 1954, **48**, 538–542.

SILVERMAN, R. E., & BLITZ, B. Learning and two kinds of anxiety. *Journal of Abnormal and Social Psychology,* 1956, **52**, 301–303.

SPIELBERGER, C. C., GOODSTEIN, L. D., & DAHLSTROM, W. G. Complex incidental learning as a function of anxiety and task difficulty. *Journal of Experimental Psychology,* 1958, **56**, 58–61.

UNDERWOOD, B. J., & SCHULZ, R. W. *Meaningfulness and verbal learning.* Chicago: Lippincott, 1960.

WOODWORTH, R. S. The influence on retention of conditions favoring quickness of learning. *Journal of Philosophy,* 1915, **12**, 246.

YAVUZ, H. S. The retention of incidentally learned connotative responses. *Journal of Psychology,* 1963, **55**, 409–418.

(Received August 12, 1964)

ARTICLE 2

STUDIES IN INCIDENTAL LEARNING: II. THE EFFECTS OF ASSOCIATION VALUE AND OF THE METHOD OF TESTING[1]

LEO POSTMAN, PAULINE AUSTIN ADAMS, AND LAURA W. PHILLIPS

University of California

Incidental learning is a selective process. Typically, the incidental learner can recall only a fraction of the materials to which he has been exposed. There appear to be two major approaches to the analysis of the conditions governing the selectivity of incidental learning. One may seek the determinants of selectivity primarily in (*a*) the perceptual characteristics of the stimulus materials, or (*b*) the response habits with which the incidental learner enters the experimental situation. A previous study (**6**), which failed to find a difference in incidental memory for crowded and isolated items, cast serious doubts on the adequacy of the perceptual approach. The present investigation focuses on *S*s' response habits as determiners of selective retention under incidental conditions.

We shall assume that the amount of incidental as well as intentional learning depends to an important degree on the differential responses which *S* makes to the individual members of the stimulus sequence. Differential responses to a series of items may include (*a*) classifying or categorizing responses such as naming or labeling; (*b*) other responses elicited by the items by virtue of stimulus generalization; (*c*) responses serving as associative links among the members of the series. Such responses are associated with the context of the experimental situation (cf. **4**). When *S*'s recall is tested, the rearousal of these differential responses mediates the recall performance.

It is our hypothesis that there are major differences between intentional and incidental learners in the frequency and intensity of differential responses to the stimulus items. Differential responses may be regarded as habits attached, largely through stimulus generalization, to the individual items of the series. The actual performance of such responses will be a function of both the strength of the associative habits and *S*'s motivation. Intentional learners, under instructions to learn the series, are more highly motivated to respond to each of the items. Assuming equal initial strengths of differential responses for both types of learners, the

[1] This research was facilitated by a grant from the Behavioral Sciences Division of the Ford Foundation.

Reprinted with permission of the authors and the publisher, the American Psychological Association. The article appeared originally in the *Journal of Experimental Psychology*, 1955, **49**, 1–10.

threshold of response will be exceeded more readily for the intentional learners. Intentional learners may, therefore, be expected to give more frequent differential responses to the stimulus items. A further difference between the two types of learners may be sought in the intensity ("amplitude") of whatever differential responses are made, i.e., responses of the intentional learner may be more explicitly verbalized, of longer duration, etc. Finally, it is probable that intentional learners rehearse their differential responses more than do the incidental learners during exposure to the stimulus materials. In short, we assume that there is no sharp qualitative break between intentional and incidental learning. The difference is a matter of degree, particularly as regards the readiness to respond differentially to the stimulus items.

This analysis implies that the difference in the amount recalled by intentional and incidental learners should be a function of the association value of the stimulus items. The association value of an item may be regarded as an index of the readiness with which it elicits differential responses. Stimuli of high association value are likely to evoke effective differential responses from both intentional and incidental learners, and both groups should learn such items well. As items decrease in association value, they are likely to evoke less effective differential responses from incidental than intentional learners. Consequently, the lower the association value of the stimuli, the greater should be the difference between the amount retained by intentional and incidental learners.

If the learning materials consist of items differing in association value, we should expect systematic differences between the distributions of associations formed under intentional and incidental conditions. Incidental learning will be selective: some strong associations will be formed, notably for the relatively familiar items, while the associations for the remaining less familiar items will be weak. The associations formed by intentional learners will be more continuously graded in strength. In addition to strong associations for relatively familiar items, intentional learners will form more associations of intermediate strength and fewer weak associations than the incidental learners. Median associative strength will, therefore, be higher under intentional than incidental conditions.

This picture of the distribution of associations suggests that the difference in performance between intentional and incidental learners should vary systematically with the difficulty of the retention test. We should expect neither a very easy nor a very difficult retention test to discriminate effectively between the intentional and incidental conditions. If a test is relatively easy, only a low degree of associative strength will be required for correct performance. The weak associations formed by incidental learners will then be as adequate as the stronger ones formed by intentional learners. If the test is relatively difficult, only associations of high strength will result in correct performance. Such a test would tap only the core of strongly learned items which we have assumed to be common to the two groups of learners. A test of intermediate difficulty, i.e., a test requiring an intermediate degree of associative strength for correct performance, should discriminate best between intentional and incidental learners. This prediction is based on the assumption that median associative strength is higher for intentional than incidental learners.

Let us assume that among possible tests of retention a test of free recall occupies a position of intermediate difficulty. It follows from the above analysis that a test of recognition, which is sensitive to low degrees of learning and hence relatively easy, should yield smaller differences between intentional and incidental learners than a test of free recall. In addition to changing from recall to recognition, one may also vary the difficulty of the retention test by manipulation of the stimulus context at the time of recall (**3**, pp. 501–505). The associative context in which retention is tested may be such as to facilitate or inhibit recall. As compared with a standard test of free recall, a facilitating context would define a relatively easy test, and an inhibitory context would define a relatively difficult test of retention. The introduction of either a facilitating or an inhibitory context should level the difference between intentional and incidental learners.

The present study presents two experiments testing the implications of our analysis. In Exp. I, items of different association value were used, and the performance of intentional and incidental learners was tested both by free recall and recognition. Experiment II is concerned with the effects of facilitating and inhibitory contexts on the recall performance of the two kinds of learners.

Experiment I

Method

Conditions of learning.—The procedure used to create conditions of intentional and incidental learning has been described in detail in a previous communication (**6**). Two individuals were used at a time, one of whom served as *E* and the other as *S*. The *E* and the *S* were seated in front of a memory drum on which a series of nonsense syllables was exposed. As each syllable appeared in the window of the drum, *E* spelled it aloud, letter by letter. The *S* repeated the syllable as soon as it had been read by *E*. The *S* was instructed to learn as many items as possible though not necessarily in the order in which they were presented. No learning instructions were given to *E*. The *S* was an intentional learner and *E* an incidental learner.

Materials.—The stimulus list consisted of 20 nonsense syllables differing widely in association value. There were five syllables each of 0, 33, 66, and 100% association value by Glaze's norms (**1**). The series was divided into five successive blocks of four syllables each. Each block contained one syllable of each association value so that the various association values were evenly distributed over different parts of the list.

The syllables were presented on a Hull-type memory drum at the rate of one every 4 sec. The list was presented only once. It was hoped that restriction to one exposure would minimize the probability of *E*'s adopting a set to learn. A group of four syllables was used to practice the experimental procedure, after which the experimental list was presented.

Retention tests.—For purposes of measuring retention, both *S*s and *E*s were divided into a Recall Group and a Recognition Group. Each group was given two tests, one immediately after presentation of the stimulus list, and the other 20 min. later. The interval between tests was filled with a reading task which was presented as a test of reading speed and comprehension. Selected passages from Plato's *Dialogues* were used for the reading task.

On both recall tests, *S*s and *E*s were instructed to write down as many syllables as they could remember, regardless of the order of original presentation. The recognition test consisted of 20 multiple-choice items. Each multiple-choice item consisted of four syllables, one of which was taken from the learning series. None of the incorrect alternatives had more than one letter in common with any of the correct syllables. The *S*s and *E*s were forced to guess if necessary, i.e., they were required to choose one of the alternatives in each of the multiple-choice items. All tests had a time limit of 5 min.

Postexperimental inquiry.—Both *S*s and *E*s were given a standard interview at the end of the experimental session. The *E*s were asked whether (*a*) they had expected the first retention test; (*b*) they had attempted to learn any of the syllables; (*c*) which of the syllables, if any, had caught their attention during the presentation of the series; (*d*) they had expected the second retention test; (*e*) they had rehearsed any of the syllables during the interval between retention tests. The *S*s were asked only questions *c*, *d*, and *e*. The *E*s who had attempted to memorize the syllables during presentation of the series or who had expected the first retention test were discarded.

TABLE 1

MEAN NUMBER OF CORRECT RECALLS AND RECOGNITIONS BY *S*s AND *E*s (EXP. I)

Group	Recall				Recognition			
	Test I		Test II		Test I		Test II	
	Mean	*SD*	Mean	*SD*	Mean	*SD*	Mean	*SD*
*S*s	3.63	1.56	3.20	1.87	12.40	2.90	11.15	3.12
*E*s	3.03	1.82	2.70	1.79	12.50	2.18	11.55	2.97

Subjects.—There were 30 *S*s and 30 *E*s in the Recall Groups and 20 pairs in the Recognition Groups. All *S*s and *E*s were undergraduate students at the University of California. They did not know the purpose of the experiment.

Results

Amount of retention.—Table 1 presents the results of the tests of recall and recognition. On Test I, the over-all recall performance of the *S*s is higher than that of the *E*s, but the difference is not statistically significant ($t = 1.36$, $p > .05$). Both groups show a significant drop in recall on Test II. Comparison of Test I and Test II yields a t of 2.87 ($p < .01$) for *S*s, and a t of 2.36 ($p = .02$) for *E*s. Analysis of covariance, which takes the original level of learning into account, shows that there is no significant difference between intentional and incidental learners in the amount of retention loss ($F = .12$).

With the amount of practice held constant, the recognition tests yield considerably higher retention scores than do the tests of free recall. The method of recognition is more sensitive than the method of free recall, i.e., the minimum associative strength required for correct performance is lower for recognition than for recall. The recognition scores of *S*s and *E*s are virtually identical on both Test I and Test II. The difference in favor of intentional learners found in free recall disappears completely when a test of recognition is used.

Both groups show drops in their recognition scores on Test II. For *S*s, comparison of Test I and Test II yields a t of 2.45 ($p = .03$); for *E*s, $t = 1.94$ ($p = .07$). Although the

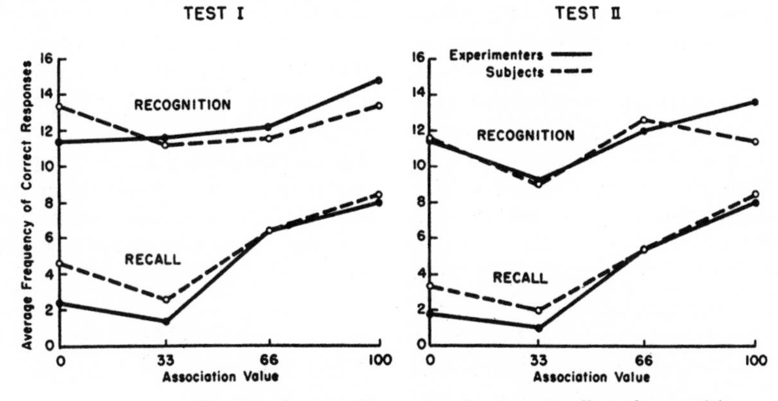

FIG. 1. Average frequency of correct recalls and recognitions by *S*s and *E*s as a function of association value (Exp. I).

percentage of loss is somewhat smaller for *E*s than for *S*s, analysis of covariance again fails to reveal a significant difference in retention loss between the two groups ($F = .42$).

Recall and recognition as a function of association value.—Figure 1 shows the average frequency of recall and recognition for syllables of different association value. Each point represents an average for five syllables distributed over different serial positions in the list.

Association value has a differential effect on the recall performance of intentional and incidental learners. Intentional learners recall more syllables of low association value than do incidental learners. The recall scores of the two groups are virtually identical for syllables of high association value.

To evaluate the significance of the relationship between condition of learning and association value, the median test (**5**, p. 394) was applied to the results of Test I. Association values were dichotomized into high (66% and 100%) and low (0% and 33%). For each *S* and *E*, the number of high-association-value syllables recalled was expressed as a proportion of the total recall score, and the median proportion was computed for the combined groups. The proportions were then divided into those greater than and equal to the median, and those falling below the median. By chance, half the members of each group should fall above the common median and half below. The null hypothesis can be rejected at a high level of confidence ($\chi^2 = 9.88$, $df = 1$, $p < .01$).

The results of Test II are substantially the same as those of Test I. It is interesting to note that both intentional and incidental learners show relatively greater retention loss for items of low association value than for items of high association value. There is no loss at all for syllables of 100% association value.

It is now apparent why the ***over-all*** difference between *S*s and *E*s fails to reach statistical significance. Comparison of the total recall scores does not take account of the selectivity of incidental learning. Intention to learn is more essential for the recall of relatively unfamiliar than of relatively familiar items.

The differential effects of association value are much less pronounced for recognition than they are for recall. For *S*s, there is little, if any, systematic relationship between association value and recognition. In the case of *E*s, recognition tends to increase as a function of association value on both tests. However, the degree of divergence between intentional and incidental learners is small. Application of the median test shows that *E*s do not surpass *S*s significantly in the selective recognition of items of high association value ($\chi^2 = 3.14$, $df = 1$, $p > .05$).

Postexperimental inquiry.—The second retention test was expected by five *S*s and three *E*s in the Recall Groups and by seven *S*s and three *E*s in the Recognition Groups. One *S* and one *E* in the Recall Groups, but none of the *S*s and *E*s in the Recognition Groups, reported rehearsing the material between retention tests. Most *S*s and *E*s mentioned at least one item which had caught their special attention during the presentation of the stimulus list. As in our previous study (**6**), virtually all items singled out by *S*s and *E*s were noticed because of their similarity to a meaningful word or symbol.

EXPERIMENT II

The results of the recognition test have shown that a test easier than free recall reduces the difference between intentional and incidental learners. It remains necessary to demonstrate that a test more difficult, as well as a test easier, than free recall results in a convergence of the two groups of learners. In addition, it is desirable to test the implications of our analysis while holding the nature of the memory performance constant. Free recall and recognition require different types of responses of the *S*. The question remains open as to whether variations in the difficulty of the retention test will have the predicted effects when only one type of performance, e.g., active reproduction, is used. In Exp. II the difficulty of the retention test was varied by manipulation of the stimulating context at the time of recall.

Method

Conditions of learning.—The learning materials consisted of 30 adjectives, taken from the list published by Haagen (2). An "orienting task" was used in order to expose both intentional and incidental learners to the stimulus materials under identical conditions. Both groups of learners were required to rate each of the adjectives with respect to the frequency with which they used it in their daily speech. A 7-point rating scale was used, with 1 standing for extremely infrequent, and 7 for extremely frequent, with the other numbers indicating intermediate degrees of frequency. The adjectives, typed in capital letters, were presented in a booklet. Each adjective appeared on a separate page of the booklet. The pages were numbered consecutively from 1 through 30. When *E* announced the number 1, *S*s turned to the first page of the booklet and made their rating by circling the appropriate number on a 7-point scale printed underneath the word. The same procedure was followed throughout the presentation of the list. The successive stimulus words were presented at the rate of one every 10 sec. A large model of the rating scale, with each of the steps labeled, was kept in full sight of the *S*s throughout the rating period. The list was presented once.

There were two forms of the booklet, each with a different random order of the stimulus words. The two orders were used equally often under all conditions of the experiment.

Intentional learners were informed that their memory for the words in the booklet would be tested later. They were asked to remember as many of the items as possible, though not necessarily in the order in which they were presented. No learning instructions were given to the incidental learners.

Retention tests.—Both intentional and incidental learners were divided into three groups for purposes of the retention test: (*a*) Free Recall Groups of 32 *S*s each, (*b*) Facilitating Context Groups of 16 *S*s each, and (*c*) Inhibitory Context Groups of 16 *S*s each. Members of the Free Recall Groups were given 5 min. in which to write down as many of the stimulus words as they could remember, regardless of the original order of presentation. They were encouraged to put down guesses as well as items of which they felt certain. The two Context Groups were provided with a series of cue words to which *S*s were instructed to respond with words from the original list. For the Facilitating Context Groups, the cue words had close associative connections with the original stimulus words. These cues were, therefore, expected to facilitate the evocation of correct responses. For the Inhibitory Context Groups, the cue words had only remote associative connections with the original stimulus words and were expected to elicit responses which would compete with the evocation of the correct items. Since the stimulus words had been taken from Haagen's list, facilitating and inhibitory cues were chosen on the basis of Haagen's "A" scales (2) which measure the "closeness of associative connection" between standard stimulus words and sets of comparison words. The range of scale separations in Haagen's tables is from .5 to 6.0. For the Facilitating Context Groups, the scale separations between the cue words and learning words were less than, or equal to, 1.5. The average scale separation was 1.2, with an *SD* of .2. For the Inhibitory Context Groups, the scale separations were equal to, or larger than, 3.0. The average scale separation was 3.8, with an *SD* of .6. Each cue word appeared on a separate page of the test booklet in which *S*s recorded their responses. The cue words were presented at the rate of one every 20 sec. For both lists of cue words there were two different random orders of presentation which were used equally often. The *S*s were encouraged to guess if they were not sure about a response word.

Postexperimental inquiry.—Following the retention test, all incidental learners were asked whether they had expected to be tested. There were no such cases, indicating that the orienting task had been quite effective in disguising the purpose of the experiment.

Association Control Groups.—In order to evaluate the effects of the cue words on retention, it was necessary to determine how many correct responses would be elicited by the cue words independently of previous learning. There were two Association Control Groups of 20 *Ss* each. One of these control groups was presented with the same cue words as the Facilitating Context Groups, the other group responded to the same cue words as the Inhibitory Context Groups. The control *Ss* were instructed to write down next to each cue word one adjective which they considered similar in meaning to the word. The cue words were again presented at the rate of one every 20 sec.

Subjects.—The *Ss* were undergraduate students at the University of California. They did not know the purpose of the experiment and were assigned to the experimental conditions at random.

Results

Retention as a function of associative context.—Table 2 shows the average number of items correctly reproduced by each of the experimental groups. In the case of the Context Groups all correct reproductions are included, regardless of whether or not the responses were made to the appropriate cues. The amount recalled varies widely as a function of the method of testing. The rank order of conditions is the same for intentional and incidental learners. The Facilitating Context Groups recall the most, the Inhibitory Context Groups the least, and the Free Recall Groups occupy an intermediate position. For both intentional and incidental learners, t tests show all differences between methods of testing to be highly significant. The values of p range from .015 to $< .0001$.

Under both conditions of learning, the Context Groups performed significantly better than the corresponding Association Control Groups. All tests of significance comparing Context Groups with the appropriate Association Control Groups yield values of t significant at the better than 1% level of confidence. All Context Groups show a significant amount of learning but the level of their performance varies markedly with the nature of the cue words.

The size and significance of the difference between intentional and incidental learners depend on the method of testing, i.e., on the stimulating conditions at the time of recall. Only the method of free recall yields a significant difference in favor of intentional learners. For both the Facilitating Context Groups and the Inhibitory Context Groups, the performance of intentional and incidental learners is virtually identical.

Free recall as a function of familiarity.—Experiment I has shown that the difference between intentional and incidental learners depends on the familiarity of the stimulus items. As the familiarity of the items increases, the performance of the two groups converges. The results of the free recall test in the present study provide further support for this relationship.

TABLE 2

MEAN NUMBER OF ITEMS CORRECTLY REPRODUCED BY THE DIFFERENT GROUPS IN EXP. II AND SIGNIFICANCE OF DIFFERENCES BETWEEN INTENTIONAL AND INCIDENTAL LEARNERS

Condition	Association Control		Intentional		Incidental		Int. vs. Incidental Learners
	Mean	*SD*	Mean	*SD*	Mean	*SD*	t
Facilitating context	9.10	3.05	17.62	4.20	18.00	4.58	0.24
Free recall	—	—	12.62	3.73	9.41	2.58	4.31*
Inhibitory context	1.05	0.80	7.19	2.13	7.38	2.44	0.23

* $p < .01$.

During the original exposure to the learning list, all *S*s rated their frequency of usage of the stimulus items on a 7-point scale. The distributions of ratings were almost identical for intentional and incidental learners. The mean rating for intentional learners was 3.91, with an *SD* of 1.58; the mean rating for incidental learners was 3.88, with an *SD* of 1.48. For both groups, the ratings showed a marked central tendency, so that the distributions were approximately normal in shape. Figure 2 shows for the two groups of learners the percentage of items correctly reproduced on the free recall test as a function of familiarity rating. Although neither the reliability nor the validity of the ratings is known, we may assume that they provide at least a crude measure of the relative frequency of usage. As Fig. 2 shows, intentional learners surpass incidental learners in the reproduction of relatively unfamiliar words, whereas there is only a small difference between the two groups in the recall of more familiar items.

Relatively unfamiliar items were recalled better than items of medium familiarity, particularly by intentional learners. It is possible that items of low and high familiarity were subject to less intraserial interference than were items of medium familiarity. Medium ratings were given more frequently than high or low ratings. To the extent that items given similar ratings were grouped and perceived as similar by the *S*s, there was more opportunity for intraserial interference among items of medium familiarity than among items of high or low familiarity.

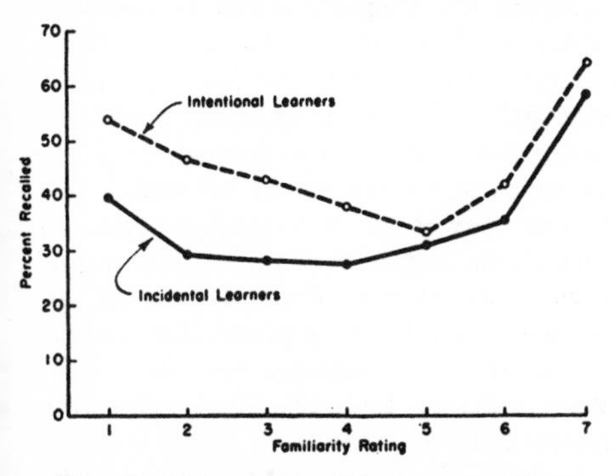

FIG. 2. Percentages of items correctly reproduced on the free recall test in Exp. II as a function of familiarity rating.

If the sag in the familiarity function is, indeed, due to intraserial interference, it is not surprising that intentional learners show the effect to a more marked degree than do incidental learners. As we have suggested in an earlier paper, incidental learners form not only fewer and/or weaker associations than intentional learners but also fewer incorrect ones. Hence the variables influencing degree of intraserial interference influence the recall performance of incidental learners less than that of intentional learners. The finding that "isolated" items are recalled better than crowded ones by intentional learners but not by incidental learners was explained along similar lines (6).

Facilitating and inhibitory effects of context.—We have suggested that the facilitating and inhibitory cues presented to the Context Groups render ineffective the difference in associative strength between intentional and incidental learners. These "leveling" effects of the contextual cues are confirmed by an analysis of the errors of the Contextual Groups. The responses of *S*s in the four Context Groups were divided into three categories: (*a*) correctly placed recalls, i.e., correct reproductions given in response to the appropriate cues, (*b*) misplaced recalls, i.e., items from the learning list given in response to other than the appropriate cues, and (*c*) importations, i.e., items which did not appear in the original learning list. Table 3 shows the percentages of responses falling into each of these

TABLE 3

Distributions of Responses Given by Context Groups Under Intentional and Incidental Conditions

(Entries are percentages of total numbers of responses)

Category of Response	Intentional		Incidental	
	Facilitating Context	Inhibitory Context	Facilitating Context	Inhibitory Context
Correctly placed	72.58	21.93	75.60	23.17
Misplaced	8.36	36.40	8.22	37.40
Importations	19.06	41.67	16.18	39.43

three categories. Facilitating and inhibitory cues produce quite different distributions of responses. In the presence of facilitating cues, the large majority of correct responses is given to the appropriate cues. The ratio of correctly placed to misplaced responses is of the order of 9:1. In the presence of inhibitory cues, the percentage of correctly placed responses is considerably smaller than the percentage of misplaced ones. The ratio of misplaced to correctly placed responses is of the order of 1.7:1. Finally, the percentages of importations are much higher for the Inhibitory Context Groups than for the Facilitating Context Groups. Most of the importations clearly consisted of words which have stronger associative connections with the cue words than do the correct responses.

The variations in the distributions of responses clearly bring out the differences between the effects of the two sets of cues. At the same time we note, however, that the distributions for intentional and incidental learners are very much alike. They differ nowhere by more than a few percentage points. The differences in associative strength between the two groups of learners, which produce significant variations on the test of free recall, are counteracted by the facilitating and inhibitory effects of the contextual cues.

Discussion

The experiments have shown that the difference between intentional and incidental learners is a function of both the association value of the stimuli and the method of measuring retention. These findings agree with the view that (*a*) degree of learning is a function of the differential responses made to the stimulus items and (*b*) intention to learn enhances the effectiveness of such responses.

The higher the association value of stimulus items, the less difference there is between intentional and incidental learners. Items of high association value are recalled equally well by intentional and incidental learners because strong differential responses presumably are evoked by these items independently of instructions to learn. Such responses are not as readily evoked by items of low association value. In the case of the latter items, instructions to learn serve to increase the frequency and intensity of differential responses to a significant degree. In general, the less the initial strength of the responses mediating acquisition, the more critical does the presence of a learning set become.

The power of a retention test for discriminating between intentional and incidental learners depends on the associative strength required for correct performance. Neither a very easy nor a very difficult test effectively discriminates between the two conditions of learning. Tests of intermediate difficulty maximize the observable effects of instructions to learn. The differences obtained by the method of free recall disappear when retention is tested by recognition or by recall in a facilitating or inhibitory context. The difficulty of a retention test, and hence its power for discriminating between intentional and incidental learners, appears to vary with the degree to which the test reinstates the original learning stimuli. The original learning items actually appear on a test of recognition; a facilitating context at recall is designed to further the reinstatement of the stimulus items. Hence, performance on both these tests requires a low degree of associative strength which can be met or exceeded with equal frequency by intentional and incidental learners. An inhibitory context at recall not only fails to reinstate the original items but also makes their reproduction difficult by evoking strong competing responses. For both groups, only a few selectively learned items exceed the threshold of recall, and again there is no difference between intentional and incidental learners. A standard test of free recall also fails to reinstate the original items but does not actively interfere with their reproduction. An intermediate degree of associative strength is, therefore, required for correct performance on the free recall test; it is only under these conditions that the difference in strength between intentional and incidental learning leads to observable differences in recall.

Summary

Differences in the amounts retained by intentional and incidental learners were compared as a function of (*a*) the association value of the stimuli and (*b*) the method of measuring retention. In Exp. I, a list of nonsense syllables covering a wide range of association values was used. Retention was measured by free recall and recognition. Intentional learners surpassed incidental learners in the recall of items of low association value but not of items of high association value. There was no significant difference in the recognition performance of the two groups.

In Exp. II, recall for a series of adjectives was measured under different stimulating conditions at the time of the retention test. Intentional and incidental learners were divided into three groups: (*a*) Free Recall Groups, (*b*) Facilitating Context Groups which were presented with cue words having strong associative connections with the learning items, and (*c*) Inhibitory Context Groups presented with cue words designed to elicit responses which would compete with the correct items. Under both conditions of learning recall was highest for the Facilitating Context Groups, lowest for the Inhibitory Context Groups, with the Free Recall Groups occupying an intermediate position. Intentional learners surpassed incidental learners on the test of free recall but under neither of the context conditions.

A major difference between intentional and incidental learners lies in the number and distribution of associations of different strengths formed during training. Both groups form some strong associations, but incidental learners form fewer associations of intermediate strength and more weak associations than do intentional learners. Hence neither a very easy test (recognition or facilitating context at recall) nor a very difficult test (inhibitory context at recall) is sufficiently sensitive to discriminate between intentional and incidental learners. A test sensitive to intermediate degrees of associative strength (free recall) allows the differences in degree of learning to produce significant differences in performance.

References

1. Glaze, J. A. The association value of nonsense syllables. *J. genet. Psychol.*, 1928, **35**, 255–267.
2. Haagen, C. H. Synonymity, vividness, familiarity and association value ratings of 400 pairs of common adjectives. *J. Psychol.*, 1948, **27**, 453–463.
3. McGeoch, J. A. *The psychology of human learning*. New York: Longmans, Green, 1942.
4. McGeoch, J. A., & McGeoch, G. O. Studies in retroactive inhibition: VI. The influence of relative serial position of interpolated synonyms. *J. exp. Psychol.*, 1937, **21**, 320–329.
5. Mood, A. M. *Introduction to the theory of statistics*. New York: McGraw-Hill, 1950.
6. Postman, L., & Phillips, L. W. Studies in incidental learning: I. The effects of crowding and isolation. *J. exp. Psychol.*, 1954, **48**, 48–56.

(Received April 14, 1954)

ARTICLE 3

THE DISTRIBUTION OF RECALLED ITEMS IN SIMULTANEOUS INTENTIONAL AND INCIDENTAL LEARNING[1]

ARNOLD MECHANIC[2]

University of California, Berkeley

Two types of incidental learning situations may be distinguished: Type I in which *S* is not instructed to learn any of the materials but is later tested; Type II in which *S* is given a circumscribed learning task and is later tested for materials to which he was exposed during learning but which are not covered by the learning instructions. In both situations, *S* is introduced to the incidental stimulus materials by means of an orienting task. This is a task which *S* is required to perform in order to insure that he is exposed to the incidental stimuli. The activities required by differing orienting tasks may vary widely as long as they insure *S*'s exposure to the incidental materials.

If instructions to learn generalize to materials not included in the instructions, amount of incidental learning should be greater in the Type II than in the Type I situation. However, such effects of generalization were not found in two previous studies using nonsense syllables. On the contrary, these studies, which will be reported in a forthcoming publication, indicated that the Type I situation produces significantly greater incidental learning. This was found to be true regardless of whether the intentional and incidental items were presented simultaneously or in temporal succession. If there were positive effects of generalization of instructions in these experiments, it would seem that they were completely countered by the negative effects of "task competition" in the Type II situation. By "task competition" we refer to the fact that the two kinds of material—the prescribed and the incidental—compete in terms of how much of the total exposure time is spent in responding to each kind of item. When *S*s are instructed to learn specific items, more of the available time will be utilized in responding to these items during exposure and in possible rehearsal thereafter. Consequently less time (or possibly no time) will be available for responding to the incidental items. The experiment to be reported in this paper studied task competition by manipulating the difficulty (meaningfulness) of both the intentional and incidental materials in a Type II situation. In addition, the effects of number of presentations were studied.

A review of the literature indicates no verbal learning data on Type II incidental learning as a function of intentional task variables. However, studies with nonverbal

[1] Based upon a thesis submitted to the Graduate School of the University of California, Berkeley, in partial fulfillment of the requirements for the PhD degree. The author is greatly indebted to his major professor, L. J. Postman, under whose direction this research was carried out and to B. J. Underwood for his suggestions in the preparation of this manuscript. This research was conducted during the author's tenure on a research fellowship (MF-9934) from the National Institute of Mental Health of the United States Public Health Service.

The manuscript was prepared during the author's tenure as a National Science Foundation Postdoctoral Fellow at Northwestern University.

[2] Now at Alameda State College, Hayward, California.

Reprinted with permission of the author and the publisher, the American Psychological Association. The article appeared originally in the *Journal of Experimental Psychology*, 1962, **63,** 593–600.

materials indicate that Type II learning varies with manipulations of the intentional task. Bahrick (1954) and Bahrick, Fitts, and Rankin (1952) found that the amount of learning irrelevant to a set is inversely related to the strength of the incentive determining that set. It might, therefore, be expected that varying the difficulty of the intentional items should also make for variations in the competition between the intentional and incidental tasks. Difficult intentional items could be expected to take up different proportions of *S*'s total learning time than would easy intentional items.

Both meaningfulness and degree of practice have been studied in the Type I situation. The studies varying meaningfulness indicate that the superiority of intentional over incidental learning decreases as the meaningfulness of the items increases (Postman, Adams, & Phillips, 1955; Postman & Phillips, 1961). These findings were explained in terms of the differential responses which *S*s make to the stimulus items. More specifically, differential responses may be regarded as habits attached to a stimulus item either through previous experience with that item or through stimulus generalization. It is assumed that learning—both intentional and incidental—depends on the performance of these differential responses to the stimuli during exposure. In this view, the major effect of learning instructions is to increase the frequency and intensity of such differential responses. It may also be assumed that the high-meaningful items will evoke strong differential responses at the outset, while the low-meaningful items will not readily evoke such responses.

As a result of the strong pre-experimental habits attached to them, many of the high-M items will be learned in the absence of learning instructions. In other words, these items should be learned quite easily by both incidental and intentional learners. The low-M items, on the other hand, could be expected to evoke only weak responses in the absence of learning instructions. Instructions to learn would be required in order to strengthen these responses to the degree that they are capable of mediating learning. Consequently, the lower the meaningfulness of the materials, the greater should be the effects of instructions to learn.

TABLE 1

STIMULUS LISTS

List A—Low	List B—Low	List C—High	List D—High
DUR	OAC	WHI	ANC
LAK	TOS	SHO	DRE
DOP	BAK	ATI	LAN
HOK	LDE	TES	GRA
FUM	DEL	OUN	ITY
HEO	LOA	HAN	ILD
ERF	KDE	RON	BLE
RHA	SYC	WER	UST
COF	WIC	UND	OVE
WYE	KAB	NES	TER
SIL	EJO	OME	OUS
ARP	MPL	EST	RES

In the Type II situation, each *S* is exposed to both intentional and incidental lists. If the differential response hypothesis is correct, the difference between intentional and incidental scores for each *S* should decrease as the meaningfulness of the items increases.

The Type I data on number of presentations indicate that this variable has only marginal effects on the number of incidental items retained (Postman & Adams, 1958). Intentional learners showed a significant upward trend as a function of presentations whereas incidental learners did not. The present experiment will provide additional data on incidental learning as a function of presentations.

METHOD

Materials.—Meaningfulness was defined in terms of language frequency of trigrams (three-letter sequences not forming words). The learning materials consisted of four 12-unit trigram lists. Two of these lists were of very high-frequency items while the other two were of very low-frequency items. Two of the lists, one high-frequency and one low-frequency, were taken from Underwood and Postman (1960). The other two lists were constructed so as to approximate the characteristics of the Underwood and Postman lists. Items were selected on the basis of the Underwood "total" frequency count. The manner in which these frequencies were derived is described by Underwood and Schulz (1960). The four lists are shown in Table 1.

There is very little overlap in frequency

between the low and high lists. On the basis of frequency per trigram in a sample of 1,035,000 English words, the frequency ranges are as follows: List A, 2–188; List B, 1–158; List C, 121–799; and List D, 127–1094. The approximate median frequencies are 5, 3, 350, and 375, respectively. None of the 48 trigrams appears in the Thorndike-Lorge (1944) word count.

The construction of these lists was governed by two criteria in addition to frequency. The first was formal intralist similarity defined in terms of duplication of letters. These lists were fairly well equated on this variable with the number of different letters for Lists A, B, C, and D being 17, 16, 13, and 16, respectively. The lower total number of letters used in List C was due to greater repetition of letters between first and second and between second and third positions.

The second criterion governing selection of items was the formal interlist similarity for all possible pairs of lists. Equating the pairs of lists on this variable was difficult because pairs of like frequency lists (H-H or L-L) tended to have more letter duplications than did pairs of mixed frequency lists (H-L or L-H). This is in all likelihood a function of different distributions of individual letters in the two populations (high-frequency trigrams vs. low-frequency trigrams). Therefore, the unmixed list pairings would be restricted to a narrower range of letters than would be the mixed pairings. Nevertheless it was possible to equate interlist similarity within reasonable limits. Duplicated letters between lists ranged from 9 to 13. Duplications in Position 1 ranged from 4 to 6; in Position 2, from 2 to 6; in Position 3, from 3 to 6. The unmixed list pairings averaged 5.5, 5.5, and 5 duplications in the three positions, respectively. The corresponding averages for the mixed list pairings were 5, 3.5, and 3.25.

Eight random orders were prepared for each of the four lists. Two of the lists were presented concurrently to each *S* during training. Each exposure of the lists involved presenting *S* with 12 pairs of items. Each pair was arranged vertically with one member in the top position and the other member directly below it. This arrangement was used to prevent the left to right chaining which might result from the reading habits of *S*s.

The top members of the pairs made up one of the stimulus lists while the bottom members made up the second list. Successive presentations of the paired lists involved different random orders for each list. As a result, the pairings of individual items from the two lists were randomly varied from trial to trial. Stimulus materials were prepared for each of the six possible pairings of the four lists. Two variations for each pairing were prepared. These reversed the top and bottom member positions but were otherwise identical.

Conditions of learning.—All *S*s were instructed to learn one of the two lists presented and were discouraged by the instructions from attempting to learn the second list. Different groups were exposed to each pair of lists for two, four, or eight presentations. The item pairings were varied from trial to trial in order to prevent learning of the incidental items through the mediation of the intentional items. The experiment was introduced as a test of the notion that words meaning the same thing in different languages tend to sound more alike than words with different meanings. The *S*s were asked to judge the phonetic similarity between the members of each pair of trigrams. These were said to be items from two different primitive languages. The *S*s were required to pronounce the members of each pair to themselves and to rate their phonetic similarity on a five-point scale. They were instructed that the top members of the pairs were always from the same language while the bottom members were always from the other language. In order to get intentional learning of only one list, *S*s were told that we also wanted to study the ease of learning of one primitive language under conditions of distraction from a second language. In this way, instructions to learn were given for either the top or bottom items exclusively.

The *S*s were given a number of paper sheets, each covered with a strip of cardboard. A window was cut out of each cardboard strip in order to allow exposure of one pair of syllables at a time in accordance with *E*'s instructions. The pairs of syllables on each sheet were numbered 1 through 12. When *E* called out the number "1," *S* slid down the window to expose the first pair of syllables and entered his rating next to the syllables. The procedure was repeated for each successive pair until all 12 pairs on the page had been rated. The pairs were presented at a 10-sec. rate, with 20 sec. between presentations of the pages. A 5-min. test of free recall was given 1 min. after the end of practice. The *S*s were requested to write down as many of the syllables as they could remember regardless of whether they appeared in the top or bottom positions of the pairs. They were told to write the syllables down in the order they were remembered, and that their scores

TABLE 2

AVERAGE NUMBER OF INCIDENTAL ITEMS RECALLED BY THE VARIOUS GROUPS

Presentations	Incidental Learning Items			
	High Meaningful		Low Meaningful	
	High Int.	Low Int.	High Int.	Low Int.
2	2.31	2.25	1.06	1.44
4	3.56	4.06	2.31	2.62
8	4.94	4.69	3.88	3.19

would depend only on the number of correct items that they wrote down. When the recall test was completed, a postexperimental inquiry was made to ascertain whether *S* understood the instructions and whether, for any reason, an attempt was made to learn the incidental items. Each *S* received two learning scores, one being the number of correctly reproduced intentional items and the other being the number of correctly reproduced incidental items.

Experimental design.—Twelve groups of 16 *Ss* each were run in a standard $2 \times 2 \times 3$ factorial design. The three independent variables were meaningfulness of the intentional items, meaningfulness of the incidental items, and number of presentations. The design was balanced for top and bottom order of lists, and for the position of the intentional items. With an overall total of six possible list combinations, two possible sequences of the items from the two lists within the pairs (i.e., A-B or B-A), two possible positions for the intentional items, and three degrees of practice, a total of 72 task variations were required for the balanced design.

Subjects.—The *Ss* were students in lower division psychology courses at the University of California. They did not know the purpose of the experiment and were assigned to the conditions by rotation. They served in groups, averaging 13 in number. Each of these groups included several different experimental conditions for which the instructions were identical but which differed with regard to the stimulus lists given to *Ss*. Of necessity, two-presentation, four-presentation, and eight-presentation conditions had to be run separately. Otherwise, the experimental conditions were assigned by rotation to the members of each laboratory group with correction for equal *N*s. The two-presentation, four-presentation, and eight-presentation treatments were assigned to the groups by rotation.

A total of 237 *Ss* were tested in order to obtain the 192 required by the experimental design. Of these, 22 indicated upon inquiry that they did not understand the instructions or that they made some attempt to learn the incidental items. They were discarded and replaced. Of these, 7 were in the two-presentation group, 8 in the four-presentation group, and 7 in the eight-presentation group. In filling out the laboratory groups during the final phase of the experiment, 23 extra *Ss* were run. Where there were extra *Ss* for any of the 72 task variations, the *Ss* to be used in the analysis were selected randomly.

RESULTS AND DISCUSSION

Incidental learning.—The incidental learning scores were analyzed in terms of the $2 \times 2 \times 3$ factorial design. The mean numbers of correctly reproduced incidental items are given in Table 2. For example, the first entry indicates that an average of 2.31 high-M items were learned incidentally, where the concurrent intentional items were also high-M, and there were two presentations. Table 3 summarizes the analysis of variance for the incidental learning data presented in Table 2. Because Bartlett's test showed significant heterogeneity of variance, the Freeman-Tukey square-root transformation $(\sqrt{x} + \sqrt{x+1})$ was used in this

TABLE 3

ANALYSIS OF VARIANCE OF INCIDENTAL SCORES

Source	*df*	*MS*	*F*
Meaningfulness (incident. items) (M_1)	1	26.85	21.46*
Meaningfulness (intent. items) (M_2)	1	.00	.00
No. of presentations (P)	2	35.25	28.17*
$M_1 \times M_2$	1	.04	.03
$M_1 \times P$	2	.29	.23
$M_2 \times P$	2	.53	.42
$M_1 \times M_2 \times P$	2	.15	.12
Error	180	(1.25)	—

* $P < .001$.

analysis, as well as in the analysis of intentional scores below. In both cases, Bartlett's test indicated that there was no significant heterogeneity in the transformed scores. It can be seen that meaningfulness of the incidental items, and number of presentations are highly significant sources of variance. The meaningfulness of the concurrently learned intentional items is not a significant source of variance in incidental learning. None of the interactions among the independent variables are significant.

If task competition is an important variable in Type II incidental learning, it might be expected that incidental learning would vary as a function of intentional-task difficulty. Therefore the question may be raised as to why incidental learning did not vary with the meaningfulness of the intentional items. The failure to find a relationship between intentional-M and incidental learning is surprising in view of the nonverbal studies which indicate that Type II incidental learning varies significantly as a function of intentional task variables (Bahrick, 1954; Bahrick et al., 1952). The considerably greater effects obtained in the nonverbal experiments become explicable when we consider the differences between the verbal and nonverbal situations. These situations differed greatly with regard to the activities required by the orienting tasks. These activities may facilitate or inhibit the performance of those differential responses which are assumed to be necessary for learning (Postman & Adams, 1956). Pronunciation of verbal items probably makes for very adequate differential responses as far as learning is concerned. In the verbal situation, the orienting task required that *S* make definite pronouncing responses to both the intentional and incidental items. Because of the nature of the orienting task, task competition could not prevent *S* from producing differential responses to the incidental items. At most, task competition could only reduce the frequency and intensity of *S*'s responses. In the case of the nonverbal experiments cited above, the situation was quite different. There was no specific orienting task which required *S* to respond differentially to the incidental stimuli. It was possible for *S* to completely ignore these stimuli while still conforming to the instructions of the experimenter. For example, *S* should be able to learn geometric forms intentionally without necessarily responding to their incidental colors. Therefore, large amounts of competition from the intentional task could result in failure to perform differential responses to the incidental materials.

It is evident from the foregoing analysis that the orienting task can be an important factor in determining the effects of task competition on incidental learning. Where the orienting task merely requires stimulus exposure of the incidental materials, the role of task competition can be great. But where the orienting task requires differential responding to the incidental materials, the role of task competition may be severely limited. In view of these considerations, it is not surprising that Bahrick's manipulations of the intentional task produced greater effects on incidental learning than did ours. We should predict that the effects of incentive upon Type II incidental learning would be sharply reduced if the orienting task required differential responses to the incidental items. Similarly, the effects of intentional-M on incidental learning should be increased by use of a less facilitating orienting task. For example, *S* might be required to assign "guessed" numbers to each incidental item instead of pronouncing it. The degree of task competition might then become an important factor in determining whether or not *S* makes appropriate differential responses to the incidental items.

Intentional learning.—The design of the analysis of intentional scores was identical to the design for the incidental scores. The means for

TABLE 4

AVERAGE NUMBER OF INTENTIONAL ITEMS RECALLED BY THE VARIOUS GROUPS

Presentations	Intentional Learning Items			
	High Meaningful		Low Meaningful	
	High Inc.	Low Inc.	High Inc.	Low Inc.
2	5.69	5.19	4.12	4.50
4	7.94	7.25	7.25	6.81
8	8.81	9.19	9.00	8.62

each condition are given in Table 4. The only significant sources of variance are meaningfulness of the intentional items ($F = 4.72$, $df = 1/180$, $P < .05$) and number of presentations ($F = 49.07$, $df = 2/180$, $P < .001$).

Differences between intentional and incidental learning.—Postman et al. (1955) and Postman and Phillips (1961) have found that the superiority of intentional over incidental learning decreases as the meaningfulness of the items increases. In the Type II situation, each *S* is exposed to both intentional and incidental lists. It is of interest to ascertain whether the difference between intentional and incidental scores for each *S* will also decrease as the meaningfulness of the items increases. Such a finding would be consistent with the Type I studies which used different groups of *S*s for intentional and incidental learning. In order to test this hypothesis, differences between intentional items recalled and incidental items recalled were obtained for each *S*. These were then divided by the *S*'s total learning in order to obtain relative difference scores for each *S* $\left(\frac{\text{Int.} - \text{Inc.}}{\text{Int.} + \text{Inc.}}\right)$. This resulted in measures of the difference between intentional and incidental learning which were comparable for different levels of overall learning. Each *S* in the experiment received one of four possible list combinations. These combinations can be ordered in terms of predicted average differences between intentional and incidental learning. Such an ordering involves two assumptions. First, that increased meaningfulness increases learning. This assumption has already been borne out by the significant *F* ratios for meaningfulness in the separate analyses of incidental and intentional learning. The second assumption is that the difference between intentional and incidental learning will decrease as the stimulus items increase in meaningfulness. On the basis of these two assumptions, the intentional-incidental differences for the four list combinations should be in the following increasing order: (1) Low Intentional-High Incidental; (2) High Intentional-High Incidental; (3) Low Intentional-Low Incidental; and (4)

TABLE 5

AVERAGE RELATIVE DIFFERENCES BETWEEN INTENTIONAL AND INCIDENTAL LEARNING FOR THE VARIOUS LIST COMBINATIONS

	List Combinations			
	(1) Low Int. High Inc.	(2) High Int. High Inc.	(3) Low Int. Low Inc.	(4) High Int. Low Inc.
Two Trials	19.23	43.94	60.04	69.58
Four Trials	34.92	42.10	45.73	51.46
Eight Trials	31.41	28.35	47.66	41.55
All Trials (two, four, & eight combined)	28.52	38.13	51.14	54.20

Note.—Means are based upon 16 *S*s for each list combination at each level of practice. The score for each *S* is: $\frac{\text{Int.} - \text{Inc.}}{\text{Int.} + \text{Inc.}} \times 100$.

High Intentional-Low Incidental. A significant gap between the second and third list combinations would indicate that the difference between the two kinds of learning varies as a function of the meaningfulness of the items.

Table 5 gives the mean relative differences for each list combination at each level of practice. The bottom row of the table gives the average differences when the three levels of practice are combined. It can be seen from this row that the differences increase in the predicted order. The largest difference is between List Combinations 2 and 3.

The data for two and four trials are also in the predicted order without any reversals. At eight trials, there are small reversals between Combinations 1 and 2 and between Combinations 3 and 4. However, Combination 3 shows a larger difference than Combination 2 at all levels of practice.

The difference scores were subjected to an analysis of variance with list combinations and number of presentations as the independent variables. Because the scores in this analysis are percentages, the arc-sine transformation (Angle = Arcsine $\sqrt{\text{Percentage}}$) was used. As hypothesized, list combinations is a highly significant source of variance ($F = 6.58$, $df = 3/180$, $P < .001$). The number of presentations does not contribute significant variance to the percentage-difference scores ($F = 1.78$, $df = 2/180$). The interaction between list combinations and presentations is also not significant ($F = 1.64$, $df = 6/180$).

In order to analyze further the significant effects of list combinations, the gap test of Tukey (1949) was utilized. The overall means of the transformed scores were tested in order to determine whether any of the differences between adjacent means were significant. These means differ from those in the bottom row of Table 5 only in that the scores have been transformed. The means for List Combinations 1–4 are 27.86, 35.16, 46.63, and 49.34, respectively. A gap as large as 10.85 between adjacent means is significant beyond the .05 level for a two-tailed test and beyond the .025 level for a one-tailed test. In view of the predicted ordering of conditions, the one-tailed probabilities are appropriate. It may be seen that the only gap larger than 10.85 ($P < .025$) is between List Combination 2 (H-H) and List Combination 3 (L-L). This indicates that the higher the meaningfulness of the items, the smaller is the difference between intentional and incidental learning.

The gap between List Combinations 1 and 2 falls short of statistical significance ($.05 < P < .10$). Therefore the application of Tukey's test divides the means into two significantly separated pairs: (*a*) the pair of mean differences when incidental items are of high meaningfulness; (*b*) the pair of mean differences when incidental items are of low meaningfulness. Differences between intentional and incidental learning are significantly greater in the case of the latter pair.

With regard to the differential response hypothesis, the crucial comparison of mean intentional-incidental differences is between the two groups with unmixed lists (H-H vs. L-L). As indicated above, the intentional-incidental difference is significantly greater when both stimulus lists are of low meaningfulness than when both are of high meaningfulness. This is a confirmation of the hypothesis using intentional-incidental differences for individual *S*s. Previous supporting data from Type I experiments have involved comparisons of groups of intentional learners with groups of incidental learners.

The role of practice.—Another finding of this experiment was that both intentional and incidental learning increased reliably as a function of presentations. These data are in contrast to a previous study on Type I incidental learning (Postman & Adams, 1958). There it was found that intentional learning showed a significant upward trend as a function of presentations whereas incidental learning did not. These different findings are probably due to the difference between orienting tasks in the two experiments. It has been shown that differences between intentional and incidental learning vary as a function of the nature of the orienting task (Postman & Adams, 1956). The earlier study of the effects of presentations required that *S* guess numbers assigned by chance to each syllable. *S*s were told that each presentation of the series would have different number assignments. The *S*s were faced with relatively novel nonsense syllables during the initial presentations of the series. With repeated presentations, there was no requirement for incidental *S*s to respond to the syllables differentially. Therefore it might be expected that practice would have only marginal effects on incidental learning while having large effects on intentional learning. The present experiment required that *S* pronounce the items to himself in order to rate phonetic similarity. Because this form of response to the incidental items was required of *S* on every presentation, it is not surprising that incidental learning increased with practice in very much the same manner as did intentional learning.

Summary

This experiment studied "task competition" by manipulating the difficulty of both the intentional and incidental materials in a Type II incidental learning situation, in which *S* is exposed to two sets of materials, instructed to learn only one of the sets, and is later tested for the materials which he was not instructed to learn.

Twelve groups of 16 *S*s each were run in a standard 2 × 2 × 3 factorial design. The three independent variables were meaningfulness of the intentional items (high vs. low), meaningfulness of the incidental items (high vs. low), and number of presentations (two, four, eight). Scores for both incidental and intentional learning were obtained from each *S*.

The first analysis of the data studied incidental learning scores in terms of the 2 × 2 × 3 factorial design described above. The meaningfulness of the incidental items was a significant source of variance in incidental learning. The meaningfulness of the intentional items did not contribute significant variance either by itself or in interaction with the other independent variables. In contrast with an earlier study, it was found that incidental learning increased significantly as a function of practice.

The second analysis of the data involved the difference scores between intentional and incidental learning for each *S*. It was predicted that differences would be greater when the items were of low meaningfulness than when they were of high meaningfulness. Analogous results have been found in the Type I situation and have been explained in terms of a differential response hypothesis. The predicted results in this Type II experiment support such an hypothesis.

References

Bahrick, H. P. Incidental learning under two incentive conditions. *J. exp. Psychol.*, 1954, **47**, 170–172.

Bahrick, H. P., Fitts, P. M., & Rankin, R. E. Effect of incentives upon reactions to peripheral stimuli. *J. exp. Psychol.*, 1952, **44**, 400–406.

Postman, L., & Adams, P. A. Studies in incidental learning: IV. The interaction of orienting tasks and stimulus materials. *J. exp. Psychol.*, 1956, **51**, 329–333.

Postman, L., & Adams, P. A. Studies in incidental learning: VII. Effects of frequency of exercise and length of list. *J. exp. Psychol.*, 1958, **56**, 86–94.

Postman, L., Adams, P. A., & Phillips, L. W. Studies in incidental learning: II. The effects of association value and of the method of testing. *J. exp. Psychol.*, 1955, **49**, 1–10.

Postman, L., & Phillips, L. W. Studies in incidental learning: IX. A comparison of the methods of successive and single recalls. *J. exp. Psychol.*, 1961, **61**, 236–241.

Thorndike, E. L., & Lorge, I. *A teacher's word book of 30,000 words.* New York: Teachers College, Columbia University, 1944.

Tukey, J. W. Comparing individual means in the analysis of variance. *Biometrics*, 1949, **5**, 99–114.

Underwood, B. J., & Postman, L. Extra-experimental sources of interference in forgetting. *Psychol. Rev.*, 1960, **67**, 73–95.

Underwood, B. J., & Schulz, R. W. *Meaningfulness and verbal learning.* Philadelphia: Lippincott, 1960.

(Received May 2, 1961)

CHAPTER 7

Acquisition as a Function of Organizational Factors

The following comments by Underwood (1964a) set the stage for the phenomena covered in this chapter.

> Theories aside, realization of the fact that we deal with nonpassive *Ss* with a vast set of habits may influence the approach we take in experimental studies of verbal learning. The preformed habits may themselves be the object of study with further attempts directed toward trying to understand how these preformed habits influence the verbal-learning phenomena under study at the moment. The fact that in rote learning we must deal in some fashion with preformed habits, and the fact that these habits are of the nature that may influence learning in many other areas lends some credence to the notion that verbal learning is a transition area between simple learning and "higher" forms of learning (p. 53).

To paraphrase Underwood, the so-called higher forms of learning, for example, concept acquisition, are commonly regarded as involving preformed or second-order habits of a conceptual nature. These preformed habits serve implicitly as mediators for the purpose of transcending the rote learning of a set of materials. For example, children learn innumerable concepts (dog, friend, etc.) as they are growing up. In each instance, the child is confronted with a variety of stimuli that are representative of a given concept. Although there may be many differences between these instances (e.g., big dogs, little dogs), there remains some underlying similarity that binds the stimuli of the concept class together. After he has learned to abstract the basis of this similarity, the child learns to attach the verbal label of the concept (e.g., the word "dog") to subsequent instances of the stimuli for that concept. Critical components of this process, then, are the abstraction of a common functional stimulus component from an array of nominally different stimuli and the association of a single response to this common cue. After years of such experiences, second-order habits of abstraction should be available for transfer to the learning of new concepts. In other words, when given a set of stimuli with some common functional cue and a common response, *S* can use his performed habits to avoid the necessity of learning rotely the separate associations between the various stimuli and the single response. His use of these conceptual habits is therefore expected to yield a sizable savings over the rote learning of the same materials.

Conceptual habits enter into many of the standard verbal learning tasks. In fact, they are not exactly strangers to the reader. In the Introduction to Chapter 2 we noted the frequent search that *Ss* have for an associative mediator to bridge the gap between unrelated *St* and *R* components of a PA list. The emphasis at that point, however, was on the nature of PA acquisition qua PA acquisition, and conceptual habits were relegated to a secondary prominence. Presently, we are concerned with conceptual habits as an area of investigation in its own right, hoping to enhance our understanding of their functioning in the complex areas of learning. The strategy will be to examine their functioning within variants of standard verbal learning tasks, such as free recall, PA acquisition, and serial learning. Insights into the principles regulating these functions and their interactions with important tasks and procedural variables cannot but help increase our understanding of analogous functions and interactions in more complex tasks. Although the complex tasks themselves may well involve manifestations of these same processes and functions, a direct attack that employs these tasks is likely to be handicapped by its unwieldiness to an analytic approach. The studies surveyed in the following sections are thus transitional experiments which span the vacuum between the rote learning of the preceding chapters and the higher mental processes. Four separate transitional areas will be discussed: Coding, Clustering, Concept Acquisition, and Contextual Organization. From the large number of articles selected for inclusion in this chapter, the reader should surmise the growing importance of the problems surveyed. With little trepidation, we may predict that the kinds of research activities represented in this chapter will forge even closer to the top of the interests of verbal learning psychologists in the near future.

Coding

The work of George Miller (e.g., 1956a,b) has played a prominent role in shaping contemporary research in verbal learning. The crux of Miller's views is apparent from the following quotation:

> In order to speak more precisely, therefore, we must recognize the importance of grouping or organizing the input sequence into units or chunks. Since the memory span is a fixed number of chunks, we can increase the number of bits of information that it contains simply by building larger and larger chunks, each chunk containing more information than before.
>
> A man just beginning to learn radio-telegraphic code hears each *dit* and *dah* as a separate chunk. Soon he is able to organize these sounds into letters and then he can deal with the letters as chunks. Then the letters organize themselves as words, which are still larger chunks, and he begins to hear whole phrases . . . . I am simply pointing to the obvious fact that the dits and dahs are organized by learning into patterns and that as these larger chunks emerge the amount of message that the operator can remember increases correspondingly. In the terms I am proposing to use, the operator learns to increase the bits per chunk.
>
> In the jargon of communication theory, this process would be called *recording*. The input is given in a code that contains many chunks with few bits per chunk. The operator recodes the input into another code that contains fewer chunks with more bits per chunk. There are many ways to do this recoding, but probably the simplest is to group the input events, apply a new name to the group, and then remember the new name rather than the original input events (1956b, p. 93).

"Encoding" or "recoding," as Miller calls it, has been an especially valuable concept in short term retention (cf. Chapter 11). It has also had considerable impact on contemporary studies on acquisition. Particularly relevant is the area of free recall where response learning is studied free of associative connections with specific intra-list stimuli. The processes of free recall, in turn, may well apply wherever response learning is called for, such as the response learning stages of SL and PA acquisition.

When the response components of a verbal list are nonsensical in form, like the trigram BJO, acquisition of the components probably requires the assimilation of independent "chunks" of information, for example, the three chunks corresponding to the letters B-J-O, for storage and future recall. An *S*, however, may encode the response component BJO into the meaningful word "Job" by readjusting the sequence of the same three letters. Being a meaningful word, Job exists as a single chunk that is easily acquired and stored for recall. Thus, encoding the component greatly facilitates acquisition of the three letters—but decoding may cause *s* to stumble at the moment recall is demanded of him. If *S* is permitted to recall the three letters in any sequence, regardless of the exact sequence given to him, there is no problem. He simply spells out J-O-B and receives credit for correct recall. But if *E* stubbornly insists that recall of the letters be in the exactly given order, then *S* may be in trouble. Having stored the sequence J-O-B, he must decode back to B-J-O. At this point, *S* may have difficulty in deciding if the component presented for study was BJO or JBO, two equally unrealistic letter sequences. Of course, if JBO is the unfortunate choice, *S* is scored as being incorrect. Time pressures on the beleaguered *S* from paced practice conditions would serve to intensify his conflict in selecting from alternatives.

Underwood and Keppel (1962b) found that encoding aids free recall when decoding is not required, especially when *Ss* are sensitized to encoding by instructions directing their attention to the nature of encoding. However, they also found the expected inhibitory effect on recall when *Ss* are forced to decode back to the originally presented sequence of letters in the trigram components. A subsequent study by Battig, Merikle, and Schild (1965) extended the Underwood and Keppel study to include the number of different orders of letters, other than the one resulting in a meaningful word, possible for each trigram in the list. They again found the expected superiority of any-order recall (including the meaningful word possibility) over exact-order (the order given for study), but they failed to find a statistically significant effect on recall for the number of available letter-order transformations.

Clustering

Clustering has come to mean the sequential organization during recall of items that are related to one another in some way—even though the items themselves are exposed in a random order during study trials. Consider a free recall list which contains, say, four equal subgroups or sets of related items. Within a subgroup the content is homogeneous (e.g., the components may all be members of the same taxonomic category—see below). Clustering is said to have occurred if there is a tendency for the related items to follow each other sequentially during recall. When clustering is present, second-order or conceptual habits are presumed to be engaged. The clustering phenomenon is largely a product of the contemporary period. Actually, several kinds of phenomena, identified by the nature of the specific conceptual habits elicited, have been investigated, each of which is described in this section.

In general, total recall scores for items in a list are higher for lists with clustering then without. This finding fits nicely into Miller's concept of encoding into chunks. Without clusters a list of *n* items is organized into a minimum of *n* chunks. With clusters the list may be encoded into considerably fewer than *n* chunks. The encoded chunks are likely to be closely related to the categories represented in the list. Assuming that *S* is able to register for future recall only a limited number of chunks on a single trial, recall should become more proficient with the presence of clustering. Nevertheless, a correlation between the degree of clustering in individual *Ss* and the amount of total recall is speculative. Bousfield and Cohen (1955a) reported a zero correlation for taxonomic clustering (see below), but Weingartner (1964) reported a moderately high correlation for associative clustering (see below).

Taxonomic Clustering

W. A. Bousfield and his colleagues have been closely identified with clustering in lists containing multiple items that are representative of distinguishable taxonomic categories. For example, four categories, such as "professions," "animals," "flowers," and "minerals," with six instances each (doctor, lawyer, Indian chief, etc., for professions) may compose an experimental list of 24 items. If *E* intends contrasting recall scores for clustered and unclustered materials, a control condition is included in which the items, by inspection, are not taxonomically related. Following the standard operating procedure, the items in each list are randomly ordered and given to the *Ss* for a paced study trial. Clustering is evident if *S* tends to recall sequentially the names of the professions, the names of the animals, etc., to an extent beyond chance expectancy. In addition, clustering is said to aid recall if the total recall score for the clustered list exceeds, with proper statistical propriety, that for the unclustered list.

Article 1 (Bousfield, 1953) will familiarize the reader with the procedures just outlined sketchily (except that Bousfield did not include a control group, thus prohibiting a test of clustering effects on total recall score) and with attempts to explain the clustering phenomenon in terms of second-order habits (i.e., the activation of superordinates). The reader will discover that the instances for each taxonomic category were selected arbitarily by the investigator himself. In a later study, the Bousfield group (Cohen, Bousfield, and Whitmarsh, 1957) compiled normative data for the frequency of occurrence of items in response to 43 specific categories (e.g., fish, insect, etc.). Thus, *E* may, if he so desires, vary the frequency of occurrence of the categorical instances on the basis of these normative data.

A number of variables have been related to the degree of clustering and frequently to total recall scores as a by-product. Bousfield and Cohen (1953) found a positive relationship between the number of list presentations (or reinforcements) and the occurrence of clustering. Clustering was found to be greater for high frequency (Thorndike-Lorge counts, see introductory section of Chapter 4,) than for low frequency words (Bousfield and Cohen, 1955b) and also for high frequency taxonomic responses (as determined by the normative data) than for low (Bousfield, Cohen, and Whitmarsh, 1958). The number of categories included in the list has been the subject of several experiments, with the emphasis being on total recall scores. We might expect recall to decrease as the number of categories increases in that the number of chunks to be assimilated also increases. However, as Mathews (1954) pointed out, a complicating factor with a list of fixed length is that as the number of categories decreases, thus increasing the incidence rate in each category, the opportunity for intra-category interference increases. Furthermore, moderate increases in the number of intra-list categories would not be expected to tax severely *S's* capacity for assimilating chunks. The net effect should be a direct relationship between the number of categories, within limits, and the amount of total recall. This has been reported by Mathews (1954) and Bousfield and Cohen (1956, their Experiment II). Dallett (1964b), however, found an inverse relationship between number of categories and recall scores. There is a strong possibility that the effect of number of categories may be confounded by the extent of intra-cluster word associations in a given list (i.e., the tendency of the words to be associates of one another). Since the extent of such associations is uncontrolled in these studies, differential amounts of associations in the lists employed may account for the disparity in findings.

Associative Clustering

Jenkins and Russell (1952; Article 2) discovered that clustering occurs when a list contains pairs of words in which one word is a common response (or word associate, see introductory section of Chapter 2) to the other as a stimulus (e.g., chair as a response to table). The list is presented in a random order during the study trials, with the associates likely to be widely scattered. Clustering here refers to the chained elicitation of the associates during recall trials. Later studies (e.g., Jenkins, Mink, and Russell, 1958; Matthews, Marcer, and Morgan, 1964) found that the degree of associative clustering is an increasing monotonic function of the associative strength existing between the word pairs (as determined by word association norms). It should also be noted that clustering takes place when sets of synonyms are incorporated into a free recall list (Cofer, 1959). The Underwood, Runquist, and Schulz study (Article 2, Chapter 2) also suggested the possibility of clustering by response synonymity in PA acquisition. There is the strong possibility that synonyms are direct associates of one another, thus accounting for their clustering in terms of direct association factors. However, as Marshall and Cofer (1963) recognized, secondary or mediated associations could also provide the basis for the clustering of synonyms.

Cofer and Bruce (1965) raised the important question of the occurrence of clustering when the categories activated by a superordinate (or naming) response contain items which are not associates of one another. In taxonomic studies (see above) intra-category items are usually related associatively as well as taxonomically. Cofer and Bruce found no evidence for clustering when they were categorized by form class (nouns, adjectives, and verbs), and the items within a form class were unrelated associatively.

Deese (1959, 1961, 1962) introduced a procedure for obtaining an index of interitem associative strength. The index measures the average relative frequency of the tendency for all the words in a list to be elicited as free associates by all the other words. To construct 15-item lists with varying degrees of associative organization, Deese (1959) selected stimulus words, such as butterfly, and 15 high-frequency associates to these stimulus words (from the Minnesota word norms). Then, using his own standardization sample of *Ss*, he determined the relative frequency of each associate to a stimulus word to elicit each of the other associates. Consider the responses "moth" and "insect" as associates of "butterfly." From Deese's own norms, the relative strength for moth to elicit insect is 2 per cent (i.e., the associate was given by 2 per cent of the sample); for insect to elicit moth as a response, the strength is 4 per cent. The average of all of these percentage scores for the 15 items in a list constitutes the list's interitem associative strength. Deese (1959) found a strikingly pronounced positive relationship between the degree of interitem associative strength extant within lists and the amount of free recall for the lists. Weingartner (1963) also found that SL proficiency increased as the degree of interitem associative strength increased.

Cofer (1965) has summarized his own research activity that has been directed toward contrasting associational and categorical bases for clustering. The methods employed compared sequential recall for categorized pairs (i.e., the words share a common category membership, such as, BED–CHAIR as items of furniture) and uncategorized pairs (e.g., BED–SLEEP) when both kinds of pairs were equated for the degree of overlapping associations. The overall results suggest that the opportunity for categorization seems to increase the degree of clustering beyond that found on an associational basis alone. Cofer ended his summary with the unfortunate, but correct, conclusion that psychologists remain largely in the dark regarding the network of processes that function to join together related items in recall, whether the relationships be by categories or by associations. As a solution he proposed an exhaustive series of experiments that would systematically manipulate situational and task variables to discover which ones aid and which ones hinder the utilization of preexperimental associations and superordinate habits.

Subjective Organization

As we discovered earlier, control lists of unrelated words serve as a contrast for the recall advantage found in clustered lists. However, there is convincing evidence (Tulving, 1962; Bousfield, Puff, and Cowan, 1964) for clustering in the recall of lists containing seemingly unrelated words, even when *E* has intentionally thwarted the presence of an organizational base within the list. Clustering in unrelated lists refers to the tendency of pairs of unrelated items to be recalled consecutively on repeated trials (again with presentation being randomized). The idiosyncratic second-order habits of *Ss* seem sufficient to provide their own organization. We obviously need to broaden our conceptualization of the clustering phenomenon and pursue further the nature of these idiosyncratic factors.

Concept Acquisition

In this section we are concerned with *S*'s ability to transfer his past experiences with the acquisition of concepts to aid in the acquisition of artificial concepts within a standardized laboratory setting. Concept acquisition (or formation) is a formidable area that challenges investigation and explanation from a variety of systematic approaches, for example, information theory, computer theory, etc. Our concern, however, is only with an approach through the procedures and processes of traditional verbal learning, with the procedures of PA acquisition being especially applicable. The following remarks by Goss (1961) describe nicely the transition from conventional PA acquisition to PA concept acquisition.

> Paired-associates learning can be regarded as referring either to a particular kind of task or to a more general *procedure* for establishing and changing stimulus-

response associations. Many concept-formation *tasks*, however, have employed the paired-associates *procedure* for strengthening associations between stimulus members and responses elicited by response members. Both conventional paired-associates tasks and such concept-formation tasks may therefore be regarded as complementary special cases of patterns of stimulus-response associations which are strengthened by the paired-associates procedure (Metzger, 1958; Richardson, 1958).

There is only one essential difference between conventional paired-associates learning tasks and concept-formation tasks in which stimulus-response associations are established by the paired-associates procedure. That difference is in the ratio of stimulus members to responses which are to be conditioned to those stimuli. For conventional paired-associates learning tasks, the ratio of stimulus members to response members has been 1 : 1; that is, separate associations are established between each of mn_s different stimulus members and each of the mn_r different responses elicited by mn_r response members.

For the formation of concepts by the paired-associates procedure, however, the ratio of stimulus members to the responses which are conditioned to those stimuli has been greater than 1 : 1, that is, for at least one, and usually for all of m subsets of stimulus members, $n_{sj} > 1$, where n_{sj} is the number of stimuli in the jth subset. Regardless of the type of sets of initiating stimuli, by increasing the numbers of responses to equal the number of initiating stimuli, concept-formation tasks in which stimulus-response associations are established by the paired-associates procedure can be transformed into conventional paired-associates learning tasks. Conversely, by decreasing the number of responses from equality with the number of initiating stimuli the latter can be transformed into concept-formation tasks (pp. 251–252).

Article 3 (Underwood and Richardson, 1956) and Article 4 (Richardson, 1958) convey the PA approach and the kinds of task materials and research hypotheses characteristic of this area of investigation. The articles also provide an adequate survey of the relevant literature prior to 1958. The concentration here will therefore be on more recent studies with the PA procedure.

Metzger (1958, his Experiment I), in a study employing systematic patterns of three or four triangles as *St* components and the digits 1 to 8 as *R* components, contrasted rote (conventional PA procedure) and concept acquisition for the same group of *St* components. In rote acquisition the number of *R* components equaled the number of *St* components (i.e., a separate digit was paired with each one of the *St* components); in concept acquisition, the number of *R* components was halved (i.e., two conceptually related *St* components—as determined by Metzger himself—were each paired with the same digit). Since the concept procedure required less response learning than the rote procedure, Metzger expected the former to yield more proficient acquisition. Instead, he failed to find a statistically significant difference between the two procedures. On the other hand, evidence is given in Article 4 for the superiority of the concept procedure over the rote when *R* components that are considerably more difficult than single digits are employed. Moreover, in a partial replication and an extension of the Metzger study, Fallon and Battig (1964) found an advantage for the concept procedure over the rote with 2-digit numbers as the *R* components. Their results also indicated that Metzger's identification of a conceptual relationship between *St* components did not coincide with the conceptual groupings perceived by the *Ss* themselves. When *Sts* were paired with *Rs* on the basis of *S*-determined groupings, acquisition was significantly more proficient than when *St-R* pairings were determined by Metzger's a priori groupings.

Richardson (1960) compared PA acquisition under concept conditions (that is, a single *R* was correct for each member of a related group of *Sts*) in which the nature of the grouping itself varied. For each class of *St* groupings he had *Ss* rate the degree of association between the individual *St* components. Although acquisition varied greatly with the class of groupings (e.g., taxonomic groupings were superior to dominance (cf. Article 3) groupings), the degree of association per se was unrelated to acquisition. Richardson interpreted his results in terms of a common mediating response for a group of related *St* components (cf. Goss, 1961, for a detailed discussion of mediation in concept acquisition) and concluded that ratings of association fail to predict the probability of occurrence of these mediating responses. In a later study, Richardson (1962) tested, with success for taxonomic groupings but not for dominance groupings, the hypothesis that the transfer within a stimulus group is based on a mediating response. This was done by means of a mediated transfer paradigm (cf. Chapter 9).

Finally, Thysell and Schulz (1964) enumerated the difficulties encountered in studying concept acquisition with normatively assessed materials, such as the dominance materials described in Article 3. As an alternative, they offered a laboratory procedure in which relevant (dominant) and irrelevant (nondominant) attributes are experimentally established.

Contextual Organization

Strings of words or paralogs have their own contextual or intrinsic organization in accordance with *S*'s past experiences with semantic and syntactic rules. As an example, consider the following three strings: "The girls jumped rope for one hour after school both yesterday and today"; "The happy chairs played darkly from a convenient tray in a large song"; "White the climbing into say an loudly boat before could entire look yet." The first string has considerable organization, both semantically and syntactically. The second string is snytactically sound but is devoid of valid semantic content. The third string, of course, has neither syntactic nor semantic form. Semantic and syntactic contextual factors each exert constraining forces that effectively monitor the organization and subsequent acquisition of verbal strings. As a result, we would expect to find strings like the first one learned more readily than either of the other strings, and the second kind of string more readily than the third.

The constraints of semantic and syntactic context serve to exclude extra-list intrusions and intra-list displacements during the acquisition of verbal strings. Thus, the sequence "jumped rope" is semantically and syntactically sound and is unlikely to be reversed in order when *Ss* practice the list; nor would extra-list words be likely to intrude on "rope" as a semantic completion of "jumped." Sequences like "played darkly" are syntactically correct but semantically meaningless. Frequent extra-list intrusions for "darkly" would not be uncommon. Sequences like "white the climbing" are syntactically nonsensical as well and are likely to be rearranged by *S* into more orderly ones, such as "climbing the white" (thus yielding frequent intra-list intrusions).

In this section the topic is that of contextual organization as an independent variable related to the free recall and serial acquisition of verbal strings. Contemporary research on this topic was greatly influenced by an important study of Miller and Selfridge (1950) in which strings of words were constructed such that they varied in their approximations to continuous English textual materials. They found that free recall was greatest for actual textual materials.

However, as the approximations began to take on many of the constraints of formal textual material, their recall did not lag far behind. Deese and Kaufman (1957; Article 5) contributed further to our understanding of contextual constraints by comparing the serial position curves for the free recall of unstructured lists (randomly selected words without semantic or syntactic form) and connected prose (both semantic and syntactic form) in their Experiment I; in their Experiment II they examined the serial position curves for strings representing Miller and Selfridge's approximations to textual materials. They concluded that serial position curves become increasingly more like those for conventional serial anticipation acquisition (cf. Chapter 1) as the degree of contextual constraint increases; or, in other words, rote SL is not as great a transgression of serial learning outside of the laboratory as the reader might have imagined.

Syntactic constraint was directly manipulated by Epstein (1961, 1962). Syntactically structured strings were learned more rapidly than unstructured, even when both strings were semantically meaningless (including paralogs that were given syntactic functions in the structured strings). This differential was true only when the entire string was perceived in toto and *S* was required to reproduce the entire string verbatim. When the serial anticipation method was used to expose the strings item by item, Epstein (1962) found no difference in acquisition rate between syntactically structured and unstructured strings. The latter finding led Epstein (1962) to conclude that the critical factor for the constraining effect of syntax is its generalized linguistic form which, in turn, serves to alter the number of chunks that require encoding, rather than specific sequential dependencies from item to item. The generalized form can be perceived only when the entire string is simultaneously presented.

Marks and Miller (1964; Article 6) manipulated semantic and syntactic constraints independently. They discovered that both sources facilitate acquisition via free recall. Normal sentences with both semantic and syntactic form gave higher recall scores than strings with syntactic form but without semantic form, or vice versa. Although the latter two were recalled considerably more than strings of random words, they did not differ markedly from one another. Slamecka (1964b) found that SL also becomes increasingly proficient as semantic constraint increases. In this study the strings were formal sentences with definite syntactic form.

The final article in this section (Mehler, 1963; Article 7) takes up the problem of learning the sense (or kernel) of a verbal message, even when grammatical details are incorrect. Miller (1962) has discussed the exciting implications of this experiment, and other related ones, for the study of language in general. Mandler and Mandler (1964) examined serial position effects for the acquisition of the core meaning of sentences. By core meaning they refer to the primary communicative content of a sentence, such as "Girls jumped rope" of our earlier example. They concluded, seemingly in disagreement with Deese and Kaufman (Article 5), that the serial learning of English sentences progresses differently than the rote learning of unrelated words. In the learning of English sentences, what words are recalled is determined largely by which ones make up the core meaning, rather than by primacy and recency effects as in rote SL (cf. Chapter 1, Article 4). Deese and Kaufman, of course, did not analyze recall in units of core meaning. Concepts like kernal and core meaning are certain to be heard more frequently as psychologists intensify their attention to the many unsolved problems in this important area.

ARTICLE 1

THE OCCURRENCE OF CLUSTERING IN THE RECALL OF RANDOMLY ARRANGED ASSOCIATES*

Department of Psychology, University of Connecticut

W. A. BOUSFIELD[1]

A. INTRODUCTION

The writer and Sedgewick (1) employed a simple technique to investigate the characteristics of sequences of associative responses. The procedure was to ask subjects to list items in specified categories, e.g., animals, birds, and cities in the United States. Inspection of the data at that time revealed a significant phenomenon which, while apparent, appeared too elusive for quantification. In the lists of birds, for example, there occurred many sequences of related items such as *hawk, eagle, vulture,* and *chicken, turkey, duck, goose.* The first three may be classed as birds of prey, and the latter as domestic fowl. We shall here refer to such groups as clusters, and define a cluster as a sequence of associates having an essential relationship between its members. An examination of kymographic records showing the temporal distribution of associates revealed an apparent tendency for the members of clusters to occur in relatively rapid succession. It turned out, however, that many of the temporally distinguishable groups of items revealed no obvious basis of relationship. For example, on one instance *hawk* was followed by *sparrow.* According to our definition this pair might be a cluster since there are several ways in which they could be related. Some hawks prey on sparrows, and sparrow hawk is the name of a bird. In this situation we cannot rely on the experimenter's subjective judgment, and we would prefer not to rely on the subject's introspections.

The purpose of this paper is to describe the results of the use of a technique for quantifying clustering as here defined. The theoretical significance of this undertaking derives in part from the assumption that clustering is a consequence of organization in thinking and recall. If clustering can be quantified, we are provided with a means for obtaining additional information on the nature of organization as it operates in the higher mental processes.

*Received in the Editorial Office on August 29, 1951.

[1]The author wishes to acknowledge the assistance of Mr. Dallas Grover in the tabulation and treatment of the data of this study.

B. Method

A consideration of the following factors determined the choice of the method: (*a*) the subjects should produce sequences of verbal responses since previous work had apparently demonstrated the occurrence of clustering in data of this type; (*b*) the sequences should be of a nature to permit clustering within a wide range; (*c*) the identification of clustering should be objective. Because of the need for objectivity it was necessary to force restrictions considerably beyond those involved in the listing of items in a single general category. The method finally chosen was that of presenting subjects a prepared list of nouns, and then having the subjects list serially as many as they could recall within a period of 10 minutes. The list used throughout the experiment comprised 60 nouns made up of 15 each of four different categories, namely, *animals, names, professions,* and *vegetables.* In order to insure at least a minimum of control over the associative values of the words, use was made of the Thorndike-Lorge tables (4). The four categories were matched as closely as possible on the basis of frequencies of occurrence per million of words in general. These words appear in Table 1. The mean frequencies of occurrence are the same for each category, and the ranges of these frequencies approximately match. We chose two-syllable words on the assumption that they would be more recognizable in an auditory presentation than would one-syllable words. Having selected the words, they were randomized in the following way. Each word was written on a small piece

TABLE 1
List of Stimulus Words

Animals		Names		Professions		Vegetables	
Word	Freq.	Word	Freq.	Word	Freq.	Word	Freq.
giraffe	1	Amos	1	milkman	1	eggplant	1
baboon	2	Gerald	1	typist	1	parsnip	1
zebra	2	Byron	3	florist	2	garlic	3
panther	5	Oswald	4	plumber	2	rhubarb	3
wildcat	5	Jason	5	diver	4	radish	4
leopard	6	Otto	5	druggist	4	melon	5
reindeer	6	Noah	6	broker	7	mustard	7
chipmunk	7	Wallace	7	printer	7	spinach	8
muskrat	7	Owen	7	dentist	9	parsley	8
woodchuck	7	Bernard	9	baker	10	carrot	9
otter	8	Adam	10	chemist	10	mushroom	10
weasel	9	Sherman	10	dancer	10	turnip	10
badger	11	Simon	11	grocer	11	lettuce	12
donkey	16	Moses	12	waiter	13	pumpkin	13
camel	18	Howard	19	blacksmith	19	cabbage	16
Mean Freq.	7.33		7.33		7.33		7.33

of cardboard, ⅛ x 1 in. These cards were then repeatedly shuffled in a box, and then drawn one by one. The original items, thus randomized, occurred in the following serial order to make up the list of stimulus words:

> Muskrat, blacksmith, panther, baker, wildcat, Howard, Jason, printer, chemist, radish, mushroom, Otto, plumber, pumpkin, chipmunk, Amos, Wallace, parsnip, milkman, druggist, leopard, woodchuck, Adam, grocer, Simon, Owen, lettuce, giraffe, turnip, garlic, rhubarb, tvpist, eggplant, Noah, zebra, donkey, Gerald, dentist, otter, parsley, spinach, Oswald, weasel, broker, waiter, florist, Bernard, dancer, reindeer, Byron, cabbage, melon, badger, mustard, diver, carrot, Sherman, camel, baboon, Moses.

The technique for obtaining data resembled that outlined in the earlier study (1) for group experimentation. The experiment took place in a large lecture room. Each subject had a piece of paper, 8½ x 11 in., and a pencil. Two groups (90 and 35 subjects respectively) of undergraduate students in psychology received the following instructions:

> I shall read you a list of words, and you are asked to recall as many of them as you can after I have completed the reading. You are to start writing the words as rapidly as possible when I say, *"Go!"* Write the words in a column at the left side of the paper that has been given you. At intervals I shall say, *"Draw a line."* On hearing this signal please draw a short horizontal line under the last word you have written, and then continue with more words. In the event you have thought of no additional words since the last instruction, *"Draw a line,"* you will draw another line just the same. Are there any questions?

After these instructions, the experimenter answered such questions as were relevant, and then read the stimulus list at a rate of three seconds per word, cues for these intervals being the barely audible click of a mechanical timing device. The signal for writing the words recalled was given three seconds after the reading of the last stimulus word. Thereafter the signals for drawing the demarcation lines were given at one-minute intervals for the period of 10 minutes. It may be noted that there was no mention in the instructions of the nature of the stimulus words. The subjects were asked only to list as many as they could recall, and to draw the demarcation lines when they heard the appropriate signal.

C. Results

From the 125 lists of recalled items, 100 were selected at random. Four of the lists thus chosen were rejected because of obvious failure to follow instructions. Substitutes for these were also chosen at random. Thus 100 lists supplied the basic data of the experiment. The first step in the statistical treatment of the data was to determine the extent to which the subjects exceeded chance in their tendency to cluster their items in the four categories inherent in the list of stimulus words. The test of randomness was a derivation from the binomial theorem. In this frame of reference the problem was to determine, on the basis of chance expectation, how often we would expect an item (*A*, animal; *N*, name; *P*, profession; or *V*, vegetable) to be followed by another item in the same category. If a subject repeats n nouns, in one-fourth of all the cases there would be, by chance, a double symbol *AA*, *NN*, *PP*, or *VV*. If we suppose there are r such repetitions, an appropriate measure of the tendency toward repetition, which we represent as y, is given by the following formula:[2]

$$y = \frac{4r}{\sqrt{3n}} - \sqrt{\frac{n}{3}}$$

We shall here refer to y as the index of repetition. In this formula, since n represents the total number of sequences, it must be the total number of items minus 1. The *4* is the number of categories in which repetitions can occur. It may be noted that y is distributed normally with unit standard deviation about zero, and that it is independent of the magnitude of n. Applying this formula to the list of randomized stimulus words, we have $n = 59$, and $r = 15$. In this case the index of repetition, y, is about .08. We are, therefore, justified in regarding the four categories of the stimulus words as randomly distributed.

The data, as expected, contained errors in the form of items not appearing in the stimulus words. When such items could be classed in the categories of the stimulus words they were labelled ***categorical intrusions;*** when they could not be so classed they were labelled ***irrelevant intrusions.*** Examples of the former were ***bear, Allen, banker, clergy;*** and of the latter, ***number, atom, order,*** and ***bourbon.*** Apparently, ***clang*** associations accounted for some of the irrelevant intrusions. In our analysis of clustering, the categorical intrusions were treated in the same way as the correct items.

Indices of repetition were computed not only for the data of the subjects, but also for data derived from a parallel artificial experiment. In this case the method involved drawing capsules at random and without replacement from a box containing 15 blue, 15 green, 15 orange, and 15 white capsules. A total of 100 such sequences were thus drawn with the number in each case matching the number of items listed by a corresponding subject.

---

[2]The author is indebted to Dr. Geoffrey Beall for his suggestion of this formula.

To test for possible bias in this method, 1,000 capsules were drawn with replacement. The result was 261 blues, 245 greens, 236 oranges, and 258 whites. These data yield a chi-square of 1.624. The corresponding probability value lies between .70 and .50 which is well within the limits of chance expectation.

The indices of repetition for the data of the subjects and for the drawings in the artificial experiment appear in Table 2. The differences between the two distributions are obvious. The mean index for the subjects is 2.38

TABLE 2
INDICES OF REPETITION FOR SUBJECTS AND FOR ARTIFICIAL EXPERIMENT

Indices	Subjects	Artificial experiment
6.25 to 6.74	1	—
5.75 to 6.24	2	—
5.25 to 5.74	—	—
4.75 to 5.24	1	—
4.25 to 4.74	9	—
3.75 to 4.24	11	—
3.25 to 3.74	7	—
2.75 to 3.24	6	—
2.25 to 2.74	16	1
1.75 to 2.24	9	3
1.25 to 1.74	9	5
.75 to 1.24	12	19
.25 to .74	11	13
— .25 to .24	4	14
— .75 to — .26	1	17
—1.25 to — .76	1	16
—1.75 to —1.26	—	9
—2.25 to —1.76	—	2
—2.75 to —2.26	—	1
	100	100

with a standard deviation of 3.11. For the artificial experiment the mean is —.04 and the standard deviation 1.03, which approximate the theoretical expectations of zero and 1.00 respectively. Thus the subjects as a group not only clustered their items beyond chance expectation, but they also showed greater variability. The correlation between the indices of repetition and the number of items listed by the subjects was .36 with a probable error of .06.

As was expected, the subjects showed appreciable variability in the number of items they listed. The range was 12 to 36, with a mean of 24.97 and a standard deviation of 5.70.

A second method for appraising clustering was that of computing a simple *ratio of repetition.* This was the fraction representing the number of repetitions of items divided by the total items listed. For the subjects as a group this ratio was .45. The corresponding ratio for the artificial experiment was .24. The subjects, therefore, made nearly twice as many repetitions as were obtained in the artificial experiment.

A third method was employed for comparing the clustering tendency of the subjects with that obtained by chance. This involved the tabulation of the incidence of single (unclustered) items, and the clusters of varying size. Table 3 shows the results of this analysis. It may be noted that whereas the subjects gave fewer single items and clusters of two than were found in the artificial experiment, they greatly exceeded the chance results in the incidence of higher order clusters.

TABLE 3
INCIDENCE OF SINGLE ITEMS AND CLUSTERS OF VARYING SIZE FOR SUBJECTS AND FOR ARTIFICIAL EXPERIMENT

	1's	2's	3's	4's	5's	6's	7's
Subjects	810	261	164	85	38	18	5
Artificial exp.	1,452	343	87	18	4	1	—

It thus appears that the use of three separate methods for appraising clustering yielded measures showing that the subjects in recall tended to cluster their items beyond chance expectation. The use of the artificial experiment was in a sense gratuitous. To the experimenter, however, this simple expedient served as a useful check on the significance of the data.

In following through the foregoing analysis the question arose of possible changes in the clustering tendency during the course of recall. From *a priori* reasoning it appeared unlikely that clustering would remain constant. It would seem reasonable to suppose that the clustering tendency should diminish as the subjects approached exhaustion of their available supplies of items. In order to investigate this problem, the Vincent method was employed by dividing each of the 100 lists of items into successive decile intervals. The ratios of repetition (repeated items to total items) for these intervals appear in Table 4 and Figure 1 for both the data of the subjects and

TABLE 4
RATIOS OF REPETITION IN SUCCESSIVE DECILES OF ITEMS FOR SUBJECTS AND FOR ARTIFICIAL EXPERIMENT

	Deciles									
	1st	2nd	3rd	4th	5th	6th	7th	8th	9th	10th
Subjects	.45	.56	.58	.61	.53	.51	.38	.35	.31	.21
Artificial exp.	.21	.23	.22	.25	.25	.22	.24	.28	.21	.26

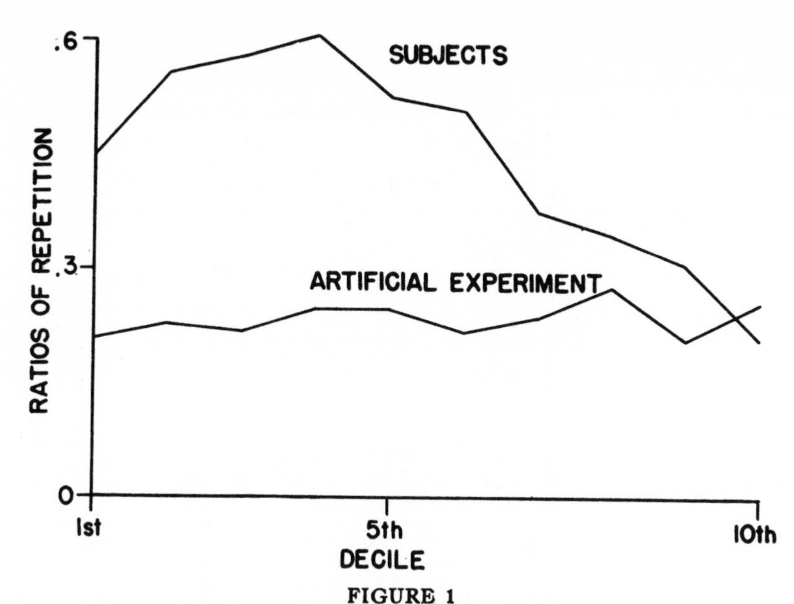

FIGURE 1
PLOTS OF RATIOS OF REPETITION IN SUCCESSIVE DECILES OF ITEMS FOR SUBJECTS AND FOR ARTIFICIAL EXPERIMENT

the data of the artificial experiment. These results reveal several interesting facts. The clustering tendency is initially above chance. It rises to a maximum in the region of the 4th decile, and then drops progressively to the range of chance. In so far as clustering represents organization in recall, this organization broke down as the subjects approached their limits of memory for the items. This trend receives interesting general confirmation from a parallel analysis of the progressions of occurrence of single items and clusters. The data from this analysis are in Table 5. This confirmation is most marked for the single items and the clusters of 3. The former, representing lack of clustering, are at a minimum in the 4th decile, whereas the clusters of 3 have their maximum incidence in the same region. It is interesting to note that clusters of 2 have a consistently higher incidence in the artificial experiment than in the data of the subjects.

It was indicated earlier that the errors appearing in the data were of two types, namely, categorical intrusions and irrelevant intrusions. The totals of the categorical intrusions were as follows: 61 names, 54 animals, 43 professions, and 21 vegetables. There were 75 irrelevant intrusions. Since the subjects listed a total of 2,497 items, 7.17 per cent of these items were categorical intrusions and 3.00 per cent were irrelevant intrusions. It

TABLE 5

PROGRESSIVE CHANGES IN THE INCIDENCE OF SINGLE ITEMS AND CLUSTERS OF VARYING SIZE FOR SUBJECTS AND FOR ARTIFICIAL EXPERIMENT

Decile	1's S's	1's A. Exp.	2's S's	2's A. Exp.	3's S's	3's A. Exp.	4's S's	4's A. Exp.	5's S's	5's A. Exp.	6's S's	6's A. Exp.	7's S's	7's A. Exp.
1st	66	142	21	26	12	7	9	1	2	1	2	—	—	—
2nd	47	152	23	31	21	5	7	4	9	1	6	—	1	—
3rd	40	146	23	30	20	9	18	1	3	—	2	—	—	—
4th	29	142	23	36	26	11	15	2	5	—	3	—	—	—
5th	55	149	23	29	23	11	12	4	4	—	1	—	1	—
6th	64	155	27	33	15	7	8	1	7	1	2	—	2	—
7th	102	141	30	44	15	6	6	1	2	—	1	—	1	—
8th	110	126	31	38	9	11	4	3	3	—	1	1	—	—
9th	119	146	34	38	12	6	4	—	2	—	—	—	—	—
10th	178	153	26	38	11	14	2	1	1	1	—	—	—	—
Totals	810	1,452	261	343	164	87	85	18	38	4	18	1	5	0

may be noted that two items classed as irrelevant intrusions were especially frequent. These were *auto* which was listed 21 times and *milk* which was listed 14 times. The former may have been a consequence of its phonemic similarity to the name *Otto* which was in the stimulus word list. This fact escaped detection until after the treatment of the data. We may further observe that the item *milk* may have derived from *milkman* which was also on the stimulus word list. Perhaps the items *auto* and *milk* should not be classed as completely irrelevant. They are irrelevant, however, to the categories of the stimulus words. The totals of all errors occurring in the successive deciles of items listed were as follows: 5, 13, 3, 15, 13, 20, 45, 32, 48, 60. It is apparent from these figures that the errors progressed at a positively accelerated rate. This trend is not changed when we subtract the irrelevant intrusions which were as follows for the successive deciles: 1, 6, 1, 3, 5, 7, 13, 6, 14, 19.

D. Discussion

The results of this study have indicated that subjects, when given a list of randomly arranged items will in their recall show a greater-than-chance tendency to group the items in clusters containing members of the same general category. This implies the operation of an organizing tendency. The results further show that the extent of clustering varies in an orderly manner as a function of the number of items already recalled. The nature of this change is indicated in Figure 1 where the ratios of repetition initially exceed chance expectation, rise to a maximum, and then drop to the level of randomness. The assumptions necessary to account for this progression present a challenging theoretical problem. The following analysis is proposed tentatively and with full realization of its speculative character. To begin with, the progressive change in the clustering tendency as revealed in our data is too complex to be attributed solely to a unitary property of dynamic interrelationships between verbal habits or solely to the habit strengths of the individual items. If a single factor were sufficient, the curve of clustering tendency should probably be monotonic, and this does not appear to be the case. We can generate the curve of clustering tendency, however, from a minimum of two monotonic functions. This in turn implies the necessity of a minimum of two basic assumptions. These assumptions should account for the probability of occurrence of individual items. At present the most plausible assumptions would appear to be the following: (*a*) Habit strength (*HS*) deriving from the reinforcement an item has received both before and during the experiment. (*b*) Relatedness increment (*RI*) which is a hypothetical increment added to habit strength. An item by virtue of its occurrence adds this increment to other items to which it is related. A tentative method for distinguishing between these two types of strength is as follows. It may be recalled that the subjects were instructed to draw demarcation lines at the end of each successive minute of the 10-minute period allowed for recall. It was thus possible to construct a curve based on the means of the cumulative totals of the items produced in successive one-minute periods throughout the period of recall. We may regard the reciprocals of the latent periods of the successive deciles of items as measures of the combined habit strengths and relatedness increments operating within these deciles. As Hull (3) has indicated, the latent period is an index of habit strength. The addition of the relatedness increment to habit strength should not invalidate the use of the latent period as an index of availability of items. The reciprocals for the successive deciles were as follows: 16.68, 6.26, 3.33, 2.00, 1.25, 0.81, 0.53, 0.33, 0.19, 0.10. The curve of these reciprocals is shown in Figure 2 where it is labelled *HS+RI*. We now make the assumption that the amount of clustering that takes place is proportional to the strengths of the verbal habits. It is also reasonable to as-

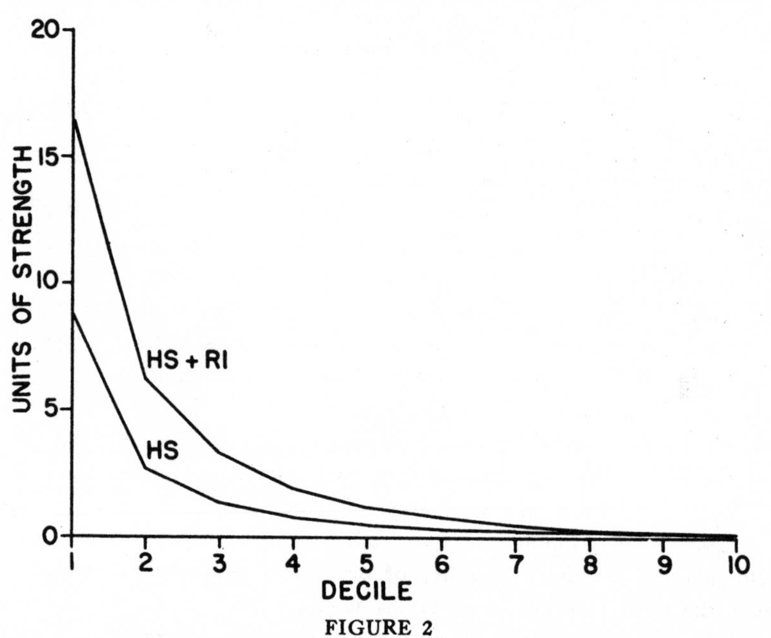

FIGURE 2

Curves of Hypothetical Strengths of Items in the Successive Deciles of Recall

The upper curve (*HS+RI*) represents habit strengths plus relatedness increments; the lower curve (*HS*) represents habit strengths alone.

sume that the habit strengths of the items are randomly distributed with respect to the categories of the items. Using the ratio of repetition as the index of clustering, we may take the step of assuming the equality of the following ratios:

$$\frac{HS+RI}{RRs} = \frac{HS}{RRc}. \tag{1}$$

In this formula HS is habit strength; RI is relatedness increment; RRs is the ratio of repetition for the decile obtained from the data of the subjects; RRc is the ratio of repetition derived by chance from the artificial experiment, and to which we assign the mean value of 0.24.

From the above formula we derive the equation for HS which is as follows:

$$HS = \frac{RRc(HS+RI)}{RRs}. \tag{2}$$

Applying this formula to the successive deciles of items, we obtain the following values for HS: 8.90, 2.68, 1.38, 0.79, 0.57, 0.38, 0.33, 0.23, 0.15, 0.11. These values for HS are plotted in Figure 2. Considering any pair of corresponding points on the curves for HS and $HS+RI$, we may describe what is assumed to happen when a subject produces an item. Suppose, for example, a hypothetical subject has just named an animal, and that he has reached the 5th decile of his productions. Competing for the next place is another animal-item with a strength ($HS+RI$) of 1.25 units and an item in a different category with an HS of 0.57 units. These strengths are supposedly subject to oscillation and their respective values may be regarded as probability weightings. It is more likely that the subject will list another animal-item than an item in a different category. The result is that the amount of clustering is raised from the chance-level of 0.24 to 0.53. Obviously HS and RI do not remain constant throughout the decile, but this does not alter the basic interpretation.

The assumptions of habit strength and relatedness increments can, it would seem, be meaningfully related to Hebb's (2) conception of cell assemblies. Within this framework full recognition is given to the necessity of stimulus-response constancy for the development of the habit strength of the assembly. On the other hand, the clustering tendency may derive from the overlap of assembly action.

This discussion may appropriately include mention of the somewhat surprising finding that the clusters made up of two similar items occurred at a lower-than-chance frequency throughout the lists. This is shown in Table 5. For the present we may venture only a partial explanation. The clustering tendency may have been so strong that the larger clusters precluded the occurrence of the small ones.

The possibilities for further research based on the measurement of the clustering tendency are extensive. There is a need for further study of the nature of the clustering tendency and the assumptions that may adequately account for it. Such research should be useful as already indicated for providing additional information on the nature of organization as it operates in higher mental processes. Among the more specific problems to which the method appears applicable are the development of verbal behavior, individual differences, consequences of emotion and frustration, consequences of mental disorders assumed to affect organization in higher mental processes, recall of different types of material, and influence of learning.

E. Summary

1. Subjects were presented a randomized list of 60 items made up of 15 each of animals, names, professions, and vegetables. Immediately following the presentation, the subjects listed serially the items they were able to recall.

2. Analysis of the data from 100 subjects on the basis of three separate indices showed that the items were clustered in groups of similar categories appreciably beyond chance as indicated by a parallel artificial experiment.

3. The clustering tendency changed with the serial positions of the items on the lists in a way to indicate that it was initially above chance expectation, rose to a maximum, and then declined to randomness.

4. The progressive change in the clustering tendency is explained on the basis of two assumptions, namely, habit strength and clustering increment.

References

1. Bousfield, W. A., & Sedgewick, C. H. W. An analysis of sequences of restricted associative responses. *J. Gen. Psychol.*, 1944, **30**, 149-165.
2. Hebb, D. O. The Organization of Behavior. New York: Wiley, 1949. Pp. 335.
3. Hull, C. L. Principles of Behavior. New York: Appleton-Century, 1943. Pp. 422.
4. Thorndike, E. L., & Lorge, I. The Teacher's Word Book of 30,000 Words. New York: Columbia University, 1944. Pp. 274.

Department of Psychology
University of Connecticut
Storrs, Connecticut

ARTICLE 2

ASSOCIATIVE CLUSTERING DURING RECALL [1]

JAMES J. JENKINS AND WALLACE A. RUSSELL
University of Minnesota

Much human behavior is inextricably associated with verbal processes. Adequate theoretical accounts of such behavior cannot be expected until the role of language is better understood. This understanding is in itself a long-range goal, to be gained by careful analysis of the complexities of language and the assiduous gathering of basic empirical data. The preliminary study reported here was undertaken as a step in this direction.

Investigations of verbal behavior have frequently encountered the intricate problem of context. This problem, of course, may be analyzed into a large number of factors. One aspect which has received attention is the tendency for words to appear in meaningfully related clusters even in the absence of the usual syntactically structured communication situation.

Bousfield, for example, has noted clustering of words during the production of discrete or individual words (1, 2) and has dealt with this phenomenon in experimental settings. In a recent experiment (3) he showed that a randomized list of words drawn from four categories (animals, vegetables, names, professions) tends to be recalled in clusters of related (i.e., same category) words. He postulates a "relatedness increment" of habit strength to account for the clustering.

The writers have also observed tendencies for discretely produced words to appear in groups or clusters. This typically occurs even when experimental instructions require the subject to say individual words and avoid sentences, phrases or counting.

Among the possible determinants of clustering as observed in these experiments is simple word-association strength. In the present study an effort was made to determine the extent to which clustering during recall is a function of such associations.

Word-association techniques have a long history of use in psychology. Typically a stimulus word is provided by the experimenter (*E*) and the subject (*S*) is asked to respond with the first word that occurs to him. Commonality of response has been so pronounced for certain stimulus words that it has been possible to develop cultural norms from which one can predict individual responses with fair accuracy (6, 7, 8). The frequency with which a particular stimulus word is followed by a given response word is considered to be an index of the associative strength of the paired words within the norm group. The predictive utility of this index when associations are elicited in somewhat different situations is not well known. There is some evidence that objects or pictures substituted for the stimulus words will evoke responses similar to those made to the stimulus words in the test (5). However, the generality of these associative phenomena when the stimulus is produced by *S* himself rather than by *E* has not been systematically investigated.

During the recall of discrete words, *S* might be expected to respond to his own verbal production as if these stimuli originated from an external source. It might be hypothesized that the associative phenomena noted in the classical word-association test would occur during the recall of word lists containing associatively related words. The clustering of words during recall thus would be expected to be, at least partially, a function of culturally determined associative strengths.

Four hypotheses emerge from this line of thinking. First, associative pairs should occur more frequently during recall than nonsystematically selected word pairs. This amounts to saying that word pairs known to occur with high frequency in word association tests will appear more often than randomly determined pairs.

Second, reverse associations should occur more frequently than nonsystematically determined pairs. That is, the response word of a strong association would be expected through its common occurrence (perhaps in varied sequence) with its stimulus word in everyday language to have some tendency to elicit its own stimulus word. This should make the frequency of response-stimulus

[1] This study is part of a larger series of studies of verbal behavior being conducted at the University of Minnesota. The series is being sponsored by the Office of Naval Research (Contract No. N8onr 66216) under its policy of encouraging basic research.

Reprinted with permission of the authors and the publisher, the American Psychological Association. The article appeared originally in the *Journal of Abnormal and Social Psychology*, 1952, 47, 818–821.

pairing somewhat greater than random pairings.

Third, forward associative pairs should occur more frequently than reverse associative pairs. Stimulus words in many association tests are selected because they show high frequencies of association with a given response. The presence of the stimulus-response order in a word list often implies that associations in that direction are greater than in the reverse direction. Little systematic research has been done with the frequencies of reversed associations since occasions for measuring such associations have seldom arisen. It would be expected that on the average forward associations would be at greater strength than reverse associations.

Fourth, persons who show high commonality of response (6) in the typical free association situation should demonstrate associative clustering in recall to a greater extent than persons who show low commonality. A high commonality index for an individual indicates the presence of many popular associative bonds. This should lead to a stronger tendency for such an individual to recall appropriate pairs of words.

The first three of these hypotheses were tested in the framework of the present experiment.

Procedure

The procedure in this study was similar to Bousfield's (3) with the exception that the word list used was made up of randomly presented stimulus and response words from the Kent-Rosanoff association test.

The pairs of stimulus and response words were selected from the list primarily on the basis of frequency. It was necessary that neither the stimulus word nor the response word of any pair be the same as the stimulus or response of any other pair. It was felt that a list of approximately 50 words would be neither too difficult nor too easy for the recall task. The 40 most frequent pairs in Schellenberg's (7) normative data for college students were selected, and subsequent eliminations on the basis of overlapping stimulus and response words reduced the list to 24 pairs. The lowest frequency pair occurred 288 times in Schellenberg's 925 *Ss*. In those cases where the same pairs appeared in the test in reverse order (e.g., black-white, white-black) the pair with the highest frequency was the pair analyzed as a forward association in the experiment. The words were randomized and the list was checked to avoid the contiguous appearance of any pair of words in the forward stimulus-response order.

Table 1 lists the pairs used. The number following each word indicates its position in the randomized list.

The word list was presented to two groups of *Ss*. Group 1 ($N=39$) was an introductory class in laboratory psychology. Group 2 ($N=62$) was an advanced class in the psychology of individual differences. The two classes were chosen for independent replication.

The *Ss* were told that they were participating in a formal research project. After they were provided with sheets of composition paper, they were given the following instructions:

I am going to read a rather long list of words. I want you to listen carefully and when I am through we will see how many you can remember.

TABLE 1

Kent-Rosanoff Pairs Used in Experiment *

Stimulus	Response	Stimulus	Response
Table (37)	Chair (17)	Eagle (24)	Bird (11)
Man (30)	Woman (18)	Lamp (33)	Light (32)
Mountain (1)	Hill (21)	Cottage (22)	House (4)
Black (36)	White (12)	Ocean (45)	Water (7)
Mutton (44)	Sheep (16)	Long (29)	Short (3)
Slow (46)	Fast (6)	Square (31)	Round (38)
Rough (25)	Smooth (40)	Butter (20)	Bread (8)
Carpet (5)	Rug (47)	Lion (13)	Animal (26)
High (14)	Low ** (27)	Bed (35)	Sleep (43)
Sour (41)	Sweet (34)	Tobacco (2)	Smoke (9)
Cabbage (23)	Vegetable (28)	Scissors (42)	Cut (10)
Hard (19)	Soft (48)	Blossom (15)	Flower (39)

* Number in parentheses refers to position of the word in the randomized list.

** In class 1 this was misread as *lion* so that in effect this class had only 23 pairs from the Kent-Rosanoff list.

The order in which the words are given or recalled is not important, but the *number* you will be able to recall is. That is, you can remember the words in any order as long as you remember as many as possible. Since the list is long, you are not expected to remember all the words. Just do the best you can. I will explain the exact procedure for the recall test as soon as I have finished the list. Are there any questions?

Listen carefully and remember all the words you can: here is the list. (Here the list was read at the rate of approximately one word per second.) That ends the list. Now take the piece of lined paper and a pencil. Do not write anything. When I give you the signal start writing as many of the words as you can remember. Write down the left-hand column of the paper. Put one word to a line, and if you complete the left hand column, start down the right-hand side with a second column. At regular intervals I will ask you to draw a line beneath the last word you have written. Do this clearly and then go right on down the page. Make a clear separate line every time I say that. Write down the words in any order that they occur to you.

Any questions? Ready, go!

After working five minutes at the recall task, *Ss* were asked to raise their hands if they had produced any words in the preceding 30 seconds. They then resumed the recall task immediately. This question was repeated every 30 seconds until no hands were raised. In the first group this occurred at seven and one-half minutes. Analysis of the data for both groups was accordingly based on this time.

In order to create a serious experimental atmosphere, the proceedings of the entire session were recorded and this fact was brought to the attention of the *Ss*.[2]

The results of the recall test were analyzed for (*a*) the number of responses, (*b*) the number of forward associations, (*c*) the number of reverse associations, and (*d*) the number of arbitrary, nonsystematic pairs.

Each occurrence of a stimulus word which was followed immediately by its response word was called a forward association. Each response word which was followed immediately by its stimulus word was called a reverse association. Arbitrary pairs were defined as those instances in which a stimulus word was followed immediately, not by its own response word, but by the response word of the pair succeeding it in Table 1 (e.g., table-woman, man-hill, etc.). There seemed no reason to expect systematic associations between words so selected. It was felt that such arbitrary pairs would provide an estimate of chance pairings.

Results

The major results relative to the hypotheses to be tested are presented in Tables 2 and 3.

The first hypothesis was that forward associative pairs would occur more frequently during recall than would arbitrarily selected word pairs. This proved to be the case. For class 1, the mean number of associative pairs was 3.41, while the mean number of arbitrary pairs was 0.26. Using a t test for related measures this difference proved to be significant far beyond the .001 level of confidence. The corresponding differences for class 2 reached a similar high level of confidence. It is obvious that in this situation associative strength is a factor influencing the clustering of words.

The second hypothesis was that reverse associative pairs would occur more frequently than arbitrary pairs. Here again appropriate t tests proved the mean differences to be significant far beyond the .001 level in both of the classes tested.

The third hypothesis was that forward associations would occur more frequently

TABLE 2

Mean and Standard Deviation of Relevant Variables in Class 1

Variable	Mean	*SD*
Forward Associations	3.41	2.05
Reverse Associations	2.85	2.01
Arbitrary Associations	0.26	0.44
Total Words Recalled	24.64	5.83

[2] Recordings on Audograph disks are available on loan from the writers.

TABLE 3

Mean and Standard Deviation of Relevant Variables in Class 2

Variable	Mean	*SD*
Forward Associations	3.61	2.53
Reverse Associations	2.47	2.23
Arbitrary Associations	.14	.31
Total Words Recalled	23.59	7.25

than reverse associations. In class 1 this difference was in the expected direction but was of only borderline significance ($t=1.81$, $.05<p<.10$). In class 2, however, the corresponding difference yielded a t of 3.37 which, of course, is significant beyond the .01 level. Taken together, it seems reasonable to conclude that the third hypothesis is also confirmed.

The importance of associative strengths is clearly evident when the combined forward and reverse associations are considered. In class 1 there are 6.26 such associations on the average and 6.08 in class 2. Since each association consists of two words, it may be seen that these associations account for slightly more than 50 per cent of all words recalled.

During the analysis of the data for class 1, it became apparent that there were sex differences in the frequency of forward associations. This difference in frequency was significant at the .02 level, with females showing the greater number of associations. This was associated with a higher absolute level of total word production of females, although differences in total production between the sexes did not reach a high level of significance ($p=.10$). In class 2, however, differences in total production reached significance at the .01 level while the differences in number of associations showed only a slight predominance in favor of the females ($.10<p<.20$). Taken together, the results from the two classes would seem to warrant the conclusion that the females recalled significantly more words and produced significantly more forward associations than the males.

It is, of course, possible that the sex differences in forward associations are a direct result of the fact that the females recalled more words and thus had greater opportunity to produce associations. However, it may be observed that in class 2, where the difference in total production is greater, the difference in associations is less significant than in class 1. This seems to imply that the relationship is not a perfect one. In order to determine whether or not differences in associations would persist when there were no differences in total production, an analysis of sex differences was made with the number of words recalled held constant at the level of the *S* recalling the fewest words (this amounted to 15 words in class 1 and 10 words in class 2). In class 1 this procedure almost eliminated any differences in associations between the sexes ($.50<p<.60$), but in class 2 the females still showed a significantly greater number of associations ($p=.01$). While combined probabilities would convincingly support the conclusion that females produce more associations even when total word production is held constant, it would seem safest, in the absence of replication, to state this only tentatively.

Discussion

While the sex differences in associative clustering were not anticipated, their appearance is perhaps explicable. Schellenberg (7) has shown that for the Kent-Rosanoff word list female college students show a significantly greater commonality of response than do male students. If our fourth hypothesis (not tested in this experiment) is correct, the sex differences found here would be expected. This hypothesis states that persons who show high commonality of response should demonstrate associative clustering in recall to a greater extent than persons who show low commonality. Studies are now under way to examine in detail the relationships between commonality of response and associative clustering in recall.

While it should be possible to manipulate average association strengths by using groups of students with different commonality indices, this is not the only way in which associative strength might be varied. Another approach would involve the use of special word lists in which the response words were those known to occur at relatively low frequencies. For example, a list using the same stimulus words as those used here but substituting secondary or tertiary response words for the primary response words should accomplish this end. With the reduction in average associative strength, the amount of associative clustering should be reduced.

Of course it is recognized that associative clustering is but one of many factors determining the order of recall. In our protocols the effects of serial order, clang associations, etc., were obvious. Nevertheless, in this situation it can be seen that once the *S* has recalled a stimulus word, the probability that a culturally frequent response will follow is far above chance. The fact that an *S* so responds to his own verbal production is of clear relevance to current formulations (4) which stress the importance of response-produced stimulation in behavior determination.

Summary

Two psychology classes recalled a word list comprised of stimulus and response pairs from the Kent-Rosanoff word list. The words were presented in random order. Both groups showed a highly significant tendency to recall the Kent-Rosanoff pairs together and in the stimulus-response sequence. Reversed associations (recall in the response-stimulus sequence) occurred significantly more than chance pairings but significantly less than the forward sequence. Females recalled more words and produced more forward associations than males. In one class females produced more forward associations even when total production was held constant.

The results are interpreted as demonstrating that associative strength is a factor in word clustering during recall.

References

1. Bousfield, W. A., & Sedgewick, C. H. W. An experimental analysis of sequences of restricted verbal associative responses. *J. gen. Psychol.*, 1944, **30**, 149–165.
2. Bousfield, W. A. An empirical study of the production of affectively toned items. *J. gen. Psychol.*, 1944, **30**, 205–215.
3. Bousfield, W. A. Frequency and availability measures in language behavior. A paper presented as part of a symposium at Amer. Psychol. Ass., Chicago, September, 1951.
4. Dollard, J., & Miller, N. E. *Personality and psychotherapy*. New York: McGraw-Hill, 1950.
5. Karwoski, T. F., Gramlich, F. W., & Arnott, P. Psychological studies in semantics: I. Free association reactions to words, drawings and objects. *J. soc. Psychol.*, 1944, **20**, 233–247.
6. Kent, G. H., & Rosanoff, A. J. A study of association in insanity. *Amer. J. Insanity*, 1910, **67**, 37–96, 317–390.
7. Schellenberg, P. E. A group free association test for college students. Unpublished doctor's thesis, Univer. of Minnesota, 1930.
8. Woodrow, H., & Lowell, F. Children's association frequency tables. *Psychol. Monogr.*, 1916, **22**, No. 5 (Whole No. 97).

Received January 21, 1952.

ARTICLE 3

VERBAL CONCEPT LEARNING AS A FUNCTION OF INSTRUCTIONS AND DOMINANCE LEVEL

BENTON J. UNDERWOOD AND JACK RICHARDSON

Northwestern University[1]

The task of *S* in the present research is that of learning how objects are related. We are concerned with two variables that influence the rate at which such learning occurs. The stimuli used consist of names of common objects. When such a stimulus is presented to *S*, it could elicit a number of different verbal responses. For example, if the stimulus word *tomato* were presented (with appropriate instructions) we might expect a series of responses such as "fruit," "red," "round," "soup," "sauce," and so on. Thus, each *S* may have a hierarchy of responses to such a stimulus, the hierarchy presumably reflecting differences in response strengths of different responses. Different *S*s may be expected to have different hierarchies to some stimuli; to others there may be not only high agreement among responses elicited but the response strengths may be highly comparable.

In the present task *S* is presented with names of four common objects and he is to discover what single characteristic can be used to describe all four of them. For example, *brick*, *cherry*, *tomato*, and *lips* can all be described as "red." We have discussed elsewhere (**2**) the rather simple proposition that concept learning (as described above) would occur more quickly the stronger the common descriptive response to the stimuli. Thus, if "red" were high in the hierarchy of responses to each of these four stimuli, learning should take place more rapidly than if it were low in the hierarchy. In the present study the strength of a given response to a stimulus, relative to the strength of other responses, is called ***response dominance***. An arithmetic definition of dominance of response to each stimulus used will be given in the procedure section. In the experiments to be reported, the effect of three levels of response dominance is studied.

As suggested above, with relatively unrestricted instructions a number of different classes of descriptive responses would be elicited by verbal stimuli. That is, with free-association instructions, *S* might give opposites, functional associations, classificatory responses, synonyms, and so on. For compelling practical reasons (which are too detailed to set forth here) we have found it necessary to

[1] This work was done under Contract N7onr-45008, Project NR 154-057, between Northwestern University and the Office of Naval Research.

Reprinted with permission of the authors and the publisher, the American Psychological Association. The article appeared originally in the *Journal of Experimental Psychology*, 1956, **51**, 229–238.

restrict sharply the class of descriptive responses by which learning of relationships among objects is studied. More specifically, we are studying the learning of relationships among objects when these relationships are based on what we call sense impressions. By this we mean relationships based on rather immediate sense data. Thus, the descriptive characteristics refer to size, shape, color, smell, feel, and so on. Since our concept-learning task is limited to a particular class of similarities among objects, it becomes quite apparent that the nature of the instructions to *S* would be an important variable. At one extreme we could actually give *S* the specific characteristics by which the objects go together. At the other we could simply tell *S* what concepts are and let him discover completely how the objects are related (according to our scheme). In spite of the obviousness of this instructional variable, we have manipulated it in the present study for three reasons. First, a demonstration of the obvious has never been made. Secondly, we wanted to know something about the magnitude of differences in learning speed produced by different instructions so that subsequent experiments could be planned more intelligently. Finally, with unrestricted instructions, we can study the process by which *S* discovers the particular class of responses required by the task as well as the particular responses within the class.

In summary, the present research is a study of concept learning as a function of (*a*) three different dominance levels of responses to verbal stimuli, and (*b*) three different sets of instructions which reflect different amounts of information concerning the nature of the concept to be learned.

Procedure

Materials.—The words used as stimuli were concrete nouns. They were taken from a list of 213 words which had been subjected to a scaling procedure to provide a measure of dominance level of various responses elicited by each stimulus. Details of the scaling procedure have been presented elsewhere (**3**), so only the critical points will be presented here. In the final procedure the nouns were presented, one at a time, to 153 *Ss* under instructions to give the first sense-impression response which occurred to them upon seeing the stimulus word. The delineation of what was meant by a sense impression was accomplished through instructions followed by a series of practice words. When *Ss* were familiar with the class of associations required, additional practice words were presented at an increasing rate of speed until the rate reached 6 sec. per word, the rate used for the experimental words.

The 153 *Ss* were run as seven groups, varying in size from 13 to 30. Each group had a different randomized order of the words in an effort to avoid bias resulting from response sets. The words were flashed on the screen and simultaneously pronounced. The *S* was instructed to write down the first sense impression which occurred to him. At the end of the 6-sec. interval another word was flashed, and so on. To each word, then, we had a maximum of 153 responses, although we did not always get a response from all *Ss* within the short interval allowed. Responses to each word were then categorized so that responses having the same general meaning, e.g., "small," "little," "tiny," were all put in the same category. The percentage of total responses in each category was determined. Categories for a response were maintained if 5% or more of the total frequency fell in that category; otherwise, the responses were placed in a miscellaneous category. An example may make this clear. To the stimulus word *cigar*, 152 responses were given. Of this total 61 (40%) said "smelly" (or equivalent), 40 (26%) said "brown," and 21 (14%) said "long." A total of 19 (12%) responses fell into the "miscellaneous" category. Dominance level of responses is defined directly in terms of percentage frequency of a particular category of response. In the above example "smelly" is the most dominant and "long" the least dominant (of those given by 5% or more of the *Ss*).

It can be seen that for each of the 213 words we have the frequency with which a particular sense-impression description was used by *Ss*. It can be seen, furthermore, that somewhat diverse stimuli may be described by the same sense impression. For example, the response "soft" was given to 35 different stimuli with 5% or greater frequency. Thus, this response was given to *banana*, *bread*, *belly*, *flannel*, *jellyfish*, *lips*, *custard*, *moccasin*, *pillow*, *sheep*, *skin*, and so on. In short, all of these objects are related because they were all described as "soft." In the concept-learning task we have chosen a limited number of such stimuli, and *S* is to discover how they are related.

Construction of lists.—The complete list of 213 words and responses to them have been published elsewhere (**3**). There are a number of rules we followed in constructing the lists for studying concept recognition. Some of these rules were purely arbitrary, while others were required in order to isolate the dominance variable. We chose first to work with six different concepts, namely, *round*, *small*, *white*, *smelly*, *soft*, and *big*. Each of these concepts was represented at what we will call high, medium, and low dominance levels. Thus, there is a total of 18 concepts on which we have learning data.

To make the task a reasonable one we arbitrarily decided that a single list would consist of 24 nouns, representing six concepts. Each concept would have four examples (instances, illustrations), and *S* was to learn to respond to these four examples in the same way. Three independent lists of 24 nouns each were constructed. Since six independent concepts were involved in each list, our 18 concepts are accounted for.

Certain considerations led us to vary dominance level within each list rather than to have a separate list for each of the three levels of dominance. For each noun we knew the frequency of various responses. However, a noun having a highly dominant response would have only a few distracting or interfering tendencies, and these should be weak, relatively. On the other hand, a response to a noun which we were using as an example of a concept of low dominance would have one or more very strong distracting or interfering tendencies. In short, number and strength of interferences and dominance level are inversely related. Now it would seem that if dominance level as defined here was directly related to concept-learning rate, the explanation could be based on the fact that high-dominant concepts had less interference than did low. Indeed, this is essentially our interpretation of the results. However, we could not place all the high-dominant concepts in one list, the medium in another, and the low in a third, and expect to get a clear interpretation. It will be remembered that the response given by *S* in the scaling procedure were sense impressions, and many nouns elicited the same sense impressions. This commonality in response was necessary in order to obtain the materials for the concept-learning studies. But, if we chose a given noun for a low-dominance list, responses to it other than the one we were calling correct may be "correct" for another concept in the list. For example, assume word A elicits response X with 15% frequency and response Y with 70% frequency. Assume further that we use A in a list as an example of a low-dominant concept X. We also choose another word, B, to which the correct concept response is Y. Thus, Y will be correct for one word and incorrect for another. We speak of this as overlap of response tendencies among concepts within a list. In our materials we cannot avoid this completely; therefore, we have to equalize this overlap. Such equalization cannot be accomplished if we put all of the high-dominant concepts in one list and low in another.

In each list we have four instances of each of two high-dominant concepts, two of medium, and two of low. Each level of dominance for a given concept appears in a different list. Thus, four instances of *round* as a high-dominant response appear in one list, four instances of *round* as a medium-dominant response in another, and four instances of *round* as a low-dominant response in a third. Since no *S* learned more than one list, we have no biases based on familiarity. The words used in each of the three lists appear in Table 1. In Table 1 we have grouped the words forming a concept although they were not presented to *S* in this manner. We have also indicated the concept involved and the mean dominance level.

Differences in dominance level can be seen by reference to Table 1. To each word in Table 1 we know the frequency with which sense-impression responses have been elicited. To the stimulus *barrel* 72% of the *S*s said "round"; to *doughnut* 70% said "round," to *knob* 68%, and to *balloon* 55%. The average of these four values is 66% as entered in the table. These values may be contrasted with those for the low dominance as seen in List 3. To the word *snail* the response "round" occurred 14% of the time; to *cherry* 14%, to *grapefruit* 12%, and to *skull*, 11%. The average is 13%.

We have said that dominance level of an arbitrarily chosen response to a noun and frequency and strength of *other* responses (having at least 5% frequency) to that noun are inversely related. The frequency measures show that for all six high-dominant concepts combined there were 25 *other* responses given with greater than 5% frequency. For the medium concepts the value is 48, and for the low, 53. The relationship apparently is not linear when expressed in frequency terms. However, the strength measures give somewhat greater linearity. If we take the average strength (average percent

TABLE 1

CONCEPT-LEARNING LISTS WITH CONCEPT AND AVERAGE DOMINANCE LEVEL INDICATED

List 1		List 2		List 3	
Noun	Concept and Dominance Level	Noun	Concept and Dominance Level	Noun	Concept and Dominance Level
Barrel Doughnut Knob Balloon	"round" high (66%)	Bracelet Derby Platter Pill	"round" medium (31%)	Snail Cherry Grapefruit Skull	"round" low (13%)
Village Minnow Crumb Germ	"small" high (75%)	Bungalow Capsule Mouse Pollen	"small" medium (45%)	Earthworm Closet Freckle Tack	"small" low (16%)
Bone Collar Frost Lint	"white" medium (37.5%)	Baseball Fang Paste Sugar	"white" low (12%)	Milk Chalk Snow Teeth	"white" high (76.5%)
Garlic Gasoline Pine Sulphur	"smelly" medium (51%)	Daffodil Goat Gym Sauerkraut	"smelly" low (19%)	Ether Garbage Gardenia Manure	"smelly" high (74.5%)
Custard Lips Moss Sheep	"soft" low (21.5%)	Bed Chamois Fur Pillow	"soft" high (76.5%)	Bread Flannel Jellyfish Moccasin	"soft" medium (42%)
Camel Forest Hospital Limousine	"big" low (15%)	Auditorium City Elephant Mansion	"big" high (80.5%)	Boulder Gorilla Ocean Zoo	"big" medium (38%)

frequency) of *other* responses, we obtain the values of 8.3%, 19%, and 31% for high, medium, and low concepts, respectively.

Three other characteristics of the lists constructed must be indicated. We have kept the total number of *other* responses fairly constant for the three lists, the values being 44, 43, and 39 for the three lists in order. The equalization of interference tendencies *among* concepts, as discussed earlier, was fairly successful, there being 8 instances of overlap in List 1, 10 in List 2, and 8 in List 3. Finally, in choosing the words for a given concept from the master list, we allowed no common *other* responses among the four words. Thus, while ***village, minnow, crumb,*** and ***germ*** all had the common description of "small" given to them, no other common descriptive terms applied to even two of the four words.

In summary: there are three lists, each list having six concepts to be learned, two each of high, medium, and low dominance. Taking all six high-dominant concepts into account, the average dominance level is 74.8%; for medium, 40.7%, and for low, 16.1%.

Presentation of the lists.—The lists were presented at a 4-sec. rate on a Hull-type memory drum. Three different orders of each list were used, being random except for the restriction that at least one other word must separate the presentation of two words which were examples of the same concept. A 4-sec. interval occurred between each presentation of the list. The lists were presented for 20 trials irrespective of performance attained.

Most concept studies in the past have required *S* to give some neutral response to indicate concept learning. Thus, a nonsense syllable might be used as an indicator that *S* knew the concept. A recent study (1) has shown that such a procedure may add a very large component of rote learning to the task. That is to say, *S* may discover rather quickly how the stimuli "go together" but it may take him considerable time to learn the nonsense syllable which is used to indicate that he has learned how they go together. In order to avoid this rote component we had *S* respond with the concept name itself. For example, to the four stimuli *village*, *minnow*, *crumb*, and *germ*, he would respond with "small" if he correctly recognized the concept.

Instructions to *S* indicated that he was to give a response to each word during the 4-sec. interval even on the first trial. After each response *E* said "right" or "wrong." All responses were recorded. The *E* used reasonable flexibility in deciding whether a response was right or wrong. Preliminary studies, however, allowed us to set up responses which were to be called "right" so that it was rare that *E* had to exercise judgment at the time *S* responded. The basic criterion, of course, for a response being called "right" was that the response given must reflect the characteristic required.

Subjects.—A total of 144 *S*s served in the experiment. These *S*s were taking elementary psychology and on this characteristic were comparable to the 153 used originally to scale the words. The 144 *S*s were divided into three groups of 48 each. Each of the three groups received different instructions (see below). Within each group of 48 there were three subgroups of 16 *S*s, each subgroup being presented with a different list. The *S*s were assigned in rotation to the lists in the order of their appearance at the laboratory. That is to say, the first *S* had List 1, the second List 2, the third List 3, the fourth List 1, and so on. It should be mentioned again that lists as such were not intended to be a variable. Our intent was to construct lists of as near equal difficulty as possible. The use of three lists allowed us to test the influence of dominance level for a single concept since all three levels of a single concept, e.g., "round," were represented when all three lists are considered.

Instructions.—Each of the three groups of 48 *S*s received instructions which differed in certain critical aspects. These three groups of *S*s were not run concurrently and we do not know that they are comparable in ability. However, all came from the courses in elementary psychology under the same system for obtaining *S*s and there is no reason to expect large sampling differences. The differences in performance as a function of instructions are so great that we do not think it is likely that these differences can be attributed exclusively to sampling bias.

The three sets of instructions differed as to the amount of information given *S* concerning the nature of the concept. First, however, we will give the essential points in the instructions which were *common* to all three groups. The following four points give the instructions in abbreviated form.

1. There are 24 nouns on the tape; four of these can be described by the same word, four others by a different word, and so on.
2. Each noun will be presented for 4 sec. and you must give a response to each one within the 4-sec. period. I will tell you "right" or "wrong" after each response.
3. We will go through the list time after time and you are to give a response to each word every time it comes up even though you know the response is wrong or even if you have been getting it right consistently.
4. If you learn the list completely you will be responding with only six different words since each response is correct for four of the nouns. These are six distinctly different words and are not in any sense synonyms.

The *unrestricted instructions* (UR) told *S* nothing about the nature of the concepts to be learned. The *S*s were instructed to respond in a free-association fashion to the words on the first trial. They were further told that it would be a good idea to vary their responses on the second trial from those given on the first, on the third from those on the second, and so on, until they started to get some responses correct.

In the *partially restricted* (PR) instructions *S*s were told the class of responses needed to form the concepts. It is probably more correct to say that *S* arrived at an understanding of the class through appropriate questioning by *E*.

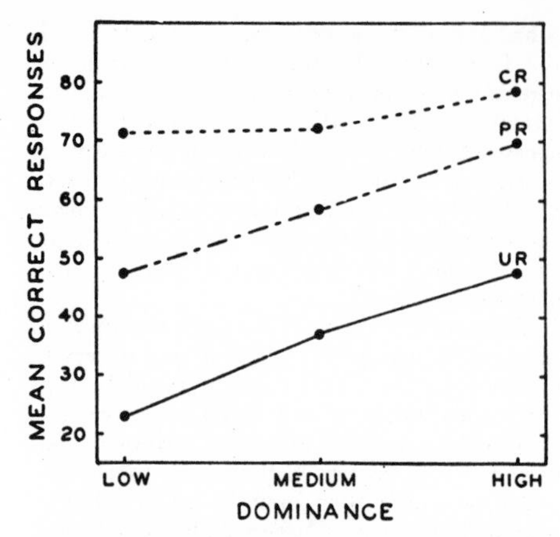

Fig. 1. Mean total correct responses over 20 trials as a function of dominance level and instructions. UR refers to unrestricted instructions, PR, partially restricted, and CR, completely restricted.

The *S* was asked about simple ways of describing common objects. The *E* prodded *S* on this matter until *S* gave sense-impression descriptions. Furthermore, we did not allow *S* to give only one or two such sense impressions; rather, we forced him to give a number of these so that a set for a particular type of sense impression did not occur. From this procedure, presumably, *S* knew the class of responses needed but did not know the particular responses within the class. It can be seen that these *S*s were instructed in the same manner as were *S*s who originally scaled the words.

In the *completely restricted* (CR) instructions *S* actually was given the six responses which were correct. He was allowed to study these until he could repeat them. Furthermore, he was given the card on which the six responses were printed and kept it in front of him during concept learning so that he could refer to it if necessary.

Results and Discussion

Over-all performance.—All *S*s were given 20 trials. The first performance measure to be considered is the mean total correct responses given on all 20 trials for the nine conditions (three dominance levels against three sets of instructions). It will be remembered that three different lists of concepts were involved, each list having two concepts at each dominance level. For this analysis performance scores for all three lists have been combined so that at each dominance level there are six different concepts involved.

Figure 1 shows the influence of the two variables. As dominance level increases, performance (number of correct responses) increases. And, the greater the amount of information given *S* by instructions, the better the performance. The statistical analysis has provided some difficulty. Variance within each instructional level UR and PR is homogeneous, but differs so much between instructional levels that we have found no way to adjust for this. Dominance within each instructional level is highly significant. However, there is a suggestion in Fig. 1 that as more information is given *S* by instructions, the influence of dominance level is reduced. Because of the great heterogeneity of variance resulting from different instructions, we have found no satisfactory way to evaluate statistically the suggested trends toward interaction. Ignoring heterogeneity, the *F* falls far short of significance.

First-trial performance.—Probably the clearest way of assessing the

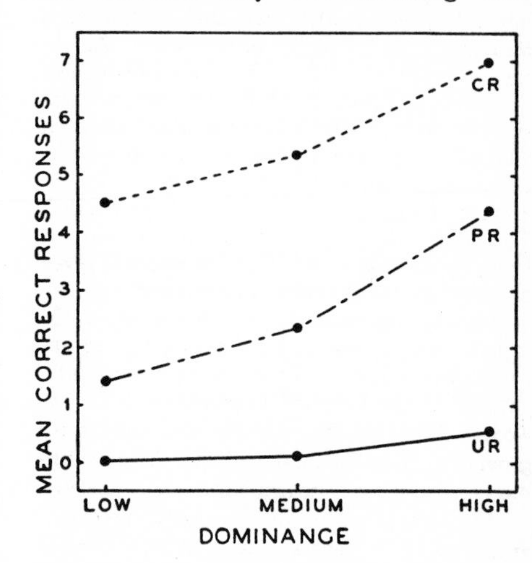

Fig. 2. Mean total correct responses on Trial 1 as a function of dominance level and instructions.

validity of our dominance measure is to examine performance on the first trial. On this trial, within the limits imposed by the instructions, the *S*s are responding most clearly on the basis of strength of response tendencies which they "brought" to the laboratory. That is, the differential reinforcement procedure has less influence on this first trial than on subsequent trials. The results for the first trial are shown in Fig. 2, where it is again clear that both variables are highly effective.

Concept attainment.—The data presented thus far give no direct evidence on attainment of a particular concept. That is, nothing has been asserted about the rate of acquisition of all four examples defining a given concept. Since the basic results when viewed in this manner are essentially the same as those presented above, and since the trends are quite comparable for the three sets of instructions, we are presenting the data for all three instructions combined. The data are shown in Table 2. We have determined on which trial the correct response was given to all four examples of a concept, and have defined this trial as the point of concept attainment. Pooling the data for all *S*s, we have indicated the number of times the concept was attained on Trials 1–5, 6–10, 11–15, and 16–20. There is a final column indicating the number of concepts not attained in the 20 trials. There are 144 *S*s, each *S* being presented two concepts at each dominance level for a total of 288. Table 2 shows that as dominance level increases, number of concepts attained on Trials 1–5 increases and number of concepts not attained in the 20 trials decreases. In general, then, this measure of performance shows quite the same picture as did measure relating number of correct responses to dominance level.

TABLE 2

NUMBER OF CONCEPTS ATTAINED ON SUCCESSIVE BLOCKS OF FIVE TRIALS FOR EACH DOMINANCE LEVEL FOR ALL INSTRUCTIONS COMBINED

Dominance	Trials				Not Attained
	1–5	6–10	11–15	16–20	
Low	92	55	50	16	75
Medium	118	59	40	31	40
High	188	40	25	13	22

Dominance level and individual concepts.—It will be remembered that each particular concept, e.g., *white*, was represented at all three levels of dominance, each level in a different list. The question may be raised as to how perfectly related are dominance level and performance for separate concepts. With the partially restricted instructions, instructions which are essentially the same as those given *S*s for the scaling procedure from which dominance levels were derived, the alignment between dominance and learning is perfect for all six concepts. That is to say, for each of the six concepts considered separately, the total correct responses given during the 20 trials was directly related to dominance level. For the unrestricted instructions and for the completely restricted instructions, there were minor reversals in the ordering. When the results for all three sets of instructions are pooled, the ordering is perfect, as shown in Fig. 3. In each case, fewer correct responses are given for low-dominance concepts than for medium, and fewer for medium than for high. Nevertheless, it can be seen that there are appreciable differences among concepts at a given level of dominance. The implication of this is that there are other factors involved in learning in addition to dominance level. Certain

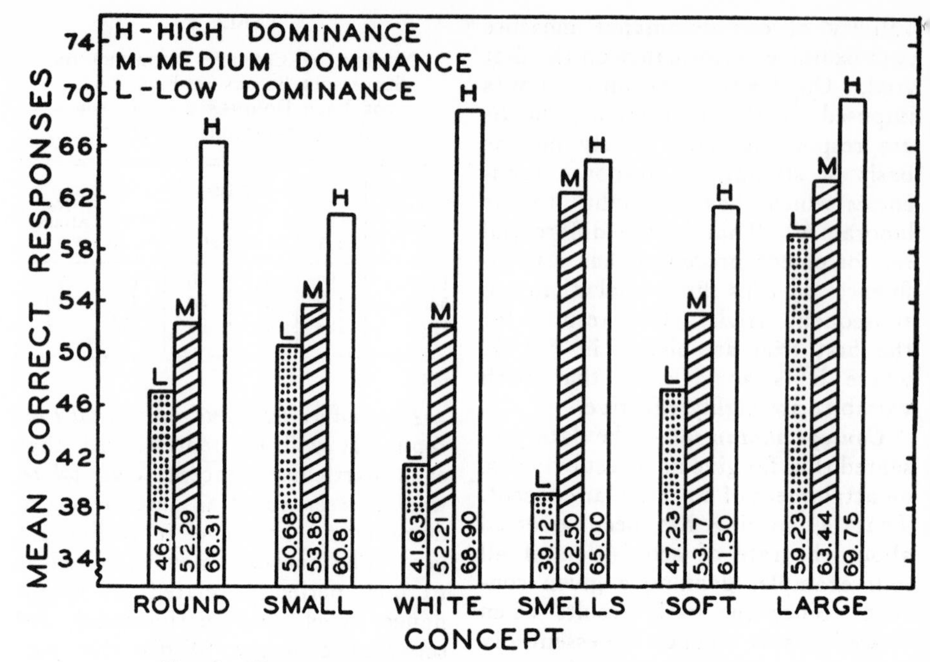

Fig. 3. Mean total correct responses over 20 trials as a function of dominance level for particular concepts.

of the responses (sense impressions) very likely have higher dominance as a descriptive response than do others. Also, it is quite likely that our procedure of having different levels of concepts in the same list introduces a source of variance. Thus, while dominance is a very important variable in the learning, it does not by any means account for all differences in rate of acquisition as this has been determined here.

Intralist interference.--We noted earlier that our conception of why

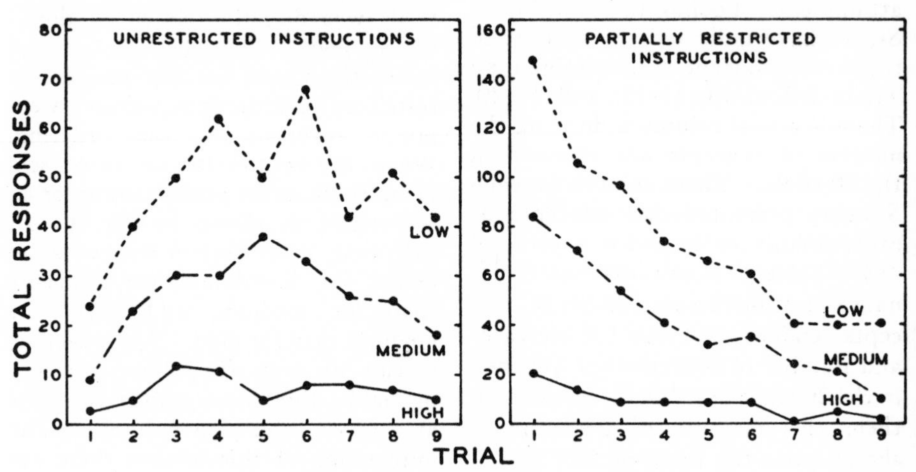

Fig. 4. Interfering responses as a function of dominance level.

dominance achieves status as an important variable is because the higher the dominance level the less the relative strength of competing response tendencies. Within limits we know what the frequency and strength of these competing response tendencies are. We shall present, therefore, some evidence of how these competing response tendencies appear in the learning records. The first set of data are shown in Fig. 4, which consists of two parts. One part concerns the experiment using unrestricted instructions, the other the partially restricted instructions. The first 9 of the 20 trials are shown along the baseline. Only these 9 trials are included since they show the essential facts. The ordinates represent the total times a known interfering response occurred. By a known interfering response we mean a response which had been given with 5% or greater frequency on the original scaling of the stimulus words.

In the experiment with unrestricted instructions it can be seen that the interfering responses are initially few in number and then increase, followed by a decrease. This is contrasted with the partially restricted instructions where the frequency decreases from an initial high. With the partially restricted instructions *S*s were told the class of responses which were correct; in the unrestricted instructions this was a part of the learning process and is reflected in the initial increase in this class of responses up to the fifth or sixth trial.

The frequency of interfering responses as plotted in Fig. 4 are inversely related to rate of acquisition as shown in earlier data. For the unrestricted-instruction experiment, for low dominance, the errors as plotted in Fig. 4 were greater in frequency than were the correct responses through the first six trials. Not until the seventh trial did the correct responses become more frequent. With partially restricted instructions the errors were more frequent than the correct responses for low dominance for only two trials. It should be clear that the errors to which we are referring are those responses which occurred with 5% or greater frequency in the original scaling, but which were incorrect responses in the concept-learning lists as constructed for this experiment. In the unrestricted-instruction experiment there were may other errors initially, since the instructions essentially asked *S* to give free associations. Errors of this nature decreased rapidly as *S* began to learn that the class of responses required were sense impressions.

TABLE 3

ERRORS AS A FUNCTION OF PERCENTAGE OF FREQUENCY (STRENGTH)

Per Cent Frequency	Number Words	Number Errors	Mean Errors Per Word
5–15	19	48	2.5
16–35	15	78	5.2
36–55	11	142	12.9
56–over	9	146	16.2

Another way to analyze the relationships among rate of learning, dominance, and interference is to determine if frequency of interfering responses is related to strength of interfering tendency. By strength we mean the percentage of times it was given on the original scaling. A sample of the findings is given in Table 3. The data come from examination of errors on the first 9 trials of low-dominance concepts for the unrestricted-instructions experiment. The first column, "Per Cent Frequency," indicates groupings of response strengths in terms of percentage of frequency of occurrence on original scaling. For example, there were 19 responses which occurred between 5% and 15% of the time in the scaling. In the present lists these are wrong responses. The third column, "Number Errors," indicates the total number of times these 19 words were given as errors in concept learning. The final column gives the mean errors based on the number of words of that grouping which could produce errors. It is quite clear from the last column that as strength (percentage of occurrence in original scaling) of interfering responses increases the greater the number of times it is given as an overt error.

Miscellaneous.—We have made a number of other analyses of our data. Most of these merely supplement the information already given and will not be presented. A few findings are worth mentioning briefly.

The three lists used did not differ widely in difficulty. If all three experiments are combined the mean total correct responses was 58.05, 53.00 and 57.99 for Lists 1, 2, and 3, respectively. List 2 appears somewhat deviant, but this deviation does not achieve statistical significance.

We have plotted a number of individual acquisition curves for the 20 trials. There are no easy generalizations which can be made about them. Some curves showed gradual increments with no more than one or two correct responses being gained from trial to trial. Others showed jumps of four to eight correct responses on a single trial. But the gradualness and the spurts were not related in any systematic fashion to fast and slow learning. Jumps in the curves occurred more frequently for *S*s in the partially restricted and restricted groups than in the group given unrestricted instructions. The group learning curves are quite smooth and provide no additional information not already presented in other ways.

Summary

The learning of concepts to verbal stimuli was studied as a function of (*a*) nature of instructions, and (*b*) three dominance levels of the concepts. Dominance level was determined by the frequency of a given restricted association elicited by the verbal stimuli in an earlier scaling procedure. The greater the frequency of a given response, the higher the dominance level. Instructions were varied (three ways) in terms of amount of information given *S* concerning the nature of the concept to be learned. Each list consisted of 24 nouns, these 24 nouns being four instances of six concepts. The *S* was to learn that the four nouns "went together" because they could be described by a single sense impression, e.g., size, shape, color, etc. The six concepts used were *large*, *small*, *white*, *soft*, *smelly*, and *round*. Each concept was used at each level of dominance and with each set of instructions. A total of 20 trials was given to 144 *S*s with the response measures being number of correct responses made in 20 trials and number of concepts attained in 20 trials. The stimuli were presented at a 4-sec. rate with *S* responding directly in terms of sense impressions, i.e., *S* would respond with "large," "small," etc., to be correct. The major results were:

1. The higher the dominance level, the greater the number of concepts learned and the greater the number of correct responses given in 20 trials.

2. The greater the amount of information given *S* concerning the nature of the concepts to be learned, the more rapid the acquisition.

3. Dominance level and number of interfering responses were inversely related, and the shape of the interfering response curves varied with the nature of the instructions. The stronger the interfering responses, the more frequently they occur in the learning records.

References

1. Richardson, J., & Bergum, B. Distributed practice and rote learning in concept formation. *J. exp. Psychol.*, 1954, **47**, 442–446.

2. Underwood, B. J. An orientation for research on thinking. *Psychol. Rev.*, 1952, **59**, 209–220.

3. Underwood, B. J., & Richardson, J. Some verbal materials for the study of concept formation. *Psychol. Bull.*, 1956, **53**, 84–95.

(Received May 9, 1955)

ARTICLE 4

THE RELATIONSHIP OF STIMULUS SIMILARITY AND NUMBER OF RESPONSES[1]

JACK RICHARDSON

Harpur College

The experimental tasks reported as examples of concept formation vary in many respects but seem to have two common characteristics which also serve to distinguish them from rote-learning tasks. The same response is correct for more than one stimulus and the stimuli which are designated by identical responses are discriminatively different but are "similar" in some way (have common elements, belong to the same class, etc.) while the stimuli designated by different responses are less similar.

Although verbalization of the basis of classification is often used as the criterion of concept attainment, there are two major methods of presenting concept examples and each has another criterion of concept learning or attainment. The first method presents single examples of each concept until the correct responses are learned and then presents a different example of each concept and requires the same response (e.g., **1, 7, 9**). The criterion of concept learning is the tendency for new examples of a concept to evoke the same response as the previous examples. This type of concept study resembles rote-learning studies of transfer in paired associates where the stimuli are similar and the responses identical (e.g., **4, 15**). Positive transfer from A-B to A′-B is expected in both, but A and A′ are examples of the same concept in the concept studies while in the transfer studies A and A′ have been rated as similar.

The second method presents several examples of a concept without requiring the correct response for the previous examples (e.g., **3, 10, 11**). The criterion for concept learning is the tendency for each example of the concept to evoke the same response. In these studies it would be possible to learn the correct response to each concept example independently, but it is assumed that assigning the same response to each example of a concept facilitates learning. Apparently there is positive transfer between examples of the same concept. To apply this method to rote-learning materials would require lists in which similar stimuli are paired with the same response.

There is some indication that similarity ratings are useful in predicting the relative difficulty of concepts (**13**). If stimulus similarity and number of responses are relevant to the differences between rote learning and concept learning then it should be possible to produce results characteristic of concept learning by manipulating rote-learning materials. The results should conform to the laws of transfer in verbal learning and at the same time show the faster learning and apparently better retention of concepts (**10, 11, 12**).

The present study is concerned with paired-associate lists in which the

[1] This research was supported by Grant G2594 from the National Science Foundation to the Research Foundation of State University of New York. Completion of this study was made possible by the cooperation of Paul Gimmie, Charles Traphagen, Malcolm Piester, and the students of Vestal Central School who served as *S*s.

Reprinted with permission of the author and the publisher, the American Psychological Association. The article appeared originally in the *Journal of Experimental Psychology*, 1958, **56**, 478–484.

number of stimuli were held constant while the similarity of the stimuli and the number of different responses were varied. Of course, the important thing is the relationship between the stimulus similarity and the number of responses rather than either isolated from the other. One of the lists resembles the second method of concept presentation in that highly similar stimuli are designated by the same response while there are different responses for low-similarity stimuli.

Method

Lists.—Nine lists of 16 pairs were constructed with adjectives from Haagen (6) as stimuli and nonsense syllables from Glaze (5) as responses. The only differences in the lists were the number of *different* syllables used as responses and the similarity of the stimuli which were paired with a response. The design may be considered factorial with three different numbers of responses and three stimulus similarity relationships. Low-similarity adjectives were used as stimuli for three of the lists and consisted of 16 adjectives with no apparent or rated similarity. The high-similarity adjectives consisted of four groups of four highly similar items and were used as stimuli in six of the lists. The nonsense syllables were of either 47% or 53% association value, of minimum formal similarity, and either 2, 4, or 8 different syllables were correct as responses for all 16 stimuli in a list.

The nine lists are presented in Table 1 with the high-similarity stimuli in Column 1, the low-similarity stimuli in Column 2, and the responses which were paired with the stimuli in Columns 3–8. The headings of the columns containing the responses designate the different lists with the number indicating the number of different responses in the list and the letters indicating that the responses in that column were paired with the low (L) or the high-similarity (Ha and Hr) stimuli. For each different number of responses there were two pairings with the high-similarity stimuli. In one there was high intraresponse stimulus similarity (Ha), i.e., the responses were assigned so there was maximum similarity between stimuli paired with the same response. In the other there was high interresponse stimulus similarity (Hr), i.e., there was maximum similarity between stimuli paired with different responses.

It should be noted that only in the lists with four responses is it possible to assign a different response to each group of similar adjectives or to assign a single adjective from each similarity group to one response.

Procedure.—The 16 pairs in each list were arranged in three random orders and presented with a 16-mm. strip-film projector. The pairs were flashed from the back of a screen so that *S* could not see either *E* or the projector during

TABLE 1

Lists

Item	Stimuli		Responses					
	High	Low	2-L 2-Ha	2-Hr	4-L 4-Ha	4-Hr	8-L 8-Ha	8-Hr
1	DOUBLE	VERBAL	BIH	BIH	BIH	BIH	BIH	BIH
2	DUAL	TWOFOLD	BIH	ZET	BIH	VOM	BIH	SUJ
3	PAIRED	HALLOWED	BIH	BIH	BIH	RUK	SUJ	VOM
4	TWOFOLD	DARING	BIH	ZET	BIH	ZET	SUJ	NAC
5	SACRED	PERFECT	BIH	BIH	VOM	BIH	VOM	BIH
6	DIVINE	DIRTY	BIH	ZET	VOM	VOM	VOM	SUJ
7	HALLOWED	REMOVED	BIH	BIH	VOM	RUK	NAC	VOM
8	HOLY	RISING	BIH	ZET	VOM	ZET	NAC	NAC
9	SPOKEN	ROBUST	ZET	BIH	RUK	BIH	RUK	RUK
10	ORAL	FLUID	ZET	ZET	RUK	VOM	RUK	YAD
11	VERBAL	PLAYFUL	ZET	BIH	RUK	RUK	YAD	ZET
12	VOCAL	GLEAMING	ZET	ZET	RUK	ZET	YAD	QIX
13	TRANQUIL	URGENT	ZET	BIH	ZET	BIH	ZET	RUK
14	PEACEFUL	OPEN	ZET	ZET	ZET	VOM	ZET	YAD
15	QUIET	STEADY	ZET	BIH	ZET	RUK	QIX	ZET
16	SERENE	LITTLE	ZET	ZET	ZET	ZET	QIX	QIX

the presentation. The stimulus of each pair was presented for 2 sec. followed by a 2-sec. presentation of the stimulus and response together. There was a 4-sec. intertrial interval.

Twenty-four different *Ss* learned each list; 12 *Ss* were college students from introductory psychology courses and 12 were junior or senior high school students. The *Ss* from each of the two groups of students were assigned to lists as they appeared at the laboratory. None of the *Ss* had previously served in a learning experiment. They were required to spell the syllables and were given the usual instructions for paired-associate learning by the anticipation method. They were not told that the same response would be correct for more than one stimulus or that the stimuli were grouped in any way for the assignment of responses.

To avoid selection due to loss of *Ss* and to approximately equate performance at the end of the first session, the lists were presented for a specific number of trials. The lists with two different responses were presented for 5 trials, those with four different responses for 10 trials, and the lists with 8 responses for 15 trials. After learning for the appropriate number of trials, *Ss* were dismissed and returned 48 hr. later for the second session. Since differential transfer was expected between items in the lists, it was important that the responses should not be presented during any test of recall. To control for intralist transfer and for warm-up, the first five trials of the second session were recall trials. During the five recall trials the lists were presented in exactly the same way as during learning except that the responses were not presented and there was no indication to *S* whether a response was right or wrong. The *Ss* were told that the responses would not appear for a few trials but that they should continue to spell as many responses as possible each time through the list. After the five recall trials the responses were again presented in the usual fashion and relearning continued to a total of 25 trials for both sessions or to a criterion of three successive perfect trials. For purposes of the analysis it was assumed that all responses would be correct after three successive perfect trials.

Results

Learning.—The mean number of correct responses on Trial 25 of each list is given in Table 2 and the analysis of variance is presented in Table 3. The college students are superior to the high school students, but there is no significant interaction of students with the other variables. The two groups are combined in Fig. 1 and the mean number of correct responses on each trial is presented for each list. The first break in each curve indicates the 48-hr. retention interval, and the second the end of the five recall trials when the responses were again presented.

Number of different responses is highly significant, but this analysis does not take into account the differential probability of guessing the correct response. The appreciable number of times *Ss* did not respond makes the value of a correction for guessing doubtful. However, the correction used by Bricker (**2**) was ap-

TABLE 2

Mean Number of Correct Responses on Trial 25

Similarity	College Students			High School Students		
	No. of Responses			No. of Responses		
	2	4	8	2	4	8
Hr	12.08	9.17	8.17	11.25	8.50	8.92
L	14.17	12.00	10.92	11.25	11.17	11.50
Ha	14.17	15.33	12.00	13.67	13.17	7.83
Combined	13.47	12.17	10.36	12.06	10.94	9.42

TABLE 3

Analysis of Variance for the Number of Correct Responses on Trial 25

Source	*df*	*MS*	*F*
Students (St)	1	77.04	7.48*
No. of Responses (NR)	2	150.04	14.58*
Similarity (Sm)	2	173.51	16.86*
NR × Sm	4	37.83	3.67*
St × Sm	2	18.76	1.82
St × NR	2	1.01	.10
St × NR × Sm	4	21.17	2.06
Within	198	10.29	

* $P = .01$.

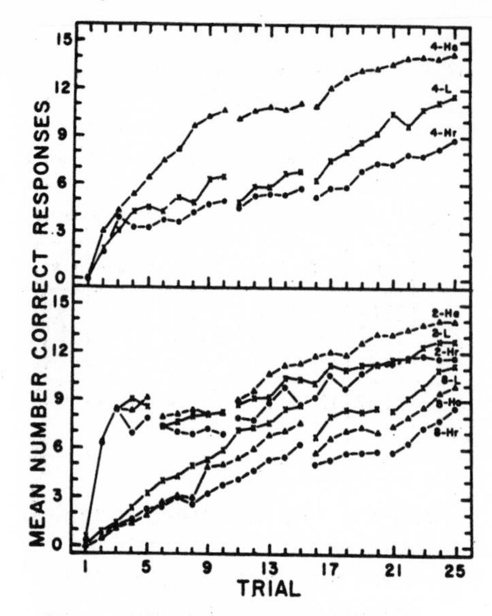

FIG. 1. Mean number of correct responses on each list as a function of trials.

plied to Trial 25 and an analysis of variance was computed on the corrected scores. This decreased the F for number of responses to .97 and reduced the F for the interaction between number of responses and similarity to 2.98. The F's for Similarity and for Students increased to 17.51 and 8.82, respectively. This correction probably overestimates the effect of guessing, but there are other indications that number of responses may not be an effective variable in learning. In Fig. 1 it is apparent that the performance level expected from guessing alone is attained in approximately the same number of trials for lists with different numbers of responses and that the differences between the 2-, 4-, and 8-response lists tend to decrease after this point. There is also a significant interaction between number of responses and similarity with the smallest differences between the low-similarity lists. In view of this, the significant effect of number of responses is attributed to guessing and to similarity relationships.

The over-all effect of similarity is highly significant with the high interresponse stimulus similarity lists being more difficult, and the high intraresponse stimulus similarity lists less difficult, than the low-similarity lists. However, the significant interaction indicates that the effect of similarity is not independent of the number of responses. Similarity as it is used here is a dimension only if considered in relation to the responses. If the number of stimuli remains constant then the relationships in the Ha and Hr lists must change as the number of responses change. If we consider intralist transfer as a function of the similarity of the stimuli then there would be little or no transfer in the low-similarity lists while each stimulus in the high-similarity list would produce transfer to three others. The direction of transfer would depend on whether the three stimuli had the same or different responses as the stimulus which is producing the transfer. Thus the

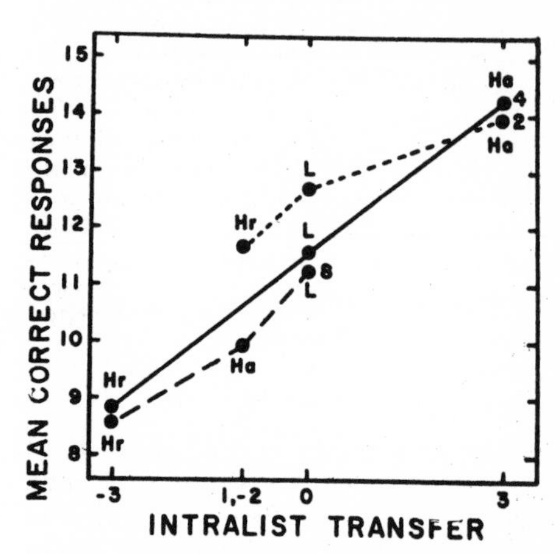

FIG. 2. Mean number of correct responses on Trial 25 as a function of the number of items within a similarity group to which the transfer would be positive or negative.

high-similarity lists would have either negative transfer to three items within a similarity group (Lists 4-Hr and 8-Hr), positive transfer to one and negative to the other two (Lists 2-Hr and 8-Ha), or positive transfer to three items (Lists 2-Ha and 4-Ha). In Fig. 2 the number of correct responses on Trial 25 is plotted as a function of the amount of transfer expected. The abscissa indicates the number of items, within a single similarity group, to which transfer is expected to be positive or negative. There is a separate curve for each of the three different number of responses and the similarity is indicated at each point. It is clear that the number of correct responses increases as the number of items to which positive transfer is expected increases. This effect is not dependent on the number of different responses in the list.

Retention.—In Fig. 1 it is apparent that there was an appreciable loss on all lists from the last learning trial to the first recall trial and, even though *S*s were given no information as to the correctness of their responses, there was a gain over the five recall trials on all except List 2-Hr. For a statistical evaluation a count was made of the number of *S*s who had more correct responses and the number of *S*s who had fewer correct responses on the second of the two trials being compared. Computation of χ^2's indicated that a significant number decreased over the 48-hr. retention interval, increased from Recall 1 to Recall 5, and that there was not a significant number of *S*s who decreased from the last learning trial to the fifth recall trial. There was a tendency for more loss over the retention interval in the low-similarity lists but there was also more gain in these lists over the five recall trials. There were no systematic differences in retention as a function of stimulus similarity relationships with the responses. The percentage of the number correct on the last learning trial which was correct on the first and fifth recall and the first relearning trial is given for each list in Table 4. It should be noted that retention is uniformly high and that it increases from Recall 1 to Recall 5.

TABLE 4

PERCENTAGE OF RETENTION AFTER 48 HR.

List	Recall 1	Recall 5	Relearn 1
2-Hr	93.1	87.2	100.5
2-L	86.3	95.6	102.0
2-Ha	86.3	89.0	98.6
4-Hr	91.5	117.8	105.1
4-L	76.1	106.4	98.1
4-Ha	94.9	104.3	102.4
8-Hr	80.5	93.3	92.0
8-L	77.8	98.6	96.6
8-Ha	75.7	92.8	98.9

Errors.—The errors on the last learning trial, the first and fifth recall trials, and the first and second relearning trials were classified as omissions (failure to make an overt response), errors from within the list, or others which included partial responses and combinations of letters which were not correct for any item in the list. There were no systematic

TABLE 5

TOTAL NUMBER OF ERRORS IN EACH CLASSIFICATION FOR ALL LISTS COMBINED

Type of Error	Last Learning Trial	Recall 1	Recall 5	Relearn 1	Relearn 2
Omissions	545	587	433	586	395
Within	1084	1183	1130	1104	1155
Other	146	244	244	96	93
Total	1775	2014	1807	1786	1643

differences in the distribution of types of errors as a function of similarity. Although there were many more errors in the Hr groups, the percentage of these that were from within the list was no greater than in the Ha groups. The number of different types of errors in the five trials for all lists combined are given in Table 5. The increase in correct responses over the five recall trials is primarily the result of the decrease in the number of omissions.

Discussion

It is apparent from Fig. 2 that rote-learning transfer principles predict the relative speed of learning when similarity relationships are varied in relation to the responses. The higher the similarity between stimuli with the same response the faster the learning, and the higher the similarity between stimuli with different responses the slower the learning. The positive intralist transfer commonly found in concept learning can be produced by manipulating stimulus similarity. List 4-Ha is most comparable to the concept lists since there is one response for each group of similar stimuli. It is here that the difference between the Ha list and the L list is greatest.

Retention does not seem to be related to similarity and this agrees with other studies in which stimulus similarity has been varied (**14**). However, the retention is high. If one considers only the 4-Ha list, there is 94.9% retention on the first recall trial and this increases to 104.3% on the fifth recall trial. Differences in number of items, degree of learning, retention interval, and procedure prohibit direct comparison with concept studies (**10, 11, 12**), but the retention of concepts is not obviously better. In view of the high degree of retention in this study it seems that a direct comparison of concept and rote materials which used the same procedure and equated the degree of learning might show no differences in retention.

The five recall trials during which the responses were not presented resulted in an increase in the number of correct responses on all lists except 2-Hr and the small increase in the 2-response lists may be due to the fact that the performance at the end of learning was at approximately the guessing level. This procedure seems similar to warm-up before recall found by Irion (**8**) but differs in that it is practice on the same task rather than some other task. On the other hand, it cannot be considered learning in the usual sense because there was no information given as to the correctness of the response. In Table 4 there seems to be little relation of the percentage of increase over the five recall trials with either similarity or number of responses. The increase is definitely related to the number of trials on recall, but the limit cannot be determined from this experiment. Further experimentation is required to relate this phenomenon to warm-up and to determine what aspects of the procedure are necessary to produce it.

Summary

This study varied the number of different responses and the similarity of the stimuli in relation to the responses in paired-associate lists. In 16-item lists either 2, 4, or 8 nonsense syllables were used as responses and either high- or low-similarity adjectives were used as stimuli. The similarity of the stimuli which had the same response was varied.

It was found that similarity was a variable in learning and that the list with a single response for each group of similar adjectives showed high positive intralist transfer characteristics of concept learning. Retention did not seem to be related to similarity, but was uniformly high.

References

1. Baum, M. H. Simple concept learning as a function of intralist generalization. *J. exp. Psychol.*, 1954, **47**, 89–94.
2. Bricker, P. D. The identification of redundant stimulus patterns. *J. exp. Psychol.*, 1955, **49**, 73–81.
3. Buss, A. H. A study of concept formation as a function of reinforcement and stimulus generalization. *J. exp. Psychol.*, 1950, **40**, 494–503.

4. Gibson, E. J. Retroactive inhibition as a function of degree of generalization between tasks. *J. exp. Psychol.*, 1941, **28**, 93–115.

5. Glaze, J. A. The association value of nonsense syllables. *J. genet. Psychol.*, 1928, **35**, 255–267.

6. Haagen, C. H. Synonymity, vividness, familiarity, and association value ratings of 400 pairs of common adjectives. *J. Psychol.*, 1949, **27**, 453–463.

7. Heidbreder, E. The attainment of concepts: VIII. The conceptualization of verbally indicated instances. *J. Psychol.*, 1949, **27**, 263–309.

8. Irion, A. L. Retention and warming-up effects in paired-associate learning. *J. exp. Psychol.*, 1949, **39**, 669–675.

9. Hull, C. L. Quantitative aspects of the evolution of concepts. *Psychol. Monogr.*, 1920, **28**, No. 1 (Whole No. 123).

10. Oseas, L., & Underwood, B. J. Studies of distributed practice: V. Learning and retention of concepts. *J. exp. Psychol.*, 1952, **43**, 143–148.

11. Reed, H. B. Factors influencing the learning and retention of concepts: I. The influence of set. *J. exp. Psychol.*, 1946, **36**, 71–87.

12. Richardson, J. Retention of concepts as a function of the degree of original and interpolated learning. *J. exp. Psychol.*, 1956, **51**, 358–364.

13. Richardson, J., & Bergum, B. O. Distributed practice and rote learning in concept formation. *J. exp. Psychol.*, 1954, **47**, 442–446.

14. Underwood, B. J. Studies of distributed practice: IX. Learning and retention of paired adjectives as a function of intralist similarity. *J. exp. Psychol.*, 1953, **45**, 143–149.

15. Yum, K. S. An experimental test of the law of assimilation. *J. exp. Psychol.*, 1931, **14**, 68–82.

(Received January 29, 1958)

ARTICLE 5

SERIAL EFFECTS IN RECALL OF UNORGANIZED AND SEQUENTIALLY ORGANIZED VERBAL MATERIAL[1]

JAMES DEESE AND ROGER A. KAUFMAN[2]

The Johns Hopkins University

One of the best established generalizations in the study of verbal learning is found in the serial position effect for the learning of homogeneous, discrete verbal items by the method of serial anticipation. Some form of the classical serial position curve is found for a considerable variety of verbal material and conditions of testing; the essential restriction seems to be that the learning and/or recall be by the method of serial anticipation or some modification of it (**5**). Several studies (**4, 8**) show that there is quite a different form of the serial position effect when free recall is the method of testing employed. With the method of free recall, the middle items are less frequently recalled, the first items are moderately well recalled, and the last items are most frequently recalled. Thus, the serial position curve for serial anticipation and that for free recall are roughly mirror images of one another. This, of course, is a qualitative comparison, since the exact form of the curves will depend upon the material and method of testing.

Recently, Bousfield, Cohen, and Silva (**2**) have noted that in free recall the order in which items are recalled depends upon their probability of being recalled. Items frequently recalled by everyone are apt to be recalled first by particular individuals. Since, in free recall, the last items are most frequently recalled, it suggests, for homogeneous material, that the last items should be recalled first and the middle items last. It is clear, however, that free recall of ordinary English textual material does not happen in this way (so perhaps it is not really free recall). We ordinarily do not recall the last words of a passage of prose first and the middle words last. In general, we recall the first words first and the last words last. Thus, our recall of ordinary prose approximates the order of recall forced by the method of serial anticipation. It seems an obvious conclusion that this is because the sequential nature of ordinary prose forces such sequential recall.

The purpose of the experiments reported here is to examine the influence of sequential structure in verbal material upon the order of recall of individual items and upon the serial position curve for frequency of recall. A formal hypothesis may be stated as follows: As increasing sequential structure is introduced into material given *S*s with instructions for free recall, the order of recall and the serial position curve for frequency of recall will change from that characteristic of free recall of unstructured material to that characteristic of the learning or recall of unstructured material by the method of serial anticipation. This implies that the serial position curve for a passage of ordinary prose in free recall, all other things equal, should be like that for nonsense material in serial anticipation.

[1] The research reported in this paper was in part supported by funds from the National Science Foundation grant NSF—61369.

[2] Now at the University of California, Berkeley.

Reprinted with permission of the authors and the publisher, the American Psychological Association. The article appeared originally in the *Journal of Experimental Psychology*, 1957, **54**, 180–187.

In Exp. I, the characteristics of free recall for serially unstructured material and for connected prose are compared. In Exp. II the effects of variation in sequential structure is examined by analyzing the changes in patterns of recall in certain of the pseudosentences employed by Miller and Selfridge (**3**) in their study of the effect of sequential structure on amount retained in immediate free recall.

Experiment I

Method.—Male undergraduate students at the Johns Hopkins University were used as *S*s in this study. Two groups of 16 *S*s each were presented with lists of words drawn randomly from the Thorndike-Lorge word list (**7**). A third group of 27 *S*s was presented with passages of connected discourse made by altering selections obtained from the 1953 World Almanac. Presentation was oral, and all *S*s were instructed to try to remember what they heard. A test for recall was obtained immediately after each list or passage was read. For the lists of randomly selected words, a verbatim transcription of recall was taken by *E*. For the passages of connected discourse, a dictophone recorded *S*'s recall and the recording was later transcribed. A tape recorder was used to present the passages of connected discourse; the same recording was used throughout. The lists of random words were read orally by *E* (two *E*s tested an equal number of *S*s each) at the rate of 1 word per sec. Both *E*s used in this and subsequent phases of the study were instructed and trained to read the material at the appropriate rate without emphasis or inflection.

One group of 16 *S*s recalled 10 lists of words 10 items in length. A second group of 16 *S*s recalled 10 lists of words 32 items in length. The order of words in the lists was randomly scrambled for each *S* and each *S* was presented the lists in a different order.

The passages of connected discourse were on three different topics, and each of these three topics was presented to 27 *S*s. The topics were respectively, "Montana," "The Museum of Science and Industry," and "Bonneville Dam." Each passage was approximately 100 words in length, consisted of 10 simple statements organized into sentences and clauses. The statements were such that, by minor rewording, they could be presented in different orders. This is important to the problem under study, since individual words and phrases in connected discourse differ greatly in their ease of being recalled, and in order to study the effects of serial order on recall it is necessary to randomize as well as possible the location of individual items. Consequently, nine different orders of statements in each passage were used. Two examples of arrangements of the passage, "The Museum of Science and Industry," are given below:

1. "The Museum of Science and Industry is devoted to exhibits of scientific and industrial processes. And it will always remain a picture of modern civilization. Many mechanical displays can be operated by the visitor, and for many years the most popular display has been an operating coal mine. Perhaps the most unusual display is a room given over to an operating radar center. Many other displays are devoted to things of historical interest, and as the techniques of industry change, the contents of the museum will change. The museum is located in South Chicago, and it was founded by Julius Rosenwald. It occupies the grounds of the old Columbian exposition."

2. "Many displays are devoted to objects of historical interest at the Museum of Science and Industry, which occupies the grounds of the old Columbian exposition. The Museum is devoted to exhibits of scientific and industrial processes, and perhaps the most unusual room is given over to an operating radar center. The Museum is located in South Chicago. It will always remain a picture of modern civilization, for as the techniques of industry change, the contents of the Museum will change. For many years the most popular display has been an operating coal mine. Many mechanical displays can be operated by the visitor. The Museum was founded by Julius Rosenwald."

The word lists were scored by number of words per position recalled correctly. The passages were scored by number of statements per position recalled correctly; some latitude in exact wording was allowed in the scoring (for example, the substitution of "exhibit" for "display"). There was, however, 100% agreement between two scorers on a sample of transcriptions of recall from five *S*s.

Results.—The curves in Fig. 1 show the mean frequency per list with which items in each position were recalled for all lists of each length. For both the 10-word lists and the 32-word lists the highest frequency of recall occurs at the end of the list. The frequency of recall for initial items is relatively higher than in an earlier

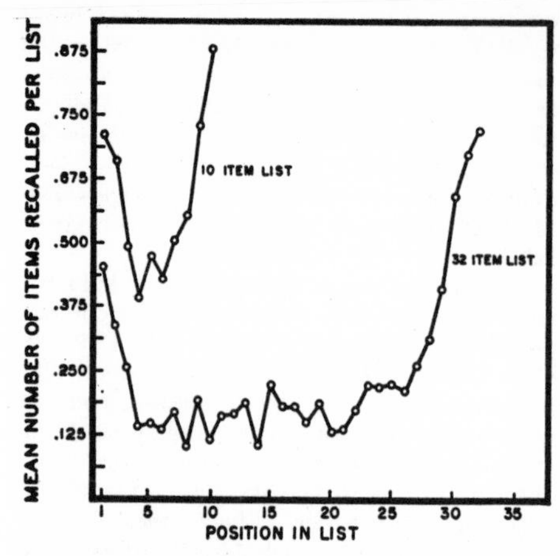

Fig. 1. Mean frequency of recall per list per *S* for lists of randomly arranged words as a function of position of items in original lists.

study (8), and this is probably because ordinary words rather than nonsense syllables were used in the present study. The mean order of recall of items as a function of position is presented in Fig. 2. Comparing Fig. 1 and 2 it appears that probability of

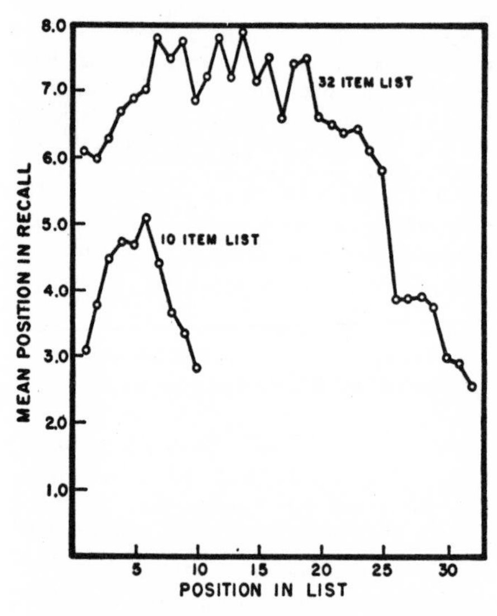

Fig. 2. Mean position of items in recall of randomly arranged words as a function of position of items in original lists.

recall and order are correlated. In general the last items are recalled first and the middle items last. Estimates of the concordance between frequency of recall and position in recall were obtained by Kendall's *tau* coefficient (6). The value of *tau* for the 10-word lists is .867 and *tau* for the 32-word list is .536. These are positive since the item at the first position of recall was assigned a rank of one and the item with the highest frequency of recall was assigned a rank of one, etc. Both obtained *taus* are significant beyond the 1% level.

The serial position curve for the free recall of statements from the passages of connected discourse is different from those presented in Fig. 1. Figure 3 shows that the serial position curve for the textual material is very much like the classical curve for the method of serial anticipation; the highest frequency of recall is at the beginning of the list, and the lowest frequency of recall is just past the middle. The result suggests that the association processes in learning by the method of serial anticipation

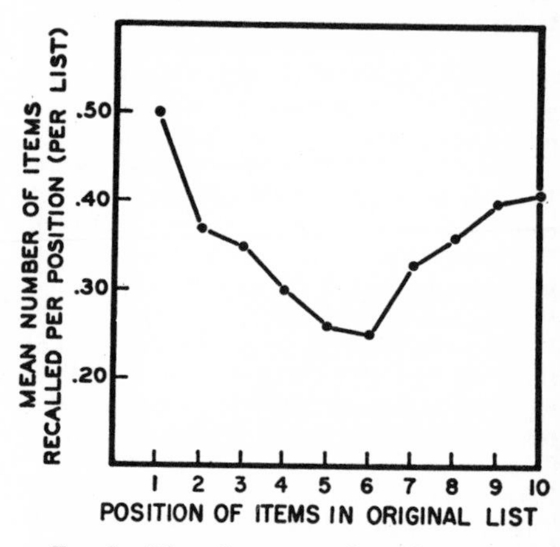

Fig. 3. Mean frequency of recall per passage per *S* for statements in textual passages as a function of position of statements in original passages.

may not be so different from the processes of ordinary language as has sometimes been supposed. The rank order of mean position in recall is perfectly correlated with the position of statements in the original passage (*tau* = 1.0).

The results of this phase of the study suggest that the variation in serial position curves for free recall is limited on one hand by free recall of disconnected material and on the other by free recall of sequentially connected passages like those used in the present study. It remains to be shown, however, that the differences between these two types of curves reflect the higher sequential organization in the passages of connected discourse. The purpose of Exp. II is to examine this question.

Experiment II[3]

Method.—Forty Johns Hopkins undergraduates were used as *S*s. The material presented to *S*s consisted of the 50-item lists of words used by Miller and Selfridge (**3**) as part of their study of the influence of sequential dependency upon the amount of immediate memory.

The Miller and Selfridge lists are made in such a way as to approximate by degrees the statistical sequential structure of ordinary prose. The lists with zero-order dependency were obtained by randomly selecting words from the Thorndike-Lorge wordbook; therefore, these lists are very much like the ones used in the first experiment. The first-order dependency lists were obtained by scrambling words from the higher order lists (in an attempt to approximate the frequencies of usage with sequential dependencies). The second-order lists were obtained by giving an *S* two words and asking him to make a sentence of them. The word *S* used following the initial two was added to the two and the first word of the two was dropped. This new group of two was given to a new *S* with instructions to make a sentence. Lists of words were then constructed by chaining together the successive words of new *S*s. Third-, fourth-, fifth-, and seventh-order lists were made in exactly the same way, except that longer chains of words were given to *S*s. In addition, Miller and Selfridge present lists of ordinary English prose, and their 50-word textual passage was used in the present experiment.

Eight lists (seven orders of approximation and textual passage) were presented to all *S*s. The order of words in the lists was, of course, fixed by the sequential dependencies in all except the zero-order list. The zero-order list was presented in a different, randomized order to each *S*. Randomization of order of presentation of the different lists was achieved by repeating five times an 8 × 8 latin square. The lists were read to *S* by *E* at the rate of 1 word per sec.; one *E* tested all *S*s. The *E* requested recall immediately after the reading of a list, and all responses made by *S*, in order, were recorded. In the analysis of recall, responses extraneous to the list being recalled were ignored.

Duplicate words appeared in all of the higher-order lists and the textual passage. Because the recall of such words would be ambiguous with respect to position, these words were not scored.

Results.—Frequency of recall as a function of order of items in the lists is presented in Fig. 4. Frequency of recall has been averaged by groups of five items in order to minimize the influence of particular high association words at unique and unalterable positions. The greater smoothness in the recall curve for the zero-order list is attributable to the fact that individual words could be randomized by position in this list.

There is an increase in the total frequency of recall with an increase in order of approximation, in confirmation of Miller and Selfridge (**3**). The *tau* between frequency of recall for each order and order of approximation is .857 ($P < .01$). Table 1 yields information on the question of where, in the lists, the increase of frequency of recall with higher-order approximations occurs. Here are presented the *tau*s for the separate

[3] Preliminary data on 30-word lists were obtained. These data are not presented here because of some irregularities in procedure. They may be found, however, in a master's essay by the junior author on deposit in the Johns Hopkins University library.

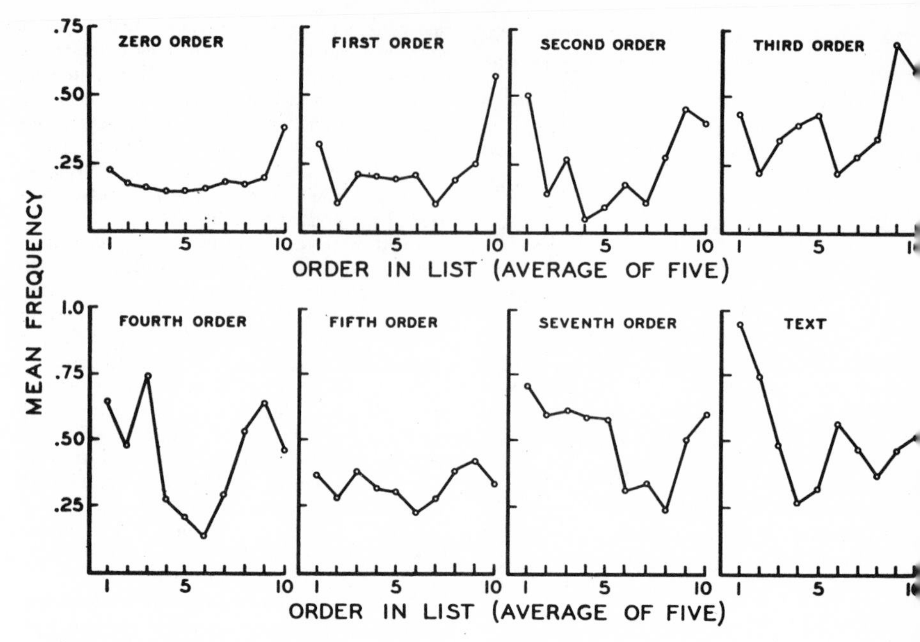

FIG. 4. Mean frequency of recall per *S* for items in lists of various degrees of sequential structure (orders of approximation) as a function of position of items in original lists (averaged by groups of five items).

positions in the lists (averaged by groups of five). All of the obtained *taus* presented in Table 1 are significant at the 5% level or beyond except those for the last three groups of five items and that for the third group of five items. Therefore, it appears that the greater portion of the increase in frequency of recall in the higher-order approximations comes from the first two-thirds of the lists.

There is also a change in the form of the serial position curves. The serial position curve for the zero-order approximation resembles the curves for free recall of random material presented in Exp. I. The curves for the higher-order appıoximations are apparently different, however. In order to obtain some estimate of the extent to which the shift in position of maximum recall is reliable, the *tau* statistic was used again. The percentage of total recall scores found in

TABLE 1

RANK-ORDER (*tau*) CORRELATIONS BETWEEN FREQUENCY OF RECALL AND ORDER OF APPROXIMATION FOR SUCCESSIVE 10THS OF THE 50-WORD LIST

Position in List.....	1–5	6–10	11–15	16–20	21–25	26–30	31–35	36–40	41–45	46–50
tau	.714**	.786**	.857**	.357	.500*	.571*	.786**	.429	.357	.214

* $.01 < P < .05$.
** $P \leq .01$.

TABLE 2

RANK-ORDER (*tau*) CORRELATIONS BETWEEN MEAN POSITION IN RECALL AND (1) FREQUENCY OF RECALL, AND (2) ORDER OF ORIGINAL LIST, FOR EACH ORDER OF APPROXIMATION

tau Between	Order of Approximation							Text
	0	1	2	3	4	5	7	
Position and Frequency	.422*	.467*	.467*	.467*	.644**	.333	.289	.289
Position and List Order	.067	−.156	−.289	−.289	.022	.067	.467*	.689**

* $.01 < P < .05$.
** $P \leq .01$.

items from the first half of the list was computed for each order of approximation. These percentages were correlated with the order of approximation, and this yielded a *tau* of .643 ($P = .01$). Thus, for the higher-order approximations a larger percentage of the total items recalled comes from the first half of the list than is the case for the lower-order approximations.

In Exp. I it was shown for the free recall of random items that the order of recall was correlated with the frequency with which the individual items were recalled. For recall of the textual material, however, the order of recall was correlated with the order of presentation of items in the lists. The implication of these results for Exp. II are, (*a*) the order of recall (position of an item in recall) should be correlated with frequency of recall for the early orders of approximation, and (*b*) the order of recall should be correlated with the position in the original list for the higher-orders of approximation.

Table 2 presents the *tau* coefficients for these two sets of correlations. The correlations between position in recall and frequency of recall are all positive (highest frequency and first position given rank one), though only those for the zero, first, second, third and fourth orders of approximation are significant beyond the 5% level. The correlations between position in recall and position in the original list are either very low or negative except for the seventh order of approximation and the textual passage, both of which are highly significant. Thus, the seventh-order and textual passages are recalled roughly in their order of presentation, while for the other passages the dominant relationship to order of recall is frequency of recall.

DISCUSSION

The results of the present experiments show that the serial position curve of frequency of recall varies with the sequential structure of the material being recalled. The variation in serial position curves with changes in sequential dependency is accompanied by variation in the order with which the items are emitted in recall. It is probable that the changes in serial position are dependent upon these changes in the order in which the items are emitted.

For material which has little or no inherent sequential structure, items are emitted in a kind of primitive order of strength during test for recall. In this connection, Bousfield, Cohen, and Silva (2) have pointed out the parallel to Marbe's law. The present study shows that for unstructured material, in which the primitive order of strength determines the order of recall, *S*s emit the last items first on the average, the beginning words next and finally the words in the middle of the list.

For material with high sequential structure the order of emission is principally determined by the order of items in the list, and furthermore, the serial position curve is much like that found in serial anticipation learning. Thus, as increasing sequential dependency is introduced into lists of words used in recall tests, *S*s do more than simply organize the words into larger and larger chunks; they reorganize their patterns of verbal behavior to conform with long established habits of dealing with the sequentially structured material of ordinary language.

The advantage gained in frequency of items recalled by the redundancy in higher-order lists seems largely to come from the beginning and middle of the lists. It is not certain, however, whether this particular location of gain in recall is associated with redundancy per se or whether it is because the recall for the higher-order lists is correlated with the order of presentation. If the same shift in order of items recalled occurred in the experiments of Miller and Selfridge (3) as occurred in the present experiment, then it is not certain that all of the gain in recall with higher-order lists is associated with the greater redundancy of these lists; it is possible that it may be associated with the change in order of emission. From data in existence at the present it is impossible to tell if this is the case or not; however, because increasing redundancy in the sequentially organized lists is associated with reorganization of the emission of items in recall, the effect of sequential structuring is more complicated than it appeared to be at first. In order to further examine this question it will be necessary to compare the effects of different methods of introducing redundancy into the lists used in tests of recall. It is possible, for example, that redundancy introduced by meaningful relationships of the sort exhibited in the study of "clustering" (1) will produce a different pattern of organization, and hence may enable us to separate the effects of redundancy and reorganized order of emission.

Summary

The results of two experiments on the immediate recall of verbal material are presented. For lists of words in which there is no sequential association between adjacent words (randomly arranged lists), *S*s recall the individual items in order of their probability of being recalled. For these kinds of lists, the last items are recalled most frequently, the first items next most frequently, and the middle items least frequently. For passages of connected discourse, the order of recall is in the order with which the material is presented, and the serial position curve of frequency of recall is like that obtained by the method of serial anticipation with nonsense material (and roughly the mirror image of that obtained with free recall of nonsense material). It is probable that the serial position curve obtained with textual material depends upon the serial order of emission during recall. It was demonstrated by the use of the orders of approximation to textual English devised by Miller and Selfridge (3) that increasing the sequential dependency from zero to that characteristic of textual English changes the order and frequency of recall from those characteristic of free recall of disconnected material to those characteristic of serial anticipation. Thus, recall of sequentially dependent material involves more than the organization of words into larger groups, it also involves the reorganization of the patterns of emission of responses and changing the relative frequency with which items in various positions are recalled.

References

1. Bousfield, W. A., & Cohen, B. H. The occurrence of clustering in the recall of randomly arranged words of different frequencies-of-usage. *J. gen. Psychol.*, 1955, **52**, 83–95.
2. Bousfield, W. A., Cohen, B. H., & Silva, J. G. The extension of Marbe's law to the recall of stimulus-words. *Amer. J. Psychol.*, 1956, **69**, 429–433.

3. Miller, G. A., & Selfridge, J. A. Verbal context and the recall of meaningful material. *Amer. J. Psychol.*, 1950, **63**, 176–187.

4. Raffel, G. Two determinants of the effect of primacy. *Amer. J. Psychol.*, 1936, **48**, 654–657.

5. Robinson, E. S., & Brown, M. A. Effect of serial position upon memorization. *Amer. J. Psychol.*, 1926, **37**, 538–552.

6. Siegel, S. *Nonparametric statistics.* N. Y.: McGraw-Hill, 1956.

7. Thorndike, E. L., & Lorge, I. The teacher's word book of 30,000 words. N. Y.: Bureau of Publications, Teacher's Coll., Columbia Univer., 1944.

8. Welch, G. B., & Burnett, C. T. Is primacy a factor in association-formation? *Amer. J. Psychol.*, 1924, **35**, 396–401.

(Received July 30, 1956)

ARTICLE 6

The Role of Semantic and Syntactic Constraints in the Memorization of English Sentences[1]

LAWRENCE E. MARKS AND GEORGE A. MILLER

Harvard University, Cambridge, Massachusetts

It has been shown by Miller and Isard (1963) that the intelligibility of strings of English words depends, at least in part, on their conformity to linguistic rules known by the listener. Other things being equal, intelligibility is highest for meaningful grammatical sentences, lower for semantically anomalous (grammatical but meaningless) sentences, and lowest for ungrammatical strings of words. Apparently, both syntactic and semantic rules provide psychologically effective constraints on the number of alternative messages that a listener expects to hear. When strings of words follow these rules, perceptual processing is facilitated and intelligibility is increased.

If adherence to syntactic and semantic rules increases the intelligibility of strings of words, it might be expected that memorizing such strings would likewise be facilitated. Miller and Selfridge (1953) reported that the recall of strings of words improves as their order of approximation to the statistical pattern of English increases. Statistical approximations to English, however, do not distinguish between the syntactic and semantic factors that underlie the sequential contingencies. In the present experiment, strings of words were constructed in which semantic and syntactic rules could be violated independently. *S*s' performance in a free-recall type of learning situation was then compared for the various types of strings. We expected that, when syntactic and/or semantic rules were disrupted, the least disrupted strings would be most easily recalled, and that specific and predictable types of errors would occur in the recall of the disrupted strings. These expectations were confirmed by the experimental data.

[1] This investigation was supported in part by grant NSF G-16486 from the National Science Foundation and in part by PHS research grant MH-05120-02, both to Harvard University, Center for Cognitive Studies. Supported also in part by funds from the Department of Defense, Advanced Research Projects Agency, Contract SD-187.

METHOD

Materials

The method of construction of meaningful grammatical sentences and semantically anomalous sentences has been described by Miller and Isard (1963), and thus will be treated here only briefly. Five normal sentences of five words each with identical syntactic structures (adjective–plural noun–verb–adjective–plural noun) were constructed. From these original sentences five more sentences were derived by taking the first word from the first sentence, the second from the second, and so on. The syntactic structure of these derivative sentences remained identical to that of the normal sentences, but, because of the word substitutions, the derivative sentences were semantically anomalous.

In addition, two other types of strings of words were derived. The first, which we shall call anagram strings, was constructed by taking each of the normal sentences and scrambling the word-order, each sentence being scrambled somewhat differently in order to avoid the possibility of *S*s noticing any pattern, with care being taken that none of the scrambled sentences was grammatical. Thus nothing was done to the semantic components of these sentences, but the normal syntactic structure was destroyed. Finally, strings of words which we shall call word-lists were similarly formed by scrambling

Reprinted with permission of the authors and the publisher, the Academic Press. The article appeared originally in the *Journal of Verbal Learning and Verbal Behavior*, 1964, **3**, 1–5.

the word-order of the anomalous sentences. The word-lists preserved neither the syntactic structure nor the semantic components of the original sentences.

Five strings of each type were formed. Two sets of materials, each containing all four types of strings, were constructed. These materials are presented in full in the Appendix. It should be noticed that the words used are not in general high-frequency words in English. As Miller and Isard pointed out, high-frequency words have multiple syntactic and semantic roles which they can play, so that scrambling or substituting them is less likely to produce ungrammatical or semantically anomalous derivatives.

Procedure

Each group of four strings was recorded on magnetic tape by one of the experimenters (LEM). They were read at the rate of about 5 words in 3½ sec, with about 2 sec between strings. Since 5 trials were run, each group of strings was recorded 5 times, the order of the strings being varied from trial to trial according to a latin-square design.

The recorded strings were played to *S*s in a quiet room. On each trial *S*s listened to all 5 strings, then had 2 min in which to write them down in any order as accurately as possible. *S*s were requested to guess if they were uncertain.

Twenty-four groups of 4 *S*s were used. *S*s were Harvard and Radcliffe undergraduates and graduate students. Each group was tested on two different types of strings, one from each of the two sets of materials. Each of the four types of string from each set was given first to three groups and was then followed by one of the other three types from the other set. Thus, each of the 24 possible combinations of two sets of strings was presented to one group of 4 *S*s.

RESULTS

There was a marked warm-up effect for all groups of *S*s from the first to the second set of materials learned. Since this effect was of secondary interest, and since the relative differences among the four types of test materials were essentially the same on both the first and the second tasks, the results of the same type of strings for the two sets were combined. The counterbalanced design of the experiment made such a combination possible.

Three alternative ways of scoring *S*s' performance were used; the results for each are given in Figs. 1–3. Figure 1 shows the median per cent of words correct on each trial for the four types of material. In order for a word to be correct, it had to be written as presented and in its correct position relative to the other words recalled in the string. Clearly, learning was most rapid for the normal sentences and most difficult for the word-lists. The curves for the anomalous sentences and for the anagram strings are almost identical.

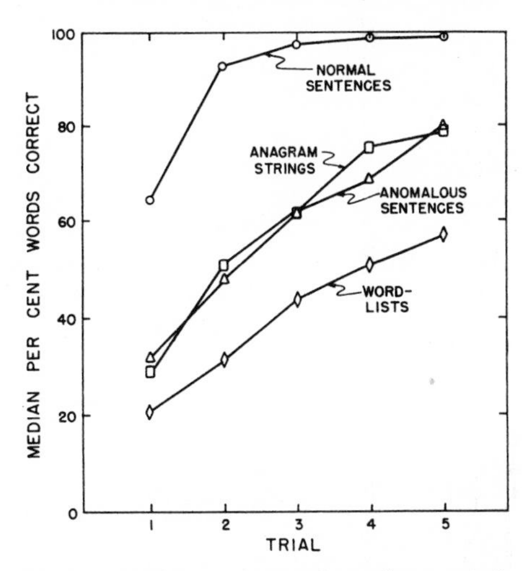

FIG. 1. Median per cent of words correct for each of the four types of strings over five trials. A word was counted as correct only if it appeared in its correct position in the string.

Figure 2 shows the median per cent of total words correct. That is to say, words counted as correct if they occurred together in a presented string, but regardless of the position in the string in which *S*s recalled them. These functions are similar to those of Fig. 1, except that the anagram strings here are slightly superior to the anomalous sentences. This difference is due to the fact that a relatively large number of inversions occurred in the responses to anagram strings.

Scores for complete strings recalled were, of course, lower than word scores, as Fig. 3 indicates. Normal sentences are far superior to the other three; word-lists are the lowest. With this method of scoring, however, ano-

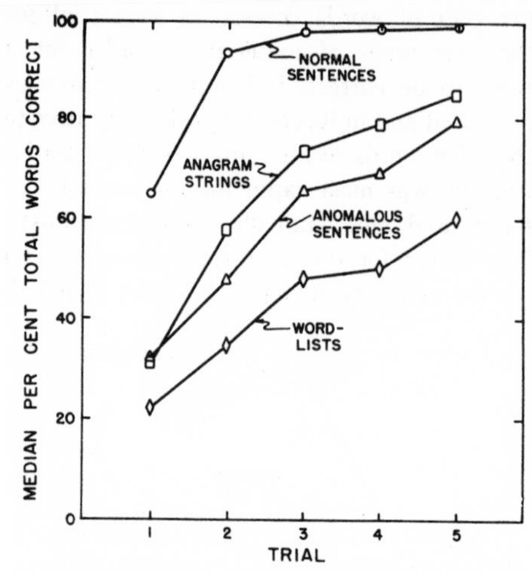

FIG. 2. Median per cent of total words correct for each of the four types of strings over five trials. A word was counted as correct regardless of its position in the string.

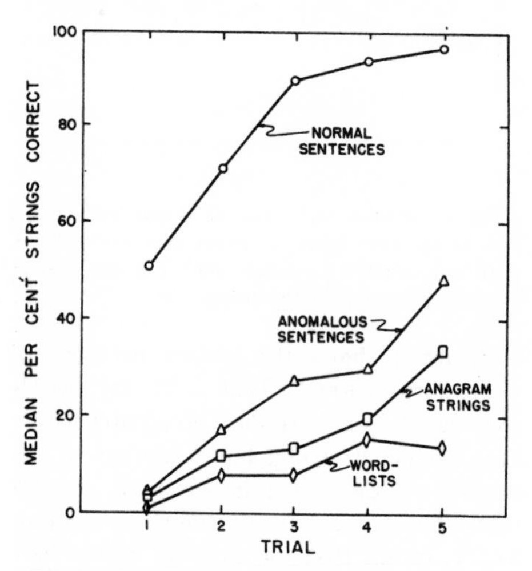

FIG. 3. Median per cent of complete strings correct for each of the four types of strings over five trials.

malous sentences were definitely better recalled than anagram strings.

Three types of errors in *S*s' responses for the five trials were analyzed: inversions, bound-morpheme errors, and intrusions. The results are summarized in Table 1.

Inversions of words within strings occurred most frequently in the case of anagram strings, rarely in the other three cases. They are somewhat more common to word-lists than to normal or anomalous sentences, and significantly so at each of Trials 2–5 (χ^2 for each $\geqslant 6.5$, $p < 0.01$). There is no significant difference in the frequency of inversions between the normal and anomalous sentences.

TABLE 1
MEDIAN NUMBER OF THREE TYPES OF ERROR FOR EACH *S* FOR THE FOUR TYPES OF STRINGS OVER FIVE TRIALS

String	Trial	Inversions	Bound-morpheme error	Intrusions
Normal sentences	1	0.15	0.75	0.19
	2	0.04	0.17	0.12
	3	0.02	0.13	0.05
	4	0.00	0.09	0.02
	5	0.01	0.06	0.06
Anomalous sentences	1	0.10	0.27	1.42
	2	0.07	0.30	1.09
	3	0.07	0.13	1.00
	4	0.04	0.25	0.83
	5	0.04	0.30	0.50
Anagram strings	1	1.39	1.61	0.42
	2	2.70	2.63	0.21
	3	2.59	2.90	0.17
	4	1.94	2.77	0.09
	5	1.15	2.50	0.10
Word-lists	1	0.08	0.63	0.83
	2	0.32	1.44	1.29
	3	0.30	1.64	1.43
	4	0.30	1.37	0.94
	5	0.25	1.61	0.90

Bound-morpheme errors refer to the omission or incorrect addition of prefixes and suffixes. The majority of these were omissions of the plural *–s*. Again, these errors are most frequent in anagram strings. They are also common to word-lists but are relatively rare in normal and anomalous sentences, except for the former on Trial 1.

The final type of error studied was intrusions. These concern the misplacing of words from one string to another in the group of strings being learned. Intrusions are most common to the word-lists and anomalous sentences, and rare in normal sentences and anagram strings. They are most frequent in word-lists, but the difference is significant only with respect to anomalous sentences at Trial 1 ($\chi^2 = 5.44$, $p < 0.01$).

Discussion

It is clear that, in this experimental situation at least, syntactic and semantic structure facilitate learning. The role of the former has previously been studied by Epstein (1961, 1962), who concluded that the facilitation is apparently the result not of constraints which reduce the number of possible alternatives, but of some sort of "chunking" according to grammatical rules (see Miller, 1956). As mentioned above, constraints due to transitional probabilities do not distinguish between semantic and syntactic factors. Yet these two seem distinguishable on the basis of error scores.

The three types of error scores may be placed into two categories: semantic and syntactic errors. Intrusions can be considered as semantic errors, related to decisions as to which words may combine in a sentence, and thus occur most frequently in anomalous sentences and word-lists, where semantic rules are violated. Bound-morpheme errors and inversions can be considered as syntactic errors: the first related to grammatical tags, the second to word-order. Both occur most frequently in anagram strings and word-lists, where syntactic rules are violated. Apparently, therefore, these errors give support to the contention that syntactic and semantic rules have psychological as well as linguistic reality.

Figure 1 indicates almost no difference between the relative frequencies of correctly placed words for anomalous sentences and anagram strings; using a more lenient scoring method that ignores order, however, the scores (Fig. 2) for anagram strings are higher. It can be argued that the similarity between the two sets of scores is in line with the conclusion reached by Epstein. If the facilitory effect on learning of syntactic and semantic structure is due to chunking, then, for these strings at least, one would conclude that the *average* size of the chunks is the same in anomalous sentences and anagram strings. However, string scores (Fig. 3) show the anomalous sentences well above anagram strings. Thus, it would seem that the chunks formed in the recall of anomalous strings are more varied in length, more nearly "all-or-none," and are more consistent in the recall of anagram strings.

Summary

Ninety-six *S*s learned normal sentences, anomalous sentences, anagram strings, and word-lists for five trials by the method of free recall. The results demonstrate a differentiation between semantic and syntactic factors and a facilitory effect of both on learning.

Appendix

The Two Sets of Materials Used in the Present Experiment

Set I

Original Sentences: Rapid flashes augur violent storms. Pink bouquets emit fragrant odors. Fatal accidents deter careful drivers. Melting snows cause sudden floods. Noisy parties wake sleeping neighbors.

Anomalous Sentences: Rapid bouquets deter sudden neighbors. Pink accidents cause sleeping storms. Fatal snows wake violent odors. Melting parties augur fragrant drivers. Noisy flashes emit careful floods.

Anagram Strings: Rapid augur violent flashes storms. Bouquets pink odors fragrant emit. Deter drivers accidents fatal careful. Sudden melting cause floods snows. Neighbors sleeping noisy wake parties.

Word Lists: Rapid deter sudden bouquets neighbors. Accidents pink storms sleeping cause. Wake odors snows fatal violent. Fragrant melting augur drivers parties. Floods careful noisy emit flashes.

Set II

Original Sentences: Furry wildcats fight furious battles. Respectable jewelers give accurate appraisals. Lighted cigarettes create smoky fumes. Gallant gentlemen save distressed damsels. Soapy detergents dissolve greasy stains.

Anomalous Strings: Furry jewelers create distressed stains. Respectable cigarettes save greasy battles. Lighted gentlemen dissolve furious appraisals. Gallant detergents fight accurate fumes. Soapy wildcats give smoky damsels.

Anagram Strings: Furry fight furious wildcats battles. Jewelers respectable appraisals accurate give. Create fumes cigarettes lighted smoky. Distressed gallant save damsels gentlemen. Stains greasy soapy dissolve detergents.

Word Lists: Furry create distressed jewelers stains. Cigarettes respectable battles greasy save. Dissolve appraisals gentlemen lighted furious. Accurate gallant fight fumes detergents. Damsels smoky soapy give wildcats.

References

Epstein, W. The influence of syntactical structure on learning. *Amer. J. Psychol.*, 1961, 74, 80-85.

Epstein, W. A further study of the influence of syntactical structure on learning. *Amer. J. Psychol.*, 1962, **75**, 121-126.

Miller, G. A. The magical number seven, plus-or-minus two: some limits on our capacity for processing information. *Psychol. Rev.*, 1956, **63**, 81-97.

Miller, G. A., and Isard, S. Some perceptual consequences of linguistic rules. *J. Verb. Learn. Verb. Behav.*, 1963., **2**, 217-228.

Miller, G. A., and Selfridge, J. A. Verbal context and the recall of meaningful material. *Amer. J. Psychol.*, 1953, **63**, 176-185.

(Received July 15, 1963)

ARTICLE 7

Some Effects of Grammatical Transformations on the Recall of English Sentences[1]

JACQUES MEHLER

Harvard University, Cambridge, Massachusetts

It is an all too common observation that we can understand the general significance of a verbal message even though we may be unable to repeat the exact words in which it was originally expressed. To give a precise account of all that goes on under these circumstances would, of course, be difficult if not impossible; yet it has been possible to isolate some aspects of the process and to study them by experiments on the memorization of connected discourse. The present paper represents an attempt to extend this general line of investigation by exploiting certain concepts that have proved useful in descriptive linguistics.

The fact that a person can often rephrase "in his own words" the general sense of a message that he has not yet memorized in precise detail would seem to indicate that semantic components of a meaningful message are generally easier to recall than are its specific grammatical details. In the present experiment, therefore, we have attempted to explore this possible difference in a systematic manner. In general terms, the strategy adopted was the following: a set of eight short sentences was presented to the S, who was instructed that he would be tested for recall. The sentences differed systematically in their grammatical forms; they might be either active or passive, affirmative or negative, declarative or interrogative. The S's responses were then scored both for semantic accuracy (did he recall one of the eight sentences, regardless of grammatical form?) and for syntactic accuracy (given that a sentence was recalled, was its grammatical form correct?). The results of a preliminary study using this general approach have already been reported by Miller (1962).

The syntactic description used here is essentially Chomsky's (1957). According to Chomsky's grammar, most sentences are derived from more fundamental ones by certain special rules, called transformations. The fundamental, or kernel (K), sentences are, in the vocabulary of traditional grammar, simple, active, affirmative, declarative sentences, such as *The boy has hit the ball, The girl has worn the jewel*, etc. Only three grammatical transformations are considered in this experiment: the negative (N), the passive (P), and the interrogative (Q). When the N transformation is applied to *The boy has hit the ball* it produces a new sentence, *The boy hasn't hit the ball*. When P is applied to the same K sentence, it produces *The ball has been hit by the boy*. The Q transformation applied to the same K sentence produces *Has the ball been hit by the boy?* These transformations may also be applied in combination to produce, for example, a passive-negative-question

[1] This research was supported by funds from the Public Health Service research grant No. M-05120-02 from the National Institutes of Health, by the National Science Foundation grant No. NSF-G-16486, and by the Carnegie Corporation of New York, to Harvard University, Center for Cognitive Studies.

I want to express my gratitude to Professor G. A. Miller for his advice on the form and content of this paper. Also I want to thank Dr. H. B. Savin for his criticism of earlier drafts and for the encouragement he gave me.

Reprinted with permission of the author and the publisher, the Academic Press. The article appeared originally in the *Journal of Verbal Learning and Verbal Behavior*, 1963, 2, 346–351.

(*PNQ*), ***Hasn't the ball been hit by the boy?***

Application of these transformations in all possible combinations will generate seven transformed sentences for each *K*. The relations between these eight sentences can be simply represented by a cube, as in Fig. 1,

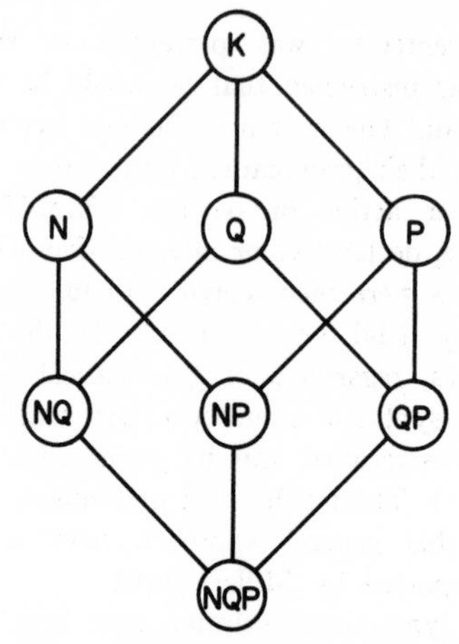

FIG. 1. Syntactic relations of the eight sentences. Each vertex corresponds to a type of sentence, and adjacent vertices correspond to pairs of sentences that differ only by one transformation.

where each vertex corresponds to a type of sentence, and adjacent vertices correspond to pairs of sentences that differ by only a singular transformation.

METHOD

Materials

The following eight kernel sentences were used: ***The man has bought the house; The boy has taken the photograph; The biologist has made the discovery; The girl has worn the jewel; The student has written the essay; The car has hit the tree; The airplane has carried the passenger;*** and ***The secretary has typed the paper.*** The eight kernel sentences, together with their seven transformations, give 64 sentences, which were divided into eight groups of eight sentences in such a way that in each group no sentence and no transformation were represented more than once. Each of the eight groups of sentences was the experimental material for one group of *S*s.

Procedure

Each set of eight sentences was presented for five successive trials, each time in a different order. Ten *S*s at a time (chosen randomly) listened to the sentences, which were recorded on magnetic tape with a separation of 2 sec. between the end of one sentence and the beginning of the next.

After each presentation, *S*s attempted to recall the sentences; they wrote their responses in a recall booklet that had five pages, one for each of the five trials. On each page were listed eight prompting words, one for each sentence; four of these prompting words were subjects and four were predicates. For example, a page in the booklet might contain the words ***man, boy, biologist, girl, tree, essay, paper, airplane,*** listed vertically on the page. The use of prompting words to improve the recall of the underlying kernel sentences is the principal methodological difference between the present experiment and the preliminary study reported by Miller (1962).

The instructions asked the *S*s to complete their recall as quickly as possible, although no definite time limit was specified.

There were 80 *S*s, all native speakers of English currently enrolled in an American university.

RESULTS

Figure 2 shows the acquisition curves for each of the various transformations, where per cent recalled correctly is plotted as a function of the trial number. The most striking fact in Fig. 2 is the greater facility with which *S*s learned the kernel sentences. At each trial the difference between *K* and all the other types of sentences is significant at least at $p < .005$ for the first and last trials and at $p < .001$ for the other three trials. In this experiment the number of words in a sentence was not a good predictor of the ease of learning; although the *P* sentences contained more words, they were somewhat better learned than the *Q* sentences.

Figure 3 presents the percentages of the various kinds of errors that occurred on successive trials. A sentence was scored by means of the following rules:

(a) A sentence is scored as *correct* if it is a verbatim reproduction of the stimulus sentence or if it differs from the stimulus sentence only by (i) the replacement of a word

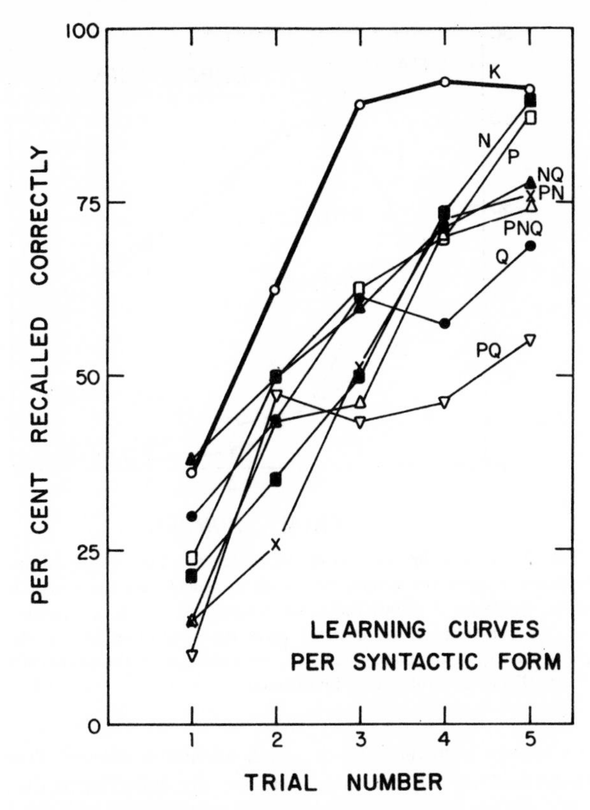

FIG. 2. Acquisition curves for each of the transformed sentences. The kernel is learned with greater facility than any of the other sentences.

TABLE 1
ERRORS IN RECALL

Stimuli	Responses								
	K	N	Q	P	NQ	NP	QP	NPQ	Totals
K	300	14	12	14	8	4	1	3	356
N	36	234	20	3	29	11	6	2	341
Q	31	16	210	1	72	2	8	12	352
P	43	3	8	243	15	10	30	13	365
NQ	29	15	31	3	221	3	7	23	332
NP	6	49	9	18	16	191	16	31	336
QP	13	5	32	27	29	15	145	60	326
NPQ	2	2	14	16	44	5	38	182	303
Totals	460	338	336	325	434	241	251	326	2711
Per cent of total number of errors	16.2	10.5	12.8	8.3	21.6	5.1	10.8	14.6	

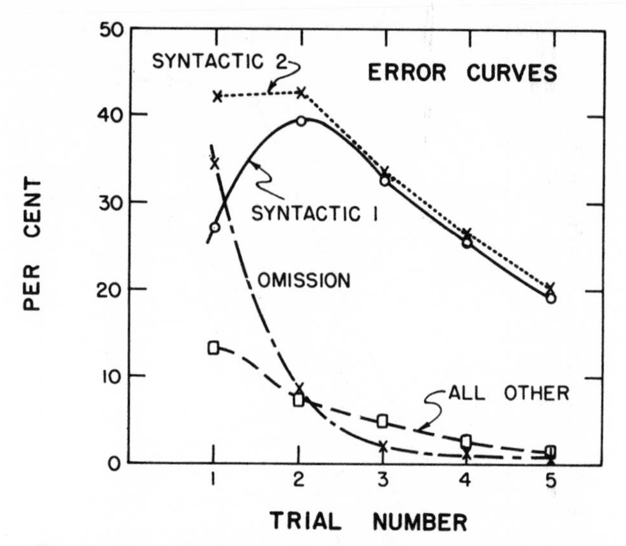

FIG. 3. Errors in free recall of sentences. The curve labeled *Syntactic 1* gives the proportion of all sentences that are syntactic errors. *Syntactic 2* shows the same proportion of actual responses that are syntactic errors. *Omitted* gives the proportion of all sentences that were completely omitted. *All others* gives the proportion of miscellaneous errors (e.g., inventions).

by a synonym; (ii) a change from the definite to the indefinite article; and/or (iii) a change in tense.

(b) A sentence is scored as a *syntactic error* if and only if it can be derived from a correct sentence [as defined in (a) above] by applying one or more of the singular transformations P, Q, or N or their inverses. If a recalled sentence is correct except for a syntactic error, then by definition its *sentence-content* is the same as the one in the original sentence.

(c) A sentence is said to be omitted when no recognizable part of it occurs in recall.

(d) All other errors are errors that do not fit any of the above categories.

Among the various types of other errors were pure inventions, partial inventions, conjugation of two sentences, etc. In Fig. 3 it can be seen that omissions drop steeply between Trials 1 and 2 and remain at a low level thereafter. Syntactic errors, however, increase to a maximum around Trial 2 and then decrease; this inflection is due, of course, to the many omissions on the first trial, as can be seen from the curve labeled SYN 2, since *S*s could not make syntactic errors on the sentences they did not remember at all.

A matrix showing the total number of syntactic confusions of each type on all five trials is given in Table 1; the rows indicate the syntactic form of the sentence that was presented, the columns indicate the syntactic form of the sentence that was recalled, and the cell entries give the raw frequencies of occurrences of each stimulus-response combination. Entries on the main diagonal, of course, indicate the number of sentences of each type that were correctly recalled. The bottom row of the matrix gives the proportion of the total number of errors of each syntactic category.

The probability of coding correctly the sentence-content of the sentences is .85. The probabilities of recalling correctly each of the transformations are respectively $p_N = .81$; $p_P = .83$; $p_Q = .86$.

Discussion

These results suggest a partial answer to the question of how *S* can remember the general sense of a sentence even when he cannot repeat it verbatim. Very roughly, the suggested answer is that *S*s do not recall the sentence verbatim, but rather that they analyze it syntactically and encode it as a kernel sentence plus appropriate transformation. For example, if the sentence is ***The ball has been hit by the boy,*** then *S* presumably codes it as an underlying kernel plus some "mental tag" that indicates that the passive transformation must be applied for recall. Exactly how the kernel is encoded, of course, is not established; it might be an image, an abstract set of symbols, or anything else capable of regenerating the kernel sentence on demand.

In support of this schema-plus-correction hypothesis, one notes a strong tendency for *S*s to simplify the syntactic structure. Not only were kernel sentences easier to recall, but from Table 1 we can count 468 syntactic errors that (in terms of Fig. 1) involve responses nearer to the kernel than was the correct response, but only 380 errors in the opposite direction. (If we ignore the more or less natural confusions between *Q* and *NQ* and between *QP* and *NPQ*, this difference becomes even more obvious: 400 to 248.) Moreover, the nature of the errors in *K* is also suggestive; the great majority of them were simple omissions.

In his report of our preliminary data, Miller (1962) suggested that there are three syntactic "footnotes" that are remembered more or less independently. This hypothesis of independence, however, is not critical for the general hypothesis that *S* stores the information after analyzing it into its separate syntactic and semantic components. In particular there is one notable exception to the proposal that the three transformations might be encoded independently: *Q* and *NQ* are frequently confused, as are *PQ* and *NPQ*. Questions, both active and passive, are more likely than nonquestions to be recalled in the negative. Thus more often than we would expect on the assumption of independence, *Q* is recalled as *NQ*, and *QP* as *NQP*. This interaction between *N* and *Q* transformations is undoubtedly related to the fact that affirmative and negative questions mean the same thing (***Has the boy hit the ball?*** vs. ***Hasn't the boy hit the ball?***), whereas affirmative and negative declarative sentences mean very different things (***The boy has hit the ball*** vs. ***The boy hasn't hit the ball***).

Fortunately, however, independence of the recall of the various transformations is not essential for a schema-plus-correction type of hypothesis. The critical point is that the great majority of the errors people made consisted of sentences that could be derived from the correct sentence by omitting or applying syntactic transformations; it would not be possible to account for this fact by any theory of recall that neglected these syntactic operations.

Moreover, if one accepts the kernel sentence as psychologically simpler and, in some sense, closer to the way we understand the meanings of sentences, then we may also have a partial explanation for the fact, reported in numerous studies of thinking and concept learning, that negative information is harder to use than affirmative information. The difficulty may be due, at least in part, to the fact that negative sentences involve an additional syntactic transformation. The validity of this explanation might be tested by investigating the use of information expressed in passive sentences or in questions.

Summary

The recall of English sentences varying systematically in syntactic structure was studied by the method of prompted recall with 80 *Ss*. Analysis of the errors indicated that most of them were due to syntactical confusions. The hypothesis is advanced that *Ss* analyze the sentences into a semantic component plus syntactic corrections when they learn them, and that this separation of semantic content from syntactic form is one reason that the general meaning of a message is generally so much easier to recall than its exact wording.

References

Chomsky, N. *Syntactic structures.* 'S-Gravenhage: Mouton, 1957.

Miller, G. A. Some psychological studies of grammar. *Amer. Psychol.*, 1962, **17**, 748-762.

(Received March 18, 1963)

Part Two

TRANSFER

CHAPTER 8

Classical St-R Paradigms

Transfer is a gross learning phenomenon that represents the effects of past on present acquisition. Like acquisition, transfer has been a focal point for verbal learning theory and research, both historically and presently. For detailed reviews of the older literature on transfer in verbal learning the reader is referred to Ellis (1965), McGeoch and Irion (1952), and Osgood (1953). The hallmark of the contemporary period has been the increasing precision of the analysis of gross transfer effects into component subphenomena or mechanisms. As a corollary of this analysis, more exact determinations of the functional relationships between relevant independent variables and gross transfer effects are rapidly accruing. By gross transfer effect we mean the overall, observable outcome of the complexity of mechanisms that may enter into any given transfer situation. Gross transfer effects vary two-dimensionally—in direction and in degree. Directionally, they range from positive to negative, with zero (i.e., no transfer effect) as the in-between point. Positive and negative refer to facilitation and hindrance, respectively, with respect to the effect of past on present acquisition; zero means that there is no observable carry-over from past to present acquisition. Degree of transfer specifies the magnitude of facilitation (positive transfer) or hindrance (negative transfer) as determined by the extent of departure from zero transfer.

Perhaps even more than acquisition, transfer reflects the centrality (cf. Overview) of verbal learning laws and processes. The inexorable progress being made in our understanding of transfer as it occurs in the verbal learning laboratory should, in turn, transfer extensively to other areas and situations of learning. Of special significance is the viability of transfer principles and laws within the framework of educational, industrial, and military training programs (cf. Ellis, 1965, Chapter 7).

In Part One it was frequently emphasized that verbal acquisition is rarely accomplished independently of past acquisition. However, experiments concerned with acquisition ordinarily relegate past acquisition to a role that is presumed, unspecified, and unmeasured; that is, the stress is on present acquisition, rather than on the contribution of past acquisition. Partial exceptions occur in some problem areas of acquisition, but even here, transfer serves mainly as the *modus operandi* for demonstrating phenomena of acquisition. For example, transfer offers an effective experimental design for testing hypotheses about such phenomena as the locus of the stimulus in SL (cf. Introduction, Chapter 1) and the nature of cue selection in PA acquisition (cf. Article

4, Chapter 2). In Part Two transfer itself is the phenomenon studied, and contemporary studies on the laws and mechanisms of transfer will be surveyed and sampled.

The content of this chapter is concerned with transfer as determined by stimulus-response relationships between two lists. The first list (or List 1) represents past acquisition, and the second list (or List 2) represents the present acquisition for which we wish to assess transfer effects. Transfer paradigms (i.e., models that symbolically describe the inter-list relationships) of the two-list variety are commonly called two stage paradigms. Two-stage paradigms may also be considered classical in the sense of their long-standing prominence in transfer theory and research. In Chapter 9 we shall turn to additional paradigms that have had a briefer history but which have, nevertheless, stimulated feverish research activity in the contemporary period. These paradigms involve three (or possibly more) lists—that is, they are three-stage paradigms. Here Lists 1 and 2 represent past acquisition, with List 3 being the present or transfer list. Three-stage variants differ from the two-stage ones in that the relationships between the first and third lists are affected by their commonality with either the stimuli or responses of the intervening second list. First-to-third list transfer is then presumed to be mediated via symbolic activity associated with this commonality. For this reason, three-stage paradigms are also called mediational paradigms. However, mediation itself, as we shall see, is a transfer mechanism frequently hypothesized to account for positive transfer effects in several two-stage paradigms. Because of the great importance of identifying the nature of inter-list stimulus-response relationships in both two and three stage paradigms, most contemporary studies on transfer have utilized PA lists rather than SL lists (recognizing once more the difficulty of identifying stimulus components in SL lists). Occasionally, however, SL lists are still being employed (e.g., Keppel, in press) when the nature of the problem dictates their use.

Nonspecific and Specific Transfer

An operational definition of transfer as a gross, comprehensive phenomenon was given in the Overview in terms of the *E*/*C* differential. Both an experimental (*E*) and a control (*C*) group practice on the same transfer or present acquisition list (identified as List 2). In addition, Group *E* receives practice on a prior acquisition list (identified as List 1) which bears some relationship, via either the stimulus or response components of the two lists, to List 2. The nature of this relationship determines the name of the paradigm represented by Group *E*. By common practice the stimuli of List 1 are called *A* terms and the responses *B* terms. Thus, List 1 becomes an *A-B* list. A number of possibilities exist for the construction of List 2 pairings, the choice being contingent on the transfer law or mechanism under investigation. We might, for example, wish to make the responses in List 2 identical with those of List 1 but have the two sets of stimuli unrelated. In this case, the List 2 pairings become *C-B* (new stimuli, old responses), and the overall paradigm is labeled the *A-B*, *C-B* paradigm. Or we might make the stimuli in List 2 identical with those of List 1 but introduce new response terms. The paradigm is then *A-B*, *A-C* (old stimuli, new responses). Other important paradigms will be introduced at a later point. Returning to our *E*/*C* definition, the treatment of Group *C* is a critical issue. The simplest treatment would be to let Group *C* practice on List 2 only, without prior practice on the List 1 given to Group *E*. The difference in proficiency of acquisition between Groups *E* and *C* on List 2 defines transfer in its broadest terms of direction and degree.

One of the major developments in contemporary research on transfer has been the recognition that two discrete sources contribute to the gross transfer effect yielded by the above simple design. These two sources, each of which may be fractionated into further subphenomenal components, are *nonspecific* and *specific* transfer. Nonspecific transfer results from practice on a list prior to the transfer task, regardless of the stimulus-response relationships between the prior and transfer lists. In other words, nonspecific transfer is independent of list content. Specific transfer, on the other hand, varies with the relationships between the stimulus and/or response components of the two lists. The underlying dimension is inter-list similarity, ranging from identity of components to relatedness (either primarily or secondarily) to neutrality, rather than intra-list similarity. The laws describing the relationships between inter-list similarity and the direction and degree of overall transfer are called primary laws. We shall return to them at a later point.

Nonspecific transfer is positive in direction; that is, a group of *Ss* given List 2, following practice on an unrelated List 1, ordinarily performs more proficiently than another group of *Ss* given List 2 practice only. Dimensional analyses of nonspecific transfer have indicated that two separate and isolable subphenomena, warm-up and learning-to-learn, are involved. Both subphenomena were well demonstrated before the contemporary period (e.g., Hamilton, 1950; Harlow, 1949; Thune, 1950). An important feature of the contemporary period, however, has been the increasing recognition given to the need to tease out the effects of both warm-up and learning-to-learn from overall transfer effects when the laws and mechanisms of specific transfer are at stake. Another feature of the contemporary period has been the inauguration by Postman of a series of experiments designed to provide a further analysis of learning-to-learn into its component mechanisms. In this analysis, an initial distinction is made between warm-up and learning-to-learn, with warm-up referring to the development of a set (e.g., postural adjustments, adoption of an optimal pacing for emitting responses, etc.) which maximizes performance proficiency, and learning-to-learn to the acquisition of various instrumental habits (e.g., acquiring effective techniques of mediation) related to mastery of the task at hand. In the first study of the series, Postman and Schwartz (1964) found that learning-to-learn transfer centers largely in the associative stage of PA acquisition. Moreover, the amount of transfer is partly dependent on the method of practice on List 1, being greater if List 1 is also a PA list than if it is a SL list, and on the class of materials for List 1, being greater if List 1 contains the same class (e.g., adjectives) as List 2 than if List 1 contains a different class (e.g., trigrams in one list and adjectives in the other). The second study (Postman, 1964b) in the series is relevant to the secondary laws of specific transfer and is reprinted as Article 7 of this chapter.

Methodological Issues in the Measurement of Specific Transfer

The basic methodology for measuring specific transfer as it is manifested above and beyond nonspecific transfer effects was given in the Overview with the *A-B*, *C-B* paradigm as the illustrative experimental condition. For further emphasis of the underlying rationale, we shall restate the method as it applies to the *A-B*, *A-C* paradigm for Group *E*. Group *E* receives *A-B* pairs on List 1 and *A-C* pairs on List 2. For Group *C*, however, there are two alternative courses of action. We might give this group practice on List 2 (the *A-C* pairings) only. In this event, the differential between Groups *E* and *C* would reflect both nonspecific positive transfer in Group *E* resulting from prior practice on the *A-B* pairs and specific negative transfer resulting from unlearning and interference (see below). The resultant observable transfer (the summation of the separate contributions) may well be close to zero. Assuming our interest is in specific transfer per se, this method confounds specific with nonspecific transfer. A more adequate method consists of requiring Group *C* to practice on *two* lists of unrelated content, thus equating List 2 for both groups in terms of nonspecific effects. Symbolically, the list conditions for Group *C* may be designated as *A-B*, *C-D*. Now the *E*, *C* difference on List 2 may be linked directly to specific transfer effects in Group *E*. Transfer studies in the contemporary era have been characterized by an increasingly greater and greater reliance on the *A-B*, *C-D* paradigm as the appropriate control condition.

A problem remains before we have assurance that the *E*, *C* difference yielded by this second method provides an unbiased estimate of specific transfer. The symbols for the *E* and *C* paradigms (*A-B*, *A-C* and *A-B*, *C-D*) imply that Groups *E* and *C* receive identical Lists 1 but different Lists 2. With variation in content for the two second lists, it is conceivable that specific transfer effects are confounded by differential difficulty of the items in the two lists (as determined, perhaps, by differences in response meaningfulness, pre-experimental strength of associations, etc.). This difference could exaggerate or attenuate the measured amount of transfer, depending on which of the two second lists is more difficult. To obviate this possibility, it has become standard practice in the last few years to make List 2 identical in item content for Groups *E* and *C*. The inter-group variations in content that define the paradigms themselves are then introduced in List 1. For our present example, the corrected paradigms for Groups *E* and *C* become *A-C*, *A-B* and *C-D*, *A-B*, respectively. Nevertheless, the reverse labels (i.e., with *A-B* listed first in every paradigm) have managed to stick stubbornly in transfer terminology, even when inappropriate.

An experiment on specific transfer will often include two or more experimental paradigms (e.g., perhaps both the *A-B*, *A-C* and *A-B*, *C-B* paradigms) which are each to be contrasted with the control or *A-B*, *C-D* paradigm. Orthodox methodology in the past called for a separate group of *Ss* for each paradigm employed. Therefore, for each group the lists used are unmixed in the sense that they enter into only one paradigm. During the contemporary period, a popular practice, stimulated by the experiment of Twedt and Underwood (1959), has been to make use of a mixed list—that is, one that is heterogeneous in content with respect to inter-list transfer relationships. For example, a single group of *Ss* could be used to compare the above three paradigms by giving the *Ss* 2 nine-pair lists in which three of the pairs bear an *A-B*, *A-C* relationship, three an *A-B*, *C-B* relationship, and three an *A-B*, *C-D* relationship. With college students as *Ss*, Twedt and Underwood (1959) discovered that the direction of specific transfer for the several experimental paradigms they tested was the same whether the unmixed or mixed list method was used. Moreover, the amount of transfer was found to be approximately the same for both methods.

The mixed list method has the obvious advantage of a considerable economy in the number of *Ss* required in an experiment. The danger remains, however, that with other populations of *Ss* the estimates of the amounts of specific transfer may vary widely for the two methods. For children, anyway, Johnson and Penney (1965) found markedly different estimates for the mixed as compared to the unmixed method. Caution in the widespread use of the mixed method seems in order.

A final methodological issue pertains to the quantification of specific transfer. Transfer for an experimental paradigm is expressed in both absolute and relative terms with respect to the control paradigm. The usual procedure is to have separate *E* and *C* groups practice on List 1 to a criterion of mastery, followed by a fixed number of trials for both groups on List 2. Both absolute and relative transfer scores may be found from the number of correct responses (or, conversely, the number of errors) made during the trials on List 2. Assume that Group *E* averages 40 correct responses and Group *C* averages 50 during 10 trials on List 2. Absolute transfer is found by simply applying the formula *E-C*, where *E* is the average number of correct responses made by Group *E*, and *C* the comparable figure for Group *C*. In our present example, the amount of absolute transfer is —10, with the minus indicating that we have negative transfer. Relative transfer has less common agreement as to a standard formula, and a number of formulas have been proposed over the years, each with advantages and shortcomings (Murdock, 1957). Murdock (1957) introduced a formula that has since received widespread acceptance. The formula estimates the precentage of transfer by the expression $(E - C/E + C)$ (100). For our current example, relative transfer is —11.1 per cent as estimated by Murdock's formula. Relative transfer found by this formula ranges from 100 per cent to —100 per cent, thus satisfying an obvious goal of quantifications. With mixed lists, the *E* and *C* figures are based on the same group of *Ss*, but the computational procedures are unaltered.

Primary Laws of Specific Transfer

The primary laws of specific transfer are a set of descriptive relationships between variations in inter-list similarity, in terms of stimulus and/or response components, and the direction and degree of resultant transfer. Osgood (1949), in a monumental integration of the existing evidence on transfer, formulated three empirical laws which attempted a synthesis of the multitude of demonstrated relationships. These laws are given in the "Results" section of Wimer's (1964) article (Article 1) and will not be restated here. Osgood also depicted the three laws in the form of a three dimensional graph, commonly known as the transfer and retroaction surface (the laws of retroaction closely parallel those of transfer; cf. Introduction, Chapter 10), which is reproduced in Figure 1.

The *St* and *R* components of the surface represent the stimuli and responses of List 2 of a transfer (and/or retroaction) paradigm. The stimuli may be seen to vary along a continuum, with respect to their List 1 counterparts, from complete identity (S_I) to varying degrees of similarity (S_s) to complete neutrality (S_n). Responses also vary dimensionally from identity (R_I) to varying degree of similarity (R_s) and on to neutrality (R_n). In addition to these points along the response continuum, Osgood also included points beyond

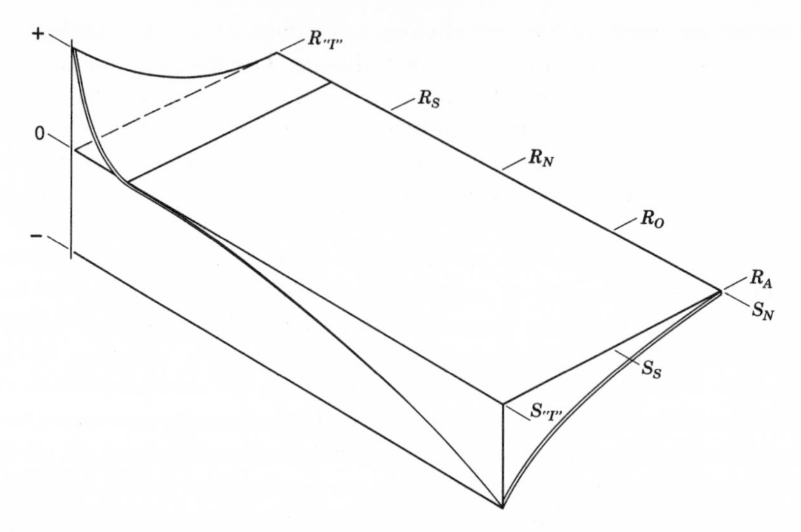

Fig. 1. Transfer and retroaction surface: medial plane represents effects of zero magnitude; response relations distributed along length of solid and stimulus relations along width. From C. E. Osgood, The similarity paradox in human learning: A resolution. *Psychological Review*, 1949, *56*, p. 140.

neutrality, ranging from responses with meaning opposite to that of the List 1 counterparts to responses with complete antonymity (R_a). By locating the appropriate coordinates, individual transfer paradigms may be placed on the surface and a prediction made concerning the expected direction and relative degree of transfer.

Specific points that are relevant to predictions from the transfer surface will be considered later when transfer mechanisms are discussed. For the moment, our concern is with contemporary efforts to validate the overall surface—that is, comprehensive tests that probe a number of critical points along the surface. Wimer's (1964; Article 1) study, using materials previously employed by Osgood (1946) himself, is especially sound and comprehensive. Earlier tests of the surface were made by Bugelski and Cadwallader (1956) and Dallett (1962). The former has the disadvantage associated with the use of different Lists 2 for the various transfer conditions and the inherent possibility of confounding task difficulty with transfer effects (cf. p. 362); the latter is less extensive in its scope than the Wimer study. Although these separate tests have confirmed large segments of the transfer surface, there nevertheless are several points where the validity of the surface is dubious, especially at points involving responses of opposite meaning and antonymity (Article 1). Wimer wisely suggested that it would behoove psychologists to conduct further validations with materials departing from those used in earlier validations.

Extensions of the Transfer Surface

Not all transfer paradigms may be fixed by locating coordinates along the axes of Osgood's transfer surface. Two unique kinds of List 1–List 2 relationships that fall outside of the surface have attracted considerable attention during the contemporary period. The two have in common the fact that they involve *R-St* associations (cf. introductory section and Article 5, Chapter 2). The first maximizes negative transfer by re-pairing in List 2 the stimuli and response components of List 1. The paradigm generated by this maneuver is symbolized as *A-B, A-Br*. The second kind of relationship is a generic one that embraces a number of possible paradigms, each of which involves an interaction between *St-R* and *R-St* associations of the two lists. For our purposes, paradigms of this kind will simply be called *R-St* paradigms.

A-B, A-Br Paradigm

The *A-B, A-Br* paradigm was introduced to verbal learning by Porter and Duncan (1953) who followed closely the procedure proposed by Gagne, Baker, and Foster (1950) as a means of producing massive negative transfer in a motor skills task. The procedure as applied to verbal materials may be illustrated by selecting three pairs from List 1, namely A_1-B_1, A_2-B_2, and A_3-B_3 and showing how they might enter into a repaired List 2. If List 2 contained A_1-B_2, A_2-B_3, and A_3-B_1, it would have stimuli and responses that are identical to those contained in List 1. However, *S* would be forced to learn new associations between these stimuli and responses.

Porter and Duncan (1953) contrasted transfer for this new paradigm with that for the standard *A-B, A-C* negative transfer paradigm. Since they did not control for nonspecific transfer, their estimate of the differential in absolute amount of specific transfer is spurious. Nevertheless, in relative terms, the negative transfer effect was considerably more pronounced for *A-Br* (for convenience we will frequently refer to a paradigm by its second list designation only) than for *A-C*.

The Porter and Duncan study employed unmixed lists. Later studies by Besch and Reynolds (1958), Kausler and Kanoti (1963), and Twedt and Underwood (1959) included both *A-Br* and *A-C* pairings in a mixed list, together with *C-D* control pairs. In each case, the absolute amount of negative transfer was greater for *A-Br* than for *A-C*.

In their interpretation of the greater negative effect in *A-Br* than in *A-C*, Porter and Duncan hinted at the probable role played by *R-St* associations. This interpretation has since become commonly accepted and elaborated on by others working within the *A-Br paradigm*. According to this view, re-paired stimuli and responses generate interference effects in both the forward (*St-R*) and backward (*R-St*) direction, whereas old stimuli paired with new responses (as in the *A-C* paradigm) generate interference in the forward direction only. Forward interference refers to the competition between the old and new response to a stimulus during List 2 practice. Returning to the symbolic List 2 pairs cited above, the A_1 stimulus on List 2 for the *A-Br* paradigm elicits two competing responses. One is B_1 which was learned as the association to A_1 during practice on List 1; the other is B_2 (carried over from List 1 but re-paired) which is now to be associated with A_1 during List 2 practice. The *R-St* associations involving B_2 as the stimulus for backward associations also enter into an interference relationship. During the acquisition of the A_1-B_2 pair of List 2, we may assume that *S* is simultaneously learning B_2-A_1 as the *R-St* association. Moreover, we may also assume that *S* had already learned B_2-A_2 as the *R-St* association for the A_2-B_2 pair of List 1. Consequently, A_1 and A_2 compete as response to B_2 as the stimulus for *R-St* associating. Now consider the counterparts for the *A-C* paradigm. The A_1-B_1 pair of list 1 becomes A_1-C_1 (with C_1 being a completely new response, unrelated to B_1) on

List 2. There remains forward interference via the competition between B_1 and C_1 as responses to A_1. However, there is no source of interference via competing *R-St* associations. The response to B_1 on list 1 is A_1, and the response to C_1 on List 2 is also A_1. The dual source of interference in the *A-Br* situation seems to be highly likely explanation for the pronounced negative transfer effect.

There is, however, an additional mechanism presumed to be operative in the *A-Br* paradigm but missing in *A-C*. This mechanism is positive in direction and should mitigate the negative transfer contributed by the dual interference; that is, the resultant, overall negative effect in *A-Br* is less than it would be without the presence of this compensatory mechanism. The positive source results from the fact that the *Br* responses in List 2 are identical to the responses contained in List 1. As a result, *S* does not have to learn new responses during his practice on List 2, assuming, of course, that response learning has already been completed during practice on List 1. For the *A-C* paradigm, *S* must learn new responses during List 2 practice. In Chapter 2 we discovered that response learning is a major contributor to PA acquisition. Thus, we should expect positive transfer for the response learning stage of List 2 acquisition. The contribution of this positive source to the overall transfer effect is a function of the difficulty of the response components. With responses of high meaningfulness, integration of the response units should progress rapidly, and the savings from prior integration on List 1 should not be great. In other words, the response learning stage for the *C-D* control condition should also progress rapidly, and the advantage of *Br* prior integration over the new integration of *D* response should not be great. On the other hand, with responses of low meaningfulness, the savings from prior integration, relative to the integration of new *D* responses, should be great. In fact, Mandler and Heinemann (1956) found a zero specific transfer effect for *A-Br* pairs when the response components consisted of trigrams of very low meaningfulness. Apparently, the positive source of transfer completely compensated for the dual sources of negative transfer. For a further discussion of these presumed operations the reader is referred to a recent analysis by Martin (1965).

R-St Paradigms

Harcum (1953) introduced two new paradigms in which the two lists entered into *A-B*, *C-A* and *A-B*, *B-C* relationships. In the *C-A* paradigm the stimuli of List 1 become the responses of List 2, and they are paired with new stimuli, unrelated to either component of List 1. In the *B-C* paradigm the responses of List 1 becomes the stimuli of List 2, and they are paired with new responses, unrelated to either component of List 1. The *C-A* paradigm is characterized by competition between the *R-St* associations of List 2 (i.e., *A-C* pairings) and the *St-R* associations of List 1 (i.e., *A-B* pairings). In this analysis the *B* and *C* components are assumed to compete with one another as responses to *A* as a stimulus in the *R-St* direction. Similarly, the *B-C* paradigm is characterized by competition between the *R-St* associations of List 1 (i.e., *B-A* pairings) and the *St-R* associations of List 2 (i.e., *B-C* pairings). Here *A* and *C* components compete as responses to *B* as a stimulus. A basic hypothesis at this point is that nonindependence between *St-R* and *R-St* associations extant during practice on a PA list (Kausler and Kanoti, 1963; Twedt and Underwood, 1959). According to this hypothesis, interference for associations in one direction will also have a deleterious effect on associations in the other direction. If the nonindependence hypothesis is valid, we should expect to find negative transfer in both the *C-A* and the *B-C* paradigm. Evidence to support this expectancy has been found by Harcum and also by Murdock (1958b) and Goulet and Barclay (1965). In addition, Goulet and Barclay found the amount of negative transfer to be significantly greater for the *C-A* than for the *B-C* paradigm.

Two other *R-St* paradigms were introduced by Murdock (1956). In one, the two lists form an *A-B, B-A* relationship in which the stimuli and responses of List 1 reverse their roles in List 2 (with the specific pairings being maintained—i.e., A_1-B_1 becomes B_1-A_1, etc.). Since *B-A* associations are likely to be learned as *R-St* associations during List 1 practice, massive positive transfer is anticipated for List 2. Murdock did discover positive transfer for the *B-A* pairs—in fact, the amount was as great as that found for a control condition in which the *A-B* pairs of List 1 were simply repeated on List 2. In the other paradigm, the two lists form an *A-B, B-Ar* relationship. Here the stimuli and responses of List 1 again reverse roles, but this time they are re-paired as in the *A-B, A-Br* stimulus-response paradigm. Murdock found as much negative transfer for his *B-Ar* pairs as he did for control *A-Br* pairs.

From the studies reviewed, it seems apparent that the transfer effects attributable to *R-St* factors are nearly as potent, if not equated, as those attributable to *St-R* factors. Parenthetically, it should be noted that this observation provides further support for the interpretation of *R-St* learning in terms of a principle of associative symmetry (cf. Introduction, Chapter 2). Despite their potency, these paradigms are not included on the conventional transfer surface. Houston (1964c; Article 2) has performed a valuable service by projecting these demonstrated relationships, and hypothetical additional ones, onto a new transfer surface which has dimensions corresponding to reversed stimulus-response roles for Lists 1 and 2. In a subsequent test of several previously untested points along these dimensions, Houston (in press) obtained impressive validating evidence for the surface.

Transfer Mechanisms in St-R Paradigms

Our analysis of transfer into its component processes began with the gross phenomenon of overt transfer effects and proceeded to the molar subphenomena of nonspecific and specific sources. Specific transfer may, in turn, be partitioned into more molecular subphenomena which are commonly called the transfer mechanisms. Two of these mechanisms, interference and transfer of response learning, were encountered in the previous section. In this section we shall pursue the examination of these mechanisms as they function in the classical *St-R* paradigms.

Two principles govern the application of these mechanisms to overall transfer effects: A given mechanism may operate in more than one paradigm, and a given paradigm may have more than one mechanism activated simultaneously. Within a single paradigm, multiple determinism is the general rule, and the resultant, or overt, transfer effect may be viewed as the algebraic summation of the effects of the separate mechanisms. As an example, consider a paradigm in which three mechanisms, *X*, *Y*, and *Z*, are active. Suppose, in addition, that the contributions of *X*, *Y*, and *Z* are all negative in direction but weak in effect. The resultant transfer may be represented by the equation $(-X_{weak}) + (-Y_{weak}) + (-Z_{weak})$, where the minus sign indicates the contribution of the separate effect to the direction of resultant transfer and the subscript indicates the degree of this contribution. The summated effect, with resultant transfer as the consequence, should be strongly negative. Suppose, however, that the effect of *X* is weakly negative, whereas the effect of both *Y* and *Z* is weakly positive. Here summation leads us to expect a weakly positive resultant transfer effect. In a similar manner, other combinations of two or more mechanisms can be summated to yield predictions regarding resultant transfer effects. The previously cited *A-Br* paradigm was presumed to involve this summation principle, with a strongly negative interference effect combining with a positive effect from response learning that may range from very low to very high. We turn now to the mechanisms presumed operative in several other important paradigms.

A-B, A-C Paradigm

As noted earlier, a potent mechanism in this paradigm is that of response interference (i.e., the competition existing between *B* and *C* responses to *A* stimuli during practice on the *A-C* pairs of List 2). This competition inhibits performance on List 2, thus contributing a large source of negative transfer. During the early trials of List 2 practice, *Ss* are faced with a variant of a familiar dilemma—to *B* or not to *B*. The conflict is eventually resolved, and the *C* responses dominate.

An intriguing question is that of the fate of the *A-B* associations; that is, are the *B* responses to the *A* stimuli simply displaced by the *C* responses and remain available for recall on demand, or are the *B* responses lost to *S* following his practice on the *A-C* pairs? Melton and Irwin (1940), in an important theory intended to explain differences in the amount of retroactive inhibition (RI) and proactive inhibition (PI) (cf. Chapter 10), proposed two factors to account for transfer and retention effects within the rubric of the *A-C* paradigm. The first factor was clearly identified as interference from the *B-C* competition to *A* stimuli during List 2 practice. The second factor, labeled "Factor X," remained vaguely identified as the unlearning of *A-B* associations. Unlearning is basically equivalent to experimental extinction as it occurs in classical conditioning experiments. According to this conception, the *A* stimuli of List 2 evoke *B* responses early in practice; however, these *B* responses are not reinforced (i.e., the *C* responses are presented instead), making the situation tantamount to nonreinforcement in conditioning studies. For a lucid evaluation of interference and unlearning theory the reader is referred to an essay by Postman (1961a).

Substantial evidence for unlearning demanded a sophisticated methodology that eluded psychologists until Barnes and Underwood (1959; Article 3), in what has become a contemporary classic, introduced a technique that has since been called the "modified modified free recall" (MMFR) method (Melton, 1961). The name is derived from the fact that the method is a modification of an earlier variant of free recall (Briggs, 1954). A wave of research on unlearning followed closely on the heels of the Barnes and Underwood study. One development has been the demonstration (Garskof, Sandak, and Malinowski, 1965; Goggin, 1963; McGovern, 1964) that the *B* responses themselves tend to become unavailable during List 2 practice; that is, *S* not only has difficulty in aligning *B* responses with their *A* stimuli from List 1, but he also finds it difficult to recall the *B* responses without regard to their matched stimuli. Garskof and Sandak (1964) also found evidence for the unlearning of *A-B* associations when measured by a recognition task rather than a recall task. A second development is the incipience of research directed toward the discovery of those independent variables which bear functional relationships with the unlearning phenomenon. Thus, Postman, Keppel, and Stark (1965) found greater unlearning of *A-B* associations when the *B* and *C* responses come from the same response class (e.g., both adjectives) than when they come from different classes (e.g., trigrams and adjectives). Competition between *B* and *C* responses to *A* stimuli should be less when the responses are from different classes—thereby reducing the necessity for unlearning the *A-B* associations. Bryk and Kausler (1966) related stimulus meaningfulness to both the unlearning of *A-B* associations and the availability of *B* responses. Their evidence indicated greater unlearning of *B* responses under high than under low meaningfulness. The effect of meaningfulness on *A-B* unlearning, however, did not approach statistical significance. Dallett and D'Andre (1965) found that instructions to use *B* as a mediator to learn the unrelated *C* response, via a chain of *A* to *B* to *C* (cf. Article 3 for a discussion of mediation in the *A-C* paradigm), increased slightly the resistance of *A-B* associations to unlearning.

Negative transfer from interference and unlearning is partly compensated for by a weakly positive mechanism—that of transfer of intra-list stimulus differentiation (Gibson, 1940; cf. Introduction, Chapter 5). In attaining mastery of the *A-B* pairs in List 1, *S* succeeds in eliminating generalization tendencies between the *A* stimulus components, thus leading to the intra-list differentiation of these components. Having already differentiated between the *A* components, *S* does not have this mildly horrendous problem added to his otherwise formidable task of resolving the *B-C* competition to *A*. Of course, control *Ss* who practice on *C-D* pairs in List 2 must attain further intra-list differentiation of stimuli. The fact that resultant transfer in the *A-C* paradigm is ordinarily quite negative suggests that the positive transfer from differentiation is considerably less pronounced than the negative transfer from interference and unlearning; that is, the summation combines a strongly negative with a weakly positive component.

An area of research in which stimulus differentiation is investigated as a mechanism relatively independently of confounding interference effects is that of "stimulus predifferentiation." The typical design employed in this research is the *A-B*, *A-C* transfer paradigm. However, the *B* and *C* responses are selected so as to be from very different response classes. The *B* responses are usually verbal components, whereas the *C* responses are usually motor components, such as pushing or pulling a lever. As noted in the comment above on the Postman, Keppel, and Stark (1965) study, interference and unlearning effects are greatly reduced, if not eliminated, when *B* and *C* responses are from discrepant classes. This discrepancy is maximized by the verbal-motor dichotomy of predifferentiation experiments. The net effect in these studies is the occurrence of resultant positive transfer, as might be expected by the summation of a weakly positive effect and a virtually zero negative transfer effect (from interference). For a succinct review of the predifferentiation literature and the issues at stake the reader is referred to Ellis (1965).

A-B, A′-C Paradigm

The *A′* indicates that the stimuli of List 2 are related to but are not identical with the stimuli of List 1; that is, the stimuli of the two lists are such that A_1' is similar to A_1 (or is, perhaps, a word associate), A_2' is similar to A_2, etc. Gibson's generalization theory (1940, 1941; cf. Introduction, Chapter 5 for a discussion of the theory) predicts negative transfer for *A′-C* pairs via generalization effects. For any given pair of stimuli from the two lists, *A′* falls along the generalization gradient of *A*. Consequently, there is the propensity for *A′* to evoke the response previously associated with *A*, which, of course, is the *B* response from List 1. Competition should therefore be present between *B* and *C* as responses to *A′*. In other words, the *A′-C* paradigm, through generalization effects, is reduced to the equivalent of the *A-C* paradigm, and negative transfer is to be expected. However, *A′-B* associations should yield less interference for *A-C* associations than should *A-B*, in that the former is only a generalized association and the latter is a direct association. Therefore, negative transfer should be more pronounced for *A-C* than for *A′-C*, with the difference in the amount of negative transfer increasing as the similarity between *A* and *A′* decreases. Although this prediction is incorporated into the transfer surface (see Figure 1, p. 364), Gibson herself found little difference in the amount of negative transfer between the *A-C* and *A′-C* paradigms. There has been little contemporary interest in the *A′-C* paradigm, probably because of the general rejection in recent years of many of the facets of Gibson's original theory (Underwood, 1961b).

A-B, A-B′ Paradigm

In this paradigm *B′* indicates that the responses of List 2 are related in some manner to those of List 1. On the transfer surface this relationship is expressed in terms of the response similarity dimension. With identical stimuli in the two lists (i.e., *A* components), the surface predicts diminishing negative transfer as the response of List 2 change from neutrality (*C* responses of the *A-C* paradigm) to increasing degrees of similarity (*B′* responses of the *A-B′* paradigm). In fact, at some unspecified degree of similarity, transfer begins to shift from negative to positive. Some studies (e.g., Bastian, 1961) have found large positive transfer effects, while others (e.g., Dallett, 1962) have reported zero or slightly negative transfer. Bastian (1961) also discovered that positive transfer is greater when *B* and *B′* are related as word associates (e.g., table-chair) than when they are related by secondary similarity (e.g., happy-elated).

Stimulus differentiation, as a source of positive transfer is, of course, as apropos to the *A-B′* paradigm as it is to the *A-C*. More important as a positive transfer mechanism in the present paradigm is the likely presence of mediation. Mediation here refers to *B* serving as a link to the elicitation of *B′*, rather than having *B* as a competitor of *B′*. Mediation as a mechanism for positive transfer is thoughtfully discussed by Barnes and Underwood (Article 3), and impressive evidence on its behalf in the *A-B′* paradigm is given. Further strong support for the mediation hypothesis was given by Jenkins, Foss, and Odom (1965) in a very carefully controlled study.

Another possibility for a source of positive transfer in this paradigm is what has been called "parasitic reinforcement" (Morgan and Underwood 1950). The processes hypothesized to be involved have been discussed fully by Young (1955) and Kincaid, Bousfield, and Whitmarsh (1962). Briefly, the main underlying process is presumed to be response generalization. During practice on List 1, *A-B* associations are reinforced. Since *B′* is highly similar to *B*, the *A-B′* association is assumed to derive generalized reinforcement at the same time *A-B* is directly reinforced. The *A-B′* associations should therefore have considerable strength before they are actually presented formally in List 2. The parasitic reinforcement hypothesis as the source of positive transfer in the *A-B′* paradigm has gradually lost favor, whereas the mediation hypothesis has been attracting more and more proponents.

A-B, C-B Paradigm

The savings from prior response learning, previously met in the *A-Br* paradigm, is also a positive mechanism in the *C-B* paradigm. The *C-B* paradigm was considered for many years to be a paragon of positive transfer (Underwood, 1949a), even though the transfer surface places it at zero transfer. Nevertheless, a number of recent studies (e.g., Kausler and Kanoti, 1963; Twedt and Underwood, 1959) have yielded statistically significant negative transfer for *C-B* pairs relative to *C-D* pairs. The mechanism which more than compensates for transfer from response learning has been hypothesized to be the competition of the *R-St* associations from the two lists; that is, the *B-A* and *B-C* backward associations are such that the *A* and *C* components compete with one another as response to *B* components as stimuli. Once more the hypothesis of nonindependence between *St-R* and *R-St* associations must be invoked, and the *R-St* interference present during List 2 acquisition is expected to have a concomitant effect on *St-R*, or, in this case, *C-B*, acquisition. Support for this *R-St* interpretation has been found by Houston (1964a), Kausler and Kanoti (1963), and Keppel and Underwood (1962a). In addition, support for the unlearning of the *B-A* (*R-St*) associations of List 1 during practice on List 2 was obtained by Ellington and Kausler (1965). Unlearning seems to be a product of the *B-A* competition with *B-C*, just as the unlearning of *A-B* is a product of the *A-B* competition with *A-C* in the *A-C* paradigm.

A-B, A′-B Paradigm

The segment of the transfer surface that traces the change from unrelated stimuli in List 2 (*C* components) to related stimuli (*A′* components), when responses are identical for the two lists, suggests increasing positive transfer as the similarity of the related stimuli increases. The study by Ryan (1960; Article 4) does report pronounced positive transfer for the *A′-B* paradigm. We have already discovered that the *C-B* paradigm is unlikely to yield positive transfer. Ryan's interpretation of positive transfer in the *A′-B* paradigm is in terms of mediation—with the *A-A′* linkage serving as the mediator. This kind of linkage is, of course, absent in the *C-B* paradigm. We should also note that *R-St* competition (the source of negative transfer in the *C-B* paradigm) is unlikely in the *A′-B* paradigm. The *B-A* and *B-A′* backward associations of the *A′-B* paradigm actually suggest another source of positive transfer via mediation of *A′* as a response, with *A* as the mediating response.

Secondary Laws of Specific Transfer

Resultant transfer for a given paradigm is not to be considered invariant. The amount, and perhaps even the direction, may be altered as relevant variables, other than those defining the stimulus-response inter-list relationships, change. These relevant variables are commonly called secondary variables, and their functional relationships with resultant transfer constitute the secondary laws of specific transfer. Secondary laws result from the fact that the contribution of a mechanism to summated resultant transfer may be weighted differently under various levels of the secondary variable. The *A-Br* paradigm previously illustrated the nature of a secondary law. Positive transfer from response learning varies inversely with response meaningfulness. Consequently, resultant transfer becomes less negative as response meaningfulness decreases.

Meaningfulness

Response meaningfulness is also an important secondary variable for several classical *St-R* paradigms. Jung (1963; Article 5) determined specific transfer effects for both the *C-B* and *A-C* paradigms under low and high degrees of response meaningfulness. Understandably, transfer for the *C-B* paradigm was more positive for responses of low meaningfulness than for response of high meaningfulness. As in the *A-Br* paradigm, we expect the positive transfer from response learning to be at its maximum when the responses are low in meaningfulness. Surprisingly, Jung also found that negative transfer in the *A-C* paradigm varied with response meaningfulness—with negative transfer being greater for responses of high meaningfulness.

In an extension of Jung's study, Goulet (1965) tested the effects of response meaningfulness on *A-C* transfer by means of a factorial research design. The meaningfulness conditions for the *B* and *C* responses, respectively, of the two lists were high-high, high-low, low-high, and low-low. In agreement with Jung's results, negative transfer was more pronounced for responses of high meaningfulness than for those of low meaningfulness—with the differential effect being more pronounced for the *B* components than for the *C* components. In addition, negative transfer was considerably less when the *B* and *C* components were heterogeneous in meaningfulness (i.e., one high and the other low) than when they were homogeneous (i.e., both high or both low). Goulet attributed the latter finding to the likelihood that heterogeneous responses permit a differentiation of the two response systems, thereby reducing confusion between *B* and *C* and their resulting competition. This interpretation closely parallels that given by Postman, Keppel, and Stark (1965) for response selected from different classes of materials.

Stimulus meaningfulness was related to transfer in the *C-B* paradigm by Dean and Kausler (1964). They reasoned that *R-St* learning should increase as the meaningfulness of nonsense syllables as stimuli increases (cf. Introductory section, Chapter 2; and Article 5), thereby magnifying negative transfer for *C-B* pairs through the enhanced competition between *B-A* and *B-C* response-stimulus associations. They failed, however, to obtain substantial support for this hypothesis.

Degree of List 1 Learning

Article 6 (Postman, 1962a) surveys earlier studies on this secondary variable and gives a penetrating discussion of the mechanisms suspected of covarying with degree of List 1 learning. Postman's own research indicated that the *A-C* and *C-B* paradigms are relatively insensitive to degree of List 1 learning, at least within the limits of List 1 practice employed in this study. There was, however, a pronounced tendency for negative transfer in the *A-Br* paradigm to increase as the degree of List 1 acquisition increased. These results were later replicated by Jung (1962). Dean and Kausler (1964), however, found that with the *C-B* paradigm positive transfer occurred under a low degree (i.e., less than mastery) of List 1 acquisition and negative transfer under a high degree (i.e., overlearning). They accounted for the discrepancy between their findings and those of the earlier studies to the different class of materials (nonsense syllables) used in their study as compared to the earlier ones (adjectives). Backward learning (the source of interference in the *C-B* paradigm) presumably increases considerably more with overlearning when nonsense syllables serve as stimuli rather than adjectives.

The question of extreme degrees of overlearning of List 1 is an interesting one. Mandler (1962) concluded, on the basis of his research (e.g., Mandler and Heinemann, 1956) and that of others (e.g., Underwood, 1949b) that with massive degrees of List 1 overlearning transfer for *A-C* pairs becomes positive. His explanation for this reversal of direction stressed what he calls the transition from associative to cognitive processes as overlearning progresses. By cognitive processes Mandler means symbolic responses which are the analogues of the overt associative responses (i.e., the responding of *B* to *A*). Analogic responses occur covertly and are recognized by *S* as being erroneous prior to the elicitation of their associative counterparts. The *A-B* associations are presumably effectively inhibited during practice on List 2 by these symbolic responses, thereby markedly reducing their power of interference with the *A-C* associations. However, recent tests of the Mandler cognitive hypothesis by Spence (1963) and Spence and Schulz (1965) failed to find evidence for the operation of such symbolic analogues. Moreover, Jung (1965b) has presented a well documented case, though aptly challenged by Mandler (1965), for a strictly associative explanation of the shift from negative to positive transfer with overlearning.

Sets of Lists

A final secondary law to be considered here is the effect of the number of sets of lists (one set being defined as the normal List 1—List 2 sequence) *S* has received prior to practice on the set in question. There might be, for example, three sets of lists, with the lists of each set bearing *A-B*, *A-C* relationships with one another. The problem becomes the changes in transfer effects from Set 1 to Set 2 to Set 3. The procedures involved and the transfer mechanisms affected are explored thoroughly in the study by Postman (1964b; Article 7).

ARTICLE 1

Osgood's Transfer Surface: Extension and Test[1]

RICHARD WIMER

The Jackson Laboratory, Bar Harbor, Maine

Osgood made two contributions to the study of transfer. First, he proposed a model for meaningful similarity and focused interest on its relation to direction and amount of transfer produced. Second, he proposed three "empirical laws" to account for all transfer phenomena in both serial and paired-associate learning. Both contributions are represented in his Transfer and Retroaction Surface (Osgood, 1949): its marginal indices of interlist stimulus and response similarity are defined and ordered according to his theory of meaningful similarity; direction and amount of transfer at the intersects are predicted on the basis of his three empirical laws. The theoretical aspects of Osgood's work are generally known, so that no detailed description is considered to be necessary.

Osgood made the initial statement and test of his theoretical model for meaningful similarity in two papers devoted to experimental tests of the effects of theoretically ordered interlist response similarity on transfer and retroaction in paired-associate learning. Using identical stimuli, he found similar responses to produce more positive transfer than either opposed or neutral ones, but failed to find the expected difference between opposed and neutral responses (Osgood, 1946). Thus, though there were differential transfer effects produced by meaningful relations of similarity and opposition, the predicted inhibitory effects associated with meaningful opposition failed to materialize. In a second study (Osgood, 1948) he failed to find any difference between similarity and opposition, except for a latency measure for early stages of second-list acquisition. Since Osgood did not include the unrelated-response condition in this second study, the significance of the findings for the inhibitory model cannot be assessed.

Osgood always varied interlist response similarity while maintaining identical stimuli. Thus, he tested but a few of the points which the Transfer and Retroaction Surface (Osgood, 1949) was intended to encompass, and based the other points on his Surface on studies by others who used a variety of materials and procedures. Subsequently, Bugelski and Cadwallader (1956) tested most of the points on Osgood's Surface for retroaction. With the exception of results for variation of response similarity, their findings were in general agreement with Osgood's Surface. For interlist response similarity, however, they found that when stimuli were identical, interference was *least* for opposed responses. Effects produced by similar and unrelated responses did not differ. Bugelski and Cadwallader state that their reported generalizations held for estimated transfer effects as well as for retroaction.

With the exception of the opposed-response condition, which he omitted, Dallett (1962) investigated for proaction the same interlist stimulus and response relations that Bugelski and Cadwallader specifically tested for retroaction. The only definite evidence for (posi-

[1] Data were collected while the author was associated with Douglass College of Rutgers University. This study was supported in part by a research grant from the Research Council of Rutgers University. The invaluable assistance of Mrs. Carol J. Richter is gratefully acknowledged.

The substance of this paper was presented at the 1963 meetings of the American Psychological Association in Philadelphia.

Reprinted with permission of the author and the publisher, the Academic Press. The article appeared originally in the *Journal of Verbal Learning and Verbal Behavior*, 1964, **3**, 274–279.

tive) transfer which Dallett found was for identical responses with similar stimuli. While he concluded that his findings were in general agreement with Osgood's Surface, it is clear from an inspection of his results that the agreement was very general and that, like Bugelski and Cadwallader, he failed to obtain a statistically reliable difference between similar- and unrelated-response conditions. While Bugelski and Cadwallader found some evidence that simultaneous variation of interlist stimulus and response similarity produced increasing interference as stimulus similarity increased, Dallett did not.

The purpose of the present experiment was to explore the transfer effects produced by a large number of combinations of interlist stimulus and response similarity relations including, but not restricted to, those suggested by Osgood (a) to test Osgood's model for transfer, and (b) to search for other possible similarity effects. More exploratory in intent and design, this study differed from those of Osgood, Bugelski and Cadwallader, and Dallett in two important ways. First, a wider range of similarity relations was used. Response-similarity relations included were identity, similarity, neutrality, opposition, and antonymity. Second, stimulus similarity was extended from relations of identity, similarity, and neutrality specified by Osgood to include opposition and antonymity. This was done so that variations of interlist stimulus similarity would be fully comparable with those for response similarity, and to permit observation of the effects of a larger variety of common interlist stimulus- and response-similarity relationships. Thus, five conditions of stimulus similarity were combined factorially with five degrees of response similarity to generate a 25-cell matrix of interlist stimulus- and response-similarity relations.

Method

Design. All *Ss* first learned a simple task to acquaint them with procedures for paired-associate learning and to provide *E* with information to equate groups on initial learning ability. Following this, *Ss* were assigned to learn one of 25 different lists of paired-associates whose stimuli were adjectives meaningfully identical, similar, unrelated, opposed, or antonymous with respect to adjective stimuli on a final common list which all groups learned; and whose responses, also adjectives, varied in meaningful relation to responses on the final common list in the same possible ways. The 5 stimulus relations were combined factorially with the 5 response relations; hence the 25 groups. All stimulus and response sets were unmixed, i.e., all stimuli or responses in a set were meaningfully similar, opposed, etc. to those on the final common list.

Materials. Stimuli and responses for the preliminary learning task were single letters of the alphabet arranged in pairs such as *w-n* and *z-h*. The materials from which the paired-associate lists for transfer were constructed are presented in Table 1. The adjective sets were originally devised by Osgood (1946). His procedure in constructing them was to select familiar words for which dictionaries of synonyms and antonyms provided entries in both categories. Osgood then personally selected other adjectives as meaningfully similar or opposed on the basis of comparability of "feeling tone" and descriptive equivalence with the standards or their antonyms (Osgood, 1946, p. 280). Judges ranked the items in these sets for similarity or opposition, and only sets for which a high degree of agreement occurred were used. This procedure resulted in 15 selected familiar adjectives for each of which there existed other adjectives similar, neutral, opposed, and antonymous in meaning. To select materials for the present experiment, two groups of seven sets each were selected from Osgood's list. One group was arbitrarily selected to serve as stimuli for constructing lists, while the other group was used for constructing responses. Column headings indicate the meaningful relation of adjectives in that column to those on the final common list; the upper half of the table presents the stimuli and the lower half the responses. The final common lists consisted of materials in the stimulus and response column labeled "identical."

Procedure. All materials were typed on tape in three different orders and presented on a Gerbrands Model M-1 memory drum. Stimuli and responses were presented at a 3-sec rate, i.e., the stimulus was presented alone for 3 sec, and the stimulus and response together for an additional 3 sec. The time interval between trials on a list was 6 sec. The interval between successive lists was approximately 2 minutes. All lists were learned to the criterion of one errorless anticipation of the entire list.

Subjects requiring more than 14 trials to reach criterion on the preliminary task (paired letters of

TABLE 1
MATERIALS USED IN CONSTRUCTING TRANSFER-PRODUCING LISTS

Relation to transfer list				
Identical	Similar	Unrelated	Opposed	Antonym
		Stimuli		
Tense	Hard	Basic	Soft	Relaxed
Skillful	Quick	Sour	Slow	Awkward
Pale	Sickly	Similar	Healthy	Brilliant
Neat	Clear	Numb	Hazy	Messy
Noisy	Excited	Equal	Calm	Quiet
Dainty	Clean	Curious	Dirty	Coarse
Robust	Solid	Long	Flimsy	Puny
		Responses		
Rounded	Graceful	Lucky	Clumsy	Angular
Drowsy	Dead	Necessary	Alive	Alert
Boorish	Rough	Near	Smooth	Gracious
Weighty	Serious	Common	Humorous	Spritely
Slender	Airy	Daily	Solid	Stout
Elated	High	Left	Low	Dejected
Distinct	Sharp	Rancid	Blunt	Blurred

the alphabet) were eliminated. The *S*s were initially assigned to experimental conditions by reaching blindly into a box containing experimental tapes. After a tape had been used, it was placed in a second box, which was sampled when the first box was emptied. After approximately 125 *S*s had been tested, a distribution of learning scores on the preliminary task by experimental group was constructed. Throughout the remainder of the study, *S*s were assigned to a group on the basis of initial performance in order to equate groups for learning ability.

Subjects. The final group of *S*s consisted of 250 male and female undergraduate students in psychology courses at Rutgers University. Ten *S*s served in each experimental condition.

RESULTS

Preliminary Task

An analysis of variance was performed on the number of trials to criterion on the preliminary paired letters of the alphabet task. It is clear that the groups were well equated, since the F obtained was less than 0.1.

Transfer-Producing Lists

An analysis of variance was performed on the number of trials to learn the various transfer-producing lists. All lists were comparable in difficulty.

Transfer List

Product-moment correlations between performance on the lists were as follows: preliminary task and transfer-producing lists, +0.26; preliminary task and transfer list, +0.28; transfer-producing lists and transfer list, +0.35. The multiple correlation of performance on the preliminary task and on the transfer-producing lists with performance on the transfer list was +0.40. All correlations reported are significant at or beyond the 0.01 level.

Table 2 presents the mean number of trials to criterion on the final common list. All means are adjusted by covariance for performance on the preliminary task and on the transfer-producing lists which, since they do not differ in difficulty, can be considered a homogeneous set of estimators of learning ability. The adjusted error mean square is 12.6.

The appropriate comparison group for determining the amounts and signs of transfer is the group for which both stimuli and responses were unrelated in the successive lists. Dunnett's t-statistic for multiple comparisons with a single control group (Winer, 1962)

TABLE 2
COVARIANCE-ADJUSTED MEAN NUMBER OF TRIALS TO LEARN TRANSFER LIST CATEGORIZED BY STIMULUS AND RESPONSE SIMILARITY RELATIONS TO PRIOR LISTS[a]

Stimulus relations	Response similarity relations				
	Identical	Similar	Unrelated	Opposed	Antonym
Identical	1.9+	9.5	11.3—	8.8	8.1+
Similar	7.1+	7.8+	9.2	6.3+	7.7+
Unrelated	10.0	9.2	*9.6*	8.3	9.9
Opposed	8.6	9.7	9.6	7.6+	6.8+
Antonym	10.0	8.2	10.0	7.8+	6.7+

[a] Plus and minus signs are used to indicate the direction of transfer suggested by the difference from the control group (italic).

was used to estimate the significance of the transfer effects. Except for the group with both stimuli and responses identical, which clearly produced a large amount of positive transfer, none of the differences from the control group approached acceptable levels of statistical significance.

Though the total number of subjects used was rather large (250), the number involved in the test for any specific interlist-similarity relation was quite small (10). A more lenient standard of significant transfer for exploratory purposes appears justifiable. In Table 2 those cell means for which the magnitude of the difference from the control mean is at least one standard error of the difference (1.6) have been marked with the sign of the transfer effect. The picture which emerges can only be suggestive.

Analyses of Osgood's Empirical Laws. (1) *When stimuli are identical and interlist response similarity is varied, the amount of negative transfer will decrease as response similarity increases.* There is no evidence of Osgood's predicted inhibitory effects associated with meaningfully dissimilar interlist response relations. When stimuli on the two lists are identical, positive transfer is suggested for both conditions of interlist response identity and antonymity, with evidence for negative transfer only for the customary condition of unrelated responses. That the similarity of transfer effects for similar and dissimilar response relations is genuine is strongly supported by the results shown in the second row of Table 2 (stimuli similar). There, the effect appears even stronger, cells for which positive transfer is suggested including those for interlist response similarity and opposition, as well as for identity and antonymity.

(2) *When responses on two lists are identical and interlist stimulus similarity is varied, positive transfer increases as interlist stimulus similarity increases.* This appears to be approximately correct, though change in transfer does not become apparent until the similar condition is reached. Note that the squares in the lower left corner of Table 2 are conspicuously unmarked. When stimuli on the transfer-producing lists are meaningfully opposed or antonymous with respect to those on the transfer list, more positive transfer appears to occur when responses are also meaningfully opposed or antonymous. For reasons not immediately apparent, comparability of interlist relation—common interlist similarity or dissimilarity of both stimuli and responses—does not appear important when stimuli are identical or similar.

(3) *When both interlist stimulus and response similarity are varied simultaneously, negative transfer will increase as stimulus similarity increases.* Cells for which both stimulus and response sets had the same similarity relation to those on the transfer list—both similar, both opposed, etc.—are used to test this. The appropriate cell means fall along the principal diagonal (upper left to lower

right) of the matrix in Table 2. Note that the ordering of the cell means is clearly contrary to Osgood's prediction, and that there is evidence for positive transfer for all conditions of relation between lists. Transfer between lists appears to increase as *relation* between lists, either similarity or opposition, increases.

Discussion

The results of the present study, taken with those obtained by Bugelski and Cadwallader (1956), would seem to deny rather conclusively the action of Osgood's inhibitory mechanisms under the conditions for which he originally proposed that they should operate, i.e., with high interlist stimulus similarity. However, results obtained under conditions of interlist stimulus opposition and antonymity, where positive transfer was indicated only if interlist response relations were also those of opposition or antonymity, suggest some inhibitory process related to Osgood's which clearly merits further investigation.

Perhaps the most important finding of long-term interest for the study of transfer is that only relatively small amounts of transfer could be produced by the very numerous and sometimes extreme combinations of interlist similarity relations used. This finding is consistent with all studies which have used Osgood's materials, including those of Osgood himself.

The similarity relations among the adjective sets devised by Osgood were determined by dictionary entries for synonymity and antonymity, or by judged comparability of feeling tone and descriptive equivalence with the standards or their antonyms. Thus, the similarity relationships presumably reflect relationships among the connotative meanings of the words. There are studies which suggest that associative similarity (the frequency with which one word occurs as a response to the other) is more closely related to the phenomenon of transfer. Thus, using identical stimuli and varying interlist response relation, Bastian (1961) found that both judged similarity and associative connection are contributors to transfer, but that associative factors may be more important. In an extension of Bastian's work, Ryan (1960) used identical responses and varied interlist stimulus relation. He also found evidence for positive transfer resulting from both types of relation, but, substantiating Bastian's findings, he found greater facilitation resulting from associative connection among the words.

In view of the number of studies now accumulated which, taken together, show (a) that variations in transfer produced by Osgood's materials tend to be small and unstable, and (b) that there are other categories of meaningful relation among words that are likely to be at least as important as judged or connotative similarity, although they may be correlated with it, it would seem that now is the time to use materials scaled on a variety of meaningful relations for extensive multidimensional analyses of relational variables producing transfer. There have been two such studies concerned with intralist factors affecting task difficulty (Higa, 1963; Wimer, 1963), but none for transfer.

Summary

The purpose of the experiment was to determine transfer effects for (a) Osgood's Surface as presently defined, and (b) additional points on the enlarged Surface resulting from extension of interlist stimulus similarity from identical, similar, and unrelated to include opposed and antonymous.

Subjects learned a final common list after learning one of twenty-five different first lists having one of five categories of interlist stimulus similarity (identical, similar, unrelated, opposed, or antonymous) combined factorially with one of the same five conditions of interlist response similarity.

Results suggested (acceptable levels of statistical significance were hardly ever achieved) were (a) when stimuli on both lists are identical or similar, positive transfer occurs for opposed and antonymous response relations as well as for those of identity and similarity; (b) when responses are identical on both lists, only high degrees of stimulus similarity produce positive transfer; (c) when stimuli are meaningfully opposed or antonymous, positive transfer occurs only when responses are also meaningfully opposed or antonymous; and (d) simultaneous variation of interlist stimulus and response similarity tends to produce increasing positive transfer as relation between lists, either similarity or opposition, increases.

References

BASTIAN, J. Associative factors in verbal transfer. *J. exp. Psychol.*, 1961, **62**, 70-79.

BUGELSKI, B. R., AND CADWALLADER, T. C. A reappraisal of the transfer and retroaction surface. *J. exp. Psychol.*, 1956, **52**, 360-366.

DALLETT, K. M. The transfer surface re-examined. *J. verb. Learn. verb. Behav.*, 1962, **1**, 91-94.

HIGA, M. Interference effects of intralist word relationships in verbal learning. *J. verb. Learn. verb. Behav.*, 1963, **2**, 170-175.

OSGOOD, C. E. Meaningful similarity and interference in learning. *J. exp. Psychol.*, 1946, **36**, 277-301.

OSGOOD, C. E. An investigation into the causes of retroactive interference. *J. exp. Psychol.*, 1948, **38**, 132-154.

OSGOOD, C. E. The similarity paradox in human learning: a resolution. *Psychol. Rev.*, 1949, **56**, 132-143.

RYAN, J. J. Comparison of verbal response transfer mediated by meaningfully similar and associated stimuli. *J. exp. Psychol.*, 1960, **60**, 408-415.

WIMER, C. C. An analysis of semantic stimulus factors in paired-associate learning. *J. verb. Learn. verb. Behav.*, 1963, **1**, 397-407.

WINER, B. J. *Statistical principles in experimental design*. New York: McGraw-Hill, 1962.

(Received November 8, 1963)

ARTICLE 2

VERBAL TRANSFER AND INTERLIST SIMILARITIES[1]

JOHN P. HOUSTON

University of California, Berkeley

Degree and direction of verbal transfer were related to first list stimulus–second list response similarity (S_1-R_2) and to second list stimulus–first list response similarity (S_2-R_1). This was accomplished through a relabeling of Osgood's transfer and retroaction surface such that the dimensions referred, not to degree of S_1-S_2 and R_1-R_2 similarity, but to degree of S_1-R_2 and S_2-R_1 similarity. When S_2-R_1 similarity is minimal transfer will be minimal, no matter what the degree of S_1-R_2 similarity. As S_2-R_1 similarity increases transfer increases until, when S_2 and R_1 are identical, maximum negative transfer will obtain when S_1-R_2 similarity is minimal and maximum positive transfer will occur when S_1 and R_2 are identical.

Although the importance of the similarity variable in relation to transfer phenomena has long been recognized there has been a tendency among psychologists to focus upon particular loci of similarity and to ignore certain others. The sets of similarity relationships which have received the most attention in the typical two list S_1-R_1, S_2-R_2 verbal transfer situation are those expressed by Osgood's (1949) transfer and retroaction surface. His three dimensional surface represents an attempt to relate direction and degree of transfer to first list stimulus–second list stimulus similarity (S_1-S_2) and to first list response–second list response similarity (R_1-R_2).

Two loci of similarity which have been virtually ignored in the study of transfer may be described as the similarity between first list stimuli and second list responses (S_1-R_2) and the similarity between second list stimuli and first list responses (S_2-R_1). What will be the influence, if any, of varying degrees of S_1-R_2 and S_2-R_1 similarity upon direction and degree of transfer? Although the verbal learning literature contains a number of examples discussed below which suggest what these influences might be, there has been no attempt to provide a general integrative statement of the relationships between transfer and the S_1-R_2 and S_2-R_1 similarity loci. The intent of the present paper is to provide this kind of a statement, based upon data, through a relabeling of the dimensions of Osgood's transfer surface such that the surface corresponds, not to the amount of transfer associated with degrees of S_1-S_2 and R_1-R_2 similarity, but to the amount and direction of transfer associated with varying degrees of S_1-R_2 and S_2-R_1 similarity. Figure 1 contains the relabeled surface.

As is true of Osgood's surface the vertical dimension represents direction and degree of transfer. The length of the horizontal plane, labeled S_1-R_2, represents degree of similarity between first list stimuli and second list responses. The width of the horizontal plane, labeled S_2-R_1, represents degree of similarity between second list stimuli and first list responses. In both cases the similarity dimension extends from maximum similarity or identity (labeled 1) to minimum similarity or neutrality (labeled 0). If the first list responses are different from and neutral with respect to the second list stimuli then, no matter what the de-

[1] This paper was written during the tenure of the author's United States Public Health Service postdoctoral fellowship at the Institute of Human Learning, University of California, Berkeley.

Reprinted with permission of the author and the publisher, the American Psychological Association. The article appeared originally in the *Psychological Review*, 1964, **71**, 412–414.

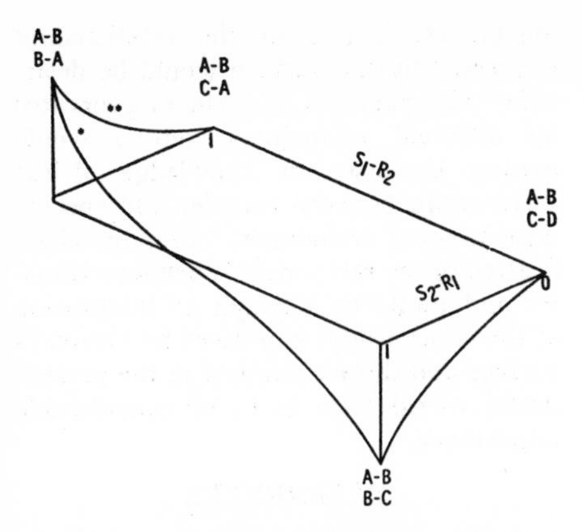

FIG. 1. Transfer as a function of S_1-R_2 and S_2-R_1 similarity.

gree of second list response–first list stimulus similarity, transfer will be minimal. As the degree of S_2-R_1 similarity increases transfer will increase until, when S_2 is identical to R_1, maximum positive transfer will obtain when R_2 is identical to S_1 and maximum negative transfer will occur when R_2 and S_1 are different and neutral.

The surface is not completely unsubstantiated. Although little attention has been given to S_1-R_2 and S_2-R_1 transfer effects per se, the verbal learning literature does contain some data which document a number of points on the surface. Murdock (1956) found that A-B learning will facilitate subsequent B-A learning. His experimental paradigm corresponded to the point of maximum positive transfer on the proposed surface where S_1 is identical to R_2 and S_2 is identical to R_1. Murdock explained this instance of positive transfer in terms of B-A strength established during the A-B learning stage. In another study Murdock (1958) has confirmed an additional point on the surface. He employed an A-B, B-C paradigm and found a negative transfer effect during second list learning. This situation corresponds to the point of maximum negative transfer where S_2 and R_1 are identical and R_2 and S_1 are different and neutral with respect to each other. Murdock proposed that the B-A connection established during A-B learning will compete with the B-C learning during the second stage.

An experiment by Young (1961), while not conforming to the usual two list transfer situation, produced some pertinent data. He constructed lists such that all items served as both stimuli and responses and found that these lists were more difficult to learn than lists whose items did not serve in the double capacity. The proposed transfer surface would predict this result. His lists were, in effect, composed of B-C pairs preceding A-B pairs and A-B pairs preceding B-C pairs. According to the surface the former sequence of pairs should produce no transfer while the latter should produce negative transfer effects through the competition of the B-A associations with the B-C associations. Thus slow overall learning would have been predicted for the double-function list.

Further documentation of the surface may be found in the field of verbal mediation. Although not strictly applicable to the similarity surface contained in Figure 1, as some of the relationships are associative, these data are at least suggestive of the kinds of results which might be obtained with similarity measures. Kjeldergaard and Horton (1962) employed two mediation paradigms which may be located on the transfer surface. The first was a C-B, B-A, A-C paradigm. If one thinks of this situation as a two stage B-A, A-C transfer paradigm with the C-B list establishing a relationship (in this case associative) between the first-stage stimuli (B) and the second-stage responses (C) then it corresponds to a transfer situation with maximum S_2-R_1 similarity (A and A) and some positive amount of S_1-R_2 relatedness (B-C). In accordance with the transfer surface prediction for such a paradigm (see * in Figure 1) Kjeldergaard and Horton found A-C facilitation or positive transfer. The second relevant paradigm was an A-B, C-B, A-C situation. Once again, if A-B is interpreted as a definition of a positive relationship between the first-stage response (B) and the second-stage stimulus (A) then the paradigm corresponds to a transfer situation in which

S_1-R_2 (C-C) is maximum and S_2-R_1 (A-B) is some positive value (see ** in Figure 1). Kjeldergaard and Horton reported A-C facilitation. The transfer surface predicts positive transfer if A-B strength is assumed to be of some minimal degree.

Thus there is some evidence or support for a number of points on the surface. Of course, the majority of the relationships depicted by the surface have never been tested and require empirical verification, particularly under constant experimental conditions.

The surface is intended as nothing more than a rough index of the relationships existing between transfer and S_1-R_2 and S_2-R_1 similarity. Presumably varying materials, experimenters, and situations will produce variations in the shape of the surface. Qualitative as well as quantitative changes in the relationships between stimuli and responses should also influence the shape of the surface. Thus, formal similarity, judged similarity, associative strength, synonymity, and associative overlap may each generate surfaces which, while conforming to the general characteristics of the Figure 1 surface, may differ from each other considerably.

The proposed surface, as a statement of the relationships between transfer and two specific similarity loci, suggests a number of directions for further study. As mentioned, a good deal of experimental verification of the relationships expressed by the surface would be desirable. Comparisons of surfaces generated by different relatedness indices would greatly increase our knowledge of the interactions between transfer and specific measurement techniques. Finally, clarification of the relationships between transfer and similarity through an integration of the relationships expressed by Osgood's surface and those contained in the present model would seem to be of considerable importance.

REFERENCES

KJELDERGAARD, P. M., & HORTON, D. L. An experimental analysis of associative factors in stimulus equivalence, response equivalence and chaining paradigms. *Studies in verbal behavior*. Report No. 3, National Science Foundation Grant, University of Minnesota.

MURDOCK, B. B. "Backward" learning in paired associates. *J. exp. Psychol.*, 1956, **51**, 213–215.

MURDOCK, B. B. "Backward" associations in transfer and learning. *J. exp. Psychol.*, 1958, **55**, 111–114.

OSGOOD, C. E. The similarity paradox in human learning: A resolution. *Psychol. Rev.*, 1949, **56**, 132–143.

YOUNG, R. K. Paired-associate learning when the same items occur as stimuli and responses. *J. exp. Psychol.*, 1961, **61**, 315–318.

(Received December 9, 1963)

ARTICLE 3

"FATE" OF FIRST-LIST ASSOCIATIONS IN TRANSFER THEORY

JEAN M. BARNES AND BENTON J. UNDERWOOD

Northwestern University

Theorists who attempt to arrive at an accounting of the facts of transfer and retroactive inhibition in verbal materials must inevitably make a decision concerning "what happens" to first-list associations when a second list is learned. The present study was designed to gather data which would make such decisions easier. Two transfer paradigms were used. One of these, A-B, A-C, is normally associated with production of negative transfer. In the other paradigm, A-B, A-B′, stimuli are identical with responses highly similar; such an arrangement normally produces positive transfer.

The data from the present study allow an evaluation of three different conceptions concerning the fate of first-list (hereafter called List 1) associations during the learning of the second list (hereafter called List 2). These three positions will be examined first as they apply to the A-B, A-C paradigm.

1. List 1 associations are unlearned or extinguished during the learning of the second list. While A-B, A-C is more comparable to the operations of counterconditioning than to extinction of conditioned responses, the term extinction will be used here in keeping with past practice. As a theoretical position, the unlearning or extinction hypothesis is associated with Melton and Irwin (1940) who used it to explain certain facts of RI. They suggested that at least part of RI could be accounted for by the loss of associative strength of List 1 responses resulting from extinction. It might also be assumed that negative transfer results from the interference accompanying the extinction process. A rather impressive amount of evidence could be marshalled in support of this extinction hypothesis. For present purposes, however, only an illustration of this evidence will be given. At various points in learning the second list, Briggs (1954) presented the stimuli common to both lists, one at a time, and asked *S* to give the first of the two responses which came to mind. The results showed that during the learning of List 2 there is a gradual decrease in frequency of List 1 responses, the curve being not unlike an extinction curve. A phenomenon analogous to spontaneous recovery of the List 1 responses was also found when retention was measured at various intervals of time after List 2 learning. Such evidence appears quite in line with the extinction hypothesis. However, as Briggs points out, a certain amount of ambiguity remains; the extinction curve does not necessarily mean that List 1 associations are extinguished in the sense that they are no longer available for recall. His results may mean only that List 2 associations become stronger than List 1 associations, hence, occur more and more frequently in recall. Such an increase in frequency of List 2 associations must necessarily be accompanied by a decrease in frequency of List 1 associations at recall. The question still remains,

Reprinted with permission of the authors and the publisher, the American Psychological Association. The article appeared originally in the *Journal of Experimental Psychology*, 1959, 58, 97–105.

therefore, as to whether or not the A-B association is available after A-C is learned and this is one question the present study attempts to answer.

2. The system of associations in List 1 (A-B) remains relatively independent and intact throughout the learning of the associations in List 2 (A-C). This will be referred to as the independence hypothesis. The verbal stimuli are, of course, identical in the A-B, A-C paradigm, but there are other possible differentiating cues (e.g., first list vs. second list) which would provide a means of having two independent response systems attached to the same apparent stimulus. Negative transfer could be said to occur in the process of establishing the independent response systems early in learning A-C. Retroactive inhibition could be attributed to loss of differentiation so that response competition occurs.

3. A third possible conception makes use of mediation. Having learned A-B in List 1, *S* retains this association so that List 2 items are learned with B as the mediator; *S* learns A—B—C. Negative transfer and RI could occur as a consequence of confusion on the part of *S* as to which response is used as the mediator and which response is mediated.

In the present study, different groups of *S*s were stopped at various points in learning List 2 and were asked to give *both* List 1 and List 2 responses to each stimulus. If (as degree of List 2 learning increases) there is an increasing inability to give List 1 responses (over and above normal forgetting), the extinction hypothesis would be favored. If there was no such loss either the independence hypothesis or the mediation hypothesis would be favored. Provisions were included in the design to choose between these latter two if it became necessary. For example, if the mediation hypothesis is tenable it should be found that B is given before C more frequently than C before B when *S* is asked to write down both responses. The independence hypothesis would not predict such an ordering in response recall.

Turning next to the paradigm in which stimuli are identical but responses highly similar (A-B, A-B′), the present study should again provide bases for choice among the three hypotheses.

1. Because retroactive facilitation is expected with this paradigm (e.g., Young, 1955) it might appear than an extinction hypothesis is not tenable. However, by the use of extinction plus other factors it is possible to account for retroactive facilitation. It is a fact that more List 1 instrusions occur in the learning of List 2 for this paradigm than for the A-B, A-C paradigm. Thus, the nonreinforcement of these responses makes extinction a very plausible mechanism. So, it could be assumed that in learning A-B′, A-B is extinguished. Retroactive facilitation could then be accounted for by mediation. It is known that highly similar items have high associative connection (Haagen, 1949). When *S* is asked to recall A-B after learning A-B′, even if A-B is extinguished the mediation sequence in recall could be A—B′—B, since there has been no extinction of the strong association between B′ and B. However, without the addition of still more factors the positive transfer in learning A—B′ cannot be accounted for. Since the results of the present procedures do not make the extinction hypothesis a reasonable one for this paradigm, no attempt will be made here to suggest the additional factors needed to account for the positive transfer produced by this paradigm.

2. The independence hypothesis, used in conjunction with a theory of response generalization (Underwood, 1951), can be employed to account for both positive transfer and retroactive facilitation in the A-B, A-B′ paradigm.

3. The mediation hypothesis also provides an attractive alternative for this positive transfer paradigm. As noted above, items which have high similarity have high associative connection. Thus, having learned A-B, the learning of A-B-B′ should be very simple since B and B′ are already strongly connected. Therefore, positive transfer should occur. In learning List 2, if mediation occurs *S* will be given additional practice on A-B; hence, this association will be further strengthened during List 2 learning, and retroactive facilitation would be expected to occur.

In summary, two paradigms are used, one associated with the production of negative transfer, the other with production of positive transfer. By requiring *S* to recall both List 1 and List 2 responses at various points in the learning of List 2, it was expected that choice could be made among three conceptions (extinction, independence, mediation) of the fate of List 1 associations during the learning of List 2.

METHOD

General.—Two parallel experiments were conducted, one using the A-B, A-C transfer paradigm and one using the A-B, A-B′ paradigm. Within each experiment there were four groups of *S*s. All *S*s learned a first paired-associate list (List 1) of eight pairs to one perfect trial. Then List 2 was presented for a specified number of trials, namely 1, 5, 10, and 20 anticipation trials for the four groups in each experiment. After the specified number of trials for a given group, the memory drum was stopped, *S* was provided a sheet of paper on which the eight stimuli were printed, and he was asked to write down the two responses (one from the first list and one from the second) which were associated with each stimulus. This written recall provided the major source of data.

Lists.—Eight nonsense syllables of from 60% to 73 % association value (Glaze, 1928) were used as stimuli for all lists. Intrastimulus similarity was low in that no consonant was repeated, and four vowels were used twice each. The responses were two-syllable adjectives taken from Haagen (1949). In the A-B, A-C lists there was no apparent interlist response similarity and intralist response similarity was as low as careful inspection procedure will produce. In the A-B, A-B′ lists the responses again had low intralist response similarity but high interlist response similarity. The responses from each list which were paired with the same stimulus had similarity ratings ranging from .9 to 1.4 by Haagen's scale. These high-similarity response pairs were as follows: *insane—crazy; barren—fruitless; complete—entire; royal—regal; double—twofold; afraid—scared; tranquil—peaceful; spoken—verbal.* Three different pairings of stimuli and responses were used for both experiments to avoid the possibility that fortuitous associations between stimulus and response would bias the results. An equal number of *S*s in each group was given each pairing. For each experiment for each condition a given list was used as List 1 for half the *S*s and as List 2 for the other half. Four orders of items were used to minimize serial learning.

The lists were presented on a Hull-type drum at a 2:2-sec. rate. The intertrial interval was 4 sec. Anticipation learning was used for List 1 and for List 2 to the point at which written recall was given (after 1, 5, 10, or 20 anticipation trials). A 1-min. interval separated the learning of the two lists.

Subjects.—A total of 192 *S*s was used. There were 24 *S*s in each condition for each experiment, the conditions being the point at which *S* was asked for written recall. All *S*s had previously served in at least one verbal-learning experiment. However, no other experiment had been run in which *S* was asked to recall responses from both lists, so there is no reason to believe that *S* anticipated that he would be asked for such recall. It should be emphasized that each *S* was asked for written recall only once so that it is not believed that *S*s made any special attempt to remember List 1 responses. In assigning *S*s, a listing of 192 entries was made such that each of the eight conditions occurred 24 times. Within these limits the ordering was random and *S*s were successively assigned in order of their appearance at the laboratory.

Written recall.—When the specified number of trials on List 2 had been given, the memory drum was stopped and the sheet for written recall given to *S*. The stimuli were listed on the sheet with two blank spaces under each. The *S*s were first instructed to write down the responses from the two lists below the appropriate stimuli. They were further told to write these down as they came to mind, and not to attempt to recall all the responses from one list first and then all those from the other. Two minutes were then allowed for this initial recall. Following this, they were instructed to go through the responses they had written, and indicate, by assigning the numbers 1 and 2, from which list the responses had come. An additional 2 min. were allowed for this. The *S*s were also told to write down any additional responses which they might think of while they were assigning list numbers.

After the recall papers were collected, a series of questions was asked to determine: (*a*) if *S* had written the responses as they came to mind or if there was deliberate attempt to recall the adjectives from a given list first, (*b*) whether or not *S* had used first-list responses to mediate the learning of the second-list responses.

Results

Transfer.—The major concern in the present paper is with the written recall results. However, it will be worthwhile to note briefly the transfer facts and to show that random assignment of *S*s to groups was effective. For all eight groups combined, the mean number of trials to learn List 1 to one perfect trial was 10.36, with the means for groups ranging from 9.17 to 12.00 trials. The *F* was less than 1. Lacking a precise control for transfer, some indication of the effects can be obtained by comparing the learning of List 1 with that of List 2. The total correct responses for the first three trials of the two lists were used as the response measure for the three groups having 5, 10, and 20 trials on List 2. For the A-B, A-B′ paradigm, more correct responses were given on List 2 than on List 1, indicating positive transfer. For all three groups combined, the mean number correct on the first list was 9.84, and for the second, 14.35. The *t* was 8.55. For A-B, A-C the mean number correct on the first list was 9.64, and on the second, 8.57. This *t* was 1.67. This result indicates that in a statistical sense no negative transfer was present, but this is not an unusual finding for this type of comparison since learning-to-learn and warm-up would counteract the negative effect. Finally, in keeping with previous studies (e.g., Underwood, 1951), the number of overt intrusions of List 1 responses during the learning of List 2 was much greater for A-B, A-B′ than for A-B, A-C.

Written recall.—There were several alternative ways by which the written recall could be scored. The most stringent method would be to count a response as correct only if it were placed with the appropriate stimulus and also correctly identified as to list. The most liberal method would be to count an adjective correct if recalled, regardless of whether it was placed with the correct stimulus and correctly identified as to list. The results for both methods are shown in Table 1. An inspection of this table will show that the differences produced by the two scoring methods are relatively small. The implication is that if *S* wrote down a response, he usually identified it correctly with stimulus and list.

TABLE 1

Mean Number of Responses Recalled From Each List for Each Transfer Paradigm as Scored by Two Methods[a]

Method	List	Point of Written Recall (Trials)			
		1	5	10	20
Paradigm A-B, A-C					
1	1	6.67	5.38	5.00	4.12
	2	3.46	6.29	7.33	7.38
2	1	6.96	5.58	5.42	4.29
	2	4.12	6.71	7.71	7.42
Paradigm A-B, A-B′					
1	1	7.67	7.21	7.12	6.92
	2	7.21	7.25	7.83	7.79
2	1	7.75	7.33	7.25	7.08
	2	7.38	7.29	7.96	7.83

[a] In Method 1 the response is counted correct only if correctly identified with stimulus and list. In Method 2 it is counted correct if merely recalled.

Turning first to the results for the A-B, A-C paradigm, the results for the stringent scoring method have been plotted in Fig. 1. As would be expected, as the number of learning trials on List 2 increases, the number of correct responses given from this list increases. Responses from the first or A-B list, however, show a gradual decline as the number of trials on List 2 increases. It is as if

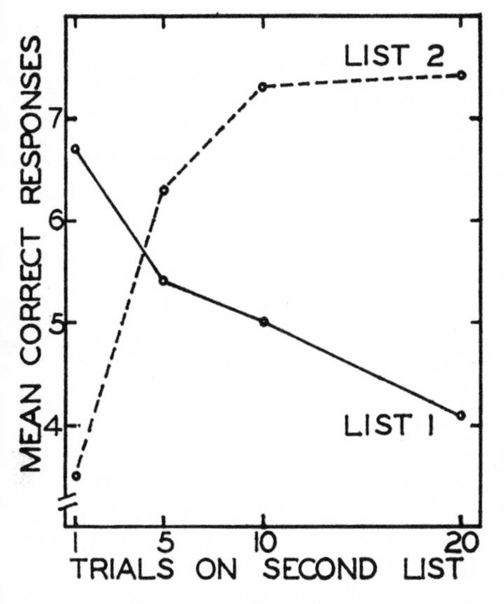

FIG. 1. Mean number of responses correctly recalled and identified with stimulus and list in the A-B, A-C paradigm.

the A-B associations are weakened or extinguished during the learning of A-C. The loss as a function of number of A-C trials cannot be attributed to a few *S*s losing many responses since most *S*s showed the decline. An analysis of variance of the four recall points for A-B gave an F of 8.86 ($F = 4.88$ for $P = .01$ with 3 and 92 *df*).

It was noted that Fig. 1 suggests that the A-B associations are extinguished. It might be suggested, furthermore, that not only are these associations extinguished, but also that the response per se is not available. This could be deduced from the fact that the two scoring methods did not differ much, implying that if *S* knew the response, he also knew what stimulus and what list it went with. However, this conclusion cannot be reached with complete confidence. The reason is that the instructions to *S* stressed the recall of the responses to the specific stimuli; he was never told to put down a response even if he didn't know with which stimulus it was paired. It is therefore possible that *S*s did not put down responses unless they were reasonably confident of its stimulus.

The objection might be raised that the decline in A-B associations seen in Fig. 1 is not to be attributed to the learning of A-C but rather represents simple forgetting. To make sure that this would not be a valid objection, a control group of 12 *S*s was run. This group learned List 1 to one perfect trial and then rested for a period of time equivalent to that spent in learning A-C by the group given 20 trials. This period was 13 min. (including the 1 min. between lists). The rest interval was filled with *S* working on a pyramid puzzle. After the rest, *S*s were given a written recall for the responses to the stimuli in the list they had learned. Counting only those responses which were appropriately paired with their stimuli, the mean recall was 7.75. Hence, it can be concluded that the decrement in recall of A-B associations as a function of trials on A-C cannot be attributed to simple forgetting, but must result from the learning of A-C.

The results for the A-B, A-B′ paradigm as given in Table 1 are quite different from those of A-B, A-C. It may first be noted that the recall of List 2 responses (A-B′) is nearly perfect after only one anticipation trial and, of course, remains high throughout 20 trials. Indeed, by both scoring methods the median recall for all groups at all points is 8.0 items. The first-list associations (A-B) show no appreciable decline. By the stringent scoring method the mean recall, even after 20 trials on A-B′, is nearly seven.

Order of recall.—The facts concerning the order of recall of the two responses can be used as evidence for or against a mediation hypothesis, as this hypothesis was discussed in the introduction. If *S* tends to recall List 1 responses first, it could be taken as evidence in support of a mediation hypothesis. Contrariwise, it would be evidence against mediation if List 2 responses tend to be recalled first. In this analysis data were not used from 12 *S*s who admitted under questioning that they attempted to write down all responses from one list first and then all from the other. Of these, seven had learned A-B, A-C, and five, A-B, A-B′. Obviously, only cases in which both responses were recalled could be used. For A-B, A-B′, there were 161, 159, 170, and 162 pairs of responses recalled for 1, 5, 10, and 20 trials, respectively. The corresponding percentages for the List 1 response being recalled before the List 2 response are 79%, 62%, 58%, and 53%. For A-B, A-C, the number of cases where both responses were recalled was 79, 113, 109, and 95 for 1, 5, 10, and 20 trials, respectively. The percentages of List 1 responses recalled first are 81%, 49%, 40%, and 43%. Assuming chance order as 50%, it can be seen that (excepting the conditions where only one trial was given on List 2 and where List 1 would be much stronger than List 2) with A-B, A-C the List 1 responses tend to be recalled first with chance or less than chance frequency. For A-B, A-B′ first-list responses are recalled with greater than chance frequency although after 20 trials this frequency has nearly reach 50%.

Subject reports.—Of the 96 *S*s who learned the A-B, A-B′ paradigm, 94 said they had used the List 1 responses to mediate the learning of List 2. These *S*s further reported that they tended to drop the use of these mediators as List 2 learning progressed. Of those 96 *S*s who had learned A-B, A-C, only two reported attempts to use the B response to mediate A-C learning; both *S*s further reported that this merely confused them.

Discussion

The A-B, A-C paradigm.—Three conceptions of what might "happen" to A-B during the learning of A-C were given in the introduction. These three conceptions were extinction or unlearning, the maintenance of two independent S-R systems, and mediation. The present data give strong support to the conception of extinction and at the same time argue against the other two conceptions. The recall of List 1 associations decreased progressively throughout the learning of A-C with nearly a 50% loss after 20 trials on A-C. A hyperbolic equation fitted to this curve predicts an asymptote at 3.46. Thus, it does not seem that all items would be extinguished, even with an extremely large number of trials on A-C. This conforms to the fact that forgetting in the RI paradigm has not been shown to be complete with very high degrees of interpolated learning. Thus, while the present data strongly support an extinction hypothesis they do not indicate why all items are not, nor are likely not to be, extinguished.

It seems reasonable to reject the independence hypothesis. If this hypothesis is to be retained, some mechanism will have to be added to account for the loss in the A-B associations over and above normal forgetting. If it is said that the A-C associations were so dominant that *S* was unable to recall the A-B associations, then the conception becomes very similar to an extinction hypothesis.

The mediation hypothesis cannot be seriously considered in light of the evidence. If List 2 responses are learned through mediation of B (A—B—C) the A-B association should not be lost from *S*'s repertoire. If it is said that the mediators drop out, then something like extinction must also be added to account for their loss from *S*'s repertoire. Furthermore, *Ss*' reports did not indicate that mediation had taken place (as was true of the reports for A-B, A-B′). All in all, the results give strong support to an extinction-like process; they do not give much support to an hypothesis of independence nor one of mediation.

It was noted that if *S* could recall a response he could usually identify it correctly as to list. On the surface, such evidence seems contrary to conceptions which say that some RI may be attributed to competition resulting from a lack of differentiation as to which response belongs in which list (e.g., Underwood, 1949). However, two additional facts must be noted which are relevant to this matter. First, in the present study essentially unlimited recall time was given so that identification of responses with lists should be more accurate than when recall is paced by a memory drum at a 2-sec. rate. Secondly, this differentiation is assumed to be very high when recall is given immediately after interpolation; differentiation is assumed to decrease as a function of time between interpolated learning and recall (Underwood, 1949). It is quite possible that the high accuracy of identifying responses with lists would be lost even with the present method if, say, a 24-hr. interval occurred between interpolation and written recall. Nevertheless, the present results would strongly suggest that nearly all RI could be accounted for by unlearning or extinction if unlimited recall time is given immediately after interpolated learning. The lack of differentiation, leading to competition between responses, should become an additional component in RI only after the passage of time since interpolated learning. Indeed, in view of the findings suggesting spontaneous recovery of extinguished associations (Briggs, 1954), it can be held that after the recovery is complete, all RI is due to competition. This two-component conception of RI will incorporate the major facts.

The A-B, A-B′ paradigm.—The data for this paradigm have shown that the A-B associations were maintained at a high level throughout the learning of A-B′. The very slight decline noted over 20 trials could be attributed to the extinction of the A-B responses for those cases in which *Ss* did not know the meaning of a word or words, hence, similarity of the responses was ineffective and the results were the same as an A-B, A-C paradigm. However, while accepting this possibility, it can be omitted from further consideration. The question still remains as to whether it is or is not likely that the A-B associations were extinguished while *S* learned A-B′ even when similarity was effective. It was noted in the introduction that such an hypothesis was a plausible one; indeed, looking only at the basic results it remains plausible.

The possibility that A-B could be extinguished and the present results still be obtained (no apparent loss in the A-B associations) may be handled by mediation in which after learning A-B′ (and extinguishing A-B), *S* recalled the B response because of its high associative connection with B′. Thus, when asked to recall, the associations were A to B′ and then B′ to B. If this took place, A-B could be extinguished and the present basic results would still be obtained. However, other findings argue against this interpretation and tend instead to support mediation in which A leads to B and B leads to B′ at recall.

1. If B is recalled via B′, B′ should be recalled before B. The data indicate that B is more often recalled first. It is true that after 20 trials B and B′ were recalled first about equally often. So, it is still possible that with high degrees of A-B′ learning, some extinction of A-B did occur.

2. Nearly all *Ss* report using B as a mediator to learn A-B′; none reported that B′ was used as a mediator in the recall of B. However, they did report that the use of B as a mediator tended to drop out as learning of A-B′ proceeded. Some extinction of A-B might have been a concomitant or cause of this drop out. But, the fact that the percentage of times in which A-B was recalled first (before A-B) never drops below 50%

suggests that if extinction was occurring it was much less in amount than that which occurred in A-B, A-C.

The conclusion is, therefore, that while the possibility of extinction of A-B in the A-B′ paradigm cannot be completely ruled out, it does not appear as compelling an interpretation as does the mediation hypothesis in which A-B mediates B′.

Finally, what about the hypothesis of independent response systems in which response generalization is used to account for positive transfer and retroactive facilitation? The use of response generalization to explain certain facts of transfer has been of considerable help in organizing the facts of transfer. One particular statement of this formulation can be briefly summarized (Underwood, 1951). It is assumed that when A-B is being learned, all responses similar to B likewise develop some associative strength to A. The amount of such strength, developed through what has been called parasitic reinforcement, is directly related to similarity of the response with the B response. Positive transfer occurs, therefore, because less learning has to occur in the second list than in the first. Thus, in the present situation, if A-B′ develops some associative strength as a consequence of learning A-B, positive transfer should occur when *S* is asked to learn A-B′. Retroactive facilitation would occur, since during the learning of A-B′ the A-B association would be further strengthened. It should be noted that this hypothesis deals only with the associations between A and B, and between A and B′; it does not deal in any way with the already well-established association between B and B′ which forms a central part of the mediation hypothesis.

The present evidence suggests that the response-generalization accounting of certain facts of transfer may well be abandoned in favor of a mediation hypothesis. The mediation hypothesis will account for the same general facts as will response generalization; furthermore, certain facts of the present experiment seem difficult to reconcile with the response-generalization hypothesis.

1. Almost without exception, *S*s report mediation. While it may be possible to extend the theory of response generalization to account for this fact that *S*s report mediation, the mediation per se can be used to account for the results, without further elaboration.

2. It was noted that after only one anticipation trial, recall of List 2 was nearly perfect. The theory of response generalization assumes a generalization gradient decreasing rather sharply as similarity decreases. The generalized association is not assumed to grow in associative strength at a rate comparable at all to the directly-reinforced association (A-B). To account for the extraordinarily rapid learning of A-B′ would mean that there is essentially no gradient between B and B′, or to say this another way, the gradient is flat. In previous experiments, no such rapid learning of A-B′ was noted; learning was more rapid than for a control condition but nothing like that shown here in the written recall. Indeed, in the present study for the groups having 5, 10, and 20 trials (before written recall), the mean number of items recalled on the second anticipation trial (comparable to the point at which written recall was asked for in the group having only 1 anticipation trial) was 5.04. This is to be contrasted with 7.75, obtained on written recall at the same point. The reason for this discrepancy, it is believed, is that under the standard procedures of anticipation learning *S* does not have time to mediate all items. Given more time, recall is nearly perfect right at the start of "learning" the second list. This finding is not compatible with the theory of response generalization.

The conclusion is that mediation of B′ through A-B is a more appropriate formulation than response generalization to account for positive effects in transfer and retention when response similarity is involved with identical stimuli. As similarity between responses decreases, the associative connection between them will likewise decrease; thus, a gradient-like phenomenon will appear in transfer. With moderate similarity between responses, the associative connection between the two will be less than in the present case, and additional strengthening of the associative connection will be necessary before mediation is completely effective. Thus, positive transfer will be less than when the responses are highly similar. It is apparent that since no evidence for mediation could be found in A-B, A-C, the mediation hypothesis must be abandoned when the responses reach a certain level of dissimilarity (or a low level of similarity). It is at this point that extinction begins to occur with consequent negative transfer.

Summary

The A-B, A-C and the A-B, A-B′ transfer paradigms were studied in order to evaluate three conceptions concerning the fate of first-list associations in learning a second list; namely: extinction of first-list associations, maintenance of two independent S-R systems, and mediation of the learning of the second-list response by the first-list association. For each paradigm, different groups of 24 *Ss* each were stopped after 1, 5, 10, or 20 anticipation trials on List 2 and were asked to write down *both* List 1 and List 2 responses to the stimuli. Both lists contained eight pairs of nonsense syllables and two-syllable adjectives. List 1 learning was carried to one perfect trial.

For the A-B, A-C paradigm there was a gradual reduction in reproduction of List 1 responses as degree of List 2 learning increased. A control condition showed that this reduction could not be accounted for by normal forgetting. No successful mediation of the C response via A-B was reported. It was concluded that of the three alternative conceptions, extinction of the List 1 responses was clearly to be preferred. It appears that nearly all retroactive inhibition measured immediately after interpolated learning may be due to extinction or unlearning of first-list responses during the learning of the second list.

For the A-B, A-B′ paradigm, the List 1 responses showed no appreciable loss over 20 trials and List 2 was given nearly perfectly after one anticipation trial. Of 96 *Ss*, 94 reported the use of the A-B association to mediate the B′ response. The rapid learning of List 2 is understandable by the mediation hypothesis, but some extinction of the A-B association in the A-B, A-B′ paradigm cannot be ruled out completely by the present data. The A-B association may be extinguished and then mediation of the List 1 response occurs via A-B′-B. However, considering all evidence, it seemed most probable that mediation occurs most frequently in the order A-B-B′. Finally, the evidence suggests that transfer effects produced by variation in response similarity can be more simply accounted for by mediation than by a theory using response generalization.

References

Briggs, G. E. Acquisition, extinction, and recovery functions in retroactive inhibition. *J. exp. Psychol.*, 1954, **47**, 285–293.

Glaze, J. A. The association value of nonsense syllables. *J. genet. Psychol.*, 1928, **35**, 255–269.

Haagen, C. H. Synonymity, vividness, familiarity, and association-value ratings for 400 pairs of common adjectives. *J. Psychol.*, 1949, **30**, 185–200.

Melton, A. W., & Irwin, J. McQ. The influence of degree of interpolated learning on retroactive inhibition and the overt transfer of specific responses. *Amer. J. Psychol.*, 1940, **53**, 175–203.

Underwood, B. J. Proactive inhibition as a function of time and degree of prior learning. *J. exp. Psychol.*, 1949, **39**, 24–34.

Underwood, B. J. Associative transfer in verbal learning as a function of response similarity and degree of first-list learning. *J. exp. Psychol.*, 1951, **42**, 44–53.

Young, R. K. Retroactive and proactive effects under varying conditions of response similarity. *J. exp. Psychol.*, 1955, **50**, 113–119.

(Received August 18, 1958)

ARTICLE 4

COMPARISON OF VERBAL RESPONSE TRANSFER MEDIATED BY MEANINGFULLY SIMILAR AND ASSOCIATED STIMULI [1]

JAMES J. RYAN

University of Nevada

In studies concerned with the process of transfer in learning, one of the factors usually considered crucial in determining the amount of transfer has been the specific relation existing between the original and subsequent stimulus or response elements. The degree of *similarity* between these elements, with respect to any of several attributes, has characteristically been represented as the basis for predicting and explaining differences in transfer. With respect to verbal materials, several studies (Haagen, 1943; Osgood, 1946, 1948; Underwood, 1951) have provided empirical support for similarity as a factor contributing to transfer. But, except for variation in the degree of similarity between subsequent stimulus and response terms in paired-associate learning, little work has been done investigating the other properties of the relationship between these verbal materials which might also facilitate transfer. However, some studies (Bulgelski & Scharlock, 1952; McClelland & Heath, 1943) have indicated that verbal habit connections existing between interlist stimulus or response words can mediate effects not unlike those which contribute to transfer effects.

Elaboration of the similarity concept in verbal materials has culminated in a theory presented by Osgood (1953) which hypothesizes that similarity in meaning has a dominant role in the mediation of verbal learning. Osgood suggests that covert meaning reactions can function as mediators in this process and also has suggested that observed positive and negative transfer effects could be explained in terms of differential mediating effects accompanying differences in meaningful similarity. In addition, Osgood and Suci (1952) have developed a scaling procedure which provides a basis for deriving a measure of the degree of connotative similarity between words.

In recent years, under the impetus of concern with communication and the psychology of language, interest has developed in intraverbal habit chains manifested by frequency of association in free-association response norms. Research investigating effects of such verbal habits on behaviors such as recall, perception, learning, and problem solving (Jenkins & Russell, 1956, 1958; Russell & Storms, 1955) has led to consideration of these pre-existing verbal habits as a basis for mediation of transfer in the traditional retroactive inhibition or response transfer paradigms. Bastian (1956) recently conducted a study directly concerned with the comparison of meaningful similarity and verbal habit connections as mediators of interlist transfer. In his study, verbal responses paired with the

[1] This article is based upon a dissertation submitted to the University of Minnesota in partial fulfillment of the requirements for the PhD degree. The author is indebted to James J. Jenkins for his helpful direction and generous advice on all phases of this study.

Reprinted with permission of the author and the publisher, the American Psychological Association. The article appeared originally in the *Journal of Experimental Psychology*, 1960, **60**, 408–415.

same stimulus terms in sequential paired-associate learning lists represented the different interlist relations being compared. He obtained significantly greater interlist transfer effects for response words having strong verbal habit connections and minimal similarity in meaning as compared with response words having high similarity in meaning and weak verbal habit connections.

The present study represents an extension of this comparison to a paradigm in which the interlist *stimulus* words are differentially related with respect to meaningful similarity and verbal habit strength. The purpose of this study was to determine the relative effectiveness of each of these verbal factors for mediating response transfer between stimulus words in two successively learned lists of paired associates and in the subsequent recall and relearning of the first list. To provide equivalence between the magnitudes of the two factors being compared, the objective was to determine the contribution of each factor independently when it is at maximum strength and other factors are of relatively minimal strength. This study differs from most previous studies concerned with similarity in meaning in that the semantic differential served as the basis for determining the degree of similarity in connotative meaning in terms of derived semantic distances (D). As in Bastian's study, free association served as the basis for inferring the pre-experimental strength of the verbal habit connections.

METHOD

Experimental Design

The experiment was designed so that one basic list of words would serve as stimulus terms in either the original list (Sequence I condition) or the transfer list (Sequence II condition). For each of these basic-list stimulus words, three other words were selected to represent one of the following types of relationship with respect to the basic-list stimulus words:

Type A (associated)—*Maximal* habit strength connections with *low* similarity in meaning.
Type S (similar)—*Weak* habit strength connections with *maximal* similarity in meaning.
Type C (control)—*Weak* habit strength connections with *low* similarity in meaning.

The necessity of having the same response paired with each of four different stimulus words required three separate paired-associate lists in addition to the basic list. Each *S* was required to learn the single set of responses to only two paired-associate lists, the basic list and one of the other three lists. The latter were made up in a counterbalanced order so that each list contained an equal number of stimulus words representing each type of relationship when the list was learned in sequence with the basic-list stimulus words. Each *S* was then exposed to an equal number of stimulus words in the transfer list representing each relationship, thereby allowing an estimate of the major experimental differences independent of subject differences.

There were six conditions in all, three in which the basic-list stimulus words occurred in the original list with *one* of the other three sets of stimulus words occurring in the transfer list (Sequence I); and three in which the basic-list stimulus words occurred in the transfer list and the other set of stimulus words occurred in the original list (Sequence II).

Selection of Materials

Stimulus words.—The indices most closely indentified with the two processes being compared served as the primary basis for selecting stimulus words representing the pre-experimental verbal relationships. Two normative studies, using a student sample from a population very similar to that from which the experimental *S*s were drawn, provided the data for these indices.

Russell and Jenkins (1954) have obtained free-association response norms for the 100 Kent-Rosanoff stimulus words. These norms indicate the primary (most frequent) response given to each stimulus word. A maximal habit strength connection is assumed to

TABLE 1

WORD RELATIONSHIPS AND LIST ASSIGNMENTS

Basic List	Stimulus Words						Response Words
	Type A		Type S		Type C		
	Words	List	Words	List	Words	List	
SLOW	FAST	3	DIM	1	FLAMING	2	CORLEP
SQUARE	ROUND	2	LONG	3	CURLED	1	TIFTON
HARD	SOFT	1	RIGID	3	MILD	2	BURBET
HEALTH	SICKNESS	3	VISION	2	ANGER	1	MERMIC
WAR	PEACE	1	DANGER	2	CALM	3	LODRAM
SWEET	BITTER	2	RIPE	1	CRUDE	3	VOLVAP
BOY	GIRL	2	FATHER	3	SISTER	1	DUNTEL
UGLY	BEAUTIFUL	3	HEARTLESS	1	CHARMING	2	WENDAN
FOOD	HUNGRY	1	CLEAN	2	WET	3	RISPUL

exist between a given word and its primary response. Jenkins, Russell, and Suci (1957) have made available a table of semantic distances (D values) between all pairs of a set of 360 words. This set includes a large number of Kent-Rosanoff stimulus words and also their primary responses as given in the Russell-Jenkins norms. The D value between a pair of words is derived from their individual semantic differential profiles and according to Osgood represents their relative degree of similarity in connotative meaning. From the set of words having data available on both indices it was possible to select the nine basic-list stimulus words such that for each of these there were three other words in the set which represented each of the desired interlist stimulus relationships. The stimulus words used are shown on Table 1.

In terms of the indices used these interlist relationships were as follows: (*a*) Type A words, for which the basic-list stimulus words were primary free-association responses and which had relatively high semantic distance values (low similarity of meaning) with respect to the basic stimulus words. (*b*) Type S words, for which the basic-list stimulus words had the lowest semantic distance values (highest similarity of meaning) and which had very low or zero frequency of occurrence as free-association responses with respect to the basic stimulus words. (*c*) Type C words, for which the basic-list stimulus words had a very low or zero frequency of occurrence as free-association responses and which had relatively high semantic distance values (low similarity of meaning) with respect to the basic stimulus words.

Each Type C word was selected to have approximately the same D value (low similarity of meaning) relative to the basic-list stimulus word as the corresponding Type A word while having the same relatively minimal degree of association strength as the corresponding Type S word. Stimulus words were also screened to include only those having high frequency of usage as indicated by the Thorndike-Lorge word count (Thorndike & Lorge, 1944); to minimize pre-experimental associative connections between Types A, S, and C words paired with the same response; and to minimize intralist interference effects.[2]

Response words.—To reduce the possibility of any associative or meaningful connections which would contribute to consistent but differential learning of a given pair or pairs of words in these lists, a set of two-syllable nonsense words (paralogs) was prepared for use as the response terms. This set of paralogs was pretested for consistent association value by including them in a free-association test and eliminating those that elicited a given response with any degree of consistency. These words were also constructed to minimize interlist and intralist orthographic similarity. The response words are shown in Table 1.

Procedure

A total of 90 male students randomly selected from sophomore general psychology courses served as *S*s. The apparatus used was a Hull-type memory drum set up for

[2] A complete description of the stimulus words in terms of the relevant measures has been presented by the author (Ryan, 1957).

paired-associate learning. The apparatus presented each stimulus word for 2 sec. after which a shutter lifted to expose the response word (together with the stimulus word) for 2 sec. before a new stimulus word appeared alone. Stimulus materials were presented through use of tapes which contained randomly ordered repetitions of stimulus and response pairs in each list. Each *S* was told that he was to engage in a learning experiment and instructed in the function of the apparatus and the specific learning procedure to be followed. The *S*s were instructed to say each stimulus word aloud as it appeared, and as soon as possible after the first trial to anticipate and say aloud each response before it appeared. If no response or an incorrect response was given, *S*s were to say the correct response aloud when it did appear. The *S*s were also told that each list would be continued until all responses had been correctly anticipated on the same trial.

As a warm-up task *S*s learned a practice list consisting of five pairs of three-letter nonsense syllables as stimuli and two-digit numbers as responses. Following the warm-up task each *S* was given a set of 45 cards each containing one of the nine paralog response words. He was asked to go through the cards twice pronouncing each word aloud, thereby providing 10 exposures to each of the response words. This procedure allowed *S*s to learn more readily the verbal response to the visual stimuli provided by these unfamiliar paralogs eliminating somewhat this additional learning process from the actual experimental learning task. The *S* was then randomly assigned to one of the six experimental conditions and the experimental learning task was begun with the original list followed by the transfer list and relearning of the original list. Prior to beginning the original list, instructions were repeated and *S* was instructed not to attempt to anticipate the correct response on the first trial but only to say the response after it appeared. Each list was continued with a 4-sec. interval between each trial. Immediately after the original list had been learned to the criterion, *S* was instructed that a new list would be learned following the same procedure. The *S* was told that there would be a different set of stimulus words with the same set of response words. The learning of the transfer list proceeded without further delay. After the transfer list had been learned to the criterion, *S* was told that the original list would be repeated and that he was to attempt to anticipate the correct responses prior to their exposure for the first as well as subsequent trials.

Results and Discussion

The primary comparison in this study concerns response acquisition during transfer-list learning as well as performance during recall and relearning of the original list. However, this comparison assumes that there are no initial systematic differences in ease of response acquisition between those sets of stimulus words representing Types A, S, and C interlist relations as they appear in the transfer and relearning lists. To check this assumption a comparison was made of performance during the original-list learning between stimulus words representing each of these relationships. The reversal of sequence of presentation permitted this comparison. Stimulus words in the original list of each sequence could be classified on the basis of the functional relationship they represented in the transfer list of the alternate sequence.

An analysis of variance using the total correct anticipations given during original-list learning for Sequences I and II separately revealed no significant differences ($F = .18$ and $.95$, respectively, $P > .05$) in ease of response acquisition between words representing the three types of relationship.[3] This result is consistent with the assumption that stimulus words representing the three types of relationship do not differ initially with respect to ease of response acquisition.

[3] Since measures of the three experimental word types were obtained from the same *S*s and were therefore intercorrelated within list conditions, an analysis of variance model presented by Collier for "Two dimensional classification with observations at one level correlated" (Collier, 1956) was used for this and all other analyses of word-type effects.

The performance measures which served as indices of the degree of transfer obtained during learning of the transfer list were the number of correct responses given on Trial 2 (first anticipation trial); the number of correct responses given on Trial 3; and the total number of correct responses given on all trials to the criterion. For each of these measures an analysis of variance was carried out for Sequences I and II separately. Each analysis of variance indicated a significant difference at the .01 level between word-type means for all measures with the exception of the total correct responses in Sequence II for which the probability was at the .05 level. Duncan's multiple range test (Duncan, 1955) was used to determine the significance of the difference between each pair of the three word-type means in each sequence. The means and *SD*s obtained for each measure are shown in Table 2.

Words representing the Type A relationship obtained a significantly greater number of correct responses on the initial anticipation trials (Trials 2 and 3) than words representing either Type S or Type C relationships. The differences between Type A and Type C words are significant at the .01 level in both sequences on Trials 2 and 3. The differences between Type A and Type S words are significant at the .01 and .05 levels, respectively, for Trials 2 and 3 in both sequences. A difference favoring the Type A words is also observed when the total number of learning trials are considered, although for this measure only the difference between Type A and Type C words is significant and this difference is at the .01 level in both sequences. The Type S words also exhibited a consistently greater ease of response acquisition than the Type C words for all measures of learning. This difference, though, is not significant for the first anticipation trial (Trial 2) of either sequence nor for subsequent trials in Sequence II. In Sequence I the difference between Type S and Type C words is significant at the .05 level for Trial 3 and at the .01 level for all trials to the criterion. These results indicate that the interlist relations between stimulus words represented by both the Type A words (strong verbal habit connections) and the Type S words (high similarity in meaning) facilitated learning to a greater extent than those for the control words. The Type A words however, exhibited greater ease of response acquisition than the Type S words as indicated by differences obtained on the initial trials. It appears then that the Type A relationship provided an initial learning advantage which carried over the subsequent trials and although the Type S relationship did not provide a reliable difference on the initial

TABLE 2

Transfer List Learning: Mean Correct Anticipations and *SD*s

Sequence	Types: A		S		C	
	Mean	*SD*	Mean	*SD*	Mean	*SD*
Trial 2						
I	1.38	.89	.98	.69	.80	.81
II	1.53	.84	1.04	.90	.93	.81
Trial 3						
I	1.93	.86	1.56	.87	1.24	.93
II	1.91	.92	1.56	.99	1.47	1.01
All Trials						
I	22.60	12.26	21.36	11.47	17.91	7.67
II	22.02	10.53	20.53	10.49	19.07	10.77

trials, it did facilitate subsequent learning at a faster rate than was obtained for the Type C words as indicated by an overall difference with respect to the latter.

An analysis was made of performance during relearning of the original list. The results of the analysis of variance of the number of correct responses on the first relearning trial, which represents a measure of recall, indicated no significant differences between word-type means. Similarly the analysis of variance for the total number of correct responses given during all trials for relearning the original list indicated no significant effect attributable to word types. The means for both measures during relearning the original list are shown in Table 3.

Since the maximum number of correct responses possible for *S* to make on a single trial for a given word type was three, it can be seen that on the recall trial there was a very high probability of correct anticipation for words representing all three interlist stimulus relationships. It is apparent that there was a minimal loss in learning due to the interpolated transfer list and that this minor loss showed no systematic relationship to the different verbal relations.

TABLE 3

RELEARNING ORIGINAL LIST: MEAN CORRECT ANTICIPATIONS AND *SD*s

Sequence	Types					
	A		S		C	
	Mean	*SD*	Mean	*SD*	Mean	*SD*
	Trial 1 (Recall)					
I	2.36	.84	2.22	.79	2.29	.82
II	2.31	.67	2.31	.70	2.16	.85
	All Trials					
I	7.96	4.60	7.91	4.97	7.58	4.20
II	9.49	7.83	9.78	7.74	8.96	6.11

On the basis of these results it can be concluded that the mediation effects of verbal habit strength (as determined by free-association response norms) and similarity in meaning (as determined by the semantic differential) can facilitate response transfer between interlist stimulus words. Further, for the sample of words used here, the mediation effects of the verbal habit connections provide greater facilitation than those provided by similarity in connotative meaning.

Since transfer effects have been obtained for words representing both verbal habit and similarity relationships, it is somewhat difficult to make any unequivocal statement favoring only one of the underlying theoretical positions. The response chaining mediation mechanism supported by Bastian (1956) and the Minnesota investigators and the representational mediating process offered by Osgood (1953) both find adequate support in terms of the transfer effected by the verbal relationships assumed to provide maximum opportunity for each of these processes to be effective. The most conservative conclusion that could be drawn at this point is that both factors, and as far as can be determined their assumed mediating processes, operate independently—each factor being a sufficient condition in itself for facilitating response transfer in a learning scheme such as that utilized here. It should be understood, however, that these results provide no indication concerning relative transfer effects of dimensions of similarity other than connotative similarity that could exist between stimulus words either separately or in combination with similarity in connotative meaning.

Although no systematic bias was apparent, the words used in this study to represent the interlist relations were not randomly sampled from the potentially large population of word pairs that could exhibit these relations, but rather were selected from those for which the appropriate normative data were available. Therefore, more extensive generalization of these results concerning the relative effectiveness of the two factors would require some qualification.

It is consistently evident, however, that the transfer obtained through the verbal habit relationships used in this study is of larger magnitude than that obtained for the similarity relationships employed here. It might be suggested that this difference has arisen through a deficiency in the sampling procedures as far as similarity is concerned. That is, it is reasonable to question whether those words selected for maximal similarity (low semantic distance) to the basic-list stimulus words did not actually exhibit as much similarity as other possible words not so selected. For example, synonyms in general usage tend to have an association frequency of measurable magnitude and therefore, even if within the set for which normative data were available, could not be included here to represent the Type S relationship. Although it is possible that the degree of similarity may have been depressed to some extent through this kind of selection it should be noted that the semantic distances for the meaningfully similar words used here tended to be only slightly larger than the test–retest difference in semantic distance of words measured by the semantic differential obtained for a separate subject sample (Norman, 1957). This suggests that the error of measurement could account for any slight differences that would separate the words used from others that might appear more similar with respect to connotative meaning.

The results in this study seem to indicate quite clearly that verbal habit strength can mediate verbal response transfer independent of the effects of connotative similarity. Further, it seems that for certain subsets of words at least, verbal habit strength provides as good if not a better basis for verbal response transfer than is provided by connotative similarity in meaning.

Summary

Similarity in connotative meaning and verbal habit strength as separate factors relating interlist stimulus words in subsequent paired-associate learning lists were compared as to their effectiveness in mediating response transfer across these lists. The *S*s learned in sequence two paired-associate lists, an original and transfer list, and relearned the original list. Three types of verbal relationship were established between the corresponding interlist stimulus words paired for learning with the same response: Type A, representing maximal habit strength connections and low similarity in meaning; Type S, representing weak habit strength connections and maximal similarity in meaning; Type C (control), representing weak habit strength connections and low similarity in meaning. These interlist relations were obtained by pre-experimental selection of stimulus word pairs on the basis of appropriate norms for semantic distance (as derived from Osgood's semantic differential), which served as an index of similarity in connotative meaning; and free-association response frequency, which served as an index of verbal habit strength. Measures of performance on the transfer list showed that both Type A words and Type S words facilitated learning to a greater extent than the Type C control words and that the Type A words facilitated learning to a greater extent than the Type S words. No systematic differences in recall or relearning of the original list were obtained. It was concluded that both verbal habit strength and connotative similarity in meaning as relations between interlist stimulus words contribute independently to the mediation of response transfer and that the mediation effects contributed by verbal habit strength connections were as good if not better than those contributed by connotative similarity within the subset of words used here. The theoretical relevance of these two factors was presented and discussed.

References

Bastian, J. R. Response chaining in verbal transfer. Unpublished doctoral dissertation, Univer. Minnesota, 1956.

Bulgelski, B. R., & Scharlock, D. P. An experimental demonstration of unconscious mediated association. *J. exp. Psychol.*, 1952, **44**, 334–338.

Collier, R. O., Jr. Experimental designs in which observations are assumed to be correlated. Unpublished doctoral dissertation, Univer. Minnesota, 1956.

Duncan, D. B. Multiple range and multiple *F* tests. *Biometrics*, 1955, **11**, 1–42.

Haagen, C. H. Learning and retention as a function of the synonymity of original and interpolated tasks. Unpublished doctoral dissertation, State Univer. Iowa, 1943.

Jenkins, J. J., & Russell, W. A. Research studies in the role of language in behavior. *ONR tech. Rep.*, 1956. (Contract N8-onr-66216, Univer. Minnesota.)

Jenkins, J. J., & Russell, W. A. The role of language in behavior. *ONR tech. Rep.*, 1958. (Contract N8-onr-66216, Univer. Minnesota.)

Jenkins, J. J., Russell, W. A., & Suci, G. J. Studies on the role of language in behavior: An atlas of semantic profiles for 360 words. *ONR tech. Rep.*, 1957. (Contract N8-onr-66216, Univer. Minnesota.)

McClelland, D. C., & Heath, R. M. Retroactive inhibition as a function of degree of association between original and interpolated activities. *J. exp. Psychol.*, 1943, **33**, 420.

Norman, W. T. The role of language in behavior: Stability characteristics of the semantic differential. *ONR tech. Rep.*, 1957, No. 19. (Contract N8-onr-66216, Univer. Minnesota.)

Osgood, C. E. Meaningful similarity and interference in learning. *J. exp. Psychol.*, 1946, **36**, 299–301.

Osgood, C. E. An investigation into the causes of retroactive interference. *J. exp. Psychol.*, 1948, **38**, 132–154.

Osgood, C. E. *Method and theory in experimental psychology.* New York: Oxford Univer. Press, 1953.

Osgood, C. E., & Suci, G. J. A measure of relation determined by both mean difference and profile information. *Psychol. Bull.*, 1952, **49**, 251–262.

Russell, W. A., & Jenkins, J. J. Studies on the role of language in behavior: The complete Minnesota norms for responses to 100 words from the Kent-Rosanoff Word Association Test. *ONR tech. Rep.*, 1954, No. 11. (Contract N8-onr-66216, Univer. Minnesota.)

Russell, W. A., & Storms, L. H. Implicit verbal chaining in paired-associate learning. *J. exp. Psychol.*, 1955, **49**, 287–293.

Ryan, J. J. An experimental comparison of response transfer facilitated by meaningfully similar and associated stimuli. Unpublished doctoral dissertation, Univer. Minnesota, 1957.

Thorndike, E. L., & Lorge, I. *The teacher's word book of 30,000 words.* New York: Bureau of Publications, Teachers College, 1944.

Underwood, B. J. Associative transfer in verbal learning as a function of response similarity and degree of first list learning. *J. exp. Psychol.*, 1951, **42**, 44–53.

(Received November 20, 1959)

ARTICLE 5

EFFECTS OF RESPONSE MEANINGFULNESS (*m*) ON TRANSFER OF TRAINING UNDER TWO DIFFERENT PARADIGMS[1]

JOHN JUNG[2]

Northwestern University

The effects of 2 levels of response meaningfulness (m) on transfer under 2 paradigms, A-B, C-B and A-B, A-C were studied using paired-associate lists of 6 pairs of items consisting of adjectives as stimuli and trigrams as responses. Since the same responses occur on both lists of the A-B, C-B paradigm, positive transfer or facilitation of 2nd list learning may result from response learning on the 1st list. Such transfer should be greater with low m responses which require more response learning than high m responses. The results supported the prediction of greater positive transfer with low m. Although negative transfer was predicted for the A-B, A-C paradigm, it was predicted to be independent of Response m. However, high m produced greater negative transfer.

The learning of paired-associate lists has been logically analyzed into two major components, a response-learning stage and an associative stage (Hovland & Kurtz, 1952; Underwood, Runquist, & Schulz, 1959). During the first stage the responses per se are learned so that they become readily available units. Secondly, these responses must be associated to the appropriate stimuli with which they have been paired.

Ellis and Burnstein (1960) have advocated extending the above analysis of the learning of a single paired-associate list to the learning of two successive paired-associate lists, i.e., the transfer of training paradigm. They analyzed the A-B, C-B paradigm (stimuli different, responses identical) accordingly. Since the responses on the two lists are identical, response learning which occurs on the first list should be readily transferred to the learning of the second list. Learning of the second list can begin with the second or associative stage since the responses necessary were already learned during training on the first list. Thus, positive transfer is possible via the response-learning stage in this paradigm.

Adding to the Ellis-Burnstein analysis, it can be seen that negative transfer may occur under this paradigm via the associative stage. This transfer task requires the learning of two different associations with the same responses and it is not inconceivable that interference may be encountered in such a situation. In fact, Twedt and Underwood (1959) obtained a slight amount of negative transfer using this paradigm. They attributed this result to possible interference of backward associations from the first list to the forward associations of the second list. Thus, whereas the response-learning stage produces an element of positive transfer under this paradigm, the associative stage leads to negative transfer effects. Transfer effects obtained under this

[1] This study is based on a PhD dissertation submitted to the Graduate School of Northwestern University. The author is indebted to Benton J. Underwood for his guidance and encouragement during the course of the investigation.

[2] Now at Long Beach State College, Long Beach, California.

Reprinted with permission of the author and the publisher, the American Psychological Association. The article appeared originally in the *Journal of Experimental Psychology*, 1963, **65**, 377–384.

paradigm will be the difference between these two opposed factors.

Ellis and Burnstein were concerned only with the A-B, C-B paradigm but it is possible to analyze similarly the A-B, A-C paradigm (stimuli identical, responses different). Unlike the A-B, C-B paradigm, no specific response-term transfer is expected in this paradigm since the responses on the two lists are dissimilar. Response learning on the second list should be independent of the response learning of the first list, except for the nonspecific transfer which occurs in proceeding from the first list to the second due to warm up and learning-to-learn. However, a measure of nonspecific transfer in this paradigm may be obtained from an appropriate control paradigm, A-B, C-D (stimuli different, responses different). As compared to the A-B, C-D paradigm, there should be no positive transfer of response learning under the A-B, A-C paradigm such as will be the case with the A-B, C-B paradigm.

On the other hand, the associative stage of the first list may affect the learning of the second list under the A-B, A-C paradigm. The A-B associations which are formed on the first list are incompatible with the A-C associations required on the second list. The tendency to respond with B, upon the presentation of A, may interfere with the acquisition of C responses to A, hence negative transfer on the second list.

In the light of the preceding analyses of two transfer paradigms, the effects of one variable, response meaningfulness (*m*), on transfer in those two paradigms will now be specified.

Before a verbal unit can be emitted as a response it must first be available in the repertoire of the *S*. Verbal units of high *m* are well integrated and readily become part of the *S*'s response repertoire; on the other hand, units of low *m* require substantial response learning before becoming well integrated and available units. Thus, in the A-B, C-B paradigm, the beneficial effects of having identical responses on the two lists depends on the extent to which response learning is necessary. The improvement in learning from the first list to that on the second in this paradigm with responses of high *m* will be small compared to the case of low *m* responses. As compared to the A-B, C-D control which receives different responses on the two lists, the advantage of having identical responses on the two lists under A-B, C-B will be greater when the responses are of low *m* which allows greater transfer of response learning.

In the A-B, A-C paradigm, Response *m* should not lead to differential transfer of response integration since the responses on the two lists are dissimilar. Furthermore, although it was hypothesized that negative transfer under this paradigm was due to associative interference between the two lists, it does not appear that this interference is a function of Response *m*. Thus, transfer in the A-B, A-C paradigm is not expected to be related to Response *m*.

METHOD

Design.—The effects of two different levels of Response *m* on the amount of transfer of training were studied under three different transfer paradigms, A-B, C-B (stimuli different, responses identical), A-B, A-C (stimuli identical, responses different), and A-B, C-D (stimuli different, responses different). Hereafter, these paradigms will be referred to as the C-B, A-C, and C-D paradigms, respectively. Although the primary interest of this study was in the effects of Response *m* under the first two paradigms, it was necessary to include the C-D paradigm as a control group in order to separate effects attributable to specific and nonspecific transfer. In other words, changes in performance between List 1 and List 2 learning may be due to specific stimulus-response relationships between the lists and also to nonspecific factors such as warm up and fatigue, etc., which are unrelated to the stimulus-response relationships between the two lists. Both sets of factors may be considered to be at work under the C-B and A-C paradigms but only the nonspecific factors may be expected under the C-D paradigm where the two lists are relatively unrelated. By comparing the results for the C-D paradigm with each of the other two paradigms, it is possible to assess the amount of transfer due to specific stimulus-response relationships between the two lists.

The two variables, Response *m* and paradigms, were studied in a 2 × 3 design which required six experimental conditions. Each condition required the learning of two different lists which were related to each other in such a way as to form one of the paradigms noted above. Under each of these paradigms, different levels of Response *m* (high and low) were employed for different groups of *S*s. The responses of both lists for any given condition were of the same level of Response *m*.

All conditions within a given level of Response *m*, regardless of paradigm, received the identical second list which may be designated as List A-B. This procedure avoids the possibility that the second lists may be unequal in difficulty.

Subjects.—The 120 *S*s used were students from introductory psychology classes at Northwestern University fulfilling course requirements. All *S*s were required to have previously served in at least one other memory drum experiment before serving in the present study. Twenty *S*s were assigned randomly to each of the six experimental conditions with the restriction that within each of the 20 successive blocks of 6 *S*s each, 1 *S* be assigned to each condition. During the course of the study, 3 *S*s were dropped for failure to learn the first list to the established criterion. These *S*s were replaced by assigning the next *S* to the same condition.

Materials.—Two paired-associate lists, each consisting of six two-syllable adjectives (Haagen, 1949) as stimulus terms and trigrams (Underwood & Schulz, 1960, Appendix F) as response terms, were used for all conditions. Intralist stimulus similarity was kept as low as possible. Similarly, for conditions requiring two sets of stimuli (A-C and C-D), the interlist stimulus similarity was low. Within any given paradigm, the same stimuli were used for both levels of Response *m*.

The two levels of Response *m* were generated from Appendix F in Underwood and Schulz (1960). The ranges of summed letter counts for the two levels of Response *m* were: low, 9–14; and high, 46–79. The mean summed letter counts for the first list responses were: low, 10.5; and high, 58.3; for the second list responses, the mean summed letter counts were: low, 10.3; and high, 57.1.

Within each list, the intralist response similarity was minimized by not allowing any duplication of letters within any given list; each list of six trigrams required 18 different letters to form the responses. For those paradigms requiring two sets of responses (A-C and C-D), interlist response similarity was minimized by not allowing any letter to occupy the same position within any two responses between lists. The response terms which appeared on the second list across paradigms are presented to illustrate these points, low *m*: SBL, MQK, OCJ, HFW, RDG, TXP; high *m*: JAK, ENT, XYW, IMP, UVR, HOS.

Procedure.—Standard paired-associate learning instructions were read to the *S*s. They were informed that there was a list of six pairs of two-syllable adjectives and three-letter units which would be presented in various orders in the window of the memory drum facing them. When the two-syllable adjective stimulus of a given pair appeared in the window, the *S* was to attempt to spell out the corresponding three-letter unit with which it was previously paired before the shutter opened 2 sec. later revealing the three-letter unit.

Learning on the first list was carried to a criterion of one perfect anticipation trial. Approximately 1 min. after the completion of List 1 learning, *S*s were told that there was a second list to be learned using the same procedures as for the first list. The second list was presented for 10 anticipation trials under all conditions.

The lists were presented on a Hull-type memory drum with a 2:2 sec. rate of presentation and with a 4-sec. intertrial interval. To minimize the possibility of serial learning, each list was presented in five different orders.

Results

List 1 learning.—The mean number of anticipation trials to meet the established criterion for learning the first list for each condition is presented in Table 1. As might be expected, the learning of the first list was more rapid under high than with low *m* under all paradigms. These differences were significant, F (1, 114) = 72.98, $p < .001$. However, there

TABLE 1

MEAN NUMBER OF ANTICIPATION TRIALS TO CRITERION ON LIST 1

Paradigm	Response m	
	High	Low
A-B, C-B	9.50	24.90
A-B, A-C	10.50	23.45
A-B, C-D	10.85	23.40

were no significant differences in first-list learning as a function of paradigms under either high m, F (2, 57) = .37, or under low m, F (2, 57) = 1.15.

List 2 learning, Trials 1–2.—Figure 1 presents the mean number of correct anticipations for each condition on the first two anticipation trials of List 2. A greater number of correct anticipations was found with high than with low m. The F for Response m of 61.80 with 1/114 df was significant at the .001 level. The relative performance of groups under the different paradigms was identical at both levels of Response m, C-B being highest, followed by C-D, and finally A-C. The differences between the paradigms was significant, F (2, 114) = 16.67, $p < .001$. The Response $m \times$ Paradigm interaction was also significant, F (2, 114) = 4.17, $p < .05$, reflecting the fact that the magnitude of the effect of Response m is not the same for all paradigms.

In order to measure specific transfer, it is necessary to partial out any nonspecific transfer effects which are derived from warm up, etc., in proceeding from the first list to the second. In the present study, this is possible by comparing the C-D control (which provides a measure of nonspecific transfer) with each of the other two paradigms (A-C and C-B). The latter paradigms may produce some transfer attributable to specific stimulus-response relationships in addition to nonspecific transfer.

Inspection of Fig. 1 indicates that

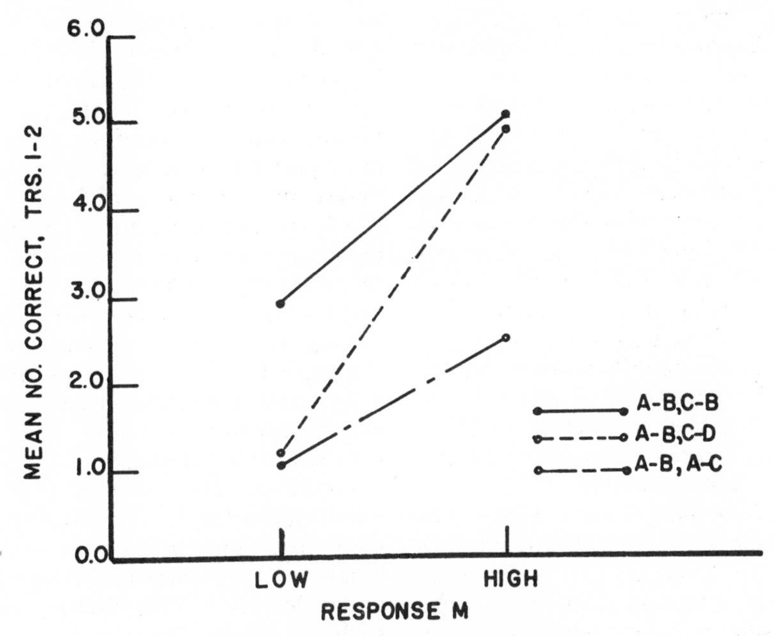

FIG. 1. Mean number of correct anticipations as a function of Response m and paradigms on Trials 1–2.

the superiority of the performance of the C-B condition to that of the C-D condition is greater with low than with high *m*. This finding shows that positive transfer under this paradigm is greater with low than with high *m*, as predicted earlier.

To determine if these differences in net transfer as a function of Response *m* were significant statistically, difference scores were obtained between the number of correct anticipations for each *S* in the C-B paradigm and the mean number of correct anticipations for the C-D condition at each level of Response *m*. First, the mean number of correct anticipations was obtained for the C-D condition at each level of Response *m*. Then, for each *m* level, the C-D mean score was subtracted from each C-B score at that level of *m*, providing two distributions of difference scores. A t of 2.63 with 19 *df* was obtained between the difference scores obtained for high and low *m* ($p < .01$).

A similar analysis was made of transfer under the A-C paradigm. Figure 1 indicates that the inferiority of the A-C condition to the C-D condition was greater with high than with low *m*. In other words, net negative transfer was obtained under the A-C paradigm and it was greater with high than with low *m*, contradicting the hypothesis that Response *m* would not differentially affect transfer under this paradigm. Statistical analysis was performed in the same manner described above for the the C-B paradigm. The difference scores obtained for each level of Response *m* differed very significantly, $t\ (19) = 5.38, p < .001$.

List 2 learning, Trials 1–10.—The mean number of correct anticipations on all 10 trials of List 2 for each condition is presented in Fig. 2. For all paradigms, better performance occurred under high than under low *m*, $F\ (1, 114) = 79.95, p < .001$. Performance also differed significantly as a function of paradigms, $F\ (2, 114) = 18.61, p < .001$. For low *m*, the highest performance came under C-B, followed by C-D, and finally by A-C; however, under high *m*, performance was highest under C-D, then C-B, and finally, A-C. This difference in the rank ordering of the paradigms as a function of Response *m* is reflected by a significant Response *m* × Paradigm interaction, $F\ (2, 114) = 10.40, p < .001$.

As in the case of the results for Trials 1–2, to obtain measures of net transfer it is necessary to compare the C-D condition with each of the other two paradigms in performance on the transfer list. Inspection of Fig. 2 indicates that the superiority of the C-B paradigm to the C-D paradigm on performance on Trials 1–10 is, as it was on Trials 1–2, greater under low than with high *m*. Actually, with high *m*, the performance of the C-B condition is inferior to that of the C-D paradigm.

Difference measures were obtained by comparing the mean number of correct anticipations for the C-D condition with the number of correct anticipations for each *S* in the C-D paradigm at each level of Response *m*. The difference scores for the high and low *m* groups were significantly different, $t\ (19) = 3.82, p < .01$. These findings are in agreement with similar findings from Trials 1–2 and support the prediction based on the response-integration hypothesis that transfer will be greater with low than with high *m* in this paradigm.

Figure 2 also indicates that the inferiority of the A-C paradigm to the C-D paradigm in performance on Trials 1–10 is greater under high than under low *m*. This finding agrees with a similar relationship found between Response *m* and net transfer

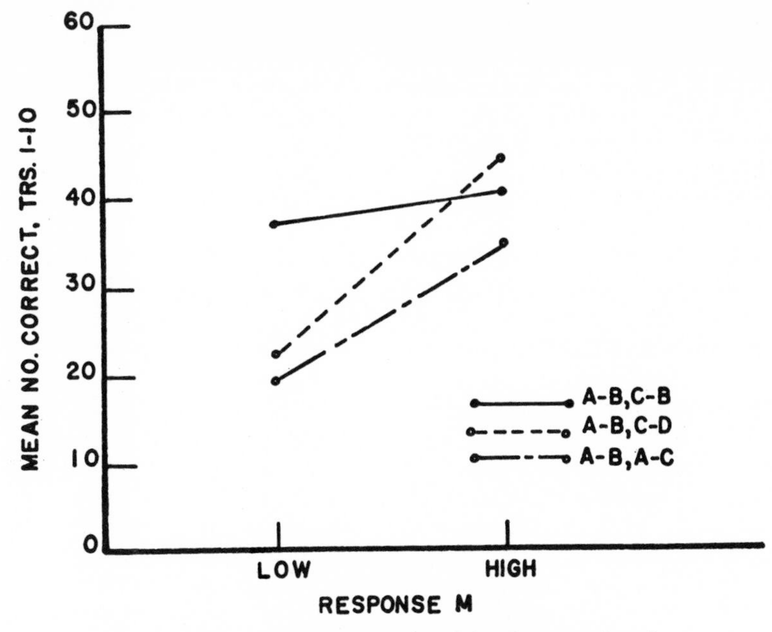

FIG. 2. Mean number of correct anticipations as a function of Response *m* and paradigms on Trials 1–10.

on Trials 1–2 although it is less striking on Trials 1–10. Difference scores were obtained to provide measures of net transfer at each level of Response *m* in the same manner used for the C-B paradigm described above. The *t* of 2.25 ($df = 19$, $p < .05$) obtained showed that net negative transfer was significantly greater with high than with low *m*. This result, like the relationship found on Trials 1–2, is incompatible with the earlier prediction that transfer under this paradigm is independent of Response *m*.

Error analysis.—In learning a paired-associate list it is reasonable to expect that as the course of training proceeds erroneous responses will increase up to some point and then decrease as learning becomes complete. The portion of training during which errors gradually increase to some peak corresponds roughly to the response-learning stage; the period of training during which errors decrease parallels the associative-learning stage.

One may analyze the transfer of training situation in terms of how the learning of a prior list affects the error-making tendencies on the learning of the second list. In the C-B paradigm, since the responses which appear on the second list have been integrated on the first list, little or no response learning is necessary at the beginning of learning of the second list. On the other hand, for the A-C and C-D paradigms, a completely different set of responses is encountered on the second list. Response learning as well as associative learning is necessary on the second list for these two paradigms.

The preceding analysis implies that the course of error committment on the transfer list for the C-B paradigm will be different from that under the A-C and C-D paradigms. To be explicit, error tendencies should be maximal at the very outset of List 2 learning for the C-B paradigm and minimal for the A-C and C-D paradigms. As List 2 training proceeds, errors will steadily decrease until they are eliminated for the C-B paradigm; on the other hand, errors will first increase to some point before decreasing and finally become eliminated for the A-C and C-D paradigms. Not only should the shapes of the error curves be different for the C-B as opposed to the A-C and C-D paradigms but these differences should be affected by the level of Response *m*. The higher the response *m*, the less should be the difference in the shapes of the error curves between the C-B and the A-C and C-D paradigms because response learning is relatively fast. In other words, the advantage of having responses on List 2 which have already been integrated on List 1 for the C-B paradigm is minimized with higher degrees of Response *m*. On the other hand, with low *m*, the differential effects of response integration should be greater and lead to the expected differences in the shapes of the error curves for the C-B as opposed to the A-C and C-D paradigms.

It is not possible to meaningfully interpret the absolute or even the relative frequencies of errors under the various conditions since the degree of learning was not equated. This problem is avoided by restricting the interpretation of errors to the shapes of the error curves. Figure 3 presents the course of intrusion errors on List 2 learning for both levels of Response *m* and for each type of paradigm (C-B compared to A-C and C-D). An intrusion is an error which is correct as a response but given to an inappropriate stimulus. As predicted, under low *m* the commitment of intrusion errors decreased over training for the C-B paradigm whereas it increased over training for the A-C and C-D paradigms. This finding is consistent with the finding of maximal positive transfer under low *m*. But as also shown in Fig. 3, the differences in the shapes of the error curves for the two types of paradigms are less striking under high *m* than they were under low *m*. Errors decreased over training for the C-B paradigm as they did under low *m*; for the A-C and C-D paradigms, errors increased at first but reached a peak quite early and began to decrease over the remainder of List 2 training whereas under low *m* errors were still increasing on the last block of List 2 trials. These findings are

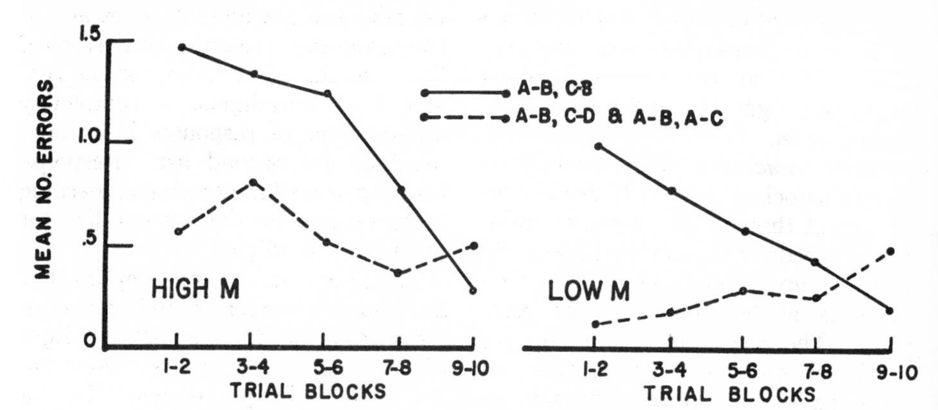

FIG. 3. Mean number of intrusions over the course of List 2 training as a function of Response *m* and paradigms.

consistent with the finding of little positive transfer under high *m*.

Discussion

The findings for the C-B paradigm offer strong support for the predictions from the response-integration hypothesis. First, greater positive transfer was obtained under low than with high *m* on both Trials 1–2 and 1–10 as shown in Fig. 1 and 2, respectively.

Under high *m*, not only was less positive transfer found on Trials 1–10 but a net negative transfer was actually obtained. This result agrees with an earlier finding (Twedt & Underwood, 1959).

The response-integration hypothesis was also supported by the analysis of errors committed in learning List 2. In the learning of a single paired-associate list, it is logical to expect that errors should increase from zero to some maximum and then decrease toward zero as learning becomes complete. If two paired-associate lists are learned, as in the transfer of training paradigm, the temporal course of errors on the second list will depend on the relationship of the responses on the two lists. For example, if the responses are dissimilar on the two lists as in the C-D and A-C paradigms, the course of errors on the second list should be rather similar to that on the first list, increasing, then decreasing. However, in the C-B paradigm where the responses are identical on the two lists, it is not necessary for response learning on the second list to start "from scratch." Due to transfer of response learning from the first list to the second list, errors should be maximal at the onset of the second list learning and decrease as learning proceeds. These expectations for the different paradigms were confirmed (Fig. 3).

Furthermore, Fig. 3 shows that under high *m* the error curves for the C-B and the other two paradigms were more similar in shape than they were under low *m*. The more similar are the shapes of the error curves, the less difference there is in the amount of response integration in the different paradigms. This fact should be reflected in any measures of transfer such that the greater the difference in the shape of the error curve for the C-B as opposed to that for A-C and C-D paradigms, the greater should be the positive transfer. This was found to be the case since more positive transfer was found with low *m* where the error curves were dissimilar in shape and less positive transfer was obtained with high *m* where the shapes of the error curves were highly similar.

The prediction for the A-C paradigm that the amount of negative transfer obtained would be independent of Response *m* was contradicted by both the results on Trials 1–2 and on Trials 1–10. These results suggest that the higher the response *m*, the greater the negative transfer. Learning of List 2 A-C associations appear to be more subject to interference from the reinstatement of List 1 A-B associations when the list responses are of high than of low *m*. Exactly why this might be the case is not apparent.

References

Ellis, H. C., & Burnstein, D. D. The effect of stimulus similarity and temporal factors in perceptual transfer of training. Technical Report No. 1, 1960, Sandia Corporation, Albuquerque, New Mexico.

Haagen, C. H. Synonymity, vividness, familiarity, and association value ratings of 400 pairs of common adjectives. *J. Psychol.*, 1949, **27**, 453–463.

Hovland, C. I., & Kurtz, K. H. Experimental studies in rote learning theory: X. Pre-learning syllable familiarization and the length-difficulty relationship. *J. exp. Psychol.*, 1952, **44**, 31–39.

Twedt, H. M., & Underwood, B. J. Mixed vs. unmixed lists in transfer studies. *J. exp. Psychol.*, 1959, **58**, 111–116.

Underwood, B. J., Runquist, W. R., & Shulz, R. W. Response learning in paired-associate lists as a function of intralist similarity. *J. exp. Psychol.*, 1959, **58**, 70–78.

Underwood, B. J., & Schulz, R. W. *Meaningfulness and verbal learning.* Chicago: Lippincott, 1960.

(Received May 24, 1962)

ARTICLE 6

Transfer of Training as a Function of Experimental Paradigm and Degree of First-List Learning[1]

LEO POSTMAN

University of California, Berkeley, California

This study investigates transfer of training in paired-associate verbal learning as a function of (*a*) the relations between the stimuli and responses in two successive lists and (*b*) the amount of practice on the first list.

A widely accepted generalization which dates back to the classical work of Bruce (1933) states that positive transfer increases with degree of first-list learning whereas negative transfer declines or shifts toward positive transfer (cf. McGeoch and Irion, 1952, pp. 336 ff.). The available data support this conclusion when transfer is measured, as it was by Bruce, against a control condition in which only a single list is learned. When the responses in the two lists are similar, the amount of positive transfer varies directly as a function of degree of first-list learning (Underwood, 1951). In studies of interserial interference using the A-B, A-C paradigm associative inhibition in the acquisition of the second list is typically superseded by associative facilitation as degree of first-list learning is increased (Atwater, 1953; Underwood, 1944, 1949). In such cases specific and nonspecific transfer effects cannot be separated, however, and it is probable that facilitation resulting from learning to learn and warm-up masks the presence of associative inhibition.

A baseline for the evaluation of specific transfer effects, with learning to learn and warm-up held constant, is provided by a control condition in which there is no systematic relation between either the stimuli or the responses of the two lists (A-B, C-D). Using such a control baseline, Mandler and Heinemann (1956) investigated the effects of overlearning on transfer in a study using digits as stimuli and consonant syllables as responses. Three paradigms of transfer were compared with the control condition in a mixed-list design: A-B, A-C (old stimuli and new responses); A-B, C-B (new stimuli and old responses), and A-B, A-Br (old stimuli and old responses repaired). There was increasing positive transfer as a function of degree of first-list learning for both A-B, C-B and A-B, A-Br, but no consistent positive or negative effects were found for A-B, A-C. Since the responses were consonant syllables, the beneficial effects of overlearning A-B on the acquisition of C-B and A-Br were attributed to progressive increases in response integration. The lack of negative transfer in A-B, A-C was ascribed by Mandler and Heinemann to the effective differentiation between correct and incorrect responses. However, the absence of negative transfer at the lower degrees of first-list learning is at variance with other findings and may have been due to the limited sample of items used—two pairs representing each of the four paradigms. Moreover, with responses of low meaningfulness such as consonant syllables, specific negative transfer effects in the control condition (A-B, C-D) cannot be ruled out. The presence of such effects would serve to reduce the measures of negative transfer and inflate the measures of positive transfer under the experimental conditions.

[1] This research was carried out under Contract Nonr 222(90) between the Office of Naval Research and the University of California. Reproduction in whole or in part is permitted for any purpose of the United States Government. This work was performed at the Center for Human Learning which is supported by a grant from the National Science Foundation.

Reprinted with permission of the author and the publisher, the Academic Press. The article appeared originally in the *Journal of Verbal Learning and Verbal Behavior*, 1962, **1**, 109–118.

There are no comparable systematic data for materials of high meaningfulness on the relationship between degree of first-list learning and transfer. There is clear evidence that the transfer effects obtained with a given paradigm may vary as a function of meaningfulness. In the study of Mandler and Heinemann A-B, A-Br was the condition yielding the highest positive transfer effects. By contrast, with paired adjectives this paradigm results in massive negative transfer which exceeds that observed under the A-B, A-C condition (Besch and Reynolds, 1958; Porter and Duncan, 1953; Twedt and Underwood, 1959). A shift from positive to negative transfer with increasing meaningfulness is also indicated for the A-B, C-B paradigm. Again in contrast to the results obtained with nonsense materials, this condition yields small but consistent amounts of negative transfer when the lists are composed of familiar adjectives (Twedt and Underwood, 1959). These results suggest that the use of old responses, whether with new or old stimuli, leads to positive transfer during the response-learning phase and to negative transfer during the associative phase of the acquisition of the second list. As meaningfulness increases, the beneficial effects of response learning become relatively small and transitory and are outweighed by associative interference. The negative transfer effects may be attributed primarily to interference from backward associations in A-B, C-B, and from both forward and backward associations in A-B, A-Br.

To the extent that negative transfer reflects the strength of competing responses, associative interference should increase directly with degree of first-list learning. However, improved differentiation between the lists (Underwood, 1945, 1949) should counteract in some measure the rises in the strength of competing associations. Depending on the relative weight of response competition and list differentiation the net result may be an increase or a decrease in negative transfer. There is no reason, however, to expect the specific transfer effects to shift from negative to positive.

The rate at which differentiation between lists increases should vary with the paradigm of transfer. Under the C-B and A-C conditions discrimination of list membership can be based on the stimulus and response terms, respectively. In A-Br the identity of neither the stimulus nor the response term provides a basis for the discrimination of list membership. Increases in the strength of competing associations are, therefore, less likely to be offset by improved differentiation between lists under the A-Br than the C-B and A-C conditions. These three paradigms as well as a control condition (A-B, C-D) were used in the present study to investigate transfer as a function of degree of first-list learning with materials of high meaningfulness.

METHOD

Lists. The learning materials were lists of 10 paired associates. Both the stimulus and response terms were two-syllable adjectives selected from Haagen's tables (1948). Intralist similarity was kept as low as possible. There were no synonyms among the items in a list and no duplications of first letters on the stimulus or the response side. Stimulus and response members had four first letters in common. The same rules were applied to minimize interlist similarity when stimulus or response members in successive lists were different.

Pairs of lists were constructed so as to conform to four different paradigms of transfer: (1) new stimuli and new responses (A-B, C-D); (2) new stimuli and old responses (A-B, C-B); (3) old stimuli and new responses (A-B, A-C); (4) old stimuli and old responses re-paired (A-B, A-Br). The second lists were the same in all conditions. Two sets of 10 adjectives were used in the construction of the second lists. Each set was used on the stimulus side for half the *S*s and on the response side for the other half of the *S*s. Under each of the two resulting arrangements there were two different pairings of stimulus and response members. Thus there were four different second lists, each of which was used equally often. The selection of items for the first lists corresponding to each of the second lists was determined by the requirements of the different paradigms of transfer.

Experimental Procedure. There were 12 independent groups representing all possible combinations of three degrees of first-list learning and four paradigms of transfer. The three degrees of first-list learning were: (1) to a criterion of 6/10; (2) to a criterion of 10/10; and (3) to a criterion of 10/10 + 50% overlearning. To achieve 50% overlearning practice was continued past the first perfect trial for half as many trials as had been required to reach criterion. The low, medium, and high degrees of first-list learning will be referred to as Conditions L, M, and H, respectively. The second list was presented 3 min. after the end of practice on the first list. The second list was learned to a criterion of 10/10 or for 10 trials, whichever took the longer.

The lists were presented at a 2:2 rate on a Hull-type memory drum with an intertrial interval of 8 sec. Four different random orders were used to minimize serial learning. Each of the four orders was used on Trial 1 equally often.

At the end of second-list learning a modified test of free recall (MMFR) was administered. A procedure developed by Barnes and Underwood (1959) was used. In the A-B, A-C and A-B, A-Br conditions the 10 stimulus terms (A) were presented one at a time, and *Ss* were required to call out both the first and second responses learned to that stimulus in the order in which they occurred to them.[2] In the A-B, C-D and A-B, C-B conditions the 20 stimuli from the two lists were presented in scrambled order, and *Ss* were required to call out the response associated with each of them. During MMFR the stimuli were presented on cards and the rate of exposure was paced by *S*. The purpose of the MMFR procedure was to determine the "fate" of first-list associations during the acquisition of the second list.

Subjects. There were 16 *Ss* in each of the 12 groups. The *Ss* were assigned to conditions in blocks of 12, with one *S* from each condition per block. The running orders within blocks were determined by means of a table of random numbers as were the assignments to specific lists and starting orders. The *Ss* were undergraduate students whose native language was English. The *Ss* were not necessarily naive to verbal learning, but those who had had experience in paired-associate learning during the same academic year were excluded.

Results

First-List Learning

Different first lists were used in each of the transfer conditions, so that variations in list difficulty could not be ruled out. As it turned out, however, there were no significant differences among the 12 groups in speed of first-list learning. All groups can be compared on the number of trials required to reach a criterion of 6/10. The over-all mean was 7.65, and the range of means for the 12 groups was 6.25 to 9.44 ($F < 1$). The groups in conditions H and M can be compared on trials to a criterion of one perfect recitation. The over-all mean was 15.60. The range of variation among groups (12.12 to 19.31) was greater than for the lower criterion, but the differences are not significant ($F = 1.29$).

Early Transfer Effects

In order to assess the course of transfer in the early phases of second-list learning, a stage analysis (Underwood and Schulz, 1960) was performed. The results of this analysis are presented in Table 1. The length of the response-recall stage is measured by the mean trial on which the responses were given anywhere in the list, i.e., either as correct anticipations or as misplaced responses. The pattern of transfer effects measured by this index shows pronounced changes as a function of degree of first-list learning. In Condition L, the group learning a new response to an old stimulus (A-C) is clearly slowest whereas there are relatively small differences between the control group and the groups for which the responses remained the same in the two lists (C-B and A-Br). As degree of first-list learning increases, the negative transfer for C-B drops out and is superseded by a small positive effect. The difference between the control condition and A-C rises to a maximum and then declines. A-Br is the only paradigm for which there is a drop in performance between Conditions M and H, and a progressive increase in negative transfer.

Analysis of variance shows that the differences among paradigms are significant ($F = 7.35$, $df = 3/180$, $P < .001$) as are the changes with degree of learning ($F = 5.42$, $df = 2/180$, $P < .01$). There is also a significant interaction ($F = 2.23$, $df = 6/180$, $P < .05$), i.e., the shifts in the pattern of differences are reliable. The fact that A-Br, in which old responses are re-paired with old stimuli, shows considerable decrements indicates that the trial of first occurrence reflects not only differences in response recall but also in *Ss*' readiness to attempt an anticipation. Under conditions of heavy associative inter-

[2] In accordance with the usage introduced by Melton (1961), a test in which *S* is required to recall the responses from both lists is designated as MMFR, as distinct from MFR in which only one response is called for.

TABLE 1
RESULTS OF STAGE ANALYSES FOR SECOND LIST

Degree of first-list learning	Paradigm of Transfer			
	A-B, C-D	A-B, C-B	A-B, A-C	A-B, A-Br
	Mean Trial of Response Recall[a]			
Low	3.41	3.81	4.72	3.86
Medium	2.95	3.08	4.56	3.61
High	2.89	2.46	3.12	4.18
	Mean Percentages of Correct First Responses			
Low	89.4	90.6	91.9	78.2
Medium	91.9	88.8	88.1	73.1
High	91.9	86.2	93.8	70.0
	Mean Trials for Associative Learning[b]			
Low	.23	.34	.33	1.36
Medium	.19	.40	.36	1.06
High	.23	.36	.24	1.05

[a] Mean trial on which response was given anywhere in the list.
[b] Mean number of trials between first occurrence and first correct placement of response.

ference even highly available responses from within the list may be withheld when the discrimination between errors and correct responses is extremely difficult.

As Table 1 shows, the percentages of correct anticipations among the first occurrences of the responses were substantially lower for A-Br than for the other paradigms. The differences among the latter are small. This finding provides additional evidence for heavy initial interference in A-Br. Following an arcsine transformation the F for paradigms is 17.62 ($P < .001$). The percentages do not vary reliably with degree of first-list learning, nor is there a significant interaction ($F < 1$ in both cases).

The difference between the trial of first occurrence of a response and the trial of first correct anticipation is used to estimate the duration of the associative stage. As was to be expected on the basis of the high percentages of correct first occurrences, the values are quite small, with the sole exception of A-Br. Paradigms is again the only significant source of variance ($F = 11.07$, $P < .001$).

Acquisition of Second List

Figure 1 shows the mean numbers of correct responses over Trials 1–5 and 6–10 on the second list. For purposes of graphic presentation Conditions L, M, and H have been placed along the abscissa according to the mean number of reinforcements during first-list learning.

On Trials 1–5 all groups except those trained on A-Br show improvements in performance as a function of degree of first-list learning. It should be noted, however, that for A-C the increase first occurs in Condition H. The upward trend in C-D may be attributed to learning to learn and warm-up. The same factors are assumed to contribute to the rises in performance under the experimental conditions. In addition, there may be progressive increases in stimulus differentiation and in response learning for the paradigms using old stimuli and old responses, respectively.

The rank order of the four paradigms remains the same for all degrees of first-list learning. All experimental groups fall below the control group. C-B yields the smallest amount of negative transfer and A-Br the greatest, with A-C occupying an intermediate position. The pattern remains substantially the same on Trials 6–10, except for a very slight upward trend in A-Br and the complete convergence of C-B and C-D in Condition H. The trends in negative transfer are sum-

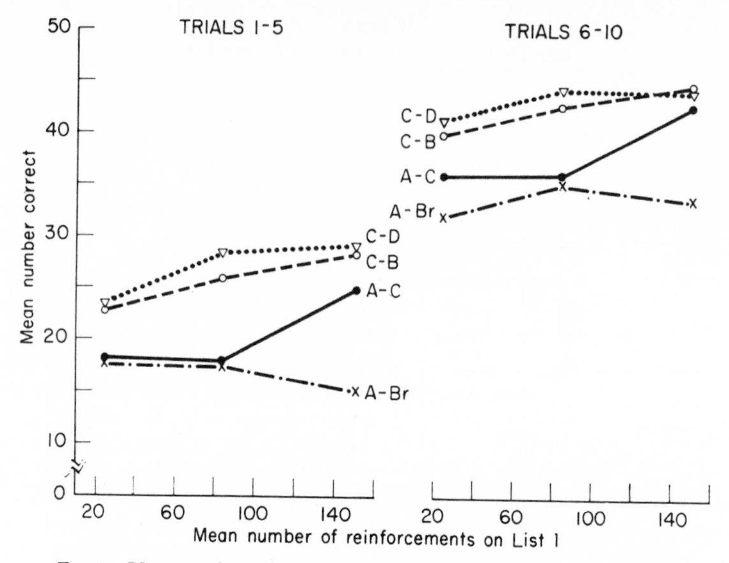

FIG. 1. Mean numbers of correct responses in 10 trials on the second list.

marized in Fig. 2 which shows the differences between the control condition (C-D) and each of the experimental conditions in the mean number of correct responses over Trials 1–10 on the second list. For C-B and A-C the amount of negative transfer first rises and then declines as a function of degree of first-list learning; for A-Br negative transfer increases steadily.

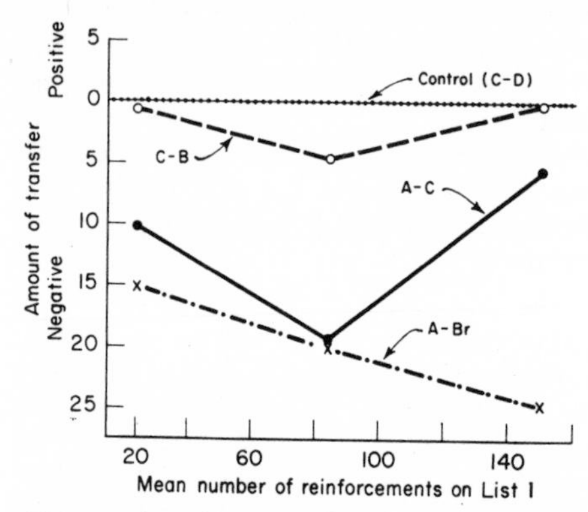

FIG. 2. Amounts of negative transfer as measured by the differences between the control condition (C-D) and each of the experimental conditions in the mean number of correct responses over Trials 1-10 on the second list.

An analysis of variance was performed on the numbers of correct responses in 10 trials of second-list learning. The differences among paradigms are highly significant ($F = 15.86$, $P < .001$). A procedure described by Snedecor (1956, pp. 251 ff.) was used to make comparisons among the individual means. Each paradigm differs significantly from the others, with the exception of the difference between C-D and C-B which is not reliable. The over-all increases as a function of degree of first-list learning are also significant ($F = 3.80$, $P < .02$). Further comparisons show that the difference between Conditions H and L is significant but that Condition M differs reliably from neither of the other two. The interaction of paradigms and degrees of first-list learning is not significant ($F = 1.04$). Although Fig. 1 suggests an increasing divergence between A-Br and the other paradigms, this shift in the pattern of differences is not statistically reliable.

Figure 3 shows the mean numbers of trials to a criterion of 10/10 on the second list. The rank order of paradigms and the pattern of differences correspond to those shown in Fig. 1. Again the negative transfer effects are smallest for C-B, intermediate for A-C and

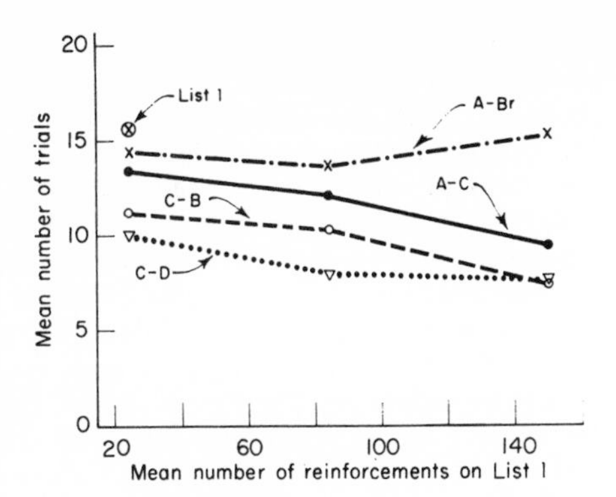

FIG. 3. Mean numbers of trials to a criterion of 10/10 on the second list.

largest for A-Br. The latter is the only paradigm for which there is no improvement as a function of degree of first-list learning. The results of an analysis of variance (following log transformation in view of the skewness of the distributions) also agree with those obtained for correct responses over 10 trials. The two main effects are significant. The F's for paradigms and degrees of learning are 12.90 ($P < .001$) and 4.94 ($P < .01$), respectively. Comparison of the individual means yields exactly the same conclusions as for the data in Fig. 1. The interaction of degree of first-list learning with paradigms again is not significant ($F = 1.02$).

The mean number of trials to a criterion of 10/10 on the first list, obtained from the data of Conditions M and H, is indicated in Fig. 3 for purposes of comparison. A precise test of the net transfer effects cannot be made since all groups learned the same second lists whereas different first lists were necessarily used for each of the four paradigms. Nevertheless it appears highly probable that the net transfer effects were increasingly positive for all paradigms except A-Br. In the latter case the criterion scores on the two lists remained of the same order of magnitude.

Intralist Errors

The mean percentages of misplaced responses during the learning of the second list to criterion are shown in Table 2. The percentages are based on numbers of opportunities (total occurrences minus correct responses). The percentages are higher when the responses are the same in the two lists (C-B and A-Br) than when they are different (C-D and A-C). Following arc-sine transformation the F for paradigms is 8.16 ($P < .01$). However, the only significant differences are those between A-Br and each of the other paradigms. There are no consistent trends as a function of degree of first-list learning ($F < 1$) and no reliable interaction ($F = 1.15$). It is interesting to note, however, that the mean percentage of misplaced responses during the acquisition of the first list, again based on the data of Conditions M and H, was 21.4. Thus, there appears to be a consistent reduction in error rate except for A-Br.

TABLE 2

MEAN PERCENTAGE OF MISPLACED RESPONSES IN ACQUISITION OF SECOND LIST

Degree of first-list learning	Paradigm of Transfer			
	A-B, C-D	A-B, C-B	A-B, A-C	A-B, A-Br
Low	14.2	16.1	11.7	24.5
Medium	9.2	18.4	13.6	18.0
High	13.1	15.9	11.1	30.0

The finding that A-Br produced a higher percentage of intralist errors than the other paradigms must be interpreted with considerable caution. It is in the nature of the A-Br paradigm that no sharp distinction can be made between misplaced responses from within the list and interlist intrusions. It is possible, however, to consider as intrusions all intralist errors which would have been correct responses in the first list. If all such intrusions are eliminated from the count of intralist errors, the mean percentages of misplaced responses for A-Br are 15.9, 9.2, and 18.0 for Conditions L, M, and H, respectively. By this measure there are no longer any clear differences between A-Br and the other paradigms. The same ambiguity arises in the evaluation of interlist intrusions which will be considered next.

Interlist Intrusions

If interlist intrusions are defined as associations which were correct in the first list, they can occur only in A-C and A-Br. The total frequencies of such errors over 10 trials of A-C were 6, 6, and 3 in Conditions L, M, and H, respectively. The corresponding frequencies for A-Br were 75, 66, and 97.

All intrusions during the acquisition of C-D were necessarily given to new stimuli. The total numbers of such occurrences over 10 trials were 8, 1, and 2 for Conditions L, M, and H, respectively. These errors may be compared with the intrusions during the learning of A-C in which the intruding response was given to a stimulus with which it had not been paired in the first list. The corresponding frequencies of such intrusions were 12, 11, and 2. Thus the number of nonspecific intrusions declined more rapidly for C-D than for A-C.

Modified Free Recall

In the MMFR test which followed the end of practice on the second list, *S*s were required to recall both first-list and second-list associations. Recall of second-list associations was uniformly high. For the 12 groups in the experiment the mean numbers of correct responses ranged from 9.00 to 9.81, and these minor variations need not be considered further. The mean numbers of first-list associations recalled correctly are shown in Fig. 4. As was to be expected, the number recalled increased steadily with degree of first-list learning. There are also pronounced differences as a function of the paradigm of transfer. In Condition L, A-C falls below the other three paradigms which yield very similar values. In Conditions M and H the paradigms in which the second-list stimuli are new (C-D and C-B) have a clear advantage over those in which they are old (A-C and A-Br). Within these two groupings, C-D is consistently above C-B and A-Br shows slower increases than does A-C so that the difference between them is reversed in Condition H.

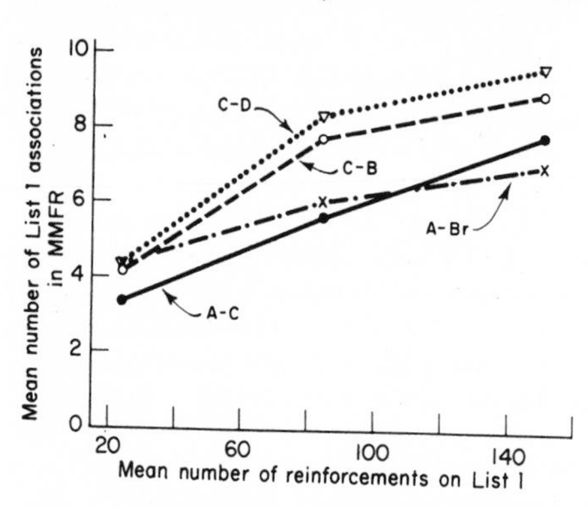

FIG. 4. Mean numbers of first-list associations recalled in MMFR test.

Analysis of variance shows both main effects to be significant. The *F*-ratios are 10.70 ($P < .001$) for paradigms and 106.60 ($P < .001$) for degrees of first-list learning. There is also a significant interaction ($F = 2.14$, $P < .05$). The interpretation of these differences is complicated by the fact that degree of learning on the second list was not strictly equated across groups. The second list was learned to a criterion of one perfect recitation or for 10 trials, whichever took the longer. The more rapid the acquisition of the second list, the larger was the proportion of *S*s for whom 10 trials constituted some overlearning. However, the resulting bias should operate against the major trends shown in Fig. 4. Under conditions of negative transfer recall of first-list associations should vary inversely with degree of second-list learning (Barnes and Underwood, 1959). In the present comparisons among the paradigms the relationship between degree of second-list learning and recall of first-list associations is predominantly direct.

For the paradigms in which the responses in the two lists are different (C-D and A-C) a further analysis was made to assess the sheer availability of first-list responses. Credit was given for all responses from the first list regardless of whether they were given to the appropriate stimulus. At successively higher degrees of first-list learning the recall scores for C-D were 4.94, 8.62, and 9.69, whereas the scores for A-C were 4.06, 6.12, and 8.25. The difference between the two paradigms is significant ($F = 26.28$, $df = 1/90$, $P < .001$), but does not interact significantly with degree of first-list learning ($F = 2.32$, $df = 2/90$). The reduction in the availability of first-list responses is reliably greater when new responses are attached to old stimuli than when both stimuli and responses are new.

Discussion

The three experimental paradigms investigated in this study all yield negative transfer effects as compared with a control condition in which neither the stimuli nor the responses in the successive lists are systematically related. The amount of associative interference is greatest for A-Br, intermediate for A-C, and least for C-B. These findings are in full agreement with the results of Twedt and Underwood (1959). The present study shows that the pattern of transfer effects remains substantially the same at successively higher degrees of first-list learning. The absolute level of performance increases with degree of first-list learning for all conditions except A-Br but there are no shifts in the relative positions of the four paradigms.

The analyses consistently show a divergence between A-Br and the other conditions of transfer as a function of degree of first-list learning. Since A-Br is the only paradigm for which there are no apparent beneficial effects of learning to learn and warm-up, its separation from the other paradigms reaches a maximum in Condition H. However, the two major measures of transfer—mean number of correct responses in 10 trials and trials to criterion—both fail to show a significant interaction between paradigms and degree of first-list learning. On the other hand, the measure of the response-recall stage does yield a significant interaction. It is reasonable to conclude that the amount of negative transfer in A-Br increases relatively to the other conditions, but that there is a substantial divergence only in the early phases of second-list learning.

In considering the stable over-all differences among the paradigms we must take account of the following sources of transfer effects: (*a*) learning to learn and warm-up; (*b*) response learning; (*c*) associative interference; and (*d*) differentiation between the lists. The observed differences represent a balance of these influences. Learning to learn and warm-up may be assumed to be equal for all paradigms. Response learning favors the conditions in which the responses remain the same in the two lists (C-B and A-Br). However, the positive factor of response learning is exceeded by the detrimental effects of associative interference since the transfer for both these paradigms is negative. The opportunities for associative interference are clearly different for each of the experimental paradigms. In C-B the occurrence of backward associations, i.e., A evoked by B, may lead to the improper rejection of the correct association (Twedt and Underwood, 1959). Given the known favorable effects of response learning (Underwood, Runquist, and Schulz, 1959), and on the assumption that indirect interference from backward associations is less damaging than competition from prior forward associations to the same stimulus, smaller negative transfer for C-B than A-C is readily predicted. The summation of interference from both forward and backward associations should maximize negative transfer in A-Br.

The absence of significant rises in negative transfer suggests that improved differentiation does, as expected, counteract the increasing strength of competing first-list associations. With highly integrated response terms the discrimination and rejection of errors may occur with sufficient speed to permit the substitution of the correct response during the anticipation interval. The increasing divergence between A-Br and the other paradigms in the response-recall stage (Table 1) may be attributed to the slow development of differentiation when neither stimulus nor response terms can be distinguished in terms of list membership. As suggested earlier, the relatively late occurrence of first responses in the learning of A-Br immediately after the end of practice on A-B cannot be a matter of low availability of responses. Rather the delays in responding reflect *S*s' inability to distinguish between first-list and second-list associations. When responses begin to be given, a substantial proportion of the initial attempts is incorrect. The high frequency of interlist intrusions during the acquisition of A-Br which rises to a maximum in Condition H, in contrast to the rare occurrence of such intrusions in A-C, is consistent with this interpretation. List differentiation can be based on the identity of the stimulus terms in C-B, and of both stimulus terms and response terms in C-D.

The results of the MMFR test throw additional light on the mechanisms of transfer characteristic of the different paradigms. Arousal of competing first-list associations during the acquisition of the second list should lead to negative transfer as well as to the unlearning of the interfering associations (Barnes and Underwood, 1959; Postman, 1962). Hence amount of negative transfer and forgetting of first-list associations should be directly related. Figure 4 shows that this is the case, except for the shift in the relative position of A-Br. Although the amount of negative transfer is consistently highest for A-Br, there is no difference between the MMFR scores for A-Br and C-D in Condition L. Thereafter the losses for A-Br and A-C are of the same order of magnitude, and in Condition H there is a perfect correlation between losses in MMFR and negative transfer. The reversals in the rank order of the paradigms on the MMFR test in Conditions L and M suggest that first-list associations which are highly effective sources of interference may be relatively resistant to unlearning as long as the interfering responses remain correct elsewhere in the list. When unlearning does occur, the availability of the responses common to the two lists necessarily remains high througout second-list learning so that the recovery of unlearned associations should occur readily. The results of the MMFR test also confirm the importance of interlist differentiation in determining the amount of negative transfer during second-list learning. For all paradigms the recall of first-list associations increased steadily with the amount of initial practice. These rises in the strength of competing associations were not accompanied by progressive increases in negative transfer, with the apparent exception of one condition (A-Br) in which interlist differentiation is extremely difficult.

SUMMARY

This study investigated transfer of training in paired-associate learning as a function of stimulus and response relationships and degree of first-list learning. Four paradigms of transfer were used, with familiar adjectives as both stimuli and responses: A-B, C-D (new stimuli and new responses); A-B, C-B (new stimuli and old responses); A-B, A-C (old stimuli and new responses); A-B, A-Br (old stimuli and old responses re-paired). Three degrees of first-list learning were used with each of the four paradigms: to a criterion of 6/10, to a criterion of 10/10, and to a criterion of 10/10 + 50% overlearning. All groups learned the same second lists whereas the composition of the first lists was varied in accordance with the requirements of the different paradigms of transfer. The second lists were learned to a criterion of 10/10 or for 10 trials, whichever took the longer. After the end of practice on the second list a modified test of free recall (MMFR) was administered in which *S*s were required to recall the responses from both lists.

As evaluated against the control condition (A-B, C-D), all paradigms yielded negative transfer effects. The amount of negative transfer was greatest for A-B, A-Br, intermediate for A-B, A-C, and least for A-B, C-B. Performance on the second list improved as a function of degree of first-list learning but the amounts of transfer did not change reliably. There was some evidence, however, for progressive increases in negative transfer for A-Br relative to the other conditions. The results of the MMFR test show that amount of negative transfer and forgetting of first-list associations tend to be directly related. This relationship is attributed to the fact that competition from first-list associations leads to negative transfer as well as to the unlearning of these associations.

REFERENCES

ATWATER, S. K. Proactive inhibition and associative facilitation as affected by degree of prior learning. *J. exp. Psychol.*, 1953, **46**, 400-404.

BARNES, J. M., AND UNDERWOOD, B. J. "Fate" of first-list associations in transfer theory. *J. exp. Psychol.*, 1959, **58**, 97-105.

BESCH, N. F., AND REYNOLDS, W. F. Associative interference in verbal paired-associate learning. *J. exp. Psychol.*, 1958, **55**, 554-558.

BRUCE, R. W. Conditions of transfer of training. *J. exp. Psychol.*, 1933, **16**, 343-361.

HAAGEN, C. H. Synonymity, vividness, familiarity and association value ratings of 400 pairs of common adjectives. *J. Psychol.*, 1948, **27**, 453-463.

McGeoch, J. A., and Irion, A. L. *The psychology of human learning.* New York: Longmans, Green, 1952.

Mandler, G., and Heinemann, S. H. Effect of overlearning of a verbal response on transfer of training. *J. exp. Psychol.*, 1956, **51**, 39-46.

Melton, A. W. Comments on Professor Postman's paper. In C. N. Cofer (Ed.), *Verbal learning and verbal behavior.* New York: McGraw Hill, 1961, 179-193.

Porter, L. W., and Duncan, C. P. Negative transfer in verbal learning. *J. exp. Psychol.*, 1953, 46, 61-64.

Postman, L. Retention of first-list associations as a function of the conditions of transfer. *J. exp. Psychol.*, 1962, in press.

Snedecor, G. W. *Statistical methods.* Ames: Iowa State College Press, 1956.

Twedt, H. M., and Underwood, B. J. Mixed vs. unmixed lists in transfer studies. *J. exp. Psychol.*, 1959, **58**, 111-116.

Underwood, B. J. Associative inhibition in the learning of successive paired associate lists. *J. exp. Psychol.*, 1944, **34**, 127-135.

Underwood, B. J. The effect of successive interpolations on retroactive and proactive inhibition. *Psychol. Monogr.*, 1945, **59**, No. 3.

Underwood, B. J. Proactive inhibition as a function of time and degree of prior learning. *J. exp. Psychol.*, 1949, **39**, 24-34.

Underwood, B. J. Associative transfer in verbal learning as a function of response similarity and degree of first-list learning. *J. exp. Psychol.*, 1951, **42**, 44-53.

Underwood, B. J., and Schulz, R. W. *Meaningfulness and verbal learning.* Philadelphia: Lippincott, 1960.

Underwood, B. J., Runquist, W. N. and Schulz, R. W. Response learning in paired-associate lists as a function of interlist similarity. *J. exp. Psychol.*, 1959, **58**, 70-78.

(Received April 20, 1962)

ARTICLE 7

Studies of Learning to Learn
II. Changes in Transfer as a Function of Practice[1]

LEO POSTMAN

University of California, Berkeley, California

Transfer effects in verbal learning are classified as either general or specific depending on whether or not the changes in performance are a function of known relationships between stimulus and response terms in successive lists. In the absence of such relationships, progressive improvements in performance are attributed to warm-up and learning to learn. The basic evidence for general transfer is provided by increases in the speed of acquisition for successive unrelated lists (Hamilton, 1950; Postman and Schwartz, 1964; Thune, 1951; Ward, 1937). The changes in performance obtained with unrelated lists provide a baseline for assessing the effects of stimulus and response similarity (e.g., Postman, 1962; Twedt and Underwood, 1959).

While general transfer is independent of the relationship between individual items, it nevertheless reflects circumscribed habits and skills which apply to a limited range of learning tasks. In accordance with this assumption, interlist improvement has been found to be maximal when the method of practice and the class of materials in the successive tasks remain unchanged (Postman and Schwartz, 1964). Thus, the amount and manifestations of general transfer vary with the conditions of prior training. These considerations point not only to the limitations of general transfer but also to the possibility that appropriate training may produce progressive improvement in tasks of a higher order than the acquisition of single lists. Such tasks are exemplified by the paradigms of specific transfer where *S*'s performance depends on the similarity relations between stimuli and responses in successive lists. Repeated experience with transfer tasks should enhance *S*'s effectiveness in responding to such similarity relations; as a result, increases in positive transfer and decreases in negative transfer would be expected.

The effectiveness of transfer skills developed through practice may be expected to vary with the nature of the paradigm. Increases in associative facilitation are likely to be greater than reductions in associative interference. The selective use of a circumscribed class of responses appropriate to a paradigm of positive transfer will produce substantial gains in the acquisition of a test list. There appear to be no equally effective and readily implemented modes of attack conducive to the reduction of negative transfer. For example, when the paradigm is A-B, A-B′ (identical stimuli, associatively related responses), speed of second-list learning increases with the tendency to give associates of B as responses to A. The more frequently *S* uses mediational chains (A-B-B′), the greater will be the amount of positive transfer. Under conditions of negative transfer,

[1] This research was carried out under Contract Nonr 222(90) between the University of California and the Office of Naval Research. Reproduction is permitted for any purpose of the United States Government. This work was done at the Institute of Human Learning, which is supported by a grant from the National Science Foundation.

Reprinted with permission of the author and the publisher, the Academic Press. The article **appeared originally** in the *Journal of Verbal Learning and Verbal Behavior*, 1964, **3**, 437–447.

rejection of previously correct associations will serve to reduce associative interference, as in the case of A-B, A-C (identical stimuli and unrelated responses) and A-B, A-Br (identical stimuli and responses re-paired). However, rejection of previously correct associations should be much less effective than the selective use of the appropriate class of responses in enhancing speed of second-list learning. It is possible that progressive gains in the acquisition of transfer tasks will develop only to the extent that the relation between successive lists permits a restriction in the range of alternative responses. Thus, if the paradigm is A-B, A-C, but *S* succeeds in establishing mediational chains linking initially unrelated responses (A-B-C), a class of appropriate responses is delimited and the mode of attack is continuous with that in A-B, A-B′. Hence, the functional conditions of transfer would become positive even though the nominal conditions remained negative (cf. Postman, 1963).

The present experiment uses four different paradigms to investigate the development of transfer skills. One of these—A-B, A-B′—represents a condition favorable to positive transfer; two others—A-B, A-C and A-B, A-Br—are known to produce negative transfer. The fourth paradigm is A-B, C-D (unrelated stimuli and unrelated responses) and provides a reference condition for the evaluation of changes in specific transfer effects. A separate group was assigned to each paradigm for purposes of training. The question to be answered by the experiment was whether and to what extent experience with the transfer tasks would produce progressive increases in positive transfer, or decreases in negative transfer, relative to the reference condition. The analysis will focus on evidence for changes in *S*'s mode of attack on the transfer tasks.

METHOD

Experimental Design. All groups learned three sets of lists. Each set consisted of two lists of paired associates, and for a given *S* the relationship between the lists always conformed to the same paradigm within each of the three sets. The second lists were the same for all groups, whereas the first lists varied in accordance with the requirements of the different paradigms. For each group, the six possible orders of the three sets were used equally often. Thus, materials were held constant in all comparisons of second-list learning within groups and between groups.

Lists. The learning materials consisted of lists of eight pairs of two-syllable adjectives. The adjectives were chosen from the lists of Haagen (1949) and Melton and Safier (Hilgard, 1951).[2] Word frequency (Thorndike and Lorge, 1944) was approximately equated for the stimulus series and the response series. Formal and meaningful similarity were minimized within lists and between lists, with the exception of the meaningful similarity of the synonymous responses within each set of Condition A-B, A-B′. Of the 24 synonymous pairs, 16 were obtained from Haagen's list and had a mean similarity rating of 1.4; the remaining 8 were taken from the list of Melton and Safier and had a mean rating of 2.65. In both cases the ratings indicate a high degree of similarity of meaning. Degree of associative connection, which is strongly correlated with similarity, was also high. The mean rating of associative connection for the items from Haagen's list was 1.4. Adjectives which have obvious synonyms may differ in difficulty from those which do not. As far as possible, therefore, the response terms of all lists were chosen from among adjectives with clear synonyms in the norms. Within the restrictions imposed by the criteria of word frequency and interitem similarity this requirement could be met for all but three response terms.

With three sets, and two lists per set, each group learned six different lists of paired associates. There were three different pairings of the stimulus and response terms of each list which were used equally often.

Procedure. The lists were presented on a Hull-type memory drum at a 2:2 rate, with a 4-sec intertrial interval. Four different random orders of presentation were used to minimize serial learning. The first list in each set was learned to a criterion of 7/8, and the second list was presented for 5 trials. The time interval between the first and second list in a set was 1 min; the interval between the end of one set and the beginning of the next was 1 min, 50 sec. Standard instructions for paired-associate learning were given at the beginning of the experiment. The

[2] A few additional stimulus terms from outside the norms were selected from the Thorndike-Lorge word lists.

Ss were given no advance information about the number of lists to be presented or about the relationship between the lists within each set.

A variant of modified free recall (MMFR) was administered to Groups A-C, A-Br, and A-B′ 15 sec after the end of the third set of lists. An extension of the procedure devised by Barnes and Underwood (1959) was used. The S was provided with a test sheet listing the 24 stimulus terms (8 in each of 3 sets of lists) and was instructed to write down the two responses which had been paired with each of them. Two spaces were provided for this purpose underneath each stimulus word. The S was requested to record the responses in the order in which they occurred to him. The test was self-paced. The stimuli were listed in two different random orders which were used equally often. In each order the arrangement of the items was random, with the restrictions that (a) successive blocks of 6 test items included 2 stimulus terms from each of the 3 sets, and (b) 2 items from the same set were never presented in succession.

Subjects. With 4 paradigms, and 18 Ss per paradigm, there were 72 Ss in the experiment. Assignment to conditions was in blocks of 4, with 1 S per condition in each block. The 6 possible orders of the 3 sets of lists were used once each in successive subgroups of 6 blocks. The running order within blocks was determined by a table of random numbers. The Ss were undergraduate students who were naive to rote learning by the anticipation method.

Results

List-1 Learning. Table 1 presents the mean numbers of trials to a criterion of 7/8 for the first lists of the three successive sets. There are substantial increases in speed of acquisition between the first and second sets, with only minor changes between the second and third sets. Analysis of variance (following log transformation to eliminate heterogeneity of variance) shows the differences among sets to be significant ($F = 83.44$, $df = 2/136$, $p < .001$). Whatever differences are present among paradigms may reflect variations in list difficulty, learning ability, or both. However, the differences among paradigms are not significant ($F < 1$), nor is the interaction of paradigms with sets ($F = 1.57$). Thus, the amounts of improvement in List-1 learning are comparable under all conditions.

Table 1

Mean Numbers of Trials to Criterion of 7/8 in Acquisition of First Lists of Successive Sets

Paradigm	Set 1	Set 2	Set 3
C-D	9.61	4.61	4.83
A-C	8.78	4.61	4.17
A-Br	13.56	4.78	4.17
A-B′	11.28	5.61	5.89

Errors in List-1 Learning. Table 2 shows the mean percentages of intralist errors during List-1 learning. The percentages are based on opportunities (total presentations minus numbers of correct responses). There is a sharp reduction in error rate between the first and second sets, which is followed by a relatively small further decline in the third set. The changes in error rate as a function of practice are significant ($F = 23.99$, $df = 2/136$, $p < 0.01$ after arcsine transformation). Neither the variation among paradigms nor the interaction of sets with paradigms is significant ($F < 1$ in both cases).

A breakdown of intralist errors into misplaced responses and stimulus intrusions is included in Table 2. A misplaced response is a correct response term given to an inappropriate stimulus; the use of a stimulus term as a response constitutes a stimulus intrusion.

Table 2

Mean Percentages of Intralist Errors in Aquisition of First Lists of Successive Sets

	Set 1			Set 2			Set 3		
Paradigm	Mispl. resp.	Stim. intr.	Total	Mispl. resp.	Stim. intr.	Total	Mispl. resp.	Stim. intr.	Total
C-D	23.3	4.0	27.3	8.0	5.0	13.0	6.9	4.0	10.9
A-C	21.0	7.2	28.2	11.0	2.3	13.3	9.2	2.6	11.8
A-Br	26.4	6.4	32.8	12.5	4.9	17.4	7.4	4.1	11.5
A-B′	17.5	6.8	24.3	8.6	4.8	13.4	8.8	1.9	10.7

Misplaced responses are considerably more frequent than stimulus intrusions, and it is the reduction in the former which is primarily responsible for the substantial changes in error rate. It should be noted that during the acquisition of the second and third sets the intrusions of items from earlier sets were rare. In List-1 learning the rate of such errors in no case exceeded a mean value of 3%.

Changes in Transfer as a Function of Practice. Figure 1 shows the mean numbers of

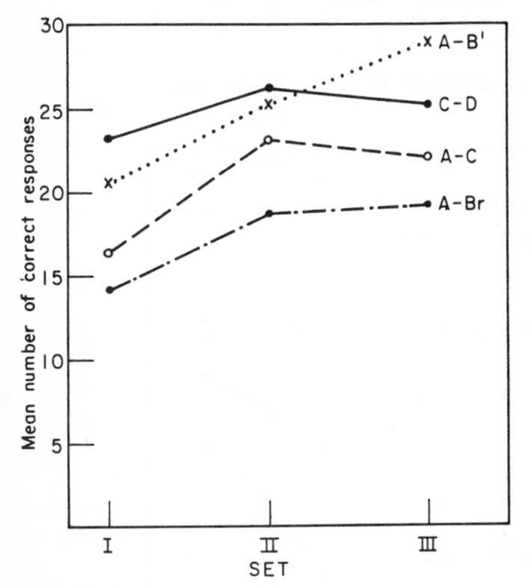

FIG. 1 Mean numbers of correct responses in 5 trials of List-2 learning as a function of set and paradigm.

correct responses given during the 5 trials of the transfer task in successive sets. The three experimental paradigms show the expected rank order, with Condition A-B′ yielding the highest scores, A-Br the lowest, and A-C occupying an intermediate position. The over-all differences among paradigms are significant ($F = 7.48$, $df = 3/48$, $p < 0.01$).[3] There is improvement as a function of practice under all conditions. The F for Sets is 31.35 ($df = 2/96$, $p < 0.001$). The amount of improvement is greater for the three experimental paradigms than for the reference paradigm. As a result, there is a shift from an initial small amount of negative transfer to positive transfer for A-B′, and a reduction in the degree of negative transfer for A-C and A-Br. The magnitude of the shift relative to the reference condition is inversely related to the level of negative transfer, i.e., it is greatest for A-B′ and smallest for A-Br.

The interaction of sets with paradigms is significant ($F = 2.38$, $df = 6/96$, $p < 0.05$), i.e., there is a reliable change in the relative positions of the paradigms. This interaction was partitioned into two orthogonal components: (a) that based on the differences between the reference paradigm on the one hand and the combined experimental paradigms on the other, which was significant ($F = 3.86$, $df = 2/96$, $p < 0.02$), and (b) that based on the differences among the experimental paradigms, which was not significant ($F = 1.64$, $df = 4/96$). For purposes of a more detailed analysis of the variations in amount of improvement over sets, the difference in linear trend between the reference paradigm and each of the experimental paradigms was evaluated by means of Dunnett's test (Winer, 1962, p. 91). The rate of improvement is significantly faster than under the reference condition for A-B′ ($p < 0.01$) and for A-C ($p < 0.05$), but not for A-Br.

Development of Transfer Effects in Acquisition. We shall consider next the temporal course of transfer during List-2 learning at successive stages of practice. Figure 2 shows the acquisition curves for List 2 of each set. In each set the greatest advantage of Condition A-B′ is on the early trials of List-2 learning; it is on these trials that there is over sets a shift from a slight amount of negative transfer to substantial positive transfer. However, as List-2 learning continues, A-B′ loses much of its initial advantage and converges on the other paradigms. The acquisition curves for A-C tend to parallel those for the reference condition. For A-Br, the amount of negative transfer tends to increase as List-2

[3] Order of test lists was included as a source of variance in the analyses of List-2 performance.

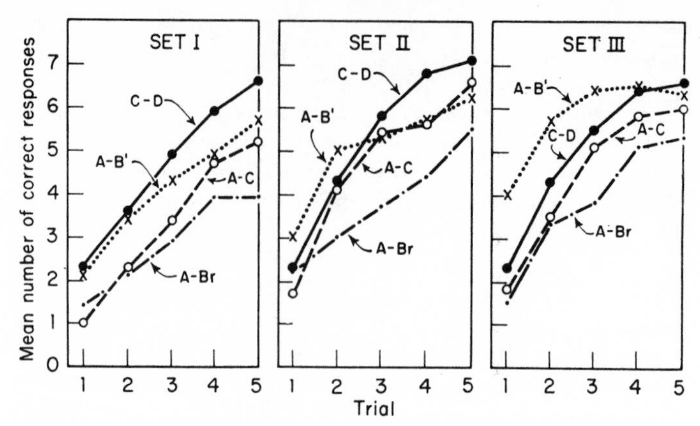

Fig. 2. List-2 acquisition curves for each paradigm in the successive sets.

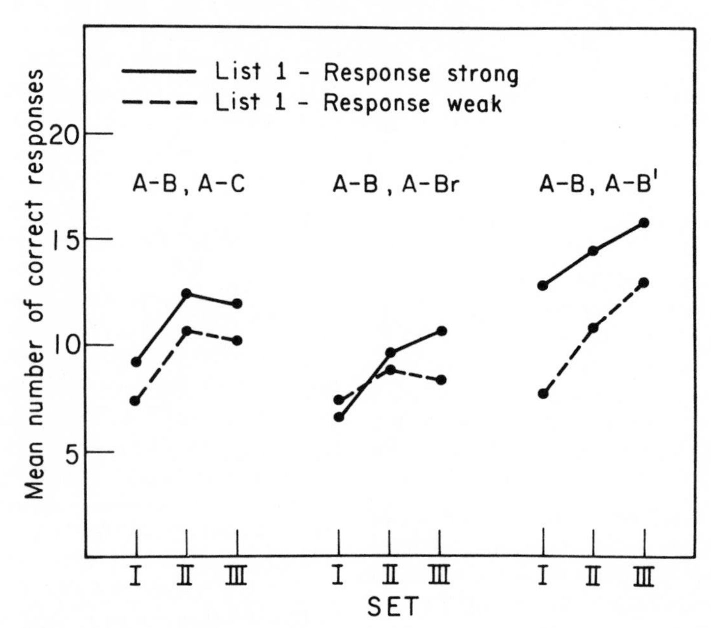

Fig. 3. Mean numbers of correct responses on List 2 as a function of List-1 strength.

learning progresses. Thus, while the levels of transfer change with practice, the differences among the paradigms continue to follow a consistent pattern as a function of trials on List 2. This conclusion is supported by a comparison of the slopes of the List-2 learning curves. Whereas the over-all differences among paradigms are significant ($F = 10.46$, $df = 3/48$), the interaction of sets with paradigms is not ($F = 1.64$, $df = 6/96$).

Interlist Correlations. Figure 3 summarizes the degree of correlation between the strength of List-1 and List-2 associations for the different paradigms at successive stages of practice. In each case the items in List 1 were evenly divided into an easy and a hard cate-

TABLE 3

MEAN PERCENTAGES OF INTRALIST ERRORS IN ACQUISITION OF SECOND LISTS OF SUCCESSIVE SETS

	Set 1			Set 2			Set 3		
Paradigm	Mispl. resp.	Stim. intr.	Total	Mispl. resp.	Stim. intr.	Total	Mispl. resp.	Stim. intr.	Total
C-D	12.5	4.8	17.3	8.5	2.5	11.0	11.4	1.7	13.1
A-C	14.6	1.9	16.5	9.2	2.3	11.5	11.8	0.8	12.6
A-Br	30.6	4.7	35.3	24.9	4.8	29.7	27.4	5.3	32.7
A-B′	8.6	0.7	9.3	11.5	0.6	12.1	10.9	0	10.9

TABLE 4

FREQUENCIES OF INTERLIST INTRUSIONS IN ACQUISITION OF SECOND LISTS OF SUCCESSIVE SETS

	Set 1				Set 2				Set 3			
	Paired		Unpaired		Paired		Unpaired		Paired		Unpaired	
Paradigm	f^a	n	f	n	f	n	f	n	f	n	f	n
C-D	—	—	1	1	—	—	1	1	—	—	4	2
A-C	—	—	4	2	1	1	1	1	5	4	2	2
A-Br	59	16	87	14	50	14	45	14	58	17	48	15
A-B′	8	5	10	7	16	10	12	7	8	5	5	3

[a] f = frequency of intrusions; n = number of *S*s contributing errors.

gory on the basis of the number of correct anticipations during the trials to criterion. The mean numbers of correct responses in List-2 learning were then determined for the two categories of items. In the first set the correlation is, in agreement with earlier studies, considerably higher for A-B′ than for A-C; there is no relationship at all for A-Br. Since increases in speed of learning serve to reduce the range of item difficulty, one would normally expect the correlation to shrink in the successive sets. Some convergence of the easy and hard categories is in fact apparent for A-B′ where the initial correlation was high. By contrast, the initial separation between the two categories of items is maintained for A-C, and there is an increase in the correlation for A-Br.

Errors in List-2 Learning. Table 3 shows the mean percentages of intralist errors during List-2 learning. Misplaced responses are again considerably more frequent than stimulus intrusions. The parallel analysis for List-1 learning (Table 2) had indicated that intralist errors decline with practice at a negatively accelerated rate. The transfer lists are the second, fourth, and sixth lists learned during the experimental session. Hence the percentages of errors for these lists do not reflect the decline from the initial level of the first list of the first set. The error rates are consistently higher for A-Br than for the other paradigms. The values for A-Br are, however, not comparable to those for the other conditions since intralist errors and interlist intrusions cannot be distinguished when old stimuli and old responses are re-paired. The inevitable confounding of both types of errors within a single category accounts for the divergence between A-Br and the other paradigms. There are no reliable differences among the latter ($F < 1$); the error rates do not change significantly as a function of practice ($F = 1.73$), nor is there a significant interaction of set with paradigm ($F = 1.71$). The absence of reliable differences between the reference paradigm and the experimental paradigms indicates that at a given stage of practice the error rates are comparable in the acquisition of new lists and of transfer lists.

The frequencies of interlist intrusions and the numbers of *S*s contributing them are presented in Table 4. The intrusions were classi-

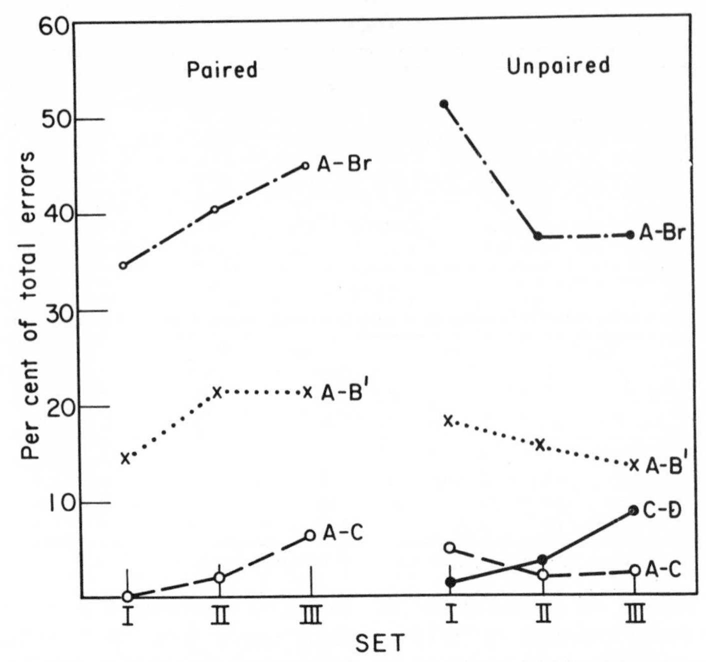

FIG. 4. Paired and unpaired intrusions as percentages of total overt errors.

fied as paired or unpaired, depending on whether or not they occurred to the appropriate stimulus terms (this distinction applies to all conditions except C-D). The entries for A-Br represent the same data as were used in the analysis of intralist errors. They were included again, primarily in order to permit an evaluation of the shifts in the relative frequencies of paired and unpaired errors.

Since the absolute frequencies of all types of errors changed as a function of paradigm and stage of practice, the numbers of the two types of intrusions were expressed as percentages of total overt errors. These percentages, which permit an assessment of changes in intrusion rates relative to the trends for all errors, are shown in Fig. 4. The proportions of both types of intrusions are substantially higher for A-B′ than for A-C. The values for A-Br are, of course, much higher still since all overt errors except for occasional importations and partial errors are included. The effects of practice on the relative frequency of paired and unpaired intrusions are consistent in each case: the proportion of paired intrusions increases whereas that of unpaired intrusions declines. While the absolute numbers are small, the fact that paired intrusions show some increase from an initial level of zero in Condition A-C is especially noteworthy. For Condition C-D only unpaired errors are possible, and these show a slight increase.

MMFR Test. Table 5 shows the mean numbers of responses recalled from both lists of each set on the MMFR test at the end of the experimental session. Before these findings are considered, some limitations of the MMFR results must be recognized: (a) The results for the three successive sets are not directly comparable because of differences in the amount of interpolated learning between original acquisition and MMFR. As one proceeds from the first to the third set, there are 2, 1, and 0 interpolated sets, respectively. (b) While the first lists were always learned

TABLE 5
MEAN NUMBERS OF LIST-1 AND LIST-2 RESPONSES RECALLED IN MMFR

Paradigm	Set 1		Set 2		Set 3	
	List 1	List 2	List 1	List 2	List 1	List 2
A-C	3.67	2.94	4.72	5.17	4.94	6.22
A-Br	3.72	3.11	5.17	4.50	5.17	5.39
A-B′	5.11	4.72	6.06	5.83	7.00	6.94

to the same criterion, degree of second-list learning varied as a function of both set and paradigm. Thus, differences in MMFR between first and second lists reflect variations in degree of learning as well as in retention interval.

A relatively unequivocal evaluation can be made of the differences among paradigms in List-1 recall, with amount of interpolated learning held constant. For the third set, in the absence of interpolated learning, Condition A-B′ shows no decline from the criterial level whereas both Conditions A-C and A-Br do. There is only a small difference between the latter two groups. These results are consistent with the assumption that List-1 associations are extinguished under conditions of negative transfer. The level of recall declines progressively from the most recent to the least recent set, but the pattern of differences among the paradigms does not change. Analysis of variance of the List-1 recall scores shows the differences among paradigms to be significant ($F = 8.71$, $df = 2/36$, $p < 0.01$), and there is also a significant decline from the most recent to the least recent set ($F = 22.77$, $df = 2/72$, $p < 0.01$). The differences among the paradigms do not vary significantly with set ($F < 1$).

While the absolute differences between List 1 and List 2 in MMFR are confounded with variations in degree of learning, it is possible to inquire to what extent there is a systematic relationship between the recall of the first and second response to the same stimulus within a given set. Table 6 presents in juxtaposition the overall probabilities of recall of List-2 responses and the conditional probabilities of List-2 recall given List-1 recall. These are designated as C_2 and $C_2{:}C_1$, respectively. A difference between the two probabilities indicates a non-random relationship between the recall of the two responses. If $C_2{:}C_1$ is greater than C_2, there is a positive relationship betwen the probabilities of List-1 and List-2 recall; if $C_2{:}C_1$ is less than C_2, the relationship is negative. For Condition A-B′ the value of $C_2{:}C_1$ consistently exceeds that of C_2, and a strong positive relationship is indicated. The fact that the absolute discrepancy between the obtained and expected value declines as a function of set is clearly attributable to a ceiling effect as recall for both lists approaches extremely high levels. By contrast, the difference between $C_2{:}C_1$ and C_2 changes from negative to positive as a function of set for both A-C and A-Br, with a larger shift for the former. Although the changes are small, they are progressive in both cases. Thus, a trend from a negative to a positive relationship between the recall of the two responses is indicated. The trend must, of course, be interpreted with caution since the total numbers of responses change from one set to the next within a given paradigm.

TABLE 6
PROBABILITY OF LIST-2 RECALL (C_2) AND CONDITIONAL PROBABILITY OF LIST-2 RESPONSES GIVEN LIST-1 RESPONSES ($C_2{:}C_1$) IN MMFR

Paradigm	Set 1		Set 2		Set 3	
	C_2	$C_2{:}C_1$	C_2	$C_2{:}C_1$	C_2	$C_2{:}C_1$
A-C	0.37	0.29	0.64	0.64	0.78	0.83
A-Br	0.39	0.34	0.56	0.52	0.67	0.70
A-B′	0.59	0.83	0.73	0.92	0.87	0.95

Discussion

Speed of learning increased significantly as a function of practice under all conditions of the experiment. At the same time there was a reduction in the rate of overt errors indicating an improved ability to discriminate and reject incorrect associations. The measures of List-1 learning permit an assessment of progressive changes in performance which are independent of specific transfer effects. Since the amount of improvement in List-1 learning did not vary reliably as a function of paradigm, it appears that the specific conditions of transfer do not influence the development of the habits and skills which are responsible for the overall upward trend in performance. It should be noted that the numbers of different stimulus and response terms to which *S*s were exposed varied with the paradigm of transfer, being largest for Condition C-D and smallest for Condition A-Br. Nevertheless there is no evidence for the accumulation of differential amounts of associative interference over the successive sets. Thus, it is likely that the reference condition, C-D, provides an unbiased baseline for the evaluation of changes in specific transfer effects.

All experimental paradigms showed greater improvement in List-2 learning than did the reference condition. Consequently, there were systematic changes in specific transfer effects as a function of practice. The most pronounced change occurred in Condition A-B′ in which there was a progressive development of positive transfer. The amount of negative transfer decreased for both A-C and A-Br, although the divergence from the reference condition was significant only in the former case. In spite of the changes in the levels of transfer, the differences among the paradigms continued to follow the same temporal pattern during List-2 learning from one set to the next. A consideration of this pattern will help to focus attention on the mechanisms of transfer characteristic of each paradigm and on the higher-order habits which may be expected to modify the effectiveness of these mechanisms.

The initial advantage of Condition A-B′ is substantially reduced as List-2 learning continues. The shift in the relative position of this paradigm is exhibited most clearly in the third set (cf. Fig. 2). On the first trial of List 2 A-B′ surpasses C-D by a considerable amount, but on the fifth trial the two conditions have fully converged. The mechanism which is most likely to be responsible for this pattern of transfer effects is mediational chaining, i.e., *S*s learn A-B-B′. Such mediation can, however, continue to be successful only as long as the forward order of the chain B-B′ remains intact. As the two associates to A approach each other in strength, failure to distinguish between the mediator and the mediated term will increase. This interpretation is supported not only by the pronounced negative acceleration of the acquisition curve but also by the fact that interlist intrusions characteristically occur more often and persist longer during the acquisition of A-B′ than of A-C. The latter condition may be assumed to provide much less opportunity for mediational chaining.

The List-2 acquisition curves for A-C in general parallel those for C-D, but at a lower level of performance. When new responses are attached to old stimuli, implicit or explicit competition from List-1 associations will delay the acquisition of the second list. These interferences are eliminated progressively as List-1 associations are extinguished and List-2 associations gain in strength. The results of the MMFR test confirm prior evidence (e.g., Barnes and Underwood, 1959) for the extinction of List-1 associations. The separation between A-C and C-D may be taken to reflect the delay in the development of List-2 associations introduced by the process of unlearning.

Negative transfer in the acquisition of A-Br increases as List-2 learning continues. Again the attachment of new responses to old stimuli leads to the extinction of List-1 associations. In agreement with the results of earlier studies (Barnes, 1960; Postman, 1962) the MMFR test indicates that such extinction occurs during List-2 learning. Since both the stimuli and responses remain identical, the failure to differentiate between List-1 and List-2 associations may be expected to become an additional major source of interference. Failures of differentiation should increase as the two systems of associations approach each other in strength. The increase in negative transfer as a function of trials is consistent with this expectation.

The question now arises in what ways practice on the successive sets of lists serves to modify the functional conditions of transfer so as to increase the positive effects in Condition A-B′ and to reduce the negative effects in Conditions A-C and A-Br. It is apparent that there is a progressive increase in the effective use of mediators under Condition A-B′. This conclusion is supported by the rapid rise in the numbers of correct responses on the initial trials of List 2 and the increase in the proportion of paired intrusions. Except for some shrinkage attributable to restriction of range, the correlation between the strength of List-1 and List-2 associations remains high, and the same is true for the interdependence of List-1 and List-2 responses in MMFR. The sharpness of the increase in the number of correct responses on the first trial of List 2 suggests the application of a systematic "strategy" of mediational chaining. It should be noted that the associative connection between the B and B′ terms was not sufficiently great to produce positive transfer in the first set. Considerably higher levels of List-2 learning are obtained when the associative connection between successive responses is maximized, e.g., by the use of items which elicit each other as primary responses in free association (Postman and Stark, 1964). Thus, the shift from negative to positive transfer which occurs with the present materials provides strong evidence for an increasingly systematic mode of attack on the transfer task.

It is only possible to speculate about the behavioral changes which are responsible for the reduction of negative transfer in Conditions A-C and A-Br. A deliberate attempt to reject all old associations might serve to improve performance. However, in the case of A-C at least, interlist differentiation is high even for inexperienced *S*s, as is shown by the low rate of intrusions in the first set. Thus, there is no independent evidence for increasing success in the recognition and rejection of old associations. The evidence on this point is indeterminate in the case of A-Br since no distinction can be made between intralist and interlist errors.

An additional, or alternative, source of improvement is suggested by some of the specific changes in performance in the successive sets, viz., that some mediational chaining occurred in the later stages of practice even when the responses were not associatively related. Since the responses were all familiar adjectives it may not have been too difficult to build up short mediational chains between them. Two lines of evidence support this possibility: (a) There was an increase in the proportion of paired intrusions, which are known to be a characteristic manifestation of mediational chaining. The fact that paired intrusions showed a rise from an initial level of zero in Condition A-C is especially significant. (b) The positive correlation between List-1 strength and speed of List-2 learning increased as a function of set for A-Br and remained constant for A-C in spite of the reduction in range. In addition, the conditional probabilities of recall in MMFR show a shift from a negative to a positive correlation between List-1 and List-2 responses. Both these correlations are clearly present for A-B′ and are to be expected between mediators and mediated terms. It must be recognized that this evidence for mediation in Conditions A-C and A-Br is highly circumstantial and based on relatively small though consistent changes in performance. To the extent that the interpretation is correct, however, it is consistent with the assumption that there was a gradual shift in the functional conditions of transfer from negative to positive.

The major result of this study is the finding that the rate at which performance on the transfer tests improves with practice is a function of paradigm. The present design does not make it possible to determine, however, to what extent these differences in improvement reflect (a) learning skills specific to each paradigm which differ in effectiveness, and (b) general transfer skills acquired as a result of practice, e.g., the ability to respond appropriately to similarity relations between lists, which are applied with varying degrees of success depending on the specific paradigm. To answer this question it will be necessary to consider the transfer of learning skills from one paradigm to another.

Summary

This study investigated changes in interlist transfer as a function of practice. Four paradigms of transfer were used, with lists of paired-associate adjectives as the learning materials: A-B, C-D (unrelated stimuli and unrelated responses); A-B, A-C (old stimuli and unrelated responses); A-B, A-Br (old stimuli and old responses re-paired), and A-B, A-B′ (old stimuli and associatively related responses). A-B, C-D served as a reference paradigm for the evaluation of specific transfer effects under the other conditions. Each *S* learned three successive sets of lists conforming to a given paradigm. Speed of first-list learning increased at comparable rates under all conditions. The degree of improvement in second-list learning varied as a function of paradigm. The amount of positive transfer for Condition A-B′ increased as a function of practice, whereas the amount of negative transfer for Conditions A-C and A-Br declined. The increase in positive transfer was greater than were the reductions in negative transfer. The results indicate systematic changes in *S*s' mode of attack on the transfer tasks.

References

Barnes, J. M. "Fate" revisited. Unpublished doctoral dissertation. Northwestern Univer., 1960.

Barnes, J. M., and Underwood, B. J. Fate of first-list associations in transfer theory. *J. exp. Psychol.,* 1959, **58**, 97-105.

Haagen, C. H. Synonymity, vividness, familiarity and association value ratings of 400 pairs of common adjectives. *J. Psychol.,* 1949, **27**, 453-463.

Hamilton, C. E. The relationship between length of interval separating two learning tasks and performance on the second task. *J. exp. Psychol.,* 1950, **40**, 613-621.

Hilgard, E. R. Methods and procedures in the study of learning. In S. S. Stevens (Ed.), *Handbook of experimental psychology.* New York: Wiley, 1951.

Postman, L. Transfer of training as a function of experimental paradigm and degree of first-list learning. *J. verb. Learn. verb. Behav.,* 1962, **1**, 109-118.

Postman, L. Does interference theory predict too much forgetting? *J. verb. Learn. verb. Behav.,* 1963, **2**, 40-48.

Postman, L., and Schwartz, M. Studies of learning to learn: I. Transfer as a function of method of practice and class of verbal materials. *J. verb. Learn. verb. Behav.,* 1964, **3**, 37-49.

Postman, L., and Stark, K. Proactive inhibition as a function of the conditions of transfer. *J. verb. Learn. verb. Behav.,* 1964, **3**, 249-259.

Thorndike, E. L., and Lorge, I. *The teacher's word book of 30,000 words.* New York: Teachers College, Columbia Univ., 1944.

Thune, L. E. Warm-up effect as a function of level of practice in verbal learning. *J. exp. Psychol.,* 1951, **42**, 250-256.

Twedt, H. M., and Underwood, B. J. Mixed vs. unmixed lists in transfer studies. *J. exp. Psychol.,* 1959, **58**, 111-116.

Ward, L. B. Reminiscence and rote learning. *Psychol. Monogr.,* 1937, **49**, No. 220.

Winer, B. J. *Statistical principles in experimental design.* New York: McGraw Hill, 1962.

(Received: December 31, 1963)

CHAPTER 9

Mediational Paradigms

Transfer in the two-stage mediational paradigms (e.g., *A-B*, *A-B′*) can be conceptualized as actually involving three stages. In this conceptualization the first (e.g., *A-B* list) and third (e.g., *A-B′* list) stages are experimentally introduced and manipulated. The second stage, or the *B* to *B′* mediating sequence, taps *S*'s natural language habits, either through associative or semantic generalization: The three stages may be related to the general concept of mediation which was tersely defined in the Overview by the symbols *A*, *B*, and *C*: *A* and *C* are unrelated verbal components that are associated together through the fact that they are both associatively connected to *B*. When so viewed, the *A-B*, *A-B′* paradigm may be translated into the three stage sequence (or paradigm) *A-B*, *B-C*, *A-C* in which *A* remains as the *St* component (*A*) of both lists, *B* becomes the *R* component (*B*) of List 1, and *C* becomes the *R* component (*B′*) of List 2. Besides the three-stage, mixed (mixed in the sense that both experimentally controlled acquisition and natural language habits enter into the stages) strategy, three other strategies have evolved as methods of demonstrating mediated transfer. These strategies are the subject of the present chapter.

The first strategy is a three-stage situation in which all three stages represent lists acquired in the laboratory under rigorous experimental control. Among the many alternatives available with this strategy is one that is analogous to the *A-B*, *A-B′* paradigm, but with all three stages (*A-B*, *B-C*, and *A-C* lists) being acquired through laboratory practice. Mediated positive transfer is inferred if the *A-C* pairs for *Ss* given this sequence are learned more proficiently than the *A-C* pairs for control *Ss* (in this case *Ss* given *A-B*, *D-C*, *A-C* as the list sequence). The second strategy is a four-stage one in which the first and fourth stages represent lists acquired in the laboratory and the second and third stages tap natural language habits—that is, a mixed strategy. The best known example of this strategy (Russell and Storms, 1955) is a paradigm in which the stages are *A-B*, *B-C*, *C-D*, *A-D*. *A-B* and *A-D* are two lists acquired sequentially in the laboratory, with identical stimuli but different responses (a condition expected to generate negative transfer through response competition and interference, if mediation from the two intervening stages were not involved). The *B-C* and *C-D* stages are word associations selected from word norms. The *B*, *C*, and *D* components are selected so that *C* is a word associate of *B* and *D* is a word associate of *C* but not of *B*. Mediated positive transfer is inferred if performance on the *A-D* pairs is superior to performance on control pairs (in this case, *A-X* pairs in the second list, with the *X* responses being unrelated by association to either the *B* or *C* components of the second and third stages). The final strategy is another four-stage one, but with all four stages being lists acquired directly in the laboratory.

Research on mediated verbal transfer with each of the above strategies has progressed rapidly during the contemporary period. In fact, prior to the present period, research on three- and four-stage mediated transfer was restricted largely to conditioning experiments involving nonverbal materials and processes. Thus, Shipley (1933), in a classical conditioning experiment, introduced the *A-B, B-C, A-C* three-stage experimental paradigm. The Shipley study was later replicated and extended by Lumsdaine (1939). In another conditioning study, Shipley (1935) demonstrated mediated transfer in a four-stage experimental paradigm.

The only early attempt to investigate three-stage (experimental stages only) mediated transfer with verbal material was by Peters (1935). This study was especially important in that it introduced the three basic paradigmatic variants for subsequent research on both three-stage and four-stage verbal transfer. These paradigmatic variants are models that simply describe the relationships between the components of the separate stages. Each model, in turn, subsumes a number of specific variants within itself. The models are chaining, stimulus equivalence, and response equivalence. A chaining model is one in which the mediating sequence relies upon some kind of link-to-link relationship between stage components. The previously cited *A-B, B-C, A-C* paradigm is a widely applied three-stage chaining paradigm in which mediation is supposedly by means of the direct *A-B-C* sequence. The identifying feature of the stimulus equivalence model is the fact that the stimulus components of two stages are each paired with the same response—presumably making the two stimuli functionally equivalent. A popular three-stage stimulus equivalence paradigm is *A-B, C-B, A-C*. The *A* components of List 1 and the *C* components of List 2 are paired with identical *B* components (e.g., A_1-B_1 in List 1 and C_1-B_1 in List 2) and are then paired with each other (e.g., A_1-C_1). The *A-B, C-B, A-D, C-D* paradigm is an example of a four-stage stimulus equivalence paradigm. Again, *A* and *C* become functionally equivalent through their association with *B*. The newly acquired *D* association to *A* (in the third stage) presumably transfers to *C* (in the fourth stage) through the equivalence of *C* to *A*. Response equivalence paradigms resemble their stimulus equivalence counterparts, but here the functional equivalence is established through the response components. *B-A, B-C, A-C* and *A-B, B-C, C-D, A-D* are examples of three- and four-stage paradigms, respectively. In the former, *A* and *C* become equivalent as responses to identical *B* stimuli. The latter is more complex and involves a chained equivalence. *B* and *D* become functionally equivalent as responses by virtue of their associative chain with *C* (*B-C-D*). Consequently, when *B* responses are learned as newly acquired responses to *A* stimuli, transfer of *D* as responses to *A* should occur through their chained equivalence with *B*.

There are eight 3-stage paradigms—four chaining, two stimulus equivalence, and two response equivalence ones. They are identified by the Roman numerals I to VIII in studies by Horton and Kjeldergaard (1961) and Peterson, Colavita, Sheahan, and Blattner (1964; Article 3). Although there are thirty-two possible four-stage paradigms, only sixteen have aroused experimental and theoretical interest (cf. Jenkins, 1963, for the rationale behind this interest and also for an identification of the specific paradigms). The paradigms are made up of eight stimulus equivalence paradigms and eight response equivalence paradigms.

The Peters (1935) study was only partly successful in demonstrating mediated verbal transfer—and then in relatively few *Ss*. For years after this study, tests of mediated transfer were largely nonverbal in nature, or were only partially verbal (e.g., combining verbal labels with instrumental responses; Birge, 1941). Finally, the existence of mediated verbal was tested again by Bugelski and Scharlock (1952; Article 1). Their marginally positive findings were followed by more convincing evidence of transfer in a multitude of subsequent experiments. Until the past few years, most of these experiments were simply tests of the null hypothesis—that is, the hypothesis of no mediated transfer. More recently, the existence of mediated verbal transfer has become generally accepted, and attention has shifted to other issues, such as the specific mechanisms held accountable for differential transfer effects for various paradigms, "awareness" as a necessary condition for mediation, and the identification of secondary variables that influence the amount of transfer.

Comprehensive attempts to explain mediated verbal transfer in terms of theoretical constructs have taken two different directions. In the one, the theoretical model is that of representational responses and their response-produced cues (e.g., Cofer and Foley, 1942; Osgood, 1953). In the other, the theory stresses associative processes that are more akin to the concept of chained word associates (e.g., Jenkins, 1955; Horton and Kjeldergaard, 1961). Both kinds of explanatory concepts are represented in the readings included in this chapter.

Three-Stage Experimental Paradigms

Evidence for and Mechanisms of Mediated Transfer

The *A-B*, *B-C*, *A-C* chaining paradigm (one of the three paradigms included in the study by Peters) was reintroduced to verbal transfer by Bugelski and Scharlock (1952; Article 1). They found positive, but weak, transfer for their experimental pairs relative to their control pairs. However, their control pairs permitted the possibility of mediated interference and resultant negative transfer. Consequently, it is impossible to tell if the positive transfer reported for the experimental pairs represents a true positive contribution or, rather, if it reflects a zero positive contribution being evaluated relative to a negative contribution from the control pairs. The nature of this confounding is carefully examined in a study by Norcross and Spiker (1958; Article 2). In their own refinement of the Bugelski and Scharlock experiments, Norcross and Spiker demonstrated both mediated facilitation and mediated interference relative to the appropriate control (nonmediation) condition. Besides strengthening his confidence in the reality of mediated transfer, the reader will profit otherwise from a careful study of Article 2. The introduction of this article provides a capsule version of the representational response theory of mediated transfer. In addition, the study indicates how verbal processes are investigated in a population (young children) considerably removed from the standard group of college-age guinea pigs.

Although the Peters study did not demonstrate mediated positive transfer in the stimulus equivalence *A-B*, *C-B*, *A-C* paradigm, a number of contemporary studies have (McCormack, 1961; Storms, 1958; Seidel, 1962). McCormack

(1961) interpreted this transfer effect in terms of associative theory. According to this view, an associative chain involving the *R-St* associations of the *C-B* list (Stage 2) mediates the transfer; that is, the *B-C* (backward) associations provide an *A-B-C* chain, comparable to that found in the *A-B*, *B-C*, *A-C* paradigm.

The entire set of eight 3-stage paradigms was investigated for mediated facilitation in two major studies (Horton and Kjeldergaard, 1961; Peterson, Colavita, Sheahan, and Blattner, 1964 (Article 3)). Horton and Kjeldergaard employed the standard method of having *S* master each list in its entirety before proceeding on to practice on the next list. Positive transfer was found for seven of the eight paradigms, with only Paradigm III (one of the chaining paradigms; cf. Article 3) yielding a null effect. The Peterson et al. study contained two interesting methodological variations. In the first variation, pairs were practiced in sets, rather than in intact lists. A set consisted of three pairs, with each pair representing, in sequence, one of the three paradigmatic stages. Practice on a set was completed before *S* was confronted with another set containing a different paradigmatic sequence. Thus, *S* might have been confronted initially by an A_1-B_1 pair, then a B_1-C_1 pair, and then an A_1-C_1 pair to complete the set. The next set could have included A_2-B_2, C_2-B_2, A_2-C_2 pairs. In their second variation, performance on the critical third stage pair was measured by a multiple choice technique rather than by the usual response anticipation method. With these two variations, Peterson et al. were able to demonstrate an overall significant facilitative effect for mediated sets versus control sets, but ancillary statistical analyses revealed that the effect was attributable to only three paradigms in their first experiment and to five in their second experiment.

Horton and Kjeldergaard (1961) had predicted not only significant positive transfer for all eight paradigms, but also significantly differential amounts between the paradigms. Their predictions of specific differences were based on an associative theory, with the directionality of chains and the contiguity between chained elements being the critical factors. Their predictions, however, were not substantiated—that is, the amount of positive transfer from paradigm to paradigm did not differ significantly. The Peterson et al. study (Article 3) contains a description of these directionality and continguity factors and the predictions based upon them. Peterson et al. confirmed these predictions in their first experiment in which trigrams of very low meaningfulness were used. Their second experiment replicated the first, but with trigrams of high meaningfulness as the *A*, *B*, and *C* components. This time the predictions based on directionality and contiguity were not confirmed. The question of meaningfulness as an important secondary variable in mediated transfer studies will be discussed below. Horton and Hartman (1963) also supported the directionality factor by finding more proficient acquisition in the third stage of a forward-chaining paradigm (Paradigm I; cf. Article 3) than in the third stage of a backward (i.e., *R-St* chained) paradigm (Paradigm IV; cf. Article 3). As in Experiment 1 of the Peterson et al. study, the *A*, *B*, and *C* components in the Horton and Hartman experiment were of low meaningfulness.

An additional mechanism, tangential to mediation per se but a factor to be considered in evaluating mediational effects in some experiments (e.g., in four-stage mixed paradigms), is described in Article 3. This is the mechanism of response availability. Increased availability of Stage 3 responses due to practice on the same responses in one of the acquisition stages contributes positive transfer to both the experimental pairs and the control pairs of many paradigms. Consequently, failure to recognize this nonmediated source of positive transfer and to adjust for it may lead to a spuriously high estimate of the amount of mediated transfer.

Secondary Variables

The results of the Peterson et al. (1964) study strongly imply that the extent of mediated transfer varies directly with the meaningfulness of the stage components. A corollary of this relationship is the increased probability of mediated transfer being demonstrated by relatively insensitive paradigms when the meaningfulness of the components increases—thus, paradigmatic differences in the amount of mediated transfer are likely to be detected under low meaningfulness but not under high. Peterson et al. were able to obtain positive transfer for Paradigms II and III under high meaningfulness but not under low. Barclay (1965) and Horton (1964; Article 4) also related meaningfulness to mediated transfer. Barclay's results indicated a significant positive effect for meaningfulness on test stage performance across three different paradigms (Paradigms I, VI, and VII) when meaningfulness was simultaneously varied for all components (*A*, *B*, and *C*). Both the *A-B*, *B-C*, *A-C* (Paradigm I) and the *B-A*, *B-C*, *A-C* (Paradigm VII) were tested by Horton under conditions in which the meaningfulness of the critical *B* component only was varied. Again, there was a direct covariation between meaningfulness level and third-stage performance.

Another important secondary variable appears to be the frequency of presenting the materials entering into the two acquisition stage (i.e., Lists 1 and 2). Peterson (1964) noted that most experiments on mediated transfer require *S* to learn Lists 1 and 2 to a higher criterion of mastery than is customarily true in other areas of PA acquisition—presumably on the basis of the untested premise that overlearning facilitates the acquisition of mediating chains. In her own studies (Peterson, 1964; Peterson and Blattner, 1963), employing the set–multiple choice methodology described above and in Article 3, Peterson found no relationship between the frequency of presenting pairs in the acquisition stages and the amount of facilitation in the test stage. Horton and Hartman (1963), with the more conventional intact list method, found some weak evidence for improving performance on the test stage as the number of trials on the acquisition stages increased. The effect was more pronounced for a backward-chaining paradigm than for a forward-chaining paradigm. Conceivably, backward chains are acquired at a slower rate than forward chains. With large doses of overlearning, the discrepancy in transfer effects often found between forward and backward paradigms would be expected to diminish and, perhaps, eventually dissipate.

Temporal variables are just beginning to be recognized as potentially powerful secondary variables. Schulz and Lovelace (1965), in a study employing a four-stage paradigm but with results having equally important implications for three-stage paradigms, varied the exposure rate during the test stage. Mediation was more conspicuous with a 4-second anticipation interval than with a 2-second interval. Their interpretation of this finding included the postulation of two different processes operating during the anticipation intervals of test-stage performance—*discovery* of the mediating chain and the actual *utilization* of this chain to aid anticipation of response terms. Longer intervals should permit the completion of both processes, whereas shorter intervals may not enable *S* to progress beyond mere discovery. Massed versus distributed practice of pairs in the acquisition stages was investigated by Peterson and Jamison (1965). They found mediated transfer under massed practice but not under distributed practice. Peterson (1965) interpolated delay intervals, ranging from 0 to 8 seconds, between either the two acquisition stages or between the second acquisition stage and the test stage. With *A*, *B*, *C* components of low meaningfulness, mediated facilitation occurred for short intervals but not for the longer 8-second interval; with components of very high meaningfulness (words), facilitation occurred regardless of the length of the delay interval.

The Horton (1964; Article 4) study has a wealth of information on three other important variables: awareness of mediation versus unawareness, individual differences in learning ability, and mixed lists (i.e., lists containing both experimental and control pairs) versus unmixed lists (i.e., lists containing only experimental pairs). Articles 1 and 3 also touch on the problem of awareness of the mediating sequence as a determining condition for mediated facilitation to take place.

Nonmediational Explanations

Not all psychologists have jumped on the mediational bandwagon. Several have attempted to incorporate mediated facilitation within the framework of the more traditional mechanisms of classical transfer (cf. Introduction, Chapter 8). In effect, the principle of parsimony is invoked. If mediated transfer can be explained without the invention of further constructs (in this case, either representational responses or associative chains), then there is no need to add these mediating mechanisms to an already overloaded stockpile.

Barclay (1961) reasoned that nonspecific or general sources of transfer could account for reported differences in test-stage performance between experimental (i.e., mediated) and control groups. His procedure for testing this hypothesis departed in one important respect from that of others active in this area. Briefly, mediation was "built in" objectively, rather than being inferred from paradigmatic relationships. His *Ss*, both experimental and control, received *B-C* pairs in List 1, *A-D* pairs in List 2, and *A-C* pairs in List 3. The *B-C*, *A-D*, *A-C* sequence is, of course, not conducive to mediated transfer. Mediation became a possibility in the experimental *Ss* by the contiguous pairing of an appropriate *B* component with a *D* response presentation during the informative feedback phase of List 2 practice—thus permitting the acquisition of *A*-[*D*]-*B* chains and the establishment of a *B-C*, *A-B*, *A-C* (Paradigm II) paradigm in the experimental *Ss*. The experimental *Ss* were subdivided into groups for which the percentage of trials on which *B* was paired with *D* varied from 25 to 100 per cent. Although the combined experimental subgroups surpassed the control group on List 3, the subgroups did not differ between themselves. The fact that mediated facilitation did not show a linear increment from 25 to 100 per cent led Barclay to conclude that the overall facilitation was attributable to some nonmediational factor. A possible factor here could be that of list differentiation. The *A-D*, *A-C* lists of Barclay's second and third stages enter into an *A-B*, *A-C* relationship of classical transfer. The presence of the contiguous component in the second list but not in the third list could serve to differentiate between these lists and lead to a reduction in negative transfer from response competition.

Interference as a causative factor has been emphasized by Mandler and

Earhard (1964; Article 5). By manipulation of interference effects they were able to demonstrate what they called "pseudomediation"—that is, facilitation in the absence of mediating conditions. The proponents of mediation have begun to answer this challenge, either by failing to find supportive evidence for hypotheses tied to Mandler and Earhard's findings (e.g., Goulet, in press) or by reporting facilitation above and beyond that attributable to pseudomediation (e.g., Schulz, Weaver, and Ginsberg, 1965).

Four-Stage Mixed Paradigms

Evidence for and Mechanisms of Mediated Transfer

The Russell and Storms (1955) study (see pp. 429–430 succeeded in demonstrating mediated positive transfer with a mixed response equivalence paradigm (*A-B, B-C, C-D, A-D,* with the *A-B, A-D* stages experimentally controlled and the *B-C, C-D* stages inferred from word association norms). Their results were later confirmed by Cofer and Yarczower (1957). Nevertheless, the validity of attributing transfer in this paradigm to mediational sources was subsequently questioned by McGehee and Schulz (1961; Article 6). They presented an alternative interpretation in terms of the heightened availability of *D* components in *S*'s response hierarchy that might result from the acquisition of *B* responses in the first list. Their carefully controlled experiments negated the availability hypothesis and provided even more convincing evidence in support of the mediation hypothesis.

Other four-stage mixed paradigms have received little empirical attention. Jenkins (1963) did report the outcome of a study in which the *A-B, C-B, A-D, C-D* stimulus equivalence paradigm (the famous Shipley four-stage paradigm) was tested for mediated facilitation. The *A-B* and *C-B* stages were language-inferred, and the *A-D* and *C-D* stages were experimentally controlled. The failure to find facilitation in this paradigm forced Jenkins to search for the probable differences in associative processes extant in the Russell-Storms and Shipley paradigms. The reader will enhance his knowledge of mediation immensely by a careful reading of Jenkin's rationale. Martin, Oliver, Hom, and Heaslet (1963) also tested the Shipley paradigm, but their *D* components were simple motor responses rather than verbal elements. They were able to find facilitation on *C-D* pairs relative to control pairs. Moreover the facilitative effect decreased with increasing practice on the *A-D* (third-stage) pairs. This inverse function was viewed as evidence for the competition between *B* and *D* as responses to *A* in the third stage and the resulting partial unlearning of *B* and partial loss as a mediator in the fourth stage.

Secondary Variables

In the Russell and Storms paradigm a secondary variable expected to be closely related to the amount of transfer is the degree of associative strength existing between the *B-C* and *C-D* connections. Jarrett and Scheibe (1962) have developed a probabilistic model in which the strength of a mediated association is predicted to be a product of the strengths of the links making up the mediated chain. Thus, if an association *A-C* is mediated by an *A-B, B-C* sequence, the probability of *A* eliciting *C* becomes the product of the separate probabilities of *A* eliciting *B* and *B* eliciting *C*. Convincing evidence for this principle was found in the learning of single lists when the pairs varied in terms of assumed intervening links. Palermo and Jenkins (1964b) tested the model further in the context of an *A-B*, *A-B′* paradigm in which both *A-B* and *B-B′* (mediating) associations had varying degrees of word associative strength, as assessed by word norms. The acquisition of *A-B′* associations was found to vary nicely with the product of the *A-B*, *B-B′* strengths. Carrying this principle over to the Russell and Storms paradigm, we would expect performance on *A-D* pairs to become increasingly more proficient as the strength of the *B-C* and *C-D* associations (again assessed from word norms) increases. Schulz and Lovelace (1965), however, failed to find this kind of sensitivity to the strength of the mediating associations.

Two other variables, rate of exposure and priming, have been applied to transfer in the Russell and Storms paradigm. One, the rate variable, has already been discussed (Schulz and Lovelace, 1965; cf. pp. 433–434). The other, priming, was part of a recent experiment by Martin and Dean (1964) in which the distinction was made between implicit and explicit mediation. Explicit mediation refers to a conscious (aware) process, implicit to an unconscious (unaware) process. Explicit mediation was varied by means of instructions which differentially primed the *C* components (the source of mediation)—that is, differentially sensitized *Ss* to the conscious awareness of *C* during *A-D* practice. They found performance on *A-D* pairs to be most proficient when *Ss* were instructed to pronounce out loud the *B* component after viewing the *A* components but before anticipating the *D* component. Presumably, pronouncing *B* increased the likelihood of *S* becoming aware of the *B-C-D* sequence, thus facilitating performance.

Four-Stage Experimental Paradigms

In an exhaustive and frustrating study, Jenkins (1963) tested sixteen different four-stage paradigms, with all four stages being experimentally acquired, for evidence or mediated transfer. In each instance the outcome was null. Jenkins proceeded to conduct a careful analysis of the probable reasons for failure. The only reported study of positive transfer in a four-stage paradigm with verbal materials is that of James and Hakes (1965) on the Shipley paradigm. Their success is likely to arouse renewed interest in four-stage experimental paradigms. Even so, these paradigms will probably remain in the "test the null hypothesis" phase for some time.

AN EXPERIMENTAL DEMONSTRATION OF UNCONSCIOUS MEDIATED ASSOCIATION

B. R. BUGELSKI AND D. P. SCHARLOCK
University of Buffalo

Some years ago McGeoch noted that "the theory of the existence of mediated associations is an old one which has generated more discussion than straightforward experimental study" (5, p. 94). In his recent revision of McGeoch's text, Irion (6) saw no good reason for altering the statement. The concept of mediation is of great potential value for the psychological analysis of learning, thinking, and insight as Hebb (2) has recently demonstrated, but unequivocal demonstration of such mediation on a verbal level is as yet lacking. There have been a number of studies of mediated association on a nonverbal level (1, 4, 8), but in these studies there is some question as to whether the mediation is a function of sensory-sensory association, stimulus generalization, or whether an intermediate response occurs and functions as a mediator. Hilgard and Marquis (3) note that in Lumsdaine's experiment the intervening eyelid response was not always present in test trials even though the response that had never been associated with the test stimulus did occur. The recent report of Wickens and Briggs (9) purports to demonstrate the need for a common response to two different stimuli as a basis for mediation. Their demonstration is not free from the criticism that the Ss may have operated under different self-instructed sets in the control experiments and, therefore, did not respond to the nonconditioned stimulus because they had discriminated the relevant and irrelevant stimuli during the preliminary training.

Peters' (7) report still remains as the only demonstration of mediation in verbal learning that Irion cites. It is important to note that Peters found such association for only a few Ss, in only two out of nine experiments, and only where Ss were able to make use of the common item "perceptually or ideationally present at the time of recall." When the common item is ideationally present, there is some question as to whether the process can be fitted into the concept of mediation as Hebb uses it: "Two concepts may acquire a latent 'association' without ever having occurred together in the subject's past experience" (2, p. 132). Certainly a broader potential application of the mediation hypothesis can be developed if such mediation operates without awareness on the part of the Ss. If, as in Peters' experiments, S specifically makes use of two previous sets of associations by which to arrive at a third, he is using something more akin to a mnemonic device than to mediated association. It should be clear to the reader that the mediation hypothesis involves two separate questions: (*a*) Does the mediation depend on the occurrence of the intermediate response as an agent for eliciting the new response? and (*b*) Must S be aware of such occurrence if it does take place?

Hebb (2) implies and Lumsdaine (4) indicates that the mediating response need not actually occur. Peters' conclusion, just cited, indicates that in verbal material, at least, awareness is necessary. The experiment to be described here deals with

Reprinted with permission of the authors and the publisher, the American Psychological Association. The article appeared originally in the *Journal of Experimental Psychology*, 1952, **44**, 334–338.

the second of the two questions. It is not expected to shed light on the answer to the first question.

Method

Experimental design.—The general outline of the experiment followed the pattern of Peters' nine experiments. The *Ss* first learned one set of paired-associate nonsense syllables so arranged that the stimulus and response syllables can be labeled A and B. They then learned another set of paired syllables with the original response syllables serving as stimuli so that the sequence B–C was established. The last stage consisted of a test for mediation in requiring *Ss* to learn the A–C pairs. Assuming that mediation has a chance to operate under these circumstances, *Ss* should learn the A–C list with comparative ease, all other factors considered equal or controlled. Because the A–C list could actually be learned more or less easily for various reasons irrelevant to the experimental hypothesis, e.g., practice, proactive inhibition, familiarity with the syllables, or even a chance selection of easy- or hard-to-learn associates in the A–C list, it was necessary to make each *S* serve as his own control and learn in his A–C list a number of paired associates which had been learned in the A–B, B–C sequence and an equal number where such an arrangement did not hold. To achieve this effect, half of the A–C list was constructed directly from the previously associated pairs, thus A–C units were made up of the A syllable and the C syllable that had been associated with a common B syllable. These A–C's will hereafter be called the experimental syllables. The other half of the A–C list was composed of the remainder of the A syllables paired at random with the remainder of the C syllables, so that no A–C pair in this half of the list had a common and specific B-syllable associate. These pairs will hereafter be called the control syllables. The arrangement of the experimental and control syllables can be appreciated from the paradigm below:

First List	Second List	Third List	
A1 — B1	B1 — C1	A1 — C1	Exper.
A2 — B2	B2 — C2	A2 — C2	
A3 — B3	B3 — C3	A3 — C4	Control
A4 — B4	B4 — C4	A4 — C3	

From the arrangement above it is obvious that if an associative inhibition is implied, the *Ss* can be expected, other things equal, to learn the experimental syllables better either because of high positive transfer from the common elements or because of associated interference operating to reduce learning for the control pairs. A high negative correlation, then, is to be expected between the learning scores for the two sets of materials.

The design, as thus far described, however, does not escape the difficulty that either of the two halves of the A–C list may, by chance, be more difficult than the other half. If the randomized half were learned more easily, it might be interpreted to mean that no mediation had been operating. To overcome this factor, half the *Ss* learned the pairs with the roles of the syllables reversed so that the formerly randomized or "control" syllables were now used to build up lists of A–B and B–C where the B was a common item, and the experimental A–C's which were previously associated with a common B were now randomized in the A–B and B–C lists. The experimental and control lists, then, consisted of exactly the same syllable pairs. They differed only in their history.

Apparatus.—Syllables for constructing the paired associates were taken from Glaze's lists of syllables with 40–50% association value. Six lists, each consisting of 16 paired associates, were prepared to fit the needs of the design just described. Thus there were A–B, B–C, and A–C lists for one group of *Ss* wherein the experimental syllables or first eight pairs of the A–C list were composed of A and C syllables with a common B associate and eight where the B associate was randomized. The other three lists were arranged so that in the A–C list the original experimental syllables now had their B associate randomized and served as control syllables while the former control syllables were systematized (associated with a common B) and served as experimental syllables. A second group of *Ss* learned the latter three lists. This arrangement permits the addition of data for both groups of *Ss* and for both groups of experimental and control syllables. It should be noted, however, that half of the *Ss* learned half of the experimental syllables and half of the control syllables, the remaining half of the *Ss* learned the other halves of the experimental and control syllables. The lists of A, B, and C syllables appear in Table 2. From this table the general arrangement of the A–B, B–C, and A–C lists can be inferred.

The syllables were block printed on 3 × 5-in. white cards and were viewed through an opening in a screen. Behind the screen a motor-driven exposure device consisting of a slotted screen was arranged to expose the stimulus half of each pair of syllables for 3 sec. and the response half for an additional 3 sec., with 4 sec. between pairs.

Procedure.—Each *S* learned three lists of paired associates; one at each of three separate learning sessions. The *Ss* learned to anticipate each correct response to a criterion of five perfect trials. As the criterion for each pair was met, that pair was eliminated to prevent differential overlearning. The cards were shuffled between trials to prevent serial learning. Learning was usually completed in 1 hr.; 48 hr. after learning the first list, *Ss* learned the second list, and 48 hr. later, the third list.

Subjects.—Twenty senior students in psychology, all of whom had nonsense syllable learning experience, served as *Ss*. Each *S* served as his own control. Half of the 20 *Ss* learned the original set of materials, i.e., the first three lists, and the other ten learned the same syllables arranged to control the factor of difficulty as described above.

Results

Because of the need for controlling the possible differential difficulty of the experimental and control syllables, the results for the two groups of ten *Ss* have been combined and treated as one lot. This procedure is justified only if the two groups are not significantly different in learning ability. The mean number of trials to learn the 16 paired associates for the two groups of *Ss* was 16.9 and 17.2, with *SD*'s of 8.3 and 4.9, indicating essential equality of the two groups of *Ss*.

Because of individual differences among *Ss* and because of unusual difficulties some *Ss* experienced with some pairs, no significant differences could be established between group results for either median or mean number of trials to learn the experimental as opposed to the control materials, although in each case the differences favored the experimental syllables. Examination of the order of learning the two sets, however, suggested that a significant difference between the two groups of syllables could be established. Accordingly, the mean rank order of learning of the experimental syllables was compared with the mean rank of the controls (see Table 1). Using a single-tail t test and taking account of the high negative correlation ($-.87 \pm .06$) in the calculation of $SD_{dif.}$, the difference between the mean rank orders is 1.2 which is significant between the .02 and .05 levels. It should be noted that 12 of the 20 *Ss* learned the experimental syllables before they learned the controls (in terms of mean rank), 2 *Ss* averaged the same, and 6 *Ss* had a lower mean rank for the control syllables. When the syllable pairs themselves are examined, the same general picture is revealed. It will be recalled from the experimental design that all 16 pairs of syllables served as experimental and control syllables (eight syllables for each group of ten subjects). When a comparison is made between the median number of trials to learn the 16 syllable pairs on their control function (see Table 2), it is found that 12 of the 16 pairs are learned more rapidly in the experimental arrangement. The mean difference between the medians is 1.7 which is significant between the .005 to .01 levels as determined by using a single-tail t test.

One additional finding of importance is that because of the combination of factors in the learning situation (large numbers of syllables to learn, 48-hr. periods between sets, and probably most important, the mixture for each *S* of experimental and control syllables so that no logical or mnemonic system could work consistently) none of the *Ss* was able to report any correct appreciation of the nature of the experiment and most assuredly did not verbalize a pattern of A–B, B–C, A–C in the learning of the third list.

TABLE 1

Mean Rank Order of Learning Experimental and Control Syllables by 20 *Ss*

Syllables	Mean	*SD*	σ_m	r exper. and control
Exper.	7.9	1.64	.38	$-.869 \pm .056$
Control	9.1	1.57	.36	

As far as can be judged by results of interrogation of the *Ss*, they learned the experimental A–C syllables more efficiently than they did the controls without the benefit of mediations that were "perceptually or ideationally present." None of the *Ss* consciously resorted to the use of the mediating B syllable in their attempts to learn the A–C list.

Discussion

The results presented appear to form a reasonably clear-cut demonstration of mediated association in the learning of verbal material. The fact that *Ss* did not consciously use the intervening common item in the more efficient learning of the experimental materials suggests that such conscious verbal interpolation is unnecessary and that it is sufficient to have had the experience to make use of it in a different connection. Whether reactions involving B syllables occurred unconsciously or at all cannot be determined from this experiment. We have, then, a sample of the type of evidence Hebb (**2**) alludes to in his automatic association of cell assemblies and phase sequences. The gratuitous learning which is assumed to have facilitated the learning of the experimental material attests to the significance of mediated association in the acquisition of new learned patterns.

Because the present findings reveal a significant amount of mediated association and Peters failed to find significant evidence of such mediation, some possible reasons for the differences might be considered. In the present study a rather high criterion was employed to insure adequate learning of the prospective mediation material. Peters generally used a criterion of two correct anticipations and this might not have been high enough. Peters also generally used an anticipation test instead of a learning test. It may be that he was using too difficult a test situation, considering his low learning criteria and the nature of his materials. A last comment concerns the order of presentation of the learning material. In the present study the order of learning the successive lists was A–B, B–C, A–C. Peters frequently used other orders such as A–B, C–B, A–C. It may well be that the reversal of the B–C may prove a more difficult condition for future mediation as it corresponds somewhat to backward conditioning which is generally recognized to be difficult to establish.

TABLE 2

The Median Number of Trials to Learn Each A–C Pair when the Same Pairs Are Learned as Experimental and Control Materials

	Syllables			Exper. Median	Control Median
	A	B	C		
1	Fuj	Mup	Qeh	6.5 (y)	7.0 (x)
2	Gud	Sif	Nal	4.0	7.0
3	Jek	Fah	Tik	6.5	6.0
4	Lud	Tek	Lix	1.5	6.0
5	Moh	Yuk	Reh	7.5	4.5
6	Pah	Baz	Tij	1.5	5.0
7	Viq	Zes	Cax	4.0	6.0
8	Weg	Vag	Puv	3.0	10.5
9	Cey	Hix	Kiv	5.0	8.5
10	Dak	Woh	Gew	3.0	3.5
11	Hax	Kor	Yob	8.5	6.0
12	Kug	Jep	Zan	8.5	7.5
13	Nof	Dal	Huy	6.5	9.5
14	Sux	Gow	Mog	5.0	8.0
15	Yob	Qur	Jax	7.5	9.0
16	Zew	Lah	Bup	*7.0*	*8.5*
Mean				5.3	7.0
SD				2.3	1.9
SD_m				0.59	0.49

Summary

1. Twenty college seniors learned three lists of paired associates so arranged as to provide a possibility of mediated association. The three lists followed the order of A–B, B–C, A–C.

2. The A–C syllables were learned significantly better than control syllables which were the exact duplicate of the experimental syllables except for different prior experience of the *S*s.

3. The *S*s benefitted from prior learning of the A–B, B–C lists without reporting any perceptual or ideational use of the material.

(Received April 7, 1952)

References

1. Brogden, W. J. Sensory preconditioning. *J. exp. Psychol.*, 1939, **25**, 323–332.
2. Hebb, D. O. *The organization of behavior.* New York: Wiley, 1949.
3. Hilgard, E. R., & Marquis, D. G. *Conditioning and learning.* New York: Appleton-Century, 1940.
4. Lumsdaine, A. A. Conditioned eyelid responses as mediating generalized conditioned finger withdrawal reactions. *Psychol. Bull.*, 1939, **36**, 650.
5. McGeoch, J. A. *The psychology of human learning.* New York: Longmans, 1942.
6. McGeoch, J. A., & Irion, A. L. *The psychology of human learning.* (2nd Ed.) New York: Longmans, 1951.
7. Peters, H. N. Mediate association. *J. exp. Psychol.*, 1935, **18**, 20–48.
8. Shipley, W. C. Indirect conditioning. *J. gen. Psychol.*, 1935, **12**, 337–357.
9. Wickens, D. D., & Briggs, G. E. Mediated stimulus generalization in sensory preconditioning. *J. exp. Psychol.*, 1951, **42**, 197–200.

ARTICLE 2

EFFECTS OF MEDIATED ASSOCIATIONS ON TRANSFER IN PAIRED-ASSOCIATE LEARNING

KATHRYN J. NORCROSS AND CHARLES C. SPIKER

Iowa Child Welfare Research Station

Several experimenters have demonstrated that a given response (R_o) may be elicited by a stimulus (S_1) to which R_o has never been conditioned, even when S_1 is physically dissimilar to any stimulus to which R_o has been conditioned (**1, 3, 6, 8, 11**). These results have been explained in terms of the principle of secondary, or mediated, generalization (**4**). Briefly, the principle states that the conditioning of a response, R_a, to each of several dissimilar stimuli (S_1, S_2, etc.) assures that on subsequent presentations of these stimuli, the stimulation, s_a, produced by R_a, will be present. Any other response, R_o, subsequently conditioned to one of these stimuli (e.g., S_2) will also be conditioned to s_a. Thus, if any other of the stimuli (S_1, etc.) is presented, R_a will tend to occur, together with s_a, and s_a will tend to elicit R_o.

The principle of mediated generalization also appears applicable to the phenomenon of mediated associations in paired-associate verbal learning. The paradigm for mediated associations provides for two preliminary lists and a third test list administered in an A-B, B-C, A-C sequence. A schematization of the analysis of this situation is presented in Fig. 1. In List I, *S* is presented with visual stimulus A, to which he makes the (overt or covert) verbalization R_A with attendant stimulation, s_a. S_B is presented in close spatial and temporal relationship with S_A and elicits R_B, which in turn produces s_b. The experimental conditioning that occurs is represented by the dotted lines in Fig. 1. As a result of List II experience, s_b comes to evoke R_C. The subsequent learning of R_C in response to S_A is facilitated through mediation by s_b.

An early series of experiments on mediated association with some positive findings was reported by Peters (**9**). Associative facilitation was investigated by Irwin (**5**) with a B-C, A-B, A-C sequence for an experimental group as compared to a D-C, A-B, A-C control sequence. A significant difference between the two groups in the learning of the A-C list was found, with the group given the B-C list superior. Bugelski and Scharlock (**2**) used an experimental design in which the third A-C list was constructed from previously associated nonsense syllables in such a way that experimental pairs were made up of an A syllable and a C syllable that had been associated with a common B

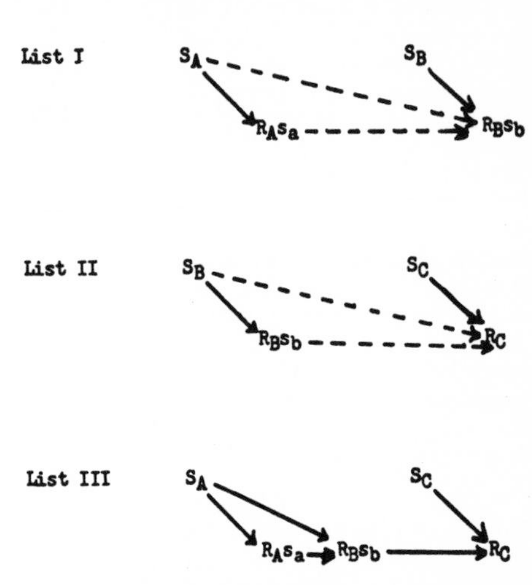

Fig. 1. A schematic analysis of mediated association in paired-associate learning.

Reprinted with permission of the authors and the publisher, the American Psychological Association. The article appeared originally in the *Journal of Experimental Psychology*, 1958, **55**, 129–134.

syllable; control pairs were composed of the remaining A and C syllables paired at random so that none had a common specific B associate. A significant difference was obtained in the mean rank order of learning the two types of pairs. Russell and Storms (**10**) have recently demonstrated mediational effects with experimentally established learning and inferred pre-existing language habits.

The differences that obtained in the latter experiments (**2, 10**) may have resulted from a combination of positive transfer for the experimental condition and negative transfer in the control condition, since mediated but incorrect response tendencies presumably exist for the "control" items. The present experiments attempt to demonstrate both positive and negative transfer in learning the third list in the mediated association design.

Experiment I

Method

Apparatus.—The apparatus used is an electrically operated visual stimulus presentation device.[1] It consists of a gray metal box 14 × 14 × 14 in. The front face of the apparatus contains a 3 × 6 in. aperture. A mechanical arrangement delivers to the aperture a 3½ × 6 in. plastic card from the bottom of a stack of cards. Mounted on each card was a pair of pictures taken from the *Golden Play Book of Picture Stamps for the Very Young*. Each picture was a colored representation of a single familiar object; e.g., a dog, horse, ice cream cone, etc. Black cloth curtains on the aperture serve as shutters to expose or conceal independently the left and right pictures on the stimulus cards. Following a presentation, the curtains close simultaneously and the card is released from the aperture and returned to the top of the stack by a conveyor belt. A system of electronic timers controls the rate of presenting the cards and the exposure times of the stimulus and response pictures.

[1] The apparatus was especially constructed by the Hunter Mfg. Co., Iowa City, Iowa. The authors are indebted to Dr. Alfred Castaneda for aid in formulating the specifications for the apparatus.

TABLE 1

Schematic Illustration of the Design for Exp. I

List I		List II		List III	
S	*R*	*S*	*R*	*S*	*R*
1	7	7	13	1	13*
2	8	8	14	2	14*
3	9	9	15	3	16**
4	10	10	16	4	15**
5	11	19	17	5	17†
6	12	20	18	6	18†

* Pairs in List III for which facilitation is predicted.
** Pairs in List III for which interference is predicted.
† Control pairs in List III.

Experimental design.—Each *S* learned three lists of stimulus-response pairs. Each list consisted of six pairs of pictures. In order that *S* might more easily comprehend the task, List I was constructed of picture pairs which were highly associated; Lists II and III were not so constructed. Table 1 illustrates the design, which provides that each *S* serve under each of three experimental conditions. For two pairs in List III, the mediational chain is expected to facilitate learning. For two other pairs, the mediational chain is expected to elicit incorrect responses and thus interfere with learning. Two other pairs have no experimentally established mediating tendencies, since the response items paired with the stimuli in List I were not presented in List II.

Subjects.—The *S*s were 30 kindergarten children.[2] Ten *S*s were randomly assigned to each of three groups. These three groups were designed to control for possible differential difficulty of the stimulus-response pairs in List III. All groups received the same form of Lists I and III. The groups differed with respect to which of three forms of List II they received. These three forms were constructed so that for a given List III pair, facilitation was predicted in one group, interference in another, and neither mediated facilitation nor interference for the third group.

Procedure.—Each *S* was given three experimental sessions separated by from two to seven

[2] The authors are indebted to Hale C. Reid, Director of Curriculum and Instructions, for permission to use subjects in the Cedar Rapids Public Schools. Special thanks are also due to Ray Churchill, Principal, and to the staff of Harrison School in Cedar Rapids, for administrative assistance and cooperation in the collection of the data of Exp. I.

days. After the child had been brought by *E* from the classroom to the experimental room in order to play a "guessing game with pictures," he was seated facing the aperture in which the stimulus cards were presented. The *E* was seated immediately beside *S* in order to control the apparatus, give appropriate verbal instructions to establish understanding of the procedure, and to record responses made in the anticipation interval.

At the beginning of training, the right half of the aperture was opened and the six response members of List I were shown once each. The *S* was asked to name them. Any reasonable name given was accepted; if necessary, a name was supplied. The same procedure was followed as the stimulus members were presented in the left half of the aperture. A second naming trial was then given with the response members. During the first paired presentation, the stimulus side of the pair was exposed while *E* asked *S* each time what he thought was behind the curtain on the other side. The stimulus and response items were then simultaneously exposed while *S* gave the response name, either voluntarily or upon request. After the first trial, *E* instructed *S* to try to guess which picture was behind the curtain each time. Presentation was continued until a learning criterion of two consecutive correct trials had been reached.

Three varying orders of presentation were used for all lists in order to control for serial learning. A 6-sec. anticipation period was followed by a 5-sec. period of joint presentation of the stimulus and response items. The between pair interval was 2.2 sec. All verbal responses occurring in the anticipation interval were recorded verbatim throughout the experiment.

On the second experimental day, List II was administered in the same way as was List I, except that a simultaneous presentation of both the stimulus and response members was given rather than the second presentation of the response items alone.

On the third day, Lists I and II were each reviewed to criterion. A short rest period of approximately 2 min. followed. List III was then introduced in the same way as List I on the first day. Five trials on List III were given, terminating the experiment.

Results and Discussion

The mean number of trials to criterion for all *S*s on List I was 2.13. The means of the number of trials for the various forms of List II did not differ significantly; the overall mean was 3.47. The more rapid learning of List I than of List II is probably due to the higher associations within pairs for List I.

An analysis of variance of correct anticipations on List III is summarized in Table 2. In this analysis, the main effect of control groups appears as a between-*S* factor and the main effect of conditions as an intra-*S* factor (**7**, p. 267, Type I). This analysis revealed that the means for the groups designed as controls for possible differential difficulty of the picture pairs did not differ significantly. The means for the facilitation, control, and interference conditions differed at better than the .001 level of significance. For all 30 *S*s combined, the mean numbers of correct responses in five trials were 7.40 for the facilitation, 4.83 for the control, and 4.40 for the interference conditions. Individual *t* tests showed that the mean differences for the facilitation and control comparison and for the facilitation and interference comparison were significant at better than the .001 level. The difference between control and interference means, although in the predicted direction, was not significant.

According to the mediation hypothesis, the learning of Lists I and

TABLE 2

ANALYSIS OF VARIANCE OF CORRECT RESPONSES ON LIST III (EXP. I)

Source	*df*	*MS*	*F*
Between *S*s	29		
Control groups (G)	2	2.98	<1.00
Error (b)	27	8.48	
Within *S*s	60		
Conditions (C)	2	78.88	28.89*
G × C	4	2.48	<1.00
Error (w)	54	2.73	
Total	89		

* $P < .001$.

II should have set up a tendency for the stimulus member of each interference pair in List III to elicit the response that was correct for the other pair. Thus, the hypothesized interference effects may be further tested by comparing the number of these within-set errors for the two interference pairs with the number that occurred for the two control pairs, the latter reflecting the chance frequency of such reversals. The mean number of reversals per *S* for the interference condition was 1.50 and for the control condition, .20. A related *t* test indicated that the mean difference was significant at the .001 level.

Thus, the results of Exp. I indicate clear-cut positive transfer with a mediating facilitation sequence. Significant overall negative transfer was not shown, but the interference condition produced significantly more within-set errors than did the control condition. This latter finding is consistent with the hypothesis that specific incorrect responses are mediated under the interference condition.

Experiment II

Experiment II was conducted to investigate further the interference effects due to the mediational sequence. It was thought that by increasing the number of pairs in the interference and control conditions and by omitting the facilitation condition, a significant overall negative transfer might be obtained for the interference condition. The apparatus was the same as that used in Exp. I. The stimulus materials were of the same type as those in Exp. I.

Method

Experimental design.—Each *S* learned three lists of stimulus-response pairs with six pairs of pictures per list, List I again being constructed of high association pairs. Table 3 illustrates the design. List III was composed of three control pairs and three pairs for which mediated interference was predicted. Thus, each *S* served in both the interference and control conditions.

TABLE 3

Schematic Illustration of the Design for Exp. II

List I		List II		List III	
S	*R*	*S*	*R*	*S*	*R*
1	7	7	13	1	14*
2	8	8	14	2	15*
3	9	9	15	3	13*
4	10	19	16	4	16**
5	11	20	17	5	17**
6	12	21	18	6	18**

* Pairs for which interference is predicted in List III.
** Control pairs in List III.

Subjects.—The *S*s were 24 first grade children.[3] Twelve *S*s were randomly assigned to each of two groups. These groups were designed to control for possible differential difficulty of the stimulus-response pairs in List III. Both groups were given identical forms of Lists I and III; the groups differed only with respect to which of two forms of List II they received. These two forms were constructed so that any given pair in List III would be a control pair for one group and an interference pair for the other.

Procedure.—The procedure for Exp. II was essentially the same as that for Exp. I. In order to adjust the difficulty of the tasks to the older first-grade *S*s, the anticipation interval was reduced from 6 sec. to 4 sec., and the joint presentation interval was reduced from 5 sec. to 2 sec.

Results and Discussion

The mean number of trials to criterion for all *S*s on List I was 1.67. The means of the number of trials for the two forms of List II did not differ significantly; the combined mean was 2.38. As in Exp. I, it should be noted that the pairs in List I were of highly associated items.

[3] Appreciation is expressed to Dr. Jerry Kuhn, Principal, University Elementary School, Iowa City, Iowa, for his permission to use the first grade class and for providing experimental facilities for Exp. II.

TABLE 4

ANALYSIS OF VARIANCE OF CORRECT RESPONSES ON LIST III (EXP. II)

Source	*df*	*MS*	*F*
Between *Ss*	23		
Control groups (G)	1	35.02	2.33
Error (b)	22	15.07	
Within *Ss*	24		
Conditions (C)	1	31.68	7.90*
G × C	1	2.53	<1.00
Error (w)	22	4.01	
Total	47		

* $P \approx .01$.

Table 4 presents a summary of the analysis of variance of correct anticipations in five trials on List III. The stimulus control groups did not differ significantly. The mean number of correct anticipations for all 24 *Ss* was 7.83 for the control condition and 6.21 for the interference condition. The difference is significant at about the 1% level.

As in Exp. I, the within-set errors were tabulated for the interference and control pairs. There were 37 such errors for the interference condition and only 9 for the control. The mean difference of 1.17 yields a *t* of 3.19 ($P < .01$).

Experiment II thus provides statistically significant evidence that the conditions designed to produce the mediation of incorrect responses result in overall negative transfer in learning List III. When both experiments are considered, it appears that, under appropriate conditions, both positive and negative associative transfer is a consequence of mediated associations.

It is of interest to compare the results of the present experiments with those of Bugelski and Scharlock (2). Their experiment is like these in that the mediational tendencies were experimentally manipulated. Their experimental condition corresponds to the facilitation condition of Exp. I, while their control condition is analogous to the interference conditions of Exp. I and II. They found no significant differences in the mean or median number of trials to criterion for the two conditions; a significant difference was found in the mean rank order of learning the pairs in the two conditions. In the present investigation, the use of a control condition, in which no mediational tendencies existed that did not also exist for the other conditions, permitted the separation of the facilitation and interference effects.

SUMMARY

This investigation proposed to study the effects of mediated associations on the positive and negative associative transfer in the paired-associate learning of kindergarten and first-grade *Ss*.

In Exp. I, a different list of six stimulus-response picture pairs was learned by each of 30 *Ss* on each of three days. The learning sequence was such that mediation would be expected to have facilitating, interfering, and no effects for each *S* in the learning of different pairs of List III. A statistically significant difference was found between the mean number of correct anticipations for the control and facilitation conditions during List III learning. The difference between the means for the control and interference conditions, although in the predicted direction, was not statistically significant.

In Exp. II, each of 24 *Ss* learned a different list of six stimulus-response picture pairs on each of three days. The first two lists were arranged so that, in the learning of List III, interference effects were predicted for three pairs relative to the other three pairs. A statistically significant difference was found in the mean number of correct anticipations for the interference and control conditions.

It was concluded that, under the appropriate conditions, mediated associations can produce both positive and negative associative transfer.

REFERENCES

1. BIRGE, J. The role of verbal responses in transfer. Unpublished doctor's dissertation, Yale Univer., 1941.
2. BUGELSKI, B. R., & SCHARLOCK, D. P. An experimental demonstration of unconscious mediated association. *J. exp. Psychol.*, 1952, **44**, 334–338.
3. EISMAN, B. S. Attitude formation: the development of a color-preference response through mediated generalization.

J. abnorm. soc. Psychol., 1955, **50**, 321–326.

4. Hull, C. L. The problem of stimulus equivalence in behavior theory. *Psychol. Rev.*, 1939, **46**, 9–30.
5. Irwin, Irl A. Associated facilitation as a function of the strength of the associative connection between first and second list response words. Unpublished doctor's dissertation, State Univer. Iowa, 1951.
6. Jeffrey, W. E. The effects of verbal and non-verbal responses in mediating an instrumental act. *J. exp. Psychol.*, 1953, **45**, 327–333.
7. Lindquist, E. F. *Design and analysis of experiments in psychology and education.* New York: Houghton Mifflin, 1953.
8. Murdock, B. B., Jr. Effects of failure and retroactive inhibition in mediating an instrumental act. *J. exp. Psychol.*, 1952, **44**, 156–164.
9. Peters, H. N. Mediate association. *J. exp. Psychol.*, 1935, **18**, 20–48.
10. Russell, W. A., & Storms, L. H. Implicit verbal chaining in paired-associate learning. *J. exp. Psychol.*, 1955, **49**, 287–293.
11. Shepard, W. O. Mediated generalization with high interstimulus similarity. Unpublished M.A. thesis, State Univer. Iowa, 1953.
12. Shipley, W. C. Indirect conditioning. *J. gen. Psychol.*, 1935, **12**, 337–357.

(Received February 11, 1957)

ARTICLE 3

Verbal Mediating Chains and Response Availability as a Function of the Acquisition Paradigm[1]

MARGARET JEAN PETERSON, FRANCIS B. COLAVITA, DREXEL B. SHEAHAN, III, AND KEITH C. BLATTNER

Department of Psychology, Indiana University, Bloomington, Indiana

Eight combinations of a three-stage mediation paradigm (A-B, B-C, A-C) are possible, as shown in Table 1. Paradigms I through IV have been identified as chaining models; Paradigms V and VI, as stimulus-equivalence models; and Paradigms VII and VIII, as response-equivalence models. The relevant experimental literature has been summarized by Horton and Kjeldergaard (1961) and Jenkins (1963). They reported that the paradigms have received varying amounts of experimental attention; however, most of the paradigms yielded positive evidence of mediation. Interestingly, no one paradigm appeared to induce consistently greater mediated facilitation than any other. In general, the equivalence paradigms produced facilitation. Cramer and Cofer (1960) and Horton and Kjeldergaard (1961) found approximately the same amount of mediated generalization for both stimulus (V, VI)- and response(VII, VIII)-equivalence models. Seidel (1962) reported facilitation with the stimulus-equivalence model V and the response-equivalence model VII, using two different measures.

The chaining models have not fared as well. Seidel (1962) found mediated facilitation with chaining models I and III; Horton and Kjeldergaard (1961), in the only study to in-

[1] These investigations were supported by research grant M 5209 from the National Institutes of Mental Health. Francis B. Colavita conducted Exp. I; Drexel B. Sheahan, III, Exp. II; and Keith C. Blattner, Exps. III and IV.

TABLE 1
THE EIGHT PARADIGMS

Stage		Paradigms: Chaining models I	II	III	IV
Acquisition	1	A-B	B-C	B-A	C-B
	Cue	A	B	B	C
	2	B-C	A-B	C-B	B-A
	Cue	B	A	C	B
Test		A-CDE	A-CDE	A-CDE	A-CDE
		Stimulus-Equivalence models V	VI	Response-Equivalence models VII	VIII
Acquisition	1	A-B	C-B	B-A	B-C
	Cue	A	C	B	B
	2	C-B	A-B	B-C	B-A
	Cue	C	A	B	B
Test		A-CDE	A-CDE	A-CDE	A-CDE

Reprinted with permission of the authors and the publisher, the Academic Press. The article appeared originally in the *Journal of Verbal Learning and Verbal Behavior*, 1964, **3,** 11–18.

vestigate all eight paradigms, reported facilitation for three of the chaining models (I, II, and IV) but not for Paradigm III. Using a chaining model (I) and a response-equivalence model (VII), Mink (1963) paired Kent-Rosanoff words and a simple motor response. The chaining model yielded evidence of mediated facilitation when the word associations were bidirectional but not when they were unidirectional, whereas the response-equivalence model showed generalization for unidirectional associations as well.

Thus the experimental literature suggested that the eight paradigms might not produce equivalent indices of mediational facilitation, although only minimal evidence of differences was found in the study which tested all eight paradigms (Horton and Kjeldergaard, 1961).

The present investigations were designed to test the eight paradigms by using a somewhat different experimental method than had been employed in the earlier studies. The meaningfulness of the materials was varied from experiment to experiment.

Experiment I

Method

Materials and Design. Consonant trigrams (CCCs) with association values of 0–33% (Underwood and Schulz, 1960) were used to construct the mediation sets (Table 1). A mediation set representing Paradigm I began with the first-stage presentation of a pair of consonant trigrams, A-B. Stimulus A was then shown alone on a cue-trial to test the retention of the preceding pair, and *S* was instructed to read off the stimulus and to give the response which had been paired with it on the previous presentation. In the second acquisition stage, the response term from the first pair, B, was shown as the stimulus with another trigram response term, C. The appropriate cue-trial, B, followed. In the test stage, the first stimulus trigram, A, was presented with the second-stage response, C, and two additional trigram response alternatives, D and E. The *S*s were instructed to pair verbally each of the response trigrams successively with the stimulus trigram, A, and then to select the response alternative which "seemed right or made the best pair" with stimulus A. The C response alternative was used 21 times in the first and in the third position among the alternatives on the test trials and was used 22 times in the second position. To equate frequency of experience with each of the test-trial alternatives over the entire group of sets, the D and E components for a particular set were C trigrams from other sets.

A control set was prepared for each mediation set by substituting a new, extraneous trigram for Stimulus B in the second-stage pair, X-C, providing a pool representing the Paradigm I format of 64 mediation sets and their respective 64 control sets.

The mediation and control sets for Paradigm I were then recast to conform with each of the other seven paradigms, yielding a total pool of 512 mediation sets and their 512 control sets. The consonant trigrams which served as A in the first set for Paradigm I was the A term for the first set for all of the other paradigms. Similarly, the B, C, D, E (and X for control) trigrams for a given set were identical for the eight paradigms so that the only difference which existed among the paradigmatic representations of different sets was the arrangement of the trigrams in the first two stages (Table 1). The materials were printed in capital letters 3/8 inches high on white, 4 × 6-inch index cards.

The experimental design was a 2 × 8 factorial with type of presentation (mediation vs. control) orthogonal to the paradigms (I, II, . . . , VIII). The resulting 16 cells were each represented 4 times among the 64 sets assigned to a particular *S*. Sixteen orders of randomized presentation of the sets were established. The *S*s were assigned to one of the 16 orders by means of a table of random numbers, subject to the restriction that 4 *S*s experience each order.

Subjects. The *S*s were 64 introductory psychology students at Indiana University who participated to fulfill a course requirement.

Procedure. S and *E* sat at a table. A screen shielded the stack of cards and the response sheet from *S*'s view. The *S*s were instructed to read aloud the letters of the trigram pairs. When only the first trigram was shown for a cue-trial, the *S*s read off the cue-trigram and then responded with the trigram that had previously been paired with the trigram on the card. If *S* erred on a cue-trial, he was shown the preceding pair again, then the cue, etc., until he responded correctly on the cue-trial. On test trials, the *S* read the A trigram with each of the response alternatives, and then stated which of the response alternatives "seemed right or made the best pair" with the A trigram.

Following two practice trials which used all different CCC trigrams in all stages, *S*s were shown the assigned 64 sets. The *S*s were asked how they selected the response to pair with A and dismissed.

Results and Discussion

The mean number of selections of C on the test trials for the two types of presentation mediation and control) and for the eight paradigms are shown in Table 2. The 16 orders of presentation were not reliably different, nor were any of the interactions involving order significant. The factor of order was therefore ignored in later analyses.

TABLE 2
MEAN NUMBERS OF SELECTIONS OF C ON TEST TRIALS; EXPERIMENTS I AND II

	Exp. I, CCCs		Exp. II, CVCs	
Paradigm	Med.	Cont.	Med.	Cont.
I	2.55	2.38	2.95	2.86
II	2.00	1.92	3.08	2.73[b]
III	1.92	1.84	2.91	2.75[a]
IV	1.94	1.77	2.61	2.61
V	1.84	1.84	2.95	2.80
VI	1.94	1.69[b]	2.53	2.23[b]
VII	2.72	2.36[b]	3.14	2.91[b]
VIII	2.25	1.81[b]	2.89	2.39[b]

[a] $p < 0.05$
[b] $p < 0.01$

Generally, more selections of the C alternative were made on test trials following mediation presentation than were made on test trials following control presentation, $F\ (1, 48) = 6.70$, $p < 0.05$, indicating that mediated facilitation had been obtained. In addition, the paradigms yielded reliably different numbers of selections of C on the test trials, $F\ (7, 336) = 11.79$, $p < 0.001$. The F for the Type of Presentation by Paradigm interaction term was less than unity, but inspection of the means in Table 2 suggested that not all the paradigms showed mediated facilitation. Consequently, the differences between individual treatment means were evaluated by the Newman-Kuels procedure (Winer, 1962). Reliable evidence of mediated facilitation was found for one stimulus-equivalence paradigm (VI, $p < 0.05$) and for the two response-equivalence paradigms (VII, $p < 0.01$, and VIII, $p < 0.01$). The other stimulus-equivalence paradigm (V), which did not show facilitation, was associated with approximately the same mean number of C selections following mediation presentation as was VI, but the mean number of C selections following control presentation was reliably greater for V than for VI ($p < 0.01$; Newman-Kuels).

The experimental technique also permitted comparison of the observed frequency of selection of C on the test trials following control presentation with an expected chance level of selection of C. Presumably, if no experience with the C item preceded its presentation as a test-trial alternative, the probability of selection of C would be 0.33. If the observed probability reliably exceeded 0.33, it seemed reasonable to asume that the experience with C during the acquisition stage had a sensitizing effect which fostered the selection of C as the favored test-trial alternative. This factor (response availability) had been noted previously when the same general experimental technique was employed (Peterson and Blattner, 1963). Deviations from the expected chance mean were evaluated for control presentations of each paradigm in the present experiment. The t-tests were significant beyond the 0.01 level, each with 63 df, which suggests the presence of a response-availability factor for each paradigm.

Since the enhancement of the test appearance of C appeared to have resulted from the recency of its acquisition-stage presentation, the following predictions were made: If the level of selections of C on the test trials following control presentation were predictable from the temporal separation existing between the acquisition stage and the test-trial appearance of the C item, I and VII would be expected to show the highest rate of control responding because C was the second-stage response; II and III would be next; then V and VIII, and lastly, IV and VI. When C was in the same position for two paradigms, e.g., I and VII, selection of C on the test trial of the control condition should be approximately the same for both paradigms. The obtained order was I, VII, II, III, V, VIII, IV, and VI. I and VII differed reliably from the others but not from each other. II was reliably above VI but did not differ significantly from III, V, VIII, and IV. V through VI did not differ. The Spearman rank-order correlation coefficient corrected for tied ranks was 0.88, which is significant beyond the 0.01 level. Predictions based on the proximity existing between the two presentations of C appeared to be related to the observed differences among paradigms in test-trial responding following control presentation.

Other factors which might produce paradigmatic differences have been discussed by Horton and Kjeldergaard (1961). Their associative model for mediated generalization took into account the directionality of habit chains and the contiguity existing between implicit and explicit members of the chain during both acquisition and test stages. They assumed that once a stimulus-response association had been formed, subsequent presentations of either the stimulus or of the response would tend to elicit the other member of the association. The tendency would be stronger for forward associations (stimulus-response) than for backward associations (response-stimulus). Using Paradigm I as an example, if the A-B association was learned during Stage 1, any later presentation of B would tend to elicit A although to a lesser extent than a later presentation of A would tend to elicit B. When B-C was presented during Stage 2, both the explicit term B and the implicit term A would be associated with the explicit term C. Then when A was encountered during the test stage, the association with C would be in the forward direction as learned during Stage 2, and the likelihood of observing mediated facilitation on the test trial would be increased over a situation in which the paradigmatic presentation fostered the learning of a backward association, C-A, during Stage 2. Recently, Horton and Hartman (1963) reported that Paradigm I (forward association) was superior to Paradigm IV (backward association) for both of two response measures. However, no control condition was run to permit an estimation of mediated facilitation per se.

An examination of the paradigms in Table 1 indicated that forward associations would be acquired with Paradigms I, II, VI, and VII, and backward associations with Paradigms III, IV, V, and VIII. The mean number of selections of C on test trials following mediation presentation for the first four paradigms (2.30) reliably exceeded the mean for the second set of four paradigms (1.99) at the 0.01 level, suggesting that the direction of the A-C association probably established during Stage 2 may have influenced test trial responding following mediation presentation.

Horton and Kjeldergaard (1961) also considered the temporal contiguity existing between the implicit and explicit terms. If the implicit term were elicited by the first explicit term presented during Stage 2, it would be temporally closer to the explicit term used as the Stage 2 response term than if it had been elicited by the response term. For Paradigm I, the expected order during Stage 2 would be explicit B, implicit A, explicit C. For Paradigm II, the order would be explicit A, explicit B, implicit C. In both cases the A-C association would be in the forward direction, but the interval separating the A and C items would be longer for Paradigm II than for Paradigm I. The prediction was made that mediated facilitation would be inversely related to the duration of the temporal interval separating the A and the C items during Stage 2. The mean of the paradigms with a minimal A-C interval in Stage 2 (I, IV, VII, VIII = 2.36) was expected to be greater than that of the paradigms with a greater interval between A and C (II, III, V, and VI = 1.93). The difference was reliable at the 0.01 level by the Newman-Kuels procedure. It should be noted that the temporal interval presumed to affect the establishment of a mediational chain involved the hypothetical linkage of A and C during the second acquisition stage, whereas the interval responsible for the variations in response availability indices separated the acquisition and test-trial presentations of C.

The same analyses were used to assess the influence of directionality and contiguity on mediated facilitation (the difference between selections of C on the test trials following mediation and following control presentation). The mean for the paradigms with forward associations was 0.22, and for the paradigms with backward associations, 0.18. This difference was not reliable, but the difference between paradigms with relatively contiguous occurrences of A and C during Stage 2 (0.28) and those with temporally diverse occurrences (0.10) was reliable beyond the 0.05 level.

Examination of the answers given by the *S*s to the post-experimental interrogation did not provide additional insight into the variables which might have operated to produce the differences among the paradigms. None of the *S*s indicated awareness of the experimental paradigms; rather, they said that one of the response alternatives had sounded better, contained some of the letters they had seen previously, or represented some other kind of idiosyncratic association.

Discrepancies between the results of the present study and earlier work summarized above may have resulted from gross differences in the methods of presentation, in the levels of meaningfulness of the learning materials, in the type of statistical design used, or from a combination of factors.

Experiment II was conducted to replicate Exp. I and to yield some information about the relative effects of meaningfulness of the materials. Peterson and Blattner (1963) found that both mediation and control responding increased when consonant-vowel-consonant trigrams (CVCs) of 100% association value were used instead of the CCC trigrams of low association value.

Experiment II

Method

Materials. The materials were prepared and presented in exactly the same way as in Exp. I, except that 100% association value CVCs (Underwood and Schulz, 1960) were used. The instructions were changed to identify the materials as nonsense syllables.

Subjects. The *S*s were 64 introductory psychology students at Indiana University. None of the *S*s had participated in Exp. I.

Results and Discussion

Means for the two types of presentation for each paradigm appear in Table 2. Mediated facilitation was shown by the greater mean number of selections of C following mediation than control presentation, F (1, 48) $= 16.11$, $p < 0.001$. The mean responses associated with the different paradigms varied reliably, F (7, 336) $= 8.43$, $p < 0.001$. In addition, lists were reliably different, F (15, 48) $= 2.24$, $p < 0.05$, but none of the interactions involving lists was reliable, nor did inspection of the data suggest any interactions between lists and the other variables; this factor was therefore ignored in further evaluations.

The difference between mediation and control presentation was tested for each paradigm by the Newman-Kuels procedure. Paradigms VIII, II, VI, VII, and III yielded evidence of mediated facilitation in order of decreasing magnitude. Thus VIII showed the most facilitation with both CCCs and CVCs. VII and VI also exhibited reliable evidence of mediation for both types of learning materials, whereas II and III gave such evidence only when CVCs were the learning materials. In neither experiment did I, IV, or V yield mediated facilitation. Other investigators demonstrated positive results for the latter with somewhat different techniques of stimulus presentation.

Reliable indices of response availability

were found for control presentation of each paradigm as in Exp. I, and the ordering of test-trial selections of C following control presentation conformed to the order predicted on the basis of the temperal interval existing between the acquisition- and test-stage presentations of C: VII, I, V, III, II, IV, VIII, VI. The Spearman rank-order correlation coefficient corrected for tied ranks with the predicted order was 0.91, $p < 0.01$.

The effectiveness of the directionality of the A-C linkage in Stage 2 was evaluated by comparing the mediation presentation mean of I, II, VI, and VII (2.92) with the mean of III, IV, V, and VIII (2.84). The difference was not statistically significant; neither was a comparison designed to evaluate the importance of the temporal contiguity of A and C during Stage 2 by a comparison of the mean for mediation presentation of I, IV, VII, and VIII (2.90) with the mean of II, III, V, and VI (2.87). This result is in contrast to the data obtained with CCCs. Analyses of the difference scores used to index mediated facilitation yielded the same results.

The results of the first two experiments suggested that increased meaningfulness of the learning materials was conducive to mediated facilitation in more of the paradigms. Contiguity of the likely A-C association in Stage 2 appeared to be related to the establishment of mediational chains with CCCs but not with CVCs. The influence of directionality was more ambiguous but also tended to be reduced when more meaningful materials were used. If these factors assume less weight as the meaningfulness of the materials increases, then even paradigms with backward associations and maximal A-C separations in Stage 2 might be expected to show mediated generalization if highly meaningful materials were used to construct the sets. Indeed, Cramer and Cofer (1960) reported that the stimulus-equivalence paradigm V, which is characterized by both a backward association and a maximal A-C separation during Stage 2, yielded mediated facilitation when Kent-Rosanoff words were used as the learning materials. In all comparable cases for the present experiments, the CVCs of Exp. II were associated with more selections of C on the test trials than were the CCC sets of Exp. I.

It was possible that two confounding effects might have been produced by the experimental design used in Exps. I and II. The mediational facilitation shown for Paradigms VI, VII, and VIII might have resulted from increased frequency of presentation of the pairs in the acquisition stages, since a pair was reshown if *S* erred on the cue-trial. The possibility seemed particularly plausible for Paradigms VII and VIII, the traditional paradigms for investigating negative transfer. Paradigm VI would have been expected to show positive transfer effects. However, differences in the numbers of errors made during acquisition presentations of each of the paradigms were minimal, as shown by *F*'s of less than unity for both experiments. Variations in the frequency of presentations in the acquisition stages did not appear to be confounded with the observed paradigmatic differences in mediated facilitation.

Intermixed presentation of both types of presentation and the eight paradigms among the sets shown to each *S* might have produced interference effects which tended to camouflage mediational facilitation. To explore this possibility, one paradigm was used alone in two experiments. Paradigm II was chosen because it yielded negative results in Exp. I and positive results in Exp. II. CCCs were employed in Exp. III, and CVCs in Exp. IV.

Experiments III and IV

Method

Materials. Thirty-six mediation sets and their controls were prepared to conform to Paradigm II. CCCs of low association values were taken from the materials of Exp. I to be the trigrams in Exp. III, and CVCs were taken from the sets used in Exp. II to construct the materials for Exp. IV. All details followed the procedures specified previously. Exp. IV was conducted after Exp. III so *S*s were not assigned randomly to the two experiments.

Subjects. The *S*s for each experiment were 36 introductory psychology students at Indiana University. None of the *S*s participated in more than one of the four experiments.

Results and Discussion

The mean numbers of selections of C on the test trials following mediation and following control presentation for the CCCs of Exp. III were 6.61 and 6.46, respectively. The difference between the means was not reliable, substantiating the results of Exp. I. In contrast, the means for the CVCs of Exp. IV were 10.11 following mediation presentation and 9.33 following control. This difference was reliable at the 0.01 level, confirming the data of Exp. II. Generally, the selections of C on the test trials for CVCs exceeded those for CCCs.

The conclusion was drawn that the differences in the amount of mediated facilitation under the various paradigms in Exps. I and II probably were stable phenomena and did not arise from some artifacts in the experimental design. Additionally, the increases in mediation associated with more meaningful material may reflect a reduction in the importance of the contiguity of the A-C linkage (within restricted limits, presumably) occurring during stage 2 and in the direction of the A-C association.

Summary

Eight mediation paradigms were evaluated by comparing test-trial responses following mediation presentation with test-trial responses following control presentation. CCCs of low association value were used as the learning materials in one experiment, and CVCs of 100% association value in a second experiment. Response-equivalence paradigms and one stimulus-equivalence paradigm yielded mediated facilitation with both types of learning materials. When CVCs were used, two chaining models also showed mediated facilitation. Forward associations and minimal temporal separation of the A and C items, as they probably existed implicitly and explicitly during the second acquisition stage, led to mediated facilitation only when CCCs were the learning materials. With more meaningful materials these two variables were considerably less potent.

Two additional experiments were performed to replicate the results of Paradigm II, which yielded negative results in Exp. I and positive results in Exp. II. The data corroborated the earlier conclusions that mediated facilitation was more likely to be observed with learning materials of higher meaningfulness.

Selections of C as the test-trial alternative which made the "best pair" with the stimulus were reliably above an *a priori* chance level for all paradigms. In addition, the eight paradigms showed significant differences in this factor (response availability) which seemed to be predictable from the temporal interval separating presentation of C in the acquisition stages and its appearance of a test-trial alternative.

References

Cramer, P., and Cofer, C. N. The role of forward and reverse associations in transfer of training. *Amer. Psychologist,* 1960, **15**, 463.

Horton, D. L., and Hartman, R. R. Verbal mediation as a function of associative directionality and exposure frequency. *J. verb. Learn. verb. Behav.*, 1963, **1**, 361-364.

Horton, D. L., and Kjeldergaard, P. M. An experimental analysis of associative factors in mediated generalization. *Psychol. Monogr.*, 1961, **75**, No. 11.

Jenkins, J. J. Mediated associations: Paradigms and situations. In C. N. Cofer and Barbara S. Musgrave (Eds.), *Verbal behavior and learning: Problems and processes.* New York: McGraw-Hill, 1963. Pp. 210-245.

Mink, W. D. Semantic generalization as related to word association. *Psychol. Rep.*, 1963, **12**, 59-67.

Peterson, M. J., and Blattner, K. C. The development of a verbal mediator. *J. exp. Psychol.*, 1963, **66**, 72-77.

Seidel, R. J. The importance of the S-R role of the verbal mediator in mediate association. *Canad. J. Psychol.*, 1962, **16**, 170-176.

Underwood, B. J., and Schulz, R. W. *Meaningfulness and verbal learning*. Philadelphia: Lippincott, 1960.

Winer, B. J. *Statistical principles in experimental design*. New York: McGraw-Hill, 1962.

(Received June 20, 1963)

ARTICLE 4

The Effects of Meaningfulness, Awareness, and Type of Design in Verbal Mediation[1]

DAVID L. HORTON

University of Kentucky, Lexington, Kentucky

During the past several years a great deal of experimental evidence has been accumulated concerning the phenomena of mediate association. The findings that have been reported leave little doubt concerning the reality of mediational effects and the wide variety of situations in which they can be observed (Jenkins, 1959; Horton and Kjeldergaard, 1961; Goss, 1961a, b). However, the majority of investigations reported thus far have been primarily concerned with the demonstration of mediation, and relatively little attention has been paid to those variables which may influence the degree of effects that can be obtained (cf. Jenkins, 1963).

Although there is undoubtedly a number of factors of potential relevance to verbal mediation, the selection of variables for the present investigation was largely determined by an interest in the variations in performance that could be obtained in a mediation situation without the introduction of "real" language associations. Within this framework particular attention was focused on those variables which appeared likely to produce in the *S* an awareness of the mediational relationship. It was reasoned that the aware *S*, particularly in view of the findings reported in the verbal conditioning literature (e.g., Dulany, 1962; Spielberger, 1962), should tend to generate maximum mediational effects within the limits imposed by the experimental conditions. In addition, the extent to which mediation effects could be produced by unaware *S*s was also of interest.

One variable which appeared to be especially relevant to the production of mediational effects in addition to *S* awareness was the meaningfulness of the common element. Although the research literature dealing with meaningfulness does not clearly specify the contribution of this variable to learning as opposed to performance, there can be little doubt about its general importance in the paired-associate case (Underwood and Schulz, 1960; Noble, 1963). In a mediation context variations in meaningfulness of the common term could increase facilitative effects either by producing stronger associations during the learning stages or by increasing the availability of the mediator during the test stage. In either case a likely result would be an increase in *S* awareness.

A second variable related to awareness effects was first observed by the writer in an earlier investigation (Horton and Hartman, 1963). This experiment involved a comparison of two mediation paradigms without the inclusion of separate control pairs. During the course of the experiment it was noted that several *S*s were aware of the mediational relation although they were apparently unaware of the differences between the paradigms. Since the absence of control pairs represented the only difference between this situation and previous ones in which awareness was not observed (cf. Horton and Kjeldergaard, 1961), this variation appeared to be a good

[1] This research was supported by a grant from the National Science Foundation. The author is indebted to Rosemary R. Hartman and Andree J. Lloyd for assistance in data collection and analysis.

Reprinted with permission of the author and the publisher, the Academic Press. The article appeared originally in the *Journal of Verbal Learning and Verbal Behavior*, 1964, 3, 187–194.

choice for further investigation. An additional but equally important consequence of this variation in design is that the exclusion of nonmediational control items makes it possible for the *S* to be reinforced for mediating on all test-stage pairs. This is in distinct contrast to the usual split-plot arrangement in which the *S* is reinforced for mediating on half of the pairs and for not mediating on the remaining pairs. In addition to the reinforcement difference the split-plot design presents the *S* with a discrimination problem in which both facilitation and interference effects are likely to be strong.

The two remaining factors included in the present investigation were learning ability of the *S*s and type of paradigm. The variable of learning ability was selected in order to examine the possibility, suggested by Horton and Kjeldergaard (1961), that learning speed may determine to some degree the magnitude of mediational effects. In addition, it seemed likely that learning ability and awareness would be related. The variation in paradigm was included to test an indication from previous, unpublished data that the relation between learning speed and mediation would interact with paradigm.

Since there was considerable doubt as to whether awareness could be obtained in a mediational setting (cf. Bugelski and Scharlock, 1952; Russell and Storms, 1955; Mednick and Freedman, 1960; Horton and Kjeldergaard, 1961), it was decided to conduct the present investigation in two parts. The first experiment was intended to maximize the likelihood of obtaining awareness while the second experiment was focused more exclusively on variables affecting the magnitude of the mediation effect.

Experiment I

This experiment was intended to provide a test of the effects of learning ability, meaningfulness of the mediating term, and paradigm in a situation in which the stimulus and response members of every test-stage pair had previously been associated with a common term.

Method

Two paradigms were used in this investigation: I: A-B, B-C, A-C; VII: B-A, B-C, A-C.[2] These paradigms are typically referred to as "simple chaining" and "acquired response equivalence," respectively. Each paradigm was tested under two levels of meaningfulness, and within each meaningfulness level the *S*s were divided into fast and slow learners.

The division of *S*s into fast and slow learners was accomplished by cutting the distribution of scores on a revised form of Part V of the Modern Language Aptitude Test (MLAT) (Carroll and Sapon, 1958) at the median. The original form of this test has been shown to predict paired-associate learning quite well (Kjeldergaard, 1962). The test was administered to a pool of introductory psychology students during a regular class period with the reduced time limits suggested by Kjeldergaard (1962).

The A and C terms of both paradigms were CVC syllables ranging from 70 to 80% association value according to the Krueger norms (see Underwood and Schulz, 1960). The common or mediating (B) terms were selected from the extremes of Noble's (1952) scale of dissyllables. A single random combination of pairings was employed in accordance with the structure of each paradigm. The terms used and the pairings are given in Table 1.

TABLE 1
LEARNING MATERIALS FOR HIGH MEANINGFULNESS (HM) AND LOW MEANINGFULNESS (LM) CONDITIONS

List A	List B-HM	List B-LM	List C
JAV	DINNER	DAVIT	FAW
FOM	WAGON	RENNET	VAD
CEB	OFFICE	NEGLAN	PIM
VOS	MONEY	KAYSEN	BIQ
HIG	ARMY	VOLVAP	NOF
BAZ	KITCHEN	WELKIN	TEP
DAK	JEWEL	TUMBRIL	CUN
NUD	HEAVEN	POLEF	GOK

The learning materials were presented by means of a Lafayette Model 303B memory drum. All letters were typed in pica capitals. The materials to be learned were exposed to the *S*s in the following order: stimulus term alone, 2 sec.; stimulus and response terms together, 2 sec.; no inter-pair or inter-trial interval was employed; five randomizations of each list of pairs were used to prevent serial learning.

[2] Paradigm numbers correspond to those used by Jenkins (1963).

Seventy-two students (28 men and 44 women) enrolled in introductory psychology classes served as *Ss*. Assignment of *Ss* to conditions was made at random in accordance with the *S*'s order of appearance for the experiment. Nine *Ss* were assigned to each combination of paradigm, meaningfulness level, and learning-ability level.

The procedure followed that of Horton and Kjeldergaard (1961), with the exception that the learning criterion employed for stages 1 and 2 was two errorless trials instead of three. In addition, the *Ss* were run for a total of five trials on the third or test stage of the experiment. The instructions were essentially the same as those typically employed with the paired-associate method of anticipation, although the *Ss* were required to pronounce both the stimulus and response terms in all stages of the experiment.

The evaluation of *S* awareness was made following the test stage of the experiment. Each *S* was asked the following question: "Did you notice any relation between the pairs you just completed and the ones you learned earlier in the experiment?" Those *Ss* indicating awareness in reply to the initial question were asked to explain whatever relations they had observed. If an *S* indicated no awareness the paradigm was illustrated with test materials and the *S* was again asked if he had noticed any relationship between the three stages. The *Ss* were then divided into three categories on the basis of their replies. Category 1 included those *Ss* who indicated no recognition of *any* relation between the three stages in response to either question. Category 2 comprised *Ss* who said that the stages were related but they either could not specify the relationships adequately or seemed confused about them. The *Ss* in this category were quite variable in their replies. At one extreme *Ss* would correctly state the paradigm but could not illustrate it. These *Ss* also stated that they had not made use of the relations. At the other extreme were *Ss* who indicated that some words were used more than once but could not specify anything further. The remaining *Ss* (Category 3) were able to specify the mediational relation and illustrate it with actual experimental materials. In addition, these *Ss* indicated an attempt to use the perceived relations.

Results

The dependent variable employed in this experiment was the number of correct anticipations on the five trials of the test stage. The mean values obtained for the eight conditions are reported in Table 2.

Analysis of variance indicated that the main effect of meaningfulness was significant beyond the 0.01 level ($F = 11.02$, $df = 1/64$). In addition, since meaningfulness and paradigm did not interact significantly ($F < 1.00$), it is clear that differences in meaningfulness of the common element resulted in differences in mediated facilitation or interference for both paradigms.

TABLE 2

MEAN NUMBER OF CORRECT ANTICIPATIONS FOR EACH COMBINATION OF PARADIGM, MEANINGFULNESS, AND LEARNING ABILITY

	Meaningfulness			
	High		Low	
Paradigm	Fast *Ss*	Slow *Ss*	Fast *Ss*	Slow *Ss*
I	23.55	13.00	18.35	9.10
VII	24.20	10.35	13.80	7.80

Examination of the learning-ability variable showed the main effect to be significant beyond the 0.01 level ($F = 35.45$, $df = 1/64$) and *t*-tests (each with $df = 34$) indicated that all comparisons between fast and slow learners, within paradigm by meaningfulness combinations, were significant at the 0.05 level or beyond ($ts \geqslant 2.76$). This finding, of course, has no necessary implications for mediation effects, and can only be interpreted as a further indication of the adequacy of the revised MLAT for predicting paired-associate learning.[3] This conclusion is also supported by the failure of any interaction to approach a statistically significant level.

The data concerning the awareness variable are presented in Table 3. Two aspects of these findings were examined. First, chi-square tests were performed to determine the effects of meaningfulness and of learning ability on the degree of awareness. These analyses indicated that meaningfulness exerts a highly significant effect on awareness ($\chi^2 = 35.30$, $df = 2$, $p < 0.001$) but learning ability does not ($\chi^2 = 2.18$, $df = 2$). Secondly, *t*-tests were per-

[3] Correlations between revised MLAT scores and trials to criterion on stage 1 for both Experiments I and II ranged from -0.39 to -0.71 with a median of -0.57.

TABLE 3
NUMBER OF *Ss* AND MEAN CORRECT ANTICIPATIONS FOR THREE LEVELS OF AWARENESS BY EXPERIMENTAL CONDITION[a]

	Condition					
	All *Ss*		High M *Ss*		Fast *Ss*	
Awareness	*N*	Mean	*N*	Mean	*N*	Mean
1.0	29	11.34	3	8.67	14	16.29
2.0	12	8.75	6	6.33	4	9.75
3.0	31	20.87	27	21.33	18	25.11

[a] Values for Low M and Slow Learners can be obtained by subtraction.

formed to determine the relationship between awareness and number of correct anticipations. For all *Ss* *t*-tests showed that the number of correct anticipations for Category 3 *Ss* was significantly different from either Category 1 *Ss* ($t = 4.89$, $df = 58$, $p < 0.01$) or Category 2 *Ss* ($t = 5.03$, $df = 41$, $p < 0.01$), although Category 1 and Category 2 did not differ significantly ($t = 1.09$, $df = 39$). Similar results were obtained for the various breakdowns. While these findings are suggestive it would seem premature to attempt any interpretation before examining the results of the second experiment.

EXPERIMENT II

This experiment was designed as a further test of the major independent variables in a situation involving both mediation and control pairs, thus providing a baseline condition against which mediation effects could be compared.

Method

The conditions of this experiment were identical to those of Experiment I with the following modifications: (1) a split-plot design was employed; (2) as control words 4 additional dissyllables were selected from Noble's (1952) list at each end of the meaningfulness range (CAPTAIN, REGION, INSECT, GARMENT—DELPHIN, GAMIN, ULNA, ATTAR). These words were substituted for the appropriate common terms in the second stage of the experiment; (3) four test-stage pairs were selected at random as mediation pairs for half of the *Ss*. The remaining pairs served as mediation pairs for the other half of the *Ss*; (4) the *Ss* were run for a total of 10 trials on the test stage. In all other respects the design and procedure followed that of Experiment I.

Eighty *Ss* (34 men and 46 women), 10 per combination of paradigm, learning ability level, and meaningfulness level, were drawn from introductory psychology classes. The cutting score on the revised MLAT was the same as that used in Experiment I.

Results

The mean number of correct anticipations for mediation pairs (E), control pairs (C), and E-C on the first five trials of the test stage are given in Table 4.[4] Analysis of variance indicated that the between-*Ss* meaningfulness effect was significant at the 0.05 level ($F = 5.13$, $df = 1/72$) and the effect of learning ability (i.e., revised MLAT score) was significant at the 0.01 level ($F = 19.89$, $df = 1/72$). These findings essentially replicate those of Experiment I.

On the within-*Ss* comparisons, analysis of variance indicated a significant mediation effect ($F = 17.37$, $df = 1/72$, $p < 0.01$) and a significant interaction between meaningfulness and mediation ($F = 4.78$, $df = 1/72$, $p < 0.05$). The latter finding of course reflects the stronger mediation effect obtained with the more meaningful common term. In fact, individual comparisons showed that the mediation effect was only significant for the high-meaningfulness condition (HM: $t = 4.45$, $df = 39$, $p < 0.01$; LM: $t = 0.60$, $df = 39$). However, the mediation effect under low meaningfulness approached significance for ten trials ($t = 1.46$, $df = 39$, $p < 0.08$ one-tailed). It is also of interest to note that the learning-ability variable did not interact

[4] The results for 5 and 10 trials did not differ significantly.

TABLE 4
MEAN NUMBER OF CORRECT ANTICIPATIONS ON MEDIATION PAIRS (E), CONTROL PAIRS (C), AND E-C FOR EACH COMBINATION OF PARADIGM, MEANINGFULNESS (M), AND LEARNING ABILITY

	Paradigm							
	I				VII			
Test	High M		Low M		High M		Low M	
Pair	Fast *S*s	Slow *S*s	Fast *S*s	Slow *S*s	Fast *S*s	Slow *S*s	Fast *S*s	Slow *S*s
E	10.5	4.7	6.9	3.4	10.0	6.5	4.7	2.1
C	6.3	4.2	5.0	3.3	4.4	3.3	4.6	2.8
E-C	4.2	0.5	1.9	0.1	5.6	3.2	0.1	—0.7

TABLE 5
NUMBER OF *S*s AND MEAN CORRECT ANTICIPATIONS ON MEDIATION PAIRS (E) AND DIFFERENCE BETWEEN MEDIATION AND CONTROL PAIRS (E-C) FOR EACH LEVEL OF AWARENESS BY EXPERIMENTAL CONDITION[a]

	Condition								
	All *S*s			High M *S*s			Fast *S*s		
Awareness	*N*	E	E-C	*N*	E	E-C	*N*	E	C-C
1.0	42	3.62	—0.33	10	3.70	—1.00	16	5.38	0.43
2.0	19	6.16	2.26[c]	13	7.15	3.08[b]	10	6.50	2.60[b]
3.0	19	11.53	6.32[c]	17	11.00	6.29[c]	14	12.14	6.07[c]

[a] Values for Low M and Slow Learners can be obtained by subtraction.
[b] $p < 0.05$
[c] $p < 0.01$

significantly with either mediation ($F = 1.50$, $df = 1/72$) or meaningfulness ($F = 0.50$, $df = 1/72$). Thus, learning ability seems to be related to learning speed but not to mediation.

The data concerning awareness are reported in Table 5. Chi-square tests indicated a significant difference in awareness due to meaningfulness level ($\chi^2 = 25.94$, $df = 2$, $p < 0.001$) and learning ability ($\chi^2 = 6.68$, $df = 2$, $p < 0.05$) with fast learners and *S*s under high meaningfulness showing greater awareness.

The effects of awareness on mediation score as well as E and C scores were evaluated by means of *t*-tests. It can readily be seen from Table 5 that the mediation effect increases with increases in awareness for the classifications presented. In all cases both the marginally aware (Category 2) and the fully aware (Category 3) *S*s show a significant mediational effect while the unaware *S*s do not. In addition, individual comparisons indicate that the three awareness groups differ significantly from one another on mediation score for all *S* classifications ($ts \geqslant 2.20$, $ps < 0.05$). Similar differences were obtained between awareness levels when correct anticipations on the mediation pairs were examined separately ($ts \geqslant 2.57$, $ps < 0.05$). However, Categories 1 and 2 only differed significantly when all *S*s were considered. When the number of correct anticipations on control pairs was examined no significant differences were obtained between awareness levels under any *S* classification. Thus, it appears that awareness is only related to the learning of mediation pairs.

In order to obtain an indication of the effect of control pairs in the test list the data from Experiments I and II were compared in the following manner. First, chi-square tests were performed to determine the effect of this variable on awareness. These analyses (see Tables 3 and 5 for the raw data) indicated a significantly higher level of awareness when only mediation pairs were employed ($\chi^2 = 6.43$, $df = 2$, $p < 0.05$). Furthermore, this increase in awareness appeared in the high-meaningfulness condition ($\chi^2 = 8.78$, $df = 2$, $p < 0.05$) and with the slow learners ($\chi^2 = 6.41$, $df = 2$, $p < 0.05$) but not in the low-meaningfulness condition ($\chi^2 = 1.14$, df $= 2$) or with the fast learners ($\chi^2 = 2.84$, $df = 2$). Second, the number of correct anticipations on the test stage of Experiment I was compared with twice the number of correct anticipations on the mediation pairs of Experiment II. Analysis of variance on these data indicated a significant difference in favor of the all-mediation-pair condition ($F = 8.84$, $df = 1/128$, $p < 0.01$). None of the interactions were significant. In addition, the advantage for the all-mediation-pair condition appeared despite the fact that the *S*s in this condition were significantly slower on the first learning stage ($F = 5.32$, $df = 1/128$, $p < 0.05$).

Discussion

The results of the present investigation clearly indicate the importance of several factors in the mediation situation. Since the major experimental variables were found to be related to both awareness and the mediation effect, the findings can be most appropriately discussed by examining the effects of the experimental variables prior to a consideration of the relationship between awareness and mediation.

Variables That Influence Mediation. It is apparent from the results presented here that variations in meaningfulness of the common term and the type of design employed are significantly related to mediated association. The meaningfulness effect, which is located solely in the mediator, may be viewed as a consequence of stronger associative connections developed during the learning stages or of greater response learning of the mediator. In either case, the mediator should be more readily available in the test stage under conditions of high meaningfulness than under low meaningfulness. This difference in availability, which may be simply a variation in response latency, could also account for the somewhat unusual weakness of the mediation effect under low meaningfulness. In any case, the present findings are indicative of an extremely important role for the meaningfulness variable even in a situation in which it does not function as an overt stimulus or response. In addition, the meaningfulness effect provides further support for the reality of mediated association and indicates the operation of an important variable in the mediation process.

The effect of the variation in type of design can probably be attributed to the difference in the tasks presented to the *S*s. In the all-mediation-pair condition the *S* is presented a homogeneous test list in which reinforcement for mediating is possible on every pair. However, in the split-plot situation the *S* can be reinforced for both mediating (on E pairs) and not mediating (on C pairs) and, until the *S* discriminates when to mediate and when not to, interference effects are likely to be particularly strong. The interpretation that the difference between the two designs is primarily due to stronger interference effects in the split-plot situation is consistent with the finding that *S*s perform better on mediation pairs in the all-mediation-pair condition than in the half-mediation-pair condition. In addition, the importance of facilitative effects in mediation is supported by the observation that good (Category 3) and poor (Category 1) mediators in Experiment II only differed significantly in correct anticipations on the mediation pairs.

Two additional factors, learning ability of the *S*s and type of paradigm, did not significantly affect the mediation score. However, it should be noted that point estimates indicated that fast learners were superior to slow learners and the effects obtained with the response-equivalence paradigm were greater than those obtained with the chaining paradigm. The latter observation is consistent with previous studies (Cramer and Cofer, 1960; Horton and Kjeldergaard, 1961).

Variables That Influence Awareness. The

results of Experiments I and II indicate that variations in meaningfulness of the common term, type of design, and learning ability produce significant differences in awareness of the mediational relations. The effect of meaningfulness was significant in both experiments but greater awareness was observed among *S*s under high meaningfulness when the test stage contained only mediation pairs. The variation in type of design also appeared to influence the relation between learning ability and awareness since learning ability was significantly related to awareness only when both mediation and control pairs were employed. The data further indicated that this interaction was due to less awareness on the part of slow learners when mediation and control pairs were both used in the test stage. These findings support the contention that degree of awareness can be significantly influenced by experimental conditions and is not entirely a matter of individual differences among *S*s. Similar findings have been reported in verbal operant conditioning by Kanfer and McBrearty (1961) and Spielberger (1962).

Awareness and Mediation. Finally, the relationship between mediation and awareness needs to be considered. The finding that significant increases in mediation score accompany increases in awareness can, of course, be viewed as evidence for an effect of awareness on mediation. However, since both awareness and the mediation effect were assessed post-experimentally, these same data can be taken as an indication that mediation occurs prior to, and contributes to, awareness. In addition, it could be argued that mediation and awareness are both independent consequences of the experimental variables. This possibility seems unlikely, however, in view of the significant relation between awareness and mediation within the high-meaningfulness condition in both Experiments I and II. While the results of the present study do not provide any further evidence concerning the relation between mediation and awareness the view that mediation occurs independent of awareness is supported by a recent study (Hartman, 1963) in which *S*s instructed as to the composition of the test list showed no greater mediation effect than an uninstructed group.

It also may be noted that previous mediation studies (e.g., Bugelski and Scharlock, 1952; Russell and Storms, 1955; Mednick and Freedman, 1960; Horton and Kjeldergaard, 1961) have consistently obtained positive findings in the absence of awareness. While this observation is not consistent with several reports from the operant conditioning literature (cf. Dulany, 1962; Spielberger, 1962), and could be attributed to a lack of systematic interviewing in previous mediation studies, the writer is more inclined toward the view that this discrepancy is due to a relation between awareness and learning or performance that depends primarily on the conditions under which the experiment is carried out. That is, when the conditions of an experiment provide cues which greatly facilitate awareness (as in the high-meaningfulness condition of the present experiment) the unaware *S* is likely to be a particularly poor performer. This lack of performance may be due to factors such as task set, strategy, or a variety of other variables which prevent some *S*s from attending to the task-relevant cues (cf. Horton and Kjeldergaard, 1961; Spielberger, 1962). However, when the experimental conditions are not particularly conducive to awareness, many of the unaware *S*s can, and frequently do, perform quite well (Dixon, 1962; Postman, 1962; Hilgard, 1962). This would also appear to be the case in the mediation studies cited above. Furthermore, the amount of learning without awareness under such conditions would appear to depend, as noted by Postman (1962), ". . . on the readiness with which the general rule governing correct responses can be applied to specific instances."

Summary

Two three-stage mediation paradigms, simple chaining and response equivalence, were used to investigate the effects of meaningfulness of the common element, type of design, and learning ability of the *S*s on mediate association and awareness of the mediational relations.

The results indicated that all of the experimental variables (except paradigm) were related to awareness and that variations in meaningfulness, type of design, and awareness were also related to the mediation effect. The results were discussed in terms of the relative independence of these variables in mediation and the issue of learning without awareness.

References

Bugelski, B. R., and Scharlock, D. P. An experimental demonstration of unconscious mediated association. *J. exp. Psychol.*, 1952, **44**, 334-338.

Carroll, J. B., and Sapon, S. M. *The modern language aptitude test.* New York: Psychological Corp., 1958.

Cramer, Phebe, and Cofer, C. N. The role of forward and reverse associations in transfer of training. *Amer. Psychologist,* 1960, **15**, 463.

Dixon, T. R. The verb as a discriminative stimulus in verbal operant conditioning. Unpublished doctoral dissertation, Washington Univer., 1962.

Dulany, D. E., Jr. The place of hypotheses and intentions: An analysis of verbal control in verbal conditioning. *J. Pers.* (*Suppl.*) 1962, **30**, 102-129.

Goss, A. E. Early behaviorism and verbal mediating responses. *Amer. Psychologist,* 1961, **16**, 285-298. (a)

Goss, A. E. Verbal mediating responses and concept formation. *Psychol. Rev.*, 1961, **68**, 248-274. (b)

Hartman, R. R. The effect of rate of presentation and task set on mediated verbal learning. Unpublished M.A. thesis, Univer. of Kentucky, 1963.

Hilgard, E. R. What becomes of the input from the stimulus? *J. Pers.* (*Suppl.*) 1962, **30**, 46-72.

Horton, D. L., and Hartman, R. R. Verbal mediation as a function of associative directionality and exposure frequency. *J. verb. Learn. verb. Behav.*, 1963, **1**, 361-364.

Horton, D. L., and Kjeldergaard, P. K. An experimental analysis of associative factors in mediated generalizations. *Psychol. Monogr.*, 1961, **75**, No. 11 (Whole No. 515).

Jenkins, J. J. A study of mediated association. *Studies in Verbal Behavior.* Rep. No. 2, NSF Grant, Univer. of Minnesota, 1959.

Jenkins, J. J. Mediated associations: Paradigms and situations. In C. N. Cofer and B. S. Musgrave (Eds.) *Verbal behavior and learning: Problems and processes.* New York: McGraw-Hill, 1963. Pp. 210-244.

Kanfer, F. H., and McBrearty, J. F. Verbal conditioning: Discrimination and awareness. *J. Psychol.*, 1961, **52**, 115-124.

Kjeldergaard, P. K. Predicting paired-associate learning speed. *Psychol. Rep.*, 1962, **11**, 353-354.

Mednick, S. A., and Freedman, J. L. Facilitation of concept formation through mediated generalization. *J. exp. Psychol.*, 1960, **60**, 278-283.

Noble, C. E. An analysis of meaning. *Psychol. Rev.*, 1952, **59**, 421-430.

Noble, C. E. Meaningfulness and familiarity. In C. N. Cofer and B. S. Musgrave (Eds.) *Verbal behavior and learning: Problems and processes.* New York: McGraw-Hill, 1963. Pp. 76-118.

Postman, L. Rewards and punishments in human learning. In L. Postman (Ed.) *Psychology in the making.* New York: Knopf, 1962. Pp. 331-401.

Russell, W. A., and Storms, L. H. Implicit verbal chaining in paired associate learning. *J. exp. Psychol.*, 1955, **49**, 287-293.

Spielberger, C. D. The role of awareness in verbal conditioning. *J. Pers.* (*Suppl.*) 1962, **30**, 73-101.

Underwood, B. J., and Schulz, R. W. *Meaningfulness and verbal learning.* Philadelphia: Lippincott, 1960.

(Received August 9, 1963)

ARTICLE 5

Pseudomediation: Is chaining an artifact?[1]

George Mandler and Bruce Earhard
UNIVERSITY OF TORONTO

Abstract

Mediated association in verbal learning has frequently been characterized by the facilitation produced in a three-stage paired-associate paradigm: A-B, B-C, A-C. Using an appropriate control group, the present experiment demonstrated facilitation in an A-B, B-C, A-E paradigm. It is argued that the usual mediation effect may be not due to mediated chaining but rather to a combination of bidirectional association and unlearning.

Problem

In the course of preparing a review of the literature on mediated association in verbal learning (Earhard & Mandler) it became increasingly obvious that previous writers, in accounting for the mediation effect, have neglected other known effects in paired-associate learning. The three-stage paradigm that has been typically used to illustrate and demonstrate mediational chaining consists of a list of A-B pairs, followed by training on B-C pairs, and tested with a list of A-C items. Such a paradigm assumes that in the testing stage A-C is facilitated because A implicitly elicits B, which in turn elicits C. The typical control paradigm for this effect consists of the stages: A-B, D-C, A-C, and the mediation effect is said to be demonstrated when the third stage of the mediation paradigm shows faster acquisition than the third stage of the control paradigm (cf. Horton & Kjeldergaard, 1961).

However, the mediation phenomenon is subject to an alternative explanation based on the mechanisms of bidirectional association and unlearning. Horton & Kjeldergaard (1961) have pointed out the importance of bidirectional or backward associations in the various mediation paradigms and Jenkins (1963) has cited relevant evidence. One can assume that when an S learns a list of A-B pairs, he is also acquiring the B-A associations. Secondly, Barnes & Underwood (1959) and others have shown that when Ss learn an A-B list and are then required to learn an A-C list, unlearning of the A-B association occurs as A-C learning proceeds. These mechanisms lead to two predictions: Stage II should show faster learning in the control paradigm and Stage III should show faster acquisition in the mediation paradigm.

Specifically, during Stage II the acquisition of a B-C list is subject to interference effects from Stage I, while the control list D-C is not. At the same time, the acquisition of B-C produces unlearning or forgetting of the B-A and, by implication, the A-B association acquired in Stage I. As a result there will be little interference in Stage III of the mediation paradigm with A-C items from implicit or explicit B items. In the control paradigm no learning of the A-B association occurs and B items can still interfere with the acquisition of A-C.

If this alternate explanation of the mediation effects holds, it should be possible to demonstate a "mediation" effect in a three-stage A-B, B-C, A-E paradigm where the effects postulated for the first two stages of the mediation paradigm hold but where mediation as conventionally conceived cannot affect the acquisition of the test list since a new response item is used.

Method

Two groups of 22 Ss each were used. Each group learned successively three lists of six paired associates. For the Experimental group the stages were: A-B, B-C, A-E; for the Control groups they were A-B, D-C, A-E.

All lists were constructed from a word pool of 30 low frequency English words; the 28 words used by Horton & Kjeldergaard (1961) plus "ingot" and "opine." Three different sets of random pairings were constructed with additional requirements that no pair of items had the same initial letter and no two words in any list started with the same initial letter. For any one list five different orders of pairs were constructed to minimize the effects of serial learning. Ss were assigned at random to one of the three sets of lists (different pairings). Lists were constructed in such a way that both the initial and the final lists were identical for Experimental and Control groups within each of the three sets of pairings.

The paired associates were presented by the anticipation method on a Stowe memory drum at a 2:2 rate with no intertrial interval. Ss pronounced both terms of a pair. Interstage intervals were as long as necessary to instruct Ss that they were to learn a new list. Instructions were standard paired-associate instructions with Ss being encouraged to guess.

All Ss learned the lists in all stages to a criterion of two correct trials. Three Ss were discarded because they required 35 trials or more to learn their first list.

Results

The data for all three stages were analyzed in terms of three dependent variables: Number of trials to a criterion of one correct trial (C1), Number of trials to a criterion of two correct trials (C2), and number of correct anticipations during the first six trials (NC).

Figure 1 shows the results for the first and third of these variables. The results for the stricter criterion were comparable with the one presented here. The data are in accord with the predictions. The Experimental group is superior in Stage III, while the Control group shows faster learning in Stage II. An analysis of variance shows a significant Group by Stage interaction, $F(2,86)$ is 6.19 ($p < .005$) for C1 and 11.39 ($p < .001$) for NC. On

Reprinted with permission of the authors and the publisher, the Psychonomic Press. The article appeared originally in *Psychonomic Science*, 1964, **1**, 247–248.

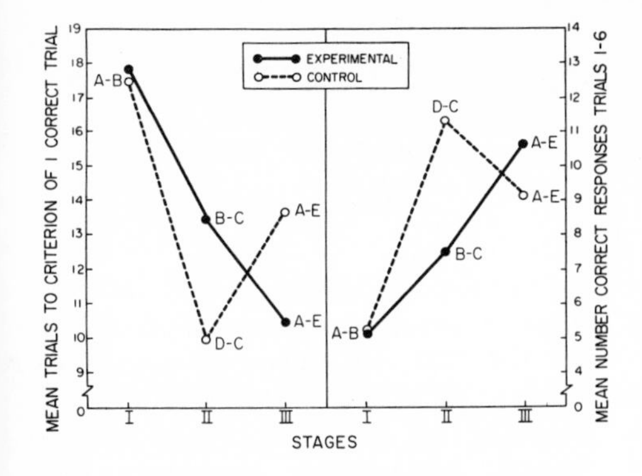

Fig. 1. Mean trials to one correct trial (C1) and mean correct responses in six trials (NC) for experimental and control groups in the three stages.

the A-E test list (Stage III) the Experimental group produces significantly faster learning under C1 ($t = 2.22$; $p < .04$); the same was found for C2 ($t = 2.10$; $p < .05$), but the difference is not significant for NC. For both C1 and NC the Control group shows significantly faster learning in Stage II ($t = 2.45$; $p < .02$, and 2.88; $p < .01$ respectively).

Discussion

The results show the expected pseudomediation effect. Given the first two stages of the mediation-chaining paradigm, the third stage showed facilitation even when a non-mediated, neutral response was used. The theoretical notions advanced above are further substantiated by the Stage II results. A B-C list was more difficult to learn than a new set of D-C pairs, suggesting associative interference in Stage II. Horton & Kjeldergaard (1961), using mixed lists, obtained similar results in Stage II of this particular paradigm.

The present argument is that the so-called mediation effect may be the result of decreased interference in the test stage due to unlearning or forgetting of the A-B association. This alternative interpretation is diametrically opposed to an argument based on associative mediation which states that the presence of the B association in Stage III facilitates acquisition. The general reasoning applies similarly to the other mediation paradigms discussed by Horton & Kjeldergaard (1961) and Jenkins (1963).

Finally, this particular analysis should not be taken as applicable to mediation studies which involve mediational processes inferred from language habits. These studies, in contrast to the associative model treated here, deal with highly overlearned language structures which, when available, function as conceptual rules. The mediating mechanism in these studies deals more with concept learning than with simple associative relations (cf. Mandler, 1963).

References

BARNES, J. M., & UNDERWOOD, B. J. "Fate" of first-list associations in transfer theory. *J. exp. Psychol.*, 1959, 58, 95-105.

EARHARD, B., & MANDLER, G. Mediated associations: Paradigms, controls, and mechanisms. in preparation.

HORTON, D. L., & KJELDERGAARD, P. M. An experimental analysis of associative factors in mediated generalizations. *Psychol. Monogr.*, 1961, 75, No. 11 (Whole No. 515).

JENKINS, J. J. Mediated associations: Paradigms and situations. In C. N. Cofer and B. Musgrave (Eds.), *Verbal behavior and learning*. New York: McGraw-Hill, 1963.

MANDLER, G. Comments on Professor Jenkins's paper. In C. N. Cofer and B. Musgrave (Eds.), *Verbal behavior and learning*. New York: McGraw-Hill, 1963.

Note

1. This research was supported by Grant GB-810 from the National Science Foundation and by Grant APA-64 from the National Research Council, Canada. The authors are most grateful to Shirley Singer for experimental assistance.

MEDIATION IN PAIRED-ASSOCIATE LEARNING

NAN E. McGEHEE AND RUDOLPH W. SCHULZ

Northwestern University *University of Iowa*

Russell and Storms (1955) have shown that language habits inferred from free-association norms are presumably capable of mediating the learning of verbal paired associates. Their *S*s learned to associate a word (B) with a nonsense syllable (A) in learning the first of two lists. The response unit B was the first word of an associative-chain (B-C-D) inferred from the norms. Following A-B learning, *S*s learned a test list consisting of A-D and A-X pairs. The A-D pairs were learned significantly faster than the A-X control pairs. However, as Russell and Storms (1955) hasten to point out, "The mere demonstration of mediational influences in learning . . . does not explain how the effect is achieved" (p. 292). One main purpose of the present experiments was to attempt to provide this explanation for the above situation.

As pointed out recently (Underwood & Schulz, 1960), it is analytically fruitful to conceive of verbal learning as a two-phase process. The first phase consists of a response-acquisition or response-recall phase where *S* is concerned with learning or recalling the response units per se. The second phase, the associative phase, involves learning to associate the response units with their appropriate stimulus units.

The usual interpretation of the Russell and Storms (1955) result has been the one that the associative phase of test-list acquisition was facilitated via the specific associative chains linking the A and D items of the respective pairs. An alternative interpretation, made apparent by the two-phase conception, is that facilitation occurred because the B items on the first list enhanced the availability of the D items during A-B learning by raising them in *S*'s response hierarchy. Moreover, this enhanced availability could facilitate test-list acquisition in the absence of any specific associative link between A and D. That is, the increased ease of response recall which would accompany heightened availability should facilitate test-list acquisition. The latter expectation is consistent with the results of a recent study in which it was found that the acquisition of paired-adjective lists was facilitated when the availability of the response units was enhanced by deliberate pretraining (Underwood, Runquist, & Schulz, 1959). The availability hypothesis was tested in Exp. I.

A second purpose of Exp. I was to compare performance under Russell and Storms' (1955) mediated and nonmediated conditions with performance under a condition in which first and test lists were unrelated (i.e., the practice control of transfer experiments). This was done to determine, in somewhat more absolute terms, the amount of facilitation which results from mediation in this situation.

The third purpose of Exp. I was to extend the generality of the Russell and Storms' (1955) results by replicating them with a design consisting of independent random groups and homogeneous lists as well as including *S*s of both sexes.

The results of Exp. I failed to

Reprinted with permission of the authors and the publisher, the American Psychological Association. The article appeared originally in the *Journal of Experimental Psychology*, 1961, **62**, 565–570.

support the availability hypothesis. However, for reasons too lengthy to detail here, we remained skeptical as to whether the failure of the availability hypothesis necessarily implied that mediation had taken place via specific associative chains. Therefore, Exp. II was undertaken to investigate the matter further. Namely, if there is specific linkage, then a test list in which the A and D items are inappropriately paired (i.e., the analogue of the S_1-R_1, S_1-R_r paradigm of conventional transfer terminology) should be more difficult to learn than the nonmediated test list. Put another way, there should be mediated interference. Indeed, Norcross and Spiker (1958) have demonstrated just such mediated interference for associative links acquired entirely in the laboratory. In Exp. II an attempt was made to demonstrate mediated interference in the present situation.

A second purpose of Exp. II was that of determining the "criticalness" of the free-association norms as predictors of the mediation effects obtained in Exp. I. That is, while the B and D items were selected so as to minimize the possibility of a *direct* free-associative link between them, the method of selection *did not* preclude the possibility of a meaningful relationship between these items (e.g., Thief-Take, Wish-Need, etc.). Similarly, it did not prevent the occurrence of interlist relationships between response units in terms of formal similarity (e.g., Smell-Stem, Memory-Matter, etc.). Hence, if the interlist relationships between response units, along dimensions *not* predictable from free-association norms, were stronger in the mediated condition than in the nonmediated condition, then the interpretation of the superior performance in the mediated condition would require revision. Therefore, Exp. II included a condition in which the first and test lists were learned in reverse order (A-D, A-B). The logic of this arrangement is based on the assumption that the associative linkage defined by the free-association norms is unidirectional (i.e., B-C-D, but not D-C-B). Thus, making A-D the first list and A-B the test list, should reduce substantially, or even eliminate, the facilitation presumed to be mediated by habits inferred from free-association norms. Contrariwise, a relationship between B and D based on interlist response similarity should be unaffected by the reversal of the lists because it would be expected to be a bidirectional relationship. Storms (1958) has proposed and tested a similar hypothesis for a situation involving a single mediating term. He found clear evidence for bidirectionality with normatively unidirectional materials.

METHOD

Lists: Exp. I.—The relationships between first and test lists define the conditions of Exp. I, and are summarized in Table 1. The first-list designations shown in Table 1 will be used as abbreviations in subsequent references to the various conditions (e.g., the mediated condition will be called Cond. A2-B, the nonmediated condition will be Cond. A2-X, etc.).

The stimulus designations A1 and A2 are used to distinguish between the two sets of 10 nonsense syllables required by the design of Exp. I. The syllables were selected so that inter- and intralist similarity would be at a minimum. Their association values ranged from 0% to 27% according to Glaze (Underwood & Schulz, 1960, Appendix A). In minimizing similarity it was impossible, with one exception, to retain the syllables used by Russell and Storms.

The B, D, and X response units were the same words as those used by Russell and Storms (1955) and are shown in Table 3 of their article (p. 290). The details regarding the selection of these words may also be found there. In brief, C was the most frequent free-association response to B, and D the most

TABLE 1

Relationships between First and Test Lists Defining Conditions of Exp. I

Condition	First List	Mediation Chain	Test List	Inferred Action
Mediated	A2-B	B-C-D	A2-D	A2 ↗ B→C ↘ D; A2- - - - - - - D
Nonmediated	A2-X	X-Y-Z	A2-D	A2 ↗ X→Y→Z; A2- - - - - - - D
Availability	A1-B	B-C-D	A2-D	A2 ↗ ?; A2- - - - - - - D
Practice control	A1-X	X-Y-Z	A2-D	A2 ↗ ?; A2- - - - - - - D

frequent free-associate of C, but D was not among the 10 most frequent responses to B, e.g., B (Trouble), C (Bad), D (Good). The members of the X-Y-Z chain are related to one another in the same manner as the members of the B-C-D chain; however, the members of the two respective chains were not related, and must not be related, to each other. Each list consisted of 10 paired associates.

Conditions A2-B and A2-X correspond to Russell and Storms' (1955) chained (A-D) and unchained (A-X) conditions, respectively. The availability hypothesis would be supported if test-list performance in Cond. A1-B is superior to that in Cond. A1-X. Similarly, comparison of A2-B with A1-X will determine if absolute positive transfer resulted from mediation.

Lists: Exp. II.—Conditions A2-B and A2-X of Exp. 1 were replicated. The lists of Cond. A2-D were the same as those of Cond. A2-B in Table 1 except that A2-D was the first list and A2-B the test list. Condition A2-Br is most easily described as follows. Let A_1-B_1, A_2-B_2, etc. represent the syllable-word pairings of the first list. Similarly, B_1 is the beginning of the free-association chain B_1-C_1-D_1. The test list represents a random re-pairing of the respective A and D items: A_1-D_4, A_3-D_{10}, A_5-D_1, etc. This test list was List A2-D—the same one used in Exp. I and in Cond. A2-B and A2-X of this study.

Mediated interference will be demonstrated if performance in Cond. A2-Br is inferior to that in Cond. A2-X. If mediation in these materials is unidirectional, performance in Cond. A2-D and A2-X should not differ.

Procedure: Exp. I and II.—Each *S* was read standard instructions for paired-associate learning prior to learning the first list. This list was then learned to a criterion of three consecutive errorless recitations. Following the completion of first-list learning all *S*s rested for 4 min. After brief instructions to proceed as before, *S*s were presented the test list for 10 anticipation trials. For those *S*s not reaching a criterion of one errorless recitation during the first 10 trials, test-list acquisition was continued until this criterion was reached. The lists were presented on a memory drum at a 2:2-sec. rate with a 4-sec. intertrial interval. The 10 pairs in each list were presented in five random orders to prevent serial learning of the response units. The experimental session was limited to 50 min. for all *S*s.

Subjects.—The *S*s, Northwestern University undergraduates, were randomly assigned to conditions, with 30 and 24 *S*s per condition in Exp. I and II, respectively. The *S*s were naive with respect to the materials used, although most of them had served in other verbal learning experiments prior to their present service. When an *S* did not complete the experiment he was replaced by the next *S* appearing at the laboratory. There was no relationship between failure to complete the experiment and conditions.

Results and Discussion

First-list acquisition: Exp. I and II.—Performance, in terms of mean number of trials to reach the criterion of three consecutive perfect recitations, did not differ significantly under the four respective conditions

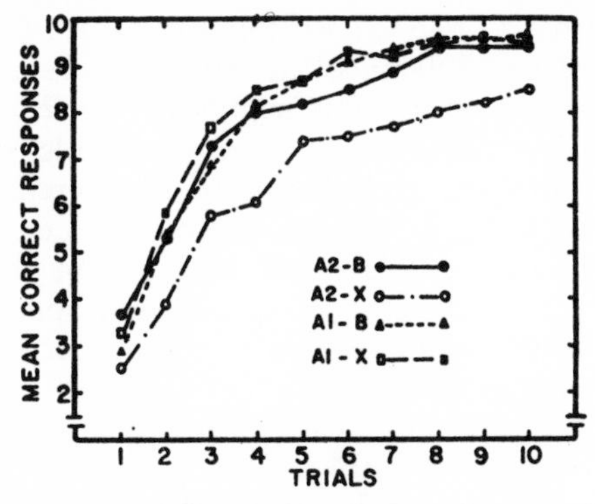

FIG. 1. Test-list performance in Exp. I as a function of various relationships between the stimulus and response units of the first and test lists. (See text for a complete description of these relationships.)

of either experiment (Exp. I: $F=1.77$, $P > .10$; Exp. II: $F < 1$). In Exp. I the means were 18.33, 19.23, 18.90, and 15.43 for Cond. A2-B, A2-X, A1-B, and A1-X, respectively. The respective means for Cond. A2-B, A2-D, A2-X, and A2-Br of Exp. II were 13.62, 14.75, 14.71, and 15.87. The comparable difficulty of Lists A2-B and A2-D as first lists permits direct comparisons of test-list performance under Cond. A2-D with the other conditions of Exp. II, since the test list for this condition was List A2-B while List A2-D served as test list for the other conditions.

Test-list acquisition: *Exp. I.*—Test list performance is shown in Fig. 1. It is apparent from Fig. 1 that performance under Cond. A2-B, A1-B, and A1-X was essentially equivalent. Performance under Cond. A2-X was consistently inferior to performance under the other three conditions. The mean total number of correct responses during Trials 1–10 was 78.23, 65.43, 79.50, and 81.30 for Cond. A2-B, A2-X, A1-B, and A1-X, respectively. The standard error of these means ranged from 1.64 to 2.75. The only reliable ($P < .01$) differences among these means are those involving a comparison between Cond. A2-X and each of the other three conditions. The results for mean number of trials to reach the criterion of one perfect recitation were in complete agreement with those for total correct responses.

From these results it seems clear that Russell and Storms' (1955) findings were reliable and of some generality. The significantly ($t = 3.79$, $P < .01$) superior performance under mediated as contrasted with nonmediated conditions in the present study represents a reproduction of their results. The interlist relationship in these two conditions—S_1-R_1, S_1-R_2—is such that negative transfer would ordinarily be expected. Hence, the failure to find negative transfer under the mediated condition and the presence of a substantial amount of negative transfer in the nonmediated condition indicates that the inhibitory effects of the interlist relationship were somehow overcome in the mediated condition. However, comparison of performance under mediated and practice-control conditions makes it clear that the facilitation produced by mediation was not of sufficient magnitude to produce absolute positive transfer (see Fig. 1).

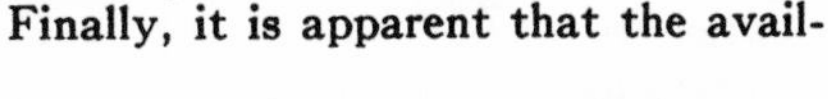

Finally, it is apparent that the avail-

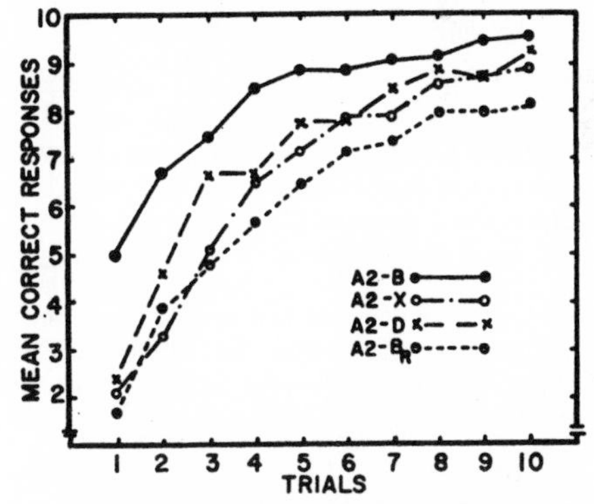

FIG. 2. Test-list performance in Exp. II as a function of various relationships between the stimulus and response units of the first and test lists. (See text for a complete description of these relationships.)

ability hypothesis was not supported by the results of the present study. That is, had the availability of the D units of the test list in Cond. A1-B been enhanced during first-list acquisition, then test-list performance under Cond. A1-B should have been superior to performance under Cond. A1-X. As can be seen from Fig. 1, it was not. Moreover, an analysis of overt errors failed to adduce any evidence indicating enhanced response availability in Cond. A1-B. Therefore, mediation effects, at least in the present situation, cannot be attributed to facilitation of the response-recall phase of test-list acquisition via enhanced response availability.

Test-list acquisition: *Exp. II*.—The performance on the test list for Trials 1–10 is shown in Fig. 2. The means for the total number of correct responses over the 10 trials were 83.04, 66.37, 71.62, and 61.54 for Cond. A2-B, A2-X, A2-D, and A2-Br, respectively. The standard error of these means ranged from 1.75 to 2.57. The overall differences among means are highly reliable ($F = 10.55$, $P < .01$).

Significant ($t = 5.12$, $P < .01$) superiority of performance in Cond. A2-B over Cond. A2-X again replicates Russell and Storms' (1955) results along with those of Exp. I.

As can be seen from Fig. 2, performance was initially comparable in Cond. A2-X and A2-Br, but after Trial 3 the curves diverge with performance under Cond. A2-X remaining consistently superior on Trials 4 through 10. The conditions did not differ significantly ($t = 1.45$, $P > .10$) in terms of total correct over Trials 1–10. However, the difference in mean performance is clearly in the expected direction. Furthermore, consistent with the divergence in the curves of Fig. 2 for these conditions, the means for the number of trials to reach the criterion of one perfect recitation were 8.92 for Cond. A2-X and 11.87 for Cond. A2-Br. This difference in trials to reach criterion is highly significant ($t = 2.65$, $P < .01$). It appears justifiable to conclude that mediated interference has been demonstrated in Cond. A2-Br. This result agrees with the one obtained by Norcross and Spiker (1958) with associative chains learned in the laboratory.

Inspection of Fig. 2 reveals a trend toward slightly better performance, at least initially, in Cond. A2-D than in Cond. A2-X. However, when the means for total correct on the 10 test-list trials for Cond. A2-D and A2-X were compared they failed to differ significantly ($t = 1.61$, $P > .10$). Indeed, in terms of mean trials to criterion Cond. A2-D was slightly inferior to Cond. A2-X. Furthermore, performance under Cond. A2-D was reliably poorer ($t = 3.51$, $P < .01$) than under Cond. A2-B.

Thus interlist response similarity along dimensions not predictable from free-association norms does not appear to be a major contributor to the facilitation of test-list performance in the present situation. This result appears to conflict with the one described earlier, which Storms (1958) obtained. However, it should be recalled that his situation differed from the present one in that it involved only a single mediating term in contrast to the present two term mediating link. Perhaps, the potency of the "recency" effect to which he attributes his results varies inversely with the length of mediating chain. If this is the case, the present contradiction would be resolved easily.

In short, the results of Exp. I and II seem to provide fairly conclusive evidence that mediation in the Russell and Storms (1955) situation can be explained in terms of the facilitation of the associative phase of test-list acquisition via specific unidirectional associative chains linking the respective A and D items of the test-list pairs. Moreover, this interlist response relationship is associated with previously acquired language habits reflected by free-association norms.

Summary

Two experiments were conducted to determine, among other things, how language habits inferred from free-association norms might mediate the learning of verbal paired associates in the Russell and Storms' (1955) situation. Their general procedure was replicated except that independent random groups and homogeneous lists as well as *S*s of both sexes were used. The interlist relationship between the stimulus syllables and response words of the first and test lists were appropriately varied to define the various conditions under which the 216 *S*s of the present experiments learned the 10-item lists on a memory drum at a 2:2-sec. rate.

From the results it was concluded that: (*a*) The response-recall phase of test-list acquisition is not facilitated in the mediated condition. (*b*) Mediated interference can be produced with the Russell and Storms' (1955) materials. (*c*) Under the mediated condition, the associative phase of test-list acquisition is facilitated via the specific associative chains linking the stimulus and response units of the respective pairs. (*d*) The free-association norms are "critical" in defining these associative chains. (*e*) Russell and Storms' (1955) results are reproducible and of considerable generality even though the facilitation produced by mediation does not result in absolute positive transfer.

References

Norcross, K. J., & Spiker, C. C. Effects of mediated associations on transfer in paired-associate learning. *J. exp. Psychol.*, 1958, **55**, 129–133.

Russell, W. A., & Storms, L. H. Implicit verbal chaining in paired-associate learning. *J. exp. Psychol.*, 1955, **49**, 287–293.

Storms, L. H. Apparent backward association: A situational effect. *J. exp. Psychol.*, 1958, **55**, 390–395.

Underwood, B. J., Runquist, W. N., & Schulz, R. W. Response learning in paired-associate lists as a function of intralist similarity. *J. exp. Psychol.*, 1959, **58**, 70–78.

Underwood, B. J., & Schulz, R. W. *Meaningfulness and verbal learning.* Chicago: Lippincott, 1960.

(Received September 2, 1960)

Part Three

RETENTION

CHAPTER 10

Long-Term Retention

In the acquisition of a list of verbal materials, *S* ordinarily practices for a number of trials before mastery is attained. Increments in acquisition obviously require retention of associations from trial to trial. The continuity of acquisition and retention is so inherent that their processes are inseparable in most studies on acquisition. As is true for transfer processes (cf. introductory section of Chapter 8), the processes of retention are simply presumed to be operative without further specification when acquisition is under study. However, a recent effort to view acquisition primarily in terms of retention processes will be noted in Chapter 11.

Retention becomes an area of independent study after *S* terminates his practice on a task, and a time period without further practice intervenes before he again utilizes his previously acquired associations. The role of retention theory and research in the psychology of verbal learning is clearly stated in the following comments by Underwood (1964b):

> A distinction must be drawn between learning and retention. It is misleading to say only that learning and retention are continuous processes. Of course, it is apparent that on any given trial in a verbal-learning experiment the performance measure includes the retention of the learning which had taken place on previous trials. But to say this, and no more, becomes absurd in view of the facts available concerning the variables which influence forgetting. In studying forgetting, hours or days elapse between any two given trials; in studying learning, the interval between any two trials involves only a few seconds. Theories of forgetting make assertions about processes which occur slowly over time so that they have little if any influence during the short intervals between learning trials but may become of great importance when the interval is, say, 24 hours. Finally, the fact is that there are variables which produce marked differences in rate of learning which have no residual influence over a long retention interval. Thus, we may ask two questions. First, we may ask about the variables which influence the rate at which an association is learned, and second, given an association learned to a given level or degree, we may ask what variables will influence the subsequent performance of that association at a later point in time when no further practice intervenes (pp. 112–113).

Empirical and theoretical studies of retention therefore concentrate on those factors that influence performance following the cessation of practice. Part Three is devoted to these factors.

Forgetting over hours or days has been an on-going research area since the early studies of Ebbinghaus (1885). This chapter is concerned with contemporary developments in long-term retention or, as it is frequently called, long-term memory (LTM) (Melton, 1963a). Contemporary psychologists have also broadened the scope of retention to include retention over much shorter time intervals, usually defined in seconds. This newer area of short-term retention or short-term memory (STM) (Melton, 1963a) will be covered in Chapter 11. However, several points are in order at this time. LTM and STM as discrete areas of study in retention are distinguishable in two principal ways. First, the duration of the time interval between the end of acquisition trials and the measurement of retention is obviously important, but the distinction between LTM and STM in time alone is not always clear-cut. An interval of several minutes may intervene in either LTM or STM studies. A second and perhaps more important distinction is the extent of original acquisition for the materials to be retained. In LTM acquisition refers to a list of verbal items, involving a multitude of stimulus-response associations mastered only after a number of practice trials; in STM acquisition refers to single verbal items, usually mastered after only one presentation.

Interference Theory and LTM

A dominant force in studies on LTM has been a set of concepts organized into what is called interference theory. The basic premise of interference theory is that we forget what we learn originally because of interferences produced by interpolated and/or prior learning experiences. Without such interferences retention should remain virtually intact over long periods of time. The interfering learning is called interpolated learning (IL) if it occurs after original learning (OL) and prior learning (PL) if it occurs before. Methodologically, the distinction between IL and PL leads to two distinct experimental designs and two different operationally defined phenomena. If the sequence of events is OL, followed by IL and then recall of OL, the design is one of retroaction. If the retention of OL is significantly lower for an experimental group given the OL, IL, OL sequence than for a control group given OL and recall of OL without the presence of IL, the obtained difference defines the phenomenon of retroactive inhibition (RI, or retroactive facilitation if the difference favors the experimental group). Similarly, the sequence PL, followed by OL and then later recall of OL, defines a proaction design, and the inferiority of this group to an OL-OL control group defines the phenomenon of proactive inhibition (PI, or proactive facilitation if the experimental group is superior to the control).

Interference theory relies heavily on the two factors—response competition and unlearning—believed to be the principal mechanisms for producing negative transfer (cf. Introduction and Article 3, Chapter 8). For this reason interference theory is also called "two-factor theory." In general, interference theory is largely an extension of the basic concepts of transfer. Thus, a third factor, list differentiation (Underwood, 1945), is also one that plays an important role in transfer theory (cf. Article 6, Chapter 8). However, a fourth factor, the spontaneous recovery over time of unlearned associations (a close cousin to spontaneous recovery in conditioning experiments), is unique to the LTM version of interference theory.

In most studies of LTM phenomena the OL and IL or PL tasks are PA lists which form the classic *A-B, A-C*, relationship of negative transfer experiments. For RI and PI the list sequence becomes *A-B, A-C, A-B* and *A-B, A-C, A-C*, respectively. Some unlearning of *A-B* associations is expected during practice on the *A-C* pairs. This unlearning contributes directly to RI and indirectly to PI. *A-B* associations that are not unlearned and unlearned *A-B* associations that recover spontaneously during the retention interval are available at the time of recall. In the RI design these *A-B* associations are the ones to be retained; in the PI design they provide the source of interference. Interference in RI consists of the blockage of *B* as a response to *A* by the competing *C* response from the *A-C* (IL) list; in PI the *C* response is blocked by the competing *B* response from the *A-B* (PL) list. Both the *B* and *C* responses may be available for recall in either the RI or PI situation, but *S*'s ability to differentiate between the two lists and assign the responses to the appropriate list tends to deteriorate with the passage of time. The relative balance between these various factors is hypothesized to change in accordance with a number of independent variables, such as the length of time separating the learning of the two lists from the recall test, the degree of acquisition for both OL and IL (or PL), etc. Article 1 (Slamecka and Ceraso, 1960) serves the dual purpose of presenting a more comprehensive treatment of interference theory than that given in the above brief sketch (cf. Postman, 1961a, for another comprehensive examination of interference theory) and reviewing thoroughly the research literature on LTM through 1959. Consequently, the remainder of this Introduction and the two other selected articles will center on developments in LTM that have occurred since 1959.

Extraexperimental Interference

The most significant development in this period has been the increasing recognition given to PI as the major determiner of forgetting in LTM, especially for PI stemming from extraexperimental sources. Classical interference theory had given RI more status than PI, primarily because of the direct unlearning of OL associations present in RI but not in PI. A number of early experiments gave strong support for the importance of RI by measuring the amount of forgetting of OL over periods of hours or days. The typical procedure consisted of having *Ss* learn OL one day and then return to the laboratory a day or two later for a measure of retention. These early experiments revealed large amounts of forgetting, supposedly attributable to RI effects from the extraexperimental experiences of normal activity during the retention interval. These interpolated experiences were held responsible for the unlearning of OL and for the source of competition during the retention test. Moreover, everyday forgetting as it occurs completely outside of the context of laboratory conditions was explained by generalizing such RI effects.

Underwood's (1957b) insightful reanalysis of these early findings augured a new era for interference theory and LTM in general. He discovered the amount of RI reported in the experiments to be a direct function of the number of prior lists *S* had practiced on before beginning his formal acquisition of OL. With naive *Ss*—that is, *Ss* without previous participation in the laboratory acquisition of verbal lists—the amount of forgetting over a period of days was found to be remarkably small. Underwood concluded that PI effects from the series of lists preceding OL accounted for most of the forgetting previously attributed to RI from outside of the laboratory.

Underwood and Postman (1960) extended the emphasis on PI to include an indentification of two major PI sources of extraexperimental interference, letter-sequence and unit-sequence interference. These sources of interference were hypothesized to be responsible, proactively, for much of the forgetting of verbal materials that takes place in everyday living. Article 2 (Postman, 1961b) describes the nature of these two sources and also illustrates how such interference may be investigated under standard laboratory conditions. In this study unit-sequence interference was manipulated by means of word frequency (cf. pp. 188–189) within SL lists. Follow-up studies by Postman (1962b, 1964c) manipulated unit-sequence interference within PA lists as well.

The concepts of unlearning and spontaneous recovery are as indispensable to PI from extraexperimental sources as they are to PI from prior lists. A simple example illustrates how these concepts may enter into letter-sequence interference. Suppose the trigram QVC is among the items included in a serial list. The acquisition of the qv sequence in this trigram is likely to encounter interference from *S*'s natural habit of following q with u, and the interfering qu habit is partially unlearned as a result. However, the natural habit should recover quickly, in time to serve as a powerful competitor for qv during recall. A recent study by Saltz (1965) provided some sorely needed independent (i.e., outside of the direct context of extraexperimental interference experiments) verification of this unlearning-spontaneous recovery progression in letter-sequence interference. Spontaneous recovery was demonstrated to be at its maximum after one hour, with very little additional recovery taking place beyond one hour. Comparable independent demonstration of unlearning and recovery for unit-sequence interference seems equally desirable.

Other Post-1959 Developments

Theoretical Issues

The summary section of Slamecka and Ceraso's review article (Article 1) lists a number of "pressing problems and empirical gaps" extant in our understanding of RI and PI. Since this review a number of studies have been directed toward many of these problems, but frequently they have created new problems and further gaps to be filled. One of the gaps included by Slamecka and Ceraso is the need for an improved measurement of the unlearning factor in interference theory. The MMFR method of Barnes and Underwood (Article 3, Chapter 8) and its subsequent modifications have largely solved this problem (cf. pp. 368–369). A related problem is the need for further tests of the validity of the spontaneous recovery hypothesis, another vital cog in interference theory. The Saltz study on recovery of letter-sequence habits is a step in this direction. The role of spontaneous recovery in the more traditional aspects of PI was examined by Koppenaal (1963; Article 3). His findings indicate that the classical view of spontaneous recovery, including its contribution to the balance of forces determining the amount of PI over time, may be erroneous. He proposed several revisions of interference theory that merit serious consideration in future studies on LTM.

Considering the current popularity of analyzing acquisition into two stages (cf. introduction and Article 2, Chapter 2), it is not surprising to discover a similar move for analyzing retention into analogous stages. Thus, Rock and Ceraso (1964) argued that forgetting in LTM, as measured by the standard method of aided recall (the *St* components of the OL list are presented on a recall trial and *S* attempts to anticipate the associated *R* components), consists of two different types. The first (item loss) refers to the decreasing availability of responses from OL without regard to their associative connections. It is, of course, the counterpart of response learning in acquisition. The second (associative loss) is the inability to match available responses with their appropriate stimuli. It corresponds to the associative stage of acquisition. Transfer research has contributed substantially to this two-type conception by identifying two kinds of unlearning, responsive and associative, following List 2 practice in the *A-B, A-C* paradigm (cf. p. 368). In a study more directly relevant to LTM, Ceraso and Henderson (1965) succeeded in teasing apart these two types of forgetting from aided recall scores under both RI and PI conditions. Over a 24-hour retention interval, RI was found to be due mainly to associative loss, whereas PI seemed to be due to both item loss and associative loss. Stage specification is likely to become an important requirement in future developments of LTM theory and research.

Functional Relationships

Slamecka and Ceraso (Article 1) pointed out the need for further study of RI and PI with paradigms other than the conventional *A-B, A-C* relationship typically used for testing implications of interference theory. Particularly acute has been the need for testing RI and PI effects when mediated associations exist between list components. The Osgood surface (Figure 1, p. 364) specifies decreasing amounts of RI as interlist response similarity increases, with some amount of RI to be expected when response similarity is less than complete identity. The studies cited in Article 1 (e.g., Bugelski and Cadwallader, 1956) generally support these predictions. The effect of interlist response similarity on PI has been less clearly demonstrated. PI, like RI, might be expected to decrease as response similarity increases, but again some amount of PI is expected when similarity is less than identity. The two studies cited in Article 1 (Morgan and Underwood, 1950; Young, 1955), however, failed to find statistically significant amounts of PI when PL and OL lists entered into an *A-B, A-B′* relationship.

Postman and Stark (1964) noted that the finding of statistically significant PI in the *A-B, A-C* paradigm but not in the *A-B, A-B′* paradigm presents a problem for interference theory. According to their analysis of the *A-B′* condition, there should be more competition at recall between similar responses (*B* and *B′* responses) than between dissimilar responses (*B* and *C* responses). Hence, they concluded that PI should be as great for the *A-B′* relationship as it is for the *A-C*. Their own experiment employed *B* and *B′* components that were word associates rather than synonymous adjectives as in the earlier experiments. In addition, they corrected a bias resulting from the rapid acquisition of the *A-B′* associations of OL (List 2). The bias consists of intensive overlearning of the *A-B′* associations, thus making them markedly resistant to PI effects. Under these conditions they were able to demonstrate PI for the *A-B, A-B′* paradigm. Further evidence for PI in the *A-B, A-B′* paradigm was obtained by Dallett (1964c) on materials in which *B* and *B′* were semantically related.

A number of independent variables conceivably affect LTM considerably, but their functional relationship with appropriate dependent variables are extremely difficult to establish because of an accompanying serious methodological problem. The problem exists because the independent variable affects acquisition as well as retention. Meaningfulness is a prototype for this kind of variable. We might wish to determine the retention of OL lists differing in the meaningfulness of their components. Most likely, we would find a pronounced positive relationship between meaningfulness and amount retained. The question arises, however, whether the effect of meaningfulness should be assigned to retention processes. Lists containing components of high meaningfulness are almost certain to be acquired more quickly than lists containing components of low meaningfulness. Correlated with this fact is the strong possibility that the associations in the high-meaningful list accrue greater strength than the associations in the low-meaningful list even though both lists are taken to the same criterion of mastery. A well-established relationship (cf. Article 1) is that between degree of OL and the amount of either RI or PI—the better the degree of OL, the smaller the amount of forgetting. The effect of meaningfulness on retention is therefore confounded with its effect on OL. Fortunately, Underwood (1964b) has devised two ingenious methods, single-entry and multiple-entry, for correcting the bias from differential associative strengths in OL. The single-entry method is to be used only when a constant number of trials is given to each OL group, the multiple-entry method only when all groups are taken to the same criterion of mastery. The availability of these methods should open the door for a renewed interest in the effects of variables like meaningfulness on LTM.

The hiatus in the literature on the RI effects of instructions to learn (cf. Article 1)—that is, RI for intentional versus incidental learning—has been greatly narrowed by the findings of Silverstein (1964). A Type I incidental learning procedure (cf. Article 1, Chapter 6) served to contrast RI effects for materials learned intentionally by one group and incidentally by another. The two groups were equated for initial acquisition by giving more trials to the incidental group than to the intentional group, with the difference in trials necessary for equating associative strength having been determined by a prior pilot study. RI over a 48-hour period was found to be equal for the intentional and incidental groups. As Silverstein indicated, this equality is in agreement with the current conceptualization of incidental learning in terms of the same processes utilized in intentional learning. Although these processes are less efficient and the criterion is reached at a slower rate in incidental than in intentional learning, the assurance of equal associative strength prior to the retention interval makes incidental learning no more susceptible to RI than is intentional learning. Underwood (1954) had earlier demonstrated that the retention of intentionally learned material is unaffected by the rate of acquisition—that is, slow learners retain as well as fast learners. This finding seems to generalize to other situations, such as the present one, where the variable in question alters only the rate of acquisition and not the final level of acquisition.

Considerable progress has been made on the problem of the differential effects of distributed practice (DP) versus massed practice (MP), another one of the issues raised in Article 1. In their first experiment, Underwood, Keppel, and Schulz (1962) contrasted DP and MP on the retention of the fourth list in a series of *A-B*, *A-C*, *A-D*, *A-E* lists (i.e., the *St* components remained the same across lists, but the *R* components were different for each list). Retention was better under the DP acquisition condition than it was under the MP condition. In their second experiment, the four successive lists were all *A-Br* variants (cf. pp. 365–366) of the same *St* and *R* components (i.e., the *St* and *R* components were given different specific pairings for each list). This time, retention of the fourth list did not differ for DP and MP acquisition conditions. The authors concluded:

> These findings indicate that DP will facilitate retention only when the response terms of previously acquired associations producing the interference are not present in the list being learned by DP. Theoretically, the results imply that DP allows for a more permanent extinction of contextual associations but does not influence specific *S-R* associations (1962, p. 363).

Contextual associations refer to the associations between *R* components and the various cues present in the learning environs, such as the memory drum, etc. In the *A-B*, *A-C*, *A-D*, *A-E* sequence the associations between these cues and the *R* components change from list to list, but in the *A-Br* sequence of lists these associations remain unaltered because the same *R* components are used repeatedly. The "permanent extinction" process is the kind discussed by Underwood in Article 5 of Chapter 3. Interference is supposedly generated by the presence of competing contextual cue-*R* associations from prior lists during practice on the fourth list. Under both DP and MP conditions these competing associations are partially extinguished, but the spontaneous recovery of these associations under DP permits a more permanent extinction than under MP. In a later study, Keppel (1964b) obtained additional evidence for the importance of the contextual cue-*R* component mechanism in determining the facilitative effect of DP over MP. However, he also found some evidence to support the importance of both *St-R* and *R-St* associations, and their extinction-recovery phases, as determiners of the facilitating effect of DP on retention.

A final variable to be considered is that of contextual constraint—one of the organizational factors known to affect the acquisition of serial lists (cf. pp. 303–304). Slamecka and Ceraso included the determination of the variables responsible for RI and PI of connected discourse among the problems deserving further attention. Subsequent research by Slamecka (1962) hinted at the possible importance of constraint factor in RI of connected discourse. However, most of the RI in his study was attributed to a nonspecific interference effect from IL, with time spent on IL being a more important determiner than the content of IL. Contextual constraint seemed to be more directly related to the kinds of intrusion errors occurring during the recall of OL than to the amount of RI. A later study by Slamecka (1964b) found that constraint had much less of an effect on retention than it did on acquisition.

ARTICLE 1

RETROACTIVE AND PROACTIVE INHIBITION OF VERBAL LEARNING[1]

NORMAN J. SLAMECKA *University of Vermont* AND JOHN CERASO *Yeshiva University*

The last review of the literature solely devoted to retroactive inhibition (RI) was Swenson's (1941) monograph whose coverage extended through 1940. The present paper extends the coverage by presenting a full bibliography and critical analysis of all published reports on the RI and proactive inhibition (PI) of verbal learning from 1941 through 1959. Studies of infrahuman *S*s and of nonverbal behavior were excluded because of considerations of length and the fact that, traditionally, RI is a concept associated with verbal behavior. Excluded also were studies using interpolated convulsive seizures or surgical procedures because such treatments are qualitatively different from intervening learning as such and require other theoretical formulations to explain their effects. Following a brief summary of the field in 1940, subsequent developments will be discussed under five general headings: Degree of Acquisition, Similarity of Materials, Extrinsic Factors, Temporal Effects, Major Theoretical Positions.

The dominant theoretical position in 1940 was a transfer theory, given its fullest exposition by McGeoch and his collaborators. In essence the theory stated that RI could be explained by the general principles discovered in the study of transfer. The failure of performance of an old association could be attributed to greater strength of the new association, a mutual blocking of old and new associations, or a confusion between the two.

This theory was capable of handling a great deal of the relevant data and depended largely upon two sources of evidence for empirical support. The first source was the evidence for the effect of similarity of materials upon RI, which supported the contention that RI could be explained by the principles of transfer. The second source was intrusion errors, which are responses from the interpolated learning offered by *S*s when they are asked for responses from the original learning. The existence of these errors supported the contention that old responses were not given because new ones had supplanted them.

Much of the subsequent history of RI can be viewed as a process of extension and enlargement of McGeoch's basic position. The four major theories discussed later on in this paper serve as leading examples. The Melton-Irwin two-factor theory enlarged the competition of response theory by postulating an unlearning process in addition to competition of response. Gibson elaborated the theory by placing it within the setting of the

[1] This work was supported in part by a grant to the senior author from the National Science Foundation (G-6192).

Reprinted with permission of the authors and the publisher, the American Psychological Association. The article appeared originally in the *Psychological Bulletin*, 1960, **57**, 449–475.

conditioning experiment, making available the conceptual apparatus of differentiation and generalization. Underwood's work has concentrated upon clarifying the nature of both unlearning and differentiation, while Osgood has stressed the communality of transfer and RI in his "transfer and retroaction surface."

A consideration of terms is now in order. RI is the decrement in retention attributable to interpolated learning (McGeoch & Irion, 1952), and the operations that define it require a comparison of the retention of some original learning (OL) between two groups that differ in some aspect of the interpolated activity (IL) (Underwood, 1949a). The experimental group has IL, and the control group engages in some nonlearning filler task. Better retention in the control group defines RI, and better retention in the experimental group defines retroactive facilitation. Since the control group almost always shows some loss of the OL after its "rest activity," to what can the decrement be attributed: to incidental learning, to loss of set, to sheer metabolic activity (Shaklee & Jones, 1959)? The impossibility of assuring that no interpolated learning takes place for that group introduces an inevitable looseness into the significance of the RI measure. The control group's decrement is sometimes assumed to be due to "natural" forgetting, as distinct from the additional decrement attributed to the specific interfering tasks given the experimental group. But if a strict interference position is to be maintained, the "natural" forgetting must also be attributed to some source of interference, albeit beyond *E*'s control. The fact that different investigators may employ different filler tasks imposes a shifting base against which experimentally induced RI is calculated and renders comparison of results difficult. Osgood (1946, 1948) has dealt with the problem by simply omitting the control group and regarding RI as the difference in performance between the end of OL and the subsequent OL relearning (RL), lumping together both the specific and nonspecific decremental variables operating during the interpolated interval. This, of course, is a measure of total forgetting. Such a straightforward procedure cannot, however, distinguish between RI and retroactive facilitation, as they are usually understood, since facilitation may involve simply less decrement in retention as compared to a control group. Another troublesome problem arises with the other methods of quantifying RI, both of which rely upon control groups. Absolute RI is simply the numerical difference between the retention of the control and experimental groups, and relative RI is the percentage difference between them:

$$\frac{\text{Rest-Work} \times 100}{\text{Rest}}$$

Each of these measures is thus dually dependent upon both the experimental and the control groups' performance, and they may not always give the same pattern of results. This problem becomes especially important in studies of degree of OL upon RI. It is often the case that as OL increases, absolute RI increases, but relative RI decreases (Postman & Riley, 1959). To illustrate, it can be seen that, when degree of OL is low, the control group's retention is low, and even slight departures from this baseline on the part of the experimental group will represent a substantial percentage difference; whereas when the control's recall is high, the same absolute difference will reflect a lesser percentage change, and the relative RI will have decreased, while absolute RI will have remained the same. At present, we can only be alerted to this source of confusion and take it into account when viewing the results of any RI study. The foregoing observations apply just as fully to the quantification of PI, to which we now turn.

The PI paradigm requires a comparison of the retention of some original learning (List 2) between two groups that differ only in some aspect of the activity preceding that learning. The experimental group learns some previous material (List 1), and the control group does not. The same problem with regard to the control group's experience applies here. Better retention in the control group defines PI, and better retention in the experimental group defines proactive facilitation. In addition, the PI design requires that a clear temporal distinction be made between the end of the acquisition phase of List 2 and its subsequent retention test. Minimally, a retention interval longer than the OL intertrial interval is needed. If this is not done, the learning and retention phases would be operationally identical, and the PI design would be indistinguishable from the transfer design.

Degree of Acquisition

Swenson's (1941) generalizations about the acquisition variables were as follows:

> [*a*] . . . susceptibility to retroaction does not tend to decrease as the amount of original activity is increased . . . (p. 17). [*b*] . . . the greater the degree of learning of the original activity, the less susceptible is the learning to retroactive inhibition (p. 18). [*c*] . . . we may retain the idea of increased retroactive inhibition with increased amount of interpolated activity (p. 19). [*d*] All measures show an increase in retroactive inhibition with early increases in the degree of interpolated learning and a decrease in retroactive inhibition with very high degrees of interpolated learning (p. 20).

These conclusions have been further amplified through subsequent work. (Unless otherwise noted, the results cited below refer to measures at recall—first relearning trial.)

Several papers have reported the effect of degree of IL upon RI either by varying the number of IL trials (Briggs, 1957; Highland, 1949; Melton, 1941; Postman & Riley, 1959; Slamecka, 1959, 1960a; Thune & Underwood, 1943; Underwood 1945, 1950b), by setting a performance criterion (Archer & Underwood, 1951; Osgood, 1948; Richardson, 1956), by varying the number of interfering lists (Underwood, 1945), or by analysis of the associative strength of any single IL list item (Runquist, 1957).

Most of the papers agreed that RI of recall showed a negatively accelerated increase with increasing IL, and studies that carried IL to very high degrees also agreed that the curve tended to flatten out or even to decrease (Briggs, 1957; Thune & Underwood, 1943; Underwood, 1945). In general, maximum levels of RI were obtained when the IL practice had somewhat exceeded the OL practice and further IL trials did not serve to increase the RI appreciably. An exception to this was Runquist's (1957) finding that RI of individual items was not a function of the strength of the corresponding interpolated items. Also, in Exp. B of Underwood's (1945) report, there were no significant recall differences among the work groups, nor was there any consistent trend toward a negatively accelerated curve of recall as a function of degree of IL. A possible explanation for this may lie in the fact that the lowest IL degree (8 trials) exceeded the mean OL trials (which averaged about 6). Under these conditions it might well be expected that increasing the IL practice would have no further decremental effect. Increasing the IL levels did, however, produce faster RI dissipation, which gives marginal support to Underwood's differentiation hypothesis. The question of whether degree of IL, measured by trials, or amount of IL, measured by the number of different interpolated lists given, is the more powerful variable in producing RI was also specifically tested by Underwood (1945). Care was taken to equate the amount and degree levels by equal total trials, and the findings showed that RI changed at a faster rate with increases in amount than with increases in degree of IL. Both relative and absolute RI grew steadily as the number of IL lists was increased, but the frequency of overt interlist intrusions remained relatively constant, regardless of the number of lists. This is also consistent with the differentiation hypothesis, since increasing the number of lists should not increase differentiation, whereas increasing the number of trials on a single list should increase it. It is urged that a further comparison of the effect of amount against degree of IL should be made, using yet lower IL levels, so as to fill out that part of the curve at which acquisition is very slight.

Degree of OL was controlled in the following studies by varying the number of trials (Briggs, 1957; Melton, 1941; Postman & Riley, 1959; Shaw, 1942; Slamecka, 1960a), setting a performance criterion (Richardson, 1956), or analyzing individual item strengths (Runquist, 1957). All reports agreed that the susceptibility of the original material to RI was inversely related to its level of acquisition. The well-designed factorial study by Briggs (1957), using four OL and five IL levels (2, 5, 10, and 20 trials OL, compared to 0, 2, 5, 10, and 20 trials IL, all paired adjectives), confirmed previous findings as well as showing that, as OL increases, the greater must the IL level be for maximal relative RI. This was also found by Melton (1941). Further, Briggs reported more significant recall differences across the various IL levels as degree of OL increased. There was no additional information concerning the effects of amount of OL within this period.

PI as a function of List 1 acquisition has been studied by varying the number of trials (Postman & Riley, 1959; Waters, 1942), the number of lists (Underwood, 1945), setting a performance criterion (Atwater, 1953; Underwood, 1949b, 1950a), and analyzing individual item strengths (Runquist, 1957). Two other studies (Greenberg & Underwood, 1950; Werner, 1947) omitted control groups and are not strictly PI designs, and a third (Peixotto, 1947) did not distinguish between learning and retention measures. When significant PI of recall was obtained, all but one of the studies agreed that it was a positive function of the degree or amount of prior learning, and there was even some indication that it leveled off at high degrees of such learning, much as with RI (Atwater, 1953). The one exception (Runquist, 1957) found that PI was not influenced by the degree of the corresponding interfering item strength. The latter is the only study that solely used such analysis and poses an important but separate question concerning the variables determining the retention of individual items per se. Underwood (1950a) found that PI was eliminated at all degrees of prior learning when recall time was extended to 8-sec. intervals. McGeoch and Underwood (1943), using paired-associates lists, found that, when the pairs were presented in fixed order, thus providing the opportunity for serial learning, significant PI was no longer obtained, as opposed to the usual method in which the order of the pairs is varied. A further indication of the sensitivity of PI to slight procedural changes was given in a report that found significant PI in a serial list at a 2-sec. rate of presentation, but not at a 2.3-sec. rate (Underwood, 1941).

One chronic problem which crops up in studies of the degree of prior learning upon PI (and also in RI designs) is that of controlling for practice and warm-up effects. Traditionally, the control group learns only List 2, whereas the experimental group has had prior practice via List 1. Taking List 2 to a common criterion does not insure equal strengths of learning since the rates of acquisition may differ. Although the problem has been recognized (McGeoch & Irion, 1952), it is not dealt with in most PI studies. Young's (1955) is the only experimental effort at such control, wherein the learning was carried to a seven-eighths criterion on the hypothetical next trial, as determined by previous pilot study data.

The only study of PI as a function of the degree of List 2 learning appeared in the extensive investigation by Postman and Riley (1959) who used serial nonsense lists and naive *S*s. This part of their work revealed a curvilinear PI (both absolute and relative) function. Maximum PI was obtained at the lowest and highest degrees of List 2 acquisition (5 and 40 trials, respectively) across all levels of List 1 training given (5, 10, 20, and 40 trials). Runquist (1957) found that the degree of PI of any individual list item is unaffected by the acquisition strength of that item—again pointing up the discrepancy between single item retention and overall list retention. The study of PI has not kept pace with the growing knowledge about RI, although recently the greater impact of long-range cumulative effects of prior learning have been brought out strikingly by Underwood (1957) who utilized data from previous retention work and showed that more forgetting is attributable to long-range PI effects than to RI. He found that, although well-practiced *S*s forgot about 75% over 24 hours, naive *S*s (no practice lists) forgot only about 30%. This large differential in retention could only be attributed to the strong PI effects of the practice material. Further experimental support was given by Seidel (1959), measuring concurrent PI and RI.

The transitory nature of RI and PI is exemplified in the common observation that these phenomena dissipate after a few relearning trials, sometimes even by the second trial (Osgood, 1948; Underwood, 1945). It follows that recall is the most sensitive measure, whereas if a relearning criterion is used, no interference effects may be demonstrable (McGeoch & Underwood, 1943; Thune & Underwood, 1943; Underwood, 1949b; Waters, 1942).

The rate at which RI dissipates is undoubtedly some function of the degree of learning, or the degree of differentiation of the two response systems involved; but the form of the function is not completely known. Dissipation rate is of importance theoretically and empirically. Melton and Irwin (1940) obtained fastest dissipation at the highest IL level used (40 trials), followed by the next highest level (20 trials). Thune and Underwood (1943) also found rapid dissipation at the highest levels (10 and 20 trials), but there was no difference in rate between them. This latter finding was incompatible with the two-factor theory of Melton and Irwin, in that it could not be explained by reference to the unlearning factor, because the great differences in overt intrusions obtained under the two conditions should have led to different rates of dissipation, favoring the highest level. This point will be considered again in the section devoted to theory. Data from Underwood (1945, Exp. B) also showed much faster dissipation at the high IL level, and the paper by Briggs (1957) suggests that RI dissipates fastest when the interfering material is well learned or overlearned, only at low and intermediate OL levels. RI persistance was generally found to be greatest at the intermediate IL levels used in the four latter studies. Further data on this point as well as comparable figures for rates of PI would be welcome.

Similarity of Materials

Swenson's (1941) summary of the earlier work on similarity was that "Robinson's theoretical curve is at least roughly accurate" (p. 13). There has since been a definite waning of interest in the Skaggs-Robinson hypothesis as a useful generalization about the effects of similarity upon RI. This is partly because of the failures to duplicate the full theoretical curve within any one experiment (the last attempt at this was made by Kennelly, 1941, and was unsuccessful) and partly because a more heuristic alternative has emerged. The trend within this period may be traced from Boring's (1941) mathematical discussion of communality; Gibson's (1940) more analytical theory reflected in Hamilton's (1943, p. 374) statement that "a two-variable hypothesis should be accepted in preference to the Skaggs-Robinson function"; through Haagen's (1943, p. 44) conclusion that "the hypothesis applies, not to any dimension of similarity, but specifically to the condition in which the continuum of similarity involves a change in the SR relationship of the tasks"; to Osgood's (1949) integration of the literature on RI and similarity in terms of his 3-dimensional transfer and retroaction surface. Ritchie (1954) argued that the Skaggs-Robinson paradox (the statement that the point of maximal OL and IL similarity is simultaneously the condition for greatest interference and also for greatest facilitation) is a pseudoproblem because of an ambiguous scoring procedure. In short, this hypothesis has been superseded by subsequent developments, to which we now turn. Studies of the effects of similarity relationships have been separated into those using paired associates and those using serial lists. The use of paired associates allows specification of the locus of the change in similarity between the lists, an advantage which is not found with serial arrangements. Three classes of change between pair items are possible: response (A–B, A–C), stimulus (A–B, C–B), and both stimulus and response changes (A–B, C–D).

The effect upon retention of learning a new response to an old stimulus has been to produce RI (Bugelski, 1942; Bugelski & Cadwallader, 1956; Gladis & Braun, 1958; Haagen, 1943;

Highland, 1949; Osgood, 1946, 1948; Young, 1955) and, also, retroactive facilitation (Haagen, 1943; Parducci & Knopf, 1958). The variable that determined the direction of the effect was the degree of similarity between the two responses. The problem of developing a rigorously objective quantitative scale of meaningful similarity along dimensions feasible for use in verbal form is a serious one, and it has not been adequately met. Usually, adjectives scaled for varying levels of synonymity to standard words were used. These levels were based upon pooled ratings by judges (Haagen, 1949; Osgood, 1946). Parducci and Knopf (1948) used geometric figures varying along some physical dimension with four-digit numerals varying in identity as the veral responses required. Their OL and recall were visual discrimination tasks, and not really paired associates. The distinction is that the correct response figure and numeral appeared on the stimulus card, whereas in the true paired associates, the response is never a part of the stimulus item. The theoretical rationale of Young's (1955) study deserves some discussion. In the A–B, A–C paradigm, learning A–B also adds to the associative strength of A–C through generalized reinforcement. The magnitude of such generalized reinforcement should be a positive function of the degree of similarity between the B and C response items. In the RI design it was hypothesized that the original list's associative strength (after the IL list was learned) would be the sum of the direct reinforcement gained during its acquisition plus the additional generalized reinforcement gained from the subsequent IL learning. The IL list, on the other hand, would already have gained some generalized reinforcement as a result of the OL training and would thus need less direct reinforcement to achieve criterion during its learning. This would leave the original list with a greater associative strength at recall than the interpolated list, and the magnitude of this difference would be determined by the degree of response similarity between lists. Therefore, it was predicted that, as response similarity between lists increased, RI would decrease and PI would increase. These predictions were tested by Young, using three lists of paired adjectives (to increase the effect) and three levels of response similarity. Results showed that RI as well as overt intrusions decreased as response similarity increased, as predicted. The PI results, as well as a reinterpretation of this entire experiment, will be taken up at the end of this section.

Osgood's (1949) generalization that as response similarity decreases from identity to antagonism, retroactive facilitation should gradually change to increasing RI, was given some empirical support within this period. However, one disturbing finding has emerged. Bugelski and Cadwallader (1956) made a comprehensive attempt to test Osgood's generalizations about similarity effects, part of which involved the use of Osgood's own word lists to define four degrees of response similarity—identical, similar, neutral, and opposed—while keeping the stimuli the same. Results showed decreasing RI with decreasing response similarity. There was more RI with similar than with opposed responses—a finding directly contrary to Osgood's prediction, and not in accord with other data. No explanation was given for these results, but they cast doubt upon the previous formulation of response similarity. In addition to Osgood's disinclination to use RI control groups, he has also relied upon an uncommon measure of retention, namely, latency scores. In one of his studies (Osgood, 1948), the significant drop in RI between opposed and similar responses was evident only with latency scores, but traditional recall showed no significant differences. In Osgood's other study (1946) there were no significant latency differences at recall, but only on the second and third relearning trials. At no time were the differences between the neutral and opposed conditions significant. All things considered, the evidence in favor of the retroaction surface is less than overwhelming as far as the right half of the response dimension goes, and indicates that a revision is needed.

Saltz (1953) hypothesized that learning A–C after A–B inhibits B. Assuming that inhibition generalizes less than excitation, presenting a slightly altered A stimulus should again tend to evoke B. When tested in a straightforward manner, the hypothesis was not confirmed. A second attempt, designed to minimize changes in set, did result in a tendency toward reappearance of B. No further RI work along these lines has been reported.

There have been two papers on the effects of response similarity on PI. One reported no differential effect (Young, 1955), although overt intrusions increased with response similarity, and the other (Morgan & Underwood, 1950) found that PI tended to decrease as response similarity increased. Osgood (1946, 1948) reported results couched in terms of PI, but his data are for List 2 acquisition and therefore are measuring negative transfer. A methodological oversight with consequent possible confounding of the results of the Young (1955) and Morgan and Underwood (1950) studies should be pointed out. They both varied similarity along the synonymity of meaning dimension. In terms of A–B, A–C, the C response varied from very high (i.e., discreet-ailing, discreet-sickly), to very low similarity, or neutrality with regard to the B response (i.e., noiseless-sincere, noiseless-latent). Each single list had all of the responses at the same similarity level. Thus, it is conceivable that *S* could "catch on" that the List 2 responses were similar in meaning to those of List 1, and thereby reduce his chances of making errors by restricting his responses to members of the synonym category, with a resulting high positive transfer and low apparent PI. This postulated shift in the pool of responses available to *S* could be made entirely without his awareness, as several studies of verbal operant conditioning have demonstrated. With lists of low similarity on the other hand, the possibility of such an occurrence would be nil, and therefore no response class restriction would be made, resulting in a drop in positive transfer and higher apparent PI. Since these studies address themselves to rote learning and retention, the possibility of such a form of concept formation is a serious confounding variable. The test of retention may not be of rote recall at all, but actually of reconstruction of the response on the basis of the general concept of synonymity. As would clearly be predicted by such a "categorization" approach, the learning of List 2 was in fact fastest with high response similarity and became progressively slower with decreasing similarity. Both studies stressed the previously discussed response generalization rationale which would lead to increasing PI with increasing similarity, because learning a similar List 2 response would add to the interfering strength of the List 1 response through generalized or "parasitic" reinforcement. These predictions were not in fact confirmed; rather, PI tended to decrease with increasing similarity (although not statistically significant), an expectation consistent with the categorization hypothesis. The magnitude of the effect is probably dependent upon the relative strength of the two lists, as well as upon the number of alternatives in the response classes, which is a task for further empirical work to verify. Such an unintended source of bias may also have been working in the Bugelski and Cadwallader (1956) study, which used a similar list construction technique. Preferably, items at varying levels of response similarity should be included within the same list, so that *S* would have no opportunity to grasp the concept of the overall list structure. Such a procedure was used for RI by Osgood (1946, 1948) who was aware of this problem. A paper by Twedt and Underwood (1959), which showed that there was no difference in transfer effects between "mixed" and "unmixed" lists, is relevant to lists differing only in formal characteristics, but does not bear upon the question of the general synonymity of the list items as a whole. The lists of the latter study were not varied in degree of meaningful response similarity and thus do not constitute a test of the categorization hypothesis. However, an important paper by Barnes and Underwood (1959) suggested a mediation rationale as another possibility. If A–B is the first list and A–B′ the second, there is a possibility of an A–B–B′ mediation occurring at recall. In view of these complications, we must conclude that the effects of varying response similarity still have not been unequivocally demonstrated or explained.

The retention effect of learning the same response to a new stimulus was reported in four studies, all of which found retroactive facilitation (Bugelski & Cadwallader, 1956; Haagen, 1943; Hamilton, 1943; Highland, 1949). Similarity was varied either by using geometric figures differing in generalizability (originally developed by Gibson, 1941) or meaningful words scaled for synonymity. The results agreed that retroactive facilitation increased with increasing stimulus similarity. The extreme of similarity is identity, and this produces the most facilitation of all since it amounts to continued practice on the original list. At levels of very low similarity there was some inhibition (Haagen, 1943), and according to Hamilton (1943, p. 375): "When the stimulus forms were of 0 degree generalization there was very little difference in retention in conditions with responses identical and with responses different."

No study has ever tested the effects of opposed or antagonistic stimulus relationships while keeping responses the same. Osgood's (1949) retroaction surface does not extend the dimension of stimulus dissimilarity beyond "neutral" or unrelated, although the response dimension does include "antagonistic" relations. The implication is that stimulus opposition is no different in its effects from stimulus neutrality, although no RI evidence is adduced for such a position. It is conceivable, however, that meaningful stimulus opposition or antonymity would actually result in facilitation of recall, based upon a mediation rationale, since such words would be related by *S*'s previous language experience. If response opposition is expected to differ in effect from response neutrality, then stimulus opposition might also. There are no corresponding paired-associates studies upon the PI effects of stimulus variation.

The effect of changing both the stimulus and response members of the interfering list is concisely stated by Osgood (1949, p. 135): "negative transfer and retroactive inhibition are obtained, the magnitude of both increasing as the stimulus similarity increases." One experiment did not vary stimulus similarity with unrelated responses (Highland, 1949), four studies did vary stimulus similarity with unrelated responses (Gibson, 1941; Haagen, 1943; McClelland & Heath, 1943; Postman, 1958), and another used three degrees of response similarity as well (Bugelski & Cadwallader, 1956). The five latter reports indicate increasing RI with increasing stimulus similarity, and the one study available shows that this holds over all levels of response similarity tested. Two studies from this group will be more fully described since they represent an intriguing departure from the use of the usual physical or meaningful similarity dimension. McClelland and Heath (1943) used as stimulus items for the original and interpolated lists, respectively, a Kent-Rosanoff stimulus word and the most frequent free-association response made to it. Thus an existing prepotent connection was deliberately introduced. Responses were unrelated, and there was no control group. Recall was significantly less under that condition as compared with the case in which there was no association between the stimuli. Since the related words were not similar in appearance or in meaning (e.g., Thirsty-Water) and since a common mediating response could not account for the directionality of the association, the authors concluded that:

> to define the relation between original and interpolated activities which determines the amount of RI, as similarity or as generalization (plain or mediated) is too narrow a conceptionalization, since it does not cover such a learned, uni-directional relation between the two activities as was demonstrated to be of importance here (p. 429).

This study was not carried far enough to prove the point. A third group is needed, for which the related OL and IL stimuli would be interchanged. If this group would display no better recall than the unrelated stimuli group, then the case for the effect of unidirectionality of relationships upon RI would be established. Postman (1958) used geometric figures as OL stimuli. The IL stimuli were either the identical figures, words describing the figures (i.e., "square"), or color names. Responses were unrelated. Both the figure and word groups showed significant RI, with the former having the largest decrement, while the color group did not. These results were explained in terms of the previously learned connections between figures and their names, with formal similarity producing greater interference than mediated equivalence. The influence of unidirectionally prepotent and mediated connections upon forgetting deserves even more attention that it has received. PI is once again slighted, for there are no paired-associates studies concerning both stimulus and response changes.

We turn now to serial list studies, divided into those employing discrete, unconnected items, and those using connected discourse or some approximation thereto. Effects of similarity relations between discrete item lists were reported in three papers which were relatively unrelated as regards their major purposes. Irion (1946) varied the relative serial positions of the original and interpolated adjectives, with some groups learning the identical words for IL, and others learning synonyms. He concluded that similarity of serial position was an effective variable only when identity of meaning was also present. Since several significant differences for IL were reported, we feel that the main variables were confounded with the uncontrolled degree of IL, rendering the results ambiguous. Melton and von Lackum (1941), in a study designed to test an important deduction from the two-factor theory, used two levels of similarity of interpolated items, and found both RI and PI greater under the high similarity condition. Kingsley (1946), with meaningful words, also found poorer retention with interpolated synonyms as opposed to antonyms. Both of the above studies support the generalization that, with serial lists, RI increases with increasing stimulus similarity, along dimensions of both identical elements and meaningfulness.

Ordinary prose or connected discourse has been, until recently, unusually resistant to demonstrable interference effects. Blankenship and Whitely (1941) studied PI of advertising material (a simulated grocer's handbill) as a function of two levels of judged List 2 similarity. Recall after 48 hours showed greater PI for the more similar condition. Their study actually did not vary degrees of similarity of prose, since one of the two lists was nonsense material, and it may be questioned whether a grocer's handbill resembles prose rather than a list of paired associates. Hall (1955) in an RI design, using a completion test, gave 30 sentences for OL, with IL being more sentences varying in two levels of similarity of topic. Results of that, and of a second, unpublished study, both showed no RI. Deese and Hardman (1954) found no RI for connected discourse under conditions of unlimited response time. Ausubel, Robbins, and Blake (1957), using the method of whole presentation, found no RI. The measure of both learning and recall was a recognition test, largely of substance retention. Peairs (1958) did find RI using a recognition procedure; Slamecka (1959), using grouped *S*s, reported that unaided written recall of a short passage was a negative function of the degree of similarity of topic the interfering passage bore to the original passage.

On the whole, these results were rather discouraging about generalizing RI findings from nonsense material to connected discourse and led to the view that prose was not susceptible to RI, or at least to the similarity variable (Miller, 1951, p. 220). We feel, however, that the difficulty was not in the characteristics of connected discourse, but rather in the methods employed. It is noteworthy that all of the above studies employed the less well-controlled techniques of group testing, whole presentation, unlimited recall times, recognition tests, and the like. When, however, connected discourse was presented in the same manner as the traditional serial list, using the serial anticipation method with individually tested *S*s, significant RI was obtained, and it was clearly shown to be a function of degree of OL and IL, as well as of similarity of OL-IL subject matter (Slamecka, 1960a, 1960b). Any presumption of the uniqueness of connected discourse with regard to these variables is no longer tenable, and the door is now open for further exploration of this area.

Errors in recognition and recall of a story were shown to be a function of the interference provided by the interpolated presentation of a picture which bore some thematic resemblance to the story (Davis & Sinha, 1950a, 1950b). Similarly, Belbin (1950) showed that an interpolated recall test concerning an incidentally present poster interfered with the subsequent recognition of the poster. If the attempted recall is viewed as interfering with the original perceptual trace, then the degree of OL and IL (recall test) similarity was determined by each *S*'s own recall performance.

Lying somewhere between the use of discrete, unconnected items and ordinary prose are two studies employing lists of various orders of approximation to English, constructed according to a method developed by Miller and Selfridge (1950). If RI is a function of contextual constraint, then the use of such materials should be appropriate.

Heise (1956) used an unrelated word list as OL, and five different IL levels of approximation to English. He found recall was best with the greatest dissimilarity between the lists. Thus, the seventh order IL list (close to English text) produced almost no interference, whereas the first order list (same order as OL) produced a great deal, again supporting the generalization concerning greater RI with greater similarity between serial lists. King and Cofer (1958) extended this technique by using OL lists at the zero, first, third, and fifth orders, with four different orders of IL at each of the OL levels. Their intent was to examine similarity effects at various levels of contextual constraint, but the results did not show an overall comprehensive pattern for RI. They suggested that the effects of contextual constraint may prove to be more complex than originally expected, and called for further investigation.

Extrinsic Factors

In this section are papers focusing upon variables actually extrinsic to the specific items being learned. In most of these studies the groups learned identical materials, and they differed only with regard to such things as the general surround, testing methods, and sets.

The striking effects of altered environment were shown by Bilodeau and Schlosberg (1951). The two groups differed only in the conditions under which IL took place. One group stayed in the same room for all phases, and the other had the IL in a dissimilar room with a different exposure device and a changed posture for *S*. Recall, done in the OL room, indicated that IL interfered only half as much when associated with a different surround. Elaborating upon this, Greenspoon and Ranyard (1957) also used two different surrounds (different rooms, posture, and exposure devices designated as A and B), in four combinations, and the results, in terms of decreasing order of recall were ABA (AAA, ABB) AAB (those within parentheses not significantly different). Although no controls were used, the findings agree with those of Bilodeau and Schlosberg. These studies support the view that, since recall takes place in some context, the cues governing a response lie not only within the learning material, but also in the general surround, and that the magnitude of RI is a partial function of such context-carried cues. The relative importance of the proprioceptive vs. the exteroceptive cues was not assessed.

Jenkins and Postman (1949) varied testing procedures for OL and IL, using anticipation (A) or recognition (R), in four combinations. Results showed a significant increase in recall when procedures were different, under only one of the comparisons (A–A, A–R). The authors concluded that using a different testing method is a change in set and "helps in the functional isolation of materials learned successively" (p. 72). Postman and Postman (1948) gave four groups the same materials, differing only in the order of the S–R items. Paired syllables-numbers for OL were followed by either paired numbers-syllables or more syllables-numbers. The changed set groups showed better recall. No control groups were used. In the second part of the same report, OL was paired words with either a compatible (doctor-heal) or incompatible (war-peaceful) relation between them. For IL, half the *S*s learned a list with the same logical relations, and half learned one with the opposite relations to OL. This latter group showed superior retention, again attributed to the dissimilar sets involved.

Comparing the effects of incidental vs. intentional learning of OL and IL, Postman and Adams (1956) found that, regardless of the OL conditions, intentional IL produced more RI than incidental IL. Both intentional and incidental learning were equally susceptible to RI when followed by IL of the same kind and strength as OL. The authors noted that: "Intentional practice resulted in the learning of a longer number of items during interpolation and hence was a more effective source of interference" (p. 328). Thus, it appears that these conditions were simply the vehicles by which degree of IL, the effective variable, was manipulated. In an earlier paper, Prentice (1943) concluded that incidental learning was more subject to RI than intentional, but when Postman and Adams (1956) corrected Prentice's data by subtracting the respective control group scores, the results agreed with the Postman and Adams findings. If incidental and intentional conditions are construed as providing different sets, or "functional isolation," then an experiment in which the degree of acquisition was equalized should be expected to give different results: the similarly treated groups should display more RI than the changed-set groups. Since this has not been done, we must conclude that the RI effects of incidental vs. intentional conditions per se are not yet known.

The effect of the emotion-arousing characteristic of the IL upon retention is an interesting question, but only one study attempted it within this period and produced inconclusive results (McMullin, 1942), probably because of a confounded experimental design. Among the truly inherent subject variables that have been investigated is the effect of the age of *S* (Gladis & Braun, 1958; Wywrocki, 1957). The former study divided *S*s into three age classes: 20–29, 40–49, and 60–72 years. There was no control group. Although a negative relationship between age and rate of learning was found, the adjusted absolute recall scores revealed no differential RI effects related to age. One might speculate that the decreased learning ability of the older *S*s was a PI effect resulting from their many years of previous learning. When the recall scores were "corrected" for this, the actually obtained negative relation between raw recall and age was eliminated. Among the more clinical subject variables, Cassel (1957) reported no differential RI susceptibility between *S*s of normal mentality and those with mental deficiency. Sherman (1957) found that psychopaths showed better retention than either neurotics or normals, measured by total forgetting scores. Livson and Krech (1955) reported a moderate positive correlation between recall and scores on the KAE (Kinesthetic Aftereffect Test, which was related to Krech's cortical conductivity hypothesis).

The importance of set factors, generally called warm-up effects, has been recognized (Irion, 1948). Thune (1958) showed that recall was significantly facilitated by a preceding appropriate warm-up. If OL was from a memory drum and IL from a filmstrip, then a memory drum warm-up facilitated recall, but a filmstrip warm-up did not. Inappropriate warm-up did facilitate later relearning trials, and Thune concluded that warm-up has both peripheral and central components, with the former more transitory. No RI control groups were used.

The effects of such extrinsic variables upon PI have not yet been investigated. This line of research should be extended, since the magnitudes of interference obtained are often considerable, and probably much of our everyday forgetting is attributable to such context-associated factors.

Temporal Effects

Swenson (1941) summarized the effects of temporal variables as follows:

[*a*] . . . interpolation immediately adjacent either to original learning or to recall of original learning is more effective in producing retroactive inhibition than is interpolated activity between those two extremes (p. 15). [*b*] . . . the more recent studies suggest an inverse relationship between length of the time interval and relative retroactive inhibition (p. 16).

Subsequent work has called for a modification of those statements.

Examination of the RI paradigm reveals three manipulable temporal intervals: end of OL—start of IL, end of IL—start of RL, and end of OL—start of RL. No single experiment, while keeping the IL learning period constant, can vary only one of these intervals without automatically changing one of the others. When the IL learning period varies (as in studies giving different numbers of IL trials) while the OL–IL and the OL–RL intervals are kept constant, then the IL–RL interval will inevitably vary. Therefore, in the study of any one of these variables, confounding is inescapable. There is no easy way out of this dilemma. The only technique approaching a solution seems to be to do several separate experiments, confounding a different pair of intervals each time, and then evaluating the results of all the experiments by determining which confoundings have no effect. This more elaborate approach has not been used in actual practice; rather, acceptance of such confounding seems to be the rule.

Varying the IL–RL interval allows for measurement of progressive changes in the strength of RI and PI, and deductions concerning the events that occur in that time. Underwood (1948a), using IL–RL intervals of 5 and 48 hr., and Briggs (1954) at 4 min. to 72 hr., report no significant changes in magnitude of RI. Deese and Marder (1957), using unlimited response times, from intervals of 4 min. to 48 hrs., and Peterson and Peterson (1957) from 0 to 15 min., both found no changes in recall. Slight RI decreases were reported by

Jones (1953) from .17 to 24 hrs. (with an increase from 24 to 144 hrs.) and by Ishihara (1951). Using the uncommon A–B, C–D design with very high levels of practice, Rothkopf (1957) found an increase in recall from 0 to 21 hrs., but no control groups were used. From the trend of these results, the best conclusion seems to be that RI remains relatively stable over time, at least up to 72 hrs.

In examining the temporal course of PI, Underwood (1949b) found no change from 20 to 75 min., but (Underwood, 1948a) did find a drop in recall from 5 to 48 hrs. (no control groups), and Jones (1953) also reported increasing PI. In a study not explicitly designed to assess PI, therefore lacking control groups, Greenberg and Underwood (1950) also found a significant drop in List 2 recall from 10 min. to 5 hrs. to 48 hrs. In spite of the lack of appropriate controls in some of these studies, the results are in sufficient agreement to allow the conclusion that PI shows a gradual increase through time, which is in accord with logical expectations, as Underwood (1948a) has pointed out.

In comparing the relative strengths of RI vs. PI through time under comparable conditions, Underwood (1948a) found that RI was greater at 5 hrs., but that there was no difference at 48 hrs. Jones (1953) and Rothkopf (1957) reported similar observations. Underwood hypothesized that the failure of List 1 recall to diminish might be due to a process of gradual recovery of OL responses after their unlearning during IL. This led to the use of the modified free recall (MFR) procedure as a method of assessing response dominance. In MFR, *S* is given a stimulus item common to both lists and asked for the first response that comes to mind. It was felt that such unrestricted, uncorrected recall would provide a fairer estimate of the relative strengths of the competing responses, although it was clearly not intended to be equivalent to the restricted recall required for RI measures. Underwood (1948b) gave MFR at 1 min., 5, 24, and 48 hrs. after IL and found no change in OL responses, a consistent drop in IL responses, and a rise in "other" responses. He concluded that:

> These data are given as further support of the interpretation of unlearning of the first list as being similar to experimental extinction. The fact that no decrease in the effective strength of the first list responses takes place over 48 hrs. suggests that a process running counter to the usual forgetting process is present. It is suggested that this mechanism may be likened to spontaneous recovery (p. 438).

Concerning OL responses, it seems unnecessary to hypothesize two opposing tendencies (recovery vs. "usual forgetting") canceling each other out, as it were, to account for a finding of no change. The usual forgetting curve might not necessarily be expected of OL responses, since the effects of IL could be such as to obliterate, through differential unlearning, more of the weak than the strong responses, leaving the strong, stable ones that are more resistant to the "usual forgetting" process, in the preponderance. List 2 responses, not so selectively eliminated, would be expected to decrease in time. In support of this alternate view we call attention to two relevant bits of evidence. Deese and Marder (1957) found that the number of items recalled after interpolation remained constant over intervals of 4 min., 2, 24, and 48 hours after IL. Also, Runquist (1957) found that resistance to RI was positively related to the degree of an original item's strength. In another MFR experiment, Briggs (1954) did obtain a rise in OL responses between 4 min. and 6 hrs., with subsequent stability through 72 hrs. Because of the discrepancy between these data and those of Underwood (1948b), another study was done in which Briggs, Thompson, and Brogden (1954) found no OL changes between 4 min. and 6 hrs. These authors concluded that "responses from original learning show no change, that responses from interpolated learning tend to decrease with time interval in a fairly regular manner, and that 'other' responses tend to increase . . . " (p. 423). From these MFR data, we tentatively conclude that the processes underlying the temporal stability of RI do not as yet clearly indicate the recovery of unlearned original responses. The spontaneous recovery hypothesis is an attractive one, but more evidence of its validity should be brought forth.

Another problem of interest is the effect of the temporal point of interpolation, which requires keeping the OL–RL interval constant and varying the OL–IL period. Unavoidably, this introduces confounding with the simultaneously varying OL–IL interval, as discussed above.

Houlahan (1941) gave IL either 0, 4, or 8 mins. after OL and found more RI for the immediate interpolation condition. However, there was no direct measure of OL; rather, the performance on some previously learned lists thought to be of equal difficulty to OL was used as a comparison. Within a 16-day OL–RL period, Postman and Alper (1946) gave IL at eight evenly dispersed intervals and found maxima of recall at 1, 8, and 15 days after OL. Degree of acquisition was uncontrolled, since fixed numbers of trials were given; and, since no acquisition data were presented, unequivocal conclusions about the temporal variable cannot be drawn.

Maeda (1951), using short intervals, reported greatest reproduction when IL directly followed OL. Newton (1955) with an A–B, C–B design, and Archer and Underwood (1951) with A–B, A–C, using a 48-hr. OL–RL period with IL at 0, 24, and 48 hrs., concluded that temporal point of interpolation was not an effective variable. Newton and Wickens (1956) noted that the Archer and Underwood study failed to control for differential warm-up, in that the group with IL immediately before RL benefitted by warm-up, whereas the other two groups had no comparable advantage. They repeated the Archer and Underwood study with the same materials, but gave a warm-up task to the 0- and 24-hr. groups. No effects of the temporal intervals were obtained, confirming the previous results. However, they also reported two additional experiments, with an A–B, C–D design, with warm-up provided. One study had a performance acquisition criterion, and the other a fixed number of trials. Results of both showed that the 48-hr. group did show significantly more RI than the other two. Those authors state that the A–B, A–C design "is a relationship which is designed to produce a maximum amount of RI, and the intensity of this condition may obscure the RI which can arise from a variable of lesser importance—as the temporal variable may well be" (Newton & Wickens, 1956, p. 153). They especially stressed the importance of generalized competition between lists, a point which shall be developed further in the theoretical section below. We tentatively conclude from the Newton and Wickens (1956) data, supported by Maeda (1951), that RI increases as the OL–IL interval increases and that the effect is thus far specific to the A–B, C–D design.

A comparable PI design would require a constant List 2–RL period, while varying the List 1–List 2 interval. We have been unable to find such an experiment in the literature within this period. Ray (1945) studied List 2 acquisition as a function of the interval since the learning of List 1. Although he speaks of PI, the design is appropriate only to conclusions about negative transfer.

Another temporal variable which has not been studied sufficiently in an RI design is the rate of presentation of the items. The only relevant retention study on this is an unpublished honors thesis by Seeler (1958). OL was a 35-word passage of prose presented via tape recording to a criterion of one perfect unaided written recall, followed by similar memorization of an IL passage, and then by OL recall. OL rates of presentation were ½, 1, and 2 secs., followed by ½; 1; or 2-second counterbalanced rates on the IL. No control groups were used. Results showed that number of trials to mastery of all original and interpolated passages was a direct function of their presentation rates, a finding consistent with acquisition reports based on nonsense materials. There was no influence of either the OL or IL presentation rates, or any of their combinations, upon recall. It might have been supposed that an IL rate different from the OL rate would have served to functionally isolate the original list and produce less forgetting, but that was not the case. The possibility of confounding rate of presentation and strength of associations at the end of OL due to differential acquisition rates (Underwood, 1949a) is not a problem in this study, since unaided recall was used. With the method of serial anticipation, however, the criterial OL trial is also another learning trial, and two groups taken to the same performance criterion may still differ on total associative strength at the termination of the last OL trial. The problem is always present whenever any variable that effects rate of acquisition (such as meaningfulness, similarity, etc.) is used along with the serial anticipation technique. The generalizability of the latter results to unconnected materials as well as the additional independent problem of the RI effects of massed vs. distributed training must await further study.

Major Theoretical Positions

In this section we shall discuss the four main theoretical positions which have influenced the period covered by this review. Two major formulations, appearing within a few months of each other (Gibson, 1940; Melton & Irwin, 1940), guided the theoretical aspects of the study of RI within the first few years covered by this review.

Utilizing the classical conditioning principles of stimulus generalization and differentiation, Gibson (1940) presented a set of postulates for verbal behavior that served to lend greater predictive specificity to the transfer or straight competition-of-response view, previously developed by McGeoch and his collaborators. Basic to Gibson's approach is the view that verbal learning and retention are matters of developing discriminations among the items to be learned. She defines her two basic constructs as follows: The construct of generalization is "the tendency for a response R_a learned to S_a to occur when S_b (with which it has not been previously associated) is presented" (p. 204). The construct of differentiation is "a progressive decrease in generalization as a result of reinforced practice with S_a–R_a and reinforced presentation of S_b" (p. 205). A curvilinear growth function of the generalization tendency as practice trials increase is stressed. Essentially, RI is related to the degree of discriminability of the two lists, such discriminability being a positive function of their respective degrees of learning, and a negative function of the time elapsed since learning. Spontaneous recovery of generalization tendencies (wrong responses) through time is assumed. From these postulates, several deductions concerning RI were presented, and some of these have been tested and confirmed: for instance, RI as a function of various similarity relations among the items (Gibson, 1941; Hamilton, 1943), and the curvilinear RI function obtained as the degree of IL increases (Melton & Irwin, 1940). Among the deductions tested but not confirmed is one bearing upon the temporal point of interpolation problem. Gibson feels that one of the reasons for the disparity of results on this question lies in the neglect of the importance of the degree of acquisition of the lists. She predicted that acquisition level would be found to interact with the temporal point of interpolation because the spontaneous recovery of generalization tendencies between lists is a function of time. This prediction was tested by Archer and Underwood (1951) using three levels of IL acquisition (6/10, 10/10, and 10/10+5 trials) and three OL–IL intervals (0, 24, and 48 hrs.), but no interaction between them was found. RI control groups were not used, and in light of the theoretical importance of this study it would seem advisable to re-examine these variables with a design adaptable to relative RI measures. The authors themselves expressed dissatisfaction with the outcome and "felt that a modification of the conditions in our design would indicate the temporal position to be a factor" (p. 289).

Considering the general reaction toward Gibson's theory in succeeding RI work, we feel that, on the whole, it has been favorably received, since it has been given a certain amount of implicit corroboration by way of being compatible with many findings (for instance, Briggs, 1957) and has potential for even further development. It has not, however, stimulated a comprehensive series of experiments aimed at testing the many RI deductions implicit within it. The reason for this is certainly not any lack of clarity in the postulates. One present weakness seems to be the lack of direct evidence for a spontaneous recovery process influencing RI.

Melton and Irwin (1940) introduced their two-factor theory within the framework of a study of RI as a function of the degree of IL. OL was 5 trials on an 18-item serial nonsense list, followed by 5, 10, 20, or 40 trials on an IL list. Relying upon a count of the overt interlist intrusions as an objective index of the degree of competition between original and interpolated responses at recall, they found that the curves of amount of absolute RI, and the number of such intrusions (multiplied by a factor of 2 to do justice to partial intrusions) were not highly correlated. (The theoretical importance of intrusion counts gained its ascendancy with this study.) Rather, interlist intrusions increased to a maximum at intermediate IL levels and then decreased markedly, whereas the curve of RI rose sharply and maintained a relatively high level, declining slightly at the highest degree of IL. That portion of the RI attributable to direct competition of responses at recall was at a maximum when OL and IL were about equal in strength. Therefore, to account for the remainder of the obtained RI not accounted for by overt competition, Melton and Irwin postulated another factor at work, tentatively identified as the direct "unlearning" of the original responses by their unreinforced elicitation or punishment, during IL. The growth of this "Factor X" was assumed to be a progressively increasing function of IL strength. Since Factor X was almost totally responsible for the absolute RI at the highest IL level, and since RI under that condition dissipated most rapidly after a few relearning trials, it was concluded that the effects of such unlearning were quite transitory. This was still a competition of response theory in the sense that the original responses were still assumed to be competing at recall with the interpolated ones, but to that was added the factor of weakening in OL response strength, if not complete extinction, through the process of unlearning.

The presence of confounding between the degree of IL, and the end of IL–start of RL interval was pointed out by Peterson and Peterson (1957) as a possible alternative account of the differences in intrusions obtained by the Melton and Irwin design. With a fixed OL–RL interval the IL–RL interval shortens, with increasing IL trials taking more time. However, another study of the effects of degree of IL did use a fixed IL–RL interval (with a correspondingly varying OL–RL interval—Osgood, 1948) and still found comparable intrusion changes.

A direct deduction from the two-factor theory is that RI, being a result of both unlearning and competition effects, should be greater than PI, which was presumed to be the result of response competition alone. This hypothesis was tested and confirmed by Melton and von Lackum (1941) in a study using five trials on each of two 10-item consonant lists, and has also been given further general support by others (Jones, 1953; McGeoch & Underwood, 1943; Underwood, 1942, 1945). Underwood (1948a) in yet another study also found greater RI than PI at 5 hrs.; but at 24 hrs. they were equal. His resulting postulation of spontaneous recovery of the OL, and the subsequent developments of that concept have been discussed above.

Later, certain other observations led to some discontent with the two-factor theory. In an experiment designed to test the generalizability of the Melton and Irwin findings to paired-adjectives lists, Thune and Underwood (1943) used an A–B, A–C design with five OL trials and 0, 5, 10, or 20 IL trials. Their results confirmed the existence of a negatively accelerated function between RI and degree of IL, as well as the fact that overt intrusions were maximal at the intermediate IL levels (10 trials) and declined sharply by the 20-trial level, while RI still remained massive. However, there was no difference in the rate of RI dissipation between the 10 and 20 trial IL levels, and therefore the transitoriness of RI at these levels could not reasonably be attributable to the unlearning construct. The two-factor theory would have been forced to predict faster dissipation at the 20 IL level, since overt intrusions were far less for it than for the 10 IL level. In addition, the curve of Factor X drawn for the Thune and Underwood data was quite different in shape from that obtained by Melton and Irwin, and it was felt to imply rather incongruous psychological properties for a curve of unlearning. In addition, an item analysis revealed that almost half of the overt intrusions took place on items where the original response had never been reinforced (or correctly anticipated) at all! Therefore, such interlist intrusions could not be legitimate indicators of response competition, since those responses had never been learned during OL, and were simply not available to be competing with anything. It is also to be expected that for original responses to be unlearned they would have to occur during IL in sufficient frequency to be subject to punishment or lack of reinforcement. Yet, as Osgood (1948) pointed out from his data, the number of related original list intrusions during IL was "infinitesimally small" and could not possibly account for much unlearning at all. This previously observed discrepancy between the assumed growth of Factor X and the lack of increase in intrusions during IL as a function of increasing IL trials should be tempered with the possibility that partial intrusions could still play a large role in determining the degree of unlearning obtained, and such intrusions are not easily detected and counted.

Thune and Underwood (1943) suggested that the ratio of overt to covert (and partial) errors need not necessarily remain constant, but may undergo progressive change as a function of the degree of IL, therefore accounting for the drop in overt intrusions by postulating an increase in implicit interference. In a subsequent paper Underwood (1945) elaborated upon this suggestion and formalized his differentiation theory.

The shift in error ratios was interpreted as a resultant of two simultaneous processes: increasing IL associative strength tending to produce more overt intrusions, but being gradually overcome by the growth of differentiation, tending to reduce the intrusions. The magnitude of the differentiation construct was held to be a positive function of the degree of learning of both lists and a negative function of the time between the end of IL and the start of RL. A decrease in overt intrusions was, in effect, the index of increasing differentiation. When the two lists are about equally well learned, intrusions are maximal and differentiation is low; but with increasing disparity between their absolute or relative acquisition levels, intrusions are reduced, indicating increased differentiation. By the same token, a short IL–RL interval should also produce higher differentiation. That this is in fact the case was shown in the Archer and Underwood study (1958) where overt intrusions declined as the IL–RL interval became shorter. The increasing differentiation allows *S* to recognize and withhold erroneous responses, resulting in fewer interlist intrusions and more covert or omission errors. Differentiation was described phenomenologically by Underwood (1945, p. 25) as being

> related to the verbally reported experience of "knowing" on the part of the subject that the responses from the interpolated learning are inappropriate at the attempted recall of the OL. Degree of differentiation in this sense is thus an indication of the degree to which the subject identifies the list to which each response belongs.

Empirical support for various aspects of this theory has come from several studies (e.g., Archer & Underwood, 1951; Osgood, 1948; Thune & Underwood, 1943; Underwood, 1945). Further, the fact that intrusion frequencies change but RI still remains constant might be simply a function of the limited recall time (usually 2 sec.) available to *S*. If this recall time was extended, then perhaps *S* would have sufficient time both to recognize the erroneous and verbalize the correct response, thus displaying a decrease in RI at high IL (differentiation) levels. Underwood (1950a, 1950b) tested this promising hypothesis, but found no dropping off of the Melton and Irwin effect, and concluded that differentiation does not change as a function of increased (8 sec.) recall time. Unlearning was therefore still retained as a useful concept; but, since it was shown that such response weakening took place only in the first "few" IL trials, as measured by associative inhibition, and because of the relatively great stress put upon the role of differentiation, Underwood's revision of the two-factor theory became an important independent influence upon subsequent RI thinking.

Certain apparent similarities between Underwood's differentiation construct and Gibson's concept of differentiation deserve to be pointed out at this time. For both theorists, differentiation is in part a positive function of degree of reinforced practice on the material, such practice serving to reduce overt intrusion errors. Secondly, temporal relationships also play a large part in determining the strength of both constructs. However, the two positions do differ with regard to certain important aspects of operation of these determiners of differentiation. Underwood's concept refers to the more global process of *S* correctly assigning the list membership of the responses, whereas Gibson speaks of discrete S–R connections in competition. Furthermore, Underwood's theory is derived from experiments based largely upon the A–B, A–C design, whereas for Gibson, generalization as defined requires that the stimulus members be similar, but not identical. For Underwood, increasing differentiation is marked by a reduction of intrusions and an increase in omissions, but no drop in RI, whereas Gibson implies that increasing differentiation will result directly in improved performance. And finally, Gibson makes spontaneous recovery an integral part of her differentiation concept, while it was not until later that Underwood suggested a spontaneous recovery process, and that was reserved for the unlearning aspect of his theory.

The last theoretical formulation to be considered was put forth by Osgood (1946). It stemmed from his investigations of the RI effects of meaningful opposed responses and involved a hypothesis about reciprocal inhibition of antagonistic reactions, wherein "simultaneous with learning any response the *S* is also learning not to make the directly antagonistic response" (Osgood, 1948, p. 150). This was clearly an application of the reciprocal inhibition concept of neurophysiology to the area of verbal behavior. In pursuing the tenability of this position, two relevant transfer studies have shown that the learning of both similar and opposed List 2 responses was equally rapid, and much easier than learning neutral responses (Ishihara & Kasha, 1953; Ishihara, Morimoto, Kasha, & Kubo, 1957), thus failing to confirm the hypothesis. Unless further support for the hypothesis is forthcoming, we must conclude that it will not become an important influence in RI work.

With regard to the question of the adequacy of the two-factor theories we are of the opinion that the concept of unlearning is a valuable one, but that an acceptable measure of its magnitude has not yet been devised. Interlist intrusions were proposed only as a partial index, but not as a complete measure of its effects, and the difficulties encountered by such an index have been enumerated above. Instructions calculated to encourage the verbalizing of errors do just that: Morrow (1954) and Bugelski (1948) found that "all that is required to obtain a large number of such errors is to ask for them" (p. 680).

Two interesting proposals have been advanced as methods for distinguishing operationally between effects of competition and effects of unlearning. Postman and Kaplan (1947) spoke of two measures of RI: error scores, and the reaction times for correct responses (residual retroaction). These two measures were found not to be correlated and are thus of necessity measures of two different processes. They suggest that: "It is possible that retention loss (error scores) reflects the effects of unlearning, whereas reaction times may depend primarily on the competition between responses" (p. 143). Their experiment did not include variation of any factor which might be expected to affect unlearning differentially and therefore the usefulness of their proposal has not yet been tested.

Later, Postman and Egan (1948) proposed that the rate of recall of correct responses be a measure of unlearning. Retention was measured by the free recall procedure, and performance was recorded both in terms of number of items recalled, as well as by the rate of emission of correct items, per 3-sec. periods. They state that

> The two types of measures—amount lost and rate of recall—may be regarded as measures of these two processes (unlearning and competition, respectively). Those aspects of OL which have been unlearned cannot be evoked on retest: unlearning leads to decrement in amount retained. Other aspects suffer competition from the IL but are not unlearned. They are potentially available but "disturbed," and manifest that in a slower rate of recall (p. 543).

These are both valid and constructive formulations deserving of further attention, but no significant efforts have as yet been made to test their usefulness in predicting data crucially relevant to the unlearning factor.

These experiments by Postman point in a new direction, suggesting that such evidence for competition of response is a result of the brief recall times used in RI studies. If competition of response results in increased latencies, then decrements in recall may come when the latency of a response exceeds the 2-sec. interval usually used. Underwood's (1950a) study, which found no PI with an 8-sec. recall interval, supports this possibility.

An experiment by Ceraso (1959) may provide further support for such a hypothesis. With an A–B, A–C design, *S*s were asked to recall both the first and second list responses and also to assign these to the proper list. Since a 20-sec. (maximum) recall interval was used, blocking due to competition of response should not be expected. An analysis of the first list responses which were correct on the last trial of OL, and were then scored as incorrect at recall, showed that the reason for the forgetting was simply the unavailability of the response. If the response was available at recall, it was also assigned to the correct list. Since competition of response should reveal itself as a misassignment of the response, it was clear that the forgetting obtained could not be accounted for by competition. Using a technique somewhat related, with an A–B, A–C design, Barnes and Underwood (1959) obtained similar results, and accordingly rejected a competition explanation.

Ceraso also found that in a large number of cases *S* could give both responses to the stimulus. But does not the unlearning hypothesis imply that learning the second list response entails the unavailability of the first list response? The answer that immediately suggests itself is that unlearning is a function of the degree of first and second list item learning. Therefore, an item analysis of the kind performed by Runquist was undertaken. The result showed that degree of learning of the second list item did not affect the retention of the first list item, thus verifying Runquist's (1957) original finding.

It seems that the latter data pose a real problem for current theories of RI, since the basic mechanism usually postulated requires interaction between associations with similar or identical stimulus items. Both the Runquist and Ceraso findings seem to indicate a nonspecific mechanism. Learning a second list affects the entire first list, regardless of the specific item interactions.

In conclusion, it appears that the major theoretical accounts of RI have remained relatively unchallenged and unchanged for the last ten years, in spite of the accumulation of considerable empirical data. It is hoped that this overview of the current state of the field will help to initiate a more vigorous and sustained effort toward an improved theory of forgetting.

Summary

For a concluding statement we feel it would be appropriate to enumerate some of the pressing problems and empirical gaps currently evident in the status of our knowledge of RI and PI. These points are presented in the order of their appearance in the foregoing review and do not reflect any opinion regarding their relative importance.

1. Reconsideration of the relative merits of RI quantification: absolute RI, relative RI, and total forgetting
2. Determinants of the RI and PI of individual items
3. Determinants of the rate of PI dissipation
4. Development of an objectively quantitative scale of similarity for use in constructing lists of items
5. Reappraisal of the right half of the response dimension of Osgood's retroaction surface
6. Effects of opposed or antagonistic stimulus relations upon RI and PI, with responses the same
7. Effects of varying response similarity upon PI, with the "categorization approach" error eliminated
8. Further study of the RI effects of mediated and unidirectional prepotent association between list items
9. PI as a function of similarity relations within the A–B, C–D design
10. Determinants of the RI and PI of connected discourse
11. Relative importance of proprioceptive vs. exteroceptive extrinsic cues for recall
12. RI effects of incidental vs. intentional acquisition conditions, with degree of acquisition controlled

13. Effects of the affective characteristics of the material upon its RI and PI

14. Better handling of the problem of confounding which arises when temporal intervals are manipulated

15. Further tests of the validity of the spontaneous recovery hypothesis

16. Examination of the point of interpolation problem as a function of other attendant variables

17. RI as a function of presentation rate, and of massing vs. distributing trials

18. Testing of the two-factor theory through an improved measure of the unlearning construct

REFERENCES

ARCHER, E. J., & UNDERWOOD, B. J. Retroactive inhibition of verbal association as a multiple function of temporal point of interpolation and degree of interpolated learning. *J. exp. Psychol.*, 1951, **42**, 283–290.

ATWATER, S. K. Proactive inhibition and associative facilitation as affected by degree of prior learning. *J. exp. Psychol.*, 1953, **46**, 400–404.

AUSUBEL, D., ROBBINS, L., & BLAKE, E., JR. Retroactive inhibition and facilitation in the learning of school materials. *J. educ. Psychol.*, 1957, **48**, 334–343.

BARNES, J. M., & UNDERWOOD, B. J. "Fate" of first-list associations in transfer theory. *J. exp. Psychol.*, 1959, **58**, 97–105.

BELBIN, E. The influence of interpolated recall on recognition. *Quart. J. exp. Psychol.*, 1950, **2**, 163–169.

BILODEAU, I. M., & SCHLOSBERG, H. Similarity in stimulating conditions as a variable in retroactive inhibition. *J. exp. Psychol.*, 1951, **41**, 199–204.

BLANKENSHIP, A. B., & WHITELY, P. L. Proactive inhibition in the recall of advertising material. *J. soc. Psychol.*, 1941, **13**, 311–322.

BORING, E. G. Communality in relation to proaction and retroaction. *Amer. J. Psychol.*, 1941, **54**, 280–283.

BRIGGS, G. E. Acquisition, extinction, and recovery functions in retroactive inhibition. *J. exp. Psychol.*, 1954, **47**, 285–293.

BRIGGS, G. E. Retroactive inhibition as a function of degree of original and interpolated learning. *J. exp. Psychol.*, 1957, **53**, 60–67.

BRIGGS, G. E., THOMPSON, R. F., & BROGDEN, W. J. Retention functions in retroactive inhibition. *J. exp. Psychol.*, 1954, **48**, 419–423.

BUGELSKI, B. R. Interference with recall of original responses after learning new responses to old stimuli. *J. exp. Psychol.*, 1942, **30**, 368–379.

BUGELSKI, B. R. An attempt to reconcile unlearning and reproductive inhibition explanations of proactive inhibition. *J. exp. Psychol.*, 1948, **38**, 670–682.

BUGELSKI, B. R., & CADWALLADER, T. A reappraisal of the transfer and retroaction surface. *J. exp. Psychol.*, 1956, **52**, 360–366.

BUXTON, C. E. List structure as a determiner of amount of retroactive inhibition. *Psychol. Bull.*, 1941, **38**, 719. (Abstract)

CASSEL, R. H. Serial verbal learning and retroactive inhibition in aments and normal children. Unpublished doctoral dissertation, Northwestern Univer., 1957.

CERASO, J. An experimental critique of competition of response and specific interference as factors in retroactive inhibition. Unpublished doctoral dissertaion, New School for Social Research, 1959.

COOPER, J. B. An attempt to measure the "tension" values of interpolated situations. *J. gen. Psychol.*, 1942, **27**, 347–351.

CRANNELL, C. W. An effective demonstration of retroactive and proactive inhibition. *Amer. J. Psychol.*, 1948, **61**, 391–395.

DAVIS, D. R., & SINHA, D. The effect of one experience on the recall of another. *Quart. J. exp. Psychol.*, 1950, **2**, 43–52. (a)

DAVIS, D. R., & SINHA, D. The influence of an interpolated experience upon recognition. *Quart. J. exp. Psychol.*, 1950, **2**, 132–137. (b)

DEESE, J., & HARDMAN, G. W. An analysis of errors in retroactive inhibition of rote verbal learning. *Amer. J. Psychol.*, 1954, **67**, 299–307.

DEESE, J., & MARDER, V. J. The pattern of errors in delayed recall of serial learning after interpolation. *Amer. J. Psychol.*, 1957, **70**, 594–599.

GIBSON, E. J. A systematic application of the concepts of generalization and differentiation to verbal learning. *Psychol. Rev.*, 1940, **47**, 196–229.

GIBSON, E. J. Retroactive inhibition as a

function of degree of generalization between tasks. *J. exp. Psychol.*, 1941, **28**, 93–115.

GLADIS, M., & BRAUN, H. W. Age differences in transfer and retroaction as a function of intertask response similarity. *J. exp. Psychol.*, 1958, **55**, 25–30.

GREENBERG, R., & UNDERWOOD, B. J. Retention as a function of stage of practice. *J. exp. Psychol.*, 1950, **40**, 452–547.

GREENSPOON, J., & RANYARD, R. Stimulus conditions and retroactive inhibition. *J. exp. Psychol.*, 1957, **53**, 55–59.

HAAGEN, C. H. Learning and retention as a function of the synonymity of original and interpolated tasks. Unpublished doctoral dissertation, State Univer. Iowa, 1943.

HAAGEN, C. H. Synonymity, vividness, familiarity, and association value ratings of 400 pairs of common adjectives. *J. Psychol.*, 1949, **30**, 185–200.

HALL, J. F. Retroactive inhibition in meaningful material. *J. educ. Psychol.*, 1955, **46**, 47–52.

HAMILTON, R. J. Retroactive facilitation as a function of degree of generalization between tasks. *J. exp. Psychol.*, 1943, **32**, 363–376.

HEISE, G. Retroactive inhibition as a function of the degree of approximation to English word order. *Amer. Psychologist*, 1956, **11**, 450. (Abstract)

HIGHLAND, R. W. Retroactive inhibition: Effects of S-R variations in relation to degree of interpolated learning. Unpublished doctoral dissertation, Ohio State Univer., 1949.

HOULAHAN, F. J. Immediacy of interpolation and amount of inhibition. *J. educ. Psychol.*, 1941, **32**, 37–44.

IRION, A. L. Retroactive inhibition as a function of the relative serial positions of the original and interpolated items. *J. exp. Psychol.*, 1946, **36**, 262–270.

IRION, A. L. The relation of "set" to retention. *Psychol. Rev.*, 1948, **55**, 336–341.

ISHIHARA, I. The process of retroactive inhibition in retention. *Jap. J. Psychol.*, 1951, **21**, 18–25.

ISHIHARA, I., & KASHA, K. The learning of response words in similar, opposite, or neutral relation: A study on the conditioning principle in verbal learning. *Jap. J. Psychol.*, 1953, **24**, 1–12.

ISHIHARA, I., MORIMOTO, H., KASHA, K., & KUBO, K. Associative directions and semantic relations in verbal learning. *Tohoku psychol. Folia*, 1957, **16**, 7–18.

JENKINS, W. O., & POSTMAN, L. An experimental analysis of set in rote learning: Retroactive inhibition as a function of changing set. *J. exp. Psychol.*, 1949, **39**, 69–72.

JONES, W. F., JR. A comparison of retroactive and proactive inhibition as a function of the time interval between original learning and the measurement of retention. Unpublished doctoral dissertation, Vanderbilt Univer., 1953.

KENNELLY, T. W. The role of similarity in retroactive inhibition. *Arch. Psychol.*, 1941, **37**, No. 260.

KING, D. J., & COFER, C. N. Retroactive interference in meaningful material as a function of the degree of contextual constraint in the original and interpolated learning. *ONR tech. Rep.*, 1958, No. 21. (Contract NONR 595 (04), Univer. Maryland)

KINGSLEY, H. L. The factors of similarity and association in retroactive inhibition. *Amer. Psychologist*, 1946, **1**, 262. (Abstract)

LIVSON, N. H., & KRECH, D. Dynamic systems, rote learning, and retroactive inhibition. *J. Pers.*, 1955, **24**, 2–19.

MCCLELLAND, D. C., & HEATH, R. M. Retroactive inhibition as a function of degree of association of original and interpolated activities. *J. exp. Psychol.*, 1943, **33**, 420–430.

MCGEOCH, J. A., & IRION, A. L. *The psychology of human learning*. New York: Longmans, Green, 1952.

MCGEOCH, J. A., & UNDERWOOD, B. J. Tests of the two-factor theory of retroactive inhibition. *J. exp. Psychol.*, 1943, **32**, 1–16.

MCMULLIN, T. E. A study of the affective nature of the interpolated activity as a factor in producing differing relative amounts of retroactive inhibition in recall and in recognition. *J. exp. Psychol.*, 1942, **30**, 201–215.

MAEDA, Y. Zur experimentellen Untersuchung über Faktoren der Reproduktionshemming: I. Über Hemmungswirkungen auf die Reproducktон. *Jap. J. Psychol.*, 1951, **21**, 1–17.

MELTON, A. W. Overt interlist intrusions and retroactive inhibition as a function of the ratio of the degrees of learning of original and interpolated verbal habits. *Psychol. Bull.*, 1941, **38**, 575.

MELTON, A. W., & IRWIN, J. McQ. The influence of degree of interpolated learning on retroactive inhibition and the overt transfer of specific responses. *Amer. J. Psychol.*, 1940, **53**, 173–203.

MELTON, A. W., & VON LACKUM, W. J. Retroactive and proactive inhibition in retention: Evidence for a 2-factor theory of retroactive inhibition. *Amer. J. Psychol.*, 1941, **54**, 157–173.

MILLER, G. A. *Language and communication.* New York: McGraw-Hill, 1951.

MILLER, G. A., & SELFRIDGE, J. A. Verbal context and the recall of meaningful material. *Amer. J. Psychol.*, 1950, **63**, 176–185.

MORGAN, R. L., & UNDERWOOD, B. J. Proactive inhibition as a function of response similarity. *J. exp. Psychol.*, 1950, **40**, 592–603.

MORROW, M. A. The relation of overt errors during learning to transfer and retroactive inhibition. Unpublished doctoral dissertation, Washington Univer., 1954.

NEWTON, J. M. Interlist similarities and point of interpolation in retroactive inhibition of verbal associations. Unpublished doctoral disertation, Ohio State Univer., 1955.

NEWTON, J. M., & WICKENS, D. D. Retroactive inhibition as a function of the temporal position of the interpolated learning. *J. exp. Psychol.*, 1956, **51**, 149–154.

OSGOOD, C. E. Meaningful similarity and interference in learning. *J. exp. Psychol.*, 1946, **36**, 277–301.

OSGOOD, C. E. An investigation into the causes of retroactive interference. *J. exp. Psychol.*, 1948, **38**, 132–154.

OSGOOD, C. E. The similarity paradox in human learning: A resolution. *Psychol. Rev.*, 1949, **56**, 132–143.

PARDUCCI, A., & KNOPF, N. B. Retroactive facilitation when new responses have been learned to old stimuli. *Amer. J. Psychol.*, 1958, **71**, 426–428.

PEAIRS, R. H. Development and analysis of retroactive inhibition in retention of meaningful connected verbal stimulus material. Unpublished doctoral dissertation, Ohio State Univer., 1958.

PEIXOTTO, H. E. Proactive inhibition in the recognition of nonsense syllables. *J. exp. Psychol.*, 1947, **37**, 81–91.

PETERSON, L. R., & PETERSON, M. J. Intrusions at recall in retroactive inhibition. *Amer. Psychologist*, 1957, **12**, 419.

POSTMAN, L. Retroctive inhibition in recall and recognition. *J. exp. Psychol.*, 1952, **44**, 165–169.

POSTMAN, L. Mediated equivalence of stimuli and retroactive inhibition. *Amer. J. Psychol.*, 1958, **71**, 175–185.

POSTMAN, L., & ADAMS, P. A. Studies in incidental learning: III. Interserial interference. *J. exp. Psychol.*, 1956, **51**, 323–328.

POSTMAN, L., & ALPER, T. G. Retroactive inhibition as a function of the time of interpolation of the inhibition between learning and recall. *Amer. J. Psychol.*, 1946, **59**, 439–449.

POSTMAN, L., EGAN, J. P., & DAVIS, J. Rate of recall as a measure of learning: I. The effects of retroactive inhibition. *J. exp. Psychol.*, 1948, **38**, 535–546.

POSTMAN, L., & KAPLAN, H. L. Reaction time as a measure of retroactive inhibition. *J. exp. Psychol.*, 1947, **37**, 136–145.

POSTMAN, L., & POSTMAN, D. L. Change in set as a determinant of retroactive inhibition. *Amer. J. Psychol.*, 1948, **61**, 236–242.

POSTMAN, L., & RILEY, D. A. Degree of learning and interserial interference in retention. *U. Calif. Publ. Psychol.*, 1959.

PRENTICE, W. C. H. Retroactive inhibition and the motivation of learning. *Amer. J. Psychol.*, 1943, **56**, 283–292.

RAY, W. S. Proactive inhibition: A function of time interval. *Amer. J. Psychol.*, 1945, **58**, 519–529.

RICHARDSON, J. Retention of concepts as a function of degree of original and interpolated learning. *J. exp. Psychol.*, 1956, **51**, 358–364.

RITCHIE, M. L. The Skaggs-Robinson hypothesis as an artifact of response definition. *Psycho. Rev.*, 1954, **61**, 267–270.

ROTHKOPF, E. Z. A deduction from an excitation-inhibition account of retroactive inhibition. *J. exp. Psychol.*, 1957, **53**, 207–213.

RUNQUIST, W. N. Retention of verbal associates as a function of strength. *J. exp. Psychol.*, 1957, **54**, 369–375.

SALTZ, E. Act of regression as a special case of retroactive inhibition and functionally related to stimulus generalization. *J. exp. Psychol.*, 1953, **45**, 394–400.

SEELER, R. A. Acquisition and retention of verbal materials. Unpublished honors thesis, Univer. Vermont, 1958.

SEIDEL, R. J. The concurrent effects of proactive and retroactive inhibition. *J. exp. Psychol.*, 1959, **57**, 397–402.

SHAKLEE, A. B., & JONES, B. E. Problems of method and theory in controlling rest activity. *J. gen. Psychol.*, 1959, **60**, 11–16.

SHAW, F. J. Influence of degree of original learning upon associative and reproductive inhibition. *Proc. Ia. Acad. Sci.*, 1942, **49**, 413–417.

SHERMAN, L. J. Retention in psychopathic, neurotic, and normal subjects. *J. Pers.*, 1957, **25**, 721–729.

SHRIVER, E. L. An artifact of retroactive inhibition. *Amer. Psychologist*, 1953, **8**, 435. (Abstract)

SLAMECKA, N. J. Studies of retention of connected discourse. *Amer. J. Psychol.*, 1959, **72**, 409–416.

Slamecka, N. J. Retroactive inhibition of connected discourse as a function of practice level. *J. exp. Psychol.*, 1960, **59**, 104–108. (a)

Slamecka, N. J. Retroactive inhibition of connected discourse as a function of similarity of topic. *J. exp. Psychol.*, 1960, **60**, 245–249. (b)

Swenson, E. J. Retroactive inhibition: A review of the literature. *Minn. Stud. Educ.*, 1941, No. 1.

Thune, L. E. Reproductive interference following appropriate and inappropriate warm-up activities. *J. exp. Psychol.*, 1958, **55**, 535–542.

Thune, L. E., & Underwood, B. J. Retroactive inhibition as a function of degree of interpolated learning. *J. exp. Psychol.*, 1943, **32**, 185–200.

Twedt, H. M., & Underwood, B. J. Mixed vs. unmixed lists in transfer studies. *J. exp. Psychol.*, 1959, **58**, 111–116.

Underwood, B. J. The effects of punishment in serial verbal learning. *Proc. Ia. Acad. Sci.*, 1941, **48**, 349–352.

Underwood, B. J. A test of the two-factor theory of retroactive inhibition by use of the paired-association technique. *Psychol. Bull.*, 1942, **39**, 593. (Abstract)

Underwood, B. J. The effect of successive interpolations on retroactive and proactive inhibition. *Psychol. Monogr.*, 1945, **59**(3, Whole No. 273).

Underwood, B. J. Retroactive and proactive inhibition after 5 and 48 hours. *J. exp. Psychol.*, 1948, **38**, 29–38. (a)

Underwood, B. J. "Spontaneous recovery" of verbal associations. *J. exp. Psychol.*, 1948, **38**, 429–439. (b)

Underwood, B. J. *Experimental psychology.* New York: Appleton-Century-Crofts, 1949. (a)

Underwood, B. J. Proactive inhibition as a function of time and degree of prior learning. *J. exp. Psychol.*, 1949, **39**, 24–34. (b)

Underwood, B. J. Proactive inhibition with increased recall time. *Amer. J. Psychol.*, 1950, **63**, 594–599. (a)

Underwood, B. J. Retroactive inhibition with increased recall time. *Amer. J. Psychol.*, 1950, **63**, 67–77. (b)

Underwood, B. J. Interference and forgetting. *Psychol. Rev.*, 1957, **64**, 49–60.

Waters, R. H. The concept of psychological disposition and retroactive inhibition. *Psychol. Bull.*, 1941, **38**, 573. (Abstract)

Waters, R. H. Degree of learning and proactive inhibition in retention. *Psychol. Bull.*, 1942, **39**, 495–496. (Abstract)

Werner, H. The effect of boundary strength on interference and retention. *Amer. J. Psychol.*, 1947, **60**, 598–607.

Wywrocki, E. H. Age difference in retroactive inhibition as a function of the degree of similarity of serial position between the original and interpolated learning. Unpublished doctoral dissertation, Univer. Pittsburgh, 1957.

Young, R. K. Retroactive inhibition and proactive inhibition under varying conditions of response similarity. *J. exp. Psychol.*, 1955, **50**, 113–119.

(Received June 20, 1959)

ARTICLE 2

EXTRA-EXPERIMENTAL INTERFERENCE AND THE RETENTION OF WORDS [1]

LEO POSTMAN

University of California

This paper reports a series of studies designed to explore extra-experimental sources of interference in the forgetting of verbal materials. When a naive *S* learns a single rote series, retention losses after an interval of time may be attributed to interference from verbal habits practiced outside the laboratory. Extra-experimental interferences may be proactive or retroactive. As Underwood (1957) has pointed out, major weight must be given to proactive rather than retroactive effects since the opportunities for acquiring verbal habits which become sources of interference are clearly greater prior to the experiment than during the limited time intervals typically used in studies of retention.

Experimental analysis of the conditions of extra-experimental interference requires specification of the verbal habits which are assumed to compete with the prescribed responses at the time of the retention test. In a recent theoretical account by Underwood and Postman (1960) two major sources of extra-experimental interference were distinguished, viz., (*a*) letter-sequence interference, and (*b*) unit-sequence interference. Linguistic usage outside the laboratory establishes transitional probabilities among sequences of letters as well as hierarchies of associations among verbal units *qua* units. Letter-sequence interference will occur to the extent that the sequences of letters making up the units in the experimental list deviate from those characteristic of the language, i.e., the amount of such interference will vary inversely with the probability of the prescribed sequences in the language. Unit-sequence interference will result when the sequence of units (e.g., syllables, words) in the list fails to conform to the associative habits established outside the laboratory. The amount of unit-sequence interference should increase with the frequency of occurrence of the units in the language. The more frequently the units are used the more likely they are to have strong associates which will interfere with the sequences reinforced in the experiment.

This conception of the sources of extra-experimental interference has testable implications for the relationship between meaningfulness and retention. The dimension of meaningfulness may be

[1] This research was supported by a grant from the National Science Foundation. The writer is grateful to Audrey Bohm, Karen Updegraff, and Margaret Boyer for their assistance.

Reprinted with permission of the author and the publisher, the American Psychological Association. The article appeared originally in the *Journal of Experimental Psychology*, 1961, **61,** 97–110.

represented by an arrangement of verbal units along a continuum extending from the least probable letter sequences to the most frequent words. Extra-experimental habits generate two intersecting gradients of interference which may be plotted against this continuum. The gradient of letter-sequence interference is at its maximum at the low end of the continuum and declines as the probability of letter-sequences increases. The gradient of unit-sequence interference rises as a function of the frequency of occurrence of the items as integrated verbal units and reaches its maximum at the high end of the continuum. Thus, interference is expected to be maximal for items at the two extremes of the continuum; it should be minimal for items toward the center which represent common sequences of letters but lack strong associations with other verbal units.

The conditions of extra-experimental interference are assumed to conform to the A-B, A-C paradigm used in formal studies of retroactive and proactive inhibition. The paradigm applies to both letter-sequence and unit-sequence interference. In the former case, the critical associations are among the letters within the individual units; in the latter case, between successive units. In both cases, acquisition of the prescribed association, A-C, will require the unlearning or extinction of a pre-experimental association, A-B. Evidence obtained in studies of interserial interference, and particularly in experiments using the method of modified free recall (Briggs, 1954; Underwood, 1948) makes it reasonable to assume that the extinguished habit, A-B, will recover as a function of time and compete with A-C at the time of recall and relearning. If the old habit is practiced after the end of the experiment, as is likely with popular linguistic associations, the process of recovery is speeded up. Retroactive and proactive effects may thus summate in producing extra-experimental interference with the retention of the prescribed list.

The results of a study by Underwood and Postman (1960) give some support to this analysis. Retention was compared for four kinds of three-letter units: high-frequency words, high-frequency trigrams, low-frequency words, and low-frequency trigrams. At each of the two levels of frequency, the probabilities of the letter sequences in words and trigrams were closely equated. A test of recall one week after learning showed only small differences in retention loss. Contrary to the usual assumption, meaningfulness did not favor retention. As measured by relearning to criterion, high-frequency trigrams were retained better than any of the other materials. Since both letter-sequence and unit-sequence interference are assumed to be minimal for high-frequency trigrams, this finding lends direct support to the present hypothesis. The pattern of errors was likewise in accord with theoretical expectations. Errors reflecting letter-sequence interference recovered more rapidly for the low-frequency than the high-frequency lists; the recovery of intralist errors attributable to unit-sequence interference was greater for lists of words than lists of trigrams.

The experiments reported in this paper focus on the operation of the gradient of unit-sequence interference in the retention of words. In the study of Underwood and Postman, the two lists of words differed greatly not only with respect to their frequency of occurrence in the language but also with respect to the probability of their letter sequences. In the present experiments, two-syllable nouns of high and low frequency of occurrence were used but there were no comparable differences in the probabilities of the letter sequences of which the two sets of words were composed. Forgetting, therefore, could be considered largely a matter of unit-sequence interference. In Exp. I the course of retention for the two kinds of materials was measured over a one-week interval by the method of serial anticipation. Since the results of that experiment failed to show superior retention of the high-frequency lists, the question arose as to whether a paced anticipation test masks a greater availability of high-frequency responses at recall. In order to explore this possibility, retention for the same materials was tested by the method of free recall in Exp. II. A mixed list, composed of words of high and low frequency in equal proportions, was used in Exp. III to test an implication of the hypothesis of unit-sequence interference. We assume that the probability of strong pre-experimental associations among the items to be learned varies directly with the number of high-frequency words in the list. Thus, the number of such associations converging on any one high-frequency item should be smaller in a mixed list than in a homogeneous list. The question investigated in Exp. III was whether the reduction in the number and strength of pre-experimental associations would lead to a shift in relative retention scores in favor of the high-frequency items.

Experiments I and II

Method

Materials.—The materials used in the construction of the experimental lists consisted of 48 two-syllable nouns. There were two groups of 24 nouns each, sampling the extremes of the frequency range in the Thorndike-Lorge word count (1944). For the low-frequency words, the number of occurrences in the "L" count was between 1 and 3 in 4.5 million; for the high-frequency words the number of occurrences ranged between 1000 and 3300. At each level of frequency, two 12-word lists were constructed which are presented in Table 1. In addition to the word frequencies, the table shows the mean frequency of the successive trigrams formed by the letters in each word. For a word composed of *n* letters, *n*-2 such trigrams can be formed. The trigram count (Underwood & Schulz, 1960) gives the number of occurrences in 1,035,000 words. Mean trigram frequencies correlate with the word frequencies but there is considerable overlap between the values for the two sets of words. The mean trigram values are relatively high even for the low-frequency words: all but two fall into the upper third of the total distribution of trigram frequencies. Thus, letter-sequence interference may be assumed to be negligible for all the lists. Table 1 also shows the mean familiarity ratings and *m*-values for each word. The latter two scores were obtained in a standardization study conducted by the writer.[2] The ratings represent the mean judgments of 1000 students at the University of California who rated the familiarity of each word on a 5-point scale, with 1 denoting minimal familiarity and 5, maximum familiarity. The *m*-values were obtained by a method similar to Noble's (1952) and represent the mean number of different associations given to each word by a sample of 96 *S*s during a 50-sec. interval. While the criterion for selection of the words was frequency of occurrence, the differences between the means of the ratings and *m*-values are consistent with the classification based on the word count. It should be noted that there is closer agreement between the word-frequency count and rated familiarity than between either measure and the value of *m*. Thus, there is some overlap between the two sets of words with respect to *m*-value but not the other two indices.

Two different serial orders were used with each of the 12-word lists. Thus, there were four different lists at each level of frequency. The different lists were used equally often under all conditions of the experiment.

Experiment I Procedure and Ss.—The lists were presented on a Hull-type memory drum at a 2-sec. rate, with an intertrial interval of 6 sec., and learned by the anticipation method to a criterion of one perfect recitation. Retention was tested by relearning to the same criterion. There were three retention intervals—30 sec., 2 days, and 7 days after the end of original learning. The 30-sec. test provides an empirical estimate of associative strength at the end of practice.

With two kinds of lists and three retention intervals, there were six groups of 16 *S*s each. The *S*s were undergraduate students at the University of California and were assigned to the conditions by means of a table of random numbers, with restriction to equal *N*s. All *S*s had English as their native language and were naive to rote-learning

[2] The complete results of the standardization procedures will be presented in a forthcoming publication.

TABLE 1

WORDS USED IN THE EXPERIMENT

List I					List II				
Item	Word Freq.[a]	Mean Trigram Freq.[b]	Mean Famili-arity Rating	m-Value	Item	Word Freq.[a]	Mean Trigram Freq.[b]	Mean Famili-arity Rating	m-Value
High-Frequency Words									
Answer	2132	131	4.73	8.37	Business	2850	309	4.51	9.49
Building	1014	337	4.64	9.83	Country	1714	156	4.40	10.65
Color	1541	49	4.56	10.99	Dinner	1266	126	4.90	10.51
Doctor	1631	125	4.32	9.96	Figure	1202	126	4.61	9.05
Garden	1036	152	4.23	12.01	Letter	1748	483	4.68	9.99
Husband	1788	253	4.45	8.83	Morning	2015	417	4.83	10.30
Moment	2396	619	4.44	7.39	Order	1477	220	4.53	8.33
Office	1640	112	4.43	9.72	Problem	1079	236	4.65	8.68
Paper	1235	190	4.85	10.81	Reason	1121	261	4.64	7.17
Story	1651	310	4.40	9.40	Shoulder	1135	337	4.23	9.49
Trouble	1180	182	4.49	7.76	Table	1325	288	4.73	10.56
Window	1564	148	4.70	9.86	Woman	2431	181	4.84	8.88
Low-Frequency Words									
Abbess	3	192	1.92	4.71	Bramble	3	134	2.13	7.04
Buffoon	2	54	2.17	6.45	Curfew	2	57	3.75	8.60
Caucus	1	59	2.64	7.50	Dotage	1	101	1.77	5.01
Decoy	2	47	3.30	7.59	Farthing	2	244	2.16	6.29
Gullet	2	119	2.35	5.94	Harem	2	284	2.86	8.01
Mermaid	3	78	2.91	10.01	Lorry	3	53	1.63	5.88
Oboe	1	2	2.51	8.48	Monsoon	2	98	2.52	8.50
Prefix	2	106	3.68	7.35	Oxide	1	119	3.53	7.69
Ramrod	2	38	2.60	6.75	Pestle	3	289	2.00	5.52
Sequel	3	72	2.76	6.60	Stanza	3	164	3.25	8.36
Tortoise	2	127	2.85	9.18	Tenure	3	191	2.54	7.02
Wicket	3	122	2.34	6.90	Wampum	1	10	2.36	7.63

[a] Occurrences in 4.5 million words.
[b] Occurrences in 1,035,000 words.

experiments. Two *S*s were replaced because of failure to learn, both of them in the 30-sec. group of the low-frequency condition. On the basis of a postexperimental inquiry *S*s who admitted to deliberate rehearsal during the retention interval were discarded and replaced. The criteria of deliberate rehearsal were (*a*) three or more attempts at oral recitation, and (*b*) one or more attempts at written reproduction. In the 2-day groups seven *S*s learning a high-frequency list and six *S*s learning a low-frequency list were replaced; in the 7-day groups there were three discarded *S*s in the high-frequency condition and two in the low-frequency condition. In view of the possibility that *S*s who rehearsed might differ in ability from those who did not, *S*s in the 30-sec. groups were retested after 7 days, and those who admitted to rehearsal were likewise replaced. There were five such cases in the high-frequency group and four in the low-frequency group. As it turned out, there was no apparent difference between rehearsers and nonrehearsers as measured by trials to criterion and performance on the 30-sec. test.

Experiment II Procedure and Ss.—The materials and conditions of learning in Exp. II were exactly the same as in Exp. I. The two studies differed, however, with respect to the method of measuring retention. In Exp. II, a 5-min. test of free recall was used. The *S*s were instructed to call out the words in any order that occurred to them and were encouraged to guess if they were uncertain about an item. Rate of response was recorded by *E* with the aid of a timer which flashed a light every 10 sec. Two retention intervals were used—30 sec. and 7 days.

With two kinds of lists and two retention intervals, there were four groups of 16 *Ss* each. The *Ss* were assigned to the conditions by means of a table of random numbers, with restriction to equal *Ns*. All *Ss* had English as their native language and were naive to rote-learning experiments. One *S* in the 7-day group learning the high-frequency lists was discarded and replaced because of deliberate rehearsal. No *Ss* were lost because of failure to learn.

Results

Original learning.—There were no significant differences among the groups in the two experiments learning a given kind of material. There were also no significant differences among the different lists used at each level of frequency. The data on original learning obtained in the two experiments have, therefore, been combined. The results for the two types of list are thus based on 80 *Ss* each (48 *Ss* in Exp. I and 32 *Ss* in Exp. II). The mean number of trials to criterion was 18.24 ($SD = 7.32$) for the high-frequency lists, and 24.08 ($SD = 9.61$) for the low-frequency lists. This difference is highly significant ($t = 4.36$, $P < .001$).

For purposes of assessing the conditions determining speed of acquisition, it is convenient to divide the total learning period into an integrative stage and an associative stage (Underwood & Postman, 1960; Underwood, Runquist, & Schulz, 1959). During the integrative stage the items in the list become available to *Ss* as responses; during the associative stage the responses are connected with the prescribed stimuli, e.g., the preceding items in a serial list. The duration of the integrative stage is estimated by the number of the trial on which the correct response is first given anywhere in the list. The length of the associative stage is measured by the number of trials between the end of the integrative stage and the first occurrence of the correct sequential association. The results of such a stage analysis for the two kinds of lists are shown in Table 2. The integrative stage is significantly shorter for the high-frequency lists ($t = 4.95$, $P < .001$). There is no comparable difference in the length of the associative stage. The mean number of trials separating first appearance of the response from the first correct placement is 2.06 for the high-frequency lists, and 1.83 for the low-frequency lists. This difference in favor of the low-frequency condition is not significant ($t = .96$). It appears that the difference in speed of learning is attributable primarily to the greater availability of the high-frequency responses. The fact that the advantage of the high-frequency items in the first stage of learning does not carry over into the second stage is consistent with the assumption that unit-sequence interference varies directly with meaningfulness. This assumption finds additional support from an analysis of the overt errors during learning.

Overt errors during original learning. The mean number of overt errors per trial during the acquisition of the high-frequency lists was 1.54

TABLE 2

MEAN TRIAL NUMBER ON WHICH RESPONSES WERE FIRST GIVEN AND FIRST PLACED CORRECTLY DURING ORIGINAL LEARNING IN EXP. I AND II

Word Frequency	First Given		First Placed	
	Mean	*SD*	Mean	*SD*
High	4.42	1.52	6.48	2.56
Low	5.93	2.25	7.76	2.85

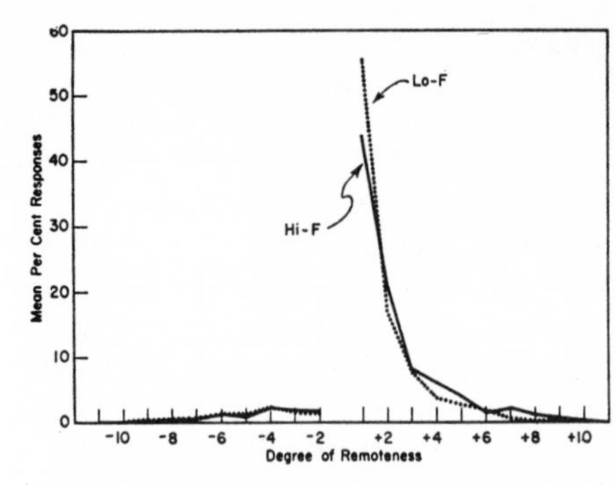

FIG. 1. Mean percentages of intralist errors of different degrees of remoteness during acquisition of lists of high and low word-frequency.

(SD = .62), and 1.14 (SD = .47) during the acquisition of the low-frequency lists. This difference in error rate is highly significant ($t = 4.54$, $P < .001$). Thus, speed of learning and rate of overt errors vary together as a function of frequency. The vast majority of the errors consisted of misplaced responses from within the list. The mean percentages that such intralist errors were of all the overt errors were 95.5 for the high-frequency lists and 92.6 for the low-frequency lists.

Figure 1 shows the mean percentages that errors of different degrees of remoteness are of the total numbers of errors. Since our concern here is with a comparison between the two types of materials, we have not corrected the percentages for opportunities, but such a correction would not change the basic relationships shown in Fig. 1. A clear separation between the two lists is brought out by the percentages of errors of the first degree of remoteness. Such associations account for the largest number of intralist errors under both conditions but the mean percentage is significantly larger for the low-frequency list ($t = 4.56$, $P < .001$). Correspondingly, the percentages of errors of higher degrees of remoteness are larger for the high-frequency lists. On the assumption that the proportion of errors of the higher degrees of remoteness reflects the probability of pre-experimental associations, the difference between the distributions of errors points to greater unit-sequence interference during the acquisition of the high-frequency lists.

Recall.—Figure 2 shows the amounts recalled by the various groups in Exp. I. We note first the difference in favor of the high-frequency list 30 sec. after attainment of the criterion. This fact supports Underwood's (1954) conclusion that the amount of post-criterial drop is related inversely to the speed of learning. Recall decreases significantly as a function of the Retention Interval ($F = 31.96$, $df = 2/90$, $P < .001$). The over-all effect of Material is not significant ($F = 1.04$). Although the drop appears to be steeper for the high-frequency list, the Retention Interval $\times$ Material interaction is not significant ($F = 1.19$). We conclude, therefore, that there is no difference in the rate of forgetting as measured by recall. The failure to find better retention of the high-frequency list is noteworthy in itself in view of the

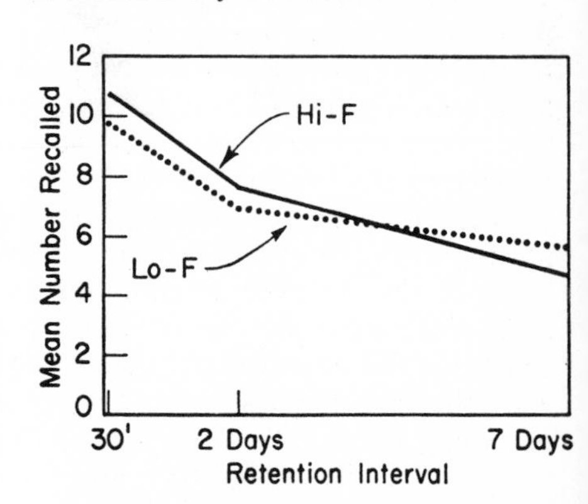

Fig. 2. Mean numbers of items recalled as a function of word-frequency and retention interval.

TABLE 3

MEAN RECALL SCORES IN EXP. I FOR ORIGINAL SAMPLE AND AFTER REPLACEMENT OF REHEARSERS

Retention Interval	High Frequency				Low Frequency			
	Original Sample		After Replacements		Original Sample		After Replacements	
	Mean	*SD*	Mean	*SD*	Mean	*SD*	Mean	*SD*
30 Sec.	10.88	1.62	10.75	1.64	9.62	2.14	9.81	2.10
2 Days	8.62	2.70	7.56	2.96	7.94	2.45	6.94	2.68
7 Days	5.44	2.95	4.62	2.59	5.31	3.29	5.56	2.92

difference in speed of learning. Thus meaningfulness favors learning, but not retention.

The effects of rehearsal.—The treatment of *S*s admitting to deliberate rehearsal presents a methodological problem in the conduct of retention experiments. In the present study such *S*s were eliminated from all groups. It is useful to compare the results obtained on this basis with those yielded by the original sample, i.e., when no *S*s are replaced because of rehearsal. Such a comparison is presented in Table 3. The differences between the two sets of recall scores are not large. On the 2-day test the means for both lists increase by an equal amount when the original sample is used. On the 7-day test there is a slight shift in favor of the high-frequency list. Analysis of variance yields the same result for both sets of scores, i.e., no significant difference in the rate of forgetting. It appears that the exclusion of *S*s admitting to rehearsal has no material effects on the experimental conclusions, at least under the conditions of the present study.

Relearning.—The mean numbers of trials to relearn to a criterion of one perfect recitation are presented in Table 4. The results are fully consistent with those of the recall test. There is a significant increase in the number of trials as a function of the Retention Interval ($F = 10.15$, $df = 2/90$, $P < .001$). While the increase is somewhat greater for the high-frequency condition, the Materials × Retention Interval interaction again is not significant ($F = 1.48$), i.e., there is no reliable difference in the rate of forgetting as measured by the speed of relearning.

Errors at recall and in relearning.—Analysis of the conditions of unit-sequence interference leads us to expect greater recovery of intralist errors for the high-frequency than the low-frequency list. Figure 3 shows the frequency of intralist errors at recall. Separate functions are plotted for errors of the first degree of remoteness and those of higher degrees of remoteness. Both types of errors are more frequent during the recall of the high-frequency lists but the difference is especially pronounced for the errors of higher degrees of remoteness. Since a large proportion of *S*s in the 30-sec. groups made no errors, the following procedure was used to evaluate the significance of the temporal trends. Each *S* in the 2-day and 7-day groups was matched with

TABLE 4

MEAN NUMBERS OF TRIALS IN RELEARNING TO CRITERION (EXP. I)

Retention Interval	High Word-Frequency		Low Word-Frequency	
	Mean	*SD*	Mean	*SD*
30 Sec.	2.31	1.65	3.44	3.39
2 Days	4.44	2.87	6.62	4.00
7 Days	6.62	3.40	6.06	2.80

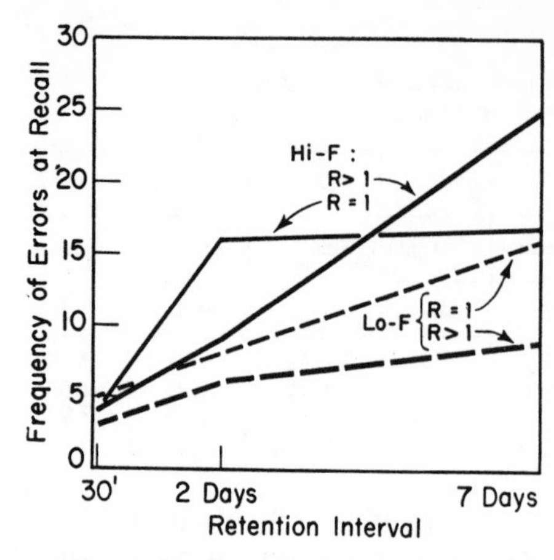

FIG. 3. Numbers of intralist errors during recall of the high- and low-frequency lists. R = 1 designates errors of first degree of remoteness, R > 1 refers to errors of higher degrees of remoteness.

an S in the 30-sec. group. Matching was by subgroups learning the same list and at random within subgroups. For each pair the difference in the number of intralist errors was determined, and the distributions of difference scores were subjected to an analysis of variance. The difference as a function of Material is significant ($F = 5.07, df = 1/60, .02 < P < .05$), indicating a differential rate of recovery. The difference between the 2- and 7-day intervals is also significant ($F = 5.80$), but the Retention Interval × Material interaction is not ($F < 1$), i.e., there is no reliable divergence in the error scores between 2 and 7 days.

Figure 4 shows the mean number of errors per trial in relearning to criterion as a function of the retention interval. Here a clear separation between the two conditions occurs only on the 7-day test. The Retention Interval × Material interaction is significant ($F = 3.22$, $df = 2/90$, $.02 < P < .05$). Both analyses agree in indicating more rapid recovery of unit-sequence interference for the high-frequency lists. It is important to note, however, that the number of importations from outside the list was negligible. Thus, it appears that there is differential recovery only of those pre-experimental associations which exist among items within the list.

Correlation between length of associative stage and retention.—It is reasonable to assume that the length of the associative stage during learning varies with the degree of unit-sequence interference. The hypothesis that forgetting is related to the recovery of unit-sequence interferences implies that in a distribution of Ss the length of the associative stage should be negatively correlated with the amount recalled. For the high-frequency lists the product-moment correlation between the length of the associative stage, as defined earlier, and the amount recalled is $-.34$ after 2 days and $-.53$ after 7 days. The latter coefficient is significant at the .05 level for $N = 16$. For the low-frequency lists the corresponding values of r are .08 and $-.21$. There is a clear inverse relationship only for the high-frequency lists which are assumed to

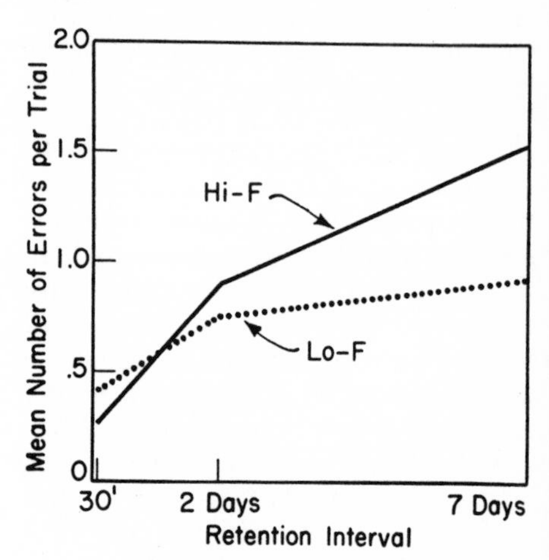

FIG. 4. Mean numbers of intralist errors per trial in relearning to criterion.

be more subject to unit-sequence interference.

Free recall.—We now turn to the results of the test of free recall in Exp. II. The mean cumulative numbers of responses obtained during the 5-min. test are plotted in Fig. 5. Recall of both lists is virtually perfect after 30 sec. The amount retained after 7 days is substantially larger than that obtained on the anticipation test in Exp. I. The mean retention loss is only 2 items. The rate of recall is, however, considerably slower after 7 days than at the end of learning. The delayed test, like the immediate test, shows little difference between the lists of high and low frequency. The amount forgotten during the 7-day period is significant ($F = 26.43$, $df = 1/60$, $P < .001$, following a Freeman-Tukey square-root transformation); neither Material nor the Retention Interval × Material interaction is significant. Thus, the change from a paced to an unpaced test results in approximately equal gains in the recall of the two kinds of materials. We conclude that the conditions of the anticipation test do not mask a greater availability of the high-frequency items.

Order of recall.—As Fig. 6 shows, there was a high degree of correspondence between the serial positions of the items in learning and the order of their appearance in free recall. The relationship is, however, less regular for the high-frequency lists than for the low-frequency lists. In order to obtain an index of serial order in free recall, the mean distance between the serial positions of successive items in recall was determined for each *S*. On the 30-sec. test, the mean index was 1.87 ($SD = .82$) for the high-frequency lists, and 1.38 ($SD = .76$) for the low-frequency lists. On the 7-day test, the corresponding means were 2.79 ($SD = .87$) and 2.23 ($SD = .89$). The rise in the index as a function of time is significant ($F = 18.80$, $df = 1/60$, $P < .001$) as is the difference between Materials ($F = 6.68$, $df = 1/60$, $.01 < P < .02$). The separation between the lists occurs on both tests and does not interact with the Retention Interval ($F < 1$). The greater disturbance of serial order in the recall of the high-frequency lists may be considered a function of unit-sequence interference and represents an effect on free recall which is parallel to the greater incidence of intralist errors on the anticipation test. These effects of unit-sequence interference appear to be present in

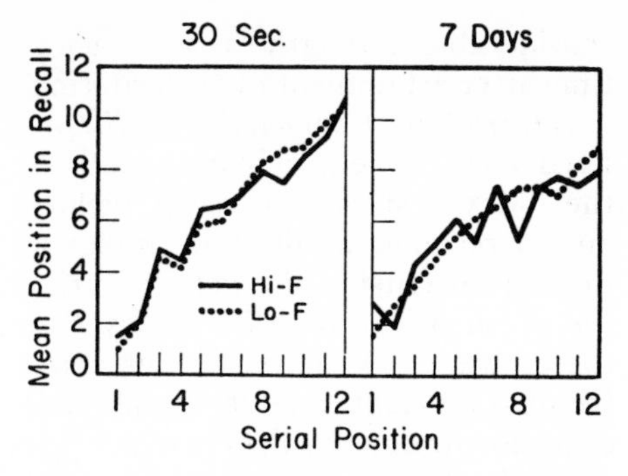

FIG. 6. Mean serial position of correct items in free recall as a function of serial position in learning.

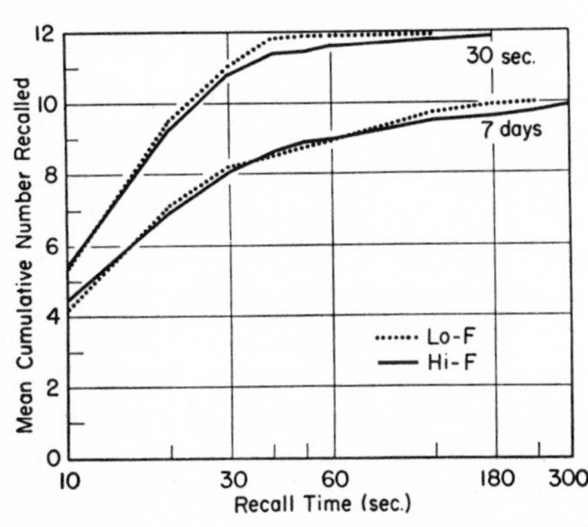

FIG. 5. Mean cumulative numbers of words reproduced in the 5-min. test of free recall.

considerable strength a very short time after attainment of the criterion.

Importations from outside the lists.—In contrast to the anticipation method, the 7-day test of free recall yielded an appreciable number of importations from outside the lists. During the recall of the high-frequency lists there were 14 importations contributed by eight *S*s; during the recall of the low-frequency lists two *S*s made a total of four such errors. The difference in the number of *S*s giving importations is significant ($\chi^2 = 5.24$, $df = 1$, $.02 < P < .05$). There were no importations on the 30-sec. test, and their appearance on the delayed test may be attributed to extra-experimental interference. In agreement with this interpretation, the importations could be readily classified as synonyms or associates of the items in the list. The fact that free recall yields more importations than an anticipation test indicates that the reinstatement of the context of the list in relearning facilitates differentiation between correct and incorrect responses. A similar difference in the probability of importations as a function of the method of measurement was reported earlier by Postman and Rau (1957).

Experiment III

Method

Materials.—The learning materials were 12-word lists. Six of the words in each list were high-frequency items, and six words were low-frequency items. The same pool of words was used as in the first two experiments (Table 1). There were eight basic lists and four different serial orders for each of these, making a total of 32 different lists. The following rules were observed in the construction of the lists: (*a*) At each serial position, a high-frequency item was used in half the lists, and a low-frequency item was used in the other half of the lists. Thus, the effects of serial position were fully counterbalanced. (*b*) No item appeared more than once in any serial position. (*c*) No forward sequence of two items was used more than once. (*d*) No more than two items from the same frequency class appeared in succession. (*e*) There was no duplication of first letters in any of the lists.

Procedure.—The lists were presented on a Hull-type memory drum at a 2-sec. rate, with an intertrial interval of 6 sec., and learned by the anticipation method to a criterion of one perfect recitation. Retention was tested by relearning either after 30 sec. or after 7 days. Relearning was for five trials or to a criterion of one perfect recitation, whichever took the longer.

Subjects.—There were 32 *S*s each in the 30-sec. and 7-day conditions. Since there were 32 lists, each *S* in a given condition learned a different list. The *S*s were assigned to the conditions in blocks of two, one each in the 30-sec. and 7-day group. The running order within each block was determined by a table of random numbers, as was the assignment of lists to *S*s within each condition. All *S*s had English as their native language and were naive to rote-learning experiments. In view of the results of the earlier studies no *S*s were replaced because of deliberate rehearsal. No *S*s had to be rejected because of failure to learn.

Results

Original learning.—The mean number of trials to criterion for the 30-sec. and 7-day groups were 18.31 ($SD = 8.47$) and 17.81 ($SD = 6.09$). The difference in speed of learning is clearly not significant ($t = .27$), and the analysis of original learning will be presented for the combined groups.

The mean number of correct responses per trial was 3.46 for the high-frequency words and 3.29 for the low-frequency words. Although this difference in the rate of correct responses per trial was small, it was quite consistent and statistically significant ($t = 5.86$, $P < .001$). Analysis of the individual records shows that serial position was the primary determinant of the rate at which individual items were learned. Nevertheless, word-frequency produced a reliable effect in the expected direction when

TABLE 5

MEAN RECALL SCORES AND MEAN NUMBERS OF CORRECT ANTICIPATIONS ON RETENTION TESTS FOR MIXED LIST IN EXP. III

Retention Interval	Recall Scores				Anticipations in Relearning			
	High Frequency		Low Frequency		High Frequency		Low Frequency	
	Mean	*SD*	Mean	*SD*	Mean	*SD*	Mean	*SD*
30 Sec.	5.12	1.32	5.00	1.30	26.56	3.18	26.56	2.50
7 Days	2.91	1.77	2.16	1.66	22.28	5.20	20.97	6.00

serial positions were fully counterbalanced. It is apparent that the influence of word-frequency on learning is less within a mixed list than between homogeneous lists.

Errors during original learning.—The mean number of overt errors per trial was 1.26 ($SD = .60$). The mean percentage of intralist errors was 91.59. The intralist errors were, in turn, classified according to the frequency values of the item eliciting the error and of the incorrect response. These criteria yield a fourfold classification of errors—S_h-R_h, S_h-R_l, S_l-R_h, and S_l-R_l—where S and R stand for stimulus and response, and the subscripts designate the frequency class of each.[3] The frequencies with which each kind of error occurred were converted into percentages of opportunities. The number of opportunities was determined for each *S* by subtracting from the total number of presentations of a given class of stimuli the number of correct responses elicited by these stimuli. The mean percentages of the four types of errors were as follows: S_h-R_h—5.72, S_h-R_l—5.35, S_l-R_h—5.39, and S_l-R_l—4.81. There is a tendency for high-frequency responses to be given as errors more often than low-frequency ones, and for high-frequency stimuli to be more effective in eliciting errors. The differences among the percentages are, however, small and not significant. As was found for correct responses, the distribution of errors during learning was primarily a function of serial position. Whatever small differences are present are consistent with the view that response availability and probability of associative connection vary with frequency of usage.

[3] Errors in the first serial position could not be included in this classification. Such errors were, however, extremely rare.

Recall.—The mean numbers of the two kinds of items recalled are presented in Table 5. High-frequency words have a slight advantage on the 30-sec. test, and a more substantial one on the 7-day test. Analysis of variance (following a Freeman-Tukey square-root transformation) shows the retention loss during the 7-day interval to be highly significant ($F = 52.98$, $df = 1/62$, $P < .001$). The over-all effect of Material is also significant ($F = 6.74$, $df = 1/62$, $.02 < P < .05$), but the Retention Interval × Material interaction is not ($F = 3.43$, whereas a ratio of 4.00 is required for $P = .05$ with 1 and 62 df). The high-frequency items have a greater advantage than was found with homogeneous lists but there still is no reliable difference in the rate of forgetting for the two kinds of items.

Relearning.—Table 5 shows the mean number of high- and low-frequency words anticipated correctly during the five relearning trials. The scores for the two kinds of items are closely similar. Thus, whatever advantage the high-frequency items had on the recall trial is quickly dissipated in the course of relearning.

Errors in recall and relearning.—A consideration of the overt errors in recall and relearning helps us to understand why the difference in the amount recalled remained so small even in a mixed list, i.e., in spite of the probable reduction in pre-experimental associations among the high-frequency items. As Table 6 shows, high-frequency responses occurred as errors more often than did low-frequency responses, and this difference increased as a function of the retention interval. Since there were very few errors of either class on the 30-sec. test, a nonparametric procedure was used to evaluate the significance of this trend. The *S*s in the two groups learning the same list were paired, and the proportions of cases in which there were increases in the two classes of errors were determined. Increases in high-frequency errors occurred in 53% of the cases whereas low-frequency errors increased in only 25% of the comparisons. The difference between the correlated proportions is significant ($CR = 2.54, P < .01$). Thus high-frequency responses recovered as errors more rapidly than did low-frequency responses. There were no comparable differences in the rate of recovery as a function of the frequency of the stimulus items. The results for the five relearning trials are fully consistent with those at recall. Having high meaningfulness in Noble's (1952) sense of the term, the high-frequency words entered readily into associations not only with other high-frequency words but with low-frequency words as well. As a result of differential recovery, there was again considerable competition among high-frequency responses at recall.

TABLE 6

NUMBER OF DIFFERENT CLASSES OF ERRORS IN RECALL AND FIVE TRIALS OF RELEARNING ON RETENTION TEST FOR MIXED LIST IN EXP. III

Class of Errors	Recall		Relearning	
	30 Sec.	7 Days	30 Sec.	7 Days
S_h-R_h	6	19	20	56
S_h-R_l	4	7	14	44
S_l-R_h	4	23	24	57
S_l-R_l	2	8	14	44
ΣR_h	10	42	44	113
ΣR_l	6	15	28	88

The assumption that response competition was more damaging to high-frequency items than to low-frequency items is supported by an additional analysis of the recall scores. In order to estimate the total number of *different* items recalled by each *S*, credit was given for anticipatory intralist errors as well as correctly placed responses. An item which occurred both as an anticipatory error and as a correct response was, of course, only counted once. The revised recall scores for the high-frequency items drop from 5.22 on the 30-sec. test to 3.19 on the 7-day test. The corresponding scores for the low-frequency items are 5.03 and 2.22. When some of the effects of unit-sequence interferences within the list are thus partialed out, high-frequency items have a distinct advantage and the Retention Interval × Material interaction is significant ($F = 5.49, df = 1/62, .02 < P < .05$). It may be noted that a similar analysis of the recall scores for the homogeneous list in Exp. I failed to produce an appreciable shift in favor of the high-frequency materials.

Discussion

To what extent do the experimental results support our conception of the conditions of extra-experimental interference? Turning to the findings on original learning first, we find in Exp. I and II that frequency of usage makes verbal units readily available as responses but at the same time favors a high rate of intralist errors. The differences between the high-frequency lists and the low-frequency lists with respect to the length of the integrative stage and the number and remoteness of overt errors provide significant evidence for the influence of pre-experimental habits on the course of acquisition. Since speed of learning and error rate are positively related, these findings do not demonstrate conclusively that pre-experimental habits are a source of interference in acquisition. The fact that the large difference between the lists during the integrative stage is not maintained during the associative stage makes it reasonable to assume, however, that the error rates reflect variations in the degree of associative interference. If this interpretation is correct, pre-experimental habits differentially retard the acquisition of the high-frequency lists. The results of Exp. III make it clear that our conclusions concerning the effects of frequency of usage on learning apply primarily to homogeneous lists. In a heterogeneous list the influence of frequency is largely masked by serial position effects. It is noteworthy, however, that whatever differences in the rate of correct responses and errors are present are consistent with those found with homogeneous lists.

The three experiments agree in failing to show a significant difference between the rates at which words of high and low frequency are forgotten. The hypothesis of unit-sequence interference would receive clear support if high-frequency items were forgotten faster than low-frequency items. This result was not found. On the other hand, the net advantage of the high-frequency materials in acquisition was not followed by comparable differences in retention. Thus, the persistent assumption that high meaningfulness necessarily favors retention can be rejected.

A larger number of overt errors is made in the recall and relearning of high-frequency items than of low-frequency items. The distributions of overt errors are consistent with the present analysis of the sources of extra-experimental interference. We assume that pre-experimental associations must be unlearned or extinguished during the acquisition of the prescribed list and that the rate at which such associations recover is a function of their initial strength. The fact that high-frequency responses appear as overt errors in recall and relearning more often than low-frequency responses bears out this expectation.

The results of the retention tests may be summarized by saying that there was no difference in the amount of forgetting for the two kinds of material in spite of the greater disturbance of serial order and the larger number of overt errors for the high-frequency items. Thus, the total pattern of responses in recall and relearning indicates that the greater initial availability of the high-frequency items is not followed by superior retention because of the rapid recovery of unit-sequence interferences. The argument in favor of our conception of extra-experimental sources of interference would, of course, be considerably more compelling if a significant difference in favor of the low-frequency lists had been found. It is possible that the rate at which pre-experimental associations recover is sufficiently slow to require longer retention intervals than those used in the present study for conclusive demonstration of differences in the amount of unit-sequence interference.

Summary

This paper reports three studies designed to explore the sources of extra-experimental interference in the forgetting of meaningful materials. In Exp. I, serial lists composed of either high-frequency words or low-frequency words were learned to a criterion of one perfect recitation, and retention was tested by relearning after intervals of 30 sec., 2 days, and 7 days. In Exp. II, the same materials were used, and retention was tested by free recall after intervals of 30 sec. and 7 days. High-frequency words were learned faster than low-frequency words but neither method of testing showed a significant difference in the amount of forgetting. The number of overt errors was larger, however, during the recall of the high-frequency items. In Exp. III, mixed lists composed of equal proportions of high-frequency words and low-frequency words were learned to criterion, and retention was tested by relearning after 30 sec. and 7 days. Speed of learning for individual items was largely determined by serial position; the high-frequency items had, however, a small but consistent advantage. There was again no significant difference in the rate of forgetting for the two kinds of items. The theoretical analysis attributes forgetting to interference from extra-experimental associations established through linguistic usage.

References

BRIGGS, G. E. Acquisition, extinction, and recovery functions in retroactive inhibition. *J. exp. Psychol.*, 1954, **47**, 285–293.

NOBLE, C. E. An analysis of meaning. *Psychol. Rev.*, 1952, **59**, 437–446.

POSTMAN, L., & RAU, L. Retention as a function of the method of measurement. *U. Calif. Publ. Psychol.*, 1957, **8**, 271–396.

THORNDIKE, E. L., & LORGE, I. *The teacher's wordbook of 30,000 words.* New York: Teachers College, Columbia Univer., 1944.

UNDERWOOD, B. J. 'Spontaneous' recovery of verbal associations. *J. exp. Psychol.*, 1948, **38**, 429–439.

UNDERWOOD, B. J. Speed of learning and amount retained: A consideration of methodology. *Psychol. Bull.*, 1954, **51**, 276–282.

UNDERWOOD, B. J. Interference and forgetting. *Psychol. Rev.*, 1957, **64**, 49–60.

UNDERWOOD, B. J., & POSTMAN, L. Extra-experimental sources of interference in forgetting. *Psychol. Rev.*, 1960, **67**, 73–95.

UNDERWOOD, B. J., RUNQUIST, W. N., & SCHULZ, R. W. Response learning in paired-associate lists as a function of intralist similarity. *J. exp. Psychol.*, 1959, **58**, 70–78.

UNDERWOOD, B. J., & SCHULZ, R. W. *Meaningfulness and verbal learning.* Philadelphia: Lippincott, 1960.

(Received January 22, 1960)

ARTICLE 3

Time Changes in the Strengths of A-B, A-C Lists; Spontaneous Recovery?[1]

R. J. Koppenaal

University of Manitoba, Winnipeg, Canada

In recent S-R transfer and interference explanations of forgetting there has been increasing emphasis on proactive interference. The increase of proactive interference with the length of the retention interval, in particular, occupies a prominent place in recent theorizing.

The time effects in question are illustrated in the case where two lists of paired-associates with the same stimulus terms but different response terms (A-B, A-C) are learned consecutively. After a short retention interval (e.g., $\frac{1}{2}$ hour) the retention of the second list learned will be far superior to the retention of the first list. This difference has been attributed to *unlearning* of the first list during second-list learning, with unlearning analogous to experimental extinction.

It is now well documented that after longer retention intervals (24 to 48 hours) there is equally good recall of first and second lists. To explain the change in relative strengths of the two lists with time, Underwood (1948a; 1948b) suggested that the first list spontaneously recovers strength lost during unlearning, extending the analogy with conditioning phenomena.

[1] This research was supported by two grants from the National Research Council of Canada, APBT-40 and APA-77, and by the University of Manitoba's Research and Publications Fund. The author is indebted to a number of students, Hannah Katz, Lorraine Wilgosh, Marcia Greenberg, and Lillian Corman, for testing subjects, and to the late Nelson O'Hara for help in the original conception of the study.

This development has brought about a fundamental change in the interference theory of forgetting. Forgetting happens over time, and for many years the variable presumed to be operating in time was interpolated learning (IL), producing retroactive inhibition (RI). Now, however, Underwood and Postman (1960) and Postman (1961a, b) have assigned the major role in forgetting to the spontaneous recovery of prior learning (PL), producing proactive inhibition (PI). Thus spontaneous recovery is the important variable operating in time.

There are two uncomfortable aspects of the explanation of the time effects in terms of spontaneous recovery. First, complete recovery would evidently be required if this concept alone is to explain the convergence of the two lists. Complete recovery would rob this concept of its analogy with conditioning phenomena. The second problem, one of parsimony, stems from Underwood's (1948b) suggestion that in addition to spontaneous recovery of the first list, both lists undergo "usual forgetting" over time. This suggestion was necessitated by the fact that while the first list increases in relative strength, it evidently does not increase in absolute strength. Therefore, two opposed processes are presumed to act on the first list over time. Spontaneous recovery increases first-list strength, while usual forgetting decreases that strength, and the two effects are largely balanced out in the resulting behavior.

Koppenaal and O'Hara (1962) suggest

Reprinted with permission of the author and the publisher, the Academic Press. The article appeared originally in the *Journal of Verbal Learning and Verbal Behavior*, 1963, **2**, 310–319.

that the time changes can be handled quite simply through the assumption of negatively accelerated unlearning. The proposition is that unlearning is a negatively accelerated, increasing function of practice on relevant IL, with the resulting retention function decreasing with positive acceleration. This notion originated in a study of short-term retention where an increase in proactive intrusions, much like that noted over time, was produced by adding a third list to the standard PI condition. In this RIP condition *S* learned A-B, A-C, A-D Lists and recalled the second list. More recent unpublished work by the author indicates that manipulation of IL in RIP conditions may produce increases in PI as well as in proactive intrusions.

In attempting to explain the similar effects of time and RIP in the same way it is immediately apparent that the notion of spontaneous recovery of the first list is inapplicable. There is no known basis for supposing that learning a third (A-D) list could aid the absolute recovery of the first (A-B) list. Instead further unlearning of the first list would be likely. Koppenaal and O'Hara suggested that the third list produced greater unlearning of the second list than of the already somewhat unlearned first list (negatively accelerated unlearning). The net result of third-list learning is a reduction in the difference betwen the strengths of the first and second lists.

Over time, it was argued, instead of a third list there is uncontrolled extra-experimental IL which produces unlearning of the two lists. However, the second list, stronger than the first following laboratory learning, loses strength at a faster rate until the two approach equal strength with time. The two central empirical time effects, relative increase of first-list responses and absolute decrease of responses from both lists, are accounted for by one process. Given that the concept of negatively accelerated unlearning can be used to account for both the time and RIP effects, and that it represents an economical explanation of the time effects alone, is there any reason to postulate spontaneous recovery of the first list?

One good reason for retaining the concept of spontaneous recovery would be direct evidence of absolute recovery. The usual specific recall employed in studies of RI and PI, and the modified free recall (MFR) of Underwood (1948b) and Briggs (1954) give results which can be attributed to either absolute or relative recovery of the first list with time. It is important in this context to formalize the differentiation of *relative* and *absolute* recovery. *Absolute* recovery refers to an increase in the absolute number of responses or associations (of a specified group) available to *S* at recall (other measures than frequency may be applicable, but this is the measure in common use). *Relative* recovery refers to an increase in the availability of one group of responses or associations in relation to another, regardless of the absolute changes in either. Recovery, of course, refers to either of the above changes taking place over an interval of time after cessation of formal learning of the responses or associations in question (hence "spontaneous").

"Availability" is a key term in the above definitions, and it is used here in the sense that Barnes and Underwood (1959) used it; i.e., availability is measured in a relatively free responding situation where *S* is encouraged and given ample time to recall all responses learned to each stimulus. This recall procedure was labelled MMFR by Melton (1961). As yet, both absolute and relative recovery, as defined, must be classed as inferred phenomena since the time effects under discussion have not been subjected to the availability measure. In using the MMFR measure, the purpose of the following study is to determine whether the recovery of the first of two A-B, A-C lists is absolute or relative, or both.

Method

Subjects and Materials. The volunteer *Ss* were 168 students of introductory psychology at the University of Manitoba. All were naive with respect to laboratory verbal learning. In one part of the study 112 *Ss*, 16 in each of seven retention-interval conditions, each learned two lists of ten paired-associate two-syllable adjectives. The lists were presented on a Gerbrand memory drum at a 3:3 sec. rate, with a 9-sec. intertrial interval, and 1 min. between lists. The learning criterion on each list was one errorless trial. Two sets of two lists each (A-B, A-C; i.e., identical stimuli, unrelated responses) were used equally often in all subconditions. In each subcondition the two lists within a set were used equally often as the first list.

The stimulus words of a set of lists, with respective responses were presented in three different orders, alternating continuously for a given *S* within and between lists over all learning trials and the recall trial.

Each set of lists was constructed so as to minimize, by careful inspection, structural and meaningful similarities between words except, of course, for the identical stimuli.

Design. The seven retention intervals, measured from the conclusion of the criterion trial on the second list to the start of the recall trial, were: 1 min, 20 min, 90 (80-100) min, 6 (5-7) hours, 24 (22-26) hours, 72 (68-76) hours, and 1 week ($\pm$ 6 hours). One MMFR-type recall trial was given to each *S* after the appropriate interval. On the recall trial the stimulus words were exposed on the memory drum in the appropriate order and *S* was instructed to give responses from both lists, and to give the responses in the order in which they occurred to him, not necessarily in the order he learned them. The *S* was allowed up to 60 sec (more than enough time by pilot data) to respond to each stimulus word on the recall trial, and was encouraged to guess.

There was one major deviation from the typical MMFR procedure. On the recall trial half of the *Ss* in each interval condition had the two correct responses exposed for 3 sec. responding to each stimulus, an adaptation of the usual anticipation-correction procedure employed in specific recall. The other half of the *Ss* received no correction information on the recall trial.

This part of the study, then, was a $2 \times 7 \times 2$ factorial, with List $\times$ Retention Interval $\times$ Correction-at-Recall, respectively. In addition another 7 groups of 8 *Ss* each learned just one list and recalled it after the various retention intervals. The four lists used in the two-list conditions were used equally often in each one-list condition. As with the two-list groups, half of each one-list group were shown the correct responses after responding on the recall trial, and half were not. No special free-recall instructions were required for the one-list *Ss* but the 60-sec. responding period and the mild encouragement to guess were maintained.

The *Ss* in the 20-min. recall conditions were given coffee, conversation, or picture magazines in a different room during the retention interval. The *Ss* in longer recall conditions were dismissed from the laboratory for the retention interval. The cooperation of all *Ss* except those with 1-min. recall was requested in not deliberately rehearsing laboratory learning during the retention interval.

The *Ss* were randomly assigned to conditions as they appeared at the laboratory. The randomization was accomplished by the use of a shuffled stack of data sheets pre-assigned to specific conditions and counterbalancings. However, an attempt was made to reassign *S* to a different retention interval if he could not possibly appear at the desired time for recall. Several devices were employed to make this an infrequent occurrence. (1) Original appointments at the laboratory were made only if *S* had at least 1½ hours free, to allow for the 20-min. interval. (2) Original learning sessions were conducted primarily in the mornings, to allow for the 6-hour interval. (3) Small deviations from the designated intervals were allowed (as indicated earlier). Reassignment was necessary in only 13 cases, and in each of these cases the next data sheet in the shuffled stack was used. Only the 1-min. interval was free of these cases, the 24- and 72-hour conditions having 3 cases each, the 20- and 90-min. and 6-hour conditions having 2 each, and the one-week condition just one case. Judging by the original learning data no sizable inequalities between conditions resulted from this virtually inescapable situation. Through care taken in reminding *Ss* of appointments, the number of failures to reappear for the recall session was negligible.

An afterthought resulted in an addition to the study after it was underway. The last 6 *Ss* in each retention interval of the two-list experiment were asked, after recalling to each stimulus, which list (first or second) each of their recalled responses was from.

Results

Original Learning. The number of trials to criterion for the two-list experiment was subjected to an analysis of variance, with Lists (within *Ss*) $\times$ Retention Interval (between *Ss*) $\times$ Correction-at-Recall (between *Ss*) as the effects. The *F* for the List main effect was 17.89 ($p < .001$); no other *F* exceeded 1.3. The mean number of trials on the first list was 12.8 ($SD = 6.75$), on the second, 10.6 ($SD = 4.90$). This small positive transfer in trials to criterion is common with the materials and procedures employed.

The mean number of trials to criterion in the one-list experiment was 11.5 ($SD = 5.87$), with no significant differences due to retention intervals or correction-at-recall.

Recall, Two-List Experiment. Since the recall scores were by nature proportions of small numbers of possible responses (10, for any one list), they were transformed to radians (Walker and Lev, 1953) before analysis of variance. The three-way analysis of the transformed scores showed the correction-at-recall variable associated with $F < 1.00$. This variable was not associated with significant variations in any other measure in this study and so will be largely ignored from this point on. Significant variations were associated with Retention Intervals ($F = 9.03$, $df = 6/98$, $p < .001$), Lists ($F = 55.00$, $df = 1/98$, $p < .001$) and the interaction of these two variables ($F = 8.25$, $df = 6/98$, $p < .001$). The mean number of responses recalled from each list at each retention interval is presented in Fig. 1. The *SD*s corresponding to these means, based on the raw scores, varied from .79 to 2.48 and were correlated with the means.

Figure 1 gives a clear indication of the nature of the interaction between lists and retention intervals. The general picture is as expected; List 2 was clearly stronger immediately following learning, with this difference diminishing over time. To lend more precision to the picture several *t*-test comparisons were made between pairs of conditions, employing overall error estimates from the analysis of variance. The differences between Lists 1 and 2 were significant beyond the .01 level at 1, 20, and 90 min., and exactly at the .05 level at 6 hours. At 24 hours, 72 hours, and one week Lists 1 and 2 did not differ significantly.

Analysis of the effect of the retention interval for the two lists separately (within-groups error estimate from the three-way analysis above) revealed significantly reduced recall of both lists over the one-week period. The finding of particular note here was that the increase in List-1 responses from 90 min. to 6 hours generated a non-significant *t* of 1.18.

Table 1 shows which list response was given first when *S* gave two responses to a stimulus, and the number of times a response from each list was the only response to a stimulus. The greater strength of the second list at short retention intervals was reflected only in a greater frequency of single responses from

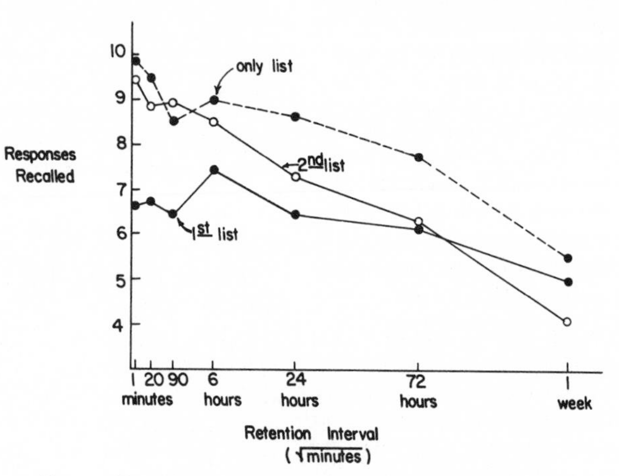

FIG. 1. Retention curves for the first, second, and only lists.

TABLE 1

MEAN NUMBER OF FIRST RESPONSES FROM EACH LIST WHEN BOTH RESPONSES WERE RECALLED, AND MEAN NUMBER OF RESPONSES FROM EACH LIST WHEN ONLY ONE WAS RECALLED: TWO-LIST EXPERIMENT

	Retention Interval						
	1 min.	20 min.	90 min.	6 hours	24 hours	72 hours	1 week
	First Response When Both Recalled						
List 1	2.94	2.75	2.88	3.25	2.69	2.94	1.44
List 2	3.25	3.19	3.07	2.81	2.06	1.00	.94
	Only Response Recalled to Stimulus						
List 1	.44	.75	.50	1.37	1.69	2.19	2.62
List 2	3.25	2.94	3.00	2.44	2.63	2.38	1.81

that list. There was no pronounced tendency for S to give the List-2 responses first when both were available. There was a tendency for List-1 responses to be given first at longer retention intervals, but since the frequencies were so small no statistical analysis was attempted.

The list-identification data (representing only the last 6 Ss run in each interval condition) were subjected to a three-way analysis of variance after transformation of the proportion scores to radians. No F exceeded 1.25, and examination of means revealed no large differences either between lists or retention intervals. The mean proportions of recalled responses which were identified with the correct list were, for the seven intervals from 1 min. to 1 week: .96, .94, .86, .95, .87, .88, .88. It has long been assumed that time decreases list differentiation and thus produces the sizable increase with time of interlist intrusions in the recall of a specific list. It should be noted, however, that in the recall of a specific list S normally has only 2 or 3 sec. to respond. The leisurely pace of the MMFR procedure may make it insensitive to changes in differentiation which do affect more hurried recall. In addition, the number of intrusions, although sometimes doubled or tripled from short to long retention intervals, is typically quite small relative to the total responses recalled. Thus even small reductions in the accuracy of list identification could contribute a substantial part of the increase of interlist intrusions with time.

Recall, One-List Experiment. The mean number of responses correctly recalled at the various intervals is presented in Fig. 1. The statistical analysis of this data is presented in the next section.

Comparison of One-List and Two-List Recall. For a statistical comparison here two simple two-way analyses of variance (Lists $\times$ Retention Intervals) were used, comparing the recall of the only list with each of the two-list recalls in turn.

The analysis comparing the only list with the second list resulted in Lists and Intervals effects significant at the .001 level (Fs $= 7.18$ and 16.33, with $df = 1/54$ and $6/154$, respectively) and the interaction significant at the .05 level ($F = 2.83$, $df = 6/154$). Comparison by t-tests at the different retention intervals showed non-significant differences between lists up to and including 6 hours, and significantly better recall of the only list at all longer retention intervals. Thus, there evidently was proactive inhibition of the second list at 24 hours and after, even under relatively free and leisurely recall.

In the comparison of the only list and the first list, some of the data were not used because of non-comparability of the actual retention intervals. That is, the "1-min." recall of the first list on the average was actually 20 min. after cessation of first-list learning.

TABLE 2
ERRORS AT RECALL FOR TWO-LIST AND ONE-LIST EXPERIMENTS

Retention interval	Two-list experiment[a] Misplaced responses	Stimulus words	Extra-experimental	One-list experiment Misplaced responses	Stimulus words	Extra-experimental
1 min.	10	1	0	1	0	0
20 min.	11.5	1.5	1	3	1	0
90 min.	9	2	3	4	0	0
6 hours	8	1.5	1	0	0	1
24 hours	15	3.5	2.5	4	1	0
72 hours	14.5	2.5	3	4	0	0
1 week	15	3	6.5	5	7	3

[a] The N per condition differed for the two experiments (two-list = 16, one-list = 8). For ease of comparison the total errors for the two-list conditions were halved.

For this analysis, then, the 1-min. recall of the first list and the 20-min. recall of the only list were matched, and the 20-min. recall of the first list and 1-min. recall of the only list were discarded. The analysis showed both the Lists and Intervals main effects significant beyond the .001 level (Fs = 33.17 and 6.21, with $df = 1/32$ and $5/132$, respectively), and the interaction non-significant ($F = 1.30$, $df = 5/132$, $p > .20$).

Errors at Recall. Table 2 gives a breakdown as to source of the overt recall errors in both experiments. The numbers in the table are per 8 *S*s. Most of the overt errors were misplaced responses; i.e., responses from the list(s) learned, but recalled to the wrong stimulus. More detailed analysis showed that at shorter retention intervals these misplaced responses tended to be primarily, though not exclusively, from the first list. At longer intervals the two lists contributed approximately equal numbers of misplaced responses.

There appears to have been some increase in all types of overt errors with increasing length of the retention interval. However, the most striking difference in overt errors was related to the number of lists learned. Misplaced responses, in particular, were rare in one-list conditions compared to two-list conditions. The difference was too large to have simply resulted because there were twice as many list responses to misplace in the two-list conditions. Learning competing A-B, A-C lists increased intralist generalization at recall.

DISCUSSION

Comment is in order on the absence of any effects of correction-at-recall under the MMFR procedure, and under the leisurely recall of a specific list in the one-list experiment. The MMFR procedure was designed with a view to explaining results obtained in the recall of specific lists (Barnes and Underwood, 1959). Recall of specific lists of paired-associates has almost universally involved the same anticipation-correction procedure as is used during learning. MMFR as used thus far has not involved any correction or knowledge of results. This difference was viewed as a possible source of error in theoretically integrating evidence from MMFR and recall of specific lists. Two theoretical points were used to predict opposite results of correction-at-recall. If seeing or rehearsing other responses in a list constitutes an important part of the stimulus context to which a response becomes associated during learning, then recall performance should be superior when the other responses are exposed on the recall trial. On the other hand, if seeing or rehearsing other responses exerts an interference effect then recall performance should be poorer with correction-at-recall. Since this variable had no discernible effect on recall it could be that these two predicted processes balanced each other out. In view of the complete lack of effects on any measure in the entire study it seems more likely that neither predicted process was in operation.

We turn now to the nature of the retention losses observed. It was indicated earlier that the 20-min. recall of the only list represents the best estimate of what the "1-min." recall of the first list would have been, had the second list not been learned. The loss of first-list strength attributable, then, to second-list learning was 2.88 of 9.50 responses, or 30%. Over the next week only an additional 1.62 first-list responses were lost (17% of 9.50). By comparison, the second list did not lose significantly in the first 20 min., but suffered greater losses than the first over the next week (53% of 20-min. recall). The effect of these different rates of loss was to reduce and finally eliminate the difference between the first and second lists. This, of course, is the time effect which has been well-documented with other measures. Consideration of other aspects of the present data, however, results in a picture of this time effect which is quite different than expected.

The most unexpected finding was the difference between the second and the only lists at longer retention intervals. In fact, this difference was probably underestimated because the second list was learned faster and therefore to a higher criterion. Under a recall procedure which has been presumed to eliminate response competition and thus proactive interference, the effects of interference from experimental prior learning appear sizable and very likely permanent. Even with recall of a specific list Underwood (1950) found that increasing the time allowed *S* for responding from 2 to 8 secs. eliminated PI. Underwood employed a 20-min. retention interval and in the present study the difference between the second and only lists appeared only at 24 hours and longer, so there is no real contradiction in the two sets of data. PI does increase with time. The present results imply that long-term PI is not due simply to the type of response competition that MMFR can be presumed to eliminate. This is a most radical suggestion. Interference theory (two-factor) has assumed that all interference effects are due to unlearning or to competition at recall. Prior learning (PL) cannot produce unlearning, as PL and unlearning are presently understood, and MMFR appears to satisfy all requirements of the operations necessary to eliminate response competition at recall.

Whatever the explanation for it, the finding of long-term PI of response availability (MMFR) augments the current emphasis on PI as the major source of forgetting. The implication relevant to the purposes of this study is that increasing PI of response availability contributes to the temporal changes in the relative strength of first and second lists. In fact, this is the only discernible process which produced the convergence of the two lists with time in this study. There is no satisfactory evidence that the first list recovered absolutely or even relatively when the standard was a proper control, the only-learned list.

While there was no clear-cut evidence of absolute recovery of the first list the retention curve (Fig. 1) does rise considerably at 6 hours. Chance ups and downs are to be expected, of course, but the observed rise is large enough to preclude a firm conclusion that there is no absolute recovery under the conditions of this study. Even if the increase in the first-list responses at 6 hours does represent actual absolute recovery, however, it is apparent that this recovery could not be considered as the only process responsible for the convergence of the first and second lists with time. In fact, the absolute recovery of, at the most, one response would represent little more than one-third of the amount of eventual recovery relative to the second list.

The lack of recovery relative to the only list is even more crucial to the understanding of the interaction of time and interference effects. The only sizable trend in the direction of relative recovery occurred at the one-week interval. It must be concluded that either the results at one week were due to error, or that recovery is extremely slow compared to that suggested by the observation of first and second lists. In view of the latter possibility, future studies of the interaction of time and interference effects would do well to explore retention intervals longer than one week. Of course, even if the recovery of the first list relative to an only list is found to occur at intervals of one week and longer, this would have little relation to the 24-48 hour convergence of first and second lists.

In order further to explore the theoretical implications of the present findings, it may be instructive to re-examine the nature of the hypotheses of spontaneous recovery and negatively accelerated unlearning. Essentially these hypotheses, both based on two-factor theory, attempted an analysis of the Time $\times$ PL interaction in the recall of a specific list by postulating a level of behaviour, response availability, where PL would have no effect. At this level time would interact with IL effects, causing temporal changes in the relative availability of first and second lists. Only when the available response competed at recall (specific or MFR) would the effects of PL and the Time $\times$ PL interaction appear. The results of this study could hardly have been more contrary to this view. Time did not interact with IL, but did interact with PL.

In order to preserve the notion that PI is due only to competition at recall it must be assumed that MMFR availability is subject to competition effects. Furthermore, the divergence of the retention curves of the second and only lists with time strongly suggests a multiplicative function involving competition and some variable operating over the retention interval. It appears reasonable and consistent with interference theory to identify the time variable as extra-experimental IL which has unlearning effects but over intervals of less than a week provides little in the way of strong responses to compete at the recall of the list. It can then be postulated that the inhibition of response availability is some multiplicative function of unlearning and response competition. For an only list the competition which interacts with unlearning over time would have to be primarily from extra-experimental sources, mostly PL, with some competition probably arising from intralist generalization. The second list would have additional strong competition from experimental PL (first list). Thus as unlearning increased with time, the inhibition of availability would increase at a faster rate for the second list.

It may be fruitful briefly to speculate on the molecular basis of this interaction of unlearning and competition. Unlearning may be viewed as a tendency to avoid an association, this tendency being built up in situations where the association is inappropriate. However, when the association is again specifically called for, the generalized avoidance tendency is effective only to the extent that there are competing responses to channel the input away from the association. If there are not, the well-directed input rapidly overcomes the generalized avoidance. The competing responses may be recognized as inappropriate and not performed. Their function is to divert the input at a stage previous to testing for appropriateness.

This interpretation has the advantage of being compatible with the interaction of experimental IL and PL reported by Koppenaal and O'Hara (1962), and of identifying the processes operating over time with experimentally manipulable variables. The disadvantage is some difficulty with the retention function of the first list over time. The immediate inhibition of the first list is not a problem, since the second-list IL produces unlearning *and* strong competing responses. However, the interference factors from experimental IL must be supposed to have had their total effect by the end of second-list learning, and not to interact with unlearning over time. The only defense for this complication is that the data insist on it; after second-list learning the first list shows no further effect of experimental IL.

There are alternative interpretations. Absolute or relative recovery of the first list could be postulated at a more fundamental level of response strength than MMFR availability, but this would result in substantial problems of balancing effects on the first list. The fact of the matter is that the only and first lists appear to be affected equally by the same time process(es). However, balancing must still be entertained seriously, as any interpretation presently available faces problems with the curve of first-list retention over time.

The interpretation in terms of an interaction of unlearning and competition, since it identifies the time processes with variables that can be manipulated somewhat independently of time, is quite amenable to investigation. For example, experimental IL that provides opportunity for substantial unlearning but does not provide strong competing responses (like time?) should produce only minor RI, but should interact with experimental PL in the manner that time did in this study. Such experimental IL could be produced by having a number of IL lists practiced for only a few trials each. On the other hand, there should not be the same pronounced interaction if the nature of PL and IL is reversed, with the poorly practiced lists as PL. Further, the speculation about the molecular nature of the interaction leads to the prediction that when the avoidance tendency (unlearning) and the diverting tendency (competition) are overcome by input which is very strongly directed to the association (e.g., a recognition test), both IL and PL should have much reduced inhibiting effects (relative to control recognition).

Summary

This study examined the availability (MMFR) of responses from two (A-B, A-C) consecutively-learned lists of paired-associate adjectives, and from an only-learned list, after seven retention intervals varying from 1 min. to one week.

As expected, the retention of the first of the two lists was far poorer than the second at short retention intervals, but the two were approximately equal after retention intervals of 24 hours and more. However, contrary to expectation, the first list showed neither absolute recovery, nor even relative recovery when the standard was the only-learned list. Comparison of the retention of the second list and the only list showed that the second list suffered proactive inhibition of response availability at longer retention intervals (24 hours and more). Both of these developments were seen as contrary to existing conceptions in two-factor interference theory, and some revisions were suggested.

References

Barnes, J. M., and Underwood, B. J. Fate of first-list associations in transfer theory. *J. exp. Psychol.*, 1959, **58**, 97-105.

Briggs, G. E. Acquisition, extinction, and recovery functions in retroactive inhibition. *J. exp. Psychol.*, 1954, **47**, 285-293.

Koppenaal, R. J., and O'Hara, G. N. The combined effect of proaction and retroaction. *Canad. J. Psychol.*, 1962, **16**, 96-105.

Melton, A. W. Comments on Professor Postman's paper. In C. N. Cofer (Ed.) *Verbal learning and verbal behavior*. New York: McGraw-Hill, 1961.

Postman, L. Extra-experimental interference and the retention of words. *J. exp. Psychol.*, 1961, **61**, 97-110. (*a*)

Postman, L. The present status of interference theory. In C. N. Cofer (Ed.) *Verbal learning and verbal behavior*, New York: McGraw-Hill, 1961. (*b*)

Underwood, B. J. Retroactive and proactive inhibition after 5 and 48 hours. *J. exp. Psychol.*, 1948, **38**, 29-38. (*a*)

Underwood, B. J. "Spontaneous recovery" of verbal

associations. *J. exp. Psychol.*, 1948, **38**, 429-39. (*b*)

UNDERWOOD, B. J. Proactive inhibition with increased recall-time. *Amer. J. Psychol.*, 1950, **63**, 594-99.

UNDERWOOD, B. J. Interference and forgetting. *Psychol. Rev.*, 1957, **64**, 49-60.

UNDERWOOD, B. J. and POSTMAN, L. Extra-experimental sources of interference in forgetting. *Psychol. Rev.*, 1960, **67**, 73-95.

WALKER, H. M., AND LEV, J. *Statistical inference.* New York: Holt, 1953.

(Received February 18, 1963)

CHAPTER 11

Short-Term Retention

Retention over short time periods has been investigated by a variety of experimental methods and tasks. The oldest method, memory span, is one with which we are already familiar through encounters with individual tests of intelligence. In tests of memory span the tester reads a series of digits at a paced rate, and the testee calls back the series, in sequence, immediately following the reading. Experimental variants of this method have been introduced in the contemporary period to investigate general phenomena of retention that are inadequately studied by simple memory span measures. In this chapter editorial license will be invoked, and only the method and findings directly relevant to verbal learning will be considered. Other methods in vogue, as well as the one considered here, have been reviewed recently by Postman (1964a).

The method of interest is one in which *S* is presented a single verbal item for a brief study period and is then asked to recall that item after some specified lapse of time, usually defined in seconds. An item may consist of one trigram, one word, one group of unrelated trigrams or words, or one pair from a PA list. Research on the retention of single verbal items began with a famous study by Peterson and Peterson (1959; Article 1) in which CCC consonant-consonant-consonant) trigrams were exposed individually for brief study. In each case exposure was followed by recall after an interval that varied from 3 to 18 seconds. The interval was filled by an irrevelant activity, counting backwards, as a means of preventing rehearsal of the item during the interval.

Despite the fact that each item was easily within *S*'s immediate span, the items were forgotten rapidly in the Peterson and Peterson study. In fact, after an interval of 18 seconds less than 10 per cent of their *Ss* were able to recall the previously exposed item. This extremely rapid rate of forgetting for trigrams was soon replicated by Murdock (1961a). Since the interpolated activity was highly dissimilar to the items, we would ordinarily expect very little, if any, of the forgetting to result from retroactive interference (cf. Article 1, Chapter 10). A potential source of interference does exist proactively, however. The procedure employed required each *S* to be tested repeatedly under each of the retention intervals. Consequently, items given early in the practice sequence may have been interfering with the retention of items occurring later. Evidence against this interpretation was given later by Peterson (1963) when he reanalyzed recall by blocks of presentation and found no trend for increasing retention losses over blocks. His conclusion was that proactive interference was an unlikely explanation for the rapid forgetting of single items.

The basic issue in short-term retention thus becomes the adequacy of interference theory, the cornerstone of explanation for LTM, to incorporate short term retention (STM). If the processes of LTM are inapplicable, separate processes need to be postulated for STM—processes that exist in some kind of blissful coexistence with those of LTM. A major alternative to interference-related processes is offered by the concepts of memory trace and decay of that trace (Hebb, 1949). According to this kind of interpretation, traces of the neural activity associated with the input from an item presentation are stored for future retrieval. These traces are viewed as decaying quickly over time, thus making the item increasingly unavailable for future recall. With repetition of the item during practice trials permanent or structural traces are formed. In STM studies repetition does not ordinarily occur, and permanent traces are not established. On the other hand, in the usual LTM study lengthy lists of items are used, and the items are repeated over and over, with permanent traces as the neural product. These permanent traces become unavailable for recall through the processes hypothesized in interference theory.

Interference Theory and STM for Trigrams and Words

RI *and* PI

Proponents of interference theory have been reluctant to accept the proposition that STM is immune to the processes operative in LTM. Their strong preference is to view both variants of retention as points along a continuum, rather than as two discrete classes of a natural dichotomy. The burden of proof, however, rests in demonstrations of the amenability of STM to the same sources of interference and to the same functional relationships with independent variables as found in LTM.

As noted above, the forgetting of single CCC trigrams does not seem to be accounted for by conventional sources of either RI or PI. Nevertheless, the absence of both RI and PI has been seriously questioned by supporters of interference theory, and these supporters have searched diligently for the hideouts of RI and PI. Postman (1964a) noted the danger of assuming that interpolated activity of any kind, even that grossly unrelated to the material to be retained, merely serves as a deterrent of rehearsal without introducing some degree of interference. He pointed out that "generalized response competition" from *S*'s tendency to continue performance on the irrelevant task at the time of recalling the item may well disrupt *S*'s recall set and serve to lower his recall score. The question of PI reappeared in a study by Keppel and Underwood (1962b; Article 2). Their careful analysis of the Petersons' (1959) procedure and findings revealed several subtle factors that may have masked PI effects in the Petersons' data. Moreover, their own results yielded firm support for PI as an important contributor to the rapid forgetting phenomenon of STM.

Intra-unit Interference

Still another potential source of interference, intra-unit interference (II), has been identified by Melton (1963b). Melton's conception of II stresses competition between the elements that make up the single item or unit. For a CCC trigram the competition is between the three consonants in that they are loosely organized into three separate chunks (cf. pp. 297–298), for a discussion of the chunk concept). Items containing fewer than three chunks are expected to generate less II than trigrams and, consequently, should display less steep slopes for their forgetting curves. The concept of II grew out of an extension of the Peterson and Peterson study (1959) by Murdock (1961a). In addition to replicating the Petersons' trigram experiment, Murdock also conducted separate experiments in which highly familiar words served as items, individually presented in one experiment and presented as triads (groups of three unrelated words) in another experiment. His findings for trigrams closely paralleled those of the Petersons. Single words, however, were susceptible to considerably less forgetting. After 18 seconds of interpolated activity close to 90 per cent of his *Ss* were able to recall the previously exposed word. Triads, on the other hand, were forgotten at about the same rate as trigrams. Since familiar words consist of one chunk, they are expected to generate much less II than either trigrams or triads, both of which consist of three chunks.

Additional support for the chunk-II coalition as a major factor in STM phenomena was provided in a series of studies by Lindley. His procedure calls for *S* to recode a three-chunk trigram into one chunk during the study period and then decode back to three chunks at the time of recall. Recoding was accomplished either by presenting word-completion cues during the study period (Lindley, 1963b) or by preceding the trigram with an associate just prior to the study period (Schaub and Lindley, 1964; Lindley and Nedler, 1965). For example, the trigram MOD might be recoded to one chunk by exposing the letters "el" in lower case type just to the right of MOD (i.e., MODel) or by preceding the study period with prior exposure to the word "model" (an associate of MOD). Recoding by both methods was found to be a highly effective means of reducing forgetting over short time periods.

An uncompromising acceptance of the chunk-II hypothesis has been handicapped by a problem that also plagues LTM—namely, the assurance of equal associative strength of items as they enter the retention interval (Keppel 1965; Underwood, 1964b; cf. p. 480 for a discussion of this problem as related to LTM). Underwood (1964b) and Keppel (1965) cautioned that items which are perfectly recalled immediately after one exposure may nevertheless differ in their associative strengths. From LTM studies we know that the rate of forgetting is inversely related to the degree of original acquisition. One-chunk and three-chunk items may appear superficially to be equal in associative strength because both are within immediate memory span, but a greater strength for the three-chunk than for the one-chunk item could be masked by the insensitivity of immediate recall to nuances of strength. Consequently, the different forgetting rates for the two kinds of items may be due to either differential II effects or to differential associative strengths or to both. Obviously what is needed for firm support of II theory is evidence of faster forgetting as the number of chunks increases even when associative strength is held constant. Houston (1965) has taken a step in this direction by demonstrating more rapid forgetting for a group of six unrelated words than for a group of five unrelated words. Comparability of associative strength following the study period was attained by use of a greater exposure interval for the six-word group than for the five-word group. A pilot study had indicated the appropriate difference in exposure rate for guarantying equality of prior associative strength.

A number of independent variables other than the number of chunks in the items per se have been related to the rate of forgetting trigrams. Hellyer (1962) determined the rate of forgetting as a function of the number of presentations (one, two, four, or eight) given an item prior to the retention interval. He found increasing resistance to forgetting with increasing number of presentations. Melton (1963b) surmised that increases in frequency of presentation serve to reduce the number of intra-item chunks, thereby lowering the amount of II during the retention interval. Association-value was related to rate of forgetting by Peterson, Peterson, and Miller (1961). Rate of forgetting was less pronounced for trigrams of high value than for those of low value. A chunk-II hypothesis is again implied—the higher the meaningfulness, the fewer the number of chunks. The importance of the nature of the interpolated activity was demonstrated by Loess and McBurney (1965). Unstructured activity was most conducive to high retention—presumably because rehearsal of the previously exposed item took place, even though *S* was instructed not to rehearse. Retention was poorest when the interpolated activity stimulated direct interference with the content of the items. In the case of trigrams this activity consisted of the active recitation of strings of random letters. The retention loss following counting backwards, the standard interpolated activity of most STM studies, fell in between that of unstructured activity and deliberate interference. An inverse relationship between retention and the similarity of the interpolated activity to the items themselves was also reported by Bruning and Schappe (1965). This inverse relationship, of course, is in agreement with studies on LTM (cf. Article 1, Chapter 10) that have manipulated the degree of similarity between the original and the interpolated learning list.

For the most part these functional relationships support the idea of a continuum for LTM and STM; that is, the relationships for STM phenomena parallel those for LTM, thus providing validation in the form of operational identification (cf. Overview), for the commonality of processes in LTM and STM. Not all of the pieces fit neatly together, however. An important exception is that for the time duration between successive tests as an independent variable. We commented earlier on the likelihood of PI resulting from the repeated use of the same *Ss* in STM experiments. Generalizing from the findings on LTM (cf. Article 1, Chapter 10), PI from one item should become increasingly more apparent on the retention of a subsequent item as the time duration separating the study-test sequences for the two items increases. Peterson and Gentile (1965) failed to find evidence for this generalization; however, some ambiguities in their data mitigate the damage to an interference-theory approach to STM.

STM for Paired Associates

STM experiments in which the single items were paired associates have been conducted by the Petersons (Peterson and Peterson, 1962; Peterson, Saltzman, Hillner, and Land, 1962) and by Murdock (1961b, 1963a, b, 1964, 1965). The procedures used fall into two general categories (Keppel, 1965). In the one (Peterson and Peterson, 1962), the retention interval is filled with irrelevant activity (e.g., counting backwards). In the other (Peterson et al., 1962; the Murdock series), the interval is filled with material (other paired associates) that is relevant to the item for which retention is to be measured.

Peterson and Peterson (1962) found that the retention of a single pair remains fairly high (84 per cent recall) after an interval of 16 seconds. Since both the *St* and *R* components of the paired associates were highly familiar words, II would not be expected to be pronounced. They also presented two pairs successively before the start of the retention interval and measured both the recall of the first pair and the recall of the second pair. Recall for both pairs was considerably less than that for single pairs, suggesting interference from both PI and RI. However, recall of the first pair was consistently greater than recall of the second pair. The presence of this primacy effect complicated their analysis in terms of specific sources of interference.

Murdock's standard procedure has been to employ what is tantamount to a PA list. For example, six pairs (A_1-B_1, A_2-B_2, etc.) are exposed successively for study periods. At the moment of recall the *St* component for one of the pairs (e.g., A_3) is given, and *S* is asked to recall the appropriate *R* component (e.g., B_3). The *A*-*B* pair had been preceded by two pairs and followed by three pairs, with the latter serving to fill in the retention interval. His procedure also calls for repeated measures on each *S*. Article 3 (Murdock, 1964) gives a detailed account of this complicated procedure. His findings have led him to reject interference sources as a means of explaining retention losses for paired associates and to accept what he calls a principle of "limited capacity" (cf. Article 3). His rejection of interference principles followed from his failure to find evidence for PI. However, Keppel (1965) has objected to the assumption that filling the retention interval with exposure to other paired associated merely passes time without generating RI effects. Keppel, in fact, interpreted Murdock's basic design as one of RIP—that is, one that introduces both retroactive and proactive sources of interference.

Acquisition Revisited

The acquisition of lists of items (e.g., paired associates) is traditionally viewed as reflecting gradual increments in the associative strength of the individual items (cf. Introduction and Article 6, Chapter 2). This gradual accruement accounts for the typical learning curve of slow but steady progress. All-or-none acquisition of the single items has been proposed (e.g., Estes, 1960), but empirical evidence gathered in the context of acquisition experiments has generally rejected this proposal (cf. Article 6, Chapter 2). However, a consideration of acquisition from within the framework of STM challenges again the validity of an incremental view. In fact, STM research has led some psychologists to reconsider seriously the very nature of acquisition. The critical fact from STM studies is the rapid forgetting of items that are within immediate memory span. Conceivably, each pair in a PA list could be learned on the very first practice trial (in an all-or-none manner) but, because of rapid intra- and inter-trial forgetting, may not be available for recall during the anticipation phase of the second trial. Broad interpretations of PA acquisition in terms of such processes of STM have been proposed by Murdock (1963c) and Tulving and Arbuckle (1963).

Why then the slow, gradual progress that is so characteristic of PA acquisition? Murdock's (1963c) data suggested that increments in acquisition over practice trials may basically be reflecting increased resistance to inter-trial forgetting rather than to increasing associative strength. Tulving and Arbuckle (1963) analyzed a typical acquisition trial into two distinct phases—a presentation or input phase and a recall or output phase—and conducted an experiment designed to separate these phases. Their results indicated to them that an interaction between input and output interference accounts for many of the conventional phenomena of acquisition. More recently, Tulving (1964) extended his approach to the phenomena of free recall. Inter-trial retention (i.e., the number of items retained from one trial to the next) was considered in addition to intra-trial functions (input and output interference). He demonstrated rather convincingly that "the traditional learning curve can be expressed as an additive function of intra-trial and inter-trial retention" (1964; p. 219).

We conclude this last introductory section with the observation that an increasing understanding of retention, in many respects the end product of acquisition, may eventually force us to revise our conceptualization of acquisition itself. Perhaps the subject matter of the terminal chapter in this book may compose the content of the initial chapter in similar future books on verbal learning. Only time, filled by the appropriate interpolated activity (namely, continuing research and theoretical analysis), will tell.

ARTICLE 1

SHORT-TERM RETENTION OF INDIVIDUAL VERBAL ITEMS [1]

LLOYD R. PETERSON AND MARGARET JEAN PETERSON

Indiana University

It is apparent that the acquisition of verbal habits depends on the effects of a given occasion being carried over into later repetitions of the situation. Nevertheless, textbooks separate acquisition and retention into distinct categories. The limitation of discussions of retention to long-term characteristics is necessary in large part by the scarcity of data on the course of retention over intervals of the order of magnitude of the time elapsing between successive repetitions in an acquisition study. The presence of a retentive function within the acquisition process was postulated by Hull (1940) in his use of the stimulus trace to explain serial phenomena. Again, Underwood (1949) has suggested that forgetting occurs during the acquisition process. But these theoretical considerations have not led to empirical investigation. Hull (1952) quantified the stimulus trace on data concerned with the CS-UCS interval in eyelid conditioning and it is not obvious that the construct so quantified can be readily transferred to verbal learning. One objection is that a verbal stimulus produces a strong predictable response prior to the experimental session and this is not true of the originally neutral stimulus in eyelid conditioning.

Two studies have shown that the effects of verbal stimulation can decrease over intervals measured in seconds. Pillsbury and Sylvester (1940) found marked decrement with a list of items tested for recall 10 sec. after a single presentation. However, it seems unlikely that this traditional presentation of a list and later testing for recall of the list will be useful in studying intervals near or shorter than the time necessary to present the list. Of more interest is a recent study by Brown (1958) in which among other conditions a single pair of consonants was tested after a 5-sec. interval. Decrement was found at the one recall interval, but no systematic study of the course of retention over a variety of intervals was attempted.

EXPERIMENT I

The present investigation tests recall for individual items after several short intervals. An item is presented and tested without related items inter-

[1] The initial stages of this investigation were facilitated by National Science Foundation Grant G-2596.

Reprinted with permission of the authors and the publisher, the American Psychological Association. The article appeared originally in the *Journal of Experimental Psychology*, 1959, **58**, 193–198.

vening. The initial study examines the course of retention after one brief presentation of the item.

Method

Subjects.—The *S*s were 24 students from introductory psychology courses at Indiana University. Participation in experiments was a course requirement.

Materials.—The verbal items tested for recall were 48 consonant syllables with Witmer association value no greater than 33% (Hilgard, 1951). Other materials were 48 three-digit numbers obtained from a table of random numbers. One of these was given to *S* after each presentation under instructions to count backward from the number. It was considered that continuous verbal activity during the time between presentation and signal for recall was desirable in order to minimize rehearsal behavior. The materials were selected to be categorically dissimilar and hence involve a minimum of interference.

Procedure.—The *S* was seated at a table with *E* seated facing in the same direction on *S*'s right. A black plywood screen shielded *E* from *S*. On the table in front of *S* were two small lights mounted on a black box. The general procedure was for *E* to spell a consonant syllable and immediately speak a three-digit number. The *S* then counted backward by three or four from this number. On flashing of a signal light *S* attempted to recall the consonant syllable. The *E* spoke in rhythm with a metronome clicking twice per second and *S* was instructed to do likewise. The timing of these events is diagrammed in Fig. 1. As *E* spoke the third digit, he pressed a button activating a Hunter interval timer. At the end of a preset interval the timer activated a red light and an electric clock. The light was the signal for recall. The clock ran until *E* heard *S* speak three letters, when *E* stopped the clock by depressing a key. This time between onset of the light and completion of a response will be referred to as a latency. It is to be distinguished from the interval from completion of the syllable by *E* to onset of the light, which will be referred to as the recall interval.

SEC. 0 1 2 3 4 5 6...
E CHJ 506
S 506 503 CHJ
|RECALL INTERVAL|←LATENCY→|

FIG. 1. Sequence of events for a recall interval of 3 sec.

The instructions read to *S* were as follows: "Please sit against the back of your chair so that you are comfortable. You will not be shocked during this experiment. In front of you is a little black box. The top or green light is on now. This green light means that we are ready to begin a trial. I will speak some letters and then a number. You are to repeat the number immediately after I say it and begin counting backwards by 3's (4's) from that number in time with the ticking that you hear. I might say, ABC 309. Then you say, 309, 306, 303, etc., until the bottom or red light comes on. When you see this red light come on, stop counting immediately and say the letters that were given at the beginning of the trial. Remember to keep your eyes on the black box at all times. There will be a short rest period and then the green light will come on again and we will start a new trial." The *E* summarized what he had already said and then gave *S* two practice trials. During this practice *S* was corrected if he hesitated before starting to count, or if he failed to stop counting on signal, or if he in any other way deviated from the instructions.

Each *S* was tested eight times at each of the recall intervals, 3, 6, 9, 12, 15, and 18 sec. A given consonant syllable was used only once with each *S*. Each syllable occurred equally often over the group at each recall interval. A specific recall interval was represented once in each successive block of six presentations. The *S* counted backward by three on half of the trials and by four on the remaining trials. No two successive items contained letters in common. The time between signal for recall and the start of the next presentation was 15 sec.

Results and Discussion

Responses occurring any time during the 15-sec. interval following signal for recall were recorded. In Fig. 2 are plotted the proportions of correct recalls as cumulative functions of latency for each of the recall intervals. Sign tests were used to evaluate differences among the curves (Walker & Lev, 1953). At each latency differences among the 3-, 6-, 9-, and 18-sec. recall interval curves are significant at the .05 level. For latencies of 6 sec. and longer these

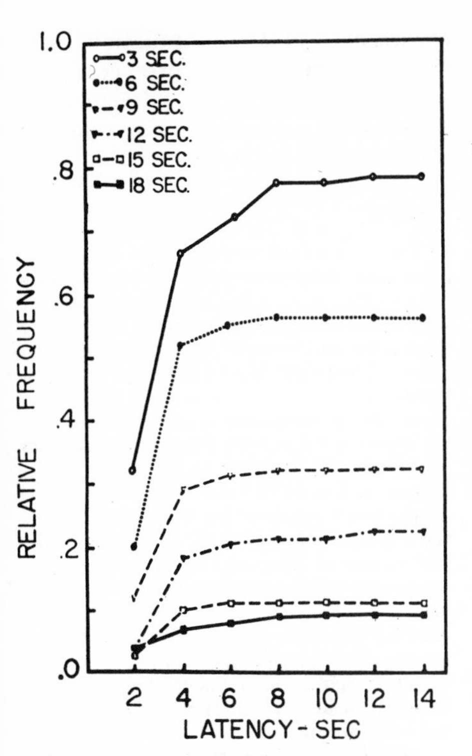

FIG. 2. Correct recalls as cumulative functions of latency.

differences are all significant at the .01 level. Note that the number correct with latency less than 2 sec. does not constitute a majority of the total correct. These responses would not seem appropriately described as identification of the gradually weakening trace of a stimulus. There is a suggestion of an oscillatory characteristic in the events determining them.

The feasibility of an interpretation by a statistical model was explored by fitting to the data the exponential curve of Fig. 3. The empirical points plotted here are proportions of correct responses with latencies shorter than 2.83 sec. Partition of the correct responses on the basis of latency is required by considerations developed in detail by Estes (1950). A given probability of response applies to an interval of time equal in length to the average time required for the response under consideration to occur. The mean latency of correct responses in the present experiment was 2.83 sec. Differences among the proportions of correct responses with latencies shorter than 2.83 sec. were evaluated by sign tests. The difference between the 3- and 18-sec. conditions was found to be significant at the .01 level. All differences among the 3-, 6-, 9-, 12-, and 18-sec. conditions were significant at the .05 level.

The general equation of which the expression for the curve of Fig. 3 is a specific instance is derived from the stimulus fluctuation model developed by Estes (1955). In applying the model to the present experiment it is assumed that the verbal stimulus produces a response in *S* which is conditioned to a set of elements contiguous with the response. The elements thus conditioned are a sample of a larger population of elements into which the conditioned elements disperse as time passes. The proportion of conditioned elements in the sample determining *S*'s behavior thus decreases and with it the probability of the response. Since the fitted curve appears to do justice to the data, the observed decrement could arise from stimulus fluctuation.

The independence of successive presentations might be questioned in the light

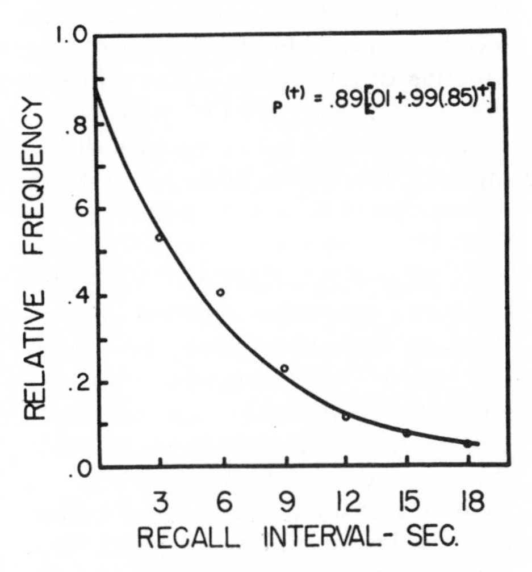

FIG. 3. Correct recalls with latencies below 2.83 sec. as a function of recall interval.

of findings that performance deteriorates as a function of previous learning (Underwood, 1957). The presence of proactive interference was tested by noting the correct responses within each successive block of 12 presentations. The short recall intervals were analyzed separately from the long recall intervals in view of the possibility that facilitation might occur with the one and interference with the other. The proportions of correct responses for the combined 3- and 6-sec. recall intervals were in order of occurrence .57, .66, .70, and .74. A sign test showed the difference between the first and last blocks to be significant at the .02 level. The proportions correct for the 15- and 18-sec. recall intervals were .08, .15, .09, and .12. The gain from first to last blocks is not significant in this case. There is no evidence for proactive interference. There is an indication of improvement with practice.

Experiment II

The findings in Exp. I are compatible with the proposition that the aftereffects of a single, brief, verbal stimulation can be interpreted as those of a trial of learning. It would be predicted from such an interpretation that probability of recall at a given recall interval should increase as a function of repetitions of the stimulation. Forgetting should proceed at differential rates for items with differing numbers of repetitions. Although this seems to be a reasonable prediction, there are those who would predict otherwise. Brown (1958), for instance, questions whether repetitions, as such, strengthen the "memory trace." He suggests that the effect of repetitions of a stimulus, or rehearsal, may be merely to postpone the onset of decay of the trace. If time is measured from the moment that the last stimulation ceased, then the forgetting curves should coincide in all cases, no matter how many occurrences of the stimulation have preceded the final occurrence. The second experiment was designed to obtain empirical evidence relevant to this problem.

Method

The *S*s were 48 students from the source previously described. Half of the *S*s were instructed to repeat the stimulus aloud in time with the metronome until stopped by *E* giving them a number from which *S* counted backward. The remaining *S*s were not given instructions concerning use of the interval between *E*'s presentation of the stimulus and his speaking the number from which to count backward. Both the "vocal" group and the "silent" group had equated intervals of time during which rehearsal inevitably occurred in the one case and could occur in the other case. Differences in frequency of recalls between the groups would indicate a failure of the uninstructed *S*s to rehearse. The zero point marking the beginning of the recall interval for the silent group was set at the point at which *E* spoke the number from which *S* counted backward. This was also true for the vocal group.

The length of the rehearsal period was varied for *S*s of both groups over three conditions. On a third of the presentations *S* was not given time for any repetitions. This condition was thus comparable to Exp. I, save that the only recall intervals used were 3, 9, and 18 sec. On another third of the presentations 1 sec. elapsed during which *S* could repeat the stimulus. On another third of the presentations 3 sec. elapsed, or sufficient time for three repetitions. Consonant syllables were varied as to the rehearsal interval in which they were used, so that each syllable occurred equally often in each condition over the group. However, a given syllable was never presented more than once to any *S*. The *S*s were assigned in order of appearance to a randomized list of conditions. Six practice presentations were given during which corrections were made of departures from instructions. Other details follow the procedures of Exp. I.

Results and Discussion

Table 1 shows the proportion of items recalled correctly. In the vocal group recall improved with repetition at each of the recall intervals tested.

TABLE 1

Proportions of Items Correctly Recalled in Exp. II

Group	Repetition Time (Sec.)	Recall Interval (Sec.)		
		3	9	18
Vocal	3	.80	.48	.34
	1	.68	.34	.21
	0	.60	.25	.14
Silent	3	.70	.39	.30
	1	.74	.35	.22
	0	.72	.38	.15

Conditions in the silent group were not consistently ordered. For purposes of statistical analysis the recall intervals were combined within each group. A sign test between numbers correct in the 0- and 3-repetition conditions of the vocal group showed the difference to be significant at the .01 level. The difference between the corresponding conditions of the silent group was not significant at the .05 level. Only under conditions where repetition of the stimulus was controlled by instructions did retention improve.

The obtained differences among the zero conditions of Exp. II and the 3-, 9-, and 18-sec. recall intervals of Exp. I require some comment, since procedures were essentially the same. Since these are between-*S* comparisons, some differences would be predicted because of sampling variability. But another factor is probably involved. There were 48 presentations in Exp. I and only 36 in Exp. II. Since recall was found to improve over successive blocks of trials, a superiority in recall for *S*s of Exp. I is reasonable. In the case of differences between the vocal and silent groups of Exp. II a statistical test is permissable, for *S*s were assigned randomly to the two groups. Wilcoxon's (1949) test for unpaired replicates, as well as a *t* test, was used. Neither showed significance at the .05 level.

The 1- and 3-repetition conditions of the vocal group afforded an opportunity to obtain a measure of what recall would be at the zero interval in time. It was noted whether a syllable had been correctly repeated by *S*. Proportions correctly repeated were .90 for the 1-repetition condition and .88 for the 3-repetition condition. The chief source of error lay in the confusion of the letters "m" and "n." This source of error is not confounded with the repetition variable, for it is *S* who repeats and thus perpetuates his error. Further, individual items were balanced over the three conditions. There is no suggestion of any difference in responding among the repetition conditions at the beginning of the recall interval. These differences developed during the time that *S* was engaged in counting backward. A differential rate of forgetting seems indisputable.

The factors underlying the improvement in retention with repetition were investigated by means of an analysis of the status of elements within the individual items. The individual consonant syllable, like the nonsense syllable, may be regarded as presenting *S* with a serial learning task. Through repetitions unrelated components may develop serial dependencies until in the manner of familiar words they have become single units. The improved retention might then be attributed to increases in these serial dependencies. The analysis proceeded by ascertaining the dependent probabilities that letters would be correct given the event that the previous letter was correct. These dependent probabilities are listed in Table 2. It is clear that with increasing repetitions the serial dependencies increase. Again combin-

TABLE 2

DEPENDENT PROBABILITIES OF A LETTER BEING CORRECTLY RECALLED IN THE VOCAL GROUP WHEN THE PRECEDING LETTER WAS CORRECT

Repetition Time (Sec.)	Recall Interval (Sec.)		
	3	9	18
3	.96	.85	.72
1	.90	.72	.57
0	.86	.64	.56

ing recall intervals, a sign test between the zero condition and the three repetition condition is significant at the .01 level.

Learning is seen to take place within the items. But this finding does not eliminate the possibility that another kind of learning is proceeding concurrently. If only the correct occurrences of the first letters of syllables are considered, changes in retention apart from the serial dependencies can be assessed. The proportions of first letters recalled correctly for the 0-, 1-, and 3-repetition conditions were .60, .65, and .72, respectively. A sign test between the 0- and 3-repetition conditions was significant at the .05 level. It may tentatively be concluded that learning of a second kind took place.

The course of short-term verbal retention is seen to be related to learning processes. It would not appear to be strictly accurate to refer to retention after a brief presentation as a stimulus trace. Rather, it would seem appropriate to refer to it as the result of a trial of learning. However, in spite of possible objections to Hull's terminology the present investigation supports his general position that a short-term retentive factor is important for the analysis of verbal learning. The details of the role of retention in the acquisition process remain to be worked out.

SUMMARY

The investigation differed from traditional verbal retention studies in concerning itself with individual items instead of lists. Forgetting over intervals measured in seconds was found. The course of retention after a single presentation was related to a statistical model. Forgetting was found to progress at differential rates dependent on the amount of controlled rehearsal of the stimulus. A portion of the improvement in recall with repetitions was assigned to serial learning within the item, but a second kind of learning was also found. It was concluded that short-term retention is an important, though neglected, aspect of the acquisition process.

REFERENCES

BROWN, J. Some tests of the decay theory of immediate memory. *Quart. J. exp. Psychol.*, 1958, **10**, 12–21.

ESTES, W. K. Toward a statistical theory of learning. *Psychol. Rev.*, 1950, **57**, 94–107.

ESTES, W. K. Statistical theory of spontaneous recovery and regression. *Psychol. Rev.*, 1955, **62**, 145–154.

HILGARD, E. R. Methods and procedures in the study of learning. In S. S. Stevens (Ed.), *Handbook of experimental psychology.* New York: Wiley, 1951.

HULL, C. L., HOVLAND, C. I., ROSS, R. T., HALL, M., PERKINS, D. T., & FITCH, F. B. *Mathematico-deductive theory of rote learning: A study in scientific methodology.* New Haven: Yale Univer. Press, 1940.

HULL, C. L. *A behavior system.* New Haven: Yale Univer. Press, 1952.

PILLSBURY, W. B., & SYLVESTER, A. Retroactive and proactive inhibition in immediate memory. *J. exp. Psychol.*, 1940, **27**, 532–545.

UNDERWOOD, B. J. *Experimental psychology.* New York: Appleton-Century-Crofts, 1949.

UNDERWOOD, B. J. Interference and forgetting. *Psychol. Rev.*, 1957, **64**, 49–60.

WALKER, H., & LEV, J. *Statistical inference.* New York: Holt, 1953.

WILCOXON, F. *Some rapid approximate statistical procedures.* New York: Amer. Cyanamid Co., 1949.

(Received September 26, 1959)

ARTICLE 2

Proactive Inhibition in Short-Term Retention of Single Items[1]

GEOFFREY KEPPEL AND BENTON J. UNDERWOOD

Northwestern University, Evanston, Illinois

In 1959 Peterson and Peterson developed a technique whereby a single verbal item was presented to *S* for a learning trial of approximately .5-sec. duration, with retention being measured over intervals of up to 18 sec. These procedures produced a very systematic relationship between length of retention interval and percentage of items correct at recall, with 78% correct after 3 sec., and 8% after 18 sec. Thus, forgetting of the single item is nearly complete after 18 sec. The reliability of this forgetting curve is demonstrated by the fact that Murdock (1961) has repeated the Peterson-Peterson experiment and obtained nearly identical results.

The present experiments were designed to obtain data which would aid in interpreting theoretically the extraordinarily rapid forgetting of the single items which has been observed in the above experiments. The nature of the interpretative problem and how it arises, requires some background discussion.

The first distinction which must be made is between short-term retention procedures and long-term retention procedures. The short-term studies, as exemplified by Peterson and Peterson, involve retention of *single* items over very short intervals, say, 60 sec. or less. The long-term retention studies involve retention of *lists* of items over much longer intervals, such as 20 min., although usually hours or days are employed. Clearly no dichotomy is possible between the two types of studies based on length of retention interval, but in actual practice a working distinction between the two exists. We may identify the short-term studies as measuring short-term memory (STM) and the long-term studies as measuring long-term memory (LTM) with the understanding that the present usage also involves memory for singly presented items versus memory for lists of items.

The critical issue is whether or not LTM and STM will require fundamentally different interpretative principles. The resolution of this issue rests primarily on determining the role which proactive inhibition (PI) plays in STM. Interference theories of LTM use PI as a cornerstone paradigm (e.g., Postman, 1961); associations learned prior to the learning of associations for which retention is being tested may interfere with recall. However, a secondary fact reported by Peterson and Peterson (1959) and by Peterson (1963) is that little or no evidence is found for PI in STM. In addition, since little or no retroactive inhibition (RI) is believed to be produced by the activity used to prevent rehearsal in the studies of STM, it would appear that an interference theory, based on PI and RI, is quite incapable of handling the extraordinarily rapid forgetting observed in the studies of STM. Thus, we are faced with a potential theoretical schism, with one set of propositions being used for LTM and another possibly wholly different set for STM. In the interests of theoretical continuity, such a schism should be avoided if possible.

As noted above, the critical issue involved is the role which PI plays in STM. If PI is operative in STM, the variables which govern magnitude of PI in LTM should also have counterparts in the laws of STM. Some of these more critical variables will now be discussed.

Number of Interfering Associations. In LTM the greater the number of previously acquired associations the greater the PI (Un-

[1] This work was supported by Contract Nonr-1228(15), Project NR 154-057, between Northwestern University and the Office of Naval Research.

Reprinted with permission of the authors and the publisher, the Academic Press. The article appeared originally in the *Journal of Verbal Learning and Verbal Behavior*, 1962, 1, 153–161.

derwood, 1945; 1957). It is the reported failure to reproduce this law in studies of STM that has led to the conclusion that there is little, if any, PI in STM. Actually, the procedure used in these studies of STM would seem to be ideal for obtaining PI. For example, in the Peterson-Peterson study, a counterbalancing technique was used in which each *S* served eight times at each of six retention intervals. Thus, each *S* at the termination of his conditions had been presented 48 different items. The items presented late in the session should be subject to a greater number of potentially interfering associations than would those items presented early in the session. Yet there appears to be little difference in the retention of items presented early in the session and those presented late in the session (but see later discussion).

Degree of Learning. In LTM the higher the degree of learning of the list to be recalled the better the recall when the PI paradigm is used (Postman and Riley, 1959). This is not to say that the absolute PI is less with higher than with lower degrees of learning (when evaluated against a control group) of the list to be recalled, for according to Postman and Riley this relationship is complex. But, given a high degree of learning of a list, its recall will be higher than will the recall of a list with a low degree of learning when the proactive interference is constant on both lists. This fact has been used by Melton (1963) indirectly to suggest that PI is indeterminate in the available studies of STM. His reasoning is that as *S* proceeds through a series of conditions the learning-to-learn will serve to increase the degree of learning of items presented. This higher degree of learning, in turn, will counteract a decrement in retention which should occur as a function of the increasing number of potentially interfering associations which have been established as practice proceeds.

There is evidence that learning-to-learn does occur in STM studies (Peterson and Peterson, 1959). That it does occur requires a distinction between learning and retention in STM, a distinction which has not, in fact, been carefully maintained in the studies to date. Normally, we may use an immediate test (say, after 1 sec.) as a measure of degree of learning. Retention for longer intervals are assessed against the scores on the immediate test to determine the retention function. However, when percentage correct for immediate retention is essentially 100%, there is no way to derive a meaningful retention function. For, in a manner of speaking, the true degree of learning may be more than 100%. Thus, if STM of common words is to be compared with that of consonant syllables, and if the immediate test for words shows 100% correct recall and that for syllables 85%, comparison of the retention of the two materials at longer intervals may be both a function of underestimated differences in degree of learning and of differences in material. Latency measures at recall might be used as subsidiary indices of forgetting which occurs when the percentage correct remains near 100% for retention intervals of increasing length, but the moment recall falls substantially below 100% we have subject selection (those who do not get an item correct are not included in the measures) which may distort the mean of the natural distribution of latencies based on all *S*s.

Length of Retention Interval. The logic of the PI situation demands an increase in PI as a function of the length of the retention interval (Underwood, 1948). So far as is known, no completely satisfactory test of this relationship has been made for LTM. Theoretically the increase in PI with increase in length of the retention interval may be accounted for by the recovery of extinguished interfering associations. Several studies strongly suggest such recovery (e.g., Briggs, 1954).

Interaction of Variables. If the facts and theory of PI in LTM hold for STM, certain interactions among the above variables will be expected. Most critical among these is the interaction between the number of potentially interfering associations and the length of the retention interval. Theoretically it is assumed that the longer the retention interval the greater the recovery of interfering associations. If there are few or none such associations little or no decrement will be observed as a function of length of retention interval (i.e., forgetting will be very slow). If there are many potential associations which could interfere proactively, the longer the retention interval the greater the forgetting, since the longer the interval the greater the number of interfering associations which will have recovered.

We may now focus on the fact that PI is said not to be involved in the rapid forgetting in STM. In the Peterson-Peterson study *Ss* were tested on 48 successive items following two practice items. It has been suggested that PI reaches some maximum level rather quickly as a function of the number of previous items and that a constant amount of PI may occur thereafter. Thus, two practice items may "throw in" the maximum amount of PI and additional items may have no further decremental effects (Postman, 1962; Melton, 1963). While it seems apparent that there must be a limit to the number of previous items which will contribute to interference in STM, it does not seem reasonable that all potential interfering associations would be established with only two items—the two practice items. It seems more reasonable to look at the Peterson-Peterson data from another point of view. If it is assumed that there is a practice effect in learning successive items, degree of learning for each successive item will be higher and higher. By principles of PI in LTM, the recall should also be higher and higher if amount of interference remains constant. But, of course, interference does not remain constant; more and more potentially interfering associations are acquired as testing continues. As noted earlier in the discussion, the question is how the positive effects of increased degree of learning with successive stages of practice balance out against the increased interference which accompanies the higher degree of learning. Some indication of the direction the answer may take is available in the Peterson-Peterson data.

These investigators divided the 48 experimental items into successive blocks of 12 items each so that Blocks 1 through 4 may reflect increasing degrees of learning of the items to be recalled and, simultaneously, increasing numbers of potentially interfering items. The percentage correct at recall by blocks was determined separately for two short intervals (3 and 6 sec.) and for two long intervals (15 and 18 sec.). The results are presented in Fig. 1. For the short reten-

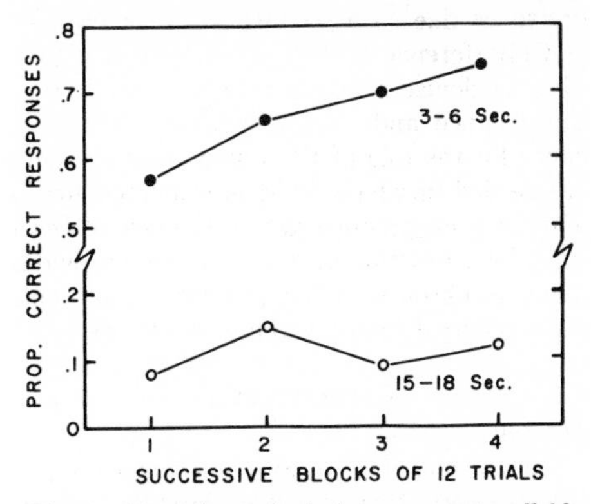

FIG. 1. Retention of single consonant syllables over short (3–6 sec.) and long (15–18 sec.) retention intervals as a function of number of preceding items. From Peterson and Peterson (1959).

tion intervals there is a consistent increase in recall from Block 1 to Block 4, the difference between the recall for the two extreme blocks being significant at the .02 confidence level. Peterson and Peterson identified this as a practice effect. Since there is no reason to believe that the practice effect occurs in the recall process it must mean that the degree of learning attained in the constant exposure period increases as trials proceed. For the longer retention interval there is no increase in recall. If only practice effects are involved, this curve should rise in exactly the same manner as the curve for shorter intervals. That it does not may indicate an increase in amount of PI as trials proceed. Thus, Fig. 1 gives indirect evidence for the critical interaction discussed earlier; that is, the interaction between amount of interference and length of the retention interval. With short retention intervals the practice effects more than compensate for increased interference; with long retention intervals the interference is of sufficient magnitude to mask the practice effects.

The evidence for the interaction between

number of previous items and length of retention interval as inferred from Fig. 1 is not entirely satisfactory. Not only is the magnitude of the interaction small, but the failure to find a change in retention over blocks for the longer retention intervals must be interpreted as due to a balance between practice and interference effects. We believe it is possible to devise situations which will destroy this balance and thus give more direct evidence for the role of PI. Furthermore, studies are needed in which STM is examined for *S*s without prior practice so that the rate of onset of PI as a function of 0, 1, 2, 3, etc., previous items is observed. The present experiments were designed to study these two issues.

Experiment 1

Method

Subjects. A total of 108 *S*s from introductory psychology classes at Northwestern University served in Exp. 1. Most *S*s had served in one or more verbal-learning experiments but in no case did an *S* have prior experience with the specific materials of the present experiment.

Procedure. Three retention intervals were used, namely, 3 sec., 9 sec., and 18 sec. A single consonant syllable was used for each retention interval. The procedure of Peterson and Peterson (1959) was followed, in which *E* spelled a syllable aloud and *S* attempted to recall it after the appropriate retention interval. The interval was timed from the moment the last letter of the syllable was spoken to the point at which *S* was instructed to recall. During the retention interval *S* counted backward by threes from a three-digit number spoken immediately after the presentation of the syllable, the rate of counting being one three-digit number per sec. Half the *S*s were given a short practice period in counting backwards prior to being given the first syllable. However, since this practice had no discernible effect on the scores, the variable has not been maintained in presenting the results.

The three trigrams or consonant syllables were KQF, MHZ, and CXJ. Each has a 4% association value in the Witmer list (Underwood & Schulz, 1960). The retention for each *S* was measured over all three intervals with, of course, a different trigram being used for each interval. The three intervals were completely counterbalanced and three different orders of the trigrams were used such that each occurred equally often as the first, second, and third trigram presented. Thus 18 *S*s are needed to fill the 18 different trigram-interval orders. Since 108 *S*s were used, the design was replicated six times.

The design allows retention to be determined for the three retention intervals after 0, 1, and 2 prior trigrams. Recall for the first trigram will be referred to as Test 1 (T-1), that of the second T-2, and the third, T-3.

Results

The results in terms of proportion of items correct for T-1, T-2, and T-3 for each retention interval are shown in Fig. 2. Each point is based on 36 *S*s. Forgetting is apparent for

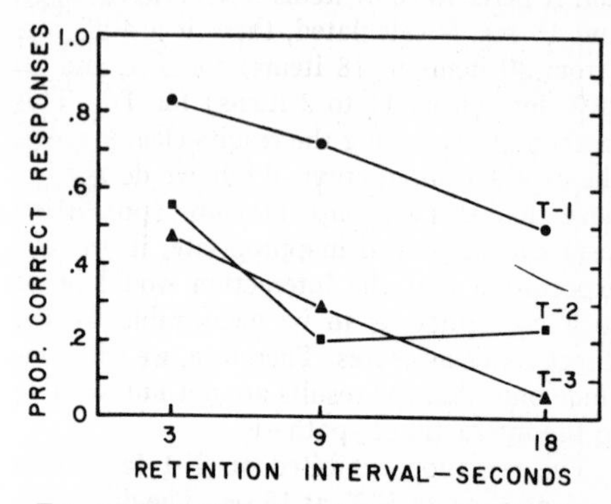

FIG. 2. Retention of single consonant syllables as a function of length of interval and number of prior syllables. Experiment 1.

all three tests. There is a large drop in proportion correct from T-1 to T-2, suggesting a severe proactive effect produced by a single prior item. There is no strong evidence that T-2 differs from T-3; thus, this may suggest a steady state or a constant amount of PI after the initial drop from T-1 to T-2. However, two facts relative to this point should be noted. First, at 3 sec. and at 18 sec., proportion correct is higher for T-2 than for T-3; only at 9 sec. is there a reversal. The fact that performance is better at 18 sec. than at 9 sec. (forgetting decreases between 9 and 18 sec.) suggests the possibility that for some unknown reason the 9 sec. T-2 estimate of retention is too low. Secondly, it is noted that the absolute number of *S*s recalling correctly at T-2 and T-3 for the 9- and 18-sec. intervals is very low. At none of these points is retention above 25% and on T-3 at 18 sec. forgetting is virtually complete. At these low levels of performance it may be very difficult to show consistent differences. Nevertheless, it must be concluded that there is no evidence for an increase in PI between T-2 and T-3. Furthermore, there is no evidence for an interaction between tests and retention intervals; the curves for T-1 and T-3 are essentially parallel, although here again it must be noted that on T-3 at 18 sec. forgetting is virtually complete, a situation which may preclude the appearance of an interaction. If, however, retention at 3 sec. is used as a base and if percentage of items lost between 3 sec. and 18 sec. is calculated, there is a 40% loss (from 30 items to 18 items) for T-1, and an 88% loss (from 17 to 2 items) for T-3. This method of evaluating the results clearly shows the expected interaction. While we do not believe that this response measure (proportion lost) can be judged inappropriate, it was our expectation that the interaction would be of such magnitude as to be measurable by the direct recall measures. Therefore, we will conclude only that the results are not unfavorable to the interaction hypothesis.

The retention exhibited on T-1 falls from 83% at 3 sec. to 50% at 18 sec. The difference between these two proportions is highly significant ($z = 3.00$). Only 83% of the *S*s could correctly reproduce the trigram shown them 3 sec. later, and this was the first trigram shown. This suggests that degree of learning was low. However, to account for this we have no evidence to choose between failure to hear the letters and letter sequence correctly, as opposed to true forgetting over 3 sec. In any event, with a low degree of learning, STM should be easily interfered with. If interference via PI is responsible for the forgetting on T-1, it must come from associations acquired in previous laboratory experiments, from conflicting letter-sequence habits, or both.

Experiment 2

Except for one major change, Exp. 2 was very similar to Exp. 1. The change made was toward increasing the degree of initial learning by using a 2-sec. visual exposure of the items for learning. As previously noted in presenting the results for Exp. 1, recall was very poor for T-2 and T-3 for the 9- and 18-sec. retention intervals. With such low recall it is doubtful that any clear interaction between tests and intervals could have been observed. Therefore, it was believed that by increasing the degree of learning a greater range of forgetting could be observed for T-2 and T-3.

Method

A total of 216 *S*s served in Exp. 2. Some had served in previous laboratory experiments on verbal learning and some had not. The three trigrams used in Exp. 1 also were employed in Exp. 2. However, each trigram was presented visually for a 2-sec. learning trial before the retention interval. Each trigram was printed with a lettering set on a 3 × 5-in. card, the letters being ½ in. high. Following the presentation of a card for 2 sec., *E* spoke a number as the card was removed and *S* counted backward by threes as in Exp. 1. Practice in number counting was given prior to presentation of the first trigram.

Each *S* again served in all three retention-interval conditions. Intervals were completely counterbalanced as were also the three trigrams; thus, 36 *S*s were required for each possible interval-trigram order.

Results

The proportions correct at each test for the three retention intervals are shown in Fig. 3. Each proportion is based on 72 *S*s. It is apparent that the level of recall is appreciably higher than in Exp. 1. This is due, we believe, to the longer exposure of the item on the learning trial. On T-1 only four responses (out of a possible 216) were incorrect; obviously, therefore, no forgetting is measurable across

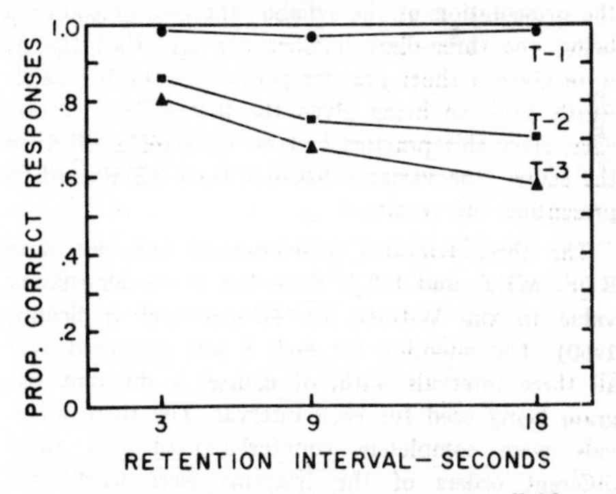

FIG. 3. Retention of single consonant syllables as a function of length of interval and number of prior syllables. Experiment 2.

intervals on T-1. Proportion correct falls sharply from T-1 to T-2, with a continued but smaller decrease from T-2 to T-3. However, the drop from T-2 to T-3 is significant statistically. For each successive block of 18 *S*s the interval order is perfectly balanced and each item has occurred equally often with each interval. Therefore, we may treat each group of 18 *S*s as an independent experiment, thus giving 12 experiments. We may determine the total correct responses on T-2 and T-3 for each experiment separately, thus deriving two distributions of 12 entries each, one distribution representing number correct on T-2 and the other on T-3. The mean total items recalled per experiment for T-2 was 13.92, for T-3, 12.42. The mean difference (1.50 $\pm$ .54) gives a t of 2.78, which, with 11 df, is significant beyond the 5% level.

Although the forgetting over time for T-2 and T-3 is not as precipitous as in Exp. 1, it is clearly evident. Since there is no forgetting on T-1, it might appear that Fig. 3 shows the expected interaction between tests and intervals. However, such a conclusion is unwarranted. Whether or not forgetting "above" 100% correct occurred across intervals for T-1 is indeterminate from the correct-response measure. In recording the scores, note was made of all correct responses with latencies of 3 sec. or less. On T-1 almost all responses had latencies shorter than 3 sec. and there was no change in frequency of such responses with increasing intervals. This might be taken to indicate no forgetting across 18 sec. for T-1, hence that the interaction apparent in Fig. 3 is real. Experiment 3 would support such an interpretation.

The fact that Exp. 2 produced a difference between T-2 and T-3 in retention indicated that no "bottom" or steady state of PI had been reached. To test more fully the course of PI as a function of number of prior items, *S*s in Exp. 3 were tested on six successive items.

Experiment 3

Method

A total of 96 *S*s was used, divided into two subgroups of 48 each. Two retention intervals were employed, 3 sec. and 18 sec. One subgroup received the retention intervals in the order 3-18-3-18-3-18, and the other in the reverse order. This procedure permitted determination of retention after 3 sec. and after 18 sec. following 0, 1, 2, 3, 4, and 5 previous items.

Six new trigrams were chosen having a Witmer association value of 21%. This was the lowest association value from which six trigrams could be chosen so that no letter was duplicated among the 18 used. The six trigrams were: CXP, GQN, HJL, KBW, SFM, and ZTD. Six different orders of the trigrams were used such that each trigram occurred equally often on each successive test and, of course, equally often with each retention interval for each subgroup. None of the *S*s used had served previously in laboratory experiments of verbal learning. The presentation procedures were exactly the same as in Exp. 2.

Results

The proportions of correct responses for both interval patterns are combined in Fig. 4. In this figure the six successive tests are given along the abscissa, with one curve representing

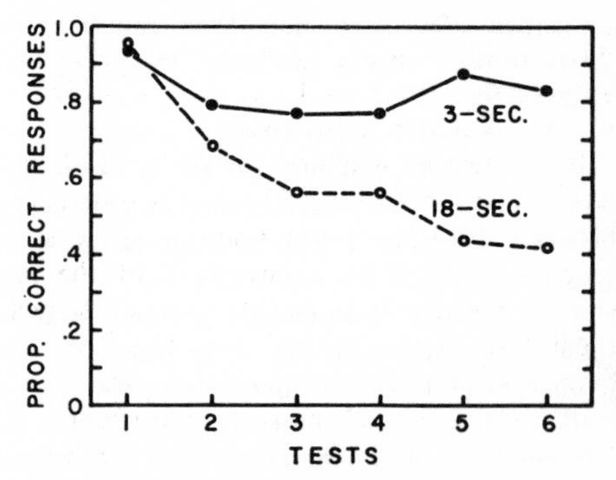

FIG. 4. Retention as a function of number of prior syllables and length of retention interval. Experiment 3.

retention after 3 sec. and the other retention after 18 sec. The trend of proactive interference which was initiated by the three tests in Exp. 2 is extended and clarified by Fig. 4. It may be noted that retention on T-1 is lower than in Exp. 2 for the 3-sec. interval. Since the procedures were identical in the two experiments, the differences must arise from the samples of *S*s and from differences in materials. Actually, the trigrams of Exp. 2 had lower association value than those of Exp. 3. Whatever the cause, it is clear that degree of learning is lower in Exp. 3 than in Exp. 2.

This unexpected turn of events, however, produces the very desirable effect of removing any problem of a "ceiling" effect in response measurement, at least for Tests 2 through 6.

It may be noted first that the recall on the very first item presented *S*s does not differ for the 3-sec. and the 18-sec. retention intervals. However, with each successive test the differences increase, thus demonstrating the interaction between tests (number of prior interfering associations) and length of retention interval. Severe PI builds up over 18 sec. with successive tests but this does not happen over 3 sec. For T-1 through T-6, the *z*'s for the difference between proportions for 3 and 18 sec. are: .47, 1.17, 2.17, 2.17, 4.51, and 4.23.

Significant forgetting is shown for the 30-sec. interval between T-1 and T-4 ($z = 2.33$). The rise between T-4 and T-5 is not significant statistically but may indicate that practice effects are more than counteracting interference effects produced by prior tests (see later).

The question as to whether a steady state of a constant amount of PI is being approached in the 18-sec. curve is not clearly answered by Fig. 4. The question can be more easily answered by replotting Fig. 4 to separate the two independent groups. That is, the 3-sec. curve in Fig. 4 is based on two different groups of *S*s, one having the 3-18-3-18-3-18 order of intervals, the other the reverse. We may, therefore, plot the 3- and 18-sec. curves separately for each group. This is done in Fig. 5. The solid lines represent the group given the 3-18 etc. order, the dotted lines representing the group given the reverse order. The filled circles represent the 3-sec. retention, the open circles the 18-sec. retention.

For the 18-sec. curves, the 3-18 Group shows no evidence of leveling off and the 18-3 Group shows only slight evidence of negative acceleration. In short, it would appear that extrapolation of these curves beyond the six tests used would give further continued larger and larger decrements in recall over 18 sec. That this is not so apparent in Fig. 4 appears to be due to the fact that this figure combines two groups of slightly different ability

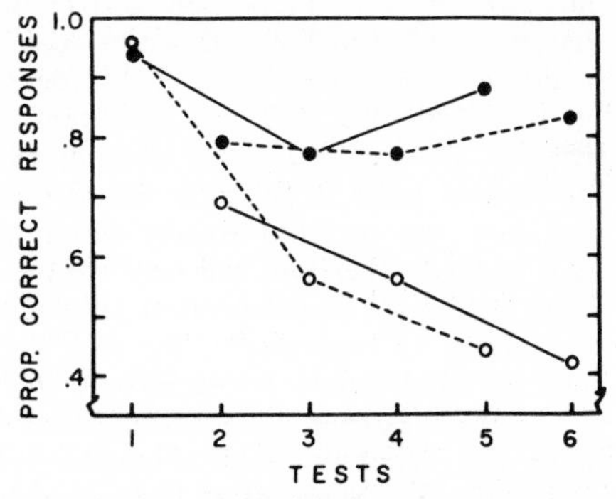

FIG. 5. Retention as a function of number of prior syllables and length of retention interval (solid circles, 3 sec.; open circles, 18 sec.) for *S*s having intervals in the order 3-18-3-18-3-18 (solid lines) and in the reverse order (dotted lines). Experiment 3.

levels. It also should be noted that for both groups there is a rise in retention between the second and third tests for the 3-sec. interval. Although neither rise is significant statistically, the trend may be reliable in view of the Peterson-Peterson data shown in Fig. 1 where performance does systematically improve as a function of successive tests for short retention intervals.

Discussion

The results of the present experiments give strong support to the presumption that short-term retention of single items and long-term retention of lists of items are subject to the same laws of proactive inhibition. The parallelism of the results for STM and LTM when common variables are manipulated may be briefly summarized.

(1) In LTM, number of potential interfering associations and amount of PI are directly related. The same relationship occurred in Exps. 2 and 3; reasons for the failure of the evidence from Exp. 1 to support the principle were discussed earlier.

(2) Length of retention interval and magnitude of PI are directly related in LTM given a constant amount of interference. This relationship was observed in all experiments except for T-1 in Exps. 2 and 3, where interference was presumed to be low, and degree of learning high.

(3) In LTM, combining the effects of the above two variables leads to an interaction between number of potential interfering associations and length of retention interval. The interaction was clearly apparent in Exp. 3.

(4) In LTM, given constant interference, magnitude of PI decreases as degree of learning of list to be recalled increases. The degree of learning was not systematically manipulated in the present studies. However, since there is no reason to believe that auditory presentation intrinsically gives more PI than visual presentation, it may be inferred that the 2-sec. visual presentation in Exp. 2 produced a higher degree of learning than did the shorter auditory presentation in Exp. 1. Greater forgetting was observed in Exp. 1 than in Exps. 2 and 3. However, this is not a "clean" result, since the degree of learning of potentially interfering items in Exps. 2 and 3 would be higher than that of comparable items in Exp. 1. Nevertheless, the forgetting on T-1 over 18-sec. in Exp. 1 may be taken as an indication that the lower the degree of learning of the item to be recalled the more retention is influenced by proactive interference from sources outside the immediate experimental situation (associations developed in previous experiments or "natural" letter-sequence associations). It is a fact that on T-1 in Exp. 1 the intrusion of letters increased from 5% to 8% to 14% of all letters given for the 3-, 9-, and 18-sec. intervals, respectively. This suggests a recovery over time of interfering associations.

No data on letter intrusions occurring for tests beyond T-1 have been given. The reason for this is simply that by the nature of the designs used it is impossible to isolate variables which may be involved in producing intrusions. In the present studies, time between successive recalls differ; degree of learning of items given previously differ for different intervals; whether or not a previously presented item was correct or incorrect at recall should influence overt intrusions on subsequent items. If systematic laws concerning evocation of letter intrusions are to be derived, experiments must be explicitly designed for the purpose. For these reasons we have not presented intrusion data.

If the conclusion of the present experiments are sound, that is, the conclusion that the laws of proaction are the same for STM as for LTM, some economy in time may be gained by working out further laws of PI on STM rather than on LTM. For example, interitem similarity (e.g., letter duplication) should clearly influence STM. But there is reason to believe that this relationship may be complex. Specifically, in the present results it was noted that many intrusions consisted of a letter from a previous item replacing a letter at recall which occupied the same serial position, e.g., the middle letter. This suggests the operation of an A-B, A-C interference paradigm in which A is the common serial position. Such intrusions also represent the evidence needed to support the notion of spontaneous recovery of extinguished or partially extinguished associations over short intervals. If, however, serial position does constitute a common stimulus from item to item, identical letters in the same position for different items may produce a positive effect—i.e., proactive facilitation may result.

Finally, it may be noted that PI measured with a short recall interval (2 sec.) in LTM may disappear with longer intervals (Underwood, 1950). In all the STM studies reported thus far, recall intervals of from 10 sec. to 14 sec. have been used. A reduction in the time allowed for recall may increase the apparent PI, thus allowing work with higher degrees of learning of single items than has been customary. With high degrees of learning and long recall intervals (as in Exp. 2), no measurement of forgetting is possible for initial items tested. Very short recall intervals might produce systematic evidence for forgetting for such degrees of learning.

Summary

Three experiments were performed to determine the relationship between certain variables influencing proactive inhibition in long-term retention of lists of verbal items and the influence of these variables on short-term retention of single items. More particularly, retention of single items over 18 sec. should, if the laws of long-term retention are applied, decrease with number of previous items to which *S* has been exposed. In addition, amount of forgetting should be a direct joint function of number of previous items and length of the retention interval.

In Exp. 1 each *S* was presented consonant syllables singly, with retention being measured after 3, 9, and 18 sec. Forgetting of the first item presented (T-1) was less than for the second (T-2) or third (T-3) item, but forgetting of the latter (T-2 vs. T-3) did not differ. On all three tests forgetting was directly related to length of retention interval, but no interaction was evident between number of previous items and length of retention interval.

In Exp. 2 a higher degree of initial learning of the items was achieved. Forgetting increased directly as a function of number of previous items presented. The predicted interaction was indeterminate since retention was essentially 100% on T-1 for all retention intervals.

Experiment 3 tested retention of six successive items over 3- and 18-sec. intervals. Retention after 3 sec. showed an initial drop and then a rise over the six tests, the rise suggesting a practice effect. Forgetting over 18 sec. increased directly from T-1 to T-6 and there was no indication that a constant amount of proactive interference had been reached. The interaction between length of retention interval and number of potential proactively interfering items was very evident.

The results were interpreted to mean that proactive inhibition in short-term memory of single items follows the same laws as proactive inhibition in long-term memory of lists of items.

References

Briggs, G. E. Acquisition, extinction and recovery functions in retroactive inhibition. *J. exp. Psychol.*, 1954, **47**, 285-293.

Melton, A. W. Discussion of Professor Peterson's paper. In C. N. Cofer (Ed.) *Problems and processes in verbal behavior and learning*. New York: McGraw-Hill, 1963.

Murdock, B. B., Jr. The retention of individual items. *J. exp. Psychol.*, 1961, **62**, 618-625.

Peterson, L. R. Immediate memory: Data and theory. In C. N. Cofer (Ed.) *Problems and processes in verbal behavior and learning*. New York: McGraw-Hill, 1963.

Peterson, L. R., and Peterson, M. J. Short-term retention of individual verbal items. *J. exp. Psychol.*, 1959, **58**, 193-198.

Postman, L. The present status of interference theory. In C. N. Cofer (Ed.) *Verbal learning and verbal behavior*. New York: McGraw-Hill, 1961.

Postman, L. Short-term memory and incidental learning. Paper read at ONR conference, Ann Arbor, Michigan, February, 1962.

Postman, L., and Riley, D. A. Degree of learning and interserial interference in retention. *Univer. Calif. Publ. Psychol.*, 1959, **8**, 271-396.

Underwood, B. J. The effect of successive interpolations on retroactive and proactive inhibition. *Psychol. Monogr.*, 1945, **59**, No. 3.

Underwood, B. J. Retroactive and proactive inhibition after five and forty-eight hours. *J. exp. Psychol.*, 1948, **38**, 29-38.

Underwood, B. J. Proactive inhibition with increased recall time. *Amer. J. Psychol.*, 1950, **63**, 594-599.

Underwood, B. J. Interference and forgetting. *Psychol. Rev.*, 1957, **64**, 49-60.

Underwood, B. J., and Schulz, R. W. *Meaningfulness and verbal learning*. Philadelphia: Lippincott, 1960.

(Received May 18, 1962)

ARTICLE 3

PROACTIVE INHIBITION IN SHORT-TERM MEMORY [1]

BENNET B. MURDOCK, JR.

University of Vermont

To study PI effects in short-term memory for paired associates, 60 Ss were tested on 6 lists of 6 pairs each. The A-B pairs consisted of common English words paired at random. After each list had been presented once, Ss were tested for retention of 1 of the 6 pairs by presenting A as the cue for recall of B. Serial position of the critical pair was counterbalanced across stage of practice. While there were changes in the serial-position curve as a function of stage of practice, when summed over all retention intervals performance did not deteriorate with practice. The results do not readily fit a PI interpretation of forgetting; instead, Broadbent's hypothesis of a limited capacity system seems more applicable.

Keppel and Underwood (1962) have recently reported results which suggest that proactive-inhibition (PI) effects develop rapidly in short-term memory (STM). Specifically, they found that, with a modification of the Peterson and Peterson (1959) technique, the retention of CCC trigrams at the longer retention intervals decreased markedly with stage of practice (i.e., number of prior items). On the other hand, PI effects do not appear to be so clear-cut with paired associates composed of common English words. In fact, in one study (Exp. VI, Murdock, 1963b) retention of naive *S*s was if anything worse than that of practiced *S*s; the one exception was a marked primacy effect for naive *S*s.

According to Keppel and Underwood (1962, p. 153), whether or not long-term and short-term memory require fundamentally different interpretative principles depends primarily upon the role of PI. Thus, if the rapid forgetting often found in STM can be shown to vary as a function of stage of practice then it becomes a reasonable presumption that interlist PI effects are involved. While such may be the case with single CCC trigrams, the study cited above suggests that such is not the case with paired associates.

However, in view of the importance of this problem (Melton, 1963) a further study seemed indicated. The main purpose of the present study, then, was to test for PI effects in STM for individual paired associates. The basic procedure was the same as that used in previous experiments (e.g., Murdock, 1963b). A list of six A-B pairs was presented once, then retention of one of the six pairs was tested by presenting A as the cue for recall of B. Each *S* was tested on six lists with serial position of the critical pair (i.e., the retention interval) counterbalanced across stage of practice. If as Keppel and Underwood suggest there is an interaction between retention interval and stage of practice, then retention of the first five pairs in the list should deteriorate with practice. Retention of the sixth pair should, as a measure of degree of original learning, either show no

[1] This study was performed while the writer held a National Science Foundation Senior Postdoctoral Fellowship at the Applied Psychology Research Unit in Cambridge, England. The author would like to thank the members of the Unit for their generous hospitality and for the stimulating atmosphere provided.

Reprinted with permission of the author and the publisher, the American Psychological Association. The article appeared originally in the *Journal of Experimental Psychology*, 1964, **68**, 184–189.

change or, perhaps, even improve over the six lists used.

METHOD

Subjects.—The *S*s were 60 British naval ratings approximately 18–25 yr. of age who had volunteered for a 2-wk. assignment to APRU to serve as experimental *S*s. Some of the *S*s may have participated in prior verbal learning experiments, but certainly not with the specific material of the present experiment and probably not with either paired-associate learning tasks or with stimulus material composed of common English words.

Materials.—With 6 lists of 6 pairs each a total of 36 pairs was needed. The pairs used were selected from a previous study (Murdock, 1963b, Exp. III) and were chosen to be of medium difficulty. Specifically, there were 156 pairs which had been tested at Serial Positions 1–3 (retention intervals of 6–10 sec.) where the retention curve is essentially flat (see Table 5, p. 438). The median number of correct recalls for the 156 pairs was 3.8 out of a maximum of 16, and there were 43 pairs which had been correctly recalled by 3 or 4 *S*s.

With 43 pairs available and 36 pairs required, seven pairs had to be eliminated; they were: FOREIGN-TRAIN, FEDERAL-DUKE, ACCOMPLISH-PHILIP, EM-INSTANTLY, RAW-CENT, HEALTHY-BELT, and DART-TAME. These seven pairs were selected as most likely to differ in associative value for American college students and English naval ratings.[2]

The remaining 36 pairs were: AGAINST-CLAIM, DISTINGUISH-EUROPE, HIGHWAY-LEAN, RIGHT-SPEAK, DELIGHTFUL-IMPORT, READING-ANGER, NOBODY-BURY, EARN-OPERATOR, AFFAIR-EXTREME, PROFIT-DISAPPOINTMENT, DUST-RESUME, HOLLAND-JAMES, SOIL-RELATE, FOLLOWER-HUNGER, SWING-ART, FROST-PRESENCE, LOAD-ACT, DECISION-COMPLAIN, THINK-DEPART, AFTERWARDS-START, SPREAD-HE, TOWER-STEADY, WAY-DELIGHT, ROYAL-BOLT, MADAM-CONTAIN, OPPOSITE-RIFLE, YOUTHFUL-TORTURE, SHAME-DISTRIBUTION, SMILE-NAIL, CRAWL-ANYHOW, DESIRE-WHERE, GAY-FACTOR, CONTINUOUS-HOTEL, SETTLE-LOUDLY, PRINCIPLE-SCHEME, and HALL-EFFECT. It was necessary to select 6 critical pairs from the list of 36; the 6 were drawn at random and were the first 6 listed above.

Procedure.—All *S*s were tested individually. At the start of the experiment they were given the following instructions to read:

> I am going to show you a set of six cards, and a pair of words will be written (typed) on each card. For instance, a pair of words might be "CAT-DOG." You will see the cards one at a time; study the pair of words on each card and try to remember it. After you have seen the six pairs I shall show you a card with the first word of one of the pairs. For instance, in the above example the card would be: "CAT—?" If you can remember the correct word (in this case "DOG") write it down on the answer sheet.
>
> The pairs will not be as easy as "CAT-DOG," but the words will be common English words. You will not have much time to study each pair—there will be about two seconds to look at each pair. You may be asked to remember the 1st pair, the 2nd pair, the 3rd pair, the 4th pair, the 5th pair, or the 6th pair, and you will not know in advance which pair you will be asked about. So just do your best to try to study each pair as it is shown and try to remember it if you can.

Then, the essential points were summarized by *E*, and care was taken to make sure *S* understood exactly the nature of the task.

As the instructions above indicate, each list consisted of six pairs, and naturally the critical pair was in no way distinguished prior to the test for recall. All *S*s were tested on six lists, and the critical pair was in a different serial position in each list. All A-B pairs were typed on individual index cards. A metronome was set at a rate of 1 beat/sec, and new cards (pairs) were presented at every other beat.

On the recall test the A word of the critical pair was presented as the cue for recall of the corresponding B word, and this A word simply followed without interruption the sixth pair in the list. The *S*s were allowed as much time for recall as they wished, but at least 20 sec. had to elapse between lists. Also, *S*s were asked to write down their responses, but were allowed to leave a blank if they "could not remember."

Design.—Each *S* was tested once at each of the six retention intervals. These six retention intervals were counterbalanced across stage of practice by means of a balanced Latin square (Edwards, 1960, p. 275). That is, for every six *S*s each retention interval occurred once at each stage of practice, and this was balanced across the whole experiment so that each retention interval was preceded and followed once by every other retention interval.

Each list consisted of one critical pair and

---

[2] The writer is endebted to Alan Baddeley for help here and in other aspects of the study.

TABLE 1

FREQUENCY OF TYPE OF RESPONSE AS A FUNCTION OF STAGE OF PRACTICE

Classification	Stage of Practice						Total
	1	2	3	4	5	6	
Correct Responses	16	25	21	21	17	17	117
Intralist A intrusions	3	5	3	3	6	7	27
Intralist B intrusions	13	13	15	20	14	19	94
Extralist intrusions	4	5	5	7	8	2	31
Omissions	24	12	16	9	15	15	91
Total	60	60	60	60	60	60	360

five irrelevent pairs. The five irrelevent pairs were determined randomly (sampling without replacement) for each *S*. That is, before each *S* was tested the 30 cards with the irrelevent pairs were thoroughly shuffled and then dealt into six equal piles, one for each of the six lists. Thus, while the critical pairs were the same for all *S*s, they were embedded in lists which were randomly determined (and hence different) for every *S*.

The ideal procedure would have been to use a Graeco-Latin square to counterbalance both critical pairs and retention interval across stage of practice. Then, not only would materials and conditions be counterbalanced across stage of practice but also each critical pair would occur equally often at each retention interval. Unfortunately this could not be done; there are no 6 × 6 Graeco-Latin squares (Fisher & Yates, 1948, p. 17). Therefore, of necessity, certain critical pairs occurred more often at some serial positions than at others.

To minimize this interaction between serial position and critical pair the Latin square was reversed for half the *S*s. That is, the assignment of critical pair to serial position was reversed within the balanced Latin square. As a result, within one complete replication of 12 *S*s the critical pairs AGAINST-CLAIM, DISTINGUISH-EUROPE, and HIGHWAY-LEAN each occurred three times at four different serial positions but never at the other two serial positions. However, the critical pairs RIGHT-SPEAK, DELIGHTFUL-IMPORT, and READING-ANGER each occurred twice at all six serial positions.

To summarize, then: Each *S* was tested on six lists. One full replication required 12 *S*s, and with 60 *S*s there were five replications in all. Within each replication each retention interval occurred equally often at each stage of practice, each critical pair occurred equally often at each stage of practice, and each critical pair occurred almost equally often at each retention interval. Finally, every retention interval preceded and followed every other retention interval equally often.

RESULTS

The main results are shown in Table 1, which presents a complete classification of all responses at each stage of practice. Grammatical vari-

TABLE 2

FREQUENCY OF CORRECT RESPONSES AT EACH SERIAL POSITION

Serial Position	Stage of Practice						Total
	1	2	3	4	5	6	
1	6	5	2	4	0	0	17
2	1	4	2	1	1	1	10
3	1	0	0	1	2	2	6
4	0	3	2	3	3	3	14
5	0	4	8	5	4	5	26
6	8	9	7	7	7	6	44
Total	16	25	21	21	17	17	117

ants (of which there were four: IMPORTANT for IMPORT three times and ANGRY for ANGER once) were considered as correct responses, primarily because they were so rare a separate classification seemed unwarranted. Intralist intrusions were A and B members of other pairs in the list. (Because irrelevant pairs were randomly distributed no record was kept of the composition of specific lists. However, in view of the fact that only about 2% of all noncorrect responses are intrusions from prior lists—see Exp. V of Murdock, 1963b—it seemed reasonable to assume that these "intralist" intrusions did in fact come from the list at hand.) Extralist intrusions were any words outside the set of words used in the experiment, and omissions were failures to response.

There is little evidence for any striking deterioration in performance as a function of stage of practice. As the first row of Table 1 shows, performance was if anything poorest on the very first list tested. Actually, a first-half vs. second-half comparison showed that 26 *S*s recalled more words on Lists 1–3, 22 *S*s recalled more words on Lists 4–6, while 12 *S*s showed equal recall. Overall, stage of practice seemed to have had little effect on retention.

A more detailed picture of the results is given in Table 2, which shows number of correct responses at each serial position as a function of stage of practice. Performance at Serial Position 1 did deteriorate with practice; a median test (with stage of practice grouped into blocks of two) showed that the difference was highly significant, χ^2 (2) = 14.88, $p < .001$. Performance at Serial Positions 2–5 either stayed constant or improved, with Serial Position 5 showing the greatest improvement. Finally, performance at Serial Position 6 (a measure of degree of original learning) showed a slight tendency to deteriorate with practice, but a median test showed that the effect was far from significant, χ^2 (2) = 1.28, $p > .50$.

Discussion

Underwood (1957) has shown that, in LTM, retention over a 24-hr. period is of the order of 75% for naive *S*s but of the order of 25% for highly practiced *S*s. Keppel and Underwood (1962) have shown that, in STM for single items, there is a marked interaction between stage of practice and retention interval (see Fig. 4, p. 158). That is, relatively speaking performance at the longer retention intervals deteriorates with stage of practice. What do the present results indicate about PI effects in STM foı individual paired associates?

The pairs in Serial Position 1 do show the expected effect, while the pairs in Serial Positions 2–5 do not. Nor does performance at Serial Position 6, a test of degree of original learning, show any convincing evidence of a learning-to-learn effect which might counterbalance a PI effect. Overall, a PI interpretation does not appear to provide a very economical description of the present results. Naive *S*s (i.e., first list tested) showed very marked forgetting, and only one of the five serial positions showed the expected deterioration.

In effect, the present experiment may be considered as a test of STM under five different conditions, with each condition utilizing a different number of prior and subsequent pairs (0–5, 1–4 . . . 4–1 for Serial Positions 1–5, respectively). The emphasis here has been on each of these five conditions separately, hence the problem of the confounding of number of prior pairs, number of subsequent pairs, and duration of the retention interval really does not arise. Actually, the confounding of prior and subsequent pairs which is inherent in this design is probably not too critical since the evidence shows that, given at least one prior pair, further increases up to eight do not decrease recall probability by more than about .10 at any retention interval (Murdock, 1963b). The use of Serial Position 6 as a measure of degree of original learning has also been discussed in this same reference; suffice it to say that the evidence shows this measure to underestimate slightly the degree of original learning for pairs early in the list. Thus, in the present design, the amount of forgetting is also slightly underestimated.

The present results corroborate those reported previously with naive *S*s (Exp. VI, Murdock, 1963b). Thus, with paired associates, there does seem to be a primacy effect which disappears with practice but is compensated for by an improvement in retention of the penultimate pair in the list. It should be noted that the magnitude of these effects is considerable; recall probability drops from about .60 to about .25 in the former case, and rises by about the same amount in the latter case. This change from primacy to recency with practice has also been found in free and in ordered recall (Dallett, 1963).

An alternative to a PI interpretation would be provided by a "swings and roundabout" principle or, more formally, Broadbent's (1958) hypothesis of a limited capacity system. That is, given a fixed limit to the amount of material that could be recalled, the p values at the individual serial positions might change markedly but these changes would tend to balance out. In addition to the evidence mentioned above, the following four studies may be cited in support:

1. Murdock (1963b) tested both naive and sophisticated *S*s under comparable conditions. As shown in Table 7 (p. 440) the sum of the p values was 2.46 for naive *S*s, 2.73 for sophisticated *S*s (Table 5, p. 438). These two numbers indicate the areas under the serial position curves and, as such, are the best overall measures of performance (Murdock, 1962). Thus, despite marked differences in the shape of the serial position curve, the overall performance of *S*s tested on 312 lists did not differ by more than 10% from those tested on one single list.

2. Tulving and Arbuckle (1963) used single-digit, category-member pairs. Under "ordered input" the pairs were presented in order (i.e., 0,1,2 . . . 9) whereas in "random input" there was no correspondence between order of presentation and A member of the pair. The serial position curve showed greater curvilinearity under ordered input conditions, but the areas under the two curves were almost identical: 5.10 and 5.00 for ordered and random input, respectively.

3. Kay and Poulton (1951) in a serial task gave instructions for recall before or after presentation. With instructions after (Cond. B_1) there was better recall at Serial Position 5, but with instructions before (Cond. C) there was a recency effect. The areas under the two curves were estimated by summing the eight data points as read from the curves of Fig. 1 (p. 36); the values (above chance level) were quite similar (1.38 and 1.62 for Cond. B_1 and C, respectively).

4. Rabbitt (1962) compared recall of two aspects of a series (colors and letters) with instructions on order of recall before and after presentation. Instructions before facilitated the first-recalled dimension, but there was a corresponding depression of the second-recalled dimension. Not only were "before" and "after" means almost the same for each of the two dimensions separately, but also the combined means for Cond. 1 and 2 were almost identical (72.8% and 71.8 %, respectively).

There is some evidence, then, that the individual has a limited capacity for the recall of a list of items presented once. Findings from studies of free recall (Murdock, 1960; Waugh, 1963) and of longer lists of paired associates (Murdock, 1963a) would be consistent with this interpretation if the limitation were on the rate at which information could be processed. The serial position curve will change with stage of practice, with conditions of presentation, and with instructions before or after presentation. However, the available evidence seems to indicate that the changes balance out; as an expression from the English fairgrounds goes, "What you gain on the swings you lose on the roundabout."

REFERENCES

BROADBENT, D. E. *Perception and communication.* New York: Pergamon Press, 1958.

DALLETT, K. M. Practice effects in free and ordered recall. *J. exp. Psychol.*, 1963, **66**, 65–71.

EDWARDS, A. L. *Experimental design in psychological research.* New York: Rinehart, 1960.

FISHER, R. A., & YATES, F. *Statistical tables for biological, agricultural and medical research.* (3rd Ed.) Edinburgh: Oliver & Boyd, 1948.

KAY, H., & POULTON, E. C. Anticipation in memorizing. *Brit. J. Psychol.*, 1951, **42**, 34–41.

KEPPEL, G., & UNDERWOOD, B. J. Proactive inhibition in short-term retention of single items. *J. verbal Learn. verbal Behav.*, 1962, **1**, 153–161.

MELTON, A. W. Implications of short-term memory for a general theory of memory. *J. verbal Learn. verbal Behav.*, 1963, **2**, 1–21.

MURDOCK, B. B., JR. The immediate retention of unrelated words. *J. exp. Psychol.*, 1960, **60**, 222–234.

MURDOCK, B. B., JR. The serial position effect of free recall. *J. exp. Psychol.*, 1962, **64**, 482–488.

MURDOCK, B. B., JR. Short-term memory and paired-associate learning. *J. verbal Learn. verbal Behav.*, 1963, **2**, 320–328. (a)

MURDOCK, B. B., JR. Short-term retention of single paired associates. *J. exp. Psychol.*, 1963, **65**, 433–443. (b)

PETERSON, L. R., & PETERSON, M. J. Short-term retention of individual verbal items. *J. exp. Psychol.*, 1959, **58**, 193–198.

RABBITT, P. M. Short-term retention of more than one aspect of a series of stimuli. *Nature*, 1962, **195**, 102.

TULVING, E., & ARBUCKLE, T. Y. Sources of intratrial interference in immediate recall of paired associates. *J. verbal Learn. verbal Behav.*, 1963, **1**, 321–334.

UNDERWOOD, B. J. Interference and forgetting. *Psychol. Rev.*, 1957, **64**, 49–60.

WAUGH, N. C. Immediate memory as a function of repetition. *J. verbal Learn. verbal Behav.*, 1963, **2**, 107–112.

(Received August 13, 1963)

References for Overview and Introductory Sections

Archer, E. J. A re-evaluation of the meaningfulness of all possible CVC trigrams. *Psychol. Monogr.* (1960), **74** (10, Whole No. 497), (4).*

Asch, S. E., & Ebenholtz, M. The principle of associative symmetry. *Proc. Amer. Philos. Soc.* (1962), **106**, 135–163, (2).

Baker, B. L., & Noble, C. E. Effects of time factors in paired-associate verbal learning. *J. verb. Learn. verb. Behav.* (1965), **4**, 437–445, (4).

Barclay, A. Objective mediators in paired-associate learning. *Amer. J. Psychol.* (1961), **74**, 373–383, (9).

Barclay, A. The influence of variations in paradigms and associative value on mediated transfer. *Psychol. Rep.* (1965), **17**, 103–106, (9).

Barnes, J. M., & Underwood, B. J. "Fate" of first-list associations in transfer theory. *J. exp. Psychol.* (1959), **58**, 97–105, (Overview, 7, 10).

Bastian, J. Associative factors in verbal transfer. *J. exp. Psychol.* (1961), **62**, 70–79, (8).

Battig, W. F. Comment on "Intralist generalization in paired-associate learning." *Psychol. Rev.* (1959), **66**, 338–339, (5).

Battig, W. F., & Brackett, H. R. Comparison of anticipation and recall methods in paired-associate learning. *Psychol. Rep.* (1961), **9**, 59–65, (3).

Battig, W. F., Brown, S. C., & Nelson, D. Constant vs. varied serial order in paired-associate learning. *Psychol. Rep.* (1963), **12**, 695–721, (3).

Battig, W. F., Brown, S. C., & Schild, M. E. Serial position and sequential associations in serial learning. *J. exp. Psychol.* (1964), **67**, 449–457, (1).

Battig, W. F., Merikle, P. M., & Schild, M. E. Anagram free-recall and recognition learning, and paired-associate transfer. *J. verb. Learn. verb. Behav.* (1965), **4**, 44–52, (7).

Battig, W. F., & Spera, A. J. Rated association values of numbers from 0–100. *J. verb. Learn. verb. Behav.* (1962), **1**, 200–202, (4).

Besch, N. F., & Reynolds, W. F. Associative interference in verbal paired-associate learning. *J. exp. Psychol.* (1958), **55**, 554–558, (8).

Bilodeau, E. A., & Bilodeau, I. M. Variation of temporal intervals among critical events in five studies of knowledge of results. *J. exp. Psychol.* (1958), **55**, 603–612, (3).

Birge, J. S. The role of verbal responses in transfer. Unpublished doctoral dissertation, Yale University, 1941, (9).

Bousfield, W. A. The occurrence of clustering in the recall of randomly arranged associates. *J. gen. Psychol.* (1953), **49**, 229–240, (7).

Bousfield, W. A., & Cohen, B. H. The effects of reinforcement on the occurrence of clustering in the recall of randomly arranged associates. *J. Psychol.* (1953), **36**, 67–81, (7).

Bousfield, W. A., & Cohen, B. H. General review of a program of research on associative clustering. *The Minnesota Conference on associative processes in verbal behavior* (1955a) 64–101, Minneapolis: University of Minnesota, Department of Psychology, (7).

Bousfield, W. A., & Cohen, B. H. The occurrence of clustering in the recall of randomly arranged words of different frequencies-of-usage. *J. gen. Psychol.* (1955), **52**, 83–95, (7).

Bousfield, W. A., & Cohen, B. H. Clustering as a function of the number of word-categories in stimulus-word lists. *J. gen. Psychol.* (1956), **54**, 95–106, (7).

Bousfield, W. A., Cohen, B. H., & Whitmarsh, G. A. Associative clustering in the recall of words of different taxonomic frequencies of occurrence. *Psychol. Rep.* (1958), **4**, 39–44, (7).

* Denotes the chapter(s) in which the reference is cited.

Bousfield, W. A., Puff, C. R., & Cowan, T. M. The development of constancies in sequential organization during repeated free recall. *J. verb. Learn. verb. Behav.* (1964), **3,** 489–495, (7).

Bowman, R. E., & Thurlow, W. R. Determinants of the effect of serial position in serial learning. *Amer. J. Psychol.* (1963), **76,** 436–445, (1).

Braun, H. W., & Heymann, S. P. Meaningfulness of material, distribution of practice, and serial-position curves. *J. exp. Psychol.* (1958), **56,** 146–150, (1, 3, 4).

Briggs, G. E. Acquisition, extinction, and recovery functions in retroactive inhibition. *J. exp. Psychol.* (1954), **47,** 285–293, (8).

Bruning, J. L., & Schappe, R. H. Type of interpolated activity and short-term memory. *Psychol. Rep.* (1965), **16,** 925–929, (11).

Bryk, J. A., & Kausler, D. H. Supplementary report: Stimulus meaningfulness and unlearning in the *A-B, A-C* transfer paradigm. *J. exp. Psychol.*, in press, (8).

Bugelski, B. R. Presentation time, total time, and mediation in paired-associate learning. *J. exp. Psychol.* (1962), **63,** 409–412, (3).

Bugelski, B. R. In defense of remote associations. *Psychol. Rev.* (1965), **72,** 169–174, (1).

Bugelski, B. R., & Cadwallader, T. C. A reappraisal of the transfer and retroaction surface. *J. exp. Psychol.* (1956), **52,** 360–366, (8, 10).

Bugelski, B. R., & Rickwood, J. Supplementary report: Presentation time, total time, and mediation in paired-associate learning: Self-pacing. *J. exp. Psychol.* (1963), **65,** 616–617, (3).

Bugelski, B. R., & Scharlock, D. P. An experimental demonstration of unconscious mediated association. *J. exp. Psychol.* (1952), **44,** 334–338, (9).

Carr, H. A. Teaching and learning. *J. genet. Psychol.* (1930), **37,** 189–218, (3).

Carroll, J. B., & Burke, M. L. Parameters of paired-associate verbal learning: Length of list, meaningfulness, rate of presentation, and ability. *J. exp. Psychol.* (1965), **69,** 543–553, (3).

Cason H. Association between the familiar and the unfamiliar. *J. exp. Psychol.* (1933), **16,** 295–305, (4).

Cassem, N., & Kausler, D. H. Supplementary report: Effects of stimulus association value and exposure duration on *R-S* learning. *J. exp. Psychol.* (1962), **64,** 94, (2).

Ceraso, J., & Henderson, A. Unavailability and associative loss in RI and PI. *J. exp. Psychol.* (1965), **70,** 300–303, (10).

Cieutat, V. J., Stockwell, F. E., & Noble, C. E. The interaction of ability and amount of practice with stimulus and response meaningfulness (*m, m'*) in paired-associate learning. *J. exp. Psychol.* (1958), **56,** 193–202, (4).

Cochran, S. W., & Wickens, D. D. Supplementary report: Rated association values of numbers from 0–100. *J. verb. Learn. verb. Behav.* (1963), **2,** 373–374, (4).

Cofer, C. N. A study of clustering in free recall based on synonyms. *J. gen. Psychol.* (1959), **60,** 3–10, (7).

Cofer, C. N. On some factors in the organizational characteristics of free recall. *Amer. Psychologist* (1965), **20,** 261–272, (7).

Cofer, C. N., & Appley, M. H. *Motivation: Theory and research.* New York; John Wiley & Sons, 1964, (Overview).

Cofer, C. N., & Bruce, D. R. Form-class as the basis for clustering in the recall of non-associated words. *J. verb. Learn. verb. Behav.* (1965), **4,** 386–389, (7).

Cofer, C. N., & Foley, J. P., Jr. Mediated generalization and the interpretation of verbal behavior: I. Prolegomena. *Psychol. Rev.* (1942), **49,** 513–540, (5, 9).

Cofer, C. N., & Yarczower, M. Further study of implicit verbal chaining in paired-associate learning. *Psychol. Rep.* (1957), **3,** 453–456, (9).

Cohen, B. H., Bousfield, W. A., & Whitmarsh, G. A. Cultural norms for verbal items in 43 categories. *Technical Report No. 22* (1957), University of Connecticut, Contract Nonr 631 (**00**), Office of Naval Research, (7).

Cohen, J. C., & Musgrave, B. S. Effect of meaningfulness on cue selection in verbal paired-associate learning. *J. exp. Psychol.* (1964), **68,** 284–291, (2).

Cook, J. O. Supplementary report: Processes underlying learning a single paired-associate item. *J. exp. Psychol.* (1958), **56,** 455, (3).

Cook, J. O., & Spitzer, M. E. Supplementary report: Prompting versus confirmation in paired-associate learning. *J. exp. Psychol.* (1960), **59,** 275–276, (3).

Dallett, K. M. The transfer surface re-examined. *J. verb. Learn. verb. Behav.* (1962), **1,** 91–94, (8).

Dallett, K. M. Implicit mediators in paired-associate learning. *J. verb. Learn. verb. Behav.* (1964a), **3,** 209–214, (2).

Dallett, K. M. Number of categories and category information in free recall. *J. exp. Psychol.* (1964b), **68,** 1–12, (7).

Dallett, K. M. Proactive and retroactive inhibition in the *A-B, A-B'* paradigm. *J. exp. Psychol.* (1964c), **68,** 190–200, (10).

Dallett, K. M. In defense of remote associations. *Psychol. Rev.* (1965), **72,** 164–168, (1).

Dallett, K. M., & D'Andre, L. Mediation instructions versus unlearning instructions in the *A-B, A-C* paradigm. *J. exp. Psychol.* (1965), **69,** 460–466, (8).

Davis, F. C. The relative reliability of words and nonsense syllables. *J. exp. Psychol.* (1930), **13,** 221–234, (4).

Dean, M. G., & Kausler, D. H. Degree of first-list learning and stimulus meaningfulness as related to transfer in the *A-B, C-B* paradigm. *J. verb. Learn. verb. Behav.* (1964) **3,** 330–334, (8).

Deese, J. Influence of inter-item associative strength upon immediate free recall. *Psychol. Rep.* (1959), **5,** 305–312, (7).

Deese, J. From the isolated verbal unit to connected discourse. In C. N. Cofer (Ed.), *Verbal learning and verbal behavior.* New York: McGraw-Hill, 1961, (1, 7).

Deese, J. On the structure of associative meaning. *Psychol. Rev.* (1962), **69,** 161–175, (7).

Deese, J., & Kaufman, R. A. Serial effects in recall of unorganized and sequentially organized verbal material. *J. exp. Psychol.* (1957), **54,** 180–187, (7).

Deese, J., & Kresse, F. H. An experimental analysis of the errors in rote serial learning. *J. exp. Psychol.* (1952), **44,** 199–202, (1).

Dollard, J., & Miller, N. E. *Personality and psychotherapy.* New York: McGraw-Hill, 1950, (2).

Dron, D. M., & Boe, E. E. *R-S* paired associate learning as a function of percentage occurrence of response members. *J. verb. Learn. verb. Behav.* (1964), **3,** 130–131, (2).

Dulsky, S. G. The effect of a change of background on recall and relearning. *J. exp. Psychol.* (1935), **18,** 725–740, (2).

Ebbinghaus, H. *Über das gedächtnis: Untersuchungen zur experimentellen psychologie.* Duncker and Humbolt, 1885, (Overview, 1, 4, 10).

Ebenholtz, S. M. Serial learning: Position learning and sequential associations. *J. exp. Psychol.* (1963), **66,** 353–362, (1).

Ellington, N. R., & Kausler, D. H. Supplementary report: "Fate" of List 1 *R-S* associations in transfer theory. *J. exp. Psychol.* (1965), **69,** 207–208, (8).

Ellis, H. *The transfer of learning.* New York: Macmillan, 1965, (8).

Epstein, W. The influence of syntactical structure on learning. *Amer. J. Psychol.* (1961), **74,** 80–85, (7).

Epstein, W. A further study of the influence of syntactical structure on learning. *Amer. J. Psychol.* (1962), **75,** 121–126, (7).

Epstein, W. The effect of stimulus and response meaningfulness when response availability is equated. *J. verb. Learn. verb. Behav.* (1963), **2,** 242–249, (4).

Epstein, W., & Platt, J. R. Free recall of paired associates as a function of meaningfulness. *J. verb. Learn. verb. Behav.* (1964), **3,** 269–273, (4).

Epstein, W., & Streib, R. The effect of stimulus meaningfulness and response meaningfulness in the absence of response learning. *J. verb. Learn. verb. Behav.* (1962), **1,** 105–108, (4).

Erickson, R. L. Relational isolation as a means of producing the von Restorff effect in paired-associate learning. *J. exp. Psychol.* (1963), **66,** 111–119, (5).

Erickson, R. L. Differential effects of stimulus and response isolation in paired-associate learning. *J. exp. Psychol.* (1965), **69,** 317–323, (5).

Estes, W. K. Learning theory and the new "mental chemistry." *Psychol. Rev.* (1960), **67,** 207–223, (2, 11).

Estes, W. K. All-or-none processes in learning and retention. *Amer. Psychologist* (1964), **19,** 16–25, (2).

Fallon, D., & Battig, W. F. Role of difficulty in rote and concept learning. *J. exp. Psychol.* (1964), **68,** 85–88, (7).

Feldman, S. M., & Underwood, B. J. Stimulus recall following paired-associate learning. *J. exp. Psychol.* (1957), **53,** 11–15, (2, 5).

Gagné, R. M. The effect of sequence of presentation of similar items on the learning of paired associates. *J. exp. Psychol.* (1950), **40,** 61–73, (5).

Gagné, R. M., Baker, K. E., & Foster, H. On the relation between similarity and transfer of training in the learning of discriminative motor tasks. *Psychol. Rev.* (1950), **57**, 67–79, (8).

Gannon, D. R., & Noble, C. E. Familiarization (*n*) as a stimulus factor in paired-associate verbal learning. *J. exp. Psychol.* (1961), **62**, 14–23, (4).

Garskof, B. E., & Sandak, J. M. Unlearning in recognition memory. *Psychonom. Sci.* (1964), **1**, 197–198, (8).

Garskof, B. E., Sandak, J. M., & Malinowski, E. W. A. Controlling the "fate" of first list associates. *Psychonom. Sci.* (1965), **2**, 315–316, (8).

Gibson, E. J. A systematic application of the concepts of generalization and differentiation to verbal learning. *Psychol. Rev.* (1940), **47**, 196–229, (5, 8).

Gibson, E. J. Retroactive inhibition as a function of degree of generalization between tasks. *J. exp. Psychol.* (1941), **28**, 93–115, (5, 8).

Gibson, E. J. Intra-list generalization as a factor in verbal learning. *J. exp. Psychol.* (1942), **30**, 185–200, (5).

Gibson, E. J. A re-examination of generalization. *Psychol. Rev.* (1959), **66**, 340–342, (5).

Glanzer, M., & Peters, S. C. Re-examination of the serial position effect. *J. exp. Psychol.* (1962), **64**, 258–266, (1, 3).

Glaze, J. A. The association value of nonsense syllables. *J. genet. Psychol.* (1928), **35**, 255–267, (4).

Goggin, J. Supplementary report: Influence of the written recall measure on first-list associations. *J. exp. Psychol.* (1963), **65**, 619–620, (8).

Goss, A. E. A stimulus-response analysis of the interaction of cue-producing and instrumental responses. *Psychol. Rev.* (1955), **62**, 20–31, (2).

Goss, A. E. Verbal mediating response and concept formation. *Psychol. Rev.* (1961), **68**, 248–274, (7).

Goss, A. E., Morgan, C. H., & Golin, S. J. Paired-associate learning as a function of percentage of occurrence of response members (reinforcement). *J. exp. Psychol.* (1959), **57**, 96–104, (2, 3).

Goss, A. E., Nodine, C. F., Gregory, B. N., Taub, H. A., & Kennedy, K. E. Stimulus characteristics and percentage of occurrence of response members in paired-associate learning. *Psychol. Monogr.* (1962), **76** (12, Whole No. 531), (4).

Gough, P. B., & Jenkins, J. J. Verbal learning and psycholinguistics. In M. H. Marx (Ed.), *Theories in contemporary psychology*. New York: Macmillan, 1963, (Overview).

Goulet, L. R. Interlist response meaningfulness and transfer effects under the *A-B*, *A-C* paradigm. *J. exp. Psychol.* (1965), **70**, 264–269, (8).

Goulet, L. R. Retroaction and the "fate" of the mediator in three stage mediation paradigms. *J. verb. Learn. verb. Behav.*, in press, (9).

Goulet, L. R., & Barclay, A. Supplementary report: A comparison of paired-associate transfer effects between the *A-B*, *C-A* and *A-B*, *B-C* paradigms. *J. exp. Psychol.* (1965), **70**, 537–538, (8).

Grant, D. A. Classical and operant conditioning. In A. W. Melton (Ed.), *Categories of human learning*. New York: Academic Press, 1964, (2).

Green, R. T. Surprise as a factor in the von Restorff effect. *J. exp. Psychol.* (1956), **52**, 340–344, (5).

Haagen, C. H. Synonymity, vividness, familiarity, and association-value ratings for 400 pairs of common adjectives. *J. Psychol.* (1949), **27**, 453–463, (5).

Hakes, D. T., James, C. T., & Young, R. K. A re-examination of the Ebbinghaus derived-list paradigm. *J. exp. Psychol.* (1964), **68**, 508–514, (1).

Hall, J. F. Learning as a function of word-frequency. *Amer. J. Psychol.* (1954), **67**, 138–140, (4).

Hamilton, C. E. The relationship between length of interval separating two learning tasks and performance on the second task. *J. exp. Psychol.* (1950), **40**, 613–621, (8).

Harcum, H. R. Verbal transfer of overlearned forward and backward associations. *Amer. J. Psychol.* (1953), **66**, 622–625, (8).

Harlow, H. F. The formation of learning sets. *Psychol. Rev.* (1949), **56**, 51–65, (8).

Hawker, J. R. The influence of training procedure and other task variables in paired-associate learning. *J. verb. Learn. verb. Behav.* (1964a), **3**, 70–76, (3).

Hawker, J. R. Supplementary report: Effects of prompting and confirmation in a serial learning task. *J. exp. Psychol.* (1964b), **67**, 99–101, (3).

Hayes, K. J. The backward curve: A method for the study of learning. *Psychol. Rev.* (1953), **60,** 269–275, (2).

Hebb, D. O. *Organization of behavior*. New York: John Wiley & Sons, 1949, (11).

Hellyer, S. Supplementary report: Frequency of stimulus presentation and short-term decrement in recall. *J. exp. Psychol.* (1962), **64,** 650, (11).

Hilgard, E. R. *Theories of learning*. New York: Appleton-Century-Crofts, 1956, (Overview).

Horowitz, L. M. Associative matching and intralist similarity. *Psychol. Rep.* (1962), **10,** 751–757, (5).

Horowitz, L. M., & Izawa, C. Comparison of serial and paired-associate learning. *J. exp. Psychol.* (1963), **65,** 352–361, (1).

Horowitz, L. M., & Larsen, S. R. Response interference in paired-associate learning. *J. exp. Psychol.* (1963), **65,** 225–232, (4).

Horton, D. L. The effects of meaningfulness, awareness, and type of design in verbal mediation. *J. verb. Learn. verb. Behav.* (1964), **3,** 187–194, (9).

Horton, D. L., & Hartman, R. R. Verbal mediation as a function of associative directionality and exposure frequency. *J. verb. Learn. verb. Behav.* (1963), **1,** 361–364, (9).

Horton, D. L., & Kjeldergaard, P. M. An experimental analysis of associative factors in mediated generalization. *Psychol. Monogr.* (1961), **75,** (Whole No. 515), (9).

Houston, J. P. *S-R* stimulus selection and strength of *R-S* association. *J. exp. Psychol.* (1964a), **68,** 563–566, (2).

Houston, J. P. Mediation in serial learning. *J. verb. Learn. verb. Behav.* (1964b), **3,** 369–370, (2).

Houston, J. P. Verbal transfer and interlist similarities. *Psychol. Rev.* (1964c), **71,** 412–414, (8).

Houston, J. P. Short-term retention of verbal units with equated degrees of learning. *J. exp. Psychol.* (1965), **70,** 75–78, (11).

Houston, J. P. Verbal transfer and interlist similarity. *J. exp. Psychol.*, in press, (8).

Hovland, C. I. Experimental studies in rote-learning theory: III. Distribution of practice with varying speeds of syllable presentation. *J. exp. Psychol.* (1938), **23,** 172–190, (1).

Hull, C. L. The meaningfulness of 320 selected nonsense syllables. *Amer. J. Psychol.* (1933), **45,** 730–734, (4).

Hull, C. L. The conflicting psychologies of learning—a way out. *Psychol. Rev.* (1935), **42,** 491–516, (1).

Hull, C. L. *Principles of behavior*. New York: Appleton-Century-Crofts, 1943, (4).

Hunt, R. G. Meaningfulness and articulation of stimulus and response in paired-associate learning and stimulus recall. *J. exp. Psychol.* (1959), **57,** 262–267, (Overview, 4).

James, C. T., & Hakes, D. T. Mediated transfer in a four-stage, stimulus equivalence paradigm. *J. verb. Learn. verb. Behav.* (1965), **4,** 89–93, (9).

Jantz, E. M., & Underwood, B. J. *R-S* learning as a function of meaningfulness and degree of *S-R* learning. *J. exp. Psychol.* (1958), **56,** 174–179, (Overview, 2).

Jarrett, R. F., & Scheibe, K. E. Association chains and paired-associate learning. *J. verb. Learn. verb. Behav.* (1962), **1,** 264–268, (9).

Jenkins, J. J. *Associative processes in verbal behavior: A report of the Minnesota Conference.* Minneapolis: University of Minnesota, Department of Psychology, 1955, (9).

Jenkins, J. J. Mediated associations: Paradigms and situations. In C. N. Cofer & B. S. Musgrave (Eds.), *Verbal behavior and learning*. New York: McGraw-Hill, 1963, (9).

Jenkins, J. J. The 1952 word association norms. In L. Postman (Ed.), *Norms of word association.* New York: Academic Press, in press, (2).

Jenkins, J. J., Foss, D. J., & Odom, P. B. Associative mediation in paired-associate learning with multiple controls. *J. verb. Learn. verb. Behav.* (1965), **4,** 141–147, (8).

Jenkins, J. J., Mink, W. D., & Russell, W. A. Associative clustering as a function of verbal association strength. *Psychol. Rep.* (1958), **4,** 127–136, (7).

Jenkins, J. J., & Russell, W. A. Associative clustering during recall. *J. abnorm. soc. Psychol.* (1952), **47,** 818–821, (7).

Jensen, A. R. Transfer between paired-associate and serial learning. *J. verb. Learn. verb. Behav.* (1962a), **1,** 269–280, (1).

Jensen, A. R. An empirical theory of the serial-position effect. *J. Psychol.* (1962b), **53,** 127–142, (1, 5).

Jensen, A. R. Temporal and spatial effects of serial-position. *Amer. J. Psychol.* (1962c), **75,** 390–400, (1).

Jensen, A. R., & Rohwer, W. D., Jr. Verbal mediation in paired-associate and serial learning. *J. verb. Learn. verb. Behav.* (1963), **1,** 346–352, (2).

Jensen, A. R., & Rohwer, W. D., Jr. What is learned in serial learning? *J. verb. Learn. verb. Behav.* (1965), **4,** 62–72, (1).

Johnson, G. J., & Penney, R. K. Transfer effects of mixed and unmixed list designs in paired-associate learning of children. *Psychonom. Sci.* (1965), **2,** 171–172, (8).

Johnson, R. C. Reanalysis of "Meaningfulness and verbal learning." *Psychol. Rev.* (1962). **69,** 233–238, (4).

Jung, J. Transfer of training as a function of degree of first-list learning. *J. verb. Learn. verb. Behav.* (1962), **1,** 197–199, (8).

Jung, J. Effects of response meaningfulness (*m*) on transfer of training under two different paradigms. *J. exp. Psychol.* (1963), **65,** 377–384, (Overview, 8).

Jung, J. A cumulative method of paired-associate and serial learning. *J. verb. Learn. verb. Behav.* (1964), **3,** 290–299, (3).

Jung, J. Two stages of paired associate learning as a function of intralist response similarity (IRS) and response meaningfulness (M). *J. exp. Psychol.* (1965a), **70,** 371–378, (5).

Jung, J. Comments on Mandler's "From association to structure." *Psychol. Rev.*, (1965b), **72,** 318–322, (8).

Kausler, D. H. Comparison of anticipation and recall methods for geriatric subjects. *Psychol. Rep.* (1963), **13,** 702, (3).

Kausler, D. H., & Kanoti, G. A. *R-S* learning and negative transfer effects with a mixed list. *J. exp. Psychol.* (1963), **65,** 201–205, (Overview, 8).

Kausler, D. H., & Lair, C. V. *R-S* ("backward") paired-associate learning in elderly subjects. *J. Gerontol.* (1965), **20,** 29–31, (2).

Kausler, D. H., Lair, C. V., & Matsumoto, R. Interference transfer paradigms and the performance of schizophrenics and controls. *J. abnorm. soc. Psychol.* (1964), **69,** 584–587, (Overview).

Keefe, K. Effects of grouping similar stimuli on paired-associate learning. Unpublished doctoral dissertation, St. Louis University, 1965, (5).

Keppel, G. Retroactive inhibition of serial lists as a function of the presence or absence of positional cues. *J. verb. Learn. verb. Behav.* (1964a), **3,** 511–517, (2).

Keppel, G. Facilitation in short- and long-term retention of paired associates following distributed practice in learning. *J. verb. Learn. verb. Behav.* (1964b), **3,** 91–111, (10).

Keppel, G. Problems of method in the study of short-term memory. *Psychol. Bull.* (1965), **63,** 1–13, (11).

Keppel, G. Unlearning in serial learning. *J. exp. Psychol.*, in press, (8).

Keppel, G., & Rehula, R. J. Rate of presentation in serial learning. *J. exp. Psychol.* (1965), **69,** 121–125, (3).

Keppel, G., & Underwood, B. J. Retroactive inhibition of *R-S* associations. *J. exp. Psychol.* (1962a), **64,** 400–404, (8).

Keppel, G., & Underwood, B. J. Proactive inhibition in short-term retention of single items. *J. verb. Learn. verb. Behav.* (1962b), **1,** 153–161, (11).

Kimble, G. A. *Hilgard and Marquis' conditioning and learning.* New York: Appleton-Century-Crofts, 1961, (1, 5).

Kimble, G. A., & Dufort, R. H. Meaningfulness and isolation as factors in verbal learning. *J. exp. Psychol.* (1955), **50,** 361–368, (4).

Kincaid, W. D., Bousfield, W. A., & Whitmarsh, G. A. The parasitic reinforcement of verbal associative responses. *J. exp. Psychol.* (1962), **64,** 572–579, (8).

Kintsch, W., & McCoy, D. F. Delay of informative feedback in paired-associate learning. *J. exp. Psychol.* (1964), **68,** 372–375, (2).

Koppenaal, R. J. Time changes in the strengths of *A-B, A-C* lists: Spontaneous recovery? *J. verb. Learn. verb. Behav.* (1963), **2,** 310–319, (10).

Krueger, W. C. F. The relative difficulty of nonsense syllables. *J. exp. Psychol.* (1934), **17,** 145–153, (4).

Lachman, R. The model in theory construction. *Psychol. Rev.* (1960), **67,** 113–129, (2).

Leicht, K. L., & Kausler, D. H. Supplementary report: Functional stimulus learning as related to degree of practice and meaningfulness. *J. exp. Psychol.* (1965), **69,** 100–101, (2).

Lepley, W. M. Serial reactions considered as conditioned reactions. *Psychol. Monogr.* (1934), **46** (Whole No. 205), (1).

Levitt, H., & Goss, A. E. Stimulus attributes and drive in paired-associate learning. *J. exp. Psychol.* (1961), **62,** 243–252, (5).

Lindley, R. H. Association value, familiarity, and pronunciability ratings as predictors of serial verbal learning. *J. exp. Psychol.* (1963a), **65**, 347–351, (4).

Lindley, R. H. Effects of controlled coding cues in short-term memory. *J. exp. Psychol.* (1963b), **66**, 580–587, (11).

Lindley, R. H., & Nedler, S. E. Supplementary report: Further effects of subject-generated recoding cues on short-term memory. *J. exp. Psychol.* (1965), **69**, 324–325, (11).

Lippman, L. G., & Denny, M. R. Serial position effect as a function of intertrial interval. *J. verb. Learn. verb. Behav.* (1964), **3**, 496–501, (3).

Lockhead, G. R. Methods of presenting paired associates. *J. verb. Learn. verb. Behav.* (1962), **1**, 62–65, (3).

Loess, H., & McBurney, J. Short-term memory and retention-interval activity. *Proceedings of the 73rd annual convention of the American Psychological Association*, 1965, Chicago, Illinois, (11).

Lumsdaine, A. A. Conditioned eyelid responses as mediating generalized conditioned finger reactions. *Psychol. Bull.* (1939), **36**, 650, (9).

Lyon, D. O. *Memory and the learning process.* Baltimore: Warwick & York, 1917, (3).

Mandler, G. Response factors in human learning. *Psychol. Rev.* (1954), **61**, 235–244, (Overview, 1, 2).

Mandler, G. Associative frequency and associative prepotency as measures of response to nonsense syllables. *Amer. J. Psychol.* (1955), **68**, 662–665, (4).

Mandler, G. From association to structure. *Psychol. Rev.* (1962), **69**, 415–427, (8).

Mandler, G. Subjects do think: A reply to Jung's comments. *Psychol. Rev.* (1965), **72**, 323–326, (8).

Mandler, G., & Campbell, E. H. Effect of variation in associative frequency of stimulus and response members on paired-associate learning. *J. exp. Psychol.* (1957), **54**, 269–273, (4).

Mandler, G., & Earhard, B. Pseudomediation: Is chaining an artifact? *Psychonom. Sci.* (1964), **1**, 247–248, (9).

Mandler, G., & Heinemann, S. H. Effect of overlearning of a verbal response on transfer of training. *J. exp. Psychol.* (1956), **51**, 39–46, (8).

Marks, L. E., & Miller, G. A. The role of semantic and syntactic constraints in the memorization of English sentences. *J. verb. Learn. verb. Behav.* (1964), **3**, 1–5, (7).

Marshall, G. R., & Cofer, C. N. Associative indices as measures of word relatedness: A summary and comparison of ten methods. *J. verb. Learn. verb. Behav.* (1963), **1**, 408–421, (7).

Marshall, M. A., & Runquist, W. N. Facilitation of performance in paired-associate learning by distributed practice. *J. verb. Learn. verb. Behav.* (1962), **1**, 258–263, (3).

Martin, C. J., & Saltz, E. Serial versus random presentation of paired associates. *J. exp Psychol.* (1963), **65**, 609–615, (3).

Martin, E. Transfer of verbal paired associates. *Psychol. Rev.* (1965), **72**, 327–343, (8).

Martin, E., & Schulz, R. W. Aural paired-associate learning: Pronunciability and the interval between stimulus and response. *J. verb. Learn. verb. Behav.* (1963), **1**, 389–391, (3, 4).

Martin, J. G., Oliver, M., Ham, G., & Heaslet, G. Repetition and task in verbal mediating-response acquisition. *J. exp. Psychol.* (1963), **66**, 12–16, (9).

Martin, R. B., & Dean, S. J. Implicit and explicit mediation in paired-associate learning. *J. exp. Psychol.* (1964), **68**, 21–27, (9).

Mathews, R. Recall as a function of number of classificatory categories. *J. exp. Psychol.* (1954), **47**, 241–247, (7).

Matthews, W. A., Marcer, D., & Morgan, E. Word association hierarchies and free recall. *J. verb. Learn. verb. Behav.* (1964), **3**, 371–375, (7).

McCormack, P. D. Backward mediated positive transfer in a paired-associate task. *J. exp. Psychol.* (1961), **61**, 138–141, (9).

McCrary, J. W., & Hunter, W. S. Serial position curves in verbal learning. *Science* (1953), **117**, 131–134, (1, 4).

McGehee, N. E., & Schulz, R. W. Mediation in paired-associate learning. *J. exp. Psychol.* (1961), **62**, 565–570, (9).

McGeoch, J. A. The influence of associative value upon the difficulty of nonsense-syllable lists. *J. genet. Psychol.* (1930), **37**, 421–426, (4).

McGeoch, J. A. *The psychology of human learning.* New York: Longmans, Green, 1942, (Overview).

McGeoch, J. A., & Irion, A. L. *The psychology of human learning.* New York: Longmans, Green, 1952, (Overview, 1, 2, 8).

McGeoch, J. A., & McKinney, F. Studies in retroactive inhibition: The influence of the relative order of presentation of original and interpolated paired associates. *J. exp. Psychol.* (1937), **20,** 60–83, (3).

McGeoch, J. A., & Underwood, B. J. Tests of the two-factor theory of retroactive inhibition. *J. exp. Psychol.* (1943), **32,** 1–16, (3).

McGovern, J. B. Extinction of associations in four transfer paradigms. *Psychol. Monogr.* (1964), **78,** (16, Whole No. 593), (8).

McGuire, W. J. A multiprocess model for paired-associate learning. *J. exp. Psychol.* (1961), **62,** 335–347, (2).

McLaughlin, B. "Intentional" and "incidental" learning in human subjects: The role of instructions to learn and motivation. *Psychol. Bull.* (1965), **63,** 359–376, (6, 10).

Mechanic, A. The distribution of recalled items in simultaneous intentional and incidental learning. *J. exp. Psychol.* (1962a), **63,** 593–600, (6).

Mechanic, A. Effects of orienting task, practice, and incentive on simultaneous incidental and intentional learning. *J. exp. Psychol.* (1962b), **64,** 393–399, (6).

Mechanic, A. The responses involved in the rote learning of verbal materials. *J. verb. Learn. verb. Behav.* (1964), **3,** 30–36, (6).

Mednick, M. T. Mediated generalization and the incubation effect as a function of manifest anxiety. *J. abnorm. soc. Psychol.* (1957), **55,** 315–321, (3).

Mednick, S. A. A learning theory approach to research in schizophrenia. *Psychol. Bull.* (1958), **55,** 316–327 (Overview).

Mehler, J. Some effects of grammatical transformations on the recall of English sentences. *J. verb. Learn. verb. Behav.* (1963), **2,** 346–351, (7).

Melton, A. W. Comments on Professor Postman's paper. In C. N. Cofer (Ed.), *Verbal learning and verbal behavior.* New York: McGraw-Hill, 1961, (8).

Melton, A. W. Comments on Professor Peterson's paper. In C. N. Cofer & B. S. Musgrave (Eds.), *Verbal behavior and learning.* New York: McGraw-Hill, 1963a, (10).

Melton, A. W. Implications of short-term memory for a general theory of memory. *J. verb. Learn. verb. Behav.* (1963b), **2,** 1–21, (11).

Melton, A. W., & Irwin, J. M. The influence of degree of interpolated learning on retroactive inhibition and the overt transfer of specific responses. *Amer. J. Psychol.* (1940), **53,** 173–203, (8).

Melton, A. W., & Safier, D. E. Meaningful similarity of pairs of two-syllable adjectives. In S. S. Stevens (Ed.), *Handbook of experimental psychology.* New York: John Wiley & Sons, 1951, (5).

Metzger, R. A comparison between rote learning and concept formation. *J. exp. Psychol.* (1958), **56,** 226–231, (7).

Miller, G. A. Human memory and the storage of information. *IRE Trans. Inform. Theory* (1956a), **IT-2,** 129–137, (7).

Miller, G. A. The magical number seven plus or minus two: Some limits on our capacity for processing information. *Psychol. Rev.* (1956b), **63,** 81–97, (7).

Miller, G. A. Some psychological studies of grammar. *Amer. Psychologist* (1962), **17,** 748–762, (7).

Miller, G. A., & Selfridge, J. A. Verbal context and the recall of meaningful material. *Amer. J. Psychol* (1950), **63,** 176–185, (7).

Morgan, R. L., & Underwood, B. J. Proactive inhibition as a function of response similarity. *J. exp. Psychol.* (1950), **40,** 592–603, (8, 10).

Murdock, B. B., Jr. "Backward" learning in paired associates. *J. exp. Psychol.* (1956), **51,** 213–215, (8).

Murdock, B. B., Jr. Transfer designs and formulas. *Psychol. Bull.* (1957), **54,** 313–326, (8).

Murdock, B. B., Jr. Intra-list generalization in paired-associate learning. *Psychol. Rev.* (1958a), **65,** 306–314, (5).

Murdock, B. B., Jr. "Backward" associations in transfer and learning. *J. exp. Psychol.* (1958b), **55,** 111–114, (8).

Murdock, B. B., Jr. The distinctiveness of stimuli. *Psychol. Rev.* (1960), **67,** 16–31, (1).

Murdock, B. B., Jr. The retention of individual items. *J. exp. Psychol.* (1961a), **62,** 618–625, (11).

Murdock, B. B., Jr. Short-term retention of single paired-associates. *Psychol. Rep.* (1961b) **8,** 280, (11).

Murdock, B. B., Jr. Direction of recall in short-term memory. *J. verb. Learn. verb. Behav.* (1962), **1,** 119–124, (2).

Murdock, B. B., Jr. Short-term memory and paired-associate learning. *J. verb. Learn. verb. Behav.* (1963a), **2,** 320–328, (11).

Murdock, B. B., Jr. Interpolated recall in short-term memory. *J. exp. Psychol.* (1963b), **66,** 525–532, (11).

Murdock, B. B., Jr. Short-term memory and paired-associate learning. *J. verb. Learn. verb. Behav.* (1963c), **2,** 320–328, (11).

Murdock, B. B., Jr. Proactive inhibition in short-term memory. *J. exp. Psychol.* (1964), **68,** 184–189, (11).

Murdock, B. B., Jr. A test of the "limited capacity" hypothesis. *J. exp. Psychol.* (1965), **69,** 237–240, (11).

Myers, G. C. A study of incidental memory. *Archives of Psychology* (1913), **4** (No. 26), (6).

Nachmias, J., Gleitman, H., & McKenna, V. The effect of isolation of stimuli and responses in paired associates. *Amer. J. Psychol.* (1961), **74,** 452–456, (5).

Newman, S. E. Effects of pairing-time and test time on performance during and after paired-associate training. *Amer. J. Psychol.* (1964a), **77,** 634–637, (3).

Newman, S. E. Supplementary report: A replication of paired-associate learning as a function of S-R similarity. *J. exp. Psychol.* (1964b), **67,** 592–594, (5).

Newman, S. E., & Buckhout, R. *S-R* and *R-S* learning as functions of intralist similarity. *Amer. J. Psychol.* (1962), **75,** 429–436, (5).

Newman, S. E., & Forsyth, G. A. Supplementary report: Isolation effects when paired associates are presented serially. *J. exp. Psychol.* (1965), **70,** 334–335, (5).

Newman, S. E., & Saltz, E. Isolation effects: Stimulus and response generalization as explanatory concepts. *J. exp. Psychol.* (1958), **55,** 467–472, (5).

Newman, S. E., & Saltz, E. Serial position as a cue in learning. *Amer. J. Psychol.* (1962), **75,** 102–108, (3).

Noble, C. E. An analysis of meaning. *Psychol. Rev.* (1952a), **59,** 421–430, (4).

Noble, C. E. The role of stimulus meaning (*m*) in serial verbal learning. *J. exp. Psychol.* (1952b), **43,** 437–446, (4).

Noble, C. E. The meaning-familiarity relationship. *Psychol. Rev.* (1953), **60,** 89–98, (4).

Noble, C. E. The familiarity-frequency relationship. *J. exp. Psychol.* (1954), **47,** 13–16, (4).

Noble, C. E. The effect of familiarization upon serial verbal learning. *J. exp. Psychol.* (1955), **49,** 333–338, (4).

Noble, C. E. Measurements of association value (*a*), rated associations (*a′*), and scaled meaningfulness (*m′*) for the 2100 CVC combinations of the English alphabet. *Psychol. Rep.* (1961), **8,** 487–521, (4).

Noble, C. E. Meaningfulness and familiarity. In C. N. Cofer & B. S. Musgrave (Eds.), *Verbal behavior and learning.* New York: McGraw-Hill, 1963, (4).

Noble, C. E., & McNeely, D. A. The role of meaningfulness (*m*) in paired-associate verbal learning. *J. exp. Psychol.* (1957), **53,** 16–22, (4).

Noble, C. E., Stockwell, F. E., & Pryor, M. W. Meaningfulness (*m′*) and association value (*a*) in paired-associate syllable learning. *Psychol. Rep.* (1957), **3,** 441–452, (4).

Nodine, C. F. Stimulus durations and stimulus characteristics in paired-associate learning. *J. exp. Psychol.* (1963), **66,** 100–106, (3).

Nodine, C. F. Supplementary report: Stimulus durations and total learning time in paired-associate learning. *J. exp. Psychol.* (1965), **69,** 534–536, (3).

Norcross, K. J., & Spiker, C. C. Effects of mediated associations on transfer in paired-associate learning. *J. exp. Psychol.* (1958), **55,** 129–134, (9).

Osgood, C. E. Meaningful similarity and interference in learning. *J. exp. Psychol.* (1946), **36,** 244–301, (8).

Osgood, C. E. The similarity paradox in human learning: A resolution. *Psychol. Rev.* (1949), **56,** 132–143, (5, 8).

Osgood, C. E. *Method and theory in experimental psychology.* New York: Oxford, 1953, (5, 8, 9).

Osgood, C. E., Suci, G. J., & Tannenbaum, P. H. *The measurement of meaning.* Urbana, Ill.: University of Illinois Press, 1957, (4).

Palermo, D. S., & Jenkins, J. J. *Word association norms: Grade school through college.* Minneapolis: University of Minnesota Press, 1964a, (2).

Palermo, D. S., & Jenkins, J. J. Paired-associate learning as a function of the strength of links in the associative chain. *J. verb. Learn. verb. Behav.* (1964b), **3,** 406–412, (9).

Peters, H. N. Mediate association. *J. exp. Psychol.* (1935), **18,** 20–48, (9).

Peterson, L. R. Immediate memory: Data and theory. In C. N. Cofer & B. S. Musgrave (Eds.). *Verbal behavior and learning.* New York: McGraw-Hill, 1963, (9).

Peterson, L. R., & Gentile, A. Proactive interference as a function of time between tests. *J. exp. Psychol.* (1965), **70,** 473–478, (9).

Peterson, L. R., & Peterson, M. J. Short-term retention of individual verbal items. *J. exp. Psychol.* (1959), **58,** 193–198, (9).

Peterson, L. R., & Peterson, M. J. Minimal paired-associate learning. *J. exp. Psychol.* (1962), **63,** 521–527, (9).

Peterson, L. R., Peterson, M. J., & Miller, A. Short-term retention and meaningfulness. *Canad. J. Psychol.* (1961), **15,** 143–147, (9).

Peterson, L. R., Saltzman, D., Hillner, K., & Land, V. Recency and frequency in paired-associate learning. *J. exp. Psychol.* (1962), **63,** 396–403, (9).

Peterson, M. J. Cue trials, frequency of presentation, and mediating responses. *J. exp. Psychol.* (1964), **67,** 432–438, (9).

Peterson, M. J. Effects of delay intervals and meaningfulness on verbal mediating responses. *J. exp. Psychol.* (1965), **69,** 60–66, (9).

Peterson, M. J., & Blattner, K. C. The development of a verbal mediator. *J. exp. Psychol.* (1963), **66,** 72–77, (9).

Peterson, M. J., Colavita, F. B., Sheahan, D. B., III, & Blattner, K. C. Verbal mediating chains and response availability as a function of the acquisition paradigm. *J. verb. Learn. verb. Behav.* (1964), **3,** 11–18, (9).

Peterson, M. J., & Jamison, S. M. Effects of distribution of practice of the acquisition pairs upon mediating responses and response availability. *J. exp. Psychol.* (1965), in press.

Porter, L. W., & Duncan, C. P. Negative transfer in verbal learning. *J. exp. Psychol.* (1953), **46,** 61–64, (7).

Postman, L. The present status of interference theory. In C. N. Cofer (Ed.), *Verbal learning and verbal behavior.* New York: McGraw-Hill, 1961a, (8, 10).

Postman, L. Extra-experimental interference and the retention of words. *J. exp. Psychol.* (1961b), **61,** 97–110, (10).

Postman, L. Transfer of training as a function of experimental paradigm and degree of first-list learning. *J. verb. Learn. verb. Behav.* (1962a), **1,** 109–118, (Overview, 8).

Postman, L. The effects of language habits on the acquisition and retention of verbal associations. *J. exp. Psychol.* (1962b), **64,** 7–19, (10).

Postman, L. One-trial learning. In C. N. Cofer & B. S. Musgrave (Eds.), *Verbal behavior and learning.* New York: McGraw-Hill, 1963, (2).

Postman, L. Short-term memory and incidental learning. In A. W. Melton (Ed.), *Categories of human learning.* New York: Academic Press, 1964a, (6, 11).

Postman, L. Studies of learning to learn: II. Changes in transfer as a function of practice. *J. verb. Learn. verb. Behav.* (1964b), **3,** 437–447, (8).

Postman, L. Acquisition and retention of consistent associative responses. *J. exp. Psychol.* (1964c), **67,** 183–190, (10).

Postman, L., Adams, P. A., & Phillips, L. W. Studies in incidental learning: II. The effects of association value and of the method of testing. *J. exp. Psychol.* (1955), **49,** 1–10, (6).

Postman, L., & Goggin, J. Whole versus part learning of serial lists as a function of meaningfulness and intralist similarity. *J. exp. Psychol.* (1964), **68,** 140–150, (3).

Postman, L., Keppel, G., & Stark, K. Unlearning as a function of the relationship between successive response classes. *J. exp. Psychol.* (1965), **69,** 111–118, (8).

Postman, L., & Schwartz, M. Studies of learning to learn: I. Transfer as a function of method of practice and class of verbal materials. *J. verb. Learn. verb. Behav.* (1964), **3,** 37–49, (2, 8).

Postman, L., & Senders, V. L. Incidental learning and generality of set. *J. exp. Psychol.* (1946), **36,** 153–165, (6).

Postman, L., & Stark, K. Proactive inhibition as a function of the conditions of transfer. *J. verb. Learn. verb. Behav.* (1964), **3,** 249–259, (5).

Primoff, E. Backward and forward association as an organizing act in serial and paired-associate learning. *J. Psychol.* (1938), **5,** 375–395, (5).

Restorff, v. H. Über die wirkung von bereichsbildungen im spurenfeld. *Psychol. Forsch.* (1933), **18,** 299–342, (5).

Ribback, A., & Underwood, B. J. An empirical explanation of the skewness of the bowed serial position curve. *J. exp. Psychol.* (1950), **40,** 329–335, (1).

Richardson, J. The relationship of stimulus similarity and number of responses. *J. exp. Psychol.* (1958), **56,** 478–484, (7).

Richardson, J. Association among stimuli and the learning of verbal concept lists. *J. exp. Psychol.* (1960), **60,** 290–298, (7).

Richardson, J. The learning of concept names mediated by concept examples. *J. verb. Learn. verb. Behav.* (1962), **1,** 281–288, (7).

Roberts, W. A. A further test of the effect of isolation in serial learning. *Amer. J. Psychol.* (1962), **75,** 134–139, (5).

Rock, I. The role of repetition in associative learning. *Amer. J. Psychol.* (1957), **70,** 186–193, (2).

Rock, I., & Ceraso, J. Toward a cognitive theory of associate learning. In C. Scheerer (Ed.), *Cognition: Theory, research, promise.* New York: Harper & Row, 1964, (10).

Rosen, H., Richardson, D. H., & Saltz, E. Supplementary report: Meaningfulness as a differentiation variable in the von Restorff effect. *J. exp. Psychol.* (1962), **64,** 327–328, (5).

Rotberg, I. C., & Woolman, M. Verbal paired-associate learning as a function of grouping similar stimuli or responses. *J. exp. Psychol.* (1963), **65,** 47–51, (5).

Rothkopf, E. Z. Stimulus similarity and sequence of stimulus presentation in paired-associate learning. *J. exp. Psychol.* (1958), **56,** 114–122, (5).

Runquist, W. N. Remarks on "Intra-list generalization in paired-associate learning." *Psychol. Rev.* (1959), **66,** 343–344, (5).

Runquist, W. N., & Farley, F. H. The use of mediators in the learning of verbal paired associates. *J. verb. Learn. verb. Behav.* (1964), **3,** 280–285, (2).

Runquist, W. N., & Freeman, M. Roles of association value and syllable familiarization in verbal discrimination learning. *J. exp. Psychol.* (1960), **59,** 396–401, (Overview).

Russell, W. A., & Jenkins, J. J. The complete Minnesota norms for responses to 100 words from the Kent-Rosanoff Word Association Test. *Tech. Rep. No. 11,* Contract N8 ONR-66216 (1954), (2).

Russell, W. A., & Storms, L. H. Implicit verbal chaining in paired-associate learning. *J. exp. Psychol.* (1955), **49,** 287–293, (9).

Ryan, J. J. Comparison of verbal response transfer mediated by meaningfully similar and associated stimuli. *J. exp. Psychol.* (1960), **60,** 408–415, (8).

Saltz, E. Response pretaining: Differentiation or availability? *J. exp. Psychol.* (1961a), **62,** 583–587, (5).

Saltz, E. Effect of induced stress on free associations. *J. abnorm. soc. Psychol.* (1961b), **62,** 161–164, (5).

Saltz, E. Compound stimuli in verbal learning: Cognitive and sensory differentiation versus stimulus selection. *J. exp. Psychol.* (1963), **66,** 1–5, (5).

Saltz, E. Spontaneous recovery of letter-sequence habits. *J. exp. Psychol.* (1965), **69,** 304–307, (10).

Saltz, E., & Newman, S. E. The von Restorff isolation effect: Test of the intralist association assumption. *J. exp. Psychol.* (1959), **58,** 445–451, (5).

Saltz, E., & Riach, W. J. The effect of stress on stimulus differentiation. *J. exp. Psychol.* (1961), **62,** 588–593, (5).

Saltz, E., & Youseff, Z. I. Role of response differentiation in forgetting. *J. exp. Psychol.* (1964), **68,** 307–311, (5).

Sauer, F. M. The relative variability of nonsense syllables and words. *J. exp. Psychol.* (1930), **13,** 235–246, (4).

Saufley, W. H., Jr., & Underwood, B. J. Cue-selection interference in paired-associate learning. *J. verb. Learn. verb. Behav.* (1964), **3,** 474–479, (2).

Schaub, G. R., & Lindley, R. H. Effects of subject-generated recoding cues on short-term memory. *J. exp. Psychol.* (1964), **68,** 171–175, (11).

Schulz, R. W., & Lovelace, E. A. Mediation in verbal paired-associate learning: The role of temporal factors. *Psychonom. Sci.* (1964), **1,** 95–96, (9).

Schulz, R. W., & Martin, E. Aural paired-associate learning: Stimulus familiarization, response familiarization, and pronounciability. *J. verb. Learn. verb. Behav.* (1964), **3,** 139–145, (3).

Schulz, R. W., & Runquist, W. N. Learning and retention of paired adjectives as a function of percentage occurrence of response members. *J. exp. Psychol.* (1960), **59,** 409–413, (2).

Schulz, R. W., & Tucker, I. F. Supplementary report: Stimulus familiarization in paired-associate learning. *J. exp. Psychol.* (1962), **64,** 549–550, (4).

Schulz, R. W., Weaver, G. E., & Ginsberg, S. Mediation with pseudomediation controlled: Chaining is not an artifact! *Psychonom Sci.* (1965), **2,** 169–170, (9).

Seidel, R. J. The importance of the *S-R* role of the verbal mediator in mediate association. *Canad. J. Psychol.* (1962), **16,** 170–176, (9).

Sheffield, F. D. The role of meaningfulness of stimulus and response in verbal learning. Unpublished doctoral dissertation, Yale University, 1946.

Shipley, W. C. An apparent transfer of conditioning. *J. gen. Psychol.* (1933), **8,** 382–391, (9).

Shipley, W. C. Indirect conditioning. *J. gen. Psychol.* (1935), **12,** 337–357, (9).

Silverstein, A. Long-term retention for intentionally and incidentally learned words. *J. verb. Learn. verb. Behav.* (1964), **3,** 236–243, (10).

Simon, S., & Wood, G. Backward learning and the stimulus-familiarization inhibitory effect. *J. exp. Psychol.* (1964), **67,** 310–315, (4).

Slamecka, N. J. Retention of connected discourse as a function of duration of interpolated learning. *J. exp. Psychol.* (1962), **63,** 480–486, (10).

Slamecka, N. J. An inquiry into the doctrine of remote associations. *Psychol. Rev.* (1964), **71,** 61–76, (1).

Slamecka, N. J. Acquisition and retention of connected discourse as a function of contextual constraint. *J. exp. Psychol.* (1964), **68,** 330–333, (7, 10).

Slamecka, N. J. In defense of a new approach to old phenomena. *Psychol. Rev.* (1965), **72,** 242–246, (1).

Slamecka, N. J., & Ceraso, J. Retroactive and proactive inhibition of verbal learning. *Psychol. Bull.* (1960), **57,** 449–475, (10).

Spear, N. E., Ekstrand, B. R., & Underwood, B. J. Association by contiguity. *J. exp. Psychol.* (1964), **67,** 151–161, (2).

Spence, J. T. Associative interference on paired-associate lists from extraexperimental learning. *J. verb. Learn. verb. Behav.* (1963), **2,** 329–338, (8).

Spence, J. T., & Schulz, R. W. Negative transfer in paired-associate learning as a function of first-list trials. *J. verb. Learn. verb. Behav.* (1965), **4,** 397–400 (8).

Spence, K. W. *Behavior theory and conditioning.* New Haven: Yale University Press, 1956, (2).

Spence, K. W., Farber, I. E., & McFann, H. H. The relation of anxiety (drive) level to performance in competitional and noncompetitional paired-associate learning. *J. exp. Psychol.* (1956), **52,** 296–305, (Overview).

Spielberger, C. D., & Levin, S. M. What is learned in verbal conditioning? *J. verb. Learn. verb. Behav.* (1962), **1,** 125–132, (Overview).

Staats, A. W., & Staats, C. K. Meaning and *m*: Separate but correlated. *Psychol. Rev.* (1959), **66,** 136–144, (4).

Storms, L. H. Apparent backward association: A situational effect. *J. exp. Psychol.* (1958), **55,** 390–395, (9).

Taylor, A. B., & Irion, A. L. Continuity hypothesis and transfer of training in paired-associate learning. *J. exp. Psychol.* (1964), **68,** 573–577, (2).

Thorndike, E. L., & Lorge, I. *The teacher's word book of 30,000 words.* New York: Columbia University Press, 1944, (4).

Thune, L. E. The effect of different types of preliminary activities on subsequent learning of paired-associate material. *J. exp. Psychol.* (1950), **40,** 423–438, (8).

Thysell, R. V., & Schulz, R. W. Concept-utilization as a function of the strength of relevant and irrelevant associations. *J. verb. Learn. verb. Behav.* (1964), **3,** 203–208, (7).

Trapp, E. P., & Kausler, D. H. A revision of Hull's table of associative values for 320 selected nonsense syllables. *Amer. J. Psychol.* (1959), **72,** 423–428, (4).

Tulving, E. Subjective organization in free recall of "unrelated" words. *Psychol. Rev.* (1962), **69,** 344–354, (7).

Tulving, E. Intratrial and intertrial retention: Notes toward a theory of free recall verbal learning. *Psychol. Rev.* (1964), **71,** 219–237, (11).

Tulving, E., & Arbuckle, T. Y. Sources of intratrial interference in immediate recall of paired associates. *J. verb. Learn. verb. Behav.* (1963), **1,** 321–334, (11).

Twedt, H. M., & Underwood, B. J. Mixed vs. unmixed lists in transfer studies. *J. exp. Psychol.* (1959), **58,** 111--116, (Overview, 8).

Uhlmann, F. W., & Saltz, E. Retention of anxiety material as a function of cognitive differentiation. *J. personal. soc. Psychol.* (1965), **1,** 55–62, (5).

Umemoto, T. On the relative weight of stimulus versus response words in rote learning. *Jap. J. Psychol.* (1951), **21,** 46–55, (2).

Umemoto, T., & Hilgard, E. R. Paired-associate learning as a function of similarity: Common stimulus and response items within the list. *J. exp. Psychol.* (1961), **62,** 97–104, (5).

Underwood, B. J. The effect of successive interpolations on retroactive and proactive inhibition. *Psychol. Monogr.* (1945), **59,** No. 3., (10).

Underwood, B. J. *Experimental psychology*. New York: Appleton-Century-Crofts, 1949a, (8).

Underwood, B. J. Proactive inhibition as a function of time and degree of prior learning. *J. exp. Psychol.* (1949b), **39,** 24–34, (8).

Underwood, B. J. Associative transfer in verbal learning as a function of response similarity and degree of first-list learning. *J. exp. Psychol.* (1951a), **42,** 44–53, (5).

Underwood, B. J. Studies of distributed practice: II. Learning and retention of paired-adjective lists with two levels of intra-list similarity. *J. exp. Psychol.* (1951b), **42,** 153–161, (5).

Underwood, B. J. Studies of distributed practice: VII. Learning and retention of serial nonsense lists as a function of intralist similarity. *J. exp. Psychol.* (1952), **44,** 80–87, (5).

Underwood, B. J. Studies of distributed practice: VIII. Learning and retention of paired nonsense syllables as a function of intra-list similarity. *J. exp. Psychol.* (1953a), **45,** 133–142, (5).

Underwood, B. J. Studies of distributed practice: IX. Learning and retention of paired adjectives as a function of intra-list similarity. *J. exp. Psychol.* (1953b), **45,** 143–149, (5).

Underwood, B. J. Speed of learning and amount retained: A consideration of methodology. *Psychol. Bull.* (1954), **51,** 276–282.

Underwood, B. J. *Psychological research*. New York: Appleton-Century-Crofts, 1957a, (Overview, 2).

Underwood, B. J. Interference and forgetting. *Psychol. Rev.* (1957b), **64,** 49–60, (10).

Underwood, B. J. Ten years of massed practice on distributed practice. *Psychol. Rev.* (1961a), **68,** 229–247, (3).

Underwood, B. J. An evaluation of the Gibson theory of verbal learning. In C. N. Cofer (Ed.), *Verbal learning and verbal behavior*. New York: McGraw-Hill, 1961b, (5, 8).

Underwood, B. J. Stimulus selection in verbal learning. In C. N. Cofer & B. S. Musgrave (Eds.), *Verbal behavior and learning*. New York: McGraw-Hill, 1963, (Overview, 1).

Underwood, B. J. The representativeness of rote verbal learning. In A. W. Melton (Ed.), *Categories of human learning*. New York: Academic Press, 1964a, (Overview, 5, 7).

Underwood, B. J. Degree of learning and the measurement of forgetting. *J. verb. Learn. verb. Behav.* (1964b), **3,** 112–129, (10, 11).

Underwood, B. J., Ham, M., & Ekstrand, B. Cue selection in paired-associate learning. *J. exp. Psychol.* (1962), **64,** 405–409, (2).

Underwood, B. J., & Keppel, G. One-trial learning? *J. verb. Learn. verb. Behav.* (1962a), **1,** 1–13, (2, 11).

Underwood, B. J., & Keppel, G. Coding processes in verbal learning. *J. verb. Learn. verb. Behav.* (1962b), **1,** 250–257, (7).

Underwood, B. J., Keppel, G., & Schulz, R. W. Studies of distributed practice: XXII. Some conditions which enhance retention. *J. exp. Psychol.* (1962), **64,** 355–363, (10).

Underwood, B. J., & Postman, L. Extra-experimental sources of interference in forgetting. *Psychol. Rev.* (1960), **67,** 73–95, (10).

Underwood, B. J., & Richardson, J. Verbal concept learning as a function of instructions and dominance level. *J. exp. Psychol.* (1956), **51,** 229–238, (7).

Underwood, B. J., Runquist, W. N., & Schulz, R. W. Response learning in paired-associate lists as a function of intralist similarity. *J. exp. Psychol.* (1959), **58,** 70–78, (2, 4, 5, 7).

Underwood, B. J., & Schulz, R. W. *Meaningfulness and verbal learning*. Philadelphia: Lippincott, 1960a, (2, 4).

Underwood, B. J., & Schulz, R. W. Response dominance and rate of learning paired associates. *J. gen. Psychol.* (1960b), **62,** 153–158, (2).

Vanderplas, J. M., & Garvin, E. A. Complexity, association value, and practice as factors in shape recognition following paired-associate training. *J. exp. Psychol.* (1959), **57,** 155–163, (4).

Wallace, W. P. Review of the historical, empirical, and theoretical status of the von Restorff phenomenon. *Psychol. Bull.* (1965), **63,** 410–424, (5).

Weingartner, H. Associative structure and serial learning. *J verb. Learn. verb. Behav.* (1963), **2,** 476–479, (7).

Weingartner, H. The free recall of sets of associatively related words. *J. verb. Learn. verb. Behav.* (1964), **3,** 6–10, (7).

Weiss, W., & Margolius, G. The effect of context stimuli on learning and retention. *J. exp. Psychol.* (1954), **48,** 318–322, (2).

Wickens, D. D. The centrality of verbal learning: Comment on Professor Underwood's paper. In A. W. Melton (Ed.), *Categories of human learning.* New York: Academic Press, 1964, (2).

Wicklund, D. A., Palermo, D. S., & Jenkins, J. J. The effects of associative strength and response hierarchy on paired-associate learning. *J. verb. Learn. verb. Behav.* (1964), **3,** 413–420, (2).

Wilcoxon, H. C., Wilson, W. R., & Wise, D. A. Paired-associate learning as a function of percentage of occurrence of response members and other factors. *J. exp. Psychol.* (1961), **61,** 283–289, (3).

Williams, J. M., & Derks, P. L. Mode of presentation and the acquisition of paired-associates that differ in pronunciability and association value. *J. verb. Learn. verb. Behav.* (1963), **2,** 453–456, (3).

Williams, J. P. Supplementary report: A selection artifact in Rock's study of the role of repetition. *J. exp. Psychol.* (1961), **62,** 627–628, (2).

Wimer, R. Osgood's transfer surface: Extension and test. *J. verb. Learn. verb. Behav.* (1964), **3,** 274–279, (8).

Witkin, H. A., Dyk, R. B., Faterson, H. F., Goodenough, D. R., & Karp, S. A. *Psychological differentiation.* New York: John Wiley & Sons, 1962, (5).

Witmer, L. R. The association value of three-place consonant syllables. *J. genet. Psychol.* (1935), **47,** 337–360, (4).

Wohlgemuth, A. On memory and the direction of associations. *Brit. J. Psychol.* (1913), **5,** 447–465, (2).

Woodworth, R. S., & Poffenberger, A. T. *Textbook of experimental psychology.* Mimeographed edition. New York: Columbia University, 1920, (1).

Young, R. K. Retroactive and proactive effects under varying conditions of response similarity. *J. exp. Psychol.* (1955), **50,** 113–119, (8, 10).

Young, R. K. A comparison of two methods of learning serial associations. *Amer. J. Psychol.* (1959), **72,** 554–559, (5).

Young, R. K. Tests of three hypotheses about the stimulus in serial learning. *J. exp. Psychol.* (1962), **63,** 307–313, (1).

Young, R. K., & Jennings, P. C. Backward learning when the same items serve as stimuli and responses. *J. exp. Psychol.* (1964), **68,** 64–70, (5).

Young, R. K., Patterson, J., & Benson, W. N. Backward serial learning. *J. verb. Learn. verb. Behav.* (1963), **1,** 335–338, (1).

Index